Volume II

The American Past

A Survey of American History

SIXTH EDITION

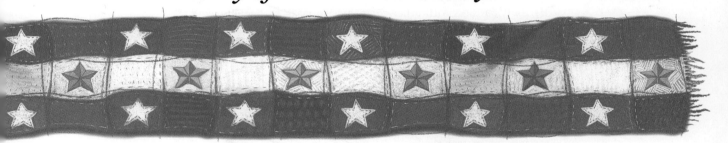

Where Learning Comes to Life

TECHNOLOGY

Technology is changing the learning experience, by increasing the power of your textbook and other learning materials; by allowing you to access more information, more quickly; and by bringing a wider array of choices in your course and content information sources.

Harcourt College Publishers has developed the most comprehensive Web sites, e-books, and electronic learning materials on the market to help you use technology to achieve your goals.

PARTNERS IN LEARNING

Harcourt partners with other companies to make technology work for you and to supply the learning resources you want and need. More importantly, Harcourt and its partners provide avenues to help you reduce your research time of numerous information sources.

Harcourt College Publishers and its partners offer increased opportunities to enhance your learning resources and address your learning style. With quick access to chapter-specific Web sites and e-books . . . from interactive study materials to quizzing, testing, and career advice . . . Harcourt and its partners bring learning to life.

Harcourt's partnership with Digital:Convergence™ brings :CRQ™ technology and the :CueCat™ reader to you and allows Harcourt to provide you with a complete and dynamic list of resources designed to help you achieve your learning goals. Just swipe the cue to view a list of Harcourt's partners and Harcourt's print and electronic learning solutions.

http://www.harcourtcollege.com/partners/

Volume II — *since 1865*

The
American
Past

A Survey of American History

SIXTH EDITION

Joseph R. Conlin

Harcourt College Publishers

Fort Worth   Philadelphia   San Diego   New York   Orlando   Austin   San Antonio

Toronto   Montreal   London   Sydney   Tokyo

Publisher	**Earl McPeek**
Executive Editor	**David Tatom**
Market Strategist	**Steve Drummond**
Developmental Editor	**Margaret McAndrew Beasley**
Project Editor	**Laura J. Hanna**
Art Director	**Burl Sloan**
Production Manager	**Linda McMillan**

Cover illustration: Kathleen Kinkopf

ISBN: 0-15-506127-5
Library of Congress Catalog Card Number: 00-104138

Copyright © 2001, 1997, 1993, 1990, 1987, 1984 by Harcourt, Inc.

© 2001 Digital:Convergence Corporation. All rights reserved.

Digital:Convergence, :C, :CRQ, :CueCat, Slant Code, the :CueCat reader, "it's your cue," "Engineering Your Digital Future" and all marks as indicated are trademarks of Digital:Convergence Corporation.

All rights reserved. No part of this publication may be reproduced or transmitted in any form or by any means, electronic or mechanical, including photocopy, recording, or any information storage and retrieval system, without permission in writing from the publisher.

Requests for permission to make copies of any part of the work should be mailed to the following address: Permissions Department, Harcourt, Inc., 6277 Sea Harbor Drive, Orlando, FL 32887-6777.

Copyrights and Acknowledgments appear on page C-1, which constitutes a continuation of the copyright page.

Address for Domestic Orders
Harcourt College Publishers, 6277 Sea Harbor Drive, Orlando, FL 32887-6777
800-782-4479

Address for International Orders
International Customer Service
Harcourt, Inc., 6277 Sea Harbor Drive, Orlando, FL 32887-6777
407-345-3800
(fax) 407-345-4060
(e-mail) hbintl@harcourt.com

Address for Editorial Correspondence
Harcourt College Publishers, 301 Commerce Street, Suite 3700, Fort Worth, TX 76102

Web Site Address
http://www.harcourtcollege.com

Harcourt College Publishers will provide complimentary supplements or supplement packages to those adopters qualified under our adoption policy. Please contact your sales representative to learn how you qualify. If as an adopter or potential user you receive supplements you do not need, please return them to your sales representative or send them to: Attn: Returns Department, Troy Warehouse, 465 South Lincoln Drive, Troy, MO 63379.

Printed in the United States of America

1 2 3 4 5 6 7 8 9   032   9 8 7 6 5 4 3 2 1

Harcourt College Publishers

To *L.V.C.*

and the Memory

of *J.R.C.*

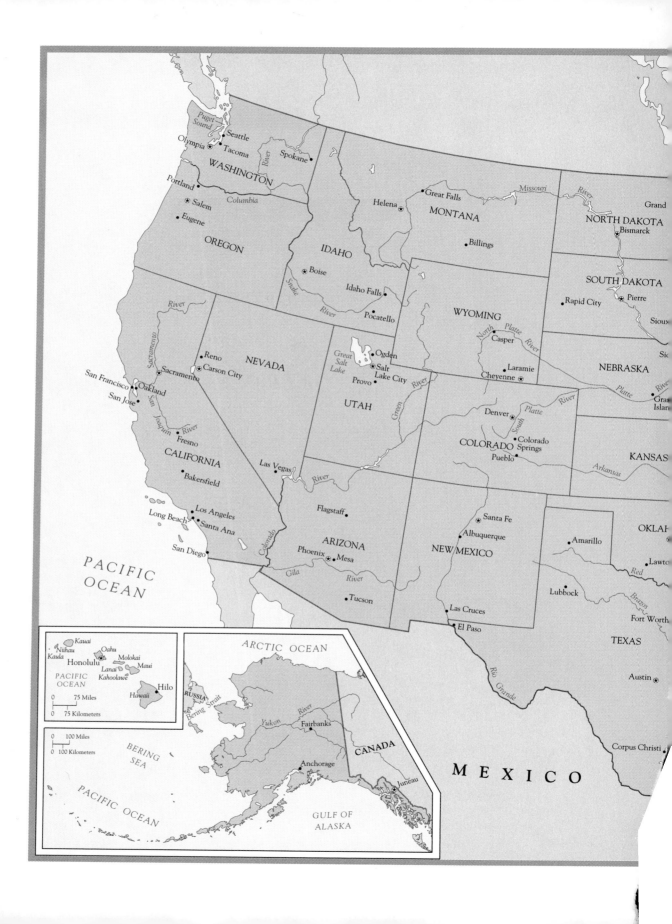

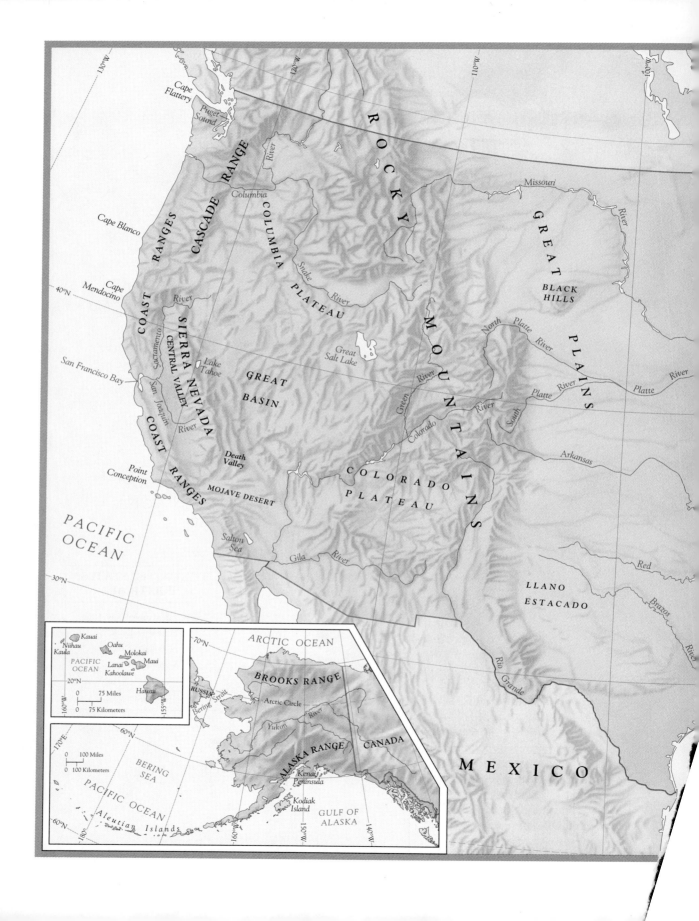

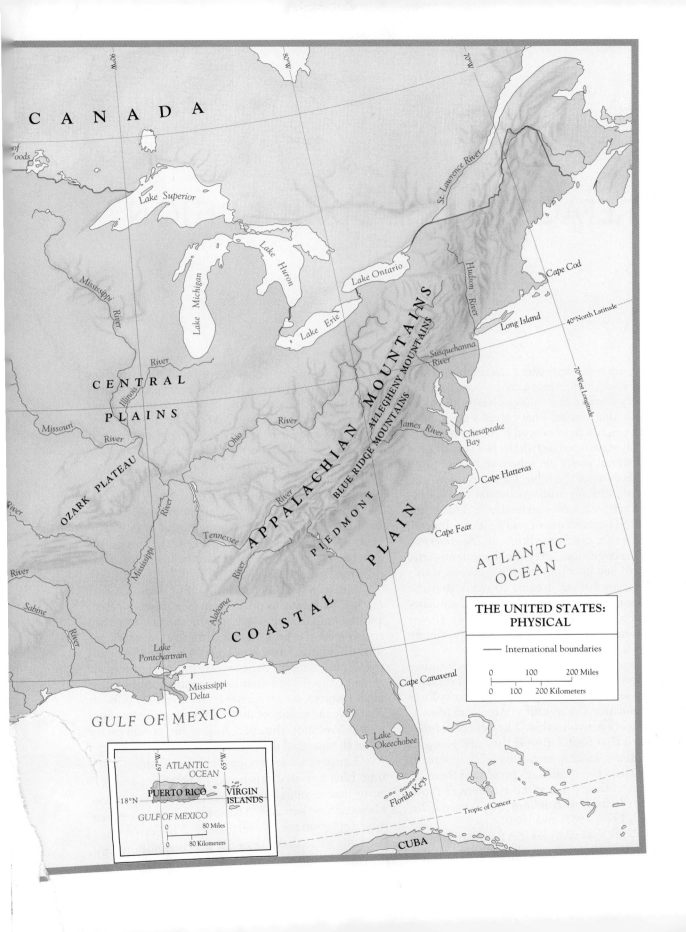

PREFACE TO THE SIXTH EDITION

There are many approaches to teaching a survey course in American history. During thirty years in the college classroom teaching principally that course, I have tried a good many of them. My courses have ranged from the prescriptive and highly structured to (when class size allowed it) open-ended seminar. One semester, inspired by a pedagogical fashion of the hour, I tried to teach U.S. History Survey with no reading material except documents—primary sources—no textbook. That lasted one semester. The experiment was a failure. Indeed, one reason I wrote the first edition of *The American Past* was my recognition, after the documents-only experiment, of just how important a textbook is to a successful survey course. I came to think that the quality of the textbook is second only to the quality of the instructor in making the U.S. History Survey a valuable—no, essential—part of undergraduate education.

The reason that the U.S. History Survey course is so important is that all but the very best of students at the most selective universities come to college lacking a foundation in the stuff of American history. A good textbook provides this. The best classroom teachers need that foundation if they are going to build in students an understanding of how human beings have faced the challenges presented them by circumstances of their times and the actions of those other human beings with whom they shared the earth in 1607, 1776, 1925, and 1980.

The textbook that provides this foundation must be, first of all, a book that is actually read. Few of the students in survey courses are budding historians willing to plow through sometimes murky documents (and scholarly prose) in order to master their subject. They are, rather, would-be accountants, ecologists, engineers, nurses, psychologists, retailers, webmasters, and zookeepers who, often enough, are enrolled in the U.S. History Survey only because they are required to do so. Such, often reluctant, students must be wooed, first by the skills and personality of the instructor, and second by the *readability* of their textbook. The book bought and put aside in favor of memorizing a crib sheet off the Internet is worthless to everyone but the individuals who profited from its purchase.

A textbook that is actually read is the kind of textbook I meant to produce in *The American Past*, and the kind of textbook I have meant to improve in revising it. Keeping in mind that my readers are not professional historians, I have painted in broad strokes, avoiding the hyper-specialization that wounds some textbooks and disturbs so many nonhistorians (and historians!) today. I have tried to clarify difficult concepts and points of interpretation with anecdote, and I have not shunned humorous commentary when the material deserved it.

There is always room for improvement. Each time I have revised this book, I have winced to discover that sections I thought adequate or even good a few years earlier needed basic rehabilitation or even total replacement. Nevertheless, *I believe I have* been more successful than not in accomplishing my goals, and with each edition moved closer to the unattainable ideal. During the two decades that *The American Past* has been in print, I have received dozens of letters—perhaps close to two hundred—from professors who have assigned the text to their classes. They have pointed out my boners, taken me to task for the slant I put on a particular topic, asked my source for one specific or another, and complimented my book. It has been gratifying that even some of the most annoyed correspondents closed their critical letters with a comment something like, **"My students really like *The American Past*. They actually read it."**

That has been the idea, and remains the guiding principle behind this Sixth Edition.

NEW TO THE SIXTH EDITION

Those familiar with *The American Past* Fifth Edition will find no major structural or organizational changes. The primary focus of this revision was updating, with a secondary emphasis on refining—of scholarship, interpretation, clarity, and pedagogical function. In the process of the revision, every sentence was reconsidered and polished as necessary. Selected notable revisions to specific chapters include: expanded treatment of Native Americans (Chapters 1–3 and 5); new material on politics and political culture (Chapter 15); new information and expanded treatment of Mormons, utopias, and Know Nothings (Chapter 17); new material on American Colonization Society (Chapter 18); more discussion of cavalry and African-American soldiers (Chapter 23); expansion of impeachment section (Chapter 25); expanded discussion of the telephone and Standard Oil (Chapter 27); modified interpretation of Southern Pacific Railroad (Chapter 28); extensive rewriting (Chapter 31); incorporation of new material on Clinton, Whitewater, impeachment proceedings, CBS and Viacom merger, presidential campaign for Election of 2000, and end of the millennium (Chapter 51); in fact, Chapter 51, the final chapter, is virtually new as a whole.

New Features: Chronologies

Based on suggestions from reviewers of the Fifth Edition, a chronology has been added to the end of each chapter. These chronologies outline the major events of the period reflected in each chapter, providing a quick reference for student review.

Thoroughly Updated "For Further Reading" Sections

The annotated bibliographies at the end of each chapter were thoroughly reviewed and include a total of nearly three hundred new entries.

New "How They Lived," "Notable People," and Sidebar Essays

The Sixth Edition includes a wealth of new social, cultural, biographical, and anecdotal material within three different types of boxed essays that have become favorite features of *The American Past* readers. "How They Lived" essays provide students with a snapshot of daily life and issues at a particular time in a particular place. "Notable People" boxes introduce students to figures of interest—some well known and others simply "ordinary" men and women with extraordinary stories. The Sidebar features are a trademark of *The American Past* and offer little gems of information that add life and dimension to the periods and events covered in the narrative.

ACKNOWLEDGMENTS

I have had splendid assistance in preparing this edition by a number of teaching historians who each read and critiqued chapters from the Fifth Edition. Among them: Scott Carter, Shasta College; Linda Cross, Tyler Junior College; Martha Kirchmer, Grand Valley State University; Jack Oden, Enterprise State Junior College; Richard H. Peterson, emeritus, San Diego State University; Nancy L. Rachels, Hillsborough Community College; William Scofield, Yakima Valley Community College; Ronald Story, University of Massachusetts; and Daniel C. Vogt, Jackson State University. I hope I have done their scrutiny justice.

In addition to reviewers commenting on the book as a whole, Donald W. Whisenhunt virtually scoured the entire Fifth Edition line by line looking for cases of poor explication, disputable interpretation, inconsistency, and typographical or factual errors. I particularly hope I have responded adequately to his observations. My thanks as well to Ronald Story who reviewed the "For Further Reading" sections and provided hundreds of new annotated entries to bring the bibliography up to date.

Once again I have benefited from the professional ministrations of a number of people at

Harcourt College Publishers. David Tatom, executive editor, has overseen the development and production of this edition, as he did the Fifth. To Margaret McAndrew Beasley, senior developmental editor, that is, the person on the floor, daily dirtying (or breaking) her fingernails as she prodded me in the right direction, I owe my fullest thanks. I am also grateful to Laura Hanna, the very able senior project editor who, herself, dirtied a few fingernails; Linda McMillan, production manager; Burl Sloan, senior art director; Steve Drummond, executive market strategist (in charge of many operations mysterious to me, yet appreciated all the more for that); and Lili Weiner, resourceful freelance photo researcher for their respective roles in the process. In a sixth edition, a book should not need much editing for clarity and style, and *The American Past* did not. It was assigned, nevertheless and to my delight, a freelance editor of the first order, Charles Naylor, whose eye for inappropriate nuances and lapses of clarity astonished me, and who also brought an extensive knowledge of American history to his task.

The American Past Web-enhanced Sixth Edition

Harcourt College Publishers brings *The American Past* to life with quick and easy access to Web-enhanced learning content. The :CueCat™ reader from Digital:Convergence makes it easy! Just a swipe of the :CueCat reader across strategically placed cues within the text immediately takes you to additional, relevant online content and resources. Many of Conlin's trademark "How They Lived" and "Notable People" boxes now include cues.

To see how it works, follow the cue. . .

CONTENTS IN BRIEF

Preface to the Sixth Edition xi

25 RECONSTRUCTION
Rebuilding the Shattered Union: 1863–1877 477

26 PARTIES, PATRONAGE, AND PORK
Politics in the Late Nineteenth Century 497

27 BIG INDUSTRY, BIG BUSINESS
Economic Development in the Late Nineteenth Century 519

28 LIVING WITH LEVIATHAN
Americans React to Big Business and Great Wealth 541

29 WE WHO MADE AMERICA
Factories and Immigrant Ships 561

30 BRIGHT LIGHTS AND SQUALID SLUMS
The Growth of Big Cities 583

31 THE LAST FRONTIER
Winning the Rest of the West 1865–1900 601

32 STRESSFUL TIMES DOWN HOME
The Crisis of American Agriculture 1865–1896 621

33 IN THE DAYS OF McKINLEY
The United States Becomes a World Power 1896–1903 641

34 THEODORE ROOSEVELT AND THE GOOD OLD DAYS
American Society in Transition 1890–1917 663

35 AGE OF REFORM
The Progressives after 1900 683

36 VICTORS AT ARMAGEDDON
The Progressives in Power 1901–1916 703

37 OVER THERE
The United States and the First World War 1914–1918 721

38 OVER HERE
World War I at Home 1917–1920 743

39 IN THE DAYS OF HARDING
Time of Uncertainty 1919–1923 763

40 CALVIN COOLIDGE AND THE NEW ERA
When America Was a Business 1923–1929 783

41 NATIONAL TRAUMA
The Great Depression 1930–1933 801

42 REARRANGING AMERICA
Franklin D. Roosevelt and the New Deal 1933–1938 817

43 HEADED FOR WAR AGAIN
Foreign Relations 1933–1942 837

44 AMERICA'S GREAT WAR
The United States at the Pinnacle of Power 1942–1945 859

45 ANXIETY TIME
The United States in the Early Nuclear Age 1946–1952 881

46 EISENHOWER COUNTRY
American Life in the 1950s 903

47 CONSENSUS AND CAMELOT
The Eisenhower and Kennedy Administrations 1953–1963 923

48 YEARS OF TURBULENCE
Conflict at Home and Abroad 1961–1968 945

49 PRESIDENCY IN CRISIS
Policies of the Nixon, Ford, and Carter Administrations 1968–1980 969

50 MORNING IN AMERICA
The Reagan Era 1980–1993 993

51 MILLENNIUM
Frustration, Anger, Division, Values 1013

Appendixes A-1

Photo Credits C-1

Index I-1

TABLE OF CONTENTS

25
RECONSTRUCTION
Rebuilding the Shattered
Union: 1863–1877   **477**
The Reconstruction Debate   *478*
The Critical Year   *482*
Reconstruction Realities and Myths   *484*
Blacks in Congress   *488*
The Grant Administration   *490*
The Twilight of Reconstruction   *493*
Chronology   *494*
For Further Reading   *495*

26
PARTIES, PATRONAGE, AND PORK
Politics in the Late
Nineteenth Century   **497**
How the System Worked   *498*
Presidents and Personalities   *504*
James Abram Garfield (1831–1881)   *506*
Issues   *509*
Politics in the City   *512*
Chronology   *516*
For Further Reading   *517*

27
BIG INDUSTRY, BIG BUSINESS
Economic Development
in the Late Nineteenth Century   **519**
A Land Made for Industry   *520*
The Field Brothers   *524*
The Railroad Revolution   *525*
The Transcontinental Lines   *528*
The Organizers   *533*
Chronology   *538*
For Further Reading   *539*

28
LIVING WITH LEVIATHAN
Americans React to Big
Business and Great Wealth   **541**
Regulating the Railroads and Trusts   *542*
The Last Dance of the Idle Rich:
The Bradley Martin Ball of 1897   *544*
Critics of the New Order   *549*
Defenders of the Faith   *551*
How the Very Rich Lived   *555*
Chronology   *558*
For Further Reading   *559*

29
WE WHO MADE AMERICA
Factories and Immigrant Ships   **561**
A New Way of Life   *562*
Who Were the Workers?   *564*
Organize!   *567*
The Immigration Experience   *570*
The Nation of Immigrants   *573*
Ethnic America   *577*
Chronology   *581*
For Further Reading   *581*

30
BRIGHT LIGHTS AND SQUALID SLUMS
The Growth of Big Cities   **583**
Cities as Alien Enclaves   *584*
Of the Growth of Great Cities   *587*
Big City Sweatshops   *588*
The Evils of City Life   *595*
Chronology   *598*
For Further Reading   *599*

31
THE LAST FRONTIER
Winning the Rest of the West 1865–1900   **601**
The Last Frontier   *602*
Punching Cows   *606*
The Cattle Kingdom   *611*
The Wild West in American Culture   *615*
The Mining Frontier   *617*
Chronology   *618*
For Further Reading   *619*

32
STRESSFUL TIMES DOWN HOME
The Crisis of American
Agriculture 1865–1896   **621**
Best of Times, Worst of Times   *622*
The New South:
The Prophet and the Builder   *628*
Protest and Organization   *630*
The Money Question   *631*
The Populists   *634*
Chronology   *638*
For Further Reading   *639*

33
IN THE DAYS OF McKINLEY
The United States Becomes
a World Power 1896–1903   **641**
Watershed   *642*
American Imperialism   *646*
The Spanish-American War   *649*

xiv

Remembering the Maine: *Soldiers in the Spanish-American War* 650
Empire Confirmed 654
Chronology 661
For Further Reading 661

34
THEODORE ROOSEVELT AND THE GOOD OLD DAYS
American Society in Transition 1890–1917 663
Middle America 664
Nellie Bly 668
A Lively Culture 672
Americans at Play 676
Sports 679
Chronology 681
For Further Reading 681

35
AGE OF REFORM
The Progressives after 1900 683
The Progressives 684
Progressivism down Home 687
Victor L. Berger (1860–1929) 692
The Fringe 694
Chronology 699
For Further Reading 701

36
VICTORS AT ARMAGEDDON
The Progressives in Power 1901–1916 703
T. R. Takes Over 704
The President as Reformer 706
A Conservative President in a Progressive Era 710
Democratic Party Progressivism 714
Coney Island: Amusement Democratized 716
Chronology 719
For Further Reading 719

37
OVER THERE
The United States and the First World War 1914–1918 721
Wilson, the World, and Mexico 722
The Great War 724
William D. Haywood (1869–1927) 728
America Goes to War 733
Chronology 740
For Further Reading 741

38
OVER HERE
World War I at Home 1917–1920 743
The Progressive War 744
Social Changes 746

Conformity and Repression 749
Wilson and the League of Nations 753
"They Dropped Like Flies":
The Great Flu Epidemic of 1918 754
Chronology 761
For Further Reading 761

39
IN THE DAYS OF HARDING
Time of Uncertainty 1919–1923 763
The Worst President 764
A Decent Man 765
How They Played the Game 766
Social Tensions: Labor, Radicals, Immigrants 769
Social Tensions: Race, Moral Codes, Religion 774
Chronology 780
For Further Reading 781

40
CALVIN COOLIDGE AND THE NEW ERA
When America Was a Business 1923–1929 783
The Coolidge Years 784
The Lone Eagle: Charles A. Lindbergh (1902–1974) 788
Prosperity and Business Culture 791
Get Rich Quick 796
Chronology 799
For Further Reading 799

41
NATIONAL TRAUMA
The Great Depression 1930–1933 801
The Face of Catastrophe 802
The Failure of the Old Order 804
Americans React to the Crisis 807
The Election of 1932 810
Weeknights at Eight 812
Chronology 814
For Further Reading 815

42
REARRANGING AMERICA
Franklin D. Roosevelt and the New Deal 1933–1938 817
The Pleasant Man Who Changed America 818
The Hundred Days 820
The New Deal Threatened; The New Deal Sustained 823
The Spellbinders 827
How the Wealthy Coped 828
The Legacy of the New Deal 831
Chronology 835
For Further Reading 835

xvi *Table of Contents*

43
HEADED FOR WAR AGAIN
Foreign Relations 1933–1942 ***837***
New Deal Foreign Policy *838*
The World Goes to War *841*
The United States and the War in Europe *845*
America Goes to War *849*
Rationing and Scrap Drives *850*
Chronology *856*
For Further Reading *857*

44
AMERICA'S GREAT WAR
The United States
at the Pinnacle of Power 1942–1945 ***859***
Stopping Japan *860*
Studying a New Kind of War *862*
Defeating Germany First *866*
The Twilight of Japan, the Nuclear Dawn *871*
Chronology *877*
For Further Reading *879*

45
ANXIETY TIME
The United States in the Early
Nuclear Age 1946–1952 ***881***
The Shadow of Cold War *882*
Jehovah's Witnesses *886*
Domestic Politics under Truman *888*
Containment in China *892*
Years of Tension *896*
Chronology *900*
For Further Reading *901*

46
EISENHOWER COUNTRY
American Life in the 1950s ***903***
Leadership *904*
Fashion and the Fifties *906*
Suburbia and Its Values *911*
Against the Grain *916*
Chronology *920*
For Further Reading *921*

47
CONSENSUS AND CAMELOT
The Eisenhower and Kennedy
Administrations 1953–1963 ***923***
Ike's Domestic Compromise *924*
The Cold War Continues *925*
Suburban Landscape *928*
1960: A Changing of the Guard *932*
Camelot *935*
Kennedy's Foreign Policy *937*
Chronology *942*
For Further Reading *943*

48
YEARS OF TURBULENCE
Conflict at Home and Abroad
1961–1968 ***945***
Lyndon Baines Johnson *946*
The Great Society *948*
Earl Warren (1891–1974) *950*
Vietnam! Vietnam! *953*
Mr. Johnson's War *955*
Troubled Years *957*
The Election of 1968 *962*
Chronology *965*
For Further Reading *967*

49
PRESIDENCY IN CRISIS
Policies of the Nixon, Ford, and
Carter Administrations 1968–1980 ***969***
The Nixon Presidency *970*
Nixon's Vietnam *973*
Nixon-Kissinger Foreign Policy *976*
Watergate and Gerald Ford *979*
Quiet Crisis *985*
The Typical American of the 1980s:
A Statistical Portrait *988*
Chronology *989*
For Further Reading *991*

50
MORNING IN AMERICA
The Reagan Era 1980–1993 ***993***
The Ayatollah and the Actor *995*
The Reagan Revolution *996*
Foreign Policy in the Eighties *1001*
The Bush Presidency *1004*
Chronology *1009*
For Further Reading *1011*

51
CENTURY'S END
Frustration, Anger, Division, Values ***1013***
Foreign Policy under Clinton *1015*
Politics Not as Usual *1018*
Scandal + Prosperity = Postitive Ratings *1024*
Millennial Society *1030*

Appendixes ***A-1***

Photo Credits ***C-1***

Index ***I-1***

LIST OF MAPS

Radical Reconstruction	484	Presidential Election 1920	760
Presidential Elections 1876–1892	499	Presidential Election 1924	786
The Great Eastern Trunk Lines 1850s–1870s	527	Presidential Election 1928	792
Transcontinental Railroads 1862–1900	529	Presidential Election 1932	814
Railroad Expansion 1870–1890	530	Presidential Election 1936	831
Northern Pacific Land Grant 1864	532	German and Italian Aggression 1934–1939	842
European Immigration 1815–1914	574	Japanese Empire 1931–1942	845
Growth of Cities 1860 and 1900	590	Allied Advances in Europe and Africa	868
Indian Reservations 1875 and 1900	603	The Pacific Theater	873
Western Economic Development in the 1870s	612	The Korean War	895
Expansion of Cultivation	623	Interstate Highway System	913
Presidential Election of 1896	646	Racial Segregation 1949	918
Presidential Election 1912	715	The Vietnam War	958
The Mexican Expedition 1916–1917	724	Population Shifts toward the "Sunbelt"	1021
European Alliances and the Road to War 1914	726	The Equal Rights Amendment 1972–1982	1035
American Operations in World War I	738		

LIST OF FEATURE BOXES

Blacks in Congress	488	"They Dropped Like Flies": The Great Flu Epidemic of 1918	754
James Abram Garfield (1831–1881)	506	How They Played the Game	766
The Field Brothers	524	The Lone Eagle: Charles A. Lindbergh (1902–1974)	788
The Last Dance of the Idle Rich: The Bradley Martin Ball of 1897	544	Weeknights at Eight	812
The Immigration Experience	570	How the Wealthy Coped	828
Big City Sweatshops	588	Rationing and Scrap Drives	850
Punching Cows	606	Studying a New Kind of War	862
The New South: The Prophet and the Builder	628	Jehovah's Witnesses	886
Remembering the Maine: Soldiers in the Spanish-American War	650	Fashion and the Fifties	906
Nellie Bly	668	Suburban Landscape	928
Victor L. Berger (1860–1929)	692	Earl Warren (1891–1974)	950
Coney Island: Amusement Democratized	716	The Typical American of the 1980s: A Statistical Portrait	988
William D. Haywood (1869–1927)	728		

Freedmen pose for a photographer in Richmond, Virginia, in 1865.

25
CHAPTER

RECONSTRUCTION

Rebuilding the Shattered Union: 1863–1877

No State shall make or enforce any law which shall abridge the privileges or immunities of citizens of the United States; nor shall any State deprive any person of life, liberty, or property, without due process of law.

—Fourteenth Amendment to the Constitution

Oh, I'm a good old rebel, that's what I am,
And for this land of freedom, I don't give a damn,
I'm glad I fought ag'in her, I only wish we'd won,
And I don't axe any pardon for anything I've done.

—Reconstruction Era Doggerel

Republicans gave the ballot to men without homes, money, education, or security, and then told them to use it to protect themselves. It was cheap patriotism, cheap philanthropy, cheap success.

—Albion W. Tourgée

478 *Chapter 25 Reconstruction*

When the guns fell silent in 1865, the people of the South looked about them to see a society, an economy, and a land in tatters. Some southern cities, such as Vicksburg, Atlanta, Columbia, and Richmond, were flattened, eerie wastelands of charred timbers, rubble, and free-standing chimneys. Few of the South's railroads could be operated for more than a few miles. Bridges were gone. River-borne commerce, the lifeblood of the states beyond the Appalachians, had dwindled to a trickle. Old commercial ties with Europe and the North had been snapped. After four years of printing paper money valued in hope alone, the South's banks were ruined.

Even the cultivation of the soil was disrupted. The small farms of the men who served in the ranks lay fallow by the thousands, many of them never to be claimed by their former owners. Great planters who abandoned their fields to advancing Union armies discovered that weeds and scrub pine were more destructive conquerors than vengeful Yankees. The people who had toiled in the great fields, the former slaves, were often gone, looking elsewhere for a place to start new lives as free men and women. Many of those who remained in their lifelong homes also made it clear they wanted nothing of the past. When a Union soldier told recently freed women in South Carolina he would bring their former master back to them, they shouted, "Don't bring him here."

"But what shall we do with him?"

"Do what you please."

"Shall we hang him?"

"If you want. . . ."

"But shall we bring him *here* and hang him?"

". . . No, no, don't fetch him here, we no want to see him nebber more again."

THE RECONSTRUCTION DEBATE

In view of the desolation and social dislocation, *reconstruction* would seem to be an appropriate description of the 12-year period following the Civil War. But the word does not refer to the literal rebuilding of the South, the laying of bricks, the spanning of streams, the reclaiming of the land, and only secondarily to the rebuilding of a society.

Reconstruction refers to the political process by which the 11 rebel states were restored to a normal constitutional relationship with the 25 loyal states and their national government. It was the Union, that great abstraction over which so many had died, that was reconstructed.

Blood was shed during Reconstruction too, but little glory was won. Few political reputations—northern or southern, white or black, Republican or Democratic—emerged from the era without blemish. It may well be that Abraham Lincoln comes down to us as a heroic and sainted figure only because he did not survive the war. Indeed, the Reconstruction policy Lincoln proposed as early as 1863 was repudiated by members of his own party, who would surely have fought the Emancipator as they fought his successor, Andrew Johnson. Lincoln anticipated the problems he did not live to face. He described as pernicious the constitutional issues with which both sides in the bitter Reconstruction debate masked their true motives and goals.

Lincoln's Plan to Restore the Union

By the end of 1863, Union armies controlled large parts of the Confederacy, and ultimate victory, while not in the bag, was reasonable to assume. To provide for a rapid reconciliation of North and South, Lincoln declared on December 8, 1863, that as soon as 10 percent of the voters in any Confederate state took an oath of allegiance to the Union, the people of that state could organize a government and elect representatives to Congress. Moving quickly, enough voters in occupied Tennessee, Arkansas, and Louisiana complied.

Congress Checks the President

Congress, however, refused to recognize the new governments, leaving the three states under the command of the military. Motives for checking Lincoln's plan varied as marvelously as the cut of the chin whiskers that politicians were now sporting, but two were repeatedly voiced. First, almost all Republican congressmen were alarmed by the broad expansion of presidential powers during the war. No president since Andrew Jackson (still an arch-villain to those Republicans who had been Whigs) had assumed as much authority as Lincoln had—at the expense of Congress. Few congressmen wished to see this trend continue during peacetime, as Lincoln's plan for Reconstruction promised to ensure.

Second, Radical Republicans, abolitionists who were at odds with Lincoln over his foot-dragging in moving against slavery, objected that the president's

Congressman Robert Elliot of South Carolina argues in the House of Representatives for a civil rights bill.

plan made no allowances whatsoever for the status of the freedmen, as the former slaves were called. These Radicals took the lead in framing the Wade-Davis Bill of July 1864, which provided that only after 50 percent of the white male citizens of a state swore an oath of loyalty to the Union could the Reconstruction process begin. Then, the Wade-Davis Bill insisted, Congress and not the president would decide when the process was complete. Wade-Davis promised to slow down a process Lincoln wanted to speed along (the 50 percent requirement) and to seize control of the process from the president.

Lincoln responded with a pocket veto and, over the following months—the last of his life—he hinted that he was ready for compromise. He said he would be glad to accept any former rebel states which opted to reenter the Union under the congressional plan and he let it be known he had no objection to giving the right to vote to blacks who were "very intelligent and those who have fought gallantly in our ranks." He urged the military governor of Louisiana to extend the suffrage to some blacks.

Stubborn Andy Johnson

Lincoln's lifelong assumption that blacks were inferior to whites and his determination to win back quickly the loyalty of southern whites prevented him from accepting the full citizenship of African Americans without reservation. However, he was willing to be flexible. "Saying that reconstruction will be accepted if presented in a specified way," he said, "it is not said that it will never be accepted in any other way." The man who succeeded him was not so accommodating.

Like Lincoln, Andrew Johnson of Tennessee grew up in stultifying frontier poverty. Unlike Lincoln, who taught himself to read as a boy and was ambitious from the start, Johnson grew to adulthood illiterate. He was working as a tailor when he swallowed his pride and asked a schoolteacher in Greenville, Tennessee, to teach him to read and write. She did, and later married him, encouraging Johnson to pursue a political career. Andrew Johnson had more political experience than Lincoln or, for that matter, than most presidents have had. Johnson held elective office on every level, from town councilman to congressman to senator and, during the war, as governor of occupied Tennessee.

Experience, alas, is rarely a substitute for natural aptitude. Whereas Lincoln was an instinctively coy politician who was sensitive to the realities of what he could and could not accomplish, Johnson was unsubtle, insensitive, willful, and stubborn.

Johnson was ill with a bad cold when he was sworn in as vice president. He bolted several glasses of brandy for strength, and took the oath of office a little drunk and thick-tongued. The incident was jested about, but Vice President Johnson had the goodwill of the Radicals because he had several times called for the harsh punishment of high-ranking Confederates. (He said he wanted to hang Jefferson Davis as a traitor.) However, after narrowly escaping death in the plot that felled Lincoln, Johnson lost the Radicals' backing in no time when, like Lincoln, he insisted that he, the president, possessed the authority to decide when rebel states were reconstructed. Thus ensued the debate over what Lincoln had called "a pernicious abstraction."

Johnson: They Are Already States

Johnson based his case for presidential supervision on the assumption that the southern states had never left the Union because it was constitutionally forbidden to do so: the Union was one and inviolable, as Daniel Webster said; it could not be dissolved. Johnson and the entire Republican party and most northern Democrats held to that principle in 1861. He stuck by it in 1865.

There had indeed been a war and an entity known as the Confederate States of America. But individuals fought the one and created the other, according to Johnson; the states had not. Punish the rebels, Johnson said—he approved several confiscations of rebel-owned lands—but not Virginia, Alabama, and the rest. They were still states, inalienable components of the United States of America. Seating their duly elected representatives in the Congress was a purely administrative affair. Therefore, the president, the nation's chief administrator, would decide how and when to do it.

Logic versus Horse Sense

There was nothing wrong with Johnson's logic; he was an excellent constitutionalist. The president's problem was his inability or refusal to see beyond constitutional tidiness to the world of human feelings, hatreds, resentments, and flesh and blood—especially blood.

Obstinate, often vulgar, Andrew Johnson was a self-taught student of the Constitution. Rigorous adherence to it, as he read it, and a reflexive distaste for the idea of black citizenship doomed his early friendly relationship with the Radical Republicans.

The fact was, virtually every senator and representative from the rebel states—Johnson was an exception—had left their seats in the winter and spring of 1861, and Congress and president had functioned as the Union through four years of war. More than half a million people were killed and a majority of northerners blamed these tragedies on arrogant, antagonistic, rich southern slave owners who, when Johnson announced that he would adopt Lincoln's plan of Reconstruction (with some changes), began to assume the leadership in their states that, as slavocrats, they had always held.

Nor did Johnson's reputation as a man who wanted to punish individual rebels hold up. By the end of 1865 he pardoned 13,000 Confederate leaders, thus making them eligible to hold public office under his plan for Reconstruction. In elections held in the fall under Johnson's plan, southern voters sent many of these rebels to Congress, including four Confederate generals, six members of Jefferson Davis's cabinet, and as senator from Georgia, former Confederate Vice President Alexander H. Stephens.

The Radicals: They Have Forfeited Their Rights

Thaddeus Stevens, Radical leader in the House of Representatives, replied to Johnson's argument that the former Confederate states had committed state suicide when they seceded. They were not states. Therefore, it was within the power of Congress, and Congress alone, to admit "Alabama," "Arkansas," and the rest. Senator Charles Sumner came to the same conclusion by arguing that the southern states were conquered provinces and therefore had the same status as the federal territories of the West.

These theories suited the mood of most northerners very well, but they were constitutionally indefensible. A rather obscure Republican, Samuel Shellabarger of Ohio, came up with the formula that appealed to angry, war-weary northerners and made constitutional sense: the rebel states had forfeited their rights as states. Congress's Joint Committee on Reconstruction found that "the States lately in rebellion were, at the close of the war, disorganized communities, without civil government, and without constitutions or other forms, by virtue of which political relations could legally exist between them and the federal government." Such a state of affairs

meant that only Congress could decide when the 11 former Confederate states might once again function as members of the Union.

The Radicals

Congress refused to seat the senators and representatives who came to Washington under the Johnson Reconstruction plan. The leaders of the resistance were Radical Republicans who, whatever constitutional arguments they put forward, were determined to crush the southern planter class they had hated for so long and, with varying degrees of idealism, wanted to help the black freedmen who had, for so long, been exploited by slave owners.

Some Radicals, like Stevens and Sumner and Benjamin "Bluff Ben" Wade of Ohio, believed in racial equality. George W. Julian of Indiana proposed to confiscate the land of the planters and divide it, in 40-acre farms, among the freedmen. With economic independence they could guarantee their civil freedom and political rights. Other Radicals wanted to grant the freedmen citizenship, including the vote, for frankly political purposes. Black voters would provide the backbone for a Republican party in the South, which did not exist before the war, and was unlikely to be more than a splinter group if only southern whites voted.

The Radicals were a minority within the Republican party. However, they were able to win the support of party moderates because of Johnson's repeated blunders and a series of events in the conquered South that persuaded a majority of northern voters that Lincolnian generosity would

---

Discouraging Rebellion

Among other provisions of the Fourteenth Amendment, the former Confederate states were forbidden to repay "any debt or obligation incurred in aid of insurrection or rebellion against the United States." By stinging foreign and domestic individuals and banks that had lent money to the rebel states, the amendment was putting future supporters of rebellion on notice of the consequences of their actions.

THE CRITICAL YEAR

The reaction of most blacks to the news of their freedom was to test it by leaving the plantations and farms on which they had lived as slaves.

Many flocked to cities, which they associated with free blacks. Others, after a period of wandering, gathered in ramshackle camps in the countryside, eagerly discussing the rumor that each household would soon be allotted 40 acres and a mule. Without a means of making a living in a stricken land, these congregations were potentially, and in some cases in fact, dens of hunger, disease, crime, and disorder.

The Freedmen's Bureau

In order to prevent chaos in conquered territory, Congress created the Bureau of Refugees, Freedmen, and Abandoned Lands, popularly known as the Freedmen's Bureau. Administered by the army under the command of General O. O. Howard, the bureau provided relief for the freedmen (and some whites) in the form of food, clothing, and shelter; attempted to find jobs for them; set up hospitals and schools run by idealistic black and white women from the northern states, sometimes at the risk of their lives; and otherwise tried to ease the transition from slavery to freedom.

When the Freedmen's Bureau bill was first enacted, Congress assumed that properly established state governments would be able to assume responsibility for these services within a year after the end of the hostilities. The Bureau was scheduled to close its doors, its job accomplished, in March 1866.

In February 1866, however, the process of Reconstruction was at a standstill. Congress refused to recognize Johnson's state governments but had not created any to its own liking. The former Confederacy was, in effect, still under military occupation. So Congress passed a bill extending the life of the bureau.

Johnson vetoed it and, a month later, he vetoed another congressional act that granted citizenship to the freedmen. Once again, his constitutional reasoning was sound. The Constitution gave the states the power to rule on the terms of citizenship within their borders, and Johnson continued to insist that the state governments he had set up were legitimate.

He might have won his argument. Americans took their constitutional fine points seriously in those days and Radical demands for black civil equality ran against the grain of white racism, which was widespread. However, the actions of the Johnson government toward blacks, and the apparent refusal of many southern whites to acknowledge their defeat in the war, nullified every point Johnson scored.

The Black Codes

Because blacks as slaves were the backbone of the southern labor force, the southern legislatures naturally expected the blacks to continue to bring in the crops after the war. The freedmen wanted the work. Far from providing farms for them, however, the Johnsonian state governments did not even establish a system of employment that treated the blacks as free men and women. On the contrary, the black codes defined a form of second-class citizenship that looked to blacks and many whites like a step or two back into slavery.

In some states, blacks were permitted to work only as domestic servants or in agriculture, just what they did as slaves. Other states made it illegal for blacks to live in towns and cities.

In no state were blacks allowed to vote or to bear arms. In fact, few of the civil liberties listed in the Bill of Rights were accorded them.

South Carolina said that African Americans could not sell goods! Mississippi required freedmen to sign 12-month labor contracts before January 10 of each year. Those who failed to do so could be arrested, and their labor sold to the highest bidder in a manner that (to say the least) was strongly reminiscent of the detested slave auction. Dependent children could be forced to work. Blacks who reneged on their contracts were not to be paid for the work that they had already performed.

The extremism of the black codes alienated many northerners who might have accepted a milder form of second-class citizenship for the freedmen. (Only a few northern states allowed African Americans full civil equality.) Northerners were also disturbed when whites in Memphis, New Orleans, and smaller southern towns rioted, killing and injuring blacks, while the Johnson state governments sat passively by.

Freedmen pose with their reading books in front of their log schoolhouse.

The Fourteenth Amendment

Perceiving the shift in mood, in June 1866, Radical and Moderate Republicans drew up a constitutional amendment on which to base congressional Reconstruction policy. The long and complex (and later controversial) Fourteenth Amendment banned from holding high federal or state office all high-ranking Confederates unless they were pardoned by Congress. This struck directly at many of the leaders of the Johnson governments in the South. The amendment also guaranteed that all "citizens of the United States and of the State wherein they reside" were to receive fully equal treatment under the laws of the states.

If ratified, the Fourteenth Amendment would preclude southern states from passing any more laws like the black codes. However, it also promised to cancel northern state laws that forbade blacks to vote, and in that aspect of the amendment Johnson saw an opportunity. Calculating that many northerners, particularly in the Midwest, would rather have ex-Confederates in the government than grant full civil equality to blacks, Johnson decided to campaign against the Radicals on the amendment issue in the congressional election of 1866.

The Radical Triumph

The first step was the formal organization of a political party. Johnson, conservative Republican allies such as Secretary of State Seward and a few senators, and some Democrats therefore called a convention of the National Union party in Philadelphia. The message of the convention was sectional reconciliation. To symbolize it, the meeting was opened by a procession of northern and southern Johnson supporters in which couples made up of one southerner and one northerner marched arm in arm down the center aisle of the hall.

Unhappily for Johnson, the first couple on the floor was South Carolina Governor James L. Orr, a huge, fleshy man, and Massachusetts Governor John A. Andrew, a little fellow with a way of looking intimidated. When Orr seemed to drag the mousy Andrew down the length of the hall, Radical politicians and cartoonists had a field day. Johnson's National Union movement, they said, was dominated by rebels and preached in the North by obsequious stooges.

In the fall, Johnson sealed his doom. He toured the Midwest seeking support—he called it his "swing around the circle"—and from the start discredited himself. Johnson learned his oratorical skills in the rough-and-tumble, stump-speaking tradition of eastern Tennessee. There, voters liked a red-hot debate between politicians who scorched each other and the hecklers that challenged them.

Midwesterners also liked that kind of ruckus, but not, it turned out, from their president. When Radical hecklers taunted Johnson and he responded gibe for gibe, Radicals shook their heads sadly that a man of so little dignity should be sitting in the seat of Washington and Lincoln. Drunk again, they supposed.

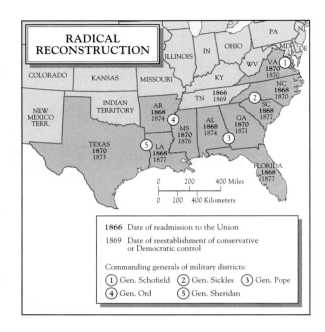

The result was a landslide. Most of Johnson's candidates were defeated. The Republican party, now led by the Radicals, controlled more than two-thirds of the seats in both houses of Congress, enough to override every veto that Johnson dared to make.

RECONSTRUCTION REALITIES AND MYTHS

The Radical Reconstruction program was adopted in a series of laws passed by the Fortieth Congress in 1867. These dissolved the southern state governments that were organized under Johnson and partitioned the Confederacy into five military provinces, each commanded by a major general. The army would maintain order while voters were registered: blacks and those whites who were not specifically disenfranchised under the terms of the Fourteenth Amendment. The constitutional conventions that these voters elected were required to abolish slavery, give the vote to adult black males, and ratify the Thirteenth and Fourteenth Amendments. After examination of their work by Congress, the reconstructed states would be admitted to the Union, and their senators and representatives could take their seats in the Capitol. The Radicals assumed that at least some of these congressmen would be Republicans.

Old Thad Stevens

Few Radical Republicans were as sincerely committed to racial equality as Thaddeus Stevens of Pennsylvania. In his will he insisted on being buried in a black cemetery because blacks were banned from the one where he normally would have been interred.

Nevertheless, even Stevens came to terms with the racism of those northern whites who refused the vote to blacks in their own states. In order to win their support for black suffrage in the South, Stevens argued that the situation was different in the South because blacks made up the majority of loyal Union men there. "I am for negro suffrage in every rebel state," he said. "If it be just, it should not be denied; if it be necessary, it should be adopted; if it be a punishment to traitors, they deserve it."

Readmission of the Southern States

Tennessee complied immediately with these terms and was never really affected by the Radical experiment in remaking the South. Ironically, it was Andrew Johnson, military governor of Tennessee during the war, and a good one, who laid the basis for a stable government in the Volunteer State.

In 1868, largely as a result of the black vote, six more states were readmitted. Alabama, Arkansas, Florida, Louisiana, North Carolina, and South Carolina sent Republican delegations, including some blacks, to Washington. In the remaining four states—Georgia, Mississippi, Texas, and Virginia—because some whites obstructed every attempt to set up a government in which blacks would participate, the military continued to govern until 1870.

In the meantime, with Congress more firmly under Radical control, Thaddeus Stevens, Charles Sumner, and other Radicals attempted to establish the supremacy of the legislative over the judicial and executive branches of the government. With the Supreme Court they were immediately successful. By threatening to reduce the size of the court or even to try to abolish it, the Radicals intimidated the justices. Chief Justice Salmon P. Chase decided to ride out the difficult era by ignoring all cases that dealt with Reconstruction issues, just what the Radicals wanted.

As for the presidency, Congress took partial control of the army away from Johnson and then struck at his right to choose his own cabinet. The Tenure of Office Act forbade the president to remove any appointed official who was confirmed by the Senate without first getting the Senate's approval of the dismissal.

The Impeachment of Andrew Johnson

Although Johnson attempted to delay and obstruct congressional Reconstruction by urging southern whites not to cooperate, the strict constitutionalist in him had come to terms with the fact of the Radicals' control of the government. He executed the duties assigned him under the Reconstruction acts. However, because of the same constitutional scruples, he decided to defy the Tenure of Office Act. To allow Congress to decide if and when a president could fire a member of his own cabinet was a clear infringement of the independence of the executive branch of the government. In February 1868, Johnson dismissed the single Radical in his cabinet, Secretary of War Edwin Stanton.

Strictly speaking, the Tenure of Office Act did not apply to Stanton's dismissal because he was appointed by Lincoln, not by Johnson. Nevertheless, the House of Representatives drew up articles of impeachment, passed them, and appointed a committee to serve as Johnson's prosecutors. The Senate acted as the jury in the trial, and the Chief Justice presided.

President on Trial

All but two of the eleven articles of impeachment dealt with the Tenure of Office Act. As expected, Johnson's defenders in the Senate argued that it did not apply to the Stanton case, and, in any event, its constitutionality was highly dubious. The other two articles condemned Johnson for disrespect of Congress. There was no doubt about this. Johnson had spared few bitter words in describing the Radical Republicans. The president was capable of civility, but not when his temper was up. However, Johnson's defenders argued with timeless merit that sharp and vulgar language did not approach being the "high crimes and misdemeanors" that the Constitution stipulates as the reason for impeachment.

The flimsiness of the charges did not matter, as they often do not when politics are on the table. The Radicals had determined to humiliate Johnson, and most moderate Republicans, sensing a turn to Radicalism in the public mood, did what successful politicians who like their jobs always do: they went along.

Conviction of an impeached federal official—removal of that person from office—requires a two-thirds majority of the Senate. In 1868, that

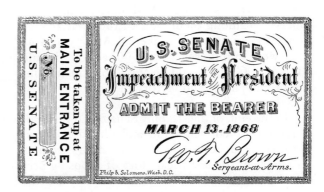

A ticket of admission to the Senate gallery to witness the impeachment of Andrew Johnson.

486 Chapter 25 Reconstruction

Was Johnson Impeached?

Andrew Johnson *was* impeached, the first American president to be so. *Impeachment* is not removal from office but the bringing of charges, the equivalent of indictment in a criminal trial. The official who is found guilty of the articles of impeachment is *convicted* and removed from office (and may be sent to prison or otherwise penalized if convicted in a subsequent criminal trial). Johnson was *not* convicted of the charges brought against him. Nor was President William Jefferson Clinton, after he was caught lying in a sex scandal in 1998. However, like Johnson, he was impeached. The House of Representatives brought charges against him and, in his case, he was fined in July 1999 by a federal judge for his dishonesty under oath.

meant 36 senators had to vote for conviction, no more than 18 for acquittal. The actual vote in Johnson's case was 35 to 19. He remained in office by a single vote.

Actually, it was not so close. Six Moderate Republican senators agreed privately that if their vote was needed for acquittal, they would vote for acquittal. They did not accept the validity of the Articles of Impeachment and they did not believe that the president should be removed from office simply because he was at odds with Congress. Moreover, if Johnson were removed from office, his successor would have been Ben Wade of Ohio, a Radical of such dubious deportment—he had a fouler mouth than Johnson—that by comparison the president was as courtly as George Washington. Finally, the sobersided among them argued, 1868 was an election year: an already weakened Andy Johnson's days were numbered. The immensely popular Ulysses S. Grant would be the Republican nominee in November and victory in November was a sure thing.

In the end, of the six, only Senator Edward Ross of Kansas joined Democrats and a handful of conservative Republicans to vote for Johnson's acquittal. To him went the historical glory of choosing principle but also, as he had been threatened by the Radicals, political death The Kansas legislature turned him out of office at the next election.

The Fifteenth Amendment

Grant easily defeated New York Governor Horatio Seymour in the electoral college by a vote of 214 to 80. However, the popular vote was much closer, a hair's breadth in some states. Nationwide, Grant won by 300,000 votes, and, some rudimentary arithmetic showed, he got 500,000 black votes in the southern states. Grant lost New York, the largest state, by a very thin margin. Had blacks been able to vote in New York (they were not), Grant would have carried the state easily. In Indiana, Grant won by a razor-thin margin. Had African Americans been able to vote in that northern state (they were not), it would not have been close.

In other words, the future of the Republican party seemed to depend on the black man's right to vote in the northern as well as the southern states. Consequently, the Moderates in Congress supported Radicals in drafting a third Civil War amendment. The Fifteenth forbade states to deny the vote to any person on the basis of "race, color, or previous condition of servitude." Because Republican governments favorable to blacks still controlled most of the southern states, the amendment was easily ratified. The Radical Reconstruction program was complete.

Legends

By the end of the nineteenth century and increasingly after 1900, a legend of Reconstruction took form in American popular consciousness. Most white people came to believe that Reconstruction was a time of degradation and humiliation for white southerners. Omnipresent northern (and African American) soldiers bullied them for a decade. They languished under the political domination of ignorant former slaves who were incapable of good citizenship, carpetbaggers (northerners who went south in order to exploit the tragedy of defeat), and scalawags (white southerners of low caste who cooperated with blacks and Yankees).

The "Black Reconstruction" governments, the legend continued, were hopelessly corrupt as well as unjust. The blacks, carpetbaggers, and scalawags looted the treasuries and demeaned the honor of the southern states. Only by heroic efforts did decent white people, through the Democratic party, redeem the southern states once they had retaken control of them. Some versions of the legend glamorized the role of secret terrorist organizations, such as the Ku Klux Klan, in redeeming the South.

The Kernel of Truth

As in most legends, there was a kernel of truth in this vision of Reconstruction. The Radical governments did spend freely. There was plenty of corruption in southern government; for example, the Republican governor of Louisiana, Henry C. Warmoth, banked $100,000 during a year when his salary was $8,000. In 1869, the state of Florida spent as much on its printing bill (a notorious budget line in which to hide thievery) as was spent on every function of state government in 1860.

Sometimes the theft was open and ludicrous. Former slaves in control of South Carolina's lower house voted a payment of $1,000 to one of their number who lost that amount in a bet on a horse race. Self-serving carpetbaggers were numerous, as were vindictive scalawags and incompetent black officials.

The Legend in Perspective

No doubt, some soldiers were rough with former rebels, especially during the first years of reconstruction. But Radical Reconstruction did not rest on military rule. There were just 15,000 Union troops in the South in 1867, only 6,600 in 1870, and a mere 3,000 in 1876. This was not the stuff of which military dictatorships are made.

As for political corruption, large governmental expenditures were unavoidable in the postwar South. Southern society was being rebuilt almost from scratch—an expensive proposition. It was the lot of the Radical state governments to provide social services—for whites as well as blacks—that had simply been ignored in the southern states before the Civil War. Statewide public school systems were not founded in the South until Reconstruction. Programs for the relief of the destitute and the handicapped were likewise nearly unknown before Republicans came to power.

Corrupt politicians are inevitable in times of massive government spending, no matter who is in charge; shady deals were not unique to southern Republican governments during the 1860s and 1870s. The most flagrant theft of public treasuries during the period was the work of Democrats in New York, strong supporters of white southerners who wanted to reduce the blacks to peonage. (New York's Tweed

> ### Birth of a Legend
>
> The legend of a South "prostrate in the dust" during Reconstruction had its origins during the Reconstruction era. In 1874, journalist James S. Pike wrote of "the spectacle of a society suddenly turned bottomside up. . . . In the place of this old aristocratic society stands the rude form of the most ignorant democracy that mankind ever saw, invested with the functions of government. It is the dregs of the population habilitated in the robes of their intelligent predecessors, and asserting over them the rule of ignorance and corruption, through the inexorable machinery of a majority of numbers. It is barbarism overwhelming civilization by physical force."

Ring also spent fabulous sums on "printing.") In fact, the champion southern thieves of the era were not Radicals but white Democrats hostile to black participation in government. After a Republican administration in Mississippi ran a clean, nearly corruption-free regime, the first post-Reconstruction treasurer of the state absconded with $415,000. This paled compared to the swag usurped by E. A. Burke, the first post-Reconstruction treasurer of Louisiana, who took $1,777,000 with him to Honduras in 1890.

As for the carpetbaggers, many of them brought much-needed capital to the South. They were hot to make money, to be sure, but in the process of developing the South, not as mere exploiters. Many of the scalawags were by no means unlettered "poor white trash," as the legend had it, but southern Whigs who disapproved of secession and who, after the war, drifted naturally, if briefly, into the Republican party that their northern fellow Whigs had joined.

Blacks in Government

The blacks who rose to high office in the Reconstruction governments were rarely ignorant former field hands. Most, at the upper level, were well-educated, refined, even rather conservative men. Moreover, whatever the malfeasances of Radical Reconstruction, the blacks could not be blamed; they never controlled the government of any southern state. For a short time, they were the majority in the legislatures of South Carolina (where blacks were the

NOTABLE PEOPLE

Blacks in Congress

Better a white crook than a black crook; better a white grafter than a black of stature and probity. Such was the view of the "Redeemers," white Democrats who wrested control of southern state governments from the Republican party during Reconstruction. They depicted black officials as incompetent, corrupt, and uninterested in the welfare of the South as a whole. With most southern whites contemptuous of the recently freed slaves, it was an effective appeal. Other issues paled into near invisibility in what seemed the blinding urgency in asserting "white supremacy."

At low levels, many black officeholders were incompetent and self-serving. A few high in state administrations were venal grafters. That their Redeemer challengers were rarely better and often worse did not, however, lend a reflective bent to southern voting behavior. Rather, race was all.

While none of the blacks who sat in Congress in the wake of the Civil War may be said to have been statesmen of the first order, as a group they were as able and worthy a lot as the era's other "ethnic delegations" in the Capitol, any random selection of farmer-congressmen or businessmen-congressmen, any northern or western state delegation of either party, any random selection of 22 Redeemers.

Between 1869 and 1901, 20 blacks served in the House, two in the Senate. South Carolina, where blacks outnumbered whites, sent eight; North Carolina four; Alabama three; and Virginia, Georgia, Florida, Louisiana, and Mississippi one each. Both black senators, Hiram K. Revels and Blanche K. Bruce, represented Mississippi, where potential black voters also outnumbered whites.

Thirteen of the twenty-two had been slaves before the Civil War, the others were lifelong free blacks. Their educational attainment compared well with that of Congress as a whole. Ten of the black congressmen had gone to college, five had graduated. Six were lawyers (rather less than among all congressmen—nothing for which to apologize); three were preachers; four farmers. Most of the others were skilled artisans, by no means "the dregs of society" as the Redeemers ritually portrayed them.

Hiram Revels was a Methodist pastor. He was born in North Carolina in 1822 but, as a free black, prudently removed to Indiana and Ohio where, during the Civil War, he organized a black regiment. The end of the war found him in Natchez where a cultivated and conservative demeanor (and a willingness to defer to white Republicans) made him an attractive candidate for the Senate.

Blanche K. Bruce was born a slave in 1841, but

Hiram Revels (left) and Blanche K. Bruce (right), both of Mississippi, were elected to the United States Congress during Reconstruction.

he was well educated: his owner leased him to a printer. In 1861, he escaped from his apparently lackadaisical master and, in the wake of the Union troops, moved to Mississippi. His record in the Senate was conservative and quiet.

The most durable of the black congressmen was J. H. Rainey of South Carolina. He sat in Congress between 1869 and 1879, winning his last election in the year of the Hayes-Tilden debacle. In most of his district, blacks outnumbered whites by 6 to 1 and 8 to 1. He was retired in the election of 1878 only as a consequence of widespread economic reprisals against black voters and some little violence.

Rainey's parents had bought their freedom long before the Civil War but, in 1862, he was drafted to work on the fortifications in Charleston harbor, a condition that was tantamount to enslavement. However, Rainey escaped to the West Indies and worked his way to the North, returning to his home state early during Reconstruction.

Rainey was indeed vindictive toward the white South, exploiting racial hostilities as nastily as any Redeemer on the other side. Most of the black congressmen were, unsurprisingly, preoccupied with civil rights issues. No doubt, had South Carolina's blacks retained the franchise, Rainey would have exploited racial hostility as destructively as his opponents.

However, Rainey was by no means oblivious to other questions. By the end of the 1870s, he used his modest seniority to work for southern economic interests that transcended the color line. He defended the rights of Chinese in California on conservative "pro-business" Republican, as well as racial, grounds and attempted to improve relations with the black republic of Haiti.

George H. White was the last black to sit in Congress from a southern state before the passage of the Civil Rights Act of 1965. Born a slave in 1852, he attended Howard University in Washington (then a black institution) and practiced law in North Carolina.

In 1896, he won election to the House of Representatives by adding a number of white Populist votes to a black Republican bloc. At the time, some southern Populists, like Thomas Watson of Georgia, preached interracial political cooperation in an attempt to build a solid agrarian front to the "Bourbons" into which the Redeemers had been transformed. Unlike the northern Populists, who fastened on the Republican party as their chief enemy, southern Populists sometimes saw allies in black Republican voters. Their issues were agrarian: almost all southern blacks tilled the soil.

This put black politicians like White in an impossible situation. Preferment in the national Republican party required him to adhere to a line that, under President William McKinley, also elected in 1896, became conservative and imperialistic. White spoke out on behalf of a high tariff—albeit on the grounds that it favored the workingman: "the ox that pulls the plow ought to have a chance to eat the fodder"—and favored the Spanish-American War.

Inevitably, his positions alienated those whites who had helped elect him. Moreover, southern Populism was undergoing a momentous transformation during the late 1890s. Shrewd Democratic party politicians like Benjamin "Pitchfork Ben" Tillman combined a populist appeal to poor whites with an incendiary hatred of blacks.

Racial hatred was the staple of demagogues like Tillman (and, soon enough, Tom Watson in Georgia). However, they also hammered on the fact that southern blacks voted overwhelmingly Republican and that meant a "plutocratic" federal government.

Conservatives like White were easy targets and, in 1898, the North Carolina Populists switched sides, supporting the Democratic candidate and almost ousting White after only one term.

He knew his political future was doomed and compensated for "an organization man's" first term by speaking out loudly during his second about what was happening in the South (while most white Republicans merely shrugged). Only after 1898 did he fasten almost exclusively on civil rights issues, describing himself as "the representative on this floor of 9,000,000 of the population of these United States."

By 1900, black voters in White's district had been reduced to a fragment. He did not even bother to stand for reelection and sure humiliation. Instead, in his farewell speech in 1901, he delivered his finest oration, an eloquent speech that served as the coda to Reconstruction's failure to integrate blacks into the American polity:

> These parting words are in behalf of an outraged, heartbroken, bruised and bleeding, but God-fearing people, faithful, industrial, loyal people, rising people, full of potential force. The only apology that I have to make for the earnestness with which I have spoken is that I am pleading for the life, the liberty, the future happiness, and manhood suffrage for one-eighth of the entire population of the United States.

majority of the population) and precisely one-half of the legislature of Louisiana. Only two blacks served as United States senators, Blanche K. Bruce and Hiram Revels, both cultivated men from Mississippi. No black ever served as a governor, although Lieutenant Governor P. B. S. Pinchback of Louisiana briefly acted in that capacity when the white governor was out of the state. Whatever Reconstruction was, its color was not black.

Redemption

The crime of Reconstruction in the eyes of most southern whites was that it allowed blacks the opportunity to participate in government. The experiment failed because black voters were denied an economic foundation on which to build their civil equality, and because northerners soon lost interest in the ideals of the Civil War.

Because few of them owned land, the blacks of the South were dependent on white landowners for their sustenance. When southern landowners concluded that it was to their interest to eliminate the blacks from political life, they could do so by threatening unemployment.

Unprotected former slaves could not command the respect of poorer whites, who provided most of the members of terrorist organizations like the Ku Klux Klan, which was founded in 1866 by former slave trader and Confederate general Nathan Bedford Forrest. These nightriders, identities concealed under hoods, frightened, beat, and even murdered blacks who insisted on voting. Congress outlawed and, within a few years, the army effectively suppressed the Klan and similar organizations like the Knights of the White Camellia, but, in the meantime, many blacks were terrorized into staying home on election day.

Congress was unable to counter the conviction of increasing numbers of white southerners that only through "white supremacy," the slogan of the southern Democratic parties, could the South be redeemed. In most southern states, where whites were the majority, an overwhelming white vote on this issue alone was enough to install legislators and governors who promptly found effective ways to disenfranchise the blacks.

In the North and West, each year that passed saw the deterioration of interest in the rights of southern blacks. At no time had more than a minority of northern whites truly believed blacks to be their equals. As an era of unprecedented economic expansion unfolded in the wake of the Civil War, and unprecedented scandals rocked the administration of Ulysses S. Grant, to whom the protection of black civil rights was entrusted, support for Reconstruction dwindled. Albion W. Tourgée, a white northerner who fought for black civil equality in North Carolina, wrote that trying to enforce the Fourteenth and Fifteenth Amendments without federal support was "a fool's errand."

THE GRANT ADMINISTRATION

Ulysses S. Grant was the youngest man to be president up to his time, only 46 years of age when he took the oath of office in 1869. In some ways, his appearance remained as unimpressive as when reporters caught him whittling sticks on the battlefield. Stoop-shouldered and taciturn in public, Grant has a peculiar frightened look in his eye in most of the photographs of him, as though he suspected he had risen above his capabilities.

In fact, Grant disliked the duties and power of the presidency. It was the perquisites of living in the White House that he fancied. He took with relish to eating caviar and tournedos sauce béarnaise and sipping the best French wines and cognac. The earthy general whose uniform had looked like that of a slovenly sergeant developed a fondness for expensive, finely tailored clothing.

Indeed, the elegant broadcloth on his back was the emblem of Grant's failure as president. Money and fame came too suddenly to a man who spent his life struggling to get by. Both he and his wife were overwhelmed by the adulation heaped on him. When towns and counties took his name, and when cities made gifts of valuable property and even cash—$100,000 from New York City alone—Grant accepted them with a few mumbled words of thanks. He never fully understood that political gift-givers were actually paying in advance for future favors. Or, if he did understand, he saw nothing wrong in returning kindness with the resources at his disposal. Among the lesser of his errors, he gave federal jobs to any of his and his wife's relatives who asked and they were not bashful about asking. Worse, Grant remained as loyal to them as he was loyal to junior officers in the army. In the military, backing up subordinates when they slip up is a virtue, essential to morale. Grant never quite learned that in politics backing up subordinates who steal is less than admirable.

Black Friday

Grant's friends, old and new, wasted no time in stealing. Unlucky in business himself, the president luxuriated in the flattery lavished on him by wealthy men. In 1869, two unscrupulous speculators, Jay Gould and Jim Fisk, made it a point to be seen in public with the president, schemed secretly with Grant's brother-in-law, Abel R. Corbin, and hatched a plot to corner the nation's gold supply.

Having won Corbin's assurance that he would keep Grant from selling government gold, Gould and Fisk bought up as much gold and gold futures (commitments to buy gold at a future date at a low price) as they could. Their apparent control of the gold market caused the price of the precious metal to soar. In September 1869, gold was bringing $162 an ounce. Gould and Fisk's plan was to dump their holdings and score a killing.

Finally grasping that he was an accomplice to a scam, on Friday, September 24, Grant dumped $4 million in government gold on the market and the price collapsed, but Gould and Fisk suffered very little. Jim Fisk simply refused to honor his commitments to buy at higher than the market price and hired thugs to threaten those who insisted. (High finance could be highly exercising during the Grant years.) But businessmen who needed gold to pay debts and wages were ruined by the hundreds, and thousands of workingmen lost their jobs. The luster of a great general's reputation was tarnished before he was president for a year.

Other Scandals

During the construction of the Union Pacific Railway in the years following the Civil War, the directors of the UP set up a dummy corporation called the Crédit Mobilier. This company charged the UP some $5 million for work that actually cost about $3 million. The difference went into the pockets of Union Pacific executives. Because the UP was heavily subsidized by the federal government, and therefore under close scrutiny, key members of Congress were cut in on the deal. Among the beneficiaries was Schuyler Colfax, who was Grant's vice president. Speaker of the House James A. Garfield also accepted a stipend.

Three of Grant's cabinet appointees were involved in corruption. Carriers under contract to the Post Office Department paid kickbacks in return for exorbitant payments for their services. The secretary of war, William W. Belknap, took bribes from companies that operated trading posts on Indian reservations under his authority. He and his subordinates shut their eyes while the companies defrauded the tribes of goods that they were due under the terms of federal treaties. Grant insisted that Belknap leave his post, but since Belknap was Grant's old crony, the president refused to punish him on behalf of cheated Indians.

Nor did Grant punish his secretary of the treasury, Benjamin Bristow, or his personal secretary, Orville E. Babcock, when he learned that they sold excise stamps to whiskey distillers in St. Louis. Whenever the president came close to losing his patience (which was considerable), Roscoe Conkling or another stalwart reminded him of the importance of party loyalty. Better a few scoundrels escape than party morale be damaged and the Democrats take over.

The Liberal Republicans

Although the full odor of the Grant scandals was loosed only later, enough scent hung in the air in 1872 that a number of prominent Republicans broke openly with the president. Charles Sumner of Massachusetts, a senator since 1851 and chairman of the Senate Foreign Relations Committee, split with the president over Grant's determination to annex the island nation of Santo Domingo to the United States.

Carl Schurz of Missouri and the British-born editor of *The Nation* magazine, E. L. Godkin, were appalled by the steamy atmosphere of corruption in Washington and the treatment of public office as a way of making a living rather than as performing a public service. Schurz and Godkin (although not Sumner) had also given up on Reconstruction, which, whatever his personal sentiments, Grant enforced. Although not necessarily convinced that blacks were inferior to whites, they concluded that ensuring civil rights for blacks was not worth the instability of government in the South, nor the continued presence of troops in the southern states. Better to allow the white redeemers to return to power.

An anti-Reconstruction cartoon depicts the South burdened by military oppression and an evil-looking Grant.

The Election of 1872

This was also the position of the man whom the Liberal Republicans named to run for president in 1872, the editor of the *New York Tribune*, Horace Greeley. He described southern blacks as "simple, credulous, ignorant men," and the carpetbaggers he once encouraged to go south "as stealing and plucking, many of them with both arms around negroes, and their hands in their rear pockets, seeing as they cannot pick a paltry dollar out of them." The freedmen, Greeley and other Liberal Republicans believed, needed the guidance of enlightened gentlemen like himself, or, better than no one, responsible southern whites.

An exciting journalist, Greeley was a terrible choice as a presidential nominee. He was a lifelong eccentric, one of the century's great "nuts." Throughout his 61 years, Greeley clambered aboard almost every reform or fad from abolitionism and women's rights to vegetarianism, spiritualism (communicating with the dead), and phrenology (reading a person's character in the bumps on his or her head).

Even in his appearance, Greeley invited ridicule. He looked like a crackpot with his round, pink face exaggerated by close-set, beady eyes and a wispy fringe of white chin whiskers. He wore an ankle-length overcoat on the hottest days, and carried a brightly colored umbrella on the driest. Sharp-eyed Republican cartoonists like Thomas Nast had an easy time making fun of Greeley.

To make matters worse, Greeley needed the support of the Democrats to make a race of it against Grant, and he proposed to "clasp hands across the bloody chasm." This was asking too much of Republican party regulars. Voters who disapproved of Grant disapproved much more of southern Democrats.

Moreover, throughout his editorial career, Greeley had printed just about every printable vilification of Democrats that the English language offered, especially of southerners. The Democrats did give him their nomination, but southern whites found it difficult to support a lifelong foe. A large black vote for Grant in seven southern states helped give the president a 286-to-66 victory in the electoral college.

Horace Greeley's (1811–1872) eccentric chin whiskers were ridiculed even in an age of fanciful beards.

THE TWILIGHT OF RECONSTRUCTION

The Liberals returned to the Republican party. For all their loathing of the unhappy Grant, upon whom the scandals piled during his second term, the Liberals found their flirtation with the Democrats humiliating. Among them, only Charles Sumner remained true to the cause of the southern blacks. His Civil Rights Act of 1875 (passed a year after his death) guaranteed equal accommodations for blacks in public facilities such as hotels and theaters and forbade the exclusion of blacks from juries. Congress quietly dropped another provision forbidding segregated schools.

The Act of 1875 was the last significant federal attempt to enforce equal rights for the races for 80 years. Not only had northerners lost interest in Civil War idealism, but southern white Democrats had redeemed most of the former Confederacy. By the end of 1875, only three states remained Republican: South Carolina, Florida, and Louisiana.

The Disputed Election

The Democratic candidate in 1876, New York Governor Samuel J. Tilden, called for the removal of troops from these three states, which would bring the white supremacy Democrats to power. The Republican candidate, Governor Rutherford B. Hayes of Ohio, ran on a platform that guaranteed black rights in the South, but Hayes was known to be skeptical of black capabilities and a personal friend of a number of white southern politicians.

When the votes were counted, Hayes's opinions seemed to be beside the point. Tilden won a close popular vote, and he appeared to sweep the electoral college by a vote of 204 to 165. However, Tilden's margin of victory included the electoral votes of South Carolina, Florida, and Louisiana, where Republicans still controlled the state governments. After receiving telegrams from party leaders in New York, officials there declared that in reality Hayes had carried their states. According to these returns, Hayes eked out a 185-to-184 electoral vote victory.

It was not that easy. When official returns reached Washington, there were two sets from each of the three disputed states—one set for Tilden, and one for Hayes. Because the Constitution did not provide for such an occurrence, a special commission was established to decide which set of returns was valid. Five members of each house of Congress and five members of the Supreme Court sat on this panel. Seven of them were Republicans; seven were Democrats; and one, David Davis of Illinois, a Supreme Court justice and once Abraham Lincoln's law partner, was known as an independent. Because no one was interested in determining the case on its merits, each commissioner fully intending to vote for his party's candidate, the burden of naming the next president of the United States fell on Davis's shoulders.

He did not like it. No matter how honestly he came to his decision, half the voters in the country would call for his scalp because he voted down their candidate. Davis prevailed on friends in Illinois to get him off the hook by naming him to a Senate seat then vacant. He resigned from the court and, therefore, the special commission. His replacement was a Republican, and the stage was set for the Republicans to steal the election.

The Compromise of 1877

The commission voted on strict party lines, eight to seven, to accept the Hayes returns from Louisiana, Florida, and South Carolina—thus giving Rutherford B. Hayes the presidency by a single electoral vote. Had that been all there was to it, there might have been further trouble. At a series of meetings, however, a group of prominent northern and southern politicians and businessmen came to an informal agreement that was satisfactory to the political leaders of both sections.

The Compromise of 1877 involved several commitments, not all of them honored, for northern investment in the South. Also not honored was a vague agreement on the part of some conservative southerners to build a lily-white Republican party in the South based on economic and social views that they shared with northern conservatives.

As to the disputed election, Hayes would be permitted to move into the White House without resistance by either northern or southern Democrats. In return, he would withdraw the last troops from South Carolina, Florida, and Louisiana, thus allowing the Democratic party in those states to oust the Republicans and destroy the political power of the blacks.

Despite the proclamations before Inauguration Day that Democrats would fight if Tilden were not elected, there was no trouble. This was not because

494 *Chapter 25 Reconstruction*

the men who hammered out the Compromise of 1877 were so very powerful. It merely reflected the growing disinterest of Americans in the issues of the Civil War and Reconstruction and their increasing preoccupation with the fabulous economic growth of the country. Southern blacks, of course, were the casualties of this watershed year, but since the price they paid was suppression, few whites heard their complaints and fewer were interested.

CHRONOLOGY

1863	Lincoln announces his plan for reconstruction
1864	Congress enacts Wade-Davis Bill, its reconstruction plan. Lincoln pocket-vetoes Wade-Davis Bill
1865	Lincoln assassinated; Andrew Johnson is president
1865–1866	Black codes enacted in former slave states; race riots in several southern cities
1866	Johnson vetoes renewal of Freedmen's Bureau Radical Republicans draw up Fourteenth Amendment National Union party formed Republicans win overwhelming victory in congressional elections
1866–1867	Congress draws up and effects reconstruction plan over presidential veto
1868	Johnson impeached and acquitted Grant elected president
1872	Grant easily reelected over Horace Greeley
1876	Uncertain results in presidential election
1877	Rutherford B. Hayes named president by special commission Reconstruction ended in last three states under Republican control

FOR FURTHER READING

James McPherson, *Ordeal by Fire: The Civil War and Reconstruction*, 1982, is the best one-volume account of Reconstruction. Also see Eric Foner, *Reconstruction: America's Unfinished Revolution*, 1988. See William A. Dunning, *Reconstruction: Political and Economic*, 1907, for the old, harshly critical view of the era's policies that dominated American historical thinking for half a century. For a rejoinder, see W. E. B. Du Bois, *Black Reconstruction*, 1935. John Hope Franklin, *Reconstruction after the Civil War*, 1961, provides a more brief, objective account, as does Herman Belz, *Reconstructing the Union*, 1969. A splendid account of the reaction of blacks to freedom is Leon F. Litwack, *Been in the Storm So Long*, 1979. Also valuable are Joel Williamson, *The Crucible of Race: Black-White Relations in the American South Since Emancipation*, 1984; and Michael Perman, *Emancipation and Reconstruction, 1862–1879*, 1987.

Valuable studies of special topics include Richard N. Current, *Three Carpetbag Governors*, 1967; Stanley Kutler, *Judicial Power and Reconstruction Politics*, 1968; George C. Rable, *But There Was No Peace: The Role of Violence in the Politics of Reconstruction*, 1984; Robert C. Morris, *Reading, 'Riting, and Reconstruction: The Education of Freedmen in the South, 1861–1870*, 1981; Willie Lee Rose, *Rehearsal for Reconstruction*, 1964; Hans A. Trefousse, *The Radical Republicans*, 1969; A. W. Trelease, *KKK: The Ku Klux Klan Conspiracy and Southern Reconstruction*, 1971; C. Vann Woodward, *Reunion and Reaction: The Compromise of 1877 and the End of Reconstruction*, 1951; and Gaines M. Foster, *Ghosts of the Confederacy: Defeat, the Lost Cause, and the Emergence of the New South*, 1987.

This political cartoon of the 1880s shows Uncle Sam weighing the Democratic and Republican parties, represented as roosters. Because they balanced, a few votes could, and did, win an election for either party.

26
CHAPTER

PARTIES, PATRONAGE, AND PORK
Politics in the Late Nineteenth Century

That . . . a man like Grant should be called—and should actually and truly be—the highest product of the most advanced society, made evolution ludicrous. One must be as commonplace as Grant's own commonplaces to maintain such an absurdity. The progress of evolution from President Washington to President Grant, was alone evidence to upset Darwin.

—Henry Adams

The prevailin' weakness of most public men is to Slop over. G. Washington never slopt over.

—Artemus Ward

We have exchanged the Washingtonian dignity for the Jeffersonian simplicity, which was in truth only another name for the Jacksonian vulgarity.

—Henry Codman Potter

If statesmanship gets the formalities right, never mind about the moralities.

—Mark Twain

The presidents of the late nineteenth century are not a heroic lot. Their portraits lined up on a gallery wall—Grant, Hayes, Garfield, Arthur, Cleveland, Harrison, Cleveland again, even McKinley, whose election ended the era—they resemble nothing so much as a line of mourners at a midwestern funeral. They were dignified and conscious of their dignity, to be sure. They were grandly bewhiskered (except McKinley). Their honesty was beyond reproach (except, perhaps, for a little slip on Garfield's part), as was their personal morality (except, perhaps, for a none too secret slip by Cleveland). They were competent to perform executive duties, sobersided and drab (except for Chester A. Arthur), and unexciting. The hosts had to amuse them at their parties, the guests at gatherings the presidents sponsored.

Their lack of charisma, their mere reticence to smile when on public view, is why early twenty-first-century Americans find them so uninteresting. In our age of ceaseless entertainment, short attention spans, and lust for scandal, it is the polished performer who has the edge in winning elections and the colorful character who garners attention.

Moreover, twenty-first-century Americans have gotten used to vigorous chief executives who seize the initiative—who *lead* both at home and abroad. In the days of Grant through William McKinley, presidents believed Congress, the legislative arm of government, should take the lead. The president's job was to represent the nation in his person, to execute laws, to steer the government, and, when necessary, to apply a constitutional brake on a hyperactive Congress.

Finally, there is no doubt that what was most vital in late nineteenth-century America lay not in politics but in the fabulous growth of the economy, the creation of big business and the development of the great "Wild West" so central to American popular culture. The historian might easily be tempted to hasten through the whole subject of politics with a few words—except for two striking facts.

First, politics was itself a business in the late nineteenth century, from White House down to brick-and-board city hall. Politics reflected the nation's preoccupation with getting ahead, with developing and organizing for material gain. Second, Americans loved the sport of politics. In no other period of American history did a higher percentage of eligible voters actually exercise their right to vote. Fully 80 percent of those who were eligible to vote

in the 1870s, 1880s, and 1890s did vote. In the late twentieth century, by comparison, fewer than half the eligible voters turned out at a typical election.

HOW THE SYSTEM WORKED

Presidential elections brought out the most voters of all. In part this was because, nationally, the two major parties were so evenly matched. A man (and in a few western states after 1890, a woman) found plenty of evidence that a vote or two really could make a difference. Between 1872, when Grant won reelection by a smashing 750,000 votes, and 1896, when William McKinley ushered in an era of Republican dominance with an 850,000-vote plurality, two presidential elections (1880 and 1884) were decided by fewer than 40,000 votes in a total of 9 to 10 million. In two elections (1876 and 1888), the winning candidates actually had fewer supporters than the losers: the winners collected their prize in the electoral college.

In fact, the only presidential candidate of either party between 1872 and 1896 to win a majority of the popular vote was Samuel J. Tilden, who lost the "stolen election" of 1876. In losing, Tilden won a larger share of the popular vote than any Democratic presidential candidate between 1832 and 1932!

Solid South and Republican Respectability

The parties were not so well balanced by region, nor among distinct social groups. With the exception of Connecticut, which was evenly divided, New England voted heavily Republican. In the section where Federalism, Whiggery, and abolitionism were strongest, distaste for the party of Jefferson, Jackson, and the old slave owners prevented Democrats from winning many elections.

The upper and middle classes of the Northeast and Midwest were generally Republican. They thought of the GOP, or the "Grand Old Party," as a bastion of morality and respectability, another legacy of the Whigs to the Republican party. Ironically, most big cities, run by cynical if not corrupt political machines, also voted Republican. (The most important exception was Democratic New York.) Finally, those blacks who retained the right to vote after Reconstruction were staunch Republicans. Although the GOP paid little more than rhetorical attention to their rights after 1877, as the party of Lincoln and

How the System Worked 499

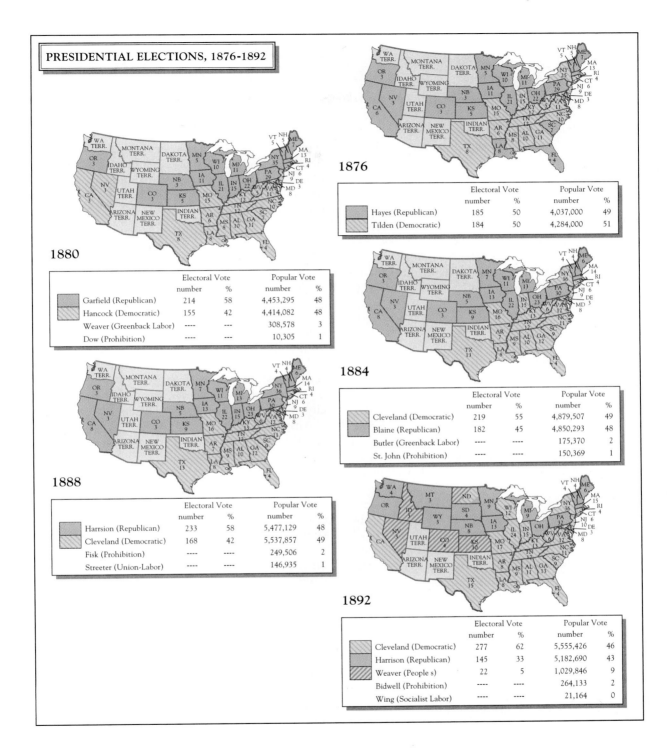

emancipation, the Republicans could count on African-American support.

The Democrats built their national vote upon the foundation of the "Solid South." Blacks and the white people of Appalachia who opposed secession formed large Republican minorities in Virginia, North Carolina, and Tennessee. But not a single former slave state, Union or Confederate, including

Yellow Dog Democrats

In eastern Texas, some white voters took pride in the name "Yellow Dog Democrats." They meant that they were so loyal to their party that if the Republican candidate for office were Jesus Christ, and the Democratic candidate an old yellow dog, they would vote for the yellow dog.

West Virginia, voted Republican in a presidential election during the late nineteenth century. The Democrats also invariably won New York City by appealing to immigrants, and they commanded a majority of the immigrant and white ethnic vote elsewhere.

Swing States

As a result of these steady voting patterns, the outcome of national elections turned on the returns from a handful of "swing states," particularly Illinois, Indiana, Ohio, and New York. In each of these states, with their large blocs of electoral votes, hard-core Republicans and Democrats were about equal in number; the decision was thus in the hands of independents who might swing either way, depending on local issues, party organization, the personalities of the candidates, or a passing whim. Several presidential elections during the period were decided in New York State, where the result depended on how big a majority the New York City Democrats could turn in to counterbalance the Republican edge upstate.

Party leaders believed that the personal popularity of a candidate in the swing states could make

One-Party Politics

When Judge M. B. Gerry sentenced Alfred E. Packer to death for murdering and eating five companions during a blizzard in Colorado in 1873, he stated as a reason for his decision: "There were seven Democrats in Hinsdale County, but you, you voracious, man-eating son of a bitch, you ate five of them."

the difference in a national election. Consequently, a disproportionate number of late nineteenth-century presidential and vice presidential nominees came from Indiana, Ohio, and New York. In the elections held between 1876 and 1892, the major parties filled 20 presidential and vice presidential slots. Eighteen of the twenty (90 percent) were filled by men from the four key states. Eight were from New York, and five more from Indiana. Neither party was primarily interested in finding the best man for the job. They wanted to win an election, and to do so they had to carry the swing states.

Bosses at Conventions

National conventions, which met every four years, played a much more important role in party politics than they do today. The difference was communications. Today, political leaders from every part of the country can discuss affairs with any other by picking up the phone, sending a fax, pecking out an e-mail, or by hopping on a plane. In the late nineteenth century, congressmen saw one another in Washington on a regular basis. However, governors and state and city political bosses, who were often the real powers in party politics, did not.

When they did gather at their quadrennial meetings, they wheeled and dealed, bargained and traded, made and broke political careers. There was no army of television reporters around to shove a microphone and camera into the midst of every circle of politicians who gathered on the floor of the barn-like convention halls. The few newspaper reporters there were could be kept away by strong-arm bodyguards, often ex-boxers, when the discussion promised to be interesting.

Today, incessantly publicized public opinion polls and primary elections inevitably assure that a party's presidential candidate will be picked long before delegates order their first drink at party conventions. In the late nineteenth century, nominations were likely to be decided at the convention, perhaps on the floor, but just as likely by bosses in hotel corridors and suites over oysters, beefsteak, and free-flowing whiskey and Vichy water. Delegates, whose livelihood depended on party bosses, did as they were told.

In the Democratic party, the most important bosses were the head of New York's Tammany Hall, who reliably delivered that city's vote, and the Bourbon leaders of the Solid South. (They were named for

How the System Worked 501

the tribes. In some federal bureaucracies like the Customs Service, there was enough paperwork to bury thousands of clerks wearing green visors and celluloid cuffs to protect their white shirts from smudges of ink and graphite.

For the most part, these positions were filled by supporters of the party in power; activists who worked to get the vote out were rewarded with government employment. In return, in election years their party assessed them a modest percentage of their income to finance the campaign. The result was politics for its own sake. The party scratched the jobholder's back; the jobholder reciprocated.

The higher ranking the party official, the more rewarding the job. Not only was corrupt income possible in some positions, most famously in the Indian Bureau, but it was possible to grow rich quite legally in government service. The post of Collector of Customs in large ports was particularly lucrative. In addition to a handsome salary, the collector was paid a share of all import duties on goods reclaimed from smugglers who were caught at their work. This curious incentive system made for a remarkably uncorrupt Customs Service; there was more to be made in catching violators than in taking bribes from them.

Thus, Collector of the Port of New York Chester A. Arthur earned an average $40,000 a year

A balloon lamp (Chinese lantern), hung at a political rally on behalf of Republican Benjamin Harrison in 1888.

their extreme conservatism, like that of the Bourbon kings of France—not after Kentucky's famous whiskey.) In the Republican party, men like Boss Matthew Quay of Pennsylvania and Boss Thomas C. Platt of New York traded the support of their delegations for the promise of a prestigious cabinet post or a healthy share of the lucrative government offices and contracts that a victorious party had at its disposal.

The Patronage

The spoils system had come a long way since the days of Andrew Jackson and William Marcy. The United States was a big country. There was a lot of patronage—government jobs for the party faithfuls—to go around: 50,000 positions in Grant's time, and 250,000 by the end of the century, compared to just 5,000 when Jackson first defended the principle of handing out government jobs to loyal party workers.

Most government jobs involved real work. There was a postmaster in every town and there were hundreds of postal employees in the cities. Indian agents administered the government's treaty obligations to

This toy scale weighed the comparative merits of Democrat Grover Cleveland and Republican Benjamin Harrison.

502 *Chapter 26 Parties, Patronage, and Pork*

between 1871 and 1874, and in one big case he shared a bounty of $135,000 with two other officials. He was the best paid government official in the country that year, earning more than even the president. And he was assessed a handsome sum for the privilege by the Republican party. On a rather more modest level, a handful of southern blacks benefited from the patronage when the Republican party was in power. Some federal appointments in the South went to African-American Republicans, postmasterships and the like.

Pork

Other party supporters were rewarded with contracts for government work in "pork-barrel" bills. At the end of each congressional session, congressional coalitions pieced together bills to finance government construction projects in each member's district — a new post office here, a government pier there, the dredging of a river channel somewhere else. The idea was not so much to get needed work done, but to reward businessmen who supported the proper party.

Thus, the River and Harbor Bill of August 1886 provided for an expenditure of $15 million to begin over 100 new projects, although 58 government projects that had been started two years earlier remained unfinished and unattended.

Of course, there was not a job or contract for every voter. In order to turn out the vast numbers they did, the parties exploited the emotional politics of memory, the very rational politics of pensions, and ballyhoo that would have horrified Washington, Adams, Jefferson, and even William Henry Harrison.

The Politics of Memory

If most Republicans suppressed thoughts about the civil rights of blacks, they remembered the Civil War. Party orators specialized in "waving the bloody shirt," reminding northern voters that Democrats had caused the Civil War. Lucius Fairchild, a Wisconsin politician who lost an arm in battle, literally flailed the air with his empty sleeve during campaign speeches. With armless and legless veterans hobbling about every sizable town to remind voters of the bloodletting, it was an effective technique.

The Civil War loomed over the period. Between 1868 and 1901, every president but the Democrat Grover Cleveland had been an officer in the Union

---

The Surplus

Many late nineteenth-century congressmen voted for dubious veterans' pensions and pork-barrel bills because spending won votes. However, there was also a profoundly good economic reason to get rid of the government's money during the 1880s. Bizarre as it seems to us today, with the federal government's huge debt, in the 1880s the United States Treasury collected about $100 million more in taxes each year than it spent. Each dollar that came to rest in the treasury was a dollar less in circulation, feeding the economy. Allowing the surplus to grow meant risking a depression.

Reducing revenue was out of the question. More than half the government's collections came from the tariff, which was backed by powerful interests. So, the government spent on pensions, often dubious internal improvements, and during the 1890s, on the construction of a large modern navy.

Even then, it took a major depression and war to wipe out the surplus. In 1899, after the war with Spain, the government had a deficit of $90 million. There have been years since when more money flowed into the treasury than out, but there has never again been cause to worry about a surplus.

Army. When Cleveland, believing that sectional bitterness was fading, issued an order to return captured Confederate battle flags to their states for display at museums and war monuments, an angry protest in the North forced him to back down and contributed to his failure to win reelection the next year.

The man who defeated Cleveland in 1888, Benjamin Harrison, was still waving the bloody shirt after 20 years and not apologizing for it. "I would a thousand times rather march under the bloody shirt, stained with the lifeblood of a Union soldier," Harrison told voters, "than march under the black flag of treason or the white flag of cowardly compromise." Dwelling on the past could not possibly be constructive, but it won elections, even for the Democrats in the South. They waved the Confederate Stars and Bars, reminding voters of the nobility of the lost cause and of the white supremacy that the Redeemer Democrats had salvaged from that cause and from the "Black Republicans."

> ### Waving the Bloody Shirt in Indiana
>
> "Every unregenerate rebel, . . . every man who labored for the rebellion in the field, who murdered Union prisoners by cruelty and starvation calls himself a Democrat. Every wolf in sheep's clothing who pretends to preach the gospel but proclaims the righteousness of man-selling and slavery; every one who shoots down negroes in the streets, burns up negro school-houses and meeting-houses, and murders women and children by the light of their own flaming dwellings, calls himself a Democrat. . . . In short, the Democratic party may be described as a common sewer and loathsome receptacle, into which is emptied every element of treason North and South, every element of inhumanity and barbarism which has dishonored the age."
>
> —Oliver Morton

Vote Yourself a Pension

In their pension policy, the Republicans converted the bloody shirt into dollars and cents. Soon after the war ended, Congress provided for pensions to Union veterans who were disabled from wartime wounds and diseases. The law was strictly worded, in fact excessively so. Many genuinely handicapped veterans did not qualify under its terms. Instead of changing the law, however, northern congressmen took to introducing special pension bills that provided monthly stipends for specifically named constituents who persuaded them that their case was just.

By the 1880s, the procedure for awarding special pensions was grossly abused. Congressmen took little interest in the truthfulness of the petitioner or the worthiness of his grievance. (One applicant for a pension had not served in the army because, he said, he had fallen off a horse on the way to enlist.) They simply introduced every bill that any constituent requested. When almost all Republicans and many northern Democrats had a few special pension bills in the hopper, the bills were rushed through collectively by voice vote. Instead of declining as old veterans died, the cost of the pension program actually climbed to $56 million in 1885 and $80 million in 1888. Pensions made up one of the largest line items in the federal budget, and a veterans' lobby, the Grand Army of the Republic (GAR), came to serve effectively as a Republican political action committee.

The GAR

In 1888, Congress passed a new general pension bill that granted an income to every veteran who served at least 90 days in the wartime army and was disabled for any reason whatsoever. An old soldier who fell off a bar stool in 1888 was eligible under its terms. "Disability" was interpreted with the generosity of a Santa Claus.

President Cleveland vetoed the law and was sustained. The Republicans ran against him that year with the slogan "Vote Yourself a Pension" and won the election. The next year, the new president, Benjamin Harrison, signed an even more generous Dependent Pensions Act and appointed the head of the GAR, James "Corporal" Tanner, to distribute the loot. "God help the surplus," Tanner said, referring to the money in the treasury. He meant it. By the end of Harrison's term, Tanner had increased the annual expenditure on pensions to $160 million. Local wits

In 1902, 40 years after Antietam and Shiloh, members of the Grand Army of the Republic were still a staple of Memorial Day parades. They were almost always Republican voters.

504 Chapter 26 Parties, Patronage, and Pork

> ### Civil War Pensions
>
> Between 1890, when pensions for veterans of the Union Army and their dependents were paid practically for the asking, and 1905, when the practice was prohibited, it was by no means uncommon for very young ladies to marry very old veterans in order to collect widow's pensions after their bridegrooms died. As late as 1983, 41 Civil War widows were still receiving a monthly check of about $70 from the federal government.

took wry notice of young women who married doddering old Billy Yanks who had a gleam in their eyes and a check in the mail.

Northern Democrats posed as the party of principle in the controversies over the bloody shirt and pensions. In the South, however, Democrats played the Civil War game in reverse. State governments provided benefits for Confederate veterans.

PRESIDENTS AND PERSONALITIES

In the wake of the Grant scandals, a presidential candidate's reputation for honesty became a popular campaign cry. In 1876, the Republicans turned to Rutherford B. Hayes, and the Democrats to Samuel J. Tilden—largely because, as governors of Ohio and New York respectively, they had never stolen a cent. Hayes and his running mate, *The Nation* editorialized, were "eminently respectable men—the most respectable men, in the strict sense of the word, the Republican party has ever nominated." When Hayes was named the victor in the "stolen election," Democrats took particular delight in calling him "His Fraudulency" or "Rutherfraud" B. Hayes.

Hayes, Integrity, and Oblivion

In truth, Hayes was an honest man, amiable and obliging within the law. A Civil War hero who was twice seriously wounded, he was the first president who traveled for pleasure rather than on military or diplomatic missions. According to drinkers, there was little pleasure to be had at White House social functions. Mrs. Hayes disapproved of alcoholic bev-

erages and would not serve them at the White House, earning the by-no-means affectionate nickname, "Lemonade Lucy."

As president, Hayes pleased Lucy but not a great many people in his own party. Old Radical Republicans were ired by his abandonment of southern blacks to Redeemer Democrats. (In fact, Hayes was obligated to do so by the Compromise of 1877.) Neither of the Republican party's two major factions, the "Stalwarts" (Grant supporters) or the "Half-Breeds" (critics of Grant) believed that Hayes allotted them as much patronage as they deserved. There never was a question of renominating him; even Hayes yearned to pack up and hit the tourist road.

Long before his term ended, two prominent Republicans announced their intention of succeeding Hayes. One was James G. Blaine of Maine, leader of the Half-Breeds. The other was Ulysses S. Grant, out of office four years, just back from a world tour, and nearly bankrupt. He needed the salary; he resented the fact that in becoming president earlier he was obligated to give up his lifetime pay as a general. And the leader of the Stalwarts, an old Radical who despised Blaine, Roscoe Conkling of New York, persuaded Grant that it was his duty to run.

Garfield: A Dark Horse

Neither Blaine nor Grant was able to win a majority of the delegates to the Republican convention. They were frustrated by the ambitions of several favorite-son candidates, men who came to Chicago backed only by the delegations of their own states. The hope of the favorite son is that there will be a deadlock be-

> ### Spiked Oranges
>
> Lucy Hayes allowed no alcoholic beverages in the White House—or so she thought. According to Washington newspapermen, a bibulous lot, they bribed White House servants to serve them punch and oranges spiked with rum—or so they thought. After he left the presidency, Rutherford Hayes insisted that the joke was on the drinkers. He said that he and his wife knew of the journalists' plan and had their servants spike the drinks and fruit with a nonalcoholic beverage that tasted like rum.

tween the front-runners, forcing the tired delegates to turn to him, the favorite son, as a compromise candidate.

After 34 ballots, the Blaine men recognized that their hero's cause was lost. However, instead of turning to one of the favorite sons, whom the Blaine backers held responsible for the senator's disappointment, they switched their votes to a man whose name was not even in nomination, James A. Garfield of Ohio. On the thirty-sixth ballot, he became the Republican candidate.

Garfield was a Half-Breed, a Blaine supporter, but he played on Roscoe Conkling's bottomless vanity by traveling to New York to seek the boss's blessing and to promise him a share of the patronage. So Garfield went to the polls with a nominally united party behind him.

The Democrats, having failed to win with an antiwar Democrat in 1868 (Seymour), a Republican maverick in 1872 (Greeley), and a rich reformer in 1876 (Tilden), tried their luck with their own Civil War general, Winfield Scott Hancock. An attractive if uninspiring man, he made the election extremely close. Garfield drew only 10,000 more votes than Hancock, just 48.3 percent of the total.

Another Presidential Murder

Garfield was a more intelligent and substantial man than his opportunistic career indicates. Whether or not he would have blossomed as president cannot be known, for he spent his four short months as an active chief executive doing little but sorting out the claims of Republican party workers to government jobs. At one point he exclaimed in disgust to Blaine, his secretary of state, that he could not understand why anyone pursued the presidency, considering all of its trivial tawdry concerns.

Garfield tried to placate both wings of the party. But when he handed the choicest plum of all, the post of collector of customs of the Port of New York to a Blaine man, Roscoe Conkling openly broke with the president. He and his protégé in the New York Republican machine, Thomas Platt, resigned their seats in the Senate. Their intention was to remind Garfield of their political power by having the state legislature reelect them.

By the summer of 1881, it appeared that Conkling and Platt had lost their battle. The Garfield-Blaine Half-Breeds succeeded in blocking their reelection. But the issue was finally resolved by two gunshots in a Washington train station. Charles Guiteau was a ne'er-do-well preacher and bill collector who worked for the Stalwarts but was not rewarded with a government job. On July 2, 1881, he walked up to Garfield as he was about to depart on a holiday and shot him twice in the small of the back. After living in excruciating pain for 11 weeks, the second president to be murdered died on September 19th.

"I am a Stalwart! Arthur is president!" Guiteau shouted after firing the fatal shots. He meant that the new president was none other than Conkling's longtime ally, Vice President Chester A. Arthur. The deranged Guiteau expected Arthur to free him from prison and reward him for his patriotic act. Once in office, however, Chester Arthur, recently the "prince of spoilsmen," proved to be an able and uncorrupt president who signed the first law to limit a party's use of government jobs for political purposes.

Civil Service Reform

The Pendleton Act of 1883 established the Civil Service Commission, a three-man bureau empowered to draw up and administer examinations for applicants for some low-level government jobs. Once in these civil service jobs, employees could not be fired simply because the political party to which they belonged lost the presidency.

At first, only 10 percent of 131,000 government workers were protected by civil service. However, the Pendleton Act empowered the president to add job classifications to the civil service list at his discretion. Because the presidency changed party every four years between 1880 and 1896, each incumbent's partisan impulse to protect his own appointees in their jobs—a violation of the spirit of civil service reform—led by the end of the century to a fairly comprehensive civil service system.

Thus, after the Democrat Grover Cleveland was elected in November 1884, but before he took office in March 1885, outgoing President Chester Arthur protected a number of Republican government employees by adding their job classifications to the civil service list. Cleveland did the same thing for Democratic government workers in 1888, Benjamin Harrison for Republicans in 1892, and Cleveland again for Democrats in 1896. By 1900, 40 percent of the federal government's 256,000 employees held civil service positions. About 30 percent of government

Notable People

James Abram Garfield (1831–1881)

Perhaps if he had lived longer, he would be better understood. As it is, James A. Garfield of Cuyahoga County, Ohio, is one of the most puzzling (and disappointing) personalities of the late nineteenth century. A man of exceptional intelligence and talent, he has gone down in history as just another lackluster politician in an age that was crowded with them. Perhaps it would have been different if he had made a mark as president. But he was fatally shot just four months after his inauguration in March 1881, the fourth president to die in office, and the second to be assassinated. And yet, even before his dark-horse nomination and election in 1880, Garfield had failed to distinguish himself from his run-of-the-mill colleagues. Perhaps, understanding the character of politics in his era, Garfield consciously strove to be a mediocrity.

James Abram Garfield was born in a log cabin, the last of the frontier presidents. Poverty-stricken then, the family was devastated when Garfield's father died and young James had to shoulder the responsibility of supporting his mother. He worked on a canal boat, developing the powerful physique that, after he was shot in 1881, enabled him to survive for two months while infection festered painfully in his body.

Like Lincoln, Garfield educated himself, not merely to read and write but well enough to gain admission to Williams College. There he distinguished himself, mastering the demanding classical curriculum that was still the rule in colleges. Although he entertained friends by simultaneously writing in Latin with his right hand and Greek with his left, Garfield's erudition was not limited to tricks. His diaries reveal a man who was familiar with history (although not with literature, save the Bible) and who understood, as did very few of his politician contemporaries, the forces of industrialization and urbanization that were changing America.

After serving as an officer in the Civil War, brevetted as a general, Garfield entered Congress as a Radical Republican. He was a leader, becoming speaker of the House, but also a straight party man who risked nothing with imaginative speeches and viewpoints, of which he seemed to have been capable. Indeed, while the details are vague, it appears that he accepted some money from the Crédit Mobilier company during Johnson's presidency.

In 1880, Garfield was elected to the Senate from Ohio and attended the Republican national conven-

---

clerks were women, an unlikely proportion at a time when jobs were given out in order to win votes.

Another provision of the Pendleton Act was the abolition of the assessment system. The parties were forbidden to require that members who held government positions donate a percentage of their salaries to political campaign chests. Until the presidency of Benjamin Harrison (1889–1893), the professional politicians were at a loss as to how to replace these revenues. Harrison's postmaster general, Philadelphia retail king John Wanamaker, came up with the solution. He levied contributions on big businessmen who had an interest, direct or ideological, in Republican victory at the polls. This method, with the Democrats finding their share of big business support, and later drawing from the treasuries of labor unions, remained the chief means of financing national political campaigns until the 1970s.

Honest Chet Arthur

Chester A. Arthur may have been president illegally. The Constitution says that only a native-born American citizen may be president and Arthur's enemies said he was born not in Fairfield, Vermont, as he claimed, but in a cabin a few miles north—across the Canadian line. However that may have been, the urbane and elegant Arthur, resplendent in his furs and colorful waistcoats compared to the gray dour look of the Republicans around him, did a good job in the White House.

Knowing that was so, Arthur wanted a second term. He tried to mend fences with the Stalwarts

tion as floor manager for presidential hopeful John Sherman. When the convention deadlocked and turned quickly to Garfield as its nominee, he remained silent. Sherman was convinced that he had been betrayed. In fact, Garfield allowed his opportunities to develop without either encouraging them or choking them off—again, standard operating procedure for a politician of the Gilded Age.

He was nominated and elected, but served only four months in good health. Ironically, this exceptional individual who forced himself to be a political hack was struck down at 50 years of age because of one of the most sordid aspects of that era's politics that Garfield tolerated—the patronage.

On July 2, 1881, the president was waiting for a train when Charles Guiteau, an insane man to whom Garfield had refused to give a government position, pumped two bullets into the small of his back. Had the wounds been inflicted in the late twentieth century, Garfield would have been up and around in a few days, the slugs would have been located by x-ray and easily removed, and the danger of infection eliminated with antibiotics. No vital organs were damaged; no bones were broken. But because one bullet was lodged against Garfield's spine, the doctors were afraid to operate. Instead, they treated the president by probing with metal rods and by "irrigating," flooding the worst wound with water. It did more harm than good. After living in excruciating pain for 11 weeks, Garfield died on September 19.

Garfield's single contribution to American political development occurred two years after his death, when Congress enacted the Pendleton Act, which instituted the civil service in the United States. Garfield was a martyr to the principle that lower-level government employees remain in their jobs no matter which party is in power. But would he have signed the bill had he been alive and well in the presidency at that time? As with almost everything about the man, it is impossible to say. On the one hand, he had lived happily with the spoils system during the two decades he had sat in Congress. On the other hand, when he was at the top, the tyranny of the patronage disgusted him. Referring to the fact that most of his time as president was spent dividing up the spoils among his supporters, Garfield exclaimed, "My God! What is there in this place that a man should ever want to get into it!"

by twice offering Roscoe Conkling (a superb lawyer) a seat on the Supreme Court. Conkling twice rejected his old crony's gesture. Arthur tried to woo the Half-Breeds by deferring to Secretary of State James G. Blaine's judgment in foreign affairs. But Blaine would have none of it and resigned from the cabinet. With Conkling's political career in eclipse, Blaine easily won the Republican nomination for the presidency, again at Chicago, in the summer of 1884.

1884: Blaine versus Cleveland

Blaine expected to win the election as well. As usual, New York State seemed to be the key to victory, and Blaine believed that he would run more strongly there than most Republicans. Some old Liberal Republicans, now known as Mugwumps (an Algonkian word for "big chief," a reference to their often pompous self-righteousness), had deserted the

> #### Conkling the Idealist
>
> Although he is chiefly remembered for his cynical attitude toward the patronage and party loyalty, Roscoe Conkling remained truer to the Radical Republican ideals of his young manhood than did most members of his party. Until his death in 1888—he froze to death in a blizzard—Conkling's extremely successful law firm was instructed to take cases from blacks at nominal or no cost.

Secretary of State Blaine aids the wounded President Garfield and identifies his assassin, Charles Guiteau.

party, announcing that the Democratic candidate, Grover Cleveland, was the more honest man.

Blaine expected to make up this defection and more by winning the Irish vote, which was usually in Democratic party pockets. He was popular in the Irish-American community because, in an era when Republican leaders frequently disdained the Catholic church, Blaine had Catholic relatives. Moreover, for reasons of his own, Blaine liked to "twist the lion's tail," taunt the British, the ancestral enemy in many unsmiling Irish eyes. Finally, news broke that seemed a bonus: it was revealed that while Grover Cleveland was a lawyer in Buffalo, he had fathered an illegitimate child. The stringent sexual code of the period seemed to dictate that such a libertine should not be president, and Republicans chanted

>Ma, Ma, Where's my Pa?
>Gone to the White House,
>Ha, ha, ha.

Cleveland nimbly neutralized the morality issue by publicly admitting the carnal folly of his youth and explaining that he tried to make amends by financially supporting the child. For a male (woe betide the errant lady who was exposed), this was enough. Indeed, the Democrats turned the scandal to their advantage when they argued that if Cleveland had been indiscreet in private life, he had an exemplary record in public office, whereas Blaine, admirable as a husband and family man, engaged in several dubious stock deals as a congressman from Maine. Put Cleveland into public office where he shined, they said, and return Blaine to the private life that he richly adorned.

Little Things Decide Great Elections

Just a few days before the election, disaster struck the Blaine campaign. The confident candidate made the mistake of dining lavishly with a group of millionaires in Delmonico's, the grandest restaurant in New York City. This was not a good idea when he was

Issues 509

Grover Cleveland (1837–1908) was the only Democratic president of the late nineteenth century, elected in 1884 and 1892. He was defeated in 1888.

> ### Ordinary People
>
> As the circumstances of Garfield's assassination show, presidents were not so remote and sheltered from the people in the late nineteenth century. When he was shot, the president of the United States was waiting for a train on a public platform.
>
> An incident that involved Rutherford B. Hayes after he left the White House illustrates the point more amusingly. While attending a GAR encampment, Hayes was stopped by a policeman, who brusquely pulled him back to a pathway, and gave him a finger-shaking lesson because he was walking on the grass. Likewise, President Grant, who never lost his love for fast horses, was written a ticket by a Washington officer for speeding.

counting on the votes of poor, class-conscious Irishmen. Then, in another group, he ignored the statement of a Presbyterian minister, Samuel Burchard, who denounced the Democrats as the party of "rum, romanism, and rebellion," that is, of the saloon, the Roman Catholic church, and southern secession.

This was pretty ordinary stuff in Republican oratory of the period, but Blaine was not fighting the campaign with an ordinary strategy. He was wooing Irish-American votes, and the Irish were sensitive about their Catholic religion. When Democratic newspapers plastered the insult "romanism" across their front pages, Blaine rushed to express his sincere distaste for this kind of bigotry and to explain that had he heard Burchard's words, he would have called him on them. But the damage was done. The Irish voters trundled back into the Democratic column and blizzards upstate snowed many Republican voters in. New York State and the presidency went to Grover Cleveland.

In 1888, four years later, Cleveland was undone in his bid for reelection by a similarly trivial incident. A Republican newspaperman, pretending to be an Englishman who was a naturalized American citizen, wrote to the British ambassador in Washington asking which of the two candidates, Cleveland or Benjamin Harrison of Indiana, would be the better president from the British point of view. Foolishly, the ambassador replied that Cleveland seemed to be better disposed toward British interests. The Republican press immediately labeled Cleveland the British candidate. Thousands of Irish Democrats in New York, who were reflexively hostile to anything or anyone the British favored, voted Republican and helped give that swing state to Harrison.

This sort of folderol, and the color and excitement of political rallies, seemed to make the difference in an era when the two parties were so evenly balanced. Unlike twenty-first-century Americans, who struggle not to drown in entertainment from a dozen media and to whom elections are just one show among many, and among the most boring, late nineteenth-century Americans enjoyed politics as a major diversion. They flocked to rallies in numbers almost unknown today in order to hear brass bands, swig lemonade or beer, and listen to speeches that were more show than statement of principle.

ISSUES

Principles and issues did play a part in late nineteenth-century politics. Within the Republican party, a shrinking minority of leaders tried to revive the party's commitment to protecting the welfare of southern blacks until as late as 1890. When President Grant tried to seize Santo Domingo in 1870, he was frustrated by the resistance of senators from his own party who were impelled by old antiexpansionist prejudices.

However, both episodes illustrate the fact that differences of principle and opinion were as likely to lie within the parties as they were to distinguish one from the other. The political party's business was to win power. Having cooperated in that effort, politicians lined up on issues with only casual or self-serving nods toward the organization to which they belonged.

Even the question of the tariff, the nearest thing to an issue that distinguished Republicans from Democrats, found members of both parties on each side. The level at which import duties were set could inspire orators to sweating, thumping, and prancing. But their position on the issue, low tariff or high protective tariff, depended on the place their constituents occupied in the economy, not on the party to which they belonged, an abstract principle, or even social class.

The Tariff

With the exception of the growers of a few crops that needed protection from foreign producers—like Louisiana's sugar cane planters—farmers inclined to favor a low tariff. Corn, wheat, cotton, and livestock were so cheaply produced in the United States that American farmers were able to undersell local growers of the same crops in large parts of Europe and Asia—if other countries did not levy taxes on American crops in response to high American duties on the goods that those countries shipped to the United States. Moreover, low duties on imported manufactured goods meant lower prices on the commodities that consumers of manufactured goods, such as farmers, had to buy.

The interest of agriculturalists in keeping import duties down meant that the Democratic party, with its powerful southern agrarian contingent, was generally the low-tariff party. However, Republican congressmen representing rural areas also voted for lower rates.

While industrialists, who wanted to protect their factories from foreign competition, were generally Republican and set the high-tariff tone of that party, equally rich and powerful railroad owners and bankers often supported lower duties. Some remained contentedly within the Republican party in the company of other wealthy capitalists; others—the grand financier August Belmont, for example—were Democrats. As far as bankers like Belmont were concerned, the more goods being shunted about the country the better, no matter whether they were foreign or domestic in origin. Railroaders had an added incentive to support a low tariff. They were huge consumers of steel for rails, which was one of the commodities that received the most protection.

In the late nineteenth century, high-tariff interests had their way. After bobbing up and down from a low of 40 percent (by no means a low tariff) to a high of 47 percent, rates were increased to 50 percent in the McKinley Tariff of 1890. That is, on the average, an imported item was slapped with a tax that was equivalent to half of its value.

When a depression followed quickly on the act, Grover Cleveland and the Democrats campaigned against the McKinley rates and won the election of 1892. But the tariff that Congress prepared, the Wilson-Gorman bill, lowered duties by only 10.1 percent—to a level of 39.1 percent of the value of imports. This rate was good enough for Cleveland's supporters in commerce and finance, but too high for the farmers who voted for him. The president's rather wishy-washy way out of his quandary encapsulates the fact that tough issues were intraparty problems, not questions that divided the two parties. Cleveland did not sign the Wilson-Gorman bill; he did not veto it; he let it become law by ignoring it.

The Great Agnostic

Robert G. Ingersoll was a rare politician for the late nineteenth century. He sacrificed a career for the sake of a principle. Acknowledged as one of the greatest orators of his time and a man of immense talent, Ingersoll was an agnostic who preached his uncertainty about the existence of God at every opportunity and with every oratorical trick he knew. As a result, despite his considerable contributions to the Republican party, the only political office that Ingersoll ever held was the comparatively minor one of attorney general of Illinois, and then for only two years.

Money

The issue that would, in the 1890s, shatter the political equilibrium of the 1870s and 1880s was money. The question was: What should be the basis of the circulating currency in America's rapidly expanding economy? Should it be gold and paper money redeemable in that metal from the bank that issued the note? Or should the supply of money be monitored and regulated by the government in such a way as to adjust to changing economic needs?

The controversy had its roots in the Civil War. In 1862, in order to help finance the war effort, the Union government authorized the printing of about $450 million in paper money that was not redeemable in gold. The greenbacks, so called because they were printed in green ink instead of gold on the obverse, were accepted at face value by the federal government. That is, their value in payment of taxes or other obligations was established in the law.

As long as the war went badly and the government's word was of dubious value, individuals involved in private transactions insisted on discounting the greenbacks, redeeming them in gold at something less than face value. Even after the war was won, bankers remained suspicious of any paper money that was not redeemable in gold. The secretaries of the treasury, who shared the conservative views of the bankers, determined to retire the greenbacks. When the notes flowed into the treasury in payment of taxes, they were destroyed and were not replaced by new bills.

The result was deflation, a decline in the amount of money in circulation and, therefore, an increase in the value of gold and of paper money that was redeemable in gold. Prices dipped, and so did wages. It took less to buy a sack of flour or a side of bacon than it had when the greenbacks flowed in profusion. That meant that the farmer who grew the wheat and slopped the hogs received less for his efforts.

Farmers, who were usually in debt, were hit hardest by deflation. They borrowed heavily to increase their acreage and to purchase machinery when the greenbacks were abundant and prices therefore high. After the treasury began to retire the greenbacks, the farmers found themselves obligated to repay these loans in money that was more valuable and more difficult to get. For example, a $1,000 mortgage taken out on a farm during the 1860s represented 1,200 bushels of grain. By the 1880s, when a farmer might still be paying off his debt, $1,000 represented 2,300 bushels.

The Greenback Labor Party

Protesting the retirement of the greenbacks as a policy that enriched banker-creditors at the expense of producer-debtors, farmers formed the Greenback Labor party in 1876. In an effort to convince industrial wage workers that their interests also lay in an abundant money supply, the party chose as its presidential candidate Peter Cooper, New York philanthropist and an exemplary, popular employer.

Cooper made a poor showing, but in the congressional race of 1878, the Greenbackers elected a dozen congressmen, and some Republicans and Democrats rushed to back their inflationary policy. However, President Hayes's monetary policy was as conservative as Grant's had been, and in 1879, retirement of the greenbacks proceeded apace. In 1880, the Greenback Labor ticket, led by a Civil War general from Iowa, James B. Weaver, won 309,000 votes, denying Garfield a popular majority but, once again, failing to affect policy.

In 1884, Benjamin J. Butler led the Greenbackers one more time, but received only one-third of the votes that Weaver won in 1880. The demand to inflate the currency was not dead. Indeed, within a decade the structure of American politics was turned upside down and inside out because of it. But the greenbacks were gone. Just as, after all the fuss and fury died down, industrialists had their way on the tariff, banking interests got the money policy they wanted. When political parties are not built around principles and issues, the best organized interest groups within the parties usually prevail.

Turkey

Roscoe Conkling was a physical-culture enthusiast. He exercised daily and was extremely proud of his exceptional physique. This provided his enemy, James G. Blaine, with an easy target when he described Conkling's "haughty disdain, his grandiloquent swell, his majestic, over-powering, turkey-gobbler strut."

POLITICS IN THE CITY

By 1896, silver had replaced the greenbacks as the talisman of those Americans who wanted to inflate the nation's money supply. Both the Republican and Democratic parties were shaken by a fierce debate in which gold and silver became sacred symbols. (See Chapter 32.) The political atmosphere was religious, evangelical, even fanatical. "Gold bugs" and "free silverites" both believed they were engaged in a holy war against the other in which there could be no compromise, no quarter. The political equilibrium of the 1870s and 1880s was no more, not to mention the minor role issues played in distinguishing the parties.

The Democratic party convention of 1896 was the most tumultuous since the party of Jefferson and Jackson destroyed itself at Charleston in 1860. Richard Croker, the leader of New York City's Democrats, was bewildered by the fury in which the members of his party were running about, arguing, and shaking their fists. He listened to an agitated gold versus silver debate and impatiently shook his head. He could not understand what the fuss was about. As far as he was concerned, gold and silver were both money, and he was all for both kinds.

The Political Machine

Urban politics in the late nineteenth century resembled national politics in some ways. Issues were of secondary importance. What counted first was winning elections. The big-city political party existed, like a business, for the benefit of those who "owned" it. The technique of election victory, therefore, was the profession of the political leader. His skill and willingness to work for "the company," and his productivity in delivering votes, determined how high he rose in an organization as finely tuned as any corporation.

The chairman of the board of the urban political company was "the boss." He was not necessarily the mayor, who was often a respectable front man. The boss coordinated the complex activities of the machine. Voters had to be aroused by the same sort of emotional appeals and hoopla that sustained national political campaigns. The machine was expected to provide small material incentives to more demanding citizens comparable to the GOP's pensions program. The party activists who worked to get the voters out to the polls (the company's "employees"), and kept them happy between elections, were "paid" with patronage and pork courtesy of the city treasury. Control of the municipal treasury was the purpose of politics, not the service of principles or the implementation of a program.

"You are always working for your pocket, are you not?" an investigator into government corruption asked Richard Croker, thinking to embarrass him. Croker snapped back, "All the time, the same as you." On another occasion, Croker told the writer, Lincoln Steffens, "Politics is business, and reporting—journalism, doctoring—all professions, arts, sports—everything is business." Candor as blunt as the prow of a ferryboat was one quality that distinguished municipal politicians from national politicians in the late nineteenth century. Another was that the control of cities that many political machines exercised was so nearly absolute that profiteering in government sometimes took the form of blatant thievery.

The Profit Column

The political machine in power controlled law enforcement. In return for regular cash payments, some politicians winked at the operations of illegal businesses: unlicensed saloons, gambling houses, opium dens, brothels, even strong-arm gangs. "Bathhouse" John Coughlan and "Hinkey-Dink" Kenna, Chicago's "Gray Wolves," openly collected tribute from the kings and queens of Chicago vice at an annual ball.

The political machine in power peddled influence to anyone willing to make a purchase. Although he was no lawyer, William Marcy Tweed of New York, the first of the great city bosses, was on Cornelius Vanderbilt's payroll as a legal adviser. What the commodore was hiring was the rulings of judges who belonged to Tweed's organization. In San Francisco after the turn of the century, Boss Abe Ruef would hold office hours on designated nights at an elegant French restaurant; purchasers of influence filed in between appetizer and entrée, and entrée and roast, and negotiated their bargains.

Kickbacks and Sandbagging

The rapid growth of cities in the late nineteenth century provided rich opportunities for kickbacks on contracts awarded by city governments. In New York, Central Park was a gold mine of padded contracts. The most notorious swindle of all was the New York County Courthouse, a $600,000 building that cost taxpayers $13 million to erect. Plasterers, carpenters, plumbers, and others who worked on the building had standing orders to bill the city two and three and more times what they actually needed to make a reasonable profit and kick back half the padding to Tammany Hall, the men's club that controlled the Democratic party in New York. For example, forty chairs and three tables cost the city $179,000. The most intriguing item was "Brooms, etc.," which cost $41,190.95.

Then it was possible to do business directly with the city at exorbitant prices. Boss Tweed was part-owner of the stationery and printing companies that supplied and serviced the New York City government at ridiculous prices—$5 for each bottle of ink, for example.

Another technique for getting rich in public office was called "sandbagging." It worked particularly well in dealing with traction companies, the street-car lines that needed city permission to lay tracks on public streets. It goes without saying that it took bribes to get such contracts in machine-run cities. Moreover, the most corrupt aldermen, such as Coughlan and Kenna in Chicago, would grant a line the rights to lay tracks on only a few blocks at a time; thus the Chicago "Traction King," Charles T. Yerkes, would be back for a further franchise at an additional cost.

Another variety of sandbagging involved threatening an existing trolley line with competition on a nearby parallel street. Rather than have their traffic decline by half, traction companies coughed up the money to prevent new construction.

It was not necessary to break the law in order to profit from public office. A well-established member of a political machine could expect to be on the city payroll for jobs that did not really exist. In one district of New York City where there were four water pumps for fighting fires, the city paid the salaries of twenty pump inspectors. Probably, none of them ever looked at the pumps. Their real job was to keep the political machine in power at taxpayers' expense.

It was even possible to hold several meaningless city jobs simultaneously. Cornelius Corson, who kept his ward safe for the New York Democratic party from an office in his saloon, was on the books as a court clerk at $10,000 a year, as chief of the Board of Elections at $5,000 a year, and as an employee of four other municipal agencies at $2,500 a

> ### *Vote Early, Vote Often*
>
> Because voter registration methods were quite lax in the nineteenth century, it was not difficult to march a group of men from one precinct house to the next, voting them in each one. When Tim Sullivan was a low-level worker in the New York machine, he used this system with his "repeaters" — unemployed men who voted "early and often" for the price of a day's wages or a day's drinking money:
>
> *When you've voted 'em with their whiskers on, you take 'em to a barber shop and scrape off the chin fringe. Then you vote 'em again with the side lilacs and a mustache. Then to a barber again, off comes the sides and you vote 'em the third time with the mustache. If that ain't enough and the box can stand a few more ballots, clean off the mustache and vote 'em plain face.*

year per job. Another ward boss, Michael Norton, held city jobs that paid him $50,000 a year.

This was a munificent income in the late nineteenth century, but the bosses at the top of the machine did much better. Altogether, the Tweed Ring, which controlled New York City for only a few years after the Civil War, looted the city treasury of as much as $200 million. (Nobody really knew for sure.) Tweed went to jail, but his chief henchman, Controller "Slippery" Dick Connolly, fled abroad with several million dollars.

Richard Croker, head of Tammany Hall at the end of the century, retired to Ireland a millionaire. Timothy "Dry Dollar" Sullivan also rose from extreme poverty to riches as well as adulation; when he

> ### *Above the Issues*
>
> The classic instance of a big-city machine politician avoiding issues occurred at a Fourth of July picnic. New York City boss Charles F. Murphy refused to sing "The Star-Spangled Banner" along with the crowd. When a reporter asked Murphy's aide for an explanation, the aide replied, "He didn't want to commit himself."

died as the result of a streetcar accident, 25,000 people attended his funeral.

Staying in Business

Big Tim's send-off illustrates that despite their generally obvious profiteering, machine politicians stayed in office. Although few of them were above stuffing ballot boxes or marching gangs of "repeaters" from one polling place to the next, they won most elections fairly; the majority of city voters freely chose them over candidates who pledged to govern honestly.

The machines acted as very personalized social services among a hard-pressed people. During a bitterly cold winter in 1870, Boss Tweed spent $50,000 on coal that was dumped by the dozens of tons at street corners in the poorest parts of the city. Tim Sullivan gave away 5,000 turkeys every Christmas. It was the duty of every block captain to report when someone died, was born, was making a first holy communion in the Catholic church, or was celebrating a bar mitzvah in the Jewish synagogue. The sensible ward boss had a gift delivered.

Ward bosses brought light into dismal lives by throwing parties. In 1871, Mike Norton treated his constituents to 100 kegs of beer, 50 cases of champagne, 20 gallons of brandy, 10 gallons of gin, 200 gallons of chowder, 50 gallons of turtle soup, 36 hams, 4,000 pounds of corned beef, and 5,000 cigars.

Ward bosses fixed up minor (and sometimes major) scrapes with the law. In control of the municipal government, the machines had jobs at their disposal, not only the phony high-paying sinecures that the bosses carved up among themselves, but jobs that

Tim "Dry Dollar" Sullivan (right), beloved New York machine politician.

required real work and that unemployed men and women were grateful to have. Boss James McManes of Philadelphia had more than 5,000 positions at his disposal; the New York machine controlled four times that number. When the votes of these people were added to those of their grateful relatives and friends, the machine had a very nice political base with which to fight an election.

The Failure of the Goo-Goos

Not everyone brimmed with gratitude. The middle classes, which paid the bills with their property taxes, periodically raised campaigns for good government—the bosses called them "Goo-Goos"—and sometimes won elections. The Tweed Ring's fall led to the election of a reform organization, and in 1894, even the powerful Richard Croker was displaced. Chicago's "Gray Wolves" were thrown out of city hall, and a major wave of indignation swept Abe Ruef and Mayor Eugene Schmitz out of power in San Francisco in 1906. But until the turn of the century, reform governments were generally short-lived. The machines came back.

One political weakness of the Goo-Goos was that they did not offer an alternative to the informal social services that the machine provided. They believed instead that honest government was synonymous with very inexpensive government. Faced with their great material problems and inclined from their European backgrounds to think of government as an institution that one used or was used by, the immigrants preferred the machines.

Indeed, Goo-Goos often combined their attacks on political corruption with attacks on the new ethnic groups, not a ploy that was calculated to win many friends among recent immigrants. In the persons of the successful machine politicians, however, the ethnics could take a vicarious pleasure in seeing at least some Irishmen, Jews, Italians, Poles, or blacks making good in an otherwise inhospitable society.

Erin Go Bragh

"The natural function of the Irishman," said a wit of the period, "is to administer the affairs of the American city." In fact, a few bosses had other lineages: Cox of Cincinnati and Crump of Memphis were WASPs; Tweed was of Scottish descent; Ruef was Jewish; and Schmitz was German. But a list of nineteenth-century machine politicians reads like a

---

Citizenship

The New York machine naturalized newly arrived immigrants almost as soon as they stepped off the boat. The record day was October 14, 1868, when a Tweed judge swore in 2,109 new citizens, three a minute. One James Goff attested to the "good moral character" of 669 applicants. Two days later, Goff was arrested for having stolen a gold watch and two diamond rings.

---

roll call of clarinetists in a St. Patrick's Day parade: Richard Connolly, "Honest" John Kelley, Richard Croker, George Plunkitt, Charles Murphy, and Tim Sullivan of New York; James McManes (unlike the others, a Republican) of Philadelphia; Christopher Magee and William Finn of Pittsburgh; and Martin Lomasney of Boston.

The Irish were so successful in politics in part because they were the first of the large ethnic groups in the cities, and in part because they were highly political in their homeland as a consequence of rule by Great Britain. Moreover, the Irish placed a high premium on eloquent oratory, which led naturally to politics, and, most important of all, the Irish spoke the English language, a head start in the race to succeed over the other major immigrant groups of the late nineteenth century.

Ethnic Brokers

The primacy of the Irish did not mean that the new immigrants were shut out of politics. On the contrary, the political machine lacked ethnic prejudice. If a ward became Italian and an Italian ward boss delivered the votes, he was welcomed into the organization and granted a share of the spoils commensurate with his contribution on election day. In many cities, while the police forces retained an Irish complexion, sanitation departments and fire departments often were predominantly Italian.

In the mid-twentieth century, it became the unwritten law among New York Democrats that nominations for the three top elective offices in the city (mayor, president of the city council, and controller) be divided among New York's three largest ethnic groups—Irish, Italians, and Jews. Later, with the arrival of Puerto Ricans and of blacks from the

South, certain public offices were assigned to their leaders—for example, president of the borough of Manhattan to a black and political leadership of the borough of the Bronx to a Puerto Rican. Other cities worked out similar arrangements.

CHRONOLOGY

1877–1881	Presidency of Rutherford B. Hayes
1881	Presidency of James A. Garfield
	Garfield assassinated
1881–1885	Presidency of Chester A. Arthur
1883	Pendleton Act reforms civil service
1885–1889	Presidency of Grover Cleveland
1889–1893	Presidency of Benjamin Harrison
1893–1897	Second presidency of Grover Cleveland
1896	William McKinley elected president

FOR FURTHER READING

The best survey of politics during "the Gilded Age," the late nineteenth century, is H. Wayne Morgan, *From Hayes to McKinley: National Party Politics, 1877–1896*, 1969. For a more jaundiced, and once the traditional, view, see Matthew Josephson, *The Politicos, 1865–1896*, 1938. Also valuable are John A. Garraty, *The New Commonwealth, 1877–1890*, 1968; Ray Ginger, *Age of Excess*, 1965; Robert H. Wiebe, *The Search for Order*, 1967; Michael E. McGerr, *The Decline of Popular Politics*, 1986; and Nell Irvin Painter, *Standing at Armageddon: The United States, 1877–1919*, 1987.

On prominent politicians and individual administrations, see Harry Barnard, *Rutherford B. Hayes and His America*, 1954; R. G. Caldwell, *Gentleman Boss: The Life of Chester A. Arthur*, 1975; D. B. Chidsey, *The Gentleman from New York: A Life of Roscoe Conkling*, 1935; Justus T. Doenecke, *The Presidencies of James A. Garfield and Chester A. Arthur*, 1981; David S. Muzzey, *James G. Blaine: A Political Idol of Other Days*, 1934; Allan Nevins, *Grover Cleveland: A Study in Courage*, 1932; and Harry J. Sievers, *Benjamin Harrison: Hoosier Statesman*, 1959.

Concentrating on specific political issues and institutions are A. B. Callow, Jr., *The Tweed Ring*, 1966; Mark W. Summers, *The Era of Good Stealings*, 1993; M. R. Dering, *Veterans in Politics: The Story of the G.A.R.*, 1952; Ari Hoogenboom, *Outlawing the Spoils: A History of the Civil Service Reform Movement, 1865–1883*, 1961; Morton Keller, *Affairs of State: Public Life in Late Nineteenth-Century America*, 1977; Paul Kleppner, *The Third Electoral System, 1852–1892*, 1979; J. Morgan Kousser, *The Shaping of Southern Politics*, 1974; Edward L. Ayers, *The Promise of the New South*, 1992; Paul Escott, *Many Excellent People: Power and Privilege in North Carolina*, 1985; R. O. Marcus, *Grand Old Party: Political Structure in the Gilded Age, 1880–1896*, 1971; Horace L. Merrill, *Bourbon Democracy of the Middle West*, 1953; Walter T. K. Nugent, *Money and American Society, 1865–1880*, 1968; D. J. Rothman, *Politics and Power: The United States Senate, 1869–1901*, 1966; Morton J. Horwitz, *The Transformation of American Law*, 1992; and Tom E. Terrill, *The Tariff, Politics, and American Foreign Policy, 1874–1901*, 1973.

The world's largest steel mill, Homestead, Pennsylvania, about 1900.

27
CHAPTER

BIG INDUSTRY, BIG BUSINESS

Economic Development in

the Late Nineteenth Century

This movement was the origin of the whole system of modern economic administration. It has revolutionized the way of doing business all over the world. The time was ripe for it. It had to come, though all we saw at the moment was the need to save ourselves from wasteful conditions. . . . The day of the combination is here to stay. Individualism has gone, never to return.

—John D. Rockefeller

The growth of a large business is merely the survival of the fittest. The American Beauty Rose can be produced in the splendor and fragrance which bring joy to its beholder only by sacrificing the early buds which grow up around it. This is not an evil tendency in business. It is merely the working out of a law of nature and a law of God.

—John D. Rockefeller, Jr.

520 *Chapter 27 Big Industry, Big Business*

In 1876, the American people celebrated the nation's centennial. It was a hundred years since the founding fathers pledged their lives, their fortunes, and their sacred honor to the causes of independence and liberty. The birthday party, called the Centennial Exposition, was held in Philadelphia, where the Declaration had been signed, and it was a roaring success. Sprawling over the gentle hills of Fairmount Park, housed in more than 200 structures, the great show dazzled ten million visitors with its displays of American history, ways of life, and products.

The emphasis was on the products and the processes for making them. The center of the fair was not the hallowed Declaration, but a building that covered 20 acres and housed the latest inventions and technological improvements: from typewriters and the telephone through new kinds of looms and lathes and a dizzying variety of agricultural machines.

Towering above all the pulleys and belts, five times the height of a man and weighing 8,500 tons, was the largest steam engine ever built, the giant Corliss. Hissing, rumbling, chugging, and gleaming in enamel, nickel plate, brass, and copper, the monster powered every other machine in the building. It was literally the heart of the exposition. It was to the giant Corliss that President Ulysses S. Grant went to open the fair. When he threw the switch that set Machinery Hall in motion, he wordlessly proclaimed that Americans were not just free and independent, but they were hitching their future to machines that made and moved things quickly, cheaply, and in astonishing quantities—industry!

A LAND MADE FOR INDUSTRY

Between 1865 and 1900, the population of the United States more than doubled from fewer than 36 million to 76 million people. The wealth of the American people grew even more rapidly than their numbers. At the end of the Civil War, the annual production of goods was valued at $2 billion. It increased more than six times in 35 years, to $13 billion in 1900.

Even in 1860, the United States was the fourth largest industrial nation in the world, with more than 100,000 factories capitalized at $1 billion. But before the Civil War there was no doubt that the United States was primarily a farmer's country. More than 70 percent of the population lived on farms or in small farm towns. In 1860, scarcely more than a million people worked in industrial jobs. Because many of them were women and children who did not vote, factory workers were an inconsequential force in politics.

By 1876, change was everywhere. Railroads were so central to the national economy that a strike by railway workers the next year shook the country to its foundations. By 1900, $10 billion was invested in American factories, and five million people worked in industrial jobs. During the first years of the 1890s, the industrial production of the United States surpassed that of Great Britain, to put the United States in first place in the world. By 1914, fully 46 percent of the world's industrial and mining economy was American, more than the combined shares of Germany and Great Britain, the second and third leading industrial powers.

An Embarrassment of Riches

Viewed from the late twentieth century, this success story seems to have been as predestined as John Winthrop's throne in paradise. All the ingredients of industrial transformation were heaped upon the United States in an abundance that no other country has enjoyed.

In contrast to the plight of undeveloped countries today, Americans were rich in capital and able to welcome money from abroad without losing control of their own destinies. Once the Union victory in the Civil War assured foreign investors that American government was stable and friendly to commercial and industrial interests, the pounds, guilders, and francs poured in. By 1900, over $3.4 billion in foreign wealth fueled the American economy. Thanks to investors from abroad, Americans had to divert only 11 to 14 percent of their national income into industrial growth, compared with 20 percent in Great Britain half a century earlier and in the Soviet Union some decades later. As a result, the experience of industrialization was far less painful in the New World than in the Old. Americans sacrificed less for the sake of the future than other industrial peoples.

The United States was also blessed in both the size and character of its labor force. The fecund and adaptable farm population provided a pool of literate and mechanically inclined people to fill the skilled jobs the new industry created. Unlike Asian and European peasants who were attached to an ancestral plot of ground and often suspicious of unfamiliar ways, American farmers were always quick to move on at opportunity's call. In the late nineteenth century, not only did the new industries beckon seductively, but the labor-saving farm machinery that factories sent back to the farm made it possible for farm families actually to increase production of crops while their sons and daughters packed themselves off to the city.

During these same years, Europe's population underwent a spurt of growth with which the European economy could not keep pace. Cheap American food products undersold crops grown at home, helping to displace European peasants. They emigrated to the United States by the hundreds of thousands each year, filling low-paying, unskilled jobs. At every level in the process of industrialization, the United States was provided a plenitude of clever hands and strong backs.

Land of Plenty

No country has been so blessed with such varied and abundant natural resources as the United States: rich agricultural land producing cheap food; seemingly inexhaustible forests supplying lumber; deposits of gold, silver, semiprecious metals; and dross such as phosphates and gravel. Most important of all in the industrial age were huge stores of coal, iron, and petroleum.

The gray-green mountains of Pennsylvania, West Virginia, and Kentucky seemed to be made of coal, the indispensable fuel of the age of steam. In the Marquette range of Michigan was a mountain of iron ore 150 feet high. The Mesabi range of Minnesota, just west of the birdlike beak of Lake Superior, was opened in the 1890s to yield iron ore richer and in greater quantity than any other iron mining region in the world.

The United States had a huge, ready-made market for mass-produced goods in its constantly growing population. And with the growth of industry (and the political influence of the industrial capitalist class), government in the United States proved quick to respond to the needs of manufacturers.

"Yankee Ingenuity"

So were inventors. Abraham Lincoln (who himself owned a patent—a device to refloat a sunken steamboat) observed that Americans have "a perfect rage for the new." An English visitor to the Centennial Exposition wrote, "As the Greek sculpted, as the Venetian painted, the American mechanizes." Actually, the new invention that turned the most heads at the great fair, the telephone, was the brainchild of a Scot who

---

Clouded Crystal Balls

The fabulous success of Americans in exploiting technology can obscure the fact that technological pioneers often faced massive resistance in selling their inventions, and often themselves failed to understand the potential of what they had done.

This has been vividly true in the communications field. Thus, in 1845, the Postmaster General rejected an opportunity to purchase the patent for the telegraph for $100,000 because "under any rate of postage that could be adopted, its revenues could [not] be made equal to its expenditures." Within a generation, a private telegraph company, Western Union, was one of the most profitable giants of American business. In 1876, Western Union's president, William Orton, turned down an opportunity to buy Alexander Graham Bell's telephone, saying "What use could this company make of an electrical toy?"

In 1899, of all people, Commisioner of the Patent Office, Charles H. Duell, announced that "everything that can be invented has been invented."

---

came to the United States via Canada, Alexander Graham Bell. Millions of people picked up the odd-looking devices he had set up and, alternately amused and amazed, chatted with companions elsewhere in the room. Young men at the fair dropped a hint of what was to come by "ringing up" young ladies standing across from them, casually striking up conversations that, lacking proper introductions, would have been unacceptable face to face.

It was probably true that only in the United States could Bell have parlayed his idea into the gigantic enterprise it became, the American Telephone and Telegraph Company.

As a writer in the *Saturday Evening Post* at the end of the century put it,

The United States is the only country in the world in which inventors form a distinct profession. . . . With us, inventors have grown into a large class. Laboratories . . . have sprung up almost everywhere, and today there is no great manufacturing concern that has not in its employ one or more men of whom nothing is expected except the bringing out of improvements in machinery and methods."

Young women quickly monopolized the profession of telephone operator when Bell's companies found "boys" to be imprudent and impolite.

The Telephone

Bell was a teacher of the deaf who, while working on a mechanical hearing aid, realized that if he linked two of the devices by wire, he could transmit voice over distance. He was unable to interest the communications giant Western Union in his telephone. "This 'telephone' has too many shortcomings to be seriously considered as a means of communication," an executive of the company wrote. So, Bell set up a pilot company in New York and the telephone seized the American imagination. Rutherford B. Hayes put a telephone in the White House in 1878. By 1880, only four years after they first heard of the thing, 50,000 Americans were paying monthly fees to hear it jangle on their walls. By 1890, there were 800,000 phones in the United States; by 1900, 1.5 million people in the tiniest hamlets knew all about exchanges, party lines, and bored, nasal-voiced operators. Bell's patent, No. 174,465, proved to be the single most valuable patent ever issued.

Edison's Oddest Invention

Alexander Graham Bell invented the telephone, but Thomas Edison invented the word Americans use when they answer a call— "Hello!" Bell wanted to use the nautical term "Ahoy!" Others proposed "What is wanted?," "Are you ready to talk?," or the sounding of a bell signifying the phone had been answered. Edison, who was hard of hearing and was used to shouting in ordinary conversation, drew on an old English word hunters used to hail people at a distance, "Halloo!" to coin a term that, previously, did not exist. Apparently, he first used "Hello!" in the summer of 1877. By 1880, it was widely enough known that Mark Twain used it in a short story. In Twain's *Connecticut Yankee in King Arthur's Court,* published in 1889, operators were known as "Hello Girls."

Narrow Gauge

The short, narrow-gauge feeder lines that snaked into canyons and around mountains to bring out ore or logs were not so colossal as the great trunk lines, but the engineering required to build them was often more demanding. For example, the California Western that brought redwood logs down to the port of Fort Bragg, California, was only 40 miles long but never ran in a straightaway for as much as a mile, crossed 115 bridges, and went through one tunnel 1,122 feet long.

Many systems were useful only locally. But as early as 1892, the eastern and midwestern cities were connected by a long distance network, and rambunctious little western desert communities noted in their directories that "you can now talk to San Francisco with ease from our downtown office." Instantaneous communication was an invaluable aid to business and, as important to some entrepreneurs, it left no written records of dubious transactions as letters and telegrams did.

The Wizard of Menlo Park

Even more celebrated than Bell was Thomas Alva Edison. Written off by his boyhood teachers as a dunce, Edison was, in fact, befuddled throughout life by people who pursued knowledge for its own sake. He was the ultimate, practical American tinkerer who looked for a need—and an opportunity to make money from that need—and he went to work. Despite an abrupt, obnoxious personality, Edison became a folk hero because of the no-nonsense all-American way with which, he said, he approached invention. He said that genius was 1 percent inspiration and 99 percent perspiration. He took pride in his work, not his thoughts. With a large corps of assistants sweating away in his research and development laboratory in Menlo Park, New Jersey, he took out more than a thousand patents between 1876 and 1900.

Most of these patents were for improvements in existing processes. (He perfected a transmitter for Bell.) However, a few of Edison's inventions were seedbeds for wholly new industries: the storage battery, the motion picture projector, and the phonograph. The most important of his inventions was the incandescent light bulb, a means of converting electricity into stable, controllable light.

Young Thomas Edison (1847–1931), already America's most honored inventor.

Electric Light

Edison solved the theoretical principle of the electric bulb—the 1 percent inspiration—almost immediately. Within a vacuum in a translucent glass ball an electrically charged filament or thread should burn (that is, glow) indefinitely. The perspiration part was discovering the fiber that would do the job. In 1879, after testing 6,000 materials, Edison came up with one that burned for 40 hours, enough to make it practical. Before he patented the incandescent light bulb early the next year, Edison improved the filament enough to make it work for 170 hours.

The financier, J. P. Morgan, who loathed the telephone, was fascinated by Edison's invention. His house and bank were among the first electrically illuminated structures in the United States. Morgan realized that many people disliked gas, the principal source of nighttime light. Although clean enough (unlike kerosene), gas could be dangerous. Hundreds

NOTABLE PEOPLE
The Field Brothers

The economic explosion of the late nineteenth century created opportunities from the bottom to the top of American society. Immigrants who had flirted with starvation in the old country found subsistence and comfort. Ordinary Americans moved up into the middle class as skilled workers, managers, and small businessmen. Scions of the old elite, of comfortably fixed, educated, and genteel families who would have been content to have been local eminences in the early nineteenth century found that, in the new America, they had a vast, national arena in which to make their marks.

The Field family of Connecticut is a case in point. Of *Mayflower* vintage, the Fields had produced generation upon generation of farmers, Congregationalist ministers, merchants, and local political leaders. The family was ancient and respectable, but quite unknown beyond its township. Opportunity for the Reverend David Field, born in 1781, meant a midlife exchange of a pulpit in tiny Haddam, Connecticut, for one in Stockbridge, Massachusetts, a scarcely larger town. Four of his six sons, by way of contrast, became national figures in the law, business, technology, and popular culture.

The eldest of them, David Dudley Field (1805–1894), was America's foremost legal reformer. As a lawyer in New York, he observed that the century-old tangle of ordinances that had worked well enough in a small commercial city were inadequate in a burgeoning metropolis and commercial empire. He labored, much of the time drawing on his own resources, to sift, reform, and codify city and state law. Late in his life, he turned to international law, particularly rules governing the conduct of nations during wartime.

New York State adopted David Dudley Field's codification of criminal law in 1881, but not the reforms of the civil code which he proposed. By the 1880s, his influence had been somewhat tarnished by his political and business associations. Field had defended "Boss" William Marcy Tweed, the head of the corrupt political machine that governed New York City during the 1860s, as well as the notorious robber barons Jim Fisk and Jay Gould. However, many of his proposals were incorporated into the English Judicature Acts of 1873-1875, which later spread to British colonies throughout the world.

David Dudley Field had the curious experience of arguing cases before the Supreme Court when his younger brother was an associate justice. Stephen Johnson Field (1816–1899), also an attorney, was a Forty-Niner, rushing off to California in search of gold or, perhaps, litigants. He settled in the boomtown of Marysville, was elected mayor and, in 1857,

of fires were caused when, in a moment of ignorance, forgetfulness, or drunkenness, people blew out the flame instead of turning off the gas. Hotel managers nervously plastered the walls of rooms with reminders that the lights were gas.

The incandescent bulb succeeded as dramatically as the telephone. From a modest start on New York's Pearl Street in 1882 with 85 customers burning 400 lamps, Edison's invention spread so quickly that by 1900, more than 3,000 towns and cities were electrically illuminated. Within a few more years, the gaslight disappeared, and the kerosene lantern survived only on farms and in the poorer sections of the cities.

No single electric company dominated the industry, as American Telephone and Telegraph controlled Bell's patents. Nevertheless, like the railroads, the great regional companies were loosely associated by interlocking directorates and the influence of the investment banks. Edison, a worse businessman than scholar, saw most of his profit go to backers like Morgan. He ended his working life as an employee of mammoth General Electric, the corporate issue of his inventive genius.

The Problem of Bigness

George Westinghouse became a millionaire from his invention of the air brake for railroad trains. By equipping every car in a train with brakes, operated from a central point by pneumatic pressure, Westinghouse solved the problem of stopping long strings of railroad cars. Not only did his air brake save thou-

was named Justice of the California Supreme Court. Stephen Field was a Democrat but also a staunch supporter of the Civil War. In 1863, Abraham Lincoln named him to the U.S. Supreme Court.

On the high court, he proved to be conservative in cases involving business, but also a defender of civil liberties. Indeed, his insistence on defending the rights of Chinese immigrants in California may have cost him further advancement in public life. He was several times considered as a favorite-son candidate for the presidency, but was denied the prize because he had offended white workingmen with his "pro-Chinese" judicial decisions.

Cyrus Field (1819–1892) was a technological visionary of extraordinary persistence. A successful paper manufacturer before he was 30, in 1854 he turned to promoting the idea of a cable between Europe and North America over which telegraphic messages could be sent. Such a device would obviously be of inestimable value to business, but the difficulties of laying such a cable seemed overwhelming. Indeed, Field's first attempt at laying a cable between Ireland and Newfoundland in 1857 broke and a second, in 1858, lasted just three weeks.

In 1865, Cyrus Field tried again, this time using the largest ship in the world, the British-built *Great Eastern*. Almost 700 feet long and 120 feet across, the "great iron ship" was an engineering marvel that was never used properly. Able to power itself by sail, paddle wheel, or screw, it could carry 4,000 passengers and 2,000 crew. Instead of exploiting its size in long voyages, such as between Britain and Australia, the *Great Eastern*'s owners put it on the Atlantic run, where it did not compete well with smaller ships. Repeatedly, its owners went bankrupt.

Cyrus Field saw the *Great Eastern* as a massive cable factory with enough power to run all the mills of Manchester. He outfitted the ship to reel out the continuous, fragile wire that would tie together Old World and New. In 1865, he lost a cable once again but, on July 27, 1866, the connection was made. Despite his achievement, Cyrus Field did not die wealthy. A bit too trusting of his business associates, including Jay Gould, he saw his fortune evaporate by the time of his death.

The youngest Field brother, Henry Martyn Field (1822–1907), was a Presbyterian minister who wrote adulatory biographies of David Dudley and Cyrus (but not, oddly, Stephen). However, he too made his mark as a communicator. During the 1890s, with the American middle class large, energetic, and curious, he wrote best-selling travel books for vicarious sojourners.

sands of lives, but it led to bigger profits for railroads by making longer trains possible.

Well established, Westinghouse turned his inventive genius to electricity and capitalized on Edison's stubborn resistance to alternating current. Edison's direct current served very well over small areas, but it could not be transmitted over long distances. By perfecting a means to transmit alternating current, Westinghouse leapt ahead of his competitor by fully utilizing massive natural sources of power at isolated places such as Niagara Falls.

Like Bell, Westinghouse's invention confronted the single impediment Americans faced in their drive toward massive industrial development. The very vastness of the country was an impediment as well as a blessing. The United States spanned a continent that was dissected by rivers, mountains, and deserts into regions as large as the other industrial nations of the time. If geography had the last word, the United States would have remained a patchwork of distinct manufacturing regions in which small factories produced goods largely for the people of the vicinity alone. Indeed, this is a fair description of manufacturing in the United States through the period of the Civil War.

THE RAILROAD REVOLUTION

The steam railroad conquered America's awesome geography. The steam-powered locomotive, belching white steam and black smoke, its whistle piercing

526 *Chapter 27 Big Industry, Big Business*

> ### *Watering Stock*
>
> Daniel Drew was notorious for watering the stock in companies he owned. A popular story about him had it that he had started young. As a young drover, Drew would bring his cattle to the New York market, where he would pen them up with salt and no water. The next morning, before he sold them, he would drive them into a creek, where the groaning beasts bloated themselves. At market, they were fat, sleek, and largely phony.

the air of city and wilderness, tied the country together on its "two streaks of rust and a right of way." Railroads made it possible for Pittsburgh steelmakers to bring together the coal of Scranton and the iron of Michigan as if both minerals were found just across the county line. Thanks to the railroad, the great flour mills of Minneapolis could scoop up the cheap spring wheat of the distant Northwest, grind it into flour, and put their trademarked sacks into every cupboard in the country.

Because so many western railroads found their way into Chicago, the Windy City quickly eclipsed river-based Cincinnati as "hog butcher to the world" and the nation's dresser of beef. Livestock fattened on rangeland a thousand miles away rolled bawling into Chicago in rickety railroad cars and then rolled out—packed in cans, barrels, and refrigerator cars— to the east coast and from there around the world.

With the possible exception of the telegraph line, the railroad was the physical manifestation of industry that most people knew. Rails and the noisy locomotives that sailed along them penetrated to the very centers of cities and reached into the most remote deserts and mountains. Where the railroad ran the landscape was forever changed by massive excavations, embankments, bridges, and tunnels.

Inefficiency and Chaos

By 1865, the United States was already the world's premier railway country with about 35,000 miles of track. With a few exceptions, however, individual lines were short, serving only the hinterlands of the cities in which they terminated. In the former Confederacy, there were 400 railroad companies with an average track length of only 40 miles each. It was

possible to ship a cargo between St. Louis and Atlanta by any of 20 routes. Competing for the business in cutthroat rate wars, not a single southern line was financially secure.

Few lines actually linked up with one another. Goods to be shipped over long distances, and therefore on several lines, had to be unloaded (hand labor added to costs), carted across terminal towns by horse and wagon (another bottleneck), and reloaded onto another train. No two of the six railroads that ran into Richmond shared a depot. Before the Civil War, Chicago and New York were linked by rail on the map, but a cargo going the entire distance had to be unloaded and reloaded six times.

Some early railroaders encouraged inefficiency in order to discourage takeovers by companies interested in consolidation. They deliberately built in odd gauges (the distance between rails) so that only their own locomotives and rolling stock could run on their tracks. As narrow as two feet apart in mountainous areas, the distance between rails ran to five feet in the South. Until 1880, the important Erie Railroad clung to a monstrous six-foot gauge. The Illinois Central, the nation's third largest railroad, employed two different gauges.

Lack of coordination among railroads presented shippers and passengers with another headache. Each railway company scheduled its trains according to the official time in its headquarters city. But local time varied even in cities just a few miles apart. When it was noon in Washington, D.C., it was 12:24 P.M. in Baltimore, 70 miles away (and 11:43 in Savannah, Georgia). The Baltimorean in Washington who tried to catch a noon train home might discover that his watch was quite right for Baltimore, but that he was nearly half an hour too late to make the trip that day. In the train station in Buffalo, which served the New York Central and the Michigan Southern, three clocks were necessary: one for each railroad, and one for local time, which was different yet. In the Pittsburgh station there were six clocks. Traveling from Maine to California on the railroad, one passed through 20 time zones. In fact, there were 80 such zones in the United States.

The Consolidators

Charles F. Dowd introduced the idea of four official time zones in 1870; his plan was enacted into law at the behest of the railroads in 1883. Long before that, men like J. Edgar Thompson of the Pennsyl-

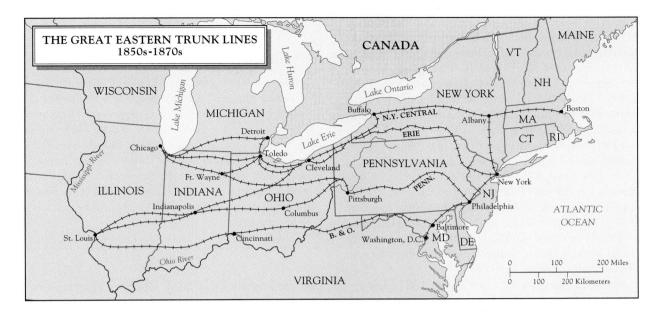

vania Railroad and Cornelius Vanderbilt of the New York Central labored outside the law, and often in conflict with it, to bring order out of the chaos of independently owned short lines.

They secretly purchased stock in small railroad companies until they had control of them, then drove other competitors out of business by means of ruthless rate wars. They built the "Pennsy" and the New York Central ever westward from New York to Chicago and, thus, connections with lines that ran to the Pacific. All along their main lines, feeders tapped the surrounding country.

Thompson was all business, a no-nonsense efficiency expert with little celebrity outside railroad and government circles. Vanderbilt, who began his working life as a ferryman in New York City's crowded harbor, was colorful and often in the news. Ferrying was a rough business, no place for a milquetoast, and as a young man, the Commodore, as Vanderbilt styled himself (dressing in a mock naval uniform), fired more than one cannon at a competitor's harbor barge.

Vanderbilt gave up brawling as his shipping empire and responsibilities grew, but he was as tough and unscrupulous behind a broad oak desk as he had been at the tiller of a ferry. Once, when a reporter suggested that he had broken the law in a conflict with a rival, Vanderbilt snapped back gruffly, "What do I care about the law? Hain't I got the power?"

He had, and he used it masterfully to crush competition. By the time of the Civil War, Vanderbilt had a near-monopoly of New York harbor commerce. He even controlled the business that hauled New York City's monumental daily production of horse manure to farms on Staten Island. Vanderbilt's waterborne transportation empire led him naturally into moving the commerce of America's greatest city overland, too.

The Commodore was never quite respectable. His rough-and-tumble origins resonated in his speech. He befriended Victoria Woodhull and Tennessee Claflin, two eccentric sisters who outraged society by preaching free love and not shunning its practice. The mention of Vanderbilt's name caused ladies and gentlemen of genteel New York society to shudder—for a while. Because he said out loud what other businessmen did quietly—that ethics and social responsibility did not always make good business—he was an easy target for moralists, hypocrites though they might have been. Vanderbilt could not have cared less. Like many of the great capitalists of the era, he regarded his fortune—$100 million when he died—as adequate justification for what he did.

Pirates of the Rails

Compared to another breed of early railroader, men like Thompson and Vanderbilt can be justified very easily. In addition to making millions for themselves, they built transportation systems of inestimable social value. The Pennsy was famous for safe roadbeds in an age of frequent, horrendous railroad accidents.

The New York Central pioneered the use of steel rails and was equipped with the lifesaving Westinghouse air brake while other lines halted (or failed to halt) their trains mechanically. The Commodore's son and heir, William Vanderbilt, was best known for saying "The public be damned!" but he also played a major part in standardizing the American gauge at the present 4 feet, 8½ inches.

In contrast, some early railroaders simply took, making their fortunes by destroying what others had built. The most famous of these pirates was a trio that owned the Erie Railroad and actually succeeded in bilking Cornelius Vanderbilt. The senior member of the Erie Ring was Daniel Drew, a pious Methodist who knew much of the Bible by heart, but put a very liberal interpretation on the verse in Exodus that said "Thou shalt not steal."

James Fisk, only 33 years old in 1867, was another sort altogether. No Bible for "Jubilee Jim," he was a stout, jolly extrovert who fancied garish clothing, tossed silver dollars at street urchins, and caroused openly in New York's gaslit restaurants and cabarets with showgirls from the vaudeville stage who, at the time, were little better than costly prostitutes. (One of them, Josie Mansfield, was his undoing; in 1872, Fisk was murdered by another one of her suitors.)

Jay Gould was a man of the shadows. When Drew went to church and Fisk slapped on cologne, Gould slipped home to his respectable Victorian family. Furtive in appearance as in fact, tight-fisted, and close-mouthed, Gould was probably the brains of the Erie Ring. Certainly he lasted the longest, becoming almost—but never quite—respectable, and marrying his daughter to a European nobleman. But when it came to making money, Gould was at one with his partners in the Erie Ring: the consequences of their piracy for others, let alone society, were quite beside the point.

The Erie War

In control of the Erie Railroad, the three men knew that Vanderbilt wanted their property and was quietly making large purchases of Erie stock. In order to separate him from as much of his capital as possible, they watered Erie's stock; that is, they marketed shares in the dilapidated railroad far in excess of the Erie's real assets, from $24 million to $78 million in a few years when virtually nothing was done to improve the line. As Vanderbilt bought, they

---

> ### *Land for Sale*
>
> In order to promote land that it owned in Nebraska, the Burlington and Missouri River Railroad offered a number of come-ons. A would-be purchaser had to pay his own fare to go out to look at the land, but the railroad would refund his fare if he bought. Once a landowner, he would receive a free railroad pass, as well as "long credit, low interest, and a twenty percent rebate for improvements." Prices were not extravagant. The Union Pacific disposed of pretty good Nebraska land at $3 to $5 an acre.

---

pocketed the money that should have gone into expanding the Erie's earning power.

The Commodore came to his senses and went to the judges, whom he regularly bribed, to indict the trio. Forewarned, Drew, Fisk, and Gould escaped to New Jersey, where they owned the judges. (It was said in the streets that they rowed across the Hudson River in a boat filled with bank notes.) A settlement was pieced together. In the meantime, the Erie amassed the worst accident record among world railroads and the company was devastated as a business. The Erie did not pay a dividend to its stockholders until the 1940s. For 70 years, what profits there were went in part to make up for the thievery of three men over six years.

THE TRANSCONTINENTAL LINES

In the Northeast and South, the creation of railroad systems was partly a matter of consolidating short lines that already existed. This movement peaked during the 1880s, when the names of 540 independent railway companies disappeared from the business registers. In the West, railroad lines were extensive, integrated transportation systems from the start. Beyond the Mississippi, creating railroad systems was a matter of construction from scratch.

Public Finance

The great transcontinental railroads were built and owned by private companies but financed by the public (with one exception, James J. Hill's Great

Northern). The sparsity of population between the Mississippi Valley and the western states of California and Oregon (and Washington after 1889) made it difficult to attract private investors to railroad projects there. It was simply too expensive. To lay a mile of track required bedding more than 3,000 ties in gravel and attaching 400 rails to them by driving 12,000 spikes. Having built that mile in Utah or Nevada at considerable expense, a railroader had nothing to look forward to but hundreds more miles of arid desert and uninhabited mountains.

With no customers along the way, there would be no profits and, without profits, no investors. The federal government had political and military interests in binding California and Oregon to the rest of the Union, and, in its land, the public domain, the government had the means with which to subsidize railroad construction.

Building the Railroads

"Track-laying is a science. A light car, drawn by a single horse, gallops up to the front with its load of rails. Two men seize the end of a rail and start forward, the rest of the gang taking hold by twos. They come forward at a run. At a word of command the rail is dropped in its place, less than thirty seconds to a rail for each gang, and so four rails go down to the minute: Close behind come the gangers, spikers, and a lovely time they make of it."

The Pacific Railway Act of 1862 granted to two companies, the Union Pacific and the Central Pacific, a right of way of 200 feet wide between Omaha, Nebraska, and Sacramento, California. For each mile of track that the companies built, they were to receive, on either side of the tracks, ten alternate sections (square miles) of the public domain. The result was a belt of land 40 miles wide, laid out like a checkerboard on which the UP and CP owned half the squares. (The rest was reserved for disposition under the Homestead Act or by direct government sale.)

The railroads sold their land, thus raising money for construction and creating customers. Or, just as important, they could use the vast real estate as collateral to borrow cash from banks. In addition, depending on the terrain, the government lent the two companies between $16,000 and $48,000 per mile of track at bargain interest rates.

The Romance of the Rails

As in the consolidation of eastern trunk lines, the business operations of the transcontinentals was sometimes a wee shady—as in the case of the Crédit Mobilier. However, the actual construction of the line was a heroic and glorious feat. The Union Pacific, employing thousands of Civil War veterans and newly immigrated Irish pick-and-shovel men, the "Paddies," laid over 1,000 miles of track. The workers lived in shifting cities of tents and freight cars built like dormitories. They toiled by day, and

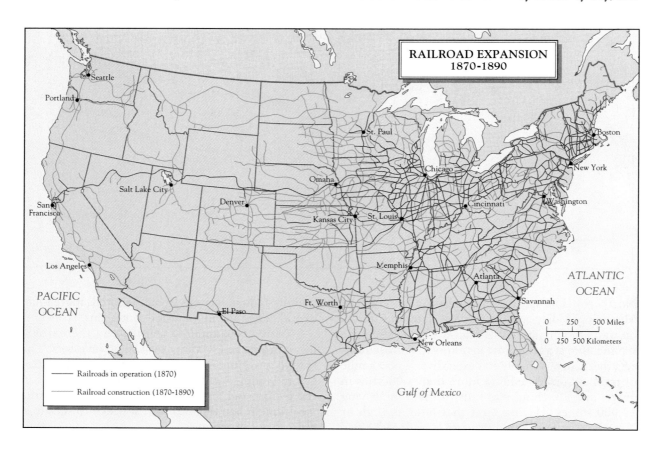

bickered and brawled with gamblers, saloon keepers, and whores by night. Until the company realized that it was more efficient to hire professional gunmen as guards, the workers kept firearms with their tools in order to fight off those Indians who may have sensed that the iron horse meant the end of their way of life.

The builders of the Central Pacific had no trouble with Indians, but a great deal with terrain. Just outside Sacramento rose the majestic Sierra Nevada. There were passes in the mountains through which the line could snake, but they were narrow and steep. Under the direction of a resourceful engineer, Theodore D. Judah, 10,000 Chinese chipped ledges into the slopes, built roadbeds of rubble in deep canyons, and bolted together trestles of timbers two feet square.

The snows of the Sierra proved to be a difficult problem, not only for the builders but for the eventual operation of the line. To solve it, the workers constructed snowsheds miles long. In effect, the transcontinental railroad crossed part of the Sierra Nevada indoors. Once on the Nevada plateau, the experienced CP crews built at a rate of a mile a day for an entire year.

The UP and CP joined at Promontory Point, Utah, on May 10, 1869. The final days were hectic. Because the total mileage that each company constructed determined the extent of its land grants, the two companies raced around the clock. The record was set by the crews of the Central Pacific. They built 10.6 miles of more-or-less functional railroad in one day (just about the same length of track the company laid down during the whole of 1864). That involved bedding 31,000 ties and connecting 4,000 iron rails to them with 120,000 spikes!

Railroad Mania

Seeing that the owners of the UP and CP became instant millionaires, other ambitious men descended on Washington in search of subsidies. In the euphoria of

Ten thousand immigrant Chinese laborers built the Central Pacific Railway across the West. Here, workers complete the Secrettown Trestle in the Sierra Nevada.

the times, Congress in 1864 was doubly generous to the Northern Pacific, which planned to build from Lake Superior to Puget Sound. In the territories, the NP received 40 alternate sections of land for every mile of railway built! The Atchison, Topeka, and Santa Fe ran from Kansas to Los Angeles. The Texas Pacific and Southern Pacific linked New Orleans and San Francisco at El Paso, Texas (Jefferson Davis's route in the days before the Kansas-Nebraska Act). In 1884, the Canadians (who were even more generous with government land) completed the first of their two transcontinental lines, the Canadian Pacific. Never before had there been such an expenditure of effort and wealth to accomplish the same purpose in so short a time.

The costs were considerable. The federal government gave the land-grant railroads a total of 131 million acres. To this, state governments added 45 million acres. Totaled up, an area larger than France and Belgium was given to a handful of capitalists. In addition, towns along the proposed routes enticed the builders to choose them as sites for depots by offering town lots, cash bounties, and exemption from taxes.

These gifts were not always offered with a glad hand. If a railroad bypassed a town, the town fathers knew the town might die, and their fortunes and status with it. Aware of this, railroaders did not hesitate to set communities against one another like roosters in a cock fight. The Atchison, Topeka, and Santa Fe, popularly known as "the Santa Fe," did not originally enter the city of that name. Nearby Albuquerque offered the better deal and got the major depot.

The Panic of 1873

Western railroaders made money by building railroads with public and borrowed money, not by actually operating them. As a result, they built too much railroad too soon. When the time came to shoulder high operating costs and to pay off loans out of fees paid by shippers and passengers, many of the new companies found that there were just not enough customers to go around. In 1872, only one railroad in three made a profit.

On September 18, 1873, a Friday, the chickens came home to roost. Jay Cooke and Company, a bank that loaned heavily to western railroads, including the richly endowed Northern Pacific, announced that the firm was bankrupt. Jay Cooke and Company was not an ordinary bank. It was the most prestigious house of finance in the United States; Cooke had been the government's chief financial agent during the Civil War. Its failure caused a panic: speculators rushed to sell their stocks and the market crashed. By the end of 1873, 5,000 businesses declared bankruptcy and a half million workers were jobless. The depression of the 1870s was the worst in American history to that time.

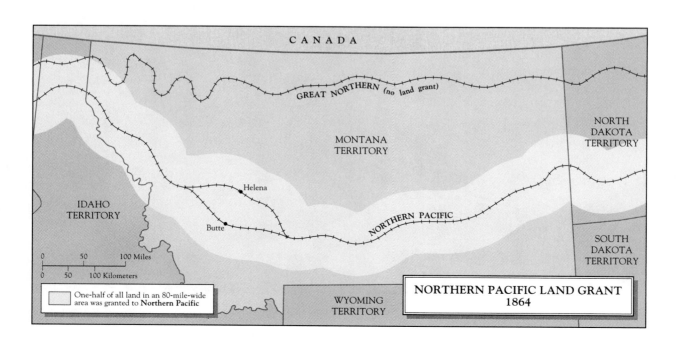

Depressions

The "most noteworthy peculiarity" of the depressions of the industrial age, wrote D. A. Wells in 1889, was their universality. There seemed no escaping the inevitable collapses of economic life. Depression afflicted nations

which have a stable currency based on gold, and those which have an unstable currency, those which live under a system of free exchange of commodities and those whose exchanges are more or less restricted. It has been grievous in old communities like England and Germany, and equally so in Australia, South Africa, and California, which represent the new; it has been a calamity exceeding heavy to be borne alike by the inhabitants of sterile Newfoundland and Labrador, and of the sunny, fruitful sugar islands of the East and West Indies; and it has not enriched those at the centers of the world's exchanges, whose gains are ordinarily greatest when business is most fluctuating and uncertain.

It would not be the last. A by-product of fabulous economic growth was a wildly erratic business cycle, the "unprecedented disturbance and depression of trade," in the words of a contemporary. For a time the industrial capitalist economy boomed, luring investment and speculation, encouraging expansion and production. Sooner or later, the capacity of railroads to carry freight, and factories to produce goods, outpaced the capacity of the market to absorb their services and products. When that happened, banks closed, investments and savings were wiped out, factories locked their gates, workers lost their jobs, and the shops they frequented went broke.

THE ORGANIZERS

In a free, unregulated economy, the cycle of boom and bust was inevitable and, since the Age of Jackson, Americans as a people were committed to the ideal of a free and unregulated economy. They believed that their country's peculiar virtue lay in the fact that competition was open to everyone having the will and wherewithal to have a go at it.

Once a businessman reached the top of the economic pyramid, however, he was apt to become disenchanted with the competitive ideal. To the entrepreneur who was no longer scrambling but in charge of a commercial or industrial empire valued at millions of dollars and employing thousands of people, freewheeling competitors threatened stability and order, like so many yapping spaniels at his heels. In the late nineteenth century, Andrew Carnegie in steel, John D. Rockefeller in oil, and other canny businessmen devoted their careers to minimizing the threat of competition. Carnegie organized his company so efficiently that he could determine the price structure of the entire steel industry without regard to what other steelmakers did. Rockefeller destroyed his competitors by fair means and foul, and simply gobbled them up.

Steel: The Bones of the Economy

Steel is the element iron from which carbon and other impurities are burned out at high temperatures. Nineteenth-century engineers were well aware of its potential in construction. Steel is much stronger than iron per unit of weight. Produced in quantity, steel could be used in buildings, bridges, and, of particular interest in the late nineteenth century, superior rails for trains. Until the mid-nineteenth century, however, the costs involved in producing this super-iron restricted steel's use to small, expensive items: blades, firearms, precision instruments, bearings for machinery, and the like.

By the time of the Civil War, working independently of each other, two iron makers, Henry Bessemer of England and William Kelly of Pennsylvania and Kentucky, developed a method by which steel could be made in quantity at a reasonable price. No one grasped the significance of their discovery more quickly than Andrew Carnegie, an immigrant from Scotland who, beginning as a telegrapher, became a high-ranking executive of the Pennsylvania Railroad. Already a rich man by the end of the Civil War as a result of speculations in oil and the manufacture of iron bridges (his company built the first span across the Mississippi), he decided to sell everything and concentrate on steel, "putting all his eggs in one basket, and then watching that basket." In 1873, he began construction of a huge Bessemer plant in Braddock, Pennsylvania, outside Pittsburgh.

A Head for Business

Carnegie knew apples as well as eggs—how to polish them. He named his factory after J. Edgar Thompson, the president of the Pennsy, which would be a

A nineteenth-century steel mill was a hellish, dirty, and dangerous workplace.

major customer of Carnegie Steel. But Carnegie also knew to locate the great works outside of Pittsburgh, which was served by the Pennsylvania Railroad alone. In Braddock, Carnegie could play several railroads against one another, winning the most favorable shipping rates. Nor was it luck that Carnegie built his mill during the depression of 1873. For the next 25 years, he took advantage of hard times, when the price of everything was down, to expand his factories, scrap old methods, and introduce new technology.

Carnegie also prided himself on spotting talent, putting it to work for him, and rewarding it. Charles Schwab, later the president of United States Steel and the founder of Bethlehem Steel, was an engineer's helper at Carnegie Steel whom Carnegie promoted and made a partner.

"Vertical Integration"

Carnegie's major contribution to business organization was his exploitation of the principle of "vertical integration." That is, in order to get a leg up on his competitors, he expanded his operation from a base of steel manufacture to include ownership of the raw materials from which steel was made and the means of assembling those raw materials at the factory. For example, Bessemer furnaces were fueled by coke, which is to coal what charcoal is to wood, a hotter-burning distillation of the mineral. Rather than buy coke from independent operators, Carnegie absorbed the 5,000 acres of coalfields and 1,000 coke ovens owned by Henry Clay Frick, who became a junior partner in Carnegie Steel. Carnegie and Frick then added iron mines to their holdings.

While never completely independent of trunk-line railroads, Carnegie controlled as much of his own shipping as he could. He owned barges that carried iron ore from Michigan and the Mesabi to his own port facilities in Erie, Pennsylvania. He owned a shortline railroad that brought the ore from Erie to Homestead. By eliminating from his final product price the profits of independent suppliers, distributors, and carriers, Carnegie was able to undersell competing companies that were not vertically inte-

> ### Steel at One Cent a Pound
>
> Just as John D. Rockefeller liked to point out that kerosene was cheaper after Standard Oil came to monopolize the refining industry, Andrew Carnegie had a neat justification of his organization of the steel industry:
>
> *Two pounds of ironstone mined upon Lake Superior and transported nine hundred miles to Pittsburgh; one pound and one half of coal, mined and manufactured into coke, and transported to Pittsburgh; a small amount of manganese ore mined in Virginia and brought to Pittsburgh—and these four pounds of materials manufactured into one pound of steel, for which the customer pays one cent.*

> ### Inc. and Ltd.
>
> In the United States, a limited liability corporation is distinguished by the word "Corporation" in its name or the abbreviation "Inc.," meaning "incorporated." In Great Britain, the comparable designation is "Ltd.," meaning "limited."

grated and, therefore, had to include the profits of independent suppliers in their final product price.

Vertical integration served Andrew Carnegie very well. His personal income rose to $25 million a year. He lived much of the time in a castle in Scotland not far from where his father had worked as a weaver, while his company steadily assumed a more dominant role in the steel business. In 1870 there were 167 iron and steel firms around Pittsburgh. By the end of the century there were 47.

In 1901, 66 years old and bored with business, Carnegie threatened to combine most of these into a behemoth that would threaten companies organized by the banker J. P. Morgan with an all-out price war. Morgan was persuaded to buy Carnegie out for $500 million, the largest personal commercial transaction ever made. Morgan then created the first billion-dollar corporation, United States Steel. From its birth, the company controlled "the destinies of a population nearly as large as that of Maryland or Nebraska," and spent more money and carried a larger debt than most of the world's nations.

The Corporation

Carnegie was progressive in many ways, always open to the new. But he organized his company as a partnership, disdaining the business structure that was the chief means of consolidation in the late nineteenth century, the corporation. Corporate structure—selling small shares in a company on the open market—was advantageous to both investors and business or-

ganizers. Widely dispersed ownership meant widely dispersed risk. The investor who owned some shares in a number of companies did not lose everything if one of those companies failed. American law also provided investors with the privilege of limited liability. That is, the corporation's legal liability was limited to the assets of the corporation, and did not extend to the assets of shareholders. (If an individually owned business or partnership went bust, creditors could seize the other assets of the owners, including home and personal property.)

These inducements made it possible for entrepreneurs to raise the huge amounts of capital needed to finance expensive industrial enterprises. However, by reserving controlling interest to themselves, they did not have to share decision making with small investors. Abuses were common enough. Pirates like the Erie Ring could drain a corporation of its assets, enrich themselves personally through their control of corporate policy, allow the company to go under, and walk away with their ill-gotten personal fortunes.

New Uses for Equal Rights

The Fourteenth Amendment to the Constitution, designed to secure equality under the law to all citizens, proved to be more valuable to corporations than to the African Americans for which it was written. After dodging the question for several years, the Supreme Court ruled in *Santa Clara County* v. *Southern Pacific Railroad* (1886) that a corporation was a "person" under the meaning of the Fourteenth Amendment. The states were forbidden to pass laws that applied specifically to corporations and not to flesh-and-blood persons because such laws denied corporate persons civil equality.

However, while corporations enjoyed the civil rights of citizens who walked and talked, it was difficult to exact the same responsibilities of them. Men and women could be sent to jail for violating the law.

Corporations could not. And the diffusion of authority within the corporate structure made nabbing flesh-and-blood culprits very difficult.

John D. Rockefeller

While thousands of businessmen organized corporations, they all fade into a crowd in the shadow of the solemn, muscular, well-dressed, and deeply religious person of John Davison Rockefeller. Beginning his career as an accountant, Rockefeller avoided service in the Civil War by hiring a substitute. He made a small fortune selling provisions to the Union Army, but a small fortune was only an appetizer. Rockefeller had a voracious appetite for riches. Outside of home and Sunday school, which he taught throughout his life, he was obsessed with business. After swinging a lucrative deal as a young man, he danced a two-step jig and exclaimed "Bound to be rich! I'm bound to be rich!"

Rockefeller disapproved of smoking and drinking, in part because of his intense Baptist faith, but in part because cigars and whiskey cost money that could be invested to make more money. He carefully recorded how he spent every dime; he spent few frivolously. He would remove his stovepipe hat and bend down to pick up a penny. John D. Rockefeller would have succeeded no matter what his business. The one he chose proved to be as basic to the modern world as steel.

Black Gold

Crude oil has been seeping to the surface of the earth since before there were human beings to step into it. Ancient Mesopotamians wrote of it in cuneiform. Europeans used it as a lubricant. In southern Poland, peasants tried to make vodka from it. And there was plenty of it in the United States. Jesuit priests in western New York in the seventeenth century reported of "a stagnant thick water that ignites like brandy, burning with bubbles of flame when fire is tossed into it." Some American Indians, like the Seneca, ate it as a laxative. That classical American huckster, the snake oil salesman, bottled the stuff, flavored it with sugar and spices and tossed in a healthy shot of alcohol, thence claiming it cured everything from "female weakness" to the threat of snow. The farmers who lived around Titusville in western Pennsylvania hated the gunk. It fouled the soil, polluted streams, and, if it caught fire, it filled the air with billows of noxious smoke.

In 1855, an organic chemist, Benjamin Silliman, discovered that one of the components into which crude oil could be broken down was kerosene, a liq-

John D. Rockefeller (1839–1937), builder of Standard Oil, philanthropist.

The Richest

Today, at the beginning of the twenty-fist century, Bill Gates of Microsoft Corporation is the richest man in the world. His edge on the nearest competition is measured in the billions.

However, if Gates's fortune is adjusted for inflation, he finishes a weak fourth in a field of nineteenth-century industrial moguls.

John D. Rockefeller	$190 billion
Andrew Carnegie	$101 billion
Cornelius Vanderbilt	$ 96 billion
Bill Gates	$ 62 billion

uid that could be safely burned to heat a house or cookstove, or illuminate the night. It was a timely discovery. In the 1850s, overharvesting had desolated the world's population of whales. Whale oil, used to illuminate middle- and upper-class homes—the poor used candles or went to bed—had soared in price. Kerosene was cheap; even the poor could afford it. In 1859, seeing the opportunity, a former army officer named Edwin Drake went to Titusville, Pennsylvania, and devised a drill-and-pump system by which, he hoped, crude oil could be extracted in commercial quantities. Late in August, Drake's driller, William A. "Uncle Billy" Smith, hit a crevice at 69 feet. He drilled six inches more and shut down. The next morning, Smith discovered oil ten feet from the surface. Easy pumping.

The Pennsylvania oil rush that followed was as wild as the gold rush of 1849. Drilling for oil, like panning for gold, required only modest capital, so thousands of men dreaming of instant riches descended on the oil fields of western Pennsylvania. John D. Rockefeller, living in nearby Cleveland, Ohio, came and looked. But he did not like what he saw, neither the social disorder and moral laxity, nor the fact that the independent drillers, competing fiercely to stay afloat, repeatedly declared price wars on one another, slashing the price at which they sold their black gold to refiners. A few drillers got rich; many more went broke. It was not Rockefeller's kind of business.

"Horizontal Integration"

Oil refining was a fragmented business, too; there were 250 companies engaged in it as late as 1870. However, operating a refinery called for rather more capital than sinking a drill bit into the ground and saying a prayer. Rockefeller recognized that, unlike drilling, which would always attract "wildcatters" who might get lucky, hit a gusher, and become a major competitor overnight, the refining end of the business was manageable. It was a kind of narrows on the river of oil that flowed from well to consumers. Like the robber barons of medieval Europe, who built castles at narrow places on the Rhine and Danube, thence deciding which boat might pass and which might not, the company that controlled the narrows of oil business—refining—would be able to determine production and prices. It did not matter how many wild-eyed visionaries roamed the countryside with a drilling rig. If there was one re-

finer, they would sell their crude oil at the price the refiner was willing to pay.

Controlling an entire industry by controlling a key phase of its process is known as horizontal integration. Instead of setting the standards for an industry by integrating a portion of the business from top to bottom, from source of raw materials to market (as Carnegie did in steel), horizontal integration meant establishing an effective monopoly across the industry.

This is what Rockefeller and his associates, his brother William, Samuel Andrews, and Maurice Clark accomplished. In 1870, their Standard Oil Company of Ohio refined 3 or 4 percent of the nation's oil. Within 20 years, Standard Oil controlled 90 percent of American refining capacity, and Rockefeller pretty much ran Standard by owning 25 percent of its stock. He worked this magic by persuading strong and cooperative competitors to throw in with them, and by driving weak and uncooperative refiners out of the business.

Rebates

Rockefeller ground some refineries down by attacking them in cutthroat rate wars. With generally superior facilities, Standard Oil was able to take losses over the short term that less efficient competitors could not bear. At one point, Standard sold crude oil at $.50 a barrel, less than a barrel of water. On another occasion, Rockefeller bought up every barrel, stave, and hoop in the oil region. Competitors could not ship their products for lack of containers. On another, a private army of 250 Standard Oil men forcefully prevented a refining company from building a pipeline to New York City.

Much more effective was the drawback or rebate. Because Standard Oil could promise railroads a fixed, large amount of oil to carry east each day, Rockefeller demanded of them and got a refund of part of their published rate list—under the table. With smaller competitors paying the published rates, Rockefeller had a huge advantage when it was time to sell. For a short period, Rockefeller got a rebate from the Erie Railroad for each carload of kerosene his competitors shipped! This was his price to the Erie for continuing to use the line himself. The rebate was particularly effective in fighting the refiners of Pittsburgh, who were served by only one railroad which, therefore, did not have to bargain.

The Standard Oil Trust

In order to win these wars, Rockefeller had to occupy a commanding position in the refining industry. At the beginning of the consolidation, however, he and his associates lacked the vast capital resources that would have been necessary to buy out other large producers. The solution, designed by Rockefeller's lawyers, Samuel C. T. Dodd and John Newlon Camden, was to adapt the ancient legal device of the trust to the running of a business.

Traditionally, the trust was the means by which the property of a minor or an incompetent was managed on his or her behalf. That property was put into the care of a trustee whose obligation was to see to it that the property was well administered. Rockefeller, Andrews and Clark, and Henry Flagler explained to their major competitors that if they surrendered control of their refineries to the Standard Oil Trust, for which they would receive trust certificates, they would be spared the duties of management and the risks of competition while, because the trustees would coordinate the use of the combined facilities, their income would soar. The wiser refiners saw the point—in the early 1870s, most refineries were running at half-capacity—they agreed to give Rockefeller control of their facilties, and they very soon became very wealthy. In 1875, Standard declared dividends of $115, more than the par value of Standard stock.

Rockefeller, once in control of a near-monopoly, was able to mop up those refiners who held out and to calculate precisely how much oil the market could absorb, how much, therefore, to produce, and at what price to sell.

The goal of the trust was not to drive prices up to extortionate levels. Rockefeller enjoyed telling hostile interrogators that with each step toward monopoly, Standard had reduced the retail price of a gallon of kerosene. The goal of the trust, he said, was economic order, not rapacious profiteering.

Rockefeller had no apologies for what he did. He remained a critic of the gospel of competition to the end of his days. However, the fact that a handful of men could dictate the doings of an entire, vital industry—Standard Oil was run by only nine trustees—aroused a storm of fear and resentment in the land.

CHRONOLOGY

1862	Pacific Railway Act
1869	First transcontinental railroad completed
1870	Standard Oil begins consolidation of petroleum refining
1873	Financial panic and depression Andrew Carnegie begins construction of steel mill at Braddock, Pennsylvania
1876	Centennial Exposition celebrates American industry Alexander Graham Bell demonstrates telephone
1879	Thomas Edison perfects incandescent light
1883	Time zones introduced at behest of railroads Northern Pacific Railroad completed
1886	*Santa Clara Co. v. Southern Pacific Railroad*
1890	U.S. industrial output exceeds Great Britain's

FOR FURTHER READING

For overviews of American economic development, see the following books: Elliott Brownlee, *Dynamics of Ascent: A History of the American Economy*, 1974; Thomas C. Cochran and William Miller, *The Age of Enterprise*, 1942; Vincent P. DeSantis, *The Shaping of Modern America, 1877–1916*, 1973; John A. Garraty, *The New Commonwealth, 1877–1890*, 1968; Samuel P. Hays, *The Response to Industrialism, 1885–1914*, 1957; Matthew Josephson, *The Robber Barons*, 1934; Glenn Porter, *The Rise of Big Business, 1860–1910*, 1973; Robert H. Wiebe, *The Search for Order*, 1967; David A. Hounsell, *From the American System to Mass Production*, 1984; and Daniel Boorstin, *The Americans: The Democratic Experience*, 1973.

Valuable special studies include Roger Burlingame, *Engines and Democracy: Inventions and Society in Mature America*, 1940; A. F. Chandler, *Strategy and Structure: Chapters in the History of the American Industrial Enterprise*, 1962, and *The Visible Hand: The Managerial Revolution in American Business*, 1977; Thomas C. Cochran, *Railroad Leaders, 1845–1890*, 1953; Robert W. Fogel, *Railroads and American Economic Growth*, 1964; Gabriel Kolko, *Railroads and Regulation*, 1965; James McCague, *Moguls and Iron Men*, 1964; Elting E. Morison, *From Know-How to Nowhere: The Development of American Technology*, 1974; David F. Noble, *America by Design: Science, Technology, and the Rise of Corporate Capitalism*, 1977; Walter T. K. Nugent, *Money and American Society, 1865–1880*, 1968; John F. Stover, *The Life and Decline of the American Railroad*, 1970; and Gavin Wright, *Old South, New South: Revolutions in the Southern Economy Since the Civil War*, 1986.

One of the finest recent biographies is Robert V. Bruce, *Alexander Graham Bell and the Conquest of Solitude*, 1973. For other personages mentioned in this chapter, see Matthew Josephson, *Edison*, 1959; Harold C. Livesay, *Andrew Carnegie and the Rise of Big Business*, 1975; Allan Nevins, *A Study in Power: John D. Rockefeller*, 1953; and J. F. Wall, *Andrew Carnegie*, 1971.

Wealthy New Yorkers celebrate their prosperity with crowns of laurel at an elegant dinner.

28
CHAPTER

LIVING WITH LEVIATHAN

Americans React to Big Business and Great Wealth

All successful men have agreed in one thing—they were causationists. They believed that things went not by luck, but by law; that there was not a weak or a cracked link in the chain that joins the first and last of things.

—Ralph Waldo Emerson

Success is counted sweetest
By those who ne'er succeed.

—Emily Dickinson

A successful man can not realize how hard an unsuccessful man finds life.

—Edgar Watson Howe

The moral flabbiness of the exclusive worship of the bitch-goddess SUCCESS. That—with the squalid cash interpretation put on the word success—is our national disease.

—William James

In *Democracy in America*, written more than 20 years before the Civil War, Alexis de Tocqueville admired the equity with which wealth was distributed in the United States. Except for slaves, of course, only a few Americans were so poor that they could not hope to improve their situation; few families were so rich that they had coalesced into an aristocracy, a distinct privileged social class permanently ensconced above the mass of the population. As a result, Tocqueville observed, the many seemed confident that their country was indeed the promised land of opportunity, where their fate lay entirely in their own hands. At the same time, many wealthy people Tocqueville met seemed haunted by the fear that one adverse stroke of fortune would send them tumbling down into the world of hard work, sore backs, and callused hands.

Today, Jacksonian America may not have apportioned its wealth quite so equitably as Tocqueville believed. Nevertheless, the gap between dirt poor and filthy rich was not nearly so yawning then as it became in the late nineteenth century. Industrialization and the growth of big business created a class of multimillionaires whose fortunes were so great that it was absurd to imagine them slipping back into the unwashed masses. Cornelius Vanderbilt amassed $100 million in his lifetime. His son, William, doubled that to $200 million in a few years. By 1900, Andrew Carnegie was able to pocket $480 million in a single transaction. John D. Rockefeller gave away such a sum within a few years, all the while his family grew richer.

To many observers, the industrial and financial aristocracy's control of technology, transportation, industry, and money made a mockery of the American dream of equality of opportunity. How could an ordinary fellow succeed against such entrenched wealth, power, and privilege? How could he realize the "American Dream"?

Social critics railed at the new elite. Substantial social movements protested the new inequities. In the end, however, Americans came to terms with a society that was both richer and poorer than the one that Alexis de Tocqueville examined.

REGULATING THE RAILROADS AND TRUSTS

Railroads were the first big business and railroads were the target of the first significant social protests of America's industrial era. Poets and philosophers saw "the machine in the garden" as a defilement of what was good and vital in American life, the nation's closeness to nature. In some cities, residents banded together to fight plans to run tracks down the streets on which they lived and shopped.

But the nay-sayers were few. Most Americans welcomed the iron horse at first, especially those who lived in isolated rural areas. To them the railroad provided the opportunity to ship their produce to market, thereby earning money with which to escape a life of mere subsistence.

A Short Honeymoon

The honeymoon was brief. It was not difficult to see that pirates like Drew, Fisk, and Gould made money only to the extent that they abused the railroad as a means of transportation. Western townspeople discovered that the railway barons' arrogance did not end with their demands for free sites for their depots and exemptions from property taxes. Along the transcontinental lines, virtually every important piece of business had to be cleared with the local railway manager. Farmers learned that the railroads were less their servants, carting their produce to market, than the masters of their fate.

California's "Big Four"—Collis P. Huntington, Leland Stanford, Mark Hopkins, and Charles Crocker—it was overstated, "owned the state" thanks to their control of the Southern Pacific Railroad, which absorbed the transcontinental Central Pacific and ran the length of the state as well. In addition to its stranglehold on transportation, the SP was, next to the federal government, California's biggest landowner. Moreover, land in California's Central Valley, or Douglas fir forests, was worth a lot more than acreage in Nevada or even Nebraska.. In just a generation, the price of much of the SP's land rose to ten times the $3 to $5 an acre charged elsewhere in the West.

The Farmers' Grievances

The farmers of the Mississippi Valley also discovered that the railroad did not necessarily usher in a golden age. The problem, as they saw it, was, as in California, monopoly. In most areas, one line handled all the traffic. Consequently, the rates at which farmers shipped their wheat, corn, or livestock to markets in the East were at the mercy of the shippers. Too often for goodwill to prevail, farmers saw their margin of profit consumed by transportation costs.

Gift for the Grangers, *a lithograph made in 1873 celebrates the Patrons of Husbandry, a farmers' organization.*

How They Lived

The Last Dance of the Idle Rich: The Bradley Martin Ball of 1897

In the winter of 1896–1897, Americans were wrestling with a depression greater than the depression of the 1870s, bad times that would be exceeded only during the Great Depression of the 1930s. Businesses had failed by the thousands. Several million people were out of work. People had been evicted from farms and homes by the hundreds of thousands. The treasuries of charitable organizations were strained to the breaking point; some had given up in despair and closed their doors. Jobless people had marched on Washington; others had rioted; yet others plodded on day by day—gathering coal along railroad tracks, or picking through the garbage pails behind expensive restaurants. In November 1896, a presidential candidate who was called the Great Commoner, William Jennings Bryan, was defeated by William McKinley, who, fairly or not, was widely described as a tool of the moneyed interests. It was an unhappy time, with class sensibilities keen, resentments explosive.

Sometime during that winter, at breakfast in his Fifth Avenue mansion, Bradley Martin, one of high society's grandest adornments, had an idea. "I think it would be a good thing if we got up something," he told his wife and brother, Frederick. "There seems to be a great deal of depression in trade; suppose we send out invitations to a concert."

Mrs. Martin complained that a concert would benefit only foreigners. Most professional musicians in the country at that time were German and Italian, and she wanted to do something for Americans. "I've got a far better idea," she said. "Let us give a costume ball at so short notice that our guests won't have time to get their dresses from Paris. That will give an impetus to trade that nothing else will."

The conversation was recorded by Frederick Townshend Martin with no intention of making his brother and sister-in-law look either vicious or ridiculous. In fact, he justified their economic theories, explaining that "many New York shops sold out brocades and silks which had been lying in their stockrooms for years."

The ball was held on February 10, 1897, in the ballroom of the Waldorf-Astoria Hotel, which had been decorated to resemble the palace of the French kings at Versailles. To the Martins' set, it was a glorious success. According to experts, there was never such a display of jewels in New York. Financier August Belmont came in gold-inlaid armor that cost him $10,000. The costumes of others were inferior only by comparison. One woman said that in order to help the particularly hard-pressed Indians, she had had Native Americans make her Pocahontas costume. Bradley Martin himself made a curious selection. As the host at Versailles, he had first claim to be Louis XIV, the Sun King, who had built the great palace and was universally conceded to be the most glorious of the French monarchs. But Bradley chose to be his great-grandson, Louis XV. He would not have wanted to be Louis XVI, who had been beheaded because of his and his predecessors' extravagance in a country where the poor suffered wretched misery.

"Everyone said it was the most brilliant of the kind ever seen in America."

Not quite everyone. Even before the first waltz, Martin and his "idle rich" friends were being vilified from pulpit, editorial desk, and political platform for their callous decadence in a difficult time. Much more significant, the ball was criticized by more than one business leader. If idle heirs such as the vapid Martin did not know that such affairs caused resentment, class hatred, and (in more than one instance in the past) social revolution, sensible businessmen did. Two years after the ball, in his book *The Theory of the Leisure Class*, economist Thorstein Veblen would give a name to Bradley Martin's lifestyle, "conspicuous consumption." However, already by that time, America's wealthy were learning to enjoy their riches quietly. Indeed, looking

---

Most infuriating was the railroads' control of storage facilities, the grain elevators that stood close to the depot in every railway town. The farmer had to pay the company storage fees until such time as the railroad sent a train to haul away his grain. Obviously, it could be to the railroad's interests to delay scheduling shipment. The company alone determined how long a farmer had to store his produce and, therefore, how large his fee was.

Extravagant parties of the type shown here became out of favor after the Bradley Martin ball.

back after several decades, two distinguished historians, Charles and Mary Beard, called the Bradley Martin ball of 1897 the "climax of lavish expenditure" in the United States. "This grand ball of the plutocrats astounded the country, then in the grip of a prolonged business depression with its attendant unemployment, misery, and starvation."

It was not only the fear of social upheaval that wrote an end to conspicuous consumption on a grand scale. To a large extent, high-society affairs like the ball were the doings of women, the wives and daughters of rich businessmen. After the turn of the century, many of them rebelled against their enforced idleness and frivolity and began to take an interest, even a leading role, in social and political causes: votes for women, of course, but also Prohibition, suppression of the white-slave racket (prostitution), amelioration of lower-class suffering, and other social programs of the Progressive Era.

Not Mrs. Bradley Martin and her husband, of course. Unreconstructable denizens of the ballroom, they carried on as before. But not in New York. The ball was so unpopular there that city hall slapped a large tax increase on the Martin mansion on Fifth Avenue. In a huff, the Martins moved to London. Brother Frederick Townshend Martin wrote of this relocation with an air of despondency; the United States had lost two valuable citizens.

Attempts to Regulate

In the early 1870s, the Patrons of Husbandry became the focus of farmer protest in the Midwest. Founded as a social and cultural organization, the society transformed itself into a political pressure group and grew like sunflowers. In 1869, there were 39 Granges, as local chapters were called; by the mid-1870s, there were 20,000, with 800,000 dues-paying members.

Pro-Grange politicians won control of the state legislature of Illinois and considerable influence in adjoining states. Allied with small businessmen, who also felt squeezed by railroads, they passed a series of Granger laws that set maximum rates that railroad companies could charge both for hauling and storing. Several other state governments followed Illinois' lead.

The railroad barons launched a legal counterattack, hiring high-powered corporation lawyers like Richard B. Olney and Roscoe Conkling to challenge state regulatory legislation before the Supreme Court. At first, the Grangers prevailed. In the case of *Munn v. Illinois* (1877), a Supreme Court dominated by old-fashioned Lincoln Republicans declared that when a private company's business affected the public interest, the public had the right to regulate that business for the common good.

Nine years later, the times and the personnel of the Supreme Court had changed. In 1886, justices on cordial terms with the new order wrote several pro-railroad doctrines into the law of the land.

The most important was handed down in the Wabash case of 1886 (*Wabash, St. Louis, and Pacific Railway Co. v. Illinois*). In this decision, the court reinterpreted the interstate commerce clause of the Constitution in such a way as to protect large railroad companies. That is, the Constitution provides that only Congress can regulate commerce between and among states. In the Wabash case, the court ruled that because the Wabash Railroad ran through several states, the Illinois legislature could not regulate freight rates even between two points within the state. The Wabash decision left state governments with authority over only short, generally insignificant local lines that were rarely exploitative in the first place.

The Interstate Commerce Commission

The *Wabash* decision was not popular. Rural politicians and urban reformers condemned the Supreme Court as the tool of the railway barons. If only Congress could bridle the iron horse, they shouted from Grange halls and from the stages of city auditoriums, let Congress do so. In 1887, Congress did, enacting the Interstate Commerce Act.

On the face of it, the law brought the national railroads under control. It required railroads to publish their rates and to charge them; under-the-table rebates were forbidden. Railroads were forbidden to charge less for long hauls along routes where there was competition than for short hauls in areas where a company had a monopoly. The act also outlawed the pooling of business by railroads, a practice by which, many shippers believed, they were controlled and fleeced. To enforce the act and to regulate rates, Congress created a permanent independent federal commission, the Interstate Commerce Commission.

The Interstate Commerce Act calmed antirailroad protest, but it did not have much effect on railroad policy. The ICC, simply, had no real power. If the commissioners wished to compel a railroad to comply with their regulations, they had to take the company to the same courts that had favored the railroads over the state legislatures. Commissioner Charles A. Prouty commented, "If the ICC was worth buying, the railroads would try to buy it. The only reason they have not is that the body is valueless in its ability to correct railroad abuses."

In fact, the railroads did not have to buy the ICC; it was given to them. The Harrison, Cleveland, and McKinley administrations—1889–1901—were all sympathetic to big business and staffed the commission with railroaders and lawyers friendly to them.

The Money Power

By the early 1890s, the trunk lines of the country were consolidated into five great systems. By 1900, these had effectively fallen under the control of two large New York investment banks, J. P. Morgan and Company and Kuhn, Loeb, and Company, the latter in league with Union Pacific president Edward H. Harriman.

This development owed to the fact that, when the government ceased to subsidize construction, the railroads had to look to other sources in order to mobilize the huge amounts of capital needed to lay second tracks, modernize equipment, and buy up competitors. The companies often needed more money than their profits provided. Capital was even more serious a problem during the recurrent business recessions of the period when income sank but fixed costs (such as maintenance) remained the same.

The traditional means of raising capital—offering shares of stock to the public—was simply not up to these needs, particularly during bad times. Into the gap stepped the investment banks. These institutions served both as sales agents, finding moneyed buyers for railway stock at a commission, and as buyers themselves. In return for these services, bankers such as John Pierpont Morgan insisted on a say in making railroad policy by placing representatives of the bank on the client's board of directors.

Because every large railroad needed financial help at one time or another—every transcontinental but the Great Northern went under during the depression of 1893 to 1897—Morgan's and Kuhn and Loeb's men soon sat on every major corporate board, creating a complex interlocking directorate. Like all bankers, their goal was a steady, dependable flow of profit, and their means to that end was to eliminate wasteful competition. They called a halt to the periodic rate wars among the New York Central, Pennsylvania, and Baltimore and Ohio railroads in the eastern states. In 1903, J. P. Morgan tried to merge the Northern Pacific and the Great Northern, two systems with parallel lines between the Great Lakes and the Pacific Northwest. Competing for traffic, he believed, hurt them both.

Banker control had many benefits. No more did unscrupulous pirates like the Erie Gang ruin great transportation systems for the sake of short-term killings. The integration of the nation's railways also resulted in a gradual but significant lowering of fares and freight rates. Between 1866 and 1897, the cost of shipping a hundred pounds of grain from Chicago to New York dropped from 65 cents to 20 cents, and the rate for shipping beef from 90 cents per hundredweight to 40 cents. J. P. Morgan's self-justification was identical to that of John D. Rockefeller. Competition was wasteful and destructive; consolidation better served the nation as a whole, as well as the cream of its capitalists.

J. P. Morgan

The control of so important a part of the economy by a few men with offices on Wall Street called into question some touted and treasured American ideals. Where was individual freedom and opportunity, many people asked, when a sinister money power headed by the imperious Morgan could decide on a whim the fate of millions of farmers and working people?

"The Scourge of the West": the railroad as arrogant exploiter backed up by the power of government.

J. P. Morgan (1837–1913) was a formidable presence. He knew it, and he liked it.

In his person, Morgan was no half-mannered robber baron. He was resplendent and cultivated. He owned yachts larger than the warships in many national navies, paintings and rare books superior to the collections in many a national library. He loved good food, the company of Episcopalian bishops, and beautiful young women, and he was not squeamish about mixing them on social occasions (to the delight of more than one bishop). He was also sickly, chronically down with a cold, it seemed, or profoundly depressed. He was not an articulate man. He seemed genuinely alarmed when faced with a telephone receiver. He sincerely answered questions about complex financial transactions he had designed by stammering, "I thought it was the right thing to do."

But his genius at such transactions was peerless and he was rarely bested. Because of his success, his power, and a too rarely disguised contempt for ordinary mortals, he was feared, held in awe, hatred, caricatured as the symbol of the Wall Street plutocracy.

Morgan shrugged off all criticism. He was sensitive only to ridicule of his most obvious frailty. Rhinophyma, an affliction of the skin, had given him a large, bulbous nose that swelled and glowed like a circus clown's when he was angry. Making fun of it, however, was the only foolproof way to aggravate it, and Morgan rarely rubbed elbows with the kind of people who would take note of his deformity. Only cartoonists and hostile journalists, whose published work fell into his hands, addressed the subject.

An Age of Trusts

In addition to bishops and railroaders, Morgan found plenty of company among the industrialists whose trusts and other devices for doing business he organized for fees of a million dollars and more. The trust was most useful in industries in which, like oil, there was a single critical stage of manufacture that involved relatively few companies. Some of John D. Rockefeller's most successful imitators were in sugar refining (the sugar trust controlled about 95 percent of the nation's facilities) and whiskey distilling. In 1890, James Buchanan Duke of Durham, North Carolina, founded the American Tobacco Company, a trust which coordinated the activities of practically every cigarette manufacturer in the United States. In effect, he dictated the terms by which tens of thousands of tobacco growers did business.

By 1890, many Americans were convinced that when a few men could control a whole industry, the principle of economic opportunity and the foundations of American democracy were in jeopardy.

The Sherman Antitrust Act

Responding to public pressure in that year, Congress passed the Sherman Antitrust Act, which stated: "Every contract, combination, in the form of trust or otherwise, or conspiracy, in restraint of trade or commerce among the several states, or with foreign nations, is hereby declared to be illegal." The Sherman Act authorized the attorney general to move against such combinations and force them to dissolve, thus reestablishing the independence of the companies that formed them.

The Sherman Act was no more successful in halting the consolidation movement than the Interstate Commerce Act was in controlling the power of the railroads. Critics said that the Sherman Act was a sham from the beginning, designed to quiet unease but not to hurt big business. In fact, the weakness of the law lay in the inability of congressmen to comprehend this new economic phenomenon. Real monopoly was so unfamiliar to the lawmakers that they were unable to draft a law that was worded well enough to be effective. The language of the Sherman Act was so ambivalent that a shrewd lawyer—and the trusts had the best—could usually find a loophole.

Moreover, while congressmen could take fright at a popular uproar, the courts were immune to it. The Wabash case was only one of a series of decisions by the Supreme Court that ensured the survival of the biggest of businesses. In the first major case tried under the Sherman Act, *United States* v. *E. C. Knight Company* in 1895, the court found that a nearly complete monopoly of sugar refining in the United States did not violate the law because manufacture, which the sugar trust monopolized, was not a part of trade or commerce, even though its sugar was sold in every state.

Nor was the executive branch keen to attack big business. President Grover Cleveland's attorney general, Richard B. Olney, was a corporation lawyer. Under Benjamin Harrison and William McKinley, the other presidents of the 1890s, the Justice Department was similarly pro-business. During the first ten years of the Sherman Act, only 18 cases were instituted and four of these were aimed not at businesses but at labor unions, which were also "conspiracies in restraint of trade."

Consequently, rather than heralding doomsday for the trusts, the years between 1890 and 1901 were a golden age of bigness. The number of state-chartered trusts actually grew from 251 to 290. More telling, the amount of money invested in trusts rose from $192 million to $326 million. By the end of the century, there was no doubt that the demands of modern manufacturing meant that massive organizations were here to stay. But whether they would continue to be the private possessions of a few Bells, Morgans, Carnegies, and Rockefellers was still open to debate.

CRITICS OF THE NEW ORDER

The Interstate Commerce and Sherman Antitrust laws were enacted by mainstream politicians who believed that the individual pursuit of wealth was a virtue. They wished only to restore competition and the opportunity to succeed that big business threatened to destroy. Outside the mainstream, sometimes radical critics of the new industrial capitalism raised their voices and wielded their pens in opposition to the new order itself. At least briefly, some of them won large followings.

Henry George and the Single Tax

A lively writing style and a knack for simplifying difficult economic ideas made journalist Henry George and his "single tax" the center of a short-lived but momentous social movement. In *Progress and Poverty*, published in 1879, George observed what was obvious, but also bewildering to many people. Instead of freedom from onerous labor, as the machine once seemed to promise, the machine had put millions to work under killing conditions for long hours. Instead of making life easier and fuller for all, the mass production of goods had enriched the few in the "House of Have," and impoverished the millions in the "House of Want."

George did not blame either industrialization or capitalism as such for the misery he saw around him. Like most Americans, he believed that the competition for comfort and security was a wellspring of the nation's energy. The trouble began only when those who were successful in the race grew so wealthy that they ceased to be entrepreneurs who built, and became parasites who lived off the income their property generated, or rent.

George called income derived from mere ownership of property unearned increment, because it required no work, effort, or ingenuity on the part of its possessors. Property grew more valuable and its owners richer only because other people needed access to it in order to survive. Such value was spurious, George said, even heinous; government had every right to confiscate unearned increment by levying a 100 percent tax on it. Because the revenues from this tax would be quite enough to pay all the expenses of government, all other taxes could be abolished. The single tax became the rallying cry of George's movement. It would destroy the idle and parasitic rich as a social class. The entrepreneurship and competition that made the country great would flourish without the handicaps of taxation.

George's gospel was popular enough that in 1886 he narrowly missed being elected mayor of New York, a city where real estate values and "unearned increment" from land ownership were higher than anywhere in the world.

Edward Bellamy Looks Backward

Another book which became the bible of a protest movement was Edward Bellamy's novel of 1888, *Looking Backward: 2000–1887*. Within two years of its publication, the book sold 200,000 copies (the equivalent of more than a million in 1990) and led to the founding of about 150 Nationalist Clubs, made up of people who shared Bellamy's vision of the future.

The story that moved them was simple, its gimmick conventional. A proper young Bostonian of the 1880s succumbs to a mysterious sleep and awakes in the United States of the twenty-first century. There he discovers that technology has produced not a world of sharp class divisions and widespread misery (as in 1887), but a utopia that provides abundance for all. Like George, Bellamy was not opposed to industrial development in itself.

Capitalism no longer exists in the world of *Looking Backward*. Through a peaceful democratic revolution—won at the polls—the American people have abolished competitive greed and idle, unproductive living because they were at odds with American ideals. Instead of private ownership of land and industry, the state owns the means of production and administers them for the good of all. Everyone contributes to the common wealth. Everyone lives decently, and none miserably or wastefully.

Bellamy's vision was socialistic. However, because he rooted it in American values rather than in the internationalism of the Marxists, he called it Nationalism. The patriotic facet of his message made his gospel palatable to middle-class Americans who, while troubled by the growth of fantastic fortunes and of wretched poverty, found foreign ideologies and talk of class warfare obnoxious and frightening.

Socialists and Anarchists

Nevertheless, Marxist ideology, including the doctrine of class conflict, found adherents in the United States. Some old stock Americans were converted to Marxian socialism. For the most part, however, Marxism found its adherents among immigrants and the children of immigrants. Briefly after 1872, the General Council of the First International, the official administration of world socialism, made its headquarters in New York, where Marx sent it to prevent the followers of his anarchist rival, Mikhail Bakunin, from winning control of it.

The Marxists taught that the capitalist system of wage slavery—workers laboring for wages in the employ of a capitalist class who owned the means of production, the factories and machines—would fall under its own weight to socialism and then communism, under which, respectively, the state and the workers themselves would own the factories and machines, administering them for the good of all.

Some Marxist socialists held that in democratic countries like the United States, this social revolution would be voted in peacefully. Social Democratic movements flourished in a number of cities, most notably in Milwaukee, where an Austrian immigrant, Victor L. Berger, built a party that, after 1900, would govern the city for several decades.

Other Marxian socialists held that the overthrow of capitalism would inevitably be violent. The most extreme of these revolutionaries were the anarchists, some of whom held that individuals could hasten the great day through "the propaganda of the deed," acts of terrorism against the ruling class. Anarchists figured prominently in an incident in Chicago in 1886 in which, ironically, they were not responsible for the bloodshed that occurred.

Haymarket

In May 1886, workers at the McCormick International Harvester Company, the world's largest manufacturer of farm machinery, were on strike. The Chicago police were blatantly on the side of the employers, and over several days they killed four workers. On May 4, a group of anarchists, mostly German but including a Confederate Army veteran of a once prominent family, Albert Parsons, held a rally in support of the strikers at Haymarket Square, just south of the city center.

The oratory was red-hot; but the speakers broke no laws, and the crowd was orderly. Indeed, the rally was about to break up under the threat of a downpour when a platoon of police entered the square and demanded that the assembly disperse. At that instant, someone threw a bomb into their midst, killing seven policemen and wounding sixty-seven. The police fired a volley, and four workers fell dead.

News of the incident fed an antianarchist hysteria in Chicago. Authorities rounded up several dozen individuals who were known to have attended anarchist meetings, and authorities brought eight to trial for the murder of the officers. Among them was Parsons and a prominent German agitator, August Spies.

The trial was a farce. No one on the prosecution team knew or even claimed to know who threw the bomb. (His or her identity remains unknown.) Nor did the prosecution present evidence to tie any of the eight to the bombing. One, a deranged young German named Louis Lingg, was a bomb maker,

> ### Belmont's Wine Cellar
>
> While many millionaires outspent August Belmont, New York associate of the Rothschild banking interests, few of them spent their money with as much panache as did the European-born banker. It was said of Belmont that his monthly wine budget was $20,000.

although even he had a plausible alibi. Several of the defendants had not been at the rally. Parsons was ill in bed that evening and, indeed, had been ill since before the rally was called.

All these facts proved to be irrelevant. Chicago was determined to have scapegoats. Although the charge was murder, the Haymarket anarchists were tried for their ideas and associations. Four were hanged. Lingg committed suicide in his cell. The remaining three were sentenced to long prison terms.

The Social Gospel

Taking a more moralistic approach to the tensions of the late nineteenth century were a number of influential Protestant clergymen. Troubled by the callousness of big business, preachers of the Social Gospel emphasized the Christian's social obligations, his duty to be his brother's keeper.

Walter Rauschenbusch began his ministerial career on the frontiers of Hell's Kitchen, then one of New York City's most dangerous slums. "One could hear human virtue cracking and crushing all around," he wrote in later years. To Rauschenbusch, poverty was the cause of the crime and sin, and mass poverty was the result of allowing great capitalists a free hand in enriching themselves. Later, as a professor at Rochester Theological Seminary, Rauschenbusch taught the obligation of the churches to work for both the relief of the poor and a more equitable distribution of wealth.

Washington Gladden, a Congregationalist, called unrestricted competition "antisocial and anti-Christian." He did not propose the abolition of capitalism, but he did call for regulation of its grossest immoralities. He was highly moralistic. Late in life, Gladden described John D. Rockefeller's fortune as tainted money and urged his church not to accept contributions from the millionaire. (The millionaire,

however, found plenty of untroubled clergymen to whom to write checks.)

The Social Gospel appealed to many of the middle-class, often modestly well-to-do themselves, who did not suffer directly from the power of the very wealthy but who were offended by the extravagance and idleness of their lives. William Dean Howells, the editor of the *Atlantic Monthly*, wrote a novel about a successful paint manufacturer (*The Rise of Silas Lapham*, 1885) who finds the idleness of wealth discomfiting. He rises, and finds purpose and happiness again, only when he loses his fortune and is forced to return to productive work. Howells even convinced an old friend from Ohio, former President Rutherford B. Hayes, to go on record late in his life as an advocate of the peaceful abolition of capitalism.

DEFENDERS OF THE FAITH

Such a barrage of criticism did not, of course, go unanswered. At the same time that great wealth was taking its knocks, it was reaping the praise of defenders. In part, like the critics, they drew on traditional American values to justify the new social system. In part, also like the critics, the defenders created new philosophies, original with the era of industrial capitalism.

> ### Private Cars
>
> Partial to yachts, J. P. Morgan never owned a private railroad car, which was one of the status symbols of the late nineteenth century. In George Gould's car, guests for dinner were expected to dress formally; Gould's liveried waiters served the food on solid gold plates. The Vanderbilt family's car, called the "Vanderbilt," could not accommodate all the guests whom they wished to entertain, so they had a new one built and called it "Duchess" after Consuelo. At Palm Beach, a favorite pleasuring ground of the rich, 20 to 30 private cars were sometimes parked in a special section of the train yard. When Morgan wished to go to a place he could not reach by water, he had to rent an opulent private car. On one occasion, he rented a whole train of private cars to transport east coast Episcopalian bishops to a conference in San Francisco.

Social Darwinism

Thoughtful and reflective people who were at peace with their era found a justification for great wealth and even dubious business ethics in a series of books, essays, and lectures by the British philosopher Herbert Spencer. Because Spencer seemed to apply Charles Darwin's celebrated theory of biological evolution to human society, his theory is known as Social Darwinism.

According to Spencer, as in the world of animals and plants, where species compete for life and those best adapted survive, the fittest people rise to the top in the social competition for riches. Eventually, in the dog-eat-dog world, they alone survive. "If they are sufficiently complete to live," Spencer wrote, "they do live, and it is well that they should live. If they are not sufficiently complete to live, they die and it is best they should die."

A Survival of the Fittest Sampler

We have unmistakable proof that throughout all past time, there has been a ceaseless devouring of the weak by the strong.

—Herbert Spencer

The ultimate result of shielding men from the effects of folly is to fill the world with fools.

—Herbert Spencer

Whatever capital you divert to the support of a shiftless and good-for-nothing person is so much diverted from some other employment, and that means from somebody else.

—William Graham Sumner

The price which society pays for the law of competition . . . is . . . great; but the advantages of this law are . . . greater still, for it is to this law that we owe our wonderful material development, which brings improved conditions in its train. But whether the law be benign or not, we must say of it . . . : It is here; we cannot evade it; no substitutes for it have been found; and while the law may be sometimes hard for the individual, it is best for the race, because it ensures the survival of the fittest in every department.

—Andrew Carnegie

The intellectual tough-mindedness of Social Darwinism made Spencer immensely popular among American businessmen who were as proud of their practicality as of their success. The Englishman was never so celebrated in his own country as he was in the United States. Although a vain man, Spencer was mortified by the adulation heaped on him at banquets sponsored by American academics and rich businessmen. Social Darwinism accounted for brutal business practices and underhanded methods, justifying them as the natural law of the jungle.

The language of Social Darwinism crept into the vocabulary of both businessmen and politicians who represented business interests. John D. Rockefeller, Jr., described the growth of a large business as the survival of the fittest. But neither he nor many other American millionaires were true Social Darwinists. The very ruthlessness of the theory— "Nature, red in tooth and claw"—made it unpalatable to men and women who, in their personal lives were, like the Rockefellers, deeply committed to traditional religious values. Moreover, businessmen are rarely intellectuals, and Spencer's philosophy and writing style were as thick and murky as Standard crude. Understanding him demanded careful study, such as businessmen have rarely had time to do. Spencer's explanation of the new society was most influential among scholars who merely envied the rich.

William Graham Sumner

The most important of these scholars was a Yale professor, William Graham Sumner. He was uncompromising in his opposition to aiding the poor, putting government restrictions on business practices, and interfering in any way whatsoever with the law of the jungle. "The men who are competent to organize great enterprises and to handle great amounts of capital," he wrote, "must be found by natural selection, not political election."

Sumner's rigorous consistency also led him to oppose the use of government to aid capital. He opposed protective tariffs. To subsidize American manufacturers by taxing imports was just as unnatural to him as was regulating the growth of trusts. If American manufacturers were not fit to compete with European manufacturers in a free market, Sumner said, they were not fit to survive. Likewise, Sumner opposed government intervention in strikes on behalf of employers. He believed that the strike was a natural test of the fitness of the employers' and the

Perhaps the most grotesque display of "conspicuous consumption" among upper-class New Yorkers was this gentlemen's (and horses') banquet at Sherry's in 1903.

workers' causes. The outcome of a strike determined which side was right.

To businessmen who used government trade policy and courts to their own purposes, Sumner's impartial applications of "natural law" were going too far. They had no objection to the right kind of government action.

After the turn of the century, the principles of Social Darwinism were turned on their head by the sociologist Lester Frank Ward of Brown University. Whereas Sumner argued that nature in society must be allowed to operate without restraint, Ward suggested that human society had evolved to a point where natural evolution could be guided by government policy. Just as farmers improved fruit trees and ranchers improved livestock through selective breeding, government could improve society by intervening in the naturally slow evolutionary process. Ward's Reform Darwinism influenced two generations of twentieth-century liberals.

The Success Gospel

The Gospel of Success had far more influence among nineteenth-century capitalists than Social Darwinism did. The United States was built on the desire to prosper, Success Gospelers said. Therefore, if competition for riches was a virtue, what was wrong with winning? Far from a reason for anxiety or evidence of social immorality, the fabulous fortunes of America's wealthy families were an index of their virtue. The Carnegies and Morgans deserved their money. John D. Rockefeller was quoted as saying of his money, "God gave it to me."

Success manuals, books purporting to show how anyone could become a millionaire, were read as avidly as the works of George and Bellamy, and by far more people. All much the same, the manuals drew on the widespread assumptions that hard work, honesty, frugality, loyalty to employers and partners, and other bourgeois virtues drawn from Benjamin

Franklin inevitably led to success. Having succeeded, America's millionaires deserved not resentment but admiration and imitation.

A Baptist minister from Philadelphia, Russell B. Conwell, made a fortune delivering a lecture on the same theme. In "Acres of Diamonds," which the eloquent preacher delivered to paying audiences more than 6,000 times, Conwell said that great wealth was a great blessing. Not only could every American be rich, but every American should be rich. If a man failed, the fault lay within him, not with society. "There is not a poor person in the United States," Conwell said, "who was not made poor by his own shortcomings." The opportunities, the acres of diamonds, were everywhere, waiting to be collected.

Conversely, those who already were rich were by definition virtuous. "Ninety-eight out of one hundred of the rich men of America are honest. That is why they are rich."

Horatio Alger and Ragged Dick

Through the 130 boys' novels written by another minister, Horatio Alger, the Success Gospel was conveyed to the younger generation. Alger's books sold 20 million copies between 1867 and 1899, and a battalion of imitators accounted for millions more.

He enjoyed this success despite the fact that he was no writer. His prose was wooden, his characters were snipped from cardboard, and his plots were variations on two or three simple themes. All assume as a given that one of the paramount goals of life is to get money. All teach that wealth is within the grasp of all because almost all Alger's heroes are lads grappling with destitution. They are also honest, hard-working, loyal to their employers, and clean-living. Ragged Dick, Alger's first hero and the prototype for Tattered Tom, Lucky Luke Larkin, and dozens of others, is insufferably courteous and always goes to church.

Curiously, Ragged Dick, et al., rarely, if ever, got rich slowly through hard work. At the beginning of the final chapter, the hero is often as badly off as he was on page one. Then, however, he is presented with what amounts to a visitation of grace, a divine gift that rewards his virtues. The child of a rich industrialist falls off the Staten Island Ferry; or a rich girl stumbles into the path of a runaway brewery wagon drawn by panicked horses; or she slips into the Niagara River just above the falls. Because the Alger hero acts quickly, rescuing her, the heroic lad is rewarded

---

> ### The Grand Tour
>
> It became almost a social necessity for wealthy Americans—the women of the family, at least—to tour western Europe and sometimes Egypt in the late nineteenth century. "The Grand Tour" was no mere two-week race-around, but lasted months, even a year or more. In 1879, when a million tourists visited Switzerland, the first "vacationland," 200,000 of them were Americans. The novelist Henry James and, to a lesser degree, Edith Wharton built their careers writing about Americans in Europe.

---

with a job, marriage to the daughter, and eventually the grateful father's fortune. While appealing to the adolescent boy's yen for adventure, the novels also touched the American evangelical belief in divine grace. Just as he did with Rockefeller, God gave Ragged Dick his money as reward for his virtues.

Philanthropy

The flaw in the Success Gospel as a justification of great fortunes was the obvious fact that many rich men got their money by practicing the opposite of the touted virtues: dishonesty, betrayal of partners and employers, reckless speculation; and they grew richer while living a life of sumptuous, even decadent ease. John D. Rockefeller's business practices were not nearly so unethical as his many enemies said, but there was no question that he cut corners. Similar suspicions surrounded practically every rich family in the country.

Perhaps in part to compensate for the negative marks on their reputations, many wealthy businessmen turned to philanthropy as a kind of retroactive justification of their fortunes. Horatio Alger supported institutions that housed homeless boys in New York City. Russell B. Conwell founded Temple University, where poor young men could study very cheaply and improve themselves. Leland Stanford built a wholly new "Harvard of the West" in California—Stanford University. Rockefeller and other industrial millionaires gave huge sums to their churches and to universities. In retirement, Rockefeller took particular interest in helping American blacks to break out of the prison that racial discrimination had built around them.

Booker T. Washington (center) won the support of many wealthy benefactors with his "Atlantic Compromise." To his left is steel magnate Andrew Carnegie at the dedication of Tuskegee Institute.

Andrew Carnegie devised a coherent theory that justified fabulous fortunes on the basis of stewardship. In a celebrated essay entitled "Wealth," he argued that the unrestricted pursuit of riches made American society vital and strong, but it also made the man who succeeded a steward, or trustee. He had an obligation to distribute his money where it would provide opportunities for poor people to join the competition of the next generation. Indeed, Carnegie said that the rich man who died rich, died a failure.

Carnegie retired from business in 1901 and devoted the rest of his life to granting money to libraries, schools, and useful social institutions. He was so rich, however, that despite his extraordinary generosity, he died a multimillionaire.

HOW THE VERY RICH LIVED

Probably nothing reconciled ordinary Americans to the existence of multimillionaires more than the sheer fascination of the multitudes with the splendor in which the very rich lived. As Thorstein Veblen, an eccentric economist observed in several books written at the end of the century, the very wealthy literally lived to spend money for the sake of proving that they had money. Veblen called this showy extravagance conspicuous consumption, and the propensity to throw it away, conspicuous waste.

Conspicuous Consumption

Having much more money than they could possibly put to good use, the very rich competed in spending it by hosting lavish parties for one another, by building extravagant palaces, by purchasing huge yachts that were good for little but show, by adorning themselves with costly clothing and jewelry, and by buying European titles for their daughters.

Some high-society parties lasting but a few hours cost more than $100,000. At one, hosted by the self-proclaimed "prince of spenders," Harry Lehr, a hundred dogs dined on "fricassee of bones" and gulped down shredded dog biscuit prepared by a French chef. The guests at one New York banquet ate their meal while mounted on horses (trays balanced on the animals' withers). The horses munched oats out of sterling silver feedbags, just possibly making more noise than their riders. At a costume affair, guests boasted that they had spent more than $10,000 each on their fancy dress.

It was the golden age of yachting. Cornelius Vanderbilt's *North Star* was 250 feet long. Albert C. Burrage's *Aztec* carried 270 tons of coal; it could steam 5,500 miles without calling at a port for fuel. As on land, J. P. Morgan was champion at sea. He owned three successively larger, faster, and more opulent yachts called *Corsair*. Morgan had a sense of humor; a corsair is a pirate's vessel.

Having Her Cake and Eating It Too

At least one American heiress actually improved her finances by marrying European aristocrats. Alice Heine, daughter of a wealthy New Orleans banker, married the French Duc de Richelieu. When the duke died in 1879, he left her $15. She later married Prince Albert of Monaco, thus becoming the wife of a prince who actually ruled and was himself quite comfortably fixed.

Consuelo Vanderbilt, the Duchess of Marlborough, the richest and one of the most beautiful American heiresses to buy herself a European title.

Nowhere was consumption more conspicuous and lavish than at upper-class resorts such as Newport, Rhode Island. A summer "cottage" of 30 rooms, used for only three months a year, cost $1 million. Coal baron E. J. Berwind spent $1.5 million to build "The Elms." William K. Vanderbilt outdid everyone with "Marble House." That cottage cost $2 million; the furniture inside, $9 million.

Those places were for vacations. At home in the cities, the millionaires created neighborhoods of mansions such as New York's Fifth Avenue, a thoroughfare given over to grand houses for 20 blocks; Chicago's Gold Coast, which loomed over the city's lakeshore; and San Francisco's Nob Hill, from which palaces looked down on the city like the castles of medieval barons.

A Lord in the Family

A fad of the very rich that aggravated many Americans was the rush during the 1880s and 1890s to marry daughters to European nobles. Nothing more

> ### Leland Stanford
> When he was president of the Southern Pacific Railroad, Leland Stanford ordered that all employees of the company stand at attention in a line along the track when his private trains passed through. All Southern Pacific locomotives traveling in the other direction were to blow their whistles in salute.

clearly dramatized the aristocratic pretensions of the new elite. Wealthy families took pride in the price that they paid to have an earl or a duke as a son-in-law.

It was a two-way bargain. An American daughter got a title to wear to Newport; an impoverished European aristocrat got money with which to maintain himself in fine wines, horses, and hounds. One aficionado of the phenomenon counted 100 titled families that embraced 100 American heiresses with dowries totaling $100 million.

Thus, heiress Alice Thaw was embarrassed on her honeymoon as countess of Yarmouth when creditors seized her husband's luggage. She had to wire her father for money to get it out of hock. Helena Zimmerman, the daughter of a coal and iron millionaire from Cincinnati, married the duke of Manchester. For 20 years their bills were paid by the father of the duchess out of the labor of workers living on subsistence wages.

The most famous American aristocrats were the heiresses of two of the original robber barons, Jay Gould and Cornelius Vanderbilt. Anna Gould became the Countess Boni de Castellane. Before she divorced him in order to marry his cousin, the higher-ranking Prince de Sagan, the count extracted more than $5 million from Jay Gould's purse. Consuelo Vanderbilt was married against her wishes into the proudest family in England. Both when Consuelo married the duke of Marlborough and when

> ### You Can Take It with You
> At the Vanderbilt family tomb on Staten Island, watchmen punched a time clock every hour on the hour around the clock. William Vanderbilt, son of the Commodore, had a deathly fear of grave robbers.

The lavish interior of "The Breakers," built by Cornelius Vanderbilt as his summer house, in Newport, Rhode Island.

she divorced him, the payoffs ran to several million. The duke may have been the only individual ever to get the better of the Vanderbilt family.

Women as Decor

The role of young heiresses in the game of conspicuous waste helps to illustrate the curious role of the women of the new social class. They were idler than their menfolk. A role in business or public life was denied them and they had none of the homemaking duties of middle-class women to occupy their time.

What, then, to do? In effect, the women of the wealthiest classes became their families' chief conspicuous consumers. The rich woman's role was to reflect her husband's accomplishment in amassing wealth; she was a glittering display piece for costly clothing and jewelry. Mrs. George Gould, daughter-in-law of the crusty Jay, went through life known for nothing but the fact that she owned a pearl necklace that was worth $500,000. No one ever mentioned Mrs. Gould in any other context. Her life revolved around the moments when she entered ballrooms, all eyes on her pearls.

Women's fashions were designed to emphasize their wearers' idleness. Indeed, fashion, by its very nature, is conspicuously wasteful. In keeping up with changes, the whole point of fashion, the wealthy woman demonstrated that it made no dent in her husband's fortune if she annually discarded last year's expensive clothing to make room in her closet for the latest from Paris.

Fashion reflects social status in other ways as well. When wealthy women laced themselves up in crippling steel and bone corsets, which made it difficult for them to move, let alone perform any physical work, they were making it clear that they did not have to do such work and were purely decorative. They had servants to care for every detail of their lives.

Men's clothing reflected social status, too. The tall silk hat, the badge of the capitalist, was a completely useless headgear. It offered neither protection nor warmth. But it did prevent a man from so much as bending down to dust his patent leather shoes. "White collar," displaying clean linen at wrist and neck, made it clear that the wearer did no work that would soil his clothing.

Unlikely Neighbors

For the most part, ordinary Americans knew of the shenanigans of the very rich only through hearsay and the popular press. Farmers and factory workers did not vacation at Newport or attend costume balls and ducal weddings at Blenheim Palace. The nature of urban life in the late nineteenth century was such, however, that the idle rich could not conceal their extravagance from the middle and lower classes.

The rich employed legions of servants to maintain their mansions. The grandeur and waste of upper-class life was well known to these poorly paid people. (Two million women worked in domestic service at the end of the century.) More important, because it was impossible to commute long distances in the congested cities, whether for business or social life, the wealthy lived not in isolated suburbs but close to the centers of New York, Boston, Philadelphia, Chicago, and other great cities.

The tradesmen who made daily deliveries of groceries, meat, vegetables and fruit, ice, coal (for heating), and other necessities, not to mention repairmen and those who delivered durable goods, were intimately familiar with the kind of wealth that their customers enjoyed. Marginal workers who were employed by the service and the light manufacturing industries of the center city walked daily past palaces and saw the rich come and go in lacquered carriages tended by flunkies in livery.

Popular Culture

In newspapers aimed at a mass readership, in popular songs, and in the melodramas favored by working people, the idleness and extravagance of the filthy rich were favorite themes. The wealthy were depicted with a mixture of envy and resentment. New York's Tin Pan Alley, the center of the sheet music industry, preached a combination of pity for the "bird in a gilded cage," the wealthy woman, and the traditional moral that because poor people worked, they were more virtuous.

In the popular melodramas of the day, simple plays with little subtlety of character and a completely predictable plot, right-living poor people were pitted against an unscrupulous rich villain. "You are only a shopgirl," said the high-society lady in a typical play.

"An honest shopgirl," replied the heroine in stilted language, "as far above a fashionable idler as heaven is above earth!" (The poor but virtuous shopgirl was often rewarded in the final act by marriage to a rich young man; she consequently took up the life of idleness that she condemned through two and a half acts.)

Juicy Scandals

Ordinary people studiously followed the scandals that periodically rocked high society. In 1872, "Jubilee Jim" Fisk was shot to death by a rival for the affections of his showgirl mistress, Josie Mansfield. Newspaper readers could find a moral in the fact that Fisk's great wealth and power could not save him from a violent death at the age of 38. Nevertheless, a good part of the story's appeal were the details of Fisk's sumptuous personal life, on which the newspapers lovingly dwelled.

Even more sensational was the 1906 murder of architect Stanford White by millionaire Harry Thaw. During his trial, Thaw accused White of having seduced his beautiful fiancée, Evelyn Nesbit. Her testimony concerning the famous White's peculiarities behind closed doors simultaneously titillated the public and served as a moral justification for the murder. (Thaw went free.) Such scandals were the stock in trade of nationally circulated periodicals, such as the *Police Gazette* and *Frank Leslie's Illustrated Newspaper*, that appealed to the working classes. By the end of the century, many large daily papers also took to bumping conventional news to the back pages when an upper-class scandal came up in the courts.

CHRONOLOGY

1867–1899	Horatio Alger publishes boys' books celebrating rags to riches
1870–1886	Grangers active in railroad regulation
1877	*Munn* v. *Illinois*
1879	Henry George publishes *Progress and Poverty*
1886	Wabash Case Haymarket Massacre
1887	Interstate Commerce Commission established
1888	Edward Bellamy publishes *Looking Backward*
1890	American Tobacco Company founded Sherman Anti-Trust Act

FOR FURTHER READING

Most of the works cited in "For Further Reading" in Chapter 27 are relevant here, particularly Vincent P. DeSantis, *The Shaping of Modern America, 1877–1916*, 1973; John A. Garraty, *The New Commonwealth, 1877–1890*, 1968; Samuel P. Hays, *The Response to Industrialism, 1885–1914*, 1957; Glenn Porter, *The Rise of Big Business, 1860–1910*, 1973; and Robert A. Wiebe, *The Search for Order*, 1967. Also see Sigmund Diamond, *The Reputation of American Businessmen*, 1959, and L. Galambos, *The Public Image of Big Business in America*, 1975. For aspects of end-of-the-century economic transformation, see Naomi Lamoreaux, *The Great Merger Movement in American Business*, 1985; and Martin J. Sklar, *The Corporate Reconstruction of American Capitalism: The Market, the Law, and Politics*, 1988.

Justifications and defenses of the new order are studied in John G. Cawelti, *Apostles of the Self-Made Man in America*, 1966; Sidney Fine, *Laissez-Faire and the Welfare State: A Study of Conflict in American Thought, 1865–1901*, 1956; Richard Hofstadter, *Social Darwinism in American Thought*, 1944; Edward C. Kirkland, *Dream and Thought in the Business Community*, 1956; and Irwin Wyllie, *The Self-Made Man in America*, 1954.

Criticisms of the new commonwealth are the focus in C. A. Barker, *Henry George*, 1955; Gabriel Kolko, *Railroads and Regulation*, 1965; Samuel T. McSeveney, *The Politics of Depression: Political Behavior in the Northeast, 1893–1896*, 1972; Andrew Sinclair, *Corsair: The Life of J. Pierpont Morgan*, 1981; John L. Thomas, *Alternative America: Henry George, Edward Bellamy, Henry Demarest Lloyd*, 1983; and an enduring classic, Thorstein Veblen's *The Theory of the Leisure Class*, 1899.

Entrance to a West Virginia coal mine.

29
CHAPTER

WE WHO MADE AMERICA

Factories and Immigrant Ships

So at last I was going to America! Really, really going at last! The boundaries burst! The arch of heaven soared! A million suns shone out for every star. The winds rushed in from outer space, roaring in my ear, "America! America!" . . .

My father found occasion to instruct or correct us even on the way from the pier to Wall Street, which journey we made crowded together in a rickety cab. He told us not to lean out of the windows, not to point, and explained the word "greenhorn." We did not want to be "greenhorns," and gave the strictest attention to my father's instructions. . . .

With our despised immigrant clothing we shed also our impossible names. A committee of our friends, several years ahead of us in American experience, put their heads together and concocted American names for us all. Those of our real names that had no pleasing American equivalents they ruthlessly discarded, content if they retained the initials. . . . As for poor me, I was simply cheated. The name they gave me was hardly new. My Hebrew name being Maryashe in full, Mashke for short, Russianized into Marya, my friends said that it would hold good in English as Mary; which was very disappointing, as I longed to possess a strange-sounding American name like the others.

—*Mary Antin*

562 Chapter 29 *We Who Made America*

Leland Stanford and James J. Hill thought of themselves as the men who built the railroads. So did most Americans. John D. Rockefeller took pride in the majesty of the Standard Oil Company as his personal creation, and, whether they liked the results or not, Americans agreed with him. Newspapers and magazines referred to Andrew Carnegie as the nation's greatest steelmaker. In the popular mind, vast industries were associated with powerful individuals, just as battles were identified with generals: Sherman had marched across Georgia; and Grant had taken Richmond. Vanderbilt ran the New York Central; Philip D. Armour and Gustavus Swift put cheap fresh meat on the dining room table. J. P. Morgan even spoke of his hobby, yachting, in personal terms. "You can do business with anyone," he huffed, "but you can only sail a boat with a gentleman."

In reality, Morgan and his friends merely decided when and where the boat was to go. It took 85 grimy stokers and hard-handed sailors to get the *Corsair* out of New York harbor and safely into Newport or Venice. In the same way, Stanford, Hill, Rockefeller, Carnegie, Swift, Armour, and other great businessmen supervised the creation of industrial America, but the edifice was built by anonymous millions of men and women who wielded the shovels and needles and tended the machines that whirred and whined in the factories and mills.

A NEW WAY OF LIFE

America's working people could not be quartered below decks like the crew of the *Corsair*. While the population of the United States rose rapidly during the last part of the nineteenth century, more than doubling between 1860 and 1900, the size of the working class quadrupled. In 1860, 1.5 million Americans made their living in workshops and mills, and another 700,000 in mining and construction. By 1900, 6 million people worked in manufacturing and 2.3 million in mining and construction, increases of 4 times and 3.3 times, respectively. Industrial workers, once a negligible minority, now constituted a large, distinct, and significant social class.

Bigger Factories, Better Technology

The size of the workplace also grew, a fact of profound importance for the quality of working people's lives. In 1870, the average workshop in the United

States employed eight people. It was owned by an individual or by partners who lived nearby and who personally supervised the business, often working at the bench beside their employees. Like it or not, generous, peevish, or cruel as they might be, such bosses were personally involved in the lives of their workers. They heard of events in their lives ranging from the birth of a child to the death of a parent, and they discussed matters such as wages, hours, and shop conditions face to face with the people who were affected by them. Even Pittsburgh's iron and steel mills, the largest factories in the country, employed on average just 90 workers.

By 1900, the average industrial worker labored in a shop with 25 employees. Plants employing 1,000 men and women were common. The average payroll of Pittsburgh steel plants was 1,600 and a few companies listed 10,000 people on the payroll. (Carnegie Steel employed 23,000.) The men who directed the affairs of such concerns might never step on the floor of a shop. They were interested in wages, hours, and conditions only insofar as they were entries in the ledgers that lined the walls of their offices and boardrooms.

The increased application of steam power and improved machinery affected workers in other ways. The highly skilled craftsman, trained for years in the use of hand tools, ceased to be the backbone of the manufacturing process. Not many crafts actually disappeared (as they would in the twentieth century). A few, like the machinist's trade, increased in importance. But in most areas, steam-powered machines took over from artisans, performing their jobs more quickly and often better.

Many machines were tended by unskilled or semiskilled men, women, and children who merely guided the device at its task. Unlike craftsmen, these workers were interchangeable, easily replaced because the jobs they did required little training. Consequently, unskilled workers could be poorly paid, and they commanded scant respect from employers, small businessmen, professionals, politicians, and skilled workers. "If I wanted boiler iron," said one industrialist, "I would go out on the market and buy it where I could get it cheapest; and if I wanted to employ men I would do the same."

Wages

In actual dollars in the pay envelope (virtually all workers were paid in cash), the wages of many workers declined during the final decades of the nineteenth century. However, real wages, or purchasing power, rose as the cost of food, clothing, and housing dropped more radically than hourly pay did. The standard of living rose. Taken as a whole, the industrial working class enjoyed almost 50 percent more purchasing power in 1900 than in 1860.

But this statistic can be misleading because the skilled "aristocracy of labor"—locomotive engineers, machinists, master carpenters, printers, and other highly trained craftsmen—improved their earnings much more than did the unskilled workers at the bottom of the pile. The average annual wage for all manufacturing workers in 1900 was only $435, or $8.37 a week. Unskilled workers were paid about ten cents an hour on the average, about $5.50 a week, a dollar a day. A girl of 12 or 13, tending a loom in a textile factory, might take home as little as $2 a week after various fines (for being late to work, for example) were deducted from her pay. As late as 1904, sociologist Robert Hunter estimated that one American in eight lived in poverty, and he probably hit below the true figure.

Hours

Hours on the job varied. Most government employees had enjoyed an eight-hour day since 1840. Skilled workers, especially in the building trades (bricklayers, carpenters, and plumbers), generally worked ten. Elsewhere, a factory worker was counted lucky if he or she worked only a 12-hour day. During the summer months, many mills ran from sunup to sundown, as long as 16 hours-with only one shift.

The average workweek was 66 hours long in 1860, and 55 hours in 1910. A big drop, but people were still on the job five and a half or six days a week;

A teenage girl in a Southern cotton mill.

564 Chapter 29 We Who Made America

a half-day Saturday was considered a holiday. In industries required to run around the clock, such as steel (the furnaces could not be switched off like an electric motor), the workforce was divided into two shifts on seven-day schedules. Each shift worked for 12 hours. At the end of a two-week period, the day workers switched shifts with the night workers. This meant a holiday of 24 hours once a month. The price of that holiday was working for 24 hours two weeks later while the other shift enjoyed its full day off.

True holidays were few. However, because of the erratic swings in the business cycle, factory workers had plenty of unwanted time off. Some industries were highly seasonal. Coal miners, for example, could expect to be without wages for weeks or even months during the summer, when city people did not heat their homes. In bad economic times, unemployment soared. During the depressions of the 1870s and 1890s, about 12 percent of the working population was jobless for extended periods.

Conditions

While some employers attended to safety conditions, a safe workplace was far from the rule in the nineteenth century. Between 1870 and 1910, there were 10,000 major boiler explosions in American factories—almost one each workday. Between 1880 and 1900, 35,000 American workers were killed on the job, about one every two days, on average. Railroads had a chilling record. Every year, one railroad worker in 26 was injured seriously, and one in 400 was killed. Textile workers lacking fingers and ex-textile workers without hands were fixtures in every mill town. In lumber mill towns, the old-timer with all his digits was a marvel deserving applause.

In many cases, injured workers and the survivors of those who were killed on the job received no compensation. In others, employer compensation amounted to little more than burial expenses. In the coalfields, mine owners thought themselves generous if they allowed a dead miner's son who was younger than the regulation age to take his father's job in the pit so that the mother and other children would not want.

Employer liability law was stacked against workers. Most courts insisted that employers were not liable for an employee's work-related injury unless the plaintiff could prove he in no way contributed to the accident in question. Short of the collapse of a factory roof or the boss's son run amok with a Colt .45,

complete lack of responsibility was difficult to prove, particularly by a worker who could not afford a skilled lawyer. Courts ruled that if an employee was hurt because his machine was dangerous and he knew it, the employer was not liable. It did no good to plead that an injured worker's co-worker had been fired because he refused to tend the device; under the law, the choice to stay on the job, and therefore part of the responsibility for his injury, was his.

Occupational diseases—the coal miner's "black lung," the cotton mill worker's "white lung," and the hard-rock miner's silicosis—were not recognized as the employer's responsibility. Poisoning resulting from work with chemicals was rarely identified as job-related.

WHO WERE THE WORKERS?

Skilled workers inclined to be males of old-stock British or, increasingly toward the end of the century, of Irish origin. Unskilled jobs were generally filled by children, women, and recent immigrants. In some industrial towns, half to three-quarters of the workforce was foreign-born.

Child Labor

In 1900, the socialist writer John Spargo estimated that 1.8 million children under 16 years of age were employed full-time. They did all but the heaviest kinds of work. Girls as young as 12 tended dangerous looms and spinning machines in textile mills. "Bobbin boys" of ten hauled heavy wooden boxes filled with spindles from spinning rooms to weaving rooms and back again. Children swept filings in machine shops. Boys of eight worked the breakers at coal mines, handpicking slate from anthracite in filthy, frigid wooden sheds.

In sweatshops in city tenements, whole families and their boarders sewed clothing, rolled cigars, or made small items by hand, and children worked as soon as they were able to master the simplest tasks. In cities, children practically monopolized messenger service work, light delivery, and some kinds of huckstering.

In part, child labor was the fruit of greed. On the grounds that children had no nonworking dependents to support, employers could pay them less than they paid adults. Even that justification was not always valid. In southern textile towns, the "Mill

A newsboy peddles papers in St. Louis, Missouri.

Daddy" became a familiar figure. Unable to find work because his own children could be hired to do his job for less, the Mill Daddy was reduced to carrying lunches to the factory and tossing them over the fence each noon.

Women in the Workforce

There was at least one woman in every occupation listed by the Census Bureau in 1890. More than 225,000 were running farms, and 1,143 listed their occupation as clergyman. Women outnumbered men as teachers and as waiters (the latter by five to one). There were 28 female lumberjacks. In all the United States, however, out of 12,856 wheelwrights (makers and repairers of wagon wheels) there was only one woman.

But the phenomenon was also an example of cultural lag. That is, children had always worked. But it took time for society to wake up to the realization that the nature of labor was something new in the world of the dynamo and factory; industrial work was different from chores on a family farm or in a small workshop. Where relations in the small shop or on the farm were personal, the sharply limited capacity of children, particularly their fatigue when set to tedious, repetitive tasks, was easy to recognize and take into account. Placed in a niche in a massive factory, the child laborer became nothing but a number on an accountant's sheet.

Women Workers

Cultural lag also played a part in the large numbers of women in industry. The first industrial workers were female, partly because the first industry was textiles and women were long the mainstay of cloth making in western culture, partly because the founders of the first American textile mills—like the Lowells—had not been able to imagine factory work as a suitable lifetime career for the head of a family. In devising the "Lowell system," the well-meaning pioneers of the factory system believed that they had reconciled industrialization with the old way of life.

The increasing demands of growing industry, and the heavy nature of much factory work, soon resulted in a workforce that was predominantly male. Nevertheless, the difficulty of supporting a family on one person's income forced working-class women to continue to labor for wages even after they married. In 1900, almost 20 percent of the total workforce was female. About half the workers in textiles were women, and the percentage in the needle trades and other home manufactures was much higher.

With few exceptions, women were paid less than men for performing the same tasks for the same number of hours, sometimes half as much. Abysmally low pay was particularly characteristic of the largest female occupation. In 1900, 2 million women were employed for subsistence wages or less in domestic service: cooking, cleaning, and tending the vanities and children of the well-to-do. In an age before cheap household appliances and other mechanical conveniences, even ordinary middle-class families had a maid or two.

No Blacks Need Apply

While a few blacks found work in southern coal mines, and factory jobs in the most menial positions—as sweepers, for example—industrial work went mostly to whites. Blacks remained concentrated in agriculture and in low-paying service occupations: domestic servants, waiters, porters, and the like. In 1900, more than 80 percent of the black population lived in the South, most of them on the land.

The industrial color line was most clearly drawn in the South. When the cotton textile industry moved south at the end of the century, the mill owners drew

A small girl working alongside her mother and scarcely older sister in a Louisiana oyster cannery.

on the poor white population for its workforce. Implicitly, and sometimes explicitly, employees were informed that if they proved troublesome (that is, if they complained about wages, hours, and conditions), the companies could always tap the South's huge and poor black population. Racism served to keep southern workers the poorest industrial laborers in the country. Rather than risk the loss of their poorly paid jobs to blacks, they accepted their low wages and standard of living.

ORGANIZE!

However poorly industrial work paid, it was preferable to other alternatives open to people on the bottom of society. The majority of workers, most of the time, tacitly accepted unattractive wages, hours, and conditions of labor. They expressed their discontent (or desperation) as toilers have done since ancient times. Absenteeism was high in factories, particularly on "Blue Monday" after beery Sunday. And in good times, when getting another menial job was not difficult, workers unable to take holidays sufficient to health and sanity simply quit on a minute's notice.

Sabotage was a word yet to be invented, but the practice was well understood. When the pace of work reached the dropping point, or a foreman stepped beyond the bounds of tolerable behavior, it was easy enough to jam or damage a machine so that it appeared to be an accident — and take a break while it was fixed. An angry worker who made up his mind to quit might decide literally to throw a monkey wrench into the works or to slash the leather belts that turned the looms, drills, stampers, or lathes that ran the entire factory. For obvious reasons, episodes of this kind of protest are impossible to number.

A Heritage of Violence

When workers were powerless to remedy their conditions through institutional channels, violence was common. During the nationwide railroad strike of 1877, an unorganized, spontaneous outbreak that had its roots in a serious depression, workers did not merely walk off the job. Mobs stormed into railroad yards and set trains and buildings on fire. In a few places they fought pitched gun battles with company guards and, toward the end of the unsuccessful strike, with troops who were called out to put them down.

At Andrew Carnegie's Homestead Works in 1892, a strike led by the Amalgamated Association of Iron and Steel Workers actually besieged the giant factory and forced the withdrawal of a barge bringing 300 armed guards into the town. Then, in 1894, came another nationwide labor crisis when a strike at the Pullman Palace Car works in Illinois led to a widespread railroad strike and the massive intervention by the federal government.

George Pullman's employees, who built ordinary bunk-bed sleeping cars for railroads—Pullmans—as well as luxurious private cars, were required as part of their job to live in a company-owned town, Pullman, Illinois. Ironically, given what was to happen, the town of Pullman was founded with idealistic intentions, and considered a model of paternalistic employer goodwill. Workers lived in well-built cottages and the town provided a full range of services for a decent life. However, when accounts confront good intentions, the best intentions usually disintegrate. A decline in business prompted George Pullman to cut wages by 25 percent, but he did not cut rents and utility bills in Pullman. Some 4,000 of his employees responded by joining the American Railway Union and a majority of them struck the Pullman plant in May.

A few weeks later, ARU members on several of the nation's major railroads voted to support the strikers by boycotting Pullman cars, which were owned by the Pullman Company. That is, they refused to hook Pullman cars to trains, or to cut them out. A federal judge ordered the boycott to cease, saying that the boycotters were interfering with the U.S. mails, when, temporarily, it was necessary for the railroad workers to sidetrack postal cars. Over the protests of Illinois Governor John Peter Altgeld, who was disgusted by the judicial sophistry, President Grover Cleveland ordered federal troops into Chicago. This enraged railroad workers from

---

Sui Generis

The population of Ireland in 1840 was estimated to have been 8 million. In 1980, the population of the country was a bit less than 4 million. Surely the Emerald Isle is the only part of the world with fewer people today than 140 years ago, let alone less than half the number. Leaving is, perhaps, the central fact of Irish culture.

> ### Irish-American Patriotism
>
> In 1835, John England, the Roman Catholic bishop of Charleston, provided an explanation of why the Irish took so adeptly to politics: "The Irish are largely amalgamated with the Americans, their dispositions, their politics, their notions of government; their language and their appearance become American very quickly, and they praise and prefer America to their oppressors at home."

Oakland, California, to the East Coast. Formerly peaceful, they rioted and destroyed millions in railroad property. Not until mid-July did the trains begin to run again. The American Railway Union was destroyed, and its leader, Eugene V. Debs, was jailed for disobeying the court's order.

Less colossal conflicts were also common, nowhere more bloody and bitter than in the coal mines of Pennsylvania and in the hard-rock gold and silver mines of the mountain West.

The Molly Maguires

During the early 1870s, many Irish coal miners in northeastern Pennsylvania gave up on the possibility of improving the conditions of their unhealthful and dangerous work through peaceful means. Within the semisecret atmosphere of a fraternal lodge, the Ancient Order of Hibernians, they formed a secret society called the Molly Maguires. The Mollys then launched an effective campaign of terrorism against the mine owners and particularly the supervisors. They systematically destroyed mine property and murdered loyal company men rather than merely beating them up (in which case, the victims could have identified their attackers).

Because of the ethnic dimension of the conflict—almost all the miners were Irish; almost all the bosses were American or Cornish—the Molly Maguires were able to maintain an effective secrecy. Their enemies did not know who they were, how numerous they were, or how much support they had in the community. To this day, historians must conjecture a good deal when discussing the Mollys.

In any case, the mine owners had the last word. They brought in an Irish-American undercover detective, James McParland, an employee of the Pinkerton Agency, which specialized in breaking up unions.

Risking his life, McParland infiltrated the Mollys and gathered evidence that led to the hanging of 19 men and the end of terrorist action in the mines.

The Union Makes Us Strong

Setting aside its evil consequences, violence is a risky mode of protest and resistance. In a stable and free society, organizing for strength seemed more appropriate and likelier to yield results. "One out of many," "in numbers there is strength," the sacredness accorded to the federal union in the Civil War—all such American mottos and ideals fed the imaginations of working people determined to improve their lot.

The first American union dated from before 1800, an association of shoemakers in Philadelphia, the Knights of St. Crispin. Workingmen's associations were the backbone of the Jacksonian political movement in the eastern states. By the early 1870s, skilled workers such as machinists, iron molders, carpenters, and locomotive engineers and firemen formed thousands of local trade groups that totaled about 300,000 members.

For the most part, these scattered organizations had little to do with one another. Developing at a time when industry was decentralized, the unions inevitably lagged behind employers in recognizing the need for national organization. By the end of the Civil War, however, the outlines of the new industrial order were sketched in. In 1866, William Sylvis, a visionary iron puddler (a man who made iron castings from molds), founded the National Labor Union and devoted the last three years of his life to its cause, traveling by foot around the northeastern states, his overcoat flecked with holes burned by flying sparks, rallying workers of every occupation in churches, in fraternal lodges, or under the stars.

Sylvis believed that the workers' future depended on political action. He formed alliances with a number

> ### Divide and Conquer
>
> A western lumber magnate explained that in order to have a tractable workforce, an employer should hire from several ethnic groups: "Don't get too great a percentage of any one nationality. For your own good and theirs mix them up and obliterate clannishness and selfish social prejudices."

of reform groups, including the woman-suffrage movement and farmers' organizations that were lobbying for a cheap currency. The National Labor party put up candidates in the presidential election of 1872 but with so poor a showing that the party and the NLU folded. From a membership of 400,000 in 1872, the NLU disappeared within two years.

The Knights of Labor

A different kind of national labor organization already had emerged to take the place of the National Labor Union. Organized in 1869 by a group of tailors led by Uriah P. Stephens, the Noble and Holy Order of the Knights of Labor spread its message much more quietly than Sylvis had done, indeed, secretly. Stephens was aware that an employer's usual reaction, when he discovered a union man in his midst, was to fire him. When the Knights announced meetings in newspaper advertisements, therefore, they did not reveal their meeting place or even their name, but identified the group as "******".

The Knights of Labor also differed from the NLU in their disinterest in political action as an organization. Members were urged to vote, but Stephens believed that the interests of working people would ultimately be served by solidarity in the workplace, not at the ballot box. He also wanted to avoid the divisions that the keen Democratic-Republican opposition of the era might engender.

Some Knights spoke as if they believed in class conflict, irreconcilable differences between producers and parasites, and workers and farmers on the one hand; and capitalists on the other. But their concept of class lines was far less precise than that of the Marxists. They barred from membership only

Women delegates to a Knights of Labor convention held in 1886.

HOW THEY LIVED

The Immigration Experience

The immigrant's trek began with a walk. Most of the people who came to the United States after 1880 were peasants, from rural villages that were far from a seaport or a railroad line. So they walked, a circumstance that put a stricter limit on the amount of baggage they could carry to America than did the rules of the steamship companies. Some might fill a handcart and sell it in a buyer's market when they reached their port of embarkation. More commonly, they carried a cheap suitcase or a bundle filled with their few possessions: clothing; a down-filled pillow or comforter; perhaps a favored cooking pot; a treasured keepsake; sometimes a vial of the soil of the native land that they would never see again.

In Italy, they usually walked all the way to the seacoast, to Genoa in the north or to Naples in the south. In Greece, which is made up of peninsulas and islands, there would usually be a ferry ride to Piraeus, the port of Athens. From deep within Russia, Lithuania, Poland, and Germany, there would be a train ride—more likely in boxcars than in passenger wagons. Even the Russians and Poles headed for a German port, Bremen or Hamburg, because while the czarist government provided both Christian peasants and Jews with excellent reasons to leave, the absence of a first-class commercial port in Russia prevented exploitation of the emigrant trade at home. Indeed, despite the threat of persecution, Russian and Polish Jews often had to enter Germany illegally, paying people who lived on the frontier to smuggle them across and secure a semblance of legal passports and exit visas.

Tickets, at least, were cheap. By the 1890s, heated competition among steamship companies in both northern and southern Europe pushed the price of transatlantic passage in steerage (the lowest class) below $20 and sometimes as low as $10. There were humiliating but important ceremonies on departure day: a rude bath and fumigation for lice on the docks, and a more than casual examination by company doctors for contagious diseases (especially tuberculosis), insanity, feeble-mindedness, and trachoma (an inflammation of the eye that leads to blindness and was common in Italy and Greece at the time). On the other side of the Atlantic, United States immigration authorities would refuse entry to anyone who suffered from these diseases, and the company that had brought them over was required to take them back. With paying passengers waiting in New York for passage home—there was a reverse migration too—captains were careful to make sure that they would not lose money on the return voyage. Moreover, while the horrors of shipboard epidemic were considerably reduced from what they had been in the age of sail, highly contagious diseases were not to be taken lightly.

The immigrants were crowded together. Immigrant ships held as many as a thousand people in steerage. There were no cabins, only large compartments formed by bulkheads in the hull. The only privacy was the minimum that could be created by hanging blankets around the few square feet of deck to which a family could enforce its claim. Bickering was constant, and fistfights were common. Except when the weather was bad, almost everyone preferred sitting on the open deck to huddling in the hold.

Most captains prohibited cooking of any kind, except perhaps the brewing of tea on the open deck. Meals were included in the price of passage and were taken in shifts; the last breakfast ran into the first dinner, and so on. Despite the efforts of the German and Italian governments to regulate the quality of food and cookery, the ship at sea was pretty much on its own, and emigrants were unlikely to complain about the quality of service once they arrived in America. Food was cheap, and the cause of constant complaint. Even when meals were good and prepared in sanitary galleys, the ship's cook could not please every passenger; the immigrants tended to be conservative in their

---

saloonkeepers, lawyers, and gamblers, hardly professions that included all the bosses of industrial America. In fact, Stephens himself disliked the idea of class conflict and looked forward to a day when all men and women of good will would abolish the wage system and establish a cooperative commonwealth.

Women were welcome in the Knights; so were African Americans and unskilled workers, who

culinary tastes, and devoted to a regional or village cuisine. Immigrant manuals recommended the smuggling on board of a sausage or two, or some fruit and vegetables, in order to escape from the poor fare.

Between meals the travelers chatted, sewed, exercised, played games, sang, danced, studied English in small groups, read and reread manuals and letters from friends and relatives who were already in the United States, exchanged information and misinformation about their new home, and worried that they might have made a mistake. Days could be interminable, but the voyage was not a long one by steamship. Depending on the port of embarkation and the size of the ship, it took from eight days to two weeks to arrive in New York harbor.

Indeed, an immigrant steamer that arrived at the same time as many others might lie at anchor in lower New York harbor for almost as long as it had taken to cross the Atlantic. In 1892, the United States Immigration Service opened a facility designed specifically for the "processing" of newcomers on Ellis Island, a landfill site in New York harbor that had served as an arsenal. Laid out so that a stream of immigrants would flow in controlled lines through corridors and examination rooms to be inspected by physicians, nurses, and officials, Ellis Island, its architects boasted, could handle 8,000 people a day. Fifteen thousand immigrants passed through on some days, and thousands more had to wait before they could be checked.

Processing at Ellis Island was an experience that few immigrants ever forgot. Crowds milled and shoved for position before they entered the maze of pipe railings that took them from station to station. Instructions boomed over loudspeakers in half a dozen languages; children wailed, and anxious parents called for their lost children. The first person to examine the immigrants was a doctor who was expected to make an instant diagnosis of afflictions for which the newcomers might be denied entry. If he saw a facial rash, he marked a large *F* on the immigrant's clothing with a piece of soft white chalk. People so marked were cut out of the herd and examined more closely. *H* meant suspected heart disease; *L* meant limp and examination for rickets (children were made to do a little dance); and a circle around a cross meant feeble-mindedness and thus immediate return to the ship. Thousands of families were faced with the awful decision, which had to be made within moments, whether to return to Europe with a relative who had been forbidden entry or to push on.

Those who pushed on were quickly examined for trachoma and other eye diseases and brusquely interviewed by an immigration officer. Everyone was prepared for the trick question: "Do you have a job waiting for you?" Immigrant manuals cautioned readers in capital letters *NOT* to reply in the affirmative. The Foran Contract Labor Law of 1885 forbade the making of pre-arrival agreements to work. Previously—and surreptitiously after 1885—labor jobbers had impressed immigrants into jobs under virtually slave-like conditions, or, at least, many immigrants believed that they had no choice but to work for what the Italians called the *padrone*, or "master."

About 80 percent of those who had entered the building were given landing cards that enabled them to board ferries to the Battery, the southern tip of Manhattan Island. The United States government was through with them, and the horde of agents who made their living by offering "services" now took charge. Again in a babel of languages, previously arrived countrymen shouted that they could offer jobs, provide train tickets, change currency, recommend an excellent boardinghouse. Some, but not many, were honest. Every large ethnic group in the United States eventually founded aid societies to provide newcomers such services and to protect them from being swindled within hours of their arrival in the land of opportunity.

usually were overlooked as union material in the nineteenth century. However, the Knights had a problem with one group that was essential to the success of any labor organization. Roman Catholics, particularly Irish-Americans, were the single largest ethnic group in the working class.

As the name of his organization implies, Stephens surrounded the Knights of Labor with the mystery, symbolism, ritual, secret handshakes, and other rigamarole that was common to American fraternal organizations. A lifelong Freemason, Stephens based the Knights' ritual on that of his own lodge. The trouble was that in Europe, the Masons were an anti-Catholic organization, and the pope forbade members of the Roman church to join secret societies of any sort. Catholic suspicion of the Knights was a serious obstacle to the Knights, and without Catholic participation, no labor organization could prosper.

Enter Terence Powderly

In 1879, Stephens was succeeded as Grand Master Workman by Terence V. Powderly, a misleadingly mousy-looking man with a handlebar mustache. Himself a Roman Catholic, Powderly brought the Knights into the open and moderated the Masonic flavor of their rituals. He then persuaded an influential Catholic bishop, James Gibbons, to prevail on the pope to remove his prohibition of Catholic membership in the union. Gibbons worked a miracle; the pope obliged him.

The Knights grew at a dazzling rate under Powderly. With 110,000 members in 1885, the organization claimed 700,000 the next year. Ironically, for Powderly disliked strikes, the major impetus of this growth was a remarkable strike victory by the Knights against Jay Gould's Missouri Pacific Railroad. Gould had vowed to destroy the union. "I can hire half the working class to kill the other half," he growled. But when he tried to cut wages, the Knights closed down his line and forced him to meet with their leaders and agree to their terms.

The easy victory and the explosive growth of the union proved to be more curse than blessing. Powderly and the union's general assembly were unable to control the new members. Instead of working together according to a national policy, which would seem to be the idea of a national labor organization, local leaders, who were often new to the concept of unionism, were encouraged by the victory in the Missouri Pacific strike to go it alone in a dozen unrelated directions. Powderly fumed and sputtered and refused to back the rash of strikes in 1885 and 1886. But he could not stop them.

Jay Gould got his revenge, completely crushing a strike against the Texas Pacific Railroad, another of his many properties. Then, in 1886, the Haymarket tragedy was unfairly but effectively imputed to the

Knights. Membership plummeted. Workers wanted union, more money, and a better life; not many wanted chaos.

Samuel Gompers and the AFL

In the same year as Haymarket, a national labor organization dedicated to union and stability for *some* workers was put together by a few dozen existing associations of skilled workers. The American Federation of Labor's guiding spirit was a cigar maker, born in London of Jewish parents from Holland, an immigrant to the United States as a boy.

Samuel Gompers astonished his fellow workers (and their employers) with his intelligence, learning, toughness in bargaining, and eloquence on the soapbox. He was a homely, even ugly man, squat and thick of body with a broad, coarse-featured face. But this uncomely character had very definite ideas about how labor organizations could not only survive in the United States, but become one of the interlocking forces that governed the country.

Practicality .

First of all, Gompers believed that only skilled craftsmen could effectively force employers to negotiate with them. When bricklayers refused to work, and all the bricklayers in a locality stuck together, the employer who needed bricks laid had no choice but to talk. When the unskilled hod carriers (workers who carried the bricks to the bricklayers) went out, however, employers had no difficulty in finding other men with strong backs and empty stomachs to take their place. Therefore, Gompers concluded, the AFL would admit only skilled workers.

Second, the goal of the AFL unions was "bread and butter"—higher wages, shorter hours, and better working conditions. Gompers had no patience with utopian dreamers, particularly socialists, to whom he took a strong dislike early in life. What counted was the here-and-now, not "pie in the sky." Unions with utopian programs not only distracted workers from the concrete issues that counted, but were easy targets for suppression by the bosses who were able (as in the Haymarket incident) to convince Americans that labor organizations threatened the very foundations of their society.

Third, while Gompers believed that the strike, as peaceful coercion, was the union's best weapon, he made it clear that AFL unions would cooperate with employers who recognized and bargained with them. Make unions partners in industry, he told employers, meaning AFL unions that supported the capitalist system, and radical anticapitalist organizations would wither and die.

The Friends of Friends

Gompers, who lived until 1924, served as president of the AFL every year but one (when AFL socialists defeated him). He did not see his hopes come to fruition, but he made a start. With his carrot-and-stick approach to dealing with employers—striking against those who refused to deal with the AFL, cooperating with those who accepted unions—he saw the AFL grow from 150,000 members in 1888 to more than 1 million shortly after 1900.

Most employers, however, continued to detest him and the AFL as dearly as they hated socialists and revolutionary labor unions. "Can't I do what I want with my own?" Cornelius Vanderbilt had asked years before about his company's policies. The majority of American industrialists continued to believe that the wages they paid and the hours their employees worked were no one's business but their own. Their argument was that the worker who did not like his pay had the right to quit. In 1893, such hard-nosed antilabor employers formed the National Association of Manufacturers to destroy unionism wherever it appeared. The NAM remained the most important antiunion organization into the twentieth century.

In 1900, a more enlightened group of manufacturers led by Frank Easley and Marcus A. Hanna, a former Rockefeller associate, came to the conclusion that labor unions were a permanent part of the American industrial scene. The choice was not between unions and no unions. The choice was (as Gompers had preached for more than a decade) between conservative, procapitalist unions that were willing to cooperate with employers and reckless, revolutionary unions that were determined to destroy capitalism.

Easley and his associates chose Gompers's AFL and joined with him in 1900 to form the National Civic Federation, which was to work for industrial peace through employer-union cooperation.

Conservative Unionism

By the turn of the century, Gompers's antiradicalism and opposition to organizing the unskilled, once practical policies, hardened into ideology and prejudice. On more than one occasion, Gompers actually

---

The Yellow-Dog Contract

Yellow-dog contracts, which were forced on employees by some companies, were meant to intimidate as much as anything else. The penalty for violating such a contract was dismissal, which employers did often enough without such documents. Employees had to agree that "in consideration of my present employment I hereby promise and agree that I will forthwith abandon any and all membership, connection, or affiliation with any organization or society, whether secret or open, which in any way attempts to regulate the conditions of my services or the payment therefor."

---

used AFL unions to destroy promising unions formed by unskilled workers.

The AFL's opposition to unrestricted immigration began as a hard-headed bread-and-butter policy—to keep wages up—and took on a racist aspect. Gompers, though himself a Jewish immigrant, denounced Jews from Eastern Europe as being incapable of becoming good American citizens. His opinions of the Japanese and Chinese on the West Coast were sometimes rabid.

AFL unions generally opposed the organization of women (20 percent of the workforce) and blacks, who were not numerically important outside of agriculture but were potentially of supreme interest to any working-class movement because they could be used as strikebreakers. The result was that while the lot of the skilled workers steadily improved in the late nineteenth and early twentieth centuries, only 3 percent of gainfully employed Americans were members of labor organizations. A union movement, the AFL was; a working-class organization, it was not.

THE NATION OF IMMIGRANTS

No one caught the thrill of moving to the New World with the exuberance of Mary Antin, whose genius with her adopted language made her a bestselling author. Americans bought 85,000 copies of *The Promised Land*, published in 1912. The book told the story of how Antin's Russian family left their homeland, fell in love with the United States, and either became what they considered to be good Americans, or were not quite able to do so.

Antin's tale had a special poignance because, as Jews, her mother and father came to the United States not merely to improve their standard of living, but to survive. In 1881, a czar who had relaxed anti-Jewish laws in Russia was assassinated. His dim-witted son, Alexander III, persecuted the Jews and encouraged Christian peasants to rampage through the *shtetls* on bloody pogroms (from the Russian word meaning "riot" or "devastation"). Frustrated by the poverty and desperation of their own lives in that oppressive and poor country, they beat and killed Jews with no fear of the law. As they had before and would again, the Jews moved on. Between about 1881 and 1914, fully one-third of the Jewish population of Russia left the country, most of them bound for the United States. It was one of the greatest relocations of a people in such a short period in the history of the world.

The Flood

And the Jews were not the largest ethnic group to come to the United States during the late nineteenth and early twentieth centuries. Between 1890 and 1914 (when the outbreak of the First World War temporarily choked off immigration), some 3.6 million Italians cleared the Immigration Service. And there were others: Irish, Scots, Welsh, English, Scandinavians, Germans—the so-called "Old Immigration" that continued in large numbers through the late nineteenth century—and Poles, Lithuanians, Ukrainians, Russians, Serbs, Croatians, Slovenes, Armenians, Greeks, and, from Asia, Chinese and Japanese.

Immigration was part and parcel of the American historical experience (and is so again today). The word itself, meaning movement into a place, was coined by an American, as more appropriate to Americans than emigration, movement from a place. Not even the Indians, the Native Americans, originated in the Western Hemisphere. Throughout most of the colonial period, immigrants were as important to American growth as the natural increase of population. The American Revolution and the uncertain period that followed slowed down the flow of newcomers, but not even the dangers of sea travel during the War of 1812 could quite close it down. After 1815, Europeans came over in numbers that

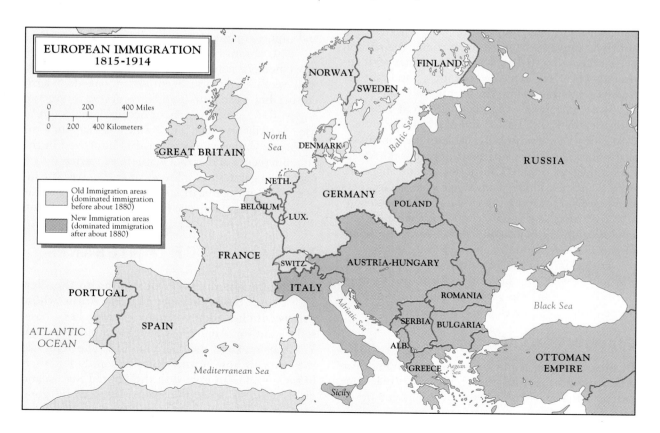

Dining hall at Ellis Island, New York. These immigrants were waiting to be "processed" and ferried to New York City.

increased almost annually. Only during serious depressions, when jobs were scarce, and during the Civil War, when a young man might be drafted before he shook down his sea legs, did the influx slow down.

From 10,000 in 1825, immigration topped 100,000 in 1845. Except for the first two years of the Civil War, the annual total never dipped below that figure. In 1854, a record 428,000 foreigners stepped ashore and it fell in 1880, when 457,000 immigrants made landfalls in Boston, New York, Philadelphia, Baltimore, New Orleans, and dozens of smaller ports. Only a crippling depression during the 1890s pushed the annual total below 300,000. After the turn of the century, during each of six years, more than a million people arrived to make homes in the United States. On one day in 1907, 11,747 immigrants were processed at one entry point alone, New York's famous Ellis Island. Always an abundant stream, sometimes swollen, immigration became a flood.

Old Immigrants, New Immigrants

But there was more to the immigration after 1880 than a mere increase in numbers. Before 1880, a large majority of immigrants listed the British Isles, Germany, or Scandinavia as their place of birth. While these northern and western Europeans continued to arrive in large numbers after 1880, an annually larger proportion of newcomers after that year originated in southern Italy: the Ottoman (Turkish) Empire; Greece; and the Slavic, Hungarian, and Romanian parts of the Austro-Hungarian Empire. And from Russia, which then included much of Poland, came both Christian and Jewish Russians, Poles, Lithuanians, Latvians, Estonians, and Finns.

Before 1880, only about 200,000 people of southern and eastern European origin lived in the United States. Between 1880 and 1910, about 8.4

million arrived. In 1896, this new immigration exceeded the old for the first time. By 1907, new immigrants were almost the whole of the influx. Of 1,285,349 legal immigrants who were registered that year, just about 1 million began their long, difficult journey in southern and eastern Europe.

Birth Pains of a World Economy

Although only parts of Europe, North America, and Japan may be described as having been industrialized in the nineteenth century, the effects of this economic revolution were felt everywhere save the most remote jungles and mountain valleys. A decline in infant mortality and an increase in life expectancy, side effects of the new technology, resulted in a giant leap in population in agricultural lands as well as in the industrial countries.

World production of foodstuffs soared too, but unequally. The biggest gains were made where agriculture was itself becoming mechanized, as in the United States. In those parts of the world where peasants remained the agricultural workforce, food production did not keep up with population growth. Thus, the grain from the broad American prairies

and increasingly from Canada undersold grain raised on small plots by peasants in countries such as Italy and Poland, the granary of eastern Europe. Even in Italy and Poland, American and Canadian grain was cheaper than the home-grown product.

The bottom fell out of the standard of living in the industrial world's hinterlands. During the latter decades of the nineteenth century, southern Italian farm workers made between $40 and $60 a year; Polish farm workers about the same. The cash income of peasants in southern China was too small to be worth calculating. When large landowners in Europe attempted to consolidate and modernize their holdings, the result was to push people off the land even more efficiently than declining incomes had.

The Jews of Russia felt the effects of the worldwide Industrial Revolution in their own way. Generally forbidden by Russian law to own land, most of them were old-fashioned artisans who handcrafted goods. Others were peddlers, some fixed in one place, others wanderers, a few scholars, professionals. Both craftsmen and peddlers found that their way of life was undercut by modernization. The shoes made by a Warsaw cobbler could not compete with cheap, machine-made shoes from England. The peddler who wandered around Russian Poland trying to sell handmade clothing learned the same lesson.

Fleeing Militarism

Finally, people on the bottom in Germany, in the Austro-Hungarian, Russian, and Ottoman empires, and in some smaller nations were cursed by the drive to build up modern military forces. In the period before the First World War, conscription into the army could mean a life sentence. Terms of service were 10 to 12 years in Austria-Hungary. A man could be on call for 25 years in Russia. And active duty in the army was brutalizing. For generations, peasants and immigrants to the United States related chilling tales of self-mutilation by young men who were trying to escape the press gangs; they chopped off their toes or fingers, or blinded an eye. Clearly it was better to go to the United States.

Promoting Immigration

Many American industrialists encouraged immigration. Until the Foran Act of 1885 made it illegal to do so, some companies paid immigrants' fares if they signed contracts agreeing to work for their patrons

---

Good Catholics

James Cardinal Gibbons used a number of arguments to persuade the pope to overcome his hostility to Catholics fraternizing with Protestants in the Knights of Labor, and to give his blessing to Catholic membership in the union. Gibbons pointed out that, whereas European union activists who were born Catholic but were now "misguided and perverted children, looking on their Mother the Church as a hostile stepmother," American Catholic workingmen were famously pious and devoted to their faith. No doubt one of the most persuasive—and oddest—of Gibbons's arguments was that, not only were Catholics already joining the Knights in droves, but they dominated the organization. "It is not in the present case that Catholics are mixed with Protestants," Gibbons wrote, "but rather that Protestants are admitted to the advantages of an association, two-thirds of whose members and the principal officers are Catholics."

when they arrived in the United States. James J. Hill plastered every sizable town in Sweden and Norway with posters that described the richness of the soil along his Great Northern Railroad. (South Dakota got its nickname the "Sunshine State" in a promotional campaign; some advertisements had palm trees swaying in the balmy Dakotan breezes.) The American Woolens Company circulated handbills in southern Italy that showed an immigrant worker with a sleek, perfumed handlebar mustache carrying a heavy sack of money from a mill to a *banco* across the street. In the West, railroaders and other employers handsomely paid Cantonese labor recruiters to import gangs of Chinese "coolies" to do heavy construction work at minuscule wages.

Employers liked immigrant labor because it was invariably cheaper than American labor, because immigrants would take menial, dirty jobs that Americans shunned, and because the newcomers were almost always more docile than old-stock Americans. So far from familiar surroundings and customs, they hesitated to complain. Since many intended to work in America only temporarily, a few months or a few years, and then return to their homelands, they were likely to accept very low wages, live on next to nothing, and take no interest in joining a union or going on strike.

From the national perspective, immigrant labor was pure asset. On the average, more than 60 percent of the arrivals on late nineteenth-century immigrant ships were able-bodied males; the percentage was higher among Italians and Greeks. The "old country" had borne the expense of supporting them during their unproductive childhood years and was still, often enough, supporting their women and children. In the United States, immigrants were producers, pure and simple. It was a very profitable arrangement.

ETHNIC AMERICA

In addition to the general push and pull that affected all immigrants to some degree, each ethnic group had its unique experience that strongly influenced both the decision to make a home in a new land and the reception that greeted them.

The Smooth Road of the British

The people of England, Scotland, Wales, and the Protestant north of Ireland continued to be among the major immigrant groups of the nineteenth cen-

tury. Between the Civil War and the turn of the century, 1.9 million Britons came to the United States. They were almost immediately at home among a people who derived primarily from their stock: in appearance they were indistinguishable from the vast majority of white Americans; they practiced the religious faiths that were most common in the United States; they were familiar with the basic culture and folkways, and they spoke the language.

To be sure, they spoke with identifiable accents that distinguished them from native-born Americans. But those accents are so rarely mentioned in the historical sources that it seems clear that the foreign birth of English, Scottish, and Welsh immigrants separated them in no meaningful way from the mainstream of American society. Andrew Carnegie, Alexander Graham Bell, James J. Hill, and several of John D. Rockefeller's associates were British, but their places of birth were of no consequence to their careers or historical images.

Among the most significant as a group in the building of the American economy were the Cornish "Cousin Jacks." Miners in their homeland in England's southwest, the Cornish brought skills that were indispensable to the development of American mining: coal, iron, lead, and precious metals. The English and Scots and Welsh eased into positions at every level in every occupation and industry.

The Catholic Irish

The story is a little different for the people of southern Ireland, then formally a part of Great Britain but far from British in sentiment. Almost all of the 3.4 million Irish who came to the United States between 1845 and 1900 spoke English, and they too were familiar with the rudiments of Anglo-American culture. However, they differed from the British in two important ways.

First, they were members of the Roman Catholic church, which many nineteenth-century American Protestants feared, even hated. In 1887 anti-Catholic prejudice was revived with the formation of the American Protective Association, which was especially strong in the Midwest. Members of the APA took an oath to "strike the shackles and chains of blind obedience" to the Roman Catholic church from the minds of communicants, but their chief activity seemed to be discrimination against ordinary Catholics.

Second, the Irish arrived not only much poorer than other Britons, but practically starved. Their land had been exploited by England for centuries. Brutalized by poverty, the Irish were considered by their English lords to be savage, stupid, and addicted to drunken riot as their recreation. Many Americans, especially the WASPs (white Anglo-Saxon Protestants) who dominated American society, culture, and economy, adopted the common English prejudice and there were many Irish immigrants happy to accommodate them: in the late 1860s and early 1870s, fully 40 percent of homicide victims in New York City were Irish-born. In fact, Irish social behavior was little different from the behavior of any people ground down by poverty; many of the idealistic Republicans who bristled when similar stereotypes were applied to blacks were the most extreme Irish-baiters. Employers hung the sign "NINA" (No Irish Need Apply) on their gates and in their shop windows.

And yet, Irish-Americans took with zest to their adopted home. Numerous enough that they could insulate their personal lives from anti-Catholic prejudice, the Irish parlayed their cohesiveness and natural bent for oratory into a formidable political force. By the time of the Civil War, the Democratic party organizations in heavily Irish cities such as Boston and New York were catering to the interests of the Irish community and reaping rewards in an almost unanimous Irish vote. By the 1880s, Irish immigrants and Irish-Americans dominated urban politics in much of the East and Midwest, and in San Francisco. Ironically, it was their considerable power on the west coast that led to the first legislation to restrict immigration—of the Chinese, for the Irish were as accomplished in bigotry as American WASPs, or anyone else who cared to step outside to settle the matter.

Guests of the Golden Mountain

In 1849, seamen brought the news to the Chinese port of Canton that a "Mountain of Gold" had been discovered in California. In a country plagued by overpopulation, flood, famine, epidemic disease, and civil warfare, the people of southern China listened avidly to the usual distortions of life across the ocean. "Americans are a very rich people," one promoter explained. "They want the Chinaman to come and will make him welcome. . . . It will not be strange company."

By the time the Chinese arrived in any numbers, the rich mines were exhausted. Accustomed to working communally, they often made a living taking over diggings that Caucasians abandoned and found employment in the menial jobs that whites disdained: cook, laundryman, farm worker, and domestic servant. By 1860, there were 35,000 Chinese immigrants in California. Most of them were young men who hoped to return home after they made their fortune; there were only 1,800 Chinese women in the state, a good many of them prostitutes. In San Francisco, Sacramento, Marysville, and most mining camps of any size, lively Chinatowns flourished.

Race and a radically different culture kept the Chinese separate. "When I got to San Francisco," wrote Lee Chew, later a wealthy businessman, "I was half-starved because I was afraid to eat the provisions of the barbarians. But a few days living in the Chinese Quarter and I was happy again."

Leaders of the Gum Shan Hok—the Guests of the Golden Mountain—also encouraged the immigrants to stick to themselves. "We are accustomed to an orderly society," explained a leader of the San Francisco Chinatown, "but it seems as if the Americans are not bound by rules of conduct. It is best, if possible, to avoid any contact with them."

Going Home

The immigrant ships were not empty when they steamed eastward across the Atlantic. Plenty of immigrants returned to Europe disillusioned, others in quite a good mood because they had intended to go home once they had made money in the land of opportunity. It is estimated that 370,697 British nationals, including Irish people, returned during the 1880s. Between 1875 and 1910, 18 percent of Swedish immigrants went home. In the depression year of 1875, about half the German immigrants to the United States turned around. Many Italian emigrants were virtual commuters known as "birds of passage." They shipped to the United States (or South America), worked for six months or so, living frugally and saving, and then returned to *bell'Italia* where they lived on their earnings until they were broke and it was time to commute once again. After the turn of the century, about one Italian returned to Italy for every three that arrived in America. The Greeks were thought to be the most likely to return. Between 1908 and 1931, about 40 percent of Greek immigrants made the trip back home.

Chinese-Americans at a Presbyterian home for girls in San Francisco pose for a photograph.

After the construction of the transcontinental railroad began in 1864, Chinese immigration stepped up. Previously about 3,000 to 6,000 a year came to California; after 1868, the annual number jumped to 12,000 and 20,000, peaking at 23,000 in 1872.

Keeping John Chinaman Out

As long as there was plenty of work, hostility to the Chinese was restrained. But in 1873, the West lapsed into a depression along with the rest of the country. In 1877, when the Chinese represented 17 percent of California's population, a San Francisco teamster named Denis Kearney began to speak to white workingmen at open-air rallies in empty sandlots. He blamed the joblessness not on impersonal economic forces but on the willingness of the Chinese to work for less than an American's living wage. Kearney led several rampages through Chinatown, but, much more important, the anti-Chinese movement inspired politicians to choke off the Asian immigration. In 1882, Congress enacted the Exclusion Act, which forbade the Chinese to come. A few hundred continued to enter legally every year (mostly women to become wives of Gum Shan Hok already here), and illegal immigration via Canada helped somewhat to augment the Chinese-American population.

To some extent, Filipinos and Japanese replaced the Chinese in the Asian immigration. Filipinos had free access to the United States after their country was made an American colony in 1898. Japanese began to trickle in, usually via Hawaii, where they were an important factor in the agricultural labor force. Caucasians resented them as much as they disliked the Chinese, but because Japan had a strong government that was sensitive to racial slights, the U.S. Congress did not adopt a Japanese exclusion law until 1924, when most immigrant groups were shut out.

The Germans and the Political Motive

In general, the large German immigration to the United States owed to the same worldwide economic forces that displaced other peasant peoples. After 1848, however, there was also a strong political dimension to the German removal. The failure of a series of liberal revolutions in several German states— revolutions aimed at establishing a democratic system and individual rights much like those that existed in the United States—forced the exile of many leading German liberals. The most famous German exile in the United States was Carl Schurz, who became a senator from Missouri and a member of Rutherford B. Hayes's cabinet.

Many of the 4.4 million ordinary Germans who came to the United States between 1850 and 1900, an average of about 100,000 a year, were also influenced by fears that life would be intolerable under the new reactionary governments in their homeland.

Because many of them were landowners in Europe, albeit not rich ones, German immigrants generally had enough money when they reached the United States to move west and take up free or cheap land. Wisconsin became heavily German in the last half of the nineteenth century. By 1900, more Milwaukeeans spoke German, at least as their first language, than spoke English. There were other heavily German areas in Missouri and Texas as well.

Adapting to America

Like the Germans, Scandinavians inclined to become farmers in the United States. Norwegians predominated in whole counties in Wisconsin and Minnesota. Swedes were numerous in other parts of Minnesota and in the Pacific Northwest. Finns, who speak an entirely different language from the Swedes but are historically tied to them in many respects, were important in yet other regions, particularly in logging country and in the iron mines of the Mesabi Range.

Ethnic groups that predominated over large areas found adaptation to the New World comparatively easy since they could approximate familiar Old World ways of life. They founded schools taught in their native languages, newspapers and other periodicals, European-style fraternal organizations (the Germans' athletically oriented *Turnverein*, or the Norwegians' musical Grieg Societies, named after their national composer), and so on. They continued to eat familiar food and raise their children by traditional rules. They were numerous enough to deal with Americans from a position of strength.

The problems that such immigrants faced were common to all settlers of a new land. Ole Rölvaag, a gloomy Norwegian-American writer, focused on the loneliness of life on the northern prairies, an experience that was shared by all pioneers there regardless of ethnic background; he did not write about cultural alienation. Indeed, he wrote in Norwegian and, like Isaac Bashevis Singer in the late twentieth century, became known as an American novelist only in translation.

Sephardic and German Jews

Other immigrant groups had a comparatively easy time adapting because they were few and cosmopolitan. The best example is the Sephardic Jews (Jews descended from and still somewhat influenced by the customs of Spanish and Portuguese forebears). Small in numbers, generally well-educated and well-fixed, they eased into middle- and upper-class society even before the Civil War, particularly in Rhode Island, New York, Charleston, and New Orleans. Considering the paucity of their numbers, they contributed a remarkable number of prominent citizens. Jefferson Davis's strongest supporter in the Confederacy was Judah P. Benjamin, a Sephardic Jew who served in three cabinet posts. Supreme Court justice Benjamin Cardozo had a Sephardic background. So did the twentieth-century financier and presidential adviser, Bernard Baruch of South Carolina.

By 1880, there was also a small German Jewish community in the United States, perhaps 150,000 people. The majority were small-scale tradesmen or businessmen—rare was the southern town without its Jewish-owned dry goods store. Some German Jews, such as the now immortalized Levi Strauss, pioneered in the founding of the ready-made clothing industry; others carved out places for themselves in finance, usually independent of the long-established American banking community, which was WASP and generally closed to outsiders. August Belmont was the most successful Jewish banker. The Guggenheim syndicate was one of the nation's leading owners of metal mines by the turn of the century.

The German Jews clung to their religious heritage, but otherwise quickly adopted American mores and customs. Indeed, led by Rabbi Isaac Mayer Wise of Cincinnati, German Jews in the United States preferred Reform religious observance, which is highly secular and closely equivalent to liberal Protestantism, over the Orthodox fundamentalist Judaism of the Jews of the new immigration.

The Trauma of the New Immigration

Adapting to their new homes was not so easy for most of the new immigrants who arrived after 1880. Very few of the newcomers from southern and eastern Europe had much money when they arrived.

Most were illiterate, and their Old World experience in peasant village and *shtetl* did not prepare them for life in the world's greatest industrial nation during its era of most rapid development.

However serious the immigrants' reasons for leaving ancestral homes, the homes were still ancestral, the rhythms of life familiar, and the customs second nature. Wherever their origins, the new immigrants were accustomed to a rural and traditional way of life that was the very antithesis of life in the United States, whether on a commercial farm or in the crowded streets of the big city.

Not only was the circle of friends and acquaintances small in the Old World, but the number of people with whom the peasant or Jewish shopkeeper dealt in the course of life was limited to a comparative few who, in any case, spoke a familiar language and thought according to similar (or, at least, well understood) values.

In the United States, however, all but a very few landsmen *(landsmänner)* or *campagni* were alien, and everyone spoke incomprehensible languages. The immigrants, at home for better or for worse in Europe or Asia, were foreigners, a minority in the United States.

Strangest of all for people who came from traditional, preindustrial cultures where life was regulated and slowed by the seasons, the weather, and the use of hand tools, American life was regulated and rushed by the tyrannical clock and powered by the relentless churning of the dynamo. In the industrial society of the late nineteenth century, Americans were even more self-driven than they were when Alexis de Tocqueville's head was set spinning by the American pace. This was particularly true in the big cities where a majority of the new immigrants settled and which, in the minds of other Americans, were intimately associated with the newcomers.

CHRONOLOGY

1866 National Labor Union organized

1869 Knights of Labor founded

1877 Nationwide railroad strike

1879 Terence V. Powderly head of Knights of Labor

1882 Chinese Exclusion Act

1886 American Federation of Labor Founded

1892 Homestead strike

1894 Pullman strike leads to national boycott

FOR FURTHER READING

The general histories listed in "For Further Reading" in Chapters 26 through 28 are all pertinent to this chapter as well. Specifically dealing with immigrants are: Rowland T. Berthoff, *British Immigrants in Industrial America*, 1953; Leonard Dinnerstein and David Reimers, *Ethnic Americans: A History of Immigration and Assimilation*, 1975; Nathan Glazer and Daniel P. Moynihan, *Beyond the Melting Pot*, 1970; Oscar Handlin, *The Uprooted*, 1951; Marcus L. Hansen, *The Immigrant in American History*, 1940; John Higham, *Send These to Me: Jews and Other Immigrants in Urban America*, 1975; Dale Steiner, *Of Thee We Sing*, 1986; and Philip A. M. Taylor, *The Distant Magnet*, 1970.

Books with a focus on working people include Bruce Laurie, *Artisans into Workers*, 1989; David Brody, *Workers in Industrial America*, 1979; Robert V. Bruce, 1877: *Year of Violence*, 1959; Leon Fink, *Workingmen's Democracy: The Knights of Labor and American Politics*, 1983; Melvyn Dubofsky, *Industrialism and the American Worker, 1865–1920*, 1975; Foster R. Dulles and Melvyn Dubofsky, *Labor in America*, 1984; Walter Licht, *Getting Work*, 1992; Herbert G. Gutman, *Work, Culture, and Society in Industrializing America*, 1976; Harold C. Livesay, *Samuel Gompers and the Origins of the American Federation of Labor*, 1978; David Montgomery, *Workers' Control in America: Studies in the History of Work, Technology, and Labor Struggle*, 1979, and *Citizen Worker*, 1993; William H. Harris, *The Harder We Run: Black Workers Since the Civil War*, 1982; Daniel Nelson, *Managers and Workers: Origins of the New Factory System in the United States, 1880–1920*, 1975; Philip Taft, *The A.F. of L. in the Time of Gompers*, 1929; and for a particular episode of owner-labor conflict, Paul Krause, *The Battle for Homestead*, 1992.

A slum in New York City at the turn of the century.

30
CHAPTER

BRIGHT LIGHTS AND SQUALID SLUMS

The Growth of Big Cities

The mobs of great cities add just so much to the support of pure government as sores do to the strength of the human body.

—Thomas Jefferson

The tumultuous populace of large cities are ever to be dreaded. Their indiscriminate violence prostrates for the time all public authority, and its consequences are sometimes extensive and terrible.

—George Washington

I have an affection for a great city. I feel safe in the neighborhood of man, and enjoy the sweet security of streets.

—Henry Wadsworth Longfellow

*O beautiful for patriot dream
That sees beyond the years
Thine alabaster cities gleam
Undimmed by human tears.*

—Katharine Lee Bates

Once in the United States, the new immigrants discovered that their ordinary practices—even the way they looked!—struck Americans of older stock as exotic. Even those WASPs who had grown accustomed to the restrained Roman Catholic worship of the Irish and the Germans found themselves troubled by the mystical Catholicism of the Poles and the public ceremonies of the Italians. Indeed, Irish bishops joined Methodists in worrying about the "paganism" implied in the magnificently bedecked statues of the Madonna and the gory, surrealistic depictions of the crucified Christ that peasants from Sicily and the Campania carried through the streets of San Francisco, Chicago, New Orleans, and New York accompanied by the music of brass bands.

The Orthodox services of the Greeks, Russians, some Ukrainians, Serbians, and other Balkan peoples seemed to feature even more ornate vestments and mystifying rituals. The Jews and the Chinese, of course, were not even Christian and therefore all the more out of line with American traditions.

The newcomers looked different from the majority of Americans, who were of northern European origin. The Greeks, Armenians, Assyrians, Lebanese, and Italians were swarthy in complexion, a formidable handicap in a nation that drew a color line. Polish women arrived clad in the colorful babushkas, billowing skirts of the eastern European peasant. The impoverished Russian Jews dressed drably enough to please the sternest American Methodist, but the men, if religious, never removed their hats. Their Saturday sabbath attracted attention because the Jews then turned Sunday into a combination holiday and major market day, which offended the sabbatarian sensibilities of some Protestants. Asians, of course, might as well have stepped from the pages of magazines.

Americans who visited immigrant neighborhoods were also unsettled because even the smells in the air were alien. Clinging to traditional cuisines, many of which employed pungent seasonings and more onion and garlic than old-stock Americans deemed humane, not to mention bizarre, the immigrants seemed determined to resist becoming American all the while they lived on American soil and shared in the national bounty.

CITIES AS ALIEN ENCLAVES

In his novel of 1890, *A Hazard of New Fortunes*, William Dean Howells sent Basil March, a genteel middle-class American, on a ride on an elevated train in New York City. March "found the variety of people in the car as unfailingly entertaining as ever" but he felt like a foreigner in his own country. Even the Irish, who ran the city, were outnumbered by "the people of Germanic, Slavonic, of Pelagic [Mediterranean], of Mongolian stock. . . . The small eyes, the high cheeks, the broad noses, the puff lips, the bare, cue-filleted skulls, of Russians, Poles, Czechs, Chinese, the furtive glitter of Italians, the blonde dullness of Germans; the cold quiet of Scandinavians—fire under ice—were aspects that he identified, and that gave him abundant suggestion for the . . . reveries in which he dealt with the future economy of our heterogeneous commonwealth."

Thomas Bailey Aldrich echoed him in verse in 1895, and wrote a foil to the famous inscription of welcome by Emma Lazarus:

Men from the Volga and the Tartar steppes,
Featureless figures of the Huang-Ho,
Malayan, Scythian, Teuton, Kelt, and Slav,
Flying the old world's poverty and scorn,
These bringing with them unknown gods and rites,
Those, tiger passions, here to stretch their claws.

A Patchwork Quilt

The cities, particularly in the Northeast and Midwest, where 80 percent of the new immigrants settled, seemed to be salients securely in the hands of

---

Race Suicide

To some Americans, the undesirable ethnicity of the immigrants would be eliminated when the newcomers intermarried with old-stock Americans and other new immigrants. Not, however, to Chester Rowell, a California editor who shivered at the prospect of racial mixing:

Castilian hidalgo mixed with Digger Indian made your servile peon. The blood of Athens and Sparta, mixed with Turk and Tatar, made your track-walking Greek. The original Aryan race, source of all the enlightenment and civilization in the world, mixed with the aboriginal black blood of India, makes your low-caste Hindu. And just these three wrecks of once proud races are being imported to repeat the same process here. It is the most dangerous possible form of race suicide, and must be stopped.

invading armies. By 1890, one-third of the population of Boston and Chicago had been born abroad, and one-quarter of Philadelphia's people. When their children, who seemed to old-stock Americans as obdurately foreign as their parents, were added to this total, the anxiety of "American" residents and visitors to the cities is easy to understand.

In fact, the immigrants threatened no one. Members of each ethnic group clustered together into ghettos that were exclusively their own. A map of New York, wrote journalist Jacob Riis, himself a Danish immigrant, "colored to designate nationalities, would show more stripes than the skin of a zebra and more colors than the rainbow." Jane Addams sketched a similar patchwork in the poor part of Chicago, where she established Hull House, a settlement house, a privately funded institution providing social services to poor immigrants. The same was true of most large eastern and midwestern cities and of many smaller industrial towns. In Lawrence, Massachusetts, a woolens manufacturing town, more than 20 languages and probably twice that many distinctive dialects were spoken.

There were ghettos within ghettos. In New York City's Greenwich Village, an Italian community, people from the region of Calabria effectively controlled housing on some streets, immigrants from Sicily on others. On such regional blocks, Italians from a specific village would sometimes be the sole occupants of an "Agrigento tenement," and so on. Grocery stores and restaurants advertised themselves not as Italian but as purveyors of Campanian or Apulian food. Priests frequently ministered to the same people whom they had known back in Italy; lawyers often represented the same clients.

The same held true for Jewish neighborhoods, where Galician Jews (Galicia was a province of Poland) looked with suspicion on Jews from Russian-speaking parts of Europe. Romanian Jews fastidiously set up their own communities, and the assimilated and better established German Jews wondered what the world was coming to. Christian Germans divided on Lutheran and Catholic lines; Serbs and Croatians, because the latter wrote their language in the Latin alphabet, the Serbs in the Cyrillic alphabet of Russia.

The Impulse to Assimilate

The desire to assimilate, to become "American," varied in intensity from group to group, and among individuals within a group. Some immigrants found solace in the familiar language, familiar customs, familiar foods, and fellowship of "Little Italy," "Jewville," and "Polack Town," and clung tenaciously to the neighborhood. The ethnic ghetto was a buffer against the prejudice of old-stock Americans and the hostility of other ethnic groups with whom its inhabitants competed for the lowest-level jobs. Even an educated immigrant from the Austro-Hungarian Empire found himself disoriented in his attempts to shift from old to new ways of thinking and reacting.

I never knew if my reactions would be in line with the new code of conduct and had to think and reflect. Whenever I decided on the spur of the moment I found myself out of sympathy with my environment. I did not feel as they felt and therefore I felt wrongly according to their standards. To act instinctively in an American fashion and manner was impossible, and I appeared slow and clumsy. The proverbial slowness of foreigners is largely due to this cause.

Others seized avidly on what they took to be American ways with an extraordinary enthusiasm. This was perhaps best illustrated in the large Jewish community of New York's Lower East Side, which in its earliest years was sharply divided between those who clung to the medieval customs of the Russian and Polish *shtetls* and the big city—wise and sophisticated younger immigrants and children of immigrants who embraced America as a new "Promised Land" and scorned their elders' greenhorn ways.

Avenues of Advancement

Hard work at menial jobs was the economic lot of most immigrants. The urban political machine, which had room at or near the top for anyone who could deliver votes, provided an avenue of advancement for a few who recognized the opportunities it provided for the "boss" of the ethnic ghetto. Others joined the American quest for material success by pursuing careers in areas that were not quite respectable, and, therefore, less attractive to members of established social groups—show business and professional sports, and also organized crime, that is, illegal business. A roster of surnames of leading entertainers, boxers, baseball players, and gangsters over a period of decades resembles the strata of a canyon that geologists read, each layer dominated by members of a new, aspiring ethnic group.

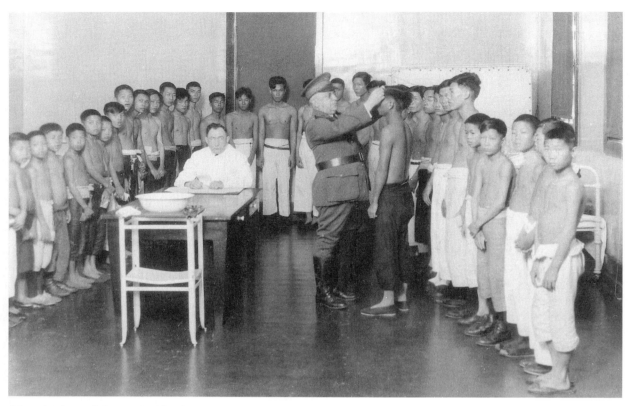

Chinese immigrants being examined for glaucoma (grounds for deportation) at Angel Island, San Francisco Bay.

Immigrant Aid Institutions

The ethnic groups themselves established institutions to assist their countrymen in adjusting to the new life. Some encouraged assimilation, some clannishness. Sephardic and German Jewish families which were comfortably established in the United States founded the Hebrew Immigrant Aid Society to minister to the needs of the penniless eastern European Jews who flocked into the cities. The Young Men's and Young Women's Hebrew Associations, dating back to 1854, expanded several times over during the last decade of the century.

Among the Catholic population, which grew from 6 million in 1880 to 10 million in 1900 (making Roman Catholicism the country's largest single denomination), traditionally charitable religious orders such as the Franciscans and the Sisters of Mercy established hospitals and houses of refuge in the slums. The St. Vincent de Paul Society functioned much like the Protestant Salvation Army, but without the military trappings, providing food, clothing, and shelter for the utterly desperate.

Curiously, a sort of ethnic prejudice helped to hamstring the older Jewish and older Catholic communities into responding to the needs of the new immigrants. Sephardic and German Jews worried that the numbers, poverty, and provincialism of the eastern European newcomers would arouse an anti-Semitic spirit among Christians that would be turned on them, too. The American Catholic church was dominated by Irish-Americans who were little more cordial toward Italians, Poles, and other new Catholic nationalities than were old-stock Protestants. Only after an encyclical of 1891, *Rerum Novarum*, in which the pope proclaimed a Catholic Social Gospel, did the church hierarchy take much interest in the material well-being of its communicants.

Then the church was torn between serving as an agency of assimilation and maintaining its high standing among Catholic immigrants—who often clung to their religion with more piety than they had in Europe—by encouraging a "fortress mentality" toward the dominant Protestant culture. Indeed, the church approved of parishes organized along ethnic rather than geographical lines. In places like Detroit

Hester Street in New York City was home to a large community of Jewish immigrants in the early 1890s.

> ### Protesting Progressive Education
>
> Like today, well-meaning middle-class progressives had their own programs for turn-of-the-century immigrants. Also like today, however, their plans did not particularly suit the people for whom they were drawn up. For example, an Italian-American woman protested permissive "child-oriented" education in schools in Greenwich Village, New York, a neighborhood shared by Italian immigrants and trendy intellectuals.
>
> *The program of that school is suited to the children of well-to-do homes, not to our children. We send our children to school for what we cannot give them ourselves, grammar and drill. . . . We do not send children to school for group activity; they get plenty of that in the street.*

and New Orleans, there might be an Italian, a Polish, a Lithuanian, and a geographical parish church—that is, an "Irish-German" church, within a few blocks of one another.

Settlement Houses

Old-stock Americans created the settlement house, patterned after Toynbee Hall in a notorious London slum, to assist immigrants in coming to terms with their new country.

During the 1880s, a number of middle-class Americans who were imbued with the New England conscience that dictated concern for others traveled to England to learn how Toynbee worked. They found that the house provided food and drink to the disinherited, as traditional charities had, but also child care for working mothers, recreational facilities, and courses of study in everything from household arts to the English language and social skills needed for self-improvement. The young men and women who worked at Toynbee Hall also told the Americans that they were morally elevated by their sacrifices and exposure to a misery that they had not known in their own lives.

The first American settlement house was the Neighborhood Guild, set up in New York City in 1886. More famous, however, because of the powerful personalities of their founders, were Jane Addams's Hull House in Chicago (1889), Robert A. Woods's South End House in Boston (1892), and Lillian Wald's Henry Street Settlement in New York (1893). From comfortable middle-class backgrounds, well-educated, and finely mannered, Addams, Woods, and Wald were exemplars of the American middle class who were determined to fight the materialism of their own people, the misery suffered by poor city dwellers, and to keep traditional American values alive. What they did not always understand was that in the great metropolises that took shape in the late nineteenth century, a new American culture and code of values was emerging.

OF THE GROWTH OF GREAT CITIES

Many Americans had an ingrained prejudice against cities that dated back to Thomas Jefferson. However, by the end of the nineteenth century, the United States was also one of the world's most

How They Lived

Big-City Sweatshops

In the early nineteenth century, four Americans in five wore clothing that had been made to order. The wealthy took their wants to the little shops in every town and city where fine garments were expertly made by hand from fabric to finished product. With great skill, tailors and seamstresses worked not from patterns, as someone interested in sewing would do today, but from fashion plates, carefully drawn pictures in magazines of people dressed in the latest styles. By the early nineteenth century, Paris was already considered the authority in such matters.

The middle classes, which began to pay more attention to "fashion" in the nineteenth century, depended on their womenfolk for their garb. That is why needlecraft learned at a mother's knee was such an important part of a young girl's education; clothing her family would be one of her most important duties as a wife and mother.

As for the poor, they made do with castoffs either scavenged or purchased from merchants who specialized in buying and reconditioning used clothing. The fact that most garments were made to fit an individual did not mean that any particular item had been made to fit the person who, at a given time, was wearing it.

Only sailors, slaves, and—after 1849—miners in the West were likely to wear clothing such as virtually everyone does today, ready-made in quantity to standard sizes and sold "off the rack." Sailors were not generally in a port long enough to be fitted and a garment sewn. (The first ready-made clothing stores were called "sailors' shops.") The slaves had no choice in the matter of what they put on their backs, and their owners, wanting to provide them some protection from the elements at a minimum cost, became an attractive market for enterprising tailors who abandoned the custom trade and took to producing rough, cheap garments in quantity. Miners, like sailors, were in a hurry, and they lived in an almost entirely masculine society. Their demand for sturdy, ready-made clothing provided the impetus for the founding in 1850 of the Levi Strauss Company of San Francisco, today perhaps the best-known manufacturer of ready-made clothing in the world.

By 1900, things had changed. Nine Americans in ten were wearing ready-made togs. A "Clothing Revolution," as historian Daniel Boorstin has called it, had taken place as a consequence of technology with, curiously, a boost from the American Civil War.

The technology was supplied by inventions such as the sewing machine, patented by Elias Howe in 1846, and powered scissors that could cut through 18 pieces of fabric at once, thus making the parts for 18 garments of exactly the same size. The standard sizes were provided by the United States government when the Civil War made it necessary to buy uniforms for hundreds of thousands of men. The army's Quartermaster Corps measured hundreds of recruits and arrived at sets of proportions that provided a fit for almost all. It was a simple step to do the same for women's sizes after the war ended, and ready-made clothing shops began to displace tailors and seamstresses. The department store, which appeared at the end of the century, was built around its selection of every kind of clothing. The great mail-order houses such as Montgomery Ward and Sears Roebuck were able, with everyone knowing his or her size, to sell garments by mail.

How were the new ready-made clothes manufactured? Not, ironically, in factories. There was little outsize machinery involved in the making of garments (sewing machines were treadle or electrically powered) and a great deal of handwork (finishing buttonholes, installing linings). Thus it was possible to farm out the work to people in their homes, just as, before the invention of cloth-making machinery, spinning and weaving had been farmed out.

urbanized countries. The proportion of city dwellers in the total population, the number of cities, and the size of cities all increased at a faster rate in the United States than in any other country in the world.

In 1790, when the first national census was taken, only 3.4 percent of Americans lived in towns of 8,000 people or more. By 1860, the eve of the Civil War, 16 percent of the population was urban, and by 1900, 33 percent. Even more striking was the

Whereas the old putting-out system usually had involved the wives and daughters of farmers, leaving people on the land, the new putting-out system engaged people who lived in city slums and who depended exclusively on needlework for their livelihood.

The system was called "sweating," and the places in which the garmentmakers worked were called "sweatshops" because of the peculiarly exploitative character of the system. A manufacturer of clothing kept a small headquarters; at the most, the material was cut to pattern in his "factory." Then, the pieces of a garment were handed out on a weekly or daily basis to people, usually Jewish or Italian immigrants, who took them home to their tenement apartments. There the whole family—perhaps some boarders, perhaps even some neighbors—sat down during all the daylight hours to make up the garments. Sometimes a household saw a coat (usually called a cloak in the nineteenth century) or a gown through from components to completion. Other households specialized in different phases of the process, such as roughing the garment in, or finishing work. Some sweatshops made buttonholes, others sewed pockets, and so on.

The key to the system was that everyone involved was paid by the piece—so much per jacket, so much per lining. A complex hierarchy of subcontracting developed in which it was to the interest of all to pay those below them in the chain as little for their work as possible. That is, a man who provided finished cloaks to the manufacturer received a fixed rate for each garment that he delivered. In order to make a profit, he had to pay less than that rate to those households that had done the work. If the head of a household sweatshop had boarders or neighbors sewing, he had to pay them even less. Everybody was "sweating" their income out of somebody else.

Moreover, just as in factories, employers were inclined to cut the piece rate as a worker's productivity increased or when someone else told the manufacturer whom he supplied (who sweated him) that others were willing to work for less. In order to compete, he sweated the people under him.

In turn, everyone in the chain had to take less for their work. The operator of a Chicago sweatshop explained the results to a congressional committee in 1893:

Q. In what condition do you get the garments?
A. They come here already cut and I make them up.
Q. What is the average wage of the men per week?
A. About $15 a week.
Q. How much do the women get?
A. About $6. They get paid for extra hours. . . .
Q. Are wages higher or lower than they were two years ago?
A. Lower. There are so many who want to work.
Q. How much do you get for making this garment?
A. Eighty cents.
Q. How much did you get for making it two years ago?
A. About $1.25.
Q. Is the help paid less now?
A. Yes, sir.

A cloakmaker, Abraham Bisno, told the same panel that he had earned about $20 a week in 1885 for completing fewer garments than he had sewn in 1890, when he had made $13 to $14 a week. In 1893, he was being paid $11 a week for even greater productivity.

As the rate per piece fell, sweatshop workers increased their hours in the unhealthful, poorly ventilated tenements. Only when urban states such as New York and Illinois passed laws that forbade such work in residences was there any improvement in conditions. But, often as not, the driving exploitation of the sweat system was merely transferred to an unhealthful, poorly ventilated factory that was little different from a tenement flat.

increase in the number of cities. In 1790, only 6 American cities boasted populations of 8,000 or more. The largest of them, Philadelphia, was home to 42,000 people. In 1860, 141 municipalities had at least 8,000 people within their limits; by 1890, 448 did, and by 1910, 778! Fully 26 cities were larger than 100,000 in 1900, and 6 of them topped 500,000. Philadelphia counted 1.3 million people at the turn of the century and, at that, had slipped to third place behind New York and Chicago.

From Country to City

Although the influx of immigrants was largely responsible for the tremendous growth of cities at the end of the century, old-stock Americans migrated from country to city, too. Dismayed by the isolation of farm life, ground down by the heavy tedious labor, and often as not reaping few rewards for their toil, they heard of well-paying jobs for literate, mechanically inclined people. Or they visited cities and were dazzled by the bright lights, the abundance of company, the stimulation of a world in constant motion, and the stories of the fortunes that might be made in business.

Parents, rural ministers, and editors of farm magazines begged, threatened, and cajoled in an effort to keep the children of the soil at home, but their efforts met with limited success. While the total number of farm families grew during the late nineteenth century, the proportion of farmers in the total population declined, and in some regions, with a nearby city beckoning, even the numbers dropped. During the 1880s, more than half the rural townships of Iowa and Illinois declined in population, while Chicago underwent its miraculous growth. In New England, while the overall population of the region increased by 20 percent, three rural townships in five lost people to the dozens of bustling mill towns that lined the fast-moving rivers and to the metropolises of Boston and New York.

For the most part, the American migration from farm to city was a white migration. Only 12 percent of the 5 million blacks in the United States in 1890 lived in cities. Nevertheless, about 500,000 blacks moved from the rural South to the urban North during the final decade of the century, foreshadowing one of the most significant population movements of the twentieth century.

Metropolis

While rapid growth was the rule in cities large and small, the most dramatic phenomenon of American urbanization in the late nineteenth century was the emergence of the gigantic metropolises, the six cities of more than 500,000 people that dominated the regions in which they sat like imperial capitals. Philadelphia doubled in size between 1860 and 1900, when William Penn's "green countrie towne" claimed 1.3 million people. New York, with 33,000 people in 1790, and over 1 million in 1860, quadrupled its

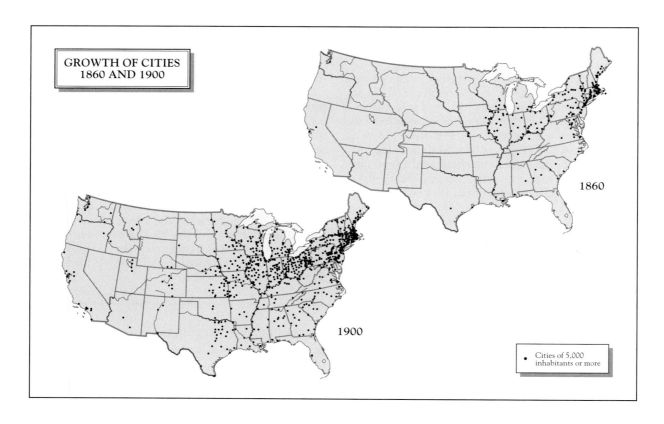

numbers until, by 1900, 4.8 million lived within its five boroughs. New York was the second largest city in the world, smaller only than London.

Chicago's crazy rate of growth as the hub of the nation's railroad system amazed Americans and foreigners alike. With only a little more than 100,000 souls in 1860, Chicago increased its size 20 times in a generation, numbering 2.2 million inhabitants in 1900.

Walking Cities

Before the 1870s, cities so populous were unimaginable. When the mass of a city's people moved around by foot or in horse-drawn conveyances, city growth was limited in area to a radius of a mile or two, as far as workers could walk to their jobs, bosses to their offices, and housekeepers to market.

To be sure, the well-to-do owned horses and carriages, but a horse at a walk moves only a little faster than a human pedestrian and rather more slowly when the streets are choked with people wending to and fro. With transportation such a major consideration, in the walking city the most desirable neighborhood was centrally located. Lots in-town were small, 20 feet wide typically, even where the well-to-do lived. Streets were narrow. With often a 12-hour day to work, there was little time for commuting and space was not to be wasted on roominess, broad avenues, or fresh air.

Except for those on the very bottom, the social classes of the walking city lived in close proximity. The wealthy needed to have their maids, butlers, and stablemen in their homes, and nearby the small businessmen who provided out-services—retailers of all kinds, coal merchants, purveyors of men, etc.—within easy reach. Small businessmen lived behind their shops, the people who worked for them nearby. Both employer and employee needed to be close to the factory or shop.

The line between city and country was clear to all. Where built-up neighborhoods, paved streets, and sewers ended, farmland began. Often, the outer edge of a large city was marked by ramshackle shantytowns inhabited by people who had not yet found a role to play in the city's life, or who were discarded by the frantic demands of a competitive society. Unlike today, when homeless people cluster in the central cores of cities, in the walking city of the nineteenth century, the limitations inherent in foot and horse travel relegated the marginal to the suburbs.

> ### Double Standard
>
> The British writer Rudyard Kipling commented on American (and Irish-American) prejudice against immigrants when visiting San Francisco in 1889: "The Chinaman waylays his adversary and methodically chops him to pieces with a hatchet. Then the Press roar about the brutal ferocity of the Pagan. The Italian reconstructs his friend with a long knife. The press complain on the waywardness of the alien. The Irishman and the native Californian in the hours of discontent use the revolver, not once but six times. The press records the fact and asks in the next column whether the world can parallel the progress of San Francisco."

Not that center city living was delightful. In fact, the congestion, pace, turmoil, noise, and dirt of urban life was such that, when the opportunity to flee presented itself, the wealthy and then the middle classes were quick to seize it, leaving center cities to the businesses that were the source of their prosperity.

Getting Around

The first device making it possible for people of means to put distance between their residences and center city was the horsecar line. With charters from city hall, entrepreneurs strung light rails down major thoroughfares on which they ran horse-drawn streetcars with seats open to the public. Fares were cheap, usually five cents, but that was still too much for working people to pay twice daily. They continued to walk to their jobs, which meant living in the old city centers, near the factories. However, well-paid skilled artisans, white-collar workers, and small businessmen took advantage of the quick, cheap transportation to move away from their places of business: north on the island of Manhattan in New York, west across the Schuylkill River in Philadelphia, north and west out of Chicago and Boston.

Making possible even more distant residential neighborhoods was the steam-powered elevated train, or El, which ran at high speeds above the crowded streets on ponderous and ugly steel scaffolding, and—in cities on large bodies of water—ferryboats catering to passengers. In 1870, New York completed the first El on Ninth Avenue, and the

Gridlock in the horse-drawn-vehicle age. Because a horse could panic or collapse, traffic jams in the late nineteenth century were often worse than they are today.

range of the trains, soon up to the northern tip of Manhattan, encouraged the middle classes to move even farther away from Wall Street and the once leafy, now crowded Bowery. In making the suburbs more accessible and desirable, the Els also served to begin the process of pushing the residents of the shantytowns into inner-city housing abandoned by the middle classes.

The steam ferry had the same effect. As early as 1850, nimble ferryboats were traveling from Manhattan to Brooklyn, across the East River, every few minutes. By 1860, 100,000 people were making the six-minute crossing each day. Brooklyn was a ferry suburb, as was Camden, New Jersey, across the Delaware River from downtown Philadelphia. San Francisco Bay, spacious as the great harbor is, was vexed by ferryboat traffic jams as wealthy and middle-class people looked to outlying areas for their homes.

Electric Trolleys

The utility of elevated trains was limited by the high cost of constructing them. Only the richest, largest (and most corrupt) cities were able and willing to shoulder the expense. Moreover, no sooner did the Els stimulate residential construction along their routes, where they ran at ground level, than the noisy, dirty, and dangerous locomotives roused the ire of the very people who rode on them to work and recreation.

Consequently, it was the electric trolley car, pioneered by inventor-businessman Frank J. Sprague, that really turned the walking city into a memory and ensured the sprawl of the great metropolises. Economical, fast but easy to stop, clean, quiet, even pleasantly rhythmic in their rattling and melodious in their ringing of bells, the trolleys were the key to the growth of big cities and assets to smaller ones.

Richmond was the first to build a system in 1887. By 1895, fully 850 lines crisscrossed American cities on 10,000 miles of track. They were as important to the urbanization of the United States as the railroads were to the settlement of the West.

Building Up

In fostering the construction of residential neighborhoods miles from city business districts, the trolleys made it possible for many more people to congregate in city centers for work, business, and entertainment. The new money-making potential of real estate in town caused property values to soar to absurd heights.

The theoretical solution was obvious enough: multiply the square footage of midtown properties by building ever taller structures, ever more stories. But there were practical problems. Masonry construction methods—piling stone on stone, laying brick on brick that, on the lower floors of an eight- or ten-story building, the weight-bearing walls had to be so thick, virtually solid like the pyramids of Egypt, as to defeat the whole purpose of building up, providing more room. What was worse, the lower levels of any building were more desirable and therefore more profitable: the more stairs a businessman had to climb to his office, or the hotel guest to his room, the less valuable the floor space.

Elisha Graves Otis's safety hoist, or elevator, solved the problem of fully exploiting the upper floors. In fact, mechanical hoists had been around since the days of the pharaohs; a steam-powered lift

A network of trolley car lines served San Francisco's transportation needs. Note "cow catchers" designed to save humans as well as errant animals from slipping beneath the wheels.

The Flatiron Building, an early skyscraper, photographed around 1905. Today it is dwarfed by its neighbors.

Safety Record

Few manufacturers can take the pride in the products that the Otis Elevator Company can. In 150 years, only one Otis elevator has fallen to the bottom of the elevator shaft, in 1943 when a plane crashed into the eighty-ninth floor of New York's Empire State Building and one elevator at the seventeenth floor plummeted to the ground. Even then, the operator survived.

was put into service in England in 1835. Until Otis, however, hoisting cables and ropes snapped so often as to make a ride on an elevator a dangerous adventure. Beginning in 1852, Otis and his equally imaginative sons developed safety systems based on ratchets. No longer were the upper stories of a building the least desirable because of the effort required to reach them. Indeed, they were more desirable because (in an Otis promotional brochure), Monsieur "makes the transit in half a minute of repose and quiet, and arriving there, enjoys a purity and coolness of atmosphere and an exemption from noise, dust, and exhalations." By 1878, the Otises' hydraulic elevators climbed at 600-800 feet per second.

Jenney and the Skyscraper

William L. Jenney solved the problem of massive weight-bearing walls. In 1885, he perfected the I-beam girder, a steel support with little mass that was so strong that it became possible to design towering skeletons of steel on which, in effect, builders hung decorative siding of cast iron or stone. The potential height of structural steel buildings seemed almost limitless; they could rise so high as to scrape the sky. Indeed, once the method was perfected, corporations competed to erect the tallest tower, as medieval cities competed to build the tallest cathedral spire.

In time, New York was to become the most dramatic of the skyscraper cities; but Chicago architects pioneered in the design of "tall office buildings," as Louis H. Sullivan, the most thoughtful of architects, rather prosaically described his graceful structures. In an article in *Lippincott's Magazine* in 1896, Sullivan explained how through the use of "proud and soaring" vertical sweeps, "a unit without a single dissenting line," the artistic form of the skyscraper reflected the essence of its construction. In the twentieth century, Sullivan's even more imaginative protégé, Frank Lloyd Wright, was to apply the principle of form following function to a wide variety of structures.

Building Over

Another technological innovation that contributed to the expansion of cities was the suspension bridge, which erased wide rivers as barriers to urban growth. Its pioneer was a German immigrant, John A. Roebling, who came to the United States in 1831 as a canal engineer and set up the first American factory for twisting steel wire into cable. Roebling's associates scoffed at his contention that if a bridge were hung from strong cables instead of built up on massive pillars that had to stand in the water, much broader rivers could be spanned. Obsessed with the concept of a suspension bridge, Roebling devoted his life to perfecting a design. Before the Civil War, he had several to his credit, including an international bridge over the Niagara River near the falls.

Roebling planned his masterpiece for the East River, separating downtown New York, which was bursting at the seams, from the roomy seaport of Brooklyn on Long Island. While working on the site in 1869, he was injured, contracted a tetanus infection, and died. Without delay, his equally devoted son, Washington A. Roebling, carried on the work. He too received serious injuries; he was crippled from the bends, later associated with deep-sea divers, as a result of working too long below water level on the foundations of the towers. Nevertheless, from a chair in a room overlooking the great span, now called the Brooklyn Bridge, with his wife taking over on-site supervision (to the consternation of many), he saw it completed in 1883. It was admired for its beauty as well as its engineering.

In providing easy access to Manhattan—33 million people crossed it each year—the bridge ignited a residential real estate boom in Brooklyn; within a few years, Brooklyn was the fourth largest city in the United States. But the bridge also spelled the end of Brooklyn as an independent city. A satellite of Manhattan in fact, Brooklyn was incorporated into the city of New York by law in 1898.

The Great Symbol

The Brooklyn Bridge was dedicated with a mammoth celebration. President Chester A. Arthur proclaimed it "a monument to democracy"; sides of beef were roasted in the streets; oceans of beer and whiskey disappeared; brass bands competed in raising a din; races were run; prizes were awarded; dances were danced; and noses were punched. A fireworks display of unprecedented magnificence topped off the festivities, illuminating the fantastic silhouette from both sides of the East River. The Brooklyn Bridge was a celebration of the city.

It was also an indictment of the city. On the morning of the gala, one dissenting newspaper editor groused that the Brooklyn Bridge had "begun in fraud" and "continued in corruption." It was no secret to anyone that much of the $15 million that the project cost had gone not into concrete, steel, and Roebling cable but into the pockets of crooked politicians.

The glories of the bridge were also marred by its cost in human lives. At least 20 workers were killed building it, and others just vanished, probably falling unnoticed. Many more were maimed. Then, just a few days after the dedication, a woman stumbled while descending the stairs that led from the causeway to the ground, and someone shouted, "The bridge is sinking!" In the stampede that followed, 12 people were trampled to death.

THE EVILS OF CITY LIFE

City people died at a rate not known in the United States since the seventeenth century. At a time when the national death rate was 20 per 1,000 annually, the death rate in New York City was 25. In the slums, it was 38, and for children under five years of age, 136 per 1,000. The figures were only slightly lower in the other big cities, and in parts of Chicago they were higher. In one Chicago slum as late as 1900, the infant mortality rate was 200; one child in five died within a year of birth. By way of comparison, the infant mortality rate in the United States today is less than 20 per 1,000, and the total death rate is less than nine.

Too Many People, Too Little Room

City people died primarily because of impossibly crowded living conditions, another consequence of high real estate values. In Philadelphia and

The newly built Brooklyn Bridge, as stunning in its design as it was revolutionary in the economy and society of New York City.

596 *Chapter 30 Bright Lights and Squalid Slums*

Horse and Buggy Days

A horse dead was a sanitation problem in big cities, but so was a horse alive. Each horse produced as much as 25 pounds of manure each day. In New York City in 1900 there were about 150,000 horses. The potential litter problem, therefore, weighed about 1,800 tons. Most manure merely dried and crumbled where it dropped, blowing or washing away in time. Some was scooped up by the city or private entrepreneurs and sold to farmers on the outskirts of the city as fertilizer.

Baltimore, the poor crowded into two- and three-story brick row houses that ran for 200 yards before a cross street broke the block. In Boston and Chicago, typical housing for the new immigrants was in old wooden structures that had been comfortable homes for one family; in the late nineteenth century, they were crowded by several families, plus boarders. In New York, the narrow confines of Manhattan Island made the crowding even worse. Former single-family residences were carved into tenements that housed a hundred and more people.

In 1866, the New York Board of Health found 400,000 people living in overcrowded tenements with no windows, and 20,000 living in cellars below the water table. At high tide, their homes filled with water. The board closed the cellars and ordered 46,000 windows cut in airless rooms; but in 1900, people whose memories dated back to 1866 said that conditions were even worse than ever.

Jacob Riis, a newspaper reporter who exposed urban living conditions in a book of 1890, *How the Other Half Lives*, estimated that 330,000 people lived in a square mile of slum; 986.4 people an acre. New York was more than twice as crowded as the London that turned Charles Dickens's stomach, and parts of it were more populous than Bombay, the Americans' image of a living hell. On one tenement block in the Jewish section of the Lower East Side, just a little larger than an acre, 2,800 people lived. In one apartment of two tiny rooms there, Riis found a married couple, their twelve children, and six adult boarders.

When architect James E. Ware designed a new kind of building to house New York's poor, he worsened the situation. His "dumbbell" tenement, named for its shape, ostensibly provided 24 to 32 apart-

ments, all with ventilation, on a standard New York building lot of 25 by 100 feet. However, when two dumbbells were constructed side by side, the windows of two-thirds of the living units opened on an air shaft, sometimes only two feet wide, that was soon filled with garbage, creating a threat to health worse than airlessness. Nevertheless, the dumbbells met city building standards, and by 1894, there were 39,000 of them in New York, housing about half the population of Manhattan.

Health

Such crowding led to epidemic outbreaks of serious diseases like smallpox, cholera, measles, typhus, scarlet fever, and diphtheria. Quarantining of patients, the indispensable first step in dealing with highly contagious diseases in the nineteenth century, was out of the question in slums: Where were the unafflicted people to go? Even less dangerous illnesses like chicken pox, mumps, whooping cough, croup, and the various influenzas were killers in the crowded cities. Common colds were feared as the first step to pneumonia.

In his famous book, Jacob Riis took readers on a tour of a tenement: "Be a little careful, please! The hall is dark and you might stumble. You can feel your way, if you cannot see it. Close? Yes! What would you have? All the fresh air that enters these stairs comes from the hall-door that is forever slamming." He paused at the entrance to a windowless apartment. "Listen! That short, hacking cough, that tiny, helpless wail. . . . The child is dying of measles. With half a chance it might have lived; but it had none. That dark bedroom killed it."

Sanitation

The crowding itself was the chief cause of poor sanitation. Whereas free-roaming scavengers—chickens, hogs, dogs, and wild birds—handily cleaned up the garbage in small towns, and backyard latrines were adequate in disposing of human wastes, neither worked when more than a hundred people lived in a building and shared a single privy. City governments provided for waste collection, but even when honestly administered (which was the exception), sanitation departments simply could not keep up.

Horses compounded the problem. They deposited tons of manure on city streets daily, and special squads could not begin to keep pace. Moreover,

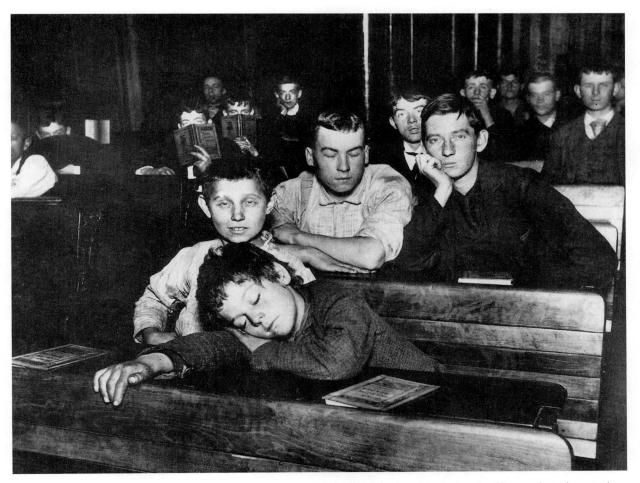

Jacob Riis photographed New York slum conditions at their worst, but also recorded attempts by private and public agencies to improve them, such as this night school.

on extremely hot and cold days, old and poorly kept horses keeled over by the hundreds; on occasion in New York the daily total topped 1,000. Although by law the owner of the dead beast was required to dispose of the carcass, this often meant dumping it into the river. More often, because the task was so formidable, owners of faltering nags cut their horses out of harness and disappeared. In summer, the corpses bloated and began to putrefy within hours.

In the poorest tenements, piped water was available only in shared sinks in the hallways, which were typically filthy. Safe water was so heavily dosed with chemicals that it was barely palatable. The well-to-do bought bottled spring water that was trucked into the cities. Other people depended on wells in the streets that were inevitably fouled by runoff.

Tenement apartments did not have bathrooms. Children washed by romping in the water of open fire hydrants or by taking a swim in polluted waterways. If you did not come home tinged gray or brown, one survivor of New York's Lower East Side remembered, you had not washed. When a bath was necessary, adults went to public bathhouses where there was hot, clean water at a reasonable price. Many of these establishments were quite respectable. Others became known as dens of immorality.

Vice and Crime

As they always are, slums were breeding grounds of vice and crime. With 14,000 homeless people in New York in 1890, many of them children—"street

Arabs"—and work difficult to get and uncertain at the best of times, many found the temptations of sneak thievery, pocket picking, purse snatching, and, for the bolder, violent robbery, too much to resist. As early as the 1850s, police in New York were vying with (or taking bribes from) strong-arm gangs who were named after the neighborhoods where they held sway: the Five Points Gang, Mulberry Bend, Hell's Kitchen, Poverty Gap, the Whyo Gang.

They sometimes struck outside their areas, robbing warehouses and the like, and preying on the middle- or upper-class fops who took to slumming in dubious neighborhoods. But the gangs' typical victims were slum dwellers struggling to survive and escape the slum: the workingman who paused for a beer before he took his pay envelope home, or the small businessmen who were forced to make regular payments or risk physical violence. Whereas the homicide rate declined in German and British cities as they grew larger, it tripled in American cities during the 1880s. Although the prison population rose by 50 percent, the streets in some sections grew more dangerous.

By the end of the century, the more sophisticated gangs moved into vice, running illegal gambling operations, opium dens, and brothels. Prostitution flourished at every level in a society where sex was repressed, and there was a plentiful supply of impoverished girls and young women who had no other way to survive. The lucky ones set themselves up as mistresses or in fancy houses that catered to the wealthy. More common was the wretched slattern who plied her trade in the slums under the protection of a gang.

An Urban Culture

And yet, for all the horror stories, which no one savored more than the people who lived in the cities, for all the lurid accounts of urban life in books, newspapers, magazines, sermons, lectures, plays, and scandalized reports by people who visited New York, Chicago, Kansas City, or other "dens of pestilence," a vital, exciting, and excited urban culture developed in American cities. City people compared rural "yokels" and "hayseeds" unfavorably to themselves. Once established, city people were unlikely to move to the country or even to be attracted by jobs beyond the municipal limits.

The cities continued to grow at an extraordinary rate, both from immigration and the influx from the towns and countryside. Indeed, had it not been for the existence of a more traditional American frontier larger than any that had gone before, it is likely that the rural population would have declined in the late nineteenth century, as it was to do in the twentieth century.

CHRONOLOGY

1883 Completion of Brooklyn Bridge

1885 Perfection of I-beam girders makes skyscraper construction possible

1886 Neighborhood Guild (first settlement house) founded in New York

1887 Richmond first city to build electric trolley company

1889 Hull House founded by Jane Addams in Chicago

1890 *How the Other Half Lives* published

FOR FURTHER READING

Again, see the "For Further Reading" sections in several of the chapters immediately preceding this one: in particular, Vincent P. DeSantis, *The Shaping of Modern America, 1877–1916*, 1973; John A. Garraty, *The New Commonwealth, 1877–1890*, 1968; Samuel P. Hays, *The Response to Industrialism, 1885–1914*, 1957. Even allowing that urbanists have been among the most productive of historians in recent decades, Arthur M. Schlesinger, *The Rise of the City, 1878–1898*, 1933, is still an essential source.

To augment and correct Schlesinger in particulars, see Robert H. Bremner, *From the Depths: The Discovery of Poverty in America*, 1956; Howard Chudakov, *The Evolution of American Urban Society*, 1975; John Higham, *Send These to Me: Jews and Other Immigrants in Urban America*, 1975; Zane Miller and Patricia Melvin, *The Urbanization of Modern America*, 1987; Thomas L. Philpott, *The Slum and the Ghetto*, 1978; Barbara Rosenkrantz, *Public Health and the State*, 1972; Stephan Thernstrom, *The Other Bostonians: Poverty and Progress in the American Metropolis*, 1973; Sam B. Warner, *Streetcar Suburbs: The Process of Growth in Boston, 1870–1900*, 1971, and *The Urban Wilderness: A History of the American City*, 1972; Morton White, *The Intellectual versus the City*, 1962; Gunther Barth, *City People: The Rise of Modern City Culture in Nineteenth-Century America*, 1980; and Roy Rosenzweig, *Eight Hours for What We Will: Workers and Leisure in an Industrial City, 1870–1920*, 1983.

Books focusing on immigrants, with a special concern for urban life, include Nathan Glazer and Daniel P. Moynihan, *Beyond the Melting Pot*, 1970; Oscar Handlin, *The Uprooted*, 1951; Leonard Dinnerstein and David Reimers, *Ethnic Americans: A History of Immigration and Assimilation*, 1975; John B. Duff, *The Irish in the United States*, 1971; Irving Howe, *World of Our Fathers*, 1976; Alan Kraut, *The Huddled Masses: The Immigrant in American Culture, 1880–1921*, 1982; Humbert Nelli, *The Italians of Chicago*, 1970; Thomas Sowell, *Ethnic America: A History*, 1981; Hasia R. Diner, *Erin's Daughters in America*, 1983; and Susan A. Glenn, *Daughters of the Shtetl: Life and Labor in the Immigrant Generation*, 1990.

One of the very last frontiers: settlers near the Verde River in Arizona, 1885.

31
CHAPTER

THE LAST FRONTIER

Winning the Rest of the West

1865–1900

American history has been in a large degree the history of the colonization of the Great West. The existence of an area of free land, its continuous recession, and the advance of American settlement westward, explain American development. . . .

To the frontier the American intellect owes its striking characteristics. That coarseness and strength combined with acuteness and inquisitiveness; that practical, inventive turn of mind, quick to find expedients; that masterful grasp of material things, lacking in the artistic but powerful to effect great ends; that restless, nervous energy; that dominant individualism, working for good and for evil, and withal that buoyancy and exuberance which comes with freedom—these are traits of the frontier, or traits called out elsewhere because of the frontier.

—Frederick Jackson Turner

In Europe, the frontier was the place where the territory of one sovereign state came to an end and the territory of another principality began. The crest of the Pyrenees Mountains marked (and marks) the frontier between Spain and France, parts of the Rhine River the eastern frontier of France and the western frontier of Germany. The novelist's and filmmaker's Old World frontier is a place of zebra-striped barricades lowered across tracks or roadway, locomotives hissing on sidings, and gruff customs guards interrogating travelers and rifling their luggage.

Traditional European history was very much the tale of moving frontiers, princes taking and losing land as a consequence of dynastic marriages, wars, and treaties. Redrawing a frontier meant detaching populated lands from one country and attaching them to another.

In North America, the word *frontier* meant something entirely different, and almost from the start. To Americans, the frontier was a vaguely demarcated zone where lands that were *settled, tamed, civilized*—by whites and, sometimes, their black slaves—came to an end and where undeveloped savage land, peopled only by Indians, began. Because the course of American expansion originated on the eastern rim of the continent, this frontier usually took the shape of a line running north to south and more or less constantly moving westward. Beyond that ever-shifting line was what Americans called "the West."

THE LAST FRONTIER

The Census Bureau's definition of settled land was not very rigorous. Americans of the twenty-first century would consider a square mile on which only two, three, or four people lived to be something on the order of howling wilderness. The Census Bureau, however, defined a square mile as settled if 2.5 persons lived there. Even at that, at the time of the Civil War, the part of the United States that was beyond the frontier comprised roughly half the nation's area. With the exception of California, Oregon, and Washington Territory on the west coast, where 440,000 people lived; the Great Salt Lake basin, where the Mormon Zion had grown to be home to a population of 40,000; and New Mexico, which was the seat of a gracious Hispanic culture, the American frontier ran north to south about 150 to 200 miles west of the Mississippi River. Settlers

had barely spilled over the far boundaries of Minnesota, Iowa, Missouri, and Arkansas. Half of the state of Texas was beyond the frontier at the end of the Civil War.

An Uninviting Land

Rather more striking in view of what was to happen in the late nineteenth century, most Americans believed that this West would never be settled. Americans thought agriculturally. Pioneering meant bringing land under tillage, and, except for isolated pockets of fertile, well-watered soil, none of the three major geographical regions of the West was suitable to agriculture.

In the middle of the last West lay the majestic Rocky Mountains, which range from Alaska to New Mexico. The snowy peaks of the Rockies were familiar to easterners from landscape paintings by artists who accompanied the transcontinental wagon trains or military expeditions, or, having learned of the natural glories of the American landscape, traveled west on their own, easel, canvases, and pigments packed in their lumbering wagons. The very grandeur of the Rockies, however, told Americans that the mountains could not support a population living as people did in the older regions.

West of the Rockies and east of California's Sierra Nevada lay the high desert and the Great Basin—the mountainous and arid home of birds, snakes, rodents, comical armadillos, cactus, creosote bush, sagebrush, and tumbleweed. The soil was rocky, thin, and usually alkaline. This region is called a basin because its rivers lose heart in their search for an outlet and pool up in the desert, disappearing into the earth and evaporating in the sun. The Mormons worked miracles in one of those sinks, the Great Salt Lake basin. But no part of the West seemed less inviting to Americans than this genuine desert.

East of the Rockies stretched the Great Plains, also a land of little rain and no trees. Short grasses carpeted the country, and rivers like the Missouri and the Platte meandered through it, making the Great Plains less forbidding than the Great Basin. Nevertheless, there was simply not enough rainfall on the plains to support staple agriculture as Americans practiced it.

The Native Peoples of the West

Some people did live in this last great "unsettled" region, of course. In addition to the Mormons and the *nuevos mexicanos*, tens of thousands of Indians continued to cling to traditional, sometimes ancient ways of life. Even the most forbidding parts of the Great Basin supported the Ute, Paiute, and Shoshone, who coped with the torrid summers by dividing into small foraging bands, finding rodents an acceptable dinner and seeking higher elevations for relief and water.

Farther south, in the seemingly more hostile environment of present-day Arizona and New Mexico, the Pima, Zuni, and Hopi were farming the desert intensively for centuries before the explorations of Francisco de Coronado. Their pueblos (a Spanish term, of course), were communal houses or groups of apartments, sometimes perched high on sheer cliffs, where a delicately integrated village culture evolved. The Navajo, more numerous than the other peoples in the desert south of the Grand Canyon (and comparative newcomers there) lived in family groups spread out over the country. The Navajo were skilled weavers of cotton when the introduction of Spanish sheep provided them with the opportunity to raise their craft into a more durable art. Both the Navajo and the Pueblo Indians feared the warlike raiders of the Apache tribes, who dwelled farther south in Mexico, but ranged widely in search of booty. Just between 1862 and 1867, Apaches killed 400 Mexicans and Anglo settlers in the borderlands, and an unknown number of other Indians.

In what was then called Indian Territory, present-day Oklahoma, the "civilized tribes," which were forced out of Georgia and Alabama during the Age of Jackson, had rebuilt their amalgam of native and European cultures: an intensive cash-crop agriculture; a town life; a written language; a school system; and newspapers.

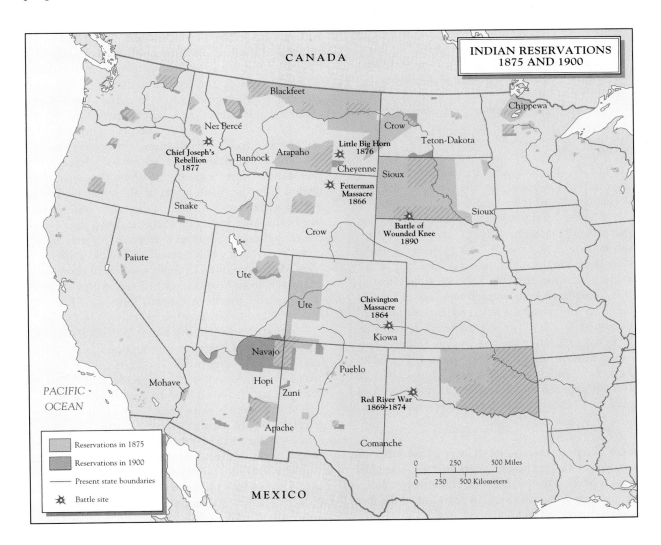

The Pony Express

The Pony Express looms large in the folklore of the American West. It would be strange if it were otherwise, the memory of lone riders trotting and even galloping across half a continent carrying a few pounds of government dispatches and very expensive private letters from "back east" to California. But it was, in fact, a short-lived enterprise, set in motion in April 1860 and shut down just 18 months later.

The "technology" of the Pony Express was primitive. Indeed, its string of some 190 relay or "stock" stations between St. Joseph, Missouri, and California represented no essential improvement on the means by which the emperors of ancient Persia communicated with their far-flung lands. Some 80 "young, skinny, wiry fellows, not over eighteen," according to the company's "Help Wanted" advertisement, "expert riders willing to risk death daily . . . orphans preferred," based at "home stations" 75 to 100 miles apart, raced against a demanding schedule with bags of dispatches and letters. Each 10 or 15 miles of their way, they changed their frothing ponies for fresh mounts at a relay station. All in all, the Pony Express kept some 500 horses in sound condition at all times.

Primitive as it was, however, the Pony Express cut 12 full days off the time it had taken for Washington to communicate with Sacramento, and vice versa (via steamship and the Isthmus of Panama).

The Pony Express was never intended as more than a stopgap until the telegraph and railroad more substantially bound East to West. However, it might have had a longer life had not the Civil War intervened in the spring of 1861. It was widely feared that Confederate raiders would so ravage the fragile line of communications as to render the Pony Express useless. Maybe so. Nevertheless, it ought to be noted that, while the ponies were running, the experiment was an extraordinary success. The Pony Express made 308 transcontinental runs covering 606,000 miles; it carried almost 35,000 pieces of mail. In 18 months, only one mail pouch was lost.

Indian Territory came to loom large in the American imagination during the first years after the Civil War because, beyond the pale of state and effective federal law, it was an attractive sanctuary for some of the most famous outlaws and badmen of the era.

But the Indians who most intrigued easterners were, curiously, those who were most determined to resist the whites and their ways, the tribes of the Great Plains. Thanks to the writings of intrepid travelers such as historian Francis Parkman and painters Alfred J. Miller, Karl Bodmer, and George Catlin, the Comanche, Cheyenne, and Arapaho peoples of the central and southern plains, and the Mandan, Crow, Sioux, Nez Percé, and Blackfoot peoples of the northern half of the grasslands were a source of awe and admiration to easterners and of apprehension to those whites who came into their country to compete with them.

Plains Culture

The lives of the Plains Indians—economy, social structure, religion, diet, dress—revolved around two animals: the native bison (or buffalo) and the European horse. The numerous bison, as many as 30 million of them in 1800, provided food and hides that were made into clothing, footwear, blankets, portable shelters (the conical teepees), bowstrings, and canvases on which artists recorded heroic legends, tribal histories, and genealogies. The bison's manure made a tolerable fuel for cooking and warmth in a treeless land where winters were harsh.

The Plains Indians were nomadic. Except for the Mandan and Pawnee, they grew no crops; they trailed after the bison herds on their horses. It was not an ancient way of life, for the horse was not native to the Americas. The Plains Indians, then farmers or pedestrian hunters, discovered the "spirit dogs" after 1680 when a revolt by Pueblo Indians in New Mexico resulted in the liberation of thousands of animals from Spanish herds. Feral mustangs were roaming the southern Great Plains by 1720 and reached Canada within 50 years.

In that short time, the Plains Indians learned to capture the wild beasts and developed their stirrupless, saddleless, and bitless mode of riding. Indian horsemanship developed independent of Mexican example and inspired awe in Americans who observed it. "Almost as awkward as a monkey on the ground," wrote painter George Catlin of a Great Plains warrior in 1834, "the moment he lays his hand upon a horse, his face even becomes handsome, and he gracefully flies away like a different being."

The wandering ways of the Plains tribes brought them frequently into contact with one another and with Indians who had developed different cultures.

While they traded and could communicate with remarkable subtlety through a common sign language, the tribes were just as likely to fight one another. Since the Indians had no concept of private ownership of land, their wars were not aimed at territorial conquest, but at capturing horses, tools, and sometimes women, and at demonstrating courage, the highest quality of which a Great Plains male could boast. The English word brave, applied to Plains warriors, was not chosen on a whim.

With only about 225,000 Native Americans roaming the Great Plains in 1860, war was not massive, but it was chronic. A permanent peace was as foreign to the Indians' view of the world as the notion that an individual could claim sole ownership of 80 acres of grassland.

By 1860, every Plains tribe knew about the "palefaces" or "white-eyes." Individuals, trappers mostly, had been adopted into most tribes. The Plains Indians were less accommodating of the more numerous whites in the wagon trains that had traversed their homeland for two decades, and they occasionally skirmished with the wayfarers. But the outsiders did move on and were welcome to the extent that they traded, abandoned, or neglected to secure their horses, textiles, iron tools, and rifles, all of which improved the Indians' standard of living.

The Destruction of the Bison

This state of coexistence began to change when Congress authorized the construction of the Pacific Railroad. The crews that laid the tracks of the Union Pacific and Kansas Pacific across the plains were not interested in staying. But unlike the California and Oregon emigrants, their presence led directly to the destruction of the bison.

The killing of the bison began harmlessly enough. In order to feed the crews building the railroad, the Union Pacific Railroad hired hunters like William F. "Buffalo Bill" Cody to harvest the herds. Numerous as they were, the workers could hardly consume enough of the lean, beef-like meat to affect the number of the Plains bison, perhaps 15 million in 1860. However, when a few of the hides were shipped back east and caused a sensation as fashionable buffalo robes, wholesale slaughter began.

A team of marksmen, an assistant who reloaded their weapons, and skinners could down and strip a thousand bison in a day. Living in huge herds, the animals were not startled by loud noises and stood

---

Just Cause

It would be a simpleton's mistake to think that all soldiers thought of the Indians as little more than vermin to be run to ground. Captain Frederick Benteen, who was at the Little Bighorn but not with Custer's doomed party, wrote of the effectiveness of the Sioux attack: "We were at their hearths and homes, their medicine was working well, and they were fighting for all the good God gives anyone to fight for."

---

grazing, pathetically easy targets, as long as they did not scent or see human beings. Buffalo Bill once killed 4,280 of the animals in 18 months. With dozens like him at work, the bison population declined at a startling rate.

The railroad companies encouraged the slaughter because, merely by crossing over the flimsy iron tracks, a herd of buffalo could obliterate the line. Other white settlers in the West linked the "Indian problem" to the abundance of bison. "So long as there are millions of buffalos in the West," a Texan told Congress, "so long the Indians cannot be controlled." As if to supply the finishing touches, wealthy eastern and European sportsmen chartered special trains and, sometimes without stepping to the ground, they shot trophies for their mansions and clubs and, in the late 1880s, extremely harsh winters wiped out huge herds at a swoop.

By 1889, when preservationists stepped in to save the species, fewer than a thousand American buffalo remained alive. (Most of today's 200,000 bison are descended from just 77 animals.) It was probably the most rapid extinction of a species in history, but no more rapid than the extinction of the culture of the people whose fate was tied to the bison. When the carnage was just underway, General Philip H. Sheridan reported that the hunters of buffalo had "done more in two years . . . to settle the vexed Indian question than the entire regular army . . . in the last thirty years."

The Army

Civil War hero Sheridan and the army went west ostensibly to enforce the Indians' treaty rights as well as to protect the transcontinental railroad and the

How They Lived

Punching Cows

It took three or four months to drive a herd of cattle from the vicinity of San Antonio, Texas, to a railhead town in Kansas and to be asked to join a trail crew was a coveted honor among the young men of the country. The wages were low, only $1 a day plus board and as good a bed as the sod of the Great Plains provided. But because a lot of money and many lives rested on every member of a crew, only those who had impressed a trail boss with their skills and reliability were invited to go.

A trail crew consisted of the trail boss, usually the owner of the cattle; his *segundo*, or assistant; a cook; a wrangler, who was in charge of the *remuda*, or herd of horses that accompanied the expedition; and a hand for each 250 to 300 cattle. Most herds were made up of between 2,500 and 3,000 cattle, so 10 to 12 cowpunchers, or buckaroos, was typical. (The "cows" were really steers, males that had been castrated at their first roundup; the "punchers" got their name because one of their jobs was to punch the cows into corrals and loading chutes—using poles.)

A herd moved about ten to fifteen miles a day, the animals grazing as they got the chance. The usual procedure for getting a herd along was for two men to ride "lead" or "point," one on either side of the milling steers; two to ride "swing" and "flank," in pairs at regular intervals alongside the herd; and two or three to ride "drag," behind the herd to hurry up stragglers.

Each position had its peculiarities and was assigned in rotation or with an eye to a particular cowpuncher's abilities or his personal standing at the moment in the trail boss's graces. Riding point was the most dangerous in the event of a stampede, but it was also the most prestigious and most pleasant in terms of dust and odor (unless there was a powerful tailwind). Conversely, riding drag was the safest but also the least desirable job, not only because of the quality of the air that 3,000 animals left behind, but also because there was not a moment in which some independent-minded "dogies" were not determined to set off on their own.

The day's drive started at first light and ended as late toward dusk as the trail boss could find satisfactory grass and water, but the cowboy's work was not done. After a big dinner at the chuck wagon, the hands had to "ride night." In two-hour shifts, pairs of riders circled the herd in opposite directions, looking out for predators and soothing the nervous steers. Some folklorists (and some old cowpunchers) say that the western singing and guitar-playing tradition developed as a means of keeping a herd calm; music soothed the generally docile if not the savage beast. Indeed, night riding was as dangerous as it was detested for its theft of sleep. Almost all stampedes started at night, tripped by a bolt of lightning, a steer dodging a coyote, or, to human reckoning, no reason whatsoever. Except for river crossings—there were four major and numerous minor watercourses between Texas and Kansas—the stampede was the most frequent cause of death written on the wooden markers that dotted the Shawnee, Chisholm, and Goodnight-Loving trails. (Indians were not a serious threat to the cowpuncher's life, although they stole his cattle when they could.)

There would be no strumming guitar in the pouring rain that came often enough. Then the night riders donned their yellow oilskin slickers that covered their whole saddle, and gently cursed, or slept. It was said that a cowpuncher who had a good night horse could sleep in the saddle, since his mount even knew to wake him at the end of the two-hour shift.

Cowboys on the long drive might bring along a horse or two of their own, but the boss supplied the tough, wiry work ponies. They were geldings, about seven to ten for each hand. (Stallions fought, and mares were considered too temperamental for the job.) Each had a unique identity and job. There

---

settlers on the frontier from the Indians. Some of these troops were captured Confederate soldiers who elected to take an oath of loyalty to the Union and serve in the West as preferable to languishing in prisoner-of-war camps. After the war, they were joined by northern whites and former slaves who enlisted and found army life preferable to hard-scrabble farming back home.

were morning horses and afternoon horses. The night horse had singular qualities already noted. The cowboy used the strong rope horse to help pull a stray out of a bog or for some other problem involving a lasso. A highly specialized but important horse was the water horse, a good swimmer on which a cowboy could count to get him across as much as a mile of strong current with steers rolling their wild, pink-rimmed eyes and thrashing about on every side. The most talented mount was the cutting horse, which knew exactly how a steer would act without the rider's instructions. The best were as agile as sheepdogs.

The cowboy's attachment to his horse, the butt of many Hollywood jokes, was nevertheless genuine. The cowpuncher was a horseman; he shunned work that had to be done on foot. Everyone had stories of crews that quit rather than slop hogs or milk dairy cows.

If passionate in general, however, the cowboy's attachment to horses in the particular was fickle. He did not own the mounts on which he worked, and at the end of the trail they were sold off along with the cattle. Only a few hands returned home to Texas overland. After they had spent most of their money on liquor, women, and cards, cowboys climbed aboard an eastbound train, rode it to the Mississippi River, and struck south by riverboat.

Some soldiers and officers learned to respect the tribes and tried to deal fairly with them. General George Crook, who is remembered as one of the ablest of the army's Indian fighters, preferred being known for his respect for his just dealings with the tribes. Some shared the values of General Sheridan, who was reputed to have told a Comanche chief at Fort Cobb in 1869, "The only good Indian is a dead Indian."

Native Americans commemorate a buffalo kill by donning ceremonial dress.

Overall, of course, the sympathies of the army were with the railroaders, miners, cattlemen, and eventually farmers who intruded on Indian lands. Whites believed in an elaboration of manifest destiny, that because the Indians, like the Mexicans, used the land so inefficiently, their claim to it was not equal to their own. From 1862, when the final wave of Indian wars began with a Sioux uprising in Minnesota, to 1890, when the military power of the Sioux was shattered at Wounded Knee, South Dakota, the United States cavalry joined with the buffalo hunters to destroy a way of life.

The Last Indian Wars

To the end, Indian war remained a war of few pitched battles and innumerable small skirmishes. Between 1869 and 1876, for example, the peak years of the fighting, the army recorded 200 distinct incidents, a number that did not include many unopposed Indian raids and confrontations between civilians and the tribes. Still, the total casualties on the army's side (and possibly that of the Indians) were less than in any of several Indian-white battles in the 1790s.

The army preferred to fight decisive battles. Such confrontations favored the soldiers' discipline and technology. But the Indians generally clung to

Moving amidst the Hostiles

A cavalry detachment in the West, unlike its movie versions, was accompanied by huge wagon trains of equipment, often 150 vehicles. In addition to a rider, each horse carried 80 to 90 pounds of equipment. With such a load, a horse needed to be rested frequently. This was accomplished without arresting progress by dividing the soldiers on the march into two troops. One troop walked until it was half a mile ahead of the plodding wagon train. Then, the soldiers dismounted to rest and graze their horses until the wagons were half a mile ahead. As they caught up, the other troop moved on ahead and repeated the maneuver. In this way, there was always a troop, in two columns, on either side of the precious supplies to warn off raiders.

traditional hit-and-run attacks that exploited their advantage—mobility—and allowed them to escape fights in which, with their inferior arms and numbers, they had little chance of prevailing. The result was frequent frustration among the soldiers and a cruelty toward the enemy such as had not been seen in the Civil War. In 1871, Commissioner of Indian Affairs Francis Walker explained that "when dealing with savage men, as with savage beasts, no question of national honor can arise. Whether to fight, to run away, or to employ a ruse, is solely a question of expediency."

By 1876, the year of the centennial, the army's victory seemed near completion. Little by little, the soldiers in their dusty blue uniforms hemmed in the wandering tribes and whittled away at their ability to subsist. The typical state of a surrendering tribe was near starvation, with a goodly proportion of the young men dead. But Indian resistance was not quite at an end.

Custer's Last Stand

In June 1876, an audacious and well-known colonel of the Seventh Cavalry, a popular hero of the Civil War, George Armstrong Custer, led 265 men into a battle with the Sioux and Cheyenne on Montana's Little Bighorn River. In a rare total victory for the Indians, every one of Custer's men was killed. Although a completely unexpected defeat, Custer's Last Stand thrilled Americans. Denied in life the advancement that he believed his record and talents merited, "Yellow Hair," as the Sioux called him, became a romantic hero in death. A brewery commissioned an imaginative painting of the Battle of the Little Bighorn by Cassilly Adams and within a few years distributed 150,000 reproductions of it.

Senior officers who disapproved of the flamboyant and impetuous Custer, and thought him to blame for the disaster, kept their mouths shut. Only in the next century would the episode be fully appreciated from the Indians' point of view, as a final great military victory brilliantly engineered by Sioux and Cheyenne war chiefs. At the time, however, the tribes' joy was short-lived. Most of the victors were under federal control within the year.

Good Intentions, Tragic Results

In 1881, a Colorado writer, Helen Hunt Jackson, published *A Century of Dishonor*, one of the decade's bestsellers. In meticulous detail and with little dis-

---

"Forgive My Country"

When artist George Catlin learned of an attack by Civil War hero Philip H. Sheridan on the Cheyenne Indians, he wrote to the general:

The American journals tell me that you have . . . killed 52 warriors, and captured 400 horses and four tons of dried buffalo meat, the only and last means of their existence. Oh mercy, mercy! A small and friendly tribe when I lived amongst them, 35 years since; where are they going? What have they done? How many of them now exist, and who have got possession of their lands, their buffalos, and wild horses? God, perhaps, may forgive my country for such cruel warfare; and oh, for my country's sake, that there could be a solvent for history, to erase such records from its pages.

---

tortion of fact, she detailed the cynicism with which the United States government had dealt with the Indians since independence. The list of Indian treaties was a list of broken treaties. Time and again, according to Jackson, "Christian" whites had cheated "savage" Indians of their land, had herded them onto reservations on lands judged to be the least useful, and then chipped away at those.

By 1876, the government ceased to make treaties with the Indians. Those Indians who did not resist American control were defined as wards of the federal government; they were not citizens but were under Washington's protection and enjoyed a few special privileges. After the publication of *A Century of Dishonor*, many easterners demanded that the government use this wardship in a just manner.

In 1887, Congress approved the Dawes Severalty Act. Intentions were of the best. Assuming that the traditional Indian way of life was no longer feasible, which was reasonable, the supporters of the Dawes Act argued that the Indian peoples must be Americanized. That is, they must become self-sustaining citizens through adoption of the ways of the larger culture. Therefore, under the Dawes Act, the tribes were dissolved and the treaty lands were distributed, homestead-style, 160 acres to each head of the family, and an additional 80 acres to each adult member of the household. Lands left over were sold to whites. In order to avoid further despoliation, remaining Indian land could not be sold or otherwise disposed of for 25 years.

A drawing of the Battle of the Little Bighorn by Red Horse, 1881.

The supporters of the Dawes Act overlooked a number of vital facts. First, few of the western Indians were farmers; traditionally they were hunters, gatherers, traders, and raiders. Second, the reservation lands were rarely suited to agriculture; they were allotted to the Indians precisely because they were unattractive to white farmers. Third, tracts of a few hundred acres in the arid West were rarely enough to support efficient white farmers, let alone novices at tillage. Finally, no western tribe outside Oklahoma thought in terms of private ownership of land as vested in a nuclear family. The tribe, which the Dawes Act aimed to relegate to the dustheap, was the basic social unit to which the Native Americans looked. The defeated Indians were demoralized by the forced disintegration of their culture and individuals too often were debauched by idleness and alcohol. When it was again permitted by law, they would be stripped of much of their land, too.

Wounded Knee

Among these desperate and demoralized people appeared a religious teacher in the tradition of Tecumseh's brother, The Prophet. Jack Wilson, or Wovoka, was a Paiute who lived with a white family and was fascinated by the Christian doctrine of redemption. Calling on Christianity and Native American practices and aspirations, he created a pan-tribal religion promising redemption for Indians on this earth. Preached throughout the West by Wovoka's disciples, the Ghost Dance religion appealed to thousands.

Geronimo and the Army

Geronimo, an Apache warrior who continued to resist in the Southwest after his tribal chief came to terms with the whites, had few followers but stunning success in eluding troops sent to pursue him. At one point, 5,000 soldiers, one fourth of the army, could not find Geronimo's band of 31.

According to Wovoka, by performing a ritual dance, the Indians, who were God's chosen people, could prevail on the Great Spirit to make the white man disappear. The Ghost Dance would also bring back to life the buffalo herds and the many Indians who were killed in the wars. The old way of life, which in the 1880s most adult Indians vividly remembered, would be restored.

This sort of belief, simultaneously edifying and heart-rending, is common among peoples who have seen their world turned upside down. In parts of the Southwest that were untouched by Wovoka's religion, defeated Indians turned to peyote, a natural hallucinogenic drug, as a way to escape a bewildering, intolerable reality.

To understand the appeal of the Ghost Dance religion, it is necessary to recall just how rapidly the culture of the Plains Indians was destroyed. The Dakota Sioux, for example, did not go to war with the whites until the end of the 1860s. Within another decade, the survivors were herded onto the Pine Ridge Reservation in South Dakota where Wovoka's message was preached by Kicking Bear and fatefully modified by Big Foot. Whereas Wovoka had preached a peaceful redemption, many of the Sioux believed their Ghost Dance shirts were "bulletproof" and carried arms in defiance of the soldiers. On Wounded Knee Creek in December 1890, when soldiers guarding Dakotas tried to take their guns away, a shoving incident led to an explosion in which about 200 people, half of them women and children, were killed. For the Indians of the Great Plains, there was no escape, not even in mysticism.

THE CATTLE KINGDOM

As the Indians lost the West, white Americans, and a few blacks, won it. Indeed, the final decades of the nineteenth century stand as the greatest era of geographic and economic expansion in American history.

The Sioux camp near Pine Ridge, South Dakota, in 1891.

In 1870, American forests yielded about 12.8 billion board feet of lumber. By 1900, this output had almost tripled to about 36 billion. Although this increase reflects in part the development of forest industries in the southern states, the region of greatest expansion was a new one, the Pacific Northwest.

In 1870, Americans were raising 23.8 million cattle. In 1900, 67.7 million head of the stupid, bawling creatures were fattening on grasslands, mostly in the West, and in western feedlots.

Annual gold production continued only slightly below the fabulous levels of the gold-rush era; until the end of the century, it was nearly double the totals of 1850. Annual silver production, only 2.4 million troy ounces in 1870, stood at 57.7 million in 1900.

The First Buckaroos

Acre for acre, cattlemen won more of the West than any other group of pioneers. They were motivated to bring the vastness of the Great Plains into the American economy by satisfying the appetite of the burgeoning cities of the East (and Europe) for cheap meat. They were encouraged in their venture by the disinterest in the rolling arid grasslands of anyone save the Indians. Their story thrills Americans to this

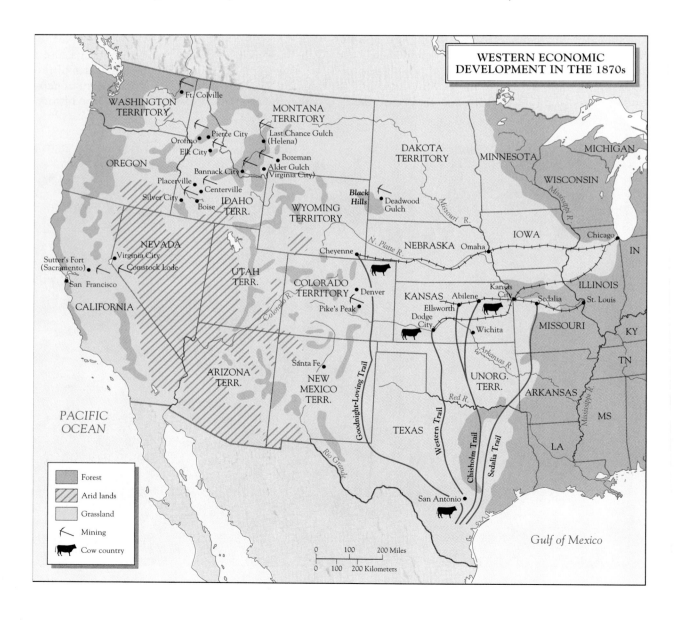

day (and other peoples) partly because it was romanticized and partly because the cattle kingdom was established so quickly and just as quickly destroyed.

The cowboy rode into American legend just before the Civil War. In the late 1850s, enterprising Texans began to round up herds of the half-wild longhorns that ranged freely between the Nueces River and the Rio Grande. They then drove them north over an old Shawnee Indian trail to Sedalia, Missouri, a railroad town with connections to Chicago. Although the bosses were English-speaking, many of the actual workers were Mexicans, who called themselves *vaqueros*, or "cowboys."

Vaquero entered the English language as "buckaroo." Indeed, while Anglo-Americans soon comprised the majority of this mobile workforce, and former black slaves were a substantial minority of it, much of what became part of American folklore and parlance about the buckaroos was of Mexican derivation. The cowboy's colorful costume was an adaptation of functional Mexican work dress. The bandana was a washcloth that, when tied over the cowboy's mouth, served as a dust screen, no small matter when a thousand cattle were kicking up alkaline grit. The broad-brimmed hat was not selected for its picturesque qualities but because it was a sun and rain shield. Extremely durable when manufactured from first-quality beaver felt, the sombrero also served as a drinking pot and washbasin.

The pointed, high-heeled boots, awkward and even painful for walking, were designed for staying in the stirrups of a saddle, where a *vaquero* spent his workday. The western saddle was an adaptation of Spanish design, and quite unlike the English tack that Americans from back east used. Chaps, leather leg coverings, got their name from chaparral, the ubiquitous woody brush against which they were designed to protect the cowboy.

Meat for Millions

The Civil War and Missouri laws against importing Texas cattle (because of hoof-and-mouth disease) stifled the cattle-driving business before it was fairly begun. However, in 1866, when the transcontinental railroad reached Abilene, Kansas, a wheeler-dealer from Illinois, Joseph G. McCoy, saw the possibilities of underselling steers raised on private pasture back east with Texas longhorns. McCoy built holding pens on the outskirts of the tiny Kansas town, arranged to ship cattle he did not then have with the Kansas Pacific Railroad, and dispatched agents to southern Texas to induce cowboys to round up and drive cattle north to Abilene on a trading route called the Chisholm Trail.

In 1867, McCoy shipped 35,000 "tall, bony, coarseheaded, flat-sided, thin-flanked" cattle to

The cowboy's "long drive" ended in a railhead town surrounded by stockyards.

Chicago. In 1868, 75,000 of the beasts, next to worthless in Texas, passed through Abilene, and Chicago meatpackers cried for more. In 1871, 600,000 "critters" passed through the pens of several Kansas railroad towns on their way to American dinner tables.

The profits were immense. A steer that cost about $5 to raise on public lands could be driven to Kansas at the cost of one cent a mile ($5 to $8) and sold for $25 or, occasionally, as much as $50. Such a business attracted investors from back east and as far as England, who established ranches that were as comfortable as the gentlemen's clubs of New York and London. The typical cattleman at Wyoming's famous Cheyenne Club never touched a gun and he sat on a horse only for a photographer. His mount was a plush easy chair, his range a fine carpet, and he puffed on Havana cigars when he discussed accounts, very often in an English accent, with his fellow buckaroos.

The railhead continued to push westward, and with it went the destination of the real cowboys, who were soon arriving from the North as well as the South. Nor did most of the citizens of old cow towns like Abilene object to the migration of the railhead. They concluded after a few seasons that the money to be made as a cattle-trading center was not worth the damage done to their own ranches and farms by hundreds of thousands of cattle. The wild atmosphere given their towns by the rambunctious cowboys, many of them bent on a blowout after months on the trail, was even less conducive to respectable civic life. As a cow town grew, its "better element" demanded churches and schools in place of saloons, casinos, and whorehouses. The stage was set for the taming of a town, which is the theme of so much treasured folklore.

Never, though, did the cowboys lack for someplace to take their herds. There were always newer, smaller towns to the west to welcome them and their wages. In Kansas alone, Abilene, Ellsworth, Newton, Wichita, Dodge City, and Hays had their wide-open period.

Disaster

The cattle kingdom lasted only a generation, ending suddenly as a result of the collaboration between human greed and natural disaster.

The short-term profits to be made in cattle were so great that exploiters ignored the long-term damage that their huge herds were doing to the grasslands. Vast as the plains were, they were overstocked and overgrazed by the mid-1880s. Unlike the wild bison, which migrated constantly in search of the lushest grass, leaving the land they grazed to recover, the cattle's wanderings were limited. They fouled clear-running springs and even trampled them into mud holes. Weeds never before noticed in the West replaced the native grasses that had invited overgrazing. Hills and buttes were scarred by cattle trails. Some species of migratory birds that once darkened the skies twice a year simply disappeared; the beefsteaks on the hoof had beaten them to their provisions.

Then, on January 1, 1886, a great blizzard buried the eastern and southern plains. Within three days, three feet of snow drifting into 20- and 30-foot banks suffocated the range. Between 50 and 85 percent of the livestock froze to death or died of hunger. About 300 cowboys could not reach shelter and died; the casualties among the Indians never were counted. When spring arrived, half the American plains reeked of the smell of death.

Drought in the summer of 1886 ruined many of the cattlemen who survived the snows. Grasses that had weathered summer droughts for millennia were unable to do so after the blizzards; they withered and died, and cattle already weakened by winter starved. Then, the next winter, the states that escaped the worst of the blizzard of 1886 got 16 inches of snow in 16 hours, followed by weeks more of intermittent snowfall.

The End of a Brief Era

The cattle industry recovered, but only when more prudent and methodical businessmen took over the holdings of the speculators of the glory days. Cattle barons like Richard King of southern Texas forswore risking all on the open range. Through clever manipulation of land laws, King built a ranch that was as large as the state of Rhode Island. If their success was not quite so spectacular as King's, others imitated his example in Texas, Wyoming, Montana, and eastern Colorado.

Even more important in ending the days of the long drive and the romantic image of the cowboy as a knight-errant was the expansion of the railroad network. When new east-west lines snaked into Texas and the states on the Canadian border, and the Union Pacific and Kansas Pacific sent feeder lines north and south into cow country, the cowboy became a ranch hand, a not-so-freewheeling employee of large commercial operations.

> ## A Century of Dishonor
>
> *It makes little difference . . . where one opens the record of the history of the Indians; every page and every year has its dark stain. The story of one tribe is the story of all, varied only by differences of time and place; but neither time nor place makes any difference in the main facts. Colorado is as greedy and unjust in 1880 as was Georgia in 1830, and Ohio in 1795; and the United States Government breaks promises now as deftly as then, and with added ingenuity from long practice.*
>
> *—Helen Hunt Jackson*

Oh, Give Me a Home

Even in the days of the long drive, the world of the cowboy bore scant resemblance to the legends that came to permeate American popular culture. Despite the white complexion of the cowboys in popular literature and in western films of the twentieth century, a large proportion of cowboys were Mexican or black. In some cases, all acted and mixed as equals. Just as often, however, the cowboys split along racial lines when they reached the end of the trail, frequenting segregated restaurants, barber shops, hotels, saloons, and brothels.

Black, white, or Hispanic, they were indeed little more than boys. Photographs that the buckaroos had taken in cow towns like Abilene and Dodge City (as well as arrest records, mostly for drunk and disorderly conduct), show a group of very young men, few apparently much older than 25. The life was too arduous for anyone but youths—days in the saddle, nights sleeping on bare ground in all weather. Moreover, the cowboy who married and had a family could not afford to be absent from his own ranch or farm for as long as the cattle drives required.

The real buckaroos were not constantly engaged in shooting scrapes such as have made western novels and movies so exciting. Their skills lay in horsemanship and with a rope, not with the less-than-accurate Colt revolver that they carried to signal coworkers far away. Indeed, toting guns was forbidden in railhead towns. With a drunken binge on every cowboy's itinerary, the sheriff or marshal in charge of keeping the peace did not tolerate shooting irons on every hip. Those who did not leave their revolvers in camp outside town checked them at the police station.

THE WILD WEST IN AMERICAN CULTURE

The legend of the cowboy as a romantic, dashing, and quick-drawing knight of the wide-open spaces was not a creation of a later era. On the contrary, all the familiar western themes were fully formed when cold, hard reality was still alive on the plains. Rather more oddly, the myths of the Wild West were embraced not only by easterners in their idle reveries, but by the cowboys themselves.

Play-Acting

The most important creator of the Wild West of legend was a none-too-savory character named E. Z. C. Judson. A former Know-Nothing who was dishonorably discharged from the Union Army, Judson took the pen name Ned Buntline. Between 1865 and 1886, he churned out more than 400 romantic, blood, guts, and chivalric novels about western heroes. Some of his characters he invented; others were highly fictionalized real people. Called pulps after the cheap paper on which they were printed, or dime novels after their price, the books by Judson and his many competitors were devoured chiefly but not exclusively by boys.

Buntline's mythical world appealed even to those who should have known better. During the 1880s, while living as a rancher in North Dakota, future president Theodore Roosevelt helped capture two young cowboys who robbed a grocery store. In their saddlebags, Roosevelt found several Ned Buntline novels that no doubt featured outlaws who were unjustly accused. The tiny town of Palisade, Nevada, on the Central Pacific railroad line, won the reputation in eastern newspapers as a den of cutthroats because brawls and gunfights broke out so regularly when passengers left the train for refreshment. In fact, Palisade may have been the first theme park: The fights were staged by locals in part to twit eastern fantasies, in part because the locals were just plain bored with the Wild West in which they lived.

American Heroes

In pulp fiction and later in films, Americans discovered that the bank and train robbers Jesse and Frank James, and several cohorts from the Clanton family, were really modern-day Robin Hoods who gave the money they took to the poor. When Jesse was murdered, his mother Zerelda (who had lost an arm in a ruction with Pinkerton detectives) made a tourist attraction of his grave, charging admission and explaining that her son had been a Christian with an inclination to read the Bible in his spare time. Jesse, according to Zerelda, examined all train passengers and did not rob those whose hands were callused because they, like he, were workingmen. Presumably, the commandment "Thou shalt not steal" did not apply to others.

Belle Starr, the moniker of one Myra Belle Shirley, was immortalized as "the bandit queen," as pure in heart as Jesse James's social consciousness. Billy the Kid (William Bonney), a Brooklyn-born homicidal maniac, was romanticized as a tragic hero who had been forced into a life of crime by an uncaring society. James Butler "Wild Bill" Hickok, a gambler and clotheshorse who killed perhaps six people before he was shot down in Deadwood Gulch, South Dakota, in 1876, was attributed with dozens of killings, all in the cause of making the West safe for women, children, and psalmbooks. Calamity Jane (Martha Cannary), later said to have been Wild Bill's paramour, wrote her own romantic autobiography in order to support a drinking problem.

Calamity Jane and other living legends of the West personally contributed to the mythmaking by appearing in Wild West shows that traveled to cities in the East and in Europe, where they dramatized great gun battles. The most famous of these shows was the creation of "Buffalo Bill" Cody, who easily made the transition from hunter to impresario. Among his featured performers was Sitting Bull, the Hunkpapa Sioux chief who had overseen the defeat of George Custer. Reality and myth were cruelly confused in Sitting Bull's life. After a successful career in show business,

Contemporary sketches of two romanticized "Queens of the Wild West."

he returned to the Rosebud Reservation where, during the Ghost Dance excitement, he was accidentally killed by two Indian policemen who were arresting him on suspicion of fomenting rebellion.

Some creators of the legendary West were conscientious realists; Frederic Remington, whose paintings and bronze statues of cowboys and Indians are studiously representative, is a fine example. Others, while romantics, were talented artists; Owen Wister, an aristocratic easterner, created the finest prototype of the western knight without armor in *The Virginian*, published in 1902. If the cowboy gave you his word, Wister wrote, "he kept it; Wall Street would have found him behind the times. Nor did he talk lewdly to women; Newport would have thought him old-fashioned."

THE MINING FRONTIER

The folklore of the precious metal-mining frontier is second only to the legend of the cowboy in American imagination. Deadwood Gulch, for example, where Wild Bill Hickok was gunned down and Calamity Jane spent much of her life, was no cow town but a gold-mining center.

Gold and Silver Rushes

After the richest of the California goldfields played out, prospectors in search of "glory holes" fanned out over the mountains and deserts of the West. For more than a generation, they discovered new deposits almost annually and very rich ones every few years. In 1859, there were two great strikes. A find in the Pike's Peak area of Colorado led to a rush reminiscent of that of 1849. At about the same time, gold miners in northern Nevada discovered that a "blue mud" that was frustrating their operations was one of the richest silver ores ever discovered. This was the beginning of Virginia City and the Comstock Lode. Before the Comstock pinched out in the twentieth century, it yielded more than $400 million in silver and gold.

In 1862, Tombstone, Arizona, was founded on the site of a gold mine; in 1864, Helena, Montana, rose atop another. In 1874, rich placer deposits were discovered in the Black Hills of South Dakota (then forbidden to whites by treaty with the Indians). The next year, silver was found at Leadville, Colorado, almost two miles above sea level in the Rockies.

During the 1880s, the Coeur d'Alene in the Idaho panhandle drew thousands of miners, as did the copper deposits across the mountains in Butte, Montana. In 1891, the Cripple Creek district in Colorado began to outproduce every other mining town. In 1898, miners rushed north to Canada's Klondike, Alaska's Yukon, and then to Nome, where the gold was on the beach. As late as 1901, there was an old-fashioned rush when the classic grizzled old prospector in a slouch hat, "his view obscured by the rear end of a donkey," Jim Butler, drove his pick into a desolate mountain in southern Nevada and found it "practically made of silver." From the town of Tonopah, founded on its site, prospectors discovered rich deposits in Goldfield, a few miles away.

Of Mining Camps and Cities

Readers of the dime novels of the time and film viewers since have avidly savored the vision of boisterous, wide-open mining towns, complete with saloons rocking with the music of tinny pianos and the shouts of bearded men. The live-for-today miner, the gambler, and the prostitute with a heart of gold are permanent inhabitants of American folklore. Nor is the picture altogether imaginary. The speculative mining economy fostered a risk-all attitude toward life and work.

However, efficient exploitation of underground (hard-rock) mining required a great deal of capital and technical expertise, both to finance the operation and to build the railroads that hauled ore out. Consequently, the mining camps that were home to from 5,000 to 10,000 people and even more within a short time of their founding were also cities with a variety of services and a social structure more like that of older industrial towns than the towns of the cattleman's frontier.

In 1877, only six years after it was founded on a vein of gold, Leadville, Colorado, boasted several miles of paved streets, gas lighting, a modern water system, thirteen schools, five churches, and three hospitals. It was hardly the tiny, false-front set that is used to represent mining towns in Hollywood films.

Camps such as Virginia City in Nevada, Deadwood Gulch in South Dakota, and Tombstone in Arizona are best remembered as places where legendary characters like Wild Bill Hickok and Wyatt Earp discharged their revolvers; but they were also the sites of huge stamping mills (to crush the ores) that towered over the landscape, and of busy exchanges where mining stocks were traded by agents of San Francisco, New York, and London bankers.

In Goldfield, the last of the wide-open mining towns, one of the most important men in the camp was the urbane Wall Street financier Bernard Baruch (who may have been outdressed by some of the locals). The Anaconda Copper Company of Butte, Montana, was one of the nation's ranking corporate giants. The Guggenheim mining syndicate was supreme in the Colorado goldfields. Rockefeller's Standard Oil was a major owner of mines in the Coeur d'Alene. If it was wild, the mining West was no mere colorful diversion for readers of dime novels, but an integral part of the national economy. In fact, the gold and silver that the hard-rock miners tore from the earth stood at the very center of a question that divided Americans more seriously than any other after the end of Reconstruction—what was to serve as the nation's money?

The miners and mine owners alone could not make an issue of the precious metals with which coins were minted, goods bought and sold, and debts incurred and paid off—or not paid off. There were too few of them. However, as the century wound to a close, the money question became of great interest to a group of people who formed a major part of the American population, and who had once been its most important segment, the farmers on the land.

CHRONOLOGY

1860–1862	Pony Express
1862	Uprising of Sioux in Minnesota inaugurates last of Indian wars
1865–1888	Ned Buntline novels romanticize West
1876	Battle of Little Big Horn Wild Bill Hickok murdered in Deadwood
1881	Publication of *A Century of Dishonor*
1886	The Great Blizzard of 1886
1887	Dawes Severalty Act
1890	Ghost Dance Massacre at Wounded Knee

Everything was movement and bustle in a mining boomtown like Deadwood, South Dakota, in 1876.

FOR FURTHER READING

Three fine books deal with the West in general from rather different perspectives: Ray A. Billington, *Westward Expansion: A History of the American Frontier*, 1967; Thomas D. Clark, *Frontier America: The Story of the Westward Movement*, 1969; and Frederick Merk, *History of the Westward Movement*, 1978. Also valuable is Robert A. Wiebe, *The Search for Order*, 1968. An essential book is that by the "founding father" of frontier history, Frederick Jackson Turner, *The Frontier in American History*, 1920. Also see Billington's *Frederick Jackson Turner*, 1973, and *America's Frontier Heritage*, 1967.

Useful special studies include Allan C. Bogue, *From Prairie to Corn Belt*, 1963; E. Dick, *The Sod-House Frontier*, 1937; Dee Brown, *Bury My Heart at Wounded Knee*, 1970; E. E. Dale, *The Range Cattle Industry*, 1930; David Day, *Cowboy Culture: A Saga of Five Centuries*, 1981; Richard Drinnon, *Facing West: The Metaphysics of Indian Hating*, 1980; Robert R. Dystra, *The Cattle Towns*, 1968; Gilbert C. Fite, *The Farmer's Frontier, 1865–1900*, 1966; William S. Greever, *The Bonanza West: The Story of the Western Mining Rushes*, 1963; Howard L. Harrod, *Renewing the World: Plains Indians Religion and Morality*, 1987; Rodman W. Paul, *The Far West and the Great Plains in Transition, 1859–1900*, 1988; J. M. Shagg, *The Cattle Trading Industry*, 1973; Fred A. Shannon, *The Farmer's Last Frontier*, 1967; Duane A. Smith, *Rocky Mountain Mining Camps*, 1967; Henry Nash Smith, *Virgin Land: The American West as Symbol and Myth*, 1950; Robert M. Utley, *Last Days of the Sioux Nation*, 1963; Wilcomb E. Washburn, *The Indian in America*, 1975; Thomas H. Watkins, *Gold and Silver in the West*, 1960; Glenda Riley, *The Female Frontier*, 1988; and Walter P. Webb, *The Great Plains*, 1931.

A recent development in the historiography of the West (exemplified in some of the titles listed above) is "the new western history," of which three principal contributors are Patricia Nelson Limerick, *Legacy of Conquest: The Unbroken Past of the American West*, 1987; Donald Worster, *Under Western Skies: Nature and History in the American West*, 1992; and Richard White, *"It's Your Misfortune and None of My Own": A History of the American West*, 1991. Limerick explains "the new western history" in *Trails: Toward a New Western History*, 1992. Two explorations by historians with different interests that illuminate this region are Ronald Takaki, *Strangers from a Distant Shore: A History of Asian-Americans*, 1989; and Richard Slotkin, *The Fatal Environment: The Myth of the Frontier in the Age of Industrialization*, 1985.

The grandeur and isolation of a plains farm are captured in this traveling photographer's masterpiece.

32
CHAPTER

STRESSFUL TIMES DOWN HOME
The Crisis of American Agriculture

1865–1896

When the lawyer hangs around and the butcher cuts a pound,
Oh the farmer is the man who feeds them all.
And the preacher and the cook go a-strolling by the brook
And the farmer is the man who feeds them all.

Farmers' song of the 1890s

They have stolen our money, have ravished our homes;
With the plunder erected to Mammon a throne;
They have fashioned a god, like the Hebrews of old,
Then bid us bow down to their image of gold.

Farmers' song of the 1890s

622 *Chapter 32 Stressful Times Down Home*

Ever since the world's first farmer poked a hole in the ground and covered a seed with dirt, tillers of the soil have understood that they were gambling with nature. Farming has always been a game of chance, betting a year's living on such uncertainties as the day of winter's final frost and summer's yield of sunshine and rain. Farmers were at the mercy of capricious insects and birds. They knew that illness or injury at harvest time could mean 12 months of privation.

But farmers have also known that their work was the bedrock on which civilization was based. After all, it was they who produced the first necessity of life after air and water. American farmers were, perhaps, particularly conscious of their role in society. They believed they were the nation's most valuable citizens, the "bone and sinew" of the republic. So they had been told by Thomas Jefferson and succeeding generations of politicians fishing for their votes. William Jennings Bryan, the American farmer's favorite politician in the 1890s, put the thought into vivid terms when he told his constituents that if their farms were destroyed, the grass would grow in every city in the nation, but destroy the cities and leave the farms, and the cities would spring up again as if by magic.

By Bryan's time, the staple farmers of the West and South needed to be reassured, for the grand old truisms were wearing as thin as knees of their overalls. In the new America of gigantic railroads, multimillion-dollar corporations, mighty investment banks, and a marketplace that extended to the obscurest corners of the earth, the powers of nature sometimes seemed to be secondary to, almost innocuous by comparison with, diabolical economic forces—and the power of people whom farmers came to think of as parasites sucking them dry. In the 1890s, welling anger and resentment down on the farm culminated in a radical political movement that shook the confidence of the conservative men who had governed the United States since the end of the Civil War.

BEST OF TIMES, WORST OF TIMES

Farmers rarely led the way on the last frontier. Miners and cattlemen and soldiers were the usual pioneers. Subsistence agriculture attracted few Americans and commercial agriculture was feasible in the West only after the railroad arrived to connect field and corral to hungry eastern and foreign cities. Once

the railroad made its appearance, however, settlers with a plow (and often little more than that) fairly inundated the last frontier.

Success Story

Never in the history of the world have people put so much new land to the plow so quickly as Americans (and immigrants) did in the final three decades of the nineteenth century. Up until 1870, Americans had brought a total of 408 million acres of land under cultivation, an average of 1.6 million acres of new farmland a year. Between 1870 and 1900, a single generation of farmers brought 431 million acres of virgin soil into agricultural production, more than between 1607 and 1870, and an average of 14.4 million acres annually.

Crop production increased even more sharply. By 1900, American farmers were producing up to 150 percent more of the staple grains—corn and wheat—than they had in 1870. Hogs, a by-product of corn, numbered 25 million in 1870 and 63 million in 1900.

The ravenous appetites of American and foreign city dwellers encouraged this amazing growth. The expansion of the railroads made it possible for crops raised by a Great Plains farmer to feed the inhabitants of Chicago and New York, even London and Warsaw.

Cool, Clear Water

American farmers and immigrants from northern Europe were accustomed to summer rains nourishing their crops. From the Atlantic seaboard to as far west as Missouri and eastern Kansas, 32 to 48 inches of rain fell each year; it was wetter in the Deep South.

West of about Wichita, Kansas, however, annual precipitation declined to 16 to 32 inches a year, with much of the year's rain falling during the winter. Yet farther west in the rain shadow of the Rocky Mountains, at about the eastern boundary of Colorado, rainfall dropped to 16 inches and less per year. This was the "Great American Desert," which an early explorer called "almost totally unfit for cultivation." The central valley of California was just as arid with, in some years, no rain at all during the summer months.

The Californians solved their problem with large-scale irrigation. They formed cooperative ditch companies that tapped the water of the San Joaquin, Sacramento, and numerous other rivers that rose in the Sierra Nevada, channeling it to their crops. Irrigation brought them into conflict with

hydraulic miners who, in washing down whole mountainsides to win their grains of gold, clogged the rivers and irrigation ditches with mud. The more numerous farmers won the contest in California's legislature and courts, shutting down the hydraulic operations.

To some extent, dry farming on the Great Plains was based on a delusion. The summers of the 1870s and early 1880s, when cultivators arrived in the region, were abnormally rainy. This convinced the settlers and some experts, such as Charles Dana Wilber, that "rain follows the plow." When they broke the primeval sod, some farmers believed, they permanently altered the climate by liberating moisture from the earth that would return indefinitely in the form of heavier rains.

There was nothing to this theory, as the devastating drought of 1887 was to demonstrate, but Great Plains farmers did make the most of what moisture was in the ground by plowing more deeply than eastern farmers did. The thick layer of dust that settled in the foot-deep furrows acted as a kind of mulch.

Large California-style ditch companies were out of the question on most of the Great Plains. The level of the largest rivers dropped too low by midsummer to be productively tapped; smaller streams dried up. Some farmers individually irrigated their fields from wells on which they mounted prefabricated windmills. However, the cost of the windmills and of drilling a well, between $1 and $2 a foot, was too much for many settlers to risk when they had no idea whether they would hit water at 25 feet or 200.

A Treeless Land

Save for groves of cottonwood along the muddy rivers, there were few trees on the Great Plains and, therefore, no wood with which to build homes or barns. Bringing in lumber by train and wagon for a respectable frame house had to be delayed until after a family harvested a few crops and squirreled away a little money. In the meantime, pioneers lived in sod houses, which were constructed of blocks cut from the tangled turf of the plains. Sod houses were rather snug in winter, but they dripped mud in the spring thaw and filled with a choking dust during the long arid summers. Many western farmers died in them after many years dreaming of clapboards and broad windows.

Building fences was more urgent. Crops needed to be protected from open-range cattle, and the settler's own livestock kept under control. But cheap as fence lumber was, the cost of ringing a 160-acre farm with wooden posts and rails was beyond the means of nearly all. The solution to the problem came in 1872 when Joseph Glidden of Illinois perfected a machine that mass-produced cheap barbed wire. With the flimsiest of scavenged fence posts, a Great Plains farmer could erect a steel hedge so efficient that a starving cow would lie down and die rather than push through it.

Barbed wire's effectiveness was the cause of numerous clashes between the farmers and small-scale cattlemen (sometimes called nesters) who used it, and open-range cattlemen accustomed to running their animals freely on the plains. When fences prevented their cattle from reaching streams and water holes, cattle barons retaliated by damming up streams above nester land, cutting fence wire into useless shreds, and, in Johnson County, Wyoming, hiring gunfighters to terrorize them.

Machines on the Land

Barbed wire was but one of dozens of technology's contributions to the fabulous expansion of American agriculture. A chilled steel plow perfected by Oliver Evans in 1877 sliced through sod and heavy soils. Disc harrows cultivated wide swaths with each pass, allowing "dry farmers" to tend more acres than they needed to do back east. Manufacturers like John Deere and International Harvester developed machines that planted seeds, shucked corn, threshed wheat, bound shocks, and shredded fodder for

---

Making a Sod House

To make a sod house, pioneers mowed about an acre of grassland, preferably when it was slightly moist, and hitched mules or oxen to a "grasshopper plow" that turned up the sod in strips about a foot wide and four to five inches thick. These were chopped into blocks with a spade and, grass side down, the "Nebraska marble" was laid like bricks. The walls of a sod house had to be two to three feet thick in order to support the roof, which was made of wooden rafters with a layer of sod grass-side up on top. Door and window frames were made from old packing crates.

A sod house was fireproof, quite snug in winter and cool in summer, but it dropped dirt and dust constantly and, in heavy rains, it might be necessary to cook, eat, and sleep with an umbrella overhead.

A couple stand with their prized possessions in front of their sod house in Custer County, Nebraska, about 1886.

livestock. The value of farm machinery in use in the United States increased from $271 million in 1870 to $750 million in 1900.

Machinery made the American farmer of the late nineteenth century the most productive in the world. He was potentially able to cultivate six times as much land as his father farmed back east before the Civil War. That is, plowing and seeding wheat by hand, harvesting it with a sickle, and threshing with a flail, a prewar farmer had to spend between 50 and 60 hours to harvest about 20 bushels of wheat per acre. With a gang plow and a horse-drawn seeder, harrow, reaper, and thresher—all of which were in widespread use by 1890—a farmer produced a much larger crop after only eight to ten hours of work per acre.

Hard Times

On the other hand, machinery carried a price that most farmers simply did not have in hand. Already short-term debtors, borrowing each year for seed and provisions during the growing season, the typical farmer of the late nineteenth century was also a long-term debtor, owing money for his machines even if he had gotten his land for free under the Homestead Act.

What was worse, beginning about 1872, the western growers of wheat, corn, and livestock watched their incomes sag and, by the 1890s, collapse. A crop that in 1872 brought a farmer $1,000 in real income (actual purchasing power) was worth only $500 in 1896. A man who was 48 years of age in 1896, still an active working farmer, had to turn out twice as many hogs or double the bushels of corn or wheat as he had produced as a young man of 24, just to enjoy the same standard of living that he had known in 1872. It was not comforting to know that a quarter-century of backbreaking toil yielded nothing but the prospect of more struggle. By the 1890s, the price of corn was so low (eight cents a bushel) that some farmers had to forgo buying coal and to burn their grain for winter warmth.

Mechanization on the farm: Horse-drawn reapers such as this did the work of many men and women.

Those who were unable to pay their debts went under. Between 1889 and 1893, some 11,000 Kansas farm families lost their homes when they failed to make their mortgage payments. In several western counties of Kansas and Nebraska during the same period, nine out of every ten farmsteads changed hands. The number of farm tenant families—those that did not own the land they worked—doubled from 1 to 2 million between 1880 and 1900, most of the increase coming after 1890. For every three landowning farm families in the North and West, there was one tenant family. For them, farming was no longer the basis of independence and hope for the future, but grinding toil for the sake of putting a meal on the table and keeping the banker from the door.

The South: Tenants and Sharecroppers

Tenancy was far more common in the South, particularly in the cotton belt. Below the Ohio River, there were as many tenant farmers as there were families working land they owned. Among African Americans, tenants and sharecroppers outnumbered landowners by almost five to one.

The South's tenancy problem originated in Reconstruction. Having freed blacks from bondage, the then-dominant Republicans failed to provide the freedmen the means to survive on their own. After some consideration, the Republicans rejected radical proposals to confiscate the large plantations and divide them into 40-acre farms for the blacks who worked them as slaves. With a few exceptions, land was left in the hands of those who owned it before the war.

But how were the crops to be got in? Wages or not, the former slaves resisted working in gangs; that was reminiscent of the patterns of life under slavery.

African-American Sodbusters

With the collapse of Reconstruction, Benjamin "Pap" Singleton, a black carpenter from Nashville, concluded that blacks could make decent lives for themselves only by doing what so many whites were doing—moving west. He came to be known as the "Moses of the Colored Exodus" by traveling throughout the South urging blacks to migrate to Kansas and found black colonies. His message touched a chord in some communities. By the end of 1878, more than 7,000 "Exodusters" took out homesteads in Kansas. In 1879, another 20,000 arrived, founding communities such as Nicodemus, which still preserves its black pioneer heritage.

At first glad for the immigrants, Kansas soon launched a campaign of discouragement to counter Singleton's work. While propagandists publicized the usual rosy lies among potential white immigrants, they told southern blacks about the hardships and risks of farming on the Great Plains (all true enough), for fear that the state would become a black refuge.

Moreover, the people who owned the land had little money with which to pay wages. They were themselves impoverished; slaves had been the southern landowner's capital.

The solution to this problem was a system of cultivation that, on the face of it, seemed fair to both landowner and worker: sharing the crop. Plantation owners partitioned their land into family farm-size plots on which cabins, usually quite rude, were constructed. In return for the use of the dwelling and the land, share-tenants, who provided their own daily bread, mule, plow, and seed, turned over to the landlord one-quarter to one-third of each year's crop. Sharecroppers were tenants who were too poor to rustle up a mule, a plow, and seed. The landlord provided everything in return for one-half of the crop.

As a means of production, the system worked. Southern cotton production reached its 1860 level in 1870 and exceeded the prewar record (1859) a few years later. As in the West, however, greater production was accompanied by a drastic decline in wholesale prices. The price of a pound of cotton fell to six cents by the 1890s, and briefly in 1893 to a nickel, $30 for a bale it took six strong men to lift.

Debt Bondage

One result of declining prices was a physically and morally debilitating poverty. Pellagra, a fatal niacin-deficiency disease unknown in slavery times, became a problem of epidemic proportions in the South. Another consequence was a form of debt bondage that, wrote Charles Oken in 1894, "crushed out all independence and reduced its victims to a coarse species of servile labor."

The victims were white as well as black. Many white farmers with modest holdings before the war lost their land to creditors, usually merchants. The ledgers of one southern merchant, T. G. Patrick,

A sharecropper's cabin in North Carolina, 1914.

NOTABLE PEOPLE

The New South: The Prophet and the Builder

In speech after speech throughout the South, he told the story of a funeral that he had attended in rural Georgia. "They buried him in a New York coat and a Boston pair of shoes, and a pair of breeches from Chicago and a shirt from Cincinnati." The coffin, continued Henry W. Grady (1851–1889), the wisecracking editor of the Atlanta *Constitution*, was made from northern lumber and hammered together with northern-forged nails. "The South didn't furnish a thing on earth for that funeral but the corpse and the hole in the ground."

Grady's point, to which he devoted most of his short life, was that the South must abandon its traditional reliance on agriculture and promote industrialization. The North's industry explained why the Confederacy had been defeated and why, in the wake of the war, the South suffered in company with the agricultural Plains. Only by accepting the realities of the modern world would the South prosper and escape its status as a backwater.

Although Grady lived to see few of his ideas come to fruition, during the very period that southern agrarians like Thomas E. Watson were vilifying urban, industrial America, southerners scored the kind of successes that Grady had called for. Beginning with a federal grant of almost 6 million acres of forest land in 1877, southern syndicates laid the basis of a thriving lumber and turpentine industry in the vast pine woods of the section. Birmingham became the "Pittsburgh of the South," the center of a booming steel industry, following the discovery of coal and iron in northern Alabama in the early 1870s. By 1890, Birmingham was making more pig iron than was Pittsburgh. ("Pigs" are iron ingots, intermediate products ready for further processing.)

The southern oil industry was largely a twentieth-century development; the great Texas gusher, Spindletop, came through in 1901. Likewise the southern textile industry. Most of the New England textile mills migrated to the South after 1900, although, even before Grady died in 1889, the trend of "bringing the factory to the fields" was to some degree underway.

The southerner who was most successful in bringing the factory to the fields was not a maker of cloth but a maker of cigarettes and bad habits. James Buchanan "Buck" Duke (1856–1925) started out as a tobacco grower, a good southern agrarian on the face of it. In 1881, he was shown a new machine that rolled cigarettes by the hundreds per minute, and his head began to spin in contemplation of its possibilities. All cigarettes were then rolled by hand, mostly by the smoker. Like a chess player, Duke had to see several moves ahead. To make money from manufacturing cigarettes, it was necessary not only to mass-

---

show that during one season he provided about $900 worth of seed, food, tools, and other necessities to a farm owner named S. R. Simonton. When, in the fall, the price of cotton dropped well below Simonton's expectations, he was able to repay only $300, leaving Patrick with a lien against his property of $600. Simonton cut his costs drastically the following year to just $400, but the accumulated debt of $1,000 was too much for Patrick to carry. He took Simonton's land and Simonton became his tenant.

Once a tenant or sharecropper, the southern farmer's debts bound him to the land almost as irrevocably as if he were a medieval serf. Tenants and sharecroppers also bought their necessities on credit from a general merchandiser, often their landlord, putting up as collateral their share of the crop. If the income from their share did not cover the year's debt, the merchandiser put a lien on the next year's harvest, quite effectively binding the cropper to work for him indefinitely. There was no quitting and moving out. In several states, to try to flee such a debt was a criminal offense punishable by imprisonment and hard labor on a chain gang, or bitter irony, leased out to a planter.

There was, of course, an element of security in debt bondage. The cropper in hock to his landlord

produce them cheaply, but also to change Americans' tobacco habits.

In the late nineteenth century, "decent" women did not smoke (at least in public), upper- and middle-class men smoked cigars or pipes, and workingmen and the lower classes in the South were inclined to chew tobacco. Cigarettes were around. The soldiers in the Civil War had taken to them because they could carry papers and a pouch of tobacco but not cigars. After the war, however, the white cylinders were considered to be effete, a boy's smoke behind the barn. Duke would have to change that image, and he did.

Buying the patent to the cigarette-rolling machine, he encouraged adolescents to cultivate the habit by selling a pack of 20 for only a nickel and by including inside each pack a "trading card" that featured pictures and brief biographies of military heroes and popular athletes, mostly boxers and baseball players. No one better understood the wisdom in putting together a long-term market than "Buck" Duke. All the while he created his consumers, he improved machinery and bought out competitors. By 1889, his company accounted for half the cigarettes sold in the United States, and Duke had only begun.

In 1890, he set up a trust along the lines laid out by John D. Rockefeller. Through it he gained control of his major competitors, R. J. Reynolds and P. J. Lorillard, and built an almost perfect monopoly. Indeed, through loose arrangements with British cigarette manufacturers, Duke had a major say in the tobacco-processing industry on two continents. Only federal antitrust action in 1911 forced him to disband his gigantic corporation. By that year, he controlled 150 factories, and, even at that, his reputation as the South's greatest home-grown business mogul was being challenged by the directors of the recently founded Coca-Cola Company of Atlanta.

Like the Yankee moguls whose methods he adopted, "Buck" Duke was a generous philanthropist. His most enduring monument is Duke University, which had been a small, local college before it received an endowment from Duke and changed its name; it is now an architecturally magnificent Gothic-style campus in Duke's hometown of Durham, North Carolina. Until the militant antismoking campaigns of the 1970s, Duke was one of the few universities in the United States where students and faculty could light up the "coffin nails" that had built the institution wherever and whenever they chose. That practice has been abandoned, but his statue, which stands in front of the university's cathedral-size chapel, portrays James Buchanan Duke gently tapping the ash from his cigar.

was not likely to be evicted. But there had been such an element of security in slavery, too.

Hayseeds

Southern black farmers needed no tutoring to know that their race excluded them from full participation in the mainstream of American politics and social life. The color line was drawn ever more clearly in the South as the nineteenth century waned. White farmers of South and West experienced a more subtle deterioration in their political power and status. Not only did the proportion of agricul-turalists in the population decline annually, but the legislators whom farmers sent to Washington and the state capitals seemed all too often to forget their grimy constituents once they made the acquaintance of back-slapping lobbyists for railroads, industry, and banks.

A newly confident urban culture depicted the man of the soil in popular fiction, songs, and melodramas as a thick-skulled yokel, a ridiculous figure in a tattered straw hat with a length of straw clenched between his teeth, a hayseed who allowed traveling salesmen to sleep with his daughter. Rather more serious chroniclers of rural life, such as Hamlin Garland, sympathized with farmers but wanted no part of their lives. In his popular book of 1891, *Main-Travelled Roads*, Garland depicted rural life as dreary and stultifying.

Tens of thousands of farmers' sons and daughters followed Garland in his flight to the city. In part, they despaired of ever making a living on the land. In part, they were lured by the social and cultural attractions of the city. "Who wants to smell new-mown hay," playwright Clyde Fitch wrote in 1909, "if he can breathe gasoline on Fifth Avenue instead?" With each son and daughter who opted for urban fumes, farmers who clung to the Jeffersonian image of themselves became further dejected, agitated, and demoralized.

PROTEST AND ORGANIZATION

To ward against jokes and jeers, farmers could repair to the good old gospel of agrarianism according to Jefferson, the assurance that they were peculiarly valuable to society. They could and did disdain the cities as sinks of iniquity and sin. In speech and sermon, and in the pages of magazines catering to country people, politicians, preachers, and journalists repeated the old shibboleths. In sturdy pillars of American popular culture, like the *McGuffey's Readers*, in which urban and rural schoolchildren alike learned their ABCs and values on their side, the ennoblement of farm life was alive and well.

Rural Renaissance

And yet, life on the western American farm was undeniably an isolated life, arduous and often dreary. The winds on the Great Plains dispatched men and women to state asylums in numbers high enough to catch the attention of the doughtiest Jeffersonian. Aside from church—which was not for everyone—and moments snatched on shopping trips to town, there was little to relieve the tedium and monotony, especially for farm women, whose lives were far more isolated than those of their menfolk. "Even my youthful zeal" in depicting the hardships of farm life, Hamlin Garland wrote, was inadequate when he tried to describe "the lives led by the women. . . . Before the tragic futility of their suffering, my pen refused to shed its ink."

In the 1870s, farm women and their husbands joined the Patrons of Husbandry, the Grange, which sponsored dances, fairs, and lecturers who spoke on everything from the date of creation to the habits of the people of Borneo. In the 1880s, new organizations—the Agricultural Wheel, the Texas State Alliance, the Southern Alliance, and the Colored Farmers' National Alliance—mushroomed all over the countryside to take over many of the same functions.

Their value was inestimable, particularly for women. A leader of the Southern Alliance, the largest of the regional organizations, declared that it "redeemed woman from her enslaved condition, and placed her in her proper sphere." Indeed, women were to play an active role in the agrarian movement at every level.

Originally, both the Grange and the Alliances were avowedly nonpolitical. Inevitably in the hard times, however, farmers getting together asked themselves what—or who—was to blame for their woes? The Grangers attacked the railroads for exploiting them, and successfully regulated their rates by electing sympathetic politicians to state legislatures. Then they saw their work wiped out by the Wabash decision of 1886. The Alliances and Wheels taught that the truculent individualism of the farmer in a highly organized society contributed to their distress and encouraged members to form cooperatives and other economic combinations.

The Co-op Movement

In consumer cooperatives, farmers banded together to purchase essential machinery in quantity and therefore more cheaply. Money pools, associations much like contemporary credit unions, sprouted all over the Midwest. Through these associations, which were capitalized by members and operated on a nonprofit basis, farmers hoped to eliminate their dependence on banks. While many survived to serve the credit needs of members for generations, money pools suffered from the hostility of bankers and the inexperience of their often amateur administrators. Farmers too often put friends rather than professionals in charge of the money pools, and the rate of mismanagement and embezzlement was sadly high.

Producer cooperatives were designed to counter the power of the railroads over farmers' lives after the Supreme Court's decision in the Wabash case of 1886 struck down the Granger laws regulating charges for storing grain. Cornbelt farmers pooled funds and built their own grain elevators in the expectation they could keep their crop off the market until they liked the selling price.

But co-ops could not remedy the problem that was at the root of agricultural distress: American staple farmers were too many and too productive for their own good. Too much land was opened to settlement by too many railroads too quickly. Improvements in farm machinery and new methods resulted in far more grain, livestock, and fiber than the market could absorb.

Sinister Forces

Some agrarian leaders recognized overproduction as a problem. Canadian-born "Sockless Jerry" Simpson of Kansas called on the federal government to carve out new markets for American farm goods abroad. Mary Elizabeth Lease of Kansas, one of the nation's first women lawyers and an orator of withering intensity, told farmers to "raise less corn and more hell." But that was a slogan, not a program. To the individual farmer, the only solution to declining prices was not to plant less corn but more, thus worsening the situation.

Moreover, few farmers believed that overproduction was the sole or even the chief cause of agrarian distress. Mother Lease herself pointed out that the streets of American cities teemed with hungry, ill-clad people while foodstuffs rotted in Kansas and cotton went unsold in Alabama. She and other agrarian leaders—Simpson, Ignatius Donnelly of Minnesota, William Peffer of Kansas, and Thomas Watson of Georgia—said that sinister, parasitical forces were at work like thieves in the night to enrich themselves at the expense of men and women who produced wealth. Their villains included the great railroaders, politicians and judges pliantly in their employ, and most of all the "money power," a conspiracy of bankers and lawyers who manipulated the nation's currency.

THE MONEY QUESTION

Money is a medium of exchange, a token that the people of a society agree represents value. It makes the exchange of goods and services more workable than simple barter: so much grain in return for a pair of shoes or so many hours of labor. Obviously, money is essential to all but the most primitive economies.

The value of money can change. At the time of the first European settlements in North America, the tribes of the eastern Woodlands used wampum, or strings of beads made of shell or stone, to represent value when they exchanged corn, hides, and other goods. Strings of wampum were difficult to make and, therefore, scarce.

When Europeans introduced glass beads in great quantity into this economy at little cost to themselves, buying valuable pelts for a pittance, but refusing to accept the beads in return when the Indians tried to purchase iron tools, weapons, and other European products, wampum was soon worthless to everyone but aficionados of art and the Indians' lost culture.

Gold and Silver

The economically sophisticated nations of the world used precious metals—gold and silver—as their medium of exchange. Gold and silver were durable and limited in supply. There was little danger that the world would suddenly be flooded with either.

Thus, the value they represented was stable and dependable. The farmer who received gold for his crop knew that the suppliers of the goods his family needed would accept the gold at the value he put on it. It did not even matter which country's emblem was stamped on a coin, and European money, especially British sterling, circulated in the U.S. to an extent astonishing in an age when Canadian quarters are looked upon as swindles. The weight of the gold in it determined its worth. In the U.S., the treasury minted coins of large denomination in gold: $5 coins, $10 coins (called eagles), and $20 coins (double eagles).

Coins of smaller denomination (dimes, quarters, and dollars) were minted in silver, which was more common than gold and therefore less valuable, but also limited in quantity. Because the supply of both metals appeared to be so stable, in 1837, Congress determined that the value of silver as money would be pegged to that of gold at a ratio of 16:1. That is, one ounce of gold was legally worth 16 ounces of silver, it being estimated that there was in the world just about 16 times as much silver as gold. Put another way, for every 16 ounces of silver a miner presented to the mint for sale, he would receive one ounce in gold. That was the law.

Large commercial transactions were carried out in paper money issued by banks pledged to redeem it in silver or gold. The value of this paper depended, of course, upon people's confidence in the ability of the bank in question to hand precious metal over the counter when presented with its own notes.

The Greenbacks

During the Civil War, finding itself with too little gold and silver to pay for the army, the Lincoln administration issued a new kind of paper money, some $433 million in bills called greenbacks because they were printed on the obverse (like our own money) in green ink. The greenbacks were not redeemable in gold or silver. Their value depended entirely upon the government's agreement to accept them in payment of most obligations, such as taxes.

Government acceptance of the greenbacks gave them value as a medium of exchange. However, no one considered them to be "as good as gold" (or silver) and their worth fluctuated, sometimes wildly, depending on the success or failure of the Union army or a twist in federal financial policy. At the end of the Civil War, a person needed $157 in greenbacks in order to buy $100 in gold or silver coin.

Inflation or Deflation

Discounted as they were, the abundant greenbacks nevertheless circulated; the Union did, after all, survive and continue to accept them. Indeed, the greenbacks won many friends because, by increasing the amount of money in circulation, they inflated wages and prices, including prices at which farmers sold their crops. The Civil War was a prosperous time down on the farm. Looking back on it in bleaker days, many farmers associated the good times with the greenbacks. They argued that the federal government should continue to use them to regulate the amount of money in circulation in order to accommodate the needs of a dynamic people, for the supply of gold and silver did not expand rapidly enough to keep up with the explosive economy of the United States.

Bankers and big businessmen thought otherwise. They dealt in large sums of money and feared having the value of their vast properties—and the money others owed to them—reduced in value by politicians seeking favor with voters. These monetary conservatives insisted that money had absolute, natural value, determined by the amount of gold in existence and, until the 1870s, by the amount of silver.

With their close ties to the executive branch of the government in the wake of the Civil War, the conservatives generally had their way. By February 1868, $45 million in greenbacks were retired from circulation; when paid to the government in taxes, they were simply burned. Money grew scarcer and therefore more valuable; deflation set in. Wages and prices, including the prices at which farmers sold their crops, declined.

A silver certificate issued in 1878. The portrait on the bill is of the Sioux chief One Papa.

Protest was so widespread that, in October 1868, Congress ordered the Treasury Department to stop retiring the greenbacks. But the inflationist victory was short-lived. In 1875, ascendant conservatives ordered that for every $100 issued by banks (money theoretically backed by gold), $80 in greenbacks be retired. In 1879, Secretary of the Treasury John Sherman ordered that all payments to the government be made in specie, or coin. This effectively destroyed the greenbacks; if the government would not accept them, who would? Between 1865 and 1878, the amount of all kinds of money in circulation in the United States shrunk from $1.08 billion to $773 million. Whereas in 1865 there had been $31.18 in circulation for every American, in 1878 there was but $16.25.

The Greenback Party

In an attempt to stem this deflation, many farmers, working people, and some small businessmen joined together to form the Greenback Labor party, which was dedicated to the single issue of inflating the currency. Like most third parties in American history, the Greenbackers attracted few voters. In 1880, Civil War General James B. Weaver of Iowa won 308,578 votes. In 1884, Greenback candidate Benjamin F. Butler won just 175,370 votes, not much more than the Prohibitionist party candidate received. By 1884, people who wanted the currency inflated had turned to another form of money for their salvation — silver coin.

Silver to the Fore

Between 1837 and 1873, the price of silver in the United States was legally pegged to the price of gold at a ratio of 16:1. During the 1860s, however, American mines produced proportionately less silver than gold, considerably less than 16 ounces for each ounce of gold. Consequently, silver mine owners preferred to sell their product not to the United States Mint, which paid the official price, but to private or foreign buyers, who were willing to pay more, an ounce of gold for just 14 ounces of silver.

In 1873, confronted with the fact that little silver was being presented to the mint for sale, Congress enacted the Demonetization Act, ceasing government purchases of silver. The silver dollar was dropped from the list of coins the government minted. Rather than money, silver became an ordinary commodity like wheat, hogs, lumber, or petticoats; its value (in gold — money!) was set not by Congress, but by the laws of supply and demand. President Grant signed the Demonetization Act without ado.

Already as the ink from his pen was drying, however, the relative supply of silver and gold was changing again. New silver strikes throughout the West and new methods of mining it were resulting in a vast increase in production of the white metal. In 1861, only $2 million worth of silver was mined in the United States compared to $43 million worth of gold. In 1873, the value of silver and gold mined was about equal, $36 million each. During the rest of the 1870s, silver production increased so rapidly that its price on the private market, the only market now open to miners, collapsed.

Politician friends of mining interests like the excitable Democrat Richard "Silver Dick" Bland of Missouri and Senator Henry W. Teller of Colorado began to denounce the Demonetization Act as "The Crime of '73." They accused the government of conspiring with bankers to punish silver miners for their very success. There was no crime of 1873; no one but the most sanguine western prospector could have anticipated the explosive increase in silver production when Congress passed the Demonetization Act.

Nevertheless, when silver production did rise, monetary conservatives were undoubtedly relieved that the government was no longer buying and minting it, thus inflating the currency and reducing the value of their property. The "Gold Bugs," as Bland and Teller called them, began to look upon abundant silver as a threat to the value of their money as serious as the greenbacks.

By themselves, mine owners and miners would not have had the power to force the government to resume the purchase and minting of silver. Even after the admission of mineral-rich Colorado in 1876, mining interests were significant in few states. However, inflationist congressmen from agricultural states — mostly southern and western Democrats, but also including Republicans — seized on silver coinage as a way to get more money in circulation. In the depression year of 1878, they forced the conservatives to agree to a compromise. The Bland-Allison Bill of that year required the secretary of the treasury to purchase between $2 and $4 million of silver each month for minting into money. The silver dollar was back.

The Sherman Silver Purchase Act

The silver dollar was back, but the principle of bimetalism (both gold and silver as money, the value of one pegged by law to the other) was not. In both the Republican and Democratic administrations of the 1880s, the treasury was safely in the hands of financial conservatives dedicated to keeping gold the sole standard of value. The government almost invariably bought the minimum $2 million in silver required by law. In effect, the silver dollars that were minted were tokens like copper cents and paper money, having money value because they would be bought or sold with gold.

The national production of silver continued to grow during the 1880s, and the market price of the metal plummeted. By 1890, it took nearly 20 ounces of silver to buy an ounce of gold. In the minds of inflationists and silver producers, the old lost ratio of 16:1 took on a mythic, sacred significance.

In 1889 and 1890, the balance of power tipped to the side of the inflationists. Two states in which silver was an important commodity (Montana and Idaho) and four in which inflationist farmers were a majority (the two Dakotas, Washington, and Wyoming) entered the Union, bringing 12 new silver senators to Washington.

The result was the Sherman Silver Purchase Act of 1890. Like the Bland-Allison Act, it was a compromise. The Sherman law required the secretary of the treasury to purchase 4.5 million ounces of silver each month, in effect the entire monthly production of the nation's silver mines at that time. However, the government bought silver at the market price, which continued to decline, from a ratio of 20:1 in 1890 to 26.5:1 in 1893. Consequently, the Sherman Act failed to relieve discontent in the mining regions and led to violent strikes as mine owners attempted to cut costs by forcing down wages.

Farmers, who favored silver coinage as a means of inflating the currency and raising prices, were also disappointed. Although he signed the Sherman Act, President Benjamin Harrison was a gold standard man. He treated silver coins as if they were tokens—paper money—instructing the secretary of the treasury to pay all the government's bills in gold. To distressed farmers already inclined to look for sinister forces at work in the night, the presidency itself seemed in the employ of the money power.

THE POPULISTS

By 1890, the Alliance movement was at flood tide. The Southern Alliance had 1.5 million members, the Colored Farmers Alliance a million, other groups combined about the same. Feeling their oats, the leaders of the various regional organizations gathered in Ocala, Florida, in December to draw up a list of grievances and consider the possibility of organizing a third party.

Hesitation

By December 1890, Kansas farmers had already organized a statewide People's party, calling themselves Populists after the Latin word for "the people," populus, and winning control of the state legislature. At Ocala, however, old Republican and Democratic loyalties were too strong, and racial anxieties too gnawing for the delegates to take the same leap.

Southern white farmers hesitated because they had made inroads in the Democratic party and feared that if they split the white vote in the South by forming a new party, blacks would regain the political equality they had held through the Republican party during Reconstruction. The leaders of the Colored Farmers Alliance were reluctant to give up their allegiance to the Republican party, which had, how-

A cartoonist uses the image of the bicycle, still a "new-fangled contraption," to argue against attempting to value silver coin on a par with gold money.

ever uncertainly, defended the civil rights of African Americans.

But events were already underway to undermine old loyalties. In July 1890, the same month the Silver Purchase Act was passed, the Republican majority in the United States Senate failed to enact the Force Bill, a law designed to protect the right of southern blacks to vote. In effect, the Republicans abandoned southern blacks to their own fate. Some black southerners called for a new party. Some southern whites like Tom Watson of Georgia, a diminutive red-headed, and hot-tempered lawyer who had been cheated out of elective office by the conservative Democratic machine, called for an alliance between black and white farmers. In a magazine article published in 1892, he told white and black farmers,

> You are kept apart that you may be separately fleeced of your earnings. You are made to hate each other because upon that hatred is rested the keystone of the arch of financial despotism which enslaves you both. You are deceived and blinded that you may not see how this race antagonism perpetuates a monetary system which beggars both.

The Omaha Convention

In February 1892, delegates from the various Alliances and Wheels, and more than a few self-appointed spokesmen for the farmers and silver miners, met in Omaha, Nebraska, to form a new party. They gladly adopted the name Populist from the Kansas party that had already sent several congressmen and Senator William Peffer to Washington.

To symbolize the fact that farmers of North and South had bridged the sectional chasm that made them enemies, the Populists nominated former Union General and Greenbacker James B. Weaver for president, and former Confederate General James G. Field for vice president. No one expected them to win, and they did not. Grover Cleveland, the Democratic candidate, won a comfortable victory in the electoral college despite carrying only 46 percent of the popular vote. And Weaver did well enough, winning more than a million votes and carrying Kansas. At Omaha, the Populists were planning for November 1896, not 1892, when they expected to restore democracy and justice to a corrupted country.

Indeed, what most impressed observers about the Omaha convention was the evangelical fervor, even

---

Conspiracy!

In the late nineteenth century, railroads allowed delegates to national political conventions to ride half-fare. However, this favor was not extended to delegates to the Populist party convention in Omaha in 1892. When one delegate referred to this oversight, another delegate from California delivered a diatribe illustrating the angry antagonism of the Populists:

The customary courtesy was denied deliberately and with insolence. I do not want this Convention to go back to the railroad company, hat in hand, and ask for any privileges whatever. The Democrats and Republicans secured half-fare, but we — not connected with railroads, but producers of the earth — have been refused equal terms. We can stand the refusal.

---

the frenzy with which the Populists addressed public questions, as if they were embarked not on a political campaign, but on a crusade against satanic evil itself. "We meet on the verge of a nation brought to the verge of moral, political, and material ruin," Ignatius Donnelly of Minnesota wrote in the preamble to the party platform. "Corruption dominates the ballot box, the legislatures, the Congress, and touches even the ermine of the bench." William Peffer, looking like a biblical prophet with his waist-length beard, railed like one about the inequities of the land. "Conspiracy" was a word on everyone's lips, the conspiracy of the great railroads to defraud the shipper, the conspiracy of politicians to destroy democracy, the conspiracy of the money power, even the conspiracy of Jews.

"The people are at bay," Mother Lease said, "let the bloodhounds of money beware." When the platform was finally approved, according to one not-too-sympathetic reporter, "cheers and yells . . . rose like a tornado . . . and raged without cessation for thirty-four minutes, during which time women shrieked and wept, men embraced and kissed their neighbors, locked arms, marched back and forth, and leaped upon tables and chairs in the ecstasy of their delirium."

A Far-Reaching Program

The atmosphere was, no doubt, disarming. And yet, the platform the Populists wrote was far from lunatic. On the contrary, it was a comprehensive program for reform that, if enacted intact, would have transformed American development, and not necessarily for the worse.

Indeed, the Populists' political reforms were (in years to come) to become the law of the land. The Pops called for the election of United States senators by popular vote, rather than by state legislatures, a reform instituted in the Seventeenth Amendment to the Constitution in 1913. They demanded the universal use of the Australian, or secret, ballot to prevent landlords and employers from intimidating their tenants and workers into voting as the bosses chose. By the early twentieth century, public ballots were abolished everywhere but in New England town meetings.

The Populists introduced the concepts of the initiative, recall, and referendum to American politics. The initiative allows voters, through petition, to put measures on the ballot independent of action by legislatures and thus, in theory, free of manipulation by professional lobbyists and their accomplices. The recall allows voters, also through petition, to force a public official to stand for election before his or her term is up. The Populists hoped that the recall would discourage politicians from backing down on campaign pledges. The referendum allows voters to vote directly on laws rather than indirectly through their representatives; it is the means by which initiative measures and recall petitions are decided. All three are accepted procedures in many states today.

The most controversial Populist demand was for the abolition of national banks and for government ownership of railroads and the telegraph. Enemies pointed to this plank as evidence that the Populists were socialists. They were not; they were landowners or tenants who aspired above all to own land. However, they believed that natural monopolies—huge enterprises that could be run efficiently only under a single management—should not be in private hands. To the Populist mind, decisions that affected the interests of all should be made democratically, not by combinations of private parties interested only in their own enrichment.

The Populists also called for a postal savings system, so that ordinary people might avoid depositing their money in privately owned banks, and for a graduated income tax. In 1892, the federal income tax was 2 percent for all; the Populists wanted the wealthy to pay a higher percentage of their income than the modest farmer or wage worker paid.

Finally—as only one plank of many—the Populists addressed the silver question. They called for an increase in the money in circulation to $50 per capita.

This inflation was to be accomplished through the free and unlimited coinage of silver, its value pegged to that of gold. In the summer of 1892, this was perhaps the mildest of the Populist demands. It represented only an adjustment of the Sherman Act then in effect. In just over a year, however, "Free Silver" was to become the Populists' obsession, nearly destroying their ardor for the rest of the Omaha platform.

The Panic of 1893

In February 1893, ten days before Grover Cleveland took the oath of office, the Reading Railroad, a major eastern trunk line, announced it was bankrupt. For two months the stock market was jittery, and then it collapsed. Hundreds of banks and thousands of businesses joined the Reading in receivership. By November, the country was sunk in a depression greater than that of the 1870s.

Needing money or fearing for the safety of their government bonds, both American and British financiers rushed to redeem them. Cleveland, who was more firmly committed to the gold standard than

---

Populist Anti-Semitism?

The hatred of farmers for bankers sometimes took the form of anti-Semitism, hatred of Jewish bankers. One book that blamed Jews particularly for the ruination of the American farmer was Ignatius P. Donnelly's novel *Caesar's Column*. One character's explanation of why Jewish bankers were exploiting farmers is curious: past anti-Semitism with a Darwinian twist:

Christianity fell upon the Jews, originally a race of agriculturists and shepherds, and forced them, for many centuries, through the most terrible ordeal of persecution the history of mankind bears record of. Only the strong of body, the cunning of brain, the long-headed, the persistent, the men with capacity to live where the dog would starve, survived the awful trial. Like breeds like; and now the Christian world is paying, in tears and blood, for the sufferings inflicted by their bigoted and ignorant ancestors upon a noble race. When the time came for liberty and fair play the Jew was master in the contest with the Gentile. . . . They were as merciless to the Christians as the Christians had been to them.

Harrison, was true to his word. He instructed the secretary of the treasury to redeem all demands in gold alone. By fall, the government's gold reserve—the actual metal in its vaults—sunk to below $100 million, the level regarded by conservatives as the absolute minimum for maintaining the government's credit.

A Most Unpopular Man

Cleveland blamed the crisis and the panic that led up to it on the Sherman Act. "To put beyond all doubt or mistake" the commitment of the United States to the gold standard, the president called for its repeal and a frightened Congress obliged him. That lost him the support of Democrats from the mining states. Then the news leaked that, at the height of the crisis, Cleveland had called on J. P. Morgan for help in increasing the government's gold reserve. Throughout the South and Midwest, more Democrats denounced him.

In 1894, Cleveland's attorney general, a former railroad attorney, Richard B. Olney, crushed the Pullman strike, turning many industrial workers against him. He blundered even in his treatment of Jacob Coxey, an Ohio businessman who led a march of unemployed men to Washington to ask for relief. Coxey was arrested for walking on the grass.

Few presidents have been so unpopular as Grover Cleveland was in his second term. When his supporters, dwindling in numbers, reminded voters of the president's unquestioned integrity, William Jennings Bryan replied, "Cleveland may be honest, but so were the mothers who threw their children in the Ganges." With each blow to Cleveland's prestige,

Coxey and his secretary leading his army to Washington, D.C.

638 *Chapter 32 Stressful Times Down Home*

the Populists celebrated. In their eyes, Cleveland's Democrats and the Republicans were indistinguishable. Both parties were the puppets of the money power. The people did indeed seem to be at bay. The Populists expected to come to power in 1896. The word revolution was being voiced in many gatherings of "the bone and sinew of the republic."

CHRONOLOGY

1872	Joseph Glidden perfects machine for making barbed wire
1873	Demonetization Act ("Crime of '73")
1877	Chilled steel plow invented
1878	Bland-Allison Act
1880, 1884	Greenback party unsuccessful in national elections
1887	Devastating drought in West
1890	Sherman Silver Purchase Act Populist party organized in Kansas
1892	Populists meet in Omaha, draft program and nominate presidential candidate
1893	Financial panic Repeal of Sherman Silver Purchase Act

FOR FURTHER READING

For background and context, see Vincent P. DeSantis, *The Shaping of Modern America, 1877–1916*, 1973, and Robert H. Wiebe, *The Search for Order, 1880–1920*, 1967. The genuinely classic studies of the subject, with contrasting visions, are Gilbert C. Fite, *The Farmer's Frontier, 1865–1900*, 1966, and Fred A. Shannon, *The Farmers' Last Frontier: Agriculture 1860—1897*, 1945. Also see Allan C. Bogue, *From Prairie to Corn Belt*, 1963; E. Dick, *The Sod-House Frontier*, 1937; and Walter P. Webb, *The Great Plains, 1931*.

On farmers' movements, see Solon J. Buck, *The Granger Movement*, 1913; Deborah Fink, *Agrarian Women: Wives and Mothers in Rural Nebraska*, 1992; Lawrence Goodwyn, *Democratic Promise: The Populist Moment in America*, 1976; Michael Kazin, *The Populist Persuasion*, 1995; the appropriate chapters of Richard Hofstadter, *The Age of Reform*, 1955; J. Morgan Kousser, *The Shaping of Southern Politics: Suffrage Restriction and the Establishment of the One-Party South, 1880–1910*, 1974; Walter T. K. Nugent, *Money and American Society, 1865–1880*, 1968, and *The Tolerant Populists: Kansas Populism and Nativism*, 1963; Norman Pollock, *The Populist Response to Industrial America*, 1966; Theodore Saloutos, *Farmer Movements in the South, 1865–1933*, 1960; William Cronon, *Nature's Metropolis: Chicago and the Great West*, 1991; and C. Vann Woodward, *The Strange Career of Jim Crow*, 1974.

P. E. Coletta, *William Jennings Bryan: Political Evangelist, 1860–1908*, 1964, and Louis W. Koenig, Bryan: *A Political Biography of William Jennings Bryan*, 1971, present somewhat different views of the man who came to personify agrarian aspirations. The model biography of the leading southern populist is C. Vann Woodward, *Tom Watson: Agrarian Rebel*, 1938.

Campaign poster, 1900: quintessentially presidential William McKinley; unknown quantity, young Theodore Roosevelt.

33
CHAPTER

IN THE DAYS OF MCKINLEY

The United States Becomes a World Power

1896–1903

God has not been preparing the English-speaking and Teutonic peoples for a thousand years for nothing but vain and idle self-contemplation. No. He made us the master organizers of the world to establish system where chaos reigned. He has given us the spirit of progress to overwhelm the forces of reaction throughout the earth. He has made us adept in government that we may administer government among savage and senile peoples. Were it not for such a force as this the world would relapse into barbarism and night. And of all our race, He has marked the American people as His chosen nation to finally lead in the redemption of the world.

—*Albert J. Beveridge*

The West Indies drift toward us, the Republic of Mexico hardly longer has an independent life, and the city of Mexico is an American town. With the completion of the Panama Canal all Central America will become part of our system. We have expanded into Asia, we have attracted the fragments of the Spanish dominions, and reaching out into China we have checked the advance of Russia and Germany. . . . The United States will outweigh any single empire, if not all empires combined. The whole world will pay her tribute. Commerce will flow to her from both east and west, and the order which has existed from the dawn of time will be reversed.

—*Brooks Adams*

Shall we go on conferring our civilization upon the peoples that sit in darkness, or shall we give those poor things a rest?

—*Mark Twain*

642 *Chapter 33 In the Days of McKinley*

Few presidential elections have been held amidst the anxiety that swirled about the election of 1896. Even as the year began, politicians were calling the contest more important than any since 1860, when the fate of the Union itself hung in the balance. This time the fissure dividing the nation was social rather than sectional — or so politicians on both sides of the split said — class arrayed against class. The terrible depression, the revolt of the hayseeds, the violent strikes, the mass demonstrations, and the passions engendered by the issue of silver versus gold lent a sense of foreboding to political discussions.

WATERSHED

The election of 1896 was in fact a political watershed. When it was decided, the political era that had begun with the end of Reconstruction was dead, and a new one was underway. No one knew what the new era would be like when the campaign began. That depended upon which party and which candidate won the electoral college in November. Thus the anxiety.

Mark Hanna and Bill McKinley

Meeting in St. Louis in June, the Republican convention was placid on the surface. Most Republican agrarians had long since bade farewell to the Grand Old Party and signed on with the Populists. A small free silver contingent from the mining states, led by Senator Teller of Colorado, caused a minor ruckus at the convention when they tried to win concessions for their cause. But the "Gold Bugs" were in charge; when they rebuked Teller's group, even though gently, he and his followers walked out. With little folderol and less fuss, the delegates who remained chose as their presidential candidate William McKinley of Ohio, a man who was a model of conservatism, prudence, respectability, sobriety, and the career politician's richest asset: he kept his ears so close to the ground, one wit said, that he had grasshoppers in them. Or, rather, as the Populists and Democrats soon claimed, the Republicans at the convention sat back and allowed a beefy Cleveland industrialist, Marcus Alonzo Hanna, to choose their candidate for them.

Bald, scowling Mark Hanna was nearly 60 years of age in 1896. An associate of the Rockefellers, he had made a fortune in coal and iron, and was known in business circles as a spokesman for moderation and flexibility in dealing with working people and labor unions. Socialists and other labor radicals were the chief villains in Hanna's book, but he railed against exploitative capitalists, too, because their pigheaded lack of vision made working people receptive to radical preachers.

Only after the descent of the depression of the 1890s did Hanna take a serious interest in national politics. He had ambitions of his own, but also the realistic good sense to know that, with America's large number of professional politicians, a man could not leap from the corporate board room to the executive mansion. Putting his personal aspirations on hold, Hanna devoted his talents and energies to promoting the presidential qualifications of fellow Ohioan, former congressman and governor William McKinley of Canton.

McKinley was a hot prospect. He was the Republican party's chief expert on the tariff, and he was himself ambitious. Theodore Roosevelt later remarked that McKinley approached every introduction and conversation with an eye on the advantage it might mean to him. And yet, without Hanna, it is unlikely that McKinley would have won the Republican presidential nomination in 1896. The issue dominating political discourse that year was not the tariff but the gold standard versus the free coinage of silver, which was not an issue that particularly interested McKinley.

Moreover, while McKinley's dignity commanded respect, he lacked excitement. He was a bit of a stiff. Journalist William Allen White quipped that McKinley "was destined for a statue in the park and he was practicing the pose for it." McKinley refused to smoke his beloved cigars in public lest he be accused of setting a bad example for America's youth. Such a politician needed a Mark Hanna behind him, a wheeler-dealer who marched into an office, cigar unashamedly ablaze, and planted a hefty haunch on the desk of the man he wanted to see. Republicans and Democrats alike assumed that McKinley was Hanna's puppet.

The Frightening Boy Bryan

The partnership of energy and solemnity proved indispensable to the Republicans in 1896 because the Democratic party candidate, nominated at a frenzied convention in July, was a tornado of energy who was plenty sober—he has a lifelong enemy of demon rum—but who singularly lacked dignity. William Jennings Bryan, scarcely beyond the 35 years of age the Constitution requires a president to be, was a two-term congressman from Nebraska, a newspaperman, and a celebrity, at least in the farm belt, because of his talents as a platform orator. Bryan's chief subject for four years had been the free coinage of silver, and he polished a single speech, the "Cross of Gold," to a mathematical perfection in phrasing, timing, and theatrical gesture. Deeply religious, Bryan enlisted God in the cause of silver coinage. He identified the gold standard with the crucifiers of Christ, silver with democracy and Christianity.

To many who heard him, Bryan was a blasphemer. But if the evangelical intensity of his oratory were set aside, he was a rather conservative man. Bryan did not approve of much of the reform program the Populists held dear except for free silver. Nevertheless, his language and youth frightened Republicans. They called him "Boy Bryan" and "the boy orator of the Platte." John Hay, a lifetime of Republican propriety behind him, sputtered that Bryan was "a half-baked little briefless jack-leg lawyer . . . promising the millennium to everybody with a hole in his pants and destruction to everybody with a clean shirt." The Democrats, committed as a party to the cause of free silver when the Chicago convention was planned, felt differently. They scheduled Bryan and the Cross of Gold to close out the debate on the currency question.

Later it would be said that Bryan's speech transformed him from a garden variety convention delegate into a presidential candidate by acclamation. In fact, Bryan and his supporters had paved the way for his nomination as carefully as Mark Hanna had engineered McKinley's. It is true, however, that Bryan's speech and the Democratic party's ringing endorsement of free silver were so electrifying that many western farmers began to celebrate a November victory in July. And the enthusiasm for "Boy Bryan" blew from Chicago to St. Louis where, a few weeks later, the Populists convened to select their standard-bearer.

When William Jennings Bryan (1860–1925) posed for this photograph just before the whirlwind campaign of 1896; he expected to win the presidency that year as both Democratic and Populist nominee.

The Cross of Gold

The following lines are the first and last from William Jennings Bryan's electrifying speech at the 1896 Democratic convention:

I would be presumptuous, indeed, to present myself against the distinguished gentlemen to whom you have listened if this were a mere measuring of abilities; but this is not a contest between persons. The humblest citizen in all the land, when clad in the armor of a righteous cause, is stronger than all the hosts of error. I come to speak to you in defense of a cause as holy as the cause of liberty—the cause of humanity. . . .

If they dare to come out in the open field and defend the gold standard as a good thing, we will fight them to the uttermost. Having behind us the producing masses of this nation and the world, supported by the commercial interests, the laboring interests, and the toilers everywhere, we will answer their demand for a gold standard by saying to them: you shall not press down upon the brow of labor this crown of thorns, you shall not crucify mankind upon a cross of gold.

The Populists Join the Democrats

Scarcely less apocalyptic than they were in 1892, the Populists faced a difficult practical decision in St. Louis. If they nominated one of their own leaders for president, the free silver vote would be split between their man and the Democrat Bryan, putting William McKinley in the White House. If they nominated Bryan—and just about everyone except Mark Hanna agreed on this in July 1896—they would easily elect a man whose style suited the Pops and whose position on free silver could not be improved on.

The trouble was, Bryan opposed just about everything in the Populist reform program except free silver. For the sake of a free silver president, the Populists would have to discard their grand plan to remake America in the interests of the common man. Moreover, once they fused their party with the older, larger Democratic party, the Populists would lose their very identity.

Urban Populists like Henry Demarest Lloyd urged the party to think in long-range terms. Lloyd told the Pops to maintain their independence and the integrity of their program, accept defeat in 1896, and work toward 1900, when many Democrats would join them! Some southern Populists like Tom Watson of Georgia had another reason for opposing fusion. In the South, the conservative enemy was not the Republican party, but the Democrats whom the Populist fusionists now wanted to marry. To join with the Democrats in the South meant party suicide, and destroying the alliance that Watson and others had been trying to forge between poor white and poor black farmers. Southern blacks would not vote for the Democratic party; it was the party of white supremacy. Bryan himself was unsympathetic to blacks. If there was fusion, African Americans would return to the Republican party that, at least, had taken some interest in their rights.

Midwestern Populists like Jerry Simpson were unmoved by any such arguments; they wanted fusion and victory. "I care not for party names," Simpson said, "it is substance we are after, and we have it in William J. Bryan." The Populists from the mining states agreed. Free silver had always been the heart of their rebellion; the rest of the Populist program was of less interest to miners (and mine owners) than a market for the ore they produced.

The fusionists won. The Populist party nominated Bryan and, to seal the partnership, nominated Tom Watson for vice president, asking the Democrats to accept him as their candidate, too. Bryan ignored the request. He accepted Populist support but made no concessions whatsoever to the party, not even the gesture of taking a Populist for vice president.

Waves against a Rock

Rallying voters was Bryan's forte. Handsome, tireless, and completely at home among ordinary, hardworking farm people—whether exhorting them to a crusade or gobbling up potato salad after a speech—Bryan revolutionized presidential campaigning in the United States.

With a few exceptions, previous presidential nominees were subdued, as if it were insulting the dignity of the office to woo votes like a candidate for town councilman in an Appalachian hollow. President Andrew Johnson's opponents had berated him successfully when he took to the hustings in 1866, but Bryan was not deterred. His speaking tour in 1896 took him more than 13,000 miles by train. He delivered 600 speeches in 29 states in only 14 weeks, more than six speeches a day. The roaring enthusiasm of the crowds that greeted him, at least in the West and South, confirmed him in his zeal and threw bankers and industrialists into a panic.

Panic was exactly what Mark Hanna wanted to see. He pressured wealthy Republicans (and more than a few conservative Democrats) into making

---

The Modern Olympics

The century ended in war for the United States, and the election of 1896 was a holy war so far as activists on both sides were concerned But 1896 was also the year, in Greece, of the first modern Olympics, an international competition in sports that, its founders hoped, would provide a bloodless alternative to war and bring nations together through athletics.

The United States team was a pickup gang of thirteen young men who, while good athletes, were recognized as "the best" by no one. They chose themselves to make the trip to Athens. Nevertheless, they won eleven gold medals, nine out of the twelve awarded in track and field. Every member of the American team won a medal except swimmer Gardner Williams who dove into the Bay of Zia for the 100-meter freestyle, shouted, "Jesus Christ! I'm freezing," and clambered out of the water.

large contributions to McKinley's campaign. By the time of the election, Hanna had spent more on posters, buttons, rallies, picnics, advertisements, and a corps of speakers who dogged Bryan's steps than was spent by both parties in every election since the Civil War. The Republicans printed five pamphlets for every American voter. Hanna was so successful a fund-raiser that, before election day, he began to return contributions he did not need.

Knowing that the phlegmatic McKinley could not rival Bryan on the stump, Hanna kept his candidate at his modest home in Canton, Ohio, instructing Republican speakers to compare McKinley's self-respect with Bryan's huckstering. In fact, although it did not show, McKinley's campaign was as frantic as Bryan's and nearly as tiring. Delegations of party faithfuls came in a steady stream to Canton, where they marched through the town behind a brass band and gathered on McKinley's front lawn. McKinley delivered a short speech from the porch, answered a few prearranged questions, and invited "all his friends" to join him for lemonade or beer, depending on the delegation's attitude toward alcohol. (This was discreetly ascertained by party workers when the visitors arrived at the railroad depot.) About 750,000 friends visited McKinley's home that summer and fall, trampling his lawn "as if a herd of buffalo had passed through."

Momentous Results

More people voted for Bryan, 6.5 million, than had voted for anyone who had ever been elected president. The election brought voters out in unprecedented numbers. However, Bryan did not win. McKinley won 7 million votes and, in the electoral college, he gathered 271 votes to Bryan's 176. It was the first time in a quarter of a century that any presidential candidate had won an absolute majority. What happened? As late as September, professional politicians believed that Bryan was well ahead.

First, although Bryan's supporters were noisy and numerous, his appeal was fatally limited to Democrats from the solid South, to hard-pressed staple farmers of the West, and to classes of people significant in only a few states, like western metal miners. McKinley swept the Northeast, including the swing states, and also the largely agricultural states of North Dakota, Minnesota, Wisconsin, Iowa, Michigan, and Illinois. Farmers whose conditions were not desperate accepted the Republican contention that Boy Bryan was a dangerous radical, and *radical* has never been a desirable label in American politics.

Nor did Bryan have much support among factory workers and city people generally. He hardly tried to win them over. Imbued with rural prejudices against big cities and the "foreigners" who lived there, he made only one speaking tour in vital New York State and was quoted as calling New York City "the enemy's country," as though the metropolis were inhabited solely by bankers and grain speculators. Fourteen of the fifteen biggest cities were controlled by Republican machines and they delivered the urban vote to William McKinley.

Some industrialists tried to intimidate their employees into voting for the Republican candidate. The Baldwin Piano Works posted notices on the eve of election day to the effect that if Bryan won, the plant would close for good the day following. But Bryan's weakness in the industrial districts was not due to such tactics. His single-issue free silver campaign offered little to factory workers. They found more convincing the Republican claims that inflation (silver coinage) would hurt them and that

Candidate William McKinley between speeches on his front porch in Canton, Ohio.

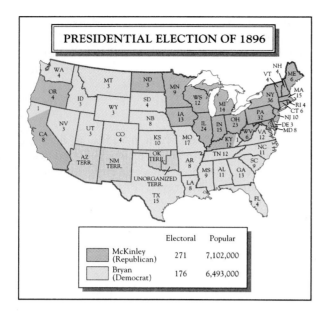

McKinley's high-tariff policy protected their jobs against cheaper foreign competitors.

Finally, Mark Hanna shrewdly judged the instincts of a newly important element in American politics, the growing middle class of small businessmen, professional people, salaried town dwellers, and highly skilled, well-paid workingmen: railroad engineers and firemen, factory foremen, and workers in the building trades. Conscious of their respectability and the social gap between them and the unskilled, considering themselves to be the bone and sinew of the industrial American republic, they were frightened by Bryan and the ragged, restive farmers whom he represented. These people committed themselves to the Republican party as "the party of decency." For 40 years after 1896, they were to make the Republican party the nation's majority party.

The End of Populism

As Watson and Lloyd feared, fusion with the Democrats meant extinction for the Populists. Having sacrificed their comprehensive reform program for the chance of winning free silver with Bryan, the Pops had nothing left when the votes were counted against him. In the South, white Populists who worked to build a party based on interracial cooperation turned against the blacks (most of whom voted Republican in 1896) to become prominent exponents of white supremacy. In the West, the party withered away, in part because of the electoral rebuke, and in part because, slowly under McKinley, the wholesale prices of farm products began to rise.

The agricultural depression lifted for a number of reasons. Newly discovered gold deposits in Canada and Alaska inflated the currency somewhat and helped raise prices. Several poor growing seasons in Europe created an increased demand for American farm products. Finally, farmers, like most of the American people, were distracted in 1898 by the McKinley administration's decision to win the United States a place among the empires of the world. A wistful Tom Watson was to say, "the blare of the bugle drowned the voice of the reformer."

AMERICAN IMPERIALISM

McKinley hoped to have a quiet presidency, watching over the retrenchment of the nation after the years of depression and agitation. His confidence in the vitality and resilience of American business convinced him that prosperity was just around the corner. All he had to do was wait patiently.

McKinley got his prosperity. Even before he was inaugurated in March 1897, the economic indicators began to improve. Peace and quiet were more elusive. Little as the role suited him, President McKinley led the American people into a series of overseas adventures that transformed a nation born in an anticolonial revolution into something of an empire, with colonies in both hemispheres.

The Myth of Isolationism

Not that the United States was isolated from world affairs before McKinley became president. Far from it. The American government maintained busy missions in all important capitals. The United States fought a war with Mexico in order to take land the Mexicans owned—the oldest kind of interaction of peoples in history—and several times came close to war in defense of American prestige. In 1889, only a typhoon that sank German and American warships near remote Samoa prevented a full-scale naval encounter with a major European power.

Trade made the United States an active participant in world affairs. American ships and sailors were a common sight in the world's most exotic ports. As early as 1844, the United States had signed a trade treaty with the Chinese Empire, as far off and foreign a place as Americans could imagine. In 1854, a naval squadron under Commodore Matthew Perry anchored off Yokohama, Japan, and threatened to bombard the city unless the Japanese agreed to abandon their country's genuine isolation and begin to purchase American goods.

By 1870, American exports totaled $320 million, mostly agricultural produce bound for Europe. By 1890, $857 million in goods were sold abroad, with American manufacturers competing with European industrialists in peddling steel, textiles, and other products in Pacific countries, Latin America, and Europe itself. No one proposed the United States purchase isolation by putting an embargo on so profitable a business. Even Populists like Jerry Simpson wanted the United States to pursue markets abroad—aggressively: "American factories are making more than the American people can consume; American soil is producing more than they can consume. . . . The trade of the world must and shall be ours."

Anticolonialism

If Americans were not isolationists, neither were they imperialists. Neither the people nor most statesmen wanted anything to do with the scramble for colonies that engrossed Europe and newly powerful Japan in the late nineteenth century. To most Americans, there was a difference between taking the West from a handful of Mexicans and Indians, and establishing suzerainty over distant and densely settled countries with long cultural traditions. Repeatedly, attempts to acquire Cuba and the Dominican Republic were squelched in Congress. With the exceptions of Alaska and the tiny Pacific island of Midway, both acquired in 1867 and neither with much population, the United States possessed no territory that was not contiguous to the states.

Two deep convictions worked against the occasional proposals that the United States take such colonies. First, the country was founded in a war against an empire. Could the heirs of the first great anticolonial rebellion take over the lands of other peoples? Second, the vastness of the American continent provided a more than adequate outlet for American energies. There was plenty of work to be done at home. William McKinley shared these assumptions. In all sincerity, he said in his inaugural address that "we must avoid the temptation of territorial expansion."

The Nature of Imperialism

But times were changing. By 1897, the United States was the single most important industrial power in the world. Consciousness of this greatness stirred many people to believe that the United States should assume its rightful place among the great nations, and in the 1890s, the great nations were imperialist nations.

The European powers were partitioning Africa so that, eventually, only two countries there maintained their independence, ancient Ethiopia and Liberia, a republic that was founded by American blacks, some of them former slaves. Indochina was a French colony. The Dutch flag flew over Indonesia. The Japanese were in the process of securing Korea and the Chinese island province of Taiwan, which they renamed Formosa. Russia had designs on northern China. Germany and Italy, latecomers to the scramble, looked in Africa and Asia for areas to annex. India, the finest prize of all, save China, was British.

The initial impulse toward empire was economic. Colonies were a source of raw materials and a market for the products of the mother country. Colonialism also generated an emotional justification of its own. Colonies were a source of pride. British imperialists took pleasure in seeing "all that red on the map." (Mapmakers traditionally colored British possessions in red.) The Germans seized parts of Africa that had little economic value to imperial masters, just for the sake of having colonies.

In England and later in the United States, this bumptious chauvinism was known as jingoism, from a British song of 1877, "We do not want to fight, But by jingo, if we do . . ." To the jingoes, being strong enough to overcome less advanced peoples was reason enough to do so. Finally, imperialism fed on itself like a sport. Nations seized colonies simply to prevent competitors from doing so.

Some young American politicians such as Henry Cabot Lodge of Massachusetts and Theodore Roosevelt of New York itched to join the scramble. They worried publicly that, in their wealth and prosperity, Americans were becoming soft and flabby. The country needed war now and then in order to toughen up. Roosevelt, a bodybuilding enthusiast,

American troops halfway around the world: marching in the Philippines.

often drew analogies between individuals and nations, between boxing matches and battles.

Anglo-Saxons

Lodge, Roosevelt, and some other expansionists were influenced by a theory of race that evolved in part out of Social Darwinism. Whereas Herbert Spencer applied his doctrine of "survival of the fittest" to relationships within a society, disciples such as Harvard historian John Fiske and Congregationalist minister Josiah Strong applied it to relationships among different races and cultures. In separate publications of 1885, Fiske and Strong wrote that the Anglo-Saxons (British and Americans) were obviously more fit to govern than were other peoples. According to Strong's *Our Country*, the Anglo-Saxons were "divinely commissioned" to spread their institutions. It was not a betrayal of American ideals to take over other lands. There was a racial and religious duty to do so.

Strong believed that inferior races would eventually die out. An influential political scientist at Columbia University, John W. Burgess, stated flatly in 1890 that the right of self-determination did not apply to dark-skinned peoples. He wrote that "there is no human right to the status of barbarism."

Alfred Thayer Mahan

Also in 1890, the expansionists found a highly calculating spokesman in naval captain Alfred Thayer Mahan. In a bestseller in both Europe and America, *The Influence of Sea Power upon History*, Mahan argued that the great nations were always seafaring nations possessing powerful navies. He chided Americans for having allowed their own fleet to fall into decay. (In 1891, jingoes who wanted war with Chile had to quiet down when they were informed the Chilean navy might make short work of the American fleet.) Mahan urged a massive program of ship construction, and Congress responded with large appropriations.

A modern steam-powered navy needed coaling stations at scattered points throughout the world. That in itself required taking colonies, even if they were mere dots on the globe like little Midway, or by building bases in ostensibly independent countries like Hawaii, where in 1887, the United States cleared a harbor at the mouth of the Pearl River on the island of Oahu.

America without a Frontier

Another theory of history that fired up the expansionist movement was based on the announcement of the director of the census in 1890 that the frontier no longer existed. In 1889, Congress opened Oklahoma to white settlement; the last large territory that was reserved for the sole use of Indians was occupied by whites literally overnight.

At the 1893 meeting of the American Historical Association, a young historian named Frederick Jackson Turner propounded a theory that the frontier was the key to the vitality of American democracy, social stability, and prosperity. Turner was interested in the past, but the implication of his theory for the future was unmistakable. With the frontier gone, was the United States doomed to stagnation, reactions, and social upheaval? To some who found Turner convincing, the only solution was to establish new frontiers abroad. Throughout the 1890s, American financiers pumped millions of dollars into China and Latin America because they felt that investment opportunities within the United States were shrinking.

By 1898, America's attitude toward the world was delicately balanced. Pulling in one direction was the tradition of anticolonialism. Tugging the other way were jingoism, Anglo-Saxonism, and apprehensions for the future. All it took to decide the direction of the leap was a sudden shove. That was provided by a war for independence just 90 miles from American shores.

THE SPANISH-AMERICAN WAR

On a map, Cuba looks like an appendage of Florida, a geographical curiosity that frequently excited the interest of American expansionists. Cuba was also a historical curiosity because, along with Puerto Rico, it had remained a Spanish colony after the revolutions that, early in the nineteenth century, established republics from Mexico to Tierra del Fuego. Not that Cubans were good Spanish colonials; rebellion was chronic on the island. But as weak as once mighty Spain had become, the archaic monarchy was able to hold fast to its last American jewel.

The uprising of 1895 was more serious than others. Cuban exiles in the United States smuggled arms and munitions in from Florida, and the rebels won the support of a large number of ordinary Cubans, perhaps the majority. An enactment of the American Congress helped spread the discontent. Until 1894, Cuba prospered, exporting sugar to the United States; but the Wilson-Gorman Tariff of that year virtually shut out Cuba's sole export and caused an economic crisis.

The Cuban rebellion was a classic guerrilla war. The Spanish army and navy controlled the cities of Havana and Santiago and most large towns. By day, Spanish soldiers moved with little trouble amongst a seemingly peaceful peasantry. By night, however, docile field-workers turned into fierce rebels and sorely punished the Spanish troops. As in most guerrilla wars, fighting was bitter and cruel. Both sides were guilty of atrocities.

Americans would have been sympathetic toward the rebels in any event. Their sympathy was whipped into near hysteria when two competing newspaper chains decided that Cuba could be used as ammunition in their circulation war.

The Yellow Press

William Randolph Hearst's New York *Journal* and Joseph Pulitzer's New York *World*, and affiliates of each in a dozen large cities, competed not only in gathering the news, but by outdoing one another in exploiting sensations and contriving gimmicks with which to woo the popular imagination. The Hearst and Pulitzer chains invented the daily comic strip (the first was called "The Yellow Kid," from which came the term "yellow press" to describe newspapers involved in such undignified antics). Colorful writers squeezed the most lurid details out of celebrated murder and sex cases, and pioneered the "invented" news story. In 1889, Pulitzer's *World* sent Elizabeth S. "Nellie" Bly around the world in an attempt to break the record of the fictional hero of Jules Verne's novel *Around the World in Eighty Days*. (She did it, completing the trip in 72 days, 6 hours, and 11 minutes.)

HOW THEY LIVED

Remembering the Maine: Soldiers in the Spanish-American War

Secretary of State John Hay called it "a splendid little war." Undersecretary of the Navy Theodore Roosevelt resigned his post in order to fight in it. William Allen White remembered the glad excitement with which the declaration of war had been received in the Midwest: "Everywhere over this good, fair land, flags were flying, . . . crowds gathered to hurrah for the soldiers and to throw hats into the air." The celebrants' favorite cry was, "Remember the *Maine*; to hell with Spain." Americans regarded the occasion as an opportunity to prove the arrival of the United States as a world power and, at home, as a chance to seal the reunion of North and South by having northern and southern boys join together to fight Spain. While McKinley would not allow political rival William Jennings Bryan to go abroad and make a military reputation, he was delighted to appoint old Confederate officers like Fitzhugh Lee and General Joseph Wheeler to active command.

But, as historian Frank Freidel points out, for the soldiers in the ranks "it was as grim, dirty, and bloody as any war in history." He adds: "Only the incredible ineptitude of the Spaniards and the phenomenal luck of the Americans" kept the Spanish-American War small and short—splendid.

While the navy proved ready to fight on an instant's notice, the army was not ready for anything. In 1898, the army was only 28,000 strong, and those troops were scattered the length and breadth of the country. Congress had authorized increasing this force to 65,700 in wartime, but despite a rush of enlistments, the army never grew this large. The young men who rallied to arms in every state preferred to join the state militias or new units of volunteers, in which enlistments were for two years unless discharged earlier (as almost all would be).

In 1898, the militias numbered 140,000 men, but regular army officers justly suspected their training and equipment and generally preferred volunteer units in the regular army. Indeed, training was generally inadequate across the board because of the rush to get into action, and supplies were worse. Companies mustering, mostly in the southern states, were issued heavy woolen winter uniforms and Civil War–vintage Springfield rifles. Much meat that was provided the recruits was tainted, and sanitary conditions in the crowded camps were such that filth-related diseases such as typhoid and dysentery ravaged them. When the dead were counted at the end of 1898, 379 men were listed as killed in combat, while 5,083 men were listed as dead of disease.

There was no difficulty in getting volunteers. While 274,000 eventually served in the army, probably an equal number were turned down. Among these rejects were Frank James, brother of the late train robber Jesse James, and William F. "Buffalo Bill" Cody, who annoyed the War Department by writing a magazine article entitled "How I Could Drive the Spaniards out of Cuba with Thirty Thousand Indian Braves." Martha A. Chute of Colorado was discouraged in her offer to raise a troop of women, as was William Randolph Hearst in his suggestion to recruit a regiment of professional boxers and baseball players. "Think of a regiment composed of magnificent men of this ilk," the editor of the New York *Journal*

It was no big jump from promotions like Nellie Bly to making hay out of Spanish atrocities. The yellow press dubbed the Spanish military commander in Cuba, Valeriano Weyler, "The Butcher" for his repressive policies, which included the establishment of concentration camps. Warring against a whole population, Weyler tried to stifle the uprising by herding whole villages into camps; everyone who was found outside the camps could be defined as enemies to be shot on sight. This strategy was inevitably brutal, and Cubans died in the camps by the thousands from malnutrition, disease, and abuse.

Real atrocities were not enough for Hearst and Pulitzer. They transformed innocuous incidents into horror stories and invented others. When Hearst artist Frederic Remington wired Hearst from Havana that everything was peaceful and he wanted to come home, Hearst ordered him to stay: "You furnish the pictures. I'll furnish the war." One sensational drawing showed Spanish soldiers and customs

wrote. "They would overawe any Spanish regiment by their mere appearance." Nevertheless, the "Rough Riders," a motley collection of cowboys, athletes, and gentlemen like Colonel Theodore Roosevelt, was mustered. But because of shipping problems, the Riders had to leave their horses in Florida when they sailed for Cuba and fight on foot.

In fact, there were few battlegrounds in Cuba or in the Philippines that were suited to cavalry attack. Both are tropical countries, and most of the fighting was done in summer and much of it in jungle. The army tried to prepare for jungle warfare by authorizing the recruitment of up to 10,000 "immunes," young men who were thought to be immune to tropical diseases. However, medicine's comparative ignorance of the nature of tropical diseases combined with racism to make the immune regiments no more serviceable than any others. Whereas the original idea had been to fill these units with men who had grown up in marshy areas of the Deep South, within months recruiters were turning away white Louisianians from the bayous and accepting blacks from the upcountry South and even urban New Jersey. They were believed to possess a genetic immunity to malaria, yellow fever, and other afflictions of the tropics.

Blacks played a large part in both the Cuban and the Philippine campaigns. When the war broke out, there were four black regiments in the regular army: two infantry and two cavalry, the Ninth and the Tenth Horse Regiments. All four saw action. In fact, while Theodore Roosevelt was describing the capture of San Juan Hill as an accomplishment of the Rough Riders, other witnesses believed that the Rough Riders would have been devastated had it not been for the Tenth Negro Cavalry, which was immediately to their left during the charge. While the Rough Riders made a lot of noise, the Tenth simply did their job. In the words of the restrained report of their commander, later to be General of the Armies, John J. "Black Jack" Pershing: "The 10th Cavalry charged up the hill, scarcely firing a shot, and being nearest the Rough Riders, opened a disastrous enfilading fire upon the Spanish right, thus relieving the Rough Riders from the volleys that were being poured into them from that part of the Spanish line."

About 10,000 blacks served in the war, 4,000 of them in the "immunes." A study done of white regiments indicates that the Spanish-American War was generally a poor man's fight and, rather more surprising, a city man's fight.

From largely rural Indiana, for example, of those volunteers who listed their occupation, only 296 were farmers. There were 322 common laborers, 413 skilled laborers, and 118 white-collar workers (clerks). Only 47 in the regiment were professional men, and 25 were merchants. A survey of a Confederate volunteer unit reveals similar figures. Several historians state that the army was far less representative of the occupations of the general population than were the armies of the two world wars.

In age, it was typical, however. The average age of the soldiers was 24. Their average height was 5 feet 8 inches, and their average weight was 149 pounds, both less than the averages today.

officials leering at a naked American woman. It was based on a real incident—except that the woman, suspected of smuggling, had been searched quite properly in private by female officers.

McKinley's Dark Hour

McKinley tried to calm tempers. Influential American businessmen had substantial investments in Cuba, about $50 million in railroads, mines, and sugar cane plantations, and they feared the revolutionaries more than the Spanish. McKinley and his advisers wanted Spain to abandon its harsh policies and placate both Cubans and bellicose Americans by liberalizing government on the island.

The Spanish responded to American pressure. In 1898, a new government in Madrid withdrew Weyler and proposed autonomy for Cuba within the Spanish Empire. McKinley's administration was satisfied.

652 *Chapter 33 In the Days of McKinley*

But the war came anyway, largely because of two unforeseeable events.

On February 9, Hearst's New York *Journal* published a letter that had been written by the Spanish ambassador in Washington, Enrique Dupuy de Lome. In it, Dupuy told a friend that McKinley was "weak, a bidder for the admiration of the crowd." It was by no means an absurd assessment of the president, but it was insulting. McKinley himself was riled.

Six days later, on February 15, 1898, the battleship USS *Maine* exploded in Havana harbor with a loss of 260 sailors. To this day, the cause of the disaster is unknown. The explosion may have been caused by a coal fire that spread to the magazine. A bomb may have been planted by Cuban rebels in an attempt to provoke the United States into declaring war on their behalf. Or the tragedy may have been the work of Spanish diehards who opposed the new liberal policy in Cuba. So charged was the atmosphere that some people suggested that William Randolph Hearst planted the bomb for the sake of a headline!

Whatever the case, there were plenty of headlines and outrage. Most Americans seemed to accept the least plausible explanation: the Spanish government, which was trying to avoid war at all costs, had destroyed the *Maine*.

McKinley continued to vacillate—for a month and a half. He bade for the approval of the crowd by flooding Spain with demands for a change of policy. As late as March 26, Mark Hanna urged him to keep the peace, and on April 9 the Spanish government gave in to every demand McKinley made on them. In the meantime, however, fearing that to continue resisting the war fever would cost the Republicans control of Congress in the fall elections, McKinley caved in. On April 11, practically ignoring the Spanish capitulation, the president asked Congress for a declaration of war and got it.

The "Splendid Little War"

Declaring war was one thing. Fighting the Spanish was quite another. The U.S. Army numbered less than 30,000 men, most of them stationed in the West, keeping an eye on Indians. Such a force, less than half the size of the army of tiny Belgium, was not up to launching an invasion even just a short sail from Florida.

The spanking new navy was ready; however, it struck first not in Cuba but halfway around the world in Spain's last Pacific colony, the Philippines. On May 1, acting on the instructions of Undersecretary of the Navy Theodore Roosevelt (the secretary of the navy was ill), Commodore George Dewey steamed a flotilla into Manila Bay and completely surprised the Spanish garrison. He destroyed most of the Spanish ships before they could weigh anchor.

But Dewey had no soldiers with which to launch an attack on land. For more than three months, he and his men sat outside Manila harbor, baking in their steel ships, while Filipino rebels struggled with the Spanish garrison in the city. Finally, in August, troops arrived and took the capital. Although they did not know it, a peace treaty had been signed the previous day: shades of the Battle of New Orleans.

For, by that time, American troops had also conquered Cuba and Puerto Rico. Secretary of State John Hay called their campaign a "splendid little war" because so few Americans died in battle. In order to celebrate so gaily, however, it was necessary that Hay overlook the more than 5,000 soldiers who died from typhoid, tropical diseases, and poisonous "embalmed beef," tainted meat that was supplied to the soldiers because of corruption or simple inefficiency.

Although the Spanish army in Cuba outnumbered the Americans until the last, both commanders and men were paralyzed by defeatism. Despite shortages of food, clothing, transport vehicles, medical supplies, ammunition, and horses, an American army

---

Dewey's Blunder

Commodore George Dewey became a national hero by virtue of his victory at Manila Bay during the Spanish-American War. A group of conservative Democrats hoped to nominate him for the presidency in 1900 in order to head off William Jennings Bryan, who was still regarded as something of a radical. At first Dewey refused because he did not believe that he was qualified for the office. He later changed his mind, explaining that "since studying the subject, I am convinced that the office of the president is not such a very difficult one to fill." As a result of his candor, Dewey lost the support of virtually everyone, and Bryan was nominated once again.

Joseph Pulitzer's World *speculated on the cause of the* Maine *disaster in the same edition in which the explosion was reported.*

of 17,000 was landed in Cuba in June and defeated the Spanish outside Santiago at the battles of El Caney and San Juan Hill. (With 200,000 soldiers in Cuba, the Spanish foolishly stationed only 19,000 in Santiago.)

The victory allowed Americans to forget the poor management of the war and gave them a popular hero. Theodore Roosevelt resigned from the Navy Department to accept a lieutenant colonelcy in a volunteer cavalry unit called the Rough Riders. It was a highly unmilitary group, made up of cowboys from Roosevelt's North Dakota ranch, show business fops, upper-class polo players and other athletes, and even some ex-convicts. The Rough Riders had to fight on foot because the army was unable to get their horses out of Tampa, Florida, but they fought bravely in the hottest action on San Juan Hill.

EMPIRE CONFIRMED

When the Spanish gave up, American troops occupied not only Manila in the Philippines and much of Cuba, but also the island of Puerto Rico, which was seized without resistance. But what should be done with these prizes? Suddenly, the colonialism controversy was no longer an academic debate. It involved three far-flung island countries that were inhabited by millions of people who spoke Spanish or Malayan languages, who clung to traditions very different from those of Americans, who were not Caucasian for the most part, and who did not want to become colonial subjects of the United States.

To the dismay of the imperialists, the independence of Cuba was guaranteed before the war had begun. In order to get money from Congress to fight

Theodore Roosevelt and his "Rough Riders" cavalry unit.

Spain, the administration accepted a rider drafted by Senator Teller of Colorado. The Teller Amendment forbade the United States to take over the sugar island. Therefore, the great debate over imperialism centered on Puerto Rico and the Philippine Islands.

The Debate

The anti-imperialists were a disparate group, and their arguments were sometimes contradictory. In Congress, they included idealistic old Radical Republicans like George Frisbie Hoar of Massachusetts, former Liberal Republicans like Carl Schurz, and much of the old Mugwump wing of the party. Some Republican regulars also opposed taking colonies. Among them was Thomas B. Reed of Maine, the no-nonsense, dictatorial speaker of the House who otherwise despised reformers. Finally, a substantial part of the Democratic party, led by William Jennings Bryan, opposed annexation of any former Spanish lands. Henry Teller himself became a Democrat in 1900 because of his opposition to imperial expansion.

The anti-imperialists reminded Americans of their anticolonial heritage. "We insist," declared the American Anti-Imperialist League in October 1899, "that the subjugation of any people is 'criminal aggression' and open disloyalty to the distinctive principles of our government. We hold, with Abraham Lincoln, that no man is good enough to govern another man without that man's consent."

Some of the anti-imperialists appealed to racist feelings. With many people ill at ease because of the nation's large black population, was it wise to bring millions more nonwhite people under the flag? When Congress finally decided to take the Philippines and pay Spain $20 million in compensation, House Speaker Reed resigned in disgust, grumbling about "ten million Malays at two dollars a head."

But racist feelings worked mostly in favor of the imperialist group. Shrewd propagandists like Roosevelt, who was now governor of New York; Henry Cabot Lodge; and the eloquent Albert J. Beveridge, senator from Indiana, preached that the white race had a duty and a right to govern inferior peoples. "God has not been preparing the English-speaking and Teutonic peoples for a thousand years for nothing but vain and idle self-contemplation and self-admiration," Beveridge told the Senate. He had made them "the master organizers of the world."

Well-grounded fears that if the United States abandoned the Philippines, Japan or Germany would seize control of them, motivated other politicians to support annexation. Such anxiety was especially significant in deciding McKinley's mind on the question. But most of all, the American people were in an emotional, expansive mood. Coming at the end of the troubled, depressed, and divided 1890s, annexation of colonies seemed a way to unite the country.

Hawaii

McKinley found it easier to come out for annexation of the Philippines and Puerto Rico because the United States already had taken its first real overseas colony. In July 1898, shortly after the Spanish-American War began, Congress annexed the seven main islands and 1,400 minor ones that made up the mid-Pacific nation of Hawaii. Shortly thereafter, Guam, Wake, and Baker islands were added to the empire as coaling stations for the navy.

The annexation of Hawaii was long in the making. Many of the descendants of American missionary families in the islands had grown rich by exporting sugar to the United States, and they won the confidence and support of the Hawaiian king, David Kalakaua. Until 1890, they were content with their independent island paradise.

Then, the McKinley Tariff of 1890 introduced a two-cent-per-pound bounty on American-grown sugar. This encouraged enough mainland farmers to produce cane or sugar beets that Hawaiian imports declined sharply. Unable to affect American tariff policy from outside, the Hawaiian oligarchy concluded that it must join the islands to the United States and benefit from the subsidy.

The plan was squelched before it got started. In 1891, Kalakaua died and was succeeded by his sister, Liliuokalani, who was determined to maintain the independence of the islands. She announced that the theme of her reign would be "Hawaii for the Hawaiians" and introduced a series of reforms aimed at undercutting *haole* or white control of the economy and legislature.

Alarmed, the oligarchy acted quickly with help from the American ambassador in Honolulu. He declared that American lives and property were in danger and landed marines from the USS *Boston*, who quickly took control. Back home, imperialists in the Senate introduced a treaty of annexation, but before

Sanford B. Dole (left), a businessman and the first governor of the territory of Hawaii, seated next to Queen Liliuokalani, the island's last monarch.

they could push it through, Grover Cleveland was sworn in as president (March 4, 1893), and he withdrew the proposal.

Cleveland was not opposed to annexation on principle. But he wanted to know how the Hawaiian people felt, and he sent an investigator, James H. Blount, to the islands. Blount reported that very few nonwhite Hawaiians wanted to be part of the United States; they wanted independence and the restoration of Queen Liliuokalani. Cleveland ordered the marines to return to their ships and to the naval base at Pearl Harbor.

The Hawaiian *haoles* had gone too far to chance restoring Queen Liliuokalani. They maintained control and declared Hawaii a republic. As long as Cleveland sat in the White House, they bided their time and quietly cultivated sympathetic Republican senators. In the excitement of the imperialist expansion of 1898, Hawaii was annexed by means of a joint resolution of the American Congress and Hawaiian legislature, the same device under which Texas had joined the Union.

Many Hawaiians continued to resent the takeover. Liliuokalani spent much time in the United States trying to win financial concessions for herself and the islands' natives. But as the white population grew and the islands attracted Japanese and Chinese immigrants, the native Hawaiians declined into a weak minority. Like the American Indians, they became foreigners in their own homeland. The famous islands' anthem, *Aloha Oe*, which was written by Liliuokalani, translates as "Farewell to Thee." It has more than one meaning.

The Philippine Insurrection

Taking over the Philippines was not so easy. If the war with Spain had been something like splendid, the war that followed was a great deal like ugly. The Philippine people were old hands at guerrilla warfare, like the Cubans. Led by Emilio Aguinaldo, a well-educated patriot who was as comfortable in the jungle as he was in the library, the rebels withdrew from the American-occupied cities to the jungle and fought only when the odds favored them.

In response, the American army of occupation was expanded to 65,000 men by early 1900, but even then the troops could make little progress outside the cities. The American commanders were unable to draw the *insurrectos* into a conventional battle in which superior firepower told the tale.

The fighting took a vicious turn. The Filipinos frequently decapitated their captives. The Americans, frustrated by their failures, the intense tropical heat, insects, and diseases, retaliated by slaughtering whole villages thought to support the rebels. The army never did defeat the Filipinos. The rebellion ended only when, in March 1901, troops under General Arthur MacArthur succeeded in capturing Aguinaldo. Weary of the bloodshed, Aguinaldo took an oath of allegiance to the United States and ordered his followers to do the same. (He lived quietly and long enough to see Philippine independence established in 1946.) More than 5,000 Americans died in the cause of suppressing a popular revolution, a queer twist in a conflict that began, three years before, in support of a popular revolution.

The China Market

The Philippines provided a superb base for Americans engaged in the China trade and investors interested in developing the large but weak and impoverished "Middle Kingdom." On the face of it, China too was ripe for imperialist plucking. The emperor had little power outside Beijing; powerful regional warlords battled one another in the provinces; and most of the imperialist nations of Europe, plus Japan, had carved out spheres of influence in China. There, their own troops maintained order and their own laws governed their resident citizens' behavior.

However, the most powerful of the powers in China, Great Britain, opposed the partition of China. Longer in the empire business and therefore more conscious than Japan, Russia, Germany, and Italy of the headaches and expense that attended imperial glory, the British believed that with their efficient industrial complex they could dominate the market of an independent China.

American businessmen disagreed with the British assessment of how economic competition in China would turn out. They believed that they would win the lion's share of the prodigious purchases 160 million Chinese were capable of making. However, this projection put them in complete agreement with the British policy of preventing the other imperialist nations from turning their spheres of influence into full-fledged colonies and shutting the door on free competition.

The Open Door Policy

Just as John Quincy Adams had outraced the British into promulgating the Monroe Doctrine, McKinley's secretary of state, John Hay, rushed ahead of Great Britain to circulate a series of memoranda called the Open Door notes. These declarations pledged the imperial powers to respect the territorial integrity of China and to grant equal trading rights in their spheres of influence to all other countries.

Anticolonialist as it was, the Open Door policy by no means established the self-determination of the Chinese people, nor ended military intervention by outsiders. In 1900, when antiforeign rebels known as Boxers (the Chinese name of their religious movement was "Righteous Harmonious Fist") besieged 900 foreigners in the British legation in Peking, American troops joined the soldiers of six other nations in defeating them. The victory encouraged beliefs in white superiority (despite the Japanese contribution to the victory) and convinced other nations that cooperation in maintaining the Open Door was the best policy in China.

McKinley Murdered

In 1900, the Democrats again nominated William Jennings Bryan to run against McKinley. Bryan tried to make imperialism the issue but the campaign fizzled. Americans were either happy with their overseas possessions or simply uninterested in the issue. McKinley sidestepped the debate and crowed about the nation's new prosperity; the Republican slogan was "Four More Years of the Full Dinner Pail." Dinner pails carried the day. Several states that voted Democratic-Populist in 1896 went Republican in 1900, including Bryan's own state of Nebraska.

A new vice president stood at McKinley's side on Inauguration Day. Theodore Roosevelt moved quickly from his exploits in Cuba to the governorship of New York. There, however, he alienated the Republican boss of the state, Thomas C. Platt, by

Old Boys

Most of Theodore Roosevelt's advisers were drawn from his own social class. They were gentlemen of old, genteel families who assumed without much reflection that they were the people intended to govern the United States. They wore their duties lightly. Cabinet meetings could seem like a clubroom full of joshing old boys.

When T. R. asked Attorney-General Philander C. Knox to prepare a legal justification of his actions in the detachment of the Isthmus of Panama from Colombia, Knox replied, "Oh Mr. President, do not let so great an achievement suffer from any taint of legality." After a long, blustering explanation of his actions to the cabinet, T. R. asked, "Well, have I defended myself?" Secretary of War, later of State, Elihu Root replied, "You certainly have, Mr. President. You have shown that you were accused of seduction and you have conclusively proved that you were guilty of rape."

refusing to take orders and even attacking some corrupt members of Platt's machine. When McKinley's vice president, the obscure Garrett Hobart of New Jersey, died in 1899, Platt saw a chance to get rid of the troublesome Rough Rider. He would banish him to the political burial ground of the vice presidency.

Mark Hanna, who was accustomed to consider all contingencies, had his reservations. What would happen to the country, Hanna asked McKinley, if something happened to him, and the manic Roosevelt became president? The president was almost 60 at a time when that was a ripe old age. "It is your duty to your country to live another four years," he told the president.

McKinley's obligations were in another man's hands. On September 6, 1901, the president paid a ceremonial visit to the Pan-American Exposition in Buffalo. Greeting a long line of guests, he found himself faced by a man who extended a bandaged hand, the gauze concealing a pistol of large bore. Leon Czolgosz, an anarchist who "didn't believe one man should have so much service and another man should have none," shot the president several times in the chest and abdomen. Eight days later, McKinley died. "Now look," Hanna shook his head at the funeral, "that damned cowboy is president."

A Flexible Imperialist

Unlike every accidental president who preceded him, Teddy Roosevelt was to leave an indelible mark on the office and the nation. The young New Yorker (42 years of age when he took office) knew only one way to do anything: rush into the lead and stay there. Nowhere was his assertive personality more pronounced than in his foreign policy, a peacetime extension of the zest that took him bellowing up San Juan Hill.

Roosevelt's actions varied according to the part of the world with which he was dealing. With the European nations he insisted that the United States be accepted as an equal, active imperial power. Although friendship between Great Britain and the United States had been long in the making, Roosevelt sped it along by responding cordially to every British request for cooperation. Toward Latin America, Roosevelt was often arrogant. He told both Latin Americans and Europeans that the whole Western Hemisphere was an American sphere of influence. Toward Asia, Roosevelt continued to practice the Open Door.

During Roosevelt's presidency, American capital poured into China. International consortia developed mines, built railways, and set up other profitable enterprises. In 1905, the president applied his policy of equilibrium in China by working through diplomatic channels to end a war between Russia and Japan. Much to the surprise of most Europeans, Japan handily defeated Russia and threatened to seize complete control of Manchuria and other parts of northern China. Through a mixture of threats and cajolery, Roosevelt got both sides to meet at Portsmouth, New Hampshire, to work out a treaty that maintained a balance of power in the area and guaranteed Chinese independence.

Big Brother

United States interventions in the Caribbean included:

Panama 1903	Mexico 1914
Cuba 1906	Haiti 1915
Honduras 1907	Dominican Republic 1916
Nicaragua 1910, 1912	

High-Handedness in Latin America

In Latin America, Roosevelt was not so compromising. He made it clear to the European nations that the United States held a special, preeminent position in the Western Hemisphere. In 1904, when several European nations threatened to invade the Dominican Republic to collect debts owed to their citizens, Roosevelt proclaimed what came to be called the Roosevelt Corollary to the Monroe Doctrine. In order to protect the independence of American states, the United States would, if necessary, exercise an international police power in the Western Hemisphere. In other words, while European nations still had to keep out of the Americas, the United States would intervene south of the border if circumstances called for such action.

Roosevelt wasted no time in putting his corollary to work. United States Marines landed in the Dominican Republic and took over the collection of customs, seeing to it that European creditors were paid off. From 1904 until the 1930s, the United States intervened in a number of Latin American countries as (according to General Smedley Butler, who was involved in several interventions) "a glorified bill collecting agency." These actions may have pleased European and American investors, but they created a reservoir of ill will among Latin Americans who felt bullied by the great *Anglo* colossus of the north. No action offended Latin Americans more than Roosevelt's high-handed seizure of the Panama Canal Zone, which the president considered his greatest achievement.

In 1911, when the construction of the canal was nearly complete, Roosevelt reflected (quite accurately) that only his decisiveness had moved the project along. "If I had followed traditional, conservative methods," he said, "the debates on it would have been going on yet. But I took the Canal Zone and let Congress debate; and while the debate goes on the Canal does also."

A Path between the Seas

Naval officers had long recognized the value of a quick route between the Atlantic and the Pacific. During the Spanish-American War, the battleship *Oregon*, stationed in San Francisco, took 67 days to steam the 12,000 miles to Cuba via Cape Horn. Had there been an isthmian canal, the voyage would have been but 4,000 miles.

A French company had started to dig a canal across Panama, then part of Colombia, in the 1880s. But the project was abandoned because of financial and engineering difficulties and the ravages of malaria and yellow fever among the builders. Three out of five Frenchmen and women in Panama died; the mortality was undoubtedly higher among the laborers, mostly blacks from Jamaica. The horrors of the French experience convinced most American experts that the path between the seas should be dug not in Panama, but in Nicaragua, which was more healthful and provided the lowest crossing of the American landmass from the Arctic to Tierra del Fuego.

It was a Nicaraguan canal that Secretary of State Hay had in mind when he negotiated a treaty with Britain, promising the United States full control of the project. Congress also favored the Nicaragua route. Then, however, two of the most effective lobbyists of all time, an agent of the French company that held rights to the Panama route, Philippe Bunau-Varilla, and an American wheeler-dealer, William Nelson Cromwell, went to work in Washington's restaurants, the cloakrooms of Congress, and in the White House itself.

Their goal was to win approval of the Panama route, then sell the assets of the French company in Panama, including an American-built railroad, to the United States. There was no good reason why their proposal should have been accepted. Even if the United States opted for the Panama route, the French company's rights on the isthmus were due to expire and most of its equipment was useless. Nevertheless, Bunau-Varilla and Cromwell somehow won over President Roosevelt and key members of Congress.

Roosevelt Takes Panama

Then the project stalled in Bogota. The Colombian government turned down the American offer to pay Colombia $10 million and an annual rental fee of $250,000. (The Colombians wanted $25 million.) Rather than take a step backward, Roosevelt conspired with Bunau-Varilla to start a revolution in Panama. On November 2, 1903, the president moved several warships to the vicinity, and the next day, the province erupted in riots and declared its independence. On November 6, the United States recognized the new Republic of Panama. On November 18, the first foreign minister of Panama,

660 Chapter 33 In the Days of McKinley

In large part, digging the Panama Canal was a transportation problem, how to get the megatonnage of excavated dirt and rock out of the excavator's way—quickly!

none other than the Frenchman Bunau-Varilla, signed a treaty with the United States that granted perpetual use of a ten-mile-wide canal zone across the isthmus on the terms that Colombia had refused.

None of Roosevelt's successors in the presidency were quite so arrogant in dealing with Latin America. For example, Roosevelt's handpicked successor, William Howard Taft, tried to replace gunboat diplomacy with dollar diplomacy, the attempt to influence Latin America (and China) through investment rather than armed force. In 1921, over the protests of Roosevelt's old ally Henry Cabot Lodge, the United States attempted to make amends to Colombia for Roosevelt's high-handed actions by paying the $25 million that the Colombians originally demanded for the right to dig the Panama Canal.

But such gestures could not change America's big brother behavior or the simmering resentment of many Latin Americans. The plunge into imperialism established intervention as an essential part of American diplomacy. Every president from Theodore Roosevelt to Herbert Hoover (1929–1933) used troops to enforce their wishes in Latin America. After 30 years of good neighbor policy, Lyndon B. Johnson (1963–1969) and Ronald Reagan (1981–1989) revived the practice.

Haiti

The high-handedness of American policy in the Caribbean should not obscure the fact that the problems of the nations of the area were often very serious. The history of Haiti, for example, was the history of a mess. In the 72 years preceding American intervention in Haiti in 1915, there had been 102 coups, revolts, and all-out civil wars. Of 22 presidents, only one served a complete term, and only four died of natural causes. At the time of the American intervention, 80 percent of the Haitian government's budget went to paying *interest* on the national debt. Many Americans opposed in principle to intervention found it easy to wink at intervention in countries with such concrete problems. Theodore Roosevelt tried to justify fomenting an uprising in Colombian Panama by arguing that his was the 53rd such insurrection since the founding of Panama.

CHRONOLOGY

1890	Publication of Alfred Thayer Mahan's *Influence of Sea Power Upon History*
1893	Frederick Jackson Turner explains American development in terms of the frontier
1895	Uprising in Cuba seeking independence from Spain
1896	Democrats and Populists nominate William Jennings Bryan for president. Republican William McKinley wins election by large margin
1898	Spanish-American War: Cuba independent, U.S. annexes Philippines U.S. annexes Hawaii
1899–1901	Insurrection in Philippines
1903	U.S. assists Panamanian rebels in winning independence from Colombia Panamanian-American Treaty lays basis for construction of Panama Canal

FOR FURTHER READING

The essential background of the political upheaval at the end of the nineteenth century can be found in Vincent P. DeSantis, *The Shaping of Modern America, 1877–1916*, 1973; H. Wayne Morgan, *From Hayes to McKinley: National Party Politics, 1877–1896*, 1971; and Ray Ginger, *The Age of Excess*, 1965.

Valuable special studies include Howard K. Beale, *Theodore Roosevelt and the Rise of America to World Power*, 1956; Robert L. Beisner, *From the Old Diplomacy to the New, 1865–1900*, 1975; C. S. Campbell, *The Transformation of American Foreign Relations, 1865–1900*, 1976; John Dobson, *America's Ascent: The United States Becomes a Great Power, 1880–1914*, 1978; Frank Freidel, *The Splendid Little War*, 1958; Lloyd Gardner, Walter R. Le Feber, and Thomas McCormick, *The Creation of the American Empire*, 1973; Ray Ginger, *Altgeld's America: The Lincoln Ideal and Changing Realities*, 1958; Paul F. Glad, *McKinley, Bryan, and the People*, 1964; S. L. Jones, *The Presidential Election of 1896*, 1964; Walter R. LaFeber, *The New Empire: An Interpretation of American Expansion, 1860–1898*, 1963; Ernest R. May, *Imperial Democ-*

racy: The Emergence of America as a Great Power, 1961; David McCullough, *The Path between the Seas*, 1977; Thomas J. Osborne, *American Opposition to Hawaiian Annexation, 1893–1898*, 1981; J. W. Pratt, *America's Colonial Experiment*, 1950; Emily S. Rosenberg, *Spreading the American Dream: American Economic and Cultural Expansion, 1890–1945*, 1982; William A. Russ, Jr., *The Hawaiian Republic, 1894–98*, 1961; and William A. Williams's provocative *The Tragedy of American Diplomacy*, 1959, and *Empire as a Way of Life*, 1982. For specific locales, see Louis A. Perez, Jr., *The War of 1898: The United States and Cuba*, 1998; and Brian M. Linn, *The U.S. Army and Counterinsurgency in the Philippines War, 1899–1902*, 1989.

See the biographies of Bryan by P. E. Coletta and Louis W. Koenig listed in "For Further Reading" in Chapter 32; Margaret Leech, *In the Days of McKinley*, 1959; Edmund Morris, *The Rise of Theodore Roosevelt*, 1979; Richard W. Turk, *The Ambiguous Relationship: Theodore Roosevelt and Alfred Thayer Mahan*, 1987; and Lewis S. Gould, *The Presidency of Theodore Roosevelt*, 1991.

The "Rough Riders," soon to win fame in the writings of Colonel Theodore Roosevelt, on a training exercise.

34
CHAPTER

THEODORE ROOSEVELT AND THE GOOD OLD DAYS

American Society in Transition

1890–1917

Don't flinch, don't foul, hit the line hard. Brutality and foul play should receive the same summary treatment given to a man who cheats at cards.

—Theodore Roosevelt

He played all his cards—if not more.

—Oliver Wendell Holmes, Jr.

The universe seemed to be spinning round, and Theodore was the spinner.

—Rudyard Kipling

That damned cowboy is President of the United States!

—Mark Hanna

And never did a President before so reflect the quality of his time.

—H. G. Wells

664 Chapter 34 *Theodore Roosevelt and the Good Old Days*

There could be no palaver about the "millennium" as the year 1900 approached, but Americans of that era made almost as much fuss about the turning of the century, about the novelty of writing so different a date on ledgers, letters, and papers for school, as the present generation did about the year 2000. Or, at least, the "media" did. There was only the press in 1900, newspapers and magazines, and the journalists and intellectuals who filled their pages. They, then as now, like religious zealots seeking signs, were always on the lookout for a hook on which to hang their opinions.

MIDDLE AMERICA

Many political historians have pointed to 1900 as the dividing line between an age of conservative hegemony—the late nineteenth century—and an age of reform, the Progressive Era of the early twentieth century. It is uncomfortable quarreling with this argument. Numerous as reformers were before 1900, they set the tone of the times only after that date. In terms of popular culture, however, 1900 is less a watershed year than the midpoint in a quarter-century era when the American middle class, as we know it, came into its own and first brimmed with confidence.

Dark Corners

To an African American, to an Indian of the Plains or a Mexican of the Southwest, to a white working-man in a marginal job, or to many of the nearly 12 million immigrants who came to the United States between 1890 and 1910, the decades that spanned the year 1900 were not rosy. During most of the 1890s, the United States languished in hard times—economic depression. In general, the Mexican Americans of the Southwest lived no better than the people of Mexico; the vast majority on both sides of the border were poor.

This was also the decade of Wounded Knee, the Pullman strike and bloody labor battles in the mountain states, and an era when the lynching of blacks in the South reached epidemic proportions. In 1899, a mob in Palmetto, Georgia, could announce in advance that a man would be burned alive so that thousands might flock aboard special trains to witness the spectacle.

Life expectancy at birth for native-born white Americans was about 45 years, lower for blacks and

> ### *Amazon.com circa 1897*
>
> Amazon.com had nothing on the Sears-Roebuck mail-order operation of the Gay Nineties. In 1897, offering just about everything for sale except books, Sears's inventory and its handlers filled a five-story building covering an entire city block in Chicago. Each day, Sears processed between 10,000 and 20,000 orders, perhaps a greater achievement of business organization than the Amazon.com of the computer age, given that these orders were read, processed, filled, and shipped using no technology more sophisticated than paper and pencil. In one other respect, Sears had it all over Amazon.com. Sears made money for those who invested in the company, not just for those who ran it.

immigrants, much lower for Indians. Infant mortality in New York City was worse than it had ever been. Nationwide, people were six times more likely to die of influenza than they are today, sixty times more likely to die of syphilis, and more than eighty times more likely to die of tuberculosis. Diseases that are minor health problems in the late twentieth century—typhoid, scarlet fever, strep throat, diphtheria, whooping cough, and measles—were common killers in the 1890s and 1900s.

And yet, when people who lived through the years around the turn of the century remembered them, they were apt to call the final decade of the nineteenth century the "Gay Nineties," to recall a decade of nickelodeon music and Coney Island, a night of vaudeville and a week at the seaside, beer gardens and ice cream parlors, the bicycle craze and winsome Gibson Girls.

The first years of the twentieth century have lived on in popular consciousness as the original "good old days." The era before World War I is the slice of time to which popular novelists and filmmakers repair when they want to portray an America that is recognizable to us but unmistakably a better place. Life was less complex in this engaging vision. The summer sun was warmer, the hot dogs tastier, the baseball more exciting, the cars adventurous, the boys more gallant, the girls prettier, and the songs lilting and cheering the heart with sprightly melody.

A Golden Age

The turn of the century has shed so alluring a glow over time because middle-class values and aspirations have dominated American culture in the twentieth century, and in the 1890s and early 1900s the modern middle class came into its own. The troubles of poor farmers, factory workers, blacks, Indians, Mexicans, and recent immigrants were real and often tragic. But they were not at the center of the culture. There was found the class of people—all but a few Caucasian—who, while not rich, did not have to struggle in order to survive. This middle class reached unprecedented numbers at the turn of the century, numerous enough to create and sustain a distinctive lifestyle and to support a bustling consumer economy and technology devoted to physical comfort, convenience, individual self-improvement, and the enjoyment of leisure time.

Increasingly well-educated, the new middle class quietly shelved the zealous, religious piety of their parents and grandparents. They embraced instead the proper pleasures of their rich nation. The people of the "good old days" were by no means oblivious to social evils. Far from it; they were also the citizens of the Progressive Era, a time of rampant reform. But progressivism was itself the manifestation of a confident people. War and revolution were not yet constant companions, unceasingly reminding of the darker side of human nature.

Teddy

The buoyant temper of the period was personified in the man who, in September 1901, succeeded William McKinley as president. Theodore Roosevelt was climbing a mountain in the Adirondacks when he received the news of McKinley's death. He rushed to Buffalo, took the oath of office, and confided to a friend, "It is a dreadful thing to come into the presidency in this way. But it would be a far worse thing to be morbid about it." Roosevelt intended to enjoy the presidency, as his fellow Americans intended to make the most of life. And no other chief executive before or since has had such a "bully" time living at 1600 Pennsylvania Avenue.

Both critics and friends of the president poked fun at his personal motto: "Walk softly and carry a big stick." They said that they observed Roosevelt wildly waving clubs around often enough, but rarely knew him to walk softly. Quite the contrary. Everything that Roosevelt did was accompanied by

On a reservation in Montana, Flathead Indians lived in a conventional western log cabin, but also retained their traditional dwellings, teepees.

fanfare. He seemed to swagger and strut about like an exuberant adolescent, hogging center stage and good-naturedly drowning out anyone who dared to compete for the spotlight. He insisted on being, as one of his own children put it, the bride at every wedding and the corpse at every funeral. You must remember, the British ambassador said, "that the president is about six years old."

Roosevelt shattered the image of solemn dignity that had been nurtured by every president since Rutherford B. Hayes. He stormed about the country far more than had any predecessor, delivering dramatic speeches, mixing gleefully with crowds of all descriptions, glutting himself almost as heroically as Bryan (a dozen eggs at a sitting), camping out, climbing mountains, and clambering astride horses and atop farm and industrial machines, all the time popping nitroglycerin pills like peanuts—for *angina pectoris*. When a motion picture photographer asked him to move for the ingenious new camera, Roosevelt picked up an ax and furiously chopped down a tree.

The Strenuous Life

Of an old aristocratic Dutch family, Roosevelt was sickly as a youth, woefully nearsighted and asthmatic. As an adolescent, however, he took up bodybuilding and revealed his tremendous inner energy. He fought on the Harvard boxing team, and rode with cowboys on his North Dakota ranch. As police commissioner of New York City, he accompanied patrolmen on night beats as dangerous as any in the world. When the war with Spain broke out, he left his office job and joined the army. In dozens of articles and books, he wrote of the glories of "the strenuous life."

Roosevelt liked to show off his large, handsome, and affectionate family with himself at stage center, a stern but generous patriarch. He sported a modest paunch (a desirable attribute in that sensible era), a close-snipped mustache, and thick pince-nez that dropped from his nose when he was excited, which was often. His teeth were odd, all seemingly incisors of the same size and about twice as many as normal. He displayed them often in a broad grin that he shed only when he took off after enemies whom middle-class Americans also found it easy to dislike: Wall Street bankers, Socialists, and impudent Latin Americans.

Unlike William McKinley, whose priggishness bemused him, Roosevelt had no compunctions about smoking cigars in public. What was the harm in a minor vice that brought a man pleasure? More than any other individual, he taught Americans to believe that their president should be a good fellow and part showman.

Symbol of His Age

Roosevelt had many critics. But most Americans, especially those of the vibrant new middle class, found him a grand fellow indeed. They called him "Teddy" and named the lovable animal doll they bought for their children, the teddy bear, after him. He was the first president to be routinely identified in newspapers by his initials, T. R. Even Elihu Root, a stodgy eastern aristocrat who served as both secretary of war and secretary of state, waxed playful when he congratulated the president on his forty-sixth birthday in 1904. "You have made a very good start in life," Root said, "and your friends have great hopes for you when you grow up."

Kansas journalist William Allen White, the archetype of the middle-class townsman, wrote that "Roosevelt bit me and I went mad." White remained a lifelong devotee of "the Colonel," as did Finley Peter Dunne, the urbane Chicagoan who captured the salty, cynical humor of the big-city Irish in his fictional commentator on current events, Mr. Dooley. Radical dissenters hated Roosevelt (who hated

Horseback riding was one of Theodore Roosevelt's many athletic pursuits.

them back with interest), but they were at a loss as to how to counter his vast popularity. Labor leaders and Socialists stuck to the issues when they disagreed with him. There was no advantage in attacking Teddy Roosevelt personally.

Although Roosevelt was a staunch believer in Anglo-Saxon superiority, he won the affection of blacks when he ignored the squeals of southern segregationists and invited Booker T. Washington to call on him in the White House. Woman suffragists, gearing up for the last phase of their long battle for votes, petitioned rather than attacked him. Elizabeth Cady Stanton addressed him from her deathbed in 1901 as "already celebrated for so many deeds and honorable utterances."

Much mischief was done during Theodore Roosevelt's nearly eight years in office. He committed the United States to a role as international policeman that damaged the nation's reputation in many small countries. He was inclined to define his opponents in moral terms, a recurring and unfortunate characteristic of American politics since his time.

But the happy symbiosis between the boyish president and the majority of the American people may be the most important historical fact of the years spanning the turn of the century. Like the man who was their president between 1901 and 1909, the worldly middle class of the Gay Nineties was confident, optimistic, and glad to be alive.

An Educated People

The foundation of middle-class vigor was wealth. American society as a whole had grown so rich that despite the disproportionate fortunes of the great multimillionaires, millions of people in the middle

President Roosevelt invited African-American educator Booker T. Washington to the White House, earning the plaudits of black organizations (and the jeers of racist groups.)

NOTABLE PEOPLE
Nellie Bly

The 1890s were a watershed decade in the public status of women in the United States. Led by the methodical Carrie Chapman Catt, the American Woman Suffrage Association began to win the vote for women where the movement of Elizabeth Cady Stanton and Susan B. Anthony had met only frustration. Social workers like Jane Addams and Lillian Wald proved too assertive and effective to be written off as eccentric spinsters. In the popular press, Charles Dana Gibson celebrated "the Gibson Girl," an assertive, independent young lady who bore little resemblance to the frail violet who had been the ideal of the Gospel of True Womanhood.

At the very beginning of the decade, Elizabeth Cochran, the orphan daughter of a Pennsylvania miller, came to personify the "new woman" while remaining rather distant from the organized woman's movement. Cochran's aloofness toward the feminists may have owed to a childhood of struggle. (Feminists were overwhelmingly middle class.) Born in 1864, she was forced by her father's death to go to work. Almost entirely self-educated, Cochran was to parlay her talents and a knack for self-promotion into international celebrity and, via an odd route, riches.

In 1885, while working at a menial job to support her mother, Cochran wrote a letter to a Pittsburgh newspaper editor who had helplessly bemoaned the fact that women who did not marry seemed useless to society. Eloquently and forcefully, Cochran called for opening employment opportunities for girls (who were "just as smart" as boys and "a great deal quicker to learn"). In that way, the single woman could prove herself, be independent, and cease to concern gentlemen like the editor of the *Pittsburgh Dispatch*.

The editor (who became a lifelong friend) was sufficiently impressed that he hired Cochran as a reporter. Using the pen name Nellie Bly (from a Stephen Foster song), she wrote a series of exposés of working and living conditions in the city ten years before the age of the muckraker is said to have begun. Nellie Bly also pioneered the technique of the undercover reporter, actually taking jobs in factories and writing her articles in the first person.

When pressure was brought on the *Dispatch* to relegate Nellie to the society pages, where women "belonged," she moved to New York and pushed her way into a job with Joseph Pulitzer's booming *World*. She was an immediate sensation when she managed to have herself committed to a municipal asylum for insane women. She lived as an inmate for ten days, and penned another blistering first-person exposé.

Nellie was sincerely interested in social reform but far from oblivious to her own interests. Her most famous project for Pulitzer was a masterpiece of self-promotion and one of journalism's first manufactured stories. As a girl, Nellie had read Jules Verne's novel

could afford to indulge interests and pleasures that had been the exclusive property of tiny elites in earlier epochs, and still were in other countries. Among these was education beyond "the three Rs"—"readin', 'ritin', and 'rithmetic." During the final third of the nineteenth century, and especially after 1890, the American educational system expanded and changed to accommodate the numbers and aspirations of the new class.

There were no more than about 300 secondary schools in the United States in 1860 (a country of 31.4 million people), and only about 100 of them were free. While girls were admitted to most public elementary schools, very few attended beyond the first few grades.

Colleges and universities—about 560 in 1870—catered to an even more select social set. They offered the traditional course in the liberal

Around the World in Eighty Days, in which a British dandy and his valet girdled the globe with unbelievable speed. A number of adventurers had tried to beat the fictional record and failed. Nellie locked herself up with train and steamship timetables and told the World that she could make the trip in 75 days. The editors were interested but said that if they financed such a project, a man would have to carry the banner. A woman on such a journey would "need a protector" anyway, her editor said. "Even if it were possible for you to travel alone, you would have to carry so much baggage that it would detain you in making rapid changes." Nellie replied, "Very well. Start the man and I'll start the same day for some other newspaper and beat him."

Nellie Bly left Jersey City under the *World*'s auspices on November 14, 1889, and, after a trip that sometimes seemed leisurely as she waited for steamships to depart, returned to her point of departure via a special transcontinental train on January 25, 1890. Her trip took 72 days.

Suffragists courted Nellie Bly for their cause, but she was uninterested. As early as 1885, when she brought herself to the attention of the *Pittsburgh Dispatch* with her plea on behalf of employment opportunities for women, she expressed oblique disdain for organized feminism. Fighting for jobs for women, she wrote, "would be a good field for believers in women's rights. Let them forego their lecturing and writing and go to work; more work and less talk." After her famous journey, Nellie declined to join the Women's Suffrage party. "If I became a suffragette," she wrote, "I would play into the hands of my critics. They may not like me, but they respect me. Joining your group would identify me as a partisan. I can help your movement more by putting into practice what you've been preaching."

Again Nellie expressed her disdain for "mere talk." She also disliked what she regarded as the feminists' lack of femininity, remembering late in life that "they looked to be neither men nor women, so queer and nondescript was their attire." She told Susan B. Anthony that "if women wanted to succeed, they had to go out as women. They had to make themselves as pretty and attractive as possible." On rather a different level, Nellie Bly was arguing for what Carrie Chapman Catt was effecting of the American Woman Suffrage Association, espousing expanded rights for women because they were different from men, rather than because they were the same.

The fact was, Nellie Bly was a loner, marching to her own drummer. Shortly after her return from her world trip, she quit journalism to marry a well-to-do manufacturer, 72 years of age to her 31. When he died in 1904, she ran his factory, designed a steel barrel, provided social and medical services and recreational facilities for her employees, and paid women the same wages received by men, a practice then almost unheard of. Unfortunately, her Iron Clad Manufacturing Company went bankrupt because of theft by an employee with whom Nellie was having an affair. She was absolved of complicity in the corruption but was soon broke herself, writing in 1919: "I have exactly $3.65 and a trunk full of Paris evening dresses." William Randolph Hearst gave her a job writing a column for the New York *Journal* but she never regained her celebrity. She died in 1922.

---

arts (Latin, philosophy, mathematics, and history) that was designed to polish young gentlemen rather than to train people for a career. The handful of "female seminaries" and colleges that admitted women before the Civil War also taught the ancient curriculum, strongly laced with evangelical religion.

After about 1880, educational facilities rapidly multiplied and changed character. By 1900, there were 6,000 free public secondary schools in the United States, and by 1915, there were 12,000, educating 1.3 million pupils. Educational expenditures per pupil increased from about $9 a year in 1870 to $48 in 1920. Secondary schools no longer specialized in preparing a select few for university, but offered a wide range of courses leading to jobs in industry and business, from engineering and accounting to agriculture and typing.

A New Kind of University

The Morrill Land Grant Act of 1862 and the philanthropy of millionaires combined with the middle class's hunger for learning to expand the opportunities for higher education. The Morrill Act provided federal land to the states for the purpose of serving the educational needs of "the industrial classes," particularly in "such branches of learning as are related to agriculture and mechanic arts." Thus it not only fostered the founding of technical schools in which middle-class youth might learn a profession, but put liberal arts training within the reach of those who sought it. Many of the great state universities of the West owe their origins to the Morrill Act.

Gilded Age millionaires competed for esteem as patrons of learning by constructing buildings and by endowing scholarships and professorial chairs at older institutions. Some even founded completely new universities. The story was told that railroad king Leland Stanford and his wife traveled to Harvard with the notion of erecting a building in memory of their son,

---

Hot Dog

The hot dog is second only to the hamburger at the center of *cuisine américaine*. Like the hamburger, its origins are hotly disputed. Not the origins of the mild sausage itself: it was being made commercially in Frankfurt, Germany, and Vienna, Austria, in the early nineteenth century. (Thus the alternative names frankfurter and wiener—Vienna in German is *Wien*.) The disputed point is: Who first put one of the things in a soft roll and provided the classic condiments of yellow mustard, chopped onion, and sweet pickle relish?

Some partisans claim that the deed was first done at the amusement park at Coney Island; hot dogs were once called "coney islands," too. Others credit Anton Feuchtwanger, who sold the sausages so quickly at the St. Louis World's Fair in 1904 that he had to add the roll so that his customers did not burn their hands. Yet others say the roll was first added at a New York Giants baseball game in April 1900 where they were first called "dachshund sausages." A popular cartoonist of the time who liked his baseball, Tad Dorgan, provided the more durable name "hot dog."

Vassar College,

For the Higher Education of Women,

POUGHKEEPSIE, NEW YORK.

J. H. RAYMOND, LL.D., President.

ADMISSION.

Applicants for admission to the College must be at least sixteen years of age, and must present satisfactory testimonials of character. None are received for a shorter period than till the close of the current collegiate year.

REGULAR STUDIES.

Mental and Moral Philosophy, The Greek, Latin, French, German and English Languages and their Literatures. Rhetoric, Mathematics, Astronomy, Physics, Natural History, Chemistry, Physiology, and Hygiene.

ART STUDIES.

Vocal, Piano and Organ Music, Painting and Drawing.
Every department of instruction is under the direction of an able Professor, assisted by competent Teachers.

THE COLLEGE HOME.

The College is situated two miles east of Poughkeepsie. Street-cars run regularly to and from the city. The Western Union Telegraph Company has an office in the College.
The College buildings are warmed by steam, lighted with gas, and supplied with an abundance of pure water. Bathing-rooms and other needful conveniences are amply provided.
All the students are members of the College family, and are subject to its regulations. The domestic and social life is under the supervision of the Lady Principal.
The grounds, embracing two hundred acres, with several miles of gravel walks, a flower-garden, lake, and the well-furnished Gymnasium, afford ample scope for healthful recreation.
A regular physician, residing in the College, devotes her entire time to the care of its health.
There are daily prayers in the Chapel, and a religious service and Bible classes every Sunday.

EXPENSES.

The uniform price of Board and Tuition for all students, whether regular, special, or preparatory, is $400 for the College year; of which $300 is payable in advance, and the balance on the first day of March following.
No extra charge is made, except for private lessons in art studies; for which the additional charges are as follows, payable three quarters in advance:

Pianoforte, two lessons a week and one
  practice period daily.................. $100 per annum.
Organ, two lessons a week and one practice period daily.... .... 100 "
Solo Singing, two lessons a week and one practice period daily........... 100 "
Thorough-Bass and Composition, two lessons a week...................... 80 "
Drawing, Painting, or Modelling, two lessons a week...................... 80 "
A nominal charge is made for medical attendance.

ENTRANCE EXAMINATIONS.

The entrance examinations for the year 1877-78 commence on Wednesday, September 19, 1877, and continue three days, from 9 a. m. until 5 p. m., with an intermission of one hour and a half for dinner.

CORRESPONDENCE.

Letters respecting departments of instruction, admission or dismission of students, etc., should be addressed to the President; Letters respecting Finances to Matthew Vassar, Jr., Treasurer; other business letters to William F. Forby, General Superintendent.
☞ CATALOGUES containing full particulars may be obtained by addressing WILLARD L. DEAN, Registrar, Poughkeepsie, N. Y.

Vassar College did not cater only to the girls of high society. This advertisement of 1877 appeared in a farmer's magazine.

who had died. As President Charles W. Eliot was explaining how much it had cost to construct each of Harvard's splendid buildings, Mrs. Stanford suddenly exclaimed, "Why, Leland, we can build our own university!" And they did; Stanford University in Palo Alto, California, was founded in 1885.

Cornell (1865), Drew (1866), Johns Hopkins (1876), Vanderbilt (1872), and Carnegie Institute of Technology (1905) were universities that bear the names of the moguls who financed them. In Philadelphia, Success Gospel preacher Russell B. Conwell established Temple University in 1884 explicitly to educate poor boys ambitious to rise in social station. John D. Rockefeller pumped millions of dollars into the University of Chicago (1890), making it within a decade one of America's most distinguished centers of learning. George Eastman, who made a fortune from Kodak cameras, gave to the University of Rochester.

The midwestern and western state universities, beginning with Iowa in 1858, generally admitted women to at least some programs. In the East, however, separate women's colleges were founded, again with the support of wealthy benefactors. Georgia Female College (Wesleyan) and Mount Holyoke dated from before the Civil War. In the later decades of the century they were joined by Vassar (1861), Wellesley (1870), Smith (1871), Radcliffe (1879), Bryn Mawr (1880), and Barnard (1889). Vassar's educational standards rivaled those of the best men's colleges, but it was necessary to maintain a kind of "head start" program in order to remedy deficiencies in the secondary education provided to even well-to-do girls.

Studying for Careers

The transformation of higher education was not simply a matter of more colleges, universities, and students. While some institutions, such as Yale, clung tenaciously to the traditional liberal arts curriculum, the majority of schools adopted the elective system that was pioneered by the College of William and Mary, Washington College in Virginia (now Washington and Lee), and the University of Michigan. The elective system was most effectively promoted by President Eliot of Harvard. Beginning in 1869, Eliot abandoned the rule that every student should follow precisely the same sequence of courses. Instead, he allowed individuals to choose their field of study. Majors included traditional subjects but also new disciplines in the social

sciences, engineering, and business administration. The new emphasis on a university education as preparation for a career reflected the aspirations of middle-class students who had not yet arrived financially and socially.

From Germany, educators borrowed the concept of the professional postgraduate school. Before the 1870s, young people who wished to learn a profession attached themselves to an established practitioner. A would-be lawyer agreed with an established attorney to do routine work in his office, sweeping floors and helping with deeds and wills, in return for the privilege of reading law in the office and observing and questioning his teacher. After a few years, the apprentice hung out his own shingle. Many physicians were trained the same way. Civil and mechanical engineers learned their professions on the job in factories. All too often, teachers received no training and were miserably paid, about $200 a year in rural states.

Women, Minorities, and the New Education

Exceptional women who were dauntless enough to shake off the sarcasm of their male classmates could be found in small numbers at every level of the new system. By the mid-1880s, the word *coeducational* and its breezy abbreviation, "coed," had become part of the American language. The first female physician in the United States, the dynamic Elizabeth Blackwell, was accredited only in 1849. In 1868, she established a medical school for women in New York City. By that date, the Woman's Medical College of Pennsylvania already was recognized, however grudgingly, as offering one of the nation's most effective programs of medical education.

Female lawyers were unusual at a time when women were not considered equal to men before the law. In 1873, the Supreme Court approved the refusal of the University of Illinois to admit women by declaring that "the paramount mission and destiny of women are to fulfill the noble and benign offices of wife and mother." By the end of the century, dozens of women practiced law, among them the Populist wife and "Mother" Mary Lease. Antoinette Blackwell, sister-in-law of Elizabeth, paved the way for the ordination of women ministers, and by the turn of the century, the more liberal Protestant denominations, such as the Unitarians and Congregationalists, had ordained some women.

Also in small numbers, well-to-do Jews and Catholics began to take advantage of the new educational opportunities. The Sephardic and German Jews were a secular people who preferred to send their sons to established institutions rather than to found their own. The Catholic church, on the other hand, the largest religious denomination in the United States but mainly a church of the lower classes, preferred to found its own colleges. Church policy was to prepare the sons and daughters of the Catholic middle class for active careers in business and the professions while simultaneously shoring up their loyalty to their faith by means of rigorous schooling in church doctrine, history, and observance.

The most famous Catholic colleges dated from before the Civil War: Notre Dame was founded in 1842; while Holy Cross (1843) and Boston College (1863) were explicitly created as foils to aristocratic and very Protestant Harvard. Thomas Jefferson's and John Quincy Adams's dream of an explicitly national university was fulfilled by the Roman Catholic Church with the founding in 1889 of the Catholic University of America in Washington, D.C. It is difficult to imagine either the Virginian or the New Englander quite happy about the sponsor.

On a much smaller scale, educational opportunities for blacks also expanded. The traditional universities in New England and many of the sectarian colleges of the Ohio Valley continued to admit a small number of very well-qualified blacks. W. E. B. Du Bois, a founder of the National Association for the Advancement of Colored People, earned a Ph.D. at Harvard. Hamilton S. Smith earned a law degree from Boston University in 1879 (the first black to do so), and when he could not make a living as an attorney, attended the Howard University School of Dentistry.

Howard was a private university educating the small but dynamic black elite. In the North as well as the South, philanthropists and state governments founded institutions for blacks only. Beginning with Lincoln University in Pennsylvania (founded as the Ashmun Institute in 1854), idealistic benefactors supported schools such as Howard in Washington (1867) and Fisk in Nashville (1866). After Booker T. Washington's Atlanta Compromise speech of 1895 and the Supreme Court's decision in *Plessy* v. *Ferguson* (1896) gave the go-ahead to segregation at all levels of education, southern state governments founded "agricultural and mechanical" schools patterned after Alabama's Tuskegee Institute (1881), at which blacks could train for manual occupations.

> ### *Pop Tunes*
>
> Two musical classics, one now international, were written in 1893. "Happy Birthday to You" began as "Good Morning to You" and was written by Patty Smith Hill, a pioneer of the kindergarten movement who taught at the Teacher's College of Columbia University. Irving Berlin tried to steal it from Hill in 1921, but she sued and won.
>
> The lyrics of "America the Beautiful" were put to the music of a hymn by Katharine Lee Bates, a professor of English at Wellesley College. Congress almost annually receives petitions demanding that the song, which celebrates American beauty and natural grandeur, replace the militaristic (and unsingable) "Star-Spangled Banner" as the national anthem.

The accomplishments of these institutions should not be underestimated. Few scientific researchers of the time were more productive than Tuskegee Institute's great botanist, George Washington Carver. Nevertheless, the educational level of blacks lagged so far behind that of whites that in 1910, when only 7.7 percent of the American population was illiterate (the figure includes the millions of recent immigrants), one black in three above the age of ten could neither read nor write.

A LIVELY CULTURE

Americans continued to buy the books of European authors and the works of the older generation of American poets—Emerson, Longfellow, Whitman, and Whittier. Emily Dickinson of Amherst, Massachusetts, a recluse all but unknown until after her death in 1886, was immediately recognized as one of the country's finest writers. But it was first of all an age when novelists flourished, some growing quite rich from the demand for their books.

Twain and James

Samuel Langhorne Clemens, or Mark Twain, was quintessentially and comprehensively American. A Missourian, he deserted a Confederate militia unit to go west to Nevada, and eventually settled in Hart-

Tuskegee students in a history class.

ford, Connecticut, when he was rich enough to choose his style of life. Brilliantly capturing both the hardships and ribald humor of frontier life in *Roughing It* (1872), he earned an international reputation with *The Adventures of Tom Sawyer* (1876) and *The Adventures of Huckleberry Finn* (1885). Readers sometimes missed the profound and subtle social criticism in Twain's work (as an old man, he grew melancholy and cynical, and quietly wrote some pornography), but they read him with pleasure for his wit and mastery of the American language.

Twain's favorite settings and themes were robustly western. The other great novelist of the period, Henry James, settled in England because he found American culture stultifying. James set most of his novels in the Old World and peopled them with cultivated, cosmopolitan characters. But like Twain, his goal was to come to grips with America. In *The American* (1877), *The Europeans* (1878), and *Daisy Miller* (1879), James dealt with the relationship of open, albeit less cultivated American characters with a jaded and decadent European culture.

Realism and Naturalism

An able novelist in his own right, William Dean Howells presided over the American literary establishment as editor of the *Atlantic Monthly*. Like *Harper's*, *Forum*, and *The Arena*, the *Atlantic* published a mix of poetry, stories, and elegant essays that sometimes dealt with contemporary issues but usually at a fastidious distance.

Howells was a realist. He had no patience with the high-flown, preposterous motives and beliefs that sentimental writers imputed to their characters. In *The Rise of Silas Lapham* (1885), a novel about a successful industrialist, when one sister loses a suitor to another, she does not react selflessly, nor does the sister who gets her man think seriously of sacrificing herself. Nevertheless, neither Howells nor the *Atlantic* would have considered dealing graphically with sexual matters or the degradation that poverty and squalor created. Because the proper upper and middle classes themselves considered such discussions unacceptable, the writings of realists like Howells are

The First Cocaine Craze

The Western world learned of the invigorating effects of chewing the coca leaf when the Spanish conquered the Inca empire in the sixteenth century. Over the next three centuries, the odd European (and American) experimented with the drug; but only after 1860, when the plant was crystallized into "cocaine," a hundred times more powerful than the leaves, did its use spread throughout society. Parke-Davis, a drug manufacturer, called it "the most important therapeutic discovery of the age, the benefit of which to humanity will be incalculable." The American Hay Fever Association praised it to the skies. Nor were the drug's social "benefits" neglected. In 1878, a magazine touted it as "the cure for young people afflicted with timidity in society." Cocaine was added to patent medicines and soft drinks.

By the end of the century, however, the addictive qualities of cocaine were dismayingly well-documented. Reformers crusaded against it, and use by the middle class sharply declined. Cocaine came to be associated with blacks, as a 1903 release by the American Pharmacological Association indicates: "The state of Indiana reports that a good many of its Negroes and a few white women are addicted to cocaine." In 1914, the police chief of Atlanta blamed 70 percent of the city's crime on cocaine. What had been almost "high fashion" became the vice of a despised underclass in a generation.

---

sometimes lumped with romanticism and sentimentalism as part of the genteel tradition.

Naturalistic writers defied the taboos, some of them with considerable success. In *Maggie: A Girl of the Streets* (1893), Stephen Crane depicted the poor not as noble and selfless but as miserable and helpless. In *The Red Badge of Courage* (1895), the Civil War is described as something other than glory, bugles, bravery, and flying colors (if anything, a more daring venture than a book about a prostitute). In *McTeague* (1899) and *The Octopus* (1901), Frank Norris dealt with people driven almost mechanically by animal motives.

The most popular of the naturalists was Jack London. His *Call of the Wild* (1903) is comparable to *Huckleberry Finn* in that it is simultaneously a grand tale of adventure (about a dog) and, at a deeper level, a profound commentary on the human condition.

Theodore Dreiser broke with a moralistic literary convention (that nevertheless survived) by allowing characters like *Sister Carrie* (1900) to enjoy rich lives despite sinful pasts. Dreiser's success was doubly remarkable because, from a midwestern German household, his treatment of the English language was adversarial at best, and often sadistic. But his mind was profound and he delved into corners of American society in which others feared to tread.

A Hunger for Words

The genteel tradition was also challenged by a new type of magazine that made its appearance in the 1880s and 1890s. Catering to the new, hungry, but not so ethereally intellectual middle classes, these periodicals illustrate the interaction of industrial technology, the larger reading public, and the emergence of modern advertising that was first exploited in 1883 by Cyrus H. K. Curtis and his *Ladies' Home Journal.*

Improved methods of manufacturing paper, printing, and photoengraving, as well as cheap mailing privileges established by Congress in 1879, inspired Curtis to found a magazine for women who were hungry for a world beyond the kitchen and parlor but found few opportunities in business and the professions. The *Ladies' Home Journal* sold for only ten cents (compared with the thirty-five-cent *Atlantic* and *Harper's*) and emphasized women's interests. It was not a feminist publication. On the contrary, editor Edward Bok preached a conservatism that reassured homemakers that their conventional prejudices were proper and right and middle-class people generally that they were a steadying influence between "unrest among the lower classes and rottenness among the upper classes."

Somewhat more daring were the new general interest magazines of the 1890s, such as *McClure's*, *Munsey's*, and *Cosmopolitan*. They too cost a dime, thus putting them within reach of a large readership. (The *Saturday Evening Post*, which Cyrus Curtis bought in 1897, sold for only a nickel.) Without stooping to sensationalism, they presented readers with a livelier writing style than the established journals and a lavish use of photographs and illustrations.

McClure's and *Munsey's* pioneered the curious but successful economics of selling their publications for less than it cost to print and mail them. They made their profit from building up big subscription lists and selling advertising to manufacturers of consumer goods wanting to reach people who had extra money to spend.

Middle- and upper-class propriety really did require genteel young ladies dressed in finery to perform tasks like tree planting.

The subscription list of *McClure's* increased from 8,000 in 1893 to 250,000 in 1895 (with $60,000 in advertising per issue), and that of *Munsey's* grew from 40,000 to 500,000 during the same two years. By 1900, the combined circulation of the four largest magazines totaled 2.5 million per month, more than all American magazines combined only 20 years earlier.

Libraries and Lyceums

The cultural hunger of the middle class was also expressed in the construction of free public libraries. Again, men suddenly grown rich gave millions to build them. Enoch Pratt donated $1 million to Baltimore for its municipal library. Wealthy lawyer and presidential candidate Samuel J. Tilden gave New York City $2 million, and William Newberry founded one of the nation's greatest collections of books and valuable manuscripts in Chicago with a munificent bequest of $4 million. Beginning in 1881, the self-taught Andrew Carnegie made libraries his principal philanthropy. Before his death in 1919, Carnegie helped found 2,800 free public libraries.

The old lyceum idea of sending lecturers on tour to speak to people who lived far from big cities was revived in 1868 by James Redpath. Offering large fees, Redpath persuaded the most distinguished statesmen, ministers, and professors of the day to deliver highly moral and usually informative addresses in auditoriums and specially erected tents in hundreds of small cities and towns.

Chautauqua

The lyceum movement was a throwback to the antebellum period, when only the very wealthy traveled away from home and the middle class still held fast to the Calvinist beliefs that constant work was the human fate and idleness such as casual travel was a sin. The lyceum scheduled programs in the evening, when the day's toil was done.

The phenomenon that was born in 1874 at Lake Chautauqua in New York's Allegheny Mountains was more characteristic of the new age. The Chautauquas originally were eight-week summer training programs away from home for Sunday school teachers. During the 1890s, however, cheap excursion fares on the trains made it feasible for people who might have little interest in active church work to make the trip for the sake of the cool mountain air and relaxation. To accommodate them, the Chautauqua organizers broadened their program to include lecturers on secular subjects.

By the turn of the century, a middle-class family spending a few weeks at Lake Chautauqua could expect to hear lectures by individuals as prominent as William Jennings Bryan and to watch "magic-lantern"

Women in Government

Just as the black cowboy virtually had been forgotten, few historians have noted that women played an important part in government long before they could vote. At the turn of the century, nearly one government worker in three was female. The federal bureaucracy was very much a woman's world.

They're Off

One spectator sport that actually declined during the "good old days," at least as an organized operation, was horse racing. There were 314 commercial racetracks in 1897, but only 25 in 1908.

What happened? An impulse to prohibit gambling happened, as part of the great progressive reform movement. State after state banned gambling in the early years of the twentieth century. Arizona and New Mexico Territories abolished it virtually as a condition of winning statehood in 1912. The last holdout was Nevada, which caved in officially in 1913 (relegalizing gaming in 1931). When gambling was prohibited in a state, horse racing as a spectator sport usually disappeared, too.

(slide) shows about the Holy Land, Persia, or China presented by professional world travelers. Distinguished professors expounded on their theories about human character, happy marriage, or child rearing. German oom-pah bands, Hawaiian dancers, trained dogs, Italian acrobats, and Indian fire-eaters provided lighter entertainment.

AMERICANS AT PLAY

Promoters founded more than 200 Chautauqua-type resorts, some in the mountains, some at the seaside. Enough people could afford to take a holiday from work that a flourishing tourist economy based on leisure time soon grew up.

Nevertheless, old assumptions died hard. Resort promoters found it advisable to provide at least the appearance of usefulness for the vacations they offered. If the middle class trekked to Lake Chautauqua or Lake George in New York and to Long Beach or Atlantic City in New Jersey primarily for rest and relaxation, they could tell others and convince themselves of the cultural and educational aspects of their holiday. They were not just wasting time.

Taking the Cure

A similar conjunction of relaxation and constructive use of time underlay the resorts that were devoted to good health. Owners of mineral springs claimed

miraculous powers for their waters. Baths in naturally heated mineral waters or in hot mud were prescribed as nostrums for dozens of afflictions. Hydropathy, a nineteenth-century medical fad, taught that virtually constant bathing in and drinking of water improved health. For decades, the wealthy made prosperous summer resorts of places like Saratoga Springs in New York and White Sulphur Springs in Virginia where "taking the cure" could be done in pleasant surroundings among congenial people. Now thousands of middle-class people followed them, again rationalizing their desire for relaxation by extolling the health benefits of their holiday.

Leisure and the Working Class

Working people could not afford to take off a week for the mountains or seaside. However, leisure came to play a part in their lives, too. Great urban greens, beginning with New York's magnificent Central Park, provided free relief on weekends for the teeming masses of the city's slums. Working people in large cities were also able to enjoy themselves at the commercial amusement parks that sprang up as a means by which trolley car companies could exploit their investments to the fullest.

Traction companies made a profit only from those parts of their lines that traversed the crowded parts of the cities, and then only on weekdays. However, the expense of center city real estate required them to build their sprawling car barns (storage and repair facilities) outside the city. If they were not required by law to run trolleys on Saturday and Sunday, they still wanted to make constant use of their expensive equipment.

In order to encourage people to ride the trolleys beyond the city centers, the traction companies encouraged the construction of amusement parks at the end of the line or, in many cases, built playlands themselves. Perhaps the most famous was New York's Coney Island, located on the ocean in Brooklyn. The fare from downtown New York was five cents, with children riding free. Once there, for a dollar or two, a large family could ride the mechanical amusements, such as George C. Tilyou's Bounding Billows, Barrel of Love, and Human Roulette Wheel. They could emulate Buffalo Bill at shooting galleries, visit sideshows and exotic Somali villages, or simply loll on the beach with a picnic lunch or "a weird-looking sausage muffled up in two halves of a roll."

These homely pleasures were as exciting to working people as was a trip to Saratoga to the new middle class. Most important, Coney Island, Philadelphia's Willow Grove, Boston's Paragon Park, and Chicago's Cheltenham Beach represented an organized industry, manufacturing, packaging, and merchandising leisure time.

Working-class leisure was more frankly devoted to simple fun than were the middle-class Chautauquas. Nevertheless, insistence that even a day at Coney Island was educational and healthful demonstrated the pervasiveness, of traditional ideals. Sordid sideshows were touted with moralistic spiels. Knocking over weighted bottles for a prize of a Kewpie doll was defined as honing a valuable skill. Even suggestive dancing by "hoochie-koochie girls" such as Fatima, the sensation of the Chicago World's Fair of 1893 who toured the country for a decade, was described as glimpses into the culture of the Turkish Empire. A writer in prim *Harper's Weekly* approved of the trolley parks because they were "great breathing-places for millions of people in the city who get little fresh air at home." In a nation not quite free of its Calvinistic past, every hour must have a purpose.

The First Fitness Craze

Good health was also the rationale for a series of sporting manias that swept over the United States at the turn of the century. To some extent, the concern for bodily health was a contribution of German immigrants, whose *Turnvereins*, clubs devoted to calisthenics, were old-country carryovers like democratic socialism and beer gardens. However, it was obvious as early as the mid-nineteenth century that the urban population walked less and got less exercise generally than had its farmer forebears. In the first issue of the *Atlantic Monthly* in 1858, Thomas Wentworth Higginson asked, "Who in this community really takes exercise? Even the mechanic confines himself to one set of muscles; the blacksmith acquires strength in his right arm, and the dancing teacher in his left leg. But the professional or businessman, what muscles has he at all?" Only a society with plenty of spare time could take Higginson's question to heart.

Croquet, archery, and tennis, all imported from England, enjoyed a vogue in the 1870s. Rollerskating was even more popular. Great rinks like San Francisco's Olympian Club, with 5,000 pairs of skates to rent and a 69,000-square-foot floor, charged nominal

Competing amusement parks line the street at Coney Island.

fees that were within reach of all but the poorest people. But no sporting fad was so widespread as bicycling.

Bicycles

Briefly during the 1860s, French "dandy horses" were seen on American city streets. These crude wooden vehicles were powered by pushing along the ground. About 1876, the "bone crusher," with its six-foot-high front wheel, made its appearance; by 1881, when the League of American Wheelmen was founded, more than 20,000 intrepid young Americans were devoting their idle hours to pedaling furiously about parks and city streets.

While some praised bicycling as a health-giving outdoor exercise, moralists condemned the sport for promoting casual relations between young people of the opposite sex. While young men and ladies might leave home for a Sunday ride in proper groups of their own sex, they found it easy to strike up acquaintanceships in parks far from the eyes of parents and chaperone aunts. More than one worried preacher thought that the bicycle was a first step toward moral chaos.

Indeed, it was on the pneumatic tires of the bicycle that many emancipated young women of the 1890s escaped into a refreshing new freedom. The safety bicycle, which had much the same design as bicycles today, reduced the risk of broken bones. On Sundays, the streets were full of them, and a goodly number carried young women in candy-striped blouses with billowing sleeves, sporty broad-brimmed hats, and full free-flowing skirts.

The Gibson Girl

The new-look woman of the 1890s took the name of the "Gibson Girl" after the popular magazine illustrator, Charles Dana Gibson, who created the style. Gibson's vision of ideal American womanhood charmed the nation from Newport high society to working-class suburbs. The Gibson Girl was by no means a feminist. She took little interest in woman suffrage or other political issues. Essentially she remained an object of adoration—fine-featured, trim, coy, flirtatious, even seductive—but an object of adoration who knew what she was about.

The Gibson Girl was novel: she was no shrinking violet. She did not faint after the exertion of climbing a staircase. She played croquet, golf, and tennis. She rode a bicycle without chaperones. She was quite able to take care of herself; one of Gibson's favorite themes was the helplessness of young men in the hands of his self-assured young ladies.

Theodore Roosevelt's daughter, Alice, who became a national sweetheart when the popular waltz "Alice Blue Gown" was named for her, might have been sculpted by Gibson, and middle-class women adopted her style. Photographs of mill girls leaving textile factories in Massachusetts and of stenographers in offices in New York reveal an air of Gibson Girl self-assurance. The new independence of women was also indicated by the fact that they were marrying later. In 1890, the average age for a woman on her wedding day was 22, two or three years older than it was in 1860.

Technology and the Lives of Women

Technology played a part in creating the new, dynamic, and independent woman. The telephone, for example, permitted a familiarity with men that was forbidden to young ladies of breeding face to face.

Also much noted by people of the time was the fact that Bell's American Telephone and Telegraph Company turned to young women to handle the job of connecting callers to each other. The company fired the young men whom it originally hired because their conversation on the wires was flippant and occasionally obscene; also anticipating the future, they took advantage of anonymity to shock or insult proper middle-class subscribers.

Unlike factory work, which was menial and dirty, a job as an operator was socially acceptable for middle-class women. In addition to finding an escape from the plush and velvet prison of the parlor, thousands of women earned an income independent of their parents and husbands. Alexander Graham Bell, unknown to both parties, was a partner with American feminists in their movement to emancipate women.

The Changing Office

Another invention that created jobs for women, and therefore independence in some, was the typewriter. Because handwriting was often illegible, and potentially costly in business, dozens of inventors had taken a stab at creating a "writing machine." But the first practical typewriter was perfected only in 1867 by Christopher Latham Sholes, and first marketed in 1874 by the Remington Arms Company, a firearms manufacturer in search of a product with which to diversify its interests.

Before the use of the machine became standard in business, almost all secretaries were men. They not only wrote letters for their employers, but they ran various errands and sometimes represented the boss. The typewriter made it possible for businessmen to split the secretarial profession into assistant and typist. Men continued to perform the more responsible and better-paid job, rising to a status that would be described as junior executive today. The mechanical task of transcribing letters and business records into type went to women.

Like the job of telephone operator, that of typist did not require the higher education that was available to only those women determined to the point of eccentricity. It was not heavy labor, an important consideration in an age that defined respectable young women as "delicate." And the job did not usually involve much responsibility, which nineteenth-century men were disinclined to allot to women. By 1890, 15 percent of clerical workers were female; by 1900 almost 25 percent.

SPORTS

The turn of the century was also a golden age of organized sport. Although football (with somewhat different rules from today) was a game played almost exclusively by university students, people of all social classes avidly followed the fortunes of the nearest Ivy League team. Basketball, which was invented in Springfield, Massachusetts, in 1891 by Dr. James Naismith, a physical education instructor who was looking for a sport that his students could play during the rigorous New England winter, was still in its infancy. The spectator sports that obsessed Americans were baseball and boxing. Both evolved from traditional folk recreations, but by the end of the nineteenth century, both already were organized as money-making enterprises.

The National Pastime

Baseball developed out of two ancient children's games, rounders and town ball, which were brought to the United States by English immigrants. According to Albert G. Spalding, a professional pitcher for clubs in Boston and Chicago, systematic rules for the sport were first drafted by Abner Doubleday of Cooperstown, New York, in 1839. The story was poppycock. There is no evidence Doubleday invested a minute thinking about the game. Spalding devised the

The typewriter created jobs for women in business, but almost all of them in subordinate clerical or secretarial roles.

tale to promote the sporting goods manufacturing company that made him a millionaire. In reality, baseball, like Topsy, "just growed"; there was little agreement on a number of important rules until after the Civil War.

While many towns organized teams to play neighbors on special occasions, the professional sport emerged from upper-class baseball clubs such as the New York Knickerbockers. Soon concerned more with defeating rivals than with enjoying an afternoon of exercise, the clubs began to hire (at first secretly and despite noisy protest) long-hitting and fast-pitching working-class "ringers" to wear their colors. In 1869, the first openly professional team, the Cincinnati Red Stockings, went on tour and defeated all comers, some by obscene scores.

Teams were focal points of civic pride. Important games often received more attention in the newspapers than did foreign wars. After Brooklyn became a borough of New York City in 1898, its baseball team, the Trolley Dodgers, became the former city's chief symbol of an independent identity, its antidote to the Brooklyn Bridge.

Boxing and Society

Watching a fight between two strong men may be humanity's oldest diversion. In 1867, because boxing was becoming a "manly art" practiced by the upper class, an English sportsman, the Marquis of Queensberry, devised a code of rules that was quickly adopted throughout Europe and the United States. The Queensberry rules hardly made for a gentle sport. One read that "all attempts to inflict injury by gouging or tearing the flesh with the fingers or nails and biting shall be deemed foul."

As with baseball, the opportunities to make money from paid admissions encouraged promoters to search out popular heroes. The first to win a national reputation was a burly Boston Irishman named John L. Sullivan, who started out by traveling the country and offering $50 and later $1,000 to anyone who could last four rounds with him. Between 1882 and 1892, "the Boston Strong Boy" bloodied one challenger after another, personally collecting as much as $20,000 a fight and making much more for the entrepreneurs who organized his bouts.

The crowds that watched great championship bouts and most baseball games included comparatively few working people. However, they followed their heroes in the new sports pages of the newspapers, which, as with baseball, devoted column after column to im-

> ### The Big Game
>
> Football was entirely a college boy's, not a professional's, game in the nineteenth and early twentieth centuries. But it was taken quite seriously both by players (18 of them were killed at games in 1905 alone) and by spectators. Thanksgiving Day, still largely a religious observance up to the time of the Civil War, became the day of the big game in a more secular, more fun-seeking United States. Harvard and Yale, the nation's two most venerable institutions of higher learning, mauled one another in New York City on Thanksgiving until Harvard's president tired of the players' off-field behavior and opted out of the rivalry. Yale had to settle for Princeton or, later, Rutgers, for a Turkey Day match. In the twentieth century, other great Thanksgiving rivalries developed: Penn–Cornell, Case–Western Reserve, Kansas–Missouri, Tulane–LSU, and Texas–Texas A&M.

portant fights. Because Sullivan and his successor as heavyweight champion, Gentleman Jim Corbett, were Irish, they became objects of ethnic pride. So entangled in the culture did the sport become that when a black boxer rose to the top, he caused an anxiety that reached into the halls of Congress.

Jack Johnson

Blacks played baseball with whites during the earliest professional years. The catcher on a team that toured the world in the 1880s was black. However, the same wave of racism that initiated the Jim Crow laws in the 1890s led to the segregation of the sport. A first baseman from Iowa, Adrian "Cap" Anson, led the fight to keep black players out of the two major leagues.

Black boxers did fight whites and, in 1908, one of them, Jack Johnson, won the heavyweight crown and proceeded to batter every challenger who stepped forth. Such a feat by a black man rankled many white Americans. Johnson aggravated the hatred for him by gleefully insulting every "great white hope" who challenged him. A tragically indiscreet man, he flaunted his white mistresses at a time when the color line was being drawn across practically every American institution.

Southern states, which had been the most hospitable to professional prize fights, forbade Johnson to fight within their borders. Politicians raved at every Johnson victory and gaudy public appearance. Congress actually passed a law that prohibited the interstate shipment of a film of Johnson's victory over former champion Jim Jeffries in Reno in 1910. Finally, in 1912, racism defeated him not in the ring but through an indictment under the Mann Act, which forbade transporting women across state lines "for immoral purposes." (Johnson had traveled with his common-law wife to another state.)

Johnson fled to Europe, but was homesick and agreed to fight the white boxer Jess Willard in Havana in 1915. He lost, and it was widely believed that he threw the match as part of a deal with the Justice Department by which he could reenter the United States without fear of arrest. A famous photograph of the knockout shows Johnson on his back, apparently relaxed and unhurt, and shielding his eyes from the Caribbean sun. Jack may have had his last jibe at good-old-days America, but the days were good enough for the white middle class that few people noticed.

CHRONOLOGY

1862 Morrill Land Grant Act lays basis for inexpensive state universities.

1867 Perfection of typewriter (effectively marketed in 1874) begins transformation of American business office, including the creation of opportunities for women

1868 Elizabeth Blackwell establishes first medical school for women

1869 "Elective system" replaces strict classical curriculum at Harvard University

1880s Rapid expansion of American educational institutions at all levels

1883 *Ladies' Home Journal* is founded

1885 Mark Twain's *Adventures of Huckleberry Finn*, a scathing attack on racism and *ante-bellum* southern society and since recognized as perhaps the greatest of American novels, is published

1893 Columbian Exposition in Chicago celebrates American culture

1899 Epidemic of lynching in South reaches symbolic climax when a Georgia mob announces hanging of African American in advance

1901 Theodore Roosevelt, the spirit of his optimistic and outgoing age, succeeds to the presidency

1908 African American boxer, Jack Johnson, wins heavyweight championship and becomes a focal point of both black pride and white racism

FOR FURTHER READING

Overviews of the era are Vincent P. DeSantis, *The Shaping of Modern America, 1877–1916*, 1973; Ray Ginger, *The Age of Excess*, 1965; William L. O'Neill, *The Progressive Years: America Comes of Age*, 1975; and Robert H. Wiebe, *The Search for Order, 1880–1920*, 1967. On general social and cultural history, students should look at Frederick Lewis Allen, *The Big Change*, 1952; Van Wyck Brooks, *The Confident Years, 1885–1915*, 1952; and the classic Mark Sullivan, *Our Times*, 1926–1935.

Studies of special topics include G. W. Chessman, *Governor Theodore Roosevelt*, 1965; Carl M. Degler, *At Odds: Women in the Family in America from the Revolution to the Present*, 1980; Kathryn Kish Sklar, *Florence Kelly and the Nation's Work: The Rise of Women's Political Culture*, 1995; Foster R. Dulles, *America Learns to Play*, 1940; Ray Ginger, *Altgeld's America: The Lincoln Ideal and Changing Realities*, 1958; Otis L. Graham, Jr., *The Great Campaigns: Reform and War in America, 1900–1928*, 1971; Jack D. Kirby, *Darkness at the Dawning: Race and Reform in the Progressive South*, 1972; James R. Barrett, *Work and Community in the Jungle*, 1987; Margaret Leech, *In the Days of McKinley*, 1959; Henry F. May, *The End of American Innocence*, 1959; Steven A. Reiss, *Touching Base: Professional Baseball and American Culture in the Progressive Era*, 1980; and Ellen Chesler, *Woman of Valor: Margaret Sanger and the Birth Control Movement*, 1992.

Fine books about "Teddy" are W. H. Harbaugh, *Power and Responsibility: The Life and Times of Theodore Roosevelt*, 1961; and Henry F. Pringle, *Theodore Roosevelt*, 1931. John Milton Cooper, *The Warrior and the Priest*, 1983, is an intriguing joint biography of TR and Woodrow Wilson.

The "whistle-stop" speech from the end of a train was a popular campaign ritual: former president Teddy Roosevelt in Kansas in 1910.

35
CHAPTER

AGE OF REFORM
The Progressives after 1900

'Tis not too late to build our young land right,
Cleaner than Holland, courtlier than Japan,
Devout like early Rome with hearths like hers,
Hearths that will recreate the breed called man.

—Vachel Lindsay

A man that'd expect to thrain lobsters to fly in a year is called a loonytic; but a man that thinks men can be tu-rrned into angels be an illiction is called a rayformer an' remains at large.

—Finley Peter Dunne

684 *Chapter 35 Age of Reform*

In 1787, when the founding fathers were writing the Constitution in Philadelphia—in part out of fear of social turmoil—Thomas Jefferson was in France, serving as United States minister there. King Louis XVI still sat on the throne; the Bastille had not yet been attacked; Paris was peaceful; and Jefferson still had the fire of 1776 in his blood. He wrote several letters in which he said that revolution was essential to the health of a free society. "A little rebellion, now and then, is a good thing," he wrote to James Madison, "as necessary in the political world as storms in the physical." To another friend a few months later he added, "The tree of liberty must be refreshed from time to time with the blood of patriots and tyrants."

Jefferson was saying that political progress depended upon violent uprising. Was he right? The history of the United States says not. During 200 years of history that, worldwide, has been marked by social convulsions and bloody carnage beyond Jefferson's imaginings, the United States has been an island of stability. The nation has been shaken by revolution only once: the secession of the southern states in 1861, and that uprising was neither progressive nor successful. Reform has been fitful in the United States, but it has also always been peaceful.

The authors of the Constitution, no revolutionaries they, wrote a mechanism for peaceable change into the document in the form of the amendment process. So, the strictest adherence to the basic instrument of government should mean a readiness to adapt to new conditions. More important, periodically in American history—in predictable cycles, some historians think—people whose means and privileges put them above the masses have them-

selves, quite without violence, attacked political and social abuses, pruning the deadwood and disease from Jefferson's tree of liberty. Such a welling of the reform spirit was the Progressive Era which spanned, roughly, the first two decades of the twentieth century.

THE PROGRESSIVES

Few of the far-reaching reforms of the early 1900s were original with the new century. The progressive movement inherited impulses and ideas from the Mugwumps, the Social Gospel, the half-century-old women's movement, from urban social workers, Populism, even from the sundry varieties of socialism expounded in the late nineteenth century. However, while the progressives' predecessors managed to appeal to but a minority of Americans, usually very small minorities, the progressives rallied the better part of a generation to their causes.

Middle America

Their chief appeal was to the new middle class of small businessmen and professionals: lawyers, physicians, ministers, teachers, journalists, social workers, and women—the wives and daughters of the middle class whose first reform was personal, to break free of the nursery, parlor, and chapel. The industrial and financial elite produced very few progressive leaders. Few progressives rose from the masses of laboring people and poor farmers, either. The movement was middle-class in its heart and head.

The progressives were acutely aware that they were in between. Eternally knocking about in the back of the progressive mind was the assumption that what was best about America was its middle class—people not so rich as to endanger the republic, not so poor as to have no stake in it. Like Thomas Jefferson and his disciples a century earlier, most progressives felt that the people in the middle were threatened by plutocrats from above, and from below by the potentially dangerous mob.

Thus, virtually all progressives were committed to destroying the immense power of the great corporations and banks or, at least, to control the manner in which that power was used. They intended that the Rockefellers and the Morgans behave in ways that were compatible with the good of society, as the progressives defined it.

> ### Reform
>
> What is reform? One dictionary defines it as "to change into a new and improved condition; removal of faults or abuses so as to restore to a former good state, or bring from bad to good." In the context of American history, *reform* has also come to mean peaceful, usually gradual change, as opposed to violent and sudden change, which Americans define as *revolution*.

Most progressives were concerned with the material and moral welfare of those below them on the social ladder. However, they also feared the masses. In the cities, progressive reformers often voiced concern that the slums were tinderboxes of anger, ready to explode in destructive anarchy. In the Midwest and West, most progressive leaders had been staunch anti-Populists because they saw the farmers' rebellion as an upheaval of the impoverished, uneducated, and unwashed. William Allen White, a leading midwestern progressive, first made his name as the author of a scathing anti-Populist manifesto called "What's the Matter with Kansas?" Years later, a little sheepishly, White explained that he wrote the piece not because an idea occurred to him in his study, but because he had been jostled on a street corner in Emporia, Kansas, by "lazy, greasy fizzles" whose crudeness and vulgarity offended him.

Many progressives saw clearly the relationship between the power of great wealth and dangerous restiveness among the exploited poor. Early in the century, Woodrow Wilson of New Jersey put the thought in a curious way when he blamed the automobile, then a plaything of the rich, for the spread of socialism. Driving their cars around recklessly, frightening horses, killing chickens, and scattering ordinary folks, Wilson wrote, the rich were bringing their arrogance to every country road in the nation.

Righteous, Optimistic, and WASP

Louis Brandeis, a Louisville, Kentucky, lawyer who helped design the Democratic party's reform program, was Jewish. Alfred E. Smith and Robert F. Wagner, progressive politicians in New York State, were Irish and German, respectively, and Roman Catholic in religion. W. E. B. Du Bois, who helped to found the National Association for the Advancement of Colored People, was an African American. But they were exceptions. Most progressive leaders were WASPs, White Anglo-Saxon Protestants from old stock; they were people whose American roots ran through several generations.

Most were urban people, brought up in cities or towns. Even those progressive politicians who represented rural states, such as Robert M. La Follette of Wisconsin and George Norris of Nebraska, grew up in small towns. As boys, they rubbed elbows with farmers, but they had not plodded behind plows or milled about anxiously next to their wagons as agents weighed, graded, and put a price on the year's crop.

Indeed, like William Allen White, La Follette was an anti-Populist during the 1890s.

Progressive political leaders inclined to be moralistic to the point of self-righteousness, ever searching for the absolute right and absolute wrong in every political disagreement. California's Hiram Johnson irked even his strongest supporters with his clenched-teeth sanctimony. Robert M. La Follette did not know what a sense of humor was. To "Fighting Bob," life was one long crusade for what was right. Theodore Roosevelt described the beginning of an election campaign in biblical terms: "We stand at Armageddon and do battle for the Lord." Woodrow Wilson, stern of visage in wing collar and pince-nez, eventually destroyed himself because he would not compromise with critics, even when doing so was the only way to save the most important cause of his life.

And yet, while their noses were ever to the wind for hint of foul odors, the progressives believed that progress was possible because human nature was intrinsically good. "Our shamelessness is superficial," wrote Lincoln Steffens, "beneath it lies a pride which, being real, may save us yet." They were optimists.

A Coat of Many Colors

Almost all progressives believed that a powerful government, active in taking the initiative and holding it, was the key to improving America. In their faith in the state, they were rather unlike earlier reformers who were more apt to consider government a part of the problem. Jane Addams, whose main work

---

Filthy Lucre

Progressives were morally appalled by money grubbing. When he was president, Theodore Roosevelt expressed this sentiment when he tried to have "In God We Trust" deleted from American coins. "It seems to me," he wrote, "eminently unwise to cheapen such a motto by use on coins, just as it would be to cheapen it by use on postage stamps and advertisements." A few coins were struck without "In God We Trust," but Congress, failing to appreciate T. R's point, restored it.

was helping the urban poor, said that private institutions like her Hull House were "today inadequate to deal with the vast numbers of the city's disinherited."

As for the corporations that threatened American ideas, the progressives believed that a powerful state was the only agency that could bring them to heel. The goals were still Jeffersonian, Herbert Croly wrote in *The Promise of American Life* (1909), the welfare of the many was determined by the will of the many. But, to Croly and most progressives, the old Jeffersonian principle of "the less government the better" was rendered obsolete by the magnitude of social problems and the vast power of the plutocrats. Croly would have Jeffersonian ends achieved through the use of Hamiltonian means, the power of the state.

Beyond a commitment to active government, progressivism was variety, a frame of mind rather than a single coherent movement. There were Democratic progressives and Republican progressives. In 1912, breakaway Republicans formed the Progressive party, while some progressives considered democratic socialists—those who rejected violent revolution as an agent of change—to be kin.

On some specific issues, progressives differed among themselves as radically as they differed from the old guard against whom they battled. For example, while many progressives believed that labor unions had the right to exist and fight for the betterment of their members, others opposed unions for the same reason that they disliked powerful corporations: organized special-interest groups were at odds with the American ideal of serving the good of the whole. On one occasion, for example, leaders of the National American Woman Suffrage Association said that women should work as strikebreakers if by so doing they could win jobs currently held by men.

Some progressives were ultranationalists. Others clung to a humanism that embraced all people of all countries. Some progressives were expansionists. Senator Albert J. Beveridge of Indiana saw no conflict in calling for broadening democracy at home while urging the United States to rule colonies abroad without regard to the will of their inhabitants. Others were anti-imperialists, even isolationists who looked on Europe as a fount of corruption.

Progressives also disagreed on the subject of laws regulating child labor. By 1907, about two-thirds of the states governed or influenced by progressives forbade the employment of children under 14 years of age. However, when progressives in Congress passed a federal child labor law in 1916, the progressive President Woodrow Wilson expressed grave doubts before signing it. Wilson worried that to forbid children to work infringed on their rights as citizens. This was essentially the same reasoning that was offered by the conservative Supreme Court in *Hammer* v. *Dagenhart* (1918), which struck down the law.

Race

Many, perhaps most, progressives could not imagine blacks as citizens equal to whites, participating fully and actively in American society. Some were frank racists, especially the southern progressives: Governor James K. Vardaman of Mississippi, Governor Jeff Davis of Arkansas, and Senator Benjamin "Pitchfork Ben" Tillman of South Carolina. As president of Princeton University, Woodrow Wilson helped to segregate the town of Princeton on racial lines,

Better known as a prominent senior citizen, Jane Addams (1860–1935) was a young woman when she founded Hull House.

including even separate "white" and "colored" water fountains. As president of the United States, he approved the introduction of "Jim Crow" practices in the federal government. Other progressives tolerated discrimination against blacks out of habit or because they feared the consequences of racial equality with 45 percent of the African-American population being illiterate, as was then the case.

Other progressives regarded racial prejudice and discrimination as among the worst evils afflicting America. Journalist Ray Stannard Baker wrote a scathing and moving exposé of racial segregation in a series of articles entitled "Following the Color Line." In 1910, white progressives, including Jane Addams, joined with the black Niagara Movement to form the National Association for the Advancement of Colored People. Except for his color, W. E. B. Du Bois, the guiding spirit of the Niagara Movement, was the progressive *par excellence:* genteel, middle-class, university-educated, he was devoted to the idea that an elite should govern. Du Bois believed that a "talented tenth" of the black population would lead the race to civil equality in the United States.

Brownsville

The limitations of progressives on matters involving race were displayed by the federal government's actions after black soldiers of the Twenty-Fifth Infantry Regiment were accused of shooting up Brownsville, Texas, in August 1906. Although no individual was found guilty of the crime, or even tried for it, progressive President Theodore Roosevelt dishonorably discharged all 167 black soldiers stationed at the fort, including six winners of the Medal of Honor.

Some circumstantial evidence indicated that a few of the men were guilty of the shooting; other evidence seemed to exonerate all of them. But Roosevelt and his progressive supporters were more interested in calming the tempers of those whites who assumed the worst of the blacks than in acting on principles of justice. The only prominent white politician to take up the cause of the African-American soldiers was a Republican conservative, Senator Joseph B. Foraker of Ohio.

Forebears

So diverse a movement had a mixed ancestry. From the Populists' Omaha Platform, the progressives took a good deal. Indeed, as William Allen White remarked, the progressives "caught the Populists in swimming and stole all of their clothing except the frayed underdrawers of free silver." They called for the direct election of senators and a graduated income tax that would hit the wealthy harder than it hit the poor and middle classes. Both reforms were enacted by constitutional amendment in 1913. Progressives also favored the initiative, referendum, and recall. Some but by no means all progressives wanted to nationalize the railways and banks. Many more believed that local public utilities such as water, gas, and electric companies, being natural monopolies, should be government-owned.

The progressives also harkened back to the "good government" idealism of the Liberal Republicans and Mugwumps. Indeed, in the progressives' intense moralism, and their compulsion to stamp out personal sin as well as social and political evils, they could sound like the evangelical preachers of the early nineteenth century.

In exalting expertise and efficiency, and in their belief that a new social order must be devised to replace the social chaos of the late nineteenth century, the progressives owed a debt to people whom they considered their enemies. Marcus A. Hanna, described as a conservative when he died in 1904, preached collaboration between capital and organized labor as an alternative to class conflict.

Frederick W. Taylor, the inventor of "scientific management," was rarely described as a progressive and personally took little interest in politics. Nevertheless, in his conviction that the engineer's approach to solving problems could be fruitfully applied to human behavior, he was a forebear of the progressive movement. The progressives believed that society could be engineered as readily as Taylor engineered machines and the shape of the shovel a workingman used to perform his job.

PROGRESSIVISM DOWN HOME

Progressivism originated in the cities. In the last years of the nineteenth century, capitalizing on widespread disgust with the corruption that became endemic to municipal government, a number of reform

Chapter 35 Age of Reform

mayors swept into office and won national notoriety. They were not, as were their predecessors in the 1870s and 1880s, easily ousted after a year or two.

Good Government

One of the first of the city reformers was Hazen S. Pingree, a shoe manufacturer who was elected mayor of Detroit in 1890. Pingree spent seven years battling the corrupt alliance between the owners of the city's public utilities and Detroit city councilmen. In nearby Toledo, Ohio, another businessman, Samuel M. Jones, ran for mayor as a reformer in 1897. Professional politicians mocked him as an addleheaded eccentric because he plastered the walls of his factory with the golden rule and other homilies. But his employees, whom Jones treated fairly by sharing profits with them, were dedicated to him, and workers in other companies admired him. As "Golden Rule" Jones, he took control of Toledo and proved to be a no-nonsense administrator. Within two years, he rid Toledo's city hall of graft.

Another progressive mayor from Ohio was Cleveland's Thomas L. Johnson. A former single-taxer, Johnson was elected in 1901. Not only did he clean up a dirty government, but he actively supported woman suffrage, reformed the juvenile courts, took over public utilities from avaricious owners, and put democracy to work by presiding over open town meetings at which citizens could make known their grievances and suggestions.

Lincoln Steffens, a staff writer for *McClure's*, called Cleveland "the best-governed city in the United States." Steffens was the expert; in 1903, he authored a sensational series of articles for *McClure's* called "The Shame of the Cities." Researching his subject carefully in the country's major cities, he named grafters, exposed corrupt connections between elected officials and dishonest businessmen, and demonstrated how ordinary people suffered from corrupt government in the quality of their daily lives.

Steffens's exposés hastened the movement for city reform. Joseph W. Folk of St. Louis, whose tips put Steffens on the story, was able to indict more than 30 politicians and prominent Missouri businessmen for bribery and perjury as a result of the outcry that greeted "The Shame of the Cities." Hundreds of reform mayors elected after 1904 owed their success to the solemn, bearded journalist.

The Muckrakers

No single force was more important in spreading the gospel of progressivism than the mass-circulation magazines. Already well established by the turn of the century thanks to their cheap price and lively style, journals such as *McClure's*, the *Arena, Collier's, Cosmopolitan*, and *Everybody's* became even more successful when their editors discovered the popular appetite for the journalism of exposure.

The discovery was almost accidental. Samuel S. McClure himself had no particular interest in reform. Selling magazines and advertising in them was his business, hobby, and obsession. When he hired Ida M. Tarbell and Lincoln Steffens at generous salaries, he did so because they wrote well, not because they were reformers. Indeed, Tarbell admitted she began the "History of the Standard Oil Company," exposing John D. Rockefeller's dubious business practices because of a personal grudge: Rockefeller had ruined her father. Steffens was looking for a story, any story, when he stumbled upon the shame of the cities.

But when Tarbell's and Steffens's sensational exposés caused circulation to soar, McClure and other editors were hooked. The mass-circulation magazines soon brimmed with sensational revelations about corruption in government, chicanery in business, social evils like child labor and prostitution, and other subjects that lent themselves to indignant, excited treatment. In addition to his series on racial segregation, Ray Stannard Baker dissected the operations of the great railroads. John Spargo, an English-born socialist, discussed child labor in "The

---

Nothing But the Facts, Ma'am

The muckrakers were keenly aware that part of the revolution they worked in American journalism was to sensationalize it. Lincoln Steffens chafed under the regime in which "reporters were to report the news as it happened, like machines, without prejudice, color, and without style; all alike." Ray Stannard Baker wrote impatiently that "facts, facts piled up to the point of dry certitude, was what the American people really wanted." Both were to remain true to high standards of journalistic integrity, but that was not true of many muckrakers.

Ida Tarbell (1857–1944) was one of the most responsible and effective muckrakers.

> ### Short-Attention-Span Journalism
>
> William Randolph Hearst, who sponsored a good deal of muckraking in his newspapers, said that
>
> *the modern editor of the popular journal does not care for facts. The editor wants novelty. The editor has no objections to facts if they are also novel. But he would prefer novelty that is not fact, to a fact that is not a novelty.*
>
> It is difficult to think of a better explanation of what went wrong with the journalism of exposure. After a few years, muckrakers were exposing scandals that existed only in their imaginations, raking muck that was more like gravel.

Bitter Cry of the Children." David Graham Phillips, who later succeeded as a novelist dealing with social themes, revealed that the United States Senate, elected by state legislatures, had become a kind of millionaires' club.

Theodore Roosevelt called the new journalists muckrakers after an unattractive character in John Bunyan's religious classic of 1678, *Pilgrim's Progress*. The writers were so busy raking through the muck of American society, he said, that they failed to look up and see the glories in the stars.

He had a point, especially when after a few years the quality of the journalism of exposure deteriorated into sloppy research and wild, ill-founded accusations made for the sake of attracting attention. During the first decade of the century, no fewer than 2,000 articles and books of exposure were published. Inevitably, the conscientious muckrakers ran out of solid material, and muckraking as a profession attracted incompetent hacks and sensation-mongers.

But the dirt could be real enough, and the early reform journalists were as determined to stick to the facts as to arouse their readers' indignation. Their work served to transmit the reform impulse from one end of the country to the other. The ten leading muckraking journals had a combined circulation of 3 million. Because the magazines were also read in public libraries and barbershops, and just passed around, the readership was many times larger.

In the Jungle with Upton Sinclair

Some of the muckrakers were explicitly pro-capitalist. Ida M. Tarbell wrote that, "as I saw it, it was not capitalism [that was the problem] but an open disregard of decent ethical business practices by capitalists." Other writers, like John Spargo, belonged to the Socialist party. Upton Sinclair, the most influential muckraker of all, was a militant, if obscure, young socialist, when, in 1906, he soared to fame because of his novel, *The Jungle*. Sinclair's theme was the transformation of a Lithuanian immigrant into a revolutionary because of ethnic prejudice and economic exploitation in Chicago.

This message did not particularly appeal to the editors of the mass-circulation magazines, and Sinclair turned to a Socialist party weekly newspaper, the *Appeal to Reason*, to run it as a serial. Even the *Appeal* had a big readership; one issue sold over 1 million copies. In its pages, *The Jungle* was a mighty success. Published as a book, it sold 100,000 copies, reaching even the desk of President Theodore Roosevelt.

Sinclair's book probably converted few Americans to socialism. In fact, its literary quality decays rapidly in the final chapters when the protagonist takes up the red flag. However, millions were moved by the

690 *Chapter 35 Age of Reform*

passages in the book that luridly described the conditions under which meat was processed in Chicago slaughterhouses. *The Jungle* publicized documented tales of rats ground up into sausage, workers with tuberculosis coughing on the meat they packed, and filth at every point along the production line.

"I aimed at the nation's heart," Sinclair later said, "and hit it in the stomach." He meant that within months of the publication of *The Jungle*, a federal meat-inspection bill that had been languishing in Congress was rushed through under public pressure and promptly signed by President Roosevelt. It, and a second Pure Food and Drug Act, which forbade food processors to use dangerous adulterants (the pet project of a chemist in the Agriculture Department, Dr. Harvey W. Wiley), expanded the power of government in a way that was inconceivable a few years earlier.

Efficiency and Democracy

In 1900, Galveston, Texas, introduced a favorite progressive municipal reform, the city manager system of government. The office of mayor was abolished. Instead, voters elected a city council, which then hired a nonpolitical, professionally trained administrator to manage the city's affairs. Proponents of the city manager system reasoned that democracy was protected by the people's control of the council. However, because the daily operations of the city were supervised by an executive who was free of political influence, they would be carried out without regard to special interests. By 1915, over 400 mostly medium-size cities followed Galveston's example.

The "Oregon system" was the brainchild of one of the first progressives to make an impact at the state level. William S. U'ren, a former Populist and single-taxer, believed that the remedy for corruption in government was simple: more democracy. The trouble lay in the ability of efficient, well-organized, and wealthy special interests to thwart the good intentions of the people. Time after time, U'ren pointed out, elected officials handily forgot their campaign promises and worked closely with the corporations to pass bad laws or defeat good ones.

In 1902, U'ren persuaded the Oregon legislature to adopt reforms pioneered in South Dakota in 1898, the initiative, recall, and referendum. The Oregon system also included the first primary law. It took the power to nominate candidates for public office away from the bosses and gave it to the voters. Finally, U'ren led the national movement to choose United States senators by popular vote rather than in the state legislatures.

U'ren lived to the ripe old age of 90, long enough to see 20 states adopt the initiative and 30 the referendum. A number of progressive states also instituted primaries of one kind or another, but until the 1970s, the primary was a less popular idea. In the South, the "white primary," by which Democratic party candidates were chosen, was used in the interests of racism: since most whites were Democrats, the primary was the contest that counted; and because the primary was an election within a private organization, blacks could be legally excluded from it.

"Fighting Bob"

The career of Wisconsin's "Fighting Bob" La Follette is almost a history of progressivism in itself. Born in 1855, he studied law and served three terms as a Republican in Congress in the 1880s. As a young man, he showed few signs of the crusader's itch. Then, a prominent Wisconsin Republican offered him a bribe to fix the verdict in a trial. La Follette flew into a rage at the shameless audacity of the suggestion, and he never quite calmed down for the rest of his life.

In 1900, he ran for governor in defiance of the Republican organization, attacking the railroad and lumber interests that dominated the state. He promised to devote the resources of the government to the service of the people and his timing was perfect. A state that recently had rebuffed the Populists was ready for reform, and La Follette was elected. As governor, he pushed through a comprehensive system of regulatory laws that required every business touching the public interest to conform to clear-cut rules and submit to close inspection of its operations.

The "Wisconsin Idea"

La Follette went beyond the negative, or regulatory powers of government to create agencies that provided positive services for the people. La Follette's "Wisconsin idea" held that in the complex modern world, people and government needed experts to work on their behalf. A railroad baron could not be kept on a leash unless the government could draw on the knowledge of specialists who were as canny as

"Fighting Bob" La Follette in an affable mood.

the railroad men. Insurance premiums could not be held at reasonable levels unless the state was able to determine when the insurance company's profit was just and when it was rapacious. The government could not intervene to determine what was fair in a labor dispute unless it had the counsel of economists.

La Follette formed a close and mutually beneficial relationship with the University of Wisconsin. In control of the state government, his organization generously supported the institution, making it one of the nation's great universities at a time when most tax-supported schools were underfunded agricultural colleges. In return, distinguished professors like Richard Ely, Selig Perlman, and John Rogers Commons put their expertise at La Follette's disposal. The Wisconsin law school helped build up the first legislative reference library in the United States so that assemblymen would no longer have to rely on lobbyists for private interests in order to draft complex laws.

The university's school of agriculture not only taught future farmers, but carried out research programs that addressed problems faced daily in Wisconsin's fields and barns. La Follette even made use of the football team. When enemies hinted there would be trouble if he spoke at a political rally, he showed up in the company of Wisconsin's burly linemen, who folded their arms and surrounded the platform. There was no trouble.

Perhaps La Follette's most original contribution to progressivism was his application of machine methods to the cause of reform. He was idealistic, but he was no innocent. In order to ensure that his reforms would not be reversed, he built an organization that was more finely integrated than Boss Tweed's. Party workers in every precinct got out the vote, and if they did not violate La Follette's exacting demands for honesty in public office, they were rewarded with government patronage.

In 1906, La Follette took his crusade to Washington as a United States senator. He held that office until his death in 1925, and made several unsuccessful tries at the presidency. In Wisconsin and elsewhere he was loved as few politicians have been. He was "Fighting Bob," incorruptible and unyielding in what he regarded as right. La Follette's mane of brown hair, combed straight back, which turned snow white with years, waved wildly during his passionate speeches. He looked like an Old Testament prophet, and, in a way, La Follette devoted his life to saving the soul of American society as Jeremiah had done for Israel.

Progressives Elsewhere

In New York State, Charles Evans Hughes came to prominence as a result of his investigation into public utilities and insurance companies. Tall, erect, dignified, with a smartly trimmed beard such as was

---

Attempted Murder?

In late May 1908, Robert La Follette led a filibuster against a financial bill of which he disapproved. He spoke for nearly 17 hours before giving up. Through much of this time, La Follette sipped a tonic of milk and raw eggs prepared in the Senate dining room. After he had been taken violently ill on the floor, it was discovered that there was enough ptomaine in the mixture to kill a man. Because no one else suffered from eating in the Senate dining room that day, many assumed that La Follette's enemies had tried to kill him.

NOTABLE PEOPLE
Victor L. Berger (1860–1929)

Victor L. Berger was born into a middle-class family in Nieder-Rehbach in the Austro-Hungarian Empire and educated at the universities of Vienna and Budapest. In 1878, he emigrated to the United States, settling briefly in Bridgeport, Connecticut. In 1881, he moved to Milwaukee, which had a large German-speaking population. A schoolteacher, Berger took an active role in the rich ethnic life of the German community, especially in the city's Old World–oriented social democratic organizations. By the early 1890s, he was the most prominent Socialist in Milwaukee, and in 1897, he became editor of the *Wisconsin Vorwarts*, the movement's newspaper.

The German bloc was the core of the Milwaukee party, but Berger concluded that in order to succeed, the Socialists had to leave European preoccupations behind and attract old-stock Americans to the movement. In 1895, he converted Eugene V. Debs, the popular and quintessentially American labor leader, to socialism. In 1897, along with Debs and several other regional Socialist leaders, Berger founded the Social Democratic party of America, a broadly based alliance of Marxist, Populist, utopian, and Christian socialist groups. In 1901, Berger helped engineer the alliance with Morris Hillquit of New York that resulted in the formation of the Socialist party of America. In the same year, he also became editor of the *Social Democratic Herald*, the new English-language organ of his Milwaukee party that signaled his concerted campaign to win non-German support in his city.

Berger deeply admired liberal American political institutions, and he was convinced that socialism could triumph in the United States only when Socialists abandoned the notion of violent revolution and won majority support. In Milwaukee, he devised a strategy that became the model for the municipal socialist movement of the early twentieth century. The Milwaukee Social Democratic party deemphasized its ultimate revolutionary goal so as not to frighten off middle-class reformers. In an age of gross municipal corruption, the Berger Socialists offered scrupulously honest and efficient government. They attracted non-Socialist members of the union movement by pledging prolabor legislation and support during strikes. The Socialists even won the support of many businessmen by promising stable labor relations. In one election campaign, Berger boasted that there would be fewer strikes when the Socialists came to power. Finally, by municipalizing public utilities (with generous compensation), Berger sought to demonstrate the workability of socialism as well as his party's competence to govern.

Following this formula, the Milwaukee party grew steadily through the first decade of the century. In 1910, it won a sweeping victory, sending Berger to Congress and electing the mayor and the majority of the city council. Other local parties, molded on Berger's design, won comparable victories in other cities—Butte, Schenectady, Berkeley—thus increasing Berger's prestige in Socialist party councils.

As a member of the party's National Executive Committee, however, Berger was not so flexible as he was in city politics. From the time the party was founded, he fought a running battle with the "revolutionist" left-wing Socialists on the issues of revolutionary militance and the party's relationship with the labor movement. The leftists scorned Berger's immediate program as "sewer socialism," and called for an unequivocally socialist plan. They argued that working for piecemeal reforms strengthened capitalism rather than hastening the day when the Socialists would take control, and they denounced Berger as nothing but a progressive. Berger, never slow to

going out of fashion at the turn of the century, he lacked the charisma of La Follette and other progressives. If they were humorless in their intensity, Hughes was "a cold-blooded creature" (in the words of the hot-blooded Theodore Roosevelt). But he was unshakably honest as governor of New York between 1906 and 1910.

William E. Borah was not elected to the Senate from Idaho in 1906 as a progressive. On the contrary, his career in politics was characterized

retaliate to criticism, said that the revolutionists' irresponsible rhetoric and policies held the party back.

Much more serious was the split between the two groups on the union question. The left wingers considered the AFL irretrievably committed to preserving capitalism and urged the party to support a truly socialist union that would organize the unskilled majority of the workforce and work toward the overthrow of the system. After 1905, they advocated an informal alliance between the Socialist party and the Industrial Workers of the World, a revolutionary industrial union that, after 1909, fought and won several well-publicized strikes.

Berger opposed the IWW from the beginning because he feared that it would damage the AFL, which, however antisocialist, was a genuine working-class organization. After 1909, he argued that the IWW endorsement of revolution and sabotage alienated the very middle-class reformist elements to whom his faction was appealing with increasing success. In 1913, Berger took the lead in engineering a divorce of the two movements by successfully removing William D. "Big Bill" Haywood from the National Executive Committee. Haywood was the chief spokesman for an alliance between party and union, and Berger forced him out on the grounds that Haywood advocated violent sabotage.

In the wake of Haywood's recall, party membership declined, and in the autumn of 1913, most of the Socialist party's electoral gains of the previous years were lost. In 1916, Berger's long-standing wish to replace Eugene V. Debs with a moderate Socialist as presidential candidate was realized with the nomination of Allen Benson. But despite an increased electorate, Benson won less than two-thirds of Debs's 1912 total.

The next year, the United States entered the world war, and the party revived in Milwaukee and nationally. The only national political body to stand unequivocally against the war, the Socialist party attracted many non-Socialist antiwar voters and thus increased its strength throughout the country. In 1918, Berger won back the congressional seat that he had lost in 1912.

By this time, however, the federal government had moved against the party for its opposition to the war. The *Milwaukee Ledger* (a Socialist daily that had been founded by Berger in 1911) lost its cheap mailing privileges, and several editions were confiscated by the Post Office. Berger was convicted of having violated the Espionage Act of 1917, a law that declared practically all antiwar agitation to be illegal. By a vote of 309 to 1, Congress refused to seat him on this basis, and after Berger won a special election to fill the seat in 1919, again turned him down.

In 1921, the Supreme Court overturned Berger's conviction. In 1923, he finally took his place in Congress and served until 1928, when he was ousted in the Republican landslide of that year. With the 1920s, however, the Socialist party was in disarray. The success of the Bolsheviks in Russia had led to the growth of a largely foreign-born Communist faction in the Socialist party, which, after Berger and Morris Hillquit expelled them in 1919, formed two Communist parties. By 1923, both Communist parties and the now almost completely reformist Socialist party were tiny sects with a combined membership that was smaller than the socialists alone had claimed before 1919.

Anti-Communist himself by this time, Berger drifted slowly but steadily away from socialism. In 1928, he supported Alfred E. Smith for president solely because the Democratic nominee was opposed to Prohibition. On July 16, 1929, Berger was struck by a streetcar in Milwaukee, and he died of his injuries three weeks later.

by a close and compliant relationship with the mining and ranching interests that ran the state. Once in the Senate, however, Borah usually voted with the growing progressive bloc. This record and his isolationism—like many westerners, Borah believed that the United States would be corrupted by close association with foreign powers—guaranteed his reelection until he died in office in 1940. Only decades later was it discovered that, unlike La Follette, Hughes, and most

694 Chapter 35 Age of Reform

progressives, Borah was not above slipping quiet gifts of cash into his pocket.

Progressivism in California

Hiram Johnson of California came to progressivism by much the same path as La Follette. A prim, tight-lipped trial lawyer from Sacramento, Johnson won fame by taking over the prosecution of the corrupt political machine of Boss Abe Ruef in San Francisco.

At first it appeared to be a garden-variety graft case. Ruef and his allies, Mayor Eugene E. Schmitz and a majority of the board of aldermen, won office by appealing to ethnic voters, collected payoffs from brothels, gambling dens, and thieves in return for running a wide-open city. In the wake of the great San Francisco earthquake and fire of 1906, Ruef set up a system by which those who wished to profit from the rebuilding had to clear their plans with him. Scarcely a street could be paved or a cable car line laid out until money changed hands. On one occasion, Ruef pocketed $250,000, of which he kept one-quarter, gave one-quarter to Schmitz, and distributed the remainder among the aldermen whose votes were needed to authorize public works. Like other city bosses, Ruef bought and sold judges in lawsuits.

But Johnson discovered that Ruef not only was associated with vice and petty graft, but was intimately allied with the most powerful corporation in the state, the Southern Pacific Railroad. The distinguished and ostensibly upright directors of the Southern Pacific, men whom Johnson admired, were tangled in a web that stretched to include profiting from the misfortune of the wretched syphilitic whores on the city's notorious Barbary Coast.

Never easygoing, Johnson was transformed into "a volcano in perpetual eruption, belching fire and smoke." In 1910, he won the governorship on the slogan, "Kick the Southern Pacific out of politics." Never again would he assume that great wealth and a varnish of propriety indicated a decent man. Indeed, his sense of personal rectitude was so great that it cost him a chance to be president. In 1920, Republican party bosses such as Johnson loathed asked him to run as vice-presidential candidate in order to balance the conservative presidential nominee, Warren G. Harding. Johnson turned them down in a huff. As a result, when Harding died in office in 1923, he was succeeded by the conservative Calvin Coolidge instead of the volcano from California.

THE FRINGE

Most progressives advocated municipal ownership of public utilities, but they were staunchly antisocialist. Indeed, progressive politicians like La Follette and Johnson warned that the reforms they proposed were necessary to preserve the institution of private property from a rising red tide in American politics.

This message had a special urgency in the early years of the twentieth century because the Socialist party of America, first fielding a presidential nominee in 1900, came very close to establishing itself as a major force in American politics. Pieced together by local Socialist organizations and frustrated former Populists, the Socialist party nominated the leader of the great Pullman strike, Eugene V. Debs, for president in 1900, and he won 94,768 votes. In 1904, running again, Debs threw a scare into progressives and conservatives alike by polling 402,460 votes. All told, he would run for president five times.

Debs and Berger

In many ways, Debs resembled a progressive politician. He was a fiery, flamboyant orator, a master of the theatrical and gymnastic style of public speaking that not only was necessary in an age when sound amplification was primitive, but was favored by Americans in their preachers and politicians. He was more a moralist than either an intellectual or a politician. Debs freely admitted that he had little patience with the endless ideological hairsplitting of which other Socialists, especially those with European ties, were fond. Personally, he was most at home in the company of ordinary working people; he shared their prejudices and foibles, as well as their lack of pretension. Unsurprisingly, Debs's followers worshiped him as progressives worshiped La Follette, Borah, and Roosevelt.

But Debs's resemblances to the progressives must not be overdrawn. He did not seek to smooth over the conflict between classes; he meant it when he exhorted working people to take charge. If he was not an ideologue, he agreed with the Marxists that the class that produced wealth should decide how that wealth was to be distributed.

Full of hope in 1908, the Socialist party chartered its own train, the "Red Special," to carry Eugene V. Debs on his presidential campaign.

Victor Berger of Milwaukee more clearly linked socialism and progressivism. An Austrian immigrant, middle-class in background, Berger forged an alliance among Milwaukee's large German-speaking population, the labor movement in that city, and the city's reform-minded middle class. His Social Democratic party (a part of Debs's Socialist party) soft-pedaled revolutionary rhetoric and promised Milwaukee honest government and efficient city-owned public utilities. Once, while he and Debs were being interviewed by a journalist, Debs said that capitalists would not be compensated when their factories were taken from them; their property was stolen from working people, and theft would not be rewarded. Berger interrupted before the interviewer finished writing: no, capitalists would be compensated for their losses. Property might well be theft; but Berger would not alienate his middle-class supporters with loose talk about confiscating it.

To radical members of the party, Berger's "sewer socialism," a reference to his emphasis on city ownership of utilities, was nothing more than progressivism. Berger thought otherwise. He insisted that by demonstrating to the American people the Socialists' ability to govern a large city, the Socialist party would win their attention to the revolutionary part of its program. In 1910, he got what seemed his chance to do just that. Berger was elected to the House of Representatives and Socialist candidates for mayor and city council were swept into power in Milwaukee.

Labor's Quest for Respectability

Berger also hoped to advance the fortunes of socialism by capturing the American Federation of Labor. Socialists were a large minority in the union movement, actually a majority among members who were not Roman Catholic. At the AFL's annual conventions, the Socialists challenged the conservative leadership of Samuel Gompers and several times came close to ousting him from the presidency.

In the end they failed. Presenting a moderate face to the American people was central to Gompers's strategy for establishing the legitimacy of the labor movement, and his version of moderation included support of progressive capitalism. His glad willingness to cooperate with employers won him many friends among progressives (and some conservatives such as Mark Hanna). In 1902, President Theodore Roosevelt intervened in the coal miners' strike. During the William Howard Taft administration (1909–1913), progressives established a Commission on Industrial Violence with a membership that was skewed in a prounion direction. Progressive Democratic President Woodrow Wilson named Samuel Gompers to several prestigious government posts and appointed a former leader of the AFL's United Mine Workers, William B. Wilson, to be secretary of labor.

The union movement grew in the favorable climate of the Progressive Era. Membership in the AFL rose from about 500,000 in 1900 to 1.5 million in 1910, with some 500,000 workers holding cards in independent organizations. However, this was a pittance among a nonagricultural labor force of almost 20 million.

The "Wobblies"

The most important unions outside the AFL were the cautious and conservative Railway Brotherhoods (of Locomotive Engineers, Firemen, Brakemen, etc.)

and the radical Industrial Workers of the World, or, as members were called, "Wobblies." Founded in 1905 by Socialists and other radicals who were disgusted by Gompers's conservatism and his reluctance to organize unskilled workers, the IWW also found friends among progressives, but more often, sent chills racing down their spines.

Progressives supported West Coast and wheat-belt Wobblies when, between 1909 and 1913, the hobo members of the union waged a series of free speech fights to protect their right to recruit members by speaking from streetcorner soapboxes. Progressive sensitivity to traditions of personal liberty and common decency was agitated when policemen assigned to destroy the union arrested Wobblies for reading publicly from the Declaration of Independence and the Constitution. In 1912, progressive organizations, particularly women's clubs, helped the IWW win its greatest strike victory among immigrant textile mill workers in Lawrence, Massachusetts. They publicized the horrendous living conditions in Lawrence, lobbied congressmen, and took the children of strikers into their homes, a masterful public-relations ploy.

The capacity of middle-class progressives to back the Wobblies could not, however, go much beyond well-wishing. The Wobblies called loudly and gaily for revolution, precisely what progressives were determined to avoid. Although the IWW officially renounced violence, including violent sabotage, individual members spoke of driving spikes into logs bound for sawmills and throwing hammers into the

---

Votes for Women? A Woman Socialist Says: Not Important

You ask for votes for women. What good can votes do when ten-elevenths of the land in Great Britain belongs to 200,000 and only one-eleventh to the rest of the 40,000,000 population? Have your men with their millions of votes freed themselves from this injustice?

Helen Keller to a British suffragist, 1911

---

works of harvesters, threshers, and balers. And, although the first blow was more often thrown by employers than workers, fistfights, riots, and even murder characterized enough Wobbly strikes to besmirch the union's reputation.

Nor were middle-class progressives alone in considering the IWW beyond the pale. No one used fiercer language in denouncing the organization than Samuel Gompers. In 1913, Victor Berger and a prominent New York Socialist, Morris Hillquit, led a movement within the Socialist party that successfully expelled the leader of the IWW, William D. "Big Bill" Haywood, from the party's National Executive Committee.

Feminism and Progressivism

Another "ism" with an ambivalent relationship to the progressive movement was feminism. In 1900, the struggle on behalf of equal rights for women was more than 50 years old. Despite the tireless work of long-lived leaders like Elizabeth Cady Stanton and Susan B. Anthony, the victories were few. In their twilight years at the beginning of the Progressive Era, Stanton and Anthony could look back on liberalized divorce laws, women voters in six western states, a movement unified for the moment in the National American Woman Suffrage Association, and the initiation of a new generation of leaders including Carrie Chapman Catt and Anna Howard Shaw, a British-born physician.

But the coveted prize, a constitutional amendment that would guarantee women the right to vote, seemed as remote as it had at Seneca Falls in 1848. Most articulate Americans, women as well as men, continued to believe that women's delicacy and fine

---

Wobblies

Members of the IWW were called Wobblies by both friends and enemies. There are several explanations of the origin of their name; according to one, they were so strike prone that they were "wobbly" workers. The story the IWW favored told of a Chinese restaurant operator in the Pacific Northwest who would give credit only to Wobblies because they could be depended on. When someone asked for a meal on credit, the restaurant owner, unable to pronounce the name of the letter *W*, asked "I-Wobbly-Wobbly?"

Under Carrie Chapman Catt, woman suffragists emphasized their respectability.

moral sense made it best that they remain in a separate sphere from men. If women participated in public life, they would be sullied as men were and lose their vital moral influence in the home.

In fact, when Anthony died in 1906, success was fewer than 15 years away. The democratic inclinations of the progressives made it increasingly difficult for them to deny the franchise to half the American people. Even progressive leaders who had little personal enthusiasm for the idea of female voters publicly supported the cause.

Changing Strategies

Much more important in accounting for the victory of the suffrage movement was a fundamental shift in its appeal. Under the leadership of Carrie Chapman Catt, the National American Woman Suffrage Association came to terms with progressive prejudices and quietly shelved the comprehensive critique of women's status in American society that the early feminists developed, including doubts about the institution of marriage. The suffragists also downplayed the traditional argument that women should have the right to vote because they were equal to men in every way.

A few "social feminists" clung to the old principles. Charlotte Perkins Gilman, an independently minded New Englander, argued in *Women and Economics* (1898) that marriage was itself the cause of women's inequality. Alice Paul, a Quaker like many feminists before her, insisted that the suffrage alone was not enough to solve "the woman question."

But most of the middle-class suffragists argued that women should have the right to vote precisely because they were more moral than men. Their votes would purge society of its evils. Not only did the suffragists ingeniously turn the most compelling anti-suffrage argument in their favor—the belief that women were the morally superior sex—but they told progressives that in allowing women to vote they would be gaining huge numbers of allies. In fact, women were in the forefront of two of the era's most important moral crusades, the struggle against prostitution and the prohibition movement.

White Slavery

To earlier generations, prostitution was an ancient evil that could be controlled, punished, or ignored by decent people, but not abolished. Most states, counties, and cities had laws against solicitation on the grounds that streetwalking "hookers" were a public nuisance. Somewhat fewer governments declared the quiet sale of sex to be a crime. Even where prostitution was nominally illegal, it was common to tolerate "houses of ill repute" that were discreetly operated (and usually made contributions to worthy causes such as the welfare of the police).

Communities in which men vastly outnumbered women — cow towns, mining camps, seaports, migrant farm-worker and logging centers — typically tolerated red-light districts in some corner of town. A stock figure of small-town folklore was the woman on the wrong side of the tracks who sold favors to those sly or bold enough to knock on her door.

In the large cities, prostitution ran the gamut from lushly furnished and expensive brothels for high-society swells, such as Sally Stanford's in San Francisco, to "the cribs," tiny cubicles rented by whores who catered to workingmen. Because their pay was so low, thousands of New York working women moonlighted as prostitutes at least part of the time. Novelists Stephen Crane (*Maggie: A Girl of the Streets*, 1892) and Upton Sinclair (*The Jungle*) both dealt with the theme of tacitly forced prostitution.

The world's oldest profession had affronted proper people long before the Progressive Era. In most places, the middle class was content to declare the trade illegal and then tolerate it out of their sight. Some cities restricted prostitution to neighborhoods far from middle-class residential areas, such as New Orleans's Storyville, San Francisco's Barbary Coast, and Chicago's South of the Loop.

The progressives, spearheaded by women's organizations, determined to wipe out the institution. During the first decade of the twentieth century, most states and innumerable communities passed strict laws against all prostitution and enforced them rigorously. In 1917, prodded by the navy when it established a big training camp nearby, even wide-open Storyville, the birthplace of jazz, was officially closed. By 1920, all but a few states had antiprostitution laws on the books. Within a few more years, only Nevada, with its stubborn mining frontier outlook, continued to tolerate the institution.

> ### *Votes for Women? T. R. Says: It Does Not Matter*
>
> *Personally, I believe in woman's suffrage, but I am not an enthusiastic advocate of it, because I do not regard it as a very important matter. I am unable to see that there has been any special improvement in the position of women in those states in the West that have adopted woman's suffrage, as compared to those states adjoining them that have not adopted it. I do not think that giving the women suffrage will produce any marked improvement in the condition of women. I do not believe that it will produce any of the evils feared, and I am very certain that when women as a whole take any special interest in the matter they will have suffrage if they desire it.*

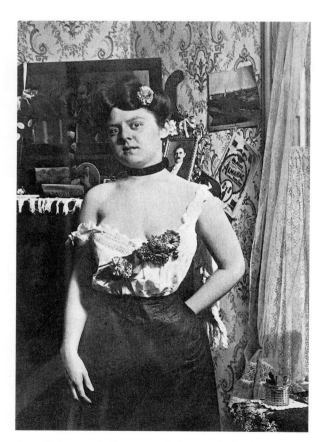

A prostitute poses for the camera. Ending prostitution became a goal of the progressives and members of the women's movement in the early 1900s.

The Limits of Progressive Moralism

Action on the federal level was more complicated. Prostitution was clearly a matter for the police powers of the states and localities. However, progressives were so convinced that government held the key to social reform and must act at every level that, in 1910, they joined with some conservatives to put the interstate commerce clause of the Constitution to work in the cause. Senator James R. Mann of Illinois sponsored a bill that struck against the probably exaggerated practice of procurers luring poor girls from one part of the country to become prostitutes elsewhere. The Mann Act forbade transporting women across state lines "for immoral purposes." It was this law under which the boxer Jack Johnson was prosecuted.

Of course, neither local, state, nor federal law abolished prostitution. The campaign may be the best example of the progressives' excessive faith in the powers of the government. Brothels continued to operate, albeit less openly and probably with more police graft than before. Streetwalkers, previously the most despised and degraded of whores, became the norm because they were less easily arrested. Wealthy men continued to maintain paid mistresses and created the "call girl," a prostitute who stayed at home until called by a hotel employee or pimp who worked the streets and hotel lobbies.

Prohibitionism

The nineteenth-century impulse to combat the evils of drink never quite died. Temperance advocates and outright prohibitionists battled back and forth with the distillers of liquor and with ordinary people who simply enjoyed a cup of good cheer. By 1900, however, antialcohol crusaders were emphasizing social arguments over their moral distaste for drunkenness and, in so doing, won widespread progressive support.

The prohibitionists pointed out that the city saloon was often the local headquarters of the corrupt political machines. Close the saloons, the reasoning went, and the bosses would be crippled. Moreover, generally overlooking the fact that poverty caused a widespread drinking problem among the working classes, the prohibitionists argued that the misery of the working classes was the result of husbands and fathers spending their wages on demon rum and John Barleycorn. Because the public bar was then an all-male institution, the temperance movement formed a close alliance with feminists.

Carrie Nation of Kansas was one woman who suffered her whole life with a drunken husband and poverty. Beginning in 1900, she launched a campaign of direct action, leading hatchet-wielding women into saloons where, before the bewildered eyes of saloonkeepers and customers, they methodically chopped the places to pieces.

Frances Willard, head of the Woman's Christian Temperance Union, opposed such tactics. She and her followers also entered saloons, but instead of breaking them up, they attempted to shame drinkers by kneeling to pray quietly in their midst. In addition, the WCTU turned to politics, supporting woman suffrage for its own sake as well as for the purpose of winning the final victory over liquor.

Increasing numbers of progressives adopted the reform. Only in the big cities, mostly in the eastern states, did socially minded politicians like Alfred E. Smith and Robert Wagner of New York actively fight the prohibitionists. The large Roman Catholic and Jewish populations of the cities had no religious tradition against alcohol; on the contrary, they used wine as a part of religious observance. Elsewhere, libertarian progressives argued that the government had no right to interfere with the individual decision of whether or not to drink.

Nevertheless, the possibilities of moral improvement, of striking a blow against poverty, and of joining battle against the political manipulations of the big distillers and brewers converted many progressives to prohibition, and in the waning days of the movement (though they were not thought to be waning at the time), they had their way.

CHRONOLOGY

1890	Hazen S. Pingree, early city reformer, elected mayor of Detroit
1897	Thomas M. Johnson elected mayor of Cleveland
1898	Publication of Charlotte Perkins Gilman's *Women and Economics*
1900	Robert M. La Follette elected governor of Wisconsin Eugene V. Debs's first of five presidential campaigns as Socialist party candidate (also 1904, 1908, 1912, and 1920)

Carry Nation begins campaign of direct action against saloons

1902 Oregon adopts initiative, referendum, and recall

1903 Lincoln Steffens's "Shame of the Cities" published in *McClure's*

1905 Founding of Industrial Workers of the World

1906 Publication of Upton Sinclair's *The Jungle*

1909 Herbert Croly's *Promise of American Life* published

1910 National Association for the Advancement of Colored People formed
Hiram Johnson elected governor of California
Milwaukee elects socialist Victor Berger to Congress

1913 Constitutional amendments authorize graduated income tax and direct election of senators.

FOR FURTHER READING

Once again, see Vincent P. DeSantis, *The Shaping of Modern America, 1877–1916*, 1973, and Robert H. Wiebe, *The Search for Order, 1880–1920*, 1967, for context. William L. O'Neill, *The Progressive Years: America Comes of Age*, 1975, is perhaps the most readable survey. However, the following general interpretations are also quite valuable: Arthur Ekirch, *Progressivism in Practice*, 1974; Lewis L. Gould, *Reform and Regulation: American Politics, 1900–1916*, 1978; Otis L. Graham, Jr., *The Great Campaigns: Reform and War in America, 1900–1928*, 1971; the appropriate chapters of Richard Hofstadter, *The Age of Reform*, 1955; Gabriel Kolko, *The Triumph of Conservatism*, 1963; Christopher Lasch, *The New Radicalism in America*, 1965; and John Milton Cooper, *Pivotal Decades: The United States, 1900–1920*, 1990.

More narrowly focused books with excellent insights about progressives are John D. Buenker, *Urban Liberalism and Progressive Reform*, 1973; D. M. Chalmers, *The Social and Political Ideas of the Muckrakers*, 1964; Carl M. Degler, *At Odds: Women in the Family in America from the Revolution to the Present*, 1980; Robert M. Crunden, *Ministers of Reform: The Progressives' Achievement in American Civilization*, 1982; Samuel T. Hays, *Conservation and the Gospel of Efficiency: The Progressive Conservation Movement*, 1890–1920, 1959; Joel Williamson, *A Rage for Order: Black/White Relations in the Urban South Since Emancipation*, 1986; David Levering Lewis, *W. E. B. DuBois: Biography of a Race*, 1993; George E. Mowry, *The California Progressives*, 1951; William L. O'Neill, *Everyone Was Brave: The Rise and Fall of Feminism*, 1969; Nancy F. Cott, *The Grounding of Modern Feminism*, 1987; J. T. Patterson, *America's Struggle against Poverty*, 1981; Jean Quandt, *From the Small Town to the Great Community: The Social Thought of Progressive Intellectuals*, 1970; James H. Timberlake, *Prohibition and the Progressive Movement, 1900–1920*, 1963; and James Weinstein, *The Corporate Ideal in the Liberal State, 1900–1918*, 1968. For the far edges of reform, see Mari Jo Buhle, *Women and American Socialism, 1870–1920*, 1982.

Important biographical studies include John M. Blum, *The Republican Roosevelt*, 1954; David McCullough, *Mornings on Horseback*, 1981; W. H. Harbaugh, *Power and Responsibility: The Life and Times of Theodore Roosevelt*, 1931; David P. Thelen, *Robert M. La Follette and the Insurgent Movement*, 1976; Nick Salvatore, *Eugene V. Debs*, 1982; and David M. Kennedy, *Birth Control in America: The Career of Margaret Sanger*, 1970.

Feminists deliver a message to diplomats from the short-lived liberal democratic government of Russia, 1917.

36
CHAPTER

VICTORS AT ARMAGEDDON

The Progressives in Power

1901–1916

America was established not to create wealth but to realize a vision, to realize an ideal — to discover and maintain liberty among men.

— *Woodrow Wilson*

Every man holds his property subject to the general right of the community to regulate its use to whatever degree the public welfare may require it.

— *Theodore Roosevelt*

Big business is not dangerous because it is big, but because its bigness is an unwholesome inflation created by privileges and exemptions which it ought not to enjoy.

— *Woodrow Wilson*

We demand that big business give the people a square deal; in return we must insist that when anyone engaged in big business endeavors to do right he shall himself be given a square deal.

— *Theodore Roosevelt*

704 *Chapter 36 Victors at Armageddon*

By 1904, the progressive movement commanded the allegiance of a large bloc of senators and congressmen from both major parties, and the president himself, Theodore Roosevelt. The irony that he, the scion of an old, rich, and privileged family should be the titular leader of a popular protest movement was not lost on T. R. In a letter to the decidedly unprogressive Senator Chauncey Depew of New York, who was also chairman of the board of directors of the New York Central Railroad, Roosevelt wrote in mock weariness: "How I wish I wasn't a reformer, Oh Senator! But I suppose I must live up to my part, like the Negro minstrel who blackened himself all over!"

Was T. R. also mocking the progressives, and his own sincerity? Perhaps in part. But then, it was not so bizarre that T. R. was willing to use his powers as president to chastise and discipline those powerful industrial capitalists whom he considered to be "malefactors of great wealth." His family's fortune and status were preindustrial; he was a member of an old American elite that sometimes felt shunted aside by the *nouveaux riches* of the late nineteenth century. Mrs. Astor reacted to the slight by creating "The Four Hundred," a list of *anciens riches* who were socially acceptable. Theodore Roosevelt reacted by going into politics and refusing to play the mouthpiece for the new elite.

Moreover, despite the sigh of resignation to duty in the letter to Depew, Roosevelt loved to be in the thick of things. During his nearly eight years in the White House, reform was where the action was.

T. R. TAKES OVER

At first, Roosevelt moved cautiously. He was well aware of the fact that the bosses of the Republican party distrusted him as a "damned cowboy." Mark Hanna openly discussed his interest in the 1904 Republican presidential nomination with party leaders like Tom Platt of New York and Matthew Quay of Pennsylvania, as if T. R. were a Democrat. And the Republican machine was beholden to the likes of them, who had created it, and not to the young and accidental president.

But no one was to contest T. R.'s claim on party leadership in 1904. Mark Hanna died suddenly in February of that year, Matt Quay a short time later. Even had they lived and been hale and hearty, they would have had to tip their hats to the cowboy. In a

little more than two years, Roosevelt built up an immense personal following, quietly replacing members of the old guard machine in government positions with his own men. Ever graceful in his maneuvers, he eased the McKinley-Hanna men who were mediocrities out of his cabinet, and won the loyalty of those he kept by giving them an authority and autonomy that they did not enjoy under McKinley.

Among the McKinley appointees he kept in office were Secretary of State John Hay; Secretary of War Elihu Root (who succeeded Hay in the State Department in 1905); Attorney General Philander C. Knox; Secretary of the Interior E. A. Hitchcock; and Secretary of Agriculture James Wilson. All were able.

Busting Taboos and Trusts

Roosevelt had no fear of ability in his subordinates. He was happy and able to delegate responsibility because there was no doubt in his or in the public's mind as to who was in charge. Thus, in April 1902, he directed Attorney General Knox, a former corporation lawyer, to have a go at the most powerful corporate organizers in the United States. His target, the Northern Securities Company, was designed by J. P. Morgan and railroaders Edward H. Harriman and James J. Hill to end struggles for control of the railroads in the northern quarter of the country. Funded by the nation's two richest banks, Northern Securities was a holding company patterned after Morgan's United States Steel Corporation.

Morgan was shocked by Roosevelt's prosecution. Under McKinley, the Sherman Antitrust Act languished, almost unused. In a pained and revealing moment, the great financier wrote to Roosevelt, "If we have done anything wrong, send your man to my man and we can fix it up." The message was not apt to appeal to the president, who read it as an invitation to sit in Morgan's waiting room.

Roosevelt blithely ignored the invitation and Knox pushed on in the courts. In 1904, they won; the Supreme Court ordered the Northern Securities Company to dissolve, and progressives cheered. When Roosevelt instituted other antitrust suits, 40 in all, of which he won 25, progressives nicknamed him the "trust-buster."

It was an overstatement. Roosevelt did not believe that bigness in business was itself an evil, and he continued to socialize among the millionaires with whom Knox was contending in the courts. Indeed, in 1907 he allowed Morgan's United States

A cartoonist makes the point that Theodore Roosevelt was not hostile to all big businesses.

Steel Company to gobble up a major regional competitor, Tennessee Coal and Iron, without public statement.

The trust-buster's criteria for determining what made one business combination good and another bad were vague. In a way, his antitrust suits were drama and symbol. Roosevelt wanted to show big business and the American people that he and the United States government were in charge. In the Tennessee Coal and Iron case, J. P. Morgan had to send his man, hat in hand, to see T. R.'s man, and not vice versa.

The Workingman's Friend

Quite as startling as trust-busting was Roosevelt's personal intervention in the autumn of 1902 in a strike by 140,000 anthracite miners. The men's demands were moderate. They wanted a 20 percent increase in pay—not so excessive, given the abysmally low wages the miners were then paid—an eight-hour day, and their employers' agreement to recognize and negotiate with their union, the United Mine Workers. The mine owners refused to yield on a single point. Theirs was a competitive, unstable business. With so many companies engaged in mining coal, the price of the commodity fluctuated radically and unpredictably. Coal mine operators traditionally avoided long-term commitments to anyone—buyers, shippers, or employees.

Most of the operators were entrepreneurs of the old hard-nosed school, easy for muckraking reporters to caricature, which they did. Their property was their property and that was that; they would brook no interference in their use of it, least of all by grimy employees. George F. Baer, the ringleader of the operators and more pious than prudent, stirred up a furious public reaction when he told a journalist that he would never deal with the UMW because God had entrusted him with his company's mines.

By way of contrast, union leader John Mitchell was depicted in the progressive press as a moderate, modest, and likable man. T. R., keenly sensitive to public opinion, knew where the applause was to be had. Moreover, Mitchell was a conservative union leader, constantly engaged in a battle with socialists in the UMW. Roosevelt was inclined to help him win his factional battle by giving him a boost in his fight with the operators. In October, the president let it be known that if the strike dragged on through the winter with no settlement, he might use federal troops to dispossess the owners and open the mines. Knowing the Rough Rider was capable of so drastic and dangerous an act, the ubiquitous Morgan stepped in and pressured the mine owners to go to Washington to work out a settlement.

The result was a compromise that rather favored the owners. The miners got a 10 percent raise and a nine-hour day; the operators were not required to recognize the UMW as the agent of the workers. (Baer and the others refused even to meet face to face with Mitchell.) Nonetheless, the miners were elated. So were people who counted on coal to ward off winter's cold. But the big winner, as in most of his chosen battles, was Theodore Roosevelt. He had reversed the tradition of using federal troops to help employers break strikes and forced powerful industrialists to bow to his will on behalf of a "square deal" for workingmen.

Teddy's Great Victory

By 1904, T. R. was basking in the sun of a nation's adulation. He was unanimously nominated and presented with a large campaign chest. The Democrats,

Coal for heating and cooking was so scarce during the spring of 1902 that poor people fished it from waters near the docks where coal barges were moored.

hoping to capitalize on the grumbling of some conservatives over the president's actions and remarks about arrogant businessmen, did a complete about-face from the party's agrarianism of 1896 and 1900. They nominated a Wall Street lawyer and judge with impeccable social credentials but also a record of sympathy for labor, Alton B. Parker, to oppose him. The urbane but colorless Parker was the antithesis of Boy Bryan and, Democratic bosses hoped, a foil to the histrionic Roosevelt.

Even the second most colorful politician in the country would have looked like a cardboard cutout next to T. R. Not even Parker's Wall Street friends voted for him. If they disliked T. R.'s antitrust adventures, they recognized that Roosevelt hewed to a conservative line when he advocated an anti-inflationary money policy and a high tariff, both of which were of more importance to big business than courtroom spats. J. P. Morgan, so recently stung in the Northern Securities case, donated $150,000 to Roosevelt's campaign.

The president won a lopsided 57.4 percent of the vote, more than any candidate since popular totals were recorded. His 336–140 electoral sweep was the largest since Grant's in 1872, and he did it without the help of the southern states. Building on the coalition of money and respectability that was put together by McKinley and Hanna in 1896, T. R. enlarged the Republican majority by appealing to progressives.

THE PRESIDENT AS REFORMER

The only sour note for the Republicans in a giddy election week was the remarkable showing of the Socialist party candidate, Eugene V. Debs. His 400,000 votes amounted to only 3 percent of the total, but represented an astonishing fourfold increase over his vote in 1900. Roosevelt did not like it either. Increasingly after 1904, he seized every opportunity—and created more than a few—to denounce anticapitalist radicals.

Perhaps his most gratuitous attack followed the arrest and (illegal) extradition late in 1905 of Charles Moyer and Big Bill Haywood, the leaders of the militant Western Federation of Miners. Charged with murder in Idaho, the two radicals were, in effect, kidnapped by authorities in Denver, Colorado. Roosevelt shrugged off the irregularity of the arrest because the two were "undesirable citizens." Moyer and Haywood's lawyer, Clarence Darrow, justifiably complained that with the president of the United States making such statements, a fair trial was not likely. (Nevertheless, both men were acquitted.)

At the same time he assailed the socialists, Roosevelt set out to co-opt them by unleashing a whirlwind of reform. He was determined to eliminate the abuses that gave the Socialists their easiest targets.

The Railroads Derailed

As they had been for 30 years, the railroads remained a focus of popular resentment. The freewheeling arrogance of their directors and the vital role of transportation in the national economy preoccupied progressives at every level of government. Prodded by regional leaders, most notably Senator Robert La Follette, Roosevelt plunged into a long, bitter struggle with the railroad companies. In 1906, he won passage of the Hepburn Act. This law authorized the Interstate Commerce Commission to set maximum rates that railroads might charge their customers, and forbade them to pay rebates to big shippers. This prohibition had been enacted before but had not been effectively enforced; the Hepburn Act gave the ICC some teeth. More than any of T. R.'s previous actions, it blasted the railroaders' traditional immunity from government interference.

Also in 1906, Congress passed an act that held railroads liable to employees who suffered injuries on the job. By European standards, it was a mild compensation law, but in the United States, it marked a sharp break with precedent, which held employees responsible for most of their injuries.

Purer Food

Affecting more people was the Pure Food and Drug Act and the Meat Inspection Act, both signed in 1906, that eliminated adulteration of foods (by large processors), enforced stringent sanitary standards on them, and put the lid on the patent medicine business, which marketed dangerous and addictive drugs as "feel-good" nostrums.

By requiring food processors to label their products with all ingredients used in making them, and providing hefty penalties for violators, the Pure Food and Drug Act eliminated sometimes toxic and often worthless preservatives and fillers from canned,

bottled, and sacked foodstuffs. The Meat Inspection Act provided for federal inspection of meatpacking plants to eliminate the abuses that Upton Sinclair detailed so gruesomely in *The Jungle*.

Big meatpackers like Armour, Swift, Wilson, and Cudahy grumbled about the federal inspectors, notebooks in hand, puttering about their abattoirs. But, in time, they learned that meat inspection worked in their favor and to the detriment of smaller regional slaughterhouses. That is, with their greater resources, the big meatpackers were able to comply with the federal standards. By way of contrast, smaller companies, able to stay in business only by slashing costs at every turn, found the expense of sanitation in an inherently gory business to be beyond their means.

The big packers actually made advertising hay of the inspection stamps on their products: the government approved of them! Small companies closed their doors or restricted their sales to the states in which they were located. (Like all national reforms, federal meat inspection applied only to firms involved in interstate commerce.) Some progressives were not pleased to be helping big business against small, but T. R. was not one of them. It was not bigness itself to which he objected, but irresponsibility in business.

War on Drugs

Proportionately, there may have been more drug addicts in the United States at the turn of the century than in the year 2000. Some were frankly hooked on

---

American Essence

Coca-Cola, which William Allen White called "the sublimated essence of all that America stands for," had its beginning as a kind of health food. An Atlanta druggist concocted it in 1886 as an alternative to alcohol. Within a year, a pious Methodist named Asa G. Candler purchased all rights to "Coke" for $2,300 and sold it as a "brain tonic," promoting its kick. Indeed, until 1902, Coke was made with coca leaves and may have been addictive; southerners called it "dope." Candler's advertising was certainly addictive. By 1908, the Coca-Cola Company had plastered 2.5 million square feet of billboard and walls with posters. By 1911, more than a million dollars a year was spent on promoting the elixir.

opium or morphine and had had minimal difficulty meeting their needs at unregulated pharmacies. Others—as many as 300,000 people—were addicted to various patent medicines advertising themselves as cure-alls. Concoctions with names such as Vin Mariani and Mrs. Winslow's Soothing Syrup were laced with cocaine. Even Lydia Pinkham's Vegetable Compound, decorously packaged and aimed in fine print at ladies suffering from "female complaints" was a rather strong alcoholic elixir laced liberally with opiates.

The Pure Food and Drug Act of 1906, which restricted the use of cocaine, cannabis, opiates, and alcohol in over-the-counter medicines, and required labeling of ingredients, undercut this dubious business. Soft drink companies were also affected, for some, including the gigantic Coca-Cola Company of Atlanta, used a by-product of cocaine processing in their beverages to give it a "kick." Coca-Cola actually introduced caffeine as its stimulant as early as 1902 but, with the passage of federal drug legislation in 1906, was able like the big meatpackers to advertise its "purity."

Natural Resources in Jeopardy

Theodore Roosevelt and his progressive allies were not always farseeing. Many of their enactments were the fruit of passionate impulse or of playing to the whims of their constituents. In their campaign to conserve natural resources, however, they looked to the distant future and created monuments for which they are rightfully honored.

As a lifelong outdoorsman, T. R. loved camping, riding, hiking, climbing, and hunting. As a historian, he was more sensitive than most of his contemporaries to the role of the wilderness in forging the American character. He actively sought and won the friendship of John Muir, the adopted Californian and Alaskan who founded the Sierra Club in 1892. Muir's interest in nature was aesthetic, cultural, and spiritual. He wanted to protect from development such magnificent areas of untouched wilderness as Yosemite Valley, which he helped to establish as a national park in 1890. Roosevelt shared these sentiments.

The motives of progressive conservationists such as T. R.'s tennis partner and America's first trained forester, Gifford Pinchot of Pennsylvania, were somewhat different. While by no means oblivious to the cultural and aesthetic values of wilderness, Pinchot's major concern was protecting forests and other natural resources from rapacious exploiters interested only in short-term profits. He wanted to ensure that future generations of Americans would have their share of nonrenewable natural resources such as minerals, coal, and oil to draw on, and the continued enjoyment of renewable resources like forests, grasslands, and water for drinking and generating power. In December 1907, T. R. told Congress:

> To waste, to destroy, our natural resources, to skin and exhaust the land instead of using it so as to increase its usefulness, will result in undermining in the days of our children the very prosperity which we ought by right to hand down to them amplified and developed.

Roosevelt had good reason to worry about the nation's natural resources. Lumbermen in the Great Lakes states had already mowed down once endless forests, moved on, and left the land behind them to useless scrub and shoddy. Western ranchers put too many cattle on delicate grasslands, turning them into deserts. Coal and phosphate mining companies and drillers for oil thought in terms of open account books and never of the fact that, in a century, the United States might run out of these vital resources. Virtually no one in extractive industries worried that they were destroying watersheds vital to urban water supplies, polluting rivers, and sending good soil into the sea.

Americans had always been reckless with the land, none more so than the pioneers. But there was a big difference between what a few frontiersmen could do to it with axes and horse-drawn plows and the potential for destruction of irresponsible million-dollar corporations.

Conservation

The National Forest Reserve, today's national forest system, dates from 1891, when Congress empowered the president to withhold forests in the public domain from private use. Over the first ten years of the law, Presidents Harrison, Cleveland, and McKinley declared 46 million acres of virgin woodland off limits to loggers without government permission.

Enforcement was desultory until, prodded by Pinchot, Roosevelt began to prosecute timber pirates who raided public lands and cattlemen who abused government-owned grasslands. Within a few years, Roosevelt added 125 million acres to the national forests, as well as reserving 68 million acres of coal deposits, almost 5 million acres of phosphate beds (vital to production of munitions), a number of oil

> ### Progressive Legacy
>
> The halt that the progressives called to the unmonitored, unregulated exploitation of natural resources has borne fruits of unmistakable measure. In terms of wildlife population, for example, in 1900, Virginia or white-tailed deer numbered about 500,000, in 1992 18.5 million; about 650,000 wild turkeys survived whilst in 1992 there were 4 million. In 1907, the government counted some 41,000 elk or wapiti in the United States; in 1992 there were 772,000.

fields, and 2,565 sites suitable for the construction of dams for irrigation and generation of electrical power.

Progressives cheered. Some of the multiple uses to which the national forests were dedicated—recreation and preservation—won the plaudits of groups like the Sierra Club. Others—flood control, irrigation, and development of hydroelectric power—pleased social planners. The principle of sustained yield, managing forests to ensure an adequate supply of lumber into the indefinite future, appealed to the big lumber companies with their huge capital investments, and encouraged them to employ foresters on their own lands.

In the West, however, an angry opposition developed. Cattlemen, clear-cut loggers, and private power companies banded together in an anticonservation movement that succeeded, in 1907, in attaching a rider to an agricultural appropriations bill that passed Congress. It forbade the president to create any additional national forests in six western states. Roosevelt had no choice but to sign the bill; the Department of Agriculture could not have functioned otherwise. But he had one last go at what he called the "predatory interests." Before he wrote his name on the bill, he reserved 17 million acres of forest land in the interdicted states.

Concern for the Farm

Theodore Roosevelt's conservation campaign remains one of the single most important contributions of his presidency. Nevertheless, his policies could hurt ordinary people as well as special interests. For example, he and Pinchot helped Los Angeles, the burgeoning metropolis of southern California, to grab the entire Owens River, 300 miles to the north, for its water supply. The president regarded the mammoth construction project, now known as the Los Angeles Aqueduct, as a showpiece of resource development and public control of electrical power. In the process, however, he helped to destroy the fertile Owens Valley. Then a land of prosperous, self-reliant small farmers, it would become by 1930 an arid region of sagebrush, dust storms, and tarantulas.

Had Roosevelt lived to see its results, he might well have regretted his action. He was a devotee of the family farm as one of the essential American institutions. He established the Country Life Commission, which lamented the steady disappearance of this way of life and submitted to Congress a number of recommendations designed to help family farmers. Conservative congressmen who soured on their progressive president refused even to publish the report.

The Reformer Retires

In two major speeches in 1908, Roosevelt called for a comprehensive, even radical, program that included federal investigation of major labor disputes and close regulation of both the stock market and businesses that were involved in interstate commerce. But Congress sidestepped virtually all of his

Theodore Roosevelt and Sierra Club founder John Muir in Yosemite National Park.

proposals because the "damned cowboy" had become a "lame duck." It was a presidential election year and, four years earlier, celebrating the great victory of 1904, T. R. impulsively declared that "a wise custom which limits the President to two terms regards the substance and not the form, and under no circumstances will I be a candidate for or accept another nomination." Having served three and a half years of McKinley's term, Roosevelt had defined himself as a two-term president.

In 1908, he almost certainly regretted his vow. Except perhaps for Ronald Reagan, Theodore Roosevelt extracted an effusive joy from his job as no other president has. Unlike Reagan, who treated the presidency as a personal homage, he was a worker and a marvelous success. He was not yet 50 years of age in 1908 and as popular as ever with the voters. He would undoubtedly have won reelection had he been willing to forget his pledge not to run.

But he kept his word and settled for handpicking his successor, which no president had been able to do since Andrew Jackson in 1836. That William Howard Taft, then secretary of war, was not the man whom either conservative or progressive Republicans would have chosen indicates just how high Roosevelt was riding.

A CONSERVATIVE PRESIDENT IN A PROGRESSIVE ERA

Taft never would have been nominated without Roosevelt's blessing. He would not have dreamed of running for president. Regularly in his correspondence he dashed off the exclamation "I hate politics!" and he meant it. He was a lifelong functionary, not a politician. His only elective post prior to 1908 was as a judge in Ohio. Taft remembered that job as the most congenial he ever held, for his temperament was judicial. Slow in thought, sober, cautious, reflective, dignified, Taft worked well in a study; he was no showman.

Amidst a people who savored Roosevelt's gymnastic style, Taft's very body militated against him. He weighed over 300 pounds in 1908, and was truly at ease only when he settled into a swivel chair behind a desk or sank into an overstuffed couch with other easygoing men. His single form of exercise, golf, did not help his image: batting a little white ball around an oversize lawn was considered a sissy's game in the early twentieth century; Taft's fondness for it identified him in many eyes with plutocrats like John D. Rockefeller (another golfer).

Taft was no reactionary. He had loyally supported Roosevelt's reforms, and T. R. calculated that he, more than anyone else, would carry out the Square Deal. So did other progressives. They supported him, as did the conservative wing of the Republican party. Anyone was preferable to the man whom they had begun to refer to privately as "the mad messiah."

The Election of 1908

The election was an anticlimax. The Democrats returned to William Jennings Bryan for their candidate, but the thrill was gone. The Boy Orator of the Platte, no longer young, was shopworn beyond his years. He had grown jowls and a paunch as penance for his lifelong vulnerability to the deadly sin of gluttony, and he was rapidly losing his hair.

Moreover, his loyal supporters, the staple farmers of the Midwest, were no longer struggling to survive. They were beginning to dress like the townsmen they jostled in 1896 and to build substantial homes. Even the issue of 1900, imperialism, was dead. Taft, who served as American governor of the Philippines, could claim credit for having transformed the anti-American Filipinos, whom he called his "little brown brothers," into a placid and apparently content colonial population. Puerto Rico was quieter. Hawaiians did the hula for increasing numbers of American tourists. Central America simmered but the specter of American power kept the lid on it. Thousands of men were digging their way across Panama under American direction, thrilling the nation.

The upshot was that a lethargic Bryan won a smaller percentage of the popular vote than in either of his previous tries. The Socialist party was also disappointed in the results. Bubbling with optimism at the start of the campaign, they chartered a private train, the "Red Special," on which candidate Debs crisscrossed the country. The crowds were big and enthusiastic. But Debs's vote was only 16,000 higher than in 1904 and represented a smaller percentage of the total. It appeared that Roosevelt's tactic of undercutting the socialist threat with a comprehensive reform program had worked.

Taft Blunders

Taft lacked both the political skills and the zeal to keep the campaign going. For example, even though he initiated 90 antitrust suits during his four years as

William Howard Taft on a Republican campaign banner in 1908.

states that supported Roosevelt returned to the Democratic column.

T. R. let Republican conservatives have their way on the tariff, placating (or distracting) progressives by pounding the tub on other reforms. By 1909, evasion was no longer possible, and Taft called Congress into special session for the purpose of tariff revision. The House of Representatives drafted a reasonable reduction of rates in the Payne Bill. In the Senate, however, Nelson Aldrich of Rhode Island, a trusty ally of industrial capitalists, engineered 800 amendments to what became the Payne-Aldrich Act. On most important commodities, the final rate was higher than under the Dingley Tariff.

Taft was in a bind. Politically, he was committed to lower rates. Personally, however, he was more comfortable with the aristocratic Aldrich and the five corporation lawyers in his cabinet than with low-tariff men in the Senate, who were Democrats or excitable Republican progressives like La Follette and Jonathan Dolliver of Iowa. After equivocating, Taft worked out what he thought was a compromise in the Roosevelt tradition. The conservatives got their high tariff but agreed to a 2 percent corporate income tax and a constitutional amendment that legalized a personal income tax. (It was ratified in 1913 as the Sixteenth Amendment.) Instead of emphasizing

president, twice as many as Roosevelt launched in seven and a half years, no one complimented him as a trust-buster. Taft managed to alienate the progressives immediately after taking office when he stumbled over an obstacle that T. R. quite nimbly evaded: the tariff.

In 1909, duties on foreign goods were high, set at an average 46.5 percent of the value of imports by the Dingley Tariff of 1897. Republican conservatives insisted that this rate was necessary in order to protect the jobs of American factory workers and to encourage industrial investment by capitalists. Some midwestern progressives disagreed. They believed that American industry was strong enough to stand up to European manufacturers in a fair competition. To maintain the Dingley rates was to subsidize excessive corporate profits by allowing manufacturers to set their prices inordinately high. Farmers were twice stung because the European nations, except Great Britain, retaliated against the Dingley Tariff by levying high duties on American agricultural products. In the election of 1908, several western

Church and State

Beginning in 1864, the motto "In God We Trust," derived from the "Star-Spangled Banner," was inscribed on most American coins. In 1907, thinking that this represented an unconstitutional entanglement of religion and government, Theodore Roosevelt ordered the motto removed. After a rare widespread public outcry against the popular president, Congress reversed his order and, in his final year in office, T. R. let the issue die.

In 1955, "In God We Trust" was added to American paper currency and, later, was declared the national motto. During the 1970s, a series of protests akin to Roosevelt's in 1907 took the issue to the Supreme Court. In 1983, Justice William Brennan, who usually took the broadest view in opposing the mixing of religion and government, approved the motto on the grounds that the words "have lost any true religious significance."

the progressive aspects of this arrangement, as T. R. surely would have done, Taft described the Payne-Aldrich Act as "the best tariff that the Republican party ever passed."

The Insurgents

This angered the midwestern Republican progressives, especially after Taft came out in favor of a trade treaty with Canada that threatened to dump Canadian crops on the American market. But they broke with the new president only when he sided with the reactionary speaker of the House of Representatives, Joseph G. Cannon of Illinois, against them.

"Uncle Joe" Cannon offended the progressive Republicans on several counts. He was so hidebound a conservative as to be a stereotype. As speaker of the House and chairman of the House Rules Committee, he put progressives on unimportant committees and loaded the meaningful ones with old guard friends. Finally, while the progressives inclined to be highly moralistic, even priggish in manner, Uncle Joe was a crusty tobacco chewer, a hard drinker who was not infrequently drunk, and a champion foulmouth.

The proper Taft also found Cannon's company unpleasant. However, the president believed in party loyalty, and when a number of midwestern Republican progressives, calling themselves Insurgents, voted with Democrats to strip Cannon of his near-dictatorial power, Taft joined with the speaker to deny the Insurgents access to party money and patronage in the midterm election of 1910. The result was a Democratic victory and Cannon was out of the speakership, never to return.

Pinchot Forces a Break

It is impossible to say how Theodore Roosevelt would have handled the quarrel between Cannon and the Insurgents. But he assuredly would not have done what Taft did in a dispute between Secretary of the Interior Richard A. Ballinger and Chief Forester Gifford Pinchot.

When Ballinger released to private developers a number of hydroelectric sites that Pinchot had persuaded Roosevelt to reserve, Pinchot protested to Taft and won the president's grudging support. However, when Pinchot leaked his evidence against Ballinger to *Collier's* magazine, which was still in the muckraking business, Taft fired him. This may have been exactly what Pinchot wanted. He acted as if he were prepared. Almost immediately, he booked

To progressives, Speaker of the House Joseph Cannon was the personification of antidemocratic and reactionary government.

passage to Italy, where his friend and patron, former President Roosevelt, was vacationing. Pinchot brought with him an indictment of Big Bill Taft as a traitor to the cause of reform.

Enter Stage Left the Conquering Hero

Roosevelt was having a bully time on his extended world tour. He left the country shortly after Taft's inauguration to give his successor an opportunity to function outside his predecessor's aura. First Roosevelt traveled to East Africa, where he shot a bloody swath through the abundant big game of Kenya and Tanganyika (Tanzania). He bagged over 3,000 animals, a good many of which he had stuffed for the trophy room of his home at Oyster Bay, Long Island.

Then he went to Europe to bask in an adulation that was scarcely less fierce than he enjoyed at home. He hobnobbed with aristocrats and politicians, who thought of him as the ultimate American, much as Benjamin Franklin was considered in eighteenth-century France. Roosevelt topped off his year-long junket by representing the United States at the funeral of King Edward VII, shining in the greatest collection of royalty ever assembled.

And yet, something was missing. Roosevelt longed for the hurly-burly of politics, and he was all too willing to believe Pinchot's accusations. When he returned to the United States in June 1910, he exchanged only the curtest greetings with the president. He spoke widely on behalf of Republican congressional candidates, at first playing down the split between regulars (conservatives) and insurgents (progressives). Then, at Osawatomie, Kansas, in September 1910, Roosevelt proclaimed what he labeled the New Nationalism, a comprehensive program for further reform. To Republican conservatives, it was frighteningly radical.

Among other proposals, Roosevelt called for woman suffrage, a federal minimum wage for women workers, abolition of child labor, strict limitations on the power of courts to issue injunctions in labor disputes, and a national social insurance scheme that resembled present-day Social Security. He struck directly at Taft's policies by demanding a commission that would set tariff rates "scientifically" rather than according to political pressures. He supported the progressive initiative, recall, and referendum, including a new twist, a referendum on judicial decisions. This was enough in itself to aggravate the legalistic Taft, but in demanding a national presidential primary law under which the people, and not professional politicians, would make party nominations, Roosevelt also hinted that he was interested in running for the presidency again.

Challenging Taft

Taft was not the only politician who worried about Roosevelt's presidential plans. Robert La Follette was preparing to seek the Republican presidential nomination in 1912, and believed he had a chance to defeat Taft, that is, if Roosevelt did not also run. Little as he enjoyed it, La Follette sent mutual friends to ask Roosevelt his intentions, implying that he would drop out if T. R. was running. Roosevelt responded that he was not interested in the White House. In January 1911, La Follette organized the Progressive Republican League to promote his own candidacy.

Most progressive Republicans supported La Follette, including Roosevelt backers who not so secretly hoped that their real hero would change his mind. In fact, Roosevelt was itching to run. When, in March 1912, La Follette collapsed from exhaustion during a speech, Roosevelt announced with unseemly haste, "my hat is in the ring."

Wilsonian Horseplay

Stern and ministerial in his public persona, Woodrow Wilson the private man was rather the opposite. On the morning after his wedding to his second wife in 1915, he was seen in a White House corridor doing a dance and singing, "Oh, You Beautiful Doll." His daughters by his first wife, Margaret, Jessie, and Eleanor, certainly showed no signs of moralistic browbeating. One of their amusements in the White House was to join tourists who were being shown around by guides and make loud remarks about the homeliness and vulgarity of the president's daughters.

La Follette was not seriously ill, and he never forgave T. R. for having, as he believed, used him as a stalking-horse. But Fighting Bob was no match for the old master when it came to stirring up party activists, and his campaign fell apart. Roosevelt swept most of the 13 state primary elections, winning 278 convention delegates to Taft's 48 and La Follette's 36. If La Follette was beaten, however, the suddenly aroused Taft was not, and he had a powerful weapon at hand.

Taft controlled the party organization. As president, he appointed people to thousands of government jobs, wedding their careers to his own success. In the Republican party, this power of the patronage was particularly important in the southern states, where there were no primaries and the party consisted of little more than professional officeholders, including many blacks, who made their living as postmasters, customs collectors, agricultural agents, and the like. While the Republicans won few congressional seats and fewer electoral votes in the South, a substantial bloc of delegates to Republican conventions spoke with a Dixie drawl. They were in Taft's pocket and, along with northern and western party regulars they vastly outnumbered the delegates Roosevelt won in the primaries.

Consequently, when the convention voted on whether Taft or Roosevelt would be awarded 254 disputed seats, Taft delegates won 235 of them. Roosevelt's supporters shouted "Fraud!" and walked out. They formed the Progressive party, or, as it was nicknamed for the battle with the Republican elephant and the Democratic donkey, the Bull Moose party.

714 *Chapter 36 Victors at Armageddon*

(In a backhanded reference to La Follette's allegedly poor health and Taft's obesity, Roosevelt said that he was "as fit as a bull moose.")

DEMOCRATIC PARTY PROGRESSIVISM

In one piece, the Republican party was unambivalently the nation's majority party, as four successive presidential elections demonstrated. Split in two, however, the GOP was vulnerable and the Democrats smelled victory. When the convention assembled in Baltimore, there was an abundance of would-be nominees ready to leap into the breach. As at the Republican convention, but for a rather different reason, the key to winning the party's presidential nomination lay in the southern state delegations.

Because the South was solid in delivering electoral votes to the Democratic column, it held a virtual veto power over the nomination. The old two-thirds rule, so important in shaping Democratic party policy before the Civil War, was reinstituted after it. In order to be nominated, a Democrat needed the vote of two-thirds of the delegates. No one could approach that total if the southern delegates opposed him as a group. A candidate with the southern delegates solidly behind him had a handsome headstart on the nomination.

Democratic Hopefuls

In 1912, none of the leading candidates was offensive to the South, and each had southern supporters; thus, the southern bloc was split. William Jennings Bryan was still popular with southerners, and he was interested. As a three-time loser, however, he was not a very attractive candidate. Bryan's only hope was a deadlocked convention when he might be selected as a compromise candidate.

Oscar Underwood of Alabama was another minor hopeful; he commanded the support of the southern Bourbon conservatives, but for that reason he was unacceptable to southern progressives, who might more accurately be described as Populists who had learned to preach racism along with attacks on big business. Some progressives supported Judson Harmon of Ohio. Others backed Champ Clark, the "Old Hound Dawg" of Missouri, which was as much a southern as a western state. In fact, Clark went into the convention confident of winning. The man who left it a winner, however, was New Jersey governor Woodrow Wilson, although it took him forty-six ballots to do it.

A Moral, Unbending Man

Wilson was a southerner himself; he was born in Virginia and practiced law in Georgia as a young man. He abandoned the law, however, earned a Ph.D. degree, and ended up as a professor of political science at Princeton University. In 1902, he was named president of Princeton, the first nonminister to hold that post at the still strongly Presbyterian school.

And yet, Wilson had more than a little of the Presbyterian clergyman in him. His father and both grandfathers were parsons. So was his wife's father. He was raised to observe an unbending Calvinist morality, and a sensitivity to the struggle between good and evil in the world. With his family and intimate friends, Wilson was fun-loving and playful, a fan of baseball and the cinema, and liable to erupt in horseplay with his daughters, who adored him. Publicly, he was formal, sometimes icy. A less talented man with such a personality would never have risen half so high as Wilson did.

In fact, his meteoric rise in politics was almost accidental. In 1910, he was merely an honored educator, the president of an Ivy League university. He transformed the college from an intellectually lazy finishing school where rich young men made social contacts into an institution that commanded intellectual respect. But Wilson's stubbornness caught up with him in a rather trivial matter. He tried to close down Princeton's eating clubs, exclusive student associations much like fraternities, and clashed with trustees and alumni dedicated to their preservation.

When he was offered the Democratic nomination for governor of New Jersey, he quit academic life. To everyone's surprise except, perhaps, Wilson's, he won the governorship in the traditionally Republican state and the upset made him a national figure overnight. He was less social reformer than an honest government progressive, and he set about cleaning up the state bureaucracy and the Democratic party. Like Teddy Roosevelt in New York a decade before, Wilson was soon at odds with the bosses of his own party in New Jersey. They were delighted when he decided to seek the presidency. Ironically, in terms of what was to follow, he offered himself to the party as a safe and sane middle-of-the-road alternative to former lunatic William Jennings Bryan and Champ Clark, a conservative.

Democratic Party Progressivism

A confident Woodrow Wilson (1856–1924) at the peak of his powers.

The Campaign of 1912

In fact, Wilson's New Freedom, as he called his program, was a decidedly less ambitious blueprint for reform than was Roosevelt's New Nationalism. Wilson emphasized states' rights to the extent that he opposed the Progressive party's comprehensive social program as strongly as Taft did. He considered Roosevelt's proposals to augur a dangerous expansion of government powers.

The two men differed even more sharply on the question of the trusts. Whereas T. R. concluded that consolidation, even monopoly, was inevitable in a modern industrial society, and that the federal government should supervise and even direct the operations of the big corporations in the public interest, Wilson condemned this vision as "a partnership between the government and the trusts." Wilson believed that competition in business was still possible in modern America. In his view, the government's task was to play watchdog over business, ensuring and restoring free competition by breaking up the trusts. In 1912, he opposed the huge, permanent government apparatus that Roosevelt endorsed.

With the Republican organization in tatters and Taft practically dropping out of the race, it would have been difficult for Wilson to lose the election. Nevertheless, he campaigned tirelessly and skillfully.

Articulate, as a college professor is supposed to be, Wilson was also inspiring, as few academics are. Lifelong dreams of winning public office flowered in eloquent speeches that left no doubt that the Presbyterian schoolmaster was a leader.

Wilson won only 41.9 percent of the popular vote but a landslide in the electoral college, 435 votes to Roosevelt's 88 and Taft's 8. Eugene V. Debs, making his fourth race as the Socialist party nominee, won 900,000 votes, 6 percent of the total. The big jump after four years of a conservative president seemed to indicate that it was necessary to reform in order to stifle the socialist challenge. Taft, the only conservative candidate, won but 23.2 percent of the total vote.

Tariffs and Taxes

T. R. had usually gotten his way by outflanking Congress, interpreting the president's constitutional powers in the broadest possible terms. Taft deferred to congressional leaders, ultimately collapsing before the most persuasive of them. Wilson's style was to act as a prime minister. He was not a member of Congress, as the British prime minister is a member of the House of Commons, but he could and did address Congress personally as though he were. He was the first president to appear personally before

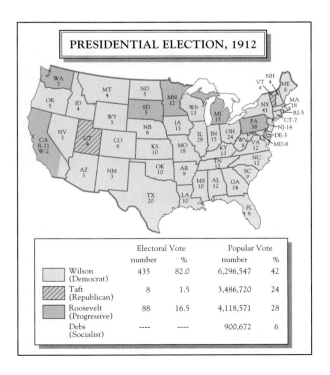

How They Lived

Coney Island: Amusement Democratized

Coney Island is a misnomer. The rabbits (coneys) were no longer particularly conspicuous when, before the Civil War, the island's broad beaches and cool ocean breezes attracted well-to-do New Yorkers, and some famous visitors, John C. Calhoun, Walt Whitman, and Daniel Webster, seeking relief from summer heat. Nor was it an island. It was separated from what was soon part of Brooklyn by a modest creek.

George C. Tilyou, born in 1862, grew up on Coney Island, with "sand in his shoes" as the local argot had it. When he was three years old, his father leased a lot on the beach and opened a hotel catering not to the rich, but to the middling sort, who were vacationing in Coney in increasing numbers, leading the very wealthy to look elsewhere for ocean breezes, like Newport, Rhode Island. Coney was strategically located for a middle-class resort, far from the congestion of New York City but close enough to be convenient for a stay of a few days, the only kind of holiday that people who had to work could imagine.

Even as a teenager, Tilyou was looking for ways to pocket vacationers' pocket change. In 1876, with the Centennial Exposition in Philadelphia attracting people from all over the nation to the East Coast, the 14-year-old filled old medicine bottles with Coney Island sea water and cigar boxes with Coney beach sand which he sold for 25 cents each. He made enough from such classic resort "gifts" with which to dabble in beachfront real estate. The township did not sell land on the beach but, instead, leased it to people who were part of the political machine, who then sublet choice business locations to others, sometimes at extraordinary profits. Because of his contacts, Tilyou was able to open a theater that featured leading vaudeville acts.

Then he made what appeared to be a fatal mistake. He broke with the political boss of Coney, John Y. McKane, who protected brothels and illegal casinos. Tilyou organized a party devoted to the policy that Coney's future rested on becoming a wholesome family resort. Tilyou denounced McKane for his grafting and when the boss weathered the attack, Tilyou found himself shut out of the profitable leasing deals.

In 1893, however, Tilyou's fortunes took an about-face. McKane was jailed for stuffing ballot boxes and Tilyou traveled to the Chicago World's Fair where, like millions of other people, he was awed by the great Ferris wheel that was the hit of the celebration. It was 250 feet in diameter, the height of a 25-story building. Suspended on the gigantic circle were 36 "cars," like railroad carriages, each of which held 60 people. When the fair closed in the fall, 1.5 million people had taken a whirl on it.

Tilyou contracted with George Ferris to build another wheel in Coney. It was only half the size of the original (no one has ever built a Ferris wheel as big as the original) but Tilyou erected a billboard: "ON THIS SITE WILL BE ERECTED THE WORLD'S LARGEST FERRIS WHEEL!" He began to make money before it was done, selling concessions around the wheel to various vendors, including one to a purveyor of a frankfurter sausage on a roll

---

Congress with his program since John Adams. Adams's successor, Thomas Jefferson, suffered from a stammer and had set the precedent of communicating with Congress only through written messages.

Wilson's brief address was aimed less at persuading congressmen than at inspiring their constituents to put pressure on them, and it worked. A number of Democratic senators who were dragging their feet on tariff revision fell into line. The Underwood-Simmons Tariff reduced the Payne-Aldrich rates by 15 percent and put on the free list several commodities that were controlled by trusts—iron, steel, woolens, and farm machinery—thus lowering prices on them.

The lower tariff reduced revenue for the government. To make up the losses, Wilson sponsored both a corporate and a personal income tax. It was not high by late twentieth-century standards. People who earned less than $4,000 a year paid no tax. On annual incomes between $4,000 and $20,000, a tidy sum in 1913, the rate was only 1 percent. People in the highest bracket, $500,000 and up, paid only 7 percent, a fraction of the low brackets today. Nevertheless, by forcing the rich to

who would claim that his "Coney Island Hot" was the first hot dog. Then Tilyou constructed a number of other "amusements," the first roller coaster, for example, a gravity device based on a gravity railroad built in the Pennsylvania coalfields to bring anthracite down a mountain. Coney's consisted of two 45-foot towers with a 450-foot run between. (Passengers embarked at the bottom of the loop, were pulled to the top of one tower by steam engine, and released to coast back and forth until they ended up where they began.)

From another Coney entrepreneur, Paul Boyton, Tilyou copied the idea of fencing in a large "amusement park" and charging a single admission fee. Coney's clientele, increasingly working-class, did not have the means for extravagant spending. Better to commit them to a whole day at Tilyou's Steeplechase Park where they would have to buy their food and other extras.

Steeplechase Park opened in 1897. Its centerpiece was a gravity-driven "horse race" ride imported from England. People mounted wooden horses—a beau and his belle could ride on the same one—which rolled on tracks over a series of "hills" and entered the central pavillion at the Park where, upon exiting, the customers were mildly abused by a clown and costumed dwarf. The biggest hit of the Steeplechase was the jet of compressed air which shot out of the floor, blowing young ladies' skirts into the air amidst great shrieking and guffawing.

Innocent sexual horseplay was the idea in many of the mechanical amusements Tilyou constructed. Airjets were everywhere. Other amusements were designed to throw young ladies in such a position that their ankles were exposed or they landed in the laps of their escorts or, perhaps, someone whom they were interested in meeting. In an age when polite society was warily trying to come to terms with sex, dwelling on it through romantic euphemisms in popular songs, Tilyou's formula worked.

He had competitors. Luna Park was opened by a former Tilyou employee in 1903. It cost $700,000 to build. On opening day, its owners had $11 among them. They had to borrow change for the box office. In seven weeks, they recouped their entire investment. In addition to amusements such as those in Steeplechase, Luna featured "real Eastern people" brought from India "for your amusement."

Dreamland, which opened in 1904, invited holidaymakers to stroll through the streets of an Egyptian city, a Somali village, among Philippine headhunters, or see the eruption of Mount Pelee, the Johnstown flood, the Galveston tidal wave, or other natural disasters.

The "nickel empire" or "poor man's paradise," as Coney was called, continued to grow throughout the early twentieth century. It enjoyed its greatest prosperity after a subway line reached the shore (now part of Brooklyn) in the 1920s. It was democratic—cheap! A newspaper reporter and his wife spent an entire day amusing themselves at Coney for $5.50.

pay proportionately more toward supporting the government, the tax provisions of the tariff law represented a triumph of progressive principles.

Wilson's Cabinet

Wilson designed his cabinet in order to unite the Democratic party behind him. The president did not like William Jennings Bryan, but he named him secretary of state because Bryan helped to nominate him and still owned the affection of many western Democrats.

Most other appointments rewarded key components of the party, especially the South and, through Secretary of Labor William B. Wilson, the labor movement, whose support the president wanted and needed. The most valuable member of the cabinet was William G. McAdoo. As secretary of the treasury, he provided the president with shrewd advice on banking policy. When McAdoo married Wilson's daughter, he became a kind of heir apparent.

Three confidants did not sit in the cabinet. Joseph Tumulty, a canny Irish politician, served as

Wilson's private secretary and reminded the president of the sometimes sordid realities involved in keeping together a political machine. Colonel Edward M. House, a Texas businessman, was a shadowy, but not sinister, figure. Self-effacing and utterly devoted to the president, House neither desired nor accepted any official position. Instead, he traveled discreetly throughout the United States and abroad, informally conveying the president's views and wants to businessmen and heads of state.

Louis D. Brandeis, a corporation lawyer become antitrust progressive, provided Wilson with both economic principles and a social conscience. The father of the New Freedom, Brandeis turned Wilson away from the limitations of the program after 1914 and toward a broader progressivism. In 1916, Wilson rewarded him by naming him to the Supreme Court, on which Brandeis served as one of the most influential liberal justices of the twentieth century. He was the first justice to consider sociological information along with legal precedent in adjudging the constitutionality of laws.

The New Freedom in Action

Two laws that reflected Brandeis's influence were the Federal Reserve Act of 1913 and the Clayton Antitrust Act of 1914. The first was designed both to bring order to the national banking system and to hobble the vast power of Wall Street. The law established 12 regional Federal Reserve Banks, which dealt not directly with people but with other banks. The Federal Reserve System was owned by private bankers who were required to deposit 6 percent of their capital in it. However, the president appointed the majority of the directors, who sat in Washington, theoretically putting the government in control of the money supply.

The greatest power of the Federal Reserve System was (and is) its control of the discount rate, the level of interest at which money is lent to other banks for lending to private investors and buyers. By lowering the discount rate, the Federal Reserve could stimulate investment and economic expansion in slow times. By raising the rate, the Federal Reserve could cool down an overactive economy that threatened to blow up in inflation, financial panic, and depression.

The Federal Reserve Act did bring some order to the national banking system. But it did not, as many progressives hoped, tame the great bankers. Indeed, because representatives of the private banks sat on the Federal Reserve Board (who else understood what was

---

Form 1040

The income tax, somewhat as it is known today, was first collected in March 1914. The original tax was designed to have well-to-do Americans pay the bulk of the federal government's bills. At a time when the average worker made $800 a year, no person earning less than $3,000 (about $35,000 in today's values) paid the tax. The rate was just 1 percent after deductions, with a surtax of 6 percent on incomes over $500,000 (about $6 million today). In part because the income tax was progressive, hitting the well-to-do harder than the tariff and excise tax did, it was quite popular at first.

During World War I, however, the need for funds lowered the minimum taxable income to $1,000. What had been a tax on the upper classes became a tax on almost all who worked. In 1990, after the tax reforms of the Reagan administration, lower- and middle-income families paid disproportionately more of the government's expenses than they did before the income tax was adopted.

---

going on?), the long-term effects of the law were to provide Wall Street with an even more efficient, albeit more accountable, control of national finance.

In 1914, Wilson pushed his antitrust policy through Congress. The Clayton Antitrust Act stipulated that corporations would be fined for unfair practices that threatened competition, forbade interlocking directorates (the same men sitting on the boards of competing companies and thereby coordinating policies), and declared that officers of corporations would be held personally responsible for offenses committed by their companies. Another bill passed at the same time created the Federal Trade Commission to supervise the activities of the trusts. This agency looked more like T. R.'s New Nationalism than the New Freedom Wilson had plumped for in 1912.

Wilson Changes Direction

After the congressional elections of 1914, Wilson shifted far more sharply toward the reforms that Teddy Roosevelt promoted. Although the Democrats retained control of both houses, many progressives returned to their Republican voting habits in 1914 and cut the Democratic margin in the House.

It was obvious to both the president and Democratic congressmen that if they were to survive the election of 1916 against a reunified Republican party, they would have to woo these progressive voters.

Consequently, Wilson agreed to support social legislation that he had opposed as late as 1914. He did not like laws that favored any special interest, farmers any more than bankers, but in order to shore up support in the West, he agreed to the Federal Farm Loan Act of 1916, which provided low-cost credit to farmers. Early in his administration, Wilson opposed a child-labor law on constitutional grounds. In 1916, he supported the Keating-Owen Act, which severely restricted the employment of children in most jobs.

The Adamson Act required the interstate railroads to put their workers on an eight-hour day without a reduction in pay. Wilson even moderated his antiblack sentiments, although Washington definitely took on the character of a segregated southern city during his tenure. Despite a lifelong opposition to woman suffrage, the president began to encourage states to enfranchise women and to hint that he supported a constitutional amendment that would guarantee the right nationwide.

By the summer of 1916, Wilson could say with considerable justice that he had pushed progressive reform further than had any of his predecessors. He enacted or supported much of Theodore Roosevelt's program of 1912, as well as his own. By 1916, however, Americans' votes reflected more than their views on domestic issues. They were troubled about their nation's place in a suddenly complicated world. Simultaneous with the enactment of Wilson's New Freedom and more than a little of T. R.'s New Nationalism, Europe was tumbling into the bloodiest war in history.

CHRONOLOGY

1901	Theodore Roosevelt becomes president
1902	Government prosecutes Northern Securities Company under Sherman Antitrust Act Roosevelt intervenes in anthracite strike sympathetic to miners
1904	Roosevelt reelected
1906	La Follette spearheads passage of Hepburn Act Pure Food and Drug Act and Meat Inspection Act become law
1907–1908	Roosevelt vastly increases acreage in National Forests
1909	Taft becomes president Payne-Aldrich Tariff increases import duties
1910	After extended trip abroad, Roosevelt returns to criticize Taft
1912	Woodrow Wilson elected president in three-way race
1913	Federal Reserve Act
1914	Clayton Antitrust Act

FOR FURTHER READING

Overviews of the era are Vincent P. DeSantis, *The Shaping of Modern America, 1877–1916*, 1973; Arthur S. Link, *Woodrow Wilson and the Progressive Era*, 1954; George E. Mowry, *The Era of Theodore Roosevelt*, 1958; William L. O'Neill, *The Progressive Years: America Comes of Age*, 1975; and Arthur Link and Richard L. McCormick, *Progressivism*, 1983.

Indeed, virtually all the books cited at the conclusion of Chapter 34 are relevant to this chapter as well. For additional biographical studies, see D. F. Anderson, *William Howard Taft: A Conservative's Conception of the Presidency*, 1973; John Morton Blum, *Woodrow Wilson and the Politics of Morality*, 1956; P. E. Coletta, *The Presidency of William Howard Taft*, 1973; John A. Garraty, *Woodrow Wilson*, 1956; and the multi-volume Arthur S. Link, *Woodrow Wilson*, 1947–65.

More specialized studies include Lewis L. Gould, *Reform and Regulation: American Politics, 1900–1916*, 1978; Stephen Skowronek, *Building a New Administrative State*, 1982; Otis L. Graham, Jr., *The Great Campaigns: Reform and War in America, 1900–1928*, 1971; Samuel T. Hays, *Conservation and the Gospel of Efficiency: The Progressive Conservation Movement, 1890–1920*, 1959; Alan Dawley, *Struggle for Justice: Social Responsibility and the Liberal State*, 1991; David Sarasohn, *The Party of Reform: The Democrats in the Progressive Era*, 1989; and Morton Keller, *Regulating a New Society: Public Policy and Social Change in America, 1900–1930*, 1994.

"Lafayette, we are here": General John J. "Black Jack" Pershing in Paris, 1918.

37
CHAPTER

OVER THERE

The United States and the First World War

1914–1918

We are fighting in the quarrel of civilization against barbarism, of liberty against tyranny. Germany has become a menace to the whole world. She is the most dangerous enemy of liberty now existing.

—Theodore Roosevelt

Our plutocracy, our junkers, would have us believe that all the junkers are confined to Germany. It is precisely because we refuse to believe this that they brand us as disloyalists.

They want our eyes focused on the junkers in Berlin so that we will not see those within our own borders.

—Eugene V. Debs

The world must be made safe for democracy. Its peace must be planted upon the tested foundations of political liberty. We have no selfish ends to serve. We desire no conquest, no dominion. We seek no indemnities for ourselves, no material compensation for the sacrifices we shall freely make.

—Woodrow Wilson

A few days before he took the oath of office in 1913, Woodrow Wilson was reminded of some difficulties in American relations with Mexico. He thought about the problem for a moment and set it aside, remarking, "It would be the irony of fate if my administration had to deal chiefly with foreign affairs."

Wilson did not fear such a challenge. His self-confidence was as sturdy as Theodore Roosevelt's. But his academic and political careers had been devoted to domestic concerns. He had paid scant attention to the thorny snarls of international relations; he was never particularly interested in them. When the Woodrow Wilson of 1913 thought about the rest of the world, he did so more on the basis of assumptions and sentiments than in the context of a coherent policy rooted in study and reflection.

WILSON, THE WORLD, AND MEXICO

Like most Americans, the president was proud that because of its population and industrial might, the United States ranked with only a handful of nations as a world power that had to be reckoned with. Also like other Americans, he believed that the United States was unique among the nations of the world. Isolated from both Europe and Asia by broad oceans, the United States needed no large standing armies in order to be secure. Instead, the nation was able to expend its resources in constructive ways. Founded on the basis of choice — coming to America from somewhere else — and on an idea in men's minds rather than on an accidental inheritance of a common culture and territory, the American nation should act toward other countries in accordance with principles rather than out of narrow self-interest.

Moral Diplomacy

Because of his moralistic views, Wilson roundly criticized Teddy Roosevelt's gunboat diplomacy. To bully small nations was to betray the principle of self-determination on which the United States was founded. He pointedly announced that his administration would deal with the weak and turbulent Latin American countries "upon terms of equality and honor." As a progressive who was suspicious of Wall Street, Wilson also disapproved of Taft's dollar diplomacy. Shortly after he took office, Wilson canceled federal support of

an investment scheme in China because it implied the government had an obligation to intervene when investors' profits were threatened. If Wall Street financiers wanted to risk money in China, that was fine for them; but they would have to risk their money, not expect Uncle Sam to guarantee against losses.

Wilson was influenced by the Christian pacifism to which Secretary of State William Jennings Bryan was more deeply dedicated. Bryan believed that war was justified only in self-defense. If nations would act cautiously and discuss their problems, they would not have to spill blood. With Wilson's approval, Bryan negotiated conciliation treaties with 30 nations. The signatories pledged that in the event of a dispute, they would wait and talk for one year before declaring war. Bryan believed that during such a "cooling-off" period, virtually every dispute between nations could be resolved without the use of force.

The Missionary

High ideals. Once in the cockpit, however, Wilson found that applying them consistently was more difficult than flying the recently invented airplane. In part, this was because of the untidy, unruly characteristics of reality. In part, it was because Wilson was also impelled by assumptions that conflicted with the moral principles by which he had been raised and the progressive principles he had adopted as an adult.

A southerner, Wilson never questioned the assumption that the white race was superior to others. He was no redneck apt to join a lynch mob. Indeed, Wilson was of the southern social class that abominated the lawlessness of southern "po' white trash." Wilson's attitudes toward blacks were those of a southern gentleman: kindly and generous but entirely patronizing, firm in insisting on the inequality of the nation's two major races and confident in the belief that segregation — separation — was the best arrangement between whites and blacks, not least because segregation minimized racial violence. The colleges and universities in which he spent his adult life were permeated with theories and pseudo-sciences assuming the white man's superiority. As president, Wilson found it difficult to act as an equal in dealing with nonwhite nations such as Japan and the racially mixed Latin Americans.

His commitment to diplomacy by good example was complicated by a missionary's impulse to prescribe proper behavior. When weaker nations did not freely emulate American ways of doing things, Wilson could wax arrogant and demanding. If other peoples did not realize what was good for them, teacher Wilson could reach for his hickory stick. "I am going to teach the South American republics to elect good men," he said in one revealing moment.

So Wilson acquiesced in a California state law that insulted race-sensitive Japan by restricting the right of Japanese immigrants to own land. In 1915, Wilson ordered the marines into black Haiti when chaotic conditions there threatened American investments; the next year, he landed troops in the Dominican Republic under similar circumstances. These actions angered Latin Americans, but they were minor irritants compared with Wilson's prolonged and blundering interference in Mexican affairs.

¡Viva Madero!

In 1911, the Mexican dictator for 35 years, Porfirio Díaz, was overthrown following a revolution supported by practically every Mexican region and social group except the tiny elite of land, mine, and factory owners that Díaz favored. Foreign investors, who reaped rich rewards by cooperating with the dictator, waited and fretted, none more so than the British and Americans. The leader of the revolution, Francisco Madero, spoke of returning control of Mexican resources to Mexicans, and Americans alone owned $2 billion in property in Mexico, most of the country's railroads, 60 percent of the oil wells, and more mines than Mexicans controlled. About 50,000 Americans lived in Mexico.

Francisco Madero was an idealist. He and Wilson might have disagreed on many matters, but they would have understood one another. Madero was cultivated, educated, and moderate, not given to acting rashly. He shared Wilson's liberal political philosophy and he admired American institutions. Mexicans out of favor with dictator Díaz had generally passed their exiles in the United States.

Madero and Wilson never had a chance to communicate. With some quiet encouragement by American diplomats during the Taft administration, a group of Díaz's generals led by no-nonsense, hard-drinking Victoriano Huerta ("he may be said to subsist on alcohol") staged a coup. The rebels struck shortly before Wilson was inaugurated and seized control of the federal government. Madero was murdered during the coup.

¡Viva Carranza!

The murder offended Wilson. He said that he would not deal with "a government of butchers," and he pressured England to withdraw its hasty recognition of the Huerta government. When peasants rebelled in scattered parts of Mexico and a Constitutionalist army took shape behind a somber, long-bearded aristocrat, Venustiano Carranza, Wilson openly approved.

In April 1914, the United States intervened directly in the civil war. Seven American sailors in Tampico were arrested by one of Huerta's colonels. Huerta freed them almost immediately. "Drunk or only half drunk (he is never sober)," Huerta was intelligent and shrewd. He wanted no trouble with the gringos. However, Huerta refused the demand of Admiral Henry T. Mayo for a 21-gun salute as the appropriate apology. Claiming that American honor was insulted (and seeking to head off a German ship that was bringing arms to Huerta), Wilson ordered troops into the important gulf port of Vera Cruz.

To Wilson's surprise, ordinary Mexicans joined the fight against the Americans, and street fighting in Vera Cruz claimed more than 400 lives. Wilson failed to understand that while Huerta was less than popular, the memory of the Mexican War was fresh in the Mexican memory. Generally, rebel groups resented gringo interference in Mexican affairs as much as Huerta did. Even Carranza, firmly in control of northeastern Mexico by now, condemned the American landing. Somewhat alarmed by the fix into which he had gotten himself, Wilson agreed to an offer by Argentina, Brazil, and Chile to mediate the crisis.

¡Viva Villa!

Before anything could be settled, Carranza ousted Huerta. However, instead of bringing stability to Mexico, he quarreled with one of his own generals, a bizarre, charismatic character who was born Doroteo Arango, but was universally known as Pancho Villa. Alternately jovial and peevish, part-time bandit and part-time social revolutionary, Villa was romanticized in the American press by a young journalist, John Reed, as "The Robin Hood of Mexico." Villa enjoyed his celebrity and played for American approval. For a time, even Wilson was convinced that Villa represented democracy in Mexico.

But Wilson wanted stability most of all. When Carranza took Mexico City in October 1915, Wilson recognized his de facto control of the government. This stung Villa, prompting him to display his

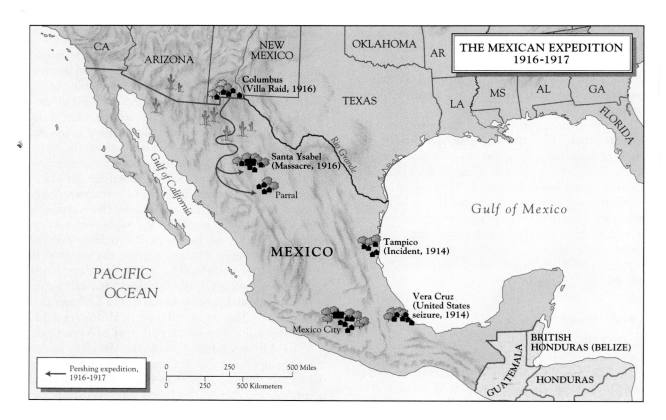

seamier side. Calculating that American intervention would create chaos in Mexico, creating an opportunity for him to seize power, Villa stopped a train carrying American engineers who were invited by Carranza to reopen mines, and shot all but one of them. Early in 1916, he also sent raiders across the border into the dusty little desert town of Columbus, New Mexico, where they killed 17 people.

Instead of allowing Carranza to root out and punish Villa, as was proper with neighboring nations that were sovereign equals, Wilson ordered General John J. Pershing and 6,000 troops, including the African-American Tenth Cavalry, to pursue and capture the bandit guerrilla. That led to another humiliation: in the arid mountainous state of Chihuahua that was his home, Villa easily evaded the American expedition, leading the soldiers 300 miles over a zigzag route during which time they never gained sight of Villa's main force. Pershing's men did, however, exchange gunfire with Carranza's troops and, in one skirmish, 40 died. While accomplishing nothing, Wilson succeeded in alienating every political faction in Mexico.

In January 1917, he gave up and ordered "Black Jack" Pershing to return home. Only because Americans were faced by a more formidable enemy than Villa, the German Kaiser, were they able to make light of their humiliation at the hands of a man whom they considered an illiterate brigand.

THE GREAT WAR

By 1917, Europe had been at war for two and a half years. In June 1914, a Serbian nationalist, Gavrilo Princip, assassinated Archduke Franz Ferdinand of the Austro-Hungarian Empire, which included among its provinces two, Bosnia and Herzegovina, that Serbia claimed as its own. At first it appeared that the incident would pass with protestations of grief and wrath. Turn-of-the-century Europe had seen an epidemic of sensational assassinations.

But Austro-Hungarian sensitivity to the disarray of its once majestic empire, obligations to one another that the great powers of Europe had written into secret treaties, the weakness of the Russian czar and the irresponsibility of the German kaiser, and the reckless arms race in which the European nations were engaged for a generation, worked together to plunge most of the continent into war.

Doroteo "Pancho Villa" Arango in his prime as a revolutionary and bandit.

Tangled Alliances

Then as now, Slavic Serbia looked to the greatest Slavic nation, Russia, for protection, and the czar backed the little country in defying Austria. Austria-Hungary looked to powerful Germany for encouragement, and got it. France, sworn to revenge a defeat by the Germans in 1870, became involved because of French fears of German industrial might, which led to secret agreements promising mutual support to Russia. England, traditionally aloof from European wrangles, was frightened by Germany's construction of a worldwide navy (larger than America's and second only to Britain's), and signed mutual assistance treaties with both France and Russia.

Many of the smaller nations of Europe were associated with either the Central Powers (Germany, Austria-Hungary, Bulgaria, and Turkey) or the Allied Powers (England, France, Russia, and eventually Italy). By August 1914, most of Europe was at war. Eventually, 33 nations would be involved.

Americans React

The American people reacted to the explosion with a mixture of disbelief and disgust. For a generation, European rulers filled the air with the sounds of saber rattling. Americans were used to that; their own Teddy Roosevelt was a master of bluff and bluster, and he fancied the military strut more than most. But T. R., it seemed, had always understood the difference between a bully display and a catastrophe. Until 1914, so had the Europeans. Even Kaiser Wilhelm II of Germany, an absurd and broadly ridiculed figure with his extravagant uniforms, gold and silver spiked helmets, comic-opera waxed mustache, and penchant for bombast, always acted prudently in the crunch. Like most Europeans, Americans concluded that the constant talk about war without going to war would continue indefinitely. They did not really believe that powerful, civilized countries would turn the twentieth century's terrifying technology for killing on one another.

Once European nations did just that, Americans consoled themselves that their country, at least, remained above the savagery. Politicians, preachers, and editors quoted and praised the wisdom of George Washington and Thomas Jefferson's warning against entangling alliances. They blamed Europe's tragedy on Old World corruptions, its kings and princes, religious intolerance, nationalistic hysteria, and insane stockpiling of armaments that were superfluous if they were not used, suicidal if they were.

Never did American political and social institutions look so grandly superior. Never had Americans

Kaiser Wilhelm II's love of militaristic finery made him an easily ridiculed figure in the United States.

What's in a Name?

The British called it the European War, and Americans were inclined to use that term until the United States intervened in April 1917. Then, a few idealistic but awkward tags were tried: War for the Freedom of Europe, War for the Overthrow of Militarism, War for Civilization, and — best known — Woodrow Wilson's War to Make the World Safe for Democracy. Only after 1918 did the Great War and the World War become standard — until 1939 when the outbreak of another great worldwide war made it World War I.

been more grateful to have turned their backs on Europe's ways. As reports of hideous carnage on the battlefield began to hum over the Atlantic cable, Americans shuddered and counted their blessings. No prominent person raised an objection when President Wilson proclaimed absolute American neutrality. However, when the president also called on Americans to be "neutral in fact as well as in name, . . . impartial in thought as well as in action," he was, as he was wont to do, demanding too much of human nature, even the nature of what Wilson called "this great peaceful people."

Sympathy for the Allies

A large proportion of Americans looked to England as their ancestral as well as their cultural motherland, and many were sympathetic to Britain's cause for that reason. Wilson was an unblushing anglophile.

Before becoming president, he vacationed regularly in Great Britain. He wrote a book in which he broadly admired the British parliamentary form of government; he even suggested adapting the British model in American government. In his first year in office, he resolved the last minor points of difference between England and the United States: a border dispute in British Columbia, a quarrel between Canadian and American fishermen off Newfoundland, and British objections to discriminatory tolls on the Panama Canal.

Hardly noted at first, but ominous in the long run, American and British capitalists were closely allied. British investments in the United States were vast, and when the cost of purchasing everything from wheat to munitions required that these holdings be liquidated, they were sold to Americans at bargain rates. Banking houses like the House of Morgan lent money to the British, at first with Wilson's disapproval, and acted as agents for Allied bond sales. By 1917, Great Britain owed Americans $2.3 billion. It was a strong tie, when compared to the meager $27 million that the Germans managed to borrow in the United States. Wall Street had good reason to favor a British victory or, at least, to pale at the thought of a British defeat.

Some Americans were also sympathetic to France. The land of Lafayette was America's oldest friend, the indispensable ally of the Revolution. Americans never had formally gone to war with the French. And France was, except for the United States, the only republic among the world's great powers constitutionally pledged to civil equality and representative institutions.

NOTABLE PEOPLE
William D. Haywood (1869–1927)

Big Bill Haywood was famous during the years before the Great War. As the head of the IWW, the Industrial Workers of the World, he came close to wielding real power as a leader of the unskilled industrial and agricultural working people so vital in the economy. But the war was to destroy Haywood's career and shatter his vision of what America should mean. Within a few years after the guns were stilled, he was a lonely exile who would never come home.

William D. Haywood was born in Salt Lake City in 1869. He became a miner in northern Nevada while still a teenager. Several times he turned to other work—cowboying, prospecting for a mine of his own, homesteading on the site of an abandoned army post. Haywood was a quintessential westerner, looking for the chance to improve himself, an implicit believer in the American gospel of opportunity that said the West was the place a man could best do such a thing.

Bad luck and the attractive wages gold and silver miners took home brought Haywood back to the mines of Silver City, Idaho. There he found his opportunity to rise within the Western Federation of Miners, the militant labor union of the miners, mill, and smelter workers of the region. His forceful personality and aptitude for running an organization brought him to the attention of the WFM's leadership in Denver. At the turn of the century, Haywood moved to the metropolis as the WFM's secretary-treasurer.

In Silver City, Haywood had supervised an orderly union local, negotiating wages and conditions across a table from the owners of the mines. Elsewhere in the West, union miners fought violent strikes with their employers, which were increasingly large corporations with headquarters in San Francisco, New York, and London.

The miners resented absentee control of the gold and silver they believed they had found and which they won from the earth. They worked daily with explosives and were apt, when pushed, to fight back with dynamite and guns. The bosses, when they sensed a chance to break the miners' unions and gain uncontested control of labor in the mining camps, were equally quick to use violence in the form of hired thugs and pliant local and state authorities. Bill Haywood found himself one of the leaders of an organization engaged in what was unmistakably class warfare. He did not disdain the role. During the 1890s, he had concluded that some form of socialism, common rather than private ownership of the means of production, was the only way to achieve social justice in the United States.

The mine owners and their allies in government considered Haywood one of an "Inner Circle" of sinister conspirators whom they held responsible for the disorder. If he could be removed from the scene, they believed they could gain the upper hand in labor relations. In 1906, when a ne'er-do-well known as Harry Orchard confessed that he had murdered a former governor of Idaho on the orders of the "Inner Circle," Haywood was brought to trial in Boise.

The prosecution's case relied heavily on the testimony of the unsavory Orchard. Haywood's lawyer, Clarence Darrow, seized on this and defended him by prosecuting Orchard's character. Haywood was acquitted.

His career in the WFM was at an end. Other leaders of the union believed Haywood's tough talk

Sympathy for the Central Powers

But Americans were by no means unanimously favorable to the Allies. One American in three was either foreign-born or a first-generation citizen, many of them with strong Old World sentiments that made them pro-German or unfriendly toward the Allies. Millions of Americans traced their roots to Germany or Austria-Hungary. Most had come to the United States for its economic opportunities; few felt any hostility to their fatherlands and fewer yet were hostile toward German culture. No serious-minded German, Austrian, or Hungarian Americans suggested that the United States take the side of the Central

was responsible for the trial (and may have believed him guilty of the crime). It mattered little to Haywood. The publicity had made him an eminent man. Intellectuals, particularly in New York's Greenwich Village, lionized him as a primal exemplar of the working masses. He lectured widely, building his image with a simple, eloquent platform manner. He was elected to the Socialist party's National Executive Committee and twice represented the party at international conferences. He became an organizer for the IWW, the revolutionary union of unskilled workers he had helped found in 1905. He was in the headlines during strikes the IWW led in Lawrence, Massachusetts, in 1912 and Paterson, New Jersey, in 1913.

In 1914, Haywood became secretary-treasurer of the IWW, in effect its leader. He introduced a degree of order to an organization that had been almost guerrilla-like in its operations. He regularized dues collections, set up an efficient national office in Chicago, and perfected a system for enrolling the dispersed casual workers who brought in the nation's grain harvest, previously a virtually unorganizable workforce.

Haywood's IWW opposed American entrance into World War I. Haywood was, however, very cautious in the issue. He believed that the workers' business lay "at the point of production," in the factory, field, forest, and mine, not in fighting causes that, however noble, were beyond their power to effect. He attempted to soft-pedal the IWW's antiwar line. He dropped bitterly sardonic antiwar lyrics from the IWW's songbook and said that it was a matter of personal choice whether or not members registered for the draft.

To no avail. In the fall of 1917, federal authorities launched nationwide raids of IWW headquarters. Either because they believed that the IWW was really treasonous, because they feared what the union's strength in the critical areas of agriculture, lumber, and copper could mean to the war effort, or simply because they saw a chance to use wartime hysteria as an opportunity to crush the anticapitalist IWW and Big Bill Haywood, the federal prosecutors did just that.

Long trials for sedition drained the IWW's resources and distracted its leaders from the business of running a union. Vigilante action against the IWW in the field reduced its membership. For all his cynical comments about the capitalist enemy, Haywood was shocked that he and more than a hundred other IWW leaders were found guilty of charges that bordered on the absurd.

By 1921 he was stunned by the shattering of the IWW. Like many American socialists, Haywood found consolation only in the success of the Bolsheviks in far-off Russia. Instead of reporting to prison, he slipped aboard a ship and sailed for the Soviet Union.

For a few years, while the Russian Communists deluded themselves that international revolution was just around the corner, Haywood acted like a leader of that campaign, appearing at ceremonies in Moscow. When the capitalist order proved far from dead in Europe and America, and the Soviet leaders engrossed themselves in domestic affairs, Haywood was first put in charge of a factory (he was apparently a failure at the job) and then pensioned off in a small apartment in the Russian capital.

He was delighted to receive American visitors but was miserable as an exile. There was no alternative. To return to the United States meant prison. In 1927, he suffered a stroke and died.

Powers. But they did hope for American neutrality, and in heavily German areas like Wisconsin and other parts of the Midwest, they said so loudly. The National German League numbered 3 million members and actively worked against intervention.

German Americans joined with Irish Americans in the German-Irish Legislative Committee for the Furtherance of United States Neutrality and the American Federation of Labor's National Peace Council. Many of the nation's 4.5 million people of Irish descent hated England. When the British crushed an Irish rebellion in 1916 (which was backed by Germany), a few prominent Irish Americans declared for the German cause.

Similarly, many Russian and Polish Jews, who suffered brutal persecution under the czars, supported Germany. To them, Germany and Austria were countries where Jews enjoyed civil equality. Socialists, an important minority within both the Jewish- and German-American communities, hated Russia above all other countries because of the cruelty of the czar's secret police.

With so diverse a population and such a tangle of conflicting loyalties, Wilson's policy of neutrality not only was idealistic, but was the only practical alternative, particularly for a Democratic party politician who depended on ethnic voters. And it might have worked if Europe's Great War (as the First World War was called until the second broke out in 1939) was fought for clearly stated and limited goals, and was concluded with an early victory by one side or the other.

The Deadly Stalemate

A quick victory was what the German General Staff had in mind. Germany's Schlieffen Plan, which dated back to 1905, was to knock the modern French army out of the war by flanking its defensive line. This meant invading France through neutral Belgium. Once in control of France's channel coast, the General Staff believed, German troops would be able to keep the British army from landing in Europe while the German army swept down on Paris, just as it did in 1870.

In the meantime, the strategists warned, weakened German forces on the eastern front would take a drubbing from the Russians. All that was expected of them was to hinder the Russian advance in parts of Germany which were, in fact, Polish in population. Once Britain was neutralized and France was defeated, troops from the western front would be sped eastward to meet the Russians on railroads designed for just that purpose.

The Schlieffen Plan failed in 1914 for two reasons. First, the Germans never committed as many troops to the attack as Von Schlieffen required. Second, instead of providing a broad avenue into France, the Belgians resisted heroically. Capturing the single fortress city of Liège took the Germans 12 days, longer than they expected to be in Belgium altogether. Frustrated, the invaders treated captured Belgian soldiers with a chilling ferocity, and civilians scarcely better. German soldiers earned a reputation as "savage Huns," which was to profoundly influence public opinion in the United States.

Henry Ford's Peace Mission

In December 1915, Henry Ford chartered an ocean liner for Europe, and attempted to fill it with celebrated Americans. He believed that if they brought their collective prestige to bear on the heads of the governments fighting the war, they could persuade them to make peace. Ford's scheme was viewed as crackbrained from the start, and he recruited more quacks and freeloading reporters who made fun of the whole business than he recruited dignitaries, most of whom left the ship of fools at its first port of call.

So disastrous was the adventure that Ford himself jumped ship before it had completed its rounds. On returning to the United States, he said, "I didn't get much peace but I heard in Norway that Russia might well become a huge market for tractors soon."

During the delay in Belgium, the Russian army advanced deeply into German Poland as Von Schlieffen had predicted. However, instead of hunkering down and absorbing the losses, the German General Staff lost its nerve. At a critical moment, the army on the western front was weakened in order to divert troops to stop the Russians in the east.

The Russians were stopped; the German army won a tremendous victory at the Battle of Tannenberg, capturing no fewer than a million soldiers. But there, and on the western front, the war bogged down into stalemate. Enemy armies dug entrenchments and earthworks and faced one another—along 475 miles in the west—across a no-man's-land of moonscape craters, spools of barbed wire, and the smell of death. Periodically for three years men on both sides would hurl themselves "over the top" and die by the tens of thousands for the sake of advancing the trenches a few miles.

The Technology of Killing

A revolution in military technology, and the slowness with which the generals comprehended it, made the war unspeakably bloody. Although the airplane, first flown at Kitty Hawk, North Carolina, in December 1903, captured the imagination of romantics, it was of minor importance in battle. (Ordinary soldiers considered pilots playboys; in fact, the life expectancy of British pilots once at the front was two weeks.) Nor was poisonous mustard gas, used by both sides, very effective. Its results were devastating, incapacitating entire divisions, but a slight shift in the wind blew the toxic fumes back on the army that had loosed it. Moreover, reasonably effective gas masks were soon issued to troops on both sides of no-man's-land.

The machine gun, by way of contrast, made the old-fashioned mass infantry charge, such as had dominated battle in the era of the American Civil War, an exercise in mass suicide. When one army charged out of its trenches, enemy machine guns filled the air with a hurricane of lead that mowed down soldiers by the thousands. On the first day of the Battle of the Somme in July 1916, 60,000 young Britons were slaughtered or wounded, the majority of them within the first half hour after they went over the top. By the time the Somme campaign sputtered to an indecisive end, British losses totaled 400,000 and the French, 200,000. The German army lost 500,000 men.

The British developed the tank as a means of neutralizing German machine guns. Armored vehicles could drive unharmed directly into gun emplacements. But the generals rarely used their edge to best advantage. They attached the tanks to infantry units, thus slowing them to a walk, rather than sending groups of the steel monsters rapidly in advance of the foot soldiers.

Incompetence at the top of every army contributed substantially to the bloodshed. Petty personal jealousies among Allied generals, especially between the English and the French, resulted in

It was impossible to romanticize trench warfare. Few tried to do so.

decisions that had little to do with the welfare of the common soldier or even the winning of the war.

The War at Sea

Americans were sickened by the news from Europe, but it was the war at sea that directly touched national interests. As in the past, naval war was economic war; it was aimed at destroying the enemy's commerce and, therefore, the enemy's capacity to carry on the fight. Naval superiority allowed Great Britain to strike first at sea, proclaiming a blockade of Germany.

According to the rules of war, all enemy merchant ships were fair game for seizing or sinking, although tradition required that crews and passengers be rescued. The ships of neutral nations, however, retained the right to trade with any nation as long as it was not carrying contraband (at first defined as war materiel).

The laws of blockade, which had caused friction between the British and the Americans in the past, were more complicated, and in 1914 Great Britain introduced several new wrinkles. The British blockaded Germany by mining some parts of the North Sea. Ships, including those of neutrals, would risk being destroyed merely by attempting to trade with Germany. The Royal Navy stopped many American ships on the high seas and took them to British ports for search. Britain also redefined contraband to mean almost all trade goods, including some foodstuffs. When neutral Holland, Denmark, and Sweden began to import goods for secret resale to Germany (pastoral Denmark, which never before purchased American lard, imported 11,000 tons of it in the first months of the war), the British slapped strict regulations on trade with those countries.

The United States protested, but measuredly, with no threat of taking action. The German market never was important to American shippers, and wartime sales to England and France rose so dramatically that few exporters needed the extra business. American trade with the Allies climbed from $825 million in 1914 to $3.2 billion in 1916, a fourfold increase in two years.

At first the Germans were indifferent to the British blockade. Their plan was to win a quick victory on land, which rendered economic warfare moot. When the war stalemated, however, the German General Staff recognized the necessity of throttling England's import economy. Germany's tool for doing this was another creation of the new military technology, the *Untersee-boot* (undersea boat, or U-boat), the submarine.

Submarine Warfare

Ironically, for it was to play a big part in dragging the United States into war, the modern submarine was the invention of two Americans, John Holland and Simon Lake. When the navy rejected their device as frivolous, they took their plans to Europe. The Germans recognized the submarine's potential and launched a large-scale construction program. By February 1915, Germany had a large enough flotilla of the vessels, each armed with 19 torpedoes, to declare the waters surrounding the British Isles to be a war zone. All enemy merchant ships within those waters were liable to be sunk, and the safety of neutral ships could not be absolutely guaranteed. Within days, several British vessels went to the bottom, and President Wilson warned the Kaiser that he would hold Germany to "strict accountability" for American lives and property lost to U-boats.

Because submarines were so fragile, the kind of warfare in which they engaged appeared to be particularly inhumane. On the surface, the submarine was helpless; a light six-inch gun mounted on the bow of a freighter was enough to blow a U-boat to bits. Because early submarines were slow in diving, British merchant vessels were instructed to ram them. Therefore, German submarine commanders had no choice but to strike without warning, giving crew and passengers no opportunity to escape. And since submarines were tiny, their crews were cramped, and there was no room to take aboard those who abandoned ship. Survivors of torpedoed boats were on their own in the midst of the ocean.

Many Americans grumbled that if the British blockade was illegal, the German submarine campaign was immoral. The British were thieves, but the Germans were murderers, drowning seamen by the score. And not only seamen. The submarine issue came to a head on May 7, 1915, when the English luxury liner *Lusitania* was torpedoed off the coast of Ireland, and 1,198 people of the 1,959 aboard were killed, including 139 Americans. What kind of war was this, Americans asked, that killed innocent travelers? The New York *Times* described the Germans as "savages drenched with blood."

Wilson Wins a Victory

The Germans replied that they had specifically warned Americans against traveling on the *Lusitania* through advertisements in newspapers in New York and Washington. They pointed out that the

Lusitania was not merely a passenger ship. It was carrying 4,200 cases of small arms purchased in the United States and some high explosives. So many people were lost because the *Lusitania* went down in only 18 minutes, blown wide open not by the torpedo but by a secondary explosion. The British were using innocent passengers as hostages for the safe conduct of war materiel.

Wilson was aware of the truth in the Germans' rationalization; he did not hold the British blameless in the tragedy. Nevertheless, Germany's military right to use the new weapon was less important to him than the principle of freedom of the seas for those not at war. He sent a series of strongly worded notes to Germany. The second was so antagonistic that the pacifistic Bryan feared it would mean war. He resigned rather than sign it, and Wilson (somewhat relieved; Bryan had begun to wear on him) replaced him in the State Department with Robert Lansing, an international lawyer.

While making no formal promises to Wilson, the Germans stopped attacking passenger vessels, and the *Lusitania* uproar faded. Then, early in 1916, the Allies announced that they were arming all merchant ships, and Germany responded that the U-boats would sink all enemy vessels without warning. On March 24, 1916, a sitting duck, a French channel steamer on a scheduled run between Dieppe and Folkestone, the *Sussex*, was torpedoed with an American among the casualties. Wilson threatened to break diplomatic relations with Germany, the last step before a declaration of war, if unrestricted submarine warfare were continued.

The German General Staff did not want the United States in the war. Plans for a major offensive on all fronts were afoot, and the German navy did not have enough U-boats to launch a full-scale attack on British shipping. In the Sussex Pledge of May 4, 1916, the German foreign office promised to observe the rules of visit and search before attacking enemy ships. This effectively meant abandoning the use of the submarine, but it kept the United States at home, which was the idea.

AMERICA GOES TO WAR

Wilson had won a spectacular diplomatic victory at the beginning of his campaign for reelection. He was enthusiastically renominated at the Democratic convention, and his campaign was given a theme that did not entirely please him. The keynote speaker built his speech around the slogan "He Kept Us Out of War."

He Kept Us Out of War — While Preparing for It

Wilson did not like the slogan because, as he confided to an aide, "I can't keep the country out of war. Any little German lieutenant can put us into war at any time by some calculated outrage." He meant that a submarine commander, acting on his own, could bark out the order that would torpedo the Sussex Pledge. Like many national leaders before and since, Wilson had trapped himself in a position where control over a momentous decision was out of his hands. He, at least, had the wisdom to know it.

Wilson began to prepare for the possibility of war as early as November 1915, when he asked Congress to beef up the army to 400,000 men and to fund a huge expansion of the navy. He was pushed into this "preparedness" campaign by his political enemy Theodore Roosevelt, who jabbed and poked at the fact that American forces totaled fewer than 100,000; that the Quartermaster Corps (entrusted with supply) had only recently begun using trucks; that at one point in 1915 the American artillery had only enough ammunition for two days' fighting with cannon that were a generation obsolete.

Wilson also had to contend with an antipreparedness Congress led by Representative Claude Kitchin of North Carolina. With widespread backing among the western and southern progressives, on whom Wilson generally depended for support, the antipreparedness forces pointed out that it had been preparedness that led to Europe going to war in the first place. If the United States had the means to fight, they argued, it was all the more likely that the United States would fight. Wilson had to settle for a compromise, less of a military buildup than the Roosevelt forces wanted, but more than Kitchin and his supporters liked.

The Election of 1916

While Wilson wrestled with the preparedness issue, the Republicans patched up their split of 1912. Progressives who were able to stomach T. R.'s bellicosity wanted to maintain the Bull Moose party's independence. They met and nominated the Colonel to run. But Roosevelt wanted to win; he wanted the Republican nomination, too. When he realized that it

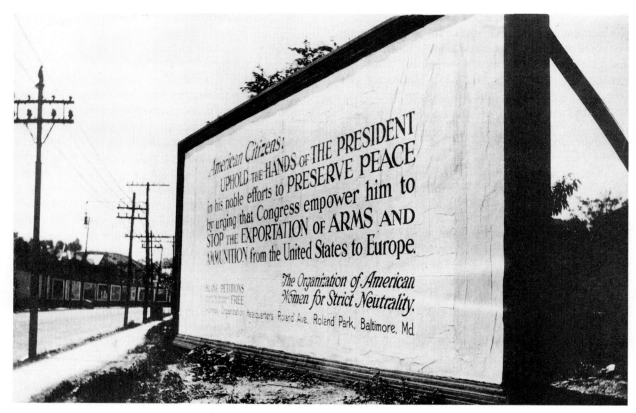

Little as Wilson liked it, Americans who opposed any involvement in World War I strongly supported him in the election campaign of 1916.

was beyond his grasp, he threw his support behind his friend, Henry Cabot Lodge. Lodge was warlike enough, but he was no progressive. In supporting him for the sake of a more aggressive war policy, Roosevelt showed just how shallow was his commitment to progressive ideals. When the Republicans actually nominated Supreme Court Justice Charles Evans Hughes, progressive in the past but a moderate on the war issue, T. R. lost heart and dropped out of the race. William Allen White wrote that the Progressives were all dressed up with nowhere to go.

Hughes's integrity was unimpeachable. In dignity and presidential bearing, he was more than a match for Wilson. His distinguished gray beard was a reminder of the simpler days before the Great War. He spoke in high-sounding phrases. But Hughes was also a dull fellow on the speaker's platform, and he lacked Wilson's toughness. Worst of all, his views on the war issue differed little from the president's; he too wanted to avoid war, but knew the United States could be forced into it. Nevertheless, thanks to Theodore Roosevelt, who stormed about the country sounding like Kaiser Bill, the Republican choice came to be known as the war candidate.

This undeserved reputation cost Hughes just enough votes to give the election to Wilson. It was a very close race. Hughes carried every northeastern state but New Hampshire and every midwestern state but Ohio. He went to bed on election night believing that he would be president. Then one antiwar western state after another turned in majorities for Wilson. When he carried California by a paper-thin margin, he was elected, 277 electoral votes to 254. The election was on Tuesday. Not until Friday did the American people know for certain who would lead them for the next four years.

Trying and Failing to Keep the Peace

Elated by the surprise but still nervous about the "little German lieutenant" who could plunge the United States into war, Wilson set out to mediate between the Allies and Central Powers. He concluded that only by ending the war in Europe could he be sure of keeping the United States out of it. During the winter of 1916–1917, he believed that he was making progress, at least with the Germans. For a time, the British seemed to be the major obstacle to peace.

On January 22, 1917, Wilson outlined his peace plan to Congress. Only a "peace without victory," a "peace among equals" with neither winners nor losers could solve the problem of European rivalries. The progressive idealist did not call for a mere cessation of hostilities. He proposed to pledge the warring powers to uphold the principles of national self-determination and absolute freedom of the seas, and to establish some kind of international mechanism for resolving future disputes.

It was all illusion. Wilson and the American people were in for a rude awakening. The president's proposal was not even half-digested when, a week later, the German ambassador informed Wilson that, as of February 1, German submarines would begin sinking neutral as well as enemy ships in the war zone around Great Britain.

What had happened?

First, 1916 was devastating for both Allies and Central Powers. A German offensive against the fortress city of Verdun cost each side more than 300,000 men. A British offensive along the Somme River killed more than a million. Even the dullest-witted general could see that the war on the ground was hopelessly stalemated. However, instead of responding to Wilson's offer to mediate, the German General Staff looked for victory in another theater.

With a fleet of 100 submarines, the German military planners believed that they could knock Great Britain out of the war within a few months. They knew that breaking the Sussex Pledge meant almost certain American intervention. However, because the United States was far from ready to intervene, the German leaders calculated that the war would be over before more than a token American force could be landed in Europe.

Wilson was crestfallen, then irate. He broke off diplomatic relations with Germany, as he threatened to do, and asked Congress for authority to arm American merchant ships. When former progressive allies such as La Follette and Borah filibustered to prevent this, he denounced them as "a little group of willful men, representing no opinion but their own."

For the first time, the president was the leader of the war party. Nevertheless, Wilson did not abandon all hope of staying out of the conflict until German submarines sent three American freighters to the bottom. On the evening of April 2, a solemn Wilson asked Congress for a formal declaration. "The right is more precious than peace," he said, "and we shall fight for the things which we have always carried nearest our hearts."

For four days a bitter debate shook the Capitol. Six senators and about fifty representatives held out against war to the end. They blamed Wilson for failing to be truly neutral; some claimed that the United States was going to spill its young men's blood in order to bail out Wall Street's loans to England and to enrich the munitions manufacturers, the "merchants of death." In one of the most moving speeches, freshman Senator George Norris of Nebraska said, "We are going into war upon the command of gold . . . We are about to put the dollar sign on the American flag."

Why America Went to War

In later years, some historians would say that Norris was right. With varying emphasis, they agreed that special interests wanted a war that did not concern the country, and methodically maneuvered the United States into it. To the extent that Wall Street favored a British victory for the sake of its own profits and that the "merchants of death" fed off the blood of soldiers, they were correct.

But to say that certain interest groups wanted to go to war is not to say that they had their way with Wilson and Congress. Woodrow Wilson was as unlikely to take a cue from Wall Street and the Dupont munitions works as he was to seek advice on a church matter from Theodore Roosevelt. To Wilson, the freedom of the seas was sacred, a right on which Americans had insisted since the 1790s. Moreover, the president shared in the profound shift in public sentiment from 1914, when virtually no American dreamed of entering the war, to the spring of 1917, when the majority favored entering the conflict. The reasons for his about-face lie in the growing belief that Germany represented a force for evil in the world and the skillful propaganda of the British and pro-British Americans in encouraging this perception.

The Hun and His *Kultur*

The depiction of Germans as barbaric "Huns" practicing a diabolical *Kultur* (merely German for "culture," but having a sinister ring to it in American

A banner headline on the New York American *reported the beginning of war between the United States and Germany, April 6, 1917.*

ears) had its origins in the German violation of Belgian neutrality. Figuratively at first, the British and French called the invasion "the rape of Belgium" and soon discovered the propaganda value of that ugly word. In fact, the German occupation of the little country, while that of a conqueror, was generally no

Patriotic posters during World War I were long on sentimentality, devoid of subtlety.

more harsh than the wartime controls the British slapped on the ever-rebellious Irish. But wall posters representing the broken body of a young girl being dragged away by a bloated, beast-like German soldier in a spiked helmet elicited all the horrible implications that rape connotes.

German insistences that their troops observed all due proprieties toward civilians were undermined in October 1915, when the German army executed Edith Cavell, the British head of the Berkendael Medical Institute in Brussels. Although Cavell was guilty of acts that were considered espionage under international law (she helped a number of British prisoners escape), the execution of a woman was profoundly stupid in an age when women were only rarely executed for murder.

The submarine war further angered Americans. Not everyone agreed with Wilson that, even in modern warfare, the rights of neutrals were absolute. But repeated incidents of unarmed merchant seamen and innocent passengers drowning in the dark cold waters of the North Atlantic touched a delicate nerve. Artists brilliantly aroused basic human fear in posters that showed seamen fighting vainly to swim while their ship sank in the moonlit background.

German saboteurs were probably not so active in the United States as British and pro-British propagandists claimed. Nevertheless, several German diplomats were caught red-handed in 1915 when a bumbling agent left incriminating papers on a train, and in 1916, the huge Black Tom munitions stores in New Jersey were completely destroyed in a suspicious "accident."

The real blockbuster was a piece of paper. On February 25, 1917, while Wilson was searching for a last chance to avoid war, the British communicated to him a message that the German foreign minister, Arthur Zimmermann, had sent to the Mexican government. In the event that the United States declared war on Germany, Zimmermann had proposed, Germany would finance a Mexican attack on the United States. Assuming Germany won, Mexico would be rewarded after the war with the return of some of the territory that it gave up in the Mexican War 70 years earlier, specifically the "lost provinces" of New Mexico and Arizona.

It was a foolish proposal. Mexico was still wracked by civil turmoil, and was in no condition to make war on Guatemala, let alone the United States. Nevertheless, with the American people already angered, the Zimmermann telegram persuaded many people that the unprincipled Hun must be stopped.

The American Contribution

The Germans provoked the American intervention on a gamble. German leaders bet that their all-out U-boat attack would starve England into surrender before the Americans could contribute to the war effort. For three months, it appeared they guessed right. In February and March 1917, German submarines sank 570,000 tons of shipping bound to and from England. In April, the total ran to almost 900,000 tons. A quarter of the British merchant fleet lay at the bottom of the sea. (All told, 203 U-boats sank 5,408 ships during the war, some 11 million tons.) At one point in April 1917, the British had enough food on hand to feed the island nation for only three weeks.

But the worst passed and the Germans lost their wager. At the insistence of American Admiral William S. Sims, merchantmen ceased to travel alone. Guarded by naval vessels, particularly the small, fast, and heavily armed destroyers (the nemesis of the U-boats), merchant ships crossed the

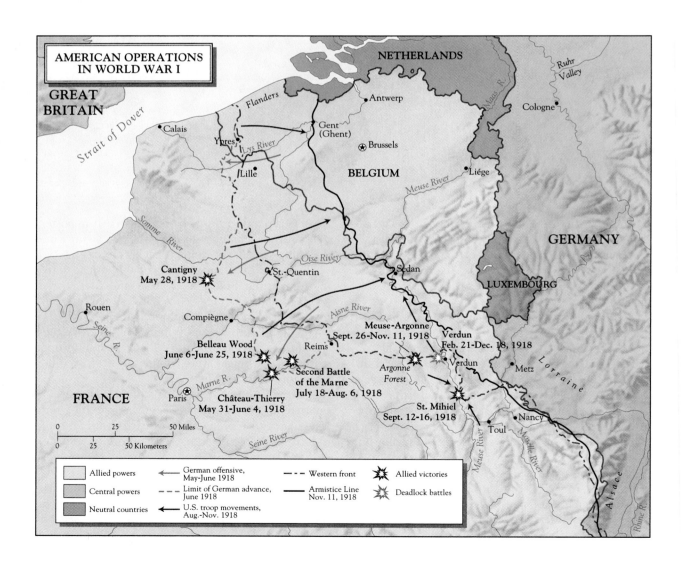

World War I Casualties

	Total Mobilized Forces	Killed or Died	Wounded	Prisoners & Missing	Total Casualties
United States	4,791,000	117,000	204,000	5,000	326,000
Russia	12,000,000	1,700,000	4,950,000	2,500,000	9,150,000
France	8,410,000	1,358,000	4,266,000	537,000	6,161,000
British Commonwealth	8,904,000	908,000	2,090,000	192,000	3,190,000
Italy	5,615,000	650,000	947,000	600,000	2,197,000
Germany	11,000,000	1,774,000	4,216,000	1,153,000	7,143,000
Austria-Hungary	7,800,000	1,200,000	3,620,000	2,220,000	7,020,000
Total	58,520,000	7,707,000	20,293,000	7,187,000	35,187,000

Atlantic in huge convoys. Over the objections of the Royal Navy (but with the support of Prime Minister David Lloyd George), Sims succeeded in building his "bridge of ships." As early as May 1917, U-boat kills dropped drastically, far below what the German navy claimed it could do. By July, the American navy took over most defense operations in the Western Hemisphere and sent 34 destroyers to Queenstown (Cobh) in Ireland to assist the British. So successful was the well-guarded convoy system that only 200 out of 2 million American soldiers sent to France in 1917 and 1918 were drowned on the way. In the meantime, by commandeering more than a hundred German ships that were in American ports at the time war was declared (including the behemoth *Vaterland*, renamed the *Leviathan*) and by launching a massive shipbuilding program, the Americans were soon producing two ships for every one that the Germans sank.

The Fighting Over There

Soldiers went too. General John Pershing, just months from frustration in Mexico, arrived in Paris in July 1917 with the first units of the American Expeditionary Force, the First Infantry Division. This was primarily a symbolic gesture. Because Pershing refused to send his poorly trained men to the front, the Germans were proved right in gambling that American reinforcements could not in themselves turn the tide. The first Americans to see action, near Verdun in October, were used only to beef up French, British, and Canadian units decimated by the fighting the previous year.

The autumn of 1917 went poorly for the Allies. The Germans and Austrians defeated the Italians in the south and, in November, knocked Russia out of the war. A liberal democratic government that deposed the czar in March 1917 proved unable to keep a mutinous Russian army supplied, and a group of revolutionary Communists, the Bolsheviks, led by Vladmir Ilyich Lenin, seized power on the basis of promises of "peace and bread." The Treaty of Brest-Litovsk, which the Germans forced on the Russians, was vindictive and harsh. News of it convinced many Americans that they did right in going to war to stop the Huns' hunger for world conquest. By closing down the eastern front, however, the Germans were able to throw a bigger army into France.

In the spring of 1918, Germany launched a do-or-die offensive. The Allies fell back to the Marne River, close enough to Paris that the shelling could be heard on the Champs Elysées. But by this time there were 250,000 fresh American troops in France, including about 27,000 at Château-Thierry, near the hottest part of the fighting. By the middle of July, when the Germans attempted one last drive toward the capital, about 85,000 Americans helped hurl them back at Belleau Wood.

The Supreme Allied Commander, Field Marshal Ferdinand Foch, wanted to incorporate American troops into exhausted British and French units. Pershing stubbornly insisted that the Yanks fight as a unit. This was important to him not only for reasons of morale, but because Wilson made it clear that the United States was not an ally of Britain and France but merely their associate. In order to ensure his "peace without victory," Wilson was determined to

740 *Chapter 37 Over There*

play an independent role at the peace conference that would follow the war. Foch had no choice but to give in and grumble.

By the summer of 1918, the Americans in France represented the margin of victory over the Germans. In September, the Americans took over the attack on a bulge in the German lines called the St.-Mihiel Salient, and succeeded in clearing it out. The final great American battle was along a 24-mile line in the Argonne Forest, a naturally rugged country just short of the border between France and Germany that had been transformed into a ghostly wasteland by four years of digging and shelling. It was in that position that over a million "doughboys" were sitting when, on November 11, 1918, the Germans surrendered.

Armistice

In the trenches and back home, Americans celebrated deliriously. Millions of people gathered in city centers throughout the country, dancing and whooping. They believed that the Yanks had won the war. After all, the Germans had stalemated the French and British until the boys went "Over There," in the title of a popular song by George M. Cohan of the time. Then, just a year after the Americans began to fight, it was over.

The American intervention was invaluable to the Allied victory. Three million boys were drafted; two million went to France. But the unmitigated joy in the United States was possible only because the American sacrifice was a comparatively minor one. Over 100,000 Americans were dead, more than half of them from disease (particularly the influenza that swept the world in 1918) rather than from bullets.

By comparison, 1.4 million French and almost 1 million British soldiers died. Three-quarters of all the Frenchmen who served in the armed forces were casualties. Both France and Britain were badly maimed. Germany and Russia were defeated. If it was not true that the United States had won the war, it was certainly true that the United States was the only belligerent nation whose people could feel they were victors.

CHRONOLOGY

1911   Francisco Madero leads successful revolution in Mexico

1913   Madero murdered

1914   American troops occupy Vera Cruz.
Franz Ferdinand assassinated; World War I begins

1915   Wilson sends marines into Haiti
Germans initiate submarine warfare
Lusitania torpedoed

1916   Germany agrees to suspend unrestricted submarine warfare
Pancho Villa raids Columbus, New Mexico
U.S. troops pursue Villa into Mexico
Easter Rebellion in Ireland
Wilson reelected

1917   Germany resumes unrestricted submarine warfare
Zimmermann Telegram published
U.S. declares war on Germany

1918   Armistice in Europe

FOR FURTHER READING

Several books cited earlier remain basic, particularly Vincent P. DeSantis, *The Shaping of Modern America, 1877–1916*, 1973; Arthur S. Link, *Woodrow Wilson and the Progressive Era*, 1954; William L. O'Neill, *The Progressive Years: America Comes of Age*, 1975; and Nell Irvin Painter, *Standing at Armageddon: The United States, 1877–1919*, 1987.

Somewhat more narrowly focused, but dealing with this era in part, are E. H. Buehrig, *Woodrow Wilson and the Balance of Power*, 1955; Foster R. Dulles, *America's Rise to World Power, 1898–1954*, 1955; Lewis L. Gould, *Reform and Regulation: American Politics, 1900–1916*, 1978; Otis L. Graham, Jr., *The Great Campaigns: Reform and War in America, 1900–1928*, 1971; P. Edward Haley, *Revolution and Intervention: The Diplomacy of Taft and Wilson with Mexico, 1910–1917*, 1970; George F. Kennan, *American Diplomacy, 1900–1950*, 1951; David Kennedy, *Over Here: The First World War and American Society*, 1980; N. G. Levin, Jr., *Woodrow Wilson and World Politics: America's Response to War and Revolution*, 1968; and A. S. Link, *Wilson the Diplomatist*, 1957, and *Woodrow Wilson: War, Revolution, and Peace*, 1979. A newer treatment is Robert H. Ferrell, *Woodrow Wilson and World War I, 1917–1921*, 1985.

Also see Ernest R. May, *The World War and American Isolation, 1914–1917*, 1959; Walter Millis, *The Road to War*, 1935; R. E. Quirk, *An Affair of Honor: Woodrow Wilson and the Occupation of Vera Cruz*, 1962; Charles C. Tansill, *America Goes to War*, 1938; Russell Weigley, *The American Way of War: History of United States Military Policy and Strategy*, 1973; and William A. Williams, *The Tragedy of American Diplomacy*, 1959. A provocative but significant specialized study is David S. Fogelsong, *America's Secret War Against Bolshevism: U.S. Intervention in the Russian Civil War, 1917–1920*, 1995.

For military history, an excellent source is the work cited above, Russell Weigley, *The American Way of War: History of United States Military Policy and Strategy*, 1973. See also A. E. Barbeau and F. Henri, *The Unknown Soldiers*, 1974; Lawrence Stallings, *The Doughboys*, 1963; Dorothy and Carl J. Schneider, *Into the Breach: American Women Overseas in World War I*, 1991; Paul F. Braim, *The Test of Battle: American Expeditionary Forces in the Meuse-Argonne*, 1987; and Gene Smith, *Until the Last Trumpet Sounds: The Life of General of the Armies John J. Pershing*, 1998.

Film star Douglas Fairbanks drumming up sales of war bonds on Wall Street.

38
CHAPTER

OVER HERE

World War I at Home

1917–1920

Once lead this people into war, and they'll forget there ever was such a thing as tolerance. To fight you must be ruthless and brutal, and the spirit of ruthless brutality will enter into the very fiber of our national life.

—Woodrow Wilson

War means an ugly mob-madness, crucifying the truth-tellers, choking the artists, sidetracking reforms, revolutions, and working of social forces.

—John Reed

When I think of the many voices that were heard before the war and are still heard, interpreting America from a class or sectional or selfish standpoint, I am not sure that, if the war had to come, it did not come at the right time for the preservation and reinterpretation of American ideals.

—George Creel

The more horrible a depersonalized scientific mass war becomes, the more necessary it is to find universal ideal motives to justify it.

—John Dewey

Woodrow Wilson called the Great War "a war to make the world safe for democracy." He sent the doughboys to Europe, and threw the industrial might of the United States behind the Allies on the understanding that there would be no victors in the traditional sense of the word, but instead a new world order dedicated to settling disputes between nations justly and peaceably. He also called World War I "a war to end all wars."

THE PROGRESSIVE WAR

The First World War was simultaneously the apogee of progressivism, when reformers had a free hand in turning their beliefs into policy, and the undoing of the progressive movement. For two years, progressive moralists and social planners of the New Nationalist stripe had their way in Washington. Within two years of the conclusion of the war, however, there was no progressive movement worth noticing, only a few, aging voices crying in the wilderness in the shape of a minority in Congress, and getting few replies but echoes from the past.

The Movement Splits

World War I split the progressives. A few of them itched to fight from the start. The most famous was Theodore Roosevelt, and he became a pathetic shrill figure in his final years. (T. R. died in 1919.) When the United States finally intervened, T. R. asked for a command in Europe. No doubt with relish, but also prudently (for this was no splendid little war on a tropical island), Wilson ignored him. In doing so, he embittered many of Roosevelt's devotees.

Other Republican progressives, mostly westerners such as La Follette, Norris, Borah, and Hiram Johnson, fought against a declaration of war to the bitter end. After the United States was in the conflict, they toned down their rhetoric in the interests of national unity. (And, so as to save their careers, some newspaper cartoonists depicted the antiwar westerners as traitors; in one cartoon they accepted medals from the German Kaiser.) Still, they never changed their opinion that going to war was a tragic blunder, or even that war was foisted on the country by munitions makers and bankers. The "willful men" prolonged the debate on the Conscription Act of 1917 for six weeks, finally forcing Congress to exempt men under 21 from the draft. Any attraction they felt to Wilson before April 1917 quickly dissipated thereafter.

That was not the case, however, with the Democratic party and some other Republican progressives. In Congress and out, the majority of them wholeheartedly supported the war. Like Wilson, they came to believe that imperial Germany was a serious threat to free institutions all over the world. Moreover, in the task of mobilizing resources in order to fight the war, and in the wave of patriotic commitment that swept the country, the progressives saw a golden opportunity to put their ideas for economic and social reform to work.

They were right on one count. It was impossible to wage modern total war and still cling to the nineteenth-century's vision of a free, unregulated economy. Armies numbering millions of men could not be supplied with food, clothing, shelter, medicine, and arms by private companies that were free to do entirely as their owners chose. France and England clamped tight controls on their factories and farms in 1914. (Germany already had them.) When America went to war, progressives believed that their government had to do the same.

Mobilizing the citizenry: At this rally, champion gardeners and canners were honored for their contributions to the war effort.

They were not disappointed. Proposals for regulation of business that were rejected in peacetime as too radical proved, in the emergency of wartime, to be less than was necessary. Although generally with a soft touch, the federal government virtually took over the direction of the economy.

Planned Economy

The federal government grew like a mushroom in the war as government spending increased tenfold. The federal bureaucracy doubled in size. Employees of the executive branch, 400,000 in 1916, numbered 950,000 in 1918.

Some 5,000 government agencies were set up during the 20 months that the United States was at war, a statistical average of more than eight new agencies a day. Some were useless and wasteful, established without careful thought; they served little purpose save to provide desks, chairs, inkwells, and salaries for the functionaries who ran them. A few agencies were just plain failures. The Aircraft Production Board was commissioned to construct 22,000 airplanes in a year. That figure was unrealistic. But the 1,200 craft and 5,400 replacement motors that the board actually delivered to France were far fewer than a hustler with a bank loan could have supplied.

Other agencies were quite successful. The Shipping Board, actually founded in 1916 before the declaration of war, produced vessels twice as fast as the German submarines could sink them. Privately run shipbuilding companies, loaded with deadwood in management, were not up to that herculean task.

The United States Railway Administration, headed by Wilson's son-in-law and secretary of the treasury, William G. McAdoo, was created early in 1918 when the owners of the nation's railroads proved incapable of moving the volume of freight the war created. The government paid the stockholders a rent equal to their earnings in the prosperous prewar years and simply took over. McAdoo untangled a colossal snafu in management within a few weeks, and reorganized the railroads into an efficient system such as the nation had never known. About 150,000 freight cars short of what was needed to do the job in 1917, American railroads enjoyed a surplus of 300,000 cars by the end of the war.

The various war production boards were coordinated by a superagency, the War Industries Board, headed by Wall Street financier Bernard Baruch. His presence at the top of the planning pyramid indicated that the progressives had not won their campaign for a directed economy without paying a price. American industry and agriculture were regulated, indeed regimented, as never before. But democratically elected officials and public-spirited experts with no stake in the profits were not in the driver's seat. Businessmen were.

Herbert Hoover: The Administrator as War Hero

The task given to Food Administrator Herbert C. Hoover was even more difficult than McAdoo's, and his achievement was daily in the public eye. Hoover's job was to organize food production, distribution, and consumption so that America's farms could feed the United States, supply the huge Allied armies, and help many European civilians to survive as well.

Only 43 years old when he took the job, Hoover already was known as a boy wonder. An orphan when still a child in Iowa, Hoover moved to California to live with relatives and worked his way through Stanford University. A mining engineer, he decided to work abroad on new strikes rather than for established mining companies at home. Hoover had his share of adventure; he and his wife were besieged in China during the Boxer Rebellion and both acquitted themselves admirably. Mostly, however, Hoover helped develop mines, made shrewd investments, and was so soon a millionaire that he was bored with money-making when still a young man.

Hoover's interests and ambitions lay in public service. Like Wilson an idealist, like Andrew Carnegie he believed that able, wealthy men had special responsibilities to society. Unlike Carnegie, who gave money away, Hoover meant to devote his talents for administration and organization to public service.

He got his chance when he happened to be in London at the outbreak of the Great War. He was asked to take over the problem of getting food to the people of devastated Belgium and he jumped at the challenge. Hoover liquidated his business interests, quickly mastered the complex and ticklish task of feeding people in a war zone, and undoubtedly saved tens of thousands, if not hundreds of thousands, of lives.

Hoover did all this without charm or personal flash. He was an intense, outwardly humorless, grim person, even in one-on-one relationships. He was all business. His method was to apply engineering principles to the solution of human problems. Progressives admired just such expertise, and the cool, methodical Hoover was a refreshing contrast to other humanitarians who moved about in a cloud of pious self-congratulation. It is an insight into the spirit of the times that he became a war hero alongside such traditional types as General "Black Jack" Pershing and America's swashbuckling ace pilot, Eddie Rickenbacker.

Hooverizing America

In one significant manner, Hoover was far from a typical progressive. He preferred voluntary programs to government coercion. Consequently, food was never rationed in the United States as it was in the combatant nations of Europe. Instead, Hoover engineered colorful publicity campaigns urging Americans, in the spirit of cooperation, to observe Wheatless Mondays, Meatless Tuesdays, Porkless Thursdays, and so on. The program worked because compliance was easy, yet psychologically gratifying. Making do without a vital commodity one day a week was no real sacrifice, but doing so made civilians feel as though they were part of the fighting machine. And when a Meatless Tuesday was observed by tens of millions, the savings were enormous.

Hoover also encouraged city dwellers to plant "victory gardens" in their tiny yards. Every tomato that was raised at home freed commercially produced food for the front. His agency promoted classes in economizing in the kitchen and distributed cookbooks on how to prepare leftovers. The impact was so great that, half-seriously, Americans invented the verb hooverize to mean economize, and they used it. Chicago proudly reported that the city's housekeepers had hooverized the monthly output of garbage down by a third.

Hoover increased farm production through a combination of patriotic boosting and cash incentives. He helped increase the acres in wheat from 45 million in 1917 to 75 million in 1919. American exports of foodstuffs to the Allies tripled over already high prewar levels. Hoover added "Miracle Man" to his list of flattering nicknames. Another young Washington administrator, Undersecretary of the Navy Franklin D. Roosevelt, was so impressed that he wanted the Democratic party to nominate Hoover for president in 1920 to carry on Woodrow Wilson's work.

Managing People

People were mobilized along with railway cars and crops, workers and ordinary citizens as well as soldiers. In May 1917, Congress passed the Selective Service Act, the first draft law since the Civil War. Registration was compulsory for all men between the ages of 21 and 45. (In 1918, the minimum age was lowered to 18.) From the 10 million who registered within a month of passage (24 million by the end of the war), local draft boards selected able-bodied recruits according to quotas assigned by the federal government. Some occupational groups were deferred as vital to the war effort, but no one was allowed to buy his way out, as had been done during the Civil War. Indeed, authority to make final selections was given to local draft boards in order to silence critics who said that conscription had no place in a democracy. The draft contributed about 3 million young men to the armed forces, in addition to 2 million who volunteered.

About 21,000 draftees claimed to be conscientious objectors on religious grounds, although, in the end, only 4,000 insisted on being assigned to noncombatant duty, as medics or in the Quartermaster Corps. Approximately 500 men refused to cooperate with the military in any way, some for political rather than religious reasons. Under the terms of the Selective Service Act, they were imprisoned and, in general, treated poorly. In Washington State, a man who claimed that Jesus had forbidden him to take up arms was sentenced to death. He was not executed, but the last conscientious objector was not freed from prison until 1933, long after most Americans had come to agree with him that the war had been a mistake.

SOCIAL CHANGES

War is revolutionary or, at least, it is an agitator. The changes impressed on American society from the top in the interests of victory inevitably affected social relationships. Some groups consciously took advantage of the government's wants, needs, and preoccupations to achieve old goals. Others were merely caught up by the different rhythms of a society at war.

Labor Takes Its Seat

In order to keep the factories humming, Wilson made concessions to the labor movement that would have been unthinkable a few years earlier. He appointed Samuel Gompers, the patriotic president of the American Federation of Labor, to sit on Baruch's War Industries Board. The postmaster general refused to deliver an issue of a socialist magazine in which

Gompers was criticized. In return for such recognition and favors, Gompers pledged the AFL unions to a no-strike policy for the duration of the conflict.

Because wages rose during the war, there were comparatively few work stoppages. Business boomed, and employers dizzy with bonanza profits did not care to jeopardize them by resisting moderate demands by their employees. Most important, the National War Labor Board, on which five AFL nominees sat, mediated industrial disputes before they disrupted production; in many cases, the board found in favor of the workers.

The quiet incorporation of organized labor into the federal decision-making process made the AFL respectable, as it never had been before, as Samuel Gompers had prayed the union would be. From 2.7 million members in 1914, the union movement (including independent unions) grew to 4.2 million in 1919.

Blacks in Wartime

Like Gompers, leaders of black organizations hoped that by proving their patriotism in wartime, African Americans would win improved civil and social status in time of peace. About 400,000 young black men enlisted or responded to the draft. Proportionately, more blacks than whites donned khaki in World War I.

It was difficult to ignore the contradiction between Wilson's ringing declaration that the purpose of the war was to defend democracy and liberty and the second-class citizenship suffered by black people. W. E. B. Du Bois, probably the best-known African-American leader after the death of Booker T. Washington, pointedly reminded the president of the dichotomy, and Wilson did go so far as to issue a stronger condemnation of lynching than he had ever done before the war. Nevertheless, mere war could not destroy deeply rooted racist sentiments. Black soldiers were assigned to segregated units and usually put to menial tasks such as digging trenches and loading trucks behind the lines. Only a few black units saw combat, although the French government awarded the African-American 369th Regiment the *Croix de Guerre* for gallantry in battle.

Military segregation held a few advantages for blacks. In order to command black units, the army trained and commissioned more than 1,200 African-American officers. This was particularly gratifying to Du Bois, who staked his hopes for the future on the creation of a colored elite.

Race Riot at Home

More important in the long run than service in the army was the massive movement of blacks from the rural and strictly segregated South to the industrial centers of the North. Before 1914, only about 10,000 blacks a year drifted from the South to cities like New York, Philadelphia, Detroit, and Chicago. After 1914, while the risks of ocean travel choked off immigration from abroad just as factories filling war orders needed more workers, 100,000 blacks made the trek each year. It was not so great a leap in miles as the European immigration, but it was just as wrenching socially and culturally. Moving from a Mississippi delta cabin to a Detroit factory and slum meant a massive change in the way of life.

Most of the blacks who moved north were young people, less conditioned than their elders to accept the daily humiliations that accompanied being black in white America. This was particularly true of the men in uniform, who believed that their service entitled them to respect. Moreover, African-American soldiers who went to France discovered a society which, if far from unprejudiced in matters of race, did not draw a color line so absolute as America did.

One consequence of the social upheaval was that 1917 was a year of violent racial conflict. There was a frightening race riot in industrial East St. Louis, Illinois. In Houston, white civilians fought a pitched battle with black soldiers, and 12 people were killed. Although both sides shared the blame for that riot, 13 black soldiers were hanged and 14 were imprisoned for life. Du Bois and the NAACP were only partly correct in their analysis of how the war would affect blacks. Society made economic concessions to African Americans in the interests of winning the war, but it did not grant civil equality.

It's a Woman's War

The woman suffrage movement, by way of contrast, skillfully parlayed wartime idealism and fears into final victory for the long-fought cause. Imitating British and French examples, the armed forces inducted female volunteers, mostly as nurses and clerical workers. More important was the same labor shortage that created opportunities in northern factories for blacks. Working-class women began doing factory work and other jobs that were entirely closed to them in peacetime. Women operated trolley cars, drove delivery trucks, cleaned streets, directed

Members of the 369th Infantry, a black regiment, returned to the United States in 1919 wearing medals given to them by the French government for gallantry in battle.

traffic, and filled jobs in every industry from aircraft construction to zinc galvanization.

Middle-class women took the lead in organizing support groups. They rolled bandages, held patriotic rallies, and filled the holds of ships with knitted sweaters, socks, and home-baked cookies for the boys in France. With women's contributions to waging the war so conspicuous, it was increasingly difficult for patriotic politicians to oppose suffrage with the argument that women belonged in the nursery minding infants and in the kitchen baking peach cobbler.

Voting at Last

By 1917, the feminist movement was split into radical and conservative wings. Curiously, while the radicals and conservatives often had harsh words for one another, their different approaches both contributed to the victory of the suffrage movement. Thus, when the aggressive Women's party led by Alice Paul demonstrated noisily in Washington, burning a copy of Wilson's idealistic Fourteen Points and chaining themselves to the fence in front of the White House, many politicians went scurrying for reassurance to the more genteel National American Woman Suffrage Association.

Led by Carrie Chapman Catt, the association shrewdly obliged them. Not only did most American women oppose such irresponsible behavior, Catt argued, but social stability and conservative government could be ensured only by granting women the vote. Their numbers would counterbalance the increasing influence of radicals and foreigners at the polls, not to mention the blacks who were demanding their Fourteenth and Fifteenth Amendment rights.

The suffrage movement was too long in the field and too large to be denied. Even Wilson, who instinctively disliked the idea of women voting, announced his support. On June 4, 1919, a few months after the Armistice, Congress sent the Nineteenth Amendment to the states. On August 18, 1920, ratification by Tennessee put it into the Constitution. "The right of citizens . . . to vote," it read, "shall not be denied or abridged by the United States or by any State on account of sex." Carrie Chapman Catt had no doubt about what put it over. It was the war, the former pacifist said, that liberated American women.

The Moral War

Another long progressive campaign had already been brought to a victorious end. Like the suffragists, the prohibitionists appeared to be stalled permanently on the eve of the war. In 1914, only one-quarter of the states had some sort of prohibition law on the books, and many of those were casually enforced at best. By the end of 1917, when a constitutional amendment prohibiting alcohol nationally was proposed, only 13 states were completely dry. And yet, within a year and a half, prohibition was the law of the land. What happened?

With American participation in the war, the antidrinking forces added several new arguments to their armory: the distilling of liquor consumed a vast quantity of grain that was needed as food. Shortly after the declaration of war, Congress passed the Lever Act, a section of which forbade the sale of grain to distilleries.

Because many breweries were run by German Americans, with their teutonic names emblazoned proudly on bottle and barrel, they were doubly handicapped in fighting against prohibition. Although Americans had developed a taste for chilled lager beer, the beverage was still associated with Germans. Moralism, hooverizing, and the popular insistence on 100 percent Americanism all combined to bring about the Eighteenth Amendment, which prohibited "the manufacture, sale, or transportation of intoxicating liquors" in the United States. The power of wartime conformism can be read in the fact that many politicians voted to ratify Prohibition because they believed it would fail, and hoped it would fail, but wanted to be on record as favoring it.

Ending Prostitution

War usually leads to relaxation of sexual morality, as young men are removed from the social restraints of family and custom. The First World War proved to be no exception. However, well-meaning moralistic progressives in Wilson's administration hoped to take advantage of the mobilization of millions in order to instill high moral standards in the young men under their control. Josephus Daniels, the deeply religious secretary of the navy, thought of his ships as "floating universities" of moral reform. He gave orders to clear out the red-light districts that were a fixture in every naval port, and the army did the same in cities near its bases.

Prostitution was not eliminated by these orders any more than drinking whiskey and beer were abolished by the Eighteenth Amendment. But the short-term victories encouraged reformers in their belief that, among the horrors, the First World War was a blessing on reformers.

CONFORMITY AND REPRESSION

It was no blessing on civil liberties. As Wilson privately predicted, white-hot patriotism scorched the traditions of free political expression and toleration

A woman welder was unthinkable before the war created a labor shortage.

of disparate ways of life. Of course, free speech, religious expression, and ethnic diversity had been violated before the First World War. But never had violation of the Bill of Rights been so widespread as during the war, and never had the federal government so stridently supported, and even initiated, repression.

The Campaign against the Socialists

The Socialist party of America was the only important national political institution to oppose American intervention. In April 1917, just as war was being declared in Washington, the party met in emergency convention in St. Louis and proclaimed "unalterable opposition" to a conflict that killed working people while paying dividends to capitalists. Rather than hurting the party at the polls, this stance earned the party an increase in votes; many non-Socialists cast ballots for Socialists as the only way to express their opposition to the war.

Government moved quickly to head off the possibility of an antiwar bandwagon. The state legislature of New York expelled seven Socialist assemblymen simply because they objected to the war. Not until after the war did courts overrule this action as unconstitutional. Victor Berger was elected to Congress from Milwaukee, but denied his seat by the House. When, in the special election to fill the vacancy, he defeated an opponent supported by both the Democratic and Republican parties, Congress again refused to accept him. Berger's district remained unrepresented until 1923 when, finally, he was allowed the seat he was elected to fill. In the meantime, the Milwaukee Socialists' *Social Democratic Herald* and many other Socialist papers were denied cheap mailing privileges by Postmaster General Albert S. Burleson. Most of them never recovered from the blow. The golden age of the American socialist press was in the past.

The most celebrated attack on the Socialists was the indictment and trial of the party's longtime leader, Eugene V. Debs, for a speech opposing conscription. In sending Debs to Atlanta penitentiary, the Wilson administration was taking a chance. The four-time presidential candidate was loved and respected by many non-Socialists. At his trial in September 1918, Debs's eloquence lived up to its reputation. "While there is a lower class I am in it; while there is a criminal element I am of it; while there is a soul in prison, I am not free," he told the jury. But in

prosecuting and jailing him and other prominent Socialists such as Kate Richards O'Hare, the government also made it clear that dissent on the war issue would not be tolerated.

The Destruction of the IWW

The suppression of the IWW was more violent. There was an irony in this because, while the radical union officially opposed the war, Secretary-Treasurer William D. "Big Bill" Haywood tried to soft-pedal the issue. For the first time since strikes in 1912 and 1913, the IWW was enrolling new members by the thousands every month, and those earlier recruits did not stick. Haywood hoped to ride out the patriotic hysteria of wartime and emerge from the war with a powerful labor organization.

However, the federal government did not decide to move against the IWW because of its paper opposition to the war. Unlike the Socialists, who numbered many articulate and politically active middle-class people among their supporters, the IWW worked among the lowest ranks of the working class, people with little influence on public opinion. By 1917, however, most of these Wobblies were concentrated in three sectors of the economy that were vital to the war effort: among the migrant harvest workers who brought in the nation's wheat; among loggers in the Pacific Northwest; and among copper miners in western towns like Globe and Bisbee in Arizona and Butte in Montana. And these workers had not agreed to a no-strike pledge such as Samuel Gompers made on behalf of the American Federation of Labor.

The IWW was crushed by a combination of vigilante terrorism and government action. In July 1917, 1,000 "deputies" wearing white armbands in order to identify one another rounded up 1,200 strikers in Bisbee, loaded them on a specially chartered train, and dumped them in the Hermanas desert of New Mexico, where they were without food for 36 hours. The next month, IWW organizer Frank Little was lynched in Butte, possibly by police officers in disguise. In neither case was any attempt made to bring the vigilantes to justice. President Wilson pointedly ignored Haywood's protest of the Bisbee deportation and his demand for federal action in the case of Little's murder.

In the grain belt, sheriffs and farmers had a free hand in dealing with suspected Wobblies. In the Sitka spruce forests of Washington and Oregon

Editors of the anti-war left-wing magazine, The Masses, *pose outside the courthouse after being indicted for sedition, 1918.*

(Sitka spruce was the principal wood used in aircraft construction), the army organized the Loyal Legion of Loggers and Lumbermen to counter the popularity of the IWW. There, at least, conditions were improved as the union was repressed, but attacks on the IWW were consistently vicious. Local police and federal agents winked at and even participated in everyday violations of civil rights and violence against Wobblies and their sympathizers.

Civil Liberties Suspended

The fatal blow fell in the autumn of 1917, when the Justice Department raided IWW headquarters in several cities, rounded up the union's leaders, and indicted about 200 of them under the Espionage Act of 1917. Along with the Sedition Act of 1918, the Espionage Act outlawed not only overt treasonable acts, but made it a crime to "utter, print, write, or publish any disloyal, profane, scurrilous, or abusive language" about the government, the flag, or the uniform of a soldier or sailor. A casual snide remark was enough to warrant bringing charges, and a few actual cases were based on little more than that.

In *Schenck* v. *United States* (1919), the Supreme Court unanimously upheld this broad, vague legislation. As if to leave no doubt as to the court's resolve, Oliver Wendell Holmes, Jr., the most liberal-minded and humane Justice on the Supreme Court, was assigned to write the opinion which established the principle that when "a clear and present danger" existed, such as the war, Congress had the power to pass laws that would not be acceptable in normal times.

Even at that, the government did not prove that the IWW was guilty of sedition. In effect, the individuals who were sentenced to up to 20 years in prison were punished because of their membership in an unpopular organization. Many liberals who had no taste for IWW doctrine but who were shocked at the government's cynical policy of repression fought

752 *Chapter 38 Over Here*

the cases. In 1920, led by Roger Baldwin, they organized the American Civil Liberties Union to guard against a repetition of the wartime experience in American judicial history.

Manipulating Public Opinion

The attack on the Socialists and the Wobblies was only one fulfillment of Wilson's prediction that modern war would bring a spirit of ruthless brutality to American life. Many otherwise ordinary people were stirred by patriotism to believe that they were part of a holy crusade against a foe with the wiles and dark powers of the devil.

Violent acts against German Americans and the very idea of German culture were not uncommon. Some incidents were spontaneous; for example, a midwestern mob dragged a German-American shopkeeper from his home, threw him to his knees, forced him to kiss the American flag, and made him spend his life savings on war bonds. But intolerance and even vigilante activity was ignored if not abetted by the national government.

The agency entrusted with mobilizing public opinion was the Committee on Public Information. Ironically, it was headed by George Creel, a progressive newspaperman who had devoted his career to fighting the very sort of intolerance and social injustice he now found himself encouraging. Creel's task was twofold. First, in order to avoid demoralization, the CPI censored the news from Europe. CPI dispatches emphasized victories and suppressed or played down stories of setbacks and the misery of life in the trenches between battles. With most editors and publishers solidly behind the war, Creel had little difficulty in convincing them to censor their own correspondents.

Second, the CPI took up the task of molding public opinion so that even minor deviations from full support of the war were branded as disloyal. Obviously, all German Americans could not be imprisoned. (Only 6,300 people were actually interned compared with 45,000 of Great Britain's much smaller German-born community.) However, the CPI could and did launch a massive propaganda campaign that depicted German *Kultur* as intrinsically evil.

The CPI issued 60 million pamphlets, sent prewritten editorials to pliant (or merely lazy) newspaper editors, and subsidized the design and printing of posters conveying the impression that a network of German spies was ubiquitous in the United States. With money

to be made in exploiting the theme, the infant film industry centered in Hollywood, California, rushed to oblige. A typical title of 1917 was *The Barbarous Hun*. (Another film company was prosecuted in 1917 for releasing a film about the American Revolution that depicted British troops in an unfavorable light.)

At movie theaters before feature films and during intermissions, some 75,000 "Four-Minute Men," all volunteers, delivered patriotic speeches of that length, 7.5 million such messages in all. Film stars like action hero Douglas Fairbanks, comic Charlie Chaplin, and Mary Pickford ("America's Sweetheart") appeared at Liberty Bond rallies and spoke anti-German lines written by the CPI.

Liberty Hounds and Boy Spies

The anti-German hysteria could take laughable form as well. Restaurants revised their menus so that sauerkraut became "liberty cabbage," hamburgers became "Salisbury steak" (after a liberal British lord), and frankfurters and wiener sausages, named after German and Austrian cities, became widely known as "hot dogs."

The real dog, the dachshund, had to be reshaped into a "liberty hound." Towns with names of German origin voted to choose more patriotic designations. German measles, a common childhood disease,

---

Profiteering

If Woodrow Wilson was America's most important single movie fan (producers were delighted to send him prints of whatever he requested), he was far from alone. Perhaps as well as any statistic, the income earned by Mary Pickford, "America's Sweetheart," the nation's favorite leading lady, gauges the storm with which movies took the United States. A Broadway actress before 1910, Mary Pickford made $25 a week. In 1910, moviemaker Carl Laemmle lured her to Hollywood with the astronomical weekly salary of $175. In 1914, Adolph Zukor of Famous Players paid Pickford $20,000, then $52,000 a year. In 1915, she demanded and got $104,000 per movie plus one-half the profits it earned. In June 1916, her price was $1 million guaranteed against half the profits.

became "patriotic measles." Hundreds of schools and some colleges dropped the German language from their course offerings. Dozens of symphony orchestras refused to play the works of German composers, leaving conspicuous holes in the repertoire. Prominent German Americans who wished to save their careers found it advisable to imitate opera singer Ernestine Schumann-Heink. She was a fixture at patriotic rallies, her ample figure draped with a large American flag and her magnificent voice singing "The Star-Spangled Banner" and "America the Beautiful."

But the firing of Germans from their jobs, discriminating against German farmers, burning of German books, and beating up German Americans were not so humorous. Nor was the treatment of other people designated as less than fully patriotic by organizations of self-appointed guardians of the national interest with names like "Sedition Slammers," "Terrible Threateners," and even "Boy Spies of America." The members of such organizations stopped young men on the streets and demanded to see their draft cards. The largest of these groups, which was responsible for hundreds of illegal acts, was the American Protective League. At one time it numbered 250,000 members, although many of these probably signed up simply to avoid having their loyalty questioned.

WILSON AND THE LEAGUE OF NATIONS

Why did Woodrow Wilson, a Jeffersonian liberal before the war, tolerate and even encourage such activity? The answer lies in the fact that the president's dream of building a new world order became an obsession. Before the war, there was an almost easygoing side to Wilson. He worked only three or four hours a day, and never on Saturday and Sunday. With the war, he scarcely ever stopped toiling.

Like no president before him (but like several since), Wilson lost interest in domestic affairs except insofar as they affected his all-consuming foreign concerns. The one-time enemy of big government presided over its extraordinary expansion. Repression of dissenters, even unjust and illegal repression, appeared to hasten the defeat of the kaiser, so Wilson abandoned values that had guided his life.

The President's Obsession

In January 1918, Wilson presented Congress with his blueprint for the postwar world. It consisted of Fourteen Points, which, Wilson insisted, were to be incorporated into the treaty that would eventually be written. Most of Wilson's program dealt with specific European territorial problems, but five general principles wove through the plan.

First, defeated Germany must be treated fairly and generously in order to avoid the festering resentments that could lead to another war. Wilson was well aware that, for more than 40 years before World War I, French politicians demanded revenge for Germany's defeat of France in 1870. In practical terms, Wilson meant that Germany must not be stripped of territory occupied by German-speaking people, and the nation must not be saddled with huge reparations payments—fines as punishment for the war—such as French politicians were at that very time telling their people they would be paid.

Second, Wilson said, the boundaries of all European countries must conform to nationality as

Poster art was an effective weapon in the hands of government propagandists.

HOW THEY LIVED

"THEY DROPPED LIKE FLIES": The Great Flu Epidemic of 1918

About 10 million people died as a result of battle during the four years of the First World War. Small wonder that the event staggered the confidence and morale of the European nations.

But the war was a modest killer compared with the "Spanish flu." During only *four months* late in 1918 and early in 1919, a worldwide flu epidemic, or pandemic, killed 21 million people. The American army in Europe lost 49,000 men in battle and 64,000 to disease, the majority of them to the flu. At home, fully 548,452 American civilians died, 10 times as many as soldiers felled in battle.

In the United States, the yet unnamed disease first appeared in March 1918, at Fort Riley, Kansas. After a dust storm, 107 soldiers checked into the infirmary complaining of headaches, fever and chills, difficulty in breathing, and miscellaneous aches and pains. Most curious to them, the illness had befallen them in an instant; one moment they were feeling fit, the next they could barely stand. Within a week, Fort Riley had 522 cases, and in a little more than a month, when the affliction abruptly disappeared, 8,000 cases. Almost 50 of the sick men died, not too disturbing a rate in an age when any number of contagious diseases forgotten today were considered deadly. Some doctors noted that these flu victims were in the prime of life and, presumably after basic training, in excellent condition. Moreover, most of them were strapping farm boys, who usually shook off such ailments as though they were colds.

It was wartime, however, and the soldiers from Fort Riley were shipped to Europe in May. The flu made a brief appearance in the cities of the eastern seaboard, but did not rival any of a number of epidemics, including a serious one in the United States in 1889 and 1890.

In Europe, the disease was far more deadly. In neutral Switzerland alone, 58,000 died of it in July. The deaths in the trenches on both sides of the line were enough, according to the German general Erich von Ludendorff, to curtail a major campaign. By June, the flu was sweeping Africa and India, where the mortality was "without parallel in the history of disease." That could be attributed to the wretched poverty of the subcontinent. But what of Western Samoa, where 7,500 of the island's 38,000 people died?

The total figures had not been calculated when the flu began a second and even more destructive tour of the world. The war had created ideal conditions for such a pandemic. People moved about in unprecedented numbers; 200,000 to 300,000 crossed the Atlantic to Europe each month, and many were carrying the unidentifiable germ. Moreover, war crowded people together so that conditions were also perfect for the successful mutation of viruses. With so many handy hosts to support propagation, the emergence of new strains was all the more likely.

That is apparently what happened in August, in western Africa, France, or Spain, which got the blame. A much deadlier variation of the original swept over the world, and this time the effects in the United States were cataclysmic.

In Boston, where it struck first, doubtless carried in by returning soldiers, 202 people died on October 1. New York City reported 3,100 cases in one day; 300 victims died. Later in the month, 851 New Yorkers died in one day, far and away the record. Philadelphia, which was particularly hard hit, lost 289 people on October 6; within one week, 5,270 were reported dead. The death rate for the month was 700 times its usual rate. Similar figures came in from every large city in the country. Just as worrisome, the disease found its way to the most obscure corners of the country. A winter logging camp in Michigan, cut off from the rest of humanity, was afflicted. Oregon officials reported finding sheepherders dead by their flocks.

Most public officials responded about as well as could be expected during a catastrophe that no one understood. Congress, many of its members laid low, appropriated money to hire physicians and nurses

---

defined by language—"self-determination." Like many other people, Wilson believed that the aspirations of people to govern themselves was a major cause of the war. No such concessions were to be made to the nonwhite peoples in Europe's colonies, however, although Wilson did call for Germany's colonies to be disposed of on some basis other than as spoils of war divided among the victors.

and set up clinics. Many cities closed theaters, bars, schools, and churches, and prohibited public gatherings such as parades and sporting events. Others, notably Kansas City, where the political boss frankly said that the economy was more important, carried on as usual. Mystifying moralists, Kansas City was no harder hit than were cities that took extreme precautions. (Nationwide and worldwide, about one-fifth of the population caught the Spanish flu, and the death rate was 3 percent.)

Several city governments required the wearing of gauze masks and punished violators with fines of up to $100. Many photographs that were taken during the autumn of 1918 have a surreal quality because of the masks. San Franciscans, their epidemic at a peak on Armistice Day, November 11, celebrated wearing gauze. Some wretched poet wrote the lines:

> Obey the laws
> And wear the gauze
> Protect your jaws
> From septic paws

Philadelphia gathered its dead in carts, as had been done during the bubonic plague epidemics of the Middle Ages. The city's A. F. Brill Company, a maker of trolley cars, turned over its woodshop to coffinmakers. The city of Buffalo set up its own coffin factory. Authorities in Washington, D.C., seized a trainload of coffins headed for Pittsburgh.

Then, once again, the disease disappeared. There was a less lethal wave (perhaps another mutation) in the spring of 1919, with President Wilson one of the victims; and a leading historian of the phenomenon, Alfred W. Crosby, suggests that another minor epidemic in 1920 may have been a fourth wave. But the worst was over by about the time that the First World War ended, leaving physicians to reflect on the character of the disease and to wonder what they could do if it recurred.

There were some things to reflect on. The first has already been noted: the Spanish flu struck very suddenly, offering individuals no way to fight it except to lie down and wait.

Second, the disease went fairly easy on those people who are usually most vulnerable to respiratory diseases, the elderly; and it was hardest on those who usually shake off such afflictions, young people. In the United States, the death rate for white males between the ages of 25 and 34 was, during the 1910s, about 80 per 100,000. During the flu epidemic it was 2,000 per 100,000. In a San Francisco maternity ward in October, 19 out of 42 women died. In Washington, a college student telephoned a clinic to report that two of her three roommates were dead in bed and the third was seriously ill. The report of the police officer who was sent to investigate was "Four girls dead in apartment." Old people died of the flu, of course, but the death rate among the elderly did not rise a point during the epidemic!

Third, people who had grown up in tough, poor, big city neighborhoods were less likely to get the disease and, if they got it, less likely to die of it than were people who had grown up in healthier environments.

These facts eventually led scientists to conclude that the Spanish flu was a mutation of a common virus that caused a flu that was nothing more than an inconvenience. It was postulated, although never proved, that the deadly germ was the issue of an unholy liaison between a virus that affected humans and another that affected hogs. Spanish flu became "swine flu."

Thus, poor city people, who were more likely to suffer a plethora of minor diseases, had developed an immunity to the virus that farm people had not. Because old people were spared in 1918 and 1919, it has been said that the Spanish or swine flu was related to the less fatal virus that had caused the epidemic of 1889 to 1890. Having been affected by it, the elderly were relatively immune to its descendant.

Third, Wilson demanded "absolute freedom upon the seas, . . . alike in peace and in war." This was a reference to the German submarine campaign that Wilson blamed for American intervention, but it also hearkened to Britain's historical inclination to use British primacy on the waves to interfere with neutral shipping.

Fourth, Wilson demanded disarmament. It was obvious to all parties that the arms race of the two

> ### Multiple-Choice Question
>
> When President Wilson spoke of national "self-determination" as a virtually sacred element of his vision of a better postwar world, his less than idealistic secretary of state, Robert Lansing, commented (not to Wilson's face): "The phrase is simply loaded with dynamite. It will raise hopes which can never be realized. It will, I fear, cost thousands of lives."
>
> Change *thousands* to *millions and counting*, and the prize for prophecy goes to (a) the secretary of state; (b) the president.

decades preceding the war was not a deterrent but a major cause of the tragedy.

Finally and most important toward avoiding another Great War, Wilson called for the establishment of "a general assembly of nations," a kind of congress of countries, to replace the alliances and secret treaties that, he believed, contributed to the tragedy of 1914. More than any other aspect of his program, the dream of a League of Nations came to obsess the president.

Wilson Fools Himself

When an Allied breakthrough in the summer of 1918 put victory within view, Wilson turned virtually all his energies to planning for the peace conference to be held in Paris. He announced that he would personally head the American delegation, the first president to take so active a part in diplomatic negotiations.

The enormity of World War I justified such an innovation, but Wilson somewhat mistook his enthusiasm for remaking the world as reflecting the mood of the American people. In the congressional elections of 1918, held just a week before the armistice, the voters returned Republican majorities of 240 to 190 to the House of Representatives and of 49 to 47 to the Senate. Not only was the new Congress Republican, but it had a decidedly unidealistic, unprogressive tinge. Old bosses and professional politicians who struggled against reform for a decade were coming back to Washington.

Not that they were all reactionaries, nor Wilson-haters: they were the kind of men who were willing to deal. It was Wilson who was uncooperative. He did not seem to recognize that, in voting for so many Republican regulars, the American people were reflecting a weariness with the idealism and rigorously active government of the Wilson administration. He did not even include a prominent Republican—not even a progressive Republican—among the delegates he took with him to Europe on December 4.

Wilson also misinterpreted his reception in England, France, and Italy. Everywhere he went he was greeted with roaring cheers and blizzards of flowers thrown by adoring crowds. With a new democratic government in Germany surrendering on the basis of the Fourteen Points, Wilson believed that the people of Europe had risen to greatness, expressing their support for a peace without victors and a postwar world organized on principles of justice.

The Peace Conference

He could not have been more mistaken. The cheering crowds were welcoming not a visionary leader, but a conqueror, the man who, Europeans believed, had tilted the stalemated war in favor of the Allies, enabling them to win it. The leaders of the Allied nations, the men with whom Wilson sat down in Paris, understood this. They knew what the four years of terribly destructive war meant to Europe. The winners wanted to avenge the bitterness of their sacrifices by tasting the fruits of victory. For four years, the other three members of the "Big Four" had promised them those sweets. Now, in 1919, they paid lip service to Wilson's ideals, but once behind the closed doors of the conference room, they put their national interests first.

> ### Prestige
>
> John Maynard Keynes, a member of the British delegation at the Versailles Peace Conference, wrote that Woodrow Wilson enjoyed a prestige and a moral influence throughout the world unequaled in history.
>
> *His bold and measured words carried to the peoples of Europe above and beyond the voices of their own politicians. The enemy peoples trusted him to carry out the compact he had made with them; and the Allied peoples acknowledged him not as a victor only but almost as a prophet.*

Indeed, Georges Clemenceau, the prime minister of France, commented wryly, "God gave us the Ten Commandments and we broke them. Wilson gives us the Fourteen Points. We shall see." Clemenceau was a cagey, tough, and nasty infighter whom a lifetime in politics, mostly in opposition, had turned into a cynic. He was determined to hang the blame for the war on Germany and to ensure that France would never again be attacked. Clemenceau wanted to strip Germany of valuable territory and saddle the German people with huge reparations payments that, on top of their massive war debt, would hobble Germany for a generation.

David Lloyd George of Great Britain was personally more cordial to Wilson. But he was a habitual backroom manipulator given to inconstancy and outright deceit; and he too had political demands to meet. His country suffered dreadfully from the bloodletting and wanted reparations. Moreover, the Royal Navy had no intention of giving up its dominance on the high seas.

Vittorio Orlando of Italy was only casually interested in the larger questions of the peace. He went to Versailles to make sure that Italy was rewarded with Austrian territory, including several regions of the Alps that were home to 200,000 German-speaking people, and the port of Fiume (Rijeka) on the Adriatic, a city that was largely Serbian in population. His program directly contradicted Wilson's ninth point. The Japanese delegate, Count Nobuaki Makino, not a member of the Big Four, was determined to retain the German colonies in the Pacific that Japan had seized. So much for Point Five.

Bit by bit the Allies drew new lines on Wilson's blueprint. When the president revealed how all-important the league was to him by insisting that its covenant (constitution) be acted on early in the proceedings, they calculated that he would give in on other questions in order to save it. He did. The Treaty of Versailles, which Wilson brought home in July 1919, bore only a passing resemblance to the Fourteen Points he took to Europe eight months earlier.

Woodrow Wilson (right) with three fellow heads of government at the Versailles Conference, (left to right) Vittorio Orlando (Italy), David Lloyd George (Great Britain), and Georges Clemenceau (France). None of these men shared Wilson's ideals.

Round Robin

A round robin is a petition or statement that is signed by several people with no one of them identified as the leader or instigator. All sign around the text of the document in order to disguise the order of signing. The intent of the round robin is precisely the opposite of John Hancock's in signing his name so prominently to the Declaration of Independence.

Article 10

Europe's rejection of Wilson's call for national self-determination in Europe and just treatment of Germany did not much concern the senators who had the constitutional responsibility to approve or reject the treaty. On the contrary, only 12 of the 49 Republican senators, mostly the western progressives who opposed going to war in 1917, announced themselves to be irreconcilable in their opposition to the pact. Still fuming because the United States went to war in the first place, they meant once again to isolate the United States from the corruptions of the rest of the world.

In March 1919, before Wilson returned from Versailles, the other 37 Republican senators signed a round robin declaring themselves to be reservationists on the treaty issue. That is, while they considered the Treaty of Versailles as it stood to be unacceptable, they let the president know that they would vote to ratify if Wilson made some changes in it or accepted their reservations. What worried them most was Article 10 of the league covenant, which pledged all member states to "preserve against external aggression the territorial integrity and . . . political independence of all members." Article 10 seemed to commit the United States to go to war if any other member of the league were attacked.

Wilson replied that Article 10 was merely a moral obligation on the part of members, and, long after his day, he would be proved correct; throughout its history, the league was unable to enforce its decisions. Nevertheless, having said that the article had little concrete meaning, Wilson refused to change a word of it in order to accommodate the worried senators. In his stubbornness, he created an opportunity for the chairman of the Senate Foreign Relations Committee, an old friend of Theodore Roosevelt who despised everything about Woodrow Wilson, to destroy his dream.

The Fight for the League

Henry Cabot Lodge was a dapper, ill-tempered senator from Massachusetts who was not very popular with his colleagues. As stubborn and demanding a man as Wilson, he lacked the aura of moral rectitude and greatness Wilson wore even during his lifetime. Nevertheless, in the battle over the League of Nations, Lodge proved to be much the shrewder, better politician. Perceiving that, as the debate took shape, Wilson was growing less flexible, Lodge became open and cooperative with senators who disliked the league less avidly than he did. Understanding that the longer the debate dragged on, the less the American people would take an interest in the league, Lodge played for time and welcomed every one of Wilson's refusals to compromise. He read the entire 264 pages of the treaty into the record of his committee's hearings, even though it already had been published and placed on every senator's desk.

Lodge guessed right, and Wilson, less reasonable with every day that passed, guessed wrong. Whereas the majority of Americans probably favored American participation in the league during the first months of 1919, their interest waned slowly but perceptibly as the year wore on.

The climax came in September. With the treaty about to come before the Senate, Wilson undertook an exhausting 8,000-mile speaking tour. He believed that by rallying the people behind him, he could bring pressure on the reservationist senators to vote for the treaty as it was. By September 25, when he moved into Colorado, the crowds seemed to be with him. At Pueblo, however, his speech was slurred, and he openly wept. Wilson either suffered a mild stroke at that time or was on the verge of a nervous breakdown. His physician hastily canceled the remainder of the tour and rushed him back to Washington. A few days later he crumpled to the floor of his White House bedroom, felled by a cerebral thrombosis, a blood clot in the brain.

The Invisible President

No one really knows just how seriously Wilson was disabled in 1919 and into 1920. His protective and strong-willed wife isolated him for six weeks from

his wits. To a senator who told him, "We've all been praying for you," he replied, "Which way, Senator?"

Wilson did not meet officially with his cabinet for six months, and photographs of that occasion show a haggard old man with an anxiety in his eyes that cannot be found in any earlier picture. Even if the clarity of his thinking was not affected, because Wilson in the best of health had refused to consider compromising with Lodge, his removal from the scene probably had little effect on the outcome of the battle.

That outcome was defeat. In November, on Wilson's instructions, the Democratic senators voted with the irreconcilables to kill the treaty with the Lodge reservations by a vote of 55 to 39. When the treaty was introduced without the reservations, the reservationists and the irreconcilables defeated it against the Democrats. In March, over Wilson's protest, 21 Democrats worked out a compromise with the reservationist Republicans and again voted on the treaty. The 23 Democrats who went along with Wilson's insistence that he get the original treaty or no treaty at all made the difference. They and the irreconcilables defeated it.

The Election of 1920

Wilson believed that he could win the Treaty of Versailles, and with it the League of Nations, in the presidential election of 1920. Incredibly, given his shattered health and the tradition against a third term, he wanted to be the Democratic party's nominee. That was too much for even the most faithful Democrats to swallow. They ignored Wilson's hints and chose Governor James M. Cox of Ohio, a lackluster party regular who looked like a traveling salesman. For vice president the Democrats nominated a staunch young Wilsonian with a magical name, the undersecretary of the navy, Franklin D. Roosevelt. The Democrats were pessimistic. But perhaps the Roosevelt name on the Democratic ticket would win enough progressive votes to put the party across; 1920 seemed an occasion when the vice presidential nomination mattered.

Still, the Republicans had better reason to expect victory. The congressional elections of 1918 had seemed to show that despite six years of Democratic government, they remained the majority party. As is common when a party's chances are promising, there was a catfight for the nomination

Senator Henry Cabot Lodge led the fight against the League of Nations.

everyone but his physicians. She screened every document brought to him and returned them with shaky signatures at the bottom. When suspicious advisers insisted on seeing the president, they discovered that his left side was paralyzed and his speech was halting. However, he appeared to be in complete control of

between General Leonard Wood, an old comrade of Theodore Roosevelt (but no progressive) and Illinois Governor Frank O. Lowden, who had a reputation as an innovative scientific farmer. Both arrived in Chicago with large blocs of votes, but neither had a majority.

Early in the proceedings, a group of reporters cornered a political wheeler-dealer from Ohio named Harry M. Daugherty and asked him who he thought would be nominated. Daugherty replied genially: "Well boys, I'll tell you what I think. The convention will be deadlocked. After the other candidates have failed, we'll get together in some hotel room, oh, about 2:11 in the morning, and some 15 men, bleary-eyed with lack of sleep, will sit down around a big table and when that time comes Senator Harding will be selected."

Senator Harding was Warren G. Harding. A crony of Daugherty, he was a handsome, likable man who was considered one of the least competent figures in Congress. Perhaps because of that, he was acceptable to almost every Republican. Because Harding had been a mild reservationist on the treaty issue, Henry Cabot Lodge (in whose smoke-filled room at the Blackstone Hotel the nomination took place) probably believed that he could control him.

The Great Bloviator

During the campaign, Harding waffled on the treaty, sometimes appearing to favor it with reservations and at other times hinting that he would let the whole thing quietly die. If there was a theme to his campaign, it was the need for the country to cool off after almost two decades of experimental reform and wartime crusading. His strategy allowed Harding to make use of his technique of "bloviation." Bloviating, as Harding was refreshingly happy to define it, was "the art of speaking for as long as the occasion warrants, and saying nothing." In Boston, in September, Harding declared that "America's need is not heroism but healing, not nostrums but normalcy, not agitation but adjustment, not surgery but serenity, not the dramatic but the dispassionate, not experiment but equipoise, not submergence in internationality but sustainment in triumphant nationality."

The acerbic journalist H. L. Mencken said that Harding's speech reminded him of "stale bean soup, of college yells, of dogs barking idiotically through endless nights." But he added that "it is so bad that a sort of grandeur creeps through it." A Democratic politician remarked that the normalcy speech "left the impression of an army of pompous phrases moving over the landscape in search of an idea."

But Harding did have an idea. The great bloviator had sensed that no specific issue, including the League of Nations, was as important to the American people in 1920 as getting back to "normalcy," and he was right. He won 61 percent of the vote, more than any candidate who preceded him in the White House since popular votes were recorded, and the record for a landslide until 1964.

Wilson lived on quietly in Washington until 1924. His wit returning on his retirement, he said, "I am going to try to teach ex-presidents how to behave." He set a good example. A semi-invalid specter out of the past, he took drives almost daily in the elegant Pierce-Arrow automobile that was his pride and joy, attended vaudeville performances and baseball games, and watched movies, of which he was an avid fan, at home.

Unlike Harding (whose funeral Wilson lived to attend), he was a giant who loomed over an age. His intelligence, dignity, steadfastness, and sense of rectitude overshadowed even those of Theodore Roosevelt, something T. R. himself must have sensed in his final years. Wilson's end was therefore more tragic than that of any other president, including

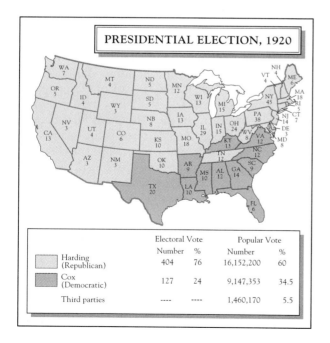

those who were assassinated. For Wilson, like the tragic heroes of great drama, was murdered not by his weaknesses, but by his virtues.

CHRONOLOGY

1916 Shipping Board established

1917 Selective Service Act passed into law
Race riots in East St. Louis and Houston
Nationwide raids on IWW headquarters
Committee on War Information founded

1918 Wilson announces Fourteen Points
U.S. Railway Administration established
War Industries Board established
Food Administration established
Eugene V. Debs found guilty of sedition

1919 Eighteenth Amendment to Constitution (Prohibition)
Nineteenth Amendment (Woman suffrage)
Wilson collapses with stroke while campaigning for League of Nations

1920 Warren G. Harding elected president

FOR FURTHER READING

The regnant study of the American home front during World War I is David Kennedy, *Over Here: The First World War and American Society*, 1980. See also Ellis W. Hawley, *The Great War and the Search for a Modern Order: A History of the American People and Their Institutions, 1914–1920*, 1979; the early chapters of William E. Leuchtenburg, *The Perils of Prosperity, 1914–1932*, 1958; and Arthur S. Link, *Woodrow Wilson: War, Revolution, and Peace*, 1979.

Worthwhile diplomatic studies include Thomas A. Bailey, *Woodrow Wilson and the Great Betrayal*, 1945; John A. Garraty, *Henry Cabot Lodge*, 1953; N. G. Levin, Jr., *Woodrow Wilson and World Politics: America's Response to War and Revolution*, 1968; Thomas J. Knock, *To End All Wars: Woodrow Wilson and the Quest for a New World Order*, 1992; the classic

Harold Nicholson, *Peacemaking: 1919*, 1939; and Ralph Stone, *The Irreconcilables: The Fight against the League of Nations*, 1970.

On economic mobilization, see Robert Cuff, *The War Industries Board: Business–Government Relations during World War I*, 1973. On social aspects of the wartime experience, see Maurine W. Greenwald, *Women, War, and Work: The Impact of World War I on Women Workers in the United States*, 1980; Frederick C. Luebke, *Bonds of Loyalty: German-Americans and World War I*, 1974; Frederick L. Paxson, *American Democracy and the World War*, 1948; Paul L. Murphy, *World War I and the Origin of Civil Liberties*, 1979; Neil A. Wynn, *From Progressivism to Prosperity*, 1986; and Ronald Shaffer, *America in the Great War: The Rise of the War Welfare State*, 1991.

These Virginia Ku Klux Klansmen (and women) made a public relations play by delivering food baskets to the needy; surely just the white needy.

39
CHAPTER

IN THE DAYS OF HARDING

Time of Uncertainty

1919–1923

Excesses accomplish nothing. Disorder immediately defeats itself.

— *Woodrow Wilson*

My candle burns at both ends;
It will not last the night;
But, ah, my foes, and, oh, my friends—
It gives a lovely light.

—*Edna St. Vincent Millay*

Grown up, and that is a terribly hard thing to do. It is much easier to skip it and go from one childhood to another.

—*F. Scott Fitzgerald*

Chapter 39 In the Days of Harding

The 1920s have come down to us with a ready-made personality, a nickname that supposes to capture the flavor of the decade. In the popular imagination, in novels and films and television shows, the 1920s are the "Roaring Twenties." The picture is familiar: worn out by the prolonged fervor of the progressive years, disillusioned by a righteous war that failed to save humanity from itself, or much of anything from anything, the American people shrugged, set out to have a little fun, and ended up by having a lot of it.

Images of the Roaring Twenties readily flood the mind: speakeasies; college boys and flapper girls defying stodgy, traditional moralists during breaks between dancing to the exciting new jazz played by carefree black musicians; and bootleggers and gangsters, somehow menacing and engaging at the same time. F. Scott Fitzgerald captured—created?—the age in his stories and novels, particularly *The Great Gatsby*.

The 1920s were the golden age of sport: Babe Ruth's Yankees and John McGraw's Giants were the superteams of baseball; Harold "Red" Grange was the saint of the regional religion of football; Jack Dempsey and Gene Tunney were prizefighters as mythic as Odysseus and Hercules. Robert T. "Bobby" Jones of Georgia made golf a popular sport for both participants and spectators, and William "Big Bill" Tilden did the same for tennis.

Radio made its debut: the first commercial broadcast told of Warren G. Harding's landslide victory in the presidential election of 1920. The movies were now a fixture of everyday life in the cities and towns, and in their golden age—with Charlie Chaplin, Rudolph Valentino, and unabashedly sexy Clara Bow, the "It" girl with the "bee-sting" lips rumored (by press agents) to entertain the entire USC football team. The automobile, the modern world's amulet of personal freedom, was everywhere, from the homely, accessible Model-T Ford to the Stutz Bearcat, Dusenberg, and Cord, still among the most glorious creations of the automaker's technology and craft.

The list could go on, but at any length it will be a distortion. Only a small proportion of the American population—the wealthy and the comfortably fixed middle classes who lived in cities and sizable towns—enjoyed even a vague semblance of the legend's roaring good times. And the gravy years were not ten—a decade—but five or six in number, beginning only after Calvin Coolidge became president in 1923.

THE WORST PRESIDENT

During the four years that preceded the tenure of "Silent Cal," between 1919 to 1923, American life was characterized less by good times than by contradictions, uncertainties, and fears. In fact, during the two years immediately before and the two following the inauguration of President Harding in March 1921, American society may be said to have been on edge, as was the man whom many historians consider to have been the worst president.

Gamaliel

A newspaperman, Warren Gamaliel Harding worked his way up in politics with a friendly smile, a firm handshake, reliable support of the Republican party line in his newspaper, the Marion *Star*; and the happy discovery by Ohio's political bosses that whenever they asked a favor, and whatever the favor they asked, Warren G. Harding said yes. Harding himself, calling on an allusion that, today, is as quaint as Clara Bow, said that if he had been born a woman, he would have been forever "in the family way," given his inability to mouth the word no.

Presidents and Baseball

In 1910, William Howard Taft instituted the custom that the president throw out the first ball of the baseball season in Washington, D.C. Perhaps the most avid presidential baseball fan was his successor, Woodrow Wilson, who drove often to Griffith Stadium where he watched the Washington Senators play from his limousine in foul territory beyond the right-field flagpole. (A spare player stood nearby to shield Wilson from errant foul balls.)

Warren G. Harding, Herbert Hoover, Franklin D. Roosevelt, and Harry S Truman were also fans, and Jimmy Carter was a pretty good softball player. Ronald Reagan had been a baseball announcer as a young man, and had portrayed the great pitcher, Grover Cleveland Alexander, in a film of 1952. As president, however, he rarely remained at a game longer than ceremony required. In April 1989, by way of contrast, newly elected George Bush took Egyptian President Hosni Mubarak to a game and both stayed to the end.

President Warren G. Harding flanked by (right) Vice President Calvin Coolidge, and Postmaster General, later Hollywood censor, Will Hayes.

For someone like Harding, the Senate, where Ohio's voters sent him in 1914, was heaven. The distinguished job suited Harding's temperament perfectly. Being a senator called for making the occasional speech—Harding was good at that; he coined the word *bloviating*—but as only one senator among 96, he was not expected to take the lead in anything. Indeed, with a surplus of prima donnas crowding the Senate floor, an obliging fellow already gratified beyond the imaginings of his ambition was bound to be popular. The Senate was a club in which members watched out for one another, across party lines as well as within the parties. No one objected that Harding helped old cronies find government jobs they were unfit to perform, and the job left the affable Ohioan with plenty of time to enjoy the all-night poker and bourbon and cigars parties with his pals that were Harding's second most favorite recreation.

Because newspaper reporters were more restrained in dealing with the private lives of public officials than they are today, Harding's treatment in the press was only slightly more censorious. Many reporters thought him the least effective senator, but they never publicized his adulterous relationships with several mistresses. Only after Harding's death did one of his lady friends, Nan Britton, go public with the story that Harding fathered her illegitimate daughter.

A Decent Man

It is difficult, looking back, not to feel sympathy for this weak man. Harding lacked cant—an extraordinary trait in politics—and he had no illusions about his intelligence and his moral capacity for leadership. He freely and openly admitted that he could not hope to be "the best president," and said he would try to be "the best-liked." Such a man did not belong in public life, but Harding was personally kind and decent. After the sour experience with the brilliant but self-righteous and imperious Wilson, the American people did not regard an ordinary mind and a self-effacing personality as handicaps.

HOW THEY LIVED

How They Played the Game

Originally, baseball was a gentleman's game, played by wealthy amateurs for the pleasure of competition. By the turn of the twentieth century, this had changed. Baseball became a business, potentially very lucrative. The players were paid for their skills by teams organized into two major leagues, the National and the American. The profits to the owners, who called themselves "sportsmen" and their properties "clubs," lay in paid admissions to games. Because the better the team, the more people willing to pay to attend, it stood to reason that club owners would seek to build winning teams. However, it did not always work that way. While the players indeed competed with one another to win games, the sportsmen did not compete with one another to win the best players.

In order to avoid bidding wars among themselves for the services of star pitchers, hitters, and fielders, the club owners devised the "reserve clause," an agreement that every player was required to sign. The reserve clause was based on the dubious assumption that a baseball player was a professional like a physician or lawyer and not a lowly employee. Unlike a machinist or miner who, of course, as industrial employers never tired of saying, were free at all times to quit their job and find another, the professional baseball player was not free to do so. In signing the reserve clause, he agreed that he could not leave to play with another team without the owner's consent. His services were reserved unless the club owner "sold" or "traded" him to another owner with whom the player then had no choice but to come to terms—if he wanted to stay in baseball.

As in other businesses, practices varied from team to team, but perhaps the most frankly businesslike of the owners was Cornelius "Connie Mack" McGillicuddy, who also managed his Philadelphia Athletics of the American League. The dominant team in baseball in the years before the First World War, the A's won six league pennants and three World Series. Mack twice built up powerhouse teams in that era and then broke them up, selling his star players off for a cash profit. And again by the end of the 1920s he created a team that was better than the New York Yankees of the era. Once again Mack cashed in, selling off his players.

There was no reconciling the concept of sportsmanship or a sense of civic responsibility with Mack's policies, and yet, simply because he continued to manage the A's into his 90s, he was touted as one of the grand old men of the "game."

Charles A. Comiskey, owner of the Chicago White Sox, was another kind of businessman. Until the First World War he was content with mediocre players to whom he paid the lowest salaries in either major league. Then, during the war, while attendance in all cities declined, the White Sox gelled behind such stars as hard-hitting outfielder Joseph "Shoeless Joe" Jackson and third baseman George "Buck" Weaver. After finishing high in the standings in 1917 and 1918, the White Sox won the American League pennant in 1919 and were regarded by most sports journalists as unbeatable in the World Series, particularly because the National League champion was an old team but an upstart champion, the Cincinnati Red Stockings.

There was trouble in the White Sox team, however. While their sterling play had caused attendance and profits to soar, Comiskey had actually taken the lead in calling for a league-wide pay cut. At a time when wages in almost every job were rising, the two leading White Sox pitchers, who won 50 games between them, were paid a combined salary of only $8,600. Adding insult to exploitation, Comiskey allowed his champion players considerably lower expenses when they were on the road than any other team in either league.

Harding displayed his humanity when, at Christmas 1921, he pardoned Eugene V. Debs and other Socialists who opposed the war. (Vindictive to the end, Wilson refused to do so.) Harding personally pressured the directors of the United States Steel Corporation, to whom he was inclined to defer in other matters, to reduce the workday in their mills to eight hours, not because he challenged the owners' asserted right to do with their property as they chose, but because he was appalled at the idea of a 12-hour day for anyone.

The White Sox lost the World Series to the Red Stockings 5 games to 3. (Only in 1922 was the Series reduced to 7 games.) An investigation during the winter and spring revealed that it was no mere upset. Eight White Sox players, including stars Weaver and Jackson, had conspired with gamblers to throw the match and make a killing on long-shot bets.

It was rumored that Comiskey had been aware of the fix all along but was willing to sacrifice the Series for the chance to intimidate future players. Indeed, although the eight accused "Black Sox" were acquitted in criminal court for lack of hard evidence, they were banned from playing professional ball for life by a newly installed commissioner with broad powers to regulate the business, Judge Kenesaw Mountain Landis. Like the head of a government commission, Landis showed no reluctance to discipline owners whose actions threatened the good of the whole, but he backed the owners in disputes with players.

Not every club ownership was so cash-oriented as Mack 'or so exploitative as Comiskey. Indeed, during the same years that Landis was brushing up baseball's reputation for honesty at the top, an ugly, pot-bellied, spindly legged, and atrociously vulgar orphan from Baltimore was revolutionizing the game and winning huge salaries from ungrudging employers, the New York Yankees.

George Herman "Babe" Ruth started in baseball as a pitcher—quite a good one—for the Boston Red Sox. In 1919, the year of the Black Sox scandal, while playing the outfield on days he did not pitch, Ruth hit 29 home runs, double that of any previous player. In fact, the major leagues did not even keep official home run statistics until 1921; baseball B.R.— before Ruth—was a game of tactics played by lithe, swift men who eked out runs one at a time with scratch hits off overpowering pitchers, and gritty base running. Tyrus J. "Ty" Cobb of the Detroit Tigers, a genuinely mean-spirited man whose specialty was sliding into second with file-sharpened cleats slicing the air, was the most respected player of the 1910s.

Now, with a single swing, the "Sultan of Swat" could put up to four runs on the scoreboard and the fans loved it. Purchased from the Red Sox by the Yankees for $100,000—itself an unprecedented windfall under the reserve clause—Ruth hit 59 home runs in 1921, the record until his own 60 in 1927. Rather than haggle with their godsend, the Yankee ownership paid him annually higher salaries. By the end of the decade, when his pay was higher than that of the president of the United States, Ruth shrugged nonchalantly, "I had a better year than he did."

Not only did he make the Yankees the best team in baseball, Babe Ruth made them the richest. In 1923, New York opened the largest baseball stadium of the era, Yankee Stadium, which was properly nicknamed "the house that Ruth built." Other owners and Commissioner Landis took notice too. If home runs sold tickets, they would have more home runs. The baseball itself was redesigned into a livelier "rabbit ball" and the slugger became the mythic figure in the game. Hack Wilson of the Chicago Cubs hit 56 home runs in 1930, setting the National League's record, and Jimmy Foxx of the Philadelphia Athletics was eclipsing Ruth himself by 1932 when he hit 58 (and was promptly sold by Connie Mack). The New York Yankees remained the team that most totally staked its fortunes on men who swung the heavy bat and the "club" that was the most liberal with a paycheck. It would not have much mattered to Connie Mack and Charles Comiskey, perhaps, but the Yankees were also, of course, the most successful team in the history of both the sport and the business.

Most striking was Harding's reaction when political enemies whispered that he had African blood in his ancestry. In an era when most white people thought in at least mildly racist terms, that kind of talk could ruin a career. Politicians contemporary with Harding would have responded with a lawsuit or an indignant diatribe that outdid their accusers in racism. But Harding merely shrugged: how did he know whether or not one of his forebears "had jumped the fence"?

Smart Geeks

Harding made some excellent appointments to his cabinet, or had them pushed on him by political expedience. As secretary of commerce, he picked Herbert Hoover. Although Franklin D. Roosevelt assumed that Hoover was a Wilsonian Democrat, he was, in fact, a Republican by inheritance, temperament, and philosophy. If he was slightly appalled by the backslapping Harding, Harding was ill at ease with the all-business Hoover. He called Hoover (not to his face) "the smartest geek I know."

As he did during the war, Hoover worked without fanfare or conspicuous self-promotion; he really did believe that merit and his achievements would take care of his career. He mollified conservative Republicans by encouraging the formation of private trade associations in industry and agriculture rather than, in the manner of the progressives, putting the government in the driver's seat. Hoover's hope was that these organizations would eliminate waste, develop uniform standards of production, and end "destructive competition."

Harding named another "smart geek," Charles Evans Hughes, as secretary of state. This was a gesture to the progressive wing of the Republican party, with which Hughes was associated. A man of moderate temperament, an able if unimaginative Supreme Court Justice between 1910 and 1916, Hughes had waffled on the issue of the League of Nations, just as Harding had done.

By 1921, that issue was dead. However, because the Senate had not ratified the Treaty of Versailles, the United States was still officially at war with Germany. Hughes ironed out that diplomatic kink by prevailing on Congress to pass a simple resolution that the war was over, and by extending recognition to the new German republic. Hughes's most important achievement as secretary of state, however, was finagling the other great naval powers of the world into reducing the size of their fleets.

The Treaty of Washington

Ignoring the League of Nations, Hughes gathered representatives of the world's most important naval powers to an international conference in Washington. The delegates, who expected the usual round of receptions and meaningless platitudes about the need for disarmament, followed by backroom horse trading, were shocked when Hughes opened the conference by proposing a detailed plan for reducing the size of the world's navies. All the naval powers were to scrap some capital ships (battleships and battle cruisers) and to cancel plans for future naval construction.

Everyone agreed that the arms race was instrumental in allowing the First World War to happen. Therefore, the delegates in Washington had little choice but to listen, particularly when Hughes reminded them that by limiting the size of their navies, their governments could save millions of dollars: The construction of even a single capital ship was a major line item in a national budget.

In the Treaty of Washington of 1921, the five major naval powers agreed to limit their fleets according to a ratio that reflected their interests and defensive needs. For each five tons that Great Britain and the United States floated in capital ships, Japan would have three, and France and Italy somewhat smaller fleets.

Each nation gave up ships, but each benefited, too. Great Britain maintained equality on the high seas with the United States, a primacy that American plans for ship construction would have destroyed. (The United States scrapped 30 battleships and cruisers that were under construction or on the drawing boards.) The American government slashed its expenditures, a high priority for the conservative Harding administration. Japan, which needed only a one-ocean navy, whereas Britain and the United States had worldwide interests, got parity (even superiority) in the Pacific, as important symbolically to the racially sensitive Japanese as it was important militarily. Italy and France, still reeling from the war, were spared the strain of an arms race that would bankrupt them, but remained dominant in the Mediterranean.

The Harding Scandals

Unfortunately, the work of Hoover and Hughes just about sums up the accomplishments of the Harding administration. The president's other appointees were either servants of narrow special interests or outright crooks. Secretary of the Treasury Andrew Mellon pursued tax policies that extravagantly favored the rich and helped bring on the disastrous depression that would end the Roaring Twenties. More dismaying in the short run were those cronies to whom Harding gave government jobs for old times' sake. No sooner were they settled in their Washington offices than they set about filling their pockets and ruining their generous friend.

Attorney General Harry Daugherty winked at violations of the law by political allies. Probably with Daugherty's connivance, Jesse L. Smith, a close friend of the president, sold favorable decisions and public offices for cold cash. Charles R. Forbes, the head of the Veterans Administration, pocketed money intended for hospital construction. The grandest thief of all, Secretary of the Interior Albert B. Fall, leased the navy's petroleum reserves at Teapot Dome, Wyoming, and Elk Hills, California, to two freewheeling oilmen, Harry Sinclair and Edward L. Doheny. In return, Fall accepted "loans" of about $300,000 from the two. Fall also tarred Harding with corruption because, some time earlier, he cajoled the president into transferring the oil reserves from the navy's authority to that of Fall's Department of the Interior.

By the summer of 1923, Harding realized that his administration was shot through with thievery. When he set out on a vacation trip to Alaska, he knew that it was only a matter of time before the scandals hit the newspapers. His health was suffering; the famous handsome face is haggard and gray in the photographs of his trip to the north. Nevertheless, he remained loyal to his treacherous pals. He allowed Forbes to flee abroad, and he took no action against the others.

Jesse Smith eventually killed himself. Albert Fall went to prison. Mercifully, perhaps, for he was personally innocent of corruption, Harding died, too, shortly after disembarking from his Alaska trip at San Francisco. Only later did the nation learn of the secrets that tormented him in his last days, from the crooks in his administration to the irregularities in his personal life. So tangled were Harding's affairs that, when Harding's wife, Florence, refused to allow an autopsy, scandalmongers suggested that she had poisoned him, and they were widely believed. Actually, while doctors disagreed on the cause of death, the president probably suffered massive heart failure.

SOCIAL TENSIONS: LABOR, RADICALS, IMMIGRANTS

If Harding's poignant tale is symbolic of his time, the social tensions that strained and snapped while he was in the White House ran far deeper than the personality of an unhappy man from Marion, Ohio.

Had Harding been a pillar of moral strength and probity—or had Woodrow Wilson or Calvin Coolidge been elected president in 1920—the years which Harding actually presided over would have been quite as troubled as they were. Indeed, the tensions of the early 1920s set in two years before Harding was inaugurated.

1919: A Year of Strikes

During the First World War, the conservative trade unions of the American Federation of Labor seemed to become part of the federal power structure. In return for recognition of their respectability, most unions agreed not to strike for the duration of hostilities. Unfortunately, while wages rose slowly during the war years (1917–1918), the prices of consumer goods, including necessities, increased quickly. Then they soared during a runaway postwar inflation. The end of the war also led to the cancellation of government contracts; tens of thousands of people in war-related jobs were thrown out of work, leading to the inevitable: 3,600 strikes in 1919 involving 4 million workers.

The "Teapot Dome" scandal threatened to bring down the Republican administration, but in the end it survived.

The strikers' grievances were generally valid, but, to the surprise of many workers, few Americans outside the labor movement were sympathetic. When employers described the strikes of 1919 as the handiwork of revolutionaries, aimed at destroying middle-class decency, much of America agreed. In Seattle, a dispute that began on the docks of the busy Pacific port turned into a general strike involving almost all the city's 60,000 working people. Most of the strikers were interested in nothing more than better pay. However, the concept of the general strike was associated in the popular mind with class war and revolution. Seattle Mayor Ole Hansen depicted the dispute as an uprising inspired by dangerous foreign Bolsheviks like those who seized power in Russia during the war. With the help of the marines, Hansen crushed the strike.

Steelworkers Walk Out

The magnates of the steel industry employed similar methods to fight a walkout in September 1919 by 350,000 workers, mostly in the Great Lakes region. The men had good reason to strike. Many of them worked a 12-hour day and a 7-day week. It was not unusual for individuals to put in 36 hours at a stretch. That is, if a man's relief failed to show, he might be told to stay on for another 12-hour shift, or lose his job. When the extra shift ended, his own began again.

For this kind of life, steelworkers took home subsistence wages. For some Slavic immigrants in the industry, that home was not even a bed to themselves. They contracted with a landlord to rent half the use of a bed. After their wearying shift and a quick meal, they rolled under blankets still warm and damp from the body of a fellow worker who had just trudged off to the mill.

These wretched conditions were well known. And yet, the heads of the industry, Elbert Gary of United States Steel and Charles Schwab of Bethlehem Steel, easily persuaded the public that the strike of 1919 was the work of revolutionary agitators like William Z. Foster. Because Foster had a radical past as a leader of the Wobblies (and a future as head of the American Communist party), and because many steelworkers had ethnic roots in Eastern Europe, the nursery of Bolshevism, the strikers were almost universally condemned. The strike ended in failure although, under pressure from President Harding, working conditions in steel were somewhat improved.

The Boston Police Strike

The Boston police strike of 1919 frightened Americans more than any other. While the shutdown of even a basic industry like steel did not immediately affect daily life, the absence of police officers from the streets caused a jump in crime as professional hoodlums, low-lifes, and desperately poor people took advantage of the situation.

Boston's policemen, mostly of Irish background, were underpaid. They earned 1916 wages, not enough to support their families decently in a city where many prices had tripled during the war. Nevertheless, they too commanded little public support for their work stoppage. When Massachusetts Governor Calvin Coolidge ordered the National Guard into Boston to take over police functions and break the strike, the public applauded. When Samuel Gompers asked Coolidge to restore the beaten workers to their jobs, the governor replied "there is no right to strike against the public safety by anybody, anywhere, anytime." It made him a national hero, and won Coolidge the Republican vice presidential nomination in 1920 when the California progressive, Hiram Johnson, refused to share the ticket with Harding.

Some of the strikes of 1919 ended in victory, but most failed and the debacle ushered in a decade of decline for the labor movement. Union membership stood at more than 5 million in 1919, but was only 3.6 million in 1929, despite the expansion of the nonagricultural workforce during the twenties.

Red Scare

Public reaction to the strikes of 1919 revealed widespread hostility toward recent immigrants and second-generation Americans. This xenophobia took its most virulent form in the Red scare of 1919. Even before the Armistice, a new stereotype replaced the "bloodthirsty Hun" as the villain Americans most loved to fear and hate: the seedy, lousy, bearded, and wild-eyed Bolshevik.

The atrocities that characterized the civil war following the Russian Revolution of 1917 were real, lurid, and numerous. Nevertheless, American newspapers exaggerated them and even invented tales of mass executions, torture, children turned against their parents, and women proclaimed the common sexual property of all men. Already uneasy because of the war, Americans were prepared to believe the worst about a part of the world from which so many immigrants had recently come.

Many Americans believed that foreign-born Communists were a threat to the security of the United States. In March 1919, the Soviets organized the Third International, or Comintern, an organization explicitly dedicated to fomenting revolution around the world. So it seemed to be no accident when, in April, the Post Office discovered 38 bombs in the mail addressed to prominent capitalists and government officials. In June, several bombs reached their targets. One bomber who was identified—he blew himself up—was a foreigner, an Italian. Then, in Chicago in September 1919, two American Communist parties were founded, with the press emphasizing the immigrant element in the membership. Many Americans concluded that the Red threat was closely related to the large number of immigrants and their children within the United States.

In reality, a tiny minority of American ethnics were radicals, and many of the most prominent Socialists and Communists boasted WASP ancestry as impeccable as Henry Cabot Lodge's. Max Eastman, the editor of the radical wartime magazine *The Masses*, was of old New England stock. John Reed, whose *Ten Days That Shook the World* remained for many years the classic English-language account of the Russian Revolution, was a Harvard boy from Portland, Oregon. Debs and William Z. Foster had no ethnic ties. William D. Haywood observed that he could trace his ancestry "to the Puritan bigots." Moreover, neither they nor the foreign-born radicals posed a real threat to established institutions. Within a few years, the combined membership of the two Communist parties and the Socialist party numbered only in the thousands.

The Palmer Raids

Nonetheless, dread of a ghost can be as compelling as fear of a grizzly bear, and Americans' fear of communism was intense in 1919. The temptation to exploit the popular anxiety was too much for President Wilson's attorney general, A. Mitchell Palmer, who tried to ride the Red scare into a presidential nomination by ordering a series of well-publicized raids on Communist headquarters.

Although an investigation found that only 39 of the hundreds Palmer arrested could be deported under the law, the attorney general nonetheless put 249 people on a steamship dubbed "the Soviet Ark"

and sent them to Russia. On New Year's Day 1920, Palmer's agents again swooped down on hundreds of locations, arresting 6,000 people. Some of them, such as a Western Union delivery boy, merely had the bad luck to be in the wrong place at the wrong time. Others were arrested while peering into the windows of Communist storefront offices. Nevertheless, all were imprisoned at least briefly.

Palmer's popularity fizzled when he predicted mass demonstrations on May Day, the international socialist and communist holiday, and nothing happened. By midsummer, the great Red scare was over, but antiforeign feeling continued to shape both government policy and popular attitudes throughout the 1920s.

Sacco and Vanzetti

The two most celebrated victims of the wedding of antiradicalism to xenophobia were Nicola Sacco and Bartolomeo Vanzetti. In 1920, the two Italian immigrants were arrested for an armed robbery in South Braintree, Massachusetts, in which a guard and a paymaster were killed. They were promptly found guilty of murder, and sentenced to die in the electric chair.

Before they could be executed, however, the newly founded American Civil Liberties Union, Italian-American groups, and labor organizations

---

Radical Eloquence

Murderer or victim of an injustice, Bartolomeo Vanzetti was a man of rare eloquence. The very mistakes he made in his adopted language added a luster to his statements. Shortly before his execution, he wrote, with foresight as well as feeling:

If it had not been for these thing, I might have live out my life talking at street corners to scorning men. I might have die, unmarked, unknown, a failure. Now we are not a failure. This is our career and our triumph. Never in our full life could we hope to do such work for tolerance, for joostice, for man's understanding of men as now we do by accident. Our words—our lives—our pains—nothing! The taking of our lives—lives of a good shoemaker and a poor fish peddler—all! That last moment belongs to us—that agony is our triumph.

publicized the fact that the hard evidence against Sacco and Vanzetti was scanty and, at least in part, invented by the prosecution. The presiding judge at their trial, Webster Thayer, had been openly prejudiced against the defendants because they were anarchists and Italians; he was overheard speaking of them as "damned dagos."

At the same time doubts were being aroused, Sacco and Vanzetti won admiration by acting with dignity, steadfastly maintaining their innocence but refusing to compromise their political beliefs. "I am suffering," Vanzetti said, "because I am a radical and indeed I am a radical; I have suffered because I was an Italian, and indeed I am an Italian . . . but I am so convinced to be right that if you could execute me two times, and if I could be reborn two other times, I would live again to do what I have done already."

The movement to save Sacco and Vanzetti reached international proportions. Even the Italian dictator, Benito Mussolini, who was savaging anarchists at home without a semblance of the trial Sacco and Vanzetti enjoyed, expressed his distaste for the verdict. Nevertheless, the two were finally executed in 1927. Although recent research has indicated that Sacco was almost certainly guilty of the Braintree murder with Vanzetti's involvement likely, that question was irrelevant to most of those engaged in the controversy during the 1920s. The majority were glad to see the two anarchists punished;

Bartolomeo Vanzetti and Nicola Sacco were executed after a long international debate about the justice of their trial.

while Sacco and Vanzetti's defenders could see nothing in the case against them except ethnic and political prejudice.

The Passing of the Great Race

In 1883, the poet Emma Lazarus wrote, "Send these, the homeless, tempest-tost to me, I lift my lamp beside the golden door." As if they heard her, European immigrants continued to pour into the United States at high levels until 1915, when all-out naval war made the Atlantic too dangerous for large numbers of people to cross. In 1918, immigration into the United States declined to 110,000.

Even before the war, many Americans of WASP and old-immigrant stock had become nervous about the large numbers of eastern and southern Europeans among them — or rather, about the immigrants who clustered in ethnic ghettos in the larger cities. Unlike earlier arrivals, including the once-despised Irish, the new immigrants seemed determined not to become Americans.

Around the turn of the century, this essentially cultural and social anxiety took on racist overtones as respected anthropologists began to describe significant genetic distinctions among the European peoples. The most important of these writers was William Z. Ripley, whose *Races of Europe* was published in 1899. Ripley divided Caucasians into the Teutonic, Alpine, and Mediterranean races. While all three had their redeeming traits (the Mediterranean Italians, for example, were credited with a finely developed artistic sense), there was no question that Teutons — Britons, Germans, northern Europeans generally — were the ones with a dependable commitment to liberty and to the American way of life. Slavic peoples got very bad reviews in this respect.

In 1916, a lawyer and natural scientist of some repute, Madison Grant, took up where Ripley left off. In *The Passing of the Great Race*, Grant maintained that, through intermarriage with old-stock Americans, the new immigrants were literally destroying, through dilution, the nation's prized genetic heritage. The book was immensely successful, running through several editions. (During the war, Grant demoted the Germans out of the great race.) After the war, when immigration soared again — to 805,000 in 1921, mostly from "lesser" stock — the time for action seemed to have come.

Immigration Restriction

There was a precedent for restricting immigration on the basis of race. In 1882, Congress had excluded the Chinese from the United States. In that same year, Congress determined that criminals, idiots, lunatics, and those likely to become a public charge (people with glaucoma, tuberculosis, and venereal disease were the chief targets) could no longer immigrate. By 1900, pressure groups such as the Immigration Restriction League began to call for an immigration law that would discriminate against other "genetic inferiors" — southern and eastern Europeans; in brief, the new immigrants.

Four times between 1897 and 1917, Congress tried to discriminate against the new immigrants by enacting a bill requiring all newcomers to pass a literacy test. Few peasants from southern and eastern Europe could read and write. Four times, however, thrice by Woodrow Wilson alone, the bills were vetoed. The importance of ethnic voters to the Democratic party, and the demand of a still-expanding industry for cheap labor, stymied the restrictionists.

Then the election of 1920 brought the Republicans to power. In 1921, Congress enacted and President Harding signed a law limiting annual immigration to 350,000 people. Each year, each European nation was entitled to send to the United States a number equal to 3 percent of the number of its nationals who were residents of the United States in the base year of 1910. In 1924, an amendment reduced the number of immigrants from outside the Americas to 150,000, the quota to 2 percent, and changed the base year to 1890. Because most southern and eastern Europeans began to emigrate to the United States after 1890, the quotas of such poor countries as Poland, Czechoslovakia, Hungary, Rumania, Yugoslavia, Bulgaria, Greece, and Italy were very low. For example, the annual quota for Italy was a minuscule 5,802, for Poland 6,524, for Russia 2,784, and for Syria 100. All were inevitably filled within the first few months of each year.

By way of contrast, the quotas for the comparatively prosperous countries of northern and western Europe, the nations of the old immigration, were generous and rarely filled. The annual quota for Great Britain under the 1924 law was 75,000, one-fifth of the total number of immigrants admitted. During the 1930s, an average of only 2,500 Britons emigrated to the United States each year.

SOCIAL TENSIONS: RACE, MORAL CODES, RELIGION

The 1920s were also a time of tension in relations between whites and blacks, between Americans who found consolation in traditional moral codes and those who rejected them, and—closely allied to the moral issue—between country and city, between rural people and urbanites.

Black Scare

Having supported the war effort enthusiastically, African-American leaders looked forward to a greater measure of equality for black people after the armistice. The 200,000 young black men who served in the army in Europe had been exposed to a white society in which their color was not a major handicap. At home, blacks who moved to northern cities experienced civil equality on paper, and a less repressive life than they knew in the rural South. They felt freer to express themselves more than was possible in the land of Jim Crow.

But the war had not changed white America's mind about the color line. In 1919, of the 78 blacks who were lynched, 10 were veterans; several were hanged while dressed in their uniforms. Race riots broke out in 25 cities with a death toll of more than a hundred. The worst of the year was in Chicago, where a young African American, swimming from a de facto segregated Lake Michigan beach, drifted into waters off the "white beach" and, when tiring, he tried to swim to shore, he was pelted with stones by whites and drowned.

The incident mushroomed into vicious racial war. White and black gangs with guns roamed the streets shooting at anyone of the opposite color across whom they stumbled. In all, 38 people were killed and more than 500 were injured.

Black Nationalism

From this charged and disillusioned atmosphere emerged a remarkable figure. Born in the British colony of Jamaica, Marcus Garvey came to the United States in 1916. He quickly concluded that, in general, whites would never accept blacks as equals, and, filled with pride in his own race, he rejected integration where it was possible. Garvey's alternative to color-blind equality on the one hand, and violent racial conflict on the other, was for blacks throughout the world to organize a powerful nation in Africa. It was nationhood, Garvey said, that won respect for a people. For proof, he pointed to the fact that protests from Japan had discouraged the state of California from putting Asians into segregated schools, as had successfully been done to African Americans in the South.

Garvey's Universal Negro Improvement Association (UNIA) was based on pride in race, the strong organizing point of all movements preaching separation. "When Europe was inhabited by a race of cannibals, a race of savages, naked men, heathens, and pagans," Garvey told cheering throngs in New York's Harlem, turning white stereotypes of blacks upside down, "Africa was peopled by a race of cultured black men who were masters in art, science, and literature."

He made little headway in the South, but in the North, many urban blacks who already were uprooted found his call for a return to Africa appealing, at least in the abstract. Estimates of UNIA membership as high as 4 million were probably exaggerated,

Marcus Garvey hoped that his grand regalia would instill a sense of nationhood among black Americans.

but many more blacks than that listened to Garvey's message with open minds and enjoyed the pageantry with which he surrounded his activities.

Garvey bedecked himself in extravagant uniforms and commissioned paramilitary orders with exotic names such as "The Dukes of the Niger" and the "Black Eagle Flying Corps." Even veterans in the fight for racial equality were influenced by Garvey's magic. W. E. B. Du Bois wrote, "The spell of Africa is upon me. The ancient witchery of her medicine is burning in my drowsy, dreamy blood."

The popularity of black nationalism unnerved whites who were accustomed to a generally docile African-American population. When Garvey ran afoul of the law with one of his many business enterprises, the authorities moved against him with an enthusiasm that bore little relation to the seriousness of his offense. Whether because of mismanagement or fraud, Garvey's Black Star Line, a steamship company, sold worthless shares through the mails at $5 a share. Some 35,000 blacks lost $750,000, a comparatively minor take during the 1920s. When prosecution took over five years to be resolved, the UNIA's resources were depleted and Garvey was deported. The movement died.

The Ku Klux Klan

Marcus Garvey's ritual, costume, and ceremony was paralleled in a white racist organization of the same era, the Ku Klux Klan. The twentieth-century KKK was founded in 1915 by William Simmons, a Methodist minister. After viewing *The Birth of a Nation*, a film that glorified the anti-black movement of the post-Civil War period, Simmons began organizing, first in the South but, by 1919, in the North and West as well.

Under Hiram Wesley Evans, the KKK gave local units and officials exotic names such as Klavern, Kleagle, Grand Dragon, and Exalted Cyclops. Evans was a more successful businessman than Garvey. The Klan's central office retained a monopoly of "official" bedsheet uniforms that all members were required to buy, and the Klan provided a cash incentive for local organizers by giving them a percentage of all money that they collected, a kind of franchised bigotry. By the mid-1920s, membership in the Klan may have risen as high as 4.5 million.

In the South, the KKK was primarily an anti-black organization. Elsewhere, KKK leaders exploited whatever hatreds, fears, and resentments were most likely to keep the bedsheet orders rolling in. In the Northeast, where Catholics and Jews were numerous, Klan leaders inveighed against them. Immigrants generally also were targets. In the Owens Valley of California, a region of small farmers whose water was drained southward to feed the growth of Los Angeles, the big city was the enemy. In the Midwest, some Klaverns concentrated their attacks on saloonkeepers who ignored Prohibition and "lovers' lanes" where teenagers flouted traditional morality the old-fashioned way on weekend nights.

Setting aside the hocus-pocus and the mercenary motives of the central office, the Klan represented the unease of generally poor, Protestant, and small-town people that the America they knew was being destroyed by immigrants, cities, and modern immorality. Nevertheless, the Klan prospered in cities, too. The twentieth-century metropolis was an unsettling phenomenon, but it continued to attract people of every kind.

Klan power peaked in 1924. In that year, the organization boasted numerous state legislators, congressmen, senators, and even governors in Oregon, Ohio, Tennessee, and Texas. In Indiana, state Klan leader David Stephenson was boss of the state. At the Democratic national convention of 1924, the Klan was strong enough to prevent the party from adopting a plank critical of its bigotry.

The KKK declined as rapidly as the UNIA. In 1925, Grand Dragon Stephenson was found guilty of second-degree murder in the death of a young woman whom he had taken to Chicago on an un-Klanlike tryst. In an attempt to win a light sentence, he turned over evidence showing that virtually the whole administration of the KKK was involved in thievery and that Indiana Klan politicians were thoroughly corrupt. By 1930, the KKK dwindled to 10,000 members.

Wets and Drys

To some extent, the Klan was a manifestation of hostility between cities on the one hand and country and small towns on the other. This social cleavage was also evident in the split that developed after the Eighteenth Amendment went into effect in 1920. Violation of Prohibition law was widespread. While some bootleggers smuggled liquor into the country from Mexico, the West Indies, and Canada,

The Ku Klux Klan adorned racial and religious hatred with the secrecy and mumbo-jumbo ceremony typical of men's voluntary organizations.

individual liquor distillers in isolated corners of rural America continued to practice their ancient craft, distilling "white lightning" and "moonshine" from local grain, and battling government agents with guns as well as stealth.

Nevertheless, there was a clear geographical and social dimension to the political battle between "drys," people who supported Prohibition, and "wets," those who opposed it. The drys were strongest in the South and in rural areas generally, where the population was largely composed of old-stock Americans who clung to fundamentalist Protestant religions. The wets drew their support from the big cities, where Roman Catholics and Jews, who generally had little understanding of or sympathy for Prohibition, were numerous.

Many wet mayors and city councils refused to help federal officials enforce Prohibition. Democratic Mayor James J. Walker of New York openly frequented fashionable speakeasies, illegal saloons. Republican "Big Bill" Thompson of Chicago ran for office on a "wide-open-town" platform and won. As a result, smuggling, illegal distilleries and breweries, and theft of industrial and medicinal alcohol were commonplace and provided the basis for an extremely lucrative, if illegal, business. In Chicago by 1927, the Alphonse "Al" Capone bootleg ring grossed $60 million by supplying liquor and beer to the Windy City's speakeasies. (Capone also made $25 million that year from gambling and $10 million from prostitution.)

Gangsters as Symbols

As far as Al Capone was concerned, he was a businessman. He supplied 10,000 drinking houses and employed 700 people. He and other gangsters

> ### Bottoms Up
>
> One argument wets marshalled against Prohibition was that forbidding drinking resulted in an actual *increase* in drinking. The statistics, while fragmentary, do not bear their assertion out. Between 1906 and 1910, per capita alcohol consumption in the United States was 2.6 gallons per year. In 1934, the first year after the Prohibition Amendment was repealed, consumption stood at 1.2 gallons. Not until 1971, a generation after Prohibition, did per capita consumption of alcohol reach pre-World War I levels.
>
> The death rate from chronic alcoholism peaked in the United States in 1907 at 7.3 per 100,000. By 1932, the last full year of Prohibition, the rate had declined to 2.5 per 100,000.
>
> One alcohol-related problem was directly the result of Prohibition, the 50,000 "jake walkers" who roamed America's streets, the object of cruel derision to boys who dogged them. "Jake walking" (also known as "jake leg") was a nervous disorder caused by drinking poisonous "jake," methyl or wood alcohol. An overdose was fatal; smaller quantities resulted in a loss of muscular control so that victims strode along in jerky steps, their toes touching the ground before their heels. Jake walkers were not known when potable ethyl alcohol was legal, but they were almost common during Prohibition.

Al Capone thought of himself not as a thug, but as an American businessman, 1920s-style.

needed the administrative acumen of a corporation executive to run their affairs and the same kind of political influence that conventional businessmen courted. "What's Al Capone done?" he told a reporter. "He's supplied a legitimate demand. . . . Some call it racketeering. I call it a business. They say I violate the Prohibition law. Who doesn't?"

With incredible profits at stake, rival gangs engaged in open, bloody warfare for control of the trade. More than 400 gangland slayings made the name of Chicago synonymous with mob violence, although other cities had only slightly better records.

Very few innocent bystanders were killed in these frays. As conscious of public relations as other businessmen of the era, Capone and his ilk tried to keep their violence on a professional level. But those

Americans who were appalled by the carnage did not overlook the fact that most prominent gangsters were "foreigners." Capone and his predecessors in Chicago, Johnny Torrio and "Big Jim" Colosimo, were Italians. Dion O'Bannion (Capone's rival), "Bugsy" Moran, and Owney Madden were Irish. Arthur "Dutch Schultz" Flegensheimer of New York was of German background. "Polack Joe" Saltis came from Chicago's Polish West Side. Maxie Hoff of Philadelphia, Solly Weissman of Kansas City, and "Little Hymie" Weiss of Chicago were Jews.

Illegal business attracted members of groups on the bottom of the social ladder because success in it required no social status or family connections, no education, and, to get started, little money. With less to lose than the respectable established people who patronized the speakeasies, ethnics with a crooked bent were less likely to be forestalled by the high risks involved. But the majority of Americans were not inclined to take a sociological view of the matter. To them, organized crime was violent, and "foreigners" were the source of it.

Anti-Semitism

The hatred of Jews that was to acquire nightmarish proportions in Germany had its counterpart in the United States, albeit never so vicious or significant as it was under Adolf Hitler. For a time during the 1920s, automobile millionaire Henry Ford sponsored a newspaper, the *Dearborn Independent*, that insisted, as Hitler did, that Jews in general were party to an "international conspiracy" to destroy Western Christian civilization. The most astonishing aspect of this kind of anti-Semitism was that it posited an alliance between wealthy, conservative Jewish bankers like the Rothschild family of Europe and their worst enemies, Socialists and Communists who were Jews.

These allegations never were taken very seriously in the United States. However, anti-Semitism was acceptable and even respectable when it took the form of keeping Jews out of some businesses (banking, ironically) and social clubs. Moreover, a number of universities applied Jewish "quotas" when they admitted students. Jews were admitted, but only up to a certain percentage of each class.

Hollywood as Symbol

Show business was also a low-status enterprise that presented few competitive advantages to wealthy and established groups. The film industry, which was booming by 1919, was dominated from the beginning by Jewish studio bosses such as Samuel Goldwyn and Louis B. Mayer. Consequently, when protest against nudity and loose moral standards in Hollywood films boiled over, it too took on an ethnic flavor. Preachers who demanded that controls be slapped on filmmakers were not above attributing immorality on the silver screen to "non-Christian" influences aimed at subverting Protestant America.

By 1922, Hollywood's nabobs feared that city and state governments were on the verge of banning their films. They headed off the censors by joining together to censor themselves. Keenly sensitive to the ethnic angle in the anti-Hollywood campaign, studio bosses hired a man who was the epitome of the small-town midwestern Protestant to be chief censor and film-industry spokesman. Will H. Hays of Indiana, postmaster general under Harding,

supervised the drafting of a code that forbade movies which allowed adultery to go unpunished or that depicted divorced people in a sympathetic light. The Hays Code went so far as to prohibit showing a married couple in bed together or, indeed, having a double bed in the background of bedroom scenes. In the movies, married couples slept in twin beds; so powerful was the medium that separate beds became fashionable in three-dimensional society, too.

The Evolution Controversy

The clash between traditional values and the worldly outlook of the twentieth century was clearest cut in the controversy that developed around the theory of the evolution of species as propounded half a century earlier by the English biologist Charles Darwin. Although many scientists and churchmen insisted that there was no contradiction between the biblical account of the creation of the world (if interpreted as literary) and Darwin's contention that species emerged and changed character over the eons, fundamentalist Protestants who insisted on the literal truth of every word of the Bible disagreed. Feeling threatened by fast-changing times and urged on by such influential leaders as William Jennings Bryan, the fundamentalists tried to prohibit the teaching of

Hooray for Hollywood

The first filmmakers set up shop wherever they happened to be. By the 1920s, however, the movie industry had become concentrated in Hollywood, one of the myriad communities that grew together to form greater Los Angeles. The official explanation of the choice of location was the weather; southern California is one of the sunniest parts of the nation, and early filmmakers depended on natural light. But there was another reason for choosing Hollywood. Like the organizers of many infant industries, filmmakers took considerable liberties with business law, particularly copyright and contract law. Everyone, it seemed, was engaged in a dozen lawsuits at all times. Hollywood was only a hundred miles from the Mexican border. If a case seemed to be getting serious, the filmmakers could make a quick dash down to Tijuana.

evolution in the public schools. In Tennessee, they succeeded in passing a law to that effect.

In the little Appalachian town of Dayton, Tennessee, in the spring of 1925, a group of friends who were arguing about evolution decided to test the new state law in the courts. One of their number, a high school biology teacher named John Scopes, agreed to violate the law in front of adult witnesses. Scopes would explain Darwin's theory, submit to arrest, and stand trial.

The motives of the men were mixed. The earnest young Scopes hoped that the law would be stricken from the books. Some of his friends wanted to see it confirmed. Yet others, Dayton businessmen, could not have cared either way. They looked on a celebrated trial as a way to put their town "on the map" and to make money when curiosity-seekers, sensation-mongers, cause-pleaders, and reporters—the more the merrier—flocked to Dayton in search of lodgings, meals, and other services.

The "Monkey Trial"

Dayton's boosters succeeded beyond their dreams. The "Monkey Trial," so called because evolution was popularly interpreted as meaning that human beings were "descended" from apes, attracted broadcasters and reporters by the hundreds; among them was the nation's leading iconoclast, Henry L. Mencken, who came to poke fun at the "rubes" of the Bible belt.

Number-one rube in Mencken's book was William Jennings Bryan, in his sixties now—he died

Clarence Darrow for the defense and William Jennings Bryan for the prosecution in the Scopes "Monkey Trial," which addressed the question of evolution and its instruction in classrooms.

780 *Chapter 39 In the Days of Harding*

shortly after the trial ended—who agreed to go to Dayton to advise the prosecution. Bryan wanted to fight the case on the strictly legal principle that, in a democracy, the people of a community had the right to dictate what might and what might not be taught in tax-supported schools. His advice was ignored. Their heads spinning from the hullabaloo and carnival atmosphere of the town, even the prosecuting attorneys wanted to debate religion versus science. Bryan caved in.

The defense, which was put together and funded by the American Civil Liberties Union, also intended to fight the case on the basis of two significant principles. Led by the distinguished lawyer and libertarian Arthur Garfield Hays, the attorneys planned to argue that the biblical account of creation was a religious doctrine and therefore could not take precedence over science because of the constitutional separation of church and state. The defense also insisted that freedom of intellectual inquiry, including a teacher's right to speak his or her mind in the classroom, was essential to the health of a democracy.

Hays was assisted by the era's leading criminal lawyer, Clarence Darrow, who loved publicity and the drama of courtroom confrontation more than he loved legal niceties. Darrow regarded the trial as an opportunity to discredit fundamentalists by making their leader, Bryan, look like a superstitious old fool. Against his better judgment, Bryan allowed Darrow to put him on the stand as an expert witness on the Bible. Under the trees—the judge feared that the tiny courthouse would collapse under the weight of the crowd—Darrow and Bryan talked religion and science. Was the world created in six days of twenty-four hours each? Was Jonah literally swallowed by a whale?

Darrow supporters rested content that Bryan turned out looking like a monkey, but they lost the case. Scopes was found guilty of violating the law and given a nominal penalty. It was a small consolation to the anti-evolutionists, who were crestfallen when Bryan admitted that some parts of the Bible may have been meant figuratively. In fact, the only winners in the Monkey Trial were Dayton's businessmen, who raked in outside dollars for almost a month, and the masters of ballyhoo. This was appropriate in itself, for by 1925, the second full year of Calvin Coolidge's "New Era," raking in money and ballyhoo were what America seemed to be all about.

CHRONOLOGY

1915 Ku Klux Klan revived

1919 Year of strikes
"Red Scare": Palmer Raids

1920 First commercial radio broadcast
Sacco and Vanzetti arrested

1921 Congress officially ends World War I
Treaty of Washington

1923 Rumors, soon confirmed, of scandals in Harding administration
Harding dies in office; Calvin Coolidge is president

1924 Immigration restriction law

1925 Scopes "Monkey Trial" in Dayton, Tennessee

FOR FURTHER READING

It is not the definitive history of the 1920s, but still is the most enjoyable to read: Frederick Lewis Allen, *Only Yesterday*, 1931. Also eminently readable and less subjective are William E. Leuchtenburg, *The Perils of Prosperity, 1914–1932*, 1958; Robert K. Murray, *The Harding Era*, 1967; George Soule, *Prosperity Decade: From War to Depression, 1917–1929*, 1947; Geofrey Perrett, *America in the Twenties*, 1982; and Lynn Dumenil, *The Modern Temper: America in the 1920s*, 1995.

On the crisis of labor in 1919 and after, see Irving Bernstein, *The Lean Years*, 1960; David Brody, *Labor in Crisis: The Steel Strike of 1919*, 1965; Robert L. Friedheim, *The Seattle General Strike*, 1965; and Francis Russell, *A City in Terror: 1919, the Boston Police Strike*, 1975. On the xenophobia that was related closely to fears of a social uprising, see John Higham, *Strangers in the Land*, 1955; Robert K. Murray, *Red Scare*, 1955; and William Preston, Jr., *Aliens and Dissenters: Federal Suppression of Radicals, 1903–1933*, 1963.

The history of African Americans during the 1920s has been the subject of several excellent books in recent decades. See Nathan J. Huggins, *Harlem Renaissance*, 1972; Gilbert Osofsky, *Harlem: The Making of a Ghetto, 1890–1930*, 1966; William Tuttle, Jr., *Race Riot: Chicago and the Red Summer of 1919*, 1970; and Theodore G. Vincent, *Black Power and the Garvey Movement*, 1971.

The response of white America to rapidly changing times is the subject of D. M. Chalmers, *Hooded Americanism*, 1965; N. J. Clark, *Deliver Us from Evil*, 1976; Ray Ginger, *Six Days or Forever*, 1958; Nancy MacLean, *Behind the Mask of Chivalry: The Making of the Second Ku Klux Klan*, 1994; Don S. Kirschner, *City and Country: Rural Responses to Urbanization in the 1920s*, 1970; Lawrence Levine, *Defender of the Faith: William Jennings Bryan, The Last Decade*, 1965; and George M. Marsden, *Fundamentalism and American Culture*, 1980 and *Religion and American Culture*, 1990.

Other social and cultural themes are treated in Loren Baritz, *The Culture of the Twenties*, 1969; Isabel Leighton, *The Aspirin Age*, 1949; Larry May, *Screening out the Past*, 1980; Humbert S. Nelli, *The Business of Crime*, 1976; John Roe, *The Road and the Car in American Life*, 1971; Andrew Sinclair, *Prohibition: The Era of Excess*, 1962; Robert Sklar, *Movie-Made America*, 1975; Roland Marchand, *Advertising the American Dream*, 1985; and Susan Smulyan, *Selling Radio: The Commercialization of American Broadcasting, 1920–1934*, 1994.

On the politics of the Harding era, see Wesley Bagby, *The Road to Normalcy*, 1962; Stanley Cohen, *A. Mitchell Palmer: Politician*, 1963; Robert K. Murray, *The Politics of Normalcy*, 1973; Burt Noggle, *Teapot Dome: Oil and Politics in the 1920s*, 1962; J. W. Prothro, *Dollar Decade: Business Ideas in the 1920s*, 1954; Francis Russell, *The Shadow of Blooming Grove: Warren G. Harding in His Times*, 1968; and Andrew Sinclair, *The Available Man*, 1965.

In cities, the first traffic jam was not long in following the first automobile.

40
CHAPTER

CALVIN COOLIDGE AND THE NEW ERA

When America Was a Business

1923–1929

Civilization and profits go hand in hand.

> —*Calvin Coolidge*

The business of America is business.

> —*Calvin Coolidge*

If you can build a business up big enough, it's respectable.

> —*Will Rogers*

The simple opposition between the people and big business has disappeared because the people themselves have become so deeply involved in big business.

> —*Walter Lippmann*

Perhaps the most revolting character that the United States ever produced was the Christian businessman.

> —*H. L. Mencken*

Chapter 40 Calvin Coolidge and the New Era

Vice President Calvin Coolidge was visiting his father in tiny Plymouth Notch, Vermont, when he received the news of Harding's death. Instead of rushing to Washington to be sworn in by the chief justice of the Supreme Court, Coolidge walked downstairs to the darkened farmhouse parlor, where his father, a justice of the peace, administered the presidential oath by the light of a kerosene lamp. To the very pinnacle of his political career, Coolidge was the epitome of unpretentious simplicity and rectitude. Or, some have suggested, of sloth and a natural flair for showmanship.

THE COOLIDGE YEARS

Coolidge was not a bit like his predecessor. Far from strapping and handsome, he was thin, with a pinched face that, even when he smiled, seemed to say that he wished he were somewhere else. Alice Roosevelt Longworth, the acidulous daughter of Theodore Roosevelt, said that Coolidge looked as though he had been weaned on a pickle.

Whereas Harding's private life was suspect, even tawdry, Coolidge was a man of impeccably proper, even dreary, personal habits. His idea of a good time was a good nap. As president, he spent 12 to 14 hours out of 24 in bed except on slow days, when he tried to sneak in a few extra winks. When in 1933 writer Dorothy Parker heard that Coolidge had died, she asked, "How could they tell?"

A Quiet Clever Man

Coolidge would have appreciated that. He may have been known as "Silent Cal," hesitant to say much of anything, but when he spoke he was often witty. In an attempt to break the ice at a banquet, a woman seated next to Coolidge told the president of a friend who had bet her that untalkative Cal would not say three words all evening. "You lose," Coolidge replied, and returned to his appetizer, resuming the bland, inscrutable gaze that was his trademark. "I found out early in life," this fabulously successful politician once noted, "that you don't have to explain something you haven't said."

And he was clever. At a meeting of American heads of state in the West Indies, Coolidge was sitting in a semicircle with his colleagues when a waiter began to walk down the line serving drinks. It was the Prohibition Era; if Coolidge took a drink while out

of the country, it would make juicy front-page news, and American reporters and photographers (who were undoubtedly enjoying their daiquiris) waited on tenterhooks for the waiter to reach Coolidge with his tray. If, on the other hand, Coolidge doughtily turned the waiter away, it would be a mild but stereotypically American insult to his hosts. Coolidge fooled everyone. The instant before the waiter tried to serve him, he bent down to tie his shoe, and remained hunched over until the waiter moved on.

In fact, Coolidge was nowhere near so laconic as he and his boosters liked to claim. In 1917, the year the United States went to war, Woodrow Wilson gave 17 speeches. In 1925, when nothing much happened to command the attention of the president, Coolidge gave 28. He also took a curious pleasure in posing for photographers in costumes that were ludicrous on him: wearing a ten-gallon hat or a Sioux Indian war bonnet; strapping himself into skis on the White House lawn; dressing as a hardworking farmer at the haying, in patent leather shoes with a Pierce Arrow waiting in the background. Perhaps the photos were Coolidge's quiet way of saying that he was at one with the American people of the 1920s in enjoying novelties and pranks. On being asked about the costuming, he said that he calculated "the American public wants a solemn ass as president and I think I'll go along with them."

He was assuredly at one with the majority of the American people in abdicating political and cultural leadership to the business community. Coolidge worshiped financial success and believed without reservation that millionaires knew what was best for the country. "The man who builds a factory builds a temple," he said, an odd piety indeed for a man who devoted not a day of his life to business—or, perhaps, it was not.

Keeping Cool with Coolidge

While Coolidge quickly rid the cabinet of the racketeers and hacks whom he inherited from Harding, he retained Harding's appointees from the business world, most notably Herbert Hoover (with whom he was as uncomfortable as Harding had been) and Secretary of the Treasury Andrew Mellon. He then sat back to preside over the most business-minded administration to his time. In return, business praised his administration higher than they built skyscrapers in New York and Chicago. The Republicans crowed about "Coolidge prosperity," the recovery from the

An old hand at grabbing publicity, Calvin Coolidge posed in an Indian headdress for photographers.

erratic postwar economy that began in 1923, and, thanks to the president's unblemished record for honesty, the GOP never suffered a voter backlash as a result of the Harding scandals.

On the contrary, the biggest of the scandals, Teapot Dome, hurt the progressive Democrats—what was left of them. The Wilsonian, William G. McAdoo, a leading contender for the Democratic nomination in 1924, had been an attorney for the oilman Edward L. Doheny. Although McAdoo knew no more of the crooked transaction than Coolidge did, people associated him more closely with the thieves than they did the Republicans. When Montana Senators Thomas J. Walsh and Burton Wheeler, who led the investigation into the oil leases, attacked the Republicans, they were squelched by the slogan "Keep Cool with Coolidge." The president's supporters chastised them for ranting and raving about past crimes that Coolidge had remedied in his quiet way. By the summer of the election year of 1924, it was clear that Coolidge had the confidence of the country.

The Election of 1924

Then the Democrats obliged by tearing themselves apart. The convention, held in New York, pitted the Empire State's favorite son, Alfred E. Smith, against William G. McAdoo, whose support came mostly from the South and the West. Smith was a Roman Catholic and had the backing of ethnics in the Northeast and urban Midwest as a symbol of their arrival in American politics. McAdoo, although no bigot himself, was supported by many southerners and westerners, who regarded Catholicism with at best distaste, and virulently anti-Catholic Ku Klux Klansmen. So bitter was the split and vicious the whisper campaign that neither candidate would yield for more than a hundred ballots, long after it was obvious neither could win the nomination.

Finally, the weary delegates settled on a compromise candidate, Wall Street lawyer John W. Davis. He did not have to neglect his lucrative practice for long. Davis won a mere 29 percent of the vote to Coolidge's 54 percent. Aged Robert La Follette, trying to revive the Progressive party in 1924, captured 17 percent of the popular vote and carried his native Wisconsin.

For four more years, Calvin Coolidge napped through good times. It was eight months after he left office, in October 1929, that what businessmen called the New Era came crashing to an end. Ironically, in view of the impending Great Depression, Coolidge retired from office with great reluctance. It was whispered that when the Republican convention of 1928 took his coy statement, "I do not choose to run for president in 1928" as a refusal to run, and nominated Herbert Hoover to succeed him, Coolidge threw himself on his familiar bed and wept.

Mellon's Tax Policies

The keystone of New Era government was the tax policy sponsored by the secretary of the treasury, Andrew Mellon of Pittsburgh. Mellon looked less like the political cartoonist's stereotype of a big businessman—a bloated, fleshy moneybags—than like a fit, sporting duke, but a moneybags he was. Trim, with chiseled aristocratic features, and dressed in deftly tailored suits and tiny pointed shoes that shone like newly minted coins, Mellon was one of the three or four richest men in the world, a banker with close ties to the steel industry.

Believing that economic prosperity depended on the extent to which capitalists reinvested their profits in economic growth, Mellon favored the rich by slashing taxes that fell most heavily on them. He reduced the personal income tax for people who made more than $60,000 a year, and by 1929, the treasury was actually shoveling taxes back to large corporations. United States Steel received a nice refund of $15 million; other big corporations were comparably blessed.

To compensate for the loss in government revenues, Mellon cut government expenditures. The costs of government that he conceded were indispensable were to be paid for in two ways. First, Mellon raised the tariff on imported products, a double benefit for industrial capitalists. In the Fordney-McCumber Tariff of 1922, import duties reached levels that were unheard of for a generation.

Andrew Mellon (1855–1937), the "Sporting Duke," as secretary of the treasury.

PRESIDENTIAL ELECTION, 1924

	Electoral Vote Number	%	Popular Vote Number	%
Coolidge (Republican)	382	72	15,725,016	54
Davis (Democratic)	138	25.5	8,386,503	29
La Follette (Progressive)	13	2.5	4,822,856	16.5
Third parties	----	----	155,833	0.5

Second, Mellon sponsored modest increases in regressive taxes, that is, taxes that fell disproportionately on the middle and lower class. The costs of some kinds of postal services increased. The excise tax was raised and a new federal tax was imposed on automobiles. Both were paid by consumers. To those who complained that these measures penalized the middle classes and to some extent the poor, Mellon replied that the burden on each individual was small, and that his overall scheme helped ordinary people as well as the rich.

Mellon contended that when businessmen reinvested their government-sponsored windfalls, they created jobs and, therefore, the means of a better standard of living for all. The share of the middle and lower classes in Coolidge prosperity would "trickle down" to them. Moreover, the inducement to get rich, encouraged by government policy, would reinvigorate the spirit of enterprise among all Americans. The argument was to reemerge in the 1980s and 1990s under Presidents Reagan and Clinton.

For six years, from late 1923 to late 1929, it appeared as though Mellon was dead right. His friends toasted him as "the greatest secretary of the treasury since Alexander Hamilton." Just how much damage his policies did to the national economy would not be known until after the collapse of the New Era in 1929. As early as 1924, however, the policy of subordinating federal policy to the short-term interests of big business and banking was helping to make a shambles of the international economy.

The Legacy of Versailles

The fundamental weakness of the international economy during the 1920s owed to the fabulous costs of World War I. The war had pushed every participant nation except the United States to the brink of bankruptcy (and Russia over the cliff). Germany, for example, spent more during four years of war than during the previous four decades of the nation's existence. Britain and France were also deeply in debt — $10 billion to the United States alone — and France bore the additional burden of having been the battlefield. Both countries demanded that Germany pay them $13 billion in reparations. In addition to fixing guilt for causing the war on the Germans, the money was earmarked for repaying the debts owed to Americans.

The result was a flow of international payments from Germany to Britain and France (and other

> ### *Racy Reading*
>
> In 1919, publisher Emanuel Haldeman-Julius sensed that there was a mass market for books if they could be priced cheaply and marketed correctly. His "Little Blue Books" were printed in a small, uniform format on cheap paper and were immensely successful. By 1951, Haldeman-Julius had published more than 2,000 titles and sold more than 500 million "Little Blue Books." Many were racy for the times or, at least, had racy come-ons. Haldeman-Julius liked to publish classics on which no royalties had to be paid, but he retitled the minor ones in order to boost sales. Thus, when he renamed Théophile Gautier's *Golden Fleece* as *The Quest for a Blond Mistress*, annual sales jumped from 600 to 50,000. Haldeman-Julius had similar results when he retitled Victor Hugo's *The King Amuses Himself* to read *The Lustful King Enjoys Himself*.

smaller countries), and from there to the United States. The trouble was that too much wealth was drained from Germany for the economy of that important industrial nation to remain healthy. The gold went abroad. At home, paper German currency inflated crazily; in time it took bundles, even wheelbarrows full of paper money to buy food. Economists warned that to continue to bleed Germany was to promote political extremism (including Adolf Hitler's Nazi party) and to threaten the economies of all the European nations.

Some British and French statesmen acknowledged the point but insisted that as long as they were obligated to make huge debt payments to the United States, they had no choice but to insist on German payments to them. The burden of finding a remedy was on Americans.

A Foreign Policy for Bankers

There were several ways out of the morass. First, the United States, the world's wealthiest nation, could invigorate European industry by importing more European products. The Fordney-McCumber Tariff, a vital part of Mellon's fiscal policy, shut the door on that idea. Alternatively, the United States could forgive Britain and France all or most of their debts, in return for which they would cancel reparations

NOTABLE PEOPLE

The Lone Eagle: Charles A. Lindbergh (1902–1974)

Raymond Orteig was a wealthy French restauranteur living in New York whose two enthusiasms were Franco-American friendship and aviation. He believed that airplanes had a much brighter future than, in 1926, seemed likely. During the 1920s, the fragile but ever improved crafts served as toys for rich hobbyists, as showpieces at state and county fairs where nomadic "barnstormers" did aerial tricks such as walking on the wing of a plane in flight, and, here and there in the United States, as vehicles to deliver "air mail," which the Post Office regarded as an experiment.

Even the prospects of military aviation were dim. Despite the publicity that had been given aerial dogfights during the First World War, planes had been more show than substance, playing no significant role in any action. In 1921 and 1923, General William Mitchell of the Air Service, a branch of the army, had proved in a series of tests that bombs dropped from planes could sink a capital ship (a captured German vessel); but in order to prove his point, Mitchell had disobeyed orders and won the enmity of his superiors. He was court-martialed, and his vision momentarily discredited.

But Orteig believed in the commercial potential, if not in the military uses, of airplanes. Partly to demonstrate the feasibility of long-distance trips, the only kind of transportation in which flying made sense, and partly because he enjoyed ballyhoo as well as most people in the 1920s, Orteig offered a $25,000 prize to the first plane to cross the Atlantic nonstop between France and the United States.

By the spring of 1927, a number of pilots, including First World War flying ace René Fonck, and polar explorer Admiral Richard A. Byrd, using huge biplanes powered by three motors, had tried and failed. Both survived their accidents, but in other attempts, including an east–west flight by two Frenchmen who almost made it to North America, six were dead and two were seriously injured.

In the meantime, in San Diego, California, another challenger for the prize had been making news. Charles A. "Slim" Lindbergh, Jr., a shy 25-year-old mail pilot from the Midwest, had a different approach to the problem. He had persuaded a group of St. Louis businessmen to finance the construction of a plane that would be capable of flying the Atlantic, and he had found a company, Ryan Aircraft of San Diego, to build it. Instead of pinning his hopes on a massive machine powered by three large (and heavy) engines and flown by a crew (more weight), Lindbergh believed that the way to get to France was with a plane of the utmost simplicity, a machine designed to carry little more than gasoline and a single pilot.

Far from being the rickety wing and a prayer, as the press described the *Spirit of St. Louis*, it was the creation of careful calculation and engineering expertise that had no commercial value, but was designed down to the last rivet to do one thing: get off the ground with a maximum load of fuel. In effect, the *Spirit* was a flying gas tank. The press would dub the young pilot "Lucky Lindbergh" when he succeeded in his mission, but most of the luck involved in the venture was in the ease with which he persuaded his backers of his idea and found a builder who shared his confidence. Indeed, in getting the *Spirit* from San Diego to the airfield on Long Island from which he would depart, Lindbergh broke two aviation records: he made the longest nonstop solo flight to date (San Diego–St. Louis) and the fastest transcontinental crossing. It was no reckless experiment.

But that was how the press of the 1920s played it. Lindbergh was mobbed wherever he went in New York, and was depicted as the simple, plucky, American frontiersman sort of hero. He was not allowed to examine his plane without the presence of thousands of well-wishers, sensation-seekers, and even hysterics who wanted to touch him as though he were a saint. Historians have compared the fuss made over him with the adoration that Americans of the 1920s lavished on movie stars and boxing champions; but it seems more accurate to describe the preflight hoopla in terms of Daniel Boorstin's definition of a celebrity: a person who is "well known for being well known."

On May 16, 1927, conditions for a takeoff were less than ideal. The airstrip was muddy from rains, which meant additional drag on the plane, and by the time that Lindbergh was ready to go, he was taking off with a tailwind, not recommended procedure even

when the craft is not loaded to the utmost of its theoretical limitations. (At the last minute, Lindbergh called for an additional 50 gallons of gasoline in the tanks.)

But Richard A. Byrd's plane was sitting at the same field, mechanically ready to go but stalled by legal complications; and another challenger was almost ready. Impatient, emotionally geared for the moment, perhaps influenced by the press notices of his singularity, Lindbergh packed five sandwiches into the tiny cockpit and took off. Once he was airborne, the riskiest part of the venture was behind him. Unless he fell asleep. That, and occasional threats of ice on the wings, which would add weight to the plane, were the worries he later recalled as most serious. At ten o'clock at night, two days after his departure, he landed amidst a screaming mob of 100,000 people at Le Bourget Field, Paris.

Americans were popular in Europe during the 1920s, and Lindbergh was exalted as the greatest of them. Back home it was the same thing: ticker-tape parades, thousands of invitations merely to appear in towns and cities. For a while, the soft-spoken hero luxuriated in the fame and money that came to him. In 1929, he married Anne Morrow, the daughter of the American ambassador to Mexico (Lindbergh was himself the son of a congressman), and as a team they continued to tour on behalf of the government and commercial aviation.

In 1932 the couple's infant son was kidnapped from their New Jersey home and, despite the payment of ransom, murdered. Police (and the Lindberghs) believed that the frenzied publicity surrounding the event contributed to the death of the child by frightening the abductor. After the trial, conviction, and execution of a carpenter, Bruno Hauptmann, which were criticized because of the relentless press coverage, the Lindberghs moved to Europe, where, they believed, they could escape the spotlight.

There, Lindbergh was impressed by the new German air force built up by Adolf Hitler and Hermann Goering, and he accepted a medal from the German dictator. After 1939, when he returned to the United States to lecture on behalf of the isolationist America First Committee, Lindbergh was criticized as being pro-Nazi. He was not, but he was an Anglophobe, and he believed that Germany would win the war that broke out in September 1939. Therefore, he opposed those who wanted to go to war before England fell.

Like most of the America Firsters, Lindbergh ceased his opposition to the war once the United States had entered it. He worked as a technical expert to aircraft companies, and, although over 40, he flew several missions in the Pacific theater. In the end, Lindbergh's accomplishment of 1927 overshadowed his politics of 1939 to 1941, and he was commissioned a general in the air force.

payments from Germany. The international economy would, so to speak, have a fresh start.

Unfortunately, an administration that was closely allied with banking interests would not do that. "They hired the money, didn't they?" Coolidge said of the French and British war debts, as though he were talking about a grocer having trouble paying for his automobile. Indeed, American bankers were profiting doubly from the European financial mess by loaning money to the Germans to, in part, subsidize their reparations payments. Interest, and a little bit of principal, was coming in from everywhere.

And that fact, bank profiteering, was good enough for the Republican administrations of the 1920s. In the Dawes Plan of 1924 (named for Charles G. Dawes) the United States agreed to a rescheduling of reparations payments. The Young Plan of 1929 (named for Owen D. Young) reduced Germany's burden from about $33 billion to $9 billion.

The circular flow of payments continued. American bankers loaned money to Germany; Germany paid about $2.5 billion in reparations to Britain and France between 1923 and 1929; Britain and France paid $2.6 billion to American creditors. The European economy was steadily, if slowly, sapped, and the American economy was indirectly damaged: capital that was supposed to be reinvested at home to trickle down was devoted to a nonproductive balancing of international books that did nothing for American workers.

Isolationism?

After the Treaty of Washington, the Harding and Coolidge administrations resisted making meaningful cooperative cause with other nations. There was no question of joining the League of Nations as more and more Americans became convinced that it had been a mistake to intervene in the war that produced it. America's international efforts on behalf of maintaining the peace were restricted to proclamations of goodwill much like William Jennings Bryan's cooling-off treaties. In 1928, Secretary of State Frank B. Kellogg joined with French Foreign Minister Aristide Briand to write a treaty that outlawed war as an instrument of national policy. Eventually, 62 nations signed the Kellogg-Briand Pact, a clear indication that, as a broad and pious statement of unenforceable sentiment, the pact was meaningless.

Because the United States refused to cooperate internationally in any meaningful way, the foreign policy of the 1920s is usually described as isolation-

---

Let's Have a Look under the Hood

Americans and Britons speak a different language when they talk about their cars. What Americans call the hood, the British call the bonnet. Some other differences:

American English	British English
clunker or junker	banger
gas	petrol
generator	dynamo
headlight	headlamp
muffler	silencer
station wagon	estate wagon
trunk	boot
windshield	windscreen

The different vocabularies provide a little case study in how languages develop. The automobile roared into history long after the United States and Great Britain had gone their separate political and cultural ways, but before instantaneous electronic communication allowed words coined on one side of the Atlantic to become immediately familiar on the other.

Because the early automobile was largely a French development, many American automotive terms were taken from the French language: *automobile* itself, *cabriolet* (later shortened to *cab*), *chassis*, *chauffeur*, *coupé*, *garage*, *limousine*, and *sedan*.

---

ist. This is, however, something of a misnomer. Towards Latin America, the Harding and Coolidge administrations were active and aggressive on behalf of the interests of American investors.

American investments in Latin America climbed from about $800 million in 1914 to $5.4 billion in 1929. The United States replaced Great Britain as the chief economic power in Latin America, particularly in the nations of the Caribbean.

The poorer Latin American nations sorely needed capital, and to that extent every dollar invested there was potentially a boon—if the population of the host countries as a whole benefited from it. Unfortunately, American businessmen had little interest in how the Latin American countries were governed until their profits were threatened by political instability. They ignored the depredations of predatory elites until they were in trouble.

President Coolidge presides over the signing of the Kellogg–Briand Pact. Coolidge believed taking part in such rituals was his major duty as president.

When dictators in the "banana republics" were unable to contain popular resentments, American investors turned to Washington for protection of their profits. By 1924, American officials directly or indirectly administered the finances of ten Latin American nations. For at least part of the decade, the marines occupied Nicaragua, Honduras, Cuba, Haiti, and the Dominican Republic. The business of the entire Western Hemisphere was the business of Coolidge's America, too.

PROSPERITY AND BUSINESS CULTURE

In the late twentieth century, it was easy to see the damage wreaked by the Coolidge administration. But the voters of the 1920s supported Silent Cal and his policies with unmistakable enthusiasm. The Republican party held comfortable majorities in every Congress between 1920 and 1930. Only in the South and some thinly populated western states, and in a few big cities, could the Democrats count on winning elections.

The Anticlimactic Election of 1928

In 1928, Hoover won 58 percent of the popular vote, more even than Coolidge won in 1924. The victorious Republican candidate was, in his energy and

---

The Tin Lizzie

Although Americans did not invent the automobile, they democratized it by putting cars within the reach of almost everyone. But striving for simplicity (shunning all "extras," including a choice of color), by adapting the assembly line to the manufacture of cars, and by refusing to change his design, Henry Ford managed to whittle the price of a brand-new Model-T to $260 in 1925. It was the cheapest new car on the market. By 1927, Ford had sold 15 million tin lizzies, as Model-T Fords were affectionately known, more than all other automakers combined.

unrestrained celebrations of business, even more an exemplar of the New Era than Silent Cal.

Hoover's opponent, Alfred E. Smith of New York, spent four years mending fences with southern and western Protestants who supported McAdoo in 1924. Smith was unable to win over the bigots, however. For the first time since Reconstruction, a number of prominent southerners, including influential Methodist Bishop James Cannon, urged voters to support the Republican party. Their reason was partly Smith's Roman Catholic religion. But they also drummed on Smith's opposition to Prohibition. Like many urban politicos, Smith not only urged repeal, but he openly flouted the law. Herbert Hoover may have disapproved of Prohibition personally, but in 1928 he called it "a great social and economic experiment, noble in motive and far-reaching in purpose." He was the "dry" candidate, Smith the "wet."

Smith also invited disdain from southern, western, and rural voters with his rasping, nasal New York accent. Heard over the radio—or "raddio" as Smith called it—his voice conjured up all the unsavory images associated with New York City for half a century.

Still, had Smith been a Kansas Presbyterian who never drank even patent medicines, he would have lost in 1928. Business and the Republican party reigned supreme because of the general prosperity of the New Era and because a great many Americans were sincerely convinced that businessmen constituted the new messiah Woodrow Wilson had tried so hard to be.

The Shape of Prosperity

Industrial and agricultural productivity soared during the 1920s, even though there was not much increase in the size of the industrial workforce, and the number of agricultural workers actually declined. Wages did not keep up with the contribution that the more efficient workers were making to the economy, however. While dividends on stock rose 65 percent between 1920 and 1929, wages increased only 24 percent.

Nevertheless, the increase in wages was quite enough to satisfy the working people who enjoyed them, particularly because consumer goods were relatively cheap and business promoted an alluring new way for a family to live beyond their means—consumer credit.

Buy Now, Pay Later

Before the 1920s, borrowing was something one did in order to build a business, get crops in the ground, or to save or improve an enterprise. In theory, borrowed money was invested in productivity, thus providing the means to retire the debt. Or, people borrowed in order to build or buy a home, in which case their debt was secured by real property. During the 1920s, for the first time, large numbers of Americans began to borrow simply in order to live more pleasingly. They went into debt not to produce but to consume and enjoy.

The chief agency of consumer borrowing during the 1920s was the installment plan. A refrigerator that sold for $87.50 could be ensconced in a corner of the kitchen for a down payment of merely $5 and monthly payments of $10. Even a comparatively low-cost item like a vacuum cleaner ($28.95) could be had for $2 down and "E-Z payments" of $4 a month. During the New Era, 60 percent of all automobiles were bought on time; 70 percent of furniture; 80 percent of refrigerators, radios, and vacuum cleaners; and 90 percent of pianos, sewing machines, and washing machines. With 13.8 million people owning radios by 1930 (up from virtually none in 1920), the Americans who basked in the glow of Coolidge prosperity were also up to their necks in hock.

Moralists pointed out that borrowing in order to consume marked a sharp break with American ideals of frugality—the axioms of Benjamin Franklin—but

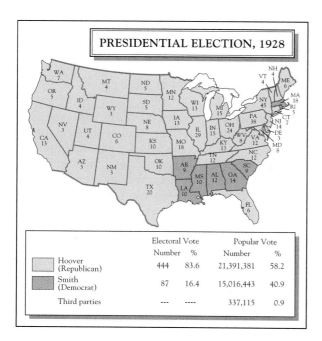

> ### Anxiety Advertising
>
> The text that follows was taken from a magazine advertisement of the 1920s for Listerine Antiseptic, a mouthwash. The illustration that accompanied it showed an elderly, attractive, poignantly sad woman sitting in a darkened parlor (with a photograph of Calvin Coolidge on the wall) poring over old letters and a photograph album.
>
> *Sometimes, when lights are low, they come back to comfort and at the same time sadden her—those memories of long ago, when she was a slip of a girl in love with a dark-eyed Nashville boy. They were the happiest moments of her life—those days of courtship. Though she had never married, no one could take from her the knowledge that she had been loved passionately, devotedly; those frayed and yellowed letters of his still told her so. How happy and ambitious they had been for their future together. And then, like a stab, came their parting . . . the broken engagement . . . the sorrow and the shock of it. She could find no explanation for it then, and now, in the soft twilight of life when she can think calmly, it is still a mystery to her.*
>
> The advertiser then went on so as to leave no doubt that "halitosis"—bad breath—was the source of the woman's tragedy.

over and over, down every column. To Bonner's surprise, the blunder did not bankrupt him; his magazine sold out in one afternoon.

The lesson was unmistakable. During the 1890s, C. W. Post, without a cent to his name, borrowed enough money to plaster an entire city with the name of his new breakfast cereal, Post Toasties, and was a millionaire within a month. Bombarded by the name in newspapers, on billboards, painted on the sides of buildings, and slipped under doors on leaflets, people bought. By the 1920s, advertisers moved on to making the extravagant claims of the snake oil salesman, telling outright lies, and bringing sexual titillation into the game: suggestive young ladies in advertisements for such products as soda pop and tickets on railroads.

Advertising became a profession and the pros styled themselves as practical psychologists. They sold goods by exploiting anxieties and, in the words of Thorstein Veblen, "administering shock effects" and others spoke louder and in more dulcet tones. They were the advertisers, members of a new profession dedicated to creating wants in people's minds—the advertising men called them needs—which people had never particularly noticed before.

Buy, Buy, Buy

The earliest advertisements, dating to antiquity, were announcements. By the eighteenth and nineteenth centuries, merchants placed tiny notices in newspapers describing goods, perhaps unusual ones, available for purchase, or special sale prices on common products.

During the 1870s, Robert Bonner, the editor of a literary magazine, the New York *Ledger*, learned by accident the curious effectiveness of repetition. He intended to place a conventional one-line ad in a newspaper—"Read Mrs. Southworth's New Story in the *Ledger*"—and the compositor misread his specification of "one line" as "one page." The line ran

A woman's thighs, a forbidden sight just a few years before, were enlisted in a campaign to sell automobiles. Note that a woman is also the driver of the Buick.

> ### A Businessman's Prayer
>
> The following is not a parody, but a "prayer" that was quite seriously recommended to those in business during the 1920s:
>
> *God of business men, I thank Thee for the fellowship of red-blooded men with songs in their hearts and handclasps that are sincere.*
>
> *I thank thee for telephones and telegrams that link me with home and office, no matter where I am.*
>
> *I thank thee for the joy of battle in the business arena, the thrill of victory and the courage to take defeat like a good sport.*
>
> *I thank thee for children, friendships, books, fishing, the game of golf, my pipe, and the open fire on a chilly evening.*
> *AMEN.*

"trading on the range of human infirmities which blossom in devout observances, and bear fruit in the psychopathic wards." In the age of Coolidge, the makers of Listerine Antiseptic, a mouthwash, invented the disease "halitosis," of which the symptoms included nothing more than a curter greeting than usual from a friend: "Even your best friend won't tell you." Listerine made millions. Fleischmann's yeast, losing its market as people began buying instead of baking their bread, advertised their product as excellent for curing constipation and adolescent pimples. The success of anxiety advertising resulted in the creation of underarm deodorants, a nicety without which humanity had functioned for millennia.

Chain Stores

With manufacturers of small-ticket items like toothpaste and mouthwash spending millions to create a demand for their products, it became advantageous to retail advertised goods on a nationwide basis, too. Individual "Mom and Pop" grocery stores and locally owned and managed haberdasheries and sundries shops sold comparatively few cans of Chef Boy-Ar-Dee Spaghetti, Arrow shirts, and tubes of Ipana toothpaste each month. Therefore, they paid the regional wholesaler a premium price. A centrally managed chain or franchise company, on the contrary, could buy the same goods for hundreds of stores at once, secure a better wholesale price, and keep shipping charges down through "vertical integration." The result was they sharply undersold "Mom and Pop," and their retail chains spread rapidly throughout the country.

By 1928, 860 grocery chains competed for the dollars of a population that was eating better. Among the biggest success stories between 1920 and 1929 were the first supermarkets: Piggly-Wiggly (from 515 to 2,500 stores), Safeway (from 766 to 2,660 stores), and A & P (Atlantic and Pacific Tea Company, from 4,621 to 15,418 stores). Chains also came to dominate the sundries trade (F. W. Woolworth and J. C. Penney), auto parts (Western Auto), and, of course, the retailing of gasoline.

Image Advertising

Image advertising—associating a product with values or a certain attractive kind of person—characterized the selling of automobiles at a time when dozens of manufacturers competed for a share of the market. Pierce Arrows and Lincolns implied, none too subtly, that possession of one of these automobiles indicated a person of high social standing. Stutz

An outlet of the retailing behemoth of the era, Sears Roebuck.

Bearcat was the car of the sport and the swell. Dodge affected a stodgy and stolid comfortable "old shoe" family image. Henry Ford insisted that his car be presented as common and democratic (and cheap!).

By the end of the decade, the number of automobile manufacturers in the United States had shrunk from 108 to 44. But there were 27 million cars registered by state departments of motor vehicles in 1929. Indeed, everything related to automobiles, from publicly financed highway construction to those new features of the American landscape, service stations and the roadside motor hotel or motel, flourished during the New Era.

The Limits of Prosperity

A few economists joined the moralistic critics of runaway consumption, pointing out that the time would come when everyone who could afford a car, a washing machine, and other consumer durables would have them. They would no longer be buying, and the consumer industries would be in trouble.

Another major weakness of the Coolidge economy was that significant numbers of Americans did not share in the good times and were, therefore, shut out completely from the buying spree. The 700,000 to 800,000 coal miners and 400,000 textile workers and their dependents suffered depressed conditions and wages throughout the decade; they were not buying many cars and radios. Staple farmers were once again struggling to stave off bankruptcy. Even those who did well often lived in places where there was no electricity; they were buying no appliances that had to be plugged in.

The southern states generally lagged far behind the rest of the country in income and standard of living. Blacks, Indians, Hispanics, and other minority groups tasted Coolidge prosperity only in odd bites.

Business Culture

But economically deprived groups are rarely politically articulate when mainstream society is at ease in its world, and in the 1920s, mainstream America was quite at ease. Business leaders hastened to take the credit for good times, and they got it.

On a local level, businessmen's clubs such as the Rotary, Kiwanis, Lions, and Junior Chambers of Commerce seized community leadership and preached boosterism: "If you can't boost, don't knock." Successful manufacturers like Henry Ford were looked to for

wisdom on every imaginable question. Any man who made $25,000 a day, as Ford did during most of the 1920s, must be an oracle on whatever subject he chose to speak about. Even that man once the most hated in America, John D. Rockefeller, now in his eighties and retired to Florida, became a figure of respect and affection, thanks to Coolidge prosperity and the skillful image building of the Rockefeller family's public relations expert, Ivy Lee.

The career of an advertising man, Bruce Barton, showed just how thoroughly the business culture dominated the way Americans thought. In 1925, Barton published a book called *The Man Nobody Knows*. It depicted Jesus as a businessman, a hale fellow well-met, a sport, an entrepreneur, and an advertising genius whose religion was like a successful company. Instead of finding Barton's vision blasphemous or laughable, Americans bought *The Man Nobody Knows* by the hundreds of thousands. It was a best-seller for two years!

Jesus as Advertising Man

He would be a national advertiser today, I am sure, as he was the greatest advertiser of his own day. Take any one of the parables, no matter which—you will find that it exemplifies all the principles on which advertising textbooks are written.

1. First of all they are marvellously condensed, as all good advertising must be. Jesus hated prosy dullness.

2. His language was marvellously simple—a second great essential. All the greatest things in human life are one-syllable things—love, joy, hope, child, wife, trust, faith, God.

3. Sincerity glistened like sunshine through every sentence he uttered. The advertisements which persuade people to act are written by men who have an abiding respect for the intelligence of their readers, and a deep sincerity regarding the merits of the goods they have to sell.

4. Finally he knew the necessity for repetition and practiced it. No important truth can be impressed upon the minds of any large number of people by being said only once.

Bruce Barton, *The Man Nobody Knows* (1925)

John Jacob Raskob of General Motors promoted the worship of business in popular magazines such as the *Saturday Evening Post*. Because the value of many kinds of property was rising throughout the 1920s under the stewardship of business, Raskob said that it was a simple matter for workingmen to save a little money and invest it, thus becoming capitalists themselves. To an astonishing degree, middle-class Americans who had a small nest egg in the bank believed him. They plunged their savings into one get-rich-quick scheme after another, feeding but at the same time dooming the speculative economy.

GET RICH QUICK

The most colorful get-rich-quick craze of the decade centered on Florida, previously a backward and isolated agricultural state. Improved train connections with eastern and midwestern population centers, retirement to Florida by such celebrities as Rockefeller and William Jennings Bryan, and the lively nationwide ballyhoo of ingenious promoters such as Samuel Flagler and Wilson Mizner put people on notice of the Sunshine State's possibilities as a vacation and retirement paradise.

The Florida Land Boom

The development of places like Fort Lauderdale and Miami Beach would take time, of course, no one denied that. The way to make money from their growth, therefore, was to buy orange groves and sandy wasteland at bargain prices and hold the land for resale to the actual builders of vacation hotels and retirement homes. The number of people rich enough to make such a long-term commitment, however, was small. In 1925, however, Florida's boosters attracted more modestly fixed people to send their money south by promoting a get-rich-quick speculative fever that fed on itself.

As had happened repeatedly in the American West, the price of Florida land rose not because development was underway and residents were pouring in by the hundreds of thousands, but because speculator bought from speculator, each planning to sell to another as quickly as possible at an even higher price. Some lots in Miami Beach on which no one dreamed of building changed hands dozens of times within a few months, the price climbing with every sale. At the height of the craze, one issue of a Miami newspaper ran more than 500 pages of advertisements of land for sale. There were over 2,000 real-estate offices in the little city.

Since the price of every acre in Florida seemed to be skyrocketing, many northerners were willing to buy sight unseen, and frauds were inevitable. More than a few snowbound dreamers in Chicago and Minneapolis purchased tracts of alligator-infested swampland from fast-talking salesmen who assured them that they were purchasing a site that Piggly-Wiggly or Woolworth's would find highly desirable. Others bought beachfront lots that were closer to the ocean than they counted on—underneath six feet of salt water at high tide. But the major fuel of the mania was not fraud. It was a foolishness born of a culture that exalted money-making above all else, much like the 1990s.

As with all speculative crazes, the day inevitably arrived when there were no more buyers, no one willing to bet on higher prices in the future. After a few months of making mortgage payments on land that was not moving, would-be land barons decided, as herd-like as they had bought, to get out of Florida real estate with their winnings, to break even, or just to cut their losses. The market was flooded with offerings at ever lower prices. The speculators who were caught holding overpriced property saw paper fortunes evaporate; the banks that lent them money to speculate failed; people who trusted those banks to invest their savings sensibly lost their accounts.

I Hear a Melody

Sales of sheet music, the staff of life for the creators of popular music before World War I, declined by a third during the 1920s. Sales of rolls for player pianos dropped as radically. With the spread of radio and phonograph ownership, the pop music business became almost synonymous with the sale of records. As early as 1921, record companies (RCA foremost among them) sold 100 million "platters" in the United States. With the stock market crash, the business collapsed as quickly as it had grown. In 1932, only 6 million records were sold.

The Florida crash was triggered by a hurricane that hit Miami and showed, as Frederick Lewis Allen put it, what a soothing tropical wind could do to a vacation paradise when it got a running start from the West Indies. The price of land plunged within weeks to dollars per acre. Citrus farmers who cursed themselves a thousand times for having sold their groves so cheaply at the beginning of the boom discovered that, thanks to a chain of defaults, they were back in possession of their orchards, the trees only a little worse for the wear of speculators tromping through it imagining hotels and happy beach loungers. Wilson Mizner, one of the architects of the boom and a big loser in the bust, was good humored about the debacle. "Always be pleasant to the people you meet on the way up," he said, "because they are always the very same people you meet on the way down." He went to Hollywood.

Buying on Margin

Middle-class America was almost as nonchalant as Mizner. Even before Florida busted, they began to fuel another speculative mania, driving up the prices of shares on the New York Stock Exchange.

Speculation in stocks had always been a game for a few very rich people. However, the prosperity of the 1920s created savings accounts for middle-class Americans, even after consumption. In order to tap their capital, stock brokers offered the possibility of purchasing stock on an installment plan in which, so it seemed, there were no installments to pay.

That is, investors with just a few hundred or thousands of dollars to risk in the market could buy stocks "on margin." They bought shares of RCA (Radio Corporation of America), the New York Central, or Illinois Gadget by paying out as little as 10 percent of the quoted price of those companies' shares. In this way, they were able to hold title to ten times as many shares as they could afford to buy with cash. A bank or broker loaned the speculator the balance of the stocks' actual price with the stocks themselves serving as collateral. This—the money the speculator owed—was "the margin." When the shares were sold, presumably at a big profit—the loan was paid off and the shrewd speculators pocketed the difference, also ten times what they would have made if they bought with cash. At least that was how the 1.5 million Americans playing the market in 1926 understood margin to work.

The Bull Market

Beginning in 1927, that was how it did work for hundreds of thousands of people. Prices of shares began to soar as more and more people rushed to buy. During the summer of 1929, values went crazy. American Telephone and Telegraph climbed from $209 a share to $303; General Motors went from $268 to $391, hitting $452 on September 3. Some obscure issues enjoyed even more dizzying rises. And with each tale of a fortune made overnight, related breathlessly or with smug self-congratulation at country club, lodge hall, community dance, or, indeed, on the porch of the church on Sunday, more people were hooked, encouraged to carry their savings to stockbrokers, whose offices were as easy to find as auto parts stores.

Historically and ideally, the value of a share in a corporation represented the earning capacity of the company. The money that a corporation realized by selling shares was to be expended, theoretically, to improve the company's plant, equipment, marketing capacity, and in other productive ways. Thus, when the price of stock in General Motors or RCA rose during the late 1920s, it represented to some extent the extraordinary expansion of the automobile and radio industries.

During the speculative Coolidge bull market, however, the prices of shares also reflected nothing more than the willingness of people to pay those prices because, as in Florida, they expected someone else to buy from them at yet greater prices. It was immaterial to such speculators that the companies in which they had put their money did not pay dividends or even use their capital to improve productive capacity. The rising prices of stocks fed on themselves. It became more profitable for companies to put their capital into speculation—making loans to margin buyers, for example—than into production. The face value of shares in the Coolidge bull market bore little relationship to the health of the American economy.

Politicians, either unable to understand what was happening or afraid to appear pessimistic in a time of buoyant optimism, reassured their constituents that there was nothing wrong. When a few concerned economists warned that the bull market was a bubble that had to burst, with calamitous consequences, others scolded them. President Coolidge told people that he thought stock prices were cheap, in effect encouraging others to rush to the broker.

The Inevitable

Joseph P. Kennedy, a Boston millionaire (and father of President John F. Kennedy), said in later years that he had sold all of his stocks during the summer of 1929 after the man who shined his shoes mentioned that he was playing the market. Kennedy reasoned that if such a poorly paid person was buying stock, there was no one left out there to bid prices higher. The inevitable crash was coming soon.

Kennedy was right. On September 3, 1929, the average price of shares on the New York Stock Exchange peaked and then dipped sharply. For a month, prices spurted up and down. Then on "Black Thursday," October 24, a record 13 million shares changed hands, and values collapsed. General Electric fell $47\frac{1}{2}$ points on that one day; other major issues dropped almost as much.

On Tuesday, October 29, the wreckage was worse. In a panic now, speculators dumped 16 million shares on the market. Clerical workers on Wall Street had to work through the night just to sort out the avalanche of paperwork. When the dust settled early the next morning, more than $30 billion in paper value had been wiped out.

It was phony value, representing little more than the irrational belief that prices could rise indefinitely. Nevertheless, the eradication of so many dollars profoundly shattered the confidence of businessmen and belief in the business culture of the 1920s. The Great Crash eventually contributed to the hardship of

Wall Street teems like a stockyard on Black Friday, 1929.

millions of people who could not have distinguished a share in Seaboard Air Lines from the label on a bottle of cognac.

Crash and Depression

The Great Crash of 1929 did not cause the Great Depression of the 1930s. That was the result of fundamental weaknesses in the economy that had little to do with the mania for speculation. But the crash helped to trigger the decline in the American economy that was well underway by New Year's Day 1930.

Middle-class families who had played the market lost their savings. Banks that had recklessly lent money to speculators went broke. When they closed their doors, they wiped out the savings accounts of frugal people who looked on a bank as a vault to protect their money from robbers.

Corporations whose cash assets were decimated shut down operations or curtailed production, thus throwing people out of work or cutting their wages. Those who had taken mortgages during the heady high-interest days of 1928 and 1929 were unable to meet payments and lost their homes; farmers lost the means by which they made a living. This contributed to additional bank failures.

Virtually everyone had to cut consumption, thus reducing the sales of manufacturers and farmers and stimulating another turn in the downward spiral: curtailed production meant layoff; increased unemployment meant another reduction in consumption by those newly thrown out of work. And so it went, from buy, buy, buy to down, down, down.

CHRONOLOGY

1922   Fordney-McCumber Tariff

1923   Calvin Coolidge becomes president

1924   Calvin Coolidge easily elected president
Dawes Plan to restructure German reparations

1927   Charles A. Lindbergh flies Atlantic solo
Beginning of Coolidge Bull Market

1928   Kellogg-Briand Pact
Herbert Hoover elected president

1929   Young Plan reduces German war debt
Stock Market collapses

1930   Great Depression begins

FOR FURTHER READING

See these general histories of the 1920s: Loren Baritz, *The Culture of the Twenties*, 1969; Paul A. Carter, *The Twenties in America*, 1968; Ellis W. Hawley, *The Great War and the Search for a Modern Order: A History of the American People and Their Institutions, 1917–1933*, 1979; William E. Leuchtenburg, *The Perils of Prosperity, 1914–1932*, 1958; and David Fromkin, *In the Time of the Americans*, 1995.

Focusing on politics are David Burner, *The Politics of Provincialism: The Democratic Party in Transition*, 1968; Otis L. Graham, Jr., *The Great Campaigns: War and Reform in America, 1900–1928*, 1971; John D. Hicks, *Republican Ascendancy, 1921–1933*, 1960; Donald Lisio, *The President and Protest*, 1974; Paula Elder,

Governor Alfred E. Smith: The Politician as Reformer, 1983; Theodore D. Saloutos and John D. Hicks, *Twentieth-Century Populism: Agricultural Discontent in the Middle West, 1900–1939*, 1951; D. R. McCoy, *Calvin Coolidge: The Quiet President*, 1967; Arthur M. Schlesinger, Jr., *The Crisis of the Old Order*, 1957; Joan Hoff Wilson, *Herbert Hoover: Forgotten Progressive*, 1975; and David Burner, *Herbert Hoover*, 1979.

On economic and financial questions, see Irving Bernstein, *The Lean Years*, 1960; C. P. Kinderberger, *The World in Depression*, 1973; J. W. Prothro, *Dollar Decade: Business Ideas in the 1920s*, 1954; David Montgomery, *The Fall of the House of Labor*, 1987; and the incomparable John K. Galbraith, *The Great Crash*, 1955.

The aftermath of a series of dust storms, South Dakota, 1936.

41
CHAPTER

NATIONAL TRAUMA

The Great Depression

1930–1933

We in America today are nearer to the final triumph over poverty than ever before in the history of any land. The poorhouse is vanishing from among us. We have not yet reached the goal, but given a chance to go forward with the policies of the last eight years, and we shall soon, with the help of God, be within sight of the day when poverty shall be banished from the nation.

—Herbert Hoover

I have no fears for the future of our country. It is bright with hope.

—Herbert Hoover

What our country needs is a good big laugh. If someone could get off a good joke every ten days, I think our troubles would be over.

—Herbert Hoover

Prosperity is just around the corner.

—Herbert Hoover

802 Chapter 41 National Trauma

The stock market crash of 1929 made headlines day after day. The depression that followed made its impact less dramatically at first. By the end of 1930, however, hard times had engulfed the nation in something far more serious than a collapse in the value of securities. And the hard times did not fully dissipate until 1939 and 1940, when the economy was jolted into prosperity by the outbreak of another world war.

The Great Depression was not only the most serious economic crisis in American history. It was, with the exception of the Civil War, a more jarring psychological and moral experience for the American people than any other event. The Great Depression was a national trauma that left marks on society still discernible at the beginning of the twenty-first century.

Millions of Americans who lived through the First World War and the Roaring Twenties found their recollections of those periods vague and even inconsequential after 1930. People who came of age during the 1930s remembered the deprivations, anxieties, and struggles of the decade more vividly than, sometimes, they remembered the Second World War, the return of prosperity, and the beginning of the nuclear age in the 1940s. So large did the memory of hard times loom in their minds that they passed on to their children, who never personally experienced the Depression, a sense that it was an important event in their own lives.

Not until the later 1960s did a generation come of age for which the Great Depression was "ancient history." Not until 1980, half a century after the Depression began, did voters in a national election decisively repudiate the liberals whom the Great Depression brought to the fore. In the early twenty-first century, political and social divisions brought to the fore by the Depression still shaped American politics, if more obscurely with each year that passed. Few observers of the incredible stock market boom of the 1990s, and the roaring "Clinton prosperity" that accompanied it, dared remind Americans of the bull market of the 1920s and of Calvin Coolidge.

THE FACE OF CATASTROPHE

Not every memory of the 1930s was a bad one. Far from it: many people were proud that when times were at their toughest, they survived and, what is more, carried on vital cultural, social, and personal lives. Whether negative or positive the memories, however, the Depression generation was the last American generation to date whose character and values were forged in an era of economic decline, material denial, and a jaundiced outlook on the future.

The Depression in Numbers

During the first year after the crash of the stock market, 4 million workers lost their jobs. By 1931, 100,000 people were being fired each week. By 1932, 25 percent of the workforce was unemployed, about 13 million people with about 30 million dependents. Black workers, "the last hired and the first fired," suffered a higher unemployment rate than whites, 35 percent. In Chicago, 40 percent of those people who wanted work could not find it. In Toledo, 80 percent were unemployed. In some coal-mining towns like Donora, Pennsylvania, virtually no one had a job.

Employees who held on to their jobs took cuts in pay. Between 1929 and 1933, the average weekly earnings of manufacturing workers fell from $25 to less than $17. The income of farmers plummeted from a low starting point. By the winter of 1933, some corn growers were burning their crop for heat—shades of the 1890s—because they could not sell it at a profit. Growers of wheat estimated that it

---

No One Has Starved

At the worst of times early in the Great Depression, it was common to say that "no one has starved." But some came close, as these two excerpts from the *New York Times* indicate:

MIDDLETOWN, N.Y., December 24, 1931.—Attracted by smoke from the chimney of a supposedly abandoned summer cottage near Anwana Lake in Sullivan County, Constable Simon Glaser found a young couple starving. Three days without food, the wife, who is 23 years old, was hardly able to walk.

DANBURY, CONNECTICUT, September 6, 1932.—Found starving under a rude canvas shelter in a patch of woods on Flatboard Ridge, where they had lived for five days on wild berries and apples, a woman and her 16-year-old daughter were fed and clothed today by the police and placed in the city almshouse.

took five bushels to earn the price of a cheap pair of shoes. The wholesale price of cotton dropped to five cents a pound, laughably low if the consequences were not so tragic.

Banks failed at a rate of 200 a month during 1932, wiping out $3.2 billion in savings accounts. When New York City's Bank of the United States went under in December 1930, 400,000 people lost their deposits. Much of the money was in small accounts that had been squirreled away by working people as a hedge against economic misfortune. When, understandably frightened, they withdrew their emergency funds, the downward spiral continued.

Hundreds of thousands of people lost their homes between 1929 and 1933 because they could not meet mortgage payments. One farm family in four was pushed off the land by 1933, mainly in the cotton, grain, and pork belts of the South and Midwest. With their customers unable to buy, more than 100,000 small businesses went bankrupt, 32,000 in 1932 alone (88 per day). Doctors, lawyers, and other professionals reported huge drops in income. Some schools closed for lack of money; in others, teachers took sharp cuts or worked without pay as the only means of keeping them open. Some teachers in Chicago were not compensated for ten years. Others never were.

What Depression Looked Like

Even people who did not personally suffer were reminded of the Depression at every turn. More than 5,000 people lined up outside of a New York employment agency each week to apply for 500 menial jobs. When the city government of Birmingham, Alabama, called for about 800 workers to put in an 11-hour day for $2, 12,000 applicants showed up. In 1931, a Soviet agency, Amtorg, announced openings for 6,000 skilled technicians who were willing to move to Russia; 100,000 Americans said they would go. Once-prosperous workers and small businessmen sold apples or set up shoeshine stands on street corners, claiming that they preferred any kind of work to accepting charity.

Charitable organizations were not up to the flood of the newly impoverished. Philadelphia's social workers managed to reach only one-fifth of the city's unemployed in order to provide $4.23 to a family for a week, not enough to buy food, let alone pay for clothing, rent, and fuel. Soup kitchens set up by both religious and secular groups offered little more than a crust of bread and a bowl of thin stew, but for three years, they were regularly mobbed by people who waited in lines that strung out for blocks. A journalist described the crowd at the Municipal Lodging House in New York City in 1930: "There is a line of men, three or sometimes four abreast, a block long, and wedged tightly together—so tightly that no passer-by can break through. For this compactness there is a reason: those at the head of the

> ### Paycut
>
> In 1929, the last year of prosperity, Lefty O'Doul had a batting average of .398 for the Philadelphia Phillies. This achievement earned him a raise of only $500. In 1930, the first year of the Depression, O'Doul hit .308, hardly a poor average. His salary was cut $1,000.

Unemployed workingman with style, 1930.

grey-black human snake will eat tonight; those farther back probably won't."

On the outskirts of most large cities (and right in the middle of New York in Central Park), homeless men and women built shantytowns out of scavenged lumber, scraps of sheet metal, flimsy packing crates, and cardboard boxes. The number of people who simply wandered the land brought the face of catastrophe to rural America. Because it was impossible to stay the flood, railroads gave up trying to keep people off the freight trains. Detectives for the Missouri Pacific railroad counted 14,000 people hopping its freights in 1928; in 1931, 186,000 rode the same rails. Rough estimates indicate that 1.5 million people were moving about in search of casual work, and others were simply moving about; railroad officials noted ever increasing numbers of children in the trek.

This revelation, plus increased desertion of their families by unemployed men, a rise in the divorce rate, and a decline in the birthrate—from more than 3 million births in 1921 to 2.4 million in 1932—convinced some moralists and sociologists that the Depression was destroying the American family. Others responded that hardship was causing families to pull together.

This was true of the tragic odyssey of the "Okies" and "Arkies." In the mid-1930s, the hardships of depression were compounded by a natural disaster in large parts of Oklahoma, Texas, Kansas, and Arkansas: dust storms literally stripped the topsoil from the land and blacked out the sun. In several counties of eastern Oklahoma, 90 percent of the population went on welfare. Some areas lost half their population as people fled across the desert to California, typically in decrepit Model-T Fords piled with ragged possessions. Novelist John Steinbeck captured their desperation, and their plucky inner resourcefulness in *The Grapes of Wrath*, a popular novel published in 1939, and in 1940 the winner of the Pulitzer Prize.

THE FAILURE OF THE OLD ORDER

Will Rogers, himself an "Okie" and the nation's most popular humorist, quipped that the United States would be the first country to go to the poorhouse in an automobile. He was trying to restore a sense of proportion to the way people thought about the Great Depression. No one was starving, President Hoover added in one of his many ham-handed attempts to ease tension.

In the broadest sense, both men were right. There was no plague or famine. Indeed, to many people the troubling paradox of America's greatest depression was that deprivation was widespread in a country that was blessed with plenty. American factories remained as capable as ever of producing goods, but they stood silent or working at a fraction of capacity because no one could afford to buy their wares. Farms were pouring forth food in cornucopian abundance, but hungry people could not afford to consume it. One of the most striking images of the early 1930s transformed a mild, white-haired California physician into an angry crusader. Early one Saturday morning, Dr. Francis E. Townsend looked out his window to see old women picking through the garbage pails of a store that was heaped high with foodstuffs. Townsend would found a network of political clubs dedicated to relieving the distress of the elderly.

The Tragedy of Herbert Hoover

Business and the Republican party had reaped credit for the soothing breezes of prosperity. Now they took the blame for the whirlwind of depression, and the recriminations were aimed particularly at the titular head of the party, Herbert Clark Hoover. The shantytowns where homeless thousands dwelled were called Hoovervilles; newspapers used as blankets by men who were forced to sleep on park benches were Hoover blankets; a pocket turned inside out was a Hoover flag; a boxcar on the railroad was a Hoover Pullman.

Still remembered as a great humanitarian when he entered the White House in 1929, Hoover was the callous tormentor of the people a year later. Celebrated for his energy and efficiency as secretary of commerce, Hoover as president was perceived to be incompetent, paralyzed by the economic crisis. When Hoover made one of his rare public appearances, a

---

A Chicken in Every Pot

The Republican party slogan in the election campaign of 1928 had been "A Chicken in Every Pot and Two Cars in Every Garage." In 1932, the advertising man who had coined it was out of work and reduced to begging in order to support his family.

With their cars loaded to overflowing, newly arrived "Okies" were a common sight in Los Angeles during the Great Depression.

motorcade through the hard-hit industrial city of Detroit, sidewalk crowds greeted him with dead silence and sullen stares. The president could not even take a brief vacation without arousing scorn. "Look here, Mr. Hoover, see what you've done," an Appalachian song had it. "You went a-fishing, let the country go to ruin."

In truth, Hoover's self-confidence decayed rapidly during his four years in the presidency. If never a warm man, Hoover had always exuded confidence, beaming smugly for photographers. Now he sat subdued, withdrawn, and embittered in the White House. Conversing with him, an adviser remembered, was like sitting in a bath of ink.

Hoover was unjustly accused when critics called him uncaring, a do-nothing president, a stooge for the Mellons and other big businessmen. The president was moved by the suffering in the country. He gave much of his income to charity and urged others to do the same. Far from paralyzed, he worked as hard at his job as James K. Polk had done. Nor was he a Coolidge, letting business do as it pleased; Hoover led government to greater intervention in the economy than had any preceding president except Wilson. It would soon be forgotten, but the man who replaced Hoover in the White House, Franklin D. Roosevelt, several times criticized Hoover for improperly expanding the powers of government. It would be forgotten because Roosevelt would recognize, as Hoover never did, that the Republican administration had not done enough.

Hoover's Program: Not Enough

Something had to be done. A good many Americans personally recollected that the somewhat less severe economic crisis of the 1890s had led to a briefly terrifying social unrest among dispossessed farmers. Now, in the 1930s, urban industrial workers—and the middle class—were suffering as they had not suffered in the depression of the 1890s.

The progressives (of whom Hoover had been considered one) established the precedent that government was responsible for guiding the economy. Only in flush times like the Coolidge era could an administration abdicate its obligations and remain popular. Indeed, Hoover promptly broke with the immediate past by cutting Mellon's regressive consumer taxes in order to encourage purchasing and, therefore, production.

Hoover also broke with the Coolidge-Mellon policies of withdrawing the government from active intervention in the economy. He spent $500 million a year on public works, government programs to build or improve government properties. These projects created some jobs that would otherwise not have existed. The most famous of them was the great Boulder Dam, now called Hoover Dam, on the Colorado River southeast of Las Vegas. The great wall of concrete was the single most massive example of government economic planning and construction to its time and provided work and relief for thousands. But, of course, the Boulder Dam project did nothing in the short run for those who were not involved in building it. (In the long term, ironically, the most conspicuous consequence of this water conservation and power-generation project was to transform Las Vegas into a pleasure dome of gambling casinos.)

In the Reconstruction Finance Corporation (RFC), established by Congress in 1932, Hoover created an agency to help banks, railroads, and other key economic institutions stay in business. The RFC lent money to companies that were basically sound but were hamstrung by the shortage of operating capital.

The trouble was that cutting consumer taxes did nothing for those who were unemployed and paying few taxes. Those who still had jobs inclined not to spend what little windfalls came their way but to save them as a hedge against the day when they might be out of work. Moreover, there was a glut in the urban middle class of the "big ticket" consumer durables like appliances and automobiles, the sale of which might have put people to work.

The RFC was a positively unpopular program. People in trouble saw it not as a recovery policy but as relief for big business while individuals were told to shift for themselves. The RFC alone looked very much like an extension of Andrew Mellon's trickle-down economics; except in the arid early years of the Great Depression, little seemed to trickle down.

The Blindness of the Rugged Individual

More was needed—massive relief to get the poor, who were growing in numbers, over the worst of the crisis. This Hoover would not authorize. A self-made man himself, he had forgotten the role of talent and good luck in getting ahead. He believed that "rugged individuals" —he used the phrase—who looked to no one but themselves, were the secret of American cultural vitality. For the federal government to encourage that trait of the national character was one thing; for the government to sponsor huge handouts was quite another. Federal relief measures were not, in Hoover's opinion, the first step in defeating the Depression, but were the first step in emasculating the American spirit. There was a difference between helping Belgians devastated by war and helping Americans deprived by economic dislocations.

Hoover also clung to certain assumptions that prevented him from realizing just how much federal guidance was needed. Failing to recognize that state boundaries had no economic significance, he wanted the states to take the lead in fighting the Depression. Viewing government as much like a business, he was particularly inflexible when it came to the ideal of a balanced budget and the government's power to manipulate the value of the currency.

Government, Hoover insisted, must spend no more money than it collected; the books must balance. As for money questions, Hoover knew that during every depression since the Civil War, only Greenbackers, Populists, and others regarded as radicals proposed increasing the supply of money (deliberately inflating prices) in order to stimulate the economy. Each time they were defeated, and each time the country emerged from hard times more prosperous than before. Hoover was positive that this cycle would be repeated if the old faith were kept: if the budget were balanced and the dollar remained rooted in gold.

The Depression Goes International

For a few months, in 1931, Hoover's prediction that "prosperity was just around the corner" seemed to be coming true. Most economic indicators made modest gains. Then the entire industrialized world followed the United States into the economic pit. In May, a major European bank, the Kreditanstalt of Vienna, went bankrupt, badly shaking other Euro-

A line of hungry men stretches beyond discerning outside a soup kitchen in New York City.

pean banks that had supported it, and toppling some. In September, Great Britain abandoned the gold standard. That is, the Bank of England ceased to redeem its paper money in gold bullion or coin. Worried that all paper money would lose its value, international investors withdrew $1.5 billion in gold from American banks, further weakening the financial structure and launching a new wave of local failures.

But the worst consequence of the European collapse was what it did to Hoover's state of mind. It persuaded him that America's depression was not the fault of domestic problems that he might help remedy, but of foreigners over whom he had no power. The most cosmopolitan president since John Quincy Adams had sunk to the ignorant provincial's easy inclination to blame others—foreigners. The result was that by 1932 his administration was paralyzed. The country was drifting as Hoover tacitly admitted that he was helpless and could only wait. And conditions worsened by the month.

AMERICANS REACT TO THE CRISIS

If Hoover's failure represented the inability of the New Era Republicans to cope with the Depression, radicals were unable to offer a plausible alternative. Critics of capitalism believed that the crisis represented the death throes of the system and that they would soon be in power. To an extent, they, like Hoover, waited for inevitable forces beyond their control to summon them to the helm.

The Not-So-Red Decade

After polling only 267,000 votes in prosperous 1928, Socialist party presidential candidate Norman Thomas won 882,000 in 1932. Communist candidate William Z. Foster doubled his vote in those four years, from 49,000 to 103,000. But the combined anticapitalist vote of less than a million was minuscule compared with the 23 million cast for the Democrats in that year and even the 16 million won by the discredited Hoover. Thomas's total in 1932 was less than the Socialists had won 20 years before, when the electorate was much smaller and the economy was in much better health.

Later in the 1930s, American Communists made some gains among intellectuals and in the leadership of the labor movement. Distinguished writers such as Lillian Hellman, Dashiell Hammett, and Granville Hicks joined the Communist party. Even F. Scott Fitzgerald, the chronicler of "flaming youth" during the 1920s, flirted with Marxist ideas that he did not really understand. Theodore Dreiser, the dean of American novelists, wanted to join the Communist party but was told by party leaders that he could do more good for the cause outside the organization than in. Perhaps they thought that if he wrote calls for revolution in his tortured version of the English language that it would all sound quite dull.

The Communist love of conspiracy and manipulation drove intellectuals out of the party as quickly as they joined. It also prevented the Communists from establishing a base in the labor movement despite making contributions to its growth that, in retrospect, can be seen to have been invaluable. Wyndham Mortimer of the United Automobile Workers, labor journalist Len De Caux, lawyer Lee Pressman, and many other Communists and "fellow travelers" (sympathizers who were not members of the party) devoted their lives to building up the union movement. However, most Communist organizers either denied or thickly camouflaged their affiliation with the party and their anticapitalist ideology. The result was that few rank-and-file union members were exposed to, let alone converted to, Communist ideas. When anti-Communist labor leaders took the offensive against the reds in the 1940s, they found it easy to oust party members from the unions.

A Curious Response

Americans simply did not interpret the Great Depression as evidence that capitalism had failed. During prosperous times, Americans believed that individual success was primarily due to individual initiative, and not to general social conditions. So their initial response to the Depression was to blame themselves for the hardships that beset them. Sociologists and journalists reported on homeless hitchhikers who apologized for their shabby clothing. A walk through any big-city park revealed unsuccessful job seekers slumped on benches, heads in hands, elbows on knees, collars drawn up, wondering where they, not the system, had failed.

The Gillette Company, a manufacturer of razor blades, exploited the feeling of personal failure by running an advertisement that showed a husband reporting shamefully to his wife that he still had not found a job. The message was that employers had turned him down not because there were no jobs available but because he presented a poor appearance with his badly shaved whiskers. A maker of underwear put the responsibility for the unemployment of a bedridden man squarely on his own shoulders. He was out of work not because 13 million others were, but because he wore an inferior brand of undershirt and so caught a cold that he well deserved.

Long after the Depression ended, it was the proud boast of many families that however bad things got, they never went "on the county," never took handouts from public welfare agencies. The unmistakable message was that coping with hard times was a personal responsibility. The implication for radicals who sought to direct anger and frustration against the system was not encouraging.

Episodes of Violence

There was violence. Hungry, angry people rioted in St. Paul and other cities, storming food markets and clearing the shelves. Wisconsin dairy farmers stopped milk trucks and dumped the milk into ditches, partly in rage at the low prices paid by processors, partly to dramatize their need for help. In Iowa, the National Farmers' Holiday Association told hog raisers to withhold their products from the market—to take a holiday—and attracted attention by blockading highways. Eat your own products, Holiday Association leader Milo Reno told the Iowans, and let the money men eat their gold.

But these incidents were isolated and exceptional. For the most part, Americans coped with the Depression peacefully and without a thought for revolution. In fact, the most violent episode of the early Depression was launched not by stricken people but by the authorities. This was the demonstration and destruction of the "Bonus Expeditionary Force" in Washington during the summer of 1932.

The Bonus Boys were 20,000 veterans of the First World War and their wives who massed in Washington to demand that Congress immediately, as a relief measure, vote them a bonus for their wartime service that was scheduled for 1945. The economic crisis, they claimed, justified making the payment immediately rather than waiting for their old age. When Congress adjourned in July 1932 without doing so, all but about 2,000 of the demonstrators left the capital. Those who remained set up a Hooverville on Anacostia Flats on the outskirts of the city, policed themselves, cooperated with authorities, and were generally peaceful.

Hoover, thoroughly frustrated by the stubbornness of the Depression and his own abysmal unpopularity, persuaded himself that the Bonus Boys were led by Communist agitators. (Actually, the most influential organization among the Bonus Boys was the militantly anticommunist American Legion.) The president sent General Douglas MacArthur to disperse them. MacArthur, a talented military man often blinded and made ludicrous by a grotesque vanity, called on armored vehicles and tear gas to make short work of the protesters. However, when an infant died from asphyxiation and Americans mulled over the spectacle of young soldiers attacking old soldiers on presidential orders, Hoover's reputation sank even lower.

Midwestern Robin Hoods

Americans displayed their disenchantment with traditional sources of leadership in other, less direct ways. Businessmen, who were almost universally lionized just a few years before, became objects of ridicule in films, on radio programs, and in the columns and comic strips of daily newspapers.

Perhaps the most curious example of cynicism toward traditional values was the admiration lavished on a new kind of criminal, the midwestern bank robbers who exploited automobiles and the wide-open highways of the Midwest to flee the scene of their dirty work. A sensationalist press transformed John Dillinger, "Pretty Boy" Floyd, "Machine Gun" Kelly, Bonnie Parker and Clyde Barrow, and "Ma" Barker and her family-centered gang into Robin Hoods.

Unlike the businessmen-gangsters of Prohibition, these Depression bank robbers were small-time, guerrilla operators who botched as many holdups as they pulled off. They were also reckless with their guns, killing bank guards and even innocent bystanders in their attempt to create an atmosphere of terror to cover their escape. But because they robbed the banks whose irresponsibility ruined many poor people and because they came from poor rural (and WASP) backgrounds themselves, the outlaws aroused a kind of admiration among midwesterners down on their luck.

Some of the gangsters themselves cultivated the image of Robin Hood. John Dillinger (who killed ten men) made it a point to be personally generous. "Pretty Boy" Floyd, who operated chiefly in Oklahoma, never had trouble finding people who would hide him from the authorities. When he was buried in Salisaw, Oklahoma, in 1934 (after being gunned down in Ohio), 20,000 people attended the ceremony. Bonnie Parker actually sent snapshots and doggerel epics celebrating the exploits of "Bonnie and Clyde" to newspapers, which greedily published them.

The Movies: The Depression-Proof Business

The film industry exploited this envy of a few who "beat the system" by making movies that slyly glamorized lawbreakers. Still fearful of censorship, the

Bonnie Parker and Clyde Barrow, bank robbers and murderers, posed for publicity shots as if they were celebrities—which they were!

studios always wrote a moral end to their gangster films: the wrongdoer paid for his crimes in a hail of bullets or seated in the electric chair. But the message was clear: criminals played by George Raft, Edward G. Robinson, and James Cagney were pushed into their careers by poverty and often had redeeming qualities.

The film industry did not suffer during the Depression. Movies flourished during the worst years, occupying the central position in American entertainment that they would hold until the popularity of television. Admission prices were cheap. Each week, 85 million people paid an average of 25 cents (10 cents for children) to see Marie Dressler, Janet Gaynor, Shirley Temple, Mickey Rooney, Jean Harlow, and Clark Gable in a dizzying array of adventures and fantasies.

The favorite themes were escapist. During the mid-1930s, Shirley Temple, an angelic if chillingly saccharine little blonde girl who sang and danced, led the list of moneymakers. Her annual salary was $300,000, and her films made $5 million a year for Fox Pictures. Royalties from Shirley Temple dolls and other paraphernalia made her a millionaire. Director Cecil B. DeMille specialized in costume epics, especially those that transported viewers into biblical times.

Choreographer Busby Berkeley made millions for Warner Brothers by staging dance tableaux featuring dozens of beautiful starlets (transformed by mirrors and trick photography into hundreds). People bought tickets to Berkeley films to escape the gray rigors of Depression life. For the same reason, they supported the production of hundreds of low-budget Westerns each year. The cowboy was still a figure of individual freedom in a world in which public events and private lives had become all too complexly interrelated.

By way of contrast, some directors specialized in didactic films on social themes that were often hardhitting. Frank Capra's métier was films that lovingly celebrated old American values and threats to them. Typically, they pitted decent ordinary men and women against indolent, parasitical, and usually crooked businessmen and politicians.

Music, Music, Music

At first almost destroyed by the Depression, the popular music business rebounded quickly to rank a close second behind the movies as the ordinary American's entertainment outside the home. Sales of records, about $50 million a year during the 1920s, collapsed in 1932 to $2.5 million. The chief casualties were the hillbilly and traditional black blues singers whose audiences were among the hardest hit social groups in the country. Companies like Columbia, Decca, and RCA discontinued their "race record" lines and only a few black and Appalachian artists, like Bessie Smith and the Carter Family, continued to make money.

The ten-inch 78-rpm record, which cost only 35 cents, and the jukebox, that provided a play for a nickel, slowly revived the business. By 1939, there were 225,000 jukeboxes in the United States scratching up 13 million records a year. Sales of records increased from 10 million in 1933 to 33 million in 1938 (and then soared, with the return of prosperity, to 127 million in 1941).

The chief beneficiaries were the big bands, which played swing, an intricately harmonized orchestral jazz music intended for dancing. For 50 cents (and even less), a young jitterbugger could dance for three or four hours to the music of Benny Goodman, Harry James, or dozens of other groups. It was not an every-evening diversion. The 50 cents needed for admission was precious enough that the big bands had to rush from city to city and to towns, too, on a series of one-night stands. Even the most popular orchestras might find themselves appearing in 30 different ballrooms in as many nights.

Nevertheless, they were lionized when they came to town. In the Palladium Ballroom in Hollywood, California, Harry James once drew 8,000 dancers in a single night, 35,000 in a week. At other capitals of swing music, like the Glen Island Casino in New Rochelle, New York, big bands earned extra revenue by playing for a radio audience. Because a good receiver could be ensconced in the parlor for $10 or $20, and operated for the cost of electricity, radio was far and away most Depression-era Americans' favorite form of entertainment. They were found in 70 percent of American households.

THE ELECTION OF 1932

The nostalgic glow that could come to surround listening to a favorite radio program, or going to a ballroom, or a movie palace decorated like a Turkish harem, meant that many people would think back about the Great Depression as quite a good time. In the summer of 1932, however, when the

Publicity photo for a "feel good" film, Now and Forever. *Left to right: Carole Lombard, Shirley Temple, Gary Cooper.*

economy hit bottom, few people took the situation with a light heart. The country's mood during the presidential election campaign of that year was somber and anxious.

A Roosevelt for the Democrats

Senator Joseph I. France of Maryland challenged Hoover for the Republican presidential nomination and actually won the primaries in New Jersey, Pennsylvania, Illinois, and Oregon. But American political parties rarely abandon incumbent presidents, even when renomination means, as it did in 1932, a sure victory for the other party. Without zest, the Republicans named President Hoover to bear the brunt of the reaction against the New Era.

Democratic hopefuls, by way of contrast, fought a hair-pulling fight to win a ticket to the White House. The chief candidates at the Chicago convention were John Nance Garner of Texas, who inherited the McAdoo Democrats from the South and West; Al Smith, the party's standard-bearer in 1928, who believed he deserved a second chance; and Governor Franklin D. Roosevelt of New York, once Smith's protégé but now a national figure in his own right.

When the beginnings of a convention deadlock brought back memories of 1924 and a bitterly divided party, a large number of Garner supporters switched to Roosevelt and gave him the nomination. With a nose for the dramatic, Roosevelt broke with tradition, according to which a nominee waited at his home to be informed of the convention's decision. He flew to Chicago (conveying a sense of urgency) and told the cheering Democrats that he meant to provide a "New Deal" for the American people. In so saying, Roosevelt simultaneously

How They Lived

Weeknights at Eight

Although commercial radio broadcasting began in 1920 and the first radio network, the National Broadcasting Company, was founded in 1926, it was during the Great Depression of the 1930s that the new medium of communication and entertainment found a place in the lives of almost all Americans. Radio receivers were found in about 12 million American households in 1930. By 1940, they were in 28 million. Fully 86 percent of the American people had easy daily access to radio sets. They were designed not to look like electronic equipment but as a prized piece of furniture, the twentieth-century equivalent of the wardrobe. Some were sleekly modern "art deco," others gothic with the pointed, vertical arches of a medieval cathedral.

Hard times themselves were a big reason for the dramatic expansion of radio. During the 1920s, the average price of a receiver was $75, far out of reach of most families. During the 1930s, a serviceable set could be bought for $10 or $20, an amount that, with sacrifices, all but the utterly destitute could scrape up.

The New Deal also played a part in the radio boom. While most cities and towns were electrified before 1933, very little of the countryside was. Private power companies were not interested in the small return to be had from stringing wire into the hinterlands. By putting the advantages of electrification for country people above profits, Roosevelt's Rural Electrification Administration brought isolated farm families into the mainstream of society. With more than 57 million people defined as living in "rural territory" in 1940, the significance of radio to American culture may be said to have owed largely to New Deal reforms. Indeed, country people depended more on the crackling broadcasts of news, music, and dramatic programs for brightening their lives than did city dwellers.

Manufacturers that produced consumer goods rushed to advertise on the three networks: the Columbia Broadcasting System; the Mutual; and the National Broadcasting Company with its two chains, the red and the blue networks. (When antitrust proceedings forced NBC to dispose of one of its networks, the American Broadcasting Company was born.) In 1935, the first year for which there are reliable statistics, networks and local stations raked in $113 million from advertisers with operating expenses at an estimated $80 million. In 1940, expenses were up to $114 million, but advertising revenues had almost doubled to $216 million.

The manufacturers of Pepsodent toothpaste got the best bargain of all. In 1928, they contracted with two white minstrel-show performers who had a program in black dialect on Chicago station WGN. "Sam 'n' Henry" agreed to pick two new names and do their show nationally on the NBC network. The new show was called "Amos 'n' Andy," and from the start it won a popularity that, comparatively speaking, has probably never been duplicated in the history of the entertainment industry.

Basically, "Amos 'n' Andy" was a blackface minstrel show set in Harlem instead of on a southern plantation.

---

slapped at Republican policies during the 1920s (the New Era) and reminded people of both major parties that he was a distant cousin of the energetic president of the Square Deal, Theodore Roosevelt.

The Campaign

Hoover's campaign was dispirited. He was in the impossible position of having to defend policies that had failed. Roosevelt, on the contrary, like any candidate who expects to win easily, avoided taking controversial stands. Any strong position on any specific question could only cost him votes. At times, indeed, Roosevelt seemed to be calling for the same conservative approach to the economic crisis that Hoover already had tested; he warned against an unbalanced budget and reassured voters that he was no radical.

The most obvious difference between the president and his challenger was Hoover's gloomy personality and Roosevelt's buoyant charm. Roosevelt

One of the two performers, Freeman Gosden of Richmond, said that he based the character of Amos Jones on a black boyhood friend. Amos was the honest, hardworking proprietor and sole driver of the Fresh Air Taxi Company—his cab had no windshield. Neither during the program's 32 years on radio nor after it had moved to television was Gosden's character offensive. However, Amos came to play a comparatively small part in the series as the program evolved. The chief protagonist was George (Kingfish) Stevens, a fast-talking con man who usually bungled his stings and ended up outsmarting himself. During the 1950s, black groups began to protest that the Kingfish, who was rather stupid underneath his pretensions and self-estimation, was an insulting stereotype.

The character of the Kingfish's usual mark, Andrew "Andy" H. Brown, also caused trouble. Andy was infinitely gullible, a character whom even the Kingfish easily swindled. He depended for survival on the con man's own ineptitude or on Amos's intervention.

Everyone in America, it sometimes seemed, listened to the program, which ran on weeknights at eight o'clock. Particularly interesting plots were discussed each day. Few needed to be told what Amos, Andy, and the Kingfish were like, or even the minor characters (also played by Gosden and his partner, Charles Correll): Lightnin', who swept up the hall of the Mystic Knights of the Sea; the shyster lawyer Algonquin J. Calhoun; Ruby Jones; and Sapphire Stevens, who made life as miserable for George as he made it for Andy.

With the emergence of television, "Amos 'n' Andy" moved to the new medium in a weekly half-hour format featuring black actors who mimicked the voices that had been created by Gosden and Correll. Already, however, the program was an anachronism. The civil rights movement was in full swing by 1960, pushing toward victory in the long campaign to establish full equality for blacks. The National Association for the Advancement of Colored People denounced "Amos 'n' Andy" as "a gross libel on the Negro."

The show's sponsors believed that blacks enjoyed the program as much as whites (which appears to have been so until the 1960s), and Gosden insisted that "both Charlie and I have deep respect for black men"; he felt that the show "helped characterize Negroes as interesting and dignified human beings." Today, it is easy to see the point. Even the most ridiculous characters on "Amos 'n' Andy" were stock comic figures in traditional comedy, and there was nothing derogatory in the depiction of Amos and Ruby Jones. Nevertheless, the NAACP had a point too. The social effects of ridiculing members of an oppressed group are mischievous at best. It is easy to shrug off ridicule when it does not relate to reality or ignore stereotypes when the stereotyped group is well established. But in the fight in which blacks were engaged in the early 1960s, such ridicule and stereotypes stood in the way of justice. After 100 episodes, "Amos 'n' Andy" went off the air.

smiled constantly. He impressed crowds who saw him as he whisked around the country as a man who knew how to take charge, liked to take charge, and was perfectly confident in his ability to lead the country out of its crisis. The theme song of Roosevelt's campaign, which was blared by brass bands or played over loudspeakers at every whistle stop and rally, was the cheery "Happy Days Are Here Again."

Only after his lopsided victory—472 electoral votes to Hoover's 59—did it become clear that Roosevelt had spelled out no program for recovery. Because Inauguration Day came a full four months after the election, there was one more long winter of depression under Herbert Hoover. The repudiated president, now practically a recluse in the White House, recognized that a void existed and attempted to persuade Roosevelt to endorse the actions he had taken.

Roosevelt nimbly avoided making any commitments either in favor of or opposed to Hoover's policies. He took a quiet working vacation. He issued no

Straight Shooting

Radio flourished during the Great Depression, playing a major role in the lives of children as well as adults. Many stations dedicated late afternoons and early evenings to juvenile programs featuring young heroes like Little Orphan Annie and Jack Armstrong, the All-American Boy, aviators and space explorers, and cowboys like the Lone Ranger and Tom Mix (who was a real person and had been a real cowboy).

Most combined strident morality and patriotism with cliff-hanging adventure, and encouraged habitual listening and consumption of the sponsor's product by offering premiums (secret decoder rings) and by forming clubs. Tom Mix's club was called the Straight Shooters and required members to swear a pledge:

I promise to shoot straight with my parents by obeying my father and mother.

I promise to shoot straight with my friends by telling the truth always, by being fair and square at work and at play.

I promise to shoot straight with myself by striving always to be my best, by keeping my mind alert and my body strong and healthy.

I promise to shoot straight with Tom Mix by regularly eating good old Hot Ralston, the official Straight Shooter cereal, because I know Hot Ralston is just the kind of cereal that will help build a stronger America.

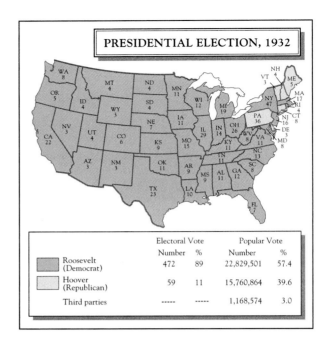

CHRONOLOGY

1929 Stock market crash

1930 United States sinks rapidly into the Depression
In December alone, 400,000 people lose savings accounts

1931 100,000 jobs lost weekly
Crisis in European banking worsens Depression in America

1932 25 percent of workforce unemployed
Banks fail at a rate of 200 each month
President Hoover sponsors creation of Reconstruction Finance Corporation to aid depressed businesses
Hoover approves destruction of "Bonus Boys" shantytown in Washington
Democratic presidential nominee Franklin D. Roosevelt easily defeats incumbent Herbert Hoover in presidential election; combined vote of anticapitalist parties less than a million

1933 One-fourth of southern and midwestern farm families forced off the land by Depression

statements of substance, but he was not idle. During this time, Roosevelt met for long hours with experts on agriculture, industry, finance, and relief. Organized by Raymond Moley, a professor at Columbia University, this "brains trust," as reporters called it, marked a rather significant shift in the personnel who ran Washington. During the 1920s, the capital was a businessman's town. Now they were turning over their apartments and selling their homes to intellectuals, men (and a few women) from universities who hungered to have a go at making policy.

FOR FURTHER READING

Arthur M. Schlesinger Jr., *The Crisis of the Old Order*, 1957, and *The Coming of the New Deal*, 1959, provide a superb overview of the critical years of the early 1930s. These should be supplemented by Robert McElvaine, *The Great Depression, 1929–1941*, 1984. See also Irving Bernstein, *The Lean Years*, 1960, and the early chapters of Michael Bernstein, *The Great Depression: Delayed Recovery and Economic Change in America, 1929–1939*, 1987; Caroline Bird, *The Invisible Scar*, 1965; Milton Friedman, *The Great Contraction*, 1965; Charles Kindleberger, *The World in Depression*, 1973; Broadus Mitchell, *Depression Decade*, 1947; Jordan A. Schwarz, *The Interregnum of Despair: Hoover, Congress, and the Depression*, 1970; and Studs Terkel, *Hard Times*, 1970.

For background, refer to Ellis W. Hawley, *The Great War and the Search for a Modern Order: A History of the American People and Their Institutions, 1917–1933*, 1979; John D. Hicks, *Republican Ascendancy, 1921–1933*, 1960; and William E. Leuchtenburg, *The Perils of Prosperity, 1914–1932*, 1958, and *The FDR Years*, 1995. Frederick Lewis Allen's *Since Yesterday*, 1940, provides the same highly individual insights as his better-known book, *Only Yesterday*.

Valuable more broadly or narrowly focused books include Roger Daniels, *The Bonus March*, 1971; John K. Galbraith, *The Great Crash*, 1955; John A. Garraty, *Unemployment in History: Economic Thought and Public Policy*, 1979; James N. Gregory, *American Exodus: The Dust Bowl Migration and Okie Culture in California*, 1989; Susan Estabrook Kennedy, *The Banking Crisis of 1933*, 1973; Donald Lisio, *The President and Protest*, 1974; Van L. Perkins, *Crisis in Agriculture*, 1969; Thomas Schatz, *The Genius of the System: Hollywood Film Making in the Studio Era*, 1988; Peter Temin, *Did Monetary Forces Cause the Great Depression?* 1976; Raymond Walters, *Negroes and the Great Depression*, 1970; and Cheryl Lyn Greenberg, *"Or Does I Explode?": Harlem in the Great Depression*, 1991.

Franklin D. Roosevelt has been the subject of numerous biographies, both political and personal. Among the most rewarding are James MacGregor Burns, *Roosevelt: The Lion and the Fox*, 1956; Frank Freidel, *Franklin D. Roosevelt*, 1952–1973; and Joseph P. Lash, *Eleanor and Franklin*, 1971. Also see H. G. Warren, *Herbert Hoover and the Great Depression*, 1956; and William Barber, *Herbert Hoover, the Economists, and American Economic Policy, 1921–1933*, 1986.

A splendid graphic capture of political moods: beaten, melancholy, outgoing, Herbert Hoover; buoyant, beaming, but of uncertain substance, Franklin D. Roosevelt.

42
CHAPTER

REARRANGING AMERICA

Franklin D. Roosevelt and the New Deal

1933–1938

The only thing we have to fear is fear itself.

— *Franklin D. Roosevelt*

This generation of Americans has a rendezvous with destiny.

— *Franklin D. Roosevelt*

I see one-third of a nation ill-housed, ill-clad, ill-nourished.

— *Franklin D. Roosevelt*

818 Chapter 42 Rearranging America

A few days before his inauguration in 1933, Franklin D. Roosevelt visited Miami. From the crowd that surged around him, a jobless worker named Joe Zangara, later found to be mentally unbalanced, stepped up and emptied a revolver. Anton Cermak, the mayor of Chicago, who was with Roosevelt, died from wounds he received. The president-elect escaped without a scratch.

The American people learned from the episode that they had chosen a leader who was cool in a crisis, who had a "first-rate character," in the words of Oliver Wendell Holmes Jr. Roosevelt barely flinched during the chaos of the shooting. But what else did they know about him? Not a great deal on March 4, 1933, and that little was not altogether reassuring.

THE PLEASANT MAN WHO CHANGED AMERICA

Holmes Jr. also called him "a second-rate intellect," Henry Cabot Lodge characterized Roosevelt as "a well-meaning, nice young fellow, but light," and Edith Galt Wilson opined that he was "more charming than able." In 1932, Walter Lippmann, a political columnist of liberal leanings, called Roosevelt "a pleasant man who, without any important qualifications, would very much like to be president." John Maynard Keynes said FDR was "an economic illiterate." Many others wondered if a person who had enjoyed so pampered and sheltered a life as Roosevelt had was capable of appreciating the difficulties and suffering that had befallen millions of Americans.

Silver Spoon

The new president was born into an old, rich, privileged, and rather idle New York family. Boyhood vacations were spent in Europe and at elegant yachting resorts in Maine and Nova Scotia. He attended the most exclusive private schools and was sheltered to the point of suffocation by an adoring mother. When Roosevelt matriculated at Harvard, Mother Sara Roosevelt packed up, followed him, and rented a house near the university so that she could keep an eye on her boy. FDR's wife, Eleanor Roosevelt, was from the same tiny and exclusive social set. Indeed, she was the president's distant cousin.

Even the charm with which Roosevelt ran his campaign—the jaunty air, the toothy smile a bit too quick to take shape, an effortless knack of putting

---

> ### Allowance
>
> Except for paychecks from the government, FDR was never gainfully employed. He paid his bills from an allowance, given him in cash each month in a plain envelope by his mother, Sara Roosevelt, until she died in 1941. FDR had then been president of the United States for two full terms, and been elected to a third.

---

people at their ease with cheery small talk—was very much a quality of the socialite who, in the 1930s, was a popular satirical target of filmmakers.

And yet, from the moment FDR delivered his ringing inaugural address—the clouds over Washington parting on cue to let the March sun through, it was obvious that he was a natural leader. From the first day, Roosevelt dominated center stage as cousin Theodore had done 30 years earlier, and without the tiresome bluster and bullying. He held 83 press conferences in 1933, 96 in 1940. (Presidents in the 1990s held four or five a year.)

Where Teddy had been liked and enjoyed, however, FDR was loved and adored. Poor sharecroppers and blacks living in big-city slums tacked his photograph on the walls of their homes next to prints of Christ in Gethsemane, and named their children for him.

Conversely, he was hated, as T. R. never was. It was said that some of the nation's wealthiest people despised him so much that they could not bear to pronounce his name. Much to the amused satisfaction of Roosevelt's supporters, they referred to him through clenched teeth as "that man in the White House," and as a "traitor to his class."

Long before FDR died in office in 1945, after winning reelection three times, he was ranked by historians as among the greatest of the chief executives along with Washington, Lincoln, and Wilson (his one-time political idol). No succeeding generation of judges has demoted him.

Roosevelt's Contribution

Roosevelt's unbounded self-confidence was a major contribution to the battle against the Depression. His optimism was infectious. The change of mood he brought to Washington and the country was

American Aristocrat

Franklin D. Roosevelt's bloodline was as aristocratic as they come in the United States. He was descended from or related by marriage to 11 previous presidents of the United States. Only one of them, Martin Van Buren, was a Democrat.

He (and Eleanor Roosevelt) had the true aristocrat's disdain for the trappings of position. Having grown up with entitlements, the Roosevelts simply did not care about them. During the Great Depression, FDR's personal staff was smaller than that of Hillary Clinton, the first lady 60 years later. Even during World War II, his staff was smaller than that of Albert Gore, when he was vice president in the 1990s.

So oblivious were the Roosevelts to their material surroundings that the White House deteriorated during their occupancy. In one visitor's words, it resembled a dingy residential hotel. FDR's successor, Harry Truman, had to move out of the White House so that structural repairs could be made.

astonishing, and shortly after assuming office he exploited his charisma by launching a series of "Fireside Chats" on the ubiquitous radio. In an informal living room manner he explained to the American people what he was trying to accomplish and what he expected of them. Millions listened avidly and trustfully.

But Roosevelt was much more than a charmer. He was not afraid to make decisions or to accept responsibility. He acted. One day after he was sworn in, he called Congress into special session for the purpose of enacting crisis legislation, and he declared a bank holiday. Calling on emergency presidential powers that are rarely used, he ordered all banks to close their doors temporarily in order to forestall additional failures. Although the immediate effect of the bank holiday was to tie up people's savings, the drama and decisiveness of his action won wide approval.

If Roosevelt was by no means brilliant, if he never fully comprehended the complex economic and social processes with which his administration had to grapple, he did not think it necessary that he should. If he were an indifferent student, he had the professors at his command. He sought the advice of experts, his "brains trust," and was open to suggestions from all quarters. But because he never doubted his responsibilities as the nation's elected

chief, he maintained complete authority over his stable of headstrong intellectuals, many of them prima donnas. He stroked their vanities when it suited his purposes, played one brain truster against another, and retained the personal loyalty of some of those whose advice he rejected. Faces changed in the White House anterooms. Friends became critics. But Roosevelt never lacked talented advisers.

In the end, Roosevelt's greatest strength was his flexibility. "The country needs bold, persistent experimentation," he said. "It is common sense to take a method and try it. If it fails, admit it frankly and try another." Roosevelt's pragmatic approach to problems not only suited the American temperament, but contrasted boldly with Hoover's insistence on making policies conform to a badly rotted ideology.

A Real First Lady

Not the least of FDR's assets was his remarkable wife, Eleanor. Only much later, in the age of anything-goes journalism, did Americans learn that their marriage was shattered by an affair between Franklin and Eleanor's one-time personal secretary, Lucy Mercer, and perhaps a lesbian relationship in Eleanor's life. Eleanor offered a divorce over Lucy; Franklin begged off; Eleanor said that Lucy had to go, and she did—at least for a time.

Not only would a divorce (not to mention publicity or unmentionable lesbianism) have likely killed Roosevelt's political career far short of the presidency, it would have denied him the services of his one aide who may be called indispensable. During the New Deal years, the homely Eleanor, her voice a shrill falsetto, was thought by friend and foe alike as the alter ego of the president. She was his legs and eyes, for FDR was a cripple, paralyzed from the waist down by polio in 1921 and unable to walk more than a few steps in heavy, painful steel leg braces, while Eleanor Roosevelt was a locomotive.

With no taste for serving tea and chucking the chins of Boy Scouts or even overseeing a household (the White House decayed during the Roosevelts' residence), she raced about the country, picking through squalid tenements, wading in mud in Appalachian hollows, and descending into murky coal mines to see how the other half made do. Whereas FDR was cool, detached, and calculating, Eleanor was compassionate, deeply moved by the misery and injustices suffered by the "forgotten" people on the bottom of society. In return, people loved her as they

820 Chapter 42 Rearranging America

The privileged and sheltered Eleanor Roosevelt had a genuine compassion for the disadvantaged.

loved her husband, but emotionally rather than abstractly. It was to Eleanor they wrote asking for a coat for winter, or a toy for a child.

She interceded with her husband to appoint women to high government positions. She supported organized labor when FDR tried to straddle a difficult question. She made the grievances of black Americans a particular interest. Much of the affection that redounded to FDR's benefit in the form of votes was earned by "that woman in the White House."

THE HUNDRED DAYS

Never before or since has the United States experienced such an avalanche of laws as Congress passed and the president signed during the spring of 1933. By nature a cautious and deliberate body, Congress was jolted by the crisis and by Roosevelt's forceful demands to enact most of his proposals without serious debate, a few without even reading the bills through. During what came to be known as the Hundred Days, Franklin D. Roosevelt and his brain trusters were virtually unopposed. Conservative congressmen simply shut up, cowed by their own failure and the decisiveness of the New Dealers.

Saving Banks and Farms

The most pressing problems were the imminent collapse of the nation's financial system, the massive foreclosures on farm and home mortgages that were throwing people out on the streets and roads, and the distress of the millions of unemployed.

The Emergency Banking Act eliminated weak banks merely by identifying them. Well-managed banks in danger of folding were saved when the Federal Reserve System was empowered to issue loans to them. Just as important, when the government permitted banks to reopen, people concluded that they were safe. They ceased to withdraw their deposits and returned funds that they had already taken home and out of circulation. Roosevelt also halted the drain on the nation's gold reserve by forbidding its export and, in April, by taking the nation off the gold standard. No longer could paper money be redeemed in gold coin that was hoarded. Instead, the value of money was based on the government's word, and the price of gold was frozen by law at $35 an ounce. ("Well, that's the end of western civilization," a Wall Street financier was quoted as saying.)

New Household Economy for Millionaires

Eleanor Roosevelt is generally attributed with being her husband's eyes and ears among ordinary people. However, when she was complimented by the *New York Times* during World War II for insisting that the ten servants in her household economize for the sake of the war effort, it was FDR who indicated that he was the one who realized that his and Eleanor's privileged past had little to do with the lives of most Americans. In a note to her, he teased: "All I can say is that your latest newspaper campaign is a corker and I am proud to be the husband of the Originator, Discoverer and Inventor of the New Household Economy for Millionaires! Please have a photo taken showing the family, the ten cooperating servants, the scraps saved from the table.... I will have it published in the Sunday *Times*."

The New Deal attempted to halt the dispossession of farmers through the establishment of the Farm Credit Administration. This agency refinanced mortgages for farmers who had missed payments. Another agency, the Home Owners' Loan Corporation, provided money for town and city dwellers who were in danger of losing their homes.

Helping the Helpless

Nothing better illustrated the contrast between Hoover's hidebound inaction and Roosevelt's flexibility than the establishment of the Federal Emergency Relief Administration. Whereas Hoover resisted federal relief measures on ideological grounds, the FERA quickly distributed $500 million to states so that they could save or revive their exhausted programs for relieving the desperate plight of the poor. The agency was headed by Harry Hopkins, an Iowa boy become New York sidewalk social worker with a cigarette dangling from his lip and a fedora pushed back on his head.

Actually, Hopkins disliked the idea of handouts. He believed that people who were able to work should be required to do so in return for help. It did not matter to him that the jobs they did were not particularly useful. His point was that government-paid jobs should not only get money into the hands of those who needed it, but give relief workers a sense of personal worth.

Nevertheless, Hopkins recognized that the crisis of 1933 was so severe that money had to be gotten out into the country quickly. Setting aside his insistence on work for pay in administering FERA, he won FDR's confidence with his able and energetic direction of the program. There was waste and bureaucratic boondoggling but FERA worked, creating hope where there had been ennui and despair.

Alphabet Soup: The CCC

New bureaucracies, with and without boondoggling, were the order of the day in 1933. With an initial appropriation of $500 million, the Civilian Conservation Corps (CCC) employed 274,375 young men between the ages of 17 and 25 in 1,300 camps. In 1935, the CCC numbered 502,000 in 2,514 camps. Eventually, some 2.9 million people served in the corps, about 10 percent of them African-American.

Signed on for six-month terms and organized into crews, they reforested land that was raped by

---

Gotcha

According to one presidential press secretary, Steve Early, FDR enjoyed looking at the tax returns of the superrich, those he called "economic royalists," and gloating over how much his tax policy was costing them. It's easy to imagine Roosevelt chuckling when one or two cases were cited, but difficult to imagine him taking a sustained interest in the matter. Roosevelt believed, after all, that the New Deal had saved capitalism and, therefore, the superrich, and he was proud of this.

---

cut-and-run lumbermen and undertook other conservation projects in national parks and forests. The CCC built 46,854 bridges, 318,076 check dams, 3,116 fire lookouts, 87,500 miles of fence, and 33,087 miles of terracing to resist erosion. For this, each was paid $30 a month of which $22–$25 had to be sent home. This policy was intended both to provide relief for the CCCers' families and as a tonic to the economy.

The CCC was one of the New Dealers' favorite and most popular programs both because of the kind of work it accomplished and because it appealed to the antiurban bias in American culture, getting city boys into the fresh air of the woods and mountains.

Alphabet Soup: CWA and WPA

Critics of the CCC fastened on the quasi-military discipline with which the army ran the program, but the idea of relief through jobs rather than through charity remained a mainstay of the New Deal. The Civil Works Administration (CWA), which Harry Hopkins headed after November 1933, put 4 million unemployed people to work within a few months. They built roads, constructed public buildings— post offices, city halls, and recreational facilities— and taught in bankrupt school systems.

When the CWA spent more than $1 billion in five months, FDR shuddered and called a halt to the program. But private investors would not or could not take up the slack, and unemployment threatened to soar once again. In May 1935, the president turned back to Hopkins and Congress to establish the Works Progress Administration (WPA).

The WPA broadened the CWA approach. In addition to basic construction, the agency hired artists to paint murals in public buildings, and writers to prepare state guidebooks that remain models of their kind. In the South, the WPA sent out workers to collect reminiscences of old people who remembered having been slaves. The WPA even organized actors into troupes that brought theater to people who never had seen a play. By 1943, when the agency was liquidated, it had spent more than $11 billion and had employed 8.5 million people. The National Youth Administration, part of the WPA, provided jobs for 2 million high school and college students.

Repeal

Roosevelt's support of the Twenty-first Amendment, the repeal of Prohibition, might be listed as one of the New Deal's relief measures. On March 13, 1933, FDR called for the legalization of weak beer, and when the amendment was ratified in December, most states quickly legalized more potent waters.

Certainly many people looked on the possibility of buying a legal drink as relief. An Appalachian song praising Roosevelt pointed to repeal of Prohibition as his most important act: "Since Roosevelt's been elected Moonshine liquor's been corrected. We've got legal wine, whiskey, beer, and gin."

The NRA

The New Deal's relief programs were a great success. Although direct benefits reached only a fraction of the people who were hurt by the Depression, they were the worst off who were helped, and the government's willingness to act in the crisis encouraged millions of other people. Nevertheless, relief was just a stopgap. FDR and the New Dealers were

The WPA was beloved by intellectuals because it put writers and artists to work, as on this mural in the California State Building in Los Angeles in 1936.

also concerned with the problem of actual economic recovery, and in this area their accomplishments were less effective.

The National Industrial Recovery Act, which created the National Recovery Administration (NRA), was a bold and controversial attempt to bring order and prosperity to the shattered economy. The NRA was headed by General Hugh Johnson, something of a blowhard but also a peerless, inexhaustible organizer and cheerleader, and a zealous believer in economic planning. Johnson supervised the drafting of codes for each basic industry and, before long, some less-than-basic industries, too.

The codes set minimum standards of quality for products and services, fair prices for which they were to be sold, and the wages, hours, and conditions under which employees in various industries would work. Section 7(a) of the National Industrial Recovery Act was pathbreaking in the area of labor relations; it required companies which signed the codes to bargain collectively with their workers through labor unions that had the backing of a majority of the company's employees.

The NRA was designed to eliminate waste, inefficiency, and destructive competition—the goal of industrial consolidators since Vanderbilt and Rockefeller. In making the federal government the referee among companies and between employers and employees, the NRA was the legatee of Theodore Roosevelt's New Nationalism of 1912 (Johnson was an old Bull Mooser), the mobilization of the economy during the First World War, and even Herbert Hoover's trade associations. The difference was that the NRA codes were compulsory. A business was bound to its industry's code not by the moral suasion that Hoover had preferred, but by the force of law. Noncompliance led to prosecution by the government.

Blue Eagle Mania

Critics of the NRA, including some within the New Deal administration, likened it to the Fascist system that was set up in Italy in 1922 by Benito Mussolini, and to the Nazi economy that was being instituted in Germany at the same time under Adolf Hitler. This was unfair. Mussolini and Hitler suppressed free labor unions; the NRA promised them a part in making industrial policy.

More to the point was the criticism that the Blue Eagle functionaries went ridiculously far. Johnson was indeed code-crazy, wanting to regiment the most peripheral and even trivial businesses. There was a

---

> ### FDR the Pragmatist
>
> In a conversation with Secretary of Commerce Daniel Roper, Roosevelt made clear his practical policymaking: "Let's concentrate upon one thing. Save the people and the nation and if we have to change our minds twice a day to accomplish that end, we should do it."

---

code for the burlesque "industry" that specified how many strippers were to undress per performance, what vestments they were to discard, and the quality of tassels and G-strings in NRA houses. Had prostitution been legal in the United States, Johnson would have risen to even more ludicrous heights.

Such extremes were possible in part because of the enthusiasm with which Americans initially took to the NRA. Rooted on by the bombastic Johnson, 200,000 people marched in an NRA parade in New York, carrying banners emblazoned with the NRA motto, "We Do Our Part." The symbol of the NRA, a stylized blue eagle clutching industrial machinery and thunderbolts, was painted on factory walls, pasted on shop windows, and adopted as a motif by university marching bands.

For a brief time, Hugh Johnson seemed as popular as Roosevelt himself. He was certainly more conspicuous. Johnson stormed noisily about the country, publicly castigating as "chiselers" those businessmen who did not fall into line. He apparently inherited his bullying personality from his mother, who at an NRA rally in Tulsa said that "people had better obey the NRA because my son will enforce it like lightning, and you can never tell when lightning will strike."

THE NEW DEAL THREATENED; THE NEW DEAL SUSTAINED

The New Deal suffered its first setback not in Congress but at the Supreme Court. It was a conservative body in 1933, with six Harding, Coolidge, and Hoover appointees and one dating back to the presidency of William Howard Taft. Out of synchronization with the revolution in government, the "nine old men," as FDR was to denounce them, declared two major pieces of New Deal legislation unconstitutional, and threatened others.

824 Chapter 42 Rearranging America

The NRA was promoted with all kinds of hoopla, like this parade, and for a time it was immensely popular.

Death of the Blue Eagle

The NRA met its death because of a suit brought by a small poultry company specializing in slaughtering chickens for use in the kosher kitchens of religious Jews. The Schechter brothers, owners of the company, found the sanitary standards required by the NRA code for their industry incompatible with the ritual requirements of kosher slaughter. They claimed that NRA regulations represented unjustifiable federal interference in intrastate commerce. (Their business was carried out almost entirely within New York State.) In 1935, the Supreme Court ruled unanimously that the Schechter brothers were right, declaring that the National Industrial Recovery Act was unconstitutional.

The fuss was minimal. Both Roosevelt's and the people's enthusiasm for the NRA had waned since 1933. Many codes were indeed so picayune as to seem impediments to economic recovery. Moreover, Congress moved promptly to salvage the one provision of the NRA codes that had widespread support, Section 7(a). In the Wagner Labor Relations Act or National Labor Relations Act of 1935, the New Dealers reinstated the requirement that employers recognize and negotiate with labor unions that claimed the support of a majority of a company's employees.

In fact, the Wagner Act went further than Section 7(a) by setting up the National Labor Relations Board to investigate unfair labor practices and to issue cease-and-desist orders to employers found responsible for them. Most important, the law guaranteed the right of unions to represent those workers who voted for those unions in NLRB-supervised elections.

Farm Policy

A similar salvage operation preserved parts of the Agricultural Adjustment Act that the Supreme Court negated in 1936. Also enacted during the Hundred Days, the Agricultural Adjustment Act established yet another agency, the Agricultural Adjustment Administration (AAA), which was to enforce the principle of parity, for which farmers' organizations had fought throughout the 1920s.

Parity meant increasing farm income from the depths it plumbed in 1933 to the ratio that it had borne to the prices of nonfarm products during the prosperous years of 1909 to 1914, a kind of golden age of agriculture, as farmers looked back on it. The AAA accomplished this by restricting farm production. Growers of wheat, corn, cotton, tobacco, rice, and hogs were paid subsidies to keep some of their land out of production. The costs of this expensive program ($100 million was paid to cotton farmers alone in one year) was borne by a tax on processors—millers, refiners, butchers, and packagers—which was then passed on to consumers in higher food, clothing, and tobacco prices.

Because the crops of 1933 were already in the ground when the AAA was established in May, it was necessary to destroy some of them. "Kill every third pig and plow every third row under," Secretary of Agriculture Henry A. Wallace said. The results were mixed. Many people were repelled by the slaughter of 6 million small pigs and 220,000 pregnant sows. Others not so sentimental wondered why food was being destroyed when millions were hungry. (In fact, 100 million pounds of the prematurely harvested pork was diverted to relief agencies and inedible waste was used as fertilizer.) Nevertheless, the AAA worked; the income of hog growers began to rise immediately.

Fully a quarter of the 1933 cotton crop was plowed under, and the fields left fallow. Unfortunately, because cotton farmers tended those fields still under cultivation more intensely, production actually rose in 1933. Within two years, however, cotton (and wheat and corn) prices rose by over 50 percent.

A less desirable side effect of AAA restrictions on production was the throwing of people off the land. Landowners dispossessed tenant farmers in order to get the subsidies that fallow land would earn. Between 1932 and 1935, 3 million American farmers lost their livelihood. Most of them were very poor black and white tenants who already were struggling to survive.

Anxious Days

Despite its negative effects, the New Dealers were devoted to the principles of the AAA. Its rejection by the Supreme Court was a far more serious blow than the loss of the Blue Eagle. Again, they salvaged what they could. In the Soil Conservation and Domestic Allotment Act, parity and the limitation of production were saved under the guise of conserving soil.

Much more worrisome was the fear that, piece by piece, the conservative Supreme Court would dismantle the entire New Deal. Roosevelt's supporters were particularly worried about the Rural Electrification Act and the law that had set up the Tennessee Valley Authority (TVA).

The Rural Electrification Administration (REA) brought electricity to isolated farm regions that were of no interest to private utility companies. It was vulnerable to court action because it put the government into the business of distributing power, indirectly competing with private enterprise. The TVA was farther-reaching yet. It was a massive government construction, flood control, and electrification project that shaped an entire region, a model of government economic and social planning.

The Regulated Society

Regulatory agencies are established by Congress and given authority to act as watchdogs over specific aspects of American life. For example, the Interstate Commerce Commission (ICC) regulates the movement of goods and people across state lines, assigning rights over certain routes to trucking companies, setting rates, settling disputes, and so on. The Federal Communications Commission (FCC) keeps an eye on the practices of radio and television broadcasters. Today, 55 major regulatory commissions in the United States government turn out 77,000 pages of decisions and rules each year.

TVA

The TVA was the brainchild and lifelong darling of Senator George Norris, a Republican progressive who advocated economic planning and regional development engineered by the government. Although he was from Nebraska, Norris had fastened on the valley of the Tennessee River, in the southern Appalachians, as the place to put his ideas to work.

Almost every year, the wild Tennessee River flooded its banks and brought additional hardship to southern Appalachia, one of the nation's poorest areas. Norris's idea was to use the stricken region as a laboratory. The government would construct a system of dams both to control the raging floods and to generate electricity. In homes, the cheap power would bring the people of Appalachia into the twentieth century. The government-generated electricity would also make possible the construction of factories, especially for the manufacture of fertilizers, which would invigorate the economy of a chronically depressed region.

Norris also pointed out that by generating electricity itself, the government would be able to determine the fairness of the prices of power demanded by other companies elsewhere in the country. Until the 1930s, the actual cost of generating electrical power was something of a mystery outside of the business.

During the 1920s, Henry Ford tried to buy key sites on the Tennessee River from the government, notably Muscle Shoals, a tumultuous rapids, in order to build a privately owned power plant. Norris fought Ford off in Congress, arguing that the Tennessee Valley provided an ideal laboratory for the testing of theories of regional planning. Fortunately for Norris, scandalous government giveaways of valuable property to profiteers like Ford, notably the oil reserves at Teapot Dome, were still alive in the public memory. However, while he was able to keep Muscle Shoals and other sites in federal hands, Norris was unable to push through his plan for government development of the Tennessee Valley until the election of FDR.

Creeping Socialism

Fiscal conservatives attacked the New Deal because of its astronomical costs. Herbert Hoover spoke of the decimal point in the government's debts "wandering around among the regimented ciphers trying to find some of the old places it used to know."

Predictably, the TVA and REA were attacked as socialistic. Big business, which had approved FDR's banking reforms and, for a time, the NRA, launched a political offensive against programs that put the government into the production and distribution of electrical power. As early as 1934, having recovered from the demoralization of 1929, some bankers and big businessmen founded the American Liberty League, which accused Roosevelt of trying to destroy free enterprise and set up a dictatorship.

Most Liberty Leaguers were Coolidge-Mellon Republicans, but they were joined by some prominent Democrats, including the party's presidential nominees of 1924 and 1928, John W. Davis and Alfred E. Smith. Davis was a corporation lawyer and found his role familiar. Smith turned against Roosevelt in part because of his peeve over losing his chance to be president to a man whose rise in politics he helped to advance. Abandoning the sidewalks of New York for seats on a number of corporate boards, the once progressive Smith took increasingly reactionary positions on public questions.

Combating such critics was like swatting mosquitoes for the able Roosevelt. A majority of Americans remained distrustful of big businessmen, even still bitter towards them. FDR labeled the Liberty Leaguers "economic royalists" and they never did have a large following.

The Supreme Court was another matter, a major threat to the New Deal. Making one of his rare political miscalculations, Roosevelt proposed a scheme to save his reforms by packing the court with additional justices who would endorse it.

Reaction in both Congress and the nation at large was hostile. The New Deal was popular but Roosevelt's court-packing scheme did indeed look like tampering with the Constitution. Roosevelt quietly retreated and the crisis passed when the court, perhaps alarmed, approved several key New Deal enactments. Then Father Time lent a hand; beginning in 1937, a series of retirements and deaths allowed Roosevelt to appoint a New Deal majority to the bench without tampering with the traditional size of the court. When FDR died in 1945, eight of the nine justices were his appointees.

THE SPELLBINDERS

FDR made his court-packing proposal in 1937, at the beginning of his second term. For a while, however, it appeared that he might not win reelection. The

A dam constructed by the Tennessee Valley Authority. The lake was once a huge gorge.

threat came not from the American Liberty League or even the Republican party but from three popular demagogues whom Roosevelt and his chief political strategist, Postmaster General James A. Farley, genuinely feared.

Father Coughlin

With the coming of depression, Charles E. Coughlin, a Canadian-born Roman Catholic priest, transformed a religious radio program into a platform for his political beliefs. At first, Coughlin enlisted his mellow, baritone voice and Irish genius with the spoken word in support of Roosevelt. He was not a man to mince. "The New Deal is Christ's deal," he said in 1933.

A year later, however, Coughlin became convinced that the key to ending the Depression was a complete overhaul of the national monetary system, including the abolition of the Federal Reserve System. Despite Roosevelt's reputation among the "economic royalists" as a radical, the president had no patience for such extreme proposals. But because Coughlin had a huge and devoted following—perhaps 10 million listeners to some programs—his scathing attacks were a source of worry to FDR, Farley, and other tacticians.

Dr. Townsend

Dr. Francis E. Townsend, a California physician, rather a different sort than the high-voltage Coughlin, was at least equally a threat to Roosevelt's majority. Himself 66 years old in 1933, Townsend was appalled by the plight of the nation's aged citizens. He proposed that the federal government pay a monthly

How They Lived

How the Wealthy Coped

The Union Cigar Company was by no means an industrial giant, but the collapse of its stock in the Great Crash of 1929 nevertheless made history. When the price of Union shares plummeted from $113.50 to $4 in one day's trading, the president of the company jumped to his death from a hotel room that he had rented for that purpose. The incident helped fuel a legend that rich men shouting "Ruined!" were hurling themselves wholesale from high buildings during late 1929 and early 1930. Cartoonists in newspapers and magazines had a field day with the theme. But it was only wishful thinking. When a historian researched the matter, he discovered that the suicide rate was higher in the months just preceding the crash than it was thereafter.

While many, perhaps most, middle-class investors and speculators were "ruined" in the collapse, the very rich suffered little more than a loss in paper wealth (relative richness) and not poverty. Still, the moneyed classes, which had been so at home during the age of Coolidge, very confident of their right and duty to govern the country, were stunned and even paralyzed by their failure. "I'm afraid," said Charles Schwab, chairman of the United States Steel Corporation, "that every man is afraid." Franklin D. Roosevelt, celestially noncommittal during his campaign for the presidency, may have had as much support from the nation's financial elite as did Hoover. Certainly the attitude of Wall Street and corporate boardroom alike was to give him a chance.

It did not last. By 1936, Roosevelt was being called "a traitor to his class" in society circles. Some of the jokes told about him and his wife, Eleanor, were vicious and ugly. Others were simply lame, as was this attack on Roosevelt's programs for putting people to work as welfare in disguise:

Q: Why is a WPA worker like King Solomon?
A: Because he takes his pick and goes to bed.

By 1937, when most people were wrestling with the recession of that year, the very wealthy were living comfortably again. Stock prices were up—although far below 1929 levels—and a new kind of social whirl made its appearance. Unlike the society of Mrs. Astor, J. P. Morgan, and Bradley Martin, with its regal ballrooms, private railroad cars, club parlors, and yachts, the café society of the late 1930s centered in Prohibition Era speakeasies that had come above ground with repeal as restaurants and as clubs in which to sit and to dance all night, to see and to be seen. In New York City, the undisputed capital of café society, the chief seats were El Morocco, the Stork Club, and the "21" Club, which reveled in its cryptic speakeasy designation.

The young always had played an important part in the social whirl. Marrying daughters to European noblemen had been a way to display wealth during the late nineteenth century; youth had set the pace of fashion during the 1920s. In café society, however, the "rich, young, and beautiful" became the center of the piece.

---

pension of $200 to all people over 60 years of age, with two conditions attached.

First, federal pensioners would be forbidden to work. Second, they would spend every cent of their pension within the month. His Townsend Plan not only would provide security for the nation's elderly, the kindly doctor told audiences all over the country, but would reinvigorate the economy by creating jobs for young men and women.

By 1936, 7,000 Townsend Clubs claimed a membership of 1.5 million. When Roosevelt rejected the plan as unworkable, Townsend went into the opposition and laid tentative plans to join his movement with those of Father Coughlin and of Roosevelt's most serious political rival, Senator Huey P. Long of Louisiana.

The Kingfish

Huey Long remains one of the most fascinating figures of the Depression decade. He rose from among the poor white farm folk of northern Louisiana to educate himself as a lawyer. He never forgot the

What was more remarkable about café society was the interest that ordinary Americans took in its doings. Whom Alfred Gwynne Vanderbilt was dating was breathlessly reported in syndicated "society columns" by hangers-on such as Walter Winchell and "Cholly Knickerbocker." It was a news item if the heiress of an industrial fortune dropped in at El Morocco several times a week in order to dance the rhumba with her "agile husband." Naughtier gossip made reference to blond hubbies dancing the rhumba with willowy debutantes.

Debutantes (or debs), young women who were "coming out" into society, when in fact they had been lounging around nightclubs since they were 15 or 16, were the queens of café society. The leading deb of 1937 was Gloria "Mimi" Baker, whose mother replied to someone who called her a decadent aristocrat: "Why Mimi is the most democratic person, bar none, I've ever known." Indeed, café society was "democratic" in ways that earlier high societies had not been. Because status depended on beauty, on what passed for wit and talent, and on simply being well known and rich, the café set admitted movie stars, athletes, and even impoverished but slickly mannered nobles from Europe. They, in turn, were delighted to rub shoulders and dance the rhumba with the very rich.

Indeed, international "playboys" jumped at the opportunity to do more than be photographed at night-clubs and racetracks they could not afford, and therein lay the great morality play of the 1930s and, possibly, part of the explanation for the fascination of many

Americans with the doings of café society. Like people who attend high-speed automobile races, they were interested in the collisions as much as in the running.

Barbara Hutton, who had to stick to spartan diets in order to keep her weight down, was sole heiress to $45 million made in the five-and-ten-cent stores (purveyors of cheap sundries) of F. W. Woolworth. In 1933, she married Alexis Mdivani, who claimed to be a dispossessed Russian prince. Almost immediately after the marriage, the debonair Mdivani began to make her miserable, railing particularly at her weight problem. Drawing on the $1 million that Barbara's father had given him as a wedding present, the prince spent much of his time in the company of other women. In 1935, Barbara won Mdivani's consent for a divorce by giving him $2 million.

Almost immediately, she married a Danish count, Kurt von Haugwitz-Reventlow. Hutton showered him with gifts, including a $4.5 million mansion in London, but divorced him in 1937. The same photographers who snapped pictures of laughing, dancing debutantes at the Stork Club rushed about to get shots of tearful Barbara Hutton, the "poor little rich girl."

Some of the people who pored over them were sympathetic. "She's made mistakes," wrote columnist Adela Rogers St. Johns, "been a silly, wild, foolish girl, given in to temptations—but she's still our own . . . an American girl fighting alone across the sea." Others took pleasure in her repeated comeuppances. "Why do they hate me?" Barbara asked. "There are other girls as rich, richer, almost as rich."

poor. He built a successful political career as a colorful and often profane orator who baited the railroad and oil industry elite that ran the state. Unlike most southern demagogues, however, Long did not resort to race-baiting to win votes. He supported segregation, but he also won the support of many of those Louisiana blacks, mostly in New Orleans, who held on to their right to vote, by providing services for them, too.

As governor of Louisiana between 1928 and 1932, Long built roads and hospitals, provided inex-

pensive or free textbooks and lunches for school-children, social benefits that were almost unknown in the South and were far from universal in the North and West. Long was an ambitious and egotistical showman. He called himself "the Kingfish" after a clownish (and devious) character on the popular radio program "Amos 'n' Andy." He was the Kingfish, and all the other politicians were little fishes. He made Louisiana State University the best public university in the South and led cheers when LSU played its great rival, the University of

Huey Long, "The Kingfish." Theatrical, able to mock himself, cynical, even brutal.

Alabama. Once, when a circus announced that it would open in Baton Rouge on the date of an important LSU game, Long killed the competition by closing down the show on the grounds that lion tamers were cruel to animals.

The New Deal Supreme

People loved Huey Long, not only in Louisiana, which he continued to run even after entering the Senate in 1933, but all over the South and Midwest. He based his national ambitions on a plan called "Share the Wealth," which called for a heavy tax on big incomes and no personal incomes of more than $1 million a year. To people struggling for the necessities, it was an appealing program.

Because Long was the virtual dictator of the Pelican State ("I'm the Constitution around here," he said with a puckish smile), Roosevelt considered him a threat to democracy as well as to his own reelection in 1936. In the end, however, the president overcame him and Townsend and Coughlin by a combination of cooptation and good luck.

A Well-Funded Campaign

In 1934, radical novelist Upton Sinclair won the Democratic party's nomination for governor of California by proposing a comprehensive social welfare program known as EPIC, "End Poverty in California." President Roosevelt was less than delighted by the emergence of another spellbinder within his own party, and pretty much sat out the campaign. The Republican party spent $4 million in the successful effort to defeat Sinclair. By way of contrast, in 1932, the Republicans had spent only $3 million nationally in the campaign to reelect President Hoover.

Roosevelt undercut Coughlin's financial program through his own moderate monetary reforms. To steal Townsend's thunder, he supported the Social Security Act of 1935. Its pensions were tiny compared with the $200 a month for which Townsend called. Nevertheless, it was a revolutionary law; for the first time, the United States government assumed responsibility for the welfare of people who were disabled or too old to work. Also in 1935, Roosevelt supported a revision of the income tax law that did not abolish huge incomes, as Long demanded, but taxed people in the upper brackets much more heavily than those in the lower.

In every case, the New Deal reforms were half a loaf. In no case was the program of the critics adopted. But so great was Roosevelt's personal popularity that his would-be rivals lost support and,

Tying Reform to Taxation

FDR insisted that Social Security pensions be paid not out of the government's general fund, but out of a special fund created by contributions to Social Security. His reasoning:

We put those payroll contributions there so as to give the contributors a legal, moral, and political right to collect their pensions and the unemployment benefits. With these taxes in there, no damn politician can ever scrap my Social Security program.

eventually, lost heart. Townsend's clubs declined slowly, as did Coughlin's radio audience. In the end, the "radio priest" discredited himself by turning to a Nazi-like anti-Semitism and praising Adolf Hitler. Long was removed from the scene by fate; in 1935, he was assassinated by a young man whose family Long had injured in his recklessness.

Thus, in the election of 1936, Roosevelt had to face only the congenial and moderate Republican governor of Kansas, Alfred M. Landon. Offering no real alternative to the New Deal, Landon was swamped, winning majorities only in Maine and Vermont.

THE LEGACY OF THE NEW DEAL

Even before the election of 1936, Roosevelt shifted the direction of his reforms. At first, he viewed the New Deal as very much a new deal for everyone. With some reason, he believed he had saved the capitalist system from the kind of political extremism that the Depression was nurturing elsewhere in the world. He felt betrayed when big business, instead of recognizing and rewarding his moderation, vilified him.

In 1935, threatened by the spellbinders and encouraged by his wife, with her ties to disadvantaged groups, FDR became, in varying degrees, the president of the people on the bottom of society. Their response in the election of 1936 only heartened him to push on. It was in this break with the classes and partisanship on behalf of the masses that the legacy of the New Deal lies. Such phenomena have occurred without revolution only rarely in history.

Blacks Become Democrats

Roosevelt emphasized the economic problems of disadvantaged groups almost to the exclusion of other problems. On the question of civil rights for blacks, for example, FDR was nearly silent. The Democratic party depended heavily on its southern bloc for support, and southern politicians were committed to white supremacy and Jim Crow segregation. As a concession to them, Roosevelt refused even to support a federal antilynching bill, and he tolerated the racial segregation of work gangs on government-supported building projects such as the TVA.

Under constant pressure from the NAACP (National Association for the Advancement of Colored People), from Eleanor Roosevelt, and from such individual African-American leaders as educator Mary McLeod Bethune, the New Dealers made sure that African Americans shared in relief programs. Black people moved into more than a third of new housing units constructed by the federal government. As a result, the 1930s saw a revolution in black voting patterns. In 1932, about 75 percent of American black voters were Republicans. They still thought of the GOP as the party of Lincoln and emancipation. For example, the only African-American congressman in 1932 was Oscar De Priest of Chicago, a member of the GOP.

By 1936, more than 75 percent of registered blacks were voting Democratic—even De Priest was defeated by a black New Dealer—and the trend continued for 30 years. The Democratic party might not have been the friend of the blacks, but it was the friend of the poor, and most blacks were just that.

The Growth of the Unions

Roosevelt also won the organized labor movement to the Democratic party. Left to his own prejudices, he would have remained neutral in disputes between unions and employers. However, when militant unionists such as John L. Lewis of the coal miners (a lifelong Republican) and Sidney Hillman and David Dubinsky of the large needle-trades unions made it

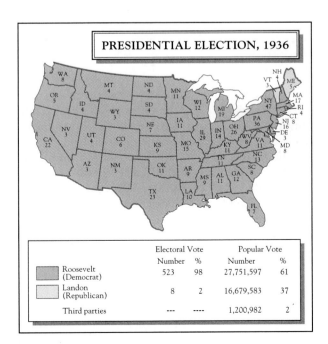

Mary McLeod Bethune, boosted by her personal friendship with Eleanor Roosevelt, won concessions for African Americans in New Deal Washington.

clear that they would throw their influence behind the president only in return for administration support, Roosevelt gave in. Lewis raised a donation of $1 million to the president's campaign for reelection in 1936. In return, Roosevelt had to be photographed accepting the check, smiling with approval on the burly, bushy-browed Lewis.

"The President wants you to join the union," the Committee on Industrial Organization told workers in basic industries after FDR signed the Wagner Act. At first a faction within the American Federation of Labor, the committee left the AFL in 1937 to form an entirely new association of unions, the Congress of Industrial Organizations (CIO). Unlike the AFL, which organized only skilled workers according to their crafts, the CIO organized unions according to the industry in which their members worked. The CIO was also more committed to broad social action than the AFL, and to massive, colorful campaigns that won recruits in unprecedented numbers.

The Steel Workers' Organizing Committee, parent organization of the United Steel Workers, was founded in 1936. By May 1937, it had 325,000 members. The United States Steel Corporation, the nerve center of antiunionism in the industry, recognized the union as bargaining agent without a strike.

The United Automobile Workers enlisted 370,000 members in a little more than a year. The story was similar among workers in other basic industries: rubber, glass, lumber, aluminum, electrical products, coal mining, the needle trades, and even textiles. "The Union" came to have a mystical signif-

As Maine Goes

In the nineteenth century, the people of Maine elected their governor in September, almost two months before the national presidential election. The saying "As Maine goes, so goes the nation" reflected the significance that was attributed to the results there. In the 28 presidential elections in which Maine voters participated, the state's record in picking the winner was 22 to 6, good but not foolproof, as Herbert Hoover learned in 1932: he won Maine, but few other states.

In 1936, Maine again looked to vote Republican. Democratic party campaign manager James Farley quipped, "As Maine goes, so goes Vermont." He was right on the button. FDR won every state that year except Maine and Vermont!

icance in the lives of many workers. Workers fought for the right to wear union buttons on the job. The union card became a certificate of honor. Old hymns were reworded to promote the cause. Professional singers like Woody Guthrie, Pete Seeger, and Burl Ives lent their talents to organizing campaigns.

Employer Violence

The sit-down strike was one of the most dramatic manifestations of worker militance. Beginning with automobile workers in the Fisher Body Plant of Flint, Michigan, in early 1937, workers shut down factories not by picketing outside the gates, but by occupying the premises and refusing to leave.

Not every employer responded so sensibly as United States Steel. Tom Girdler of Republic Steel called the CIO "irresponsible, racketeering, violent, communistic" and threatened to fight the union with armed force. In this heated atmosphere occurred the "Memorial Day Massacre" of 1937, so called because Chicago police attacked a crowd of union members, killing ten and seriously injuring about a hundred.

Although he eventually came to terms with the United Automobile Workers, Henry Ford at first responded to the new unionism as did Girdler. He employed an army of toughs from the underworld and fortified his factories with tear gas, machine guns, and grenades. At the "Battle of the Overpass"

in Detroit, Ford "goons" (as antiunion strong-arm forces were called) beat organizer Walter Reuther and other UAW officials until they were insensible. Violence was so common in the coalfields of Harlan County, Kentucky, that the area became known in the press as "Bloody Harlan."

But such incidents, well documented in photographs and newsreel films, redounded to the benefit of the union movement, and by the end of the Depression decade, organized labor was a major force in American life. In 1932, there were 3.2 million union members. In 1940, there were 9 million, and by 1944, more than 13 million.

The Bottom Line

The greatest positive accomplishment of the New Deal was to ease the economic hardships suffered by millions of Americans and, in so doing, to preserve their confidence in American institutions. In its relief measures, particularly those agencies that put jobless people to work, Roosevelt's administration was a resounding success.

As a formula for economic recovery, however, the New Deal failed. When unemployment dropped to 7.5 million early in 1937 and other economic indicators brightened, Roosevelt began to dismantle many expensive government programs. The result was renewed collapse, a depression within a depression. The recession of 1937 was not so serious as that of 1930 to 1933. But it provided painful evidence that for all their flexibility and willingness to experiment and spend, the New Dealers had not unlocked the secrets of maintaining prosperity during peacetime. Only when preparations for another world war led to massive purchases of American goods from abroad (and to rearmament at home) did the Great Depression end. By 1939, the economy was clearly on the upswing. By 1940, with Europe already at war, the Great Depression was history.

Through such programs as support for agricultural prices, rural electrification, Social Security, insurance of bank deposits, protection of labor unions, and strict controls over the economy, the federal government came to play a part in people's daily lives such as had been inconceivable before 1933. In the TVA, the government became an actual producer of electrical power and commodities such as fertilizers. It was not socialism, as conservative critics of the New Deal cried, but in an American context it was something of a revolution.

The Ohio National Guard moves against striking automobile workers in 1934.

Perhaps the most dubious side effect of the new system was the extraordinary growth in the size of government. Extensive government programs required huge bureaucracies to carry them out. The number of federal employees rose from 600,000 in 1930 to a million in 1940, a total that would rise more radically during the Second World War. To the extent that bureaucracies are concerned above all with their own survival and expansion, leading to the squandering of tax moneys and to aggravations in dealing with government, the New Deal contributed to American life, with its many blessings, a phenomenon that has, at one time or another, vexed every citizen to near distraction.

A Political Revolution

Between 1896 and 1933, the Republican party was the nation's majority party. The only Democratic president during that era, Woodrow Wilson, won election only when the Republicans split and the Great War in Europe unsettled American politics at the bottom. During the 36 years before Roosevelt's election, the Democrats controlled the House of Representatives only ten years, the Senate six.

The Great Depression and the New Deal changed everything. FDR and Jim Farley forged a new majority of the solidly Democratic South, northern and western liberals, blue-collar workers (particularly urban white ethnics), and blacks, with substantial support among western farmers and ranchers. The New Deal alliance was not without problems. Beginning in 1937, old-fashioned small-government southern Democrats who disapproved of even the New Deal's minimal gestures toward blacks and the prominence in Washington of "Yankee" liberals, sometimes voted with Republicans against New Deal measures.

Roosevelt's charm and his refusal to push civil rights for blacks, plus grass-roots support for the New Deal among southern whites, prevented the crack from widening into a real split during his presidency. The Democratic majority forged during the 1930s lasted for half a century. During the 50 years between 1930 and 1980, Republicans occupied the White House for 16 years, but those presidents

(Eisenhower, Nixon, and Ford) were moderates who made their peace with New Deal institutions.

In Congress, the Democratic majority was even more striking. During the same 50 years between 1930 and 1980, Republicans held majorities in the Senate for only six years and in the House of Representatives for only four. Between 1930 and 2000, more than two-thirds of a century, the Republican party simultaneously controlled presidency, Senate, and House for just two years (1953 to 1955).

CHRONOLOGY

1933   Franklin D. Roosevelt inaugurated; pledges a "New Deal" for the American people; declares "bank holiday" (temporary closure of American banks) in order to reform financial system

"The Hundred Days": During the first hundred days of the Roosevelt administration Congress enacts a dizzying number and variety of anti-depression laws. Prohibition is repealed. Government by "alphabet agency" is instituted

1935   Supreme Court declares the National Industrial Recovery Act, keystone of the "first New Deal," unconstitutional
Beginning with Wagner Labor Relations Act, Congress and FDR institute the "second New Deal," more hostile to big business than the first
Social Security system instituted

1936   FDR re-elected in smashing electoral college landslide. African-American voters begin to shift from Republican to Democratic party

1937   Series of often violent strikes in heavy industry

FOR FURTHER READING

First of all, see the biographical studies and general works listed in "For Further Reading" in Chapter 41. Other basic studies of the New Deal are Paul Conklin, *The New Deal*, 1975; William E. Leuchtenburg, *Franklin D. Roosevelt and the New Deal, 1932-1940*, 1963; Arthur M. Schlesinger Jr., *The Coming of the New Deal*, 1959, and *The Politics of Upheaval*, 1960; Anthony J. Badger, *The New Deal: The Depression Years, 1933-1940*, 1989, which stresses the unambitious character of New Deal reforms; and Alan Brinkley, *The End of Reform: New Deal Liberalism in Recession and War*, 1995, which stresses their impermanence. An outstanding recent survey is David Kennedy, *Freedom from Fear: The American People in Depression and War, 1929–1945*, 1999.

On the immediate crises faced by FDR and the New Dealers, see Susan Estabrook Kennedy, *The Banking Crisis of 1933*, 1973; C. P. Kinderberger, *The World in Depression*, 1973; Roy Lubove, *The Struggle for Social Security, 1900–1935*, 1968; Thomas K. McCraw, *T.V.A., and the Power Fight, 1933–1939*, 1971; Michael Parrish, *Security Regulation and the New Deal*, 1970; E. E. Robinson, *The Roosevelt Leadership*, 1955; Elliott Rosen, *Hoover, Roosevelt, and the Brains Trust*, 1977; Theodore D. Saloutos and John D. Hicks, *Twentieth Century Populism: Agricultural Discontent in the Middle West, 1900–1939*, 1951; and Studs Terkel, *Hard Times*, 1970.

On Roosevelt's critics, see Alan Brinkley, *Voices of Protest: Huey Long, Father Coughlin, and the Great Depression*, 1982; Harvey Klehr, *The Heyday of American Communism*, 1984; D. R. McCoy, *Angry Voices: Left of Center Politics in the New Deal Era*, 1958; David A. Shannon, *The American Socialist Party*, 1955; C. J. Tull, *Father Coughlin and the New Deal*, 1965; and T. Harry Williams, *Huey Long*, 1969.

On the labor movement, see Irving Bernstein, *Turbulent Years: A History of the American Worker, 1933–1941*, 1970, and *A Caring Society: The New Deal, the Worker, and the Great Depression*, 1985. Sidney Fine, *Sit-Down: The General Motors Strike of 1936–1937*, 1969; Lizbeth Cohen, *Making a New Deal: Industrial Workers in Chicago, 1919–1939*, 1990; and Steven Fraser, *Labor Will Rule*, 1991, a biography of Sidney Hillman. Other insightful monographs include Frank Freidel, *F.D.R. and the South*, 1965; Paul A. Kurzman, *Harry Hopkins and the New Deal*, 1974; Richard D. McKinzie, *The New Deal for Artists*, 1973; Richard Polenberg, *Reorganizing Roosevelt's Government: The Controversy over Executive Reorganization, 1936–1939*, 1966; Harvard Sitkoff, *A New Deal for Blacks*, 1978; and George Tindall, *The Emergence of the New South, 1914–1945*, 1967.

A woman in Redding, California, buys a special edition of the news of Pearl Harbor.

43
CHAPTER

HEADED FOR WAR AGAIN

Foreign Relations

1933–1942

When an epidemic of physical disease starts to spread, the community approves and joins in a quarantine of the patients in order to protect the health of the community against the spread of the disease. . . .

War is a contagion, whether it be declared or undeclared. It can engulf states and peoples remote from the original scene of hostilities. We are determined to keep out of war, yet we cannot insure ourselves against the disastrous effects of war and the dangers of involvement.

—*Franklin D. Roosevelt*

I shall say it again and again and again: Your boys are not going to be sent into any foreign wars.

—*Franklin D. Roosevelt*

We must be the great arsenal of democracy.

—*Franklin D. Roosevelt*

When you see a rattlesnake poised to strike, you do not wait until he has struck before you crush him.

—*Franklin D. Roosevelt*

I ask that the Congress declare that since the unprovoked and dastardly attack by Japan on Sunday, December seventh, a state of war has existed between the United States and the Japanese Empire.

—*Franklin D. Roosevelt*

In 1933, the year Franklin D. Roosevelt became president, Germany also got a new leader. Adolf Hitler, the head of the extreme right-wing National Socialist, or Nazi, party, was named chancellor of the Weimar Republic's parliamentary government by the elderly President Paul von Hindenburg. The two paid little attention to each other during their first years in office. FDR had his hands full fighting the Great Depression; Hitler faced the same challenge. He was also working from the first day he took office to destroy Germany's democratic constitution and seize absolute power.

The character and values of the two men could hardly have differed more. The patrician Roosevelt was a liberal, dedicated to democratic principles. The vulgar Hitler despised democracy and was contemptuous of individual freedoms. Nevertheless, comparisons were inevitable. Pundits noted that both men were virtuosos in using the radio and other modern forms of communication as a means to persuade. Roosevelt was at his best as a soothing voice in his "Fireside Chats," quietly reassuring Americans that through reform they could preserve what was of value in their way of life. Hitler was at his best through loudspeakers, exhorting frustrated Germans to hatred of the humiliations visited upon Germany by the Versailles Treaty, and people whom he defined as enemies within: Socialists, Communists, and Jews.

Roosevelt and Hitler would eventually confront each other and clash, but only after Americans had experimented with a foreign policy designed to avoid entanglement in another foreign war.

NEW DEAL FOREIGN POLICY

When he first took office, Roosevelt seemed to be as casual as Woodrow Wilson about foreign policy. Like Wilson, he passed over professional diplomats in naming his secretary of state. Roosevelt made a political appointment, a senator from Tennessee, Cordell Hull, whose courtly bearing belied his log cabin origins.

Hull and Roosevelt were generally content to follow the guidelines charted by Hoover and his secretary of state, Henry L. Stimson. Where they departed from this unacknowledged blueprint, their purpose was to reinforce the New Deal program for economic recovery at home.

The Good Neighbor

Roosevelt and Hull even embraced Hoover's phrase "good neighbor" to describe the role that they meant the United States to play in Central and South America. Following through on Hoover's announced intentions when he left office, Roosevelt withdrew U.S. Marines from Nicaragua, the Dominican Republic, and Haiti, where they were keeping order. Like Hoover, he refused to intervene in Cuba despite the chronic civil conflicts that plagued the island republic or to exercise America's legal entitlement, under the Platt Amendment, to send in troops in times of trouble.

In 1934, when peace returned to Cuba under a pro-American president who later became dictator, Cordell Hull formally renounced the Platt Amendment. No longer would the "Colossus of the North" be a bully, using its overwhelming power to force its way in the Caribbean. As a result of the about-face, no United States president was ever so well liked in Central and South America as was Roosevelt. Even when, in 1938, Mexico seized the properties of American oil companies and offered little compensation to the former owners, Roosevelt kept cool and took a conciliatory stand. A few years later, he worked out a friendly settlement with Mexico, acceptable to all but a few wealthy oilmen.

By then, the Good Neighbor Policy was reaping concrete benefits for the United States. The Second World War had begun, but despite German efforts to win a foothold in the Western Hemisphere, most Latin American nations backed the United States, and the few neutrals that cozied up to Hitler were

---

Two Different Worlds

In December 1940, Adolf Hitler told Germans that there could be no reconciliation between Germany, on the one hand, and Great Britain — *and the United States* — on the other. They were "different worlds."

The next month, President Roosevelt accepted Hitler's dichotomy and said that his world was devoted to the Four Freedoms, "freedom of speech and expression, freedom of worship, freedom from want, freedom from fear."

very cautious. Had even a single South American country permitted Nazi Germany to establish bases on its soil, it would have inhibited the American contribution to the war in Europe and Asia, and would even have necessitated opening a front in the Western Hemisphere.

The Stimson Doctrine

Toward Asia, New Deal diplomacy also moved along paths that were staked out during the Hoover administration. The problem in the East, as policy makers saw it, was to maintain Chinese independence and American trading rights in China—the Open Door Policy—in the face of an ambitious and expansion-minded Japan. China's government, headed by Generalissimo Chiang Kai-shek, was disorganized, inefficient, and increasingly corrupt.

Late in 1931, taking advantage of the chaos, Japanese military officers detached the province of Manchuria from China and set up a puppet state they called Manchukuo. Hoover considered but rejected Stimson's proposal that the United States retaliate against Japan by imposing severe economic sanctions, denying Japan the American products that were vital to its industry and navy, particularly oil. Instead, Hoover announced that the United States would not recognize the legality of any territorial changes resulting from the use of force. Curiously, this policy became known as the Stimson Doctrine.

The Stimson Doctrine was little more than a rap on the knuckles, one of those inexpensive and painless statements of moralistic disapproval that come regularly from critics of foreign policy, but not from those responsible for making it. Japanese militarists, driven by a compelling sense of national destiny,

Scenes of Japanese brutality toward the Chinese in Shanghai in 1937 aroused American public opinion, but few claimed the United States should come to China's aid.

shrugged it off. In 1932, they launched an attack on Shanghai and tyrannized the population. In 1937, the Japanese bombed the city, one of the first massive bombings of a civilian population.

Nevertheless, Roosevelt went no further than Hoover had in 1932. He (and the League of Nations) responded to Japanese aggression with words alone. With economic problems so serious at home, no western country would risk war with Japan for the sake of a China so dubiously governed and divided.

Recognition of the Soviet Union

When Roosevelt and Hull parted ways with Hoover and Stimson, the cause was that all-pervasive reality, the Depression at home. For example, in May 1933, Roosevelt scuttled an international conference meeting in London for the purpose of stabilizing world currencies. Delegates of 64 nations gathered with Hoover's approval and, so they assumed, with Roosevelt's as well. Before discussions actually began, however, Roosevelt announced that he would not agree to any decisions that ran contrary to his domestic recovery program, specifically his decision to take the United States off the gold standard. The conference collapsed.

In November 1933, Roosevelt formally recognized the Soviet government, which four presidents had refused to do. In part this was a realistic decision that was long overdue. For good or ill, the party dictatorship headed by Joseph Stalin was firmly in control of the Soviet Union and its traditional territories. But Roosevelt was also swayed by the argument that the Soviet Union would provide a large and profitable market for ailing American manufacturers. This proved to be an illusion. Soviet Russia was too poor to buy much of anything from anyone. Nevertheless, it was the hope of stimulating economic recovery at home that made possible the end of a pointless 16-year policy of nonrecognition.

New Directions, Old Strictures

Increased trade was also the motive behind Secretary of State Cordell Hull's strategy of reducing tariff barriers through reciprocity. With a southern Democrat's distaste for high tariffs, Hull negotiated reciprocal trade agreements with 29 countries. The high Republican rates of the 1920s were slashed by as much as half in return for other nations' agreements to lower their barriers against American exports.

Roosevelt probably would have liked his administration to take a more active part in the affairs of nations than the United States did. He admired his cousin Theodore Roosevelt's forcefulness, and both he and Hull were old Wilsonian internationalists. FDR enthusiastically supported the League of Nations when it was first proposed and, while recovering from his polio attack during the early 1920s, he studied and wrote about foreign policy.

But FDR was first and foremost a politician who thought about voters at every turn. He knew that it was political suicide for an elected official to wander too far from popular prejudices in any matter, and according to an authoritative public opinion poll of 1935, 95 percent of all Americans were isolationists. They believed that the United States had no vital interests to protect in either Europe or Asia and wanted their government to act accordingly.

Suspicion of Europe was reinforced by the theory that the economic collapse of the Old World was responsible for the Great Depression in America. This feeling intensified between 1934 and 1936, when Senator Gerald Nye of North Dakota began a series of investigations into the political machinations of the munitions industry. Nye insisted that the United States was maneuvered into the First World War by "merchants of death" such as the giant Du Pont Corporation and other companies, which were only too willing to see young men slaughtered for the sake of bigger sales. This belief was popularized in a best-selling book of 1935, *The Road to War* by Walter Millis, and many academic historians took a similarly jaundiced view of the reasons why, in 1917, Americans had gone "over there."

Neutrality Policy

In a series of Neutrality Acts passed between 1935 and 1937, Congress said "never again" with an exclamation point. Taken together, the three laws warned American citizens against traveling on ships flying the flags of nations at war (no *Lusitanias* this time) and required belligerent nations to pay cash for all American goods they purchased and to carry them in their own ships. There would be no United States flagships sunk even by accident, and no American property lost because of a war among Europeans. Finally, belligerent nations were forbidden to buy arms in the United States and to borrow money from

Better Public Relations through Chemistry

As the nation's biggest munitions manufacturer, E. I. Du Pont de Nemours and Company had a serious public relations problem during the 1930s. The Nye Committee investigations into American entrance into World War I often centered on the Du Ponts as "merchants of death." The coming of World War II and the nation's renewed need for munitions redeemed the Du Ponts. Even earlier, however, Du Pont's creation of nylon, the first completely synthetic textile and a miracle fabric in its versatility, created a new benign image for the company.

This was not dumb luck. Nylon was the fruit of Du Pont's extremely expensive program of pure research, launched in 1928 in the hope that scientists pursuing their own interests would find new salable products. Company president Lammont Du Pont made the most of what was done when nylon was introduced to the public at the New York and San Francisco World's Fairs of 1939.

American banks. This law was designed to prevent the emergence of an active lobby of munitions makers and bankers with a vested interest in the victory of one side in any conflict.

Critics of the Neutrality Acts argued that they worked to the disadvantage of countries that were the innocent victims of aggression. Such nations would be unprepared for war, whereas aggressor nations would equip themselves in advance. This was certainly the message of Fascist Italy's invasion of Ethiopia in 1935 and of Japan's huge purchases of American scrap iron. But until 1938, Americans were interested only in avoiding a repetition of the events that took them into war in 1917. The majority wanted no part of trying to influence international behavior if it meant American involvement.

THE WORLD GOES TO WAR

Each year brought new confirmation that the world was drifting into another bloodbath. In 1934, the Nazi government of Adolf Hitler began rearming Germany. In 1935, Hitler introduced universal military training and Italy invaded Ethiopia, one of but two independent nations in Africa. In 1936, Francisco Franco, a reactionary Spanish general, started a rebellion against the unstable democratic government of Spain and received massive support from both Italy and Germany, including combat troops who treated the Spanish Civil War as a rehearsal for a bigger show.

In July 1937, Japan sent land forces into China and quickly captured Beijing (then called Peiping) and most of the coastal provinces. In March 1938, Hitler forced the political union or *Anschluss* of Austria to Germany, increasing the resources of what Hitler called the Third Reich, or third empire. In September, claiming that he wanted only to unite all Germans under one flag, Hitler demanded that Czechoslovakia surrender the Sudetenland to him.

The Sudetenland was one of the places that made a mockery of Woodrow Wilson's "national self-determination." It was largely populated by people of German language and culture. But it was also the mountainous natural defense line for Czechoslovakia, the only democratic state in central Europe. Nevertheless, in the hope that they could win peace by appeasing Hitler, England and France agreed to the takeover; Hitler mocked their misplaced goodwill within months. In March 1939, he seized the rest of Czechoslovakia, where the people were Slavic in language and culture and were generally fearful of or hostile to Germans.

The Aggressor Nations

In some respects, the three aggressor nations of the 1930s were very different. Japan was primarily motivated to expand into China for economic reasons. A modern industrial nation, Japan was poor in basic natural resources like coal and iron. China was rich in these raw materials, and Japanese leaders hoped to displace the United States and Great Britain as the dominant imperial power on the Asian mainland.

Until the summer of 1941, Japanese policy makers were split between fanatical militarists who believed they must have war with the United States (and looked forward to it) and moderates who believed they could best serve their country's purposes by coming to an understanding with the United States. American trade was important to Japan; indeed, the Asian nation was the third largest customer of the United States, importing vast quantities of American cotton, copper, scrap iron, and oil.

Italy under the Fascists seemed chronically locked into poverty. Dictator Benito Mussolini, a strutting buffoon in his public posing but ruthless in his use of power, made do with the appearance of wealth and might. Ethiopia was an easy touch, a destitute and backward country that had to send men with antiquated muskets and even spears to combat Mussolini's tanks. Only so weak a country could have fallen to Italy's poorly trained and ill-equipped army. Mussolini's tanks were designed more for parades than for war. Some were made of sheet metal that could be dented with a swift kick. By itself, Mussolini's Italy represented no real threat to world peace, and Americans either applauded what progress the Italian economy made under Fascist rule or laughed at newsreel films of Mussolini's slapstick antics.

Beyond his Charlie Chaplin mustache, there was nothing comical about the Nazi dictator of Germany. Adolf Hitler's strutting was all too serious because his theater was a potentially rich and powerful nation. Moreover, Hitler was far more cunning and deliberate than Mussolini. He knew what he wanted and said as much in an autobiography entitled *Mein Kampf*, or *My Struggle*; he wanted German domina-

tion of the continent of Europe. While his strategy was not without flaws, Hitler seemed brilliantly to grasp just how much he could get away with in dealing with the other European powers and the United States. Or, as some have suggested, he was very lucky.

Perverted Nationalism

In other ways, the three aggressor nations were similar. Japanese militarists, Italian Fascists, and German Nazis were all stridently antidemocratic. They sneered at the ideals of popular rule and individual liberties, regarding them as the sources of the world's economic and social problems. In the place of traditional principles of democratic humanism, they exalted the totalitarian state as mystically personified in a single person: Hirohito, the divine emperor of Japan; Mussolini, the Italian *Duce;* and Hitler, the German *Führer*.

The aggressor nations were militaristic. They worshiped armed force as the best means of serving their national purposes. If militarism could be less than ominous when practiced by a poor country like Italy, it was frightening when combined with fanatical Japanese nationalism or Nazi racism. The Japanese considered Asia to be their garden, off limits to westerners who had dominated the Eastern Hemisphere for a century. Japanese soldiers were sworn to solemn oaths to die serving emperor and homeland.

Nazi racism was criminal from its inception. Calling on ancient Germanic mythology and nineteenth-century pseudoscience, as well as populist anti-Semitism, it taught that non-Aryans were subhuman degenerates who had no claims on the master race save to serve it. After disposing of, exiling, or silencing the German Communists, Socialists, and Democrats, Nazi paramilitary organizations routinely brutalized German Jews. Hitler's government stripped Jews of civil rights and eventually, during the war, murdered those who remained in extermination camps along with millions of Jews from conquered lands, Gypsies, congenitally handicapped people, political dissidents, homosexuals, and those bold or foolish enough to resist the Nazis.

And the War Came

Hitler repeatedly pushed the Western democracies and got his way. In September 1939, when he invaded Poland, ostensibly to secure a German-speaking part of the country, Britain and France

Mussolini on his favorite perch, in the Piazza Venezia, Rome.

drew the line, declaring war. However, neither nation had prepared adequately to help Poland, and Hitler had neutralized the Soviet Union by signing a nonaggression pact with Communist dictator Joseph Stalin. Stalin knew that Russia was on Hitler's list but he distrusted England and France. His defenders said he was buying time to prepare to fight Germany.

Plus territory for a buffer: while Hitler's legions invaded Poland from the west, Russian soldiers streamed into eastern Poland, and the tiny Baltic Sea states of Latvia, Lithuania, and Estonia.

An uneasy quiet fell on Europe during the winter of 1939–1940. Journalists spoke of a "phony war" in which neither side attacked the other with force. In fact, the French and British were committed to defensive war, remembering the terrible loss of life in World War I when the men went over the top. They huddled behind the Maginot Line, a system of fortifications to which the French had dedicated vast resources throughout the 1930s.

The Germans had other plans. Appreciating better than the British and French what the motor vehicle meant to armed conflict, they were preparing for *blitzkrieg* (lightning war): massive land, sea, and air attacks with which, in the spring, the crack German armed forces overran Denmark, Norway, Luxembourg, Belgium, and the Netherlands. In June 1940, France collapsed, and the British managed to evacuate their troops and some French units from the little port of Dunkirk only by mobilizing virtually every ship and boat that was capable of crossing the English Channel. The motley fleet returned nearly 340,000 men to England to await a German invasion. They were demoralized, but they were not in German prison camps.

Hitler (right) shakes the hand of Francisco Franco, the pro-Nazi dictator of Spain, 1940.

The Invasion of Russia

"We shall fight on the beaches, we shall fight on the landing grounds, we shall fight in the fields and in the streets, we shall fight in the hills; we shall never surrender," said the new British prime minister, Winston Churchill, and his eloquence inspired Americans as well as Britons. But few were truly confident that the British alone could withstand a German onslaught.

Instead of invading Great Britain with land forces, Hitler ordered relentless aerial bombardment of the country while Germany expanded its power to the south. Mussolini's Italy joined the war against France (forming with Germany the Rome-Berlin Axis) and faced British and Anzac (Australian and New Zealand Army Corps) troops in Libya in North Africa. Then in June 1941, the Führer made what is widely regarded as his greatest strategic blunder: he invaded the Soviet Union.

Stalin, who would later depict himself as the savior of Russia, was unprepared for the onslaught. Soviet armies disintegrated before the German *Wehrmacht* until the autumn when, miraculously, thanks to the emergence of superb Russian generals, the Red Army held. The fighting was barbaric on both sides. Hitler lost 750,000 men in the first year in Russia, more than in the entire war to that point.

Nevertheless, the *Wehrmacht* nearly surrounded Leningrad in the north and threatened Moscow. The next year, 1942, the Germans advanced farther, with

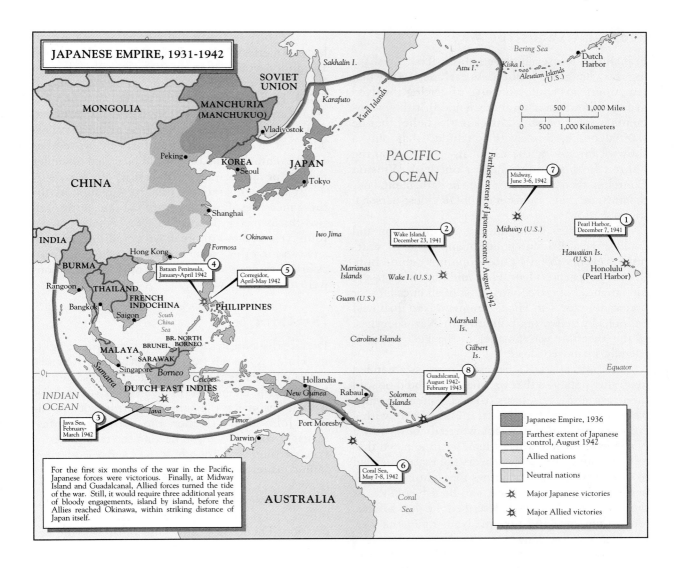

Stalingrad in the south the chief objective. There the campaign was halted.

THE UNITED STATES AND THE WAR IN EUROPE

The fall of France, the heroic resistance of Britain, and to a lesser extent the invasion of Russia changed American attitudes toward neutrality. With the exception of neutral Sweden, Switzerland, and Eire, Britain and France were the last democracies in Europe. (There were only about a dozen democracies in the world in 1940.) France was "America's oldest friend," and Britain, if the nation's oldest enemy, was nevertheless the cultural motherland with whom her daughter had reconciled.

Moreover, ugly pro-Axis and racist rhetoric in the United States by small but noisy Nazi organizations such as William Dudley Pelley's Silver Shirts and Fritz Kuhn's German-American Bund, as well as German machinations in Latin America, persuaded Americans that Hitler had no intention of stopping in Europe. During the "phony war" in March 1940, only 43 percent of Americans thought that a German victory in Europe would threaten them in any way. By July, almost 80 percent thought so. They viewed Hitler as a madman who wanted to conquer the world.

Roosevelt Leads the Way

Franklin D. Roosevelt played no small part in shaping this change of opinion. As early as 1938, when few Americans could conceive of getting involved in a foreign war, and the French and British governments were appeasing Hitler in the belief that he wanted peace, Roosevelt concluded that only a show of force—or the use of it—would stop the Führer. In this opinion he was one with Winston Churchill, then a bellicose gadfly in Parliament, later the wartime prime minister and FDR's close personal friend.

But whereas Churchill was in opposition and could snipe at Britain's policy of appeasement, waiting for events to rally public opinion behind him, Roosevelt was president. He could not afford to get too far ahead of the country, least of all in calling for preparation for war. His technique was to float trial balloons by delivering militant anti-Nazi speeches. If the reaction was hostile, he backed down; if friendly, he moved ahead.

In 1939, at FDR's behest, Congress amended neutrality policy so that war materials could be sold on a cash-and-carry basis (that is, American ships were still banned from the trade). In 1940, with a large majority of Americans worried about how a Nazi victory would affect them, he announced that he was trading 50 old destroyers the British needed to counter German submarines for eight naval bases in Bermuda, Newfoundland, and British colonies in the Caribbean. Roosevelt described the deal as a defensive measure and not involvement in the war, which, strictly speaking, was so.

Preparedness was also the justification for the Burke-Wadsworth Act of September 1940, which appropriated $37 billion to build up the navy and army air corps and instituted the first peacetime draft law in American history. It was a lottery. More than 16 million young men were registered in just 14 hours, with each given a number between 1 and 8,500. Henry L. Stimson picked the first number (#158) and the other 8,499 were drawn in order so that each knew in what sequence he would be called. The first draftees were in uniform by November 1940; eventually, 900,000 would be called up under the law for one-year terms of service.

It was comparatively easy to win support for these measures. Even the draft had the approval of two-thirds of the population. Nevertheless, when Roosevelt decided to break with tradition in 1940 and run for a third term as president, he felt it necessary to assure the American people that their sons were not going to war.

The Third Term

Despite the shift in public opinion in favor of fighting Hitler, Roosevelt feared that an antiwar Republican candidate might eke out a victory against another less eminent Democrat. (The alternatives to FDR were uninspiring: the tobacco-spitting vice president, John Nance Garner; Jim Farley, a political manager without a vision beyond the techniques of vote-getting; and Joseph P. Kennedy, a playboy liquor dealer who was sympathetic to Nazi Germany.)

So, Roosevelt blithely ignored the two-term tradition, and the Democrats were delighted with his decision. The Republicans chose a man who did not disagree with Roosevelt on any essentials. Indeed, utilities magnate Wendell Willkie was a Democrat most of his life. An attractive and personable Indianan who relocated to Wall Street, Willkie made it clear that he differed only in degree from the popular incumbent.

Thus, Willkie criticized the undeniable waste of many New Deal programs without calling for their abolition. He assailed the vast presidential powers that Roosevelt had assumed as bordering on dictatorship, but he did not propose to dismantle the huge executive apparatus that the New Deal created. Willkie claimed that he was the better bet to keep the United States out of war, but he did not oppose either arming for defense or aiding Great Britain. In short, he offered Americans the kind of choice that was better resolved by sticking to the leader who was already tested.

Military Pushover

One thing the United States was not between the two world wars was militaristic. The peacetime army numbered only 130,000 officers and men. At one point, the world's wealthiest and potentially most powerful nation had an army that ranked seventeenth in the world. Czechoslovakia, Spain, Turkey, Yugoslavia, Poland, and Romania all had larger armies.

Willkie ran a strong race. He captured Maine, Vermont, and eight midwestern states and more popular votes than any losing candidate to that time, 45 percent of the total. But Roosevelt's popularity was too great to overcome. The president ran an incumbent's campaign. He did his job while the exuberant challenger barnstormed the country. His landmark third-term reelection, which broke the tradition established by Washington and Jefferson and had been challenged by only Grant and Theodore Roosevelt, was an anticlimax, and it did not interrupt the nation's drift toward war.

Undeclared War on Germany

A few weeks after the election, Roosevelt responded to Winston Churchill's plea for additional aid by sending the Lend-Lease bill to Congress. As enacted, Lend-Lease provided that the United States would serve as the "arsenal of democracy," turning out arms of all sorts to be "loaned" to Britain. Eventually, with Lend-Lease extended to the Soviet Union, such aid totaled $54 billion.

Because no amount of aid in matériel could help the British defend their shipping against "wolf packs" of German submarines, Roosevelt proclaimed a neutral zone that extended from North American waters to Iceland. He sent troops to Greenland, a

---

Lend-Lease

Britain could not afford to pay for the destroyers that Winston Churchill requested at the end of 1940. Britain had spent $4.5 billion in the United States for arms, and in December 1940 had only $2 billion in reserve. Roosevelt explained what he called a "loan" of the ships to Britain with the following parable:

Suppose my neighbor's house catches fire, and I have a length of garden hose. If he can take my garden hose and connect it up with his hydrant, I may help him to put out the fire.

Now what do I do? I don't say to him before that operation, "Neighbor, my garden hose cost me $15; you have to pay me $15 for it." What is the transaction that goes on? I don't want $15—I want my garden hose back after the fire is over.

---

possession of conquered Denmark, and ordered American destroyers to patrol the sea lanes, warning British ships of enemies beneath the waves. This permitted the British to concentrate their navy in the waters around their home islands.

The United States was at war in everything but name. In August 1941, Roosevelt met with Churchill on two ships, the British *Prince of Wales* and the American *Augusta*, a cruiser, off the coast of Newfoundland. There they adopted what amounted to mutual war aims patterned after Wilson's Fourteen Points.

The Atlantic Charter called for self-determination of nations after the war; free trade and freedom of the seas; the disarmament of aggressor nations; and some new means of collective world security, a provision that would evolve into the United Nations.

It was only a matter of time before guns were fired. After a few ambivalent incidents involving German submarines and American destroyers, the USS *Reuben James* was sunk in October 1941 with a loss of 100 sailors. Prowar sentiment flamed higher.

A Nasty Debate

Roosevelt still did not ask Congress for a formal declaration of war. He hoped that Britain and the Soviet Union could defeat Germany without the expenditure of American lives, a commodity with which every wartime American president since Lincoln was cautious. More important, Roosevelt did not want to go to war without a unified nation behind him. By the autumn of 1941, he had his majority. Most Americans concluded, without enthusiasm but with resolve, that Hitler must be stopped at any cost. Even the Communist party, which opposed American intervention until Hitler invaded the Soviet Union, was now in the prowar camp, and much of the eastern big business establishment concluded that Hitler represented a threat to American commercial primacy in the world.

There was, however, an opposition. Roosevelt did not worry about the antiwar agitation of extremist Hitler supporters such as Father Coughlin and members of the Bund and Silver Shirts, or even about Socialist leader Norman Thomas and labor leader John L. Lewis, who opposed the draft. But he was concerned about the old-fashioned isolationists who formed the well-financed and active America First Committee. Former president Herbert Hoover, ex–New Dealer Hugh Johnson, and

FDR and Winston Churchill became good friends during the war, although there was no question that FDR was the more powerful.

progressive intellectuals such as Charles A. Beard despised Hitlerism. Whatever hostility toward Great Britain they harbored was aimed at British imperialism; they feared that the United States would go to war to protect the British Empire, an unworthy goal in their eyes. Their priority in supporting the America First Committee was to avoid making the mistake of 1917 as they saw it—pulling British chestnuts out of the fire. The America First Committee also had celebrity backing: aviators Charles Lindbergh and Eddie Rickenbacker, film actress Lillian Gish, and Alice Roosevelt Longworth, FDR's cousin and Teddy's daughter.

The America First Committee's case was weakened because most of its members agreed that the United States should arm for defense. Roosevelt and the rival Committee to Defend America by Aiding the Allies described every contribution to the British cause in just such terms, and this justification confounded the isolationists. Nevertheless, Roosevelt hesitated. He confided to Winston Churchill that he would not ask for war until some dramatic incident—in other words, a direct attack on the United States—rallied the America Firsters to his cause.

As it turned out, the bitter debate over intervention missed the point. Both sides in the argument trained their eyes on Europe and the Atlantic as the crisis area. The dramatic incident was to occur in the Pacific, where Japan moved into the former French colonies of Indochina and continued its war against the indecisive government of Chiang Kai-shek. War in Asia was an old story. It seemed reasonable to conclude that it would go on indefinitely without a decisive turn in either direction. If Roosevelt took a tougher line toward Japan after the occupation of Indochina, negotiations with Tokyo continued, too, into the summer and autumn of 1941.

AMERICA GOES TO WAR

All the while the Japanese "peace party," headed by Prince Fumimaro Konoye, continued to negotiate during the summer of 1941, the prowar faction of the imperial government, headed by General Hideki Tojo, increased its influence. When he was named premier in October 1941, Tojo gave the negotiators until early November to come up with a formula for peace that the United States would accept. But the minimum Japanese demand that Japan be recognized as the dominant economic power in China could not be reconciled with the Open Door Policy, to which the United States was committed.

Pearl Harbor

Curiously, the Japanese and American governments concluded on the same day that they were unlikely to resolve their differences peacefully. Talks continued, but Secretary of State Hull told the War Department that it should take over responsibility for Japanese-American relations, and military commanders in the Pacific were warned that hostilities could begin at any minute. In fact, the Japanese had initiated preparations for attack that could not easily be reversed.

On December 7, 1941, it was launched. Admiral Isoroku Yamamoto, a tragic figure who admired the United States and feared the result of a Japanese-American war, engineered a tactically brilliant attack from the air on Pearl Harbor, the huge American naval base on Oahu in the Hawaiian Islands where

---

Line-Ups

The United States had 96 ships docked at Pearl Harbor, and 394 planes on the ground. Admiral Yamamoto's flotilla consisted of six aircraft carriers, two battleships, two heavy cruisers, one light cruiser, nine destroyers, three submarines, and 432 planes.

Old Pals

Kichisaburo Nomura, the Japanese ambassador to the United States during 1941, had known President Roosevelt personally for 25 years. Nomura had been naval attaché at the Japanese embassy during the First World War, when Roosevelt had been Undersecretary of the Navy.

---

the Pacific Fleet was based. His planes sank or badly damaged 8 battleships, 7 other vessels, and 188 airplanes, and killed or wounded 3,435 servicemen. Yamamoto did not fully join in the celebrations that swept over his fleet and the people of Japan. The three American aircraft carriers that he believed would be at Pearl Harbor were at sea when the assault force arrived and thus escaped unscathed.

Yamamoto understood that air power was the key to war in the broad Pacific, and fretted about Japan's bad luck. As a one-time resident of the United States, he also appreciated better than did the Tojo group how great American industrial might was compared with Japan's. "I fear we have only awakened a sleeping giant," he told his officers, "and his reaction will be terrible."

The Reaction

The wounded giant awakened with a start. Pearl Harbor was attacked on Sunday. The next day, Roosevelt went before Congress and described December 7, 1941, as "a date that will live in infamy." He got his unanimous vote, or very nearly so. Of both houses of Congress, only Representative Jeannette Rankin of Montana, a pacifist who also voted against entry into the First World War, refused to endorse the declaration of war.

In every city in the nation during the next several weeks, the army's and navy's enlistment offices were jammed with stunned and angry young men. Pearl Harbor was so traumatic an event in the lives of Americans that practically every individual remembered exactly what he or she was doing when news of the attack was announced.

Quietly at the time, more publicly later, Roosevelt's critics accused him and other top officials of having plotted to keep Pearl Harbor and nearby Hickham Field, an air base, completely unprepared

How They Lived

Rationing and Scrap Drives

German submarines set a pair of four-man saboteur teams ashore in Florida and on Long Island. (They were immediately captured.) Japanese subs ran a few torpedoes up on California beaches and attempted to shell a refinery; several Japanese paper bombs, explosives held aloft and pushed by winds, ignited a forest fire in Oregon and even detonated over Texas. Otherwise, the continental United States was physically untouched by the war that devastated most of Europe, half of China, and the cities of Japan. Considering the colossal scale of the American contribution to the war, it is a remarkable testament to the nation's wealth that people on the home front experienced the war only in the form of shortages in consumer commodities and then not to a degree that could be called sacrifice.

Because the Japanese quickly gained control of 97 percent of the world's rubber-tree plantations in Malaya, automobile tires were the first consumer goods to be taken off the market. Washington froze the sale of new tires and forbade recapping early in 1942; the armed forces badly needed tires, and the national stockpile of rubber was only 660,000 tons, or just about what civilians consumed in a year. Huge quantities were collected in a scrap drive. One Seattle shoemaker contributed 6 tons of worn rubber heels that he had saved, and a Los Angeles tire dealer provided 5,000 tons of trade-ins. People cleared closets of old overshoes, and the secretary of the interior took to picking up rubber doormats in federal office buildings. Unfortunately, reclaimed rubber was not suitable to tire manufacture, and doormats were usually made of previously reclaimed rubber, so they were not particularly suitable even for new doormats.

It was fear of a rubber rather than a gasoline shortage that accounted for the first controls on driving, although, on the east coast, which was dependent on tanker imports, gasoline was also short by the summer of 1942. The president proclaimed a nationwide speed limit of 35 miles per hour, and pleasure driving was banned. (Zealous officials of the Office of Price Administration jotted down license numbers at picnics, racetracks, concert halls, and athletic events.) In addition, the miles a car could be driven was limited by the category of sticker issued to

each owner. Ordinary motorists received "A" cards, entitling them to four gallons of gasoline a week, later three, and for a short time only two. A "B" card added a few gallons; these were issued to workers in defense plants for whom driving to work was necessary. Physicians and others whose driving was essential got "C" cards, a few more gallons. Truckers ("T") got unlimited gas, as did some others, including political bigwigs who got "X" cards (a source of resentment). Counterfeiting and selling of gas cards (usually "C" category) were common, as was theft from government warehouses. The OPA discovered that 20 million gallons' worth of cards were stolen in Washington alone.

Surplus gasoline could not be collected, but just about every other commodity that was vital to the war effort could be and was. Community organizations like the Boy Scouts sponsored scrap drives through 1942 and 1943, collecting iron, steel, brass, bronze, tin, nylon stockings (for powder bags), bacon grease (for munitions manufacture), and waste paper. Many of these campaigns were more trouble than they were worth, but not those that collected iron, steel, tin, and paper. Scrap iron and steel made a significant contribution to the national output, and about half of the tin and paper products came not from mines and forests but from neighborhood drives. So assiduous were the Boy Scouts in their scrap-paper drive of 1942 that in June the government had to call a halt to it; the nation's paper mills simply could not keep up with the supply of "raw materials."

The tin shortage was responsible for the rationing of canned goods. In order to buy a can of corn or sardines, a consumer had to hand the grocer ration stamps as well as money. Ration stamps were actually first printed in 1938, a rare example of government foresight. However, they were issued regularly in books beginning in May 1942. Sugar was the first food item rationed (and the last removed from the list). By the end of 1942, coffee, chocolate, and ice cream were on the list. See's Candy, a popular candy manufacturer in California, often had to shut down sales after just an hour or two of open doors.

Ration stamps served as a second, parallel currency. In order to buy a pound of hamburger (meats, cheese, and butter were added to the list in 1943), a shopper needed stamps worth 7 "points" as well as the purchase price. A pound of butter cost 16 points; a pound of cheese, 8 points; and so on. The tiny stamps—which were color-coded red (meat, butter), blue (processed food), green, and brown—were a tremendous bother. More than 3.5 billion of them changed hands every month. In order to restock shelves, a grocer had to turn in the stamps to a wholesaler, who, in turn, had to deposit them with a bank in order to make additional purchases.

Everyone had a complaint of one sort or another, although, except for butter, the allotments were not stringent. For example, the weekly sugar ration was 8 ounces a person, about as much as a dentist would wish on a patient in the best of times. In 1943, the standard of living was 16 percent higher than it had been in 1939, and by 1945, despite rationing, Americans were eating more food and spending more money on it than ever before. Among the major foods, only butter consumption dropped appreciably, from 17 to 11 pounds per capita per year, and some home economists believed that because of butter rationing, a larger proportion of the population was eating it.

In fact, the OPA noticed a curious fact about consumer habits in the cases of coffee and cigarettes. Coffee was rationed because of the shortage of ships available to carry it from South America. When rationing began in November 1942 (one pound per person per five weeks), people began to hoard it. At restaurants, some diners would trade their dessert for an extra cup. When rationing of coffee was dropped in July 1943, sales of coffee dropped! Then, in the autumn of 1943, when a coffee stamp was accidentally included in ration books, Americans anticipated that coffee would be rationed again and stripped the market shelves bare. When the OPA announced that there would be no coffee ration, sales dropped again.

Cigarettes were rationed because 30 percent of the industry's production was reserved for the armed forces, which comprised only 10 percent of the population. The government was, in effect, subsidizing the smoking habit among the men and women in the service. At home, the operation of the principle that scarcity equals status may also have caused an increase in the incidence of the bad habit.

A much more salutary consequence of wartime shortages was the popularity of gardening. There was no shortage of fresh vegetables, and they were never rationed. But because canned vegetables were and because truck and train space was invaluable, the government encouraged the planting of Victory Gardens. Some 20.5 million individuals and families planted them, and by 1945, consumers were raising between 30 and 40 percent of all the vegetables grown in the United States. Nutritionists recognized that this was paying dividends in the national diet, but when the war was over, Americans quickly shed their good taste. By 1950, they had returned to canned vegetables and to the frozen products of Clarence Birdseye.

Destruction of the American fleet at Pearl Harbor, December 7, 1941.

for the attack. It was said that Washington knew the assault was coming but withheld vital intelligence from Hawaii, sacrificing thousands of American lives for the political purpose of getting the United States into the war.

In truth, the lack of preparation at Pearl Harbor was stupid and shameful. As early as 1924, air power advocate Billy Mitchell pointed out Pearl Harbor's vulnerability to air attack. In 1932, Admiral Harry Yarnell snuck two aircraft carriers and four cruisers to within bombing range of Oahu before he was detected. Had his force been hostile, an attack comparable to that of December 7, 1941, would have ensued. In early December 1941, numerous indications that something was brewing either were ignored or reached the appropriate commanders after unjustifiable delays. At Hickham Field, fighter planes were drawn up wing tip to wing tip so that they could be protected against sabotage on the ground. This made destruction from the air all the simpler, and, even after the attack began, it was difficult to get the fighters into the air.

But to say that there was a conspiracy among the highest ranking officials in the United States government was absurd, an example of the paranoia that periodically taints American political discourse. The blunders of the military in Hawaii were just another example of the chronic incompetence inherent in all large organizations, and the key to the stunning Japanese victory was the brilliant planning behind it, and an element of old-fashioned good luck.

Nevertheless, there is no doubt that Roosevelt was relieved to get officially into the conflict with a united people behind him. He was completely convinced by December 1941 that the survival of democracy, freedom, and American influence in the world depended on the total defeat of the aggressor nations, which only American might could ensure.

Getting the Job Done

Of all the nations that went to war, only Japan, whose participation in the First World War was nominal, celebrated at the start of it. In Europe and the United States, there was very little of the exuberance with which people greeted the first days of the fighting in World War I. Among Americans, the attitude was that there was a job to be done.

The popular songs of the period were concerned with getting home again. There was a melancholy tenor to "I'll Be Seeing You" and "I'll Never Smile Again." The lyrics told of the sadness of separation, however necessary it might be. Few people were attracted by the foot-stomping patriotism of George M. Cohan's "Over There," the American anthem during the First World War.

Once in the service, soldiers and sailors referred to the conflict as "W-W-2," a sardonically mechanical description of a war that was reminiscent of the name of a New Deal public works project. Indeed, because the country had been through it before, and because the New Deal reforms introduced the idea of government-supervised order to the national economy, mobilization of resources and people was far more orderly and effective than it was 25 years earlier.

Organizing for Victory

The mobilization of fighting capacity began before Pearl Harbor. By December 1941, more than 1.5 million men were in uniform. By the end of the war, the total number of soldiers, sailors, and airmen, and women in auxiliary corps in every service climbed to 15 million.

The draft accounted for the majority of these GIs, a name that referred to the government-issued designation of uniforms and other equipage. Boards made up of local civic leaders worked efficiently and with comparatively few irregularities to fill the armed forces. The "Friends and Neighbors" who informed young men of their fate with the salutation "Greetings" exempted only the physically disabled and those with work skills designated as essential to the war effort, including farmers and agricultural

workers. As time passed, another sad category of those exempted was adopted: "sole surviving sons," men of draft age all of whose brothers were killed in action. In the windows of homes having men in the service hung small red, white, and blue banners, with blue stars enumerating the number of sons in the service. When such soldiers were killed, blue stars became gold. The lady of the house was called a "Gold Star Mother."

Money was mobilized, too. When the war began, the government was spending $2 billion a month on the military. During the first half of 1942, the expenditure rose to $15 billion a month. By the time Japan surrendered in August 1945, the costs of the war totaled more than $300 billion. In less than four years, the American government spent more money than it had spent during the previous 150 years of national existence. The national debt, already considered high in 1941 at $48 billion, doubled and redoubled to $247 billion in 1945.

A few businessmen continued to oppose government policy, particularly the wartime labor laws. One of the most graceless was Sewell L. Avery, head of the huge retail chain store Montgomery Ward. Roosevelt's policies saved his company from bankruptcy, and during the war, full employment in the workforce resulted in bonanza profits for retailers like him. But Avery had to be carried bodily to jail for refusing to obey a law that guaranteed his employees the right to join a union.

He was not typical. Most big businessmen, including former opponents of the administration, accepted unionization and rushed to Washington to assist the government. They were responding in part to the need for national unity. Corporation executives also recognized that wartime expenditures meant prosperity. General Motors, for example, received 8 percent of all federal expenditures between 1941 and 1945, $1 of every $12.50 that the government spent.

Few criticisms came from the General Motors boardroom. Indeed, General Motors President William S. Knudsen was one of the most prominent "dollar-a-year men," business executives who worked for Roosevelt in effect without pay. He headed the War Resources Board (WRB), which was established in August 1939 to plan for the conversion of factories for military production in the event of war. There was a bit of cynical palaver about the patriotic sacrifice dollar-a-year men were making but the country did need their organizational skills.

New Alphabet Agencies

After the congressional elections of 1942, which brought many conservative Republicans to Washington, Roosevelt announced that "Dr. New Deal" had been dismissed from the country's case and "Dr. Win-the-War" engaged. He explained that since there was now full employment, social programs were no longer necessary.

However, the New Dealers' practice of establishing government agencies to oversee public affairs was vastly expanded. In addition to Knudsen's WRB, the Supplies Priorities and Allocation Board (SPAB), under Donald M. Nelson of Sears Roebuck and Company, was commissioned to ensure that raw materials, particularly the scarce and critical ones, were diverted to military industries. The Office of Price Administration (OPA) had the task of controlling consumer prices so that the combination of high wages and scarce goods did not lead to runaway inflation.

After Pearl Harbor, a National War Labor Board (NWLB) was set up to mediate industrial disputes. Its principal purposes were to guarantee that production was not interrupted and that wage increases were kept within government-set limits. This offended many of Roosevelt's former supporters in the labor movement, none of them more importantly than John L. Lewis of the United Mine Workers, who returned to the Republican party. But the NWLB also worked to ensure that employees were not gouged by avaricious employers. The board was reasonably successful. There were strikes, including a serious one led by Lewis in 1943, but labor relations were generally good, and union membership continued to rise.

The Office of War Mobilization (OWM) was the most important of the new alphabet agencies. Theoretically, it oversaw all aspects of the mobilized economy, as Bernard Baruch did during the First World War. It was considered to be sufficiently important that James F. Byrnes of South Carolina resigned from the Supreme Court to head it as a kind of "assistant president." Many believed that Byrnes's contribution to the war effort earned him the right to a presidential nomination.

Success

In essentials, Dr. Win-the-War's treatment was an overwhelming success. The size of the federal government swelled at a dizzying rate, from 1.1 million civilian employees in 1940 to 3.3 million in 1945. (State governments grew at almost the same rate.) Inevitably there was waste (agencies doing the same thing), inefficiency (agencies fighting at cross-purposes with one another), and corruption (many unessential jobs). But with national unity and military victory constantly touted as essential, the few critics of wartime problems, such as Senator Robert A. Taft of Ohio, sounded petty and were unable to carry the day. Taft was a carper. The most effective check on waste, inefficiency, and corruption, the Senate War Investigating Committee, was headed by a Democratic New Dealer, Senator Harry S Truman of Missouri.

The lessons learned during the First World War and the administrative skills of dollar-a-year businessmen and bureaucrats trained in the New Deal worked wonders on production. New factories and those formerly given to the manufacture of America's automobiles canceled civilian production and churned out trucks, tanks, the versatile jeeps, and amphibious vehicles in incredible numbers. In 1944

Henry J. Kaiser produced cheap Liberty ships that permitted the United States to fight a two-theater war.

alone, 96,000 airplanes (260 per day) rolled out of American factories. Industrialist Henry J. Kaiser perfected an assembly line for producing simple but serviceable freighters, the so-called Liberty ships. By 1943, his mammoth yards were christening a new one every day. Altogether, American shipbuilders sent 10 million tons of shipping down the ways between 1941 and 1945.

Such statistics would have been regarded as pipe dreams before the war. But they were duplicated in every basic industry, including steel, rubber, glass, aluminum, and electronics.

Liberty Ships

In one sense, *mass production* means making something no better than it has to be in order to function. The idea is to turn the product out in vast numbers, quickly and cheaply. Mass production is, obviously, the basis of the high standard of living enjoyed by the masses of people in the United States and other advanced nations. However, one of the most amazing applications of the principle was not in the manufacture of consumer goods, but of the "Liberty ship," a freighter built to carry the goods of war.

Liberty ships were "no frills" boxcars of the seas, 441 feet long, 57 feet across the beam, with a rudimentary engine. Some 800 of them were lost during the war, most to enemy action, but more than a few as the victims of storms. Because they were welded rather than riveted together, Liberty ships were not the sturdiest of vessels.

But welding was what made it possible for American shipyards employing men and women who had never before built ships to float a Liberty ship in as few as 40 days after the keel was laid. Some 2,700 were built between 1941 and 1944. Liberty ships were so cheap that if one completed a single voyage (carrying freight enough to fill 300 railroad cars), it paid for itself. Their design was such a masterpiece of simplicity that, with just a few old salts aboard, inexperienced crews of 45 (plus 35 navy gunners) could sail them.

The Workers

Unemployment vanished as a social problem. Instead, factories running at capacity had difficulty finding people to fill jobs. There was a significant shift of population to the West Coast as the demands of the Pacific war led to the concentration of defense industries in such ports as Seattle, Oakland, San Diego, and Long Beach. Among the new Californians (the population of the Golden State rose from 6.9 million in 1940 to 10.5 million in 1950) were hundreds of thousands of African Americans. Finding well-paid factory jobs that previously were closed to them, blacks also won a sense of security, which was unknown to earlier generations, because of the generally antiracist policies of the young CIO unions and FDR's executive order in 1941 that war contractors observe fair practices in employing blacks.

Economic equality for blacks remained a long way in the future. Everywhere they went they found resentments and discrimination, and serious race riots erupted in 1943. Nevertheless, prodded by Eleanor Roosevelt and pressured by influential black leaders such as A. Philip Randolph of the Brotherhood of Sleeping Car Porters, FDR issued an executive order forbidding racial discrimination in companies that benefited from government contracts.

Women, including many of middle age who never had worked for wages, entered the workforce in large numbers. The symbol of the woman performing "unwomanly" work was "Rosie the Riveter," assembling airplanes and tanks with heavy riveting guns. Indeed, women did perform just about every kind of job in the industrial economy. Rosie dressed in slacks, tied up her hair in a bandanna, and left her children with her mother. But off the job, she remained reassuringly feminine by the standards of the time.

Curiously, these genuinely independent women did not turn to traditional feminism. Comparatively little was heard of demands for equality during the war. On the contrary, woman after woman told newspaper reporters that she looked forward to the end of the war, when she could quit her job to return home as wife and mother within the traditional family system. There were exceptions, of course. Many women enjoyed the economic and social freedom. For the most part, however, the female wartime workers were an ideal wartime workforce: intelligent, educated, energetic, impelled by patriotism, and generally

856 Chapter 43 Headed for War Again

uninterested in competing with the soldiers who eventually would come back and take their jobs.

Prosperity at a Price

Labor shortages inevitably produced a demand for higher wages. The unions grew stronger; membership rose from 10.5 million to 14.7 million. With a few exceptions, however, strikes were short and did not disrupt production. The NWLB mediated disputes, generally keeping raises within the limit of 15 percent over prewar levels that the government set as an acceptable standard. This made the task of the OPA all the easier.

The success of the OPA was remarkable. Coveted consumer goods—coffee, butter, sugar, some canned foods, meat, shoes, liquor, silk, rayon, and nylon—were scarce because of rationing, but high wages gave workers the money to spend on what there was. (Real wages rose 50 percent during the war.) There was a black market, or illegal sale of rationed goods, but it never got out of control, and prices rose only moderately between 1942 and 1945. Instead of consuming wholesale, Americans pumped their wages into savings accounts, including $15 billion in loans to the government in the form of war bonds. It became a point of patriotic pride with some women to paint the seam of a nylon stocking on the calf of a naked leg (although a pair of stockings remained a treasure).

There was an element of good-humored innocence in the way Americans fought the Second World War. If they did not believe that a world free of problems would follow victory, which few doubted lay ahead, Americans were confident that they and their allies were in the right. By the time the fighting was over, 290,000 Americans were dead. But shocking as that figure is at first glance, and bloody as some individual battles were, American suffering was insignificant compared with that of other nations. Indeed, keeping the casualty list short was one of Roosevelt's priorities throughout the conflict, and he succeeded. If Winston Churchill was right in describing the year 1940, when the British stood alone against Nazism, as "their finest hour," the Second World War was an hour of confidence and pride for Americans, too, particularly in view of the difficult Depression era that preceded the war and the age of anxiety that was to follow.

CHRONOLOGY

1933	Adolf Hitler, head of totalitarian Nazi party, is named chancellor of Germany
	FDR scuttles international conference in London designed to preserve gold standard
	United States formally recognizes Soviet Union
1933–1934	FDR and Secretary of State Cordell Hull announce end of military intervention in Latin America—the "Good Neighbor" policy
1934–1938	Victories by totalitarians in Europe stimulate the growth of isolationist sentiment in the United States
1935	Fascist Italy invades Ethiopia
1936	Spanish Fascists launch eventually successful civil war against republican government
1937	Japan sends military forces into China
1938	With French and British acquiescence, Hitler seizes Sudetenland, largely German parts of democratic Czechoslovakia, and adds Austria to German Empire
1939	Germany absorbs all of Czechoslovakia and invades Poland, beginning World War II in Europe
	United States agrees to sell war matériel to democratic nations on a "cash and carry" basis
1940	Nazi Germany controls most of Western Europe
	Congress enacts first peacetime draft law in American history
	FDR elected to an unprecedented third term as president
1941	Germany invades the Soviet Union
	United States in undeclared naval war with Germany; Anglo-American "Atlantic Charter" establishes democratic goals for war
	Japan attacks Pearl Harbor, leading to war with Japan and Germany within days

FOR FURTHER READING

General studies of foreign policy during the 1930s are numerous. The following are among the most useful: Selig Adler, *Uncertain Giant: American Foreign Policy between the Wars*, 1966; Robert Dallek, *Franklin D. Roosevelt and American Foreign Policy, 1932–1933*, 1957; and John E. Wiltz, *From Isolationism to War, 1931–1941*, 1968. A book that has profoundly influenced the writing of diplomatic history in the United States in our time is William A. Williams, *The Tragedy of American Diplomacy*, 1962. See also David Kennedy's massive, magisterial *Freedom from Fear*, 1999.

More intensely focused are Warren Cohen, *America's Response to China*, 1971; W.S. Cole, *America First: The Battle against Intervention*, 1953; Roger Dingman, *Power in the Pacific*, 1976; Robert A. Divine, *The Illusion of Neutrality*, 1962; Lloyd C. Gardner, *Spheres of Influence*, 1993; Walter Johnson, *The Battle against Isolationism*, 1944; Manfred Jonas, *Isolationism in America, 1935–1941*, 1966; Warren F. Kimball, *The Most Unsordid Act: Lend-Lease, 1939–1941*, 1969; Melvin P. Leffler, *The Elusive Question: America's Pursuit of European Stability*, 1979; Basil Rauch, *Roosevelt: From Munich to Pearl Harbor*, 1950; E. E. Robinson, *The Roosevelt Leadership*, 1955; Bryce Wood, *The Making of the Good Neighbor Policy*, 1961; Warren Kimball, *Forged in War: Roosevelt, Churchill, and the Second World War*, 1997; and Robert E. Herzstein, *Roosevelt and Hitler: Prelude to War*, 1994.

Unsurprisingly, American–Japanese relations in the years leading up to Pearl Harbor have been studied extensively and yet remain a highly controversial subject. Just a few of the books on the subject are Robert J. Burtow, *Tojo and the Coming of War*, 1961; Herbert Feis, *The Road to Pearl Harbor*, 1950; Akira Iriye, *After Imperialism: The Search for a New Order in the Far East, 1921–1933*, 1965, and *The Globalizing of America, 1913–1945*, 1993; Gordon W. Prange, *At Dawn We Slept:The Untold Story of Pearl Harbor*, 1981, and *Pearl Harbor: The Verdict of History*, 1986.

Biographical studies of key players in making foreign policy in this era are James MacGregor Burns, *Roosevelt: The Soldier of Freedom*, 1970; Wayne S. Cole, *Gerald P. Nye and American Foreign Relations*, 1962; Richard N. Current, *Secretary Stimson: A Study in Statecraft*, 1954; Elting E. Morison, *Turmoil and Tradition: A Study of the Life and Times of Henry L. Stimson*, 1960; and J. W. Pratt, *Cordell Hull*, 1964.

American troops approaching a beach in the Pacific during the Second World War.

44
CHAPTER

AMERICA'S GREAT WAR

The United States at the Pinnacle of Power

1942–1945

We are now in this war. We are all in it—all the way. Every single man, woman, and child is a partner in the most tremendous undertaking of our American history.

—Franklin D. Roosevelt

More than any other war in history, this war has been an array of the forces of evil against those of righteousness. It had to have its leaders and it had to be won—but no matter what the sacrifice, no matter what the suffering of populations, no matter what the cost, the war had to be won.

—Dwight D. Eisenhower

Sixteen hours ago an American airplane dropped one bomb on Hiroshima, an important Japanese Army base. That bomb had more power than 20,000 tons of TNT. . . . It is an atomic bomb. It is a harnessing of the basic power of the universe. The force from which the sun draws its powers has been loosed against those who brought war to the Far East.

—Harry S Truman

860 Chapter 44 America's Great War

Nazi Germany was defeated by British pluck, Russian blood, and American industrial might. By holding out alone against Hitler in 1940 and 1941, Churchill's Britain prevented him from establishing an impregnable Nazi "Fortress Europe" in the West. The British saved the foothold that made an invasion of Western Europe possible. While sustaining sickening casualties—26 million people dead—the Soviet Union slowly sapped the might of the German *Wehrmacht*. The contribution of the United States was to keep both Britain and Russia afloat with Lend-Lease and, beginning in 1942, to turn the tide with the full force of the world's most powerful economy. The Pacific war against Imperial Japan—a huge effort in itself—was almost entirely an American show.

American strategists designed most of the formula that won World War II. American military administrators oversaw the huge and intricate apparatus of two military operations of unprecedented scale. Without the full participation of the United States, Germany and Japan might have been fought to a negotiated settlement. But they could not have been totally defeated. World War II was America's "Great War," the victory one of the great contributions of the United States to Western civilization.

STOPPING JAPAN

As in World War I, the United States itself was not a battlefield in World War II, but Americans knew that they were in a fight between December 1941 and August 1945. Adults of the era were to remember—were to mark passages in their lives—by the dramatic events of the conflict: the day Pearl Harbor was attacked, D-Day when the invasion of Nazi-dominated Europe began, the day Franklin D. Roosevelt died, and V-E Day and V-J Day, when Germany and Japan finally surrendered. The memories ended up sweet, sustaining a generation with the belief that their lives had meaning; but the memories began with defeat.

Humiliation and Anger

The first months after Pearl Harbor brought nothing but bad news. Immediately after Admiral Yamamoto paralyzed the American Pacific Fleet, the Japanese army advanced easily into Malaya, Hong Kong, the Philippines, Java, and Guam. Within a few weeks, the dramatic Japanese battle flag, rays emanating from the rising sun, snapped in the breezes of British Singapore and Burma, and the Dutch East Indies, present-day Indonesia.

There was heroism in the disaster. On the principal island of the Philippines, Luzon, 20,000 GIs under General Douglas MacArthur and a larger force of Filipinos fought valiantly on the Bataan Peninsula and the rocky island of Corregidor in Manila Bay. At first the men, most of them professional soldiers, thought they would be relieved or evacuated. Slowly the sickening truth sank in: they were quite alone, isolated by an ocean from a navy in disarray. They were the doomed "battling bastards of Bataan." Nevertheless, they grimly accepted the thankless, hopeless task of delaying the Japanese.

General MacArthur did not stay. Once President Roosevelt realized that the Philippines must fall, he ordered the nation's best-known general to flee to Australia. FDR must have been tempted to let MacArthur fall into Japanese hands. He disliked and distrusted the general; as early as 1934 the president named MacArthur as one of the two most dangerous men in the United States, a threat to constitutional government. Indeed, outside a coterie of doggedly devoted aides, MacArthur riled much of the American military establishment. He was an egomaniac and a posturer, carefully cultivating an image complete with props—sunglasses and corncob pipe—a cooler WASP version of Benito Mussolini. "I studied dramatics under MacArthur," General Dwight D. Eisenhower wryly remarked.

Nevertheless, MacArthur was one of the army's senior professionals and strategists; FDR believed him essential to winning the war against Japan. The general's connection with the Philippines was lifelong, intimate, and genuinely affectionate. It was in many ways his home. His father had been military governor of the colony, MacArthur the creator of the Philippine military. When MacArthur fled the islands, he promoted his mystique and inspired the Philippine resistance, which proved to be heroic, with a radio message that concluded, "I shall return."

On May 6, the last ragged defenders of Corregidor surrendered. Humiliation in the worst military defeat in the nation's history gave way to furious anger when reports trickled into the United States of Japanese cruelty toward the prisoners on the infamous Bataan Death March. Of 10,000 men forced to walk to a prison camp in the interior of Luzon, 1,000

American soldiers surrender to the Japanese on the Philippine island of Corregidor in one of the most bitter military defeats in U.S. history.

died on the way. (Another 5,000 of the captives died in the camps before the war was over.)

Japanese Strategy

While the siege of Corregidor dragged on, the Japanese piled up victories elsewhere in South Asia and Oceania. Under the command of Admiral Yamamoto, Japanese strategy was to establish a defense perimeter of fortified islands distant enough from Japan that the Americans, upon recuperating from Pearl Harbor, could not bomb Japan's home islands or force a battle in which the Japanese could be decisively defeated. Then, Japanese policy makers believed, they could negotiate a peace that left Japan in control of the resources of China and South Asia.

By early May 1942, the first phase of the plan—establishment of a distant perimeter—seemed near completion. Japanese soldiers occupied the Solomon Islands and most of New Guinea. At Port Moresby, however, Australian and American forces halted the advance, preventing, for the time being, any serious assault on Australia. Yamamoto then moved his fleet, as yet unscarred, to the Coral Sea off Australia's northeastern coast. His object was to cut supply lines between Hawaii and Australia, thus choking off the resistance in New Guinea.

The Coral Sea and Midway

On May 6 and 7, 1942, the Japanese and American fleets fought a standoff battle. The Battle of the Coral Sea was a unique naval encounter in that the ships of the opposing forces never caught sight of one another. Carrier-based aircraft did the fighting, against one another and against enemy vessels. The Japanese lost fewer ships and planes than the Americans, but the battle was no Japanese victory. Yamamoto was forced to abandon his plan to cut the

How They Lived

Studying a New Kind of War

"Tarawa was not a very big battle, as battles go," wrote G. D. Lillibridge, the historian who was a second lieutenant there in November 1943, "and it was all over in seventy-two hours." The casualties totaled only 3,300 U.S. Marines, about the same number of elite Japanese Special Naval Landing Forces, and 2,000 Japanese and Korean laborers who doubled as soldiers. A few months earlier, by comparison, half a world away in the Stalingrad campaign, the German *Wehrmacht*, lost 500,000 men.

And yet, like Stalingrad, "Bloody Tarawa" was a landmark, even a turning point, of the Second World War. If the numbers were trivial, the incidence of the casualties was appalling, especially for a nation whose wartime leaders, since Lincoln and Grant, have thought of minimizing losses in battle as a major determinant of strategy. Lillibridge's 39-man platoon lost 26; 323 of 500 drivers of landing craft died; overall, more than one-third of the American attackers were killed or wounded. The figures stunned the admirals who planned the battle and the people at home who read about it.

So did the fanaticism of the Japanese defenders. Americans had heard that the Japanese fighting man considered surrender under any circumstances to be shameful. That was in the abstract. Few were prepared to learn that only 17 of 5,000 Japanese on the tiny atoll of Betio were captured, most of them because they were too seriously wounded to commit suicide.

This willingness to die for nothing but a code of honor incomprehensible to Americans was not something that could be taught in a training film. It was bred into Japan's young men from infancy. In his reflections on the battle, something of an attempt to exorcise demons that had haunted him for 25 years, Lillibridge remembered a Japanese man his platoon had trapped during the mopping-up operation. Another Japanese marine was moaning in agony from his wounds. The defender would reassure his dying friend, then hurl challenges and insults at Lillibridge's platoon,

> his voice raised against us in the raging pitch that comes from fear and anger and then lowered to a soothing tone as he sought to comfort his mortally wounded companion.... Doomed and knowing he was doomed, he never lost control of himself and remained in command of the situation until the end.

Betio, only two miles long and 800 yards wide—half the size of New York's Central Park—was the largest of the 25 islands of the Tarawa atoll, a coral formation in the sprawling Gilbert Islands. The Japanese airstrip there was the chief strategic objective of the American assault. Japanese planes based in Tarawa could worry American supply lines between Hawaii and Australia. In a way, by November 1943, Tarawa represented the final fragment of Japanese offensive capability.

It was a tiny fragment. Just as important as the airstrip to Admirals Chester W. Nimitz and Raymond Spruance was to use Tarawa to test their theories of amphibious assault before what was anticipated to be far more difficult fighting in the Marshall Islands early in 1944 and, after that, an island-by-island advance toward Japan.

"There had to be a Tarawa, a first assault on a strongly defended coral atoll," an American officer explained. An amphibious assault against an entrenched, waiting enemy was a new kind of war for the American military, or at least an untried technique. Ironically, the Americans thought that Tarawa would be easy, more training-exercise than battle. They had no illusions about the fierceness of Japanese troops. However, Betio was small; the Japanese had been digging in there a comparatively short time; the American assault force was huge, covering eight square miles of the Pacific; and officers awed by the destructiveness of naval bombardment were sure they would "obliterate the defenses on Betio." Taking his cue from his superiors, Lieutenant Lillibridge told his platoon that "there was no need to worry, no necessity for anyone to get killed, although possibly someone might get slightly wounded."

In fact, the pre-dawn bombardment did destroy Rear Admiral Keiji Shibasaki's communications with most of his troops. However, the network of concrete blockhouses, coconut-log pillboxes, and underwater barricades he had built in just a few months, what one analyst called a "complete defensive system," was substantially untouched by the big guns and aerial bombs. The willingness of the Japanese marines and even common laborers to die more than compensated for their isolation from Shibasaki's bunker.

Nature more than compensated for the massiveness of the American attack. The tide was lower than hoped and the larger American landing crafts could not clear the reef that fringed Betio. This meant that all but the first wave of marines had to wade, breast deep, 800 yards to shore.

This was the element of amphibious attack in the Pacific that was really tested at Tarawa. Could men with no more armor than "a khaki shirt," no way to defend themselves, and in effect no support while they were slogging half a mile in water, even get to the beach, let alone establish enough of a base from which to displace enemies who, during this same critical time, were free to wreak havoc on them?

Getting to the beach was the first horror that would haunt the survivors of Tarawa and subsequent Pacific landings for the rest of their lives. Men remembered it as a "nightmarish turtle race," run in slow-motion. It was "like being completely suspended, like being under a strong anesthetic." "I could have sworn that I could have reached out and touched a hundred bullets." "The water never seemed clear of tiny men."

It was their tininess, perhaps, that enabled the Americans to reach the beach through a storm of machine gun and cannon fire. They had to push through the floating corpses of their comrades, hundreds of thousands of fish killed by the bombardment, stepping on other dead marines. The lagoon was literally red with blood for hours.

The second nightmare waited on the beach. Shibasaki had constructed a sea wall of coconut logs, three to five feet high. At first it seemed to be a shelter. The exhausted marines threw themselves under it. In fact, Japanese mortars had been meticulously registered to batter the long thin line, while to peek above the palisade meant to draw the fire of 200 perfectly positioned Japanese machine guns. More than one marine remembered that he was capable of moving beyond the sea wall only because to remain there meant certain death. About half the American casualties were suffered in the water, most of the rest on the beach. The carnage was condensed in such a way as to leave lifelong psychological scars.

One by one, almost always at close quarters, the blockhouses and pillboxes were wiped out. Betio was taken in three days, only one more than called for by commanders who thought it would be a "walkover." The aftermath was as morally devastating as the battle. Like at the Wilderness and the Marne, the vegetation that had covered the island was literally destroyed. Hundreds of bodies floating in the surf and festering in the blockhouses bloated and rotted in the tropical heat. The triumphant marines looked like anything but victors. They sat staring, exhausted, just beginning to comprehend what they had been through, as if they had been captured by their enemies. "I passed boys who . . . looked older than their fathers," General Holland Smith said, "it had chilled their souls. They found it hard to believe they were actually alive."

Smith and the other commanders learned a great deal from the "training exercise" at Tarawa, not the least of which lessons was not to gamble on tides over coral reefs. Not until the last months of the Pacific War, when the close approach to the Japanese homeland made larger forces of Japanese defenders even fiercer in their resistance, would the extremity of Tarawa's terror be repeated.

The Pacific commanders also learned that while the vast American superiority of armament and firepower was essential and telling, taking the Pacific island was much more personal and human an effort than twentieth-century military men had come to assume. With a grace rare in a modern officer, General Julian Smith frankly asserted,

> There was one thing that won this battle . . . and that was the supreme courage of the Marines. The prisoners tell us that what broke their morale was not the bombing, not the naval gunfire, but the sight of Marines who kept coming ashore.

Soldiers in the European theater, Americans at home, and more than a few troops in the Pacific Campaign, looked on the Pacific war as a picnic. G. D. Lillibridge and others remembered the idyllic holiday quality, however involuntary the vacation was, of the long months between battles spent in Hawaii, Australia, or New Zealand. Correspondent Robert Sherrod, who lived through Tarawa, wrote of "the brilliant sunlight, the far-reaching, incredibly blue Pacific, the soft breezes at evening and the Southern Cross in the sky." The idyll became a part of American popular culture with the publication of James Michener's *Tales of the South Pacific*, and the Rodgers and Hammerstein musical comedy, *South Pacific*, that was based on it. Hawaii enjoyed a second great tourist boom (the first followed annexation) as a result of the Americans' rediscovery of the islands during the war.

But if life between battles was idyllic—and the whole Pacific war a pleasure to noncombat troops—the ferocity of battle was, as Lillibridge writes in another place, perhaps the greatest in the conflict.

864 Chapter 44 America's Great War

southern shipping lanes between Hawaii and Australia. The allies had won.

Yamamoto now looked to the central Pacific where Japanese supply lines were more secure. His object was the American naval and air base on the island of Midway, about a thousand miles northwest of Hawaii. There, between June 3 and June 6, 1942, the Japanese suffered a critical defeat. The American fleet under Admirals Raymond A. Spruance and Frank J. Fletcher lost the carrier *Yorktown* to Japanese dive bombers and torpedoes. However, American planes destroyed four Japanese carriers.

It was far more than a one-for-four trade. Japan was able to produce only seven fleet, four light, and three escort carriers during the war while the United States churned them out as if they were jeeps. Japan simply lacked the wealth, natural resources, and industrial capacity to fight a long, devouring conflict. Midway meant that Japan's offensive capacity was smashed just seven months after Pearl Harbor. Moreover, by holding the island, the Americans controlled the central Pacific, an essential Japanese goal. Much earlier than he planned, and closer to Japan than he hoped, Yamamoto had to shift to defending what the Japanese had won.

The great commander did not live to see the disastrous end of the war that he had, in effect, predicted. In 1943, the Americans cracked the Japanese navy's communications code and learned that Yamamoto would be flying over Bougainville in the Solomon Islands. They shot down his plane, and Yamamoto was killed. Japan never produced another naval commander of his sagacity nor, during the war, another high-ranking statesman so sensible. It is easy to imagine an earlier end to the war had Yamamoto lived.

Anti-Japanese Hysteria

Not even the megalomaniacs among Japan's leadership seriously entertained the possibility of invading the United States. Nevertheless, the stunning Japanese victories of early 1942 and the success of a few submarines in torpedoing ships off the beaches of Oregon and California caused ripples of invasion hysteria to wash over the Hawaiian Islands and the Pacific states. Newspaper magnate William Randolph Hearst, who had baited the Japanese with racial insults for 50 years, deluded himself into believing that his person was a prime Japanese target. He hurriedly moved out of San Simeon, his fantastic castle on an isolated stretch of the central California

---

The Comic Book War

The comic book was in its infancy in World War II, but various superheroes, the greatest of whom was Superman, all joined in the battle against the Germans and Japanese: Captain Aeor, Batman, Green Mantle, Ajax, Captain America, Tarzan, and The Fighting Yank, whose motto was "No American can be forced into evil." None of the wartime comics ever explained why, with this fighting force, the conflict took so long to resolve.

---

coast, for safer haunts inland. Humbler but equally nervous citizens organized patrols to keep an eye on the surf from the Canadian border to San Diego. For a few days, parts of Los Angeles were in a panic.

In many California, Oregon, and Washington communities, anger over Pearl Harbor coalesced with long-standing racial hostility toward Japanese Americans to result in spontaneous outbreaks of violence. Gangs of teenage hooligans (and grown men) beat up Japanese and other Asians. People of Chinese and Korean descent took to wearing buttons identifying their origins in order to avoid problems.

West coast politicians called for the imprisonment of Japanese-born noncitizens, known as *issei*, and even their native-born children, the *nisei*. (Third-generation Japanese Americans were called *sansei*.) At first, officials of the Justice Department resisted them. Various investigations before the war revealed that only a handful of Japanese Americans, most of whom were known to the Federal Bureau of Investigation, were disloyal and might represent a threat of sabotage. Even the Japanese consul in Los Angeles advised Tokyo that no help could be expected from the Japanese-American community.

But when the attorney general, soon to be governor of California, Earl Warren, and the commanding general at San Francisco's Presidio, John W. DeWitt joined the anti-Japanese clamor, Roosevelt gave in. DeWitt argued preposterously that "the very fact that no sabotage has taken place to date is a disturbing and confirming indication that such action will be taken." President Roosevelt's Executive Order 9066 defined coastal areas as forbidden to "Japanese" residence, including American citizens. About 9,000 nisei tried to leave the zone but many were thwarted by prejudice, turned back at the Nevada line, or prevented from buying gasoline. In the first months of 1942, the federal government forcibly removed 110,000 Japanese Americans from their homes, interning them in camps in seven states, from inland California to Arkansas.

Many liberals and more than a few government officials were appalled by the idea of American concentration camps. Because the criteria for relocation were ancestry and race, the federal government seemed clearly to be in violation of the Fourteenth Amendment to the Constitution. But feelings were too high for constitutional niceties. "If the Japs are released," Earl Warren said in June 1943 when there was talk of closing the camps, "no one will be able to tell a saboteur from any other Jap." In the case of *Korematsu* v. *the United States* in 1944, a Supreme Court dominated by New Deal liberals voted 6 to 3 to uphold an action that cost 110,000 people their freedom for several years and about $350 million in lost property.

A Better Record

In Hawaii, ironically, where about one-third of the population was of Japanese ancestry, the nisei were treated brusquely but not grossly abused. A few thousand known sympathizers with Japan were arrested, but, as a vital part of the islands' workforce, Japanese-Hawaiians had to cope with only informal prejudice and the inconvenience of martial law. After repeated requests for a chance to prove their loyalty, 17,000 Hawaiian nisei and some from the mainland fought against the Germans in Italy, turning in one of the war's best unit records for bravery. Others acted as interpreters in the Pacific theater.

Treatment of conscientious objectors and the few individuals who opposed the war on political

A Japanese-American family interned at Manzanar in July 1942.

grounds was exemplary in comparison with the treatment of Japanese Americans. Never did government action approach the ugliness of the First World War period. Some 40,000 men were classified 4E, religious conscientious objectors; 13,000 of them were imprisoned because they refused to perform any service whatsoever (almost one-third of these were Jehovah's Witnesses).

While some 1,700 known Nazis and Fascists were arrested, German Americans and Italian Americans were not persecuted as a people. In retrospect, this might appear to be surprising since the war against Japan was essentially a war for economic domination of Asia, whereas Nazi Germany was palpably a criminal state that—it was clear by 1943—was practicing genocide against Europe's Jews.

But the Japanese were of a different race from most Americans and had a vastly different cultural attitude toward war. Americans found it easier to hate the enemy in Asia and to shrug off mistreatment of their cousins in the United States.

DEFEATING GERMANY FIRST

Even before the Japanese were stopped at the Battle of Midway, President Roosevelt and his advisers concluded that, in Chief of Staff Marshall's words, "Germany is still the prime enemy and her defeat is the key to victory. Once Germany is defeated, the collapse of Italy and the defeat of Japan must follow." Their reasoning was sound. Japan did not threaten the Western Hemisphere, but Germany did. The Nazis had ideological bedmates in power in several

---

Saboteurs

The Germans attempted to put several teams of saboteurs in the United States from submarines, and there may have been some successful attempts at sabotage at defense plants. However, of 19,649 reported cases, the FBI was unable to trace a single one to enemy action. Between 1938 and 1945, the FBI arrested about 4,000 people, mostly German aliens, who were accused of espionage activities. Only 94 were convicted.

South American republics and there were large German populations in Brazil, Uruguay, and Argentina.

More important, American strategists understood that, in time, Japan must inevitably buckle under the sheer weight of superior American power; there was no need to rush in the Pacific. By way of contrast, if either Russia or England collapsed, or if Hitler were allowed too much time to entrench his regime on the continent of Europe, it might be impossible to defeat him. Already in 1942, the Germans were so firmly entrenched in Western Europe that Allied leaders could not agree on how best to challenge them.

Friction among the Allies

Roosevelt and British Prime Minister Winston Churchill sometimes disagreed, but the two men were bound together by social class, affection, admiration, and trust. Their relations with Soviet Premier Stalin, by way of contrast, were marred by suspicion that, on Stalin's part, bordered on paranoia. Churchill was a staunch anti-Communist before the war and made no bones about the fact that the Russian alliance was a marriage of convenience. Roosevelt actually had a soft spot for Stalin personally, and believed he could allay the Russian's suspicions that he and Churchill wanted to sit the ground war out while Germany and the Soviet Union bled each other to exhaustion.

In order to weaken the German onslaught in Russia, the United States Army Air Corps (later the independent air force) joined the British in nearly constant day and night bombing raids over Germany. Eventually, 2.7 million tons of bombs would level German cities. Roosevelt also dispatched massive shipments of arms and other supplies to Russia and, on an impulse, told Stalin that, before 1942 was out, the British and Americans would open a second front on the ground in Europe, easing the horrendous pressure on the Soviets.

But a second front was out of the question in 1942. American industry was only in the process of converting to wartime production. The best the two Western Allies could muster was an attack on German and Italian forces in North Africa.

The African Campaign and Stalingrad

The British and Anzacs (Australians and New Zealanders) had fought a seesaw stalemate in Libya and Egypt with Italian troops and German Field

Marshal Erwin Rommel's *Afrika Korps* since the beginning of the war. In mid-1942, the Germans and some Italian desert forces held the forward line not far from Alexandria, threatening the Suez Canal, Britain's link with India.

In October, under the command of British General Bernard Montgomery, their arsenal beefed up by Sherman tanks from the United States, the British launched a counterattack at El Alamein. Montgomery sent the Germans reeling and, in November 1942, as he advanced from the east, Americans commanded by General Dwight D. Eisenhower landed far to the west in French North Africa.

Making a deal with French forces, who were under the thumb of the Germans, Eisenhower moved eastward and, at Kasserine Pass in February 1943, American tank forces fought the first major American battle in the European theater. It was a stinging defeat for the United States but, soon thereafter, Hitler recalled Rommel, "the Desert Fox," to Germany. Without him at the helm, and overwhelmed by Allied matériel superiority, the *Afrika Korps* collapsed.

Almost simultaneously, deep within the Soviet Union, the Russians won one of the pivotal victories of the war when they surrounded and captured 250,000 seasoned German soldiers at Stalingrad. There seemed little doubt in any Allied capital that the course of the war had been turned against the Germans. Roosevelt told Churchill that "Uncle Joe," as he called Stalin, "is killing more Germans and destroying more equipment than you and I put together."

The Invasion of Italy

In July 1943, an American, British, and Anzac force opened what they hoped might be a second front by invading Sicily. They conquered the island in six weeks and Americans got a colorful hero to crow about: the eccentric General George Patton, who rallied his troops in coarse "blood and guts" language and was a personally brave, even reckless commander of tanks, a cavalry officer from out of the past. (In fact, Patton believed in reincarnation and thought he had been any number of fabled soldiers in past lives.)

Under General Mark Clark, Allied troops promptly moved into Italy proper and knocked the Italian army out of the war. Already beset by guerrilla action behind the lines by anti-Mussolini Italian partisans, mostly Socialists and Communists, Mussolini was ousted by the conservative Field Marshal Pietro Badoglio who believed, quite correctly, that his country had become Hitler's pawn.

Nevertheless, the victories in Italy soon soured. Hitler rescued Mussolini from his captors and established him as the puppet head of the "Republic of Salo" in northern Italy. To take the place of the Italian troops who went over to the Allies, he withdrew German units to easily defended strongholds south of Rome. It was ruggedly mountainous country, and only after eight months of bloody, almost constant battle did the Americans reach the capital.

Then, once again, the Germans held. Despite massive bombardment that plunged Italian cities into famine, Hitler was able to establish a defensive line across the Italian boot with very few troops. Germany itself would fall to the Allies before they made much headway against the *Wehrmacht*'s positions in the south. Italy was not the second front that Stalin and Roosevelt wanted to give him.

Ike

Churchill wanted to send an invasion force into the Balkans, which he called "the soft underbelly of Europe." Roosevelt and his advisors disagreed, believing that the mountains of Greece and Yugoslavia would provide the Germans with the same natural defenses they found in Italy. Moreover, they regarded the problem of supplying an army in the eastern Mediterranean as unnecessarily difficult. Their plan, slated for 1944, was to attack Hitler's Fortress Europe from Britain, across the English Channel into France.

"Operation Overlord" was to be the largest amphibious invasion in history. To direct it, Roosevelt made a choice of commander that was surprising to many. Along with Chief of Staff George C. Marshall, the president selected General Dwight D. Eisenhower, known universally as "Ike." Eisenhower had had a respectable career in the peacetime army. He had been an able enough field commander in North Africa but by no means an outstanding one. He was not a colorful figure like MacArthur, nor particularly popular with the troops like his friend, Omar Bradley. Eisenhower was a desk general, an executive; but just such a man, an organizer, was precisely what was called for by an enterprise of the scale of Operation Overlord.

Eisenhower had another indispensable talent. He was a natural diplomat. He had a temper; close

868 Chapter 44 America's Great War

aides were terrified by his tirades in private. But when the doors opened and colleagues entered, he was supremely affable, smiling, conciliatory, willing to bend on nonessentials, pleasantly firm in pushing through plans on which his superiors had agreed. Eisenhower had a genius for smoothing over differences among headstrong associates, with whom he was surrounded. Churchill was a great man and aware of it. Field Marshall Montgomery was hideously vain and peevish, the very opposite of Eisenhower. The leader of the Free French in England, Charles de Gaulle, would not accept the fact

General Dwight D. Eisenhower briefs a group of paratroopers about to leave for the coast of France where they would be among 1 million Allied troops who began liberating that country from Nazi control, June 6, 1944.

that he was a principal in making plans more out of courtesy than because of the forces at his disposal. Eisenhower even forged a friendly working relationship with Soviet Marshal Georgi Zhukov.

D-Day

Most important, Eisenhower was cautious and thorough, knowing that if the invasion of France failed, the war in Europe might well be lost. His task was immense beyond imagining. He had to find and mobilize 4,000 vessels, 11,000 aircraft, tens of thousands of motor vehicles and weapons of various sorts, as well as billeting and training more than 2 million soldiers. Such a massive operation could not go unnoticed by the Germans, of course, but the British and Americans successfully kept secret the date of D-Day and, rather more remarkably, the place of the invasion.

The date was June 6, 1944, and the place was Normandy in northwestern France. Eisenhower's caution and meticulous planning of every detail paid off. The Allied troops—1 million men—marched across France and into Paris on August 25. Immediately thereafter they entered Belgium. By September, they were across the German border, farther than the Allies had penetrated by the end of the First World War.

Politics and Strategy

The British and Americans disagreed about how to finish off Germany. Montgomery wanted to concentrate all Allied forces on one narrow thrust into the

Ike's Contingency Plan

Knowing that he would be busy on D-Day, General Eisenhower scribbled out the following note to be dispatched to Washington in the event that the invasion of Europe was a failure:

Our landings in the Cherbourg-Havre area have failed to gain a satisfactory foothold and I have withdrawn the troops. My decision to attack at this time and place was based upon the best information available. The troops, the air corps and the navy did all that bravery and devotion to duty could do. If any blame or fault attaches to the attempt it is mine alone.

heart of Germany, a traditional strategy that had much to recommend it. Tactfully, Eisenhower overruled him. In part his decision was military, reflecting his innate cautiousness and perhaps his study of the American Civil War, in which such concentrated assaults were repeatedly stymied. Eisenhower feared that creating too long and weak a flank, not to mention a single extended supply line, would tempt the Germans into a massive counterattack that might lead to disaster, a much longer war, even the necessity of negotiating a peace. He preferred to exploit the overwhelming Allied superiority in arms and men by advancing slowly on a broad front that extended from the North Sea to the border of Switzerland.

Diplomatic and political considerations entered into Eisenhower's decision, too. Still absorbing tremendous casualties as they slowly pushed the Germans westward, the Russians remained suspicious of American and British motives. Stalin jumped at every rumor that his allies were considering a separate peace. Some American diplomats feared that too rapid an American and British thrust would only arouse Stalin's suspicions that, when Germany was finished off, the Allies would turn on Russia. On an earthier level, Eisenhower worried about spontaneous trouble between his soldiers and the Red Army if an orderly rendezvous were not arranged in advance. Finally, the risky single-thrust strategy was Montgomery's; he would command it. Eisenhower did not share his British colleague's confidence in his own abilities and worried how the American public would take to a British general managing the European war.

The Bulge and the End

For a while in 1944, it appeared that Eisenhower's strategy of advancing slowly was a mistake. In the summer, V-2 rockets from sanctuaries inside Germany began to rain down on London, killing 8,000 people. The V-2s were not decisive weapons from a military point of view, but with the end of the war apparently in sight, their psychological effect was disheartening to civilians. There was no advance warning from a V-2, as there was in conventional aerial attack—only a whine high in the air, a few seconds of silence, and an explosion.

Much more demoralizing was a German military counteroffensive in Belgium in the bitter cold and snowy December of 1944. In the Battle of the Bulge, German troops pushed the Americans and British back, creating a bulge in the lines and threatening to split the Allied forces in two. But a division under General Anthony McAuliffe that was isolated at Bastogne refused to surrender ("Nuts!" McAuliffe replied to the German commander), weakening the German offensive as the Belgians had done at Liège in 1914. Then, a break in the weather allowed the Allies to exploit their air superiority and, after two weeks, they advanced again. One by one German defenses collapsed.

Along with his oldest and closest Nazi party associates, a Hitler close to breakdown withdrew to a bunker under the streets of Berlin where he presided over the premature disintegration of his "Thousand-Year Empire." To the end, he thought in terms of the perverted romanticism of his ideology. It was *Götterdämmerung*, the mythical final battle of the Norse gods; the German people deserved their disaster for letting the Führer down. On April 30, 1945, Hitler committed suicide after having named Admiral Karl

Have You Heard the One About . . . ?

In the final days of the war, with tens of millions of people dead and Germany in ruins, an army officer with Hitler joked about the sound of Russian artillery in the suburbs of Berlin, that soon it would be possible to travel from the eastern front to the western front by trolley car. Hitler chuckled.

Doenitz his successor as Führer. A few days later, Doenitz surrendered.

Wartime Diplomacy

Eisenhower's sensitivity to Russian suspicions reflected President Roosevelt's policy. At a personal meeting with Stalin at Teheran in Iran late in 1943, and again at Yalta in the Crimea in February 1945, FDR did his best to assuage the Russian dictator's fears by acquiescing or, at least, by not strenuously resisting Stalin's proposals for the organization of postwar Europe.

In later years, when the Soviet Union was the Cold War enemy and Americans had come to lament Russian domination of Eastern Europe, Yalta became a byword for diplomatic blunder and even, to a few extremists, for treasonous sellout to Communism. It was at Yalta that Roosevelt and Churchill tacitly consented to Stalin's insistence that the Soviet Union had special interests in Eastern Europe, that is, governments friendly to the Soviet Union.

Right-wing extremists were later to say that FDR betrayed the Poles, Czechs, Hungarians, Romanians, and Bulgarians because he was himself sympathetic to Communism. Other less hysterical analysts suspected that the president's weariness and illness, obvious in the haggard face and sagging jaw of the official photographs, caused him to reason poorly in dealing with the calculating Stalin.

Whatever effect Roosevelt's failing health had on his mental processes, there was nothing irrational about his concessions to Russia. Roosevelt and Churchill did not give Stalin anything at Yalta that he did not already have. In February 1945, the Red Army was racing over and occupying the very countries that Stalin envisioned as buffer states against renewed German aggression or other threats from the West. No doubt Churchill and FDR expected the postwar states of Eastern Europe to have greater independence than Stalin was willing to allow.

THE TWILIGHT OF JAPAN, THE NUCLEAR DAWN

Also influencing Roosevelt at Yalta was his desire to enlist the Soviet Union in the war against Japan in order to save American lives in the final battles. While agreeing that the Red Army would attack Japanese forces in China, Stalin insisted on delaying action until the Soviet Union felt secure in Europe.

Pacific Strategy

After Midway in June 1942, American strategy in the war against Japan involved three distinct campaigns. First, just as the United States pumped matériel into Russia, supplies were flown into China from India, "over the hump" of the Himalayas, in order to keep the Chinese in the war. Unfortunately, Chiang Kai-shek was no Stalin, and his Kuomintang troops were no Red Army.

Chiang hated and feared his Chinese Communist allies as much as he hated the Japanese. He diverted hundreds of thousands of troops to battling them, and never forced the kind of battle on the Japanese that the Americans needed in order to weaken Japanese defenses in the Pacific. Inefficiency and corruption in Chiang's government resulted in gross misuse of American supplies.

General Joseph W. "Vinegar Joe" Stilwell, the gritty American commander in China, despised Chiang. He poured out an avalanche of warnings to Washington about the incompetence of "the monkey," as he called the Generalissimo, and the corruption of his political allies. But when Stilwell tried to get command of the Chinese army for himself, Roosevelt recalled him. Somewhat to Churchill's amazement, Roosevelt was convinced that Chiang was a valuable ally.

The second and third prongs of the attack on Japan were more successful, but extremely bloody. After driving the Japanese out of the Solomons in order to ensure Australia's security, one force under MacArthur began to push toward the Japanese homeland via New Guinea and the Philippines. Another, commanded by Admiral Chester W. Nimitz, struck through the central Pacific, capturing islands from which aircraft could reach and bomb Japan.

Island Warfare

To soldiers slogging through the mud and frigid cold of Italy and France, the troops in the Pacific seemed to be on a picnic, basking in a lovely climate and only periodically meeting the enemy in battle. Ernie Pyle, considered the best newspaper correspondent of the war, made this comparison in his celebration of the American fighting man in Europe.

Winston Churchill, Franklin D. Roosevelt, and Joseph Stalin pose for photographers at Yalta, February 1945.

(Ironically, Pyle survived Europe and was killed by Japanese machine gun fire on Ie Shima in the closing months of the war.)

Life behind the lines in the Pacific could be pleasant, but it could be miserable, too. "Our war was waiting," novelist James Michener wrote. "You rotted on New Caledonia waiting for Guadalcanal. Then you sweated twenty pounds away in Guadal waiting for Bougainville.... And pretty soon you hated the man next to you, and you dreaded the look of a coconut tree."

But capturing islands that were specks on the map meant battles more vicious than those in Europe, "a blinding flash ... a day of horror ... an evening of terror," in Michener's words. The Japanese soldier was a formidable fighter. He was indoctrinated with a fanatical sense of duty and taught that it was a betrayal of national and personal honor to

The Twilight of Japan, The Nuclear Dawn

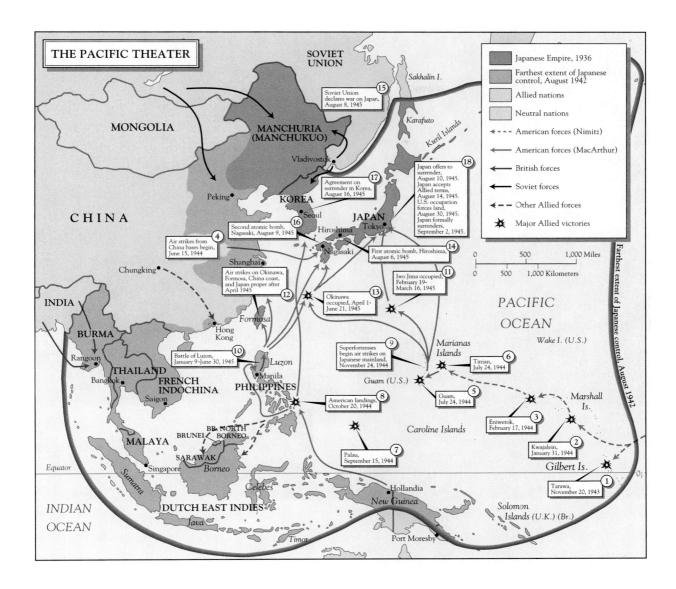

surrender, even when his army was clearly defeated. Japanese soldiers were sworn to fight to the death, taking down as many of the enemy as they could.

To an astonishing degree, this was how they fought. It took the Americans six months to win control of microscopic Guadalcanal in the Solomons beginning in August 1942, even though the defenders did not have time to complete their fortifications.

In New Guinea and along the route through the Gilbert, Marshall, and Marianas islands that Nimitz was to follow, the concrete bunkers and gun emplacements were stronger than in the Solomons, and the resistance of the Japanese was chillingly effective. Marines discovered at places like Tarawa in the Gilberts in November 1943 that when a battle was over, they had few prisoners. They had to kill almost every Japanese on the island at high cost to themselves.

As MacArthur and Nimitz moved closer to Japan, the fighting grew tougher. Attacking the Marianas and the Philippines in 1944, both American forces were hit hard. But MacArthur's dramatic return to Luzon boosted morale, and Nimitz's capture of the Marianas enabled larger land-based American planes to bomb the Japanese homeland at will. The wooden cities of Japan went up like tinder when hit by incendiary devices. A single raid on Tokyo on March 9, 1945, killed 85,000 people and destroyed 250,000 buildings.

Battles in the Pacific were sometimes brief, but hideously bloody.

Fighting to the Last Man

Not all the Japanese-occupied islands were retaken. Both MacArthur and Nimitz advocated island hopping, leaving less-important Japanese positions alone, to wither as they were cut off from supplies. Island hopping meant an ongoing Japanese threat from the American rear, of course, but it enabled the campaign to proceed much more quickly, and with fewer casualties, than a conventional advance. When the war finally ended, there were still some Japanese units operating in New Guinea, the point of farthest Japanese penetration in the South Pacific.

Fighting to the Last Man

By the spring of 1945, Japan's situation was hopeless. Germany was defeated, thus freeing hundreds of thousands of battle-hardened soldiers for combat in the Pacific. Japan's leaders correctly calculated that the Soviet Union was on the verge of declaring war on them. After the huge Battle of Leyte Gulf in October 1944, the Japanese navy ceased to exist as a fighting force, while the Americans cruised the seas with 4,000 ships, shelling the Japanese coast at will. United States submarines, which were more effective than German U-boats ever were, destroyed half of the island nation's vital merchant fleet within a few months.

Some Japanese leaders put out peace feelers via the Russians, with whom Japan was not yet at war. But the high command was divided. Fanatics high in the government prevented an open appeal for peace. They were themselves victims of the extreme nationalistic fervor they instilled in their men, and they had 5 million soldiers in uniform. There were 2 million in Japan itself, and about the same number in China, where Chiang's half-hearted war making was just enough to forge them into first-rate soldiers without inflicting heavy casualties.

With so many soldiers fighting to the death, the taking of islands close to Japan resulted in hundreds of thousands of casualties. On Saipan, in three weeks' fighting, there were more than 16,000 American casualties. Some 30,000 Japanese soldiers were killed, almost all the defenders of the island. Between 6000 and 8000 Japanese civilians committed suicide, leaping from cliffs, rather than fall into American hands. Iwo Jima, a desolate tiny volcano needed for a landing strip, cost 4,000 American lives. The invasion of Okinawa, considered part of Japan, killed or wounded 80,000 Americans. In the same fighting, more than 100,000 Japanese died, and only 8,000 surrendered. Planners guessed that the invasion of Japan itself, scheduled for November 1, 1945, would cost 1 million casualties, as many as the United States had suffered in over three years of fighting in both Europe and the Pacific.

A Birth and a Death

This chilling prediction helped to make the atomic bomb so appealing to policy makers. The Manhattan Project, code name of the group that built the bomb, dated from 1939, when the German-Jewish physicist Albert Einstein wrote to President Roosevelt that it was possible to unleash inconceivable amounts of energy by nuclear fission, splitting an atom. Einstein was a pacifist, but he was also a refugee from Nazism who believed that German science was capable of producing a nuclear bomb. Such a device in Hitler's hands was an appalling prospect.

Einstein was too prestigious to ignore and the government secretly allotted $2 billion to the Manhattan Project. Under the direction of J. Robert Oppenheimer, scientists' work on Long Island, underneath a football stadium in Chicago, and at isolated Los Alamos in New Mexico progressed steadily and, by April 1945, they told Washington that they were four months away from testing a bomb.

The decision whether or not to use it did not fall to President Roosevelt. Reelected to a fourth term in 1944 over Thomas E. Dewey, the governor of New York, Roosevelt died of a massive stroke on April 12, 1945. He was at Warm Springs, Georgia, sitting for a portrait painter when he said, "I have a terrific headache," slumped in his chair, and died.

Sands of Iwo Jima

Iwo Jima was a volcanic island two and a half by five miles in size, hardly worth military mapping except that, as an air base, it was 400 miles closer to Japan than any other occupied island in February 1945. Iwo Jima was also unbelievably well-fortified with 642 blockhouses called "pillboxes" commanded by the able General Tadamachi Kuribayashi. American generals and admirals, led by Holland M. "Howlin' Mad" Smith, expected to take the island in five days with an invasion force of 60,000 marines attacking 22,000 Japanese. Occupying Iwo Jima took five weeks. A third of the American forces were killed and wounded. but the most instructive number was that only 1,000 Japanese survived. Along with Saipan and Okinawa, wretched, desolate Iwo Jima taught the Americans just how literal the Japanese were when they said they would fight to the death.

The outpouring of grief that swept the nation at the loss of the man who was in office longer than any other president was real and profound. Silent crowds lined the tracks to watch the train that brought FDR back to Washington for the last time. People wept in the streets of every city. But in Washington, the sorrow was overshadowed by apprehensions that his

---

KAMIKAZE

The most famous Japanese suicide weapon was the Kamikaze plane, named "divine wind" after a storm that had destroyed a Mongol invasion of Japan centuries before. These were planes loaded nose to tail with explosives. Their pilots' mission was to crash into American warships. Most were shot down before they were able to strike, although dozens of American vessels were damaged or sunk.

Oka ("cherry blossms") were manned rockets, dropped from a mother plane, and then piloted toward American ships. They were not effective. *Kaiten* ("turn toward heaven") were piloted torpedoes launched from submarines that had surfaced. *Kaiten* sunk only two allied ships.

876 Chapter 44 America's Great War

successor, Harry S Truman, was not up to being president.

Truman, "Little Boy," and "Fat Man"

Truman was an honest politico who rose as a dependable and hard worker for the Kansas City machine of Boss Thomas J. Pendergast. He proved his abilities as chairman of an important Senate committee during the war, but impressed few as the caliber of person to head a nation. Unprepossessing in appearance and manner, bespectacled, something of a midwestern dandy (he once operated a haberdashery), and given to salty language, Truman was nominated as vice president in 1944 as a compromise candidate. Democratic conservatives wanted the left-liberal vice president elected in 1940, Henry A. Wallace, out of the number two spot, but they could not force conservative James J. Byrnes on the liberals. The two wings of the party settled on Truman.

Truman was as shocked by his accession as anyone else. "I don't know whether you fellows ever had a load of hay or a bull fall on you," he told reporters on his first full day in office, "but last night the moon, the stars, and all the planets fell on me." If he joined others in being unsure of his abilities, Truman knew how to make difficult decisions and never doubted his responsibility to lead. A plaque on his desk read "The Buck Stops Here"; as the president of the United States, he could not "pass the buck" to anyone else.

Truman met with Churchill and Stalin at Potsdam in July 1945, but to Stalin only alluded to the bomb. When some—not all—of his advisors in-

---

The Costs of War

The Second World War was the most expensive war that the United States ever fought:

Revolutionary War	$149	million
War of 181	124	million
Mexican War	107	million
Civil War (Union only)	8	billion
Spanish-American War	2.5	billion
First World War	66	billion
Second World War	560	billion
Korean War	70	billion
Vietnam War	121.5	billion

---

formed him that the alternative to using it was a conventional invasion of Japan and horrendously high American casualties, he opted as Roosevelt always had—to avoid them. On August 6, an atomic bomb nicknamed "Little Boy" was dropped on Hiroshima, killing 100,000 people in an instant and dooming another 100,000 to death from injury and radiation poisoning. Two days later, "Fat Man" was exploded over Nagasaki.

Incredibly, the Japanese high command still wanted to fight on. Had they known that the Americans had no more atomic bombs in their arsenal, they might have carried the debate. But Emperor Hirohito stepped in and agreed to surrender on August 15, 1945, if he were allowed to keep his throne. Because the Americans valued him as a symbol of social stability in Japan, they agreed. The war ended officially on the decks of the battleship *Missouri* on September 2.

Was the Bomb Necessary?

At first there was only wonder at a weapon that could destroy a whole city, and joy that the war was over. Within a few years, however, many Americans began to debate the wisdom and morality of having used the atomic bomb. When novelist John Hersey's *Hiroshima* detailed the destruction of that ancient city in vivid, human terms, some of Truman's critics stated that he was guilty of a war crime worse than any the Japanese had perpetrated, and exceeded only by the Nazi murder of 6 million European Jews. Truman and his defenders replied that the nuclear assaults on Hiroshima and Nagasaki were humane

---

World War II Casualties

	Total Mobilized	Killed or Died	Wounded
United States	16,113,000	407,000	672,000
China	17,251,000	1,325,000	1,762,000
Germany	20,000,000	3,250,000	7,250,000
Italy	3,100,000	136,000	225,000
Japan	9,700,000	1,270,000	140,000
USSR	—	6,115,000	14,012,000
United Kingdom	5,896,000	357,000	369,000
Total	72,060,000	12,860,000	24,430,000

A view of Hiroshima after it was flattened by an atomic bomb, August 6, 1945.

acts since millions of Japanese as well as Americans would have been killed had Japan been invaded.

When other critics said that the Japanese surrender could have been forced by a demonstration of the bomb on an uninhabited island, as Secretary of War Stimson had earlier suggested, defenders pointed out that no one was positive that the device would actually work. An announced demonstration that fizzled would have encouraged the Japanese diehards to fight all the harder.

Much later, a group of historians known as revisionists suggested that "Little Boy" and "Fat Man" were dropped not so much to end the war with Japan but to inaugurate the Cold War with the Soviet Union. In bombing Japan, the revisionist argument went, Truman was showing the Russians that the United States held the trump card in any postwar dispute. Because history is not a science, capable of absolute proof, the debate over the use of the bomb will continue indefinitely. Only two things are certain: the atomic bomb ended the Second World War decisively and ahead of schedule, and it ushered in a new and dangerous epoch in world affairs, the nuclear age.

CHRONOLOGY

1941   United States declares war on Japan and Germany

1942   Japan occupies Malaya, Hong Kong, Philippines, Java, Guam, much of New Guinea, and most islands of western Pacific

878 *Chapter 44 America's Great War*

American and Japanese navies fight to a standoff in Battle of Coral Sea. Sea lanes to Australia remain open

American navy defeats Japanese fleet at Midway, securing the central Pacific and forcing Japan to take the defensive

Japanese Americans living in western states are interned by presidential order

Americans win Guadalcanal in Solomon Islands after six months of vicious battle

American strategists conclude that war with Germany must take precedence over war with Japan

Army Air Corps commences bombing of Germany

American troops land in North Africa

1943 American troops invade Sicily and Italy

FDR, British Prime Minister Winston Churchill, and Soviet Premier Josef Stalin meet personally at Teheran, Iran

In the Pacific, horrendous losses in defeating Japanese on Tarawa dramatize the high costs of amphibious attacks

1944 D-Day: Allied troops establish beachhead in Normandy and begin push on Paris

Battle of Leyte Gulf effectively destroys Japanese naval power

Battle of the Bulge: tremendous German counteroffensive inflicts great losses on Allied forces and temporarily pushes front lines back

1945 FDR, Churchill, and Stalin meet at Yalta to plan for postwar world

Germany surrenders

FDR dies; Harry S Truman becomes president

Truman meets with Stalin and British Prime Minister Clement Atlee at Potsdam

United States drops atomic bombs on Hiroshima and Nagasaki; Japan surrenders

FOR FURTHER READING

The standard history of America's Great War is Albert R. Buchanan, *The United States and World War II*, 1962. More comprehensive studies include Martha Hoyle, *A World in Flames: A History of World War II*, 1970, and Gerhard Weinberg's extraordinary *A World at Arms*, 1994; but, of course, the literature is exhaustive, with a great number of excellent popular histories. Although hardly a study in objectivity, Winston Churchill, *The Second World War*, 1948–1953, will be rewarding to every student.

On diplomatic and political issues, see Robert Beitzell, *The Uneasy Alliance: America, Britain, and Russia, 1941–1943*, 1972; Robert Dallek, *Franklin D. Roosevelt and American Foreign Policy, 1932–1945*, 1979; Robert A. Divine, *Roosevelt and World War II*, 1969; Norman A. Graebner, *The Age of Global Power: The United States since 1938*, 1979; Gabriel Kolko, *The Politics of War: The World and United States Foreign Policy, 1943–1945*, 1968; Joseph P. Lash, *Roosevelt and Churchill*, 1976; Warren Kimball, *The Juggler: Franklin Roosevelt as Wartime Statesman*, 1991; and Doris Kearns Goodwin, *No Ordinary Time. Franklin and Eleanor Roosevelt: The Home Front in World War II*, 1994.

Military history is the major focus of Stephen Ambrose, *The Supreme Commander: The War Years of General Dwight D. Eisenhower*, 1970; Eric Larrabee, *Commander in Chief: Franklin Delano Roosevelt, His Lieutenants & Their War*, 1987; William Manchester, *American Caesar: Douglas MacArthur, 1880–1960*, 1978; Charles B. McDonald, *The Mighty Endeavor: American Armed Forces in the European Theater of World War II*, 1969; Samuel Eliot Morison, *The Two-Ocean War: A Short History of the United States Navy in the Second World War*, 1963; Cornelius Ryan, *The Longest Day*, 1959; John Toland, *The Last Hundred Days*, 1966, and *The Rising Sun: The Decline and Fall of the Japanese Empire*, 1970; and Russell F. Weigley, *The American Way of War: A History of United States Military Strategy and Policy*, 1973. For the Asian theater, see John Dower, *War without Mercy: Race and Power in the Pacific War*, 1986; and Christopher Thorne, *The Issue of War*, 1985. For aspects of the European conflict, see Ronald Shaffer, *Wings of Judgment: American Bombing in World War II*, 1985; and David Wyman, *The Abandonment of the Jews*, 1984.

Books on the home front include John M. Blum, *V Was for Victory*, 1976; Roger Daniels, *Concentration Camps USA*, 1971; some chapters of Carl M. Degler, *At Odds: Women and the Family in America from the Revolution to the Present*, 1980; William O'Neill, *A Democracy at War*, 1993; Richard Polenberg, *War and Society: The United States, 1941–1945*, 1972; Michi Weglyn, *Years of Infamy: The Untold Story of America's Concentration Camps*, 1976; Nelson Lichtenstein, *Labor's War at Home: The CIO in World War II*, 1982; and Michael C. C. Adams, *The Best War Ever*, 1994.

The reasons for dropping the atomic bomb on Japan in 1945 are hotly argued in Gar Alperovitz, *Atomic Diplomacy: Hiroshima and Potsdam*, 1965; Herbert Feis, *The Atomic Bomb and World War II*, 1966; and Greg Herken, *The Winning Weapon*, 1980. See also John Hersey's classic, *Hiroshima*, 1946; Richard Rhodes, *The Making of the Atomic Bomb*, 1987; and Martin Sherwin, *A World Destroyed*, 1975.

A radioactive mushroom cloud covers Bikini Atoll following a test of the atomic bomb.

45
CHAPTER

ANXIETY TIME

The United States in the Early Nuclear Age
1946–1952

The release of atomic energy constitutes a new force too revolutionary to consider in the framework of old ideas.

—Harry S Truman

Science has brought forth this danger, but the real problem is in the minds and hearts of men.

—Albert Einstein

The world has achieved brilliance without wisdom, power without conscience. Ours is a world of nuclear giants and ethical infants.

—Omar Bradley

Nature is neutral. Man has wrested from nature the power to make the world a desert or to make the desert bloom. There is no evil in the atom, only in men's souls.

—Adlai Stevenson

Chapter 45 Anxiety Time

Few wars have ended so abruptly as the Pacific theater of the Second World War. Determined to fight block to block and village to village one week, divided the next, and then shattered by the news of the atomic bomb, the Japanese government collapsed overnight.

Never was a new historical era so unmistakably proclaimed as by the fireballs over Hiroshima and Nagasaki. Slowly during the final months of 1945, it dawned on Americans and other peoples that the world had undergone a major passage, that old rules and guidelines would not necessarily help them to negotiate the future.

THE SHADOW OF COLD WAR

But they had not left the past behind. History is legacy. The consequences of past actions live on whether or not people choose to recognize them. Three great legacies of the Second World War were so profound that they fostered anxieties that loom menacingly over the United States and the world to this day.

Legacies

The first legacy of the Second World War was, of course, the powerful weapon that ended it. Nuclear bombs meant that it was technologically possible for humanity to destroy civilization, perhaps even the natural world as we know it. Such a circumstance was, to say the least, novel in history.

A second legacy of the war was the realization that human beings were morally capable of using such a technology in monstrous ways. It was not so much President Truman's decision to use the atomic bomb. However justified that decision may have been, neither Truman nor his advisors understood

quite how horrible a weapon nuclear fission was. Very few people could imagine the thousands of maimings and lingering deaths from radiation poisoning in Hiroshima and Nagasaki.

Also, in the spring of 1945, Allied troops discovered that reports of genocide in Nazi Europe were not exaggerated. The Nazis had systematically exterminated 6 million Jews and probably 1 million other people, many of them in camps specifically designed for killing people and disposing of their bodies on a mass scale. The photographs and films of the walking skeletons of Dachau, Belsen, Auschwitz, and Buchenwald; the "shower baths" where the victims were gassed; the cremation ovens; the human garbage dumps, arms and legs protruding obscenely from heaps of corpses like discarded furniture: these shocking spectacles mocked human pretensions to enlightenment and decency such as not even the slaughter of the First World War had done.

World War I, at least, was mindless. Nazi genocide was deliberate, calculated, and systematic. Never again would it be possible for thoughtful people to assume, as most of Western civilization assumed for more than a century, that reason, science, technology, and efficiency were moving the human race toward an ever better future.

The third legacy of the war was that only two nations emerged from it as genuine victors—the United States and the Soviet Union—and that, once the Nazis were defeated, they had little in common. For about two years after the war, Russian and American leaders tried to preserve the wartime alliance or, at least, to maintain the pretense of friendship. By 1947, however, the two great powers were in a "cold war," a state of belligerence without violent confrontation.

At first Americans were more annoyed than frightened by what they believed was Soviet ingratitude and treachery. Their nation held the trump card, the atomic bomb. Then, in September 1949, the Soviets successfully tested a nuclear device. The holocaust of which the race had proved itself capable seemed likely to be ignited sooner or later.

Roots of Soviet-American Animosity

The origins of the Russo-American Cold War lay in irreconcilable values and 30 years of history. The American commitment to democratic government, the maximum possible liberty for individuals, and a capitalist economy were incompatible with the conviction of the Bolsheviks of 1917 that they could

---

Landscaping

A pamphlet of 1950 about bomb shelters, "How to Survive an Atomic Bomb," advised: "Things are probably going to look different when you get outside. If the bomb hit within a mile and a half of where you are, things are going to look very different."

Prisoners in a Nazi concentration camp await their release in this 1945 photo by Margaret Bourke-White.

overcome the "sluggishness of history" and achieve their revolution by the creation of a dictatorial, repressive, and ruthless state power.

Obnoxious as Soviet tyranny was to Americans, however, it cannot in itself explain American hostility to the Soviets. The United States often found it convenient to come to terms with non-Communist dictators, even to assist them. Opposition to Communism in government also owed to the American commitment to maintaining an open door for trade and investment everywhere in the world. This principle—free competition for trade—was incompatible with the Soviets' determination to exclude capitalist economic penetration in those parts of the world they controlled, and Soviet determination to export Communist revolution and expand the USSR's political sway.

With such contradictory values and goals, the Soviet Union and the United States could marry only when there was a shotgun at their backs, which Nazi Germany provided between 1941 and 1945. Even then, despite cordial personal relations between Roosevelt and Stalin, neither American nor Russian policy makers deluded themselves that the conflict of interests had disappeared. People high in the American government, such as James Byrnes and Harry S Truman continued to find Russian Communism intolerably noxious. The Russians, Stalin foremost among them, remained suspicious of the intentions of the United States and Great Britain. For a decade and more after 1917, the Western nations had isolated Russia and threatened to destroy the revolution of the Bolsheviks. Then Stalin fidgeted and seethed when Roosevelt and Churchill were slow to

The Surplus

For half a generation after World War II, a fixture on the American retail landscape was the "Army-Navy Store." This was a business made possible by the huge production of goods for the military that, after August 1945, were simply not needed. At the end of the war, the government actually had more war matériel in stockpile than had been consumed during four years of conflict. It was disposed of for pennies on the dollar.

Neighborhood Army-Navy stores specialized in clothing (from uniforms to government-issued underwear), tools, "camping gear," gasoline cans, ammunition boxes and bags in which, for more than a decade, tens of thousands of children carried their schoolbooks. The stores eventually purchased and retailed 25 million folding chairs, 7 million tubes of toothpaste, and a million gallons of olive drab paint from Washington.

War surplus not purchased by Army-Navy stores included 1,300 war production factories, among them 94 chemical and munitions plants (any one of which was capable of supplying the nation's peacetime needs in TNT), 6,000 vessels, 21,000 tanks, 125,000 trucks, and 1,800 prefabricated religious chapels. Many a small business dated its origins to the cheapness of expensive equipment after the war. And big businesses too. One B-29 superfortress that cost half a million dollars to build sold for $350.

establish a second front in Europe. The Americans and the British worried that, after the war, Communist Russia would be a great power for the first time, in a position to dominate its neighbors.

An Insoluble Problem

Roosevelt apparently believed he could ensure that the nations bordering the Soviet Union would be truly independent while accommodating Stalin's repeated insistence that they be "friendly" to the Soviet Union. Although it is difficult to imagine what kind of arrangement he had in mind, Roosevelt apparently thought he could ensure that Poland, Czechoslovakia, and the Balkan countries would be democratic, open to American cooperation and trade while posing no threat to Soviet security.

At best, this was naive. Political democracy, as it was defined in Roosevelt and Churchill's Atlantic Charter, was alien to Eastern European history and culture. Moreover, some Eastern European countries, particularly Poland, were historically enemies of Russia. If the Western Allies suppressed the memory that the Soviet Union had joined Nazi Germany in invading Poland in 1939, the Poles did not. Indeed, Polish hatred for the Russians was given new life in 1943, when the Germans released persuasive evidence that the Red Army secretly massacred 5,000 captured Polish officers at Katyn in 1940.

Then, late in the war, with Russian troops advancing rapidly toward Warsaw, the Polish government-in-exile in London called for an uprising behind the German lines. At this point, Stalin abruptly halted the Russian advance, and the unpressured Germans were able to butcher the poorly armed Polish partisans. Red Army soldiers were as brutal toward Polish civilians as they were toward Germans. A democratic Poland could not be subordinate to Russia in the sense that Stalin demanded Poland be. A Poland friendly to Russia could not be democratic.

Roosevelt's confidence that he could iron out these wrinkles on the basis of his personal cordiality with Stalin also required that he defy his own mortality, to which he should have been very sensitive in early 1945; his health was rapidly and visibly deteriorating. Nevertheless, he continued to treat diplomacy as a personal endeavor. When he died before the war was over, he left an inexperienced and uninformed Harry S Truman to make a settlement with Stalin.

Truman Draws a Line

Truman was not the sly manipulator Roosevelt was. His virtues as a man and as president were his frankness, bluntness, and willingness to make and stick by a decision. On the subject of the Soviet Union he had made a decision decades earlier. Like most Americans he did not like the Russians. Even before he first met Stalin at Potsdam, he summoned Soviet Ambassador V. M. Molotov to the White House and scolded him so harshly for several apparent Russian policy turns that Molotov exclaimed, "I have never been talked to like that in my life!" For a man who was so close to Stalin, a sadistic bully, this was surely not the truth, but that Molotov said it indicates how hard-nosed Truman was with him.

By 1946, it was obvious that the Russians were not going to permit free elections in Poland. While

Truman remained cautious in his official pronouncements on the subject, he gave advance approval to Winston Churchill's speech in Fulton, Missouri, in March 1946. An "iron curtain" had descended across Europe, the former prime minister said, and it was time for the Western democracies to call a halt to the expansion of atheistic Communism.

In September 1946, Truman again signaled the confrontational turn of his Soviet policy. He fired Secretary of Commerce (and former vice president) Henry A. Wallace, the one member of his cabinet who called openly for accommodating the anxieties of the Soviet Union.

Containment and the Truman Doctrine

By 1947, Truman had a policy that went beyond merely "getting tough with the Russians." First, in a series of confidential memoranda, and then in an article signed by "Mister X" in the influential journal *Foreign Affairs*, a Soviet expert in the State Department, George F. Kennan, argued that because of the ancient Russian compulsion to expand to the west and the virtually pathological Soviet suspicion of the Western nations, it would be impossible to come to an amicable settlement with Stalin in the near future. American policy must therefore be to contain Russian expansionism by drawing clear limits as to where the United States would tolerate Russian domination, namely, those parts of Europe that already were under Russian control, and no more.

In Kennan's view, the Soviets would test American resolve; however, Russian history, recent and remote, seemed to show they would do so very cautiously. While the Soviets wanted to extend their sway to the west as far as possible, they did not want all-out war any more than did the United States. If American policy makers made it unmistakably clear that they would tolerate no more Russian gains, the Soviets would stop. Kennan envisioned a long period of tense, suspicious relations. In time, however, when the Russians felt secure, it would become possible to deal diplomatically with them and establish a genuine peace. In the meantime, "cold war" was preferable to bloodletting and the possibility of world destruction.

At the same time the containment policy was being leaked to the public, Truman was presented with an opportunity to put it into practice. In early 1947, the Soviets stepped up their support of Communist guerrillas in Greece and Communist political parties in Italy and France. On March 12, Truman asked Congress to appropriate $400 million in military assistance to the pro-Western governments of Greece and Turkey. This principle of decisively supporting anti-Communist regimes with massive aid came to be known as the Truman Doctrine.

The Marshall Plan

On June 5, 1947, Secretary of State George C. Marshall proposed a much more ambitious program, the Marshall Plan. The United States would invest vast sums of money in the economic reconstruction of Europe. Not only would the former Western European Allies be invited to apply for American assistance, but defeated Germany (then divided into British, French, American, and Soviet zones of occupation), and even neutral nations such as Sweden and Switzerland, would be eligible for aid. Indeed, Marshall invited the Soviet Union and the nations behind Churchill's Iron Curtain to participate.

Marshall and Truman calculated that Russia and its satellite states would reject the offer. By late 1947, Stalin's troops were firmly in control of the countries of Eastern Europe, including the one nation there with a strong democratic tradition, Czechoslovakia. Already in June 1946, Stalin had made it clear that he would brook no Western

---

Learning from Past Mistakes

In a number of ways, FDR and Harry S Truman pointedly departed from American policy toward Europe after the First World War. In sponsoring the United Nations, the United States departed radically from the American boycott of the League of Nations. Unlike Woodrow Wilson, who named no prominent Republican to his peace commission at Versailles, thus contributing to American opposition to the League, Roosevelt made Republican Senator Arthur H. Vandenberg, a former isolationist, a member of the American delegation that wrote the Charter of the United Nations.

With the Marshall Plan, President Truman recognized the folly of the Coolidge administration of the 1920s in refusing to help Europe economically by arranging for a significant modification of the flow of reparations from Germany and debt payments by Britain and France.

How They Lived

Jehovah's Witnesses

During the Truman years, millions of Americans were introduced to the Jehovah's Witnesses for the first time. Rather than preaching from streetcorner soapboxes, as the sects they seemed to resemble did, the Witnesses showed up on the thresholds of grand homes, middle-class tract houses, and declining urban apartments and row houses alike. Always neatly dressed, always in pairs, often racially mixed, they clutched briefcases or handbags stuffed with their books, tracts, and copies of two monthly magazines, *The Watchtower* and *Awake!* The Witnesses were never jolly nor backslapping in one well-known American evangelical tradition. Their manner was solemn, grim, thin-lipped. Their ice-breaking question was blunt and cheerless: did the householder (usually a housewife during the daytime hours) think that all was well with the world?

The Second World War left in its wake the lingering smell of the extermination camps and Hiroshima, the shock of the lowering of the Iron Curtain and the Communist triumph in China, news of cold war spies and the cries of subversion in Washington. In the vague but general sense that the war had created a more threatening world than it destroyed, the Jehovah's Witnesses won many invitations to come in and talk. The sect that was 70 years old in 1949, but still tiny, began to grow, and the numbers of its full-time walkers of streets and ringers of doorbells became more conspicuous. In 1978, the Witnesses numbered more than 600,000 in the United States, 2 million worldwide. Their Watchtower Tract Society was one of the largest publishing houses in the world. *Awake!* alone had a circulation of 8 million in 34 languages.

The Witnesses took shape during the 1870s in Allegheny City, Pennsylvania, in the midst of the iron and steel belt that epitomized industrial progress to some, a hell of soot, smoke, sparkling flame, and social insecurity to others. The founder, Charles Taze Russell, was a Presbyterian who, like many troubled believers before him, found grievous flaws in the traditional faiths, and styled himself "God's Mouthpiece."

At first, the Witnesses seemed like just another variant on the fundamentalist, millenarian, catastrophe-minded groups that have sprung up in times of trying social ferment. They taught that the Bible was "inspired and historically accurate," a single, reassuring absolute in a world of whirling flux and instability. In the 1980s, the American Witnesses' street ministers were probably nimbler in finding the apt biblical citation for an occasion than the deans and doyennes of America's most prestigious divinity schools.

Like the Millerites of the 1840s, the Witnesses said that "the end of the world" was nigh. In 1876, Russell predicted that Armageddon—the final battle between good and evil—would occur in 1914. When the First World War, with its unprecedented horrors, erupted in that year, Witness membership jumped. Russell's successor named 1918, the end of the Great War. Others have set the date at 1925, 1941, 1975, and 1984. In times of anxiety like the late 1940s and early 1950s, it often happens that many people think the world itself is soon to end, particularly those whom society has rejected, despised, or merely left behind. Like other fundamentalist groups, the Witnesses were most successful among the poor, downtrodden, and uneducated.

---

interference in these countries. He turned down a proposal by elder statesman Bernard Baruch to outlaw nuclear weapons because the plan involved enforcement on the scene by the United Nations, which was formed in 1945 under a charter that evolved from the agreements of the various wartime Allied conferences.

The Soviets did condemn the Marshall Plan. Massive American aid went to 16 nations, in some of which a political purpose was served—overcoming the economic and social chaos in which Communism flourished—but also in countries where there was no communist threat, such as Switzerland, the Netherlands, Ireland, and Norway. Winston

However, the Witnesses were unique fundamentalists and millenarians in several ways. Hardly inclined to be "right-wingers" preaching anti-Semitism and antiblack racism, the Witnesses totally rejected racial discrimination of any kind. As a consequence, they have been immensely successful proselytizers among African Americans.

Hardly uncritical superpatriots, the Witnesses considered all governments—America's included—as evil. Their meetinghouses, called "Kingdom Halls," indicate that they consider themselves subjects of God's (Jehovah's) realm. They merely submit to those powers of the state that do not conflict with Jehovah's law. They do not participate in government or politics.

As a result of their refusal to serve in the armed forces, thousands of Witnesses were imprisoned during World War II. They puzzled authorities by their passivity and self-enforced order in prison, and also by their disdain for other political and conscientious objectors to military service. In fact, the Witnesses considered their fellow prisoners as misguided "instruments of Satan," too. The Witnesses were not pacifists in any but the functional sense of the word. They looked forward with zest to Armageddon when they will themselves take up arms for Jehovah and exterminate those who have rejected their message and witness.

The Jehovah's Witnesses are also peculiar in that they do not believe in hell. When Jehovah's reign begins, the "instruments of Satan" will simply cease to exist. A material universe will be ruled by 144,000 Witnesses who alone, with Jesus, will reside in heaven.

In their vision of the post-Armageddon earth, the importance of the Truman years in the development of the organization can be seen in a most curious way. Pictorial depictions of Jehovah's kingdom in *Awake!* and *The Watchtower* show lions lying down with lambs (the ancient biblical image), but the restored Eden is a broad, weedless lawn mowed as closely as a golfing green surrounding a sprawling "ranch-type" house such as was the beau-ideal, the "good life," for millions of Americans in the late 1940s and early 1950s. Smiling, loving, neatly and conventionally dressed and barbered suburbanites (no wings and halos), albeit of all races, populate this paradise. Often, guests are arriving for a backyard barbecue.

The Witnesses' paradise bears a close resemblance to the consumer paradise that advertisers of automobiles, television sets, furniture, and carpets pictured during the postwar years; even the style of the artwork is similar. Such aspirations in a time of increasing affluence allowed most Americans to cope with the anxieties of the Truman era. To the Witnesses, such things represented the post-millennial universe.

In the 1990s, when much of society has questioned the suburban ideal of the 1950s, the Witnesses are still loyal to it, perhaps because so few of them have achieved it. The organization also shows signs of evolving into a large, wealthy, well-established, and increasingly bureaucratized body headquartered in Brooklyn, New York. Its chief official, William Van De Wall, said in 1984 that "we do not know the day or the hour, but we do feel that we are in the time of the end. We are living in the general time period." It was such an accommodation—a dodging of specific predictions that lead to crises—that in the nineteenth century transformed disreputable Millerites into acceptable Seventh-Day Adventists.

Churchill called the Marshall Plan "the most unsordid act in history."

Freezing the Lines

Containment policy worked. Neither Greece and Turkey fell to pro-Russian guerriillas nor Italy and France to Communist parties. The policy received its most severe test in June 1948, when Stalin blockaded West Berlin, deep within Communist East Germany, in an attempt to take the city without force. Unable to provision the city of 2 million by overland routes, the United States could have given up Berlin or invaded East Germany. Instead, a massive airlift was organized. For a year, C-47s and huge

A C-54 carrying supplies flies into West Berlin following Soviet measures blocking overland routes to that city from West Germany.

C-54s flew in the necessities and a few of the luxuries that the West Berliners needed in order to hold out. By this action, the Truman administration made it clear that the United States did not want war, but neither would it tolerate further Soviet expansion.

The Soviets responded quite as George Kennan predicted. Instead of invading West Berlin or shooting down the airlift planes, they watched. In May 1949, having determined that the United States would not give in, the Soviets lifted the blockade.

By that time, the Cold War had entered a new phase. In April 1949, with Canada and nine European nations, the United States signed a treaty that established the North Atlantic Treaty Organization (NATO), the first peacetime military alliance in American history. The NATO countries promised to consider an attack against any of them as grounds for going to war together.

The Soviets then wrote the Warsaw Pact, an alliance of the nations of Eastern Europe. In September 1949, the Soviet Union exploded its first atomic bomb, and soon thereafter the United States perfected the hydrogen bomb, a much more destructive weapon. The nuclear arms race was underway.

DOMESTIC POLITICS UNDER TRUMAN

All the while Harry S Truman was articulating and effecting a decisive foreign policy, he was struggling to cope with postwar domestic problems. These were considerable: rapid inflation, a serious shortage of housing, and a series of bitter industrial disputes. At first Truman seemed to founder. Professional politicians and ordinary voters alike began to suspect his competence. In his predecessor's gigantic shadow, Truman cut a second-rate figure. Compared with dynamic Eleanor Roosevelt, who was even more active in liberal causes after her husband's death, Bess Truman was a plain, frumpy homebody. The deadly serious nuclear age seemed to have caught the United States without a leader up to its challenges.

The Republican Comeback of 1946

Capitalizing on such anxieties, the Republicans ran their congressional election campaign of 1946 on a simple but effective two-word slogan, "Had Enough?" Apparently the voters had. They elected Republican majorities in both houses of Congress for the first time since 1930. One freshman Democratic senator who bucked the landslide, J. William Fulbright of Arkansas, suggested that Truman resign in favor of a Republican president. The Republicans did not take this proposal seriously, but, positive that they would elect their nominee in 1948, they set out to prepare that undesignated candidate's way by dismantling as many New Deal reforms as they could.

One of their most striking successes was the Taft-Hartley Labor-Management Relations Act of 1947. This law, enacted over Truman's veto, reversed the New Deal's active support of the union movement that was enshrined in the Wagner Act of 1935. Taft-Hartley emphasized the rights of workers not to join labor organizations, most notably by abolishing the closed shop. That is, under the New Deal, employees of a company who recognized a union as the workers' bargaining agent—the body that negotiated wages and hours with the company—were required to belong to that union as a condition of employment; employment was closed to all but union members. Taft-Hartley guaranteed the right of individuals not to join a union.

The 52-20 Club

Members of the 52-20 Club of 1945 and 1946 were demobilized soldiers and sailors who were allowed $20 a week for 52 weeks or until such time as they found a job. Although many were accused of avoiding work because of this payment, the average length of membership in the club was only three months.

The GI Bill

The government was generous with the veterans of World War II. The "GI Bill of Rights" provided them unprecedented educational opportunities. Of 14 million men and women eligible to attend college free under the GI Bill, 2.2 million actually did. Colleges and universities swelled in size. The University of Wisconsin had 9,000 students in 1945, 18,000 in 1946. Elite Stanford University went from 3,000 to 7,000 in the same year.

The GI Bill educated 22,000 dentists, 67,000 physicians, 91,000 scientists, 238,000 teachers, 240,000 accountants, and 450,000 engineers. Unfortunately, some veterans abused the bill and became college professors.

The Taft-Hartley Act was not a "slave labor" law, as Truman called it in his veto message; nor did it cripple the union movement. Indeed, its chief effect was to arouse organized labor, now more than 10 million strong, to rally behind Truman. This unexpected support (for Truman when a senator had not been considered especially friendly to organized labor) showed the president a way to fight the Republican Eightieth Congress. He vetoed 80 of its anti-New Deal enactments, thus converting himself into a crusading liberal. When Republican critics mocked his homey manners and common appearance, he turned the tables on them by becoming the common man, denouncing his enemies in Congress as stooges of the rich and privileged. Coining his own slogan, the Fair Deal, he sent to Capitol Hill proposal after proposal that expanded social services. Among his programs was a national health insurance plan such as most European nations had adopted.

Civil Rights

The Truman health plan failed, as did the president's demand that Congress act to mitigate discrimination against blacks. In 1947, the Presidential Committee on Civil Rights reported to Truman on racial discrimination in the United States, particularly as it related to employment practices and the continued condoning of the lynching of blacks in the South. Truman sent its far-reaching recommendations to Congress, where an alliance of complacent Republicans

890 Chapter 45 Anxiety Time

and southern Democrats killed them. Truman responded with an executive order that banned racial discrimination in the army and navy, in the civil service, and in companies that did business with the federal government.

Truman's civil rights program was moderate. He did not attack "Jim Crow," the system of strict social segregation that provided for separate public facilities for the white and black races in the southern and border states, including Truman's home state of Missouri. But he went much further than Roosevelt dared, and his program was politically very shrewd. Hundreds of thousands of blacks had moved out of the South, where they were politically powerless, into big cities in northern and midwestern states with large electoral votes. For a Democratic president to continue to support segregation was to risk throwing these big states to the Republicans, especially because the leading contenders for the Republican presidential nomination, Robert Taft and New York Governor Thomas E. Dewey, had been friendly to black aspirations.

Four Candidates

By the spring of 1948, Truman's popularity was on the upswing. Americans were getting accustomed to, even fond of, the president's hard-hitting style. Nevertheless, no political expert gave Truman a chance to survive the presidential election in November. The

---

Planning Ahead

So confident were the Republicans that they were going to win the election of 1948 that the Republican Congress made a record appropriation for the inauguration festivities on January 20. The benefactor of the lavish parade, of course, was the Democratic president whom the Republicans despised, Harry S Truman.

Democrats had been in power 16 years, longer than any party since the Virginia dynasty of Jefferson, Madison, and Monroe. The inefficiency of many New Deal bureaucracies was undeniable, and rumors of corruption were persistent.

Then, to turn worse into impossible, the party split three ways. Henry A. Wallace led left-wing liberals into the newly formed Progressive party. He claimed to be the true heir of New Deal liberalism and insisted that there was no reason to abandon the nation's wartime friendship with the Soviet Union. Democrats from the Deep South, angry at Truman's civil rights reforms and a strong plank condemning racial discrimination in the party platform written by the young liberal mayor of Minneapolis, Hubert H. Humphrey, formed the States' Rights, or "Dixiecrat," party. They named Strom Thurmond of South Carolina as their candidate.

Thurmond had fewer illusions of winning the election than did Wallace, who had a mystical streak that sometimes insulated him from obvious realities. Thurmond's purpose was to take credit for denying Truman the election, thus impressing on northern liberal Democrats the necessity of sticking to their traditional alliance with southern segregationists.

Presented with what looked like a gift victory, the Republicans passed over their leading conservative, Senator Robert A. Taft of Ohio, the son of President William Howard Taft. Robert Taft was the leader of the onslaught on the New Deal and Truman, but he was often peevish, driven as much by resentment as by principle; and he was not personally likable. Republican moderates calculated that if any candidate would send voters who had "had enough" back to the Democrats for more, it was Taft. Instead, they chose the safe Thomas E. Dewey, their candidate in 1944, to take on Truman.

Margaret's Dad

Harry Truman believed that politicians, and presidents most of all, should be thick-skinned when it came to criticism. "If you can't stand the heat," he said, "get out of the kitchen." However, he did not think this principle applied to concert singers, particularly when the singer was his daughter, Margaret. When her recital was panned by the music critic of the *Washington Post* ("She is flat a good deal of the time"), Truman wrote to the critic: "You sound like a frustrated old man who never made a success, an eight-ulcer man on a four-ulcer job, and all four ulcers working. I never met you, but if I do you'll need a new nose and a supporter below."

Give 'Em Hell, Harry

Dewey adopted an election strategy that was tried and true. Every poll showed him winning with ease. Therefore, as FDR had done when a sure victor in 1932, Dewey ran a low key, noncommittal campaign. He would not jeopardize his lead by saying anything that might alienate any group of voters.

Truman, faced with certain defeat, had nothing to lose by speaking out. "Give 'em hell, Harry," a supporter shouted at a rally, and Truman did. During the summer of 1948, he called Congress into special session and a corps of assistants led by Clark Clifford sent bill after bill to the Republican Congress. As the Republicans voted down his proposals, Truman toured the country, blaming the nation's problems on the "no-good, do-nothing Eightieth Congress." Did Americans want four more years of that sort of thing under a lackluster Thomas E. Dewey?

On election night, the editors of the Republican Chicago *Tribune* glanced at the early returns, which favored Dewey, and decided to scoop the competition by publishing an edition declaring the New Yorker to be the new president. The next day, Harry Truman took great pleasure in posing for photographs while pointing to the *Tribune's* headline, for Dewey had not won. Truman narrowly squeaked out victories in almost all the large industrial states and the majority of farm states. His popular vote was under 50 percent, and he lost several Gulf states to Dixiecrat Thurmond. But he was president by a whopping 303 to 189 electoral vote margin.

Following his narrow victory in 1948, Harry Truman gleefully displays a newspaper that relied on early returns to predict his defeat by Republican presidential candidate Thomas Dewey.

CONTAINMENT IN CHINA

The Fair Deal did not fare so well as its author did. Like many presidents who had other things in mind, Truman found himself preoccupied with such serious problems abroad that domestic reforms seemed insignificant by comparison. Also like other presidents who had to become diplomats, Truman discovered that he was not chief executive in world affairs, but only one player in a game in which the rules defied the power at his disposal and even his own understanding of them.

In Asia, only the Philippines and Japan were firm American allies. Given independence in 1946, the Philippines remained beholden to American financial aid and responded with pliant friendship. In Japan, a capitalist democracy was slowly emerging as a consequence of massive Marshall Plan–type assistance and the enlightened military occupation of the country under Douglas MacArthur. Understanding Japanese traditions better than he understood American, MacArthur established himself as a shogun, or a dictator who ruled while the emperor reigned. The shogun was a familiar figure in Japanese history, and the Japanese were comfortable with a new one.

Rejected Option

In China, however, the Truman administration failed because the president ignored the advice of his best advisors and tried to adapt to the Asian mainland the policy of containment that was working in Europe. The trouble was that the Soviet expansionism responsible in part for the Cold War in Europe did not lie at the bottom of Communist successes in China. Nor were, at least until after the Second World War, the Chinese Communists necessarily opposed to an understanding with the United States. Pundit Walter Lippmann pointed out that Kennan's containment policy could not apply to Asia (or the Middle East) because of the lack of shared values there, and Kennan himself understood the difference between Russia and China. However, Truman, the State Department, and the American public did not listen.

During and after the Second World War, two governments claimed to represent the will of the Chinese people: the Kuomintang, or Nationalist, regime of Chiang Kai-shek, and the powerful Communist party and military force behind Mao Zedong. Some Americans who were familiar with China urged Washington not to oppose Mao but to come to terms with him. During the war, General Joseph W. Stilwell repeatedly warned Roosevelt that the people around Chiang were corrupt and unpopular, while Mao appeared to command the loyalty of China's largest social class, the peasantry.

After the war, acting as a special envoy to China, George C. Marshall suggested that the Chinese Communists were not necessarily tools of the Soviets but could be encouraged to chart an independent course through cooperation and friendship. Mao was bent on revolutionary change at home, particularly in regard to land, which was in the hands of an elite allied to Chiang. Marshall, like many others who were familiar with the Nationalists, did not find Mao's program unattractive since the Kuomintang party included palpable thieves who misappropriated American material aid for their own profit.

The China Lobby

But Chiang had his American friends, an active, articulate, and well-connected "China Lobby" organized and headed by his brilliant wife, Madame Chiang, who spent much of her time in the United States. This group drew support from conservative congressmen; influential church leaders such as the Catholic archbishop of New York, Francis Cardinal Spellman; and much of the press, most importantly Henry L. Luce, the publisher of *Time* magazine, and Clare Boothe Luce, a Republican congresswoman and eloquent speaker.

Through 1949, the China Lobby bombarded Americans with information, some of it false: most Chinese supported Chiang; Chiang was defeating Mao's forces on the battlefield; and Mao was a Soviet stooge like the puppet leaders of Eastern Europe. So effective was the campaign that Americans were shocked at the end of 1949 when Chiang suddenly fled the mainland for the island province of Taiwan (then better known by its Portuguese/Japanese name of Formosa). They thought that Chiang was winning the war. Instead of admitting that they were wrong, at least in regard to the power of the Nationalists, the China Lobby insisted that Chiang was not repudiated but merely betrayed by inadequate American support. They urged that aid be increased and that Chiang be unleashed for an assault on the mainland.

Truman and his new secretary of state, Dean Acheson, knew better than to unleash Chiang Kai-shek. To have done so would have meant either humiliation when he was defeated or American involvement in a war on the mainland of Asia, which every military strategist, from Douglas MacArthur on down, warned against. Whether Truman and Acheson ever rued the fact that they had ignored the advice of Stilwell, Marshall, and others to come to terms with Mao Zedong's Communists is not clear. Whether American friendship would have significantly changed the course of Chinese history under Mao is also beyond certain knowledge. What is known is that China as a foe was dangerous and unpredictable precisely because China was not, as many Americans continued to believe, a Soviet satellite.

Containment Policy Falters

Truman and Acheson were applying the principle of containment to East Asia when events left them behind. No one, including themselves, was quite certain about where the United States would accept Communist control and where the line of containment was to be drawn. Japan was off limits, of course, but what of Quemoy and Matsu, tiny islands off the coast of China that, like Taiwan, were occupied by Chiang's Nationalists? And what of the Republic of Korea, set up by the United States in the southern half of the former Japanese colony of Chosen? Was the little country, bordered on the north by the thirty-eighth parallel (38° north latitude), to be protected like the nations of Western Europe?

Feeling the sting of the China Lobby's attacks, Truman was indecisive. In a similar situation in 1914, the mischievousness of two weak countries started a war and that was what happened in 1950. The Communist government of North Korea and the pro-American government of Syngman Rhee in South Korea exchanged ever more serious threats. In June, ostensibly responding to South Korean troop movements, the North Korean army swept across the thirty-eighth parallel and quickly drove Rhee's ROK (Republic of Korea) troops, and fragments of the American Eighth Army, to the toe of the peninsula.

The Korean Conflict

Truman already had stationed an American fleet in Korean waters, and he responded immediately and forcibly. Thanks to the absence of the Soviet delegation to the United Nations, he was able to win the vote necessary to make the UN the sponsor of a "police action" on the peninsula. With the United States

providing almost all the "police," General MacArthur took command of the expedition.

In a daring maneuver that might have served as the capstone of a brilliant military career, MacArthur engineered an amphibious landing at Inchon, deep behind North Korean lines, cutting off and capturing 100,000 enemy troops. The Americans and ROKs then surged rapidly northward, crossing the thirty-eighth parallel in September 1950. By October 26, they had occupied virtually the whole peninsula. At one point, a few American soldiers stood on the banks of the Yalu River, which divides Korea from Chinese Manchuria.

The headiness of winning so quickly prevented Truman and the UN from reflecting on MacArthur's assurances that the Chinese would not intervene in the war. He was wrong. With its coal and iron deposits, Manchuria was vital to Mao's plans to industrialize China. Furthermore, the northeastern province had, twice before, been the avenue through which the Celestial Kingdom was invaded. Mao threw 200,000 Chinese "volunteers" into Korea. By the end of 1950, these veterans, still hardened by the wars with Chiang, drove MacArthur back to a line that zigzagged across the thirty-eighth parallel.

There, whether because the Chinese were willing to settle for a draw or because American troops found their footing and dug in—historians differ—stalemate ensued. For two years, the Americans, ROKs, and token delegations of troops from other United Nations countries fought the North Koreans and Chinese over forlorn hills and ridges that did not even have names, only numbers. Even after armistice talks began, first at Kaesong and then in a truce zone at Panmunjom, the war dragged on. The Chinese had won their goal, which was to protect their borders, and the Americans had ensured the independence of the Republic of Korea. In the days when the objects of war were clear and concrete, that was the point at which wars were ended. But in the Cold War, with ideological rivalry taking on a religious significance on both sides, neither side knew quite what to do. Some days at Panmunjom, the negotiators simply sat at the table facing one another, saying nothing.

MacArthur's Debacle

With good reason, the American people were frustrated. Not five years after the Second World War, the Korean War put 5.7 million young men in

Matériel piles up at the massive, daring American landing at Inchon, Korea, 1950. The invasion flummoxed the North Korean Army.

uniform, killed 34,000 of them, and wounded 100,000. Defense expenditures soared from $40 billion in 1950 to $71 billion in 1952. Truman and Acheson said that the goal was containment, but having contained, they were unable to conclude hostilities. What was wrong?

In the early spring of 1951, General MacArthur offered an answer. Forgetting his own warning against a war with the Chinese on the Asian mainland, his ego perhaps bruised by the stalemate, he complained to reporters that the only reason he had not won the war was that Truman would not permit him to bomb the enemy's supply depots in Manchuria. Later, MacArthur went further; he sent a letter to Republican Congressman Joseph W. Martin in which he wrote that "there is no substitute for victory" and directly assailed the commander-in-chief for accepting a stalemate. In April, Martin went public with the letter.

This attack on civilian command of the armed forces, a constitutional principle, appalled Truman's military advisors, and on April 11, with their support, the president fired MacArthur. The American people, remembering the general's accomplishments in the Second World War and reckoning that he knew better how to fight than Truman did, cheered the old warrior upon his return to the United States. He was feted with ticker tape parades in every city he visited, and addressed Congress in a broadcast speech that was listened to by more people than had tuned into Truman's inaugural address in 1949.

MacArthur concluded his congressional appearance by quoting a line from an old barracks song, "old soldiers never die; they just fade away," but he had no intention of fading anywhere. Establishing

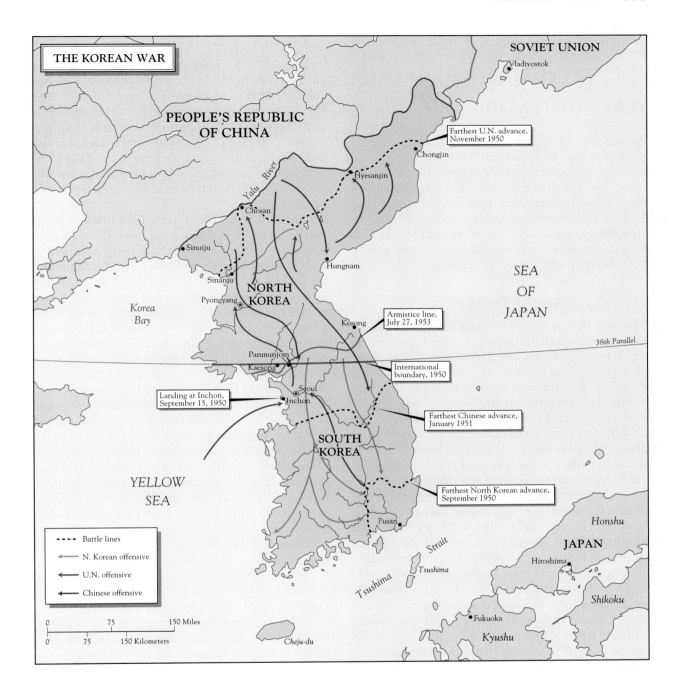

residence and a kind of command headquarters at New York's Waldorf-Astoria Hotel, he continued to issue political proclamations. He wanted the Republican nomination for the presidency in 1952; then he would battle Truman's containment policy with his promises of victory in the Cold War.

But the good general was a poor politician. He had spent half his life outside the country, and he was handicapped by a messianic vision of himself: the people would come to him. They did not. As the very clever politician Harry S Truman calculated when he dismissed the general, enthusiasm for MacArthur faded within a few months. Like Woodrow Wilson, MacArthur was left to spend his final years in an

YEARS OF TENSION

Periodically in American history, during times of great political or social stress, many people have turned to conspiracy theories to explain their anxieties. The era of the Korean War was just such a time. Substantial numbers of Americans came to believe that their failure to achieve a sense of security after the glorious victory in the Second World War must be the result of sinister forces working quietly but effectively within the United States.

"Twenty Years of Treason"

The view that, at Yalta, President Roosevelt sold out Eastern Europe to Stalin was an early expression of this paranoid streak, the belief that betrayal explained American frustrations. Then, in March 1947, President Truman inadvertently fueled anxieties by ordering all government employees to sign loyalty oaths, statements that they did not belong to the Communist party or to other groups suspected of disloyalty. Eventually, 30 states followed this example, requiring an oath even of people who waxed the floors of state university basketball courts.

Truman also promoted the belief that there was treason in government by allowing his supporters to "red bait" Henry Wallace in the 1948 presidential campaign. Wallace was an eccentric (he played with all sorts of bizarre religious ideas), and he was badly mistaken in his analysis of Soviet intentions in 1948. And Communists supported him. But he was no willing Communist party stooge. In calling him one, as many Democratic speechmakers did, they created a political tactic that, in the end, could only work against them. If there were traitors in high places, the Democratic party was responsible, for, as of 1952, they had been running the country for 20 years.

Long before 1952, frustrated right-wing Republicans such as John Bricker of Ohio, William F. Knowland of California, and Karl Mundt of North Dakota raised the specter of "twenty years of treason." The two chief beneficiaries of the scare were Richard M. Nixon, a young first-term congressman from southern California, and Joseph McCarthy, the junior senator from Wisconsin.

Alger Hiss and Richard Nixon

Richard M. Nixon built the beginnings of his career on the ashes of the less illustrious but still distinguished career of a former New Dealer named Alger Hiss. A bright young Ivy Leaguer during the 1930s when he went to Washington to work in the Agriculture Department, Hiss had risen to be a middle-level aide to Roosevelt at the time of the Yalta Conference. He was aloof and fastidious in his manner, rather the snob, and he was in his public persona a militant liberal.

In 1948, a journalist named Whittaker Chambers, who confessed to having been a Communist during the 1930s, accused Hiss of party membership and of having helped him funnel classified American documents to the Soviets. At first his testimony aroused little fuss. Chambers had a reputation for erratic behavior and, indeed, making things up. From a legal point of view, there seemed scant reason to pursue the matter; all the acts of which Hiss was accused had transpired too long in the past to be prosecuted, and he was no longer in government service in 1948. It was Hiss who forced the issue to a reckoning. He indignantly swore under oath that everything Chambers said was false. Indeed, Hiss insisted, he did not even know Chambers.

To liberals, the well-spoken Hiss, with his exemplary record in public service, was obviously telling the truth. The seedy Chambers, with his background in Henry L. Luce's *Time* magazine, was a liar. But many ordinary Americans, especially working-class ethnics and citizens of western farming states, were not so sure. With his nasal aristocratic accent and expensive tailored clothing, Hiss represented the Eastern Establishment, traditionally an object of suspicion, and the long-entrenched New Deal bureaucracy, of which they had grown weary.

Congressman Nixon shared these feelings and, following little more than a hunch, pursued the Hiss case when other Republicans lost interest. Nixon persuaded Chambers to produce microfilms that seemed to show that Hiss had indeed retyped classified documents for some reason, and, in cross-examination at congressional hearings, poked hole after hole in Hiss's defense.

Largely because of Nixon's efforts, Hiss was convicted of perjury. Additional thousands of Americans wondered how many other bright New Dealers were spies. More than one Republican pointed out that Hiss was a friend of none other than the "no-win" Secretary of State Dean Acheson and that the men resembled each other in their manners and appearance. Indeed, Acheson's style grated even more harshly than Hiss's. He favored London-made tweeds and sported the bristling waxed mustache associated with British blimps. Richard Nixon, whose social awkwardness and furtiveness at work might otherwise have obscured him for life, looked good by comparison.

Senator Joe McCarthy

Senator Joseph McCarthy of Wisconsin was another unlikely character to play a major role in the governing of a nation. Not only awkward and furtive, he was a crude, sometimes bullying man insensitive to the cruelty with which he could act. McCarthy was facing an election in 1952 in which he feared he would be defeated; his record in the Senate was lackluster. Groping for an issue, he rejected friends' suggestions that he focus on the advantages the proposed St. Lawrence Seaway would bestow on Wisconsin, a Great Lakes state. Instead, almost by accident, he discovered that anxiety about Communist subversion was his ticket to political celebrity and success.

In 1950, McCarthy told a Republican audience at Wheeling, West Virginia, that he possessed a list of 205 Communists who were working in the State Department with the full knowledge of Secretary of State Acheson. In other words, Acheson himself, as

---

Flying Saucer Scare

In 1947, a commercial pilot over the state of Washington sighted a cluster of "saucer-like things" and reported them to the federal government. By 1950, 600 Americans a year were seeing flying saucers. No one ever proved if the sightings were frauds, the fruit of mass hysteria, evidence of visitors from outer space, or of some new top-secret air force plane. The movie industry, looking for a kind of film with which to combat television, had no trouble making a choice. The early 1950s were years of dozens of movies about extraterrestrial creatures — usually, but not always, bent on destruction — who visited Earth.

Bureaucratic Cleansing

During World War II, about 100 federal employees were fired, and another 30 resigned, as a result of background investigations. Between 1947 and 1956, there were 2,700 dismissals and 12,000 resignations described as "security-related."

---

well as other high-ranking government officials, actively abetted Communist subversion.

McCarthy had no such list. Only two days later, he could not remember if he had said the names totaled 205 or 57. He never released a single name, and never fingered a single Communist in government. Because he was so reckless, interested in nothing but publicity, McCarthy probably was headed for a fall from the moment he stepped into the limelight. But the tumultuous response that met sensational accusations was an alarming symptom of just how anxious American society had become.

When a few senators publicly denounced his irresponsibility, McCarthy showed just how sensitive was the nerve he had touched. Senator Millard Tydings was a conservative whose family name gave him practically a proprietary interest in a Maryland senate seat. In 1950, McCarthy threw his support behind Tydings's unknown opponent, fabricated a photograph showing Tydings shaking hands with American Communist party leader Earl Browder, and the senator went down to defeat.

McCarthyism

Following Tydings's defeat, senators who disliked McCarthy's smear tactics were afraid to speak up lest they suffer the same fate. By 1952, McCarthy was so powerful that Republican presidential candidate Dwight D. Eisenhower, whose military career had been sponsored by George C. Marshall, and who detested McCarthy personally, refrained from praising Marshall in Wisconsin because the former secretary of state was one of McCarthy's "traitors."

In the meantime, liberal Democrats in Congress rushed to prove their loyalty by voting for dubious laws such as the McCarran Internal Security Act, which effectively outlawed the Communist party, by defining dozens of liberal lobby groups as "Communist fronts," and even by providing for the establishment

Senator Joe McCarthy in 1954, near the end of his career as the scourge of Communist subversion in the United States.

of concentration camps in the event of a national emergency. The Supreme Court fell into line with its decision in *Dennis et al. v. United States* (1951). By a vote of six to two, the court agreed that it was a crime to advocate the forcible overthrow of the government, a position that Communists were defined as holding by virtue of their membership in the party.

At the peak of McCarthy's power, only a very few opinion makers outside politics, such as cartoonist Herbert Block and television commentator Edward R. Murrow, and a few universities, including the University of Wisconsin in McCarthy's home state, refused to be intimidated by the senator's bullying. Not until 1954, however, did McCarthy's career come to an end. Failing to get preferential treatment for an intimate draftee friend of his chief aide, Roy Cohn, McCarthy accused the United States Army of being infiltrated by Communists. This recklessness emboldened the Senate to move against him. He was censured in December 1954 by a vote of 72 to 22. It was only the third time in American history that the nation's most exclusive club had turned on one of its own members.

Ironically, the release of Russian intelligence documents in the 1990s revealed that there were plenty of Communists working in federal government agencies. If they were not spies or subverters, it was only because they had access to no information of value to the Soviet Union, or were not in positions from which they could subvert more than an office picnic. They were there, nevertheless and despite McCarthy's unending accusations and expensive investigations, he never found a one. He did not really care. Like many politicians, he had discovered a line that meant political success and that was good enough.

The Making of a Politician

Nixon and McCarthy built their careers on exploiting and aggravating anxieties. Indirectly, the leader of the conservative wing of the Republican party, Senator Robert A. Taft of Ohio, did the same. Although personally less than electrifying and cultivating an image of rectitude, Taft encouraged his party's hell-raisers as a way of chipping at the Democrats.

But the American people turned to no mover and shaker to guide them through the 1950s. Instead, they chose a man with no background in party politics, whose strength was a warm personality and whose talent was a knack for smoothing over conflict.

After World War II, General Dwight David Eisenhower wrote his memoirs of the war, *Crusade in Europe*, and, early in 1948, he accepted the presidency of Columbia University. Leaders of both parties approached him in his uptown New York office with offers to nominate him as president. Truman himself told Ike that if he would accept the Democratic nomination, Truman would gladly step aside.

Eisenhower was not interested. He was a career military man who, unlike MacArthur, believed that soldiers should stay out of politics. It is not certain that Eisenhower ever bothered to vote before 1948, and he identified with neither party. But he did not identify with university life either. Ike's intellectual interests ran to pulp western novels and, after a lifetime accustomed to military order and expecting instructions to be carried out, he found the chaos of shepherding academics to be intolerable.

As one of New York City's most eminent citizens, however, Eisenhower drifted into close professional and personal association with the wealthy eastern businessmen who dominated the moderate wing of the Republican party. They showered him with gifts such as had turned General Grant's head, and financial advice that, uncannily, was inevitably sound. As an administrator himself, something of a businessman in uniform, Eisenhower found it easy to assimilate their politics.

In 1950, Ike took a leave of absence from Columbia to take command of NATO troops in Europe. There, because the Korean War dragged on to no conceivable end, MacArthur's insubordination (which shocked him), and the rise of demagogues like McCarthy, he grew increasingly receptive to the pleas of his moderate Republican friends that he run for president. Like them, Eisenhower felt no obsession to return the United States to the pre-New Deal free-enterprise idyll that Taft fantasized. He and his advisors had come to terms with the basic reforms of the Roosevelt era. What disturbed Ike and the moderates was corruption in the Truman administration, excessive government expenditures, and bureaucratic waste. Gradually, Eisenhower came to concede that he could defeat any Democrat by virtue of his tremendous personal popularity while, with Senator Taft as the party's nominee, the Republicans might well go down to defeat.

The Campaign of 1952

Indeed, many conservative Republicans who admired Taft also wanted Eisenhower to run. They were more interested in victory at the polls than in honoring their veteran leader. They agreed with the Eisenhower moderates that Taft's uncompromising conservative stands would alienate voters who had benefited from the New Deal, but who were otherwise weary of the long Democratic era. Eisenhower's lack of a political record was a positive advantage. Eisenhower did not excite people; he reassured them. But that was precisely what, Republican leaders guessed, the nation craved in 1952.

Eisenhower's Democratic opponent was the governor of Illinois, Adlai E. Stevenson. He was a liberal, but he had taken no part in the now unpopular Truman administration. Stevenson was also a superb campaigner, personable, witty, and as attractively modest in manner as Eisenhower. For a few weeks late in the summer of 1952, it appeared as though Stevenson were catching up with Ike. He enchanted reporters covering the election with his eloquence while Eisenhower, who functioned best in small groups, seemed to bumble on the podium.

But Stevenson labored under too many handicaps, and Eisenhower's shrewd campaign managers made the most of them. They actually turned Stevenson's intelligence and glibness on the rostrum against him, pointing out that "eggheads" (intellectuals) were precisely the people who were responsible for "the mess in Washington," thus associating Stevenson with Truman. In October, Eisenhower administered the *coup de grâce*. While Stevenson defended the policy on which the limited war in Korea was based, Eisenhower promised that, if he were elected, he would "go to Korea" and end the aimless war. Nothing could have better reminded voters that Eisenhower was the director of the successful war in Europe.

Landslide

Stevenson won nine southern states. Although a supporter of civil rights for African Americans, he brought the Dixiecrats back into the Democratic party by naming as his running mate a southern moderate whose support of segregation was conventional and without spleen, John Sparkman of Alabama. Otherwise, Eisenhower swept the nation, winning 55 percent of the popular vote and 442 electoral votes to Stevenson's 89.

In December, before he was inaugurated, Eisenhower kept his promise to go to Korea. He donned military gear, and was filmed sipping coffee with soldiers on the front lines. He had long recognized that an all-out conventional offensive was foolish. Now, by threatening to use the atomic bomb to end the stalemate — probably a bluff he had no intention of carrying out — he dragooned the Chinese and North Koreans to agree to an end to hostilities in July 1953.

It was an auspicious beginning. Indeed, in March 1953, the *bête noire* of postwar American frustrations, Soviet dictator Joseph Stalin, died. The first summer of the Eisenhower presidency was scarcely underway when Americans could feel with reason that they were embarked on a new age of normalcy.

CHRONOLOGY

1945   Yalta Conference: Soviets and Allies make ambiguous agreements about the fate of postwar Europe

1946   Churchill's "Iron Curtain" speech: former prime minister publicly notes Soviet suppression of non-Communist elements in Eastern European nations
Republicans elect majorities in Congress for first time since onset of Depression

Iowa 1952: The classic image of Ike, smiling, fatherly, utterly trustworthy.

1947 Diplomat George Kennan defines and justifies the "containment" of Soviet power
Marshall Plan: Secretary of State George Marshall proposes massive material aid to European nations devastated by war
Taft-Hartley Act reverses many gains made by organized labor during New Deal
President Truman orders end to racial segregation in armed forces

1948 Soviet Union blockades all overland access to West Berlin; Berlin Airlift follows, to be terminated with success in May 1949
Once-prominent New Dealer, Alger Hiss, accused of spying for the Soviet Union; investigation brings California Congressman Richard M. Nixon to prominence
In a four-way election, President Truman wins surprising victory

1949 United States, Canada, and nine European nations form NATO, the North Atlantic Treaty Organization. Soviet Union responds with Warsaw Pact, an alliance of Soviet satellites
Chinese Communists under Mao Zedong (Tse-tung) drive Nationalist government from mainland China to Taiwan

1950 Communist North Korea attacks United States–supported South Korea
Senator Joseph McCarthy of Wisconsin wins prominence by stating that the United States government harbors numerous Soviet spies

1952 Republican candidate Dwight D. Eisenhower defeats Democrat Adlai Stevenson in presidential election

FOR FURTHER READING

There are a surprising number of good general histories treating the immediate postwar era. Among the most recent are William L. O'Neill, *American High: The Years of Confidence, 1945–1960*, 1987; James Gilbert, *Another Chance*, 1984; and James Patterson's comprehensive *Grand Expectations*, 1996. But see also Godfrey Hodgson, *America in Our Time: From World War II to Nixon*, 1976; William E. Leuchtenburg, *A Troubled Feast: American Society since 1945*, 1979; and the introductory sections of C. C. Alexander, *Holding the Line: The Eisenhower Era, 1952–1961*, 1975.

On Truman and his administration, see that articulate president's own *Memoirs*, 1955–1956, and a remembrance by his daughter, Margaret Truman, *Harry S Truman*, 1973; William C. Berman, *The Politics of Civil Rights in the Truman Administration*, 1970; Bert Cochran, *Truman and the Crisis Presidency*, 1973; Susan Hartmann, *Truman and the Eightieth Congress*, 1971; R. F. Haynes, *The Awesome Power: Harry S Truman as Commander in Chief*, 1973; James T. Paterson, *Mr. Republican: A Biography of Robert A. Taft*, 1975; Allen Yarnell, *Democrats and Progressives: The 1948 Election as a Test of Postwar Liberalism*, 1974; David McCullough, *Truman*, 1992; and Melvyn P. Leffler, *A Preponderance of Power*, 1992, on Truman's foreign policy.

The trying diplomatic problems of the times are treated in Herbert Feis, *From Trust to Terror: The Onset of the Cold War, 1945–1950*, 1970; John L. Gaddis, *The United States and the Origins of the Cold War, 1941–1947*, 1972; Norman A. Graebner, *The Age of Global Power: The United States since 1938*, 1979; Gabriel Kolko, *The Limits of Power: The World and United States Foreign Policy, 1945–1954*, 1972; Walter Le Feber, *America, Russia, and the Cold War, 1945–1980*, 1981; Thomas G. Paterson, *Cold War Critics: Alternatives to American Foreign Policy in the Truman Years*, 1972; Michael Hogan, *The Marshall Plan*, 1987; Stephen Rabe, *Eisenhower and Latin America: The Foreign Policy of Anticommunism*, 1988; and again, William Appleman Williams, *The Tragedy of American Diplomacy*, 1962.

On Korea: William Manchester, *American Caesar: Douglas MacArthur*, 1978; G. D. Paige, *The Korean Decision*, 1968; and John W. Spanier, *The Truman–MacArthur Controversy*, 1965. McCarthyism and other manifestations of the red scare of the early 1950s are treated in David Caute, *The Great Fear: The Anti-Communist Purge under Truman and Eisenhower*, 1978; Stanley Cutler, *The American Inquisition*, 1982; Norman D. Markowitz, *Rise and Fall of the People's Century: Henry A. Wallace and American Liberalism, 1941–1948*, 1974; Victor Navasky, *Naming Names*, 1980; Thomas C. Reeves, *The Life and Times of Joe McCarthy*, 1982; Walter and Miriam Schneir, *Invitation to an Inquest*, 1972; and Allen Weinstein, *Perjury! The Hiss–Chambers Conflict*, 1978. American culture is covered in William Graebner, *The Age of Doubt*, 1995; and Paul Boyer, *By the Bomb's Early Light*, 1985.

The suburban communities that sprang up across the United States during the 1950s were characterized by rows of nearly identical single-family houses.

46
CHAPTER

EISENHOWER COUNTRY
American Life in the 1950s

I Like Ike.

— *Eisenhower Campaign Slogan, 1952*

I Still Like Ike.

— *Eisenhower Campaign Slogan, 1956*

904 Chapter 46 Eisenhower Country

The voters of 1952 wanted no upheaval. They wanted a change of pace. Most Americans accepted the inevitability of the ongoing Cold War with Communism, but they wanted an end to the stalemate in Korea. Most Americans approved of the basic reforms that the Roosevelt and Truman administrations had carried out; they did not want to return to the days of Coolidge and Hoover. After a generation of government by the Democratic party, however, they were ready for new faces in Washington.

Most of all, Americans wanted to cool off. They were weary of world-saving crusades—all the moral demands of reform and war. There was a sense of 1920 about the election of 1952, voters opting for a calmer, reassuring America in which they could savor the rewards of living in the world's richest nation.

LEADERSHIP

Reassurance is what Dwight D. Eisenhower gave them. The grinning, amiable Ike was a perfect regent. He kept the peace through two full terms in office. He replaced the jaded political pros, do-gooder intellectuals, and *apparatchik* liberal reformers of the Roosevelt-Truman era with cool-headed administrators like himself, and with the wealthy businessmen who had become his friends.

Ike's aides were neither colorful nor exciting. "Eight millionaires and a plumber," a scornful Democrat sniffed about Eisenhower's cabinet, and Secretary of Labor Martin Durkin, the leader of the AFL plumbers' union, resigned within a year of his appointment to be replaced by another rich businessman. When Congress created the cabinet-level Department of Health, Education, and Welfare, Eisenhower's choice to head it was not a social worker with a cause to serve, but Oveta Culp Hobby. She had been the no-nonsense head of the Women's Army Corps during the Second World War. She was an able military bureaucrat like Ike himself.

Ike's Style and Its Critics

Eisenhower's style was calculated to soothe. Rather than leaping into political catfights with claws flashing, which had been Truman's way, Ike sidled away from disputes and left the shouting to subordinates. His special assistant, Sherman Adams, former governor of New Hampshire, screened every person who applied to see the president. Adams turned away those who would aggravate Ike, involve him in a controversy, or trick him into making an embarrassing statement. Adams also studied every document that was to cross the president's desk, weeding out those he thought trivial and summarizing the rest. Except for western novels, his favored literature, Eisenhower disliked reading more than a page or so on any subject. He wanted to see briefs such as he had dealt with in the army, and ask questions about the additional information he believed he needed to know.

Critics claimed that Adams was more powerful than an appointed official should be. They said that he made many presidential-level decisions himself, and he probably did. But there was never any doubt that the flinty New Englander had Eisenhower's complete confidence. In 1958, when it was learned that Adams rigged some government decisions to favor a long-time friend, businessman Bernard Goldfine, and accepted at least an expensive coat from Goldfine in return, he was forced to resign his post. Eisenhower let him go, but he bitterly resented the loss of an aide who had served him so well.

The president delegated considerable power to the members of his cabinet. They were expected to study the details of issues, report to him, and, if they disagreed among themselves, to debate the question. Ike, the commander with ultimate responsibility, listened and handed down the decision. Whenever possible, he preferred compromise to choosing one obdurate adviser's position over another's. That was

---

Elevator Music

"Elevator music," deliberately bland background music played at low volume in restaurants, hotels, offices, shops—and elevators—is heard by 80 million Americans a day. It was originally called "furniture music" by its creator, a composer named Eric Satie, who said in 1920 that it would "fill the same role as light and heat—as *comfort*." Satie urged Americans, "Don't enter a house which does not have furniture music," but the concept caught on only after 1934, when the name "Muzak" was coined.

Muzak is played in the Pentagon and in the White House. President Lyndon Johnson pumped Muzak all over his ranch in Texas by mounting speakers on trees.

also how he had worked in London during the Second World War.

Liberal Democrats and intellectuals, outsiders in Washington during the 1950s, poked fun at what seemed Eisenhower's losing battle with the English language at press conferences. Never happy before large audiences, Eisenhower lapsed into gobbledygook under pressure. He spoke in disjointed phrases or his sentences meandered endlessly, trailing off in a scratch of the head without quite touching on the question he was asked. Some of Eisenhower's aides suggested that Ike knew exactly what he was doing when he appeared to be incoherent: he deliberately confused questioners when it did not suit him to answer them. They may well have been right; Eisenhower was quite a good writer. His memoir of the war, *Crusade in Europe*, was deservedly a best-seller.

Eisenhower's love of relaxation also aroused critics. The nation was drifting, they said, while Ike relaxed at his gentleman's farm on the battlefield at Gettysburg, and took too many vacations in climes where the golf courses were always green and the clubhouses air-conditioned.

> ### *Stupid Question, Stupid Answer*
>
> Eisenhower was at his best in confusing the press when a reporter asked him if he had been "lacking in courage and boldness" in dealing with an economic recession.
>
> *Listen, there is no courage or any extra courage that I know of to find out the right thing to do. Now it is not only necessary to do the right thing, but to do it in the right way and the only problem you have is what is the right way to do it. That is the problem. But this economy of ours is not so simple that it obeys to the opinion or bias or pronouncements of any particular individual, even to the president. This is an economy that is made up of 173 million people and it reflects their desires: they're ready to buy, they're ready to spend, it is a thing that is too complex and too big to be affected adversely or advantageously just by a few words or any particular—say a little this and that, or even a panacea so alleged.*

We're in the Money

But the critics never got through to the majority of Americans. People did not object to a president who took it easy. In 1956, when Ike ran for reelection against Adlai Stevenson, a year after suffering a serious heart attack and just a few months after undergoing major abdominal surgery, the voters re-elected him by an even larger margin than in 1952. Better easygoing Ike in questionable health than a healthy Stevenson forever calling on them to roll up their sleeves, right wrongs, and finish up the New Deal.

For a majority of Americans, the 1950s were good times, an age of unprecedented prosperity. There had not been a shift in the distribution of wealth. The poor remained about as numerous as they were for decades. The lowest-paid 20 percent of the population earned the same 3 to 4 percent of the national income that they earned during the 1920s. The very rich held on to their big slice of the economic pie: the wealthiest 20 percent of the population continued to enjoy 44 to 45 percent of the national income. Proportionately, therefore, the middle 60 percent of the population, the great American middle class, were no better off than before.

What made the difference in the 1950s was the size of the pie from which all were taking their slices. America was vastly richer as a result of the extraordinary economic growth of the Second World War decade.

Dwight D. Eisenhower, "Ike," personified America in the 1950s.

How They Lived

Fashion and the Fifties

In 1840, the British consul in Boston noted with distaste that Americans did not observe social propriety in the way they dressed. Instead of wearing clothes that were appropriate to their station in life, as an English gentleman thought should be done, Americans dressed more or less the same, and the democracy of dress did not mean a drabbest common denominator. On the contrary, servant girls were "strongly infected with the national bad taste for being over-dressed; they are, when walking the streets, scarcely to be distinguished from their employers." In other words, they were *fashionable*.

By the twentieth century, the democratization of fashion in the United States was complete. The wealthy had a monopoly of the latest from Paris for only as long as it took the American garment industry to copy designs and mass-produce cheap versions of expensive "originals." Indeed, the insistence of American women of almost every social class on their right to dress as the arbiters of fashion pleased accelerated the natural life cycle of a style. The only way the wealthy woman could conspicuously display her capability to spend freely was to move rapidly from one new look to another, always one frantic step ahead of the power shears and sewing machines of the New York garment district.

In 1940, very soon after the Great Depression, the American clothing industry was doing $3 billion in business annually. By the end of the 1950s, it was by some criteria the third largest industry in the United States. Also during those two decades, American dress designers established partial independence from Paris, the capital of fashion, but not from the social preoccupations and values that were neatly reflected in the garments they produced.

The fashions of the years of the Second World War were a product of four forces: the effective shutdown of the design business in occupied Paris; the rationing of materials; the unprecedented prominence of the military in daily life; and the entry of women into the professions and jobs previously held by men.

Because they had been so dependent on Paris for ideas, American fashion designers were disoriented by the fall of France and able on their own to come up with only a variant on the 1930s styles. One of the factors that forced some change was the government's restrictions on the amount of fabric that might go into clothing. Skirts could be no larger than 72 inches around. Belts more than two inches wide, more than one patch pocket on blouses, and generous hems were forbidden, as were frills, fringes, and flounces. The result was a severe look in women's dress, accentuated by the fact that with so many uniforms on

---

Thanks to New Deal tax reforms and the powerful labor unions that protected one worker in three, indirectly helping another third, Americans in the middle found themselves with a great deal of income for discretionary spending, money that was not required in order to provide the immediate necessities of life. In 1950, discretionary income totaled $100 billion compared with $40 billion in 1940. This sum increased steadily throughout the decade.

Traditional values of thrift and frugality dictated that such extra money be saved or invested. However, with a generation of daily denial behind them—the hard times of the Great Depression and the shortages of the Second World War—newly affluent Americans itched to spend their riches on goods and services that made life more comfortable, varied, and stimulating. A host of new consumer-oriented industries cropped up to urge them on.

Enjoy Yourself

"Enjoy yourself," a popular song went. "It's later than you think." Americans did. They lavished their extra money on a cornucopia of goods and

the streets, civilian clothing took on a military look. It also took on a "masculine look," according to fashion historians; the silhouette of women's clothing was straight and angular, with padded shoulders that emulated the male physique.

In 1947, Christian Dior, a Paris designer, reestablished French primacy in the fashion world. His "New Look" celebrated the end of wartime shortages with long, full, and flowing skirts. More interesting, Dior proclaimed a new femininity in fashion. "Your bosoms, your shoulders and hips are round, your waist is tiny, your skirt's bulk suggests fragile feminine legs," an American fashion editor wrote. Dior blouses were left unbuttoned at the top, and more formal bodices were cut in a deep V or cut low to expose shoulders.

The Frenchman either was very lucky or was a very shrewd psychologist. In the United States, the chief market for fashion in the postwar years, women were opting in droves for the home over the office, factory, and public life. As Betty Friedan would later explain, the new domesticity of the 1950s led to a halt and even a drop in the numbers of women entering the professions and other spheres that were traditionally the preserve of men.

But the domesticity of the 1950s was not the domesticity of a hundred years earlier. Thanks to labor-saving home appliances and the money to buy them, a yen for recreation after the austere years of rationing, and the steady relaxation of moral codes, the 1950s housewife was able to be "fashionable" to a degree previously open only to the doyennes of high society.

Another consequence of the new domesticity of the postwar years was the great baby boom, which in turn affected women's fashion. Just as the numerical dominance of young people led to the prominence of juvenile themes in films and popular music, the two-thirds of the female population that was under 30 years of age affected the way women dressed. "For the first time in fashion," wrote Jane Dormer, the British student of the subject, "clothes that had originally been intended for children climbed up the ladder into the adult wardrobe." While Dior and the Parisian couturiers continued to decree what was worn on formal occasions, American teenagers set the standards for casual wear, not only for themselves but for women of all but advanced age. The most conspicuous of these styles was that of the ingénue: "childlike circular skirts," crinolines, hoop skirts, frilled petticoats that were seen not only at junior high school dances but at cocktail parties on mothers of five. Girls and women began to wear their hair loose and flowing or in ponytails, both styles then closely associated with juveniles.

Hollywood both responded to and fed this kind of fashion by coming up with actresses such as Audrey Hepburn, Debbie Reynolds, and Sandra Dee, who specialized in innocent, naïve, little-girlish parts. Well into their thirties, these women clung to what clothing historian Anne Fogarty has called the "paper doll look." Not until the 1960s, when women adopted new values, would this fashion, like all fashions of another era, look ridiculous.

---

services—some trivial, some momentous in their cultural consequences, and most designed to amuse and entertain economically secure people in their spare time. The middle classes upgraded their diets, eating more meat and vegetables and fewer of the bulky, starchy bread and potatoes that sustained their parents. Mass-produced convenience foods such as frozen vegetables became staples of middle-class diet. If July-in-January came with a sacrifice of quality, frozen vegetables could be cooked in five or ten minutes, freeing people to enjoy additional leisure time.

Fashion in dress, buying clothes in order to be in style, became a diversion in which tens of millions rather than just a handful of very rich people could indulge. Mass-producers of clothing imitated the creations of Paris couturiers with affordable department store versions of "the latest." The designers encouraged the impulse to be a step ahead of neighbors by changing styles annually. In 1953, more people could identify and more or less explain the significance of Christian Dior (a French clothing designer) than the plumber in Eisenhower's cabinet.

Faddism

The 1950s were a good time for fads, frivolous behavior in which people participated for no better reason than they could afford to do so and others already were. In late 1954, a Walt Disney television program about the nineteenth-century frontiersman and politician Davy Crockett inspired a mania for coonskin caps (usually made from rabbit, cat, or even synthetic fur), lunch boxes decorated with pictures of Davy shooting bears, and plastic "long rifles" and bowie knives reasonably safe for use in backyard Alamos. Virtually any homely object with the magic name of Crockett printed on it became a best-seller. In less than a year, Americans bought 10 million coonskin caps and spent $100 million overall in commemoration of a Tennessee adventurer and Whig politician a hundred years dead.

In 1958, a toy manufacturer brought out a plastic version of an Australian exercise device, a hoop that was twirled about the hips by means of hula-like gyrations. Almost overnight, 30 million "hula hoops" were sold for $1.98, and 100 million within six months. Four converted Wham-O factories (a "Wham-O" was a wooden paddle with a rubber ball attached by means of a rubber band) could not keep up with demand and at least two instances of parents highjacking trucks carrying hula hoops were reported.

Within a year, the hoops could be had for as little as 50 cents. A more durable product was Mattel Corporation's "Barbie," an anatomically not-quite-correct doll of a voluptuous young woman in her physical prime. About ten inches high, Barbie was herself a voracious consumer, the very ideal of the 1950s. The parents of her preteen owners purchased so much clothing and accessories for Barbie that Mattel was soon the nation's fourth largest manufacturer of "women's clothing" with nine full-time designers on the payroll. Barbie was no fad. Fifty years later, in numerous incarnations, she was still a best-selling toy.

To some extent, the numerous manias of the 1950s were instigated and promoted by the advertising industry. For example, a chemical compound, chlorophyll, became the rage of the early 1950s when manufacturers of more than 90 products, ranging from chewing gum through dog food, said that the green stuff improved the odor of the breath and body of those who ate it, chewed it, shampooed or bathed with it, and rubbed it into the armpits. Americans responded by spending $135 million on chlorophyll products. The boom may have busted when the American Medical Association pointed out that goats, notoriously hard on the nose, consumed chlorophyll all day, every day. More likely, as with all fads, chlorophyll simply ran its course.

Other fads profited no one but the newspapers and magazines that reported them. College students competed to see how many of them could squeeze into a telephone booth or a minuscule Volkswagen automobile, challenging others to top their record. Such behavior worried social critics. They concluded that inane faddism revealed the emptiness of lives based on material consumption: people defined themselves in terms of what they could buy. Others were distressed by the conformism of which fads were only the most bizarre example. The American people, it seemed, would do anything and think anything that they were told to do and think, or that others were doing and thinking. But they were afraid of the eccentric, the unpopular, and the adventurous.

The Boob Tube

The most significant new consumer bauble of the 1950s, to become a major force for conformism, was the home television receiver. Developed in workable form as early as 1927, and introduced as a broadcast medium in 1939, "radio with a picture" remained a toy of electronics hobbyists and the very wealthy until after the Second World War. In 1946, there were only 8,000 privately owned TV sets in the United States, about one for every 18,000 people. Marketing the receivers was geared to elegant buyers.

Then, gambling that middle-class Americans were ready to spend their extra money on a new kind of entertainment, the radio networks plunged into television, making more extensive programming

Television in America

	Number of TV Households	Percentage of American Homes with TV
1945	5,000	—
1950	3,880,000	9.0
1955	30,700,000	64.5
1960	45,750,000	87.1
1970	59,550,000	95.2
1978	72,900,000	98.0

available. Manufacturers of sets, like Dumont, peddled their product as a healthy social innovation: "There is great happiness in the home where the family is held together by this new common bond—Television!"

By 1950, almost 4 million sets had been sold, one for every 32 people in the country. By 1960, the skeletons of obsolete small-screen receivers were conspicuous in dumps even in rural states. By 1970, more American households were equipped with a television set than had refrigerators, bathtubs, or indoor toilets. Rarely in history did a whole society fall so suddenly and hopelessly in love with a device.

At first, high-minded network executives and retooled radio reporters such as Edward R. Murrow hoped that television would be an agent of education and uplift. Corporations making consumer products agreed, and sponsored programs bringing serious plays, both classics and dramas written especially for television, to the small screen. Playwrights such as Paddy Chayefsky and Rod Serling got their start writing for shows such as *Playhouse Ninety* and *Studio One*.

But American television, like American radio, was a private enterprise that depended on advertisers for its profits, and advertisers soon learned that a mass audience wanted light entertainment. Americans made a multimillionaire of "Mr. Television," Milton Berle, who had been but a fair-to-middling burlesque comic and occasional Hollywood clown. Rather more remarkable, a New York gossip columnist utterly lacking in a stage personality, Ed Sullivan, became a national celebrity by hosting a variety show that surrounded one celebrity singer or comedian with trained dog acts, trained bird acts, trained seal acts, and ventriloquists.

> ### *Television and the Movies*
> In 1946, 82 million Americans went to the movies each week. Ten years later, only about half that many did. The others were at home watching television.

Cowboys and Quiz Shows

Beginning in 1955, Americans watched westerns. The networks launched about 40 different dramas set in an imaginary Wild West and, by 1957, one-third of television prime time, the evening hours between suppertime and bedtime, was devoted to horses, sheriffs, badmen, and saloon girls with hearts of gold. In New York City, with seven channels, it was possible to watch 51 western shows a week, in Los Angeles 64 hours of westerns each week.

One of the first, *Gunsmoke*, ran through 635 episodes; it was estimated that one-quarter of the world's population saw at least one program in which Marshall Matt Dillon made Dodge City, Kansas, safe for decent law-abiding citizens. Another popular show, *Death Valley Days*, revived the career of actor Ronald Reagan, and set him off on a trail that led to the White House.

Late in the decade, quiz shows offering huge prizes—$64,000 and up—caught the popular imagination. Millions watched avidly as intense intellectuals and idiot savants rattled off the names of opera characters and kings of Poland. Then, in 1959, it was revealed that Charles Van Doren, a Columbia University professor and scion of a distinguished academic family, had been fed the correct answers before broadcasts of *The $64,000 Question*. He agonized like a soap opera heroine on camera as he pretended to retrieve some obscure morsel of knowledge from deep within his brain. Intellectuals said they were shocked by Van Doren's betrayal of academic

Children born in the 1940s and 1950s were the first generation of Americans to grow up with television.

Disneyland

Neither television nor any other competitor kept Americans from flocking to Disneyland, a slick, glossy, squeaky-clean amusement park that opened in Anaheim, California, on July 17, 1955. By 1958, annual admissions to the "Magic Kingdom" exceeded visitors to Yellowstone, Yosemite, and Grand Canyon National Parks combined. By 1965, one-fourth of the population of the United States (statistically) had gone to Disneyland.

integrity. Many quiz shows went off the air. Ordinary folks just changed the channel. *Gunsmoke* was still going strong, although its writers admitted some strain in coming up with plots. "We've used up de Maupassant," said one, "and we're halfway through Maugham."

Social and Cultural Consequences

The social and cultural consequences of America's marriage to "the tube" are still not fully appreciated. In the short run, television seemed to kill off other kinds of popular entertainment such as the movies, social dancing, and radio. Hollywood studios that specialized in churning out low-budget films went bankrupt when empty neighborhood theaters closed their doors. However, prestigious movie companies such as Metro-Goldwyn-Mayer, Columbia Pictures, and Warner Brothers survived and prospered by concentrating on expensive, grandiose epics that could not be duplicated on the small black-and-white home screen; by experimenting with themes that were thought unsuitable for showing in homes; and, beginning in the 1960s, accepting the inevitable and producing shows for television. (In the 1990s, several Hollywood studios founded their own networks, trading in precisely the mass-production of lowbrow programs for which they had disdained TV in the 1950s.)

The big bands that had toured the country playing for local dances since the 1930s broke up when deserted dance halls closed. But the recorded music industry survived in the age of television by emphasizing individual ballad singers, such as Perry Como, Jo Stafford, Patti Page, Tony Bennett, and Frankie Laine, who promoted sales of their recordings on television. Radio stations adapted to the big change by scrapping the dramatic and comedy shows that

television could do with pictures, and offering instead a format of music, news, and weather aimed at people who were driving their cars or working and could not, during those hours, watch television.

Curiously, the "one-eyed monster" did not much change the reading habits of older Americans. Americans were soon staring into the flickering blue light for three hours a day. However, the time they devoted to magazines and newspapers declined very little, and purchases of books, particularly cheap paperback editions, rose 53 percent over what they had been during the 1940s.

What older Americans cut out in order to watch TV was socializing with one another. Instead of evening chats with neighbors or with other members of their families, instead of meeting at dances, clubs, soda fountains, even outside the movie theater, Americans barricaded themselves in their homes, hushing up and resenting all interruptions. The frozen food industry invented the "TV dinner," a complete meal that could be put in and taken out of the oven during commercials or station breaks and eaten in silence in front of the set on a "TV table," a metal tray on folding legs, one for each member of the nuclear family, perhaps an extra one or two for when grandparents, equally agog before the tube, paid a visit.

Fears for the Future

Rather more worrisome was the passive enthusiasm with which children born in the television age were addicted to the tube. Networks and local stations filled late-afternoon hours and much of Saturday and Sunday mornings with programs aimed at children and avidly sponsored by toy makers and manufacturers of breakfast cereals and sweets. If adults who grew up before the advent of television continued to read, children did not. In 1955, a book by Rudolf Fleisch called *Why Johnny Can't Read* presented Americans with disturbing evidence that they were raising a generation of functional illiterates.

Nevertheless, and regardless of class, race, occupation, or region, Americans took television to their hearts. For good or ill, they were exposed at the same moment to the same entertainment, commercials, and even speech patterns. National businesses discovered that they could compete with local merchants thanks to the hypnotic influence of television advertising.

Because the network and even local news programs preferred announcers who spoke standard

"Mad Man" Muntz

Just as has happened when other completely new consumer goods attracted the fancy of Americans—automobiles, radio receivers, miniaturized calculators, computers—the early television industry was a competitive free-for-all, with dozens of manufacturers hoping to establish themselves as giants of the industry. One of the most intriguing companies was Muntz TV, which promoted its inexpensive sets as if the item were a dubious gadget being hawked at a county fair. "Mad Man" Muntz said that he got his name—he said it on TV as well as on billboards and in magazine advertisements—because he wanted to give his sets away but his wife wouldn't let him, "She says I'm crazy." Also, as in the cases of radios, calculators, and computers, the era of all-out competition passed. After the "shake-out," a comparatively few TV set manufacturers remained, mostly old, large electronics makers. In their turn they were displaced by Japanese imports in the 1970s.

American English, regional variations in speech declined. City people and country people, who were sharply divided by hostile worldviews in the previous generation, came to look, speak, and think alike. However, neither country folk nor city folk set the cultural tone of the age of Eisenhower. The people who did were pioneers of a new kind of American community, the middle-class suburb.

SUBURBIA AND ITS VALUES

The essence of the good life, to Americans of the 1950s, was to escape from the cities (and the country) and set up housekeeping in single-home dwellings in the suburbs. In part, this massive movement of population in the late 1940s and 1950s was a vestigial expression of an antiurban bias that dates back to the nation's rural beginnings.

Flight from the Cities

In part, young couples of the postwar period had little choice as to where they would live. The Second World War forced millions of them to delay marrying and starting a family for up to four years. In 1945 and 1946, they rushed into marriage, childbearing, and searching for a place to live. But because of the stagnation of the domestic construction industry during the Depression and the war, when young couples looked for housing in the cities, they found impossibly high rents and real estate prices.

To demolish old neighborhoods as the first step of new construction meant temporarily aggravating an already critical housing shortage. The solution was the rapid development of entirely new tracts or subdivisions on the outskirts of cities, far enough from the centers that the price of land was cheap, but close enough that breadwinners could get to their jobs. Of the 1 million housing starts in 1946 and the 2 million in 1950 (compared with 142,000 in 1944), the vast majority were in the suburbs.

The first of the great suburban developments was Levittown, New York, the brainchild of a family company that adapted the assembly line to home building. In order to keep the selling prices low, the Levitt brothers used cheap materials and only a few different blueprints. The houses of suburbia were identical, constructed all at once and very quickly. Armies of workers swarmed over the tract, grading thousands of acres at a sweep, and laying out miles of gently curving streets within a few days. Practically before they were done, battalions of men laid down water, gas, sewer, and electrical lines, while teams of carpenters erected hundreds of simple, identical shells.

Then came waves of roofers, plumbers, electricians, carpet layers, painters, decorators, and other craftsmen, each finishing their specialized task on a given house within hours or even minutes. Buyers were so anxious to move in that they were happy to take care of the cleaning up and landscaping themselves. Within four years, Levittown, New York, was transformed from a potato farm into a city of 17,000 homes. On the outskirts of most large cities, developers who imitated the Levitts worked similar miracles. The population of suburbs, never more than a small fraction of the whole, soared. By 1960, as many Americans lived in suburbs as in large cities.

Conformists . . . ?

In the age of McCarthyism, William Levitt found it easy to impute profound political portent to mass-produced housing. "No man who owns his own

912 *Chapter 46 Eisenhower Country*

home and lot," he said, "can be a communist. He has too much to do."

There was something to Levitt's linking of home ownership and conservative conformism. No sooner did suburbia take shape than it attracted social and cultural criticism. Novelists and sociologists pointed out that the population of the new communities was distressingly homogeneous: 95 percent white, young (20 to 35 years old), married couples with infant children, all of whom made roughly the same income from similar skilled and white-collar jobs.

Not only did the flight from the city center leave urban centers to the elderly, the poor, and the racial minorities—an implausible tax base—but it segregated the suburbanites too, cutting them off from interaction with other ages, classes, and races of people. Homogeneous communities were narrow-minded communities, critics said; suburbia's values were timid, bland, and superficial.

In politics, people whose comforts and security were made possible by New Deal reforms were afraid to experiment. The suburbanites were staunch supporters of the Eisenhower equilibrium. They swelled the membership lists of churches and synagogues, but insisted on easy, undisturbing beliefs. Rabbi Joshua Liebman, Catholic Bishop Fulton J. Sheen, and the Reverend Norman Vincent Peale tacitly (sometimes explicitly) told the people of the three major faiths that the purpose of religion was to make them feel good: they, in effect, were at the center of the universe. The Reverend Billy Graham established himself as the country's leading revivalist by shunning the fire and brimstone of earlier evangelists. A survey of Christians showed that while 80 percent believed that the Bible was the revealed word of God, only 35 percent could name the authors of the four Christian gospels and 50 percent could not name one. Among Jews, highly secular and social Reform Judaism displaced Conservative Judaism. Outside of urban communities of Jews who clung to Polish and Russian pasts, Orthodox synagogues were hard to find.

Suburban life was isolated and fragmented, in part because of television, in part because the new communities were built with little thought for social services—schools, shops, parks, and professional offices. When such traditional social centers were constructed, they were miles from residences; thus suburbanites had to drive some distance even to buy so little as a quart of milk. As a result, the suburban single-family dwelling became a kind of fortress that residents left only to hop into a car and drive somewhere else and back again. The supermarkets encouraged weekly rather than daily shopping expeditions, thus eliminating another traditional occasion of social life.

. . . Or Social Pioneers?

Such criticisms made little impression on the people at whom they were aimed. Suburbanites wanted homes they could afford, and they found the physical roominess of life outside the cities well worth the social isolation and cultural blandness. If the houses were cheaply constructed and identical, they were far better than no houses.

Moreover, the new suburbanites, thrown into brand-new towns with no roots and traditions, were great creators of institutions. Lacking established social services and governments, they formed an intricate network of voluntary associations that were entirely supported by private funds and energies. There were the churches and synagogues built from scratch, thousands of new chapters of political parties, garden clubs, literary societies, and bowling leagues. Most important of all were programs that revolved around their children: dancing schools, Cub Scouts and Brownies, little leagues, and community swimming pools.

Since everyone was a stranger in town, the informal cocktail party became an efficient means by which to introduce people to one another. Because guests milled around the stand-up parties at will, it was not awkward to invite the most casual supermarket or little league grandstand acquaintances to come on over. Alcohol lubricated easy conversation among strangers, and statisticians noticed a change in American drinking habits toward the consumption of neutral spirits such as gin and vodka, which could be disguised in sweet soda pop or fruit juices. The conclusion was that people who did not like to drink were drinking to make themselves more comfortable and because it was the thing to do.

Insolent Chariots

The suburb could not have existed without the readily available family automobile. In turn, the growth of suburbia made the automobile king, a necessity of life and in some ways a tyrant. Each family needed a car because suburbanites worked at some distance from their homes and public transportation to many of the new communities did not exist. Because it was necessary for a suburban housewife and mother to cover considerable distances each day, the two-car family became a common phenomenon: one suburban family in five owned two vehicles.

Sales of new cars rose from none during the Second World War to 6.7 million in 1950, and continued to maintain high levels throughout the 1950s. In 1945, there were 25.8 million automobiles registered in the United States. By 1960, with the population increased by 35 percent, car ownership more than doubled, to 61.7 million vehicles.

The automobile was the most important means by which people displayed their status. Unlike the size of paychecks and bank accounts, the family car showed; it sat in the driveway for all to see. Automobile manufacturers devised and encouraged finely honed images for their chariots. The family that was "moving up" was expected to trade up from a low-priced Ford, Plymouth, or "Chevy" to a Dodge, Pontiac, or Mercury, and aspire to eventual ownership of a Chrysler, Lincoln, or Cadillac. Indeed, the easy availability of credit made it possible for people to "keep up with the Joneses" by buying beyond their means, going deeply into debt for the sake of appearances. From 1946 through 1970, short-term loans—money borrowed in order to buy consumer goods—increased from $8 billion to $127 billion!

The Automobile Economy

Virtually universal car ownership among the middle classes fueled the growth of businesses devoted to cars or dependent on them. Service stations (gasoline consumption doubled during the 1950s), parts stores, car washes, motels, drive-in restaurants, and drive-in movie theaters blossomed on the outskirts of residential suburbs. The suburban shopping mall rivaled city and town centers as the middle-class American marketplace. In 1945, there were eight automobile-oriented shopping centers in the United States. In 1960, there were almost 4,000.

Automobiles demanded roads. In 1956, Washington responded with the Interstate Highway Act, under which the government began pumping a total of $1 billion a year into road construction. (By 1960, this expenditure rose to $2.9 billion a year.) Over 41,000 miles of new roads ran cross-country, but

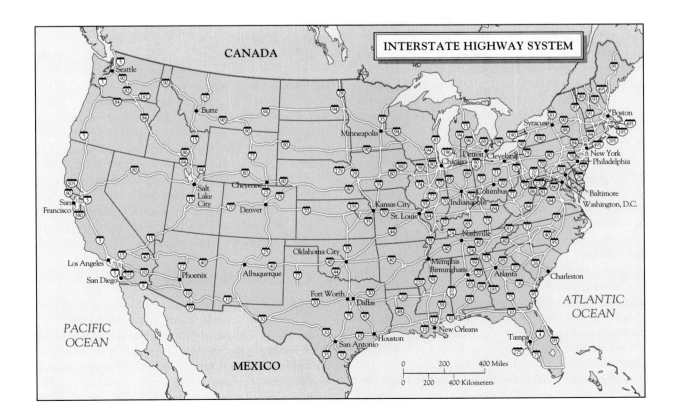

5,000 miles of freeway were urban, connecting suburbs to big cities.

Not only did this road network encourage further urban sprawl, but it made the cities less livable. Already sapped of their middle classes, once lively urban neighborhoods were carved into isolated residential islands that were walled off from one another by the massive concrete abutments of the freeways. Suburbanite cars roared in on them daily, clogging the streets, raising noise to unprecedented levels, and fouling the air for those who could not afford to move out. Progressively poorer without a middle-class tax base, cities deteriorated physically and suffered from neglected schools and hospitals and rising crime rates. During the 1960s, faced with these problems, the center city department stores and light industries joined the suburban movement, relocating in shopping centers or on empty tracts near the residential suburbs. When they left, they took not only their tax contributions, but jobs previously available to city dwellers.

Baby Boom

During and immediately after the Second World War, the number of births in the United States took a gigantic leap. While about 2.5 million babies were born in each year of the 1930s, 3.4 million saw the light of day in 1946 and 3.8 million in 1947. Population experts expected this. The Depression and war had forced young couples to put off starting families. After a few years of catching up, demographers said, the low birthrate typical of the first half of the century would reassert itself.

They were wrong. The annual number of births continued to increase until 1961 (4.2 million) and did not drop to lower levels until the 1970s. The same young couples who were buying unprecedented numbers of new homes and automobiles were having larger families than their parents.

Although all social groups participated in the "baby boom," children were most noticeable in suburbia, where, because most adults were young, children were proportionately more significant. Beginning about 1952, when the first boom babies started school, massive efforts were required to provide educational and recreational facilities for them. Businesses oriented toward children, from toy makers to diaper services, sprouted and bloomed.

As the boom babies matured, they attracted attention to the needs and demands of each age group

they swelled. By the end of the 1950s, economists observed that middle-class teenagers were a significant consumer group in their own right. They had $10 billion of their own to spend each year, and all of it was discretionary! Their necessities were provided by their doting parents.

Magazines that appealed to young people prospered, including *Seventeen* (clothing and cosmetics for girls) and *Hot Rod* (automobiles for boys). Film studios made movies about adolescents and their problems. Beginning in the early 1950s, a new kind of popular music swept the country. Rock 'n' roll was based on the rhythms of black music as it evolved in the mid-twentieth century, but was usually performed by whites, often teenagers themselves. On the one hand, it was rebellious. Elvis Presley, a truck driver from Memphis, scandalized the country with an act that included suggestive hip movements which he said (probably truthfully) he was helpless to control. On the other hand, it was juvenile. Whereas popular songs previously dealt with themes that were more or less adult, the new music's subjects were high school senior proms, double-dating, and teenage lovers lost tragically while racing to beat the Twentieth Century Limited to the crossing. A new kind of record, the compact and nearly unbreakable 45-rpm disk that sold for only 89 cents, became a medium of competition for teenage dollars.

What worried social critics was that older people, seemingly outnumbered by the young, often adopted adolescent ideals and role models. By the end of the decade, one of television's most popular programs was *American Bandstand*, an afternoon show on which teenagers rock 'n' rolled to recorded music and discussed adolescent problems. Adolescents watched it, of course, but so did housewives at their irons and kitchen sinks. Adults discussed the relative merits of their favorite pubescent dancers. Never before had adult society taken much notice of teenage culture. The baby-boom generation seemed to be proclaiming the society's cultural standards.

A New Role for Women

Middle-class America's twin obsessions with enjoying life and catering to its children caused a significant, if temporary, shift in the status of women. Since the beginning of the century, women of all social classes had been moving into occupations and professions that previously were considered masculine monopolies. Throughout the 1940s, increasing numbers of women finished high school, attended college, studied medicine, the law, and other professions, and took jobs that would have been unthinkable for women before 1900. The Second World War seemed to hasten this blurring of the lines between what the two sexes could do as women took the place of men in heavy and dirty industrial jobs.

When the war ended, however, many women willingly left those jobs and enthusiastically embraced the traditional roles of wife, homemaker, and mother. By the 1950s, middle America once more assumed that woman's place was in the home. However, the new woman was not the shrinking violet of the nineteenth century. If she was not employed, the woman of the 1950s was constantly out and about, the backbone of an active social whirl. Because the moral code that required that women be sequestered had long since withered, the modern American girl, wife, and mother were expected to be active and attractive.

Wives were considered partners in furthering their husbands' careers as sociable hostesses and companions. Women's magazines such as *Cosmopolitan* and *Redbook* first hinted, then shouted that wives should be "sexy."

Sexiness also got a boost from two books published by University of Indiana Professor Alfred Kinsey, *Sexual Behavior in the Human Male* (1948) and *Sexual Behavior in the Human Female* (1953). Although Kinsey studiously dressed the conclusions of some 18,000 interviews in scientific language, his revelation that premarital and extramarital sexual intercourse, unorthodox sexual practices, and homosexuality were fairly common made for sensational reading and discussion.

The ideal of American womanhood in the 1950s was the loving mother and homemaker.

916 *Chapter 46 Eisenhower Country*

Kinsey was condemned as a promoter of immoral and unnatural practices and unspeakable acts, and even of encouraging Communism, a ubiquitous accusation during the 1950s. His methods also came under attack from fellow researchers, and the fact that he described as "human" behavior findings based on a rather narrow segment of humanity: white, generally middle-class America. But that was humanity in suburbia, and white middle-class Americans were the people who bought and read his books and, no doubt, were often inspired by them. Only half a century later would it be discovered that Kinsey was not quite the detached observer of sexual practices that he claimed to be.

AGAINST THE GRAIN

There would be no significant challenge to the new sexy domesticity until 1963, when Betty Friedan published *The Feminine Mystique*. In this best-seller, Friedan pointed out that American women had lost ground in their fight for emancipation since 1945. She depicted the home as a prison, woman as sex object as demeaning, and said that women should move out into the world of jobs, politics, and other realms that she defined as productive. Criticism of other aspects of the culture of the 1950s, however, was widespread even during the age of Eisenhower.

Dissenters

As early as 1942, Philip Wylie's *Generation of Vipers* told the country that indulgence of children, particularly by their mothers ("Momism"), was creating tyrannical monsters. When juvenile delinquency rates soared during the 1950s, even in the well-to-do suburbs, other writers elaborated on Wylie. John Keats attacked the sterility of suburban life, especially the social irresponsibility of the developers who left new developments without vital social centers. Later, in *Insolent Chariots*, he turned his attention to the automobile as an economic tyrant and a socially destructive force.

In *The Organization Man* (1956), William H. Whyte, Jr., fastened on the workplace, arguing that jobs in the huge corporations and government bureaucracies that dominated the American economy placed the highest premium on anonymity, lack of imagination and enterprise, and generally just fitting in. Sociologist David Riesman suggested in *The Lonely Crowd* (1950) that Americans were becoming "other-directed." They no longer took their values from their heritage or their parents, least of all from within themselves, but thought and acted according to what was acceptable to those around them.

Sloan Wilson fictionalized the conformism and cultural aridity of suburban life in *The Man in the Gray Flannel Suit* (1955), a novel about a suburban commuter who works in the advertising industry. In *The Hidden Persuaders* (1957), Vance Packard reinforced the assault on advertising by pointing out that all Americans were manipulated by advertisements that played not on the virtues of the product for sale but on people's feelings and insecurities.

Beatniks and Squares

The beat generation, or "beatniks" as people called its exemplars, offered a less articulate critique of Eisenhower tranquility. Originally a literary movement centered around novelist Jack Kerouac and poet Allen Ginsberg, "beat" evolved into a bohemian lifestyle with capitals in New York's Greenwich Village, San Francisco's North Beach, and Venice, California, near Los Angeles.

Beatniks rebelled against what they considered to be the intellectually and socially stultifying aspects of 1950s America. They shunned mainstream employment. They took no interest in politics and public life. They mocked the American enchantment with consumer goods by dressing in T-shirts and rumpled khaki trousers, the women innocent of cosmetics and the intricate hairstyles of suburbia. They made a great deal of the lack of furniture in their cheap walk-up apartments, calling their homes "pads" after the mattress on the floor.

The beatniks were highly intellectual. They prided themselves on discovering and discussing obscure writers and philosophers, particularly exponents of an abstruse form of Buddhism called Zen. They rejected the ostensibly strict sexual morality of the "squares" and lived together without benefit of marriage; a few were homosexual or dabbled in homosexual practices. Their music was jazz as played by blacks, whom they regarded as free of the corruptions of white America.

Beatniks simultaneously repelled, amused, and fascinated conventional American society. Traditional moralists demanded that police raid beatnik coffeehouses in search of marijuana (which beatniks

A "beatnik" coffeehouse of the 1950s. The fare was black coffee, unfiltered cigarettes, jazz, the reading of poetry, and (not so openly) marijuana.

introduced to white America) and amateur poets reading sexually explicit verse. Preachers in the traditional churches inveighed against the moral decay that the beatniks represented.

But sexual mores were changing in suburbia, too. To be divorced was no longer to be shunned as a moral pariah. The courts approved the publication of books formerly banned as obscene, with celebrated cases revolving around D. H. Lawrence's *Lady Chatterley's Lover* and Henry Miller's *Tropic of Cancer.* The furor over Ginsberg's long poem *Howl* (1955), which included a few racy lines, made it a best-seller. Suburbanites, the favorite targets of beat mockery, flocked to Greenwich Village and North Beach on weekends to dabble in beatnik fashions. Like most cultural rebels, the beatniks did not really challenge society's basic assumptions. They merely provided another form of entertainment.

The Awakening of Black America

The protest against racial discrimination was an altogether different matter. Rather than sniping at trivialities such as lifestyle, America's blacks during the 1950s demonstrated to whites that the mansion they built included a cellar in which civil rights were systematically denied to 15 million people.

For more than half a century, black leaders such as W. E. B. Du Bois, Mary McLeod Bethune, A. Philip Randolph, and Bayard Rustin fought a frustrating battle against racial prejudice. Their most important organization, the National Association for the Advancement of Colored People, won some significant victories in the courts. Lynching, once a weekly occurrence in the South and only rarely punished, almost disappeared in the 1950s. Under Truman, the armed forces were desegregated (black recruits were no longer placed in all-black units), and the Supreme Court ordered several southern states to admit blacks to state-supported professional schools because the segregated medical and legal training they offered blacks was not equal in quality to that provided for whites.

Nevertheless, when Eisenhower moved into the White House, all the former slave states plus Oklahoma retained laws on the books that segregated parks, movie theaters, waiting rooms, trains, buses, and schools. Four more states legally permitted one form or another of racial segregation. (Fifteen states explicitly prohibited it.)

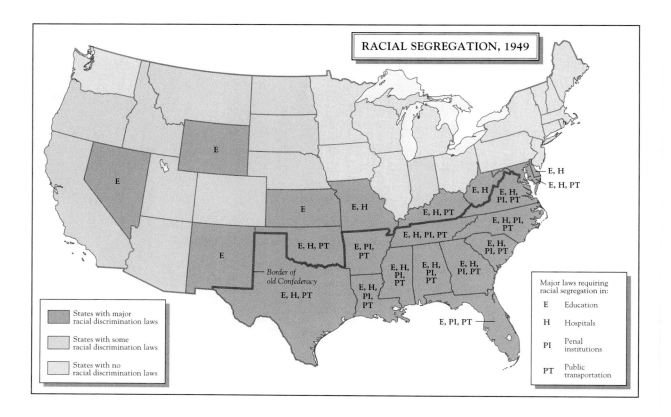

In the Deep South, public drinking fountains were labeled "white" and "colored," and some states actually provided different Bibles in court for the swearing in of witnesses. This strict color line had had federal sanction since 1896, when, in the case of *Plessy v. Ferguson*, the Supreme Court declared that racially separate public facilities were constitutional as long as they were equal in quality. This was rarely the case. In education, for example, few school districts provided the same quality facilities and education to black children as they did to white. In the late 1940s, for example, West Memphis spent $144 per year on each white pupil, $20 on each African-American child.

The Brown Case

Still, it was the doctrine of "separate but equal" that the NAACP and other African-American groups wanted to correct, not the violation of it. In 1954, Thurgood Marshall, the NAACP's legal strategist, argued before the Supreme Court that racially separate educational facilities were intrinsically unequal because segregation burdened blacks with a constant reminder of their inequality. In *Brown* v. *Board of Education of Topeka* (1954), the court unanimously agreed.

In many parts of the South, school administrators complied quickly and without incident. Southern white distaste for Jim Crow was quiet, but it did exist. However, in Little Rock, Arkansas, in September 1957, an angry mob of white adults greeted the first black pupils to enroll in Central High School with shouts, curses, and rocks. Claiming that he was protecting the peace, but actually currying the favor of white racists, Governor Orval Faubus called out the Arkansas National Guard to prevent the black children from enrolling.

Eisenhower blamed the turmoil on both Earl Warren, the new chief justice, and Orval Faubus. Sharing the belief of many Americans that there was no great harm done by segregation, Eisenhower regarded the *Brown* decision as a mistake. If nothing else, by arousing black Americans to protest, it disturbed the tranquility that Ike treasured, and he did not believe that laws could change people's feelings. He later said that his appointment of Earl Warren to the Supreme Court was the worst decision that he had ever made.

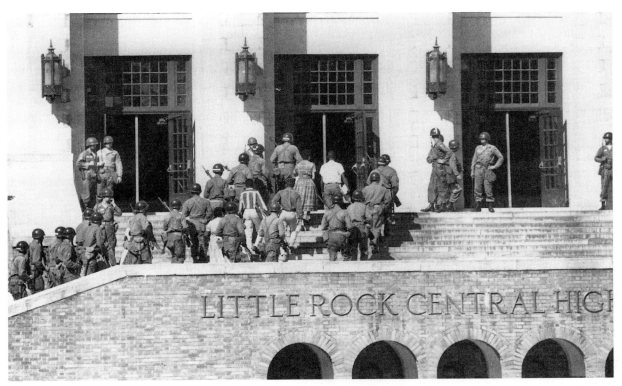
Little Rock, Arkansas, became the center of the nation's attention when it took the National Guard to enroll African-American students in the city's white Central High.

Nevertheless, the Supreme Court had spoken and Ike was a constitutionalist. To him, the court's ruling had the force of federal law, and Faubus was defying it. Eisenhower superseded the governor's command of the National Guard and ordered a thousand paratroopers to Little Rock to enforce the integration of Central High. Overnight, the mission of the Arkansas National Guard was reversed.

From the Courts to the Streets

The battle to integrate the schools continued for a decade. Beginning in 1955, however, the civil rights movement ceased to be a protest of lawyers and lawsuits and became a peaceful revolution by hundreds of thousands of blacks who were no longer willing to be second-class citizens.

The leader of the upheaval was Martin Luther King Jr., a young preacher in Montgomery, Alabama. In December 1955, Rosa Parks, a black seamstress, refused to give up her seat on a bus to a white man, as city law required, and King became the spokesman for a black boycott of the Montgomery buses. When the city tried to defend the color line, the dispute attracted journalists and television reporters from all over the country.

King's house was bombed, and he explained his strategy for ending racial discrimination from the wreckage of his front porch. Nonviolent civil disobedience, King said, meant refusing to obey morally reprehensible laws such as those that sustained segregation, but without violence. When arrested, protesters should not resist. Not only was this the moral course of action—King hated violence of all kinds—but it was politically effective. When decent people were confronted with the sight of southern police officers brutalizing peaceful blacks and their white supporters simply because they demanded their rights as citizens, they would, King believed, force politicians to support civil rights.

Although it led to considerable suffering by demonstrators and to several deaths, King's strategy worked. A few important labor leaders such as Walter Reuther of the United Automobile Workers marched with the young minister and helped finance the Southern Christian Leadership Conference

920 Chapter 46 Eisenhower Country

(SCLC), which King founded to spearhead the fight for equality. After 1960, when SCLC's youth organization, the Student Nonviolent Coordinating Committee (SNCC) peacefully violated laws that prohibited blacks from eating at lunch counters in the South, white university students in the North picketed branches of the offending chain stores in their hometowns. When white mobs burned a bus on which white and black "freedom riders" were defying segregation, the federal government sent marshals south to investigate and prosecute violent white racists.

Although King fell out of favor with some younger blacks in the late 1960s, he loomed over his era as only President Eisenhower did. After his assassination in 1968, several states made his birthday a holiday, and in 1986 it became an official federal holiday. But King and black Americans only began their fight for equality during the age of Eisenhower. It was the next decade, the troubled 1960s, which saw the end of civil discrimination on the basis of race.

CHRONOLOGY

1954 "Davy Crockett" merchandizing mania demonstrates the centrality of television to American culture

In *Brown* v. *Board of Education of Topeka*, Supreme Court declares racial segregation in schools unconstitutional

1955 African-American boycott of segregated bus system in Montgomery, Alabama, brings the Rev. Martin Luther King Jr. to national prominence

1956 Eisenhower easily defeats Stevenson for re-election to presidency
Interstate Highway Act inaugurates American interstate highway system

1958 Eisenhower loses valued aide Sherman Adams after revelations Adams had accepted gifts from a wealthy businessman

1959 Popular television quiz shows exposed as "fixed," leading to television's first major scandal

1961 "Baby Boom" births peak at 4.2 million

1963 Publication of Betty Friedan's *Feminine Mystique* signals beginning of a new wave of feminism

FOR FURTHER READING

Solid general histories of the period include C. C. Alexander, *Holding the Line: The Eisenhower Era, 1952–1961*, 1975; James Gilbert, *Another Chance: America since 1945*, 1984; Godfrey Hodgson, *America in Our Time: From World War II to Nixon*, 1976; William E. Leuchtenburg, *A Troubled Feast: American Society since 1945*, 1979; William L. O'Neill, *American High: The Years of Confidence, 1945–1960*, 1987; and especially James Patterson, *Grand Expectations*, 1996; and Warren I. Cohen, *America in the Age of Soviet Power, 1945–1991*, 1993.

The following books are good on American society in the 1950s: Daniel Boorstin, *The Image*, 1962; John Kenneth Galbraith, *The Affluent Society*, 1958; William Chafe, *The American Woman: Her Changing Social, Economic, and Political Roles*, 1988; Paul Goodman, *Growing Up Absurd*, 1960; Eugenia Kaledin, *Mothers and More: American Women in the 1950s*, 1984; E. Larrabee, *The Self-Conscious Society*, 1960; David Riesman, *The Lonely Crowd: A Study of the Changing American Character*, 1950; the appropriate chapters of Sheila M. Rothman, *Woman's Proper Place: A History of Changing Ideas and Practices, 1870 to the Present*, 1978; C. Taeubner, *The Changing Population of the United States*, 1958; William H. Whyte, *The Organization Man*, 1956; and Robert C. Woods, *Suburbia*, 1959. The bohemian dissenters of the era are treated in Bruce Cook, *The Beat Generation*, 1971.

Racial Segregation and its crumbling have been extensively studied. See James Baldwin, *The Fire Next Time*, 1963, and Martin Luther King Jr. *Stride toward Freedom*, 1958, for profound insight into black resentments and aspirations. Also see Archibald Cox, *The Warren Court: Constitutional Decision as an Instrument of Reform*, 1968; Richard Kluger, *Simple Justice: The History of* Brown v. Board of Education *and Black America's Struggle for Equality*, 1975; Philip B. Kurland, *Politics, the Constitution, and the Warren Court*, 1970; Taylor Branch, *Parting the Waters: America in the King Years, 1954–1963*, 1988; Nicholas Lemann, *The Promised Land*, 1991, on postwar African-American migration patterns; and an early classic, C. E. Silberman, *Crisis in Black and White*, 1964.

President Eisenhower's reputation among historians generally has risen in recent years, although it still is hotly argued. The standard biography is Stephen Ambrose, *Eisenhower*, 1983–1984, but also see Chester Pach Jr. and Elmo Richardson, *The Presidency of Dwight D. Eisenhower*, 1991; Dwight D. Eisenhower, *The White House Years*, 1965; and Peter Lyon, *Eisenhower: Portrait of a Hero*, 1974. Biographical studies of other notables of the 1950s include Townshend Hoopes, *The Devil and John Foster Dulles*, 1973; John Bartlow Martin, *The Life of Adlai E. Stevenson*, 1976–1977; Stephen B. Oates, *Let the Trumpet Sound: The Life of Martin Luther King, Jr.*, 1982; James T. Paterson, *Mr. Republican: A Biography of Robert A. Taft*, 1975; Thomas C. Reeves, *The Life and Times of Joe McCarthy*, 1982; John D. Weaver, *Warren*, 1967; and G. Edward White, *Earl Warren: A Public Life*, 1982.

Confident elegance: the Kennedy image during the brief era JFK supporters called "Camelot."

47
CHAPTER

CONSENSUS AND CAMELOT

The Eisenhower and Kennedy Administrations

1953–1963

The middle of the road is all of the usable surface. The extremes, right and left, are in the gutters.

—Dwight D. Eisenhower

We stand today on the edge of a new frontier — the frontier of the 1960s — frontier of unknown opportunities and perils — a frontier of unfulfilled hopes and threats.

—John F. Kennedy

Almost half a century has elapsed since Dwight D. Eisenhower became president in 1953. We are as far in time from "Ike" as Eisenhower was from Teddy Roosevelt. Most of the prominent figures of that era are dead. Many of the issues over which political leaders quarreled, sometimes bitterly, have long since been resolved. Others have been adjudged trivial. The times seem remote to a people who were, overwhelmingly, not yet born during the 1950s and early 1960s. With the sophisticated electronic means of recording and communicating at the beginning of the twenty-first century, the preservation of the events of the 1950s and 1960s in grainy black-and-white film enhances the sense that this is the stuff of "ancient history."

In fact, the age of Eisenhower and Kennedy is recent history, "only yesterday," to borrow the title of Frederick Lewis Allen's classic. Its concerns are still vivid in the memories of the elderly. Historians still lack the perspective on the era that genuine remoteness provides. There are too many strands of continuity, personal and general, linking the 1950s and 1960s to our own day. What was important? What was not? Who can say with a justifiable confidence?

One characteristic of the decade of Dwight D. Eisenhower and John F. Kennedy does stand out in high relief. Both presidents enjoyed something like a consensus of optimism, a general accord that almost all was well in the American corner of the world. There were dissidents and malcontents, militant African Americans, liberal intellectuals, beatniks. But most Americans of the 1950s and early 1960s felt that however serious a problem might be, they were in the hands of leaders who were, at least, well intentioned.

IKE'S DOMESTIC COMPROMISE

In his heart and soul, Dwight D. Eisenhower was an old-fashioned conservative. As a career soldier, he was insulated from the mainstream of political development. He thought of government in terms of his small-town childhood in Kansas and Texas at the turn of the century, and the gruff platitudes about free enterprise he swapped with the rich businessmen who befriended him after the Second World War.

The tremendous expansion of federal power during the New Deal and the Second World War disturbed him. Perhaps because the peacetime army in which he served between the wars was so stingily financed (between the world wars, the U.S. Army ranked seventeenth in the world), Ike shuddered at the size of the government's budget after World War II, and at the very notion of annual deficits piling up into a mountain of national debt. He believed that businessmen in the private sector were better qualified to manage the economy than were the bureaucratic agencies created under Roosevelt and Truman. They, after all, did not survive if they did not watch their income and outlay. He criticized the Tennessee Valley Authority, the liberal's model of regional economic and social planning, as "creeping socialism" and suggested that its facilities be sold off to private power companies, what would come to be called privatization.

The Best Laid Schemes o' Mice an' Men . . .

Some of Ike's advisers, such as Secretary of Agriculture Ezra Taft Benson of Utah, were downright reactionary in their hostility to government regulation and social welfare programs. Given his own way, Benson would have rampaged through the big Washington bureaucracies that implemented them like an avenging angel.

Secretary of Defense Charles Wilson sounded like a ghost of the Coolidge era when he gave his opinion of the role that corporations should play in framing national policy. In what was only in part a slip of the tongue, Wilson told a Senate committee that "what was good for the country was good for General Motors and vice versa." (Wilson came to government from the General Motors board of directors.)

When Dr. Jonas Salk perfected a vaccine that promised to wipe out polio, then a scourge of children, Secretary of Health, Education, and Welfare Oveta Culp Hobby warned that even though an immunization program might well eradicate the disease, for the government to sponsor such a program would be socialistic. This was the ghost of Calvin Coolidge speaking.

. . . Gang Aft Agley

And that was no doubt how many of Ike's advisers truly felt. When it came time to take action, however, the president himself was moderate, pragmatic, and realistic. He was able to face up to the fact that

> ### Vanishing Farmers
>
> There were 5.7 million farms in the United States in 1900. This number rose to 6.5 million in 1920, declined to 6.3 million in 1930 but then, in a "back to the land" movement caused by Great Depression unemployment, reached an all-time high of 6.8 million in 1935.
>
> The 1950s saw the single largest decline of farms in a decade. In 1950, there were 5.4 million farms in the United States, in 1960 just 3.7 million. Steady decline reduced the number of farms to 1.9 million in 1992, fewer than there were at the outbreak of the Civil War in 1860. This despite relatively generous federal farm-aid programs.

the America of his Kansas boyhood was gone forever and that, in the complicated world of the mid-twentieth century, the federal government had to assume some responsibility for economic and social welfare. His administration did sponsor a polio immunization program.

Eisenhower also discovered the risks in trusting too closely to his businessmen friends when he supported a private company, Dixon-Yates, in a dispute with the TVA over which of them would construct a new generating facility for the Atomic Energy Commission. Rather than the contest between "free enterprise" and "creeping socialism" that was described to him, Ike discovered that Dixon-Yates executives were mired deeply in collusion with friendly AEC officials in what amounted to a raid on the treasury — "socialism for the rich." He withdrew his support of Dixon-Yates and accepted a face-saving compromise in which the city of Memphis, in the public sector but not federal, built the plant.

Even Ezra T. Benson had to swallow his distaste for the agricultural-subsidy programs that he wanted to abolish. The 1950s were years of moderate distress in the farm belt, and the application of free-market principles would have transformed them into years of catastrophe. As agricultural productivity continued to increase but neither domestic consumption nor foreign demand kept pace, grain piled up in volcano-shaped cones in the streets of farm towns throughout the Midwest. Farm income dipped, and farm families left the land for city and town jobs in numbers not seen since the 1920s.

But food production never lagged; big agribusiness corporations gobbled up and consolidated family farms, operating them like any other industry. One reason they were able to profit where farm families could not was that the Eisenhower administration quietly expanded the subsidy programs against which Benson railed.

The Soil Bank Act of 1956 authorized the payment of money to landowners for every acre they took out of cultivation in order to reduce production. Within ten years, $1 of every $6 that farmers and agricultural corporations pocketed at harvest time came not from sales but from the federal government — for crops that were never planted. Eisenhower also adopted New Deal-like policies when he introduced programs under which the federal government purchased surplus crops for school lunches and foreign-aid programs. As late as 1999, 38 percent of farm income came from the federal government.

Dynamic Conservatism

The clearest indication that "dynamic conservatism" (as Eisenhower called his political compromise) included taking responsibility for the health of the economy came when the sharp reduction of military expenditures after the Korean War threatened to push the country into a depression. Eisenhower responded by asking Congress to lower taxes, and he persuaded the Federal Reserve Board to loosen credit restrictions so as to put more money into the hands of consumers, that is, to make it easier for them to borrow and spend.

In 1957 and 1958, a somewhat worse recession threw 7 percent of the workforce out of jobs. Ike responded with several large public works projects like the New Deal programs that he earlier condemned. In the area of social welfare, over 10 million names were added to the lists of people who received Social Security payments during Eisenhower's presidency.

THE COLD WAR CONTINUES

The Cold War continued under Eisenhower. Indeed, every president after Harry S Truman had to design foreign policy around the overwhelming fact that the United States was locked into a competition with the Soviet Union that left very little room to maneuver.

The Nature of the Beast

Because the United States and the USSR were nuclear superpowers, the contest between them could not rationally be resolved by the timeless test of decisive war. Already by the age of Eisenhower, it was obvious that armed conflict between the United States and the Soviet Union would lead to vast physical devastation in both countries and the death of tens of millions of people. By 1961, when Ike retired, nuclear technology was advanced to the point that world war could readily lead to the destruction of civilization and, conceivably, the earth's capacity to support human life. Every president from Ike to Jimmy Carter clearly understood and stated that there would be no winners in a nuclear war.

Therefore, until the United States and the Soviet Union trusted each other enough to agree on disarmament, policy makers had to live with the balance of terror and compete with their rivals under the threat of it. The history of American foreign relations between the 1950s and the 1990s is the story of how a succession of presidents and secretaries of state coped with these restraints.

America Underground

For a time in the 1950s, fear of Soviet nuclear attack spawned a minor building boom in "fallout shelters," covered pits in backyards to which, upon hearing the sirens, families would repair and thus survive the atomic bomb. Although magazines such as *Popular Science* and *Popular Mechanics* suggested fairly cheap do-it-yourself models, a professionally built shelter, carpeted and painted beige, cost $3,000. Even if her family never used their shelter, a suburban Los Angeles woman said, it "will make a wonderful place for the children to play in." Other people pointed out that shelters were useful storage areas. In the theological journals, ministers and priests argued about a person's moral justification in shooting neighbors and relatives who had not been so prudent in building their own shelters and, in the moment of crisis, were trying to horn in. One manufacturing concern in Texas was named "The Peace O' Mind Shelter Company."

More Bang for a Buck

Although Dwight D. Eisenhower spent much of his life in an army uniform, he wanted to be remembered as a man of peace. "I have seen enough war," he said, and as president he acted with moderation in crisis situations. By the time he left office, Eisenhower appeared to distrust the motives of his generals and the business leaders who supported him. In his farewell address of 1961, Ike told Americans to beware of the "military-industrial complex," the intimate and self-serving alliance of the Pentagon (the Defense Department) and the big corporations that made their money by selling weapons to the government. Along with like-minded intellectuals in the universities and think tanks, with their ivory-tower theories of how to fight the Cold War, Ike said, the military establishment and arms industry were apt to be reckless in the use of armed force.

Eisenhower's fiscal conservatism also played a role in his defense policy. If he were to balance the federal budget—to spend no more money in a year than the Treasury collected in taxes—he had to cut military expenditures, the biggest single item in the budget. Effective disarmament, such as Ike knew between the two world wars, was out of the question during the Cold War. Instead, Eisenhower adopted a comparatively inexpensive plan for maintaining national security, the "more bang for a buck" policy.

Encouraged by penny-pinching Secretary of the Treasury George Humphrey, the president cut spending on the conventional army and navy and concentrated on building up America's nuclear deterrent: atomic and hydrogen bombs and the sophisticated ships, planes, and missiles capable of delivering them to Soviet targets. This purely defensive policy threatened no one, Ike told the world. The United States would never start a nuclear war, but the Soviet Union, unless it were deterred by the threat of massive retaliation, might very well do so.

Critics claimed that the policy meant all or nothing. The United States could destroy the world, but could the nation respond in proportion to minor Soviet provocations? Secretary Humphrey was not impressed. With the frustrations of the limited war in Korea fresh in his mind, he growled that the United States had "no business getting into little wars. . . . Let's intervene decisively with all we have got or stay out."

Other Eisenhower supporters said that the reduced army and navy were more than adequate to act in minor crises. In 1958, when Eisenhower suspected that Communists intended to take over Lebanon, he was able to send marines into the Middle Eastern nation to stabilize a government friendly to the United States. It was only a long, expensive, and demoralizing conventional war like Korea for which he did not choose to prepare.

Peaceful Coexistence

The United States was directly involved in no armed conflicts of note during Eisenhower's eight years in office. In part this may have been due to a significant change in Soviet leadership. Joseph Stalin, suspicious to the point of mental imbalance late in life, died in 1953. After a few years of figurehead leaders and murky maneuvering in the Kremlin, he was succeeded by an altogether different kind of strongman, a rotund, homely, and very clever Ukrainian named Nikita Khrushchev.

Khrushchev bewildered American Kremlinologists, as Soviet experts came to call themselves. And that may have been one of his purposes. At times he seemed to be a coarse buffoon who habitually drank too much vodka and showed it. Visiting the United Nations, he stunned the assembly of dignitaries by taking off his shoe and banging it on the desk in front of him to protest a speaker of whom he disapproved. At other times Khrushchev was witty and charming, almost slick.

The new premier could issue frightening warlike challenges to the United States. But he was also the man who denounced Stalinist totalitarianism at home in 1956 and called for peaceful coexistence with American capitalism. Khrushchev claimed that the Cold War would be resolved by historical forces rather than by armed conflict. "We will bury you," he told American capitalists. It was taken by some as a military threat but Khrushchev meant that the world would peacefully choose the Soviet way of life but militant anti-Communists in the United States quoted the phrase as an example of Khrushchev's bellicosity.

Kitchen Debate

A comparison of American and Soviet societies in the 1950s and 1960s mocked Khrushchev's boast, and helped to explain his interest in slowing down the arms race. If the terror associated with Stalin receded, Soviet citizens remained under tight political controls with Khrushchev; the secret police was not dissolved. The Soviet economy was sluggish. Because a country inestimably poorer than the United States had to match American spending on armaments, daily life in Russia was drab. Long lines of people at shops waiting not only for the most modest of luxuries but for basic foodstuffs were hardly an appealing alternative to the American consumer cornucopia.

Vice President Richard M. Nixon understood the drama of the contrast when he visited Moscow in 1959. He engaged Khrushchev in a capitalism versus communism debate in front of a mock-up of an appliance-filled American kitchen, pointing out that there was nothing like it in Russia. Khrushchev was annoyed at being sandbagged by Nixon on his own ground—American photographers were carefully placed for the "kitchen debate" —but the yawning gulf between daily life in the two superpowers was a major reason he wanted some sort of rapprochement with the United States. Only by cutting the cost of the arms race could Soviet agriculture and consumer industries be built up.

However, Khrushchev had one edge in the salesmanship contest with American spokesmen. He was flexible, opportunistic, even cynical, while the chief foreign representative of the United States under Eisenhower, Secretary of State John Foster Dulles, was a man of firm principle, petrified mind, and the charm of the bullfrog he resembled.

Dull, Duller, Dulles

On the basis of his credentials, Dulles should have been a grand success. He was related to two earlier secretaries of state, and he began his diplomatic career half a century earlier. During the years he was out of government, Dulles practiced international law with a firm that was considered the best in the business. At the top of that business in 1953 when Eisenhower named him secretary of state, Dulles turned out to be handicapped by an impossible personality for a diplomat and a simplistic view of the world.

He was a pious Presbyterian of an antiquated school, as self-righteous, intolerant, and humorless as any Puritan of old New England. "Dull, Duller, Dulles," the Democrats intoned. He believed that Communists were evil incarnate, veritable agents of Satan. He was unable to respond when Khrushchev hinted that he wanted to ease tensions, and he found

How They Lived

Suburban Landscape

Until the 1950s, most American cities were densely populated and quite compact. Crowded urban neighborhoods of tenements and row homes abutted directly on farmland or other open country. Indeed, as late as 1940, there were 10,000 acres of cultivated land *within* the city limits of Philadelphia.

There were suburbs, but they did not much resemble the classic American suburban community of today. Before the Second World War, suburbs radiated out from city centers in ribbons, along the commuter train lines that made them possible. Prewar suburbs were themselves rather compact villages of two- and three-story homes and even apartment blocks of five and six stories. Suburbanites may have fled the dirt, noise, traffic, and crowding of city life, but they had no choice but to live near the railway station that was the lifeline of their community. The typical breadwinner's work remained in the city, and all but the wealthiest commuters had to walk from their homes to the train. Shops, markets, banks, public buildings, movie theaters, and other commercial services clustered conveniently near "the station."

This suburban landscape was reshaped beyond recognition during the late 1940s and 1950s. The architect of the change was the automobile in the possession of millions of modestly fixed people who formerly had only dreamed of owning one. In the age of mass automobile ownership, getting to work and just getting around the suburbs no longer depended on a combination of shoe leather and the commuter railway. Instead of radiating out from cities in ribbons of population, postwar suburbs sprawled over what had been farmland or wasteland without reference to traditional transportation networks.

Even the least pretentious of the new communities, such as the several Levittowns, were spacious tracts, with modest blue-collar homes built on lots of a quarter-acre. To young couples accustomed to three-room apartments or a bedroom in the home of a parent, they were veritable greenswards. To celebrate their liberation from urban congestion, many of the new suburbanites demanded a kind of domestic architecture they had learned from Hollywood films to associate with the wide open spaces of the Far West and the glamour of southern California.

The ranch house was the brainchild of architect Clifford May of San Diego. A designer of grand homes for well-to-do clients during the 1930s, May was inspired by the traditional single-story dwellings of the Hispanic Southwest, where the weather was mild (or hot), where acreage had always been plentiful, and where adobe construction discouraged building walls too high. During the Depression, May designed some 50 homes in southern California that were, in his words, "about sunshine and informal outdoor living." His ranch houses featured courtyards and rooms that opened wide to the clement outdoors.

Such a lifestyle was impossible in the Northeast and Midwest, where winters were long and cold. However, single-story construction came to be a status symbol by the end of the Second World War. May himself built tracts of "Yankee Version" ranch houses with board and batten or clapboard siding instead of stucco, and a roof of shingles instead of tile. There were no courtyards in ranch houses built "back East," but picture windows let the sight of the outdoors in without its weather. Much of Levittown, Pennsylvania, was built in ranch houses costing between $9,900 and $15,500.

Such suburbs had no focal point like the prewar suburb's railroad station. However, new landmarks of the good life, once exotic curiosities like the ranch house, became commonplace in postwar suburbia. The supermarket, a huge self-service grocery store

it difficult to deal with neutral nations that maintained friendly relations with the Soviets. Photographs of Dulles with neutral national leaders like Jawaharlal Nehru of India reveal a man who fears he will be defiled if he sits too closely.

Such undiplomatic manners made him unpopular not only in the Third World (countries aligned with neither the United States nor the Soviet Union), but among the diplomats who represented America's allies. To make matters worse, Dulles

providing just about everything needed to keep house, dated from 1930 when Michael Cullen opened a "warehouse grocery" on Long Island, New York. Cullen patented a shopping cart that could hold a week's worth of groceries and touted himself "The World's Greatest Price Wrecker." He kept costs down by locating his supermarkets in factories and warehouses that had been closed by the Depression. Landlords were delighted to sign long leases with him at minimal rents. Cullen lured shoppers to his stores by offering about 300 of the 1,000 items he stocked at his own cost.

Still, in order to exploit the supermarket's bargains, a shopper needed a car. Although more costly, the long-established and conveniently located "Mom and Pop" grocery, to which marketers could walk daily, remained the norm of food retailing in suburbs as well as in the cities during the 1930s. By 1940, there were only 6,000 supermarkets in the United States, about one for every 22,000 people.

By 1950, however, with automobile suburbs sprawling on the outskirts of every large city, there were 14,000 supermarkets nationwide, one for each 11,000 people. Throughout 1951, new ones opened at the rate of three each day. By 1960, the supermarket was by far the chief source of the American family's daily bread—purchased weekly. In 33,000 markets (one per 5,400 people, just about the saturation point), Americans purchased 70 percent of the foods they consumed at home. Car-owning suburbanites had transformed the American means of food distribution as well as the very landscape through which they drove daily.

The first drive-in theater opened on June 6, 1933, in Camden, New Jersey, on a busy highway leading from Philadelphia to the seashore. Richard Hollingshead had had the idea while showing home movies in his backyard during hot summer evenings. He laid out a tract of wasteland into 50-foot-wide aisles, built ramps so that viewers could see over the cars in front of them, sunk the projection pit, and charged 25 cents per person, a maximum of $1 per car, to watch old movies (the only ones distributors would rent to him or other drive-in operators). Originally, Hollingshead used a few huge speakers to bring the soundtrack to his customers. However, this system meant he had to shut down during cold weather, when customers could not be expected to leave their car windows open. In the 1940s, operators of drive-ins solved the problem of seasonal closings by developing the individual in-car speaker.

The drive-in theater was ready-made for the suburbs. It could be profitable only where land was cheap, and the population of the postwar suburbs was composed largely of young couples with small children, for whom going to a traditional movie theater was inconvenient. Early drive-ins were advertised as family centers where people bored with the film could chat, kids could frolic safely in playgrounds built directly under the towering screens, and "inveterate smokers could smoke without offending others." There were only 10 drive-in theaters in the United States in 1939. Between 1945 and 1950, as the suburbs mushroomed, 5,000 were built. (In 1994, only 900 survived.)

The drive-in soon lost its image as a family center. Indeed, a writer for *Motion Picture Daily* commented when Hollingshead opened the first drive-in, "the Romeos who lost out in the back seats of picture houses when West Point ushers . . . came into deluxe houses are waking up in a new world." As the "passion pit," however, the drive-in theater continued to prosper in suburbia, for the tots in the playground in the 1940s soon became the lusty teenagers of the 1950s.

insisted on representing his policies in person. He flew 500,000 miles on the job, demoralizing American ambassadors by converting them into mere ceremonial figures who greeted his plane and then disappeared.

In his conception of the emerging nations of the Third World and of revolutionary movements in the republics of Latin America, Dulles's limitations were even more damaging. The old colonial empires of the European nations were falling apart during the

Vice President Richard Nixon debates with Soviet Premier Nikita Khrushchev in front of a mock-up of a typical American kitchen in Moscow, 1959.

1950s as new Asian and African countries were founded almost annually. Often committed at least in word to radical social reform, including socialist institutions, the leaders of these countries were rarely pro-Soviet. They needed American friendship because they wanted American financial aid. In many parts of Latin America, revolutionaries determined to oust reactionary and repressive dictatorships had by necessity and principle to reduce American economic power in their countries. But all but the infantile ideologues among them recognized the advantage of having good relations with the nation that had sponsored the Marshall Plan.

Picking the Wrong Friends

Instead of exploiting the widespread goodwill toward the United States or, at least, the cordiality of necessity, Dulles divided the world into "us" and "them," with "us" defined as those nations that lined up behind the United States in every particular. He wrote off all independently minded national leaders and all revolutionary movements as Communist inspired. Along with his brother, Allen Dulles, who headed the semisecret Central Intelligence Agency (CIA), he threw American influence behind reactionary regimes, including repressive and often brutal dictatorships in Portugal, Nicaragua, the Dominican Republic, and Cuba, simply because they were pro-American, "us."

Dulles wasted no time in implementing his simplistic views. In 1953, the United States helped the unpopular shah of Iran overthrow a reform-minded prime minister, Mohammed Mossadegh, despite the fact that, with its border on the Soviet Union and long-standing fear of Russian domination, Iran could not afford to cozy up too closely to Russia no matter who was in power. In 1954, the CIA took the lead in overthrowing a democratically chosen prime minister in Guatemala, Jacobo Arbenz Guzmán, because he expropriated American-owned banana plantations.

Also in 1954, Dulles refused to sign the Geneva Accords, which ended a long and tragic war in Vietnam between France and a Communist-led independence movement that, because of the historical Vietnamese hostility toward China, may have been open to cooperation with the United States.

Dulles's actions in Iran, Latin America, and Southeast Asia were to redound in setbacks to American foreign policy for four decades. Dulles said, in effect, that the United States opposed social progress in those parts of the world where change was most sorely needed. His blindness provided Khrushchev with the opportunity to play the friend of anticolonialism, freedom, and reform. The pretense ill-suited the imperialist, dictatorial, and ideologically hidebound Soviet Union, but Khrushchev and Dulles worked together to make it look plausible.

Brinkmanship and Massive Retaliation

Eisenhower, by conviction or default, backed up Dulles's policies in the Third World. He shuddered, however, at the secretary's advocacy of brinkmanship and massive retaliation in relations with the Soviet Union and, because the Chinese Communists were defined as Soviet flunkies, the People's Republic of China.

Dulles rejected containment as immoral because George Kennan and the Truman administration had called for merely holding the line against the spread of Communism in the hopes that, in the future, the Soviets would prove amenable to a settlement based on trust and goodwill. Dulles could not imagine accepting Communist states as a permanent part of the world community and said that it was not necessary that the United States do so. America would win the Cold War by going to the brink. Brinkmanship Dulles defined as "the ability to get to the verge without getting into war." He would do this, Dulles said, by threatening massive retaliation, full-scale nuclear attack, when the Soviets did something that countered American foreign policy.

Indeed, Dulles meant to provoke disputes that would enable him to put brinkmanship into action. In 1953, when the Korean War just concluded, Dulles hinted that he would support Chiang Kai-shek if the exiled Nationalist Chinese leader invaded the People's Republic. In the same year, with the So-

viet leadership in a state of flux following Stalin's death, Dulles led the peoples of the satellite states of Eastern Europe to believe that Americans would come to their aid if they rebelled against Russian domination.

Moderation in Practice

However, when the Chinese Communists began to shell two tiny islands controlled by Chiang, Quemoy and Matsu, Ike backed off, forcing Dulles to do the same. Eisenhower stated clearly that it was only Taiwan the United States would defend, a reaffirmation of containment policy. The artillery exchanges between the two Chinas soon developed into a ritual worthy of the Mandarins, a far more limited war than Korea. At one point, the Communists insisted only on the right to shell Quemoy and Matsu on alternate days of the month.

In Hungary in 1956, Dulles's talk of rolling back the iron curtain contributed to a more tragic event. Anti-Soviet Hungarians rebelled and took control of Budapest. The Soviets hesitated, as though waiting to see what the Americans would do. They regarded Hungary as vital to their security, but feared all-out war on the issue. When Eisenhower did nothing, Soviet tanks and infantry rolled into Budapest, easily quashing the revolution. The net effect of the episode was to undercut confidence in Dulles's bold words throughout the world.

Also in 1956, Eisenhower and Dulles angered three important allies by first appearing to encourage them to take action against increasingly pro-Soviet Egypt, and then refusing to back them. Britain, France, and Israel invaded Egypt to prevent the government of President Gamal Abdel Nasser from taking control of the Suez Canal. When Khrushchev threatened to send Russian "volunteers" to Egypt's aid, Eisenhower announced his opposition to the allied assault. Humiliated, the British, French, and Israelis withdrew. They could not carry on without American support.

Summitry and the U-2

When Dulles resigned a month before he died of cancer in 1959, Eisenhower took personal charge of foreign policy. Curiously, given the fact that he allowed so much rein to Dulles for six years, he was rather well equipped to administer foreign relations. Of all American presidents, only Hoover and John Quincy Adams had spent more of their lives abroad than he had. Eisenhower lived for long periods in France, England, the Philippines, Panama, and Algeria. His experience in dealing with American allies during World War II demanded the utmost in diplomatic tact.

For a time, Ike seemed to be easing Soviet-American tensions. With Dulles out of the way, he and Khrushchev outdid one another with statements of goodwill, and they agreed to exchange friendly visits. Khrushchev made his tour of the United States in 1959 and scored a rousing personal success. In the flesh and on his best behavior, he captivated many Americans with his unpretentious manner and interest in everyday things. Khrushchev even drew laughter when, having been refused admission to Disneyland for security reasons, he explained that the real reason was that the amusement park was a disguise for rocket installations.

Eisenhower's visit to Russia was scheduled for May 1960. Because Eisenhower had been a hero in the Soviet Union during the Second World War, there was every reason to expect another amicable tour. Then, on May 5, Khrushchev announced that the Russians had shot down an American plane in their air space. It was a U-2, a top-secret high-altitude craft designed for spying. Assuming that the pilot was killed in the crash (or had committed suicide, as U-2 pilots were provided the means to do), Eisenhower said that it was a weather-monitoring plane that had flown off course.

Khrushchev pounced. He revealed that the U-2 pilot, Francis Gary Powers, was alive and had confessed to being a spy. Possibly because he hoped to salvage Eisenhower's forthcoming trip to Russia, Khrushchev hinted in the wording of his announcement that Ike should lay the blame on subordinates.

Ike refused to do so. Smarting under Democratic party attacks that he had never been in charge of foreign policy, he acknowledged his personal approval of all U-2 flights. Khrushchev attacked Eisenhower as a warmonger and canceled his invitation to tour Russia. The Cold War was suddenly chillier than at any time since the truce in Korea.

1960: A CHANGING OF THE GUARD

The chill in Soviet-American relations perfectly suited the strategy of the Democratic presidential nominee in 1960, John Fitzgerald Kennedy. A 42-year-old senator from Massachusetts, Kennedy's chief criticism of the Eisenhower administration was his contention that Ike had, with his stingy spending policies, let American defenses and the power to deter Soviet aggression slip dangerously low. Kennedy hammered on about a dangerous missile gap, a gross disparity between the rockets the Soviets had available to assault the United States, and those in the American arsenal. This was colossal nonsense but, such matters as numbers of missiles being secret, neither Eisenhower nor the Republican candidate for president, Richard M. Nixon, could convincingly respond.

Times Change

Eisenhower was still very popular in 1960. Had the Twenty-second Amendment to the Constitution, adopted by Republicans in 1951 as a posthumous rebuke of FDR, not forbidden a third term, the 70-year-old president would likely have been reelected. Americans still liked Ike.

And yet the country was a little tired of the 1950s. The American population was younger than at any time in the twentieth century and restless under the cautious style of the dead decade. As prosperous as the age of Eisenhower was, it was a stale and boring time in the opinion of an increasing number of Americans. The books of social critics such as Whyte and Packard had been best-sellers. Although they were out of power, the Democratic liberals had loudly and relentlessly criticized Eisenhower's lethargy in journals like *The Nation* and the *New Republic*. Liberal university professors were effective propagandists, spreading their views among young people. And although it was not a liberal majority, the Democrats had controlled both houses of Congress for six of Eisenhower's eight years in office.

> ### Silent Generation
>
> Looking back from the vantage of 1994, novelist John Updike remembered, "My generation, coming into its own, was called Silent, as if, after all the vain and murderous noise of recent history, this was a bad thing."

American pilot Francis Gary Powers (right) embarrassed President Eisenhower when he confessed to piloting a spy plane over the Soviet Union.

As 1960 approached, the feeling that it was time "to get the country moving again" was in the air. In 1959, *Life*, the favorite magazine of the middle classes, published a series of articles by prominent Americans ranging from Adlai Stevenson to Billy Graham on the subject of the national purpose. Almost all the contributors expressed an uneasiness that a sense of purpose was just not there.

John F. Kennedy

Kennedy was a politician who knew how to exploit this apprehension of drift. As Eisenhower was tailor-made for the 1950s, Kennedy seemed to fit the spirit of the emerging new decade. He was rich and attractive, breezy and witty. He had distinguished himself for bravery during the Second World War (although not for the best of military sense, which he cheerfully admitted). He also had an attractive young wife, and was ambitious.

Kennedy had weaknesses that would have destroyed a political career 20 years later. He was constantly seeking out women, boasting to friends of the number of his one-night conquests, and maintaining longer relationships with several mistresses, including actress Marilyn Monroe and one Judith Flexner, who had personal connections with organized crime.

But he was generally discreet and 1960s journalists were more restrained than the next generation would be, regarding such matters as sexual habits a man's or woman's own business.

Kennedy was unbeatable in Massachusetts politics. He had won election to the House and the Senate in years that were not kind to Democrats, and in 1956, he made a bid for the Democratic party's vice-presidential nomination. He lost, but that turned out to be a blessing—Kennedy did not share in the

President Kennedy was at his best at the podium, an orator who understood his times and audience.

humiliation of the party's trouncing that year, but by putting up an exciting fight on national television (the only contest in a dull political year), he made his name known in every corner of the country.

The avalanche of publicity in 1956 did another favor for Kennedy by initiating discussion of his religion. The senator was a Roman Catholic, and conventional wisdom was that too many people would vote against any Catholic for a member of that church to be elected to national office. The longer the question was examined, however, the less attractive the anti-Catholic position looked. When Martin Luther King Jr.'s father (a Baptist minister) expressed old-fashioned prejudices on the score, the civil rights leader so hastily dissociated himself from his father's views that he became, in the process, virtually committed to the Democratic nominee.

Kennedy and his team of advisers, which he started to assemble in 1957, understood the importance of manipulating the mass media, especially television, in creating a favorable image of their candidate. The campaign that he launched was calculated to convince younger Americans that he was more flexible, more open to change, than any of his rivals.

The Democratic Campaign

Kennedy's competition for the nomination included Adlai Stevenson, shopworn in an age that craved novelty, but still hoping to be drafted; Lyndon B. Johnson of Texas, the effective leader of the Senate Democrats, but as easy to label in his western manners as Kennedy in his religion; Hubert H. Humphrey of Minnesota, a leading liberal; and several minor candidates who hoped for a deadlocked convention.

Humphrey was the only one to challenge Kennedy head-on in the primary elections, and he was quickly eliminated. By edging him in Wisconsin, which neighbors Minnesota, Kennedy established himself as a national figure. Kennedy then won in West Virginia, a heavily Protestant Bible-belt state where, experts said, anti-Catholic feeling would wipe Kennedy out. Humphrey dropped out of the contest, and Kennedy's forces talked old-time political bosses like Governor Mike Di Salle of Ohio and Mayor Richard E. Daley of Chicago, who were straddling the fence as bosses do, into supporting him as the most likely to win in November. By the time of the convention, Lyndon Johnson was outraced and Kennedy won on the first ballot.

Kennedy then chose Johnson as his vice-presidential running mate. He expected and wanted to be turned down, but knew he needed Johnson's goodwill to win votes in the South. When Johnson shocked him by accepting, Kennedy's good manners turned out to be the shrewdest move of a brilliantly played game. Although Johnson's syrupy Texas drawl excited some ridicule in the Northeast, he was popular in the southern states where Kennedy was weak. Single-handedly, Johnson won Texas for the Democrats, a key to a close election. In the North, Kennedy's religion actually helped him by winning back many upwardly mobile Catholics who were drifting toward the Republicans as the party of respectability.

A Modern Election

The Republican standard-bearer was Vice President Richard M. Nixon, who easily fought off a challenge by New York Governor Nelson Rockefeller. Nixon had a difficult assignment. In order to keep the

Republican organization behind him, he had to defend Eisenhower's policies. But he also had to appeal to the new spirit of youth and change.

Nixon handled this juggling act remarkably well, but not without cost. Emphasizing his experience in the executive branch, he created an image of the responsible diplomat that did not mesh with his past reputation for free-swinging smears and dirty tricks. Reporters revived the nickname "Tricky Dicky" and the line, "Would you buy a used car from this man?" Kennedy wisecracked that Nixon played so many parts that no one knew who the real Nixon was, including the vice president himself.

Mistrust was to dog Richard Nixon to the end of his career, but in 1960 he almost won the election. The totals gave Kennedy a wafer-thin margin of 118,574 votes out of the almost 70 million cast. His 303 to 219 electoral vote margin, apparently more comfortable, concealed narrow scrapes in several large states. Many analysts believed that Illinois went Democratic only because of fraudulent vote counts in Richard E. Daley's Chicago. Republicans urged Nixon to demand a thoroughgoing investigation into the state's polls.

Other commentators said that Kennedy won because his wife was more glamorous than Pat Nixon, who abhorred public life, or because the Massachusetts senator looked better in the first of four nationally televised debates with Nixon. Kennedy was tan, healthy, confident, and assertive, while Nixon's nervousness showed, and an inept make-up job failed to cover his five-o'clock shadow.

It is impossible to know how much the appearances of the candidates affected the decisions of 70 million people. After 1960, however, many politicians and political scientists came to believe that in the age of television a candidate's image, rather than issues, was the key to winning elections. By 1990, no major politician would dream of running a campaign without the advice—even the control—of a high-priced advertising firm.

CAMELOT

As president, Kennedy remained a master at projecting an attractive image. Although no more an intellectual than Eisenhower (his favorite writer was Ian Fleming, creator of the British superspy, James Bond), the new president won the hearts and talents of the intelligentsia with friendly gestures. He invited the venerable poet Robert Frost to read his verse at the inauguration, and cellist Pablo Casals to perform at the White House. Genuinely athletic and competitive, Kennedy appealed to young suburbanites by releasing photographs of his large family playing rough-and-tumble touch football at their Cape Cod vacation home.

There were plenty of Kennedy haters, but the vigor of his administration (*vigor* was a favorite Kennedy word) and his undeniable charm, wit, and self-deprecating humor captivated a good many Americans. Inspired by the blockbuster musical of the early 1960s, *Camelot*, they spoke of the Kennedy White House as though it were an idyll, like King Arthur's reign in the mythical past.

Like Eisenhower, Kennedy seemed to be assembling a consensus that excluded only the lunatic fringe and, somewhat to Kennedy's dismay, southern segregationist Democrats. Just as in the Arthurian legend, however, the Kennedy Camelot was short-lived. One Mordred outside the house of the Round Table was quite enough to bring him down.

The New Frontier

Historically, John F. Kennedy is more important as an inspiration for the reforms (and tragedies) of the 1960s than for what he actually accomplished. His inaugural address was eloquent and moving. "The torch has been passed to a new generation of Americans," he warned the world, and to Americans he said, "Ask not what your country can do for you; ask what you can do for your country." He sent Congress a pile of legislation that was more innovative than

---

The Kennedy Wit

"When we got into office, the thing that surprised me most was to find that things were just as bad as we'd been saying they were."

"Washington is a city of Southern efficiency and Northern charm."

"It has recently been observed that whether I serve one or two terms in the presidency, I will find myself at the end of that period at what might be called an awkward age—too old to begin a new career and too young to write my memoirs."

any presidential program between the time of FDR's Hundred Days and Ronald Reagan's conservative agenda of 1981.

The New Frontier, as Kennedy called his program, included federal aid to education (both to institutions and in the form of low-interest student loans), assistance to chronically depressed Appalachia and the nation's decaying center cities, and help for the poor, the ill, and the aged. In 1962, Kennedy proposed a massive space research and development program to overtake the Soviet Union, which beat the United States in orbiting: the first artificial satellite in 1957 and the first human space traveler in 1961. Kennedy meant to send an American to the moon by 1970.

In Congress, however, despite comfortable Democratic majorities, the president was frustrated. Not only did most Republicans oppose the New Frontier, but Kennedy was unable to swing the powerful bloc of southern Democrats behind his program. The southerners traditionally opposed big government spending on anything but defense and public-works projects located in the South, and they were angered when the president and his brother, Attorney General Robert F. Kennedy, made friendly overtures to the growing civil rights movement.

Consequently, Kennedy was able to push through only a few of his proposals, such as the Peace Corps (volunteers working in underdeveloped countries in

A Peace Corps volunteer at a school in the Philippines.

Latin America, Asia, and Africa) and the space program (which brought money to the South).

We Shall Overcome

Kennedy wanted southern congressmen on his side and was willing to go slow in accommodating the growing civil rights movement. But blacks and increasing numbers of white allies would not be put off for the sake of Kennedy's legislative program. Martin Luther King Jr.'s Southern Christian Leadership Conference, its offshoot, the Student Nonviolent Coordinating Committee (SNCC), and other older groups like the Congress of Racial Equality (CORE) were energized by the election of 1960. They struck out at racial discrimination on a dozen fronts, sponsoring demonstrations, protests, and nonviolent civil disobedience throughout the South.

White mobs pummeled black and white demonstrators and law officers turned high-pressure fire hoses on them, unleashed vicious attack dogs, and tortured demonstrators with electric cattle prods. Black churches, the typical meeting place of civil rights workers, were firebombed and several children were killed. A bus carrying CORE "freedom riders" was burned to the ground. In April 1963, Medgar Evers, the moderate leader of the NAACP in Mississippi, was shot to death in the driveway of his home.

Kennedy and Attorney General Robert F. Kennedy could not ignore such violence. However, they were forced to take decisive and dramatic federal action only when two southern governors, Ross Barnett of Mississippi and George Wallace of Alabama said that they would personally prevent the integration of their state universities and tacitly encouraged mobs to riot. Unable to reason with the governors by phone, the Kennedys sent 400 marshals, 300 soldiers, and spent $4 million to ensure that James Meredith was admitted to the University of Mississippi. Governor Wallace, after making a show to appeal to segregationists in his state, stepped aside without violence.

The March on Washington

What wedded the Kennedys to the civil rights movement, however, was a massive demonstration, the March on Washington of August 1963, organized and led by Martin Luther King Jr. Believing that the time had come for decisive federal action, King led

200,000 supporters to the Lincoln Memorial in Washington, where he delivered the greatest sermon of his life. "I have a dream today," he began,

> I have a dream today that one day . . . little black boys and black girls will be able to join hands with little white boys and white girls and walk together as sisters and brothers. . . . When we let freedom ring, when we let it ring from every village and every hamlet, from every state and every city, we will be able to speed up that day when all of God's children, black men and white men, Jews and Gentiles, Protestants and Catholics, will be able to join hands and sing, in the words of that old Negro spiritual, "Free at last! Free at last! Thank God Almighty, we are free at last!"

Concluding that he had no choice but to choose between racist Democrats in the South (who were not supporting him on much of anything) and the large black vote in the North, which was strategically located in the cities of the states with the most electoral votes, Kennedy announced his support of a sweeping civil rights bill to be debated in Congress in 1964.

KENNEDY'S FOREIGN POLICY

Kennedy was committed to fighting the Cold War with the Soviet Union and he could sound like a young John Foster Dulles in saying so: "Freedom and Communism are in deadly embrace; the world cannot exist half-slave and half-free." Acting on his campaign claim that a missile gap between the Soviet Union and the United States threatened American security, he lavished money on research programs designed to improve the rockets with which, in case of war with Russia, nuclear weapons would be delivered.

Flexible Response

However, Kennedy's foreign policy advisers, mostly intellectuals from universities and think tanks, such as Walt W. Rostow and McGeorge Bundy, were critics of Dulles brinkmanship, threatening massive retaliation with nuclear weapons at every Soviet provocation. Instead, updating containment policy to apply to a world theater, they advocated a policy of flexible response. The United States would respond to Soviet actions in proportion to their seriousness.

Martin Luther King Jr. delivers his famous "I Have a Dream" speech in which he prays for an America in which race does not count.

For example—what was to prove a fatal example—if the Soviets were suspected of funding or actively aiding guerrilla movements against regimes that were friendly to the United States or sought American aid, the United States would fund the military forces of those regimes and offer expert advisers to help them. If the Soviets were suspected of subverting elections in the Third World, the United States would launch its own covert operations to manipulate events on disputed turf.

Toward these ends, Kennedy sponsored the development of elite antiguerrilla units in the army, most notably the Special Forces or Green Berets, and he increased funding of the spy network maintained by the Central Intelligence Agency.

Into the Third World

In contrast to Eisenhower, who thought in traditional terms that wealthy Europe and Japan were the areas that counted in the Cold War competition, Kennedy stated that "the great battleground for the defense and expansion of freedom today is the whole southern half of the globe—Asia, Latin America, Africa, and the Middle East—the lands of the rising peoples."

He preferred to back democratic reform movements in the developing countries. Kennedy took the lead in organizing the Alliance for Progress in the Western Hemisphere, a program that offered economic aid to friendly Latin American nations in the hope that they would adopt free institutions.

However, the choice in the volatile Third World was rarely between liberal-minded reform movements and pro-Communist dictatorships. Envy of American riches, the common perception that the United States reflexively supported exploitative dictators, the flexibility and opportunism of the Soviets, and the romantic zaniness common in revolutionary movements meant that most liberation movements were at best suspicious of American intentions and willing to overlook the Russian record because of Soviet revolutionary rhetoric. Consequently, Kennedy and his successors often found their only friends among reactionaries hostile to reform.

The Bay of Pigs

Cuba was the first Third World battleground to come to Kennedy's attention, and his flexible response proved to be a disaster. Since 1959, Cuba had been under the control of a revolutionary regime headed by Fidel Castro. Constantly baiting the United States in interminable but impassioned speeches, Castro began, during 1960, to expropriate American property before negotiating compensation. He had riled Eisenhower, who approved a CIA project to arm and train 2,000 anti-Castro Cubans in Florida and Central America.

They were ready to invade Cuba when Kennedy took over and, despite misgivings, Kennedy decided to go ahead. The Central Intelligence Agency assured him that Castro was unpopular with the Cuban people. At the sound of the first shot, anti-Castro rebellions would break out all over the island.

On April 17, 1961, the anti-Castro forces waded ashore at the Bahía de Cochinos, the Bay of Pigs, on Cuba's southern coast. The invasion was a disaster from the start. There was no uprising. Castro's troops, seasoned by three years of revolution, made short work of the battle and Castro's popularity soared at home for having resisted what he called imperialist aggression.

Kennedy, instead of ousting an anti-American but still perhaps flexible revolutionary leader, pushed Castro into the arms of the Soviets for fear of another assault. Indeed, Kennedy was denounced all over Latin America, and, on national television, he assumed full responsibility for the fiasco.

The Vienna Summit

The Bay of Pigs disaster heartened Soviet leader Nikita Khrushchev to take a harder line toward the United States than he had through most of the 1950s. Perhaps he sensed that the youth and inexperience of the new president provided rare opportunities for easy limited victories in the game of maneuver at which Khrushchev was so deft.

At a summit meeting in Vienna in June, Kennedy found himself outwitted and upstaged by Khrushchev. The Russian tongue-tied him in private and, when they were before reporters, treated him like a nice boy who only needed teaching. A man of perhaps too much self-confidence, Kennedy returned home seething with anger, and Khrushchev was encouraged to act more recklessly. The Soviets resumed nuclear testing in the atmosphere and ordered the sealing of the border between East and West Berlin.

The Berlin Wall

The Communist regime of East Germany was plagued by the defection of their citizens, particularly highly trained technologists who could double and triple their incomes in West Germany's booming economy. This brain drain threatened to cripple East German industry, and the Communists winced at each defection as a Western propaganda victory, people "voting with their feet." To put an end to it, Khrushchev built a wall through the city that was as ugly in reality as it was symbolically.

Kennedy allowed the Berlin Wall to stand, and he was immediately attacked by critics who said that he could have bulldozed it without interference from the Russians. The proposition was arguable but Kennedy was no man of the brink—until October 1962.

The Big Crunch

In October 1962, a U-2 flight over Cuba revealed that the Soviets were constructing installations for nuclear missiles aimed at the United States. Such a threat based a mere hundred miles from the United States was, Kennedy knew, something the American people would not tolerate. Before revealing his discovery, he met with a committee specially constituted to analyze the crisis.

Quickly, Kennedy rejected a proposal by Dean Acheson and others that bombers be dispatched to destroy the missile sites. He also rejected a proposal for an American invasion of the island. Although the president did not know it at the time, this was a wise decision. While the CIA had reported (blundering again) that there was only a handful of Soviets on the island, in fact there were 40,000 Russian troops. The CIA also grossly underestimated the size of the Cuban army, which numbered 270,000 men and women.

Instead, President Kennedy adopted his brother's more moderate and flexible approach. Announcing the discovery of the missiles to the American people, he simultaneously proclaimed a naval blockade of Cuba and demanded that the sites be dismantled and any nuclear weapons on the island be removed.

Castro panicked (it was learned in 1989), fleeing to a bunker beneath the Soviet Embassy and demanding a Russian nuclear strike on the United States. No doubt, the Cuban's rashness gave Khrushchev pause but, for four days, he refused to

JFK was a master of communicating via television, and often used the medium.

budge. Work on the sites continued, and Soviet ships loaded with 20 missiles continued on their way to Cuba to be added to the 20 already there. Americans gathered solemnly around their television sets, apprehensive that the nuclear holocaust would begin any hour. Secretary of State Dean Rusk revealed that the White House was nervous, too. "We're eyeball to eyeball," he said.

Rusk added, "I think the other fellow just blinked." The Cuba-bound freighters first stopped in mid-ocean and then turned around. On October 26, Khrushchev sent a long conciliatory letter to Kennedy in which he agreed to remove the missiles if the United States pledged never to invade Cuba. The next day, a second letter said that the Soviets would withdraw their nuclear weapons if the United States would remove its missiles from Turkey, which bordered the Soviet Union.

Before the Cuban missile crisis began, Kennedy was considering dismantling the Turkish missile sites as a gesture of friendship. Calculating that the difference in the two Soviet offers indicated indecision in the Kremlin, he saw a chance for a prestigious victory. Kennedy ignored Khrushchev's second note and accepted the terms of the first. On October 28, Khrushchev accepted.

Relations Improve

The president thought that the Cuban missile crisis was the turning point of his presidency. He made commemorative gifts to everyone who advised or merely stood by him during that tense October. In fact, both Kennedy and the Soviets were shaken by their flirtation with catastrophe and acted more responsibly after 1962. A "hot line" was installed in both the White House and the Kremlin so that, in future crises, Russian and American leaders could communicate instantly with one another. Then, following a Kennedy speech, the Soviet Union joined the United States and the United Kingdom in signing a treaty that banned nuclear testing in the atmosphere. (France and China, the only other nuclear powers, did not sign.)

The Assassination

By the fall of 1963, Kennedy had regained the confidence he exuded in the campaign of 1960. He had scored a major diplomatic victory in the Cuban missile crisis and was no longer so uncomfortable about his decision to embrace the civil rights movement and write off southern white extremists. He believed that the Civil Rights Act he proposed for 1964 would ensure the electoral votes of the populous northeastern states in the presidential election that year, and began to make plans to convince southern moderates that they should accept the civil rights revolution.

Toward this end, he agreed to accompany Vice President Johnson on a major political tour in Texas. It began with cheering crowds, and Kennedy was reassured. Then, as the long motorcade passed through Dealey Plaza in downtown Dallas, the president's head was blown open by rifle fire. Within a short time, Dallas police arrested Lee Harvey Oswald, a ne'er-do-well ex-marine and hanger-on of left-wing causes who worked in a textbook clearinghouse overlooking the plaza.

Kennedy's murder unleashed a storm of pent-up anxieties and conspiracy theories. Because Dallas, where Kennedy was killed, was a hotbed of often paranoiac right-wing political organizations, including the John Birch Society, which held that Dwight D. Eisenhower was a conscious agent of international Communism, liberals were inclined to blame Kennedy's loss on such unhealthy extremism. Stories circulated of Dallas schoolchildren cheering when they heard the news.

As a grief-stricken America watched on television, Lyndon B. Johnson, his wife to his right and Jacqueline Kennedy to his left, takes the oath of office aboard Air Force I, November 22, 1963.

But Oswald's own political associations were entirely with left-wing organizations. Indeed, he had lived for a time in the Soviet Union and tried to renounce his American citizenship. Right-wingers were confirmed in their theories that Communist agents were everywhere. Others posited a Mafia connection, yet others attributed the murder to the Central Intelligence Agency.

Lee Harvey Oswald was not able to clear (or further muddy) things up. Two days after the assassination, he was murdered in the basement of the Dallas police headquarters by a not-too-savory nightclub operator named Jack Ruby, who claimed to have been unhinged by the death of a president he idolized.

A blue-ribbon investigating commission headed by Chief Justice Earl Warren found that Oswald acted alone; he was not assisted in his act. Simply put, he was a misfit. However, sloppy evidence gathering and soft spots in one or another of the Warren Commission's conclusions continued to serve as grist for literally hundreds of articles and books that espoused theories about how the murder took place. In 1988, on the twenty-fifth anniversary of the Kennedy assassination, a large majority of Americans stated that they did not accept the official account of the murder as the true story. In 1991, a Hollywood film about the assassination implicated numerous government agencies in the killing and was a huge commercial success. However, painstaking, nonideological examination of the evidence and the many theories surrounding the assassination always returned to a scenario pretty much like the one the Warren Commission spun at the time of the crime.

Beginning of an Era

John F. Kennedy was not a great president. He accomplished little at home and his policy of intervening directly in what was, in 1961, a minor war in Southeast Asia, was to poison American life and squander the international goodwill the United States had banked in World War II and its aftermath.

But his assassination was a great tragedy, far more momentous in its consequences than even the murder of Abraham Lincoln nearly a hundred years earlier. For Lincoln's work was largely done when he died. Kennedy, if not particularly successful in pushing through the legislation his administration sponsored during the Thousand Days of his presidency, had just begun. He was building a basis of political support such as had allowed Dwight D. Eisenhower to govern with authority, and doing so by appealing to the better instincts of the American people. His untimely death not only created a climate in which conspiracy theories about it flourished, but it left a void of idealism, confidence, and goodwill that has not yet been filled.

CHRONOLOGY

1953 United States aids shah of Iran in consolidating power in opposition to leftist prime minister

1954 Eisenhower administration refuses to sign Geneva Accords ending French role in Indochina

1956 Soviet leader, Nikita Khrushchev, publicly denounces excesses and brutalities of Stalin regime
United States refuses to aid Britain, France, and Israel when Egypt seizes control of Suez Canal

1957 Minor depression, lasting into 1958, throws 7 percent of labor force out of work

1959 Eisenhower embarrassed and goodwill visit to Soviet Union canceled when a U-2, a spy plane, is shot down over the Soviet Union and its pilot is captured

1960 John F. Kennedy wins Democratic presidential nomination and narrowly defeats Richard M. Nixon in general election

1961 In "farewell address," President Eisenhower warns nation of "military-industrial complex," an informal alliance of armed forces and defense contractors
President Kennedy approves abortive and humiliating invasion of Cuba by Cubans hostile to pro-Communist government of Fidel Castro

1962 Kennedy and Khrushchev narrowly avoid war when Khrushchev backs down on his program to place missiles in Cuba

1963 Martin Luther King Jr. leads massive march in Washington demanding an end to racial discrimination
President Kennedy is assassinated in Dallas, Texas. Lyndon Johnson becomes president

FOR FURTHER READING

Overviews of the 1950s and 1960s include John Brooks, *The Great Leap*, 1966; William Chafe, *The Unfinished Journey*, 1986; James Gilbert, *Another Chance: America since 1945*, 1984; Eric Goldman, *The Crucial Decade and After*, 1961; Godfrey Hodgson, *America in Our Time: From World War II to Nixon*, 1976; William E. Leuchtenburg, *A Troubled Feast: American Society since 1945*, 1979; and James L. Sundquist, *Politics and Policy: The Eisenhower, Kennedy, and Johnson Years*, 1968.

On the Eisenhower years, see C. C. Alexander, *Holding the Line: The Eisenhower Era, 1952-1961*, 1975; Stephen Ambrose, *Eisenhower the President*, 1984; see also Eisenhower's own *The White House Years*, 1965; P. A. Carter, *Another Part of the Fifties*, 1983; B. W. Cook, *The Declassified Eisenhower*, 1981; T. Hoopes, *The Devil and John Foster Dulles*, 1973; Peter Lyon, *Eisenhower: Portrait of a Hero*, 1974; Richard M. Nixon, *Six Crises*, 1962; William L. O'Neill, *American High: The Years of Confidence, 1945-1960*, 1987; H. G. Vatter, *The U.S. Economy in the 1950s*, 1963; and David F. Noble, *Forces of Production*, 1984.

The era of John F. Kennedy's brief presidency has been studied as intensively as Eisenhower's. See Ronald Berman, *America in the Sixties*, 1968; Bruce Miroff, *Pragmatic Illusions: The Presidential Politics of John F. Kennedy*, 1976; Richard Reeves, *President Kennedy: Profile of Power*, 1993; L. G. Paper, *The Promise and the Performance: The Leadership of John F. Kennedy*, 1975; Herbert Parrnet, *Jack: The Struggle of John Fitzgerald Kennedy*, 1980, and *JFK: The Presidency of John Fitzgerald Kennedy*, 1983; and Arthur M. Schlesinger Jr., *A Thousand Days*, 1965. On Kennedy's election, see the first in a series of such studies by Theodore H. White, *The Making of the President 1960*, 1961. The president's assassination has been the subject of so many books—some crackbrained, many insightful—that it is impossible to be representative and name but a few. Perhaps the one with which to begin a study of that tragic event is William Manchester, *Death of a President*, 1967. For a summing up, see Gerald Posner, *Case Closed*, 1993.

The decisions of Chief Justice Earl Warren's Supreme Court were as important in shaping the American politics of the future as presidential and congressional policies. See Archibald Cox, *The Warren Court: Constitutional Decision as an Instrument of Reform*, 1968; Philip B. Kurland, *Politics, the Constitution, and the Warren Court*, 1970; and for the other side of the bar, Mark Tushnet, *Making Civil Rights Law: Thurgood Marshall and the Supreme Court*, 1994.

Antiwar poster of the Flower Children era: earnest, idealistic, heartwarming.

48
CHAPTER

YEARS OF TURBULENCE

Conflict at Home and Abroad

1961–1968

We have a problem in making our power credible, and Vietnam is the place.

—John F. Kennedy

The battle against Communism must be joined in Southeast Asia with strength and determination.

—Lyndon B. Johnson

Let me be quite blunt. Our fighting men are not going to be worn down; our mediators are not going to be talked down; and our allies are not going to be let down.

—Richard M. Nixon

In the final analysis, it is their war. They are the ones who have to win it or lose it. We can help them, . . . but they have to win it, the people of Vietnam.

—John F. Kennedy

Our one desire and our one determination is that the people of Southeast Asia be left in peace to work out their destinies in their own ways.

—Lyndon B. Johnson

What the United States wants for South Vietnam is not the important thing. What North Vietnam wants for South Vietnam is not the important thing. What is important is what the people of South Vietnam want for South Vietnam.

—Richard M. Nixon

946 *Chapter 48 Years of Turbulence*

In classical drama, the tragic hero overcomes great obstacles to rise to lofty heights, not always by the most delicate of means. Then, at the pinnacle of his achievement and glory, he is destroyed, not so much by his enemies (although they are always on hand to sweep away the pieces) as by flaws in the hero's own character.

Lyndon Baines Johnson and Richard Milhous Nixon were tragic figures in this tradition. Both rose to win their nation's highest prize and honor, presidency of the United States (not always by delicate means). Both savored the exercise of power. Both were masters of the spheres in which they preferred to labor: Johnson as a domestic reformer in the footsteps of his idol, Franklin D. Roosevelt, Nixon as a diplomat, an arranger of affairs among nations, which he regarded as the twentieth-century president's principal job.

And both were cast down in disgrace, Johnson because he clung stubbornly to a cause both lost and unpopular, and Nixon because of behavior that was not only unworthy of a president, but explicable only as a reflection of a flawed character. Johnson's undoing came about in foreign policy, which had never particularly interested him, and Nixon's on the domestic front, which he believed could take care of itself.

LYNDON BAINES JOHNSON

Lyndon Johnson—LBJ—so much liked the FDR-style initials that he named his two daughters and nicknamed his wife so that they were all "LBJ," Lady Bird, Lucy Baines, Lynda Bird. He came out of what people call "the sticks," the rural Pedernales River country of central Texas. His family's means were middling; although the distinguished University of Texas was nearby, Johnson was able to attend only a teacher's college. He taught school for a year, but found the life dull compared to the hubbub, machinations, and possibilities of Texas politics, which he knew through his father's interests. In 1931, LBJ went to Washington as a congressman's aide, became a devoté of the New Deal whose faith in government never wavered, and returned to Texas to win a special election to Congress in 1937.

Johnson served in World War II and, in 1948, he won the Democratic nomination to the Senate in a controversial primary. Because his margin was a handful of somewhat dubious votes, Texans joshed him as "Landslide Lyndon." Nonetheless, in the Lone Star State in the 1940s, the Democratic nomination, however secured, was tantamount to election and the voters did their duty. Back in Washington as a senator in 1949, Johnson's rise was meteoric. Taken in tow by Sam Rayburn, a legendary wheeler-dealer as Speaker of the House of Representatives, Johnson was named party whip in 1951 and majority leader of the Senate in 1955.

The "Johnson Treatment"

Johnson owed Rayburn for the speed of his rise to power but he held fast to it because he was very good at what he did. He was the master assembler of Senate majorities. By turns, he administered large doses of folksy charm, bargained with senators who were pursuing pet projects, twisted arms, and, so it was said, blackmailed those who could not be cajoled with allusions to dubious facets of their personal lives. The rumor was that Johnson had something on every Democrat and most of the Republicans in the Senate; he was not a man to be crossed when he was after something. Whether that was true or not, it was enough that a great many legislators believed it.

These political skills enabled President Lyndon B. Johnson to push through Kennedy's New Frontier and much more, a comprehensive program of national reform that he called the Great Society. Oddly (except in political terms), this very expensive program began with a tax cut. By reducing Kennedy's budget for 1964 by a mere $3.6 billion, Johnson was able to win congressional support for a $10 billion tax cut, always a crowd-pleaser. After so popular a start, Johnson moved on to what was to be his great monument, a revolution in the civil status of African Americans and the beginnings of a social revolution in relations between the races. In the Civil Rights Act of 1964, Johnson put the Fourteenth Amendment to the Constitution, somewhat in abeyance for a century, to work.

A Southerner Ends Segregation

Between 1955 and 1965, when civil rights activists were fighting to end racial segregation in the South, a few faint voices suggested that when the Jim Crow laws were gone, as they must go, white and black southerners of both races would enjoy better, more human relations than black and white northerners would. Observers of this stripe reasoned that while legal segregation was a southern institution, interac-

All-Time Champion Filibuster

To filibuster means to attempt to defeat or modify a bill before a legislature having overwhelming support by taking possession of the floor and speaking indefinitely (about anything) until the majority tires, or is required to adjourn, and therefore drops its bill or agrees with the filibusterers to modify it.

Filibustering was, because of Senate rules, most likely to succeed in that assembly and has been called into service there a number of times. The great Progressive, Robert M. LaFollette, was an indefatiguable filibusterer, once injuring his health by speaking for so long.

However, the champion of the sport was Senator Strom Thurmond of South Carolina who, in late August 1957, spoke for 24 hours and 18 minutes in an attempt to kill a civil rights bill. Thurmond's speech filled 96 pages of fine print in the *Congressional Record*. Like most filibusters, Thurmond's failed. (Most filibusters were intended to impress voters back home with the speechifier's dedication to their interests.) The Civil Rights Bill of 1957 passed the Senate by a vote of 60–15.

tion between blacks and whites in the South was personal and even intimate. In the North, by way of contrast, while blacks suffered few to no legal disabilities, comprehensive residential segregation in the big cities isolated the two races as if they were two nations.

With some southern police forces routinely brutalizing black protesters during those years, and some high-ranking southern white politicians huffing and puffing that they would fight to the death to save white supremacy, few could take such notions seriously. But it was Lyndon Johnson, a southerner and (formally) a proponent of segregation as late as 1960, who wrote an end to Jim Crow. In fact, Johnson had personally and philosophically found segregation distasteful and reactionary for a long time. He accepted it publicly, and intoned the compulsory mantras, to win election in Texas. However, he told an aide in 1960, "I'll tell you what's at the bottom of it"—of racial segregation—"if you can convince the lowest white man he's better than the best colored man, he won't notice you're picking his pocket. Hell, give him somebody to look down on, and he'll empty his pockets for you."

By 1964, like the Kennedys, Johnson was convinced that the days of Jim Crow were numbered and that the future of the Democratic party might depend on black votes in large northern cities and in the South. By means of shrewd bargaining and "the Johnson treatment," he pushed through the Civil Rights Act of 1964, effectively outlawing legal segregation and the "white" and "colored" signs on public accommodations that had marked everyday life in the South for more than half a century. The act also created the Equal Employment Opportunity Commission to work towards ending a large unemployment gap between the white and black workforces.

Nor was Johnson done. When Mississippi extremists took irregular and violent action against a civil rights campaign in that state in 1964—the Mississippi Freedom Summer—Johnson responded with another civil rights bill, the Voting Rights Act of 1965—that ensured the right of African Americans to vote.

Freedom Summer

Rural white Mississippians may have been the most stubborn of segregationists. The symbol of the Mississippi Democratic party was a white cock and the words "white supremacy." Because the state was perceived as Jim Crow's sturdiest redoubt, the Student Nonviolent Coordinating Committee, a loose alliance of black and white university students committed to racial equality, chose Mississippi in the summer of 1964 as the focus of a campaign to register African Americans to vote. If Mississippi could be cracked, they reasoned, racial barriers would crumble all over the South.

The Freedom Summer was a disillusioning experience to many of the idealistic young liberals who descended on Mississippi from northern states. Instead of finding a black population as articulate, idealistic, and militant as their black colleagues back home, they found a people as provincial and as wary of outsiders as "the rednecks" around them were, and cautious to the marrow after several generations of suffering the daily humiliation of the color line.

The African Americans of Mississippi resented their oppression, but they knew that when the bright-faced northern students, black and white, went back to school in September, and the newspaper reporters went with them, they would still be there, vulnerable to economic manipulation and, despite the disappearance of lynching, violence. Many blacks did register to vote—or tried to do so. Others sat on the porches of their cabins silently rocking, gave the earnest SNCC militants a glass of ice water, thanked them for stopping by, and sent them on their way.

Indeed, the presence of northern civil rights workers and dozens of reporters did not stay violence even during the summer of 1964. SNCC workers were harassed as a matter of daily routine, tailed by cars full of men, and regularly terrorized. The most celebrated case occurred near Philadelphia, Mississippi, when one African-American SNCC worker and two whites were kidnapped and murdered with the connivance of law enforcement officials.

Amidst atrocities and fear, some Mississippi blacks and a few white allies, led by a forceful militant, Fannie Lou Hamer, organized the Mississippi Freedom Democratic party and sent a delegation to the 1964 Democratic party convention in Atlantic City, New Jersey. The Freedom Democrats, supported by most northern state delegates, demanded that they, not the segregationist regular Democrats, be recognized by the national party.

Working through longtime liberal and civil rights advocate Hubert Humphrey, whom LBJ selected to be his vice-presidential running mate, Johnson tried to work out a compromise, dividing Mississippi's convention votes between the rival groups. The Freedom Democrats were not happy with "half a loaf," but the segregationists were furious. They walked out of the convention, announcing that they would vote Republican in November. Their secession seemed inconsequential at the time; it proved to be the beginning of a revolution in American party politics.

THE GREAT SOCIETY

The Atlantic City convention was a turning point for the Democratic party. It marked the party's transformation into an unequivocally liberal party and, for

The Reverend Martin Luther King Jr. and his wife, Coretta Scott King, walked in the vanguard of a famous civil rights march in Selma, Alabama in 1964.

the moment, a triumphant one. Johnson and the Democratic leadership had no choice but to let the die-hard southern segregationists go. In shedding them, they not only lost the faction of the party that stood in the way of wooing black voters, but they discarded southern Democrats who had traditionally opposed liberal legislation of all kinds.

The Election of 1964

The election of 1964 seemed to prove the "black strategy"—appealing to African-American voters in northern urban states—to have been wise. Lyndon Johnson's Republican challenger, Senator Barry Goldwater of Arizona, was personally a tolerant man but racists and other extremists of the far right had made him their hero. Their fanaticism, amplified by Democratic campaign propaganda, helped transform his lifelong conservatism into a carping, vindictive negativism based on hatred, fear, and frighteningly simple solutions to problems that, so the Democrats said, threatened democracy and the rights of the weak.

Republican moderates cringed when Goldwater, accepting the party's nomination, said that "extremism in the pursuit of liberty is no vice." Worst of all in an age of a nuclear balance of terror, the grandson of a gun-toting frontier merchant sounded like a warmonger when he spoke on foreign policy. He seemed to say that the Cold War with the Soviet Union was a matter of which country was tougher. Democratic strategists were able to depict Goldwater as a man who would rush for the red button in times of crisis. A Democratic television commercial depicted a little girl playing in a field of wildflowers, then dissolved into a film of a nuclear blast.

The Democrats won in a landslide. Johnson won 61 percent of the popular vote and majorities in all but six states: five states of the Deep South plus Goldwater's native Arizona. More important than the prestige of the big victory was the fact that Johnson's coattails pulled into Washington 70 first-term Democratic congressmen from normally Republican districts. The party's edge in the House was 295 to 140, in the Senate 68 to 32. The congressional logjam that stymied Kennedy was blasted into toothpicks and Johnson did not hesitate to move. He sent waves of legislation rolling down Pennsylvania Avenue to the Capitol, not only rounding out the civil rights revolution, but enacting his Great Society, the creation of a government that assumed responsibility for social welfare on a massive scale.

The Voting Rights Act of 1965

The Voting Rights Act of 1965 put the federal power of law enforcement behind the rights of blacks to vote. Secure in this right for the first time in almost a century, southern blacks rushed to register. In only ten years after Martin Luther King Jr. had led his boycott against segregation on buses in Montgomery, the legal obstacles to black equality fell. Before long, southern white politicians who had built their careers on race baiting were showing up at black gatherings—beaming, shaking hands, kissing babies, and talking about unfortunate misunderstandings.

A former SNCC worker named Julian Bond was elected to the Georgia state assembly. He was amused that businessmen who once denounced him as a dangerous radical now took him out to lunch, cozening him for favors. By the early 1970s, all southern Democrats were courting black votes, however awkward it must have felt for some. In Alabama's gubernatorial election of 1982, George Wallace, the southern symbol of resistance to integration in the early 1960s, not only courted black votes, but owed his election to them: Alabama blacks found his Republican opponent by far the worse choice.

Even southern Republicans stopped expressing the sentiments that had originally taken them into the GOP. Strom Thurmond of South Carolina, a deft practitioner of the race-baiting school of southern politics who became a Republican because of the increasing liberalism of the Democratic party, was addressing black audiences by 1982. If most Palmetto State blacks continued to vote against him, it was because of his conservatism, not race-baiting on Thurmond's part.

The Voting Rights Act of 1965 also prompted an increase in black voting in the northern and western states. Not only Atlanta and New Orleans, but Newark, Gary, and Detroit elected black mayors during the 1970s. By 1984, the nation's second and third largest cities, Chicago and Los Angeles, plus Philadelphia, had black mayors. Tom Bradley of Los Angeles, a former policeman, just missed winning the governorship of California in 1982.

Johnson's Dream

If LBJ's sponsorship of full civil rights for blacks was partly forced on him by partisan calculations, his concern for the poor and disadvantaged of all races was sincere and deeply felt. He had had to struggle

How They Lived

Earl Warren (1891–1974)

For 16 years, Earl Warren of California was chief justice of the Supreme Court. Appointed by Eisenhower in 1953, he served long enough to inaugurate another Republican Californian, whom he did not much like, Richard Nixon. In the meantime, he led a Supreme Court that was more active in making decisions that shaped American historical development than any since the Marshall court of the early nineteenth century. And Warren was the most controversial Chief Justice since Roger B. Taney and his divisive Dred Scott decision of 1857.

Earl Warren was born in Los Angeles in 1891, attended the University of California at Berkeley, and, when he graduated from law school, remained in northern California. After service in the army during the First World War, he made his home in Oakland and, in 1925, was elected district attorney of Alameda County.

He appeared to be satisfied with a career in county politics, remaining district attorney for 14 years and virtually unknown elsewhere. However, a tough policy toward organized rackets brought him to the attention of the state's Republican bosses, and Warren was nominated for and elected California attorney general in 1939. The post traditionally was a stepping stone to the governorship in that state, and Warren's career took off. Fighting organized crime at the state level enabled him to win the Republican nomination for governor in 1942 and, quite easily, the election. Warren was so popular that, in 1946, because statewide nominations were made in a popular primary, he won both the Republican and Democratic nominations for governor and received 92 percent of the popular vote. This victory caught the eye of the national leadership of the Republican party, and in 1948, Warren was tapped to run for vice president with Thomas E. Dewey of New York. The Republicans believed that they were winners in 1948, so Warren, just 57 years old, seemed to be headed for the White House. Unfortunately, Dewey was defeated in one of the great presidential upsets. Nevertheless, Warren was easily reelected to the California governorship in 1950.

As governor, Warren was aligned with neither the conservative nor the liberal wings of the Republican party. In fact, while less shrill than William Knowland, the right-wing senator from California, Warren had been responsible for orders during the Second World War that allowed the seizure of property from Japanese Americans who had been interned by the federal government. There was little in his career to anticipate what he would do after President Eisenhower named him chief justice in 1953.

What he did was to assume immediately the leadership of the Supreme Court liberals—most of the justices had been appointed by Franklin D. Roosevelt—and spearhead a rash of decisions that overturned long-entrenched policies and practices in racial segregation, apportionment of legislative districts, and police procedure.

He is best remembered for having written the unanimous decision that forbade racial segregation in the schools, *Brown* v. *Board of Education of Topeka* (1954). A series of similar decisions regarding segregation by race paved the way for congressional approval of the Civil Rights Act of 1964 and the Voting Rights Act of 1965. They also made Warren the target of critics not only among segregationists but also among judicial conservatives who believed that the Warren court had made its decision in the *Brown* case not on legal but on sociological grounds. (They had a point, but the Warren court was not the first Supreme Court to do so.)

Warren won enemies among professional politicians as a result of a series of decisions on the issue of representation in elections to the House of Representatives and to state legislatures. It was common in states that were both urban and rural for rural voters to be "overrepresented." Because district lines had been drawn before cities had grown to house so many people, farm areas got to elect more legislators and congressmen than did city voters. In Virginia, for example, 84 rural voters had the same representation as 100 city voters. In 1946, the Supreme Court had refused to intervene in this practice on the grounds that it was a political matter, which indeed it was: rural state assemblymen refused to give up their privileged position.

In *Baker* v. *Carr* (1962), however, the Warren court ordered that states redraw the lines of congressional districts on the basis of "one man, one vote," all districts to contain approximately the same population. In *Westberry* v. *Sanders* (1964) and *Reynolds* v. *Sims* (1964), the court went further. The justices ruled that "one man, one vote" also applied to state legislatures, and to *both houses*. Because the upper houses of most state legislatures were patterned on the United States Senate, with each member representing a county, these decisions revolutionized state government. A five-to-four majority of the court said that whereas the Constitution provided for unequal representation in the Senate, state legislatures did not have the same mandate. In a sense, these decisions made the upper houses of state legislatures superfluous: they, like the lower houses, would be based on population.

The most controversial area in which the Warren court "legislated," as critics averred, was in police procedure. Three cases mark the development of what many people of the 1960s and 1970s regarded as court insistence on coddling criminals. In *Mapp* v. *Ohio* (1961), the Supreme Court ruled that police could not use as a basis for criminal prosecution evidence that had been seized without a warrant. In the abstract, the decision was unexceptional, but in specific cases, it seemed to protect violators of the law. Mapp, for instance, was a woman whose house had been raided on suspicion that she dealt in drugs. No evidence to that effect was discovered, but police did discover obscene materials, which were used in court against her. The court's decision in the matter seemed to rule out prosecution in any cases when the evidence used was not the specific object of a warranted search.

In *Escobedo* v. *Illinois* (1964), the court overturned a conviction. While the defendant, Danny Escobedo, was obviously guilty of the crime of which he had been convicted, he had been refused the right to see his lawyer when police were questioning him. Much more offensive to the growing anti-Warren forces who called for "law and order" was *Miranda* v. *Arizona* (1968), in which Warren himself wrote that a suspect in a crime must be informed immediately of his rights (particularly under the Fifth Amendment, which protects against self-incrimination), or any conviction secured could be in jeopardy. To many police officers and some civilians, the necessity of repeating a legally foolproof litany of constitutional rights in heated arrest situations was making the war against crime impossible and putting the rights of suspected criminals above those of victims. An "Impeach Earl Warren" movement sprang up during the 1960s, but never grew large enough to threaten the chief justice's job.

Immediately after President Kennedy's assassination in 1963, a reluctant Warren gave in to Lyndon Johnson's insistence that he head a commission to investigate the murder. He may have had a premonition that no possible findings would go unattacked. He was right. Despite the voluminous report (26 volumes of testimony from 552 witnesses, with an 888-page summation of evidence and conclusions), the Warren Commission was criticized for slipshod work and even of a "cover-up" in its conclusions that Lee Harvey Oswald was the sole killer and that the murder of Oswald by Jack Ruby was also unconnected to any conspiracy. Nevertheless, no conclusive evidence to the contrary has since been presented.

Warren tried to resign his post when Johnson was still president so that his successor would also be a liberal. However, when Johnson tried to give the chief justiceship to an old friend, Associate Justice Abe Fortas, enemies in the Senate dug up some irregularities in Fortas's record and prevented the appointment. Warren remained in office until 1969, when Richard Nixon replaced him with Warren Burger, a more conservative jurist whose revisions of the Warren court decisions did not turn them around as much as many Warren critics had hoped. Warren died in 1974.

Julian Bond went from being a civil rights worker to one of the South's most famous politicians.

himself as a young man and, in Texas politics, was regarded as a friend of Mexican Americans, most of whom were poor and treated scarcely better than blacks were. Johnson worshiped Franklin D. Roosevelt and wanted to be remembered in history as the president who completed what the New Deal had started. He envisioned an America

> where no child will go unfed and no youngster will go unschooled; where every child has a good teacher and every teacher has good pay, and both have good classrooms; where every human being has dignity and every worker has a job; where education is blind to color and employment is unaware of race; where decency appeals and courage abounds.

Johnson's War on Poverty, which was directed by the new Office of Economic Opportunity, funded a Job Corps that retrained unemployed people for the new kinds of jobs available in high-technology industries. The OEO recruited boys and girls from impoverished families for catch-up education in special Head Start schools and young men and women for placement in universities. Other programs provided financial help and tutoring in order to compensate for the economic and cultural handicaps of growing up in poverty. Volunteers in Service to America (VISTA) was a domestic Peace Corps, sending social workers and teachers into decaying inner cities and poor rural areas. Medicare provided government-funded health insurance for the elderly, chronically ill, and very poor.

Nor did the Great Society neglect the middle and working classes. Generous funding of schools, colleges, and universities and extremely cheap student loans made it possible for hundreds of thousands of young people to secure an education otherwise closed to them.

Some of these acts were legislated before the lopsided election of 1964. But it was after his great victory, thanks to the hordes of freshman Democratic congressmen beholden to Johnson's landslide for their seats, that the program was completed.

VIETNAM! VIETNAM!

"Were there no outside world," the political journalist Theodore H. White wrote in 1969, just five years after Lyndon Johnson's great electoral triumph, "Lyndon Johnson might conceivably have gone down as the greatest of twentieth-century presidents." It was an overstatement; Franklin D. Roosevelt is surely the century's most important president. Still, obvious in his remark, White had written off the possibility of LBJ finishing high in the rankings.

So had all but a few of the president's devotees. By 1969—by 1967!—virtually no one was saying as, just a few years earlier, LBJ's aide Jack Valenti did without embarrassment, "I sleep each night a little better, a little more confidently because Lyndon Johnson is my president." More typical by 1967 was the statement of Senator Eugene McCarthy, a member of Johnson's own party: "We've got a wild man in the White House, and we are going to have to treat him as such."

What happened? A war happened. The builder of the Great Society at home mired the United States in a war in a Southeast Asian country which, before 1964, few Americans could have found on a map. Johnson inherited the American presence in Vietnam from Kennedy—and to an extent from Eisenhower and Dulles. But it was he who made the decisions that transformed a minor problem of foreign policy (and one that, with historian's hindsight, could probably have been easily resolved), into a cancer that spread into every organ of the American body politic.

A Long Way from the Pedernales

During the nineteenth century, the French established firm imperial control over most of Indo-China, the peninsula that hangs down from the Asian mainland east of India and includes the present-day nations of Vietnam, Laos, and Cambodia. As elsewhere in their empire, the French fostered the development of a native elite that embraced French culture and, for the most part, the Roman Catholic religion. This Indochinese elite prospered and was favored by the French both economically and with a share in governing the colony.

However, the majority of Vietnamese, Cambodians, and Laotians remained peasants or menial laborers, perhaps treated the worse because their rulers were foreign, perhaps not, but in any case, many resented the French presence and wanted them out. One such nationalist was Ho Chih Minh, who went to Paris during World War I and, while working at a variety of jobs and educating himself, became a founding member of the French Communist party. Ho then lived in Russia and China until World War II, when he returned to Vietnam to organize a guerrilla movement, the Viet Minh, to fight the Japanese who occupied the country after the defeat of France in Europe.

Partly because of Ho Chih Minh's contribution to the war effort in harassing the Japanese, partly because of his distaste for French imperialism, President Roosevelt favored setting up an independent Vietnam after the war. Knowing this, Ho, with the support of many non-Communists as well as reds, proclaimed the Republic of Vietnam in 1945. Later, when French forces returned, he agreed to keep Vietnam within the French imperial community so long as the nation was a self-governing commonwealth.

The French government, its pride wounded by France's collapse during World War II, refused to cooperate with Ho. Instead, it set up a puppet regime and the Viet Minh took once again to the jungles and rice paddies where they launched a guerrilla war that lasted eight years. In 1950, having defined Ho's movement as part of world Communist expansionism, the United States began to funnel aid to the French. However, after a decisive defeat in the battle of Dien Bien Phu in 1954, the French gave up and left. According to the Geneva Accords signed that same year, Vietnam was (like Korea had been) divided into two zones at the seventeenth parallel. Ho's Viet Minh would govern the northern half of the country from Hanoi; a non-Communist government would administer the southern part of the country from Saigon. After two years, when the bitterness and tumult of the long war abated, democratic elections would determine the nation's future.

It was all a long way from the Pedernales River. What did the United States have to do with a war between Indochinese demanding independence and

Ho Chi Minh founded the Viet Minh to fight for an independent Vietnam.

a weak and divided France trying to salvage an unsalvageable empire?

American Involvement

The Cold War and John Foster Dulles's determination to roll back Communist influence involved the United States in Vietnamese affairs. Dulles was blind to the fact that, although a Communist, Ho Chih Minh had initially looked to the United States for help. Ho was aware that FDR had favored an independent Vietnam and he patterned Vietnam's Declaration of Independence on the American document of 1776. Although it is impossible to know Ho's long-term intentions during the long war with the French, his Viet Minh included substantial non-Communist elements. Some evidence hints that Ho counted on American economic aid to build up the Vietnamese nation. To any Vietnamese nationalist, China, not the United States, was the chief foreign threat.

Instead of feeling Ho out, Dulles pumped millions of dollars into the French war effort and even considered using nuclear weapons to lift the Viet Minh's siege of the French at Dien Bien Phu. Eisenhower vetoed that proposal, as he usually did when Dulles's fervor overheated, and the United States attended the Geneva conference that ended French rule. Dulles refused to sign the Geneva Accords, but the United States announced that it would do nothing to interfere with its provisions, including the election to be held in 1956.

Events and propaganda by the China Lobby altered American policy. About a million anti-

Communist North Vietnamese fled to below the seventeenth parallel between 1954 and 1956, and there were several instances of mistreatment of Roman Catholics in the north. A Vietnamese nationalist who lived in exile in the United States, Ngo Dinh Diem, returned to the south and was portrayed in the United States as his nation's George Washington. The Eisenhower administration gave Diem $320 million in aid in 1955 and supported his refusal to hold elections in 1956. Instead, he proclaimed the Republic of Vietnam in the south.

Viet Cong

For several years, Diem appeared to succeed. Then, in 1960, opposition groups, led by South Vietnamese Communists, formed the National Liberation Front and launched, yet again, a guerrilla war aimed at unifying the country. The NLF attacked isolated patrols of Diem's soldiers, murdered village officials loyal to the regime, bullied and terrorized some villagers, and curried the favor of others. The NLF actually set up local governments in many parts of South Vietnam, collecting taxes and administering justice.

Diem described his enemies as Viet Cong, Vietnamese Communists, although many non-Communists belonged to the NLF during this era. Diem claimed that the guerrilla movement was inspired, aided, and abetted by North Vietnam, which was quite true, but obscured the fact that virtually all of the Viet Cong's 15,000 soldiers in 1960 were South Vietnamese peasants. Both the Eisenhower and Kennedy administrations pumped millions of dollars into his regime.

Kennedy's Uncertainty

Kennedy's military advisers urged him to send 10,000 American troops to help Diem, telling him that the essence of the problem in Vietnam was military. Kennedy was unconvinced. He had just been stung by CIA advice at Cuba's Bay of Pigs and wondered why Diem's ARVN (Army of the Republic of Vietnam), which numbered 250,000, could not handle 15,000 mostly part-time guerrillas. He compromised by sending 3,000 Green Berets, U.S. Army Special Forces experts in counterinsurgency and fighting guerrillas, to advise the ARVN. Slowly, the American presence increased. By the end of 1962, there were 11,000 American military advisers in South Vietnam.

By mid-1963, however, Kennedy soured on Diem. Isolated from the people of the country as he shambled around the presidential palace day and night, surrounded and dominated by corrupt relatives, Diem approved of repressive policies, high taxes, and favoritism toward Roman Catholic Vietnamese. In a few short years, the George Washington of Vietnam had become a peevish, unpopular dictator. Buddhist monks led protests in Saigon, Hue, and other cities, a few setting themselves aflame in intersections. Capitalizing on the unrest, the NLF stepped up its campaign in the countryside. During the day, Diem's regime more or less governed South Vietnam. Once the sun had set, the Saigon government controlled little more than the capital, other major towns, and part of the fertile rice-growing Mekong River delta. Elsewhere, NLF guerrillas moved freely.

Kennedy may have given up on the possibility of military victory. At least, he planned to reduce the American contingent in the country, 16,000 strong by the fall of 1963. When some advisers protested, insisting that another increase in American manpower would win the war, he replied that to get involved more deeply was like "taking a drink. The effect wears off, and you have to take another."

Perhaps hoping to arrange a political settlement—like much recent history, the story is muddled and hotly contested—Kennedy agreed to tolerate a coup d'état by high-ranking ARVN officers that would remove Diem from the scene. An American plane was reserved to take Diem and his family out of the country but, in November 1963, when the ARVN struck, Diem was assassinated. A month later, Kennedy was dead. While the United States was undergoing a period of mourning and transition, South Vietnam was plunged into political instability as one general toppled another and the NLF increased its power in the countryside.

MR. JOHNSON'S WAR

President Johnson ordered modest increases in the number of American military advisers in early 1964. But he, like Kennedy, seemed at first to want out of the war. Through intermediaries, he offered economic aid to North Vietnam in return for peace talks. The North Vietnamese replied that they could not speak for the NLF. The NLF, which Johnson, like Diem, referred to as the Viet Cong, refused to negotiate until all American soldiers were withdrawn from the country.

The President's Vision

This Johnson refused to do. Although he was no John Foster Dulles, LBJ's view of the Cold War was shaped in the 1950s by the belief that Communism was monolithic, an international movement directed ultimately from the Kremlin. Just enough men and supplies reached the NLF from the north to convince him that the war in Vietnam was not a civil conflict, but a war of subversion dependent on outside interference. He vowed that he was "not going to be the President who saw Southeast Asia go the way China went."

Johnson subscribed to the domino theory of Communist expansion propounded none too gracefully by President Eisenhower several years earlier: "You knock over the first one, and what will happen to the last one is the certainty that it will go over very quickly." When Johnson looked at Southeast Asia, he saw a line of fallen dominoes stretching from Russia through China to North Vietnam, and a line of standing dominoes beginning in South Vietnam, Laos, and Cambodia and extending to the Philippines and even Japan. As early as 1961, he said, "We must decide whether to help these countries to the best of our ability or throw in the towel in the area and pull back our defenses to San Francisco."

The Tonkin Gulf Resolution

As late as October 1964 (shortly before Johnson faced the saber-rattling Goldwater in the presidential election), the president assured Americans that "we are not about to send American boys nine or ten thousand miles away from home to do what Asian boys ought to be doing for themselves." In reality, he was thinking about widening the war by means of a massive American military effort as early as the summer of 1964. In August, he was informed that North Vietnamese patrol boats had attacked American destroyers in the Gulf of Tonkin. He then asked Congress for authority "to take all necessary measures to repel any armed attack against the forces of the United States and to prevent future aggression."

Only two senators voted against the Gulf of Tonkin Resolution, Wayne Morse of Oregon, a lifelong maverick who had been elected as a Republican, an Independent, and as a Democrat, and Ernest Gruening of Alaska. Gruening said that he would not vote for "a predated declaration of war." In fact, whatever Johnson's motives at the time, he was to call on the Gulf of Tonkin Resolution to turn the Vietnam conflict into a major war. By the end of 1964, the American military contingent in South Vietnam increased to 23,000, all, however, still described as advisers.

Escalation

Then, in February 1965, the Viet Cong attacked an American military base near Pleiku. Citing the Tonkin Gulf Resolution, Johnson sent in 3,500 marines, the first official combat troops, to South Vietnam. In April, 20,000 more troops arrived. By the end of 1965 there were 200,000 American troops in South Vietnam. This number doubled by the end of 1966 and reached 500,000 by the end of 1967.

Between 1965 and 1968, the U.S. Air Force carried out heavy bombing of North Vietnam. To deprive the Viet Cong of shelter in the South Vietnam jungle, planes sprayed defoliants over tens of thousands of acres, killing trees, underbrush, and crops. American soldiers then moved in on search-and-destroy missions.

Johnson's policy of step-by-step increases in the intensity of the war was known as escalation. His object was to prove to the enemy that fighting the American military machine was a hopeless cause. Briefly in 1965 and 1967, he stopped bombing and offered peace terms to North Vietnam.

Both proposals were rejected. Instead, North Vietnam matched each American escalation with an escalation of its own. Beginning in 1964 and escalating in 1966, North Vietnam sent its own soldiers into the war to replace dead Viet Cong. Within two years, 100,000 North Vietnamese were in the south. Step by step, a civil war between two groups of South Vietnamese became very largely a war between Americans and North Vietnamese.

China and the Soviet Union also escalated their contributions to the war. Both countries supplied North Vietnam with ground-to-air missiles and other sophisticated weapons as well as economic aid.

The Tet Offensive

Nevertheless, at the beginning of 1968, the American commander, General William Westmoreland, told LBJ that victory was within reach. His words

Tanks were not a major element in Vietnam. On the ground it was an infantryman's war.

had scarcely been reported in the newspapers when, in the midst of the celebrations of Tet, Vietnam's traditional lunar New Year, 70,000 Viet Cong and North Vietnamese launched attacks on 30 South Vietnamese cities. For several days they controlled much of the city of Hue. In Saigon, enemy commandos attacked the American embassy itself. The Viet Cong took back jungle areas the search-and-destroy missions had cleared.

The Americans regrouped and, when the Tet Offensive was over, the Viet Cong and North Vietnamese had suffered horrendous casualties. By any traditional definition, the battle was an American victory. In May, North Vietnam agreed to begin peace talks in Paris. However, the American people's confidence in the war was severely shaken by an enemy offensive they had been told was out of the question. The number of American boys dead, reported each evening on television, soared from an average 26 a week in 1965 to 96 a week in 1966 and 180 a week in 1967. In 1968, more than 280 Americans were killed in Vietnam each week. The cost of the war had risen to $25 billion a year, nearly $70,000,000 a day!

Despite this tremendous effort and loss of life, victory seemed as distant as ever. In just a few weeks after the Tet Offensive, public approval of Johnson's handling of the war dropped from 40 percent to 26 percent. LBJ was badly shaken, "tormented" and "paranoid," according to an aide, Bill Moyers. He "would just go within himself, just disappear—morose, self-pitying, angry." He and another aide secretly consulted psychiatrists about him.

TROUBLED YEARS

Johnson in possession of himself craved consensus, a word he used as often as Kennedy called for vigor. In making his plea for civil rights legislation, he

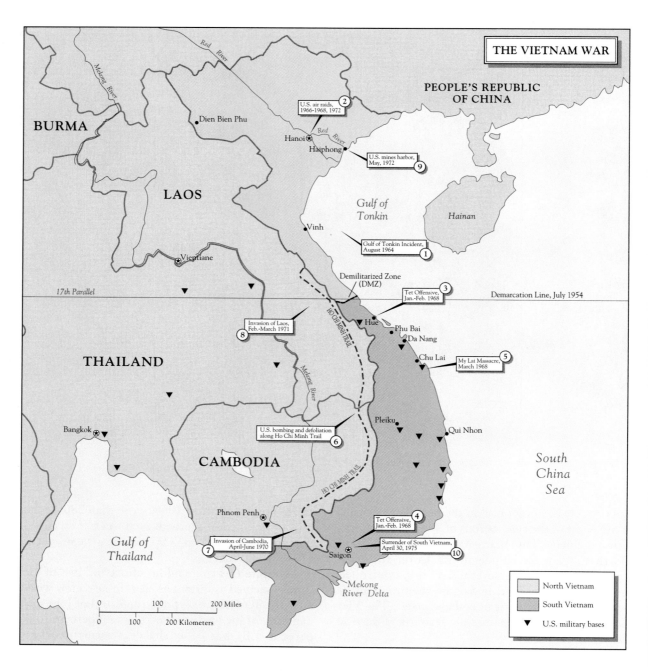

adopted the slogan of the movement, "We Shall Overcome." He meant that all Americans would rise above the blight of racial hatred and discrimination. Another favorite presidential saying was a quotation from the biblical book of Isaiah, "Let us come together." The old manipulator of votes was not, as president, content with a majority, not even so large a one as he won in 1964. He wanted a unity of Americans behind him and his vision of a Great Society.

What LBJ got was a people divided more bitterly than at any time since, perhaps, the Civil War. The major cause of the social divisions of the 1960s was the war in Vietnam.

Hawks and Doves

Until 1965, the chief criticism of Johnson's Vietnam policy came from conservative Republicans like Barry Goldwater, some retired military men, and extremists like members of the John Birch Society. They said that in moving so cautiously, Johnson was making the same mistake President Truman made in Korea. He was fighting for a limited purpose, a negotiated peace, rather than for total victory. Known as hawks, these critics wanted to use American military might to crush the Viet Cong and North Vietnamese. Former Air Force Chief of Staff Curtis LeMay called for bombing North Vietnam "into the Stone Age." Future president Ronald Reagan said "we should declare war on North Vietnam. We could pave the whole place over by noon and be home by dinner."

After LBJ escalated the war, becoming a hawk himself, his chief critics were the doves, people who called for an end to the fighting or, at least, more serious efforts to negotiate a peace. As the war dragged on and the casualty lists mounted, this antiwar movement grew in size and militance.

Most doves were liberal Democrats, members of LBJ's own party. Doves included members of Congress, university professors and schoolteachers, ministers, priests, and nuns, some working people, many middle-class professionals, and even several retired generals. College students, although most were immune to the draft that sent young men to Vietnam, were attracted to the antiwar movement in great numbers.

Mass demonstrations made for good television news features and put the antiwar movement at the center of public attention. In October 1965, 100,000 people attended demonstrations in 90 cities. In April 1967, about 300,000 Americans marched in opposition to the war in New York and San Francisco. Some young men burned their draft cards and went to jail rather than into the army. Some 40,000 went into exile, especially Canada and Sweden. Draft dodgers with influential social and political connections could join the National Guard in order to avoid combat service.

Antiwar Arguments

Doves opposed the war for many different reasons, some contradictory. A few were members of radical groups such as the Progressive Labor party, which admired Mao Zedong. They openly hoped that Ho Chih Minh would defeat the "imperialist capitalist" United States. Many youthful romantics, who knew little about Communism, were enchanted by the spectacle of the outnumbered, poorly equipped Viet Cong resisting American power.

Demonstration Decade

Between 1963 and 1968, according to the National Commission on the Causes and Prevention of Violence, there were

- 369 civil rights demonstrations
- 239 black riots and disturbances
- 213 white terrorist attacks against civil rights workers
- 104 antiwar demonstrations
- 91 student protests on campus
- 54 segregationist clashes with counterdemonstrators
- 24 anti-integration demonstrations

Other doves, like the famous pediatrician, Dr. Benjamin Spock, were anti-Communists. However, they believed that the United States was fighting against the wishes of a majority of the Vietnamese people and, therefore, was in the wrong. They disapproved of the fact that their powerful nation was showering terrible destruction on a small, poor country.

Religious pacifists like the Quakers opposed the war because they opposed all wars. Other morally concerned people, who agreed that some wars were justified, felt that the war in Vietnam was not one of them. They objected to the fact that, with no clear battle lines, American troops were making war on civilians as well as on enemy soldiers.

Bombs and defoliants took many innocent lives. In addition, a few American soldiers were guilty of deliberate atrocities. The most publicized occurred at the village of My Lai in March 1968 when American troops killed 347 unarmed men, women, and children. The Viet Cong were guilty of similar crimes but that, doves said, did not justify Americans in stooping to the same level.

Some critics of the war emphasized politics and diplomacy. They pointed out that the United States was exhausting itself fighting in a small, unimportant country while the power of China and the Soviet Union was untouched. Diplomat George Kennan and Senator William Fulbright of Arkansas argued that the United States was neglecting its commitments elsewhere in the world. Senators Gaylord Nelson of Wisconsin and Wayne Morse of Oregon pointed out that the American war effort was

960 *Chapter 48 Years of Turbulence*

alienating other Third World nations and even America's most trusted allies.

Black Separatism

The antiwar movement was not the only expression of discontent in the Great Society. Most remarkable about the troubles of the 1960s, anti-Johnson protest was noisiest among the very groups that most benefited from LBJ's reforms.

Some of the fiercest anti-Johnson rhetoric came from young blacks, for whom the president believed he did so much. While the majority of black people supported the Great Society, many younger militants, particularly in the North, attacked the president's integrationist policies in the name of the black power movement.

Black power meant many things. To civil rights campaigner Jesse Jackson, and to some intellectuals such as sociologist Charles Hamilton, it meant pressure politics in the time-honored tradition of American ethnic groups: African Americans demanding concessions for their race on the basis of the votes they could either deliver to or withhold from a political candidate. (It was Jackson who, in the 1990s, revived the term *African American* in part to define blacks as an ethnic voting bloc.) To a tiny group of black nationalists, it meant demanding a part of the United States for the formation of a separate nation for blacks only. To the great majority, the slogan was reduced to little more than fashion, dressing up in dashikis, wearing hairstyles called "Afros," and avoiding friendships and even casual social relationships with whites.

Black power was not a political program, but a cry of anguish and anger against the discrimination of the past and the discovery that civil equality of itself did little to remedy the social and psychological burdens from which American blacks suffered: poverty, high unemployment, inferior educational opportunities, health problems of a severity whites did not know, high crime rates in black neighborhoods, and a sense of inadequacy bred over three centuries of oppression.

Malcolm X and Violence

The most formidable spokesman for black separatism was Malcolm Little, an ex-petty criminal from Detroit who styled himself Malcolm X, stating that a slave owner had stolen his real African name. An adherent of a religious sect known as the Nation of Islam, or Black Muslims (for Christianity was said to be a "white man's religion"), Malcolm was a spellbinding preacher. He said that black people should reject Martin Luther King Jr.'s call to integrate into American society and, instead, separate from whites and glory in their blackness. Many young blacks, particularly in the North, were captivated by this message of defiance. One convert was a West Indian immigrant, Stokely Carmichael, who expelled all whites from the Student Nonviolent Coordinating Committee in 1966. "If we are to proceed toward true liberation," Carmichael said, "we must cut ourselves off from white people." He took SNCC out of the civil rights movement and soon into extinction; Carmichael himself married a popular folk singer and emigrated to Ghana, where he was briefly celebrated for wearing a pearl-handled revolver.

Malcolm X's admonition to meet white racist violence with black violence appealed to former civil rights workers who were beaten by police and to teenage blacks in the urban ghettos. Carmichael's successor as the head of SNCC, Hubert Geroid "H. Rap" Brown, proclaimed as his motto, "Burn, Baby, Burn." In Oakland, California, two community college students, Huey P. Newton and Bobby Seale, formed the Black Panther Party for Self-Defense. They were immediately involved in violent confrontations with police because of their insistence that they be allowed to patrol black neighborhoods with firearms.

Violence haunted black America during the 1960s. Malcolm X fell out of favor with the Black Muslims and, in 1965, was gunned down by assassins associated with the Nation of Islam. Also in 1965, a riot in the Watts district of Los Angeles resulted in 34 deaths and $35 million in property damage. In 1966 and 1967, black riots raged in the ghettos of many cities. When Martin Luther King Jr. was killed by a white racist, James Earl Ray, in 1968, the smoke from buildings set afire by rioters in Washington wafted into the White House itself.

The Student Movement

Just as troubling was discontent among another group that was favored by Johnson's Great Society reforms, university students. By 1963, it already was clear that the baby-boom generation was not so passive in its political expression as the youth of the 1950s had been. Students demonstrated against

Malcolm X (Malcolm Little), the reformed felon who inspired and energized young African Americans (Malcolm X preferred "blacks").

capital punishment, protested against the violations of civil liberties by groups like the House Un-American Activities Committee, and worked in the civil rights movement. In 1963, a new national youth organization, Students for a Democratic Society (SDS), issued the Port Huron Statement, a comprehensive critique of American society written by a graduate of the University of Michigan, Tom Hayden. The SDS called for young people to take the lead in drafting a program by which the United States could be made genuinely democratic and a force for peace and justice.

Like the advocates of black power, the New Left, as SDS and other organizations came collectively to be called, was not so much a political movement as an explosion of anger and frustration. Tom Hayden and a few other youth leaders tried to channel student energies into concrete concerns like civil rights for blacks, the problems of the poor, and the power of large corporations in American society. But most of the campus riots of the late 1960s were unfocused, aimed at local grievances such as student participation in setting university rules, or directed against the war in Vietnam, a matter beyond the competence and influence of university presidents and local merchants (major targets of student rebellion) to solve.

Massive protests on campuses began at the University of California at Berkeley with the founding of the Free Speech Movement in 1964. By 1968, protest took a violent turn with students at Columbia University seizing several buildings and refusing to budge until they were forcibly removed by police.

The Counterculture

By 1966, many young people, high school as well as college students, were dropping out of politics to pursue a personal rebellion. In the Haight-Ashbury

---

Marketing Malcolm

The unifying American faith is that everything in the world can be sold. The great American equalizer is the search for the secret to selling commodities that consumers have not yet discovered. In 1991 and 1992, marketers found a way to make money out of Malcolm X, whose name was fading into obscurity in the quarter century following his assassination. Sensing that a new generation of black (and white) young people would appreciate Malcolm's militance, Spike Lee, a movie director with a genius for promotion, made a long biographical film in which Malcolm X was depicted as a hero, El-Hajj Malik El-Shabazz, "king of the African Americans."

Lee and others marketed Malcolm X baseball hats, X T-shirts, X coffee mugs, X brand potato chips ("We dedicate this product to the concept of X," that is, the unknown heritage of African Americans), even X air fresheners for cars ("this is the lowest-priced item for Afro-Americans to show their support"). Warner Brothers, the company that released Lee's film, protested: "The last thing we want is a poor product dragging down the image of Malcolm X." The Indianapolis company that marketed Malcolm also managed the images of cult actors Humphrey Bogart and James Dean, and baseball player Babe Ruth.

The Berkeley campus of the University of California became the center of baby boomer student protest in 1966.

district of San Francisco and in the East Village of New York, thousands of teenagers gathered to establish what they called a counterculture, a new way of living based on promiscuous sex, drugs (particularly marijuana and a synthetic hallucinogen, LSD), and extravagant colorful clothing.

They called themselves "flower children," free of the pressures and preoccupations of American materialism. Other Americans called them "hippies" and were alternately amused by them, or condemned them as lazy, immoral "long-haired kids." In both New York and San Francisco, tour buses took curiosity seekers through hippie neighborhoods as though they were exotic foreign countries. When tourists from small towns snapped shots of counterculture fauna, some good-humored hippies whipped out cameras and took pictures of the "squares."

When commercialization seemed to be destroying the vitality of the counterculture, some flower children retreated to communes in the California mountains and New Mexico desert. But because the self-fulfillment of individuals was the principal goal of the phenomenon, and because drugs played a large part in the culture, the communes were doomed from the start. Commonly, the most fundamental matters of procuring the necessities of health and sanitation were neglected.

THE ELECTION OF 1968

No president can survive a serious economic depression in a year that he must stand for reelection. Lyndon Johnson, able to shout gleefully while striding through an airplane in 1964, "I am the king! I am the king!" discovered in 1968 that a reigning monarch cannot survive a serious social, cultural, and moral depression.

Eugene McCarthy

In 1967, Eugene McCarthy was in his second term as senator from Minnesota. He was a tall man with a gray solemnity about him; he was glum. His record as a liberal workhorse was solid, but no one thought of him as a mover and shaker. Minnesota already had its walking earthquake of energy and exuberance in Vice President Hubert Humphrey. McCarthy seemed just right to stay at home, anchoring Minnesota's long liberal tradition in middle western bedrock.

But McCarthy was anguished by the issue that the vice president had to dodge, the war in Vietnam. Late in 1967, he announced that he would stand as a candidate for the Democratic presidential nomination, challenging Lyndon B. Johnson on that issue.

Political pundits admired McCarthy's principle and pluck. A few were enchanted by his diffidence: with plenty of mediocrities lusting unashamedly after public office, he seemed genuinely to believe that a public servant should serve a cause. But the experts gave him little chance. McCarthy's only base of support was within the largely middle-class antiwar movement. The labor unions, vital to Democratic party success at the polls, remembered votes he had cast against their legislative programs; he struck no chord among either black or ethnic minorities (despite his somewhat mystical Roman Catholic religion); and he positively disdained big city mayors like Chicago's Richard E. Daley. A portion of the educated, cultured, affluent liberal middle class was not, the professionals said, a foundation on which to build an electoral majority.

Johnson Retires

Time was to prove them right. In 1968, however, antiwar activists were so aroused that, like Barry Goldwater's right-wing shock troops in the Republican party in 1964, they were able to turn the Democratic party upside down. At McCarthy's call, thousands of university students dropped their studies and rushed to New Hampshire, scene of the first presidential primary. They agreed to get "clean for Gene," shearing their long hippie hair, shaving their beards, and donning neckties, brassieres, and dresses so as not to alienate the people of the conservative state from the issue at hand — the war. Sleeping on the floors of McCarthy storefront headquarters, they rang door bells, handed out pamphlets at supermarkets, and stuffed envelopes.

President Johnson knew enough of the country's anxiety over the war to be concerned. He kept his name off the ballot. Instead, the governor of New Hampshire ran as his proxy. The vote was evenly split, but such a rebuke of an incumbent president in a traditionally cautious and conservative state

promised bigger McCarthy victories elsewhere. Johnson knew it. On national television, he announced that he would retire when his term expired.

The Democrats: Who Will End the War?

Johnson's announcement caught everyone by surprise. Vice President Humphrey, in Mexico on a goodwill tour, rushed back to Washington to throw his hat in the ring. He had an immediate edge on McCarthy because of long-standing ties with labor, blacks, big city Democratic machines, the party's professionals, and contributors generous with a dollar.

The McCarthy backers expected Humphrey to run and welcomed the contest. What they could not foresee was that in the wake of Johnson's withdrawal, Robert F. Kennedy also rushed to enter the race. Kennedy was a real threat to both McCarthy and Humphrey. Johnson had eased him out of his cabinet as soon after John Kennedy's death as it was seemly to do so. LBJ did not like "Bobby," whose presence kept him in the Kennedy shadow. In fact, RFK looked on Johnson almost as a usurper of a Kennedy property. After methodical public opinion polls typical of the Kennedy clan showed that he could win a Senate seat in New York despite his lack of association with the state, Robert Kennedy ran, won, and became a critic of the war and a leading liberal spokesman.

His connections with minorities were as strong as Humphrey's. He was a personal friend of Cesar Chavez, leader of the mostly Hispanic farm workers' union in California and the Southwest. Even with blacks, on whose behalf Humphrey had labored since the 1940s, Kennedy was popular. When Martin Luther King Jr. was assassinated on April 4, 1968, Bobby's response seemed more sincere and was better received than the respects of any other Democrat. He had maintained his connections with the old-line party professionals and the labor movement. Indeed, within the Democratic party, his political realism and opportunism made him anathema only to the group that continued to support McCarthy. They attacked him as avidly as they attacked Johnson and Humphrey, as an exemplar of the old politics.

Kennedy ran strong, although not without setbacks. For example, McCarthy won the next-to-last primary in Oregon. Then, on the very night he won the last of the primaries in California, Robert Kennedy was assassinated, shot point-blank in the

The Prophet of '68

No one understood more the meaning of the election of 1968—even before it was held—than then Republican party strategist Kevin Phillips, the designer of the plan that would make the Republican party the dominant party of the end of the twentieth century. "Sure, Hubert [Humphrey] will carry Riverside Drive in November," Phillips said, referring to a New York City neighborhood fashionable among intellectuals and other well-to-do liberals. "La-de-dah. What will he do in Oklahoma?"—among frustrated working people. Even George Wallace's candidacy was helping the Republicans in the long run.

We'll get two-thirds to three-fourths of the Wallace vote in 1972. I'd hate to be the opponent in that race. When Hubie loses [Eugene] McCarthy and [Congressman Allard] Lowenstein backers are going to take the party so far to the left they'll just become irrelevant. They'll do to it what our economic royalists did to us in 1936.

head by Sirhan B. Sirhan, a Jordanian who disliked Kennedy's support for the Jewish state of Israel.

The tragedy demoralized the antiwar Democrats and undoubtedly contributed to the week-long riots in Chicago that made a mockery of the Democratic national convention. Many Kennedy supporters found it impossible to swing behind McCarthy and backed Senator George McGovern of South Dakota instead. With a divided opposition, Humphrey was able to win the Democratic nomination on the first ballot. As a gesture toward blue-collar ethnics whose aspirations were aroused by John F. Kennedy, and who seemed to be supporting Bobby, Humphrey chose a Roman Catholic running mate, Senator Edmund B. Muskie of Maine.

Nixon and Wallace

Richard M. Nixon easily won the Republican nomination at a placid convention in Miami Beach. Although the former vice president had retired from politics in 1962, after losing an election for governor of California, he had doggedly rebuilt his position in the GOP. He firmed up his support among eastern moderate Republicans and won over Republican

conservatives by working hard for Goldwater in 1964. After 1964, Nixon attended every local Republican function to which he was invited, no matter how small the town, insignificant the occasion, or tawdry the candidate he was to endorse. By making himself readily available to the party's grass-roots workers, the far from charismatic Nixon built up energetic, active cadres of supporters.

The Democrats were badly split. Many in the antiwar wing of the party announced that they would vote for the pacifist pediatrician Benjamin Spock. Humphrey tried to woo them back by hinting that he would end the war but, as Johnson's vice president, he could not repudiate LBJ's policy. The Democratic split and Humphrey's ambiguity enabled Nixon to waffle on the war issue. He espoused a hawkish military policy at the same time that he reminded voters that a Republican president, Dwight D. Eisenhower, had ended the war in Korea.

The chief threat to a Nixon victory seemed to come from the American Independent party, founded by Governor George Wallace when he calculated that he had no chance to win the Democratic nomination. A diminutive, combative man—reporters called him a bantam fighting cock—Wallace barnstormed the country and attempted to forge an odd alliance of Republican right-wing extremists and blue-collar working people who felt that the Democratic party had forgotten them in its anxiety to appeal to the blacks. This "white backlash" vote appeared to grow after Robert Kennedy was killed. Already indifferent to McCarthy, many blue-collar white ethnics who liked Kennedy personally found Wallace much more to their taste than civil rights pioneer Hubert Humphrey.

A Close Call

It was obvious that Wallace could not win the election. His purpose was to win enough electoral votes from both Humphrey and Nixon to throw the election into the House of Representatives. Because each state casts one vote when a president is selected in the House, anti-integration southern congressmen under Wallace's leadership, so Wallace imagined, could make a deal with Nixon: a reversal of Democratic party civil rights policies in return for their support.

Fearing this possibility, Humphrey called on Nixon to pledge with him that neither of them would deal with Wallace. Instead, Humphrey proposed, he

Minutes before he was assassinated, Senator Robert Kennedy celebrates his victory in the California Democratic primary.

and Nixon should pledge that in the case that neither won in the electoral college, each would direct his supporters in the House to vote for whomever of the two finished with the most votes.

Nixon, competing with Wallace for votes, evaded the challenge. And in the end it did not matter. Although Wallace did better than any third-party candidate since 1924, winning 13.5 percent of the popular vote and 46 electoral votes, Nixon eked out a plurality of 500,000 votes and an absolute majority in the electoral college. It was close. A rush of blue-collar workers back to Humphrey during the final week of the campaign indicated to some pollsters that he would have won had the election been held a week or two later. Some Democratic strategists quietly blamed the loss of Johnson who, peevish towards his loyal vice president almost to the end, did little to help Humphrey. Or the explanation of Nixon's victory may well have been those antiwar Democrats who could not bring themselves to vote for Humphrey. In time, their New Age politics would transform the great political alliance forged by Franklin D. Roosevelt into a party for whom the presidency was an elusive prize.

CHRONOLOGY

1962 Under President Kennedy, United States makes small military commitment in support of South Vietnamese government against Communist-dominated Viet Cong rebels

1963 Shortly before President Kennedy's murder, unpopular South Vietnamese leaders are assassinated in coup to which United States is accomplice

1964 President Johnson launches the "Great Society," a massive program, based on the New Deal, to reform inequities in American society
Civil Rights Act of 1964 effectively ends legal discrimination in public accommodations based on race

966 *Chapter 48 Years of Turbulence*

Student Nonviolent Coordinating Committee, a trans-racial organization dedicated to civil rights, sponsors "Freedom Summer" in Mississippi, an attempt to register blacks to vote
President Johnson is reelected in a landslide over conservative Republican Barry Goldwater, who is tainted as an extremist
Southern white voters begin steady shift to Republican party

1965 Voting Rights Act puts power of federal government behind right of southern blacks to vote
Malcolm X, charismatic leader of black separatists, gunned down in New York City
200,000 American troops in South Vietnam by year's end

1966 400,000 American troops in South Vietnam

1967 "Summer of Love": thousands of "flower children" or "hippies" congregate in San Francisco celebrating drugs and sex
500,000 American troops in South Vietnam

1968 Viet Cong–North Vietnamese "Tet Offensive" fails but effectiveness of enemy belies reports of United States government to American people
Massacre of villagers in My Lai by American soldiers contributes to burgeoning unpopularity of Vietnam War
Surprisingly successful campaign for Democratic presidential nomination by antiwar Senator Eugene McCarthy prompts Lyndon Johnson to announce he will not run for reelection
Martin Luther King Jr. and antiwar presidential candidate Robert F. Kennedy assassinated
Democratic National Convention in Chicago marred by riots
Republican Richard M. Nixon defeats Vice President Hubert Humphrey in presidential election

FOR FURTHER READING

Consult the "For Further Reading" sections of Chapters 46 and 47 for overviews of the 1960s. In addition, see Robert Caro, *The Years of Lyndon Johnson*, 1982; Jim F. Heath, *Decade of Disillusion: The Kennedy–Johnson Years*, 1975; Doris Kearns, *Lyndon Johnson and the American Dream*, 1976; David Farber, *The Age of Great Dreams*, 1994; and Theodore H. White, *The Making of the President, 1964*, 1965, and *The Making of the President, 1968*, 1969.

There is a huge amount of literature dealing with the Vietnam War, its causes, and its consequences. Among the most useful books are Frances Fitzgerald, *Fire in the Lake*, 1972; G. C. Herring, *America's Longest War*, 1986; G. M. Kahn, *Intervention: How America Became Involved in Vietnam*, 1986; Gabriel Kolko, *Anatomy of a War*, 1985; Michael Beschloss, *The Crisis Years*, 1990; Lloyd Gardner, *Pay Any Price: Lyndon Johnson and the Wars for Vietnam*, 1995; Garry Wills, *The Kennedy Imprisonment*, 1980; and Thomas G. Patterson, *Kennedy's Quest for Victory*, 1989.

On the antiwar and related agitations of what was called "The Movement," see Joseph R. Conlin, *The Troubles: A Jaundiced Glance Back at the Movement of the 1960s*, 1982; Morris Dickstein, *Gates of Eden: American Culture in the Sixties*, 1977; Todd Gitlin, *The Whole World Is Watching*, 1981; David Burner, *Making Peace with the 60s*, 1996; and Irwin Unger, *The Movement*, 1974.

On the more significant civil rights movement, see D. Garrow, *Bearing of the Cross*, 1986; Alex Haley, *The Autobiography of Malcolm X*, 1965; Sam A. Levitan et al., *Still a Dream: The Changing Status of Blacks since 1960*, 1975; Anthony Lewis, *Portrait of a Decade*, 1964; David Lewis, *King: A Critical Biography*, 1970; Stephen B. Oates, *Let the Trumpet Sound*, 1982; James T. Patterson, *America's Struggle against Poverty, 1900–1980*, 1981; H. Sitkoff, *The Struggle for Black Equality*, 1981; and Harold Zinn, *SNCC*, 1965.

Gerald Ford, the "accidental president" who won affection but could not master inflation and economic stagnation.

49
CHAPTER

PRESIDENCY IN CRISIS

Policies of the Nixon, Ford, and Carter Administrations

1968–1980

In a country where there is no hereditary throne nor hereditary aristocracy, an office raised far above all other offices offers too great a stimulus to ambition. This glittering prize, always dangling before the eyes of prominent statesmen, has a power stronger than any dignity under a European crown to lure them from the path of straightforward consistency.

—James Lord Bryce

Americans expect their presidents to do what no monarch by Divine Right could ever do— resolve for them all the contradictions and complexities of life.

—Robert T. Hartmann

The American democracy must discover a middle ground between making the President a czar and making him a puppet.

—Arthur M. Schlesinger, Jr.

969

The heroes of Greek myth were constantly pursuing Proteus, the herdsman of the seas, for he could foresee the future and, once captured, he had no choice but to reveal what he knew. But Proteus was rarely caught. His also was the power to assume the shape of any creature or thing, thus easily wriggling out of a captor's grasp.

Richard Milhous Nixon, so his critics said, was never captured because he was never in his own shape. John F. Kennedy, who ran against him for the presidency in 1960, said that Dick Nixon pretended to be so many different people that he had forgotten who he was and what he stood for. Liberals called him "Tricky Dicky." At several turns in his career, even Republican partisans felt constrained to assure Americans that the "Old Nixon" was no more; it was a "New Nixon" who was running for office.

But the "Real Nixon," like the real Proteus, remained elusive to the end. Senator Barry Goldwater said that Richard M. Nixon was "the most complete loner I've ever known."

THE NIXON PRESIDENCY

Nixon will be a compelling figure so long as the history of the United States is written. He lacked the personal qualities the pundits said were essential to succeeding in late twentieth-century politics: he was not attractive physically; he lacked grace, wit, and presence. Nixon was shy lifelong; his manner was furtive and his discomfort in public often came off as insincerity. When, in the 1950s, Democrats joked, "Would you buy a used car from this man?" everyone, including Republicans, laughed. Perhaps even Nixon did. He was aware of his public *persona*, regretted it, eventually faced up to the fact that it would never be shed.

Privately, Nixon was unpresidential to an extent that is shocking even in an era that has witnessed the disintegration of personal propriety and dignity. If John Kennedy and William Clinton were distasteful in their satyriasis, Nixon's habitual language was filthy, as reliant on four-letter words as conversation in a county jail. It took the disaster of Vietnam to make Lyndon Johnson paranoid; Nixon's associates were shocked by his conviction he was persecuted when his career was flying high. If other presidents have betrayed bigotries, Nixon's antisemitism was the stuff of Nazi street thugs.

"The Jews are all over the government," he told aides (and his own tape recorder), and "most Jews are disloyal." He assigned a task force "to look at any sensitive areas [of the government] where Jews are involved. You can't trust the bastards." One Jew who served in the Nixon administration shrugged off the publication of the president's views. He said that Nixon was "an equal opportunity hater," hardly a justification of a national leader's sentiments that fall somewhere between comedic and vile.

Odd Duck

The liberals' hatred for him had the intensity of an obsession, but people who despised the liberals did not love Nixon. Dwight D. Eisenhower came within a hair of dumping Nixon as vice presidential nominee in 1952, and he considered doing so again in 1956. In 1960, when Nixon was running for the presidency, Ike humiliated him by saying he was unable to recall a single instance in which Nixon contributed to a presidential decision, while the right-wing Republicans Nixon served well for more than two decades accepted his leadership without quite trusting him. When Nixon arrived at the end of his political life, his aides, whose careers Nixon had made, raised a deafening clamor in their haste to desert and turn on him. All was forgiven at his funeral years later: his eulogists centered on his admirable accomplishments; but no one there, at Nixon's boyhood home in Whittier, California, spoke of him as beloved.

And yet, what a story! Richard Nixon clawed his way from a modest middle-class background in southern California to the top of the heap through hard work and the tenacity of a police dog. Although he overstated it in his autobiographical *Six Crises*, he overcame tremendous obstacles and repeated humiliations. If the self-made Horatio Alger boy is an American hero, Nixon should be ensconced in a pantheon for, unlike the Alger heroes, Nixon was all pluck and little luck. Whatever else may be said of Richard Nixon, he earned everything he ever got.

Political Savvy

As president, Nixon took only grudging interest in domestic matters. He believed that "the country could run itself domestically without a president." He left important decisions and directives to two young White House aides, H. R. Haldeman and John Ehrlichman. Brassy where their boss was secretive, Haldeman and Erlichman insulated Nixon from Congress and even his own cabinet as effectively as Sherman Adams had once for Ike. With their undisguised arrogance, however, they were themselves unpopular, even with Republican politicians; they did nothing to shore up political support for the Nixon administration. Like Nixon, they would have few friends when the tides of fortune turned against them.

Politicking, which Nixon never enjoyed, he left to Vice President Spiro T. Agnew, a former governor of Maryland who was named to the ticket to attract blue-collar and white-ethnic voters who might otherwise vote for George Wallace. Agnew was an energetic campaigner and, once elected, Nixon's chief cheerleader: He stormed around the country on speaking tours. He delighted conservatives by flailing student antiwar protesters, permissive educators who tolerated their disruptive activities, liberal Supreme Court justices, and the national news media. Agnew was fond of tongue-twisting alliteration, and his partisan audiences loved it. His masterpiece was "nattering nabobs of negativism," that is, journalists.

Agnew's liberal-baiting provided Nixon with a superb smoke screen for, despite his many denunciations of big-spending liberal government, the president was not interested in dismantling the New Deal or even the Great Society. His only major modification of the liberal welfare state he inherited was the New Federalism, a policy of turning federal tax monies over to the states to spend on social programs.

On other fronts, Nixon might have been a middle-of-the-road Democrat. He sponsored a scheme for welfare reform, the Family Assistance Plan, that was to provide a flat annual payment to poor families in return for the agreement by heads of households to register with employment agencies. (It failed in Congress.) When, in 1971, inflation threatened his reelection campaign, Nixon slapped on wage and price controls, a Republican anathema for half a century. By setting aside government contracts for businesses owned by minorities—a *new* liberal concept—he changed the character of affirmative action and

Richard Nixon in the Oval Office with aides Robert Haldeman (left, seated) and John Erlichman (center, seated).

unknowingly set the stage for bitter debates at the end of the century. Nixon knew what liberals did not: by helping the expansion of the African-American middle class, he was creating Republicans.

And yet, conservative yelping was muted. Quite shrewdly, Nixon understood that the grass-roots conservatives he called the "Silent Majority" were repelled far less by liberal economic policy than by the myriad noneconomic causes that liberals came to emphasize by the 1970s: what many whites perceived as kid-gloves treatment of African Americans, the sometimes ludicrous demands of feminists and advocates of gay rights, the antiwar movement's shrill antipatriotism, and the decisions of the Warren court that seemed to expand the rights of accused criminals and hobble police in enforcing the law.

Reshaping the Supreme Court

Thanks to a mistake by Lyndon Johnson in the waning days of his administration, Nixon was able to move immediately to reshape the Supreme Court. Elderly Chief Justice Earl Warren (an old Nixon nemesis) offered to retire while Johnson was still president. LBJ could then name another liberal ac-

---

Affirmative Action

Originally, as the liberal Lyndon B. Johnson imagined it, affirmative action meant vigorous recruitment of members of minority races (and women) by universities and employers of people in desirable jobs. By the 1980s, it was often to mean *preferential treatment* of members of classes previously discriminated against, and resentment of such policies hurt liberals in politics and helped conservatives.

Ironically, it was the Republican President Richard M. Nixon who initiated the reinterpretation of affirmative action. It was during his presidency that the federal government began to favor businesses owned by members of minorities in doling out federal contracts, and pressuring other federal contractors to do the same. Republican strategists understood (as liberal Democratic strategists did not) that in helping to create a larger number of wealthy African-American and Hispanic businesspeople, they were creating conservative Republicans.

---

tivist in his place. Johnson picked an old Texas crony already on the court, Abe Fortas, who was immediately revealed to have accepted payments for public appearances that were petty but of dubious propriety. Johnson had to back down and Warren retired only after Nixon was sworn in.

Nixon's choice to replace him was Warren Burger of Minnesota. Burger was conservative but, as an advocate of judicial restraint rather than of antiliberal activism, he was somewhat disappointing to the right wing of the Republican party. When the battered Fortas himself left the court in 1970, Nixon tried to mollify southern Republicans and rightwingers by naming a judge from South Carolina to the court with several prosegregation decisions in his portfolio. Senate Democrats rejected him.

An angry Nixon then named a mediocrity from Florida whose knowledge of the law was problematical. When he too was rejected by the Senate, the president had to turn to a friend of Burger from Minnesota, Harry A. Blackmun who would, in short time, turn out to be a liberal. Nixon's two additional appointments, Lewis F. Powell and William H. Rehnquist (later chief justice) were more conservative in the eyes of the "Silent Majority."

Just as Nixon left the outlines of the welfare state intact, the Burger court merely moderated Warren court rulings. On the domestic front, Nixon seemed to achieve just what he wanted, an equilibrium enabling him to concentrate on what he believed to be the modern president's chief responsibility and his ticket into the history books: foreign relations.

NIXON'S VIETNAM

No foreign problem was so pressing as the ongoing war in Vietnam. Nixon knew well that Lyndon Johnson's political career was prematurely snuffed out by the agonizing, endless conflict. "The damned fool" Johnson had, in the words of a protest song of the era, mired himself "hip deep in the Big Muddy" and been helpless to do anything but to tell the nation to "push on." Nixon wanted out of the war. But how to turn the trick?

Vietnamization

Nixon was vice president when Eisenhower freed the nation from another quagmire in Korea. But Ike's course of action in 1953 was not available in

1969. Eisenhower had threatened the Chinese and North Koreans with nuclear weapons; that was not an option in the era of the nuclear balance of terror. Ike settled the Korean War on the basis of an independent South Korea with American troops on the scene to ensure security. In 1969, the Viet Cong and North Vietnamese insisted that they would not conclude hostilities as long as there were American troops in South Vietnam. Finally, Eisenhower did not have to deal with a militant antiwar movement at home.

Nixon's scheme was of necessity more subtle. First, to neutralize the antiwar movement, Nixon set out to reduce the sickening casualty lists that weekly provided the protesters with new recruits. In July 1969, he promulgated the Nixon Doctrine, stating that while the United States would "participate in the defense and development of allies and friends," Americans would no longer "undertake all the defense of the free nations of the world."

In Vietnam, the Nixon Doctrine translated as the Vietnamization of the war. "In the previous administration we Americanized the war in Vietnam," he said, "in this administration we are Vietnamizing the search for peace." The large but unreliable ARVN was thoroughly retrained to replace American men on the bloody front lines. As South Vietnamese units were deemed ready for combat, American troops came home. At about the same speed that LBJ escalated the American presence, Nixon de-escalated it. From a high of 541,000 American soldiers in South Vietnam when Nixon took office, the American force declined to 335,000 in 1970 and 24,000 in 1972.

Nixon returned the American ground war to where it was in 1964 and, so it seemed at first, he reduced the militant antiwar movement to a hard core of pacifists and New Left anti-imperialists whom Agnew denounced as traitors and Nixon as "bums." Democrats in Congress who defended Johnson's war demanded that Nixon make more serious efforts to negotiate an end to it. But the president plausibly replied that a truculent North Vietnam, and not he, was the major obstacle to peace.

Children hit by napalm flee in agony in Trangbang, South Vietnam, June 8, 1972.

974 *Chapter 49 Presidency in Crisis*

Expanding the War

Politically, Nixon could not afford simply to pull out of Southeast Asia, to declare victory, as dovish Republican Senator George Aiken suggested, and come home. He was beholden for his election to a hard core of "hawks" who believed that Johnson failed in Vietnam simply because he had not been tough enough. Nixon reassured such supporters: "We will not be humiliated. We will not be defeated." Much as he and his chief foreign policy adviser, Henry A. Kissinger, wanted to be rid of the war, they had to salvage the independence of South Vietnam in order to save face.

Consequently, all the while he reduced the American presence in Vietnam, Nixon attempted to bludgeon the enemy into meaningful negotiations by expanding the scope of the war. In the spring of 1969, Nixon sent air force bombers over Cambodia to destroy sanctuaries where about 50,000 North Vietnamese troops rested after battles. For a year, the American people knew nothing of these attacks. Then, in 1970, Nixon sent ground forces into Cambodia, an attack that could not be concealed.

The result was a thunderous uproar. Critics condemned the president for attacking a "neutral" nation. Several hundred university presidents closed their campuses for fear of student violence, and events at two colleges proved their wisdom in doing so. At Kent State University in Ohio, members of the National Guard opened fire on demonstrators. Four persons were killed and eleven wounded.

Congress reacted to the widening of the war by repealing the Tonkin Gulf Resolution which gave the president authority to fight it. Nixon responded that the repeal was immaterial. As commander in chief, he said, he had the right to take whatever military action he believed necessary. Nonetheless, when the war was further expanded into Laos in February 1971, ARVN troops carried the burden of the fighting.

Falling Dominoes

Vietnamization did not work. Without American troops by their side, the ARVN was humiliated in Laos. The Communist organization in that country, the Pathet Lao, grew in strength until 1975 when it seized control of the country. Tens of thousands of refugees who feared Communist rule fled.

In Cambodia, the consequences of expanding the war were far worse. Many young Cambodians were so angered by American bombing that they flocked to join the Khmer Rouge, once scarcely large enough to stage a soccer game. The Khmer Rouge increased in size from a mere 3,000 in 1970 to 30,000 in just a few years. In 1976, the head of the force, Pol Pot, came to power and created a regime as criminal as the Nazi government of Germany. In three years, Pol Pot's fanatical followers murdered as many as 3 million of their own people out of a population of 7.2 million! If Hitler's campaign of genocide against the Jews of Nazi-occupied Europe was proportional to Pol Pot's, the toll in the Nazi death camps would not have been 6 million, but something on the order of 150 million.

Eisenhower's Asian dominoes had fallen, but not because the United States was weak in the face of a military threat. They toppled because the United States had escalated and expanded a war that, in 1963, was little more than a gang brawl. In the process, Southeast Asian moderates and neutrals like Cambodia's Prince Sihanouk were undercut. By the mid-1970s, North Vietnam was dominated by militarists and Cambodia by a monster. Laos was in the hands of a once-tiny Communist movement.

Finis

In South Vietnam, the fighting dragged on until the fall of 1972 when, after suffering 12 days of earth-shaking bombing, the North Vietnamese finally faced up to the fact that, at best, the war was a stalemate. Foreign Minister Le Duc Tho met with Kissinger and arranged a cease-fire. The Paris Accords they signed went into effect in January 1973. The treaty required the United States to withdraw all its troops from Vietnam within 60 days while the North Vietnamese released all prisoners of war. Until free elections were held, North Vietnamese troops could remain in the country.

South Vietnamese president Nguyen Van Thieu regarded the settlement as a sellout. It enabled Nixon to save face while Thieu was faced with a massive enemy force within South Vietnamese borders. For two years, the country simmered. Then, in April 1975, the ARVN collapsed and the North Vietnamese moved on a virtually undefended Saigon. A short time later, North and South Vietnam were united and Saigon was renamed Ho Chih Minh City.

Ironically, Cambodia's nightmare was brought to an end only when the North Vietnamese invaded

Vietnamese refugees flee from the fierce fighting in the old imperial capital of Hue in 1975.

the country and overthrew Pol Pot. Rather more remarkable, as late as 1990 the United States insisted that Pol Pot was the legitimate ruler of Cambodia and, in 1991, engineered a settlement in which the Khmer Rouge shared in the government of the nation. So bitter was the taste of North Vietnamese victory that the United States preferred a murderer to a victorious old enemy with, at least, as Hamilton said of Jefferson, pretensions to character.

Bottom Line

The long war ravaged a prosperous corner of the world. Once an exporter of rice, Vietnam remained short of food through the 1980s. About a million ARVN soldiers lost their lives, the Viet Cong and North Vietnamese about the same number. Estimates of civilian dead ran as high as 3.5 million. About 5.2 million acres of jungle and farmland were ruined by defoliation. American bombing also devastated hundreds of cities, towns, bridges, and highways. The air force dropped more bombs on Vietnam than on Europe during World War II.

The vengefulness of the North Vietnamese victors (and Pol Pot) caused a massive flight of refugees. About 10 percent of the people of Southeast Asia fled their homelands after the war. Some spent everything they owned to bribe venal North Vietnamese officials to let them go. Others piled into leaky boats and cast off into open waters, untold numbers to die. To the eternal credit of the United States, some 600,000 Vietnamese, Laotians, Cambodians, Chinese and other ethnic minorities like the Hmong and Mien (whom every government in Southeast Asia mistreated) were admitted to the United States as immigrants.

The war cost the United States something like $150 billion, more than any other American war except World War II. Some 2.7 million American men and women served in the conflict; 58,000 of them were killed or died of illness, and 300,000 were wounded. Many men were disabled for life. Some lost limbs; others were poisoned by Agent Orange, the toxic defoliant the army used to clear jungle. Yet others were addicted to drugs or alcohol. Mental disturbances and violent crime were alarmingly common among Vietnam veterans.

And yet, for ten years, Vietnam veterans were ignored, shunned, even discriminated against. Politicians, not only liberals who opposed the war, but also the super-patriotic hawks who wanted the troops to fight on indefinitely, neglected to vote money for government programs to help them. Only in 1982, almost a decade after the war ended, was a monument to the soldiers erected in Washington, D.C. Not until 1991, after the stunning success of the American military in Iraq, did then-President George Bush feel that the "Vietnam Syndrome"—skittishness about the use of military force—was put to rest.

NIXON-KISSINGER FOREIGN POLICY

Nixon called the Vietnam War a sideshow. Henry A. Kissinger said that it was a mere footnote to history. Both men wanted to bring the conflict to an end so that they could bring about what, quite rightly, they regarded as a revolution in world diplomacy, a complete reordering of relations among the world's great powers.

The revolutionary concept of the Vietnam Memorial in Washington disturbed some traditionalists, but emotionally moved Vietnam veterans as no other monument has.

The Long Crusade

It is impossible to say just how much of the Nixon-Kissinger foreign policy was Nixon's and how much was Kissinger's, and apportioning credit is not very important. The fact was that both men envisioned a new relationship among the great powers that flew in the face of American assumptions since the dawn of the Cold War.

That is, for more than 20 years before the Nixon presidency, virtually all American policy makers and shapers of public opinion described the world as divided into two inevitably hostile camps: the United States and its allies, most importantly Western Europe and Japan; and the Soviet Union and its client states, particularly the gigantic People's Republic of China. Few so eagerly looked forward to a showdown between the two camps as John Foster Dulles had done, but diplomats and politicians who favored détente—a relaxation of tensions—had to phrase their views very carefully or have their courage and patriotism questioned.

The pre-presidential Richard M. Nixon consistently played on the theme of inevitable superpower hostility and the disloyalty of those who were soft on Communism. But at some point during Nixon's eight years as a private citizen, he ceased to believe in his own rhetoric. Privately, Nixon came to two important conclusions quite at odds with the anti-Communist crusade.

Premises of Détente

First, Nixon concluded that the nuclear balance of power made a superpower showdown unthinkable. Therefore, to continue to incite high tension between the Soviets and Americans was to waste resources while indefinitely running the risk of accidental world war.

Second, Nixon recognized that the old bipolar view of geopolitics on which the Cold War was predicated was nonsense. Japan, once a docile American client, was now the world's third largest economic power. The nations of Western Europe, groping toward unity, were openly trying to define an independent economic, political, and military role for themselves. The People's Republic of China, if ever subservient to the Soviet Union, was no longer so. Reports reached the West of Sino-Soviet battles on their 2,000-mile border.

Nixon thought of himself as a hardheaded realist. He meant to win his place in history by effecting

---

> ### Kissinger on the Cold War
>
> *The superpowers often behave like two heavily armed blind men feeling their way around a room, each believing himself in mortal peril from the other whom he assumes to have perfect vision. . . . Each tends to ascribe to the other side a consistency, foresight and coherence that its own experience belies. Of course, over time even two blind men can do enormous damage to each other, not to speak of the room.*
>
> Henry A. Kissinger, *The White House Years* (1979)

---

a diplomatic revolution in which the great powers dealt with one another not as Hatfields and McCoys but as interested parties rationally making deals for the benefit of each, and to ensure peace. In 1971, he said, "It will be a safer world and a better world, if we have a strong and healthy United States, Europe, Soviet Union, China, Japan—each balancing the other, not playing one against the other, an even balance."

Nixon's views were influenced and reinforced by Henry Kissinger. A witty, urbane, brilliant, and cheerfully conceited refugee from Naziism, Kissinger never quite lost his German accent nor his taste for Realpolitik, the amoral, opportunistic approach to diplomacy of one of his historical idols, Count Otto von Bismarck. Kissinger believed that the leaders of the Soviet Union and China were as little concerned with ideology and crusades as he and Nixon were, and only needed encouragement to launch a new era. His calculation was dramatically confirmed in 1971 at a time when the Vietnam War was raging and, officially, the ripest of denunciations were flying among Chinese, Russians, and Americans.

Rapprochement with China

In 1971, an American table tennis team on a tour of Japan was startled to receive an invitation from the People's Republic of China to cross over to mainland Asia and play a series of games there before they returned home. Sports writers noted wryly that the Chinese picked a sport in which they would trounce the Americans (they did), but diplomats recognized the implications of the apparently trivial event. For more than 20 years, the United States and China had had no open contact with one another, the leaders of both nations ritually denouncing the other as mortal enemies.

Kissinger virtually commanded the Ping-Pong players to go to China and shortly thereafter opened talks with Chinese diplomats. He flew secretly to Beijing where he arranged for a goodwill tour by Nixon himself in February 1972. Only then was the amazing news announced: the lifelong scourge of Red China would tour the Forbidden City and Great Wall and sit down with chopsticks at a Mandarin banquet with Mao Zedong and Zhou Enlai, drinking toasts to eternal Sino-American amity with fiery Chinese spirits.

Nixon's meeting with Mao was ceremonial; the Chairman was senile and fading (and mired in deplorable debaucheries). However, discussions with Zhou, who had long advocated better relations with the West and his protégés, Hua Guofeng (who was to succeed Mao in 1976) and Deng Xiaoping, who had done time in prison for advocating capitalistic reforms of China's moribund economy, reassured Nixon that he had calculated correctly.

Almost overnight, Sino-American relations warmed. The United States dropped its opposition to China's demand for a seat in the United Nations and established a legation in Beijing. (In 1979, the two countries established full diplomatic relations.)

Chinese students were invited to study in American universities and China opened its doors to American tourists, who came by the tens of thousands, clambering up the Great Wall and buying redribboned trinkets. American industrialists involved in everything from oil exploration to the bottling of soft drinks flew to China, anxious to sell American technology and consumer goods in the market that had long symbolized the traveling salesman's ultimate territory.

Soviet Policy

For many years, China was not much of a customer. The Chinese population was huge, but the country was poor and in economic chaos; there was neither money nor goods with which to pay for the expensive high-technology exports in which American industry was supreme. Nor were the new leaders of China interested in resuming the status of a colonial market or in embracing wide-open political institutions. Their principal motive in courting American friendship was diplomatic, to win some edge of security in their conflict with the Soviet Union. They were "playing the American card."

That was all right with the realistic Nixon and Kissinger. They were "playing the China card," putting the fear of a closer Sino-American relationship into the Soviets, who represented a genuine threat to American security. Their gambit worked. In June 1972, just months after his China trip, Nixon flew to the Soviet Union and signed a preliminary agreement in the opening series of Strategic Arms Limitation Talks (SALT), the first significant step toward a slowdown of the arms race since the Kennedy administration.

At home, the photos of Nixon clinking champagne glasses with Mao and hugging Soviet boss Leonid Brezhnev bewildered his conservative supporters and flummoxed his liberal critics. In fact, as Nixon knew, undoubtedly savoring the fact, only a Republican with an impeccable cold warrior past could have accomplished what he did. Had a liberal Democratic president shared Peking Duck with Mao Zedong, Nixon himself would have held the noose at the demonstrations outside the White House.

Shuttle Diplomacy

Nixon was grateful to Kissinger and, in 1973, named him secretary of state. Well into 1974, Kissinger's diplomatic successes piled up. His greatest triumph came in the Middle East after the Yom Kippur War of 1973, in which Egypt and Syria attacked Israel and, for the first time in the long Arab-Israeli conflict, inflicted terrible casualties on the Israelis and fought them to a draw.

Knowing that Israel was not inclined to accept less than victory, and fearing what a prolonged war in the oil-rich Middle East would mean for the United States, Kissinger shuttled seemingly without sleep among Damascus, Cairo, and Tel Aviv, carrying proposal and counterproposal for a settlement. Unlike Dulles, who also represented American interests on the fly, Kissinger was a brilliant diplomat. He ended the war and the terms he prevailed on all the warring powers to accept actually increased American influence in the region. He won the gratitude and friendship of Egyptian President Anwar Sadat, while not alienating Israel.

After 1974, however, Kissinger lost his magic touch, in part because of revived world tensions that were not his doing. Soviet Premier Leonid Brezhnev may have wanted to reduce the chance of direct conflict between Russia and the United States. However, he was enough of an old bolshevik to continue aid-

President and Mrs. Nixon at the Great Wall of China. All Americans were amazed; some of Nixon's supporters were disgusted.

ing guerrilla movements in Africa and Latin America. Cuba's Fidel Castro, with a large army to keep paid and in trim, exported advisers and combat troops to several countries, most notably to Angola in southwestern Africa.

But Nixon and Kissinger were also willing, even anxious, to fight the Cold War by proxy in the Third World, competing with the Soviets for spheres of influence. While right-wing Republicans opposed to détente stepped up their attacks on Kissinger, he was actually pursuing their kind of confrontational policies in strife-torn countries like Angola.

The most damaging mark on Kissinger's record as the diplomat-in-chief of a democratic country came in 1974. It was revealed that, the previous year, he was aware of and may have instigated and aided militarists in Chile who overthrew and murdered the president, Salvador Allende. Allende was a championship-caliber bungler; but he was also Chile's democratically elected head and his American-backed successor, Augusto Pinochet, while stabiliz-

ing Chile, did so by means of repression and brutality marked by torture and murder of opponents.

WATERGATE AND GERALD FORD

By 1974, when news of the Pinochet connection broke in the United States, Kissinger was no longer serving Richard Nixon. The crisis of the presidency that began when Lyndon Johnson was repudiated took on a new dimension of gravity when Nixon was forced to resign in disgrace. The debacle had its beginnings in the election campaign of 1972 in which, thanks to a transformation of the Democratic party, victory was in Nixon's hip pocket from the start.

Redefining Liberalism

Between 1968 and 1972, activist middle-class liberals won control of several key Democratic party committees and remade party machinery according

980 Chapter 49 Presidency in Crisis

to their ideals. They enacted new procedures and standards for selecting convention delegates that penalized old party stalwarts: the labor unions, the big city machines, those southern "good old boys" who had not already gone Republican, and other political pros. The McGovern reforms (named for the liberal, antiwar senator from South Dakota) guaranteed representation of women and minority groups at party conventions.

The Election of 1972

As an immediate result of the reforms, the Democratic delegates who gathered in Miami in the summer of 1972 formed the youngest convention in political history; they counted more women and members of racial minority groups among them than any other convention; and they were militantly antiwar. This convention nominated Senator McGovern and adopted a platform calling for a negotiated end to the Southeast Asian war (then Vietnamized but still raging), and supporting the demands of some women's organizations that the decision as to whether or not a fetus should be aborted belonged to the pregnant woman herself, and no other person or institution.

A sincere, decent man who was profoundly grieved by the war, McGovern tried to distance himself from the radicals in his party, particularly gay rights advocates who loudly touted homosexuality as an alternative lifestyle "as good as" heterosexual marriage. McGovern understood they were not likely to win the affection of working-class people who traditionally voted Democratic. He emphasized peace in Vietnam, a popular issue by 1972, tax reform that would benefit middle- and lower-income people, and his integrity compared with Nixon's long-standing reputation for deviousness.

But virtually no labor unions supported him and many Democratic pros sat on their hands. The Republicans, by way of contrast, ran an effective campaign. They depicted McGovern as a bumbling and indecisive radical. When McGovern first defended his running mate, Senator Thomas Eagleton, who had undergone psychiatric treatment for depression several years earlier, and then forced Eagleton to drop out because of his problem, his race was doomed.

Nixon won 60.8 percent of the popular vote and carried every state but Massachusetts and the District of Columbia. In only eight years, he had

---

Persistence

When Richard Nixon ran for reelection in 1972, he became the seventh person to run for president three times as a nominee of one of the two major parties. (Only Franklin D. Roosevelt ran four times.*) The seven and the dates of their campaigns, with winning campaigns in bold face, are:

Thomas Jefferson: 1796, **1800, 1804**
Andrew Jackson: 1824, **1828, 1832**
Henry Clay: 1824, 1832, 1844
Grover Cleveland: **1884,** 1888, **1892**
William Jennings Bryan: 1896, 1900, 1908
Franklin D. Roosevelt: **1932, 1936, 1940, 1944**
Richard M. Nixon: 1960, **1968, 1972**

*Technically, John Adams was a four-time nominee because presidential and vice presidential candidates were not listed on separate ballots before 1804. Adams was certainly a vice presidential "running mate" of George Washington in 1788 and 1792 but officially listed as a presidential nominee. Adams won election in 1796, lost in his attempt at reelection in 1800.

---

reversed the Republican humiliation of 1964. Democratic bumbling helped, but his achievement was nonetheless remarkable. Still, Nixon's days of glorious triumph were, like Lyndon Johnson's in 1964, to be few.

Covering Up a Burglary

On June 17, 1972, early in the presidential campaign, Washington police arrested five men who were trying to plant electronic eavesdropping devices in Democratic party headquarters in a Washington apartment and office complex called the Watergate. Three of the suspects were on the payroll of the Committee to Re-elect the President (an unwisely chosen name inasmuch as it abbreviated as CREEP), and McGovern tried to exploit the incident as part of his integrity campaign. But the ploy fizzled when Nixon and his campaign manager, Attorney General John Mitchell, denied any knowledge of the incident and denounced the burglars as common criminals.

In fact, Nixon probably knew nothing about the break-in in advance. However, he learned shortly thereafter that the burglars acted on orders from his own aides. He never considered reporting or disciplining his men. Instead, almost nonchalantly, he instructed his staff to find money to hush up the men in jail. However, two of them, James E. McCord and Howard Hunt, refused to take the fall; they informed Judge John Sirica that they had taken orders from highly placed Nixon administration officials.

Rumors began to fly. Two reporters for the *Washington Post*, Robert Woodward and Carl Bernstein, made contact with an anonymous source who fed them information. A special Senate investigating committee headed by Sam Ervin of North Carolina picked away at the tangle from yet another direction, slowly tracing not only the Watergate break-in and cover-up but other illegal acts to the White House itself.

The Imperial Presidency

Each month that passed, dramatic insights into the inner workings of the Nixon presidency were revealed. On Nixon's own orders, an enemies list was compiled. On it were journalists, politicians, intellectuals, and even movie stars who made statements criticizing Nixon. One Donald Segretti was put in charge of a dirty-tricks campaign, planting half-truths, rumors, and lies to discredit critics of the administration. G. Gordon Liddy, who was involved in the Watergate break-in, had proposed fantastic schemes involving yachts and prostitutes to entrap political enemies. The dirty-tricks campaign grew so foul that not even J. Edgar Hoover, the never squeamish head of the FBI, would touch it.

Watergate, it turned out, was just one of several surreptitious entries sponsored by the administration. Nixon's aides also engineered the burglary of a Los Angeles psychiatrist's office to secure information about Daniel Ellsberg, a Defense Department employee who published confidential information about the prosecution of the war in Vietnam.

Observers spoke of an "imperial presidency." Nixon and his advisers had become so arrogant in their possession of power that they believed they were above the law. Indeed, several years later, Nixon himself was to tell an interviewer on television, "When the president does it, that means it is not illegal."

If imperial in their pretensions, however, "all the president's men" were singularly lacking in a sense of nobility. One by one, Nixon aides abandoned ship, each convinced that he was being set up as the sole fall guy for his colleagues. Each deserter named others and described their roles in the cover-up and dirty-tricks campaign. A snarl of half-truths and lies descended on the president himself.

In the midst of the scandal, Vice President Spiro Agnew pleaded no-contest to income tax evasion and charges that he accepted bribes when he was governor of Maryland. Agnew was forced to resign from the vice presidency in October 1973. He was replaced under the Twenty-fifth Amendment by Congressman Gerald Ford of Michigan.

Resignation

Then came Nixon's turn and he was, as the old saw has it, hoist with his own petard. He had kept tape recordings of conversations in his Oval Office that clearly implicated him in the Watergate cover-up (and revealed him as having a rather foul mouth: the transcripts of the tapes were peppered with "expletive deleted"). After long fights in the courts, the president was ordered to surrender the tapes to investigators.

Why Nixon did not destroy the incriminating recordings early in the Watergate crisis remains a mystery. It was suggested that greed—the money that the electronic documents would bring after he left the presidency—accounts for his fatal blunder. Others saw the preservation of the tapes as another manifestation of Nixon's imperial megalomania. He could not conceive of the fact that a court could order the president of the United States to abide by laws that applied to mere citizens.

After the House of Representatives Judiciary Committee recommended impeaching Nixon, he threw in the towel. On August 9, 1974, on national television, he resigned the presidency and flew to his home in San Clemente, California.

A Ford, Not a Lincoln

Gerald Ford was not a particularly intelligent man. Lyndon Johnson once told reporters, to high hilarity, that Ford had played center on the University of Michigan football team (which he had) without a helmet. Others quipped that he could not walk and chew gum at the same time. After he ascended to the presidency, news photographers fairly lay in wait to ridicule him by snapping shots of him bumping his head on door frames, tumbling down the slopes of the Rockies on everything but his skis, and slicing golf balls into crowds of spectators.

Indeed, with a safe Republican seat in the House of Representatives from Michigan, Ford rose to be minority leader on the basis of little more than

Richard Nixon forces a smile as he departs Washington after his resignation.

seniority and dutifully toeing the Republican party line. His political ambition was to be speaker of the House. He spoke stark, simply Middle Western truth when, in 1999, he said of the presidency "I never asked for it. I never wanted it. But I never was afraid of it."

Nor was he. Ford's private statement in a cabinet meeting that he could no longer support the administration was critical in Nixon's decision to resign. Ford's simplicity and forthrightness in his first days in the White House were a relief after Nixon's squirming and deception. He told the American people that fate gave them "a Ford, not a Lincoln," and he had no pretensions. Democrats howled "deal" when Ford pardoned Nixon of all crimes he may have committed, but Ford's explanation, that the American people needed to put Watergate behind them, was plausible and in character. Two very nearly successful attempts to assassinate him by unbalanced women in California helped to win sympathy for the first president who had not been elected to any national office.

Despite his unusual route to the White House, Gerald Ford had no more intention of being a caretaker president than John Tyler when he became the first president to succeed to the office by reason of death. But it was Ford's misfortune, as it had been Tyler's, to face serious problems without the confidence and support of an important segment of his party. The Republican party's right wing, informally led by former California Governor Ronald Reagan, did not like détente nor Nixon's (then Ford's) refusal to launch a frontal attack on government regulation and the liberal welfare state.

Running on Half-Empty

The most serious of the woes facing Ford struck at one of the basic assumptions of twentieth-century American life: that cheap energy was available in unlimited quantities to fuel the economy and support the freewheeling lifestyle of the middle class.

By the mid-1970s, 90 percent of the American economy was generated by the burning of fossil fuels: coal, natural gas, and petroleum. Fossil fuels are nonrenewable sources of energy. Unlike food crops, lumber, and water—or, for that matter, a horse and a pair of sturdy legs—they cannot be called on again once they have been used. The supply of them is finite. While experts disagreed about the extent of the world's reserves of coal, gas, and oil, no one challenged the obvious fact that one day they would be no more.

The United States was by far the biggest user of nonrenewable sources of energy. In 1973, while comprising about 6 percent of the world's population, Americans consumed fully 33 percent of the world's annual production of oil. Much of it was burned with little thought as to what was vital, what trivial, a human trait dating to the Olduvai Gorge. Americans overheated and overcooled their offices and houses. They pumped gasoline into a dizzying variety of purely recreational vehicles, some of which brought the roar of the freeway to the wilderness and devastated fragile land. Their worship of the wasteful private automobile meant that few taxes were spent on public mass transit systems. They packaged their consumer goods in throwaway containers of glass, metal, paper, and petroleum-based plastics; supermarkets wrapped lemons individually in transparent plastic and fast-food cheeseburgers were cradled in styrofoam caskets that were discarded within seconds of being handed over the counter. The bill of indictment went on but, resisting criticism and satire alike, American consumption increased.

OPEC and the Energy Crisis

About 61 percent of the oil that Americans consumed in the 1970s was produced at home, and large reserves remained under native ground. But the nation also imported huge quantities of crude, and in

---

> ### *Cleanup*
>
> In 1912 the Chicago Sanitation Department cleared the streets of the carcasses of 10,000 dead horses. In 1968 the Chicago Police Department cleared the streets of 24,500 carcasses of dead automobiles.

> ### *Constitutional Contradiction?*
>
> Gerald Ford was appointed to the vice presidency under the provisions of the Twenty-fifth Amendment, ratified in 1967, which stipulates that "whenever there is a vacancy in the office of the Vice President, the President shall nominate a Vice President. . . ." When he succeeded to the presidency, he appointed Nelson A. Rockefeller to the vice presidency. Neither the president nor the vice president held office by virtue of election. However, as some constitutional experts were quick to point out, Article II, Section 1 of the Constitution provides that the president and vice president are to "be elected."
>
> In fact, the contradiction was always there, if never put to the test. The U.S. Constitution and laws hold that the secretary of state and the speaker of the House were next in line to the presidency after the vice president. A case could be made that the speaker was elected, but not the secretary of state.

October 1973, the United States discovered that Americans had little control over the 39 percent of their oil that came from abroad.

In that month, the Organization of Petroleum Exporting Countries (OPEC) temporarily halted oil shipments and announced the first of a series of big jumps in the price of their product. One of their justifications was that the irresponsible consumption habits of the advanced Western nations, particularly the United States, jeopardized their future.

OPEC leaders reasoned that if the oil-exporting nations continued to supply oil cheaply, consuming nations would continue to burn it profligately, thus hastening the day the wells ran dry. On that day, if the oil-exporting nations had not laid the basis for another kind of economy, they would be destitute. Particularly in the oil-rich Middle East, there were few alternative resources to support fast-growing populations. Therefore, by raising prices, the OPEC nations would earn capital with which to build for a future without oil, while simultaneously encouraging the consuming nations to conserve, thus lengthening the era when oil would be available.

From a geopolitical perspective, the argument made sense, but ordinary Americans, like ordinary Belgians, Arabs and Yanomami, rarely thought geopolitically. They were stunned when they had to wait in long lines in order to pay unprecedented prices for gasoline. In some big cities and Hawaii, gasoline for private cars was not to be had for weeks.

The price of gasoline never climbed to Japanese or European levels, but it was shock enough for people who were accustomed to buying "two dollars' worth" to discover that $2 bought a little more than enough to drive home. Moreover, the prices of goods that required oil in their production climbed too. Inflation, already a problem under Nixon, worsened from 9 percent a year when Ford became president to 12 percent.

Whip Inflation Now!

Opposed to wage and price controls such as Nixon employed, Ford launched a campaign called WIN!, for "Whip Inflation Now!" He urged Americans to slow down inflation by refusing to buy exorbitantly priced goods and by ceasing to demand higher wages from their employers. The campaign was ridiculed from the start, and within a few weeks Ford quietly retired the WIN! button that he was wearing on his lapel. He had seen few others in his travels about the country and began to feel like a man in a funny hat.

Instead, Ford tightened the money supply in order to slow down the economy, which resulted in the most serious recession since 1937, with unemployment climbing to 9 percent. Ford was stymied by the same vicious circle that caught up his predecessor and successor: slowing inflation meant throwing people out of work; fighting unemployment meant inflation; trying to steer a middle course meant stagflation, mild recession plus inflation.

Image Problems

As a congressman, Ford had been a hawk on Vietnam. So, when the North Vietnamese launched their attack on Saigon early in 1975, his first impulse was to intervene with American troops. Congress refused

The lines at gas stations stretched for blocks during the gasoline shortage in 1979.

to respond and Henry Kissinger, who stayed on as secretary of state, talked Ford out of presidential action. Ford tried to display his determination to exercise American armed might in May 1975, when Cambodian Communists seized an American ship, the *Mayaguez*. Ford ordered in the marines. But in order to have 39 seamen returned to their homes, 38 marines died.

Kissinger savored the reports that the president hung breathlessly on his every word, but such stories only further enraged the right wing of the Republican party, which hated Kissinger, and made it easier for the Democrats to mock Ford as being not bright enough to handle his job.

Early in 1976, polls showed Ford losing to most of the likely Democratic candidates. Capitalizing on this news, Ronald Reagan, the sweetheart of the right-wing Republicans, launched a well-financed campaign to replace him as the party's candidate. Using his control of party organization, Ford beat Reagan at the convention but the travails of his two years in office took their toll. He could not overcome the image that he was the most accidental of presidents, a person who had never been elected to national office. His full pardon of Nixon came back to haunt him and, in November, he lost narrowly to a most unlikely Democratic candidate, James Earl Carter of Georgia, who called himself Jimmy. The Democrats were back, but the decline in the prestige of the presidency continued.

QUIET CRISIS

Since Eisenhower, every president had been identified closely with Congress, the arena of national politics. The day of the governor candidate seemed to be in the past. Then Jimmy Carter came out of nowhere to win the Democratic nomination in 1976. His political career consisted of one term in the Georgia assembly and one term as governor.

Indeed, it was Carter's lack of association with the federal government that helped him win the nomination and, by a slim margin, the presidency. Without a real animus for Gerald Ford, many Americans were attracted to the idea of an outsider, which is how Carter presented himself. "Hello, my name is Jimmy Carter and I'm running for president," he told thousands of people face to face in his softly musical Georgia accent. Once he started winning primaries, the media did the rest. When television

commentators said that there was a bandwagon rolling, voters dutifully responded by jumping on it.

Inauguration Day, when Carter and his shrewd but uningratiating wife, Rosalyn, walked the length of Pennsylvania Avenue, was very nearly the last entirely satisfactory day of the Carter presidency. Whether the perspective of time will attribute his failure as chief executive to his unsuitability to the office, or to the massiveness of the problems he faced, it is difficult to imagine future historians looking at the Carter era other than it is now remembered, dolefully.

The Panama Treaty

Carter had his successes, especially in foreign relations. Among his achievements was defusing an explosive situation in Central America where Panamanians and others had long protested American sovereignty over the Panama Canal Zone. The narrow strip of U.S. territory bisected the small republic and seemed to be an intolerable insult in an age when nationalist sensibilities in small countries were as touchy as boils.

American diplomats saw no need to hold on to the canal zone in the face of Panamanian protests. The United States would be able to occupy the canal within hours in case of an international crisis. After several false starts at working out a treaty under Johnson and Nixon, in 1978 the Senate narrowly ratified an agreement with Panama to guarantee the permanent neutrality of the canal itself while gradually transferring sovereignty over it to Panama, culminating on December 31, 1999.

By signing the treaty, Carter muted Latin American denunciations of *"yanqui imperialismo."*

Jimmy Carter and the Segregationists

Future president Jimmy Carter had an unusual record for a white southerner of his age on the segregation issue. In the 1950s, as a successful businessman in Plains, Georgia, he had been asked to join the anti-black White Citizens' Councils, whose membership fee was only $5. Carter replied, "I've got $5 but I'd flush it down the toilet before I'd give it to you."

Nevertheless, right-wing politicians, led by Ronald Reagan, who began to campaign for the presidency as soon as Carter was inaugurated, denounced the treaty. In the tradition of Joseph McCarthy, Reagan called it yet another retreat from national pride and greatness by a weak president.

Peacemaking

Carter's greatest achievement was to save the rapprochement between Israel and Egypt that began to take shape in November 1977. Egyptian President Anwar Sadat, risking the enmity of the entire Arab world, had flown to Israel and addressed the Israeli

---

Minority Presidents

When Jimmy Carter won the forty-eighth presidential election by just a hair under 50 percent of the popular vote, it was the sixteenth time the victor had the support of less than half the voters:

President	Year	Percent
John Quincy Adams	1824	30.5
James K. Polk	1844	49.6
Zachary Taylor	1848	47.4
James Buchanan	1856	45.3
Abraham Lincoln	1860	39.8
Rutherford B. Hayes	1876	48.0
James A. Garfield	1880	48.5
Grover Cleveland	1884	48.5
Benjamin Harrison	1888	47.9
Grover Cleveland	1892	46.1
Woodrow Wilson	1912	41.9
Woodrow Wilson	1916	49.4
Harry S Truman	1948	49.5
John F. Kennedy	1960	49.9
Richard M. Nixon	1968	43.4
Jimmy Carter	1976	50.0

Lincoln would surely not have won the election of 1864 by an absolute majority (or at all) had the southern states not been in rebellion. Three victorious candidates had fewer popular votes than their defeated opponents: John Quincy Adams in 1824, Rutherford B. Hayes in 1876, and Benjamin Harrison in 1888. In the three-way race in 1992, Arkansas Governor Bill Clinton won a substantial electoral vote victory with only 43 percent of the popular vote.

Knesset, or parliament, calling for a permanent peace in the Middle East. Rather than cooperate with Sadat, Israeli Prime Minister Menachem Begin, a former terrorist, seemed to sabotage Sadat's peacemaking efforts by refusing to make concessions commensurate with the Egyptian president's high-stakes gamble.

In 1978, Carter brought Sadat and Begin to meet with him at Camp David, the presidential retreat in the Maryland woods outside Washington. There, Sadat grew so angry with Begin's refusal to compromise that he actually packed his suitcases. Although Carter was unable to persuade Begin to agree that the West Bank of the Jordan River, which Israel had occupied in 1967, must eventually be returned to Arab rule, he did bring the two men together. In March 1979, Israel and Egypt signed a treaty.

In the United States, the political effect of this dramatic diplomatic turn was to swing American sympathies in the dispute in the direction of Sadat. Begin was unpopular even among American Jews, who traditionally were staunch supporters of Israel, and Jewish contributions to Israeli causes dropped sharply. Carter himself betrayed impatience and annoyance with the Begin government and sympathy for the Palestinian refugees. Carter deserved the Nobel Peace Prize for pulling off the Camp David Accords.

The End of Détente

The Nobel Committee may have snubbed him because, while Carter advanced the cause of peace in the Middle East, he shattered the policy of détente that Nixon, Kissinger, and Ford had nurtured. Like Nixon, Carter virtually ignored his first secretary of state, a professional diplomat, Cyrus Vance, and depended on a White House adviser, Zbigniew Brzezinski, for advice.

Unlike the flexible and opportunistic Kissinger, Brzezinski was an anti-Soviet ideologue. Himself a Polish refugee from Communism, Brzezinski's distrust of the Soviet Union blinded him to opportunities to improve relations between the nuclear superpowers, and even prompted him to sabotage Soviet overtures. Moreover, whereas Kissinger was a charmer, Brzezinski was tactless and crude in a world in which protocol and manners can be as important as substance. The foreign ministers of several of America's allies discreetly informed the State Department that they would not deal with him under any circumstances.

Anwar Sadat, Jimmy Carter, and Menachem Begin shake hands following the signing of the Camp David Accords in 1978.

But Carter was as obsessively hostile to the Soviet Union as Brzezinski and pre-Nixon policy makers. He denounced the Soviet Union for trampling on human rights while neglecting to mention the far more brutal policies of American allies such as Iran, Chile, and several Central American states.

In March 1977, Carter interrupted and set back the Strategic Arms Limitation Talks with completely new proposals. Eventually, a new SALT-II treaty was negotiated and signed, but Carter withdrew it from Senate consideration when the Soviet Union invaded Afghanistan to prop up a client government in December 1979. By the end of Carter's term of office, détente was dead.

Plus C'est la Même Chose

Inflation reached new heights under Carter, almost 20 percent during 1980. By the end of the year, $1 was worth only 15 cents in 1940 values. That is, on the average, it took $1 in 1980 to purchase what in 1940 cost 15 cents. The dollar had suffered fully half of this loss during the 1970s.

Carter could not be faulted for the energy crisis. After the crunch of 1974, Americans became more energy conscious, replacing their big "gas guzzlers" with more efficient smaller cars. Even this sensible turn contributed to the nation's economic malaise, however. American automobile manufacturers repeatedly refused to develop small energy-efficient cars. For a while in the 1960s, after the success of the Germans' Volkswagen "Beetle," Ford, General Motors, and Chrysler made compact cars. But within a few years, compacts had miraculously grown to be nearly as large as the traditional full-sized car. Now, in the crunch of the 1970s, American automakers had nothing to compete with a flood of Japanese imports: Toyotas, Datsuns, Hondas, and many others. The automobile buyer's dollars sailed across the Pacific.

Even then, by 1979, oil consumption was higher than ever, and an even higher proportion of it was

How They Lived

The Typical American of the 1980s: A Statistical Portrait

The statistical American of the year 1980 was a Caucasian female, a little more than 30 years old, married to her first husband, with one child and about to have another. She was a shade over 5 feet 4 inches tall and weighed 134 pounds. Statisticians are not sure of the color of her hair and eyes, but they were probably on the brownish side. Statisticians are sure that she had tried marijuana when she was younger, but no longer used it in the 1980s (although some of her friends still did). She did not smoke cigarettes, but at least had tried them in the past; she still drank, just this side of moderately.

The statistical American adult female of the 1980s considered herself middle class, and had attended college but had not necessarily graduated. She was likely to work outside the home, but economic conditions during the first half of the decade made her opportunities uncertain. Her household income was about $20,000 a year; she and her husband were watching their budget closely, which they were not accustomed to doing. It is a toss-up whether or not she voted in 1984 (or at all during the 1970s). She was decreasingly interested in feminism as the 1980s progressed and the failure of the ERA faded into memory. She was marginally more likely to be registered as a Democrat than as a Republican, but she was more likely to have voted for Ronald Reagan in 1984 than in 1980.

More than half of the statistical American's female friends were married. Most of her friends who have been divorced have married again within three years. The statistical American of the 1980s attached no stigma to divorce, and experienced only a slight sense of unease with people who lived with members of the opposite sex without benefit of marriage. But she found it difficult to agree that homosexuality is nothing more than an alternate lifestyle on a moral parity with heterosexuality. She was both amused and repelled by the culture of the gay communities about which she read, but by 1985 was not so indulgent as she had been because of the quantum leap in the spread of deadly AIDS.

She almost certainly had sex with her husband before they married, and almost as likely with at least one other man. There is a fair chance that she had a brief fling since marriage, probably during a trial separation.

The statistical American was more likely to be Protestant than Catholic. However, she was more likely to be Catholic than a member of any other *individual* denomination. If a Catholic, she practiced birth control, most likely using the pill, in defiance of church directives. Moreover, Catholic or Protestant, she attended church services far less frequently than had her mother.

The statistical American was in excellent health; she saw a dentist and a doctor more than once a year, and paid a little less than half of the cost of health care (state and federal government picked up about the same, private industry and philanthropy the rest). She had a life expectancy of almost 78 years, and would outlive her husband by eight years, with the prospects that her dotage would be economically trying.

The statistical American lived in a state with a population of about 3 million people—Colorado, Iowa, Oklahoma, Connecticut—and in a city of about 100,000 people—Roanoke, Virginia; Reno, Nevada; Durham, North Carolina.

Or perhaps, she lived at the population center of the United States, which in 1980 was west of the Mississippi River for the first time in American history. It was located "one mile west of the De Soto City Hall, Jefferson County, Missouri." An equal number of people in the continental United States lived east of that point as west, as many north of it as south.

As the question about her state and city of residence indicates, the statistical American is a somewhat absurd contrivance, distilled out of the majorities, means, and medians of the United States Census Bureau; the responses to surveys taken by a number of public-opinion experts; and, simply, the probabilities of the educated guess.

The virtue of the United States remains rooted in its diversity of people as well as of resources and in the survival of those people's right to change their minds as many times as they wish. And, as far as matters of public policy are concerned, to form majorities and effect their wishes. For a nation that has reached its third century, that is not so bad an accomplishment. In the star-crossed history of the human race, it has not been done in many other places.

being imported than in 1976. American oil refiners actually cut back on domestic production, which led many people to wonder if the crisis was genuine or was just a cover while the industry reaped windfall profits, which it did. As prices soared, all the refiners reported dividends of unprecedented size.

The price of electricity also rose, by 200 percent and more, because so much of it was generated by burning fossil fuels. The utility companies called for the construction of more nuclear power plants in anticipation of even higher rate increases. But Americans had become apprehensive about nuclear energy as an alternative to fossil fuels following an accident and near-catastrophe at the Three Mile Island nuclear plant near Harrisburg, Pennsylvania; the release, at about the same time, of *The China Syndrome*, a film that portrayed a similar accident; the discovery that a California reactor that was about to open was crisscrossed with flaws, and built astride a major earthquake fault; and the tremendous costs needed to build safe nuclear power plants.

Malaise

Carter was repeatedly embarrassed by his aides and family, and himself had a talent for boners. Genuinely suspicious of the Washington establishment, he surrounded himself with cronies from Georgia who did not or would not understand the etiquette and rituals of the capital. Banker Bert Lance, whom Carter wanted as budget director, was tainted by petty, unacceptable loan scams, while his ambassador to the United Nations, former civil rights activist Andrew Young, met secretly with leaders of the Palestine Liberation Organization (PLO), an anti-Israel terrorist organization that the United States did not recognize. Carter had to fire him.

The national press, stimulated by its role in uncovering the Watergate scandal to constant muckraking, leaped on every trivial incident—a Carter aide tipsy in a cocktail lounge; the president's "down-home" brother Billy's outrageous opinions—to embarrass the president. The deeply religious Carter himself frankly but foolishly told an interviewer for *Playboy* magazine, "I've looked on a lot of women with lust. I've committed adultery in my heart many times." Tittering journalists did not allow him to forget it. In 1980, when Carter's career was on the line, his mother told a reporter, "Sometimes when I look at all my children, I say to myself, 'Lillian, you should have stayed a virgin.'"

A much more serious handicap was the Carter administration's lack of direction. "Carter believes fifty things," one of his advisers said, "but no one thing. He holds explicit, thorough positions on every issue under the sun, but he has no large view of relations between them." In this, Carter was not unlike most Americans. He had the engineer mentality that is often described as the American way of thinking: as it arises, face each specific problem and work out a specific solution.

Such pragmatism worked for Franklin D. Roosevelt. It did not work for Jimmy Carter. With him at the helm, pragmatic government resembled a ship without a rudder, drifting aimlessly. Carter was sensitive to what journalists called a national malaise, but he only embarrassed himself when he tried to address the amorphous problem. He called 130 prominent men and women from every sector of American life to Washington; having heard from them, he was able to announce only that there was "a crisis of the American spirit," right back where he started from.

CHRONOLOGY

1969	"Nixon Doctrine": United States would no longer "undertake the defense of all the nations of the free world." "Vietnamization": President Nixon sponsors replacement of American combat soldiers in Vietnam with well-trained Vietnamese units U. S. Air Force bombs North Vietnamese sanctuaries in Cambodia
1971	Nixon resorts to wage and price controls to battle inflation Visit of American table-tennis team to China inaugurates regularization of American relations with Communist China
1972	President Nixon visits China Nixon signals détente with Soviet Union by signing SALT (Strategic Arms Limitation Treaty) in Moscow Paris Accords, effective January 1973, provide for withdrawal of American troops from Vietnam and release of all American prisoners of war

Antiwar Democrats dominate Democratic convention and nominate Senator George McGovern
Burglars linked to Nixon reelection committee arrested breaking into Democratic National Headquarters in Watergate apartment complex, Washington

1973 Vice President Spiro T. Agnew resigns in wake of revelations of corruption during his governorship of Maryland. Gerald R. Ford of Michigan is appointed to succeed him
Severe shortages of gasoline and other petroleum products when OPEC (Organization of Petroleum Exporting Countries) restricts world production

1973–1974 Progressively incriminating revelations involve many high officials, including President Nixon, in Watergate burglary

1974 With vote to impeach imminent, Richard Nixon resigns from presidency to be succeeded by Gerald R. Ford, who pardons Nixon of any crimes connected to Watergate break-in

1974–1976 "Stagflation": economic stagnation accompanied by inflation vexes Ford administration

1976 Comparative Democratic unknown, Jimmy Carter of Georgia, defeats Gerald Ford in presidential election

1978 Carter signs treaty providing for transfer of Panama Canal to Panama before 2000
At Camp David, Maryland, Carter brokers peace agreement between leaders of Israel and Egypt

1979 China and the United States establish full diplomatic relations
Carter terminates détente with Soviet Union when Russian forces invade Afghanistan

FOR FURTHER READING

James Gilbert, *Another Chance: America since 1945*, 1984, provides a general overview of this period; Godfrey Hodgson, *America in Our Time*, 1976, deals with the first part of it. See also Paul Boyer, *Promises to Keep*, 1995. Many contemporary historians were themselves participants and partisans during these years. Many of the major players are still around, trying to shape their posterity.

Some have written memoirs, perhaps as much for monstrous advances from publishers as for self-justification. These accounts can, nevertheless, be useful and are, in any case, valuable sources. See *The Memoirs of Richard Nixon*, 1978; George McGovern, *Grassroots*, 1977; *A Time to Heal: The Autobiography of Gerald Ford*, 1979; Henry A. Kissinger, *White House Years*, 1979, and *Years of Upheaval*, 1982; Jimmy Carter, *Keeping Faith*, 1982; and Rosalynn Carter, *First Lady from Plains*, 1984. A fascinating study of Nixon written before his fall is Garry Wills, *Nixon Agonistes*, 1970; but see also Stephen Ambrose, *Nixon*, 1988. On Kissinger, see Robert Morris, *Uncertain Greatness: Henry Kissinger and American Foreign Policy*, 1977.

Carl Bernstein and Robert Woodward, *All the President's Men*, 1974, is by the two reporters for the *Washington Post* who doggedly investigated the Watergate affair and helped bring about Nixon's fall. Perhaps the most insightful early analysis of what happened is Arthur M. Schlesinger Jr., *The Imperial Presidency*, 1973. For more recent studies, see Stanley Kutler, *The Wars of Watergate*, 1990; and Melvin Small, *Johnson, Nixon, and the Doves*, 1998.

On national politics and policy during the 1970s, see David Broder, *The Party's Over*, 1972; Samuel Lubell, *The Hidden Crisis in American Politics*, 1970; A. J. Reichley, *Conservatives in an Age of Change: The Nixon and Ford Administrations*, 1981; and Theodore H. White, *The Making of a President, 1972*, 1973. On George Wallace, see Dan Carter, *The Politics of Rage*, 1996. See Henry Kissinger's memoirs listed earlier for foreign policy and, on specific issues, R. L. Garthoff, *Détente and Confrontation*, 1985; A. E. Goodman, *The Lost Peace: America's Search for a Negotiated Settlement of the Vietnam War*, 1978; on Central America, R. A. Pastor, *Condemned to Repetition*, 1987; W. B. Quandt, *Decade of Decision: American Foreign Policy toward the Arab–Israeli Conflict*, 1978; and G. Sick, *All Fall Down: America's Tragic Encounter with Iran*, 1985. For an overview, see Warren Cohen, *America in the Age of Soviet Power, 1945–1991*, 1993.

Five presidents—Bush, Reagan, Carter, Ford, and Nixon—gather to dedicate the Ronald Reagan Library in California. Carter remarked, "At least all of you have met a Democratic president. I haven't had that honor." In January 1993, he would have that chance.

50
CHAPTER

MORNING IN AMERICA

The Reagan Era

1980–1993

For many years now, you and I have been shushed like children and told there are no simple answers to the complex problems that are beyond our comprehension. Well, the truth is there are simple answers. There are just not easy ones.

—Ronald Reagan

I have long believed there was a divine plan that placed this land here to be found by people of a special kind, that we have a rendezvous with destiny. Yes, there is a spirit moving in this land and a hunger in the people for a spiritual revival. If the task I seek should be given to me, I would pray only that I could perform it in a way that would serve God.

—Ronald Reagan

994 Chapter 50 Morning in America

Republican conservatives looked forward to the election of 1980. Democrat Jimmy Carter had been elected in 1976 by the slimmest of margins and his popularity had not increased during his four years in office. "Stagflation" and an impression of ineffectiveness, the undoing of his predecessor, Gerald Ford, dogged Jimmy Carter too. The Camp David Agreement was a foreign policy triumph comparable to Nixon's breakthrough in relations with China but other Carter diplomatic achievements, such as the Panama Canal treaty, were poorly received by many Americans. Then the roof fell in.

The Ayatollah and the Actor

Carter believed that Reza Pahlavi, the pro-Western shah (emperor) of Iran, was popular with the Iranian people. Indeed, Carter described Iran as an "island of stability" in the chaotic Middle East.

He was mistaken. During his long reign, the shah alienated almost every important element of Iranian society except wealthy landowners and the westernized middle and upper classes of the cities. The country was stable on the surface. But urban workers felt exploited by their employers. Leftists and liberals educated in Western ideals lived in fear of SAVAK, the shah's secret police. The peasantry— uneducated, pious, and numerous—was mesmerized by reactionary mullahs (Muslim preachers) who believed the shah's modernization policies were blasphemous.

The Iranian Tragedy

Discontent built until, in January 1979, the shah fled Iran and the mullahs, led by Ayatollah Ruhollah Khomeini, seized power. In October, when Carter admitted the shah to the United States for treatment of cancer, Iranian student supporters of the ayatollah seized the United States embassy in Teheran, taking 66 diplomats hostage. They demanded that Carter hand over the shah for trial. Most of the women and the African Americans among the hostages were quickly freed. However, for more than a year, 53 languished in confinement. Not until January 20, 1981, the day Jimmy Carter left the White House, were they released.

Sympathy for the ayatollah's revolution was short-lived in the United States. His regime executed political opponents and "moral offenders" (in-

cluding people possessing videotapes of Hollywood movies) on a scale that made the shah look like Good King Wenceslas. Khomeini's fanaticism helped prolong an eight-year war with Iraq that killed 200,000 Iranians, including boys dispatched on suicide attacks. In 1989, Khomeini issued a *fatwah*, a proclamation promising salvation (and money) to any Muslim who killed a British–Indian author, Salmon Rushdie, for writing a book judged insulting to Islam. Khomeini embarrassed many pious Muslims, but his power in Iran was unquestioned. And, in holding the American hostages, he wrote an end to the political career of Jimmy Carter.

The Republican nominee was Ronald Reagan, the darling of the party's conservatives. He easily defeated middle-of-the-road Republicans George Bush and Illinois Congressman John Anderson in the primary elections. Then, he and his campaign managers proceeded to play every campaign issue, including the hostage crisis, brilliantly. When defeated John Anderson announced he would run for president as an independent, Reagan shrewdly placated Republican moderates by naming Bush his running mate. The hope was that Anderson would steal as many votes from Carter as from the Republicans.

The Reagan Campaign

To have attacked Carter directly on the hostage issue might have aroused sympathy for the president. Carter was clearly in agony at their continued imprisonment. Instead, Reagan supported the president's efforts in Iran in the name of patriotic solidarity, while blasting Carter's foreign policy in general terms. He pointed to America's low prestige abroad, attributing it to Carter's "softness" with the Soviets and his failure to back up foreign friends. Toughness and a massive military buildup, Reagan said, were needed to end the slide of American influence, prestige, and pride.

Domestically, Reagan focused on the weak economy. He promised to reduce regulation of business which, he said, destroyed initiative. He would bring a stop to inflation, increase employment, cut government spending (except on the military), and balance the federal budget by 1984.

Fundamentalist preacher-politicians such as the Reverend Jerry Falwell organized independent PACs (Political Action Committees) to promote the notion that liberal social and cultural policies were responsible for a decline in American morality. Falwell's

Iranian militants demonstrate at the ill-starred American embassy in Teheran.

Moral Majority blamed the Democrats for everything from the high divorce rate to the increase of violent crime in big cities. They successfully appealed to many traditional Democratic blue-collar workers and white southerners who were bewildered by attacks on traditional values from within their party.

The Mandate

Most experts predicted a close election. Several said the winner might be decided by the outcome in California, the last of the big states to report returns. In fact, the election of 1980 was over two hours before the polls closed on the West Coast. Reagan won an electoral college landslide, 489 votes to just 49 for Carter. He won 43.9 million popular votes to Carter's 35.5 million, with 5.7 million going to John Anderson. Apparently, voters had lied to the pollsters. Many were embarrassed to say they were going to vote for Reagan, but vote for him is what they did.

The half-century-old Democratic party coalition lay in tatters. The Irish-American and Italian-American vote, always dependably Democratic, went to Reagan. In all but three states, Slavic Americans voted for him. Jews, who had once been 80 percent Democratic, split about evenly, as did labor union members. Reagan won 60 percent of the elderly who—conventional wisdom had it—would always vote for their Social Security, which meant voting liberal Democratic. Young people, lionized by liberals since the 1960s as intrinsically good and idealistic (which meant, among other things, liberal) cast 60 percent of their votes for the aged Republican candidate.

996　Chapter 50　Morning in America

> ### Priorities in the 1980s
>
> In 1983, the United States spent 57 cents per capita on public broadcasting, as compared to $10 per capita in Japan, $18 in Great Britain, and $22 in Canada. In the private sector, the cost of making one episode of the television program *Miami Vice* was $1.5 million. The annual budget of the vice squad in the real city of Miami, Florida, a major clearinghouse for imported drugs, was just $1.1 million.

The conservative PACs also defeated half a dozen liberal Democratic senators, including 1972 presidential nominee George McGovern. For the first time in nearly 30 years, the Republicans had a majority in the Senate. The Democrats still held the House of Representatives. However, a number of conservative Democrats, startled by the election results, announced they would support the president. Reagan had a working majority in both houses. A new era had begun.

THE REAGAN REVOLUTION

Reagan turned 78 before he left the White House in 1989. He was the oldest person ever to hold the presidency. A few years after his retirement, he was laid low by Alzheimer's disease and unable to recognize close friends. And yet, this ancient actor, whom some observers believed was slipping mentally before he left office, stamped his personality and values on the 1980s as indelibly as Franklin D. Roosevelt had stamped his on the 1930s. Ronald Reagan must be rated one of a handful of most effective presidents, those who significantly shaped their country, who ever served. To call him, therefore, one of the "greatest" presidents, in a league with FDR, is no partisan claim.

Man of the Decade

"He has no dark side," an aide said of Reagan, "What you see is what you get." By 1980, Americans had seen a good deal of Ronald Reagan for more than 40 years. He was a movie star in the 1940s and 1950s, and then the host of a popular television show. Al-

ways intensely political—a New Deal liberal as a young man!—Reagan became a tireless and eloquent campaigner for conservative causes in the 1960s. He was governor of California between 1967 and 1975 and very nearly won the Republican presidential nomination in 1976.

Few people disliked Reagan personally. If he was a zealot for his ideas, his personality was the polar opposite of fanatical. He was a cheerful raconteur, a walking *People* magazine with a treasury of show-business stories. He conveyed his good humor to both large audiences and small groups, around a table and on the airwaves. He won the admiration of even some political critics when, shortly after his inauguration, an unbalanced young man shot him in the chest and Reagan cracked jokes while on the operating table. Reagan was called "the Great Communicator" for his ability to sell himself and his policies. He was also known as "the Teflon president." He was so well liked personally that nothing messy stuck to him, neither his own bad decisions, an administration that brimmed with scandal, nor when former aides ridiculed him. Such are economic "good times" in the United States. When the American people are making money, there is little in political leaders they will not tolerate. The final president of the century, William Clinton, was to enjoy this phenomenon. So did Ronald Reagan.

The Teflon President

The criticisms that did not stick to Reagan were legion. After a lifetime in the Babylon of Hollywood and evincing no interest in religion, he presented himself as a born-again Christian and got away with it. Former aides said that he was interested largely in the honor and ceremony of being president, little in the complexities of government. When he first ran for governor, an aide said, "He knew zero about California when we came in, I mean zero." As president, Reagan repeatedly made preposterous gaffes— Alaska had more oil than Saudi Arabia; Bolivians spoke Portuguese; the Soviet Union planned to invade the United States through Mexico—and he repeated his illusions after his aides quietly corrected them. There was no significant public reaction.

Critics were shocked by his habit of sleeping long hours each day. They said that Reagan dozed off at cabinet meetings and came to life only while watching old movies. The public shrugged. Nothing could alienate the majority of Americans. After the

Vietnam tragedy, the Watergate scandal, and the foundering of the Carter years, Ronald Reagan's breezy cheerfulness and optimism restored confidence in the presidency. He flummoxed the Democrats.

Social Policies

Like other conservatives, Reagan believed that, under the domination of liberals, the Supreme Court had become result-oriented. With social, cultural, or political ends in view, the justices *legislated* in their judicial decisions in order to achieve them The consequences were the social ills Reagan saw around him, such as the "coddling" of lawbreakers.

During his eight years in office, a series of vacancies allowed him to continue the transformation of the Supreme Court into the more restrained body that Richard Nixon had envisaged. Reagan's first appointee was Sandra Day O'Connor of Arizona, a protégée of Nixon's most conservative appointee, William Rehnquist. By naming her, the first woman on the court, Reagan pleased feminists while adding a generally conservative vote. In 1986, Reagan made the forceful Rehnquist chief justice and added Antonin Scalia, a brilliant arch-conservative with a biting writing style, to the high court. Only in 1988, at the end of his term, did Reagan run into trouble getting his nominees confirmed. The Senate rejected Robert Bork, who ranked with Scalia as a scholar of the law but who also had been, unlike Scalia, highly political. A second Reagan appointee was dumped when it was revealed he had smoked marijuana while in law school.

That episode was embarrassing to Reagan because he made a good deal of political hay out of his "War on Drugs." Nancy Reagan headed a campaign to fight the use of drugs among American teenagers. Stung by criticism that she cared for little but expensive evening gowns, Mrs. Reagan devoted long hours to the antidrug crusade known as "Just Say No!"

Reaganomics

Reagan's popularity owed in part to good luck. Some of the problems that hobbled Ford and felled Carter resolved themselves during Reagan's presidency. A vicious war between Iran and Iraq prevented the ayatollah from vexing Americans further. In the Soviet Union, the senility of party leader Leonid Brezhnev and, after his death in November 1982, three years

of caretaker leadership by equally doddering old Bolsheviks meant that the Cold War adversary was almost without direction until 1985. OPEC, which had dictated world energy policies in the 1970s, began quarreling within and oil prices collapsed.

But the keystone of Reagan's popularity was the fact that, after two difficult years, his presidency was a time of steadily increasing prosperity for middle- and upper-class Americans. The good times, Reagan believed, were due to his economic policies, which critics mocked as "Reaganomics."

During the campaign of 1980, Reagan promised to restore prosperity by ending inflation and unemployment, reducing government regulation of business, and balancing the budget. Part of his program was based on "supply-side" economics, which called for emphasizing the nation's supply of goods and services while allowing the distribution of wealth—each person's share of the wealth—to take care of itself. There was little new in "supply side." Coolidge's secretary of state, Andrew Mellon, would have yawned with bored familiarity, when it was explained to him.

Thus, Reaganomics meant cutting the taxes of upper- and middle-income Americans, just as Mellon had done. Whereas poorer people would spend any tax savings on consumer goods, supply-siders argued, the affluent already had a comfortable life. Therefore, they would invest their tax savings, supplying capital to the economy. Economic growth would result, creating jobs for those on the bottom. People formerly unemployed would be supporting themselves and paying taxes. The expensive social welfare programs previously needed to sustain the poor could be slashed, making government cheaper. It would then be easy to balance the budget and end inflation.

Urban Decay

In New York City every day between 1977 and 1980, 600 to 2,100 subway cars were out of service because of age, mistreatment, and vandalism. Between 80 and 300 trains had to be canceled each day. There were 2,200 to 5,000 fires in the New York subway system each year. In 1980, it took 40 minutes to take a trip on the subway that required 10 minutes in 1910.

President Reagan and Chief Justice Warren Burger with the Supreme Court's first woman justice, Sandra Day O'Connor, 1981.

Prosperity in Practice

At Reagan's behest, Congress reduced taxes by 25 percent over three years. The drop, for those with good incomes, was considerable. An upper-middle-class family making $75,000 a year paid federal income taxes of 52.9 percent during the 1950s and 39.3 percent during the 1970s. By 1985, after the Reagan tax cut, such a family was taxed only 29.6 percent of its income. The rich did even better. The average tax bill for an annual income of $500,000–$1 million in 1981 was $301,072. By the time Reagan left office it was cut to $166,066.

Government revenues dropped by $131 billion, which Reagan said he would make up by slashing expenditures on bureaucracy and social programs. He cut 37,000 jobs from the federal payroll and reduced spending on education, medical research, food stamps, and other programs instituted during the 1960s to aid the poor. Federal spending on low-income housing dropped from $32 billion in 1980 to $7 billion in 1988.

The Deficit Mushrooms

During the Reagan years, however, the prosperity of the 1980s did not trickle down to all, as supply-siders had predicted it would. Too much of the upper- and middle-class tax break went not into investment but into consumption of luxury goods. By 1986, investment in manufacturing was only 1 percent higher than it had been in the recession year of 1982. By way of contrast, sales of high-priced homes boomed. Expensive imports such as Jaguar and Mercedes-Benz automobiles soared.

The money that fed the consumption binge of the 1980s came from abroad; it was borrowed. West German and Japanese investors pumped money into the United States, buying real estate, corporations, banks, stocks, and U.S. Treasury bonds in huge blocks. Then they made their money back as Americans spent on imported consumer goods. From being the world's largest creditor nation when Reagan took the oath of office, the United States became the world's greatest debtor nation. In 1981, foreign-

"The Homeless," armies of social rejects, were an anomalous, sometimes overwhelming, presence of the prosperous 1980s and 1990s.

ers owed Americans $2,500 for each American family of four. By 1989, Americans owed foreigners $7,000 for each family of four.

The federal deficit—the government's annual debt—grew worse. The costs of Social Security, pensions, and especially Reagan's military buildup were immense. Moreover, all the while the president called for a constitutional amendment mandating a balanced budget, the Reagan administration spent and borrowed at levels that smashed all records. In 1981, the federal government owed $738 billion, about 26 cents on each dollar produced and earned in the United States that year. In 1989, the debt was $2.1 trillion, about 43 cents on each dollar produced and earned. The president who criticized Jimmy Carter's borrowing policies borrowed more money in eight years than 39 previous presidents had borrowed in two centuries!

Deregulation

Since the New Deal—since the beginning of the century!—the federal government had closely regulated many aspects of national economic life. This regulation, Reagan said, discouraged the spirit of enterprise. As president, he weakened the regulatory agencies by abolishing some and cutting the budgets of others. To head other agencies, Reagan appointed officials who simply neglected to do what their job descriptions directed. Airlines, trucking companies, banks, and brokers selling stocks and bonds found there was no longer a federal watchdog outside their doors.

Profits increased and so did abuses. Airlines closed down routes that made too little money and raised fares on well-traveled air lanes. In 1981, a person could fly from San Francisco to Los Angeles on an unrestricted ticket for $36. In 1989, the same ticket cost $148. Consumer advocates claimed that the deregulated airlines sent unsafe planes and unqualified pilots aloft. Similar criticisms were made of the condition of trucks and the qualifications required of truck drivers.

The Environment

Some of Reagan's appointees to environmental agencies despised the people they called "tree huggers,"—members of conservation and environmentalist organizations. The head of the Environmental

Protection Agency, Ann Burford, was forced to resign in 1983 when it was revealed she had actively interfered with the enforcement of her agency's regulations. The president vetoed a Clean Water Act aimed at stopping the dumping of toxic industrial wastes. His first secretary of the interior, James Watt of Colorado, tried to open protected scenic coastline to offshore oil drillers.

Watt was a spokesman for the "sagebrush rebels," western businessmen who wanted the federal government to turn public lands over to the states which would then open them to exploitation by private mining, logging, and grazing companies. Watt's cynicism and tactlessness resulted in the runaway growth of environmental groups. The Wilderness Society claimed 48,000 members in 1981, 240,000 in 1989. The Natural Resources Defense Council increased its membership from 85,000 to 170,000 during the 1980s. The World Wildlife Fund had 60,000 members in 1982, 1 million in 1990. The Sierra Club and Audubon Society made similar gains.

Financial Fraud

Deregulation of financial institutions led to irresponsible and sometimes corrupt practices in banks and savings and loan associations. In 1988 alone, 135 savings and loans had to be bailed out or closed by the Federal Savings and Loan Insurance Corporation (FSLIC).

This agency, like the Federal Deposit Insurance Corporation (FDIC) for banks, guaranteed savings accounts. Before the Reagan deregulation, however, the FSLIC and FDIC also enforced strict management standards on the people who ran financial institutions. During the Reagan years, supervision was virtually nil and shoddy practices abounded.

Time Flies

A study by a scientific management firm in the late 1980s revealed that the average American living to his or her life expectancy will spend seven years in the bathroom, six years eating, five years waiting in lines, four years cleaning house, three years in meetings, one year "looking for things," eight months opening junk mail, and six months waiting at red lights.

The champion wheeler-dealer of the 1980s was probably Michael Milken, who saddled deregulated savings and loans with billions of dollars in "junk bonds," loans that promised to pay high interest precisely because no prudent investor would touch them. Milken, who in one year collected $550 million in commissions, eventually went to jail. So did several prominent figures on Wall Street, the nation's financial center. Freed of close supervision by the Securities and Exchange Commission (SEC), respected stockbrokers turned to fraud. By paying bribes to executives in large corporations, they learned before the general public of important decisions that affected the price of stocks. Using this insider information, they bought and sold shares at immense profit.

Through it all, the Reagan administration continued to approve corporate mergers and takeovers that did little but enrich a few individuals. In 1970, there were 10 corporate reshufflings paying fees of $1 million or more to those who arranged them. In 1980, there were 94, in 1986, 346. In 1988, the government approved a deal between tobacco giant R. J. Reynolds and the Nabisco Company despite the fact that, even the principals admitted, the only consequences would be higher prices for consumers, fewer jobs in the two companies, and personal profits of $10 million for a handful of shareholders.

The Election of 1984

In 1984, Walter Mondale of Minnesota, vice president under Jimmy Carter, won the Democratic party nomination by beating back challenges from Senator Gary Hart of Colorado and the Reverend Jesse Jackson, a civil rights activist and orator in the tradition of the black churches from which he had emerged. Hart was the "New Age" liberal candidate, popular among fashionable, generally affluent people in their twenties and thirties who, while largely oblivious to the social and economic views of old-line Democrats, defined themselves as liberal on the basis of their cultural sentiments.

Mondale, an old-style New Dealer, hoped that labor union support and what he called the "sleaze factor," the widespread corruption in the Reagan administration, would be enough to help him overcome prosperity and the president's personal popularity. But he was unable to bring back the traditionally Democratic voters who had gone for Reagan in 1980. Mondale was widely perceived as a pork-barrel politician, promising undeliverable benefits to

Michael Milken, financial wizard and probably the greatest profiteer of the Reagan years, went to jail because of some of his operations.

every constituent group. In fact, he was gloriously clumsy when it came to traditional politics. Thus, Mondale named a woman, Geraldine Ferraro, as his running mate. Even as a symbol of female equality, this "first" had already been diluted by Reagan's glad willingness to put women in high office. Moreover, feminists and New Age liberals were not going to vote Republican under any circumstances and conservative Republican women were not moved by appeals to sisterhood. Mondale gained no voters not already in his pocket by nominating Ferraro and he threw away a chance to use the vice presidential slot to appeal to former Democrats who were seduced by the Great Communicator.

Reagan's popularity was at flood tide in 1984. He won by a landslide, carrying 59 percent of the vote and every state except Mondale's Minnesota and the District of Columbia. He announced that the theme of his second term was "Morning in America."

FOREIGN POLICY IN THE EIGHTIES

Reagan was a Cold Warrior. In 1982, he called Russia an "evil empire . . . the focus of evil in the world." As late as 1985, he promulgated the Reagan Doctrine—pretty much the preachment of John Foster Dulles 30 years earlier—that the United States would support any anti-Communist struggle anywhere.

By the time he left office in 1989, however, Reagan scored a major breakthrough in nuclear arms reduction and set the stage for an historic rapprochement between the United States and the Cold War enemy. His policies towards other parts of the world were also sometimes surprising.

South Africa and the Middle East

Reagan criticized South Africa's policy of apartheid (strict legal segregation of races), but he resisted calls for economic sanctions designed to force the South African regime to change. He supported rebels in Angola who were fighting a government backed by the Soviet Union and Cuba.

Reagan continued Jimmy Carter's policy of aiding anti-Russian rebels in Afghanistan despite the fact that they were Muslim fundamentalists like those who kept Khomeini in power in Iran and looked on the United States as a fount of moral evil along with state-of-the-art weaponry. In 1983, he sent marines to Lebanon, which was torn by a multi-sided war involving religion and foreign intervention. When a suicide bomber driving an explosive-laden truck killed 241 sleeping marines, Reagan withdrew the force. His Teflon worked as ever. Reagan was not widely criticized either for sending the marines in or for withdrawing them in failure. He had it both ways.

In 1986, Reagan won applause by bombing Libya. The Libyan leader, Muammar Qadaffi, had long been suspected of financing terrorists. When American intelligence gathered evidence of a direct

---

Citizen Consumers

Immigrants sworn in as United States citizens at Santa Fe in April 1985 received a gift packet including the Preamble to the Constitution, a pamphlet describing etiquette toward the American flag, directories to the Safeway supermarket and Motel 6 chains, discount coupons from local businesses, and membership in the Radio Shack "battery club."

1002 Chapter 50 Morning in America

> ### Cutthroat Competition
>
> In 1984, it was revealed that the Defense Department paid General Dynamics $7,417 for an alignment pin that cost 3 cents at a hardware store, McDonnell-Douglas $2,043 for a nut priced elsewhere at 13 cents, Pratt and Whitney $118 for 22-cent plastic stool leg covers, and Hughes Aircraft $2,543 for a $3.64 circuit-breaker. A congressman went to a hardware store and purchased 22 tools found in a military repair kit. His price was $92.44; the government's price for the same kit was $10,186.56.

link between Qadaffi and terrorists in West Germany, American bombers raided several Libyan cities. Public opinion approved the expedition. Reagan also took action in the long bloody war between Iran and Iraq. In May 1987, to ensure that oil tankers moved safely in the Persian Gulf, he sent American warships to protect the seaways.

Central America

The president also applied the Reagan Doctrine in the Caribbean and Central America. In October 1983, he ordered a surprise attack on Grenada, a tiny island nation of just 110,000 people. The island was in chaos after the assassination of a Marxist leader, and Cuban workers were extending airstrips, a worrisome project. Although critics feared that one such invasion would lead to others, the president's action was popular.

His policy in Central America was more controversial. Many liberal critics opposed the United States's support of a repressive government in El Salvador and its opposition to the revolutionary Sandinista government of Nicaragua. When, in 1983, El Salvador elected a moderate over an extreme rightist as president, criticism of Reagan's policy in that country faded too.

However, many members of Congress continued to oppose American support of the Nicaraguan *contras*, guerrillas fighting the leftist Sandinista government of the country. Some said that the United States was causing turmoil and misery in an already wretched and misgoverned country by keeping it at war. Others said that the contras were reactionary and antidemocratic. Still others feared that the

United States would become involved in another Vietnam quagmire. Beginning in October 1984, a worried Congress attached the Boland Amendments to a number of bills providing money for foreign aid. These prohibited the government from directly aiding military actions in Nicaragua.

The Iran-Contra Affair

Rather than live with this restriction, in February 1985 Reagan told top aides "to figure out a way to take action." They embarked on a bizarre adventure that mocked the president's view of world politics as a competition between good and evil. Two National Security Advisers, Robert McFarlane and John Poindexter, and a marine lieutenant colonel, Oliver North, secretly sold 18 Hawk missiles to the Ayatollah Khomeini's Iran. Some of the huge profits from the deal simply disappeared into someone's pocket. The balance was given to the contras.

The roles of Defense Secretary Caspar Weinberger and the president in the affair were never clearly defined. Weinberger was indicted for withholding information and Reagan changed his story several times. The evidence indicates that he did not explicitly sanction violation of the Boland law; he simply did not know what was going on in his own administration. Even after his own advisers explained to Reagan what they had done, he seemed unable to articulate it himself.

Liberals screamed bloody murder. But Ronald Reagan was no ordinary political target. Times were good; stocks and real estate values were rising; the American public seemed not to notice. Colonel North, convicted in 1989 on 3 of 12 criminal counts, was later pardoned and went on to become a darling of the Republican right. In 1994, he narrowly missed election to the Senate from Virginia.

Changing Policies

Even before the Iran-Contra affair broke in the news, Reagan's foreign policy underwent significant changes. Rather than defend an anti-Communist dictator in Haiti in 1986, American agents played an important role in persuading him to go into exile. The United States also played a central role in the ouster of the pro-American but corrupt president of the Philippines, Ferdinand Marcos. When Marcos declared himself the victor in a disputed election, riots broke out throughout the country. Fearing a

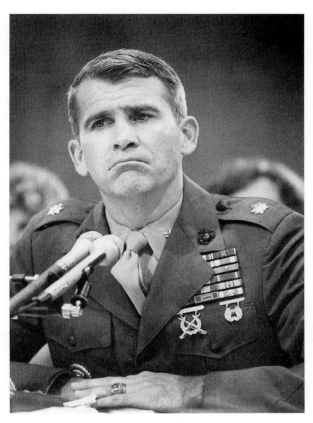
Oliver North was accused of violating federal law in the Iran-Contra affair.

civil war, the United States supported his opponent, Corazón Aquino. Marcos was given asylum in Hawaii to get him out of the Philippines.

Reagan was unsuccessful in his attempt to ease out Manuel Noriega, the military dictator of Panama. Evidence indicated that Noriega was deeply involved in smuggling cocaine and other drugs into the United States. He was indicted in the United States, and Reagan cut off the flow of American dollars to Panama. However, Noriega's hold on the Panamanian army was strong, and he rallied public support by baiting the United States, always a crowd-pleaser in Latin America.

Weapons Buildup

The most important of Reagan's foreign policy shifts was in his view of the Soviet Union. During his first years in office, he destroyed the spirit of détente that had originated under Richard Nixon. Calling the SALT-II treaty a "one-way street" with Americans making all the concessions, he refused to submit it to the Senate for ratification. In 1986, Reagan announced that the United States would no longer be bound by SALT-I.

In the meantime, the president sponsored the greatest peacetime military buildup in the nation's history, spending $2 trillion on both old and new systems. Battleships were taken out of mothballs and put to sea, and Reagan revived the MX missile, which he renamed the Peacekeeper. When it was announced that the Peacekeepers were to be installed in old Minuteman missile silos, critics said that Reagan was planning a first strike against the Soviets. The Russians, they said, had long mapped and targeted the Minuteman. Therefore, they were useless unless the missiles in them were to be fired to begin a war.

In 1983, Pershing II missiles were installed in West Germany, in places where they could hit Soviet targets in five minutes. The Russians responded by increasing their strike capability. A new arms race seemed to be underway. By 1985, the two superpowers had more than 50,000 nuclear warheads between them.

The most controversial of Reagan's weapons proposals was SDI, the Strategic Defense Initiative, mockingly called "Star Wars" after a popular movie. SDI was a system by which, in theory, satellites orbiting the earth would be equipped with lasers fired at missiles by computer. Reagan claimed that the

---

Weapons

Ronald Reagan roundly criticized his predecessor, Jimmy Carter, for neglecting the American military and, in fact, increased Carter's defense budget by 28 percent. However, weapons systems developed during the Carter administration, such as the Tomahawk Cruise Missile, the F-117 Stealth Fighter, and the HARM antiradar missile, proved to be keys to victory in the Gulf War against Iraq, while Reagan era innovations had dubious outcomes. Star Wars died. The battleships Reagan recommissioned were put back into mothballs within a few years. And the B-1 bomber was a $30 billion flop. Just 97 planes were built; they were cursed by engine failure and icing on wings.

system would create an umbrella preventing a successful missile attack on the United States.

Criticism of Star Wars took several forms. Some scientists said that SDI simply would not work. Military experts pointed out that low-flying missiles and planes would not be affected by lasers in space. Financiers worried that the astronomical costs of the project would bankrupt the United States. Antiwar groups said that SDI was actually an offensive, not a defensive, weapon. By making the United States safer from nuclear attack, it would encourage a reckless president to attack the Soviet Union. Others said that the Soviets would simply develop countermeasures, which had always been the case in military technology.

Turning toward Disarmament

Still, it was not criticism that led President Reagan to reverse direction. During his second term, the hawkish Caspar Weinberger resigned as secretary of defense and the more statesmanlike secretary of state, George Schultz, the dove of the Reagan administration, won greater influence over the president.

White House insiders said that Nancy Reagan also played a big part in persuading the president to turn toward disarmament. Deeply devoted to her husband, she grew concerned about his place in history as his term in office drew near an end. Nancy Reagan knew that presidents who worked for peace had higher historical reputations than those dubbed warmongers, as her husband was.

The concerns of allies in Europe also influenced the president. Antinuclear protesters swarmed around American bases in Germany, Britain, and Spain. Chancellor Helmut Kohl of West Germany, President François Mitterand of France, and Prime Minister Margaret Thatcher of Great Britain remained loyal to the NATO alliance. However, all made it clear that they were unnerved by some of Reagan's more reckless speeches. Most important, the Soviet Union underwent profound changes during the 1980s.

Mikhail Gorbachev

In 1985, Mikhail Gorbachev emerged as head of both the Soviet government and Communist party. At home, Gorbachev tried to institute far-reaching economic and political reforms. His policy of *pere-stroika* (restructuring) was designed to revive the Soviet economy, which had been moribund under strict government controls. *Glasnost* (opening) promised political and intellectual freedoms unheard of in the Soviet Union.

If his reforms were to succeed, Gorbachev needed to divert Soviet resources from the military to the domestic economy. Doing that depended on American cooperation. At first, Reagan resisted Gorbachev's proposals to end the arms race. Then, in Washington in December 1987, the two men, all smiles and handshakes, signed a treaty eliminating many short-range and medium-range missiles. The Soviets destroyed 1,752 missiles and the Americans 867. These represented only 4 percent of the nuclear missiles in existence. Nevertheless, nuclear power 32,000 times the force of the Hiroshima bomb was wiped out.

THE BUSH PRESIDENCY

The Democrats approached the presidential year 1988 with high hopes. They believed that the Reagan presidency was an aberration, the personal triumph of a fabulously popular individual, not the first chapter of a Republican ascendancy. A majority of governors were Democrats. The Democratic party enjoyed a comfortable grip on the House and had regained control of the Senate in 1986. Why should not the Democrats regain the presidency, too?

The Seven Dwarfs

As always when election victory seems likely, the Democrats were swamped with would-be standard bearers. The front-runner in the early going was Gary Hart, the former senator from Colorado who had given Mondale a tough race in the 1976 primaries. However, in a bizarre sequence of events, including publication of a photo showing the married Hart with a beautiful young model on his lap aboard a yacht called *Monkey Business*, political analysts suggested that the candidate's judgment was, perhaps, less than what was called for by the presidency.

When Hart withdrew from the race, the remaining candidates were ridiculed as "the seven dwarfs" for their deficiency of presidential stature. In fact, several of the dwarfs were able men, and Jesse Jackson remained, as he had been in 1976, an exciting orator.

Some party professionals hoped that Senator Sam Nunn of Georgia, a thoughtful and respected expert on national defense, would jump into the 35 primary election races for the nomination; or that Governor Mario Cuomo of New York, another inspiring orator whose thoughtful humanism was tempered by hard-headed political realism, would run.

But neither did, and the nomination went to Governor Michael Dukakis of Massachusetts. The son of Greek immigrants, Dukakis was a successful governor, balancing budgets while the Reagan administration spent and borrowed. During his administration, a state with serious economic difficulties became a prosperous center of finance and high-tech industry. For vice president, Dukakis chose the courtly Senator Lloyd Bentsen of Texas, reminding voters of the Massachusetts–Texas combination that won the election of 1960.

Bush for the Republicans

The Republican nominee was Vice President George Bush, who handily defeated Senator Robert Dole of Kansas in the primaries. Bush was a wealthy oilman who held a number of appointive positions in government before becoming vice president under Reagan, and the administration's chief cheerleader. He attracted ridicule for his conversion to right-wing politics, but Bush's change of heart enabled him to establish ties with Republican conservatives who, earlier, had looked on him as practically a liberal.

As his running mate, Bush chose Senator Dan Quayle of Indiana, a congenial young man whose achievements since first tying his shoes seemed to owe to his father's wealth and influence. Quayle admitted he had "majored in golf" at university. There was also evidence that he had dodged military service during the Vietnam War when his father's friends created a place for him in the National Guard. Quayle's political career was built on his movie star good looks and careful programming by political handlers. During the campaign of 1988, they made sure that he spoke mostly to screened groups of the party faithful.

The Campaign

Dukakis attacked Bush's judgment in picking Quayle, but Dukakis's public persona was drab and mechanical. Pundits joked of "Zorba the Clerk." By way of contrast, winning the Republican nomina-tion, his first election victory since 1968, seemed to liberate Bush. As Dukakis grew grayer, Bush exuded confidence and authority, promising both to continue the policies of the Reagan–Bush administration and to usher in "a kinder, gentler America."

While Bush took the high road, Republican strategists smeared Dukakis because a murderer paroled during his governorship killed again. They hammered on the fact that Dukakis was a member of the American Civil Liberties Union, which had become a citadel of New Age liberalism, defending pupils wearing T-shirts emblazoned with obscene messages to school. Dukakis was put on the defensive, forced to point out that he was not responsible for Massachusetts parole policies and that he disagreed with many ACLU preachments. But he never gained the initiative. Bush overcame a Dukakis lead early in the campaign and won 54 percent of the popular vote.

The Collapse of Communism

In May of 1989, thousands of student demonstrators gathered in Tiananmen Square, the huge plaza at the center of the Chinese capital, demanding glasnost-like reforms in China. Within two days, there were a million people in the square. The drama was played out "live" on American television, for two news bureaus were in Beijing to cover a diplomatic visit by Soviet Premier Gorbachev. Americans even caught some glimpses of the brutal suppression of the rebellion in June, which resulted in at least 500 and possibly, according to some sources, 7,000 deaths.

Communist hard-liners succeeded in holding onto power in China. In Eastern Europe, however, the countries that had been satellites of the Soviet Union since World War II exploited Gorbachev's relaxation of controls to oust their Communist rulers. Poland elected a non-Communist government in mid-1989. By the end of the year, Czechoslovakia followed suit. In October, Erich Honecker, the Communist chief of East Germany, resigned. The next month, a festive crowd breached the Berlin Wall. In December, the much-hated dictator of Romania, Nicolae Ceausescu, was murdered by revolutionaries. In April 1990, Hungary elected an anti-Communist government. In a few astonishing months, a European order almost half a century old was liquidated with minimal violence. The "evil empire" simply collapsed.

President George H. Bush, 1989–1993.

Communist party control of the Soviet Union also dissipated. Glasnost had successfully opened up Soviet society, but perestroika had not succeeded in bringing vitality to the Soviet economy. Food shortages in cities led to increasing protests. On May Day, 1990, the holiday of Communism, Gorbachev and his colleagues were roundly jeered as they reviewed the traditional parade. A few days later, Boris Yeltsin, a critic of Gorbachev, was elected president of the Russian Republic, the largest constituent of the Soviet Union. For the next year and a half, Yeltsin increased his following at Gorbachev's expense by calling for a free market economy and supporting claims to independence in many of the other 14 republics. At the end of 1991, the Soviet Union was formally dissolved.

Successes in Latin America

George Bush could crow that Republican policies had won the Cold War, and he did. Reagan's get-tough policy and especially the fabulously expensive arms race laid bare the fatal weaknesses of the Communist system. The United States spent the Soviet Union into destruction. Rather more important, with the leaders of the Soviet Union preoccupied by the specter of chaos at home, Bush and his secretary of state, James Baker, were able to win a series of victories in both the corridors of diplomacy and on the battlefield.

In December 1989, Bush succeeded in toppling Manuel Noriega from power in Panama. After an

More than any other single event, the fall of the Berlin Wall symbolized the collapse of Communism in Europe.

American military officer was shot in Panama City, Bush unleashed 24,000 troops. Within a few days, with little loss in American lives, Noriega was out of power and a client government installed.

In February 1990, as Soviet and Cuban aid to Nicaragua dried up, the Sandinistas were voted out of power by a political alliance backed by the United States. A less desirable right-wing party took control of El Salvador but, thanks to American prodding, moderated its policies and signed an armistice and agreement with leftist rebels, ending the long war in that country. World affairs were going well for the president.

Crisis in the Middle East

Bush's greatest success abroad was in the Middle East. The Gulf War was precipitated in August 1990 by an Iraqi invasion of Kuwait, a small sheikdom virtually floating on oil. Fearing that Iraqi President Saddam Hussein would next invade Saudi Arabia, the Bush administration secured a unanimous vote in the United Nations Security Council calling for a boycott of all foreign trade with Iraq. Although rich in oil, Iraq needed to import virtually all the rest of the materials needed to support a modern economy.

But Bush and Secretary of State Baker did not believe economic sanctions would resolve the problem. They feared, with plenty of precedent to support them, that as time went on, the boycott would disintegrate. That fear, and apprehensions for the security of Saudi Arabia, prompted Bush to send a token American military force to Saudi Arabia on August 7. Far from buckling, Hussein grew more defiant, annexing Kuwait. Bush then sent more than 400,000 troops to Arabia. Other nations, notably Britain and France, also sent contingents.

The Hundred Hours' War

In January, after Saddam Hussein ignored a United Nations ultimatum that he evacuate Kuwait, the American-led force launched a withering air attack that, in little more than a week, totaled 12,000 sorties. With an American television reporter in Baghdad, the world was presented with the phenomenon of watching a war from both sides.

In the face of this onslaught, Hussein sent most of his air force to neighboring Iran, leaving the skies to American planes. Probably, like some Americans, he believed that his huge army, dug in behind formidable defenses, could turn back any ground assault. He was wrong. His army was large but poorly trained. The air war not only devastated Iraqi communications and the transportation system, but terrified front-line Iraqi troops. When the ground attack came on February 23, 1992, most surrendered without resistance. In just a few days, the Iraqi army was routed by a daring flanking action designed by Commanding General Norman Schwarzkopf. However, fearing that a move on Baghdad, while bound to succeed, would completely destabilize Iraq, Bush ordered a halt to the ground war when it was 100 hours old. Surely, Saddam Hussein could not survive such a humiliation. But he did. What remained of the army, the "Republican Guard," remained loyal to him. In Iraq, that was enough.

Disappointing Results

Even the promising fact that the United Nations had moved decisively against an errant member, and been effective, proved to have little meaning. Briefly,

1008 *Chapter 50 Morning in America*

it appeared that dictators of small countries were put on warning that mischief-making would not be tolerated. However, when a vicious ethnic war broke out in Yugoslavia, neither the UN, nor NATO, nor yet the European Community took decisive action to end it. For three years, while the United States and the nations of Western Europe issued empty threat after empty threat, Bosnian Serbs, Croatians, and Muslims battled one another with tribal savagery.

Nor did the Gulf War preserve George Bush, as he believed it would. He proclaimed that, under his leadership, Americans had put the "Vietnam Syndrome," a demoralized army and defeatism at home behind them. The president's ratings in public opinion polls soared in early 1991. In the excitement of watching a miraculously successful war on television, Americans seemed to forget their serious economic problems at home. But it was only for a season. By 1992, a presidential election year, a tenacious recession virtually relegated the Hundred Hours' War to the realm of ancient history.

Primary Elections, 1992

Bush was challenged in the Republican primaries by a right-wing television commentator, Patrick Buchanan, an isolationist who had vociferously opposed the Gulf War. Buchanan won no early primaries, but by taking almost 40 percent of the Republican votes in some states, he signaled that Bush was in trouble in his own party.

In its first months, the Democratic party's primary campaign proved to be unlike any other in recent history. Instead of one candidate in the field pulling ahead early and coasting to the nomination, several of the would-be nominees won the convention delegates of at least one state. Senator Thomas Harkin of Iowa, a liberal with a populist tinge, won his own state. Paul Tsongas of Massachusetts won New Hampshire and Maryland. Senator Robert Kerrey of Nebraska won South Dakota. Most surprising of all, former California Governor Jerry Brown, despite a sticky reputation for bizarre beliefs—he was nicknamed "Governor Moonbeam"—won most of the delegates from Colorado.

Then, however, Governor William Clinton of Arkansas rushed to the head of what humorist Russell Baker called "the march of the Millard Fillmores." He rode out a past as a Vietnam War draft evader, accusations of adultery, and claims that he

---

> ### *Election Oddities*
>
> Clinton's 44.9 million votes in 1992 were the most ever won by a Democratic party candidate. He won a majority of the votes only in Arkansas and the District of Columbia. Bush's 39.1 million votes were 15.2 million fewer than Ronald Reagan had won in 1984. He did not win a majority in any state. Perot's 19.7 million votes were twice the total won by any previous third-party candidate. He won a plurality in no state.

---

was too slick to be trusted, to sew up the convention before it met. Clinton's strategy was to woo Gary Hart's New Age liberals by speaking up for liberal lifestyle issues (abortion, affirmative action, legitimization of homosexuality) while appealing to moderates with an economic policy that emphasized growth.

Election

It looked as if the Reagan coalition was no more. Some populist conservatives who had never liked the aristocratic Bush swarmed wholesale to the independent candidacy of H. Ross Perot, a self-made Texas billionaire. Although he offered little in the way of a program, hundreds of thousands of uneasy Americans formed local "Perot for President" organizations, and the candidate himself pledged to spend millions of his own money in the cause. In July, polls showed him leading both Bush and Clinton.

On the day in July Clinton was to accept the Democratic nomination, Perot was on the ballot in 24 states. Then he quit the race, claiming that he and his daughter had been threatened by assassins. Many of Perot's supporters lost heart, but others continued to gather signatures on petitions. Perot jumped back into the contest and was even thought to have won the first debate among the three candidates. His 19 percent in the general election was more than any third-party presidential candidate had won since Theodore Roosevelt in 1912.

Perot's candidacy almost certainly helped Bill Clinton carry several mountain states that had not gone Democratic since 1964. Clinton also won California, a Republican stronghold for decades. In electoral votes, the entire Northeast and several south-

Independent Ross Perot briefly looked like a serious contender for the presidency in 1992.

ern states also went Democratic. Although Clinton won only 43 percent of the popular vote—the fourth lowest total for a winning president—he had 370 electoral votes to Bush's 168.

CHRONOLOGY

1979 Pro-American shah of Iran overthrown by Muslim fundamentalists. Carter admits shah to United States for medical treatment. Iranian student militants seize American embassy in Teheran, taking some 50 diplomats hostage

1980 Carter's failure in Iranian hostage crisis and his image of ineffectiveness contribute to election of conservative Republican Ronald Reagan as president. Prominent liberal Democratic senators, including George McGovern, are defeated

1982 Longtime Soviet premier Leonid Brezhnev dies

1984 President Reagan easily reelected over former vice president Walter Mondale

1985 Despite rising federal deficit, President Reagan sponsors massive tax cut bill favoring upper income groups
President Reagan implicitly approves violation of Boland Amendments by authorizing aid to "contras," anti-leftist rebels in Nicaragua. Operation is financed by selling arms to Iran
Mikhail Gorbachev, reformer committed to opening Russian political system and economy, is named premier of Soviet Union

1010 *Chapter 50 Morning in America*

1986   United States bombs Libya in retaliation for terrorist activities
Almost 300 U. S. Marines killed by suicide bomber in Lebanon
U. S. troops occupy Grenada to end chaos and to oust Cubans constructing an airstrip

1988   Vice President George Bush defeats Democratic nominee, Michael Dukakis, in presidential election

1989   Student protesters in Tiananmen Square, Beijing, are brutally routed by government troops
Soviet control of Eastern Europe collapses. Cold War effectively ends

1991   In a war of 100 hours American troops rout Iraqi forces occupying Kuwait, but fail to destroy regime of Iraqi dictator Saddam Hussein

1992   William Jefferson Clinton of Arkansas defeats President Bush in his bid for reelection

FOR FURTHER READING

Surely the most likely candidate as shrewd observer of his times is Garry Wills, whose *Reagan's America: Innocents at Home*, 1987, is as provocative as his contemporary study of Nixon. Also useful in understanding the symbol of the 1980s is Reagan's own *Where's the Rest of Me?* 1965, an account of his conversion from youthful liberalism to the conservative politics for which he will be remembered. Also on this subject, see Lou Cannon, *President Reagan: The Role of a Lifetime*, 1991; and Haynes Johnson, *Sleepwalking through History*, 1991. See also P. Steinfels, *The Neoconservatives*, 1979; S. Blumenthal, *The Rise of the Counter-Establishment*, 1986; and William C. Berman, *America's Right Turn*, 1994.

On foreign policy during the 1980s: R. L. Garthoff, *Détente and Confrontation: American–Soviet Relations from Nixon to Reagan*, 1985, which does not, however, deal with Reagan's turn toward accommodation with the Soviets late in his last term. On covert operations, see G. F. Treverton, *Covert Action*, 1987, and B. Woodward, *Veil: The Secret Wars of the C.I.A., 1981–1987*, 1987. P. Kennedy, in *The Rise and Fall of the Great Powers*, 1987, may offer an explanation of why contemporary Americans find their nation's place in the world so perplexing. See, however, Henry R. Nau, *The Myth of America's Decline: Leading the World Economy*, 1990; and for an alternative perspective, Kevin Phillips, *Boiling Point: Democrats, Republicans, and the Decline of Middle-Class Prosperity*, 1993.

For George Bush, see Stephen Graubard, *Mr. Bush's War: Adventures in the Politics of Illusion*, 1992; and the relevant chapters of Stephen Ambrose, *Rise to Globalism*, Seventh ed., 1993.

A fence, and mounted border guards, mark the Mexican-American frontier near San Diego, California.

51
CHAPTER

MILLENNIUM

Frustration, Anger, Division, Values

History never looks like history when you are living through it. It always looks confusing and messy, and it always feels uncomfortable.

—John W. Gardner

To me, recent history is not history at all. It won't even be the stuff from which history is written for years to come. It's impressions, opinions, the product of penchants. It should be credited as only a little more reliable than the interpretation of a National Football League game by a tribesman of the tropical rain forest airlifted to Green Bay, Wisconsin, to view, after two days without sleep, the Packers host the Philadelphia Eagles. I have seen assessments of recent events by experts I profoundly respect discredited so many times, and watched my own understandings of recent events change so often and so quickly, that I can ask no more of readers than tolerant entertainment of my take on the years of the recent past.

—The Author

1014 *Chapter 51 Millennium*

President Clinton was, like Ronald Reagan, preternaturally lucky. He too wore "Teflon" and, in his case, the mud that failed to stick to him was not largely of his aides' making, but of his own. Flawed, even squalid in moral character, Clinton nevertheless enjoyed voter approval (although not admiration) virtually throughout his two-term presidency.

In part, Clinton's political success owed to his brilliance as a politician. Since his teenage years (when he already aspired to the presidency), Clinton played almost every card dealt him with uncanny skill. He had a gift for knowing when to hold, when to fold, and when to excuse himself for a few hands. Equals as an opportunist have, perhaps, also been president. But it is difficult to name one who was so successful, who shrugged off setbacks with more panache, who proceeded from the pit of personal shame to a pious sermon from a pulpit without a blink, stammer, or blush. He was a master.

Even more important in accounting for Clinton's success as a president was the familiar one: good times, fabulously unprecedented good times. Fueled by high technology ventures, securities doubled in value and doubled again during the 1990s, further burying the well-to-do in their already disproportionate share of the national wealth and enriching the ever larger portion of the middle class that was "in the market." (By 1998, half of American households were directly involved in the stock market, up from 37 percent in a mere six years.) And, in the 1990s, prosperity trickled down to those low on the

---

Trend?

Conservative newspaper columnist George Will was not surprised by the election results in 1992. He saw a Republican trend in the numbers dating from 1952. Will pointed out that in presidential balloting since 1856 (the first year the Republican and Democratic parties faced one another), Republicans won 51.8 percent of the popular vote. Since 1952, however, the Republican party had carried 53.3 percent of the popular vote, and since 1968, 55.1 percent.

The Republicans had won 69 percent of the electoral votes since 1952, and 79 percent of the electoral votes since 1968.

Will did not explain why the figures should have been so, or if he was just amusing himself by compiling them.

---

economic ladder, as it had never quite trickled during the 1920s and 1980s.

Clinton's First Term

Legislatively, Bill Clinton broke even during his first term. Twice he pulled victories out of Congress by margins thin as onionskin. His foreign policy (by Clinton's own admission his weak suit), was as ambiguously productive as George Bush's, if less spectacular. The economy, moribund in Bush's last year—Bush's undoing—improved slowly but steadily on Clinton's watch, then soared. The Democrat Clinton actually reduced the federal deficit, something Republicans Bush and Reagan talked about endlessly while driving it ever higher.

Even at that, a cloud of distrust hung over the young president, and a shadow of dislike followed his active wife, Hillary Rodham Clinton. In the midterm election of 1994, Republicans won majorities to both Houses of Congress for the first time in 40 years. Not even that sorcerer of vote-getting, Ronald Reagan, persuaded Americans to give Republicans the House of Representatives. Half of the American population had not been born when Republicans previously controlled both houses of Congress.

Within a year of the election, however, "Slick Willie" (as Clinton's Republican detractors called him) was wriggling out of his difficulties.

Who's Got What?

In 1929, the year of the Great Crash, the richest 1 percent of Americans owned 44 percent of the nation's net household wealth. This lopsided distribution of wealth was widely believed to have been a major cause of the economic crisis of the 1930s.

By 1976, in large part because of federal policies, the richest 1 percent's share of the nation's wealth was reduced to 20 percent. By 1989, the year Ronald Reagan left office, the top 1 percent owned 48 percent of the nation's net wealth, more than in 1929.

Foreign Policy

Clinton entered the White House lacking a foreign policy. His administration articulated no clear vision of what goals should drive the nation's use of its prestige, wealth, and military power in dealing with other nations. In part, this lack of direction was the inevitable consequence of the end of the Cold War. During the era of bipolar nuclear standoff, every foreign initiative and response had first to be assayed with the Soviet Union as the most important weight in the balance. With the old Soviet Union no more, whomever the president in the 1990s—King Solomon himself—he or she would have faced the challenge of building on uncharted ground.

Still, Clinton was, perhaps, particularly ill-equipped for international relations. As a youth, he had opposed that costly American adventure, the Vietnam War. Like many anti-Vietnam protesters in their later years, he concluded that having been morally correct on Vietnam was itself a credential as a director of foreign policy. When, in his memoirs, the Vietnam era Secretary of Defense, Robert McNamara, wrote that the war had been wrong, Clinton exclaimed to aides, "See! We were right." Clinton seemed to conclude that good intentions righteously effected would produce a successful foreign policy.

In his rhetoric, Clinton posed a moral goal for foreign policy: The United States would restore and keep the peace, and protect human rights in the world. Ironically but inevitably, actions based on this ideal inspired critics to accuse the president of playing "policeman to the world," getting involved in ructions that were none of America's concern. It was exactly the same criticism anti-Vietnam protesters had leveled at President Lyndon B. Johnson.

Somalia: Tragedy in a Distant Land

Somalia, an arid nation bereft of natural resources, is strategically located on the Horn of Africa. However, the superpowers had long since settled on sites

President William Jefferson Clinton, 1993–2001, loathed by his political enemies, enjoyed unprecedented prosperity during the 1990s.

elsewhere from which to watch over the Middle East. During the Cold War, Somalia was a minor plaything. It was a Soviet chip in the game for many years, then an American client, and after 1989 and the end of the Cold War, of no importance to either side.

The consequence for Somalia, after years of abundant foreign aid, with the usual complement lost to corruption, was chronic civil war between clans headed by warlords. By May 1992, vicious fighting had reduced the capital of Mogadishu to a shambles. Somalia's infrastructure—urban water supply, electrical service, telephones, police—all virtually vanished. The bureaucrats who had operated these services were either killed or forced to flee the country. Teenage thugs with sophisticated weapons and a gang mentality terrorized the streets. In the countryside, starvation was widespread. Once again, televised pictures of emaciated women and children made a little-known part of the world an agonizing concern in American living rooms.

With United Nations approval, American troops intervened to allay the massive human distress and to restore peace. As a relief mission, the intervention was successful. By the time Clinton was inaugurated as president, Somalia's famine and the worst of its plagues were over.

Unfortunately, when American troops attempted to capture the most mischievous of the Somali warlords, General Mohammed Farah Aidid, fighting broke out anew, this time with American and other foreign troops in the middle. Aidid survived and Clinton had to eat crow. He negotiated merely to get American soldiers out of Somalia without further casualties. Except for the humanitarian contribution, the U.S. intervention in Somalia ended having had no particular point to it. Clinton's critics condemned him for indecisiveness.

Haiti: The Curse of History

The humanitarian impulse underlying Clinton's Somalia policy also contributed to his intervention in Haiti. Always the poorest, often the most corrupt, state in the Western Hemisphere, Haiti was, by the 1990s, on the verge of the same chaos that consumed Somalia. However, Haiti's close proximity to the United States gave its crisis an urgency beyond unpleasant pictures on the evening news.

When the Haitian army deposed elected President Jean-Bertrand Aristide, Aristide fled to the United States where he organized a "Haitian Lobby" among fellow exiles, American liberals, and in the media. A furor reminiscent of the hubbub that, in 1898, demanded American intervention in Cuba brought pressure to bear on Clinton, just as the *Cuba Libre* forces had pressured President McKinley.

In fact, Clinton's situation was less enviable than McKinley's. McKinley did not have to contend with an American people nervous about tens of thousands of impoverished refugees fleeing to the United States. Many Haitians were so desperate to get out that they set to sea in overcrowded craft that had no chance of making it to American shores. Their pathetic hope was that they would be picked up in international waters by American vessels whence they could petition for political asylum.

Most of the refugees were fleeing the island's horrendous poverty, not political oppression. Therefore, they were not legally eligible for special admission to the United States. However, their numbers disturbed the large proportion of the population already nervous about massive immigration. They and Clinton's own liberal supporters urged the president to "do something."

Success out of Failure

After an embarassing attempt in October 1993 to land soldiers in Port-au-Prince (the American ship was turned back by a crowd of a few hundred rowdies organized by Haiti's military), Clinton assembled a prestigious diplomatic team headed by former President Jimmy Carter and General Colin Powell. They persuaded Haiti's dictators to restore constitutional government peacefully.

In September 1994, some 3,000 American troops landed in Haiti, returned Aristide to the presidency, and began the training of the police, army, and bureaucracies the country needed in order to function. In 1996, Haitians elected a new president and, in an event almost unprecedented in the nation's history, power was transferred constitutionally and peacefully.

With a legacy of corruption and conflict as old as the nation, disillusioning experiences with constitutional government, and a burden of crushing poverty, Haiti's photogenic new era was short-lived. By 2000, the country was mired again in its ancient problems. By then, however, Clinton was packing in preparation for the move to his retirement home.

Bosnia: Latent Nationalism

Somalia and Haiti, at least, were nations, populations sharing common territory, languages, traditions, histories, and a sense of identity. In Bosnia-Herzegovina, a province of the former Yugoslav republic, the ethnic groups that lived on the land had been able to coexist peacefully only when forced to do so by no-nonsense Communist dictatorship and foreign imperial rulers, Austrians and Turks before them.

But hatreds among Serbs, Croats, and Bosnian Muslims were suppressed, not obliterated. After the disintegration of Communist authority in the 1980s, Bosnia fell into vicious ethnic warfare. Bosnian Serbs feared they would be savaged by Croats, or dominated by the Bosnian Muslims, the largest ethnic group in the country. Both Bosnian Croats and Bosnian Serbs drew on generous aid from independent Croatia and Serbia so the Bosnian Muslims, without a supportive neighbor, suffered most. Consequently, they attracted the sympathy of most Americans.

What to do about their sympathies, however, divided Americans. Some argued that the United States should stay out of the conflict entirely: ethnic hatreds were as intrinsic to Balkan life as cabbage; nothing could overcome the effects of hatred but the triumph of one of the cultural groups. Others said that the wealthy and powerful European nations should deal with a European problem for a change. Some called for massive military intervention, as George Bush had intervened in Panama and Iraq. Others wanted to supply the beleaguered Muslims with weapons.

Clinton vacillated, although in doing so, he acted no differently than the European democracies, Russia, the United Nations, the European Community, and NATO. Repeatedly, truces and agreements among the warring groups were violated, sometimes within hours of signing. By the end of 1995, a combination of American air strikes and economic pressure on Serbia to rein in the Bosnian Serbs established a peace long enough to permit American and European troops to move in as peacekeepers. There they remained at the end of Clinton's presidency.

Kosovo

In March 1998, well into Clinton's second term, similar ethnic hatreds in neighboring Kosovo, turned violent. Although 90 percent Albanian in population, Kosovo remained a part of Serbia and, in 1989, the Serbian government repealed Kosovo's autonomy. The result was a separatist movement that, in 1998, began attacking government institutuions and the Serbian minority. Serbia's president, Slobodan Milosevich, tacitly encouraged Serb paramilitary groups, and even regular army units in a campaign of terrorism, destruction, and mass murder of Albanian Kosovars. The Albanians fled; eventually some 400,000 were living in camps in neighboring countries.

Milosevich ignored American and European threats until, in 1999, the United States and several allies launched an air war that targeted not only military sites in Kosovo but in Serbia proper. Military experts, including several American generals, did not believe an air war would in itself force Milosevich to back down. Pundits predicted that, when American ground troops moved in, as move in they must, the fight would degenerate into a morass, Clinton's "Big Muddy."

They were wrong. Under immense pressure at home, Milosevich caved in. He withdrew Serbian troops from Kosovo, and a multinational "police force" occupied the country. Its chief job was to protect Serbian Kosovars from vengeful Albanians. It appeared as if Clinton would leave office before he had to face up to the problem of how to end the occupation.

Mexico

Within North America, Clinton was decisive. With the cooperation of Republican party leaders, he pushed NAFTA (the North American Free Trade Agreement) through Congress against an oddly assorted opposition that included much of the labor movement, Ross Perot, and unabashed isolationists like television commentator Pat Buchanan.

NAFTA provided for the elimination, over a 15-year period, of tariffs and other trade barriers among Canada, the United States, and Mexico. Clinton believed that, as the creation of the European Community had been an economic boon in Western Europe, the free trade zone NAFTA created would benefit all three North American countries.

In 1994, after the Democrats lost their majority in Congress, Clinton bypassed Congress to put together a financial package to rescue the collapsing Mexican economy. Harsh critics, like the new Republican speaker of the House, Newt Gingrich of Georgia, who boasted that he had seized leadership

Ethnic Albanians seeking protection from "ethnic cleansing" in Kosovo.

of the nation, sat back and watched with consternation as the theretofore indecisive Clinton seized the initiative.

> ### What's Imported?
>
> Even without NAFTA and GATT (the General Agreement on Tariffs and Trade, also signed by Clinton), it was difficult in the global village of the 1990s to say offhand just what was a domestic product and what was imported. The Ford Crown Victoria automobile, for example, was assembled in Canada; the Mercury Grand Marquis included parts made in six different countries. Forty percent of all "Japanese" cars sold in the United States actually were manufactured in the United States by American workers. Television sets bearing the grand old American trademark Zenith were, in fact, Mexican products. Mitsubishi TVs were manufactured in Santa Ana, California.

POLITICS NOT AS USUAL

Bill Clinton knew that presidents who ushered prosperous voters to the polls rarely returned home defeated. His own popularity as governor of Arkansas had been based on good times. George Bush's 90 percent approval rating, won by the war with Iraq, dissipated by the time of the 1992 election because the economy went sour.

Clinton had no intention of attempting to jump-start the economy by reviving the free-spending Great Society. He called himself a "new Democrat," by which he meant that he was not (the Republicans' preferred term) a "tax-and-spend liberal." Nevertheless, he repeatedly said that social justice demanded the reinvigoration of some of the social programs that had been neglected or subverted during the Reagan–Bush era.

Although Clinton promised to end legislative gridlock in Washington in his 1992 campaign, and he had Democratic majorities in Congress in 1993 and 1994, he never was able to swing a united party

President Clinton addresses Congress, applauded by Vice President Albert Gore and Clinton's most powerful adversary in 1995, House Speaker Newt Gingrich.

behind him. His most important domestic political victories, a tax bill and a gun-control bill, barely eked their way through Congress.

Health Care

Clinton's biggest domestic setback was the defeat of his plan for national health insurance. In keeping with his claims to moderation, his advisors designed a middle-of-the-road solution to the soaring costs of medical care and the fact that 39 million Americans had no medical insurance at all. Clinton repudiated the virtually unregulated *status quo:* generally good private insurance for those who could afford it, the government picking up the costs of generally inadequate health care for the poor. Clinton also rejected the other extreme, the "single-payer plan" like

> ### Millennial Ghetto
>
> The largest Vietnamese-American community in the United States looked no more like the congested urban "Little Italy" or "Lower East Side" of the early twentieth century than the United States of the 1990s resembled the nation of the 1900s. "Little Saigon" stretched a mile and a half along Bolsa Avenue in Orange County, California. Some 80,000 Vietnamese and their American-born children lived in the area. On weekends, between 20,000 and 50,000 Vietnamese shoppers descended on the 800 Vietnamese shops and restaurants that lined Bolsa Avenue, many of them arriving in automobiles.

Canada's in which the government paid all citizens' medical bills according to a scale established by law. Clinton's health-care plan had the federal government rigorously regulating private insurance companies and seeing to it that those who were unable to buy insurance were apportioned for coverage among the private providers.

Politically, the Clinton plan was handicapped because it was complicated beyond the compehension of an ordinary citizen, running to more than 1,300 pages of the "fine print" every American learned as a child to distrust. It was difficult to explain clearly just how it was to work. Critics claimed that, as another clumsy government program, it would lead to more bureaucracy, waste, profiteering, and outright corruption.

To make things worse, Clinton put his wife, Hillary, in charge of the campaign to rally support for the plan. Undeniably talented and viewing herself as a kind of co-president (during the campaign of 1992, Clinton was quoted, "you get two for the price of one"), Hillary Rodham Clinton was not up to the job of managing a massive national campaign. Winning over Americans from across the political spectrum was not the same as finding consensus among friends over (a favorite Republican image) "white wine and Brie."

The opposition outflanked Mrs. Clinton at every turn. While insisting that they too wanted reform, Republicans, financed by insurance companies, picked away at the Clinton proposal, amending it so radically that it little resembled the president's original proposal. Clinton added to his reputation for indecisiveness when he repeatedly made concessions

Hillary Rodham Clinton headed the effort to enact her husband's health-care legislation. Here she addresses the American Medical Association, which opposed the Clinton scheme.

> ### King Bureaucracy
> Some critics of Clinton's medical insurance proposals said that they would result in a huge health-care bureaucracy diverting money away from actual care. In fact, the phenomenon was already well underway, and a cause of the health-care crisis.
>
> Between 1983 and 1998, the number of physicians in the United States increased 50 percent. The number of health-care "managers" increased 683 percent.

to his critics. An already complicated plan became impenetrable. In 1994, Clinton allowed his health-care program to die rather than risk defeat on a mutated program that no one liked.

The Mid-term Election of 1994

Liberal Democrats hoped to revive the health-care fight after the congressional elections of 1994. All bets were off, however, when the party lost control of Congress. Republicans won the Senate 52 to 48 and, more surprisingly, they won a 230-to-204 majority in the House. The sitting Democratic Speaker of the House, Thomas Foley, was defeated, as were two Democratic governors of national stature, Mario Cuomo of New York and Ann Richards of Texas. Only a few prominent liberals survived what the new speaker of the House, pugnacious right-winger Newt Gingrich, called a revolution. Within a year of the election, nationwide, 137 Democratic officeholders, including several senators and congressmen, switched to the Republican party. Among them was the Democrats' Native American trophy senator from Colorado, Ben Nighthorse Campbell.

What Happened?

What happened? In part, the Democrats, who styled themselves the party of ordinary people, ran afoul of an angry and burgeoning populist mood among just those ordinary people. In part, after decades of experimentation, the Republicans hit upon a successful formula for appealing to middle- and upper-middle-class taxpayers who believed the government was soaking them on behalf of special interests. In part, the Clintons personally inspired suspicion and distaste among a substantial number of voters.

Conservative Republican strategists like the brilliant Kevin Phillips had long recognized that the Democrats, in reaching out to racial, ethnic, and lifestyle minority groups, such as African Americans, Mexican Americans, and feminists and homosexuals, were discomfiting their traditional supporters among white southerners, urban working-class voters, and particularly westerners—the people of the "sunbelt."

Opining that a party of minorities must be a minority party or impossibly contentious, Phillips and others urged Republicans to tap into the unease and resentment of Democratic middle- and working-class voters, groups which, combined with traditional Republican voters, promised to constitute a national majority.

The strategy was populist. That is, it was couched in the rhetoric of equality and the salt-of-the-earth values of ordinary people. It aimed its barbs at privilege, not the ancient privilege of the rich, but at what many people regarded as the liberal

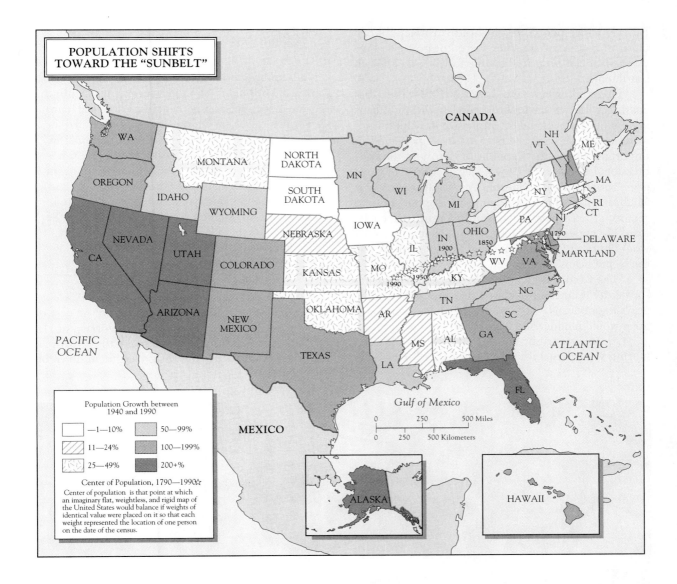

Democrats' special treatment of ethnic minorities, women, homosexuals, and even convicted criminals.

Seizing the Center

The Republican attack on the Democrats also aimed at the high taxes that were required to pay for big, costly government. However, if the party pointed to specific programs as the cause of high taxes, Republicans frightened off voters who depended on those programs.

Republicans concluded that it was safe to attack "welfare" programs that aided the poor, and it did not hurt if they implied that members of minority groups were disproportionately represented on the welfare rolls. Poor white folk, African Americans, and Mexican Americans were less likely to vote than was the population generally.

However, if the Republicans attacked government spending on Social Security and Medicare—old age pensions and help with medical bills—they alienated the large elderly population and its powerful lobby, the American Association of Retired Persons. Unlike the poor and African Americans, old people did incline to vote, piling into chartered buses in retirement communities to drive to the polls.

Elderly white people might hold with Republican cultural conservatism; they were not going to give up their Social Security benefits for the sake of such sentiments.

The trick was to avoid, as far as possible, discussing which government programs Republicans planned to reduce, and to emphasize how high taxes were under the Democrats. This strategy played an important part in the Republican victory in the congressional elections of 1994. Once in control of Congress, however, the Republicans began to snipe at Medicare and Clinton recognized his opportunity to restore at least partially the old Democratic coalition. He appealed to those whom Republican cuts would hurt and pointed out that Social Security was the Republicans' next target.

"The Comeback Kid" was back again. Occupying the center, Clinton calculated that the zealous Gingrich Republicans who were setting the tone in Congress would blunder and scare voters back to him.

Clinton was right He was rarely wrong in estimating voter behavior. House Speaker Newt Gingrich, who lacked a likable personality on the best of days, grew daily more arrogant and worrisome. In 1995, just at Christmastime to make things worse, his Congress virtually shut the government down by

> ### Slick Jesse
> No Republican politician of the 1980s and 1990s played both sides of the government spending game more audaciously than Senator Jesse Helms of North Carolina. On the one hand, he called for a government budget of Jeffersonian minimalism. On the other, he defended as a sacred cause subsidies to tobacco farmers (an important bloc in North Carolina politics). At the same time the government was warring against tobacco use, and Jesse Helms was inveighing against spending to help the poor, payments to keep tobacco growers in business flourished.

Elderly people, particularly through their lobby, the American Association of Retired Persons, formed one of the most politically potent forces of the 1990s.

refusing to vote appropriations for the government's running expenses. Clinton was not blameless for the crisis, but polls showed that most Americans blamed Gingrich and the Republicans.

The Election of 1996

The favorite to win the Republican nomination in 196 was Senator Robert Dole of Kansas, a party stalwart for almost half a century. Dole had run for vice president with Gerald Ford in 1976, and he was majority leader of the Senate. His chief handicaps were his age, 72, his undisguised distaste for the personal humiliations of campaigning, and his spontaneous, sometimes self-deprecating honesty in answering reporters' questions.

Believing that Dole's support was "a mile wide but only inches deep"—without enthusiasm—a flock of rivals opposed him in the state primaries and caucuses. The most important were Pat Buchanan, a perennial spokesman for one branch of the Republican party's right wing, and Steve Forbes, the heir to a publishing fortune who ran a one-issue campaign. Forbes's "flat tax" proposed to eliminate all income-tax deductions and to tax all Americans a flat 17 percent of their salaries or wages (but not their profits from investments).

Forbes and Buchanan each defeated Dole in several states. However, alarmed that Buchanan's increasingly shrill appeals to the right would shatter the party, Republican voters, beginning in March, fell in behind the senator. Forbes quit the race, but Buchanan remained officially a candidate even after Dole had pocketed a majority of convention votes.

Dole never threatened Clinton. Unemployment had dropped radically since 1992 and the values of securities had begun an upward climb that would become manic during his second term. Ross Perot ran again, as the candidate of the Reform party, but he aroused only a fraction of the interest he claimed in 1992.

House Speaker Newt Gingrich's strategy of undercutting President Clinton by closing the government down backfired on the Republicans.

Once again, Clinton failed to win the support of half the voters. He won 49 percent of the total, Dole 41 percent, and Perot 9 percent. The Republicans continued to control both houses of Congress. There was bound to be trouble with a substantial number of right-wing Republican congressmen "Clinton haters" and even party moderates bewildered that "Slick Willie" should continue to live in the White House. Trouble there was when the president provided his opponents with lots of ammunition.

SCANDAL + PROSPERITY = POSITIVE RATINGS

Personally, the Clintons had annoyed conservatives from the beginning. Although himself the scion of Arkansas "white trash" and as self-made a man as any nineteenth-century "robber baron," Clinton impressed populist right wingers as belonging to the Eastern elite he had aspired to join when he attended Georgetown University, Yale Law School, and Oxford. It was a group they had detested since the days of Dean Acheson and Alger Hiss.

Clinton was far from insensitive to the culture and values of "Middle America." He played the Southern Baptist and "good old boy" when the situation demanded. Hillary Clinton, however, had neither the knack for nor the training in that art. In a television interview she said contemptuously that she was not the type to stay home and bake chocolate chip cookies or to "stand by my man," a lyric from a popular country and western song sung by Tammy Wynette. That sort of thing titillated the people with whom Hillary Clinton mixed. It did not appeal to housewives, their cookie-eating husbands, and the kind of people who believed Ms. Wynette had articulated a desirable social and moral value.

Slip-Ups

When the president tried to appoint a friend of Hillary, Lani Guinier, herself of an elite African-American family, to a high position in the Justice De-

Senator Bob Dole of Kansas weathered several unnerving challenges before sewing up the Republican presidential nomination in 1996.

partment, he was embarrassed by the discovery that she had written favorably of giving members of minority groups multiple votes in order to compensate for discrimination in the past. Such silliness was publishable in academic journals but did not play well in "Peoria," the Republicans' emblem of ordinary America.

President Clinton also had to withdraw the nominations of two potential Attorneys General when it was revealed that they had employed domestic servants and not paid their Social Security taxes. It seemed as if the practice was the norm among successful liberal jurists. Finally, he appointed childless Janet Reno, a prosecutor from Florida, to be the first woman attorney general. She was never popular (Clinton came to dislike her), but she remained in office for eight years, a long time for an attorney general. Clinton's surgeon general, Jocelyn Elders, the first woman in that post, was forced to resign when she suggested the possibility of teaching schoolchildren how to masturbate. Again, such titillating "new morality" offended traditionally minded Americans.

Clinton eased away from "New Age" controversies that harmed him politically. He backed off from a pledge to force the military to accept avowed homosexuals in the ranks. In his State of the Union speech in January 1995, he conspicuously failed to mention a single one of the "New Age" issues that he formerly embraced. In March 1996, after polls showing that a large majority of Americans resented preferential hiring practices, he quietly suspended most of the federal government's affirmative action programs. He shrewdly arrogated the political center for his administration in cultural maters too, hoping to force the Republicans back to the politics of the extreme right.

Whitewater

Try as they did, the Clintons could not shake accusations that they had been involved in influence-peddling and misuse of official powers when Clinton was governor of Arkansas and Mrs. Clinton an attorney with a prestigious Little Rock law firm.

Attorney General Janet Reno was a magnet for criticism but stoically served eight years as the first woman in that office.

In 1978, using borrowed money, the Clintons invested in a 230-acre vacation home development in Arkansas dubbed "Whitewater." Slowly but inexorably, the speculation went sour. In an effort to save it, critics of the Clintons said, the governor steered business (that is, state money) in the direction of his wife's law firm while she secured favors for financial institutions involved in the Whitewater project. On the advice of one interested party, Mrs. Clinton herself turned a tiny investment in commodities into a huge profit.

Whitewater was a minor issue in the campaign of 1992, and not very effective for the Republicans. However, after July 1993, when the Clinton family lawyer who was handling Whitewater matters committed suicide, Republican Senator Alphonse D'Amato of New York resuscitated the issue. An independent investigation, headed by a respected but frankly conservative lawyer, Kenneth Starr, was set up to look into the affair. Although Hillary Clinton was caught in several evasions about her role in Whitewater, the Starr Commission never found a serious criminal irregularity in the Clintons' finances. Starr soon turned his attention to a facet of President Clinton's life that had nothing to do with Whitewater and, in every way but good political sense, little to do with a president's job.

Ladies' Man

Virtually everyone intuited that Gennifer Flowers, who said during the 1992 campaign that she had had an affair with Clinton in Arkansas, was telling the truth. However, Clinton talked his way out of the scandal before it was fairly started. Except in tabloids that specialized in sightings of the long-dead Elvis Presley, it was forgotten.

After Clinton's reelection in 1996, however, another Arkansas woman, Paula Jones, said that when she was a state employee, Governor Clinton had invited her to a hotel room where he exposed himself and asked her to perform fellatio on him. Discovered and funded by a Conservative Republican foundation, Jones initiated legal actions that would drag out until 1999. Clinton denied her accusations.

Jones's allegations (and Republican frustration) inspired the Starr Commission to look into the president's sex life; no matter it had nothing to do with Whitewater. Several women came forward to say that Clinton had propositioned them too. But Starr's big catch was Monica Lewinsky who, at age 22 in July 1995, had gone to work in the White House as an unpaid intern. Lewinski had spoken to friends of an affair with the president consisting solely of oral sex. One of these confidantes, Linda Tripp, recorded several of their phone conversations. Testifying in the Paula Jones proceedings, Lewinski denied under oath any irregular relationship with the president. This, when evidence to the contrary began to pile up, was her—and the president's—undoing. It enabled the Starr Commission to threaten Lewinsky with prosecution for perjury while offering her immunity in return for telling all about the president.

Lewinsky's tale meant more than embarrassment for Clinton. As in the cases of Flowers and Jones, he had several times publicly denied a sexual relationship with "that woman," Lewinsky, once while brimming with righteous indignation. Worse, he had denied the relationship under oath. Moreover, Lewinsky had been eased out of her White House job by Clinton aides who suspected the worst and, later, she was sent to Clinton's good friend, Vernon Jordan, who found a job for her in New York City. Only when physical evidence surfaced, a dress stained with Clinton's semen, did the president admit "inappropriate sexual contact" with Ms. Lewinsky. He had been "legally accurate" in his previous testimony, Clinton insisted (leading to serious discussions among somber Democratic intellectuals as to whether or not fellatio constituted sexual relations); he simply "did not volunteer information."

The Starr Report and Impeachment

The confession was too contrived and too late. Starr's lengthy report was issued in Sepember 1998. Whitewater was virtually forgotten but each of the president's sexual encounters with Lewinsky was described in exquisite detail. Clinton's supporters denounced this as pornography; they said that a simple summary of Lewinsky's testimony would have sufficed, trying to shift the focus of public anger to Starr. In fact, excepting the far right, few Americans approved of Starr's obsession to "get" the president any which way, and even fewer approved of the $50 million he spent. Starr was not a popular figure.

Starr replied that detail was essential in order to cinch the case against Clinton. His Commission concluded that the president had lied under oath, attempted to obstruct justice, and misused the powers of his office to cover up his affair, all impeachable offenses.

Scandal + Prosperity = Positive Ratings 1027

Monica Lewinsky became famous because of her sexual liaison with President Clinton.

On October 9, 1998, the House of Representatives instituted an investigation preparatory to impeach (as if further delving was necessary after the exhaustive Starr Report). On December 19th, after throwing out several accusations, the House impeached the president on counts of perjury and obstructing justice. The indictment then went to the Senate where, as the Constitution provides, and as had been the case in the impeachment of Andrew Johnson, a committee of Representatives served as prosecutors, the Senate was the jury, and the Chief Justice of the Supreme Court sat as presiding judge. Clinton chose his defense team but, like Andrew Johnson, he did not attend the proceedings.

Acquittal

The prosecution maintained that Clinton had committed the "high crimes and misdemeanors" the Constitution states as grounds for impeachment. Clinton's defenders responded that evidence of obstruction of justice was ambivalent at best and that lying about his sex life was far from being a "high crime."

But superior splitting of legal hairs was not to determine the outcome. Again as in the Andrew Johnson case, politics was. From the start, it was clear the prosecution did not have the two-thirds of the Senate necessary in order to convict Clinton, 67 votes. There were only 55 Republicans, not all of them happy about the impeachment. With this simple arithmetic obvious, Clinton's supporters argued that to bring charges was just another incident in the House Republicans' obsessive hatred of the president, a hatred that had preoccupied Congress and the public for almost a full year.

In the end, the prosecution could not win even a simple majority of the Senate. In the matter of perjury, ten Republican senators joined the Democrats to vote to acquit, 55-45. In the matter of obstruction of justice, five Republicans bolted; the poll was 50-50. It was over. Clinton did not gloat but pointed out that, through it all, while his domestic program was stalled, he continued to administer a generally

President Clinton before (almost) admitting he had lied under oath about his sexual adventures in the White House.

successful foreign policy, including an air attack on Iraq. Foreign policy was now in the hands of the first woman to be secretary of state, Madeleine Albright. Only late in 1999, when the Senate refused to ratify a nuclear test ban treaty, did Clinton suffer a setback in foreign policy.

The Democrats in 2000

No one's reputation emerged enhanced from the Lewinsky scandal except, curiously, Hillary Rodham Clinton's. Never loved, as some first ladies are, not even liked outside social circles similar to her own, Mrs. Clinton was showered with sympathy with each revelation or rumor of her husband's philandering and his deception of her. Mrs. Clinton won admiration when she weathered the mess with silent dignity; contrary to her disdain six years earlier for "stand by your man" women, she did just that. Hillary had the best press of her life and enjoyed it. Early in 2000, at the behest of leading state Democrats and after a long exploratory campaign, Mrs. Clnton announced that she was a candidate for the Senate from New York.

Vice President Gore, who also suppressed his moral revulsion during the scandal and stood behind the president, had long prepared to win the Democratic presidential nomination in 2000. He had the party establishment behind him, but faced a challenge in the primary elections (numerous by 2000, although as obsolete as party conventions) by former Senator Bill Bradley. Bradley had been a principled and competent senator from New Jersey (and earlier the best college basketball player of his generation). His handicap as a politician was a wooden public persona, but Vice President Gore was himself the subject of jokes on that count.

Bradley had to fight both the party machinery and the fact that his policies differed little from Gore's. All he could offer primary voters was the promise of a new face unassociated with the Clinton administration. After a few early victories, Bradley lost the interest of the media (and thereby the public) and Gore easily defeated him in primary after primary. On March 7, "Super Tuesday" (named after a professional football game, the "Super Bowl"), Gore swept primaries in 15 states, winning up to 60 percent of the vote, including big majorities among African Americans and Hispanics.

The Republicans

Bill Bradley's promise of "change" fell flat because John McCain, a Republican senator from Arizona, made a better case for the fact that he was the man to bring change, reform, and integrity to the White House.

McCain came out of almost nowhere. The Republican nomination appeared from the first to belong to Governor George W. Bush of Texas, the son of President George W. H. Bush. "Dubya," "W," as the press called him to distinguish him from his father, was the pick of the Republican establishment and the party's big money contributors. Before the primary campaign began, he owned a campaign treasury of $70 million, an astronomical sum.

At first, McCain was a lesser-noticed member of a herd of Republicans challenging Bush: Elizabeth Dole, who had long experience as an executive administrator; Steve Forbes and Pat Buchanan again; and several new faces, including Alan Keyes, an electrifyingly eloquent African-American speaker who, at every debate, ground into hamburger the safe,

Contenders for the 2000 Democratic presidential nomination: Former Senator Bill Bradley, Vice President Al Gore. In America 2000, even would-be presidents went by their nicknames.

bland, banal pronouncements of all of his conventional rivals. Keyes could be politely ignored because he spoke for a far right tendency that was unabashedly Christian. He was mesmerizing, but he was unelectable.

Slow-starting John McCain was a Vietnam War hero—five years a prisoner of war in Hanoi—personable, blunt-spoken, and politically shrewd. He sat out or neglected state primaries where only registered Republicans could vote (most of them were in Bush's pocket) and concentrated on states where he could woo independents and Democrats to cross over and vote in the Republican primary.

As the other challengers dropped out, McCain pounced nimbly on Bush's weaknesses and blunders: Bush's presumed debts to big money interests; Bush's less than gleaming intelligence (a radio interviewer set Bush up with a quiz of general knowledge which the governor badly failed; in January 2000, Bush told a group of students, "One of the great things about books is sometimes there are some fantastic pictures"); and Bush's appearance at Bob Jones University, a frankly anti-Catholic fundamentalist institution where interracial dating was forbidden. McCain won or effectively tied Bush in several primaries and polls by winning non-Republican votes. He argued that his appeal to Democrats and Independents showed that he could win the general election in November whereas Bush, increasingly, looked like he would need a stock market crash and incipient depression to defeat the increasingly popular Gore. On "Super Tuesday," however, McCain won in only four New England states while Bush's remobilized juggernaut swept the other primaries, including California, with the single largest bloc of delegates.

The Reform Party: Parlous Times

In 1992, Ross Perot won 19 percent of the electorate as Reform Party presidential candidate, enough to augur a promising future for the third party. In 1996, a shopworn Perot won only 8 percent. Two years later, however, a flamboyant and erratic former

George W. Bush, son of a president, raised astronomical sums of money before launching his quest for the Republican presidential nomination of 2000.

wrestler, Jesse ("The Body") Ventura seemed to revive the Reform party when he won the governorship of Minnesota. Ventura had no intentions of running for president in 2000 but he meant to name the candidate. He fought (and defeated) Perot loyalists for control of the party.

Then, Pat Buchanan dropped out of the Republican primary race and announced he would seek the Reform nomination; if he would not be president, he would have a national audience for his increasingly eccentric and antagonisic views. Ventura, while hardly mealy-mouthed (he called religion "a sham"), disliked Buchanan's right-wing imprecations and announced his choice for the nomination, a man more preposterous than either he or Buchanan, a fatuous and ludicrously vain billionaire, Donald Trump, who reveled in the sequence of beautiful models he wrapped around his arm for public consumption.

Things went crazy. Movie stars Cybil Shepherd (a liberal) and Warren Beatty (a *left* liberal!) expressed their interest in the Reform nomination. Television celebrity Oprah Winfrey was mentioned. The Reform party looked to be as freakish an assemblage as the Populists in 1892, and a good deal more diverse. The fact was, prosperity had killed the federal deficit—Perot's hobbyhorse—as an issue, and McCain and Bradley had co-opted campaign finance reform. The party had no center, neither a program nor, early in 2000, a compelling personality at its head, when Governor Ventura announced he was quitting Reform.

MILLENNIAL SOCIETY

President Jimmy Carter did not actually use the word *malaise* to describe the widespread uneasiness he perceived in the American people in the 1970s. Journalists foisted the word on him as shorthand for what Carter actually called "a crisis of confidence . . . that strikes at the very heart and soul and spirit of our national will."

Ronald Reagan brought plenty of heart and will to American government. However, liberal commentator Garry Wills may well have been correct when he called Reaganism a "bedazzlement" that would evanesce. When the Great Communicator left the White House, George Bush could not sustain the spell. Bill Clinton (a baby boomer, he called malaise "funk") enjoyed prosperity and his "job approval rating" remained high. That was America's riches reporting. Clinton was never respected. The society of the 1990s was dynamic, but only a judge ignorant of historical comparisons could call it morally healthy.

Narcissism

To some observers, Americans were a caricature of self-indulgence in the final third of the twentieth century. Writer Tom Wolfe called the 1970s the "Me Decade." Historian Christopher Lasch wrote of a culture of narcissism. Ronald Reagan presided over a change of mood, but his presidency did not challenge the cultural obsession with self-serving. Reaganism merely redirected it from mystical mumbo-jumbo in the direction of amassing wealth, a cultural totem that retained the devotion of the American people under President Clintoin.

"The Movement" of the 1960s had a motto: "You can't trust anyone over thirty." In the 1970s, the people who had invoked those words celebrated their thirtieth birthdays. In the 1990s, they were feeling the aches and pangs of middle age.

Through the process of life, however, the baby boomers remained the "do your own thing" generation and, thanks to their numbers, they continued to dictate much about the national style. Their "thing" changed with age. They grew bored with political action and moral outrage as a means of self-gratification and looked elsewhere.

In the 1970s, baby boomer self-indulgence took on commercial shape. One raging consumer fad followed another, with some of the biggest profits made by companies selling products that combined fun and physical exercise. Americans spent billions of dollars on ski equipment, tennis paraphernalia, tenspeed bicycles, hang gliders, backpacking gear, and on shopping malls full of sporting impedimenta. Jogging became a national mania, claiming as its devotees one adult in five by 1980. The most primitive form of exercise was the basis of a multimilliondollar industry!

In the 1980s and 1990s, the boomers' "thing" was money: income and property. Plenty of former hippies and New Leftists voted for Ronald Reagan and remained Republicans. Greed was at its most blatant, at the top of the economic pyramid. In 1990, before the Clinton bull market, when corporate profits were down 7 percent, pay for chief executive officers increased 7 percent. Chrysler gave its CEO a 25 percent raise in a year in which the company's earnings dropped 17 percent.

The rapacity intensified in the final decade of the century. The pay of a chief executive officer in Japan was 17 times the pay of the average worker in his corporation, in France and Germany about 25 times, in Britain 35 times. In the United States CEOs typically made 85 to 100 times what the average worker in their corporation was paid. In September 1999, when Viacom and CBS merged, the two CEOs who arranged the deal rewarded themselves with $90 million each.

Such grotesqueries were enhanced by the tax structure. According to the Washington *Post*, in the mid-1990s, a $1,000 raise in pay added $356 to the tax bill of a $27,000-per-year mechanic, $483 to the taxes of a plumber and his wife earning $86,000 a year, and only $180 to the taxes of a banker making $200,000 per year.

The Sexual Revolution

A revolution in sexual mores long in the making reached its climax in the 1970s when several factors combined to relax inhibitions to casual sexual

---

Disposable America

Each year, Americans throw out of their homes (not their places of work) some 160 to 180 million tons of what they variously call trash, garbage, or rubbish. This amounts to a half ton per person per year.

Much of the total is made up of products designed to be disposable. Every day, on average, each American discards almost five pounds of "disposables." On a given day, Americans throw away 123 million paper and plastic cups, 44 million paper and plastic diapers, 5.5 million razor blades and disposable razors, 4.4 million disposable pens, and nearly a million disposable cigarette lighters.

> ### By the Numbers
>
> Before the Civil War, the only personal number an American needed to know was his or her date of birth. In 1863, the Post Office introduced a second, numbered street addresses. Telephone numbers made their appearance in 1879. The Social Security number now the principal means of identifying individuals, was introduced in 1936. (Grace Owen of New Hampshire was assigned number 001-01-0001, which was easy to remember.) ZIP codes date from 1963. In 1971, the first Automatic Teller Machine was hung on the wall of a bank in Atlanta, Georgia. A PIN (Personal Identification Number) was necessary to use it.

activity. The widespread use of "the pill," a reliable birth-control device, allayed women's fear of pregnancy, and more effective antibiotic control of venereal disease eliminated dread of infection. More controversially, a third factor may have been a ruling by the Supreme Court that pornography—explicit, clinically detailed depictions of sexual acts—was protected by the constitutional right of free speech. While standards of enforcement varied from state to state and city to city, sexually explicit books and films—"porn"—became freely available after the 1970s. The number of pornographic movie houses declined radically during the 1990s, but that was because pornography could be accessed more discreetly at videotape rental shops and on the Internet. In 2000, "adult entertainment" was the type of Internet Web site receiving more "hits", visits, than any other category of Web site.

Sumner Redstone and Mel Karmazin, who merged the communications companies they headed, paying themselves the equivalent of a small country's Gross National Product for their labors.

"Singles bars," places to meet a sexual partner for a "one-night stand," were fixtures in every big city and many towns in the 1970s and 1980s. "Adult motels" suspended mirrors on ceilings and pumped pornographic movies to TV sets in perfumed rooms. Some landlords converted apartment complexes to accommodate "swinging singles" with party rooms, saunas, and hot tubs. Marriage patterns could hardly remain unaffected. The divorce rate soared from 2.5 divorces per 1,000 marriages in 1965 to 5.3 per 1,000 in 1979. The illegitimate birth rate tripled during the 1960s and 1970s, and the number of abortions increased at a comparable rate.

Homosexuality

Homosexuals—"gays" in new parlance—benefited from the relaxation of sexual attitudes. The 1960s and 1970s saw the emergence of numerous gay and lesbian groups, as homosexuals began "coming out of the closet," proclaiming that their sexuality was an important part of their individual identity rather than a perversion to be hidden. Psychologists and psychiatrists hastened to oblige the new consciousness by removing homosexuals from their lists of deviants. In the political realm, gay and lesbian groups began to pressure governments to enact laws prohibiting discrimination in housing and employment solely on the basis of sexuality. Although they had gained important political power by the early 1990s, especially within the Democratic party, gay activism was met with determined hostility, especially by conservative religious organizations. State referenda prohibiting all discrimination against homosexuals or legalizing "same sex marriages" failed as often as not. Homosexual lobbies did better in the courts, government bureaucracies, and even the corporate world than they did at the polls.

Flies in the Ointment

If medical control of venereal disease helped to ignite the sexual revolution, disease played a role in cooling it down after 1980. A penicillin-resistant strain of gonorrhea made the rounds among "swingers," and herpes, an old, relatively minor venereal infection, reached epidemic proportions. More serious was an entirely new affliction, Acquired Immune Deficiency Syndrome—AIDS—which slowly and agonizingly kills its victims.

The human immunodeficiency virus (HIV), according to most medical authorities, is the cause of AIDS. It is transmitted by the introduction into a person's bloodstream of infected blood, semen, or other bodily fluids. The disease was first identified in the early 1980s.

Because early AIDS cases were limited almost solely to gay men, the disease became a political and cultural, as well as a medical, issue. Gay activists charged that, in response to conservative pressure groups, the Reagan and Bush administrations were placing a low priority on AIDS research that would check its spread or find a cure. In fact, more money was spent on AIDS research during the 1980s and 1990s than on most killer diseases. By the end of the century, for reasons not understood, the incidence of new cases in the United States sharply declined.

Drugs

In the 1970s, use of recreational drugs spread both among the middle class and the urban poor. LSD, the hallucinogenic celebrated by hippies in the 1960s, lost popularity, but marijuana remained a staple of yuppie (young urban professional) home life. Cocaine enjoyed a reign as a high-status euphoric drug because it was expensive and thought to be harmless when "snorted" (absorbed through the mucous membranes of the nose).

When cocaine was revealed to be highly addictive, it lost some of its luster among educated Americans. However, a cheap form of the drug that could be smoked or injected, "crack," flooded American cities, sold openly on street corners and in parks.

Decade of Greed?

Critics of Reaganism associated his decade, the 1980s, with selfishness and greed. Curiously, in terms of charitable giving, the 1980s were less "greedy" than the "New Age" 1970s. During the 1970s, contributions to charities grew at an annual rate of two percent, in the 1980s at 5.2 percent. Charitable contributions declined from 2.5 percent to 2.1 percent of Gross National Product during the 1970s. By 1989, the percentage was up to a record 2.7 percent.

Greed in the Universities

In the 1960s and 1970s and even later, universities were hotbeds of protest against social injustices. They embraced the causes of affirmative action and multiculturalism, and campaigned against such things as sexual harassment.

In the 1980s and 1990s, on the other hand, universities might be better remembered for the zest of academics to better themselves financially at the expense of both institution and society.

Few were more adept at this than David Gardner who, at age 59 in 1992, retired as president of the University of California. He was due to collect a pension of $60,000 a year. However, in the months before Gardner's departure, an aide—whose principal job was to whip up exciting retirement packages for academic administrators—arranged for the state to present Gardner with a check for $797,000 and an annual payment of $126,000. In addition, the university purchased Gardner's home at a profit to him above market values of about $100,000.

The regents of the university tried to keep the arrangement confidential and were furious when one of their number went public. Gardner's public explanation for his early retirement was that his wife had died recently and he could not continue without her. Fortunately, he found a job with an $825-million foundation for which his helpmeet's companionship was not vital.

Few academics openly criticized such boondoggles. To make a fuss was to ensure that one was not himself initiated into the circles where the booty was apportioned. The American university at the turn of the millennium more than casually resembled the Irish urban political machine in its use of the resources entrusted to it.

Crack had plenty of middle-class buyers, but its chief victims were the urban poor. Not only was crack use heaviest among the poor, pestilential "crack houses" and reckless shootings by rival retailers turned merely poor neighborhoods into war zones. Drug-related violence was so out of hand in some big cities that it affected the actuarial tables. By 1990, violent death was the chief cause of death among black males 15 to 34 years of age.

Another epidemic killer drug of century's end was widely abused in non-urban areas—methamphetamine, "speed"—a central nervous system stimulant that, unlike other such drugs, was easily manufactured in garage or cabin "laboratories."

The Women's Movement

In the 1970s, only one social movement of note achieved a large following, a new wave of feminism. In 1966, after her book *The Feminine Mystique* (1963) received a rousing response, Betty Friedan organized the National Organization for Women (NOW), a political group designed to secure legal and social equality for women. At first, "women's lib" was widely ridiculed because of the antics of fringe elements such as SCUM, the Society for Cutting Up Men. But the essence of the new feminism was too serious to be ignored and the influence of NOW too great to sidestep.

NOW's early victories were deceptively easy. Archaic state laws preventing married women from borrowing money or opening bank accounts without the approval of their husbands were quickly repealed. Divorce laws were changed to provide for equal division of property between alienated spouses. Legal action or social pressure forced many corporations to pay men and women equally for equal work, and women won entrance to jobs that had been restricted to men, particularly in manual and dangerous work such as construction and firefighting.

The women's movement also created an awareness of bias in gender-specific words like *fireman*, *postman*, and *chairman*. Rather quickly, businesses and government began speaking of *mail carriers* and *chairpersons*. On the example of Gloria Steinem, the editor of *Ms.* magazine, women began addressing themselves as Ms. rather than Miss or Mrs. To the new feminists, the traditional titles of Miss and Mrs. denied a woman an identity apart from a man, either her father or her husband. It is the task of a generation of historians yet to come to adjudge these readily accepted linguistic reforms as portentous, decadent, or trivial.

ERA and Abortion Rights

NOW's biggest setback was the failure of the Equal Rights Amendment (ERA), which forbade all legal and social discrimination on the basis of sex. Congress sent the ERA to the states for ratification in

1972 and, within a few years, it was approved by all but a handful of the 38 states needed to make it a part of the Constitution.

Then, seemingly from nowhere, rose a ground swell of opposition led by longtime conservative Republican writer, Phyllis Schlafly. She cautioned that the ERA would lead to the loss of certain privileges that women enjoyed, such as exemption from military conscription. Her boldness encouraged hundreds of state legislators to fight the women's movement. When the 1979 deadline for ratification was reached, the ERA was still three states short of approval. Congress then extended the deadline to 1982 but the net result was that three states rescinded their earlier votes in favor of ratification. Whether these rescissions were constitutional was never determined by the courts. The ERA won ratification in no additional states, and died with or without the backsliding states.

NOW and other women's groups next turned to "abortion rights" as their chief goal. In 1973, the then liberal Supreme Court had declared in *Roe* v. *Wade* that state governments could not prohibit a pregnant woman from having an abortion. At first, conservatives saw the decision as just another example of liberal wrongheadedness. By the end of the decade, however, spearheaded by fundamentalist Protestants, Mormons, and Roman Catholics, the "Right to Life" movement made prohibition of most or all abortions, into a sacred cause. Feminists and most liberals took up the challenge under the banner of "Choice."

"Choice" versus "Right to Life" remained a bitterly divisive issue through the year 2000. Colloquy between the two sides was unknown; debate consisted of imprecations shouted across picket lines, and violence, bombing of abortion clinics and the murders of several abortionists.

Sexual Harassment and Affirmative Action

By 1990, the issue of sexual harassment joined abortion rights as the chief concern of the feminist movement. Strictly defined, sexual harassment meant the proposition, by a person having power in the matter, to trade job security, promotion (or, in universities, a good grade) for sexual favors. In practice—clear-cut,

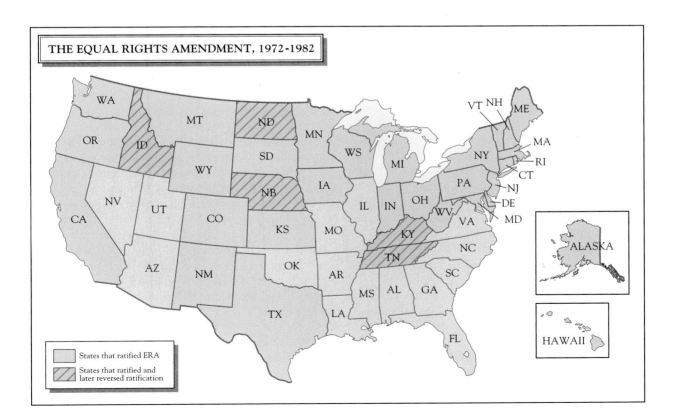

THE EQUAL RIGHTS AMENDMENT, 1972–1982

enforceable legal definitions being abhorrent to late twentieth-century America—sexual propositions and even flirtations in workplace or university were often considered to be sexual harassment. In 1991, Clarence Thomas, a nominee to the Supreme Court, was the center of a sensational inquest when a woman who had worked for him a decade earlier, Anita Hill, accused Thomas of using crude language and discussing pornographic movies in her presence. A few years later, Senator Robert Packwood of Oregon, who was accused of sexual advances by more than twenty women, albeit none of them dependent on him for their jobs, was forced to leave the Senate in disgrace.

"Sexual harassment" lost resonance as a tocsin by the end of the century. When an eight-year-old boy was suspended from elementary school for, shades of Tom Sawyer and Becky Thatcher, "stealing a kiss" from a classmate, virtually everyone laughed at the authorities who punished him. More notably, feminist leaders were silent when Paula Jones accused President Clinton of sexual harassment, when the president's sordid affair with decidedly subordinate intern Monica Lewinsky was revealed, and even when a woman claimed, with some corroboration, that Clinton had forced her to have sex with him in a Little Rock hotel room, physically wounding her in the process. As with so many other moral crusades, institutional feminism had become a political adjunct of the Democratic party, embracing the ancient rule of "what's a principle among friends?"

Anita Hill, a University of Oklahoma law professor, accused Supreme Court nominee Clarence Thomas of improperly making remarks of a sexual nature when Thomas was her superior in a federal bureaucracy. After heated hearings, Thomas was confirmed.

Affirmative Action

Another legacy of the social activism of the 1960s and 1970s that seemed to be foundering at the end of the century was affirmative action. Originally in the 1960s, the term referred to mandating that colleges and professional schools and public and private employers actively recruit blacks, Hispanics, women, and others in groups that had suffered from past discrimination.

In practice, affirmative action often came to mean establishing quotas and, when forced to choose between white males and women or minorities, to give preference to the latter even when their qualifications were not equal to those of the white males in the mix. In 1994, the United States Forest Service virtually told white male applicants for jobs not to bother applying. Universities discriminated in favor of members of protected groups in various ways.

Affirmative action programs had critics from the beginning, particularly among groups that had long warred against quotas in hiring and in admissions to professional schools. Beginning with the *Bakke* case of 1978, the Supreme Court dealt several major blows to such programs. In 1989, the Court threw out programs in several cities by which a percentage of municipal contracts were reserved for minority firms that did not have to bid against firms owned by white males.

By the 1990s, right-wing Republicans like Pat Buchanan and popular radio–television commentator Rush Limbaugh were joined in their opposition to affirmative action by many mainstream Americans. Every Republican candidate in the presidential primary campaign of 1996 opposed preferential policies. In California, the anti-affirmative action CCRI, the California Civil Rights Initiative, won by a wide margin. After invoking the slogan "Mend it, don't end it," President Clinton himself eased away from his administration's support for affirmative action policies, and in *Hopwood* v. *Texas*, a federal judge forbade universities in three states to use race or ethnicity in determining admissions to their institutions.

Racial Tensions

Affirmative action was but one ingredient of the social, political, and economic pot of the 1990s that contributed to a worsening of white–black relations. When, in 1995, Orenthal "O.J." Simpson, a black former football hero, was tried for the murder of his white wife and her white companion, opinions as to his guilt correlated with race: a large majority of whites believed him guilty, a majority of blacks celebrated when he was acquitted. The vision that race would cease to matter in the United States looked more unreal in the 1990s than it had in the 1960s when Martin Luther King Jr. dreamt it.

Hostility and resentment in the African-American community may have become more general than ever before in American history. In October 1995, hundreds of thousands of black men marched in Washington, D.C., despite the fact that the demonstration was organized by Louis Farrakhan, the head of the Black Muslim organization that advocated black self-sufficiency and moral responsibility but also lapsed frequently into anti-white and antisemitic messages. Even when, early in 1996, Farrakhan visited and praised the regimes of Syria, Iran, and Libya, which financed terrorist activities, while condemning the United States, more than a few African Americans praised his message.

Coda

As the twentieth century—the second millennium—came to an end, there was no confident assessment of the near future possible, as was easy for Americans

The "Million Man March" of 1995 brought African-American men from all over the country to Washington, D.C.

> ### Ancestors
>
> In 1982, the Census Bureau reported that 51.6 million Americans traced their ancestry to Germany compared with 43.7 million who claimed an Irish background and 40 million who had English forebears. But if Scotch-Americans and Welsh-Americans were added to the English as being of British origin, that would have been the largest group. About 16 million claimed African ancestors; and 2.8 million, Asian.

of 1900 to make. On the one hand, there was a boom economy in full swing. On the other, that boom economy resembled the flawed and ill-fated prosperity of the 1920s in many ways. On the one hand, American society weathered the personal humiliation and impeachment of a president with as much nonchalance as the president himself. On the other, the very fact that Clinton instilled nothing worse in Americans in his last two years in office than "fatigue," boredom with the Clinton name in the headlines itself may be reason for apprehension. Are a people who shrug their shoulders at any kind of moral misbehavior so long as they are growing richer fit inheritors of the legacy of those who tamed a wilderness, won independence, destroyed slavery, and fought World War II?

APPENDIX

The Declaration of Independence

*The Constitution of the
United States of America*

Admission of States

Population of the United States

Presidential Elections

*Presidents, Vice Presidents,
and Cabinet Members*

Justices of the U.S. Supreme Court

*Political Party Affiliations
in Congress and the Presidency*

Harcourt Online Documents

The Declaration of Independence

THE UNANIMOUS DECLARATION OF THE THIRTEEN UNITED STATES OF AMERICA,

When in the Course of human events it becomes necessary for one people to dissolve the political bands which have connected them with another, and to assume among the Powers of the earth, the separate and equal station to which the Laws of Nature and of Nature's God entitle them, a decent respect to the opinions of mankind requires that they should declare the causes which impel them to the separation.

We hold these truths to be self-evident, that all men are created equal, that they are endowed by their Creator with certain unalienable Rights, that among these are Life, Liberty and the pursuit of Happiness. That to secure these rights, Governments are instituted among Men, deriving their just Powers from the consent of the governed. That whenever any Form of Government becomes destructive of these ends, it is the Right of the People to alter or to abolish it, and to institute new Government, laying its foundation on such principles and organizing its Powers in such form, as to them shall seem most likely to effect their Safety and Happiness. Prudence, indeed, will dictate that Governments long established should not be changed for light and transient causes; and accordingly all experience hath shewn, that mankind are more disposed to suffer, while evils are sufferable, than to right themselves by abolishing the forms to which they are accustomed. But when a long train of abuses and usurpations, pursuing invariably the same Object evinces a design to reduce them under absolute Despotism, it is their right, it is their duty, to throw off such Government, and to provide new Guards for their future security. Such has been the patient sufferance of these Colonies; and such is now the necessity which constrains them to alter their former Systems of Government. The history of the present King of Great Britain is a history of repeated injuries and usurpations, all having in direct object the establishment of an absolute Tyranny over these States. To prove this, let Facts be submitted to a candid world.

He has refused his Assent to Laws, the most wholesome and necessary for the public good.

He has forbidden his Governors to pass Laws of immediate and pressing importance, unless suspended in their operation till his Assent should be obtained; and when so suspended, he has utterly neglected to attend to them.

He has refused to pass other Laws for the accommodation of large districts of people, unless those people would relinquish the right of Representation in the Legislature, a right inestimable to them and formidable to tyrants only.

He has called together legislative bodies at places unusual, uncomfortable, and distant from the depository of their Public Records, for the sole Purpose of fatiguing them into compliance with his measures.

He has dissolved Representative Houses repeatedly, for opposing with manly firmness his invasions on the rights of the People.

He has refused for a long time, after such dissolutions, to cause others to be elected; whereby the Legislative Powers, incapable of Annihilation, have returned to the People at large for their exercise; the State remaining in the mean time exposed to all the dangers of invasion from without, and convulsions within.

He has endeavoured to prevent the Population of these States; for that purpose obstructing the Laws for Naturalization of Foreigners; refusing to pass others to encourage their migrations hither, and raising the conditions of new Appropriations of Lands.

He has obstructed the Administration of Justice, by refusing his Assent to Laws for establishing Judiciary Powers.

He has made Judges dependent on his Will alone, for the tenure of their offices, and the amount and payment of their salaries.

He has erected a multitude of New Offices, and sent hither swarms of Officers to harass our People, and eat out their substance.

He has kept among us, in times of peace, Standing Armies without the Consent of our legislatures.

He has affected to render the Military independent of and superior to the Civil Power.

He has combined with others to subject us to a jurisdiction foreign to our constitution, and unacknowledged by our laws; giving his Assent to their Acts of pretended Legislation:

Text is reprinted from the facsimile of the engrossed copy in the National Archives. The original spelling, capitalization, and punctuation have been retained. Paragraphing has been added.

For Quartering large bodies of armed troops among us:

For protecting them, by a mock Trial, from Punishment for any Murders which they should commit on the Inhabitants of these States:

For cutting off our Trade with all parts of the world:

For imposing Taxes on us without our Consent:

For depriving us in many cases, of the benefits of Trial by Jury:

For transporting us beyond Seas to be tried for pretended offences:

For abolishing the free System of English Laws in a neighbouring Province, establishing therein an Arbitrary government, and enlarging its Boundaries so as to render it at once an example and fit instrument for introducing the same absolute rule into these Colonies:

For taking away our Charters, abolishing our most valuable Laws, and altering fundamentally the Forms of our Governments:

For suspending our own Legislatures, and declaring themselves invested with Power to legislate for us in all cases whatsoever.

He has abdicated Government here, by declaring us out of his Protection, and waging War against us.

He has plundered our seas, ravaged our Coasts, burnt our towns, and destroyed the lives of our people.

He is at this time transporting large Armies of foreign Mercenaries to compleat the works of death, desolation and tyranny, already begun with circumstances of Cruelty and perfidy scarcely paralleled in the most barbarous ages, and totally unworthy the Head of a civilized nation.

He has constrained our fellow Citizens taken Captive on the high Seas to bear Arms against their Country, to become the executioners of their friends and Brethren, or to fall themselves by their Hands.

He has excited domestic insurrections amongst us, and has endeavoured to bring on the inhabitants of our frontiers, the merciless Indian Savages, whose known rule of warfare, is an undistinguished destruction of all ages, sexes and conditions.

In every stage of these Oppressions We have Petitioned for Redress in the most humble terms: Our repeated Petitions have been answered only by repeated injury. A Prince, whose character is thus marked by every act which may define a Tyrant, is unfit to be the ruler of a free People.

Nor have We been wanting in attentions to our British brethren. We have warned them from time to time of attempts by their legislature to extend an unwarrantable jurisdiction over us. We have reminded them of the circumstances of our emigration and settlement here. We have appealed to their native justice and magnanimity, and we have conjured them by the ties of our common kindred to disavow these usurpations, which, would inevitably interrupt our connections and correspondence. They too have been deaf to the voice of justice and of consanguinity. We must, therefore, acquiesce in the necessity, which denounces our Separation, and hold them, as we hold the rest of mankind, Enemies in War, in Peace Friends.

WE, THEREFORE, the Representatives of the UNITED STATES OF AMERICA, in General Congress, Assembled, appealing to the Supreme Judge of the world for the rectitude of our intentions, do, in the Name, and by Authority of the good People of these Colonies, solemnly publish and declare, That these United Colonies are, and of Right ought to be FREE AND INDEPENDENT STATES; that they are Absolved from all Allegiance to the British Crown, and that all political connection between them and the State of Great Britain, is and ought to be totally dissolved; and that, as Free and Independent States, they have full Power to levy War, conclude Peace, contract Alliances, establish Commerce, and to do all other Acts and Things which Independent States may of right do. And for the support of this Declaration, with a firm reliance on the protection of divine Providence, we mutually pledge to each other our Lives, our Fortunes and our sacred Honor.

The Constitution of the United States of America

We the People of the United States, in Order to form a more perfect Union, establish Justice, insure domestic Tranquility, provide for the common defence, promote the general Welfare, and secure the Blessings of Liberty to ourselves and our Posterity, do ordain and establish this Constitution for the United States of America.

Article. I.

Section. 1. All legislative Powers herein granted shall be vested in a Congress of the United States, which shall consist of a Senate and House of Representatives.
Section. 2. The House of Representatives shall be composed of Members chosen every second Year by the People of the several States, and the Electors in each State shall have the Qualifications requisite for Electors of the most numerous Branch of the State Legislature.

No Person shall be a Representative who shall not have attained to the Age of twenty five Years, and been seven Years a Citizen of the United States, and who shall not, when elected, be an Inhabitant of that State in which he shall be chosen.

Representatives and direct Taxes[1] shall be apportioned among the several States which may be included within this Union, according to their respective Numbers, which shall be determined by adding to the whole Number of free Persons, including those bound to Service for a Term of Years, and excluding Indians not taxed, three fifths of all other Persons.[2] The actual Enumeration shall be made within three Years after the first Meeting of the Congress of the United States, and within every subsequent Term of ten Years, in such Manner as they shall by Law direct. The Number of Representatives shall not exceed one for every thirty Thousand, but each State shall have at Least one Representative; and until such enumeration shall be made, the State of New Hampshire shall be entitled to chuse three; Massachusetts eight; Rhode Island and Providence Plantations one; Connecticut five; New York six; New Jersey four; Pennsylvania eight; Delaware one; Maryland six; Virginia ten; North Carolina five; South Carolina five; and Georgia three.

When vacancies happen in the Representation from any State, the Executive Authority thereof shall issue Writs of Election to fill such Vacancies.

The House of Representatives shall chuse their Speaker and other Officers; and shall have the sole Power of Impeachment.
Section. 3. The Senate of the United States shall be composed of two Senators from each State, chosen by the Legislature thereof, for six Years; and each Senator shall have one Vote.[3]

Immediately after they shall be assembled in Consequence of the first Election, they shall be divided as equally as may be into three Classes. The Seats of the Senators of the first Class shall be vacated at the Expiration of the second Year, of the second Class at the Expiration of the fourth Year, and of the third Class at the Expiration of the sixth Year, so that one third may be chosen every second Year; and if Vacancies happen by Resignation, or otherwise, during the Recess of the Legislature of any State, the Executive thereof may make temporary Appointments until the next Meeting of the Legislature, which shall then fill such Vacancies.[4]

No Person shall be a Senator who shall not have attained to the Age of thirty Years, and been nine Years a Citizen of the United States, and who shall not, when elected, be an Inhabitant of that State for which he shall be chosen.

The Vice President of the United States shall be President of the Senate, but shall have no Vote, unless they be equally divided.

The Senate shall chuse their other Officers, and also a President pro tempore, in the Absence of the Vice President, or when he shall exercise the Office of President of the United States.

The Senate shall have the sole Power to try all Impeachments. When sitting for that Purpose, they shall be on Oath or Affirmation. When the President of the United States is tried, the Chief Justice shall preside:

Text is from the engrossed copy in the National Archives. Original spelling, capitalization, and punctuation have been retained.

[1]Modified by the Sixteenth Amendment.

[2]Replaced by the Fourteenth Amendment.

[3]Superseded by the Seventeenth Amendment.

[4]Modified by the Seventeenth Amendment.

And no Person shall be convicted without the Concurrence of two thirds of the Members present.

Judgment in Cases of Impeachment shall not extend further than to removal from Office, and disqualification to hold and enjoy any Office of honor, Trust or Profit under the United States: but the Party convicted shall nevertheless be liable and subject to Indictment, Trial, Judgment and Punishment, according to Law.

Section. 4. The Times, Places and Manner of holding Elections for Senators and Representatives, shall be prescribed in each State by the Legislature thereof, but the Congress may at any time by Law make or alter such Regulation, except as to the Places of chusing Senators.

The Congress shall assemble at least once in every Year, and such Meeting shall be on the first Monday in December, unless they shall by Law appoint a different Day.[5]

Section. 5. Each House shall be the Judge of the Elections, Returns and Qualifications of its own Members, and a Majority of each shall constitute a Quorum to do Business; but a smaller Number may adjourn from day to day, and may be authorized to compel the Attendance of absent Members, in such Manner, and under such Penalties as each House may provide.

Each House may determine the Rules of its Proceedings, punish its Members for disorderly Behaviour, and, with the Concurrence of two thirds, expel a Member.

Each House shall keep a Journal of its Proceedings, and from time to time publish the same, excepting such Parts as may in their Judgment require Secrecy; and the Yeas and Nays of the Members of either House on any question shall, at the Desire of one fifth of those Present, be entered on the Journal.

Neither House, during the Session of Congress, shall, without the Consent of the other, adjourn for more than three days, nor to any other Place than that in which the two Houses shall be sitting.

Section. 6. The Senators and Representatives shall receive a Compensation for their Services, to be ascertained by Law, and paid out of the Treasury of the United States. They shall in all Cases, except Treason, Felony and Breach of the Peace, be privileged from Arrest during their Attendance at the Session of their respective Houses, and in going to and returning from the same; and for any Speech or Debate in either House, they shall not be questioned in any other Place.

No Senator or Representative shall, during the Time for which he was elected, be appointed to any civil Office under the Authority of the United States, which shall have been created, or the Emoluments whereof shall have been encreased during such time; and no Person holding any Office under the United States, shall be a Member of either House during his Continuance in Office.

Section. 7. All Bills for raising Revenue shall originate in the House of Representatives; but the Senate may propose or concur with Amendments as on other Bills.

Every Bill which shall have passed the House of Representatives and the Senate shall, before it become a Law, be presented to the President of the United States; If he approve he shall sign it, but if not he shall return it, with his Objections to that House in which it shall have originated, who shall enter the Objections at large on their Journal, and proceed to reconsider it. If after such Reconsideration two thirds of that House shall agree to pass the Bill, it shall be sent, together with the Objections, to the other House, by which it shall likewise be reconsidered, and if approved by two thirds of that House, it shall become a Law. But in all such Cases the Votes of both Houses shall be determined by yeas and Nays, and the Names of the Persons voting for and against the Bill shall be entered on the Journal of each House respectively. If any Bill shall not be returned by the President within ten Days (Sundays excepted) after it shall have been presented to him, the Same shall be a Law, in like Manner as if he had signed it, unless the Congress by their Adjournment prevent its Return, in which Case it shall not be a Law.

Every Order, Resolution, or Vote to which the Concurrence of the Senate and House of Representatives may be necessary (except on a question of Adjournment) shall be presented to the President of the United States; and before the Same shall take Effect, shall be approved by him, or being disapproved by him shall be repassed by two thirds of the Senate and House of Representatives, according to the Rules and Limitations prescribed in the Case of a Bill.

Section. 8. The Congress shall have power To lay and collect Taxes, Duties, Imposts and Excises, to pay the Debts and provide for the common Defence and general Welfare of the United States; but all Duties, Imposts and Excises shall be uniform throughout the United States;

To borrow Money on the credit of the United States;

To regulate Commerce with foreign Nations, and among the several States, and with the Indian Tribes;

To establish an uniform Rule of Naturalization, and uniform Laws on the subject of Bankruptcies throughout the United States;

---

[5]Superseded by the Twentieth Amendment.

To coin Money, regulate the Value thereof, and of foreign Coin, and fix the Standard of Weights and Measures;

To provide for the Punishment of counterfeiting the Securities and current Coin of the United States;

To establish Post Offices and post Roads;

To promote the Progress of Science and useful Arts, by securing for limited Times to Authors and Inventors the exclusive Right to their respective Writings and Discoveries;

To constitute Tribunals inferior to the Supreme Court;

To define and punish Piracies and Felonies committed on the high Seas, and Offences against the Law of Nations;

To declare War, grant Letters of Marque and Reprisal, and make Rules concerning Captures on Land and Water;

To raise and support Armies, but no Appropriation of Money to that Use shall be for a longer Term than two Years;

To provide and maintain a Navy;

To make Rules for the Government and Regulation of the land and naval Forces;

To provide for calling forth the Militia to execute the Laws of the Union, suppress Insurrections and repel Invasions;

To provide for organizing, arming, and disciplining, the Militia, and for governing such Part of them as may be employed in the Service of the United States, reserving to the States respectively, the Appointment of the Officers, and the Authority of training the Militia according to the discipline prescribed by Congress;

To exercise exclusive Legislation in all Cases whatsoever, over such District (not exceeding ten Miles square) as may, by Cession of particular States, and the Acceptance of Congress, become the Seat of the Government of the United States, and to exercise like Authority over all Places purchased by the Consent of the Legislature of the State in which the Same shall be, for the Erection of Forts, Magazines, Arsenals, dock-Yards, and other needful Buildings;—And

To make all Laws which shall be necessary and proper for carrying into Execution the foregoing Powers, and all other Powers vested by this Constitution in the Government of the United States, or in any Department or Officer thereof.

Section. 9. The Migration or Importation of such Persons as any of the States now existing shall think proper to admit, shall not be prohibited by the Congress prior to the Year one thousand eight hundred and eight, but a Tax or duty may be imposed on such Importation, not exceeding ten dollars for each Person.

The Privilege of the Writ of Habeas Corpus shall not be suspended, unless when in Cases of Rebellion or Invasion the public Safety may require it.

No Bill of Attainder or ex post facto Law shall be passed.

No Capitation, or other direct, Tax shall be laid, unless in Proportion to the Census or Enumeration herein before directed to be taken.

No Tax or Duty shall be laid on Articles exported from any State.

No Preference shall be given by any Regulation of Commerce or Revenue to the Ports of one State over those of another: nor shall Vessels bound to, or from, one State, be obliged to enter, clear, or pay Duties in another.

No Money shall be drawn from the Treasury, but in Consequence of Appropriations made by Law, and a regular Statement and Account of the Receipts and Expenditures of all public Money shall be published from time to time.

No Title of Nobility shall be granted by the United States: And no Person holding any Office of Profit or Trust under them, shall, without the Consent of the Congress, accept of any present, Emolument, Office, or Title, of any kind whatever, from any King, Prince, or foreign State.

Section. 10. No State shall enter into any Treaty, Alliance, or Confederation; grant Letters of Marque and Reprisal; coin Money; emit Bills of Credit; make any Thing but gold and silver Coin a Tender in Payment of Debts; pass any Bill of Attainder, ex post facto Law, or Law impairing the Obligation of Contracts, or grant any Title of Nobility.

No State shall, without the Consent of the Congress, lay any Imposts or Duties on Imports or Exports, except what may be absolutely necessary for executing its inspection Laws: and the net Produce of all Duties and Imposts, laid by any State on Imports or Exports, shall be for the Use of the Treasury of the United States; and all such Laws shall be subject to the Revision and Controul of the Congress.

No State shall, without the Consent of Congress, lay any Duty of Tonnage, keep Troops, or Ships of War in time of Peace, enter into any Agreement or Compact with another State, or with a foreign Power, or engage in War, unless actually invaded, or in such imminent Danger as will not admit of delay.

Article. II.

Section. 1. The executive Power shall be vested in a President of the United States of America. He shall hold his Office during the Term of four Years, and, together with the Vice President, chosen for the same Term, be elected, as follows:

Each State shall appoint, in such Manner as the Legislature thereof may direct, a Number of Electors, equal to the whole Number of Senators and Representatives to which the State may be entitled in the Congress: but no Senator or Representative, or Person holding an Office of Trust or Profit under the United States, shall be appointed an Elector.

The Electors shall meet in their respective States, and vote by Ballot for two Persons, of whom one at least shall not be an Inhabitant of the same State with themselves. And they shall make a List of all the Persons voted for, and of the Number of Votes for each; which List they shall sign and certify, and transmit sealed to the Seat of the Government of the United States, directed to the President of the Senate. The President of the Senate shall, in the Presence of the Senate and House of Representatives, open all the Certificates, and the Votes shall then be counted. The Person having the greatest Number of Votes shall be the President, if such Number be a Majority of the whole Number of Electors appointed; and if there be more than one who have such Majority, and have an equal Number of Votes, then the House of Representatives shall immediately chuse by Ballot one of them for President; and if no Person have a Majority, then from the five highest on the List the said House shall in like Manner chuse the President. But in chusing the President, the Votes shall be taken by States, the Representation from each State having one Vote; A quorum for this Purpose shall consist of a Member or Members from two thirds of the States, and a Majority of all the States shall be necessary to a Choice. In every Case, after the Choice of the President, the Person having the greatest Number of Votes of the Electors shall be the Vice President. But if there should remain two or more who have equal Votes, the Senate shall chuse from them by Ballot the Vice President.[6]

The Congress may determine the Time of chusing the Electors, and the Day on which they shall give their Votes; which Day shall be the same throughout the United States.

No Person except a natural born Citizen, or a Citizen of the United States, at the time of the Adoption of this Constitution, shall be eligible to the Office of President, neither shall any Person be eligible to that Office who shall not have attained to the Age of thirty five Years, and been fourteen Years a Resident within the United States.

In Case of the Removal of the President from Office, or of his Death, Resignation, or Inability to discharge the Powers and Duties of the said Office, the Same shall devolve on the Vice President, and the Congress may by Law provide for the Case of Removal, Death, Resignation or Inability, both of the President and Vice President, declaring what Officer shall then act as President, and such Officer shall act accordingly, until the Disability be removed, or a President shall be elected.[7]

The President shall, at stated Times, receive for his Services, a Compensation, which shall neither be encreased nor diminished during the Period for which he shall have been elected, and he shall not receive within that Period any other Emolument from the United States, or any of them.

Before he enter on the Execution of his Office, he shall take the following Oath or Affirmation:—"I do solemnly swear (or affirm) that I will faithfully execute the Office of President of the United States, and will to the best of my Ability, preserve, protect and defend the Constitution of the United States."

Section. 2. The President shall be Commander in Chief of the Army and Navy of the United States, and of the Militia of the several States, when called into the actual Service of the United States; he may require the Opinion, in writing, of the principal Officer in each of the executive Departments, upon any Subject relating to the Duties of their respective Offices, and he shall have Power to grant Reprieves and Pardons for Offences against the United States, except in Cases of Impeachment.

He shall have Power, by and with the Advice and Consent of the Senate, to make Treaties, provided two thirds of the Senators present concur; and he shall nominate, and by and with the Advice and Consent of the Senate, shall appoint Ambassadors, other public Ministers and Consuls, Judges of the supreme Court, and all other Officers of the United States, whose Appointments are not herein otherwise provided for, and which shall be established by Law; but the Congress may by Law vest the Appointment of such inferior Officers, as they think proper, in the President alone, in the Courts of Law, or in the Heads of Departments.

The President shall have Power to fill up all Vacancies that may happen during the Recess of the Senate, by granting Commissions which shall expire at the End of their next Session.

Section. 3. He shall from time to time give the Congress Information of the State of the Union, and recommend to their Consideration such Measures as he

---

[6]Superseded by the Twelfth Amendment.

[7]Modified by the Twenty-fifth Amendment.

shall judge necessary and expedient; he may, on extraordinary Occasions, convene both Houses, or either of them, and in Case of Disagreement between them, with Respect to the Time of Adjournment, he may adjourn them to such Time as he shall think proper; he shall receive Ambassadors and other public Ministers; he shall take Care that the Laws be faithfully executed, and shall Commission all the Officers of the United States.

Section. 4. The President, Vice President and all civil Officers of the United States, shall be removed from Office on Impeachment for, and Conviction of, Treason, Bribery, or other high Crimes and Misdemeanors.

Article. III.

Section. 1. The judicial Power of the United States, shall be vested in one supreme Court, and in such inferior Courts as the Congress may from time to time ordain and establish. The Judges, both of the supreme and inferior Courts, shall hold their Offices during good Behaviour, and shall, at stated Times, receive for their Services, a Compensation, which shall not be diminished during their Continuance in Office.

Section. 2. The judicial Power shall extend to all Cases, in Law and Equity, arising under this Constitution, the Laws of the United States, and Treaties made, or which shall be made, under their Authority;—to all Cases affecting Ambassadors, other public Ministers and Consuls;—to all Cases of admiralty and maritime Jurisdiction;—to Controversies to which the United States shall be a Party;—to Controversies between two or more States;—between a State and Citizens of another State;[8]—between Citizens of different States,—between Citizens of the same State claiming Lands under Grants of different States, and between a State, or the Citizens thereof, and foreign States, Citizens or Subjects.

In all Cases affecting Ambassadors, other public Ministers and Consuls, and those in which a State shall be Party, the supreme Court shall have original Jurisdiction. In all the other Cases before mentioned, the supreme Court shall have appellate Jurisdiction, both as to Law and Fact, with such Exceptions, and under such Regulations as the Congress shall make.

The Trial of all Crimes, except in Cases of Impeachment, shall be by Jury; and such Trial shall be held in the State where the said Crimes shall have been committed; but when not committed within any State, the Trial shall be at such Place or Places as the Congress may by Law have directed.

Section. 3. Treason against the United States, shall consist only in levying War against them, or in adhering to their Enemies, giving them Aid and Comfort. No Person shall be convicted of Treason unless on the Testimony of two Witnesses to the same overt Act, or on Confession in open Court.

The Congress shall have Power to declare the Punishment of Treason, but no Attainder of Treason shall work Corruption of Blood, or Forfeiture except during the Life of the Person attainted.

Article. IV.

Section. 1. Full Faith and Credit shall be given in each State to the public Acts, Records, and judicial Proceedings of every other State. And the Congress may by general Laws prescribe the Manner in which such Acts, Records and Proceedings shall be proved, and the Effect thereof.

Section. 2. The Citizens of each State shall be entitled to all Privileges and Immunities of Citizens in the several States.

A Person charged in any State with Treason, Felony, or other Crime, who shall flee from Justice, and be found in another State, shall on Demand of the executive Authority of the State from which he fled, be delivered up, to be removed to the State having Jurisdiction of the Crime.

No Person held to Service or Labour in one State, under the Laws thereof, escaping into another, shall, in Consequence of any Law or Regulation therein, be discharged from such Service or Labour, but shall be delivered up on Claim of the Party to whom such Service or Labour may be due.

Section. 3. New States may be admitted by the Congress into this Union; but no new State shall be formed or erected within the Jurisdiction of any other State, nor any State be formed by the Junction of two or more States, or Parts of States, without the Consent of the Legislatures of the States concerned as well as of the Congress.

The Congress shall have Power to dispose of and make all needful Rules and Regulations respecting the Territory or other Property belonging to the United States; and nothing in this Constitution shall be so construed as to Prejudice any Claims of the United States, or of any particular State.

Section. 4. The United States shall guarantee to every State in this Union a Republican Form of Government, and shall protect each of them against Invasion; and on Application of the Legislature, or of the Executive (when the Legislature cannot be convened) against domestic Violence.

[8]Modified by the Eleventh Amendment.

Article. V.

The Congress, whenever two thirds of both Houses shall deem it necessary, shall propose Amendments to this Constitution, or, on the Application of the Legislatures of two thirds of the several States, shall call a Convention for proposing Amendments, which, in either Case, shall be valid to all Intents and Purposes, as Part of this Constitution, when ratified by the Legislatures of three fourths of the several States, or by Conventions in three fourths thereof, as the one or the other Mode of Ratification may be proposed by the Congress; Provided that no Amendment which may be made prior to the Year One thousand eight hundred and eight shall in any Manner affect the first and fourth Clauses in the Ninth Section of the first Article; and that no State, without its Consent, shall be deprived of its equal Suffrage in the Senate.

Article. VI.

All Debts contracted and Engagements entered into, before the Adoption of this Constitution, shall be as valid against the United States under this Constitution, as under the Confederation.

This Constitution, and the Laws of the United States which shall be made in Pursuance thereof; and all Treaties made, or which shall be made, under the Authority of the United States, shall be the supreme Law of the Land; and the Judges in every State shall be bound thereby, any Thing in the Constitution or Laws of any State to the Contrary notwithstanding.

The Senators and Representatives before mentioned, and the Members of the several State Legislatures, and all executive and judicial Officers, both of the United States and of the several States, shall be bound by Oath or Affirmation, to support this Constitution; but no religious Test shall ever be required as a Qualification to any Office or public Trust under the United States.

Article. VII.

The Ratification of the Conventions of nine States, shall be sufficient for the Establishment of this Constitution between the States so ratifying the Same. **Done** in Convention by the Unanimous Consent of the States present the Seventeenth Day of September in the Year of our Lord one thousand seven hundred and Eighty seven and of the Independence of the United States of America the Twelfth. **In witness** whereof We have hereunto subscribed our Names,

Articles in Addition to, and Amendment of, the Constitution of the United States of America, Proposed by Congress, and Ratified by the Legislatures of the Several States, Pursuant to the Fifth Article of the Original Constitution.

Amendment I[9]

Congress shall make no law respecting an establishment of religion, or prohibiting the free exercise thereof; or abridging the freedom of speech, or of the press; or the right of the people peaceably to assemble, and to petition the Government for a redress of grievances.

Amendment II

A well regulated Militia, being necessary to the security of a free State, the right of the people to keep and bear Arms shall not be infringed.

Amendment III

No Soldier shall, in time of peace, be quartered in any house, without the consent of the Owner, nor in time of war, but in a manner to be prescribed by law.

Amendment IV

The right of the people to be secure in their persons, houses, papers, and effects, against unreasonable searches and seizures, shall not be violated, and no Warrants shall issue, but upon probable cause, supported by Oath or affirmation, and particularly describing the place to be searched, and the persons or things to be seized.

Amendment V

No person shall be held to answer for a capital or otherwise infamous crime, unless on a presentment or indictment of a Grand Jury, except in cases arising in the land or naval forces, or in the Militia, when in actual service in time of War or public danger; nor shall any person be subject for the same offence to be twice put in jeopardy of life or limb; nor shall be compelled in any criminal case to be a witness against himself, nor be deprived of life, liberty, or property, without due process of law; nor shall private property be taken for public use, without just compensation.

---

[9] The first ten amendments were passed by Congress September 25, 1789. They were ratified by three-fourths of the states December 15, 1791.

Amendment VI

In all criminal prosecutions, the accused shall enjoy the right to a speedy and public trial, by an impartial jury of the State and district wherein the crime shall have been committed, which district shall have been previously ascertained by law, and to be informed of the nature and cause of the accusation; to be confronted with the witnesses against him; to have compulsory process for obtaining witnesses in his favor, and to have the Assistance of Counsel for his defence.

Amendment VII

In suits at common law, where the value in controversy shall exceed twenty dollars, the right of trial by jury shall be preserved, and no fact tried by a jury, shall be otherwise reexamined in any Court of the United States, than according to the rules of the common law.

Amendment VIII

Excessive bail shall not be required, nor excessive fines imposed, nor cruel and unusual punishments inflicted.

Amendment IX

The enumeration in the Constitution, of certain rights, shall not be construed to deny or disparage others retained by the people.

Amendment X

The powers not delegated to the United States by the Constitution; nor prohibited by it to the States, are reserved to the States respectively, or to the people.

Amendment XI[10]

The Judicial power of the United States shall not be construed to extend to any suit in law or equity, commenced or prosecuted against one of the United States by Citizens of another State, or by Citizens or Subjects of any Foreign State.

Amendment XII[11]

The Electors shall meet in their respective States and vote by ballot for President and Vice-President,

one of whom, at least, shall not be an inhabitant of the same State with themselves; they shall name in their ballots the person voted for as President, and in distinct ballots the person voted for as Vice-President, and they shall make distinct lists of all persons voted for as President, and of all persons voted for as Vice-President, and of the number of votes for each, which lists they shall sign and certify, and transmit sealed to the seat of the government of the United States, directed to the President of the Senate;—The President of the Senate shall, in the presence of the Senate and House of Representatives, open all the certificates and the votes shall then be counted;—The person having the greatest number of votes for President, shall be the President, if such number be a majority of the whole number of Electors appointed; and if no person have such majority, then from the persons having the highest numbers not exceeding three on the list of those voted for as President, the House of Representatives shall choose immediately, by ballot, the President. But in choosing the President, the votes shall be taken by states, the representation from each state having one vote; a quorum for this purpose shall consist of a member or members from two-thirds of the states, and a majority of all the states shall be necessary to a choice. And if the House of Representatives shall not choose a President whenever the right of choice shall devolve upon them, before the fourth day of March next following, then the Vice-President shall act as President, as in the case of the death or other constitutional disability of the President.—The person having the greatest number of votes as Vice-President, shall be the Vice-President, if such number be a majority of the whole number of Electors appointed, and if no person have a majority, then from the two highest numbers on the list, the Senate shall choose the Vice-President; a quorum for the purpose shall consist of two-thirds of the whole number of Senators, and a majority of the whole number shall be necessary to a choice. But no person constitutionally ineligible to the office of President shall be eligible to that of Vice-President of the United States.

Amendment XIII[12]

SECTION 1. Neither slavery nor involuntary servitude, except as a punishment for crime whereof the party shall have been duly convicted, shall exist within the United States, or any place subject to their jurisdiction.

---

[10]Passed March 4, 1794. Ratified January 23, 1795.

[11]Passed December 9, 1803. Ratified June 15, 1804.

[12]Passed January 31, 1865. Ratified December 6, 1865.

SECTION 2. Congress shall have power to enforce this article by appropriate legislation.

Amendment XIV[13]

SECTION 1. All persons born or naturalized in the United States, and subject to the jurisdiction thereof, are citizens of the United States and of the State wherein they reside. No State shall make or enforce any law which shall abridge the privileges or immunities of citizens of the United States; nor shall any State deprive any person of life, liberty, or property, without due process of law; nor deny to any person within its jurisdiction the equal protection of the laws.

SECTION 2. Representatives shall be apportioned among the several States according to their respective numbers, counting the whole number of persons in each State, excluding Indians not taxed. But when the right to vote at any election for the choice of electors for President and Vice-President of the United States, Representatives in Congress, the Executive and Judicial officers of a State, or the members of the Legislature thereof, is denied to any of the male inhabitants of such State, being twenty-one years of age, and citizens of the United States, or in any way abridged, except for participation in rebellion, or other crime, the basis of representation therein shall be reduced in the proportion which the number of such male citizens shall bear to the whole number of male citizens twenty-one years of age in such State.

SECTION 3. No person shall be a Senator or Representative in Congress, or elector of President and Vice-President, or hold any office, civil or military, under the United States, or under any State, who, having previously taken an oath, as a member of Congress, or as an officer of the United States, or as a member of any State legislature, or as an executive or judicial officer of any State, to support the Constitution of the United States, shall have engaged in insurrection or rebellion against the same, or given aid or comfort to the enemies thereof. But Congress may by a vote of two-thirds of each House, remove such disability.

SECTION 4. The validity of the public debt of the United States, authorized by law, including debts incurred for payment of pensions and bounties for services in suppressing insurrection or rebellion, shall not be questioned. But neither the United States nor any State shall assume or pay any debt or obligation incurred in aid of insurrection or rebellion against

the United States, or any claim for the loss or emancipation of any slave; but all such debts, obligations, and claims shall be held illegal and void.

SECTION 5. The Congress shall have the power to enforce, by appropriate legislation, the provisions of this article.

Amendment XV[14]

SECTION 1. The right of citizens of the United States to vote shall not be denied or abridged by the United States or by any State on account of race, color, or previous conditions of servitude—

SECTION 2. The Congress shall have power to enforce this article by appropriate legislation.

Amendment XVI

The Congress shall have power to lay and collect taxes on incomes, from whatever source derived, without apportionment among the several States, and without regard to any census or enumeration.

Amendment XVII[15]

The Senate of the United States shall be composed of two Senators from each State, elected by the people thereof, for six years; and each Senator shall have one vote. The electors in each State shall have the qualifications requisite for electors of the most numerous branch of the State legislatures.

When vacancies happen in the representation of any State in the Senate, the executive authority of such State shall issue writs of election to fill such vacancies: *Provided,* That the legislature of any State may empower the executive thereof to make temporary appointments until the people fill the vacancies by election as the legislature may direct.

This amendment shall not be so construed as to affect the election or term of any Senator chosen before it becomes valid as part of the Constitution.

Amendment XVIII[16]

SECTION 1. After one year from the ratification of this article the manufacture, sale, or transportation of intoxicating liquors within, the importation thereof into, or the exportation thereof from the United States and all territory subject to the jurisdiction thereof for beverage purposes is hereby prohibited.

---

[13]Passed June 13, 1866. Ratified July 9, 1868.

[14]Passed February 26, 1869. Ratified February 2, 1870.

[15]Passed May 13, 1912. Ratified April 8, 1913.

[16]Passed December 18, 1917. Ratified January 16, 1919.

SECTION 2. The Congress and the several States shall have concurrent power to enforce this article by appropriate legislation.

SECTION 3. This article shall be inoperative unless it shall have been ratified as an amendment to the Constitution by the legislatures of the several States, as provided in the Constitution, within seven years from the date of the submission hereof to the States by the Congress.

Amendment XIX[17]

The right of citizens of the United States to vote shall not be denied or abridged by the United States or by any State on account of sex.

Congress shall have power to enforce this article by appropriate legislation.

Amendment XX[18]

SECTION 1. The terms of the President and Vice-President shall end at noon on the 20th day of January, and the terms of Senators and Representatives at noon on the 3d day of January, of the years in which such terms would have ended if this article had not been ratified; and the terms of their successors shall then begin.

SECTION 2. The Congress shall assemble at least once in every year, and such meeting shall begin at noon on the 3d day of January, unless they shall by law appoint a different day.

SECTION 3. If, at the time fixed for the beginning of the term of the President, the President elect shall have died, the Vice-President elect shall become President. If a President shall not have been chosen before the time fixed for the beginning of his term, or if the President elect shall have failed to qualify, then the Vice-President elect shall act as President until a President shall have qualified; and the Congress may by law provide for the case wherein neither a President elect nor a Vice-President elect shall have qualified, declaring who shall then act as President, or the manner in which one who is to act shall be selected, and such person shall act accordingly until a President or Vice-President shall have qualified.

SECTION 4. The Congress may by law provide for the case of the death of any of the persons from whom the House of Representatives may choose a President whenever the right of choice shall have devolved upon them, and for the case of the death of any of the persons from whom the Senate may choose a Vice-President whenever the right of choice shall have devolved upon them.

SECTION 5. Sections 1 and 2 shall take effect on the 15th day of October following the ratification of this article.

SECTION 6. This article shall be inoperative unless it shall have been ratified as an amendment to the Constitution by the legislatures of three-fourths of the several States within seven years from the date of its submission.

Amendment XXI[19]

SECTION 1. The eighteenth article of amendment to the Constitution of the United States is hereby repealed.

SECTION 2. The transportation or importation into any State, Territory, or possession of the United States for delivery or use therein of intoxicating liquors, in violation of the laws thereof, is hereby prohibited.

SECTION 3. This article shall be inoperative unless it shall have been ratified as an amendment to the Constitution by conventions in the several States, as provided in the Constitution, within seven years from the date of the submission hereof to the States by the Congress.

Amendment XXII[20]

No person shall be elected to the office of the President more than twice, and no person who has held the office of President, or acted as President, for more than two years of a term to which some other person was elected President shall be elected to the office of the President more than once.

But this Article shall not apply to any person holding the office of President when this Article was proposed by the Congress, and shall not prevent any person who may be holding the office of President, or acting as President, during the term within which this Article becomes operative from holding the office of President or acting as President during the remainder of such term.

Amendment XXIII[21]

SECTION 1. The District constituting the seat of Government of the United States shall appoint in such manner as the Congress may direct:

---

[17] Passed June 4, 1919. Ratified August 18, 1920.

[18] Passed March 2, 1932. Ratified January 23, 1933.

[19] Passed February 20, 1933. Ratified December 5, 1933.

[20] Passed March 12, 1947. Ratified March 1, 1951.

[21] Passed June 16, 1960. Ratified April 3, 1961.

A number of electors of President and Vice President equal to the whole number of Senators and Representatives in Congress to which the District would be entitled if it were a State, but in no event more than the least populous State; they shall be in addition to those appointed by the States, but they shall be considered, for the purposes of the election of President and Vice President, to be electors appointed by the State; and they shall meet in the District and perform such duties as provided by the twelfth article of amendment.

SECTION 2. The Congress shall have power to enforce this article by appropriate legislation.

Amendment XXIV[22]

SECTION 1. The right of citizens of the United States to vote in any primary or other election for President or Vice President, or for Senator or Representative in Congress, shall not be denied or abridged by the United States or any State by reason of failure to pay any poll tax or other tax.

SECTION 2. The Congress shall have power to enforce this article by appropriate legislation.

Amendment XXV[23]

SECTION 1. In case of the removal of the President from office or of his death or resignation, the Vice President shall become President.

SECTION 2. Whenever there is a vacancy in the office of the Vice President, the President shall nominate a Vice President who shall take office upon confirmation by a majority vote of both Houses of Congress.

SECTION 3. Whenever the President transmits to the President pro tempore of the Senate and the Speaker of the House of Representatives his written declaration that he is unable to discharge the powers and duties of his office, and until he transmits them a written declaration to the contrary, such powers and duties shall be discharged by the Vice President as Acting President.

SECTION 4. Whenever the Vice President and a majority of either the principal officers of the executive department or of such other body as Congress may by law provide, transmit to the President pro tempore of the Senate and the Speaker of the House of Representatives their written declaration that the President is unable to discharge the powers and duties of his office, the Vice President shall immediately assume the powers and duties of the office of Acting President.

Thereafter, when the President transmits to the President pro tempore of the Senate and the Speaker of the House of Representatives his written declaration that no inability exists, he shall resume the powers and duties of his office unless the Vice President and a majority of either the principal officers of the executive department or of such other body as Congress may by law provide, transmit within four days to the President pro tempore of the Senate and the Speaker of the House of Representatives their written declaration that the President is unable to discharge the powers and duties of his office. Thereupon Congress shall decide the issue, assembling within forty-eight hours for that purpose if not in session. If the Congress, within twenty-one days after receipt of the latter written declaration, or, if Congress is not in session, within twenty-one days after Congress is required to assemble, determines by two-thirds vote of both Houses that the President is unable to discharge the powers and duties of his office, the Vice President shall continue to discharge the same as Acting President; otherwise, the President shall resume the powers and duties of his office.

Amendment XXVI[24]

SECTION 1. The right of citizens of the United States, who are eighteen years of age or older, to vote shall not be denied or abridged by the United States or by any State on account of age.

SECTION 2. The Congress shall have power to enforce this article by appropriate legislation.

Amendment XXVII[25]

No law, varying the compensation for the service of the Senators and Representatives, shall take effect, until an election of Representatives shall have intervened.

---

[22] Passed August 27, 1962. Ratified January 23, 1964.

[23] Passed July 6, 1965. Ratified February 11, 1967.

[24] Passed March 23, 1971. Ratified July 5, 1971.

[25] Passed September 25, 1989. Ratified May 7, 1992.

Admission of States

Order of admission	State	Date of admission	Order of admission	State	Date of admission
1	Delaware	December 7, 1787	26	Michigan	January 26, 1837
2	Pennsylvania	December 12, 1787	27	Florida	March 3, 1845
3	New Jersey	December 18, 1787	28	Texas	December 29, 1845
4	Georgia	January 2, 1788	29	Iowa	December 28, 1846
5	Connecticut	January 9, 1788	30	Wisconsin	May 29, 1848
6	Massachusetts	February 6, 1788	31	California	September 9, 1850
7	Maryland	April 28, 1788	32	Minnesota	May 11, 1858
8	South Carolina	May 23, 1788	33	Oregon	February 14, 1859
9	New Hampshire	June 21, 1788	34	Kansas	January 29, 1861
10	Virginia	June 25, 1788	35	West Virginia	June 20, 1863
11	New York	July 26, 1788	36	Nevada	October 31, 1864
12	North Carolina	November 21, 1789	37	Nebraska	March 1, 1867
13	Rhode Island	May 29, 1790	38	Colorado	August 1, 1876
14	Vermont	March 4, 1791	39	North Dakota	November 2, 1889
15	Kentucky	June 1, 1792	40	South Dakota	November 2, 1889
16	Tennessee	June 1, 1796	41	Montana	November 8, 1889
17	Ohio	March 1, 1803	42	Washington	November 11, 1889
18	Louisiana	April 30, 1812	43	Idaho	July 3, 1890
19	Indiana	December 11, 1816	44	Wyoming	July 10, 1890
20	Mississippi	December 10, 1817	45	Utah	January 4, 1896
21	Illinois	December 3, 1818	46	Oklahoma	November 16, 1907
22	Alabama	December 14, 1819	47	New Mexico	January 6, 1912
23	Maine	March 15, 1820	48	Arizona	February 14, 1912
24	Missouri	August 10, 1821	49	Alaska	January 3, 1959
25	Arkansas	June 15, 1836	50	Hawaii	August 21, 1959

Population of the United States (1790–1996)

Year	Total population (in thousands)	Number per square mile of land area (continental United States)	Year	Total population (in thousands)	Number per square mile of land area (continental United States)
1790	3,929	4.5	1829	12,565	
1791	4,056		1830	12,901	7.4
1792	4,194		1831	13,321	
1793	4,332		1832	13,742	
1794	4,469		1833	14,162	
1795	4,607		1834	14,582	
1796	4,745		1835	15,003	
1797	4,883		1836	15,423	
1798	5,021		1837	15,843	
1799	5,159		1838	16,264	
1800	5,297	6.1	1839	16,684	
1801	5,486		1840	17,120	9.8
1802	5,679		1841	17,733	
1803	5,872		1842	18,345	
1804	5,065		1843	18,957	
1805	6,258		1844	19,569	
1806	6,451		1845	20,182	
1807	6,644		1846	20,794	
1808	6,838		1847	21,406	
1809	7,031		1848	22,018	
1810	7,224	4.3	1849	22,631	
1811	7,460		1850	23,261	7.9
1812	7,700		1851	24,086	
1813	7,939		1852	24,911	
1814	8,179		1853	25,736	
1815	8,419		1854	26,561	
1816	8,659		1855	27,386	
1817	8,899		1856	28,212	
1818	9,139		1857	29,037	
1819	9,379		1858	29,862	
1820	9,618	5.6	1859	30,687	
1821	9,939		1860	31,513	10.6
1822	10,268		1861	32,351	
1823	10,596		1862	33,188	
1824	10,924		1863	34,026	
1825	11,252		1864	34,863	
1826	11,580		1865	35,701	
1827	11,909		1866	36,538	
1828	12,237		1867	37,376	

Figures are from *Historical Statistics of the United States, Colonial Times to 1957* (1961), pp. 7, 8; *Statistical Abstract of the United States: 1974*, p. 5, Census Bureau for 1974 and 1975; and *Statistical Abstract of the United States: 1988*, p. 7.

(continued)

Population of the United States (*continued*) (1790–1996)

Year	Total population (in thousands)	Number per square mile of land area (continental United States)	Year	Total population (in thousands)[1]	Number per square mile of land area (continental United States)
1868	38,213		1907	87,000	
1869	39,051		1908	88,709	
1870	39,905	13.4	1909	90,492	
1871	40,938		1910	92,407	31.0
1872	41,972		1911	93,868	
1873	43,006		1912	95,331	
1874	44,040		1913	97,227	
1875	45,073		1914	99,118	
1876	46,107		1915	100,549	
1877	47,141		1916	101,966	
1878	48,174		1917	103,414	
1879	49,208		1918	104,550	
1880	50,262	16.9	1919	105,063	
1881	51,542		1920	106,466	35.6
1882	52,821		1921	108,541	
1883	54,100		1922	110,055	
1884	55,379		1923	111,950	
1885	56,658		1924	114,113	
1886	57,938		1925	115,832	
1887	59,217		1926	117,399	
1888	60,496		1927	119,038	
1889	61,775		1928	120,501	
1890	63,056	21.2	1929	121,700	
1891	64,361		1930	122,775	41.2
1892	65,666		1931	124,040	
1893	66,970		1932	124,840	
1894	68,275		1933	125,579	
1895	69,580		1934	126,374	
1896	70,885		1935	127,250	
1897	72,189		1936	128,053	
1898	73,494		1937	128,825	
1899	74,799		1938	129,825	
1900	76,094	25.6	1939	130,880	
1901	77,585		1940	131,669	44.2
1902	79,160		1941	133,894	
1903	80,632		1942	135,361	
1904	82,165		1943	137,250	
1905	83,820		1944	138,916	
1906	85,437		1945	140,468	

[1]Figures after 1940 represent total population including armed forces abroad, except in official census years.

Appendix A-17

Year	Total population (in thousands)[1]	Number per square mile of land area (continental United States)	Year	Total population (in thousands)[1]	Number per square mile of land area (continental United States)
1946	141,936		1972	209,896	
1947	144,698		1973	211,909	
1948	147,208		1974	213,854	
1949	149,767		1975	215,973	
1950	150,697	50.7	1976	218,035	
1951	154,878		1977	220,239	
1952	157,553		1978	222,585	
1953	160,184		1979	225,055	
1954	163,026		1980	227,225	64.0
1955	165,931		1981	229,466	
1956	168,903		1982	232,520	
1957	171,984		1983	234,799	
1958	174,882		1984	237,001	
1959	177,830[2]		1985	239,283	
1960	180,671	60.1	1986	241,596	
1961	183,691		1987	234,773	
1962	186,538		1988	245,051	
1963	189,242		1989	247,350	
1964	191,889		1990	250,122	
1965	194,303		1991	254,521	
1966	196,560		1992	245,908	
1967	198,712		1993	257,908	
1968	200,706		1994	261,875	
1969	202,677		1995	263,434	
1970	205,052	57.5	1996	266,096	
1971	207,661		1997	267,744	
			1998	270,299	
			1999	274,114	

[1]Figures after 1940 represent total population including armed forces abroad, except in official census years.

[2]Figures after 1959 include Alaska and Hawaii.

Presidential Elections
(1789–1832)

Year	Number of states	Candidates[1]	Parties	Popular vote	Electoral vote	Percentage of popular vote[2]
1789	11	**George Washington***	**No party designations**		**69**	
		John Adams			34	
		Minor Candidates			35	
1792	15	**George Washington**	**No party designations**		**132**	
		John Adams			77	
		George Clinton			50	
		Minor Candidates			5	
1796	16	**John Adams**	**Federalist**		**71**	
		Thomas Jefferson	Democratic-Republican		68	
		Thomas Pinckney	Federalist		59	
		Aaron Burr	Democratic-Republican		30	
		Minor Candidates			48	
1800	16	**Thomas Jefferson**	**Democratic-Republican**		**73**	
		Aaron Burr	Democratic-Republican		73	
		John Adams	Federalist		65	
		Charles C. Pinckney	Federalist		64	
		John Jay	Federalist		1	
1804	17	**Thomas Jefferson**	**Democratic-Republican**		**162**	
		Charles C. Pinckney	Federalist		14	
1808	17	**James Madison**	**Democratic-Republican**		**122**	
		Charles C. Pinckney	Federalist		47	
		George Clinton	Democratic-Republican		6	
1812	18	**James Madison**	**Democratic-Republican**		**128**	
		DeWitt Clinton	Federalist		89	
1816	19	**James Monroe**	**Democratic-Republican**		**183**	
		Rufus King	Federalist		34	
1820	24	**James Monroe**	**Democratic-Republican**		**231**	
		John Quincy Adams	Independent Republican		1	
1824	24	**John Quincy Adams**	**Democratic-Republican**	**108,740**	**84**	**30.5**
		Andrew Jackson	Democratic-Republican	153,544	99	43.1
		William H. Crawford	Democratic-Republican	46,618	41	13.1
		Henry Clay	Democratic-Republican	47,136	37	13.2
1828	24	**Andrew Jackson**	**Democratic**	**647,286**	**178**	**56.0**
		John Quincy Adams	National Republican	508,064	83	44.0
1832	24	**Andrew Jackson**	**Democratic**	**687,502**	**219**	**55.0**
		Henry Clay	National Republican	530,189	49	42.4
		William Wirt	Anti-Masonic	33,108	7	2.6
		John Floyd	National Republican		11	

[1]Before the passage of the Twelfth Amendment in 1804, the Electoral College voted for two presidential candidates; the runner-up became vice president. Figures are from *Historical Statistics of the United States, Colonial Times to 1957* (1961), pp. 682–83; and the U.S. Department of Justice.

[2]Candidates receiving less than 1 percent of the popular vote have been omitted. For that reason the percentage of popular vote given for any election year may not total 100 percent.

*Note: Boldface indicates the winner of each election.

Presidential Elections
(1836–1888)

Year	Number of states	Candidates	Parties	Popular vote	Electoral vote	Percentage of popular vote[1]
1836	26	**Martin Van Buren**	**Democratic**	**765,483**	**170**	**50.9**
		William H. Harrison	Whig		73	
		Hugh L. White	Whig	739,795	26	
		Daniel Webster	Whig		14	
		W. P. Mangum	Independent		11	
1840	26	**William H. Harrison**	**Whig**	**1,274,624**	**234**	**53.1**
		Martin Van Buren	Democratic	1,127,781	60	46.9
1844	26	**James K. Polk**	**Democratic**	**1,338,464**	**170**	**49.6**
		Henry Clay	Whig	1,300,097	105	48.1
		James G. Birney	Liberty	62,300		2.3
1848	30	**Zachary Taylor**	**Whig**	**1,360,967**	**163**	**47.4**
		Lewis Cass	Democratic	1,222,342	127	42.5
		Martin Van Buren	Free Soil	291,263		10.1
1852	31	**Franklin Pierce**	**Democratic**	**1,601,117**	**254**	**50.9**
		Winfield Scott	Whig	1,385,453	42	44.1
		John P. Hale	Free Soil	155,825		5.0
1856	31	**James Buchanan**	**Democratic**	**1,832,955**	**174**	**45.3**
		John C. Frémont	Republican	1,339,932	114	33.1
		Millard Fillmore	American	871,731	8	21.6
1860	33	**Abraham Lincoln**	**Republican**	**1,865,593**	**180**	**39.8**
		Stephen A. Douglas	Democratic	1,382,713	12	29.5
		John C. Breckinridge	Democratic	848,356	72	18.1
		John Bell	Constitutional Union	592,906	39	12.6
1864	36	**Abraham Lincoln**	**Republican**	**2,206,938**	**212**	**55.0**
		George B. McClellan	Democratic	1,803,787	21	45.0
1868	37	**Ulysses S. Grant**	**Republican**	**3,013,421**	**214**	**52.7**
		Horatio Seymour	Democratic	2,706,829	80	47.3
1872	37	**Ulysses S. Grant**	**Republican**	**3,596,745**	**286**	**55.6**
		Horace Greeley	Democratic	2,843,446	2	43.9
1876	38	**Rutherford B. Hayes**	**Republican**	**4,036,572**	**185**	**48.0**
		Samuel J. Tilden	Democratic	4,284,020	184	51.0
1880	38	**James A. Garfield**	**Republican**	**4,453,295**	**214**	**48.5**
		Winfield S. Hancock	Democratic	4,414,082	155	48.1
		James B. Weaver	Greenback-Labor	308,578		3.4
1884	38	**Grover Cleveland**	**Democratic**	**4,879,507**	**219**	**48.5**
		James G. Blaine	Republican	4,850,293	182	48.2
		Benjamin F. Butler	Greenback-Labor	175,370		1.8
		John P. St. John	Prohibition	150,369		1.5
1888	38	**Benjamin Harrison**	**Republican**	**5,477,129**	**233**	**47.9**
		Grover Cleveland	Democratic	5,537,857	168	48.6
		Clinton B. Fisk	Prohibition	249,506		2.2
		Anson J. Streeter	Union Labor	146,935		1.3

[1]Candidates receiving less than 1 percent of the popular vote have been omitted. For that reason the percentage of popular vote given for any election year may not total 100 percent.

[2]Greeley died shortly after the election; the electors supporting him then divided their votes among minor candidates.

Presidential Elections
(1896–1932)

Year	Number of states	Candidates	Parties	Popular vote	Electoral vote	Percentage of popular vote[1]
1892	44	**Grover Cleveland**	**Democratic**	**5,555,426**	**277**	**46.1**
		Benjamin Harrison	Republican	5,182,690	145	43.0
		James B. Weaver	People's	1,029,846	22	8.5
		John Bidwell	Prohibition	264,133		2.2
1896	45	**William McKinley**	**Republican**	**7,102,246**	**271**	**51.1**
		William J. Bryan	Democratic	6,492,559	176	47.7
1900	45	**William McKinley**	**Republican**	**7,218,491**	**292**	**51.7**
		William J. Bryan	Democratic; Populist	6,356,734	155	45.5
		John C. Wooley	Prohibition	208,914		1.5
1904	45	**Theodore Roosevelt**	**Republican**	**7,628,461**	**336**	**57.4**
		Alton B. Parker	Democratic	5,084,223	140	37.6
		Eugene V. Debs	Socialist	402,283		3.0
		Silas C. Swallow	Prohibition	258,536		1.9
1908	46	**William H. Taft**	**Republican**	**7,675,320**	**321**	**51.6**
		William J. Bryan	Democratic	6,412,294	162	43.1
		Eugene V. Debs	Socialist	420,793		2.8
		Eugene W. Chafin	Prohibition	253,840		1.7
1912	48	**Woodrow Wilson**	**Democratic**	**6,296,547**	**435**	**41.9**
		Theodore Roosevelt	Progressive	4,118,571	88	27.4
		William H. Taft	Republican	3,486,720	8	23.2
		Eugene V. Debs	Socialist	900,672		6.0
		Eugene W. Chafin	Prohibition	206,275		1.4
1916	48	**Woodrow Wilson**	**Democratic**	**9,127,695**	**277**	**49.4**
		Charles E. Hughes	Republican	8,533,507	254	46.2
		A. L. Benson	Socialist	585,113		3.2
		J. Frank Hanly	Prohibition	220,506		1.2
1920	48	**Warren G. Harding**	**Republican**	**16,143,407**	**404**	**60.4**
		James N. Cox	Democratic	9,130,328	127	34.2
		Eugene V. Debs	Socialist	919,799		3.4
		P. P. Christensen	Farmer-Labor	265,411		1.0
1924	48	**Calvin Coolidge**	**Republican**	**15,718,211**	**382**	**54.0**
		John W. Davis	Democratic	8,385,283	136	28.8
		Robert M. La Follette	Progressive	4,831,289	13	16.6
1928	48	**Herbert C. Hoover**	**Republican**	**21,391,993**	**444**	**58.2**
		Alfred E. Smith	Democratic	15,016,169	87	40.9
1932	48	**Franklin D. Roosevelt**	**Democratic**	**22,809,638**	**472**	**57.4**
		Herbert C. Hoover	Republican	15,758,901	59	39.7
		Norman Thomas	Socialist	881,951		2.2

[1]Candidates receiving less than 1 percent of the popular vote have been omitted. For that reason the percentage of popular vote given for any election year may not total 100 percent.

Presidential Elections
(1936–1992)

Year	Number of states	Candidates	Parties	Popular vote	Electoral vote	Percentage of popular vote[1]
1936	48	**Franklin D. Roosevelt**	**Democratic**	**27,752,869**	**523**	**60.8**
		Alfred M. Landon	Republican	16,674,665	8	36.5
		William Lemke	Union	882,479		1.9
1940	48	**Franklin D. Roosevelt**	**Democratic**	**27,307,819**	**449**	**54.8**
		Wendell L. Willkie	Republican	22,321,018	82	44.8
1944	48	**Franklin D. Roosevelt**	**Democratic**	**25,606,585**	**432**	**53.5**
		Thomas E. Dewey	Republican	22,014,745	99	46.0
1948	48	**Harry S Truman**	**Democratic**	**24,105,812**	**303**	**49.5**
		Thomas E. Dewey	Republican	21,970,065	189	45.1
		J. Strom Thurmond	States' Rights	1,169,063	39	2.4
		Henry A. Wallace	Progressive	1,157,172		2.4
1952	48	**Dwight D. Eisenhower**	**Republican**	**33,936,234**	**442**	**55.1**
		Adlai E. Stevenson	Democratic	27,314,992	89	44.4
1956	48	**Dwight D. Eisenhower**	**Republican**	**35,590,472**	**457**	**57.6**
		Adlai E. Stevenson	Democratic	26,022,752	73	42.1
1960	50	**John F. Kennedy**	**Democratic**	**34,227,096**	**303**	**49.9**
		Richard M. Nixon	Republican	34,108,546	219	49.6
1964	50	**Lyndon B. Johnson**	**Democratic**	**43,126,506**	**486**	**61.1**
		Barry M. Goldwater	Republican	27,176,799	52	38.5
1968	50	**Richard M. Nixon**	**Republican**	**31,785,480**	**301**	**43.4**
		Hubert H. Humphrey	Democratic	31,275,165	191	42.7
		George C. Wallace	American Independent	9,906,473	46	13.5
1972	50	**Richard M. Nixon**	**Republican**	**47,169,911**	**520**	**60.7**
		George S. McGovern	Democratic	29,170,383	17	37.5
1976	50	**Jimmy Carter**	**Democratic**	**40,827,394**	**297**	**50.0**
		Gerald R. Ford	Republican	39,145,977	240	47.9
1980	50	**Ronald W. Reagan**	**Republican**	**43,899,248**	**489**	**50.8**
		Jimmy Carter	Democratic	35,481,435	49	41.0
		John B. Anderson	Independent	5,719,437		6.6
		Ed Clark	Libertarian	920,859		1.0
1984	50	**Ronald W. Reagan**	**Republican**	**54,281,858**	**525**	**59.2**
		Walter F. Mondale	Democratic	37,457,215	13	40.8
1988	50	**George H. Bush**	**Republican**	**47,917,341**	**426**	**54**
		Michael Dukakis	Democratic	41,013,030	112	46
1992	50	**William J. Clinton**	**Democratic**	**44,908,254**	**370**	**43.0**
		George H. Bush	Republican	39,102,343	168	37.4
		H. Ross Perot	Independent	19,741,065		18.9
1996	50	**William J. Clinton**	**Democratic**	**47,402,357**	**379**	**49**
		Robert J. Dole	Republican	39,198,755	159	41
		H. Ross Perot	Reform	8,085,402		8

[1]Candidates receiving less than 1 percent of the popular vote have been omitted. For that reason the percentage of popular vote given for any election year may not total 100 percent.

Presidents, Vice Presidents, and Cabinet Members

President	Vice President	Secretary of State	Secretary of Treasury	Secretary of War	Secretary of Navy
George Washington 1789–1797	John Adams 1789–1797	Thomas Jefferson 1789–1794	Alexander Hamilton 1789–1795	Henry Knox 1789–1795	
		Edmund Randolph 1794–1795 Timothy Pickering 1795–1797	Oliver Wolcott 1795–1797	Timothy Pickering 1795–1796 James McHenry 1796–1797	
John Adams 1797–1801	Thomas Jefferson 1797–1801	Timothy Pickering 1797–1800 John Marshall 1800–1801	Oliver Wolcott 1797–1801 Samuel Dexter 1801	James McHenry 1797–1800 Samuel Dexter 1800–1801	Benjamin Stoddert 1798–1801
Thomas Jefferson 1801–1809	Aaron Burr 1801–1805 George Clinton 1805–1809	James Madison 1801–1809	Samuel Dexter 1801 Albert Gallatin 1801–1809	Henry Dearborn 1801–1809	Benjamin Stoddert 1801 Robert Smith 1801–1809
James Madison 1809–1817	George Clinton 1809–1813 Elbridge Gerry 1813–1817	Robert Smith 1809–1811 James Monroe 1811–1817	Albert Gallatin 1809–1814 George Campbell 1814 Alexander Dallas 1814–1816 William Crawford 1816–1817	William Eustis 1809–1813 John Armstrong 1813–1814 James Monroe 1814–1815 William Crawford 1815–1817	Paul Hamilton 1809–1813 William Jones 1813–1814 Benjamin Crowninshield 1814–1817
James Monroe 1817–1825	Daniel D. Tompkins 1817–1825	John Quincy Adams 1817–1825	William Crawford 1817–1825	George Graham 1817 John C. Calhoun 1817–1825	Benjamin Crowninshield 1817–1818 Smith Thompson 1818–1823 Samuel Southard 1823–1825
John Quincy Adams 1825–1829	John C. Calhoun 1825–1829	Henry Clay 1825–1829	Richard Rush 1825–1829	James Barbour 1825–1828 Peter B. Porter 1828–1829	Samuel Southard 1825–1829

Appendix **A-23**

Postmaster General	Attorney General
Samuel Osgood 1789–1791	Edmund Randolph 1789–1794
Timothy Pickering 1791–1795	William Bradford 1794–1795
Joseph Habersham 1795–1797	Charles Lee 1795–1797
Joseph Habersham 1797–1801	Charles Lee 1797–1801
Joseph Habersham 1801 Gideon Granger 1801–1809	Levi Lincoln 1801–1805 John Breckinridge 1805–1807 Caesar Rodney 1807–1809
Gideon Granger 1809–1814 Return Meigs 1814–1817	Caesar Rodney 1809–1811 William Pinkney 1811–1814 Richard Rush 1814–1817
Return Meigs 1817–1823 John McLean 1823–1825	Richard Rush 1817 William Wirt 1817–1825
John McLean 1825–1829	William Wirt 1825–1829

(continued)

Presidents, Vice Presidents, and Cabinet Members (*continued*)

President	Vice President	Secretary of State	Secretary of Treasury	Secretary of War	Secretary of Navy	Postmaster General
Andrew Jackson 1829–1837	John C. Calhoun 1829–1833 Martin Van Buren 1833–1837	Martin Van Buren 1829–1831 Edward Livingston 1831–1833 Louis McLane 1833–1834 John Forsyth 1834–1837	Samuel Ingham 1829–1831 Louis McLane 1831–1833 William Duane 1833 Roger B. Taney 1833–1834 Levi Woodbury 1834–1837	John H. Eaton 1829–1831 Lewis Cass 1831–1837 Benjamin Butler 1837	John Branch 1829–1831 Levi Woodbury 1831–1834 Mahlon Dickerson 1834–1837	William Barry 1829–1835 Amos Kendall 1835–1837
Martin Van Buren 1837–1841	Richard M. Johnson 1837–1841	John Forsyth 1837–1841	Levi Woodbury 1837–1841	Joel R. Poinsett 1837–1841	Mahlon Dickerson 1837–1838 James K. Paulding 1838–1841	Amos Kendall 1837–1840 John M. Niles 1840–1841
William H. Harrison 1841	John Tyler 1841	Daniel Webster 1841	Thomas Ewing 1841	John Bell 1841	George E. Badger 1841	Francis Granger 1841
John Tyler 1841–1845		Daniel Webster 1841–1843 Hugh S. Legaré 1843 Abel P. Upshur 1843–1844 John C. Calhoun 1844–1845	Thomas Ewing 1841 Walter Forward 1841–1843 John C. Spencer 1843–1844 George M. Bibb 1844–1845	John Bell 1841 John C. Spencer 1841–1843 James M. Porter 1843–1844 William Wilkins 1844–1845	George E. Badger 1841 Abel P. Upshur 1841–1843 David Henshaw 1843–1844 Thomas Gilmer 1844 John Y. Mason 1844–1845	Francis Granger 1841 Charles A. Wickliffe 1841–1845
James K. Polk 1845–1849	George M. Dallas 1845–1849	James Buchanan 1845–1849	Robert J. Walker 1845–1849	William L. Marcy 1845–1849	George Bancroft 1845–1846 John Y. Mason 1846–1849	Cave Johnson 1845–1849
Zachary Taylor 1849–1850	Millard Fillmore 1849–1850	John M. Clayton 1849–1850	William M. Meredith 1849–1850	George W. Crawford 1849–1850	William B. Preston 1849–1850	Jacob Collamer 1849–1850
Millard Fillmore 1850–1853		Daniel Webster 1850–1852 Edward Everett 1852–1853	Thomas Corwin 1850–1853	Charles M. Conrad 1850–1853	William A. Graham 1850–1852 John P. Kennedy 1852–1853	Nathan K. Hall 1850–1852 Sam D. Hubbard 1852–1853
Franklin Pierce 1853–1857	William R. King 1853–1857	William L. Marcy 1853–1857	James Guthrie 1853–1857	Jefferson Davis 1853–1857	James C. Dobbin 1853–1857	James Campbell 1853–1857

Attorney General	Secretary of Interior
John M. Berrien 1829–1831 Roger B. Taney 1831–1833 Benjamin Butler 1833–1837	
Benjamin Butler 1837–1838 Felix Grundy 1838–1840 Henry D. Gilpin 1840–1841	
John J. Crittenden 1841	
John J. Crittenden 1841 Hugh S. Legaré 1841–1843 John Nelson 1843–1845	
John Y. Mason 1845–1846 Nathan Clifford 1846–1848 Isaac Toucey 1848–1849	
Reverdy Johnson 1849–1850	Thomas Ewing 1849–1850
John J. Crittenden 1850–1853	Thomas McKennan 1850 A. H. H. Stuart 1850–1853
Caleb Cushing 1853–1857	Robert McClelland 1853–1857

(continued)

Presidents, Vice Presidents, and Cabinet Members *(continued)*

President	Vice President	Secretary of State	Secretary of Treasury	Secretary of War	Secretary of Navy	Postmaster General
James Buchanan 1857–1861	John C. Breckinridge 1857–1861	Lewis Cass 1857–1860 Jeremiah S. Black 1860–1861	Howell Cobb 1857–1860 Philip F. Thomas 1860–1861 John A. Dix 1861	John B. Floyd 1857–1861 Joseph Holt 1861	Isaac Toucey 1857–1861	Aaron V. Brown 1857–1859 Joseph Holt 1859–1861 Horatio King 1861
Abraham Lincoln 1861–1865	Hannibal Hamlin 1861–1865 Andrew Johnson 1865	William H. Seward 1861–1865	Salmon P. Chase 1861–1864 William P. Fessenden 1864–1865 Hugh McCulloch 1865	Simon Cameron 1861–1862 Edwin M. Stanton 1862–1865	Gideon Welles 1861–1865	Horatio King 1861 Montgomery Blair 1861–1864 William Dennison 1864–1865
Andrew Johnson 1865–1869		William H. Seward 1865–1869	Hugh McCulloch 1865–1869	Edwin M. Stanton 1865–1867 Ulysses S. Grant 1867–1868 John M. Schofield 1868–1869	Gideon Welles 1865–1869	William Dennison 1865–1866 Alexander Randall 1866–1869 William M. Evarts 1868–1869
Ulysses S. Grant 1869–1877	Schuyler Colfax 1869–1873 Henry Wilson 1873–1877	Elihu B. Washburne 1869 Hamilton Fish 1869–1877	George S. Boutwell 1869–1873 William A. Richardson 1873–1874 Benjamin H. Bristow 1874–1876 Lot M. Morrill 1876–1877	John A. Rawlins 1869 William T. Sherman 1869 William W. Belknap 1869–1876 Alphonso Taft 1876 James D. Cameron 1876–1877	Adolph E. Borie 1869 George M. Robeson 1869–1877	John A. J. Creswell 1869–1874 James W. Marshall 1874 Marshall Jewell 1874–1876 James N. Tyner 1876–1877
Rutherford B. Hayes 1877–1881	William A. Wheeler 1877–1881	William M. Evarts 1877–1881	John Sherman 1877–1881	George W. McCrary 1877–1879 Alexander Ramsey 1879–1881	R. W. Thompson 1877–1881 Nathan Goff, Jr. 1881	David M. Key 1877–1880 Horace Maynard 1880–1881
James A. Garfield 1881	Chester A. Arthur 1881	James G. Blaine 1881	William Windom 1881	Robert T. Lincoln 1881	William H. Hunt 1881	Thomas L. James 1881
Chester A. Arthur 1881–1885		F. T. Frelinghuysen 1881–1885	Charles J. Folger 1881–1884 Walter Q. Gresham 1884 Hugh McCulloch 1884–1885	Robert T. Lincoln 1881–1885	William E. Chandler 1881–1885	Thomas L. James 1881 Timothy O. Howe 1881–1883 Walter Q. Gresham 1883–1884 Frank Hatton 1884–1885

Attorney General	Secretary of Interior
Jeremiah S. Black 1857–1860 Edwin M. Stanton 1860–1861	Jacob Thompson 1857–1861
Edward Bates 1861–1864 James Speed 1864–1865	Caleb B. Smith 1861–1863 John P. Usher 1863–1865
James Speed 1865–1866 Henry Stanbery 1866–1868 O. H. Browning 1866–1869	John P. Usher 1865 James Harlan 1865–1866
Ebenezer R. Hoar 1869–1870 Amos T. Akerman 1870–1871 G. H. Williams 1871–1875 Edwards Pierrepont 1875–1876 Alphonso Taft 1876–1877	Jacob D. Cox 1869–1870 Columbus Delano 1870–1875 Zachariah Chandler 1875–1877
Charles Devens 1877–1881	Carl Schurz 1877–1881
Wayne MacVeagh 1881	S. J. Kirkwood 1881
B. H. Brewster 1881–1885	Henry M. Teller 1881–1885

(continued)

Presidents, Vice Presidents, and Cabinet Members *(continued)*

President	Vice President	Secretary of State	Secretary of Treasury	Secretary of War	Secretary of Navy	Postmaster General
Grover Cleveland 1885–1889	T. A. Hendricks 1885	Thomas F. Bayard 1885–1889	Daniel Manning 1885–1887 Charles S. Fairchild 1887–1889	William C. Endicott 1885–1889	William C. Whitney 1885–1889	William F. Vilas 1885–1888 Don M. Dickinson 1888–1889
Benjamin Harrison 1889–1893	Levi P. Morton 1889–1893	James G. Blaine 1889–1892 John W. Foster 1892–1893	William Windom 1889–1891 Charles Foster 1892–1893	Redfield Procter 1889–1891 Stephen B. Elkins 1891–1893	Benjamin F. Tracy 1889–1893	John Wanamaker 1889–1893
Grover Cleveland 1893–1897	Adlai E. Stevenson 1893–1897	Walter Q. Gresham 1893–1895 Richard Olney 1895–1897	John G. Carlisle 1893–1897	Daniel S. Lamont 1893–1897	Hilary A. Herbert 1893–1897	Wilson S. Bissel 1893–1895 William L. Wilson 1895–1897
William McKinley 1897–1901	Garret A. Hobart 1897–1899 Theodore Roosevelt 1901	John Sherman 1897–1898 William R. Day 1898 John Hay 1898–1901	Lyman J. Gage 1897–1901	Russell A. Alger 1897–1899 Elihu Root 1899–1901	John D. Long 1897–1901	James A. Gary 1897–1898 Charles E. Smith 1898–1901
Theodore Roosevelt 1901–1909	Charles Fairbanks 1905–1909	John Hay 1901–1905 Elihu Root 1905–1909 Robert Bacon 1909	Lyman J. Gage 1901–1902 Leslie M. Shaw 1902–1907 George B. Cortelyou 1907–1909	Elihu Root 1901–1904 William H. Taft 1904–1908 Luke E. Wright 1908–1909	John D. Long 1901–1902 William H. Moody 1902–1904 Paul Morton 1904–1905 Charles J. Bonaparte 1905–1906 Victor H. Metcalf 1906–1908 T. H. Newberry 1908–1909	Charles E. Smith 1901–1902 Henry C. Payne 1902–1904 Robert J. Wynne 1904–1905 George B. Cortelyou 1905–1907 George von L. Meyer 1907–1909
William H. Taft 1909–1913	James S. Sherman 1909–1913	Philander C. Knox 1909–1913	Franklin MacVeagh 1909–1913	Jacob M. Dickinson 1909–1911 Henry L. Stimson 1911–1913	George von L. Meyer 1909–1913	Frank H. Hitchcock 1909–1913
Woodrow Wilson 1913–1921	Thomas R. Marshall 1913–1921	William J. Bryan 1913–1915 Robert Lansing 1915–1920 Bainbridge Colby 1920–1921	William G. McAdoo 1913–1918 Carter Glass 1918–1920 David F. Houston 1920–1921	Lindley M. Garrison 1913–1916 Newton D. Baker 1916–1921	Josephus Daniels 1913–1921	Albert S. Burleson 1913–1921

Attorney General	Secretary of Interior	Secretary of Agriculture	Secretary of Commerce and Labor	
A. H. Garland 1885–1889	L. Q. C. Lamar 1885–1888 William F. Vilas 1888–1889	Norman J. Colman 1889		
W. H. H. Miller 1889–1893	John W. Noble 1889–1893	Jeremiah M. Rusk 1889–1893		
Richard Olney 1893–1895 Judson Harmon 1895–1897	Hoke Smith 1893–1896 David R. Francis 1895–1897	J. Sterling Morton 1893–1897		
Joseph McKenna 1897–1898 John W. Griggs 1898–1901 Philander C. Knox 1901	Cornelius N. Bliss 1897–1898 E. A. Hitchcock 1898–1901	James Wilson 1897–1901		
Philander C. Knox 1901–1904 William H. Moody 1904–1906 Charles J. Bonaparte 1906–1909	E. A. Hitchcock 1901–1907 James R. Garfield 1907–1909	James Wilson 1901–1909	George B. Cortelyou 1903–1904 Victor H. Metcalf 1904–1906 Oscar S. Straus 1906–1909	
G. W. Wickersham 1909–1913	R. A. Ballinger 1909–1911 Walter L. Fisher 1911–1913	James Wilson 1909–1913	Charles Nagel 1909–1913	

			Secretary of Commerce	Secretary of Labor
J. C. McReynolds 1913–1914 T. W. Gregory 1914–1919 A. Mitchell Palmer 1919–1921	Franklin K. Lane 1913–1920 John B. Payne 1920–1921	David F. Houston 1913–1920 E. T. Meredith 1920–1921	W. C. Redfield 1913–1919 J. W. Alexander 1919–1921	William B. Wilson 1913–1921

(continued)

Presidents, Vice Presidents, and Cabinet Members *(continued)*

President	Vice President	Secretary of State	Secretary of Treasury	Secretary of War	Secretary of Navy	Postmaster General
Warren G. Harding 1921–1923	Calvin Coolidge 1921–1923	Charles E. Hughes 1921–1923	Andrew W. Mellon 1921–1923	John W. Weeks 1921–1923	Edwin Denby 1921–1923	Will H. Hays 1921–1922 Hubert Work 1922–1923 Harry S. New 1923
Calvin Coolidge 1923–1929	Charles G. Dawes 1925–1929	Charles E. Hughes 1923–1925 Frank B. Kellogg 1925–1929	Andrew W. Mellon 1923–1929	John W. Weeks 1923–1925 Dwight F. Davis 1925–1929	Edwin Denby 1923–1924 Curtis D. Wilbur 1924–1929	Harry S. New 1923–1929
Herbert C. Hoover 1929–1933	Charles Curtis 1929–1933	Henry L. Stimson 1929–1933	Andrew W. Mellon 1929–1932 Ogden L. Mills 1932–1933	James W. Good 1929 Patrick J. Hurley 1929–1933	Charles F. Adams 1929–1933	Walter F. Brown 1929–1933
Franklin Delano Roosevelt 1933–1945	John Nance Garner 1933–1941 Henry A. Wallace 1941–1945 Harry S Truman 1945	Cordell Hull 1933–1944 E. R. Stettinius, Jr. 1944–1945	William H. Woodin 1933–1934 Henry Morgenthau, Jr. 1934–1945	George H. Dern 1933–1936 Harry H. Woodring 1936–1940 Henry L. Stimson 1940–1945	Claude A. Swanson 1933–1940 Charles Edison 1940 Frank Knox 1940–1944 James V. Forrestal 1944–1945	James A. Farley 1933–1940 Frank C. Walker 1940–1945
Harry S Truman 1945–1953	Alben W. Barkley 1949–1953	James F. Byrnes 1945–1947 George C. Marshall 1947–1949 Dean G. Acheson 1949–1953	Fred M. Vinson 1945–1946 John W. Snyder 1946–1953	Robert P. Patterson 1945–1947 Kenneth C. Royall 1947	James V. Forrestal 1945–1947	R. E. Hannegan 1945–1947 Jesse M. Donaldson 1947–1953

Secretary of Defense

James V. Forrestal 1947–1949
Louis A. Johnson 1949–1950
George C. Marshall 1950–1951
Robert A. Lovett 1951–1953

President	Vice President	Secretary of State	Secretary of Treasury	Secretary of Defense		Postmaster General
Dwight D. Eisenhower 1953–1961	Richard M. Nixon 1953–1961	John Foster Dulles 1953–1959 Christian A. Herter 1957–1961	George M. Humphrey 1953–1957 Robert B. Anderson 1957–1961	Charles E. Wilson 1953–1957 Neil H. McElroy 1957–1961 Thomas S. Gates 1959–1961		A. E. Summerfield 1953–1961

Attorney General	Secretary of Interior	Secretary of Agriculture	Secretary of Commerce	Secretary of Labor	Secretary of Health, Education, and Welfare
H. M. Daugherty 1921–1923	Albert B. Fall 1921–1923 Hubert Work 1923	Henry C. Wallace 1921–1923	Herbert C. Hoover	James J. Davis 1921–1923	
H. M. Daugherty 1923–1924 Harlan F. Stone 1924–1925 John G. Sargent 1925–1929	Hubert Work 1923–1928 Roy O. West 1928–1929	Henry C. Wallace 1923–1924 Howard M. Gore 1924–1925 W. J. Jardine 1925–1929	Herbert C. Hoover 1923–1928 William F. Whiting 1928–1929	James J. Davis 1923–1929	
J. D. Mitchell 1929–1933	Ray L. Wilbur 1929–1933	Arthur M. Hyde 1929–1933 Roy D. Chapin 1932–1933	Robert P. Lamont 1929–1932 William N. Doak 1930–1933	James J. Davis 1929–1930	
H. S. Cummings 1933–1939 Frank Murphy 1939–1940 Robert Jackson 1940–1941 Francis Biddel 1941–1945	Harold L. Ickes 1933–1945	Henry A. Wallace 1933–1940 Claude R. Wickard 1940–1945	Daniel C. Roper 1933–1939 Harry L. Hopkins 1939–1940 Jesse Jones 1940–1945 Henry A. Wallace 1945	Frances Perkins 1933–1945	
Tom C. Clark 1945–1949 J. H. McGrath 1949–1952 James P. McGranery 1952–1953	Harold L. Ickes 1945–1946 Julius A. Krug 1946–1949 Oscar L. Chapman 1949–1953	C. P. Anderson 1945–1948 C. F. Brannan 1948–1953	W. A. Harriman 1946–1948 Charles Sawyer 1948–1953	L. B. Schwellenbach 1945–1948 Maurice J. Tobin 1948–1953	
H. Brownell, Jr. 1953–1957 William P. Rogers 1957–1961	Douglas McKay 1953–1956 Fred Seaton 1956–1961	Ezra T. Benson 1953–1961	Sinclair Weeks 1953–1958 Lewis L. Strauss 1958–1961	Martin P. Durkin 1953 James P. Mitchell 1953–1961	Oveta Culp Hobby 1953–1955 Marion B. Folsom 1955–1958 Arthur S. Flemming 1958–1961

(continued)

Presidents, Vice Presidents, and Cabinet Members *(continued)*

President	Vice President	Secretary of State	Secretary of Treasury	Secretary of Defense	Postmaster General[1]	Attorney General
John F. Kennedy 1961–1963	Lyndon B. Johnson 1961–1963	Dean Rusk 1961–1963	C. Douglas Dillon 1961–1963	Robert S. McNamara 1961–1963	J. Edward Day 1961–1963 John A. Gronouski 1961–1963	Robert F. Kennedy 1961–1963
Lyndon B. Johnson 1963–1969	Hubert H. Humphrey 1965–1969	Dean Rusk 1963–1969	C. Douglas Dillon 1963–1965 Henry H. Fowler 1965–1968 Joseph W. Barr 1968–1969	Robert S. McNamara 1963–1968 Clark M. Clifford 1968–1969	John A. Gronouski 1963–1965 Lawrence F. O'Brien 1965–1968 W. Marvin Watson 1968–1969	Robert F. Kennedy 1963–1965 N. deB. Katzenbach 1965–1967 Ramsey Clark 1967–1969
Richard M. Nixon 1969–1974	Spiro T. Agnew 1969–1973 Gerald R. Ford 1973–1974	William P. Rogers 1969–1973 Henry A. Kissinger 1973–1974	David M. Kennedy 1969–1970 John B. Connally 1970–1972 George P. Schultz 1972–1974 William E. Simon 1974	Melvin R. Laird 1969–1973 Elliot L. Richardson 1973 James R. Schlesinger 1973–1974	Winton M. Blount 1969–1971	John M. Mitchell 1969–1972 Richard G. Kleindienst 1972–1973 Elliot L. Richardson 1973 William B. Saxbe 1974
Gerald R. Ford 1974–1977	Nelson A. Rockefeller 1974–1977	Henry A. Kissinger 1974–1977	William E. Simon 1974–1977	James R. Schlesinger 1974–1975 Donald H. Rumsfeld 1975–1977		William B. Saxbe 1974–1975 Edward H. Levi 1975–1977

[1]On July 1, 1971, the Post Office became an independent agency. After that date, the Postmaster General was no longer a member of the Cabinet.

Secretary of Interior	Secretary of Agriculture	Secretary of Commerce	Secretary of Labor	Secretary of Health, Education, and Welfare	Secretary of Housing and Urban Development	Secretary of Transportation
Stewart L. Udall 1961–1963	Orville L. Freeman 1961–1963	Luther H. Hodges 1961–1963	Arthur J. Goldberg 1961–1963 W. Willard Wirtz 1962–1963	A. H. Ribicoff 1961–1963 Anthony J. Celebrezze 1962–1963		
Stewart L. Udall 1963–1969	Orville L. Freeman 1963–1969	Luther H. Hodges 1963–1965 John T. Connor 1965–1967 Alexander B. Trowbridge 1967–1968 C. R. Smith 1968–1969	W. Willard Wirtz 1963–1969	Anthony J. Celebrezze 1963–1965 John W. Gardner 1965–1968 Wilbur J. Cohen 1968–1969	Robert C. Weaver 1966–1968 Robert C. Wood 1968–1969	Alan S. Boyd 1966–1969
Walter J. Hickel 1969–1971 Rogers C. B. Morton 1971–1974	Clifford M. Hardin 1969–1971 Earl L. Butz 1971–1974	Maurice H. Stans 1969–1972 Peter G. Peterson 1972 Frederick B. Dent 1972–1974	George P. Shultz 1969–1970 James D. Hodgson 1970–1973 Peter J. Brennan 1973–1974	Robert H. Finch 1969–1970 Elliot L. Richardson 1970–1973 Caspar W. Weinberger 1973–1974	George W. Romney 1969–1973 James T. Lynn 1973–1974	John A. Volpe 1969–1973 Claude S. Brinegar 1973–1974
Rogers C. B. Morton 1974–1975 Stanley K. Hathaway 1975 Thomas D. Kleppe 1975–1977	Earl L. Butz 1974–1976	Frederick B. Dent 1974–1975 Rogers C. B. Morton 1975 Elliot L. Richardson 1975–1977	Peter J. Brennan 1974–1975 John T. Dunlop 1975–1976 W. J. Usery 1976–1977	Caspar W. Weinberger 1974–1975 Forrest D. Matthews 1975–1977	James T. Lynn 1974–1975 Carla A. Hills 1975–1977	Claude S. Brinegar 1974–1975 William T. Coleman 1975–1977

(continued)

Presidents, Vice Presidents, and Cabinet Members *(continued)*

President	Vice President	Secretary of State	Secretary of Treasury	Secretary of Defense	Attorney General	Secretary of Interior	Secretary of Agriculture
Jimmy Carter 1977–1981	Walter F. Mondale 1977–1981	Cyrus R. Vance 1977–1980 Edmund S. Muskie 1980–1981	W. Michael Blumenthal 1977–1979 G. William Miller 1979–1981	Harold Brown 1977–1981	Griffin Bell 1977–1979 Benjamin R. Civiletti 1979–1981	Cecil D. Andrus 1977–1981	Robert Bergland 1977–1981
Ronald W. Reagan 1981–1989	George H. Bush 1981–1989	Alexander M. Haig, Jr. 1981–1982 George P. Shultz 1982–1989	Donald T. Regan 1981–1985 James A. Baker 1985–1988 Nicholas F. Brady 1988–1989	Caspar W. Weinberger 1981–1987 Frank C. Carlucci 1987–1989	William French Smith 1981–1985 Edwin Meese 1985–1988 Richard Thornburgh 1988–1989	James G. Watt 1981–1983 William P. Clark 1983–1985 Donald P. Hodel 1985–1989	John R. Block 1981–1986 Richard E. Lyng 1986–1989
George H. Bush 1989–1992	J. Danforth Quayle 1989–1992	James A. Baker 1989–1992 Lawrence S. Eagleburger 1992	Nicholas F. Brady 1989–1992	Richard Cheney 1989–1992	Richard Thornburgh 1989–1990 William Barr 1990–1992	Manuel Lujan 1989–1992	Clayton Yeutter 1989–1990 Edward Madigan 1990–1992
William Clinton 1993–	Albert Gore 1993–	Warren M. Christopher 1993–1996 Madeleine K Albright 1997–	Lloyd Bentsen 1993–1994 Robert E. Rubin 1994–1999 Lawrence H. Summers 1999–	Les Aspin 1993–1994 William J. Perry 1994–1996 William S. Cohen 1997–	Janet Reno 1993–	Bruce Babbitt 1993–	Mike Espy 1993–1994 Dan Glickman 1994–

Appendix **A-35**

Secretary of Commerce	Secretary of Labor	Secretary of Health, Education, and Welfare	Secretary of Housing and Urban Development	Secretary of Transportation	Secretary of Energy	Secretary of Veterans' Affairs
Juanita Kreps 1977–1981	F. Ray Marshall 1977–1981	Joseph Califano 1977–1979 Patricia Roberts Harris 1979–1980	Patricia Roberts Harris 1977–1979 Moon Landrieu 1979–1981	Brock Adams 1977–1979 Neil E. Goldschmidt 1979–1981	James R. Schlesinger 1977–1979 Charles W. Duncan, Jr. 1979–1981	

		Secretary of Health and Human Services	Secretary of Education			
		Patricia Roberts Harris 1980–1981	Shirley M. Hufstedler 1980–1981			
Malcolm Baldridge 1981–1987 C. William Verity, Jr. 1987–1989	Raymond J. Donovan 1981–1985 William E. Brock 1985–1987 Ann Dore McLaughlin 1987–1989	Richard S. Schweiker 1981–1983 Margaret M. Heckler 1983–1985 Otis R. Bowen 1985–1989	Terrell H. Bell 1981–1985 William J. Bennett 1985–1988 Lauro Fred Cavazos 1988–1989	Drew Lewis 1981–1983 Elizabeth H. Dole 1983–1987 James H. Burnley 1987–1989	James B. Edwards 1981–1982 Donald P. Hodel 1982–1985 John S. Harrington 1985–1989	Samuel R. Pierce, Jr. 1981–1989
Robert Mosbacher 1989–1991 Barbara Franklin 1991–1992	Elizabeth H. Dole 1989–1992 Lynn Martin 1992	Louis Sullivan 1989–1992	Lamar Alexander 1990–1992	Jack Kemp 1989–1992 1990–1992	Samuel Skinner 1989–1990 Andrew Card	James Watkins 1989–1992	Edward J. Derwinski 1989–1992
Ronald H. Brown 1993–1996 Mickey Kantor 1996–1997 William M. Daley 1997–	Robert B. Reich 1993–1997 Alexis M. Herman 1997–	Donna E. Shalala 1993–	Richard W. Riley 1993–	Henry G. Cisneros 1993–1997 Andrew M. Cuomo 1997–	Frederico F. Peña 1993–1997 Rodney Slater 1997–	Hazel O'Leary 1993–1997 Frederico F. Peña 1997–1998 Bill I. Richardson 1998–	Jesse Brown 1993–1998 Togo D. West, Jr. 1998–

Justices of the U.S. Supreme Court

Chief Justices appear in bold type

	Term of Service	Years of Service	Appointed by
John Jay	1789–1795	5	Washington
John Rutledge	1789–1791	1	Washington
William Cushing	1789–1810	20	Washington
James Wilson	1789–1798	8	Washington
John Blair	1789–1796	6	Washington
Robert H. Harrison	1789–1790	—	Washington
James Iredell	1790–1799	9	Washington
Thomas Johnson	1791–1793	1	Washington
William Paterson	1793–1806	13	Washington
John Rutledge[1]	1795	—	Washington
Samuel Chase	1796–1811	15	Washington
Oliver Ellsworth	1796–1800	4	Washington
Bushrod Washington	1798–1829	31	J. Adams
Alfred Moore	1799–1804	4	J. Adams
John Marshall	1801–1835	34	J. Adams
William Johnson	1804–1834	30	Jefferson
H. Brockholst Livingston	1806–1823	16	Jefferson
Thomas Todd	1807–1826	18	Jefferson
Joseph Story	1811–1845	33	Madison
Gabriel Duval	1811–1835	24	Madison
Smith Thompson	1823–1843	20	Monroe
Robert Trimble	1826–1828	2	J. Q. Adams
John McLean	1829–1861	32	Jackson
Henry Baldwin	1830–1844	14	Jackson
James M. Wayne	1835–1867	32	Jackson
Roger B. Taney	1836–1864	28	Jackson
Philip P. Barbour	1836–1841	4	Jackson
John Catron	1837–1865	28	Van Buren
John McKinley	1837–1852	15	Van Buren
Peter V. Daniel	1841–1860	19	Van Buren
Samuel Nelson	1845–1872	27	Tyler
Levi Woodbury	1845–1851	5	Polk
Robert C. Grier	1846–1870	23	Polk
Benjamin R. Curtis	1851–1857	6	Fillmore
John A. Campbell	1853–1861	8	Pierce
Nathan Clifford	1858–1881	23	Buchanan
Noah H. Swayne	1862–1881	18	Lincoln
Samuel F. Miller	1862–1890	28	Lincoln
David Davis	1862–1877	14	Lincoln
Stephen J. Field	1863–1897	34	Lincoln
Salmon P. Chase	1864–1873	8	Lincoln
William Strong	1870–1880	10	Grant
Joseph P. Bradley	1870–1892	22	Grant
Ward Hunt	1873–1882	9	Grant

[1]Acting Chief Justice; Senate refused to confirm appointment.

Chief Justices appear in bold type

	Term of Service	Years of Service	Appointed by
Morrison R. Waite	1874–1888	14	Grant
John M. Harlan	1877–1911	34	Hayes
William B. Woods	1880–1887	7	Hayes
Stanley Matthews	1881–1889	7	Garfield
Horace Gray	1882–1902	20	Arthur
Samuel Blatchford	1882–1893	11	Arthur
Lucius Q. C. Lamar	1888–1893	5	Cleveland
Melville W. Fuller	1888–1910	21	Cleveland
David J. Brewer	1890–1910	20	B. Harrison
Henry B. Brown	1890–1906	16	B. Harrison
George Shiras, Jr.	1892–1903	10	B. Harrison
Howell E. Jackson	1893–1895	2	B. Harrison
Edward D. White	1894–1910	16	Cleveland
Rufus W. Peckham	1895–1909	14	Cleveland
Joseph McKenna	1898–1925	26	McKinley
Oliver W. Holmes, Jr.	1902–1932	30	T. Roosevelt
William R. Day	1903–1922	19	T. Roosevelt
William H. Moody	1906–1910	3	T. Roosevelt
Horace H. Lurton	1910–1914	4	Taft
Charles E. Hughes	1910–1916	5	Taft
Willis Van Devanter	1911–1937	26	Taft
Joseph R. Lamar	1911–1916	5	Taft
Edward D. White	1910–1921	11	Taft
Mahlon Pitney	1912–1922	10	Taft
James C. McReynolds	1914–1941	26	Wilson
Louis D. Brandeis	1916–1939	22	Wilson
John H. Clarke	1916–1922	6	Wilson
William H. Taft	1921–1930	8	Harding
George Sutherland	1922–1938	15	Harding
Pierce Butler	1922–1939	16	Harding
Edward T. Sanford	1923–1930	7	Harding
Harlan F. Stone	1925–1941	16	Coolidge
Charles E. Hughes	1930–1941	11	Hoover
Owen J. Roberts	1930–1945	15	Hoover
Benjamin N. Cardozo	1932–1938	6	Hoover
Hugo L. Black	1937–1971	34	F. Roosevelt
Stanley F. Reed	1938–1957	19	F. Roosevelt
Felix Frankfurter	1939–1962	23	F. Roosevelt
William O. Douglas	1939–1975	36	F. Roosevelt
Frank Murphy	1940–1949	9	F. Roosevelt
Harlan F. Stone	1941–1946	5	F. Roosevelt
James F. Byrnes	1941–1942	1	F. Roosevelt
Robert H. Jackson	1941–1954	13	F. Roosevelt
Wiley B. Rutledge	1943–1949	6	F. Roosevelt

(continued)

Justices of the U.S. Supreme Court *(continued)*

Chief Justices appear in bold type

	Term of Service	Years of Service	Appointed by
Harold H. Burton	1945–1958	13	Truman
Fred M. Vinson	1946–1953	7	Truman
Tom C. Clark	1949–1967	18	Truman
Sherman Minton	1949–1956	7	Truman
Earl Warren	1953–1969	16	Eisenhower
John Marshall Harlan	1955–1971	16	Eisenhower
William J. Brennan, Jr.	1956–1990	34	Eisenhower
Charles E. Whittaker	1957–1962	5	Eisenhower
Potter Stewart	1958–1981	23	Eisenhower
Byron R. White	1962–1993	31	Kennedy
Arthur J. Goldberg	1962–1965	3	Kennedy
Abe Fortas	1965–1969	4	Johnson
Thurgood Marshall	1967–1991	24	Johnson
Warren E. Burger	1969–1986	18	Nixon
Harry A. Blackmun	1970–1994	24	Nixon
Lewis F. Powell, Jr.	1971–1987	15	Nixon
William H. Rehnquist[2]	1971–	—	Nixon
John P. Stevens III	1975–	—	Ford
Sandra Day O'Connor	1981–	—	Reagan
Antonin Scalia	1986–	—	Reagan
Anthony M. Kennedy	1988–	—	Reagan
David Souter	1990–	—	Bush
Clarence Thomas	1991–	—	Bush
Ruth Bader Ginsburg	1993–	—	Clinton
Stephen G. Breyer	1994–	—	Clinton

[2]Chief Justice from 1986 (Reagan administration).

Political Party Affiliations in Congress and the Presidency, 1789–1995*

Congress	Year	House* Majority Party	House* Principal Minority Party	House* Other (except Vacancies)	Senate* Majority Party	Senate* Principal Minority Party	Senate* Other (except Vacancies)	President and Party
1st	1789–1791	Ad-38	Op-26	—	Ad-17	Op-9	—	F (Washington)
2nd	1791–1793	F-37	DR-33	—	F-16	DR-13	—	F (Washington)
3rd	1793–1795	DR-57	F-48	—	F-17	DR-13	—	F (Washington)
4th	1795–1797	F-54	DR-52	—	F-19	DR-13	—	F (Washington)
5th	1797–1799	F-58	DR-48	—	F-20	DR-12	—	F (John Adams)
6th	1799–1801	F-64	DR-42	—	F-19	DR-13	—	F (John Adams)
7th	1801–1803	DR-69	F-36	—	DR-18	F-13	—	DR (Jefferson)
8th	1803–1805	DR-102	F-39	—	DR-25	F-9	—	DR (Jefferson)
9th	1805–1807	DR-116	F-25	—	DR-27	F-7	—	DR (Jefferson)
10th	1807–1809	DR-118	F-24	—	DR-28	F-6	—	DR (Jefferson)
11th	1809–1811	DR-94	F-48	—	DR-28	F-6	—	DR (Madison)
12th	1811–1813	DR-108	F-36	—	DR-30	F-6	—	DR (Madison)
13th	1813–1815	DR-112	F-68	—	DR-27	F-9	—	DR (Madison)
14th	1815–1817	DR-117	F-65	—	DR-25	F-11	—	DR (Madison)
15th	1817–1819	DR-141	F-42	—	DR-34	F-10	—	DR (Monroe)
16th	1819–1821	DR-156	F-27	—	DR-35	F-7	—	DR (Monroe)
17th	1821–1823	DR-158	F-25	—	DR-44	F-4	—	DR (Monroe)
18th	1823–1825	DR-187	F-26	—	DR-44	F-4	—	DR (Monroe)
19th	1825–1827	Ad-105	J-97	—	Ad-26	J-20	—	C (J. Q. Adams)
20th	1827–1829	J-119	Ad-94	—	J-28	Ad-20	—	C (J. Q. Adams)
21st	1829–1831	D-139	NR-74	—	D-26	NR-22	—	D (Jackson)
22nd	1831–1833	D-141	NR-58	14	D-25	NR-21	2	D (Jackson)
23rd	1833–1835	D-147	AM-53	60	D-20	NR-20	8	D (Jackson)
24th	1835–1837	D-145	W-98	—	D-27	W-25	—	D (Jackson)
25th	1837–1839	D-108	W-107	24	D-30	W-18	4	D (Van Buren)
26th	1839–1841	D-124	W-118	—	D-28	W-22	—	D (Van Buren)
27th	1841–1843	W-133	D-102	6	W-28	D-22	2	W (Harrison) W (Tyler)
28th	1843–1845	D-142	W-79	1	W-28	D-25	1	W (Tyler)
29th	1845–1847	D-143	W-77	6	D-31	W-25	—	D (Polk)
30th	1847–1849	W-115	D-108	4	D-36	W-21	1	D (Polk)
31st	1849–1851	D-112	W-109	9	D-35	W-25	2	W (Taylor) W (Fillmore)
32nd	1851–1853	D-140	W-88	5	D-35	W-24	3	W (Fillmore)
33rd	1853–1855	D-159	W-71	4	D-38	W-22	2	D (Pierce)
34th	1855–1857	R-108	D-83	43	D-40	R-15	5	D (Pierce)
35th	1857–1859	D-118	R-92	26	D-36	R-20	8	D (Buchanan)
36th	1859–1861	R-114	D-92	31	D-36	R-26	4	D (Buchanan)
37th	1861–1863	R-105	D-43	30	R-31	D-10	8	R (Lincoln)
38th	1863–1865	R-102	D-75	9	R-36	D-9	5	R (Lincoln)
39th	1865–1867	U-149	D-42	—	U-42	D-10	—	R (Lincoln) R (Johnson)
40th	1867–1869	R-143	D-49	—	R-42	D-11	—	R (Johnson)
41st	1869–1871	R-149	D-63	—	R-56	D-11	—	R (Grant)
42nd	1871–1873	R-134	D-104	5	R-52	D-17	5	R (Grant)
43rd	1873–1875	R-194	D-92	14	R-49	D-19	5	R (Grant)
44th	1875–1877	D-169	R-109	14	R-45	D-29	2	R (Grant)
45th	1877–1879	D-153	R-140	—	R-39	D-36	1	R (Hayes)
46th	1879–1881	D-149	R-130	14	D-42	R-33	1	R (Hayes)
47th	1881–1883	R-147	D-135	11	R-37	D-37	1	R (Garfield) R (Arthur)
48th	1883–1885	D-197	R-118	10	R-38	D-36	2	R (Arthur)

*Letter symbols for political parties. Ad—Administration; AM—Anti-Masonic; C—Coalition; D—Democratic; DR—Democratic-Republican; F—Federalist; J—Jacksonian; NR—National-Republican; Op—Opposition; R—Republican; U—Unionist; W—Whig.

Source: *Historical Statistics of the United States: Colonial Times to the Present*, Various eds. Washington, D.C.: GOP.

A-39

Political Party Affiliations in Congress and the Presidency, 1789–1995 (continued)

Congress	Year	House* Majority Party	Principal Minority Party	Other (except Vacancies)	Senate* Majority Party	Principal Minority Party	Other (except Vacancies)	President and Party
49th	1885–1887	D-183	R-140	2	R-43	D-34	—	D (Cleveland)
50th	1887–1889	D-169	R-152	4	R-39	D-37	—	D (Cleveland)
51st	1889–1891	R-166	D-159	—	R-39	D-37	—	R (B. Harrison)
52nd	1891–1893	D-235	R-88	9	R-47	D-39	2	R (B. Harrison)
53rd	1893–1895	D-218	R-127	11	D-44	R-38	3	D (Cleveland)
54th	1895–1897	R-244	D-105	7	R-43	D-39	6	D (Cleveland)
55th	1897–1899	R-204	D-113	40	R-47	D-34	7	R (McKinley)
56th	1899–1901	R-185	D-163	9	R-53	D-26	8	R (McKinley)
57th	1901–1903	R-197	D-151	9	R-55	D-31	4	R (McKinley) R (T. Roosevelt)
58th	1903–1905	R-208	D-178	—	R-57	D-33	—	R (T. Roosevelt)
59th	1905–1907	R-250	D-136	—	R-57	D-33	—	R (T. Roosevelt)
60th	1907–1909	R-222	D-164	—	R-61	D-31	—	R (T. Roosevelt)
61st	1909–1911	R-219	D-172	—	R-61	D-32	—	R (Taft)
62nd	1911–1913	D-228	R-161	1	R-51	D-41	—	R (Taft)
63rd	1913–1915	D-291	R-127	17	D-51	R-44	1	D (Wilson)
64th	1915–1917	D-230	R-196	9	D-56	R-40	—	D (Wilson)
65th	1917–1919	D-216	R-210	6	D-53	R-42	—	D (Wilson)
66th	1919–1921	D-240	D-190	3	R-49	D-47	—	D (Wilson)
67th	1921–1923	R-301	D-131	1	R-59	D-37	—	R (Harding)
68th	1923–1925	R-225	D-205	5	R-51	D-43	2	R (Coolidge)
69th	1925–1927	R-247	D-183	4	R-56	D-39	1	R (Coolidge)
70th	1927–1929	R-237	D-195	3	R-49	D-46	1	R (Coolidge)
71st	1929–1931	R-267	D-167	1	R-56	D-39	1	R (Hoover)
72nd	1931–1933	D-220	R-214	1	R-48	D-47	1	R (Hoover)
73rd	1933–1935	D-310	R-117	5	D-60	R-35	1	D (F. Roosevelt)
74th	1935–1937	D-319	R-103	10	D-69	R-25	2	D (F. Roosevelt)
75th	1937–1939	D-331	R-89	13	D-76	R-16	4	D (F. Roosevelt)
76th	1939–1941	D-261	R-164	4	D-69	R-23	4	D (F. Roosevelt)
77th	1941–1943	D-268	R-162	5	D-66	R-28	2	D (F. Roosevelt)
78th	1943–1945	D-218	R-208	4	D-58	R-37	1	D (F. Roosevelt)
79th	1945–1947	D-242	R-190	2	D-56	R-38	1	D (Truman)
80th	1947–1949	R-245	D-188	1	R-51	D-45	—	D (Truman)
81st	1949–1951	D-263	R-171	1	D-54	R-42	—	D (Truman)
82nd	1951–1953	D-243	R-199	1	D-49	R-47	—	D (Truman)
83rd	1953–1955	R-221	D-211	1	R-48	D-47	1	R (Eisenhower)
84th	1955–1957	D-232	R-203	—	D-48	R-47	1	R (Eisenhower)
85th	1957–1959	D-233	R-200	—	D-49	R-47	—	R (Eisenhower)
86th	1959–1961	D-283	R-153	—	D-64	R-34	—	R (Eisenhower)
87th	1961–1963	D-263	R-174	—	D-65	R-35	—	D (Kennedy)
88th	1963–1965	D-258	R-177	—	D-67	R-33	—	D (Kennedy) D (Johnson)
89th	1965–1967	D-295	R-140	—	D-68	R-32	—	D (Johnson)
90th	1967–1969	D-247	R-187	1	D-64	R-36	—	D (Johnson)
91st	1969–1971	D-243	R-192	—	D-58	R-42	—	R (Nixon)
92nd	1971–1973	D-255	R-180	—	D-54	R-44	2	R (Nixon)
93rd	1973–1975	D-242	R-192	1	D-56	R-42	2	R (Nixon, Ford)
94th	1975–1977	D-291	R-144	—	D-61	R-37	2	R (Ford)
95th	1977–1979	D-292	R-143	—	D-61	R-38	1	D (Carter)
96th	1979–1981	D-277	R-158	—	D-58	R-41	1	D (Carter)
97th	1981–1983	D-242	R-192	—	R-54	D-45	1	R (Reagan)
98th	1983–1985	D-266	R-167	2	R-55	D-45	—	R (Reagan)
99th	1985–1987	D-252	R-183	—	R-53	D-47	—	R (Reagan)
100th	1987–1989	D-258	R-177	—	D-55	R-45	—	R (Reagan)
101st	1989–1991	D-262	R-173	—	D-57	R-43	—	R (Bush)
102nd	1991–1993	D-267	R-167	1	D-57	R-43	—	R (Bush)
103rd	1993–1995	D-256	R-178	1	D-56	R-44	—	D (Clinton)
104th	1995–1997	R-230	D-204	1	R-52	D-48	—	D (Clinton)
105th	1997–1999	R-228	D-206	1	R-55	D-45	—	D (Clinton)
106th	1999–2001	R-223	D-211	1	R-55	D-45	—	D (Clinton)

CREDITS

Chapter 25
Reproduced from the Collections of the Library of Congress, **476;** Reproduced from the Collections of the Library of Congress, **479;** Reproduced from the Collections of the Library of Congress, **480;** The Valentine Museum, **483;** North Wind Picture Archives, **485;** Reproduced from the Collections of the Library of Congress, **488** left; Reproduced from the Collections of the Library of Congress, **488** right; Culver Pictures, Inc., **492** bottom; Culver Pictures, Inc., **492** top.

Chapter 26
Harcourt Picture Collection, **496;** University of Hartford Collection, **501** bottom; The Smithsonian Institution, Negative #46685D, **501** top; Keystone-Mast Collection, UCR / California Museum of Photography. University of California, Riverside, **503;** Culver Pictures, Inc., **508;** Reproduced from the Collections of the Library of Congress, **509;** Culver Pictures, Inc., **514.**

Chapter 27
Culver Pictures, Inc., **518;** #CN312, University of Oregon Library, **522;** U.S. Dept. of the Interior, National Park Service, Edison National Historic Site. Photo taken by Matthew Brady, 1878, **523;** #X462, Southern Pacific Transporation Company, **531;** Culver Pictures, Inc., **534;** Culver Pictures, Inc., **536.**

Chapter 28
Photograph by Byron. The Byron Collection, Museum of the City of New York, **540;** Reproduced from the Collections of the Library of Congress, **543;** North Wind Picture Archives, **545;** Courtesy of The New-York Historical Society, New York City, **547;** North Wind Picture Archives, **548;** Photograph by Bryon, The Byron Collection, Museum of the City of New York, **553;** Keystone-Mast Collection, UCR / California Museum of Photography. University of California, Riverside, **555;** The Granger Collection, **556;** The Preservation Society of Newport County, Newport, RI, **557.**

Chapter 29
Reproduced from the Collections of the Library of Congress, **560;** Culver Pictures, Inc., **563;** Reproduced from the Collections of the Library of Congress, **565;** #RiisEE, photograph by Lewis Hine. The Jacob A. Riis Collections, Museum of the City of New York, **566;** Reproduced from the Collections of the Library of Congress, **569;** AP / Wide World Photos, **575;** San Francisco: Chinatown; Chinese Presbyterian Girls Home: Stellman Collection. California History Section, California State Library, **579.**

Chapter 30
Corbis / Bettmann, **582;** National Archives, **586;** Print Archives, Museum of the City of New York, **587;** Chicago Historical Society, **592;** Keystone-Mast Collection, UCR / California Museum of Photography. University of California, Riverside, **593;** Reproduced from the Collections of the Library of Congress, **594;** Reproduced from the Collections of the Library of Congress, **595;** Photograph by Jacob A. Riis, The Jacob A. Riis Collection, Museum of the City of New York, **597.**

Chapter 31
Courtesy of the American Museum of Natural History, New York. neg. #127375, **600;** Reproduced from the Collections of the Library of Congress, **607;** Oklahoma Historical Society, **608;** Smithsonian Institution, Bureau of American Ethnology, **610;** Reproduced from the Collections of the Library of Congress, **611;** Swift & Company, Chicago, Ill., **613;** AP / Wide World Photos, **616;** Corbis / Bettmann, **618.**

Chapter 32
National Archives, **620;** #B983-1048, Solomon D. Butcher Collections, Nebraska State Historical Society, **625;** Reproduced from the Collections of the Library of Congress, **626;** Reproduced from the Collections of the Library of Congress, **627;** AP / Wide World Photos, **632;** Corbis / Bettmann, **634;** Reproduced from the Collections of the Library of Congress, **637.**

Chapter 33
Reproduced from the Collections of the Library of Congress; #27184-3986, **640;** North Wind Picture Archives, **643;** Reproduced from the Collections of the Library of Congress, **645;** U.S. War Department General Staff, photo #165-UM-26 in the National Archives, **648;** The New York Public Library, **653;** National Park Service, Sagamore Hill National Historic Site. 0654; Hawaii State Archives, **656;** UPI / Corbis–Bettmann, **660.**

Chapter 34
Harvard Historical Society, **662;** North Wind Picture Archives, **665;** Reproduced from the Collections of the Library of Congress, **666;** The Smithsonian Institution, Neg. #73628, **667;** AP / Wide World Photos, 668; The American Agriculturist; April, 1877, **670;** Reproduced from the Collections of the Library of Congress, **673;** Corbis, **675;** Print Archives, Museum of the City of New York, **677;** Corbis / Bettmann, **679.**

Chapter 35
The Kansas State Historical Society, Topeka, Kansas, **682;** AP / Wide World Photos, **686;** Corbis / UPI-Bettmann, **689;** Corbis / UPI-Bettmann, **691;** #2730C75, Tamiment Library, New York University, **695;** Reproduced from the Collections of the Library of Congress, **697;** Providence Public Library, **698.**

Chapter 36
Corbis / Bettmann, **702;** The Granger Collection, New York City, **705;** North Wind Picture Archives, **706;** Corbis / Bettmann, **709;** The Smithsonian Institution, **711;** AP / Wide World Photos, **712;** Reproduced from the Collections of the Library of Congress, **715.**

Chapter 37
National Archives, **720;** Corbis / Bettmann, **725;** Corbis / Bettmann, **727;** North Wind Picture Archives, **728;** Corbis / Bettmann, **731;** U.S. War Department General Staff photo #165-WW-165-1 in the National Archives, **734;** The

C-1

C-2 Credits

New York Public Library, **736;** Reproduced from the Collections of the Library of Congress; #43025/1, **737.**

Chapter 38
U.S. War Department General Staff photo #165-WW-240F1 in the National Archives, **742;** Corbis / Bettmann, **744;** #165-WW-127-8, in the National Archives, **748;** #11-SC-35757 in the National Archives, **749;** Photo no. 165-WW-164B-4 in the National Archives, **751;** U.S. Signal Corps photo #111-SC8523 in the National Archives, **753;** #158964 U.S. Army Photo, **757;** AP/ Wide World Photos, **759.**

Chapter 39
Corbis / Bettmann, **762;** Reproduced from the Collections of the Library of Congress; #33809-26, **765;** Corbis / Bettmann, **769;** Corbis / UPI-Bettmann, **772;** Corbis / UPI-Bettmann, **774;** Corbis / UPI-Bettmann, **776;** AP / Wide World Photos, **777;** AP / Wide World Photos, **779.**

Chapter 40
Culver Pictures, Inc., **782;** AP / Wide World Photos, **785;** Corbis / UPI-Bettmann, **786;** Corbis / Bettmann, **789;** Corbis / Bettmann, **791;** Corbis / Bettmann, **793;** Courtesy of Sears, Roebuck & Company, **794;** Corbis / UPI-Bettmann, **798.**

Chapter 41
Exhibit 133, in the National Archives, **800;** © Radio Times Hulton Picture Library, London. Liaison Agency, Inc., **803;** Corbis / UPI-Bettmann, **805;** Corbis / UPI-Bettmann, **807;** AP / Wide World Photos, **809;** John Springer / Corbis–Bettmann, **811.**

Chapter 42
Franklin D. Roosevelt Library / The New Yorker, **816;** AP / Wide World Photos, **820;** Corbis / UPI-Bettmann,

822; AP / Wide World Photos, **824;** Tennessee Valley Authority, **827;** Corbis / Bettmann–UPI, **830;** Ebony Magazine, **832;** National Guard, **834.**

Chapter 43
Reproduced from the Collections of the Library of Congress, **836;** AP / Wide World Photos, **839;** Corbis / UPI-Bettmann, **843;** U.S. Army Photograph, **844;** Corbis / UPI-Bettmann, **848;** Corbis / UPI-Bettmann, **850;** AP / Wide World Photos, **852;** #69023-2, Kaiser Graphic Arts, **854.**

Chapter 44
The National Archives, **858;** AP / Wide World Photos, **861;** AP / Wide World Photos, **865;** U.S. Army Photograph, **869;** U.S. Army Photograph, **872;** U.S. Navy Photo in the National Archives, **874;** U.S. Army Photo, **877.**

Chapter 45
U.S. Army Photograph, **880;** Margaret Bourke-White. Life Magazine © Time, Inc., **883;** Corbis / Bettmann, **888;** Corbis / UPI-Bettmann, **891;** AP / Wide World Photos, **894;** Corbis / UPI-Bettmann, **898;** AP / Wide World Photos, **900.**

Chapter 46
#7663, Carnegie Library, Pittsburgh, **902;** AP / Wide World Photos, **905;** AP / Wide World Photos, **906;** Corbis / UPI-Bettmann, **909;** Corbis / UPI-Bettmann, **915;** AP / Wide World Photos, **917;** Corbis / UPI-Bettmann, **919.**

Chapter 47
Corbis / UPI-Bettmann, **922;** AP / Wide World Photos, **930;** AP / Wide World Photos, **933;** U.S. Army Photograph, photo by I. C. Rapoport, **934;** AP / Wide World

Photos, **936;** Corbis / UPI-Bettmann, **938;** AP / Wide World Photos, **940;** CBS, **941.**

Chapter 48
Gino Beghe, **944;** Corbis / Bettmann, **948;** AP / Wide World Photos, **952;** AP / Wide World Photos, **954;** AP / Wide World Photos, **957;** AP / Wide World Photos, **961;** Corbis / UPI-Bettmann, **962;** Corbis / UPI-Bettmann, **965.**

Chapter 49
Official White House Photo, **968;** Official White House Photo, **971;** AP / Wide World Photos, **973;** AP / Wide World Photos, **975;** Corbis / Bettmann–UPI, **976;** AP / Wide World Photos, **979;** AP / Wide World Photos, **982;** AP / Wide World Photos, **984;** AP / Wide World Photos, **987.**

Chapter 50
The White House / David Hume Kennerly, **992;** AP / Wide World Photos, **995;** AP / Wide World Photos, **998;** AP / Wide World Photos, **999;** AP / Wide World Photos, **1001;** AP / Wide World Photos, **1003;** Reuter / Corbis–Bettmann, **1006;** AP / Wide World Photos, **1007;** AP / Wide World Photos, **1009.**

Chapter 51
AP / Wide World Photos, **1012;** AP / Wide World Photos, **1015;** AP / Wide World Photos, **1018;** © Jeff Markowitz / Sygma, **1019;** AP / Wide World Photos, **1020;** © Les Stone / Sygma, **1022;** AP / Wide World Photos, **1023;** © B. Kraft / Sygma, **1024;** AP / Wide World Photos, **1025;** AP / Wide World Photos, **1027;** AP / Wide World Photos, **1028;** AP / Wide World Photos, **1029;** AP / Wide World Photos, **1030;** AP / Wide World Photos, **1032;** AP / Wide World Photos, **1036;** © Tannenbaum / Sygma, **1037.**

INDEX

Page numbers in italics refer to illustrations, maps, and photographs.

AAA. *See* Agricultural Adjustment Act (AAA)
ABC, 812
Abilene, Kan., 613–614
Abortion, 1008, 1033, 1035
Acheson, Dean, 892–893, 897, 939
ACLU. *See* American Civil Liberties Union (ACLU)
"Acres of Diamonds," 554
Adams, Brooks, 641
Adams, Henry, 497
Adams, Sherman, 904, 971
Adamson Act, 719
Addams, Jane, 585, 587, 668, 685–686, *686*, 687
Adventures of Huckleberry Finn (Twain), 673
Adventures of Tom Sawyer (Twain), 673
Advertising, 793–795, *793*, 908, 910, 911, 916
AEC. *See* Atomic Energy Commission (AEC)
Affirmative action, 971–972, 1008, 1025, 1036–1037
Afghanistan, 987, 1001
AFL, 572–573, 695, 746–747, 832
Africa
    European colonies in, 647
    Liberia, 647
    Libya, 1001–1002, 1037
    Somalia famine, 1015–1016
    South Africa, 1001
    in World War II, 844, 866–867
African Americans, use of term, 960. *See also* Blacks
Afrika Korps, 866–867
Agent Orange, 976
Agnew, Spiro T., 971, 973, 981
Agricultural Adjustment Act (AAA), 825
Agricultural Wheel, 630
Agriculture. *See also* Food; and specific crops
    acres of land under cultivation, 622, *623*
    chronology on, 638
    co-op movement and, 630–631
    crop production statistics, 622
    and debt bondage of farmers, 627–629
    deflation and farmers in late nineteenth century, 511
    in early twentieth century, 792, 795
    economic difficulties in late nineteenth century, 625–626
    farm machinery, 624–625, *626*
    farmers' grievances against railroads, 542–546
    during Great Depression, 802–803, 808
    in Great Plains, 624, *625*, 626
    irrigation for, 622–624
    in late nineteenth century, *620*, 621–638
    map of, *623*
    money question and, 631–634
    New Deal and, 820, 825
    overproduction as problem in, 631
    population of rural areas, 520, 590, 925
    Populists and, 634–638
    protest and organization by farmers, 542–546, 630–631, 634
    T. Roosevelt's support for family farm, 709
    in South, 626–629
    stereotype of farmers as "hayseeds," 629–630
    subsidy programs for, 808, 925
    tenants and sharecroppers in South, 626–629, *627*
    in twentieth century, 925
    Wilson's program for, 719
    during World War I, 746
Agriculture Department, U.S., 690, 709, 896
Aguinaldo, Emilio, 657
Aidid, Mohammed Farah, 1016
AIDS, 988, 1033
Aiken, George, 974
Air brake for railroad trains, 524–525, 528
Air force
    during Reagan administration, 1003
    in World War I, 730–731, 745, 788
    in World War II, 789, 852, 866
Airline deregulation, 999
Airplanes, 730–731, 745, 788–789, 855
Alabama
    Montgomery bus boycott, 919, 949

readmission of, during Reconstruction, 485
Selma civil rights march, *948*
Alaska, 617, 646, 647
Albanian Kosovars, 1017, *1018*
Albert of Monaco, Prince, 555
Albright, Madeleine, 1028
Alcohol
    Belmont's wine budget, 551
    consumption of, 777
    death rate from alcoholism, 777
    Hayes White House and, 504
    "jake walking" and, 777
    in 1950s, 912
    progressivism and, 699
    prohibition of, 699, 749, 775–777, 784, 792
    temperance movement and, 699
    whiskey distilling trust, 548
Aldrich, Thomas Bailey, 584
Alexander, Grover Cleveland, 764
Alger, Horatio, 554, 970
"Alice Blue Gown," 678
Allen, Frederick Lewis, 797, 926
Allende, Salvador, 648, 979
Alliance for Progress, 938
Altgeld, John Peter, 567
Alzheimer's disease, 996
Amazon.com, 664
America. *See* Canada; Latin America; and specific U.S. states
America First Committee, 789, 847–848
"America the Beautiful," 672, 753
American (James), 673
American Anti-Imperialist League, 655
American Association of Retired Persons, 1021
American Civil Liberties Union (ACLU), 752, 771–772, 780, 1005
American Communist party, 770, 771, 807–808, 897–898
American Federation of Labor (AFL), 572–573, 695, 746–747, 832
American Historical Association, 649
American Legion, 809
American Liberty League, 826
American Medical Association, 908
American Protective Association (APA), 577
American Protective League, 753
American Railway Union (ARU), 567–568
American Telephone and Telegraph Company, 521, 524, 678, 797
American Tobacco Company, 548
American Woman Suffrage Association, 668, 669
"Amos 'n' Andy," 812–813, 829
Amusement parks, 676–677, *677*, 716–717, 910
Anarchists, 550–551, 658
Anderson, John, 994
Andrew, John A., 484
Andrews, Samuel, 537, 538
Anglo-Saxonism, 648, 649, 655
Angola, 979
Animals
    bison, 605, *608*
    cattle, 606–607, *607*, 611–615, *612*, *613*
    deer, 709
    elk, 709
    hogs, 622, 808
    horses, 596–597, 604
    protection of wild animals, 709
    wild turkeys, 709
Anson, Adrian "Cap," 680
Anthony, Susan B., 696, 697
Antin, Mary, 561, 573–574
Antisemitism, 778, 842
Antitrust activities. *See* Trusts
APA. *See* American Protective Association (APA)
Apache, 603, 610
Apartheid in South Africa, 1001
Appalachia, 826, 936
Appeal to Reason, 689
Aquino, Corazón, 1003
Arab-Israeli conflicts, 978, 986, *987*, 989
Aristide, Jean-Bertrand, 1016
Arizona, *600*, 617

Arkansas
    desegregation of Little Rock schools, 918–919
    dust storms in, 804
    readmission of, during Reconstruction, 485
"Arkies," 804
Armour, Philip D., 562
Army. *See* Military
Army-Navy stores, 884
Around the World in Eighty Days (Verne), 649, 668–669
Arthur, Chester A., 498, 501–502, 505, 506–507, 595
ARU. *See* American Railway Union (ARU)
Ashmun Institute, 672
Asia. *See* specific countries
Asian Americans, 1038. *See also* Chinese immigrants and Chinese Americans; Japanese immigrants and Japanese Americans
Assassinations
    of Ceausescu, 1005
    of Garfield, 505, *508*
    of John Kennedy, 941–942
    of Robert Kennedy, 963–964
    of King, 920, 960, 963
    of Lincoln, 942
    of McKinley, 657–658
Assimilation, 585–587
Astor, Mrs., 704, 828
Atchison, Topeka, and Santa Fe railroad, 532
Atlanta, Ga., 949
Atlanta Compromise, 672
Atlantic Charter, 847, 884
Atlantic Monthly, 551, 673, 674, 677
Atomic bomb, 859, 875–877, *877*, *880*, 882, 888, 926
Atomic Energy Commission (AEC), 925
Audubon Society, 1000
Austria-Hungary, 576, 724, *726*
Automobiles and automobile industry, 685, 764, *782*, 790, 791, 792, 794–795, *805*, 832, 833, 912–914, *913*, 916, 987, 1018
Avertising, 908
Avery, Sewell L., 853
Aviation. *See* Airplanes

B&O Railroad, 547
Babcock, Orville E., 491
Baby boom and baby boomers, 914, 1031
Baer, George F., 705
Baker, Gloria "Mimi," 829
Baker, James, 1006, 1007
Baker, Ray Stannard, 687, 688
Baker, Russell, 1008
Baker Island, 655
Baker v. Carr, 951
Bakke case, 1036
Bakunin, Mikhail, 550
Baldwin, Roger, 752
Ballinger, Richard A., 712
Baltimore, 596
Baltimore and Ohio railroad, 547
Banks and banking
    deregulation in 1980s, 1000
    Federal Reserve Banks, 718
    during Great Depression, 803
    New Deal and, 820
    railroads and, 546–547
    robberies of banks, 809
    and war debts after World War I, 787, 790
Baptists, 554
Barbed wire, 624
Barbie dolls, 908
Barker, "Ma," 809
Barnard College, 671
Barnett, Ross, 937
Barrow, Clyde, 809, *809*
Barton, Bruce, 795
Baruch, Bernard, 618, 745, 746, 854, 886
Baseball, 670, 679–680, 764, 766–767, 803
Basketball, 679
Bataan Death March, 860–861
Bates, Katharine Lee, 583, 672
Battles. *See* specific wars and battles
Bay of Pigs, 939
Beard, Charles A., 545, 848

I-1

I-2 Index

Beard, Mary, 545
Beatniks, 916–917, *917*
Beatty, Warren, 1030
Begin, Menachem, 986, *987*
Belknap, William W., 491
Bell, Alexander Graham, 521–522, 577, 678
Bellamy, Edward, 549–550
Belmont, August, 510, 544, 551, 580
Benjamin, Judah P., 580
Bennett, Tony, 910
Benson, Ezra Taft, 924, 925
Benteen, Frederick, 605
Bentsen, Lloyd, 1005
Berger, Victor L., 550, 692–693, 695, 696, 750
Berkeley, Busby, 810
Berle, Milton, 909
Berlin, Irving, 672
Berlin Wall, 939, 1005, *1006*
Bernstein, Carl, 981
Berwind, E. J., 556
Bessemer, Henry, 533
Bethlehem Steel, 770
Bethune, Mary McLeod, 831, *832*, 917
Beveridge, Albert J., 641, 655, 686
Bible, 778, 780, 912, 958
Bicycles, *634*, 678
Big band music, 810, 910
Big business. *See* Business
Bill of Rights, U.S., A-9 to A-10
Billy the Kid, 616
Birmingham, Ala., 803
Birth control, 988, 1032
Birth of a Nation, 775
Birth rates, 914, 1033. *See also* Population
Bismarck, Otto von, 977
Bisno, Abraham, 589
Bison, 605, *608*
Black codes, 482
Black Friday, 491
Black nationalism, 774–775, 1037
Black Panther Party for Self-Defense, 960
Black power movement, 960–961
Black separatism, 960–961
Blackmun, Harry A., 972
Blacks. *See also* Civil rights movement
    and "Amos 'n' Andy" program, 812–813
    in cities, 590
    as cowboys, 615
    in Democratic party, 831
    education of, *483*, *555*, 672, *673*, 918–920, 950
    employment of, 566–567
    as "Exodusters" in Kansas, 624
    Freedmen's Bureau for, 482
    freedmen during Reconstruction, *476*, 478–490
    during Great Depression, 802
    higher education for, *555*, 672, *673*
    life expectancy of, 664
    lynching of, 664, 747, 774, 917
    migration to cities, 747
    in military, 687, 747, *748*, 774
    nationalism of, in early twentieth century, 774–775
    New Deal and, 831
    in 1950s, 917–920
    in 1990s, 1037
    in political office during Reconstruction, 487–490
    population of, 1038
    in Republican party, 481, 486, 644, 646, 831
    in Spanish-American War, 651
    in sports, 680–681
    as tenant farmers and sharecroppers, 626–627, *627*
    violent death among young black males, 1034
    voting rights for, 484, 947, 949
    in World War I, 747, *748*, 774
    during World War II, 855
Blackwell, Antoinette, 671
Blackwell, Elizabeth, 671
Blaine, James G., 504–505, 507–509, *508*, 511
Bland, Richard "Silver Dick," 633
Bland-Allison Bill, 633
Block, Herbert, 898
Bloviation, 760, 765
Bly, Nellie, 649, 650, 668–669, *668*
Boats. *See* Ships and boats

Bodmer, Karl, 604
Bogart, Humphrey, 961
Bok, Edward, 674
Boland law, 1002
Bolsheviks, 739, 882–883
Bomb shelters, 882
Bombs. *See* Atomic bomb
Bond, Julian, 949, *952*
Boni de Castellane, Countess, 556
Bonner, Robert, 793
Bonney, William "Billy the Kid," 616
Bonus Expeditionary Force, 808–809
Book publishing, 787
Boorstin, Daniel, 588, 788
Bootleggers, 775–776
Borah, William E., 692–694, 735, 744
Bork, Robert, 997
Bosnia, 1017
Boston
    immigrants in, 585, 596
    police strike in, 770
    poverty in, 596
    settlement house in, 587
Boston College, 672
Boulder Dam, 806
Bount, James H., 656
"Bourbons," 489, 500–501
Bow, Clara, 764
Boxer Rebellion, 657, 745
Boxing, 680–681, 764
Boy Scouts, 850–851
Bradley, Bill, 1028, *1029*
Bradley, Omar, 867, 881
Brandeis, Louis D., 685, 718
Brennan, William, 711
Brest-Litovsk Treaty, 739
Brezhnev, Leonid, 978, 997
Briand, Aristide, 790
Bricker, John, 896
Bridges, 594–595, *595*
Brinksmanship, 931
Bristow, Benjamin, 491
Britain. *See* Great Britain
British immigrants, 577, 578, 773, 1038
Brooklyn Bridge, 594–595, *595*
Brotherhood of Sleeping Car Porters, 855
Browder, Earl, 897
Brown, Hubert Geroid "H. Rap," 960
Brown, Jerry, 1008
Brown University, 553
Brown v. *Board of Education of Topeka*, 918, 950
Brownsville, Tex., 687
Bruce, Blanche K., 488, *488*, 490
Bryan, William Jennings
    Chautauqua lectures by, 675
    on Cleveland, 637
    "Cross of Gold" speech by, 643
    death of, 779–780
    and evolution trial, 779–780, *779*
    on farms, 622
    imperialism and, 655, 657
    peace efforts of, 790
    photographs of, *643*, *779*
    as presidential candidate, 544, 642–646, *646*, 657, 710, 714, 980
    retirement of, 796
    as secretary of state, 717, 722
    Spanish-American War and, 650
Bryce, James Lord, 969
Bryn Mawr College, 671
Brzezinski, Zbigniew, 986–987
Buchanan, Patrick, 1008, 1023, 1028, 1030, 1036
Buddhism, 916
Budget, balanced, 994, 999
Budget deficit, 998–999, 1030
Buffalo. *See* Bison
Bulge, Battle of, 870–871
Bull Moose party, 713–714, 733
Bunau-Varilla, Philippe, 659–660
Bundy, McGeorge, 937
Buntline, Ned, 615
Bunyan, John, 689
Burford, Ann, 1000

Burger, Warren, 951, 972, *998*
Burgess, John W., 648
Burke, E. A., 487
Burke-Wadsworth Act, 846
Burleson, Albert S., 750
Burrage, Albert C., 555
Bush, George W., 1028–1029, *1030*
Bush, George W. H., 764, 976, *992*, 994, 1004–1009, *1006*, 1031
Business. *See also* Industry and industrialization
    advertising by, 793–795, *793*
    CEO salaries, 1031
    chain stores, 794
    consumer borrowing, 792–793
    corporate mergers and takeovers, 1000, 1031
    corporate structure of, 535–536
    culture of, in 1920s, 795–796
    Fourteenth Amendment and, 535–536
    "horizontal integration" of, 537
    Jesus as advertising man, 795
    in late nineteenth century, 533–538, 542–549
    New Deal and, 826
    office work for women, 678–679, *679*
    prayer of businessman, 794
    and prosperity of 1920s, 791–798
    regulation of railroads and trusts, 542–549
    scientific management and, 687
    taxes on corporations, 786, 787
    "vertical integration" of, 534–535
    World War II and, 853
Butler, Benjamin F., 511, 633
Butler, Jim, 617
Butler, Smedley, 659
Byrd, Richard A., 788, 789
Byrnes, James F., 854, 876, 883

Cabinet members. *See also* specific persons
    list of, A-22 to A-35
Cagney, James, 810
Calamity Jane, 616
Calhoun, John C., 716
California. *See also* Los Angeles; San Francisco
    agriculture in, 622–623
    boundary between Mexico and, *1012*
    California Civil Rights Initiative (CCRI) in, 1037
    Chinese immigrants in, 525, 578–579
    during Great Depression, 804, 830
    and Japanese Americans during World War II, 864–865
    Japanese immigrants in, 723
    population of, 855
California Civil Rights Initiative (CCRI), 1037
Call of the Wild (London), 674
Cambodia, 974–975, 985
Camden, John Newlon, 538
Camelot, 935
Cameron, Donaldina, *579*
Camp David Accords, 986, *987*, 994
Campbell, Ben Nighthorse, 1020
Canada
    gold in, 646
    NAFTA and, 1017
    NATO and, 888
    Taft on trade with, 712
Candler, Asa G., 707
Cannary, Martha (Calamity Jane), 616
Cannon, James, 792
Cannon, Joseph, 712, *712*
Capitalism. *See* Business
Capone, Alphonse "Al," 776–777, *777*
Capra, Frank, 810
Cardozo, Benjamin, 580
Carmichael, Stokely, 960
Carnegie, Andrew, 533–535, 536, 552, 555, *555*, 562, 567, 577, 675, 745
Carnegie Institute of Technology, 671
Carnegie libraries, 675
Carnegie Steel, 534–535
Carole Lombard, *811*
Carpetbaggers, 487
Carranza, Venustiano, 723–724
Carter, Billy, 989
Carter, Jimmy, 764, 985–989, *992*, 994, 1003, 1031

Carter, Lillian, 989
Carter, Rosalyn, 985
Carter Family, 810
Carver, George Washington, 672
Casals, Pablo, 935
Castro, Fidel, 939, 979
Catholic University of America, 672
Catholicism
  higher education and, 672
  immigrant aid institutions and, 586–587
  of Irish immigrants, 577–578
  of Kennedy, 934
  Knights of Labor and, 571–572, 576
  in 1980s, 988
  prejudice against, 584
  Prohibition and, 776
  of Alfred E. Smith, 785, 792
Catlin, George, 604, 609
Catt, Carrie Chapman, 668, 669, 696, 697, *697*, 748–749
Cattle and cattle industry, 606–607, *607*, 611–615, *612*, *613*
Cavalry, 608–609, 651, 724
Cavell, Edith, 737
CBS, 812, 1031, *1032*
CCC. *See* Civilian Conservation Corps (CCC)
Ceausescu, Nicolae, 1005
Censorship of movies, 778
Census Bureau, 602, 649. *See also* Population
Centennial Exposition (1876), 520, 521, 716
Central Intelligence Agency (CIA), 930, 938, 939
Central Pacific Railroad, 530–531, *531*, 542
Century of Dishonor (Jackson), 609
Cermak, Anton, 818
Chain stores, 794
Chambers, Whittaker, 896
Chaplin, Charlie, 752, 764
Charitable giving, 1033. *See also* Philanthropy
Chase, Salmon B., 485
Chautauqua, 675–676
Chavez, Cesar, 963
Chayefsky, Paddy, 909
Chew, Lee, 578
Cheyenne Indians, 609
Chiang Kai-shek, 839, 848, 871, 875, 892–893, 931
Chiang, Madame, 892
Chicago
  cleanup of streets in, 983
  gangsters in, 776–777
  Gold Coast in, 556
  Great Depression in, 802, 803
  Haymarket riot in, 550–551, 572
  Hull House in, 585, 587, 686
  immigrants in, 585, 596
  libraries in, 675
  livestock industry in, 526, 614
  "Memorial Day Massacre" in, 833
  political machine in, 512, 513, 515
  population of, 589, 591
  poverty in, 596
  prostitution in, 698
Child labor, 564–565, 686
Children
  immigrant children in cities, 597–598
  infant mortality, 664
  in labor force, 564–565, 686
  in 1950s, 912, 914–915, *915*, 916
  polio vaccine for, 924
  television and, 910–911
  in Vietnam War, *973*
Chile, 648, 979
China
  Boxer Rebellion in, 657, 745
  Communism in, 892–893, 931, 1005
  Dulles's policy toward, 931
  Japan's aggression against, 839–840, 841
  Nixon-Kissinger policy toward, 977–978
  Nixon's trip to, 978, *979*
  nuclear test ban and, 940
  Open Door policy and, 657, 658, 839, 849
  T. Roosevelt and, 658
  F. Roosevelt's policy toward, 839–840
  Tiananmen Square demonstration, 1005

trade between U.S. and, 647, 657
  Truman's containment policy for, 892–893
  Vietnam War and, 956
  Wilson's policy on, 722
  in World War II, 871, 875
China Lobby, 892–893, 954–955
China Syndrome, 989
Chinese immigrants and Chinese Americans, 489, 525, 531, *531*, 573, 578–579, *579*, *586*, 591, 773, 864
Chisholm Trail, 606, 613
Chlorophyll products, 908
Cholera, 596
Christianity. *See* Religion
Church of Jesus Christ of the Latter-Day Saints. *See* Mormons
Churches. *See* Religion; and specific churches
Churchill, Winston, 844, 846, 847, *848*, 856, 860, 866, 868, 871, *872*, 876, 883–885
Chute, Martha A., 650
CIA, 930, 938, 939
Cigarette smoking, 628–629, 851. *See also* Tobacco
Cincinnati, 526
CIO, 832
Cities. *See also* specific cities and towns
  blacks in, 590
  bridges and, 594–595, *595*
  buildings in, 593–594
  chronology on, 598
  cow towns, 613–614
  crime and vice in, 597–598
  crowding in, 595–596
  culture of, 598
  evils of city life, 595–598
  growth of, 587–595
  health problems in, 596
  immigrants in, 584–587
  kickbacks and sandbagging in, 512–514
  in late nineteenth century, 584–598
  maps of, *590*
  as metropolis, 590–591
  migration from rural areas to, 590, 747
  mining camps and cities, 617–618, *618*
  political machines in, 512–516
  and politics in late nineteenth century, 512–516
  population of, 588–591
  progressivism and municipal government, 687–688, 690
  sanitation in, 596–597
  settlement houses in, 585, 587
  skyscrapers in, 594, *594*
  slums of, 551, *582*, 595–598
  suburbs and, *902*, 911–916, 928–929
  transportation within, 591–593, *592*, *593*
  walking in, 591
Citizenship for immigrants, 515
Civil disobedience, 919
Civil Rights Act of 1875, 493
Civil Rights Act of 1964, 941, 946, 950
Civil rights movement
  black separatism and, 960–961
  Civil Rights Act of 1964, 941, 950
  demonstrations in 1960s, 959
  under Eisenhower administration, 917–920
  "freedom riders," 920, 937
  Freedom Summer, 947–948
  during Johnson administration, 946–949, 952–953
  during Kennedy administration, 936–937
  March on Washington (1963), 937, *938*
  in 1950s, 917–920
  school desegregation, 917, 918–920, 937
  Selma, Ala., march, *948*
  during Truman administration, 889–890, 917
  violence and, 920, 937, 948, 960
  Voting Rights Act of 1965, 947, 949, 950
Civil Service, 505–506, 507
Civil War, 502–504, 511
Civil Works Administration (CWA), 821–822
Civilian Conservation Corps (CCC), 821
Clanton family, 615
Clark, Champ, 714
Clark, Maurice, 537, 538
Clay, Henry, 980

Clayton Antitrust Act of 1914, 718
Clean Water Act, 1000
Clemenceau, Georges, 757, *757*
Clemens, Samuel Langhorne. *See* Twain, Mark
Clerical workers, 678–679, *679*
Cleveland, Grover
  on Confederate battle flags, 502
  gold standard and, 636–637
  Harrison compared with, *501*
  Hawaii annexation and, 656
  portrait of, *509*
  presidency of, 498, 502, 505, 510, 546, 549, 567, 637–638, 656
  in presidential election of 1884, 505, 508–509, 980
  in presidential election of 1888, 980
  in presidential election of 1892, *499*, 635, 980
  unpopularity of, 637–638
Cleveland, Ohio, 688
Clifford, Clark, 891
Clinton, Bill
  domestic policies of, 1019–1023, 1037
  foreign policy of, 1015–1018, 1028
  impeachment of, 486, 1026–1028
  photograph of, *1015*, *1019*, *1028*
  presidential appointments of, 1024–1025
  in presidential election of 1992, 1008
  in presidential election of 1996, 1023–1024
  prosperity during presidency of, 1014, 1031
  sexual behavior of, 1026, 1036
  Whitewater and, 1025–1026
Clinton, Hillary Rodham, 819, 1019–1020, *1020*, 1024, 1025–1026, 1028
Clothing
  Army-Navy stores, 884
  of Beatniks, 916
  black power movement and, 960
  of cowboys, 613
  in 1950s, 906–907, *906*
  ready-made clothing, 588–589
  of wealthy in late nineteenth century, 557–558
Coal mining, 521, *560*, 564, 568, 577, 695, 705, *706*, 795
Cobb, Ty, 767
Coca-Cola Company, 629, 707, 708
Cocaine, 674, 708, 1033
Cochran, Elizabeth. *See* Bly, Nellie
Cody, William F. "Buffalo Bill," 605, 616, 650
Cohan, George M., 740
Cohn, Roy, 898
Coins. *See* Money
Cold War. *See also* Vietnam War
  Bay of Pigs, 939
  beginnings of, 882–888
  Berlin Wall, 939, 1005
  brinksmanship and massive retaliation, 931
  Carter administration and, 986–987
  chronology on, 901
  containment in China, 892–893
  Cuban missile crisis, 939–940
  détente policy, 977–979, 986–987, 1003
  Dulles and, 927–931
  Eisenhower administration and, 925–932
  end of, 1005–1006, *1007*
  "hot line" between White House and Kremlin, 940
  "iron curtain" speech of Churchill, 885
  Kennedy administration and, 937–940
  "kitchen debates" and, 927, *930*
  Korean War and, 893–896, *895*, 899, 900
  loyalty oaths in U.S., 896
  McCarthyism and, 897–898, *898*
  and Nixon-Kissinger foreign policy, 977–979
  during Reagan administration, 997, 1001–1004
  roots of Soviet-American animosity, 882–884
  U-2 incident, 932, *933*
  Vienna Summit (1961), 939
Colfax, Schuyler, 491
College of William and Mary, 671
Colleges and universities. *See* Higher education; and specific colleges and universities
Collier's, 688, 712
Colombia, 659–660
Colorado, 617, 633
Colored Farmers' National Alliance, 630, 634–635

I-4 Index

Colosimo, "Big Jim," 777
Columbia University, 648, 672, 814, 899, 961
Comintern, 771
Comiskey, Charles A., 766–767
Committee on Public Information (CPI), 752
Committee to Re-elect the President (CREEP), 980
Commons, John Rogers, 691
Communism and anti-Communism. *See also* American
  Communist party; Cold War; Soviet Union
  anti-Communism in U.S. in early twentieth
    century, 770–711
  Chinese Communism, 892–893, 1005
  collapse of Communism, 1005–1006, *1007*
  containment policy against Communism, 885,
    887–888, 892–893
  Cuban Communism, 939
  domino theory of Communism, 956
  Dulles on Communism, 937
  "fellow travelers," 808
  Hiss case, 896–897
  loyalty oaths in U.S., 896
  McCarthyism, 897–898, *898*
  Nixon Doctrine, 973
  Palmer raids, 771
  Reagan Doctrine, 1001–1002
  Red scare of 1919, 770–771
  Third International (Comintern), 771
  Truman Doctrine, 885
  Vietnamese Communism, 955
Como, Perry, 910
Compromise of 1877, 493–494
Concentration camps, 882, *883*
Coney Island, 670, 676–677, *677*, 716–717
Confederate States of America, pardon of leaders of,
  481
Congregationalism, 551, 671
Congress of Industrial Organizations (CIO), 832
Congress of Racial Equality (CORE), 937
Congress, U.S.
  blacks in, during Reconstruction, 488–489
  filibusters in, 947
  impeachment and trial of Johnson by, 485–486, *485*
  impeachment of Clinton by, 486, 1026–1028
  Kennedy's programs and, 935–937
  League of Nations and, 756, 758
  Neutrality Acts (1935–1937) of, 840–841, 846
  New Deal legislation and, 820–823
  political party affiliations in, A-39 to A-40
  Reconstruction plan of Radicals, 478–490
  representation issue in elections to, 950–951
  shut-down of government in 1995, 1022–1023, *1023*
  Versailles Treaty and, 758, 759, 768
  Wilson's relationship with, 715–716
Conkling, Roscoe, 491, 504, 505, 507, 511, 546
Connolly, Richard, 513, 515
Conscientious objectors, 865–866
Conscription Act of 1917, 744
Conservation, 708–709, *709*. *See also* Environmental
  issues
Conservatives
  Eisenhower's "dynamic conservatism," 924, 925
  Nixon's "Silent Majority," 972
Constitution, U.S. *See also* Constitutional
  amendments; and specific amendments, such as
  Fourteenth Amendment
  Bill of Rights in, A-9 to A-10
  text of, A-4 to A-13
  writers of, 684
Constitutional amendments. *See also* specific
  amendments, such as Fourteenth Amendment
  Bill of Rights, A-9 to A-10
  text of, A-9 to A-13
Consumer borrowing, 792–793
Containment policy, 885, 887–888, 892–893
Contras, 1002
Conwell, Russell B., 554, 571
Cooke, Jay, 532
Coolidge, Calvin
  on business, 783
  as governor of Massachusetts, 770
  personality of, 784
  photographs of, *785*, *791*
  presidency of, 694, 764, 780, 784–791, 797–798

in presidential election of 1924, 785–786, *786*
  as vice president, 765
Co-op movement, 630–631
Cooper, Gary, *811*
Cooper, Peter, 511
Coral Sea, battle of, 861, 864
Corbett, Gentleman Jim, 680
Corbin, Abel R., 491
CORE. *See* Congress of Racial Equality (CORE)
Corn, 622
Cornell University, 671
Cornish immigrants, 577
Coronado, Francisco de, 603
Corporations, 535–536. *See also* Business
Corregidor, siege of, 860, *861*
Correll, Charles, 813
Corruption. *See* Scandals and corruption
Corson, Cornelius, 513
Cosmopolitan, 674, 688, 915
Cotton, 627, 825
Coughlan, John, 512, 513
Coughlin, Charles E., 827, 830–831, 847
Counterculture, 961–962, 1033
Country Life Commission, 709
Cow towns, 613–614
Cowboys, 606–607, *607*, 612–613, 615
Cox, James M., 759–760, *760*
Coxey, Jacob, 637, *637*
CPI. *See* Committee on Public Information (CPI)
Crack, 1033–1034
Crane, Stephen, 674, 698
Crédit Mobilier scandal, 491
Creel, George, 743, 752
CREEP. *See* Committee to Re-elect the President
  (CREEP)
Crime
  in cities in late nineteenth century, 597–598
  gangsters, 776–777, *777*, 809, *809*
  during Great Depression, 809
  juvenile delinquency, 916
  organized crime, 933, 942
  outlaws of West, 615–616
  police expenditures, 996
  police procedure with criminals, 951
Croats in Bosnia, 1017
Crocker, Charles, 542
Crockett, Davy, 908
Croker, Richard, 512, 513, 515
Croly, Herbert, 686
Cromwell, William Nelson, 659
Crook, George, 607
Crosby, Alfred W., 755
"Cross of Gold" speech, 643
Crusade in Europe (Eisenhower), 899, 905
Cuba
  Castro in, 939, 979
  Dulles's policy on, 930
  missile crisis in, 939–940
  F. Roosevelt's policy on, 838
  Spanish-American War in, 649–655
  U.S. interest in acquisition of, 647
  U.S. intervention in, 658, 791, 930
Cuban missile crisis, 939–940
Cullen, Michael, 929
Cuomo, Mario, 1005, 1020
Curtis, Cyrus H. K., 674
Custer, George Armstrong, 605, 609, 616
Customs Service, 501–502
CWA. *See* Civil Works Administration (CWA)
Czechoslovakia, 885, 1005
Czolgosz, Leon, 658

Daisy Miller (James), 673
Daley, Richard E., 935, 963
D'Amato, Alphonse, 1026
Darrow, Clarence, 707, 728, 779, 780
Darwin, Charles, 552, 778–779
Daugherty, Harry, 769
Daugherty, Harry M., 760
Davis, David, 493
Davis, Jeff (governor of Arkansas), 686
Davis, Jefferson, 480
Davis, John W., 786, *786*, 826

Dawes, Charles G., 790
Dawes Plan of 1924, 790
Dawes Severalty Act, 609–610
D-Day, 869
De Caux, Len, 808
De Gaulle, Charles, 868–869
De Priest, Oscar, 831
De Sagan, Prince, 556
Dean, James, 961
Debs, Eugene V., 568, 692, 693, 694, *695*, 706, 710,
  715, *715*, 721, 750, 766, 771
Debt
  during Reagan administration, 998–999
  of Spanish-American War, 502
Declaration of Independence, A-2 to A-3
Deer, 709
Defense Department, 1002
Defense Department, U.S., 926, 981
Deflation, 511, 632–633
DeMille, Cecil B., 810
Democracy in America (Tocqueville), 542
Democratic party. *See also* headings beginning with
  Presidential election
  blacks in, 831
  Compromise of 1877 and, 493–494
  in elections of 1980, 995–996
  Freedom Democrats, 948
  in late nineteenth century, 498–516
  liberalism of, beginning in 1960s, 948–949, 979–980
  political cartoon on, *496*
  political machines and, 512–516
  Populists and, 644, 646
  progressivism and, 714–719
  Redeemers in, 488, 489, 502
  in twentieth century, 834–835, 1014, 1020–1023
  in 2000, 1028
  white supremacy and, 490
  World War I and, 744–745
  "Yellow Dog Democrats," 500
Demonetization Act, 633
Demonstrations, 959–961, *962*, 974, 1004
Dempsey, Jack, 764
Deng Xiaoping, 978
Dennis et al. v. United States, 898
Dependent Pension Act, 503
Depew, Chauncey, 704
Depressions. *See also* Great Depression
  in 1870s, 532–533
  in 1890s, 544
Deregulation, 999, 1000
Desegregation. *See* Civil rights movement; Integration
Détente policy, 977–979, 986–987, 1003
Detroit
  automobile industry in, 833
  black mayor in, 949
  progressivism in, 688
Developing countries. *See* specific countries
Dewey, George, 652
Dewey, John, 743
Dewey, Thomas E., 890–891, 950
DeWitt, John W., 864
Díaz, Porfirio, 723
Dickens, Charles, 596
Dickinson, Emily, 541, 672
Diem, Ngo Dinh, 955
Diet. *See* Food
Dillinger, John, 809
Dingley Tariff of 1897, 711
Dior, Christian, 907
Diphtheria, 596, 664
Discrimination. *See* Civil rights movement; Segregation
Diseases
  AIDS, 988, 1033
  in cities, 596
  in early twentieth century, 664
  flu epidemic of 1918, 754–755
  of immigrants, 570, 571, 596
  Panama Canal and, 659
  polio, 924
  Spanish-American War and, 652
  venereal disease, 664, 1032
  in World War I, 740
Disneyland, 910, 932

Disposable products, 1031
District of Columbia. *See* Washington, D.C.
Divorce, 804, 917, 988, 1033, 1034
"Dixiecrat" party, 890, 899–900
Dixon-Yates, 925
Doctors. *See* Medicine
Dodd, Samuel C. T., 538
Doenitz, Karl, 870–871
Doheny, Edward L., 769, 785
Dole, Elizabeth, 1028
Dole, Robert, 1005, 1022–1023
Dole, Sanford B., *656*
Dolliver, Jonathan, 711
Domestic servants, 558, 566
Dominican Republic, 647, 658, 659, 723, 791, 838, 930
Domino theory of Communism, 956
Donnelly, Ignatius, 631, 635
Dorgan, Tad, 670
Dormer, Jane, 907
Doubleday, Abner, 679
Dowd, Charles F., 526
Draft laws, 744, 746, 846, 853
Drake, Edwin, 537
Dreamland, 717
Dred Scott v. *Sandford*, 950
Dreiser, Theodore, 674, 808
Dressler, Marie, 810
Drew, Daniel, 526, 528, 542
Drew University, 671
Drive-in theaters, 929
Drug use and drug trade, 674, 707–708, 916–917, 962, 996, 997, 1003, 1033–1034
Du Bois, W. E. B., 672, 685, 687, 747, 775, 917
Du Pont Corporation, 840, 841
Dubinsky, David, 831
Duell, Charles H., 521
Dukakis, Michael, 1005
Duke, James Buchanan "Buck," 548, 628–629
Duke University, 629
Dulles, John Foster, 927–931, 937, 954
Dunne, Finley Peter, 666, 683
Dupuy de Lome, Enrique, 652
Durkin, Martin, 904
Dust storms, *800*, 804

Earp, Wyatt, 617
Easley, Frank, 573
East Germany, 887–888, 939, 1005. *See also* Germany
East St. Louis, Ill., 747
Eastern Europe
    Bosnia, 1017
    collapse of Communism in, 1005
    Dulles's policy toward, 931
    immigrants from, 773
    Kosovo, 1017, *1018*
    F. Roosevelt's policy on, 884
    Soviet Union and, 871, 884–888, 896
    Warsaw Pact and, 888
    Yalta Conference and, 871, 896
Eastman, George, 671
Eastman, Max, 771
Economy. *See* Debt; Depressions; Great Depression; Inflation; Prosperity; Taxes
Edison, Thomas Alva, 522, 523–524, *523*
Education. *See also* Higher education
    of blacks, *483*, 672, *673*, 918–920, 937, 950
    desegregation of, 917, 918–920, 937, 950
    Head Start, 952
    illiteracy statistics, 672
    of immigrants, 580, *597*
    during Johnson administration, 952
    in late nineteenth century, 667–669
    progressive education, 587
    segregation of, 672, 918
Edward VII, King of Britain, 712
Egypt, 931, 978, 986, *987*
Ehrlichman, John, 970–971, *971*
Eighteenth Amendment, 749, 775–776
Einstein, Albert, 875, 881
Eisenhower, Dwight D.
    Cold War policies of, 925–932, 955
    as Columbia University president, 899
    domestic policy of, 924–925

Korean War and, 899, 900, 964, 972–973
on MacArthur, 860
as NATO commander, 899
on Nixon's vice presidency, 970
presidency of, 904–905, 923, 924–932, 955
in presidential election of 1952, 897, 899–900, *900*, 903, 970
in presidential election of 1956, 903, 905
press conferences and, 905
in World War II, 859, 867–871, *869*
El (elevated train), 591–592
El Alamein, battle of, 867
El Caney, battle of, 654
El Salvador, 1002, 1007
Elderly, 1021–1022, *1022*
Elders, Jocelyn, 1025
Elections. *See* Voting; and headings beginning with Presidential election
Electric trolleys, 592–593, *593*
Electricity and electrification, 523–524, *525*, 712, 812, 825–826, 989
Elevator music, 904
Elevators, 593–594
Eliot, Charles W., 671
Elk, 709
Elliot, Robert, *479*
Ellis Island, 571, 575, *575*
Ellsberg, Daniel, 981
Ely, Richard, 691
Emergency Banking Act, 820
Emerson, Ralph Waldo, 541, 672
Energy crisis, 982–984, 987, 989
England, John, 568
England. *See* Great Britain
Entertainment. *See* Leisure; Movies; Music; Radio; Television
Environmental issues, 708–709, *709*, 999–1000
Environmental Protection Agency, 999–1000
Epidemics. *See* Diseases
Equal Employment Opportunity Commission, 947
Equal Rights Amendment (ERA), 1034–1035, *1035*
Erie Railroad, 528, 537, 547
Ervin, Sam, 981
Escobedo v. *Illinois*, 951
Espionage Act of 1917, 693, 751
Ethiopia, 647, 841, 842
Ethnic groups. *See* Immigration; Racial and ethnic groups
Europe. *See* specific countries
European Community, 1008, 1017
European frontier, 602
Europeans (James), 673
Evans, Hiram Wesley, 775
Evans, Oliver, 624
Evers, Medgar, 937
Evolution controversy, 778–780
Excise tax, 787
Exclusion Act of 1882, 579
Executions of Sacco and Vanzetti, 771–773
Expansionism. *See* Frontier; West
Exports. *See* Trade

Factories. *See* Industry and industrialization
Faddism, 908, 1031
Fair Deal, 889, 892
Fairbanks, Douglas, *742*, 752
Fairchild, Lucius, 502
Fall, Albert B., 769
"Fallout shelters," 926
Falwell, Jerry, 994–995
Families. *See also* Marriage
    during Great Depression, 804
    in 1950s, 911–916, *915*
Family Assistance Plan, 971
Farley, James, 833, 834, 846
Farm Credit Administration, 821
Farming. *See* Agriculture
Farrakhan, Louis, 1037
Fashion. *See* Clothing
Fatima, 677
Faubus, Orval, 918
FBI, 864, 866, 981
FCC. *See* Federal Communications Commission (FCC)

FDIC. *See* Federal Deposit Insurance Corporation (FDIC)
Federal budget. *See* headings beginning with Budget
Federal Bureau of Investigation (FBI), 864, 866, 981
Federal Communications Commission (FCC), 825
Federal Deposit Insurance Corporation (FDIC), 1000
Federal Emergency Relief Administration (FERA), 821
Federal Farm Loan Act of 1916, 719
Federal Reserve Act of 1913, 718
Federal Reserve System, 718, 827
Federal Savings and Loan Insurance Corporation (FSLIC), 1000
"Fellow travelers," 808
Feminine Mystique (Friedan), 916, 1034
Feminism. *See* Women's rights
FERA. *See* Federal Emergency Relief Administration (FERA)
Ferraro, Geraldine, 1001
Ferries, 592
Ferris, George, 716
Ferris wheel, 716
Feuchtwanger, Anton, 670
Field, Cyrus, 525
Field, Rev. David, 524
Field, David Dudley, 524
Field, Henry Martyn, 525
Field, James G., 635
Field, Stephen Johnson, 524–525
Fifteenth Amendment, 486, 490
52–20 Club, 889
Filibusters, 947
Filipinos, 579
Film industry. *See* Movies
Finn, William, 515
First World War. *See* World War I
Fisk, James, 491, 524, 528, 542, 558
Fisk College, 672
Fiske, John, 648
Fitch, Clyde, 630
Fitness craze, 666, *666*, 677–678
Fitzgerald, F. Scott, 763, 764, 808
Flagler, Henry, 538
Flagler, Samuel, 796
"Flat tax," 1023
Flegensheimer, Arthur "Dutch Schultz," 777
Fleisch, Rudolf, 910
Fleming, Ian, 935
Fletcher, Frank J., 864
Flexner, Judith, 933
Florida, 485, 795, 796–797
Flowers, Gennifer, 1026
Floyd, "Pretty Boy," 809
Flu. *See* Influenza
Flying saucers, 897
Foch, Ferdinand, 739–740
Fogarty, Anne, 907
Foley, Thomas, 1020
Folk, Joseph W., 688
Fonck, René, 788
Food. *See also* Agriculture
    advertising of, 793
    frozen food, 851, 907, 910
    grocery chains and supermarkets, 794, 928–929
    hot dog, 670, 716–717, 752
    legislation on, 690, 707
    meat consumption, 613–614, 808
    rationing of, during World War II, 851
    TV dinner, 910
    "victory gardens" for, 746, 851
    during World War I, 745–746, 752
Football, 679, 680, 764
Foraker, John B., 687
Foran Contract Labor Law, 571, 576
Forbes, Charles R., 769
Forbes, Steve, 1023, 1028
Ford, Gerald, *968*, 981–985, *992*, 1023
Ford, Henry, 730, 778, 791, 795, 826, 833
Fordney-McCumber Tariff of 1922, 786, 787
Forest industries, 612, *612*, 628, 750–751
Forests, 708–709
Formosa, 647
Forrest, Nathan Bedford, 490
Fortas, Abe, 951, 972

I-6 *Index*

Foster, Stephen, 668
Foster, William Z., 770, 771, 807
Four Freedoms, 838
Four Hundred, 704
Fourteen Points, 748, 753–756
Fourteenth Amendment, 477, 481, 483, 490, 535–536, 865, 946
Foxx, Jimmy, 767
France, Joseph I., 811
France
 Communist party in, 885, 887
 nuclear test ban and, 940
 at Versailles Conference after World War I, 757
 Vietnam and, 931, 953–954
 war debt from World War I, 787, 790
 in World War I, 725–740
 in World War II, 841–849, 860, 866–871
Franco, Francisco, 841, *844*
Franklin, Benjamin, 553–554, 792
Franz Ferdinand, Archduke, 724
Free blacks. *See* Blacks
Free Speech Movement, 961
Freedmen. *See* Blacks
Freedmen's Bureau, 482
Freedom Democrats, 948
"Freedom riders," 920, 937
Freedom Summer, 947–948
Freidel, Frank, 650
French. *See* France
Frick, Henry Clay, 534
Friedan, Betty, 907, 916, 1034
Frontier. *See also* West
 end of, 649
 European versus American definition of, 602
 in late nineteenth century, 602–618
 mining frontier, 617–618, *618*
Frost, Robert, 935
FSLIC. *See* Federal Savings and Loan Insurance Corporation (FSLIC)
Fulbright, J. William, 889, 959
Fundamentalists
 Jehovah's Witnesses, 886–887
 Moral Majority, 994–995
 Muslim fundamentalism, 1001

Gable, Clark, 810
Galveston, Tex., 690
Gambling, 776
Gangs, 598
Gangsters, 776–777, *777*, 809, *809*
GAR. *See* Grand Army of the Republic (GAR)
Garbage, 1031
Gardner, David, 1034
Gardner, John W., 1013
Garfield, James A., 491, 498, *499*, 504–507, *508*, 511
Garland, Hamlin, 630
Garner, John Nance, 811, 846
Garvey, Marcus, 774–775, *774*
Gary, Elbert, 770
Gary, Ind., 949
Gasoline
 prices of, 984
 rationing of, in World War II, 850, *850*
 shortage of, in 1970s, 984, *984*
Gates, Bill, 536
GATT (General Agreement on Tariffs and Trade), 1018
Gautier, Théophile, 787
Gaynor, Janet, 810
Gays. *See* Homosexuality
General Agreement on Tariffs and Trade (GATT), 1018
General Dynamics, 1002
General Electric, 524
General Motors, 796, 797, 853, 924
Generation of Vipers (Wylie), 916
Geneva Accords, 931, 954
George, Henry, 549
Georgia, 485
German-American Bund, 845
German immigrants and German Americans
 in nineteenth century, 579–580
 prohibition and, 749
 return of, to home country, 578
 statistics on, 1038

 during World War I, 752–753
 World War I and, 729
German-Irish Legislative Committee for the Furtherance of United States Neutrality, 729
Germany
 Anschluss and, 841
 East Germany, 887–888, 939, 1005
 Hitler in, 778, 787, 789, 823, 831, 838, 841–844, *844*
 reparations payments following World War I, 787, 790
 Weimar Republic in, 838
 West Germany, 998
 in World War I, 724–740
 in World War II, 789, 841–845, *842*, 847, 860, 866–871
Geronimo, 610
Gerry, M. B., 500
Ghost Dance religion, 610–611, 617
GI Bill, 889
Gibbons, James, 572, 576
Gibson, Charles Dana, 668, 678
Gibson Girl, 668, 678
Gillette Company, 808
Gilman, Charlotte Perkins, 697
Gingrich, Newt, 1017–1018, *1019*, 1020, 1022–1023
Ginsberg, Allen, 916, 917
Girdler, Tom, 833
Gladden, Washington, 551
Glasnost, 1004, 1006
Glidden, Joseph, 624
Godkin, E. L., 491
Goering, Hermann, 789
Goff, James, 515
Gold
 Black Friday during Grant administration, 491
 in Canada and Alaska, 646
 mining of, in late nineteenth century, 612, 617
 money question and, 631–633, 636–637
Goldfine, Bernard, 904
Goldwater, Barry, 949, 956, 958, 963, 964, 970
Goldwyn, Samuel, 778
Golf, 710, 764, 905, *905*
Gompers, Samuel, 572–573, 695, 696, 746–747, 770
Goodman, Benny, 810
Goodnight-Loving Trail, 606
"Goo-Goos," 515
GOP. *See* Republican party
Gorbachev, Mikhail, 1004, 1005, 1006
Gore, Albert, *1019*, 1028, *1029*
Gosden, Freeman, 813
Gospel of Success, 553–554
Gould, Anna, 556
Gould, George, 551
Gould, Jay, 491, 524, 525, 528, 542, 556, 572
Gould, Mrs. George, 557
Government agencies. *See also* specific agencies
 of New Deal, 820–826, 833–834
 regulatory legislation and agencies, 542–549, 707, 710–711, 718, 719, 825, 999, 1000
 during World War I, 745
 during World War II, 853–854
Government employment
 affirmative action for, 1025, 1037
 of Communists, 897–898
 desegregation of, 890
 firings and resignations of, 897
 loyalty oaths for, 896
 New Deal and, 834
 segregation in, 687
 women in, 675
 during World War I, 745
 during World War II, 854
Grady, Henry W., 628
Graham, Rev. Billy, 912, 933
Grand Army of the Republic (GAR), 503–504
Grand Tour of Europe, 554
Grange, *543*, 545–546, 630
Grant, Harold "Red," 764
Grant, Madison, 773
Grant, Ulysses S., 486, 490–493, 498, 504, 510, 520, 633
Grapes of Wrath (Steinbeck), 804

Great Britain
 colonies of, 647
 immigrants to U.S. from, 577
 navy of, 732, 739, 768
 nuclear test ban and, 940
 Treaty of Washington and, 768
 at Versailles Conference after World War I, 757
 war debt from World War I, 787, 790
 Wilson's relationship with, 727
 in World War I, 725–740
 in World War II, 841–849, 860, 866–871
Great Depression. *See also* New Deal
 American Communist party and, 807–808
 Americans' early reactions to, 807–810
 chronologies on, 814, 835
 crime during, 809
 Hoover's response to, 801, 804–807, 809
 impact of generally, 802
 international impact of, 806–807
 movies, during, 809–810, *811*
 music during, 810
 personal hardship during, 802, 803–804, *807*, 808
 and presidential election of 1932, 810–814, *814*
 radio and, 812, 814, 819
 statistics on, 802–803
 and stock market crash of 1929, 799
 violence during, 808
 wealthy during, 828–829
Great Eastern, 525
Great Gatsby (Fitzgerald), 764
Great Northern Railroad, 547, 577
Great Plains, 602, 604–605, 624, *625*, 626
Great Salt Lake, 604
Great Society, 948–953, 958
Great War. *See* World War I
Greece, 885, 887
Greek immigrants, 578
Greeley, Horace, 492, *492*
Green Berets, 938, 955
Greenback Labor party, 511, 633
"Greenbacks" (money), 511, 632–633
Grenada, 1002
Grocery chains, 794, 928–929
Gruening, Ernest, 956
Guam, 655
Guatemala, 930–931
Guinier, Lani, 1024–1025
Guiteau, Charles, 505, 507
Gulf War, 1003, 1007–1008
Guns. *See* Weapons
Guthrie, Woody, 833
Guzmán, Jacobo Arbenz, 930–931

Haiti, 658, 661, 723, 791, 838, 1002, 1016
Haldeman, H. R., 970–971, *971*
Haldeman-Julius, Emanuel, 787
Hamer, Fannie Lou, 948
Hamilton, Charles, 960
Hammer v. Dagenhart, 686
Hammett, Dashiell, 808
Hancock, John, 758
Hancock, Winfield Scott, 505
Hanna, Marcus A. (Mark), 573, 642, 644–646, 652, 658, 663, 687, 695, 704
Hansen, Ole, 770
"Happy Birthday to You," 672
Harding, Florence, 769
Harding, Warren G., 694, 760, *760*, 764–769, *765*, 770, 773, 784
Harkin, Thomas, 1008
Harlow, Jean, 810
Harmon, Judson, 714
Harper's Weekly, 674, 677
Harriman, Edward H., 546, 704
Harrison, Benjamin, 498, *499*, *501*, 502, 503, 505, 506, 509, 546, 549
Hart, Gary, 1000, 1004
Hartmann, Robert T., 969
Harvard University, 680
Haugwitz-Reventlow, Kurt von, 829
Hauptmann, Bruno, 789
Hawaii
 annexation of, by U.S., 655–656

harbor on Oahu, 649
Japanese Americans in, during World War II, 865
Pearl Harbor bombing, *836*, 849, 852–853, *852*, 860
tourism in, 863
Hay, John, 643, 650, 652, 659, 704
Hayden, Tom, 961
Hayes, Lucy, 504
Hayes, Rutherford B., 493, 498, *499*, 504, 511, 522, 551
Haymarket riot, 550–551, 572
Hays, Arthur Garfield, 780
Hays, Will H., *765*, 778
Hays Code, 778
Haywood, William D. "Big Bill," 693, 696, 706–707, 728–729, *728*, 750
Hazard of New Fortunes (Howells), 584
Head Start, 952
Health. *See also* Diseases
fitness craze, 666, *666*, 677–678
in 1980s, 988
polio vaccine, 924
"taking the cure" at mineral springs, 676
Health care reform, 1019–1020
Health, Education, and Welfare Department, U.S., 904, 924
Hearst, William Randolph, 649, 650–652, 669, 689
Heine, Alice, 555
Hellman, Lillian, 808
"Hello," invention of word, 522
Hepburn Act, 707
Hepburn, Audrey, 907
Hersey, John, 876
Hickok, Wild Bill, 617
Hicks, Granville, 808
Hidden Persuaders (Packard), 916, 932
Higginson, Thomas Wentworth, 677
Higher education. *See also* Education
affirmative action in, 1036, 1037
athletics and, 679, 680
of blacks, *555*, 672
Catholic colleges, 672
desegregation of, 937
elective system in, 671
greed in, during 1980s–1990s, 1034
during Johnson administration, 952
land-grant colleges, 670
in late nineteenth century, 554, 629, 668, 670–672
philanthropists' support of, 554, 629, 670–671
professional postgraduate schools, 671
progressivism and, 691
student protest during 1960s–1970s, 960–961, 974, 1005, 1031, 1034
for women, 669, *670*, 671
Highways. *See* Roads
Hill, Anita, 1036, *1036*
Hill, James J., 528–529, 562, 577, 704
Hill, Patty Smith, 672
Hillman, Sidney, 831
Hillquit, Morris, 692, 693, 696
Hippies, 962, 1033
Hirohito, Emperor, 842, 876
Hiroshima (Hersey), 876
Hiroshima bombing, 876, *877*, 882
Hispanic farmworkers, 963
Hiss, Alger, 896–897
Hitchcock, E. A., 704
Hitler, Adolf, 778, 787, 789, 823, 831, 838, 841–847, *844*, 866, 867, 870
HIV, 1033
Ho Chi Minh, 953–954, *954*, 959
Hoar, George Frisbie, 655
Hobart, Garrett, 658
Hobby, Oveta Culp, 904, 924
Hoff, Maxie, 777
Hogs, 622, 808
Holland, John, 732
Hollingshead, Richard, 929
Hollywood movies. *See* Movies
Holmes, Oliver Wendell, Jr., 663, 751, 818
Holy Cross College, 672
Home Owners' Loan Corporation, 821
Homeless, 804, *999*
Homestead Act, 530, 625
Homosexuality, 988, 1008, 1025, 1033

Honduras, 658, 791
Honecker, Erich, 1005
Hookers (prostitutes), 698–699, *698*, 749, 776
Hoover Dam, 806
Hoover, Herbert
as baseball fan, 764
biography of, 745
as Food Administrator during World War I, 745–746
Great Depression and, 801, 804–807, 809
on New Deal, 826
personality of, 745, 812, *816*
presidency of, 660, 804–807, 839
in presidential election of 1928, 791–792, *792*
in presidential election of 1932, 810–814, *814*
as secretary of commerce, 768, 784
World War II and, 847
Hoover, J. Edgar, 981
Hooverville, 809
Hopkins, Harry, 821
Hopkins, Mark, 542
Hopwood v. Texas, 1037
"Horizontal integration" of business, 537
Horse racing, 676
Horses, 596–597, 604
Hot dog, 670, 716–717, 752
Hot Rod, 914
House, Edward M., 718
House of Representatives, U.S. *See also* Congress
Cannon as Speaker of, 712
Gingrich as Speaker of, 1022–1023
impeachment of Clinton by, 486, 1026–1027
impeachment of Johnson by, 485
Rayburn as Speaker of, 946
representation issue in elections to, 950–951
Houston, Tex., 747
How the Other Half Lives (Riis), 596
Howard, O. O., 482
Howard University, 672
Howe, Edgar Watson, 541
Howe, Elias, 588
Howells, William Dean, 551, 584, 673–674
Howl (Ginsberg), 917
Hua Guofeng, 978
Huerta, Victoriano, 723
Hughes, Charles Evans, 691–692, 734, 768
Hughes Aircraft, 1002
Hugo, Victor, 787
Hula hoops, 908
Hull, Cordell, 838, 840, 849
Hull House, 585, 587, 686
Human rights
U.S. Bill of Rights, A-9 to A-10
violations of, 987
Humphrey, George, 926
Humphrey, Hubert H., 890, 948, 963–964
Hundred Days of New Deal legislation, 820–823
Hungary, 931, 1005
Hunt, Howard, 981
Hunter, Robert, 563
Huntington, Collis P., 542
Hurricanes, 797
Hussein, Saddam, 1007
Hutton, Barbara, 829
Hydrogen bomb, 888, 926

"I Have a Dream" speech, 937, *938*
ICC. *See* Interstate Commerce Commission (ICC)
Idaho, 617, 634, 692–694
Illegitimate birth rate, 1033
Illinois. *See* Chicago
Illnesses. *See* Diseases
Image advertising, 794–795
Immigration. *See also* specific groups of immigrants, such as Irish immigrants and Irish Americans
and adaptation to U.S., 580–581
advancement for immigrants, 585–587
assimilation of immigrants, 585–587
cities as home for immigrants, 584–587, 595–598
citizenship for immigrants, 515
consumer products for immigrants in 1980s, 1001
in early twentieth century, *574*, 575–576, 773
education of immigrants, 580, *597*

employment of immigrants, 577, 585
ethnic groups of immigrants, 577–581
Exclusion Act of 1882, 579
lifestyle of immigrants, 570–571
map of, *574*
in nineteenth century, 570–571, 573–581, *574*
"Old Immigration" before nineteenth century, 574–576, *574*
political machines and, 515
population of immigrants, 575–576, 773
promotion of, 576–577
restrictions on, 579, 773
return of immigrants to home countries, 578
settlement houses for immigrants, 585, 587
from Southeast Asia, 975
trauma of, 580–581
WASPs' views of, 584
Immigration Restriction League, 773
Impeachment
of Clinton, 486, 1026–1028
definition of, 486
of Johnson, 485–486, *485*
Imperialism. *See also* specific colonies and countries
and Anglo-Saxon superiority, 648, 649, 655
anticolonialism of U.S. in nineteenth century, 647
arguments against, 655
Caribbean and, 658–659
chronology on, 661
Hawaii and, 655–656
jingoism and, 647, 649
nature of, 647–648
Open Door policy and, 657, 658, 839, 849
Philippines and, 654–657
Puerto Rico and, 654, 655
T. Roosevelt and, 658–661
sea power and, 648–649
Spanish-American War and, 649–654
Imports. *See* Trade
"In God We Trust" on money, 685, 711
"Inc.," use of, 535
Income tax, 636, 786, 830, 998
India, 647
Indian Territory, 603–604, 649
Indians
and army in late nineteenth century, 605–609
Dawes Severalty Act and, 609–610
of Great Plains, 604–605
in late nineteenth century, 602–611
life expectancy of, 664
and Little Bighorn Battle, 609, *610*
population of, 605
religion of, 610–611
reservations of, 491, *603*, 611, *665*
warfare on frontier, 608–609
of West, 603–611
Indochina, 647, 848, 849
Industrial Workers of the World (IWW), 693, 696, 728–729, 750–752, 770
Industry and industrialization. *See also* Labor movement; Working class
foreign investment in, 520
hours of factory work, 563–564
inventions and, 521–525
in late nineteenth century, 520–525, 533–538, 562–573
"putting out" system, 589
resources for, 520–525
size of factories, 562
and size of working class, 562
sweatshops and, 588–589
wages for workers, 562–563, 566
women as industrial workers, 563, *563*, 565–566, *566*, 747–748, *749*, 855
working conditions in factories, 564
during World War II, 854–855
Infant mortality, 664
Infantry, 651, 739. *See also* Military
Inflation, 632–633, 636, 971, 984, 987, 989, 994
Influence of Sea Power upon History (Mahan), 648–649
Influenza, 664, 740, 754–755
Ingersoll, Robert G., 510
Insolent Chariots (Keats), 916
Installment plan for consumer purchases, 792–793

I-8 *Index*

Insurgents, 712, 713
Integration. *See also* Civil rights movement
  of education, 917, 918–920, 937, 950
  of government employment, 890
  of military, 890, 917
Interior Department, U.S., 769
Internal improvements. *See* Transportation
International Harvester, 624–625
Interstate Commerce Act, 546, 548
Interstate Commerce Commission (ICC), 546, 707, 825
Inventions
  industrialization and, 521–525
  in late nineteenth century, 521–525
  ready-made clothes and, 588
  typewriter, 678–679, *679*
  "Yankee ingenuity" and, 521
Iowa, 808
Iran, 930, 931, 994, *995*, 997, 1002, 1037
Iran hostage crisis, 994
Iran-Contra Affair, 1002
Iraq, 976, 997, 1003, 1007, 1028
Ireland
  population of, 567
  rebellion of 1916 in, 729
  return of immigrants to, 578
Irish immigrants and Irish Americans
  Catholicism of, 577–578
  gangsters, 777
  as immigrants, 577–578
  and late-nineteenth-century politics, 508–509, 515–516
  as miners, 568
  patriotism of, 568
  political machines and, 515–516
  return of immigrants to Ireland, 578
  statistics on, 1038
  track-laying by, 530
  World War I and, 729
Iron ore, 521
Irrigation, 622–624
Isolationism
  myth of, in late nineteenth century, 646–647
  after World War I, 789, 790–791
Israel, 964, 978, 986, *987*, 989
Issei, 864
Italian immigrants and Italian Americans, 586, 587, 771–773, 777
Italy
  Communist party in, 885, 887
  immigrants from, 578
  invasion of Ethiopia by, 841, 842
  navy of, 768
  Treaty of Washington and, 768
  at Versailles Conference after World War I, 757
  in World War II, 841, 842, *842*, 844, 867
Ives, Burl, 833
Iwo Jima, battle of, 875
IWW. *See* Industrial Workers of the World (IWW)

Jackson, Andrew
  in presidential election of 1824, 980
  in presidential election of 1828, 980
  in presidential election of 1832, 980
Jackson, Helen Hunt, 609, 615
Jackson, Jesse, 960, 1004
Jackson, Joseph "Shoeless Joe," 766, 767
"Jake walking," 777
James, Harry, 810
James, Henry, 673
James, Jesse and Frank, 615–616, 650
James, William, 541
James, Zerelda, 616
Japan
  aggression against China, 839–840, 841
  atomic bombing of, 876–877, *877*, 882
  attack on Shanghai by, *839*, 840
  capitalist democracy in, after World War II, 892
  Hirohito as emperor of, 842
  imperialism of, 647
  investment in U.S. by, 998
  navy of, 768, 861, 864, 874
  in nineteenth century, 647

Pearl Harbor bombing by, *836*, 849, 852–853, *852*, 860
  F. Roosevelt's policy toward, 839–840
  scrap iron purchase by, 841
  Treaty of Washington and, 768
  war with Russia, 658
  in World War II, 841, *845*, 848–849, 852–853, *858*, 860–866, *861*, 871–877, *873*, *874*, 877
Japanese immigrants and Japanese Americans, 573, 579, 723, 864–866, *865*
Jazz, 916
Jefferson, Thomas, 583, 587, 622, 684, 980
Jeffries, Jim, 681
Jehovah's Witnesses, 886–887
Jenney, William L., 594
Jesus, as advertising man, 795
Jews
  antisemitism against, 778, 842
  in concentration camp, *883*
  from Eastern Europe, 573
  in film industry, 778
  gangsters, 777
  German Jews, 580, 672
  higher education for, 672
  immigrant aid institutions for, 586
  as immigrants, 573–574, 580, 585
  Nazi murder of, 842, 866, 876, 882, 974
  in New York City, 585, *587*, 596
  Nixon on, 970
  Prohibition and, 776
  religion of, 580, 912
  of Russia, 576
  Sephardic Jews, 580, 672
  World War I and, 730
Jim Crow laws. *See* Segregation
Jingoism, 647, 649
Job Corps, 952
John Birch Society, 941, 959
John Deere, 624
Johns Hopkins University, 671
Johnson, Andrew, 479–486, *480*
Johnson, Hiram, 685, 694, 744, 770
Johnson, Hugh, 823, 847
Johnson, Jack, 680–681, 699
Johnson, Lyndon B.
  civil rights and, 946–949, 952–953
  Great Society of, 948–953, 958
  Muzak and, 904
  photograph of, *941*
  political career of, 946
  presidency of generally, 660
  in presidential election of 1964, 949
  presidential oath of office, after Kennedy's death, *941*
  retirement of, 963
  Supreme Court and, 951, 972
  Vietnam War and, 945, 953, 955–959
Johnson, Thomas L., 688
Jones, Paula, 1026, 1036
Jones, Robert T. "Bobby," 764
Jones, Samuel M., 688
Jordan, Vernon, 1026
Judah, Theodore D., 531
Judaism. *See* Jews
Judson, E. Z. C., 615
Julian, George W., 481
Jungle (Sinclair), 689–690, 698, 707
Justice Department, U.S., 549, 751, 1024–1025
Juvenile delinquency, 916

Kaiser, Henry J., 855
Kalakaua, David, 655
Kamikaze, 875
Kansas, 613–614, 624, 804
Kansas City, 777
Kansas Pacific Railroad, 605, 613, 614
Karmazin, Mel, *1032*
Kasserine Pass, battle of, 867
Kearney, Denis, 579
Keats, John, 916
Keller, Helen, 696
Kelley, John, 515
Kellogg, Frank B., 790

Kellogg-Briand Pact, 790, *791*
Kelly, "Machine Gun," 809
Kelly, William, 533
Kenna, "Hinkey-Dink," 512, 513
Kennan, George F., 885, 888, 892, 931, 959
Kennedy, Jacqueline, *922*, 935, *941*
Kennedy, John F.
  assassination of, 941–942
  Bay of Pigs and, 939
  Cuban missile crisis and, 939–940
  foreign policy of, 937–940
  New Frontier of, 935–937
  personality of, 935
  photographs of, *922*, *934*, *940*
  political career of, 933–934
  presidency of, 923, 935–942
  in presidential election of 1960, 932, 934–935, 970
  sexual behavior of, 933
  Vietnam War and, 945, 955
Kennedy, Joseph P., 798, 846
Kennedy, Robert F., 936, 937, 963–964, *965*
Kent State University, 974
Kerouac, Jack, 916
Kerrey, Robert, 1008
Keyes, Alan, 1028–1029
Keynes, John Maynard, 756, 818
Khmer Rouge, 974, 975
Khomeini, Ayatollah Ruhollah, 994, 997, 1001, 1002
Khrushchev, Nikita, 927, *930*, 931, 932, 939–940
Kickbacks, 512–513
Kidnapping, 789
King, Coretta Scott, *948*
King, Martin Luther, Jr.
  assassination of, 920, 960, 963
  "I Have a Dream" speech by, 937, *938*
  Kennedy and, 934
  and Montgomery bus boycott, 919, 949
  nonviolent civil disobedience by, 919
  photographs of, *938*, *948*
  significance of, 1037
  and Southern Christian Leadership Conference (SCLC), 919–920
King, Richard, 614
Kinsey, Alfred, 915–916
Kipling, Rudyard, 591, 663
Kissinger, Henry A., 973, 974, 976–979, 985, 986
Kitchen, Claude, 733
"Kitchen debates," 927, *930*
KKK. *See* Ku Klux Klan
Klan. *See* Ku Klux Klan
Knights of Labor, 569–572, *569*, 576
Knights of St. Crispin, 568
Knights of the White Camellia, 490
Knowland, William F., 896, 950
Knox, Philander C., 658, 704
Knudsen, William S., 853
Kodak, 671
Kohl, Helmut, 1004
Konoye, Prince Fumimaro, 849
Korea, 647
Korean Americans, 864
Korean War, 893–896, *894*, *895*, 899, 900, 964, 972–973
Korematsu v. United States, 865
Kosovo, 1017, *1018*
Ku Klux Klan, 490, *762*, 775, 776
Kuhn, Fritz, 845
Kuhn, Loeb, and Company, 546, 547
Kuribayashi, Tadamachi, 875
Kuwait, 1007

La Follette, Robert M., 685, 690–691, *691*, 707, 711, 713–714, 735, 744, 786, *786*, 947
Labor movement. *See also* Working class
  American Federation of Labor (AFL), 572–573, 695, 746–747, 832
  Communist ideas and, 808
  Congress of Industrial Organizations (CIO), 832
  conservative unionism, 573
  in early nineteenth century, 568
  in early twentieth century, 769–770
  for Hispanic farmworkers, 963
  Industrial Workers of the World (IWW), 693, 696, 750–752, 770

Index **I-9**

Knights of Labor, 569–572, *569*, 576
  in late nineteenth century, 567–573
  Molly Maguires and, 568
  National Industrial Recovery Act and, 823
  and National Labor Relations Board (NLRB), 824–825
  New Deal and, 831–833
  number of union members, 568, 569, 572, 747, 833, 856
  progressivism and, 695–696
  T. Roosevelt and, 705
  sit-down strike, 833
  strikes and, 567–568, 572, 637, 695, 696, 705, 729, 750, 769–770, 833, 854
  Taft-Hartley Act and, 889
  violence and, 567–568, 833, *834*
  Wagner Act and, 824–825, 832, 889
  during World War I, 746–747
  World War II and, 854, 856
Ladies Home Journal, 674
Lady Chatterley's Lover (Lawrence), 917
Laemmle, Carl, 752
Laine, Frankie, 910
Lake, Simon, 732
Lance, Bert, 989
Land-grant colleges, 670
Landis, Commissioner, 767
Landon, Alfred M., 831, *831*
Languages
  British versus American English, 790
  gender-specific words, 1034
Lansing, Robert, 756
Laos, 974
Lasch, Christopher, 1031
Latin America. *See also* specific countries
  Alliance for Progress and, 938
  "banana republics" in, 791
  Bush's policies on, 1006–1007
  Carter's policies on, 985–986
  Clinton's policies on, 1016, 1017–1018
  Coolidge's policy on, 790–791
  Dulles's policy toward, 930–931
  Harding's policy on, 790–791
  Kennedy's policy toward, 938–939
  Nixon-Kissinger policy toward, 979
  Reagan's policies on, 1002, 1003
  T. Roosevelt's policy on, 658–661
  U.S. investments in, 723, 790–791
  Wilson's policy on, 722–724, *724*
  during World War II, 866
Latter-Day Saints. *See* Mormons
Lawrence, D. H., 917
Laws. *See also* specific laws
  criminal law codification in New York State, 524
  divorce laws, 1034
  women's rights in 1970s, 1034
Lazarus, Emma, 773
League of Nations, 753–760, 768, 840
Lease, Mary Elizabeth, 631, 671
Lebanon, 927, 1001
Lee, Fitzhugh, 650
Lee, Ivy, 795
Lee, Spike, 961
Legal profession, 524–525, 631, 671
Lehr, Harry, 555
Leisure. *See also* Movies; Music; Radio; Television
  amusement parks, 676–677, *677*, 716–717, 910
  middle class and, 676, 678
  spectator sports, 678–681
  "taking the cure" at mineral springs, 676
  working class and, 676–677
LeMay, Curtis, 959
Lend-Lease, 847, 860
Lenin, Vladimir Ilyich, 739
Lever Act, 749
Levitt, William, 911–912
Levittown, 911, 929
Lewinsky, Monica, 1026, *1027*, 1028, 1036
Lewis, John L., 831–832, 847, 854
Leyte Gulf, Battle of, 874
Liberia, 647
Liberty ships, *854*, 855
Libraries, 675

Libya, 1001–1002, 1037
Liddy, G. Gordon, 981
Liebman, Rabbi Joshua, 912
Life expectancy, 664, 988
Life magazine, 933
Lifestyle
  amusement parks, 716–717
  baseball players, 766–767
  cowboys, 606–607
  fashion in 1950s, 906–907
  flue epidemic of 1918, 754–755
  immigrants, 570–571
  Jehovah's witnesses, 886–887
  meat consumption, 613–614
  radio, 812–813
  Spanish-American War soldiers, 650–651
  suburbs, 928–929
  Supreme Court Justice Earl Warren, 950–951
  sweatshops, 588–589
  time usage for daily living activities, 1000
  wealthy in Great Depression, 828–829
  wealthy in late nineteenth century, *540*, 544–545, *545*, 551, *553*, 554–558
  World War II rationing and scrap drives, 850–851
  World War II soldiers, 862–863
Light bulb, 523–524
Liliuokalani, Queen, 655–656, *656*
Lillibridge, G. D., 862, 863
Limbaugh, Rush, 1036
Lincoln, Abraham
  anti-imperialists' quoting of, 655
  assassination of, 942
  inventions and, 521
  Reconstruction plan of, 478–479
Lincoln University, 672
Lindbergh, Anne Morrow, 789
Lindbergh, Charles A., 788–789, *789*, 848
Lindsay, Vachel, 683
Lingg, Louis, 550–551
Lippmann, Walter, 783, 818, 892
Literature. *See* specific authors and titles
Little, Frank, 750
Little, Malcolm. *See* Malcolm X
Little Bighorn, Battle of, 609, *610*
Little Rock schools, 918–919
Livestock. *See* Animals
Lloyd, Henry Demarest, 644, 646
Lloyd George, David, 739, 757, 757
Lodge, Henry Cabot, 647, 655, 660, 734, 758, 759, *759*, 760, 818
Lomasney, Martin, 515
London, Jack, 674
Lonely Crowd (Riesman), 916
Long, Huey, 828–830, *830*
Longfellow, Henry Wadsworth, 583, 672
Longworth, Alice Roosevelt, 678, 784, 848
Looking Backward (Bellamy), 549–550
Lorillard, P. J., 629
Los Angeles, 709, 778, *822*, 960
Louis XVI, King of France, 684
Louisiana. *See also* New Orleans
  corruption in government of, 487
  Huey Long in, 828–830, *830*
  readmission of, during Reconstruction, 485
  Reconstruction in, 490
Louisiana State University (LSU), 829–830
Lowden, Frank O., 760
Loyalty oaths, 896
LSD, 962, 1033
LSU. *See* Louisiana State University (LSU)
"Ltd.," use of, 535
Luce, Clare Boothe, 892
Luce, Henry L., 892, 896
Lumber industry. *See* Forest industries
Luna Park, 717
Lusitania, 732–733
Lyceums, 675
Lynchings, 664, 747, 750, 774, 917

MacArthur, Arthur, 657
Macarthur, Douglas, 809, 860, 871, 873–874, 892–896, 899
Mack, Connie, 766, 767

Madden, Owney, 777
Madero, Francisco, 723
Madison, James, 684
Mafia, 942
Magazines, 674–675, 914, 915, 926. *See also* specific magazines
Magee, Christopher, 515
Maggie: A Girl of the Streets (Crane), 674, 698
Mahan, Alfred Thayer, 648–649
Mail-order catalogs, 588, 664
Main-Travelled Roads (Garland), 630
Maine, 833
Maine explosion, 650, 652, *653*
Malaria, 659
Malcolm X, 960, 961, *961*
Man in the Gray Flannel Suit (Wilson), 916
Man Nobody Knows (Barton), 795
Manchuria, 839, 893
Manhattan Project, 875
Manila Bay, battle of, 652
Mann, James R., 699
Mann Act, 699
Mansfield, Josie, 528, 558
Manufacturing. *See* Industry and industrialization
Mao Tse-tung, 892–893, 959, 978
Mapp v. *Ohio*, 951
March on Washington (1963), 937, *938*
Marcos, Ferdinand, 1002–1003
Marianas, 873
Marijuana, 916–917, 962, 1033
Marines, 655, 659, 791, 838, 862, 873, 875, 1001
Marlborough, Duke of, 556–557
Marriage. *See also* Families
  in 1960s–1980s, 988, 1033
  same sex marriage, 1033
  between wealthy American women and European nobles, 555, 556–557, *556*, 829
  women's age on wedding day, 678
Marshall, George C., 866, 867, 885–886, 892, 897
Marshall Plan, 885–887
Martin, Mr. and Mrs. Bradley, 544–545, 828
Martin, Frederick Townshend, 544, 545
Martin, Joseph W., 894
Marxism, 550, 694. *See also* Communism and anti-Communism; Socialism
Masons, 572
Massachusetts. *See* Boston
Masses, 771
Mattel Corporation, 908
May, Clifford, 929
Mayaguez, 985
Mayer, Louis B., 778
Mayo, Henry T., 723
Mayors, 688, 949
McAdoo, William G., 717, 745, 785, 792
McAuliffe, Anthony, 870
McCain, John, 1028–1029
McCarran Internal Security Act, 897–898
McCarthy, Eugene, 962–964
McCarthy, Joseph, 897–898, *898*, 899, 986
McCarthyism, 897–898, *898*
McClure, Samuel S., 688
McClure's, 674–675, 688
McCord, James E., 981
McCormick International Harvester Company, 550
McCoy, Joseph G., 613–614
McDonnell-Douglas, 1002
McFarlane, Robert, 1002
McGillicuddy, Cornelius "Connie Mack," 766, 767
McGovern, George, 964, 980, 996
McGraw, John, 764
McKane, John Y., 716
McKinley, William
  assassination of, 657–658
  photograph of, *645*
  presidency of, 498, 510, 546, 549, 646, 649–6658
  in presidential election of 1896, 489, 544, 642–646, *646*
  in presidential election of 1900, *640*, 657
  presidential inaugurations of, 647, 657
  Spanish-American War and, 649–654
  tariff and, 510, 655

I-10 *Index*

McKinley Tariff, 510, 655
McManes, James, 515
McNamara, Robert, 1015
McParland, James, 568
McTeague (Norris), 674
Mdivani, Alexis, 829
Measles, 596, 664, 752–753
Meat consumption, 613–614, 808
Meat Inspection Act, 707
Meat packers, 562, 707
Medicare, 952, 1021–1022, *1022*
Medicine, 671, 1019–1020
Mein Kampf (Hitler), 842
Mellon, Andrew, 768, 784, 786–787, *786*, 806, 997
Melodramas, 558
Memorial Day parades, *503*
Mencken, H. L., 760, 779, 783
Mercer, Lucy, 819
Meredith, James, 937
Mesabi Range, 521
Methamphetamine, 1034
Mexico
    Clinton's policies on, 1017–1018
    NAFTA and, 1017
    Pershing expedition in, 724, *724*
    F. Roosevelt's policy toward, 838
    U.S. interests in, 723, 838
    U.S. intervention in, 658
    vaqueros from, 613, 615
    Wilson's policy on, 723–724, *724*
    and Zimmermann telegram in World War I, 737–738
Miami, Fla., 996
Michener, James, 863, 872
Michigan. *See* Detroit
Microsoft Corporation, 536
Middle class
    Chautauqua and, 675–676
    clothing of, 588–589
    good government and, 515
    in late nineteenth and early twentieth centuries, 664, 667–668
    leisure and, 676, 678
    libraries and lyceums for, 675
    magazines for, 674–675
    in 1950s, 905–907
    progressivism and, 684–685
    taxes and, 787
Middle East. *See also* specific countries
    air attack on Iraq by Clinton administration, 1028
    Arab-Israeli conflicts in, 978, 986, *987*, 989
    Bush's policies on, 1007
    Camp David Accords, 986, *987*, 994
    Eisenhower's policy on, 927
    Gulf War, 1003, 1007–1008
    Iran-Contra Affair, 1002
    Iran hostage crisis, 994
    marines in Lebanon under Reagan, 1001
    OPEC in, 983–984, 997
    Palestine Liberation Organization (PLO) in, 989
    Reagan's policies on, 1001
    war between Iran and Iraq, 997
    Yom Kippur War in, 978
Midway, battle of, 864
Midway Island, 647
Military. *See also* Navy; Warfare; and specific wars and battles
    blacks in, 687, 747, *748*, 774
    desegregation of, 890, 917
    draft laws, 744, 746, 846, 853
    expenditures of, in 1980s, 1002
    homosexuals in, 1025
    Reagan's policies on, 1003–1004
    in Spanish-American War, 650–651, 652
    U.S. peacetime army between world wars, 846
    women in, 904
Military-industrial complex, 926, 1002
Milken, Michael, 1000, *1001*
Millay, Edna St. Vincent, 763
Miller, Alfred J., 604
Miller, Henry, 917
Million Man March, 1037, *1037*
Millionaires. *See* Wealth

Millis, Walter, 840
Milosevich, Slobodan, 1017
Mineral springs, 676
Mining, 521, *560*, 564, 568, 577, 612, *612*, 617–618, *618*, 633, 695, 705, 728, 795
Mining camps and cities, 617–618, *618*
Minuteman missiles, 1003
Miranda v *Arizona*, 951
Mississippi
    Freedom Summer in, 947–948
    military government of, during Reconstruction, 485
    Reconstruction in, 487
Missouri, 876
Missouri Pacific Railroad, 572
Missouri River Railroad, 528
Mitchell, Billy, 852
Mitchell, John, 705, 980
Mitchell, William, 788
Mitterand, François, 1004
Mizner, Wilson, 796, 797
Moley, Raymond, 814
Molly Maguires, 568
Molotov, V. M., 884
Mondale, Walter, 1000–1001, 1004
Money
    agriculture and money question, 631–634
    coins, 631, 685, 711
    gold and silver, 631–634, *634*, 636–637
    "greenbacks," 511, 632–633
    "In God We Trust" on, 685, 711
    and inflation or deflation, 511, 632–633, 636
    in late nineteenth century, 511
"Monkey Trial," 779–780, *779*
Monroe, Marilyn, 933
Monroe Doctrine, Roosevelt Corollary to, 659
Montana, 617, 618, 634, *665*
Montgomery, Bernard, 867–870
Montgomery bus boycott, 919, 949
Montgomery Ward, 588, 853
Moral Majority, 994–995
Moran, "Bugsy," 777
Morgan, J. P., 523–524, 535, 546–548, *548*, 551, 555, 562, 637, 704–706, 828
Mormons, 602
Morrill Land Grant Act, 670
Morrow, Anne, 789
Morse, Wayne, 956, 959–960
Mortimer, Wyndham, 808
Morton, Oliver, 503
Mossadegh, Mohammed, 930
Mount Holyoke College, 671
Movies, 752, 764, 778, 809–810, *811*, 907, 909, 910, 929, 961, 996
Moyer, Charles, 706–707
Moyers, Bill, 957
Ms magazine, 1034
Mubarak, Hosni, 764
Muckrakers, 688–689
Mugwumps, 507–508, 687
Muir, John, 708, *709*
Municipal government, 687–688, 690
Munitions industry, 840, 841, 884
Munn v. *Illinois*, 546
Munsey's, 674–675
Muntz TV, 911
Murphy, Charles F., 513, 515
Murrow, Edward R., 898, 909
Music
    "Alice Blue Gown," 678
    "America the Beautiful," 672, 753
    big band music, 810, 910
    Bradley Martin ball of 1897, 544–545, *545*
    elevator music, 904
    by Stephen Foster, 668
    during Great Depression, 810
    "Happy Birthday to You," 672
    jazz, 916
    of labor movement, 833
    Muzak, 904
    of 1950s, 920
    phonograph records, 796, 810
    rock 'n' roll, 914
    sheet music, 558, 796

"Star-Spangled Banner," 513, 672, 753
    Tin Pan Alley, 558
    of World War I, 740
    of World War II, 853
Muskie, Edmund B., 964
Mussolini, Benito, 772, 823, 842, *843*
Muzak, 904
MX missiles (Peacekeepers), 1003
My Lai massacre, 959

NAACP, 672, 685, 687, 747, 813, 831, 917, 918, 937
Nabisco Company, 1000
NAFTA (North American Fair Trade Agreement), 1017
Nagasaki bombing, 876, 882
Naismith, James, 679
NAM. *See* National Association of Manufacturers (NAM)
Napalm, *973*
Narcissism, 1031
Narrow-gauge railroad, 523
Nasser, Gamal Abdel, 931
Nast, Thomas, 492
Nation, Carry, 699
Nation magazine, 932
National American Woman Suffrage Association, 686, 696, 697, 748
National Association for the Advancement of Colored People (NAACP), 672, 685, 687, 747, 813, 831, 917, 918, 937
National Association of Manufacturers (NAM), 573
National Civic Federation, 573
National debt. *See* Debt
National Forest Reserve, 708–709
National German League, 729
National Guard, 770, 918–919, *919*
National Industrial Recovery Act, 823–824
National Labor party, 569
National Labor Relations Board (NLRB), 824–825
National Labor Union (NLU), 568–569
National Organization for Women (NOW), 1034, 1035
National Recovery Administration (NRA), 823–825, *824*, 826
National Socialism. *See* Nazism
National Union party, 483–484
National War Labor Board (NWLB), 854, 856
National Youth Administration, 822
Nationalist Clubs, 550
Native Americans. *See* Indians
NATO, 888, 899, 1004, 1008, 1017
Natural resources. *See* Environmental issues
Natural Resources Defense Council, 1000
Naturalism in literature, 674
Navajo, 603
Navy
    British Royal Navy, 732, 739, 768
    of Italy, 768
    of Japan, 768, 861, 864, 874
    in Spanish-American War, 650, 652
    Treaty of Washington on, 768
    in World War I, 732, 738–739
    before World War II, 846
    in World War II, *836*, 849, 852–853, *852*, 860, 864
Nazism, 838, 842, 845, 866, 876, 882, 974. *See also* Hitler, Adolf
NBC, 812
Nelson, Donald M., 854
Nelson, Gaylord, 959–960
Nesbit, Evelyn, 558
Neton, Huey P., 960
Neutrality Acts (1935–1937), 840–841, 846
Nevada, 617
New Deal. *See also* Great Depression
    blacks and, 831
    chronology on, 835
    criticisms of, 826–831, 846–847
    foreign policy and, 838–841
    Hundred Days of legislation for, 820–823
    labor movement and, 831–833
    legacy of, 831–835
    radio and, 812, 819, 838
    Supreme Court and, 823–824, 826
    use of term, 811–812
New Federalism, 971

Index **I-11**

New Freedom, 715, 718–719
New Frontier, 935–937
New Left, 961
New Nationalism, 713, 718
New Orleans
  black mayor in, 949
  prostitution in, 698
  Storyville in, 698
New Republic, 932
New York Central railroad, 527–528, 547, 562, 704
New York City. *See also* New York State
  Bradley Martin ball of 1897, 544–545, *545*
  Brooklyn Bridge in, 594–595, *595*
  café society in 1930s, 828–829
  Central Park in, 676
  Coney Island in, 670, 676–677, *677*, 716–717
  counterculture in East Village of, 962
  El (elevated train) in, 591–592
  Fifth Avenue in, 556
  gangsters in, 777
  during Great Depression, 803–804, *807*
  Greenwich Village in, 585, 587, 916–917
  Hell's Kitchen in, 551
  Hester Street in, *587*
  immigrants in, 585, *587*, 596
  Jewish community in, 585, *587*, 596
  kickbacks and sandbagging in, 512–513
  libraries in, 675
  political machine in, 500–501, 513–516
  population of, 589, 590–591
  settlement houses in, 587
  skyscrapers in, 594
  slums of, 551, *582*, 596
  subway system in, 997
  Tin Pan Alley in, 558
  Wall Street in, *798*
New York State. *See also* New York City
  Hillary Clinton as candidate for U.S. Senate from, 1028
  progressivism in, 691–692
New York Stock Exchange. *See* Stock market
Newark, N.J., 949
Newberry, William, 675
Newport, R.I., 556, *557*
Niagara Movement, 687
Nicaragua, 658, 659, 791, 838, 930, 1002, 1007
Nimitz, Chester W., 862, 871, 873–874
Nineteenth Amendment, 749
Nisei, 864–865
Nixon, Pat, 935, *979*
Nixon, Richard M.
  in Congress, 896–897
  foreign policy of, 976–979
  Hiss and, 896–897
  in "kitchen debates," 927, *930*
  pardon for, 985
  personality of, 970
  photographs of, *930, 971, 979, 992*
  presidency of, 970–980
  in presidential election of 1960, 932, 934–935, 970, 980
  in presidential election of 1968, 964–965, 980
  in presidential election of 1972, 980
  resignation of, 981, *982*
  as vice president, 927, 970
  Vietnam War and, 945, 972–976
  Watergate scandal and, 980–981
Nixon Doctrine, 973
NLRB. *See* National Labor Relations Board (NLRB)
NLU. *See* National Labor Union (NLU)
Nomura, Kichisaburo, 849
Nonviolent civil disobedience, 919
Noriega, Manuel, 1003, 1006–1007
Norris, Frank, 674
Norris, George, 685, 735, 744, 826
North, Oliver, 1002, *1003*
North Africa, 844
North America. *See* Canada; and specific U.S. states
North American Free Trade Agreement (NAFTA), 1017
North Atlantic Treaty Organization (NATO), 888, 899, 1004, 1008, 1017
North Carolina, 485
North Korea, 893–896, *895*, 900

North Vietnam. *See* Vietnam War
Northern Pacific Railroad, 532, *532*, 547
Northern Securities Company, 704, 706
Norton, Michael, 513, 514
Notre Dame, 672
NOW. *See* National Organization for Women (NOW)
NRA. *See* National Recovery Administration (NRA)
Nuclear arms race. *See also* Atomic bomb
  antinuclear protests, 1004
  beginning of, 888
  Cuban missile crisis, 939–940
  Eisenhower administration and, 926–927
  "fallout shelters" and, 926
  nuclear test ban, 940
  Reagan administration and, 1003–1004
  SALT-II, 987, 1003
  Strategic Arms Limitations Talks (SALT), 978, 987, 1003
Nuclear energy accidents, 989
Nunn, Sam, 1005
NWLB. *See* National War Labor Board (NWLB)
Nye, Gerald, 840, 841
Nylon, 841

O'Bannion, Dion, 777
Occupational diseases, 564
O'Connor, Sandra Day, 997, *998*
Octopus (Norris), 674
O'Doul, Lefty, 803
OEO. *See* Office of Economic Opportunity (OEO)
Office of Economic Opportunity (OEO), 952
Office of Price Administration (OPA), 850, 854, 856
Office of War Mobilization (OWM), 854
Office work, 678–679, *679*
O'Hare, Kat Richards, 750
Oil industry, 535, 536–538, 628, 983–984, 987, 989, 997, 1000
Oken, Charles, 627
"Okies," 804, *805*
Oklahoma, 603–604, 649, 804, 809
Olney, Richard B., 546, 549, 637
Olympics, 644
Omaha Convention, 635, 687
OPA. *See* Office of Price Administration (OPA)
OPEC, 983–984, 997
Open Door policy, 657, 658, 839, 849
Oppenheimer, J. Robert, 875
Orchard, Harry, 728
Oregon, 690, 864
Oregon battleship, 659
"Oregon" system, 690
Organization Man (Whyte), 916, 932
Organization of Petroleum Exporting Countries (OPEC), 983–984, 997
Orlando, Vittorio, 757, *757*
Orr, James L., 484
Orteig, Raymond, 788
Orton, William, 521
Oswald, Lee Harvey, 941–942, 951
Otis, Elisha Graves, 593–594
Our Country (Strong), 648
OWM. *See* Office of War Mobilization (OWM)

Pacific Railway Act of 1862, 530
Packard, Vance, 916, 932
Packer, Alfred E., 500
PACs (Political Action Committees), 994, 996
Page, Patti, 910
Pahlavi, Reza, 994
Palestine Liberation Organization (PLO), 989
Palmer, A. Mitchell, 771
Palmer raids, 771
Pan-American Exposition (1901), 658
Panama, 658, 659–660, 985–986, 1003, 1006–1007
Panama Canal, 659–660, *660*, 985–986, 994
Panama Treaty, 985–986, 994
Panic of 1873, 532–533
Panic of 1893, 636–637
Parker, Alton B., 706
Parker, Bonnie, 809, *809*
Parker, Dorothy, 784
Parkman, Francis, 604
Parks, Rosa, 919

Parks, 676
Parsons, Albert, 550–551
Passing of the Great Race (Grant), 773
Patent medicines, 708
Patent Office, 521. *See also* Inventions
Pathet Lao, 974
Patrick, T. G., 627–628
Patriotism
  of Irish-Americans, 568
  during World War I, 752–753
Patronage, 501–502
Patrons of Husbandry, *543*, 545–546, 630
Paul, Alice, 697, 748
Payne-Aldrich Act, 711–712, 716
Peace Corps, 936–937, *936*
Peacekeepers (MX missiles), 1003
Peale, Rev. Norman Vincent, 912
Pearl Harbor bombing, *836*, 849, 852–853, *852*, 860
Peffer, William, 631, 635
Pelley, William Dudley, 845
Pendleton Act of 1883, 505–506, 507
Pennsylvania, 537. *See also* Philadelphia
Pennsylvania Railroad, 526–527, 533–534, 547
Pensions, 503–504
Perestroika, 1004
Perlman, Selig, 691
Perot, H. Ross, 1008, *1009*, 1017, 1023–1024, 1029, 1030
Perry, Matthew, 647
Pershing, John J. "Black Jack," 651, 720, 724, *724*, 739, 746
Pershing II missiles, 1003
Philadelphia
  Centennial Exposition (1876) in, 520, 521, 716
  gangsters in, 777
  during Great Depression, 803
  immigrants in, 585
  population of, 589, 590
  poverty in, 595–596
Philanthropy, 554–555, 629, 670–671, 675
Philippines, *648*, 651, 652, 654–657, 860, 873, 892, 1002–1003
Phillips, David Graham, 689
Phillips, Kevin, 964, 1020
Phonographs records, 796, 810
Physicians. *See* Medicine
Pickford, Mary, 752
Pike, James S., 487
Pinchback, P. B. S., 490
Pinchot, Gifford, 708, 709, 712–713
Pingree, Hazen S., 688
Pinkerton Agency, 568, 616
Pinochet, Agostin, 979
Pioneers. *See* Frontier; West
Placer mining, 617
Plains Indians, 604–605
Platt, Thomas C., 501, 505, 657–658, 704
Platt Amendment, 838
Playboy, 989
Plessy v. Ferguson, 672, 918
Plunkitt, George, 515
Poindexter, John, 1002
Pol Pot, 974, 975
Poland, 884–885, 1005
Police procedure, 951
Police strike, 770
Polio vaccine, 924
Political machines, 512–516
Political parties. *See also* Democratic party; Republican party
  affiliations in Congress and presidency, A-39 to A-40
  American Communist party, 770, 771, 807–808, 897–898
  "Dixiecrat" party, 890, 899–900
  Greenback Labor party, 511, 633
  in late nineteenth century, 498–516
  national conventions of, 500–501
  National Labor party, 569
  National Union party, 483–484
  partonage and, 501–502
  Progressive Labor party, 959
  Progressive party, 686, 713–714, 786, *786*

I-12 Index

Political parties (continued)
    Reform party, 1023, 1029–1030
    Social Democratic party, 692–693, 695
    Socialist party, 689, 692–695, 706, 771, 807
Pony Express, 604
Population
    ancestry of, 1038
    of Asian Americans, 1038
    of blacks, 1038
    of cities, 588–591
    of immigrants, 575–576, 773
    of Indians, 605
    of Ireland, 567
    of rural areas, 520, 590, 925
    shifts toward Sunbelt, 1020, 1021
    of United States, 520, 562, 914, A-15 to A-17
Populists, 489, 634–638, 644, 646, 647, 687
"Pork-barrel" bills, 592
Pornography, 1032, 1036
Port Huron Statement, 961
Portugal, 930
Post, C. W., 793
Post Office, U.S., 491, 693, 750, 771, 788
Potsdam Conference, 876
Potter, Henry Codman, 497
Poverty. See also Great Depression
    in cities, 551, 582, 595–598
    crack use by poor, 1033–1034
    in 1890s, 544
    of Irish immigrants, 577–578
    Johnson's War on Poverty, 952
    in 1920s, 795
    in 1950s, 905
    during Reagan administration, 998, 999
    Social Gospel and, 551
Powderly, Terence, 572
Powell, Lewis F., 972
Powers, Francis Gary, 932, 933
Pratt, Enoch, 675
Pratt and Whitney, 1002
Presidential election of 1868, 486
Presidential election of 1872, 492
Presidential election of 1876, 493, 499
Presidential election of 1880, 499
Presidential election of 1884, 499, 507–509
Presidential election of 1888, 499, 509
Presidential election of 1892, 499, 635
Presidential election of 1896, 512, 642–646, 646
Presidential election of 1900, 640, 657, 695
Presidential election of 1904, 694, 706
Presidential election of 1908, 695, 710
Presidential election of 1912, 713–715, 715
Presidential election of 1916, 733–734, 734
Presidential election of 1920, 694, 759–760, 760
Presidential election of 1924, 785–786, 786
Presidential election of 1928, 786, 791–792, 792
Presidential election of 1932, 810–814, 814
Presidential election of 1936, 831, 831
Presidential election of 1940, 846–847
Presidential election of 1948, 890–891, 891, 899
Presidential election of 1952, 897, 899–900, 900, 903, 970
Presidential election of 1956, 903, 905
Presidential election of 1960, 932, 934–935, 970
Presidential election of 1964, 949
Presidential election of 1968, 962–965
Presidential election of 1972, 980
Presidential election of 1976, 985
Presidential election of 1980, 994–996
Presidential election of 1984, 1000–1001
Presidential election of 1988, 1004–1005
Presidential election of 1992, 1008
Presidential election of 1996, 1023–1024, 1037
Presidential election of 2000, 1028–1030, 1029, 1030
Presidential elections
    in late nineteenth century, 498–504, 499
    list of, A-18 to A-21
    top-running presidential nominees, 980
    "whistle-stop" campaigning, 682
Presidents. See also specific presidents
    list of, A-22 to A-35
    political party affiliations of, A-39 to A-40
    two-term tradition of, 710, 932

Presley, Elvis, 914
Pressman, Lee, 808
Princeton University, 680, 686, 714
Princip, Gavrilo, 724
Progress and Poverty (George), 549
Progressive Labor party, 959
Progressive party, 686, 713–714, 786, 786
Progressive Republican League, 713
Progressivism. See also Reform
    active government and, 685–686, 806
    in California, 694
    child labor and, 686
    conservation, 708–709
    efficiency and democracy, 690
    feminism and, 696–697, 697, 698
    forebears of, 687
    in Idaho, 692–694
    labor movement and, 695–696
    limits of moralism of, 699
    middle class and, 684–685
    muckrakers and, 688–689
    municipal government and, 687–688, 690
    in New York State, 691–692
    prohibition and, 699, 749
    prostitution and, 698–699, 749
    race and, 686–687
    reforms, 665, 684–700
    of T. Roosevelt, 685, 687, 698, 703, 704–710, 713
    state government and, 690–694
    in Wisconsin, 690–691
    woman suffrage and, 686, 696–697, 697, 698, 719, 748–749
    World War I and, 744–746
Prohibition
    constitutional amendment on, 749, 775–776, 784
    Coolidge and, 784
    progressivism and, 699, 749
    repeal of constitutional amendment, 822
    Smith's opposition to, 792
    violation of constitutional amendment, 775–777
Promised Land (Antin), 573–574
Promises of American Life (Croly), 686
Promontory Point, Utah, 531
Propaganda during World War I, 735–737, 737, 752, 753
The Prophet, 610
Prosperity
    during Clinton administration, 1014, 1031, 1038
    of 1920s, 791–798
    of 1950s, 905–907
    during Reagan administration, 997–998
Prostitution, 698–699, 698, 749, 776
Protestantism. See specific churches
Prouty, Charles A., 546
Publishing of books, 787
Pueblo Indians, 603, 604
Puerto Rico, 649, 652, 654, 655
Pulitzer, Joseph, 649, 650, 653, 668
Pullman, George, 567
Pure Food and Drug Act, 690, 707, 708
"Putting out" system, 589
Pyle, Ernie, 871–872

Qadaffi, Muammar, 1001–1002
Quakers, 697, 959
Quay, Matthew, 501, 704
Quayle, Dan, 1005
Queensberry, Marquis of, 680
Quiz shows, 909–910

R. J. Reynolds, 1000
Race riots, 747, 959, 960
Race theories
    Anglo-Saxonism, 648, 649, 655
    European races, 773
    Grant on Passing of the Great Race, 773
    immigration restrictions, 773
    imperialism defense, 648, 649, 655
Races of Europe (Ripley), 773
Racial and ethnic groups. See also Civil rights movement; Immigration; and specific groups, such as Blacks

of immigrants, 577–581, 773
    race suicide and, 584
Radcliffe College, 671
Radical Republicans, 478–490, 484
Radio, 764, 796, 810, 812–813, 814, 819, 838, 910
Raft, George, 810
Railroads. See also specific railroads
    air brake for, 524–525, 528
    consolidation of, 526–528
    construction of line for transcontinental railroads, 530–531, 531
    Crédit Mobilier scandal and, 491
    Erie War and, 528
    farmers' grievances against, 542–546
    during Great Depression, 804
    inefficiency and chaos in, 526
    land grants to, 531–532, 532
    land sales and, 528
    maps of, 527, 529, 530, 532
    narrow-gauge railroads, 523
    Panic of 1873 and, 532–533
    political campaigning on, 682, 695, 710, 715
    political cartoon on, 547
    private railroad cars for the wealthy, 551
    public finance for transcontinental railroads, 528–530
    regulation of, 545–547, 707, 719
    T. Roosevelt and, 707
    strikes against, 520, 567–568, 572, 637
    transcontinental railroads, 528–533, 529, 531, 532, 547, 605
    during World War I, 745
Railway Brotherhoods, 695
Rainey, J. H., 488–489
Ranch house, 929
Randolph, A. Philip, 855, 917
Rankin, Jeanette, 849
Raskob, John Jacob, 796
Rationing during World War II, 850–851
Rauschenbusch, Walter, 551
Ray, James Earl, 960
Rayburn, Sam, 946
RCA, 796, 797, 810
Reagan, Nancy, 997, 1004
Reagan, Ronald
    Alzheimer's disease and, 996
    baseball and, 764
    criticisms of, 996–997
    foreign policy of, 997, 1001–1004
    as governor of California, 982, 996
    and Panama Treaty, 986
    personality of, 996–997
    photographs of, 992, 998
    presidency of, 660, 936, 996–1004, 1031
    in presidential election of 1976, 985
    in presidential election of 1980, 994–996
    presidential election of 1984, 1000–1001
    quotations by, 993
    Supreme Court and, 997
    on Vietnam War, 959
Reaganomics, 997
Reagan Doctrine, 1001–1002
Realism in literature, 673–674
Rebates in oil industry, 537
Reconstruction
    black codes during, 482
    "Black Reconstruction" governments, 486–490
    cartoon on, 492
    chronology on, 494
    Civil Rights Act of 1875 during, 493
    debate on, 478–482
    definition of, 478
    Fifteenth Amendment and, 486
    Fourteenth Amendment and, 477, 481, 483
    freedmen during, 476, 478–490
    Freedmen's Bureau and, 482
    Johnson's plan for, 479–481
    legends of, 486–487
    Lincoln's plan for, 478–479
    Radical Republicans' plan for, 478–490, 484
    Redemption and, 490
    twilight of, 493–494
Reconstruction Finance Corporation (RFC), 806

Index   I-13

Record companies, 796, 810
Red Badge of Courage (Crane), 674
Redbook, 915
Redeemers, 488, 489, 490, 502
Redpath, James, 675
Redstone, Sumner, *1032*
Reed, John, 723, 743, 771
Reed, Thomas B., 655
Reform. *See also* Progressivism
    child labor and, 564–565, 686
    chronology on, 699–700
    definition of, 684
    in late nineteenth century, 549–551
    in municipal government, 687–688, 690
    in Progressive Era, 665, 684–700
    prostitution, 678, 698–699, 749
    Social Gospel and, 551
    socialists and anarchists, 550–551
    in state government, 690–694
    temperance movement, 699
Reform party, 1023, 1029–1030
Refugees from Southeast Asia, 975
Regulatory legislation and agencies, 542–549, 707,
    710–711, 718, 719, 825, 999, 1000
Rehnquist, William H., 972, 997
Religion. *See also* Catholicism
    Baptists, 554
    Buddhism, 916
    Congregationalism, 551, 671
    of Indians, 610–611
    Jehovah's Witnesses, 886–887
    Judaism, 580, 912
    in 1950s, 912
    in 1980s, 988
    Unitarians, 671
    women ministers, 671
Remington, Frederic, 617
Remington Arms Company, 678
Reno, Janet, 1025, *1025*
Reno, Milo, 808
Republican party. *See also* headings beginning with
    Presidential election
    blacks in, 481, 486, 644, 646, 831
    Compromise of 1877 and, 493–494
    "Half-Breeds," 504–505, 507
    in late nineteenth century, 498–516
    Liberal Republicans, 491–493, 687
    Mugwumps, 507–508, 687
    political cartoon on, *496*
    progressivism and, 713
    Radical Republicans, 478–490, *484*
    "Stalwarts," 504, 507–508
    in twentieth century, 834–835, 1014, 1020–1023
    in 2000, 1028
    World War I and, 744–745
Reservations for Indians, 491, *603*, 611, *665*
Reuben James, 847
Reuther, Walter, 833, 919
Revels, Hiram, 488, *488*, 490
Reynolds, Debbie, 907
Reynolds, R. J., 629
Reynolds v. Sims, 951
RFC. *See* Reconstruction Finance Corporation (RFC)
Rhee, Syngman, 893
Rhode Island, 556, *557*
Richards, Ann, 1020
Richelieu, Duc de, 555
Richmond, Va., *476*
Rickenbacker, Eddie, 746, 848
Riesman, David, 916
Rights. *See* Human rights; Women's rights
Riis, Jacob, 585, 596, *597*
Riots. *See* Violence
Ripley, William Z., 773
Rise of Silas Lapham (Howells), 551, 673
River and Harbor Bill of 1886, 502
Road to War (Millis), 840
Roads, 913–914, *913*
"Roaring Twenties," 764
Robinson, Edward G., 810
Rock 'n' roll, 914
Rockefeller, John D., 519, 535–538, *536*, 547, 548,
    551, 553, 554, 562, 577, 618, 671, 688, 710, 795

Rockefeller, John D., Jr., 519, 552
Rockefeller, Nelson, 934, 983
Rockefeller, William, 537
Rocky Mountains, 602
Rodgers and Hammerstein, 863
Roe v. *Wade*, 1035
Roebling, John A., 594–595
Roebling, Washington A., 595
Rogers, Will, 783, 804
Roller coaster, 717
Roman Catholicism. *See* Catholicism
Romania, 1005
Rommel, Erwin, 866–867
Rooney, Mickey, 810
Roosevelt, Alice, 678, 784, 848
Roosevelt, Eleanor, 818, 819–820, *820*, 831, 855, 889
Roosevelt, Franklin D. *See also* New Deal
    assassination attempt against, 818
    as baseball fan, 764
    "brains trust" of, 814
    death of, 875
    "Fireside Chats" of, on radio, 819, 838
    foreign policy of, 838–841, 884
    Four Freedoms of, 838
    Hoover and, 746, 768, 805
    as Navy Undersecretary, 746, 849
    New Deal of, 811–812, 817–835
    personality of, 812–813, *816*, 818–819
    photographs of, *848*, *872*
    polio and, 819
    in presidential election of 1932, 810–814, *814*, 980
    in presidential election of 1936, 831, *831*, 980
    in presidential election of 1940, 846–847, 980
    in presidential election of 1944, 980
    significance of, 818–819
    Supreme Court and, 823–824, 826, 950
    as vice presidential candidate, 759
    wealth and aristocratic heritage of, 818, 819
    World War II and, 837, 846–856, 859, 871
Roosevelt, Sara, 818
Roosevelt, Theodore
    athletic and outdoor pursuits of, 666, *666*, 708,
        709, 712
    Cabinet of, 658, 704
    campaign poster of, *640*
    cowboys and, 615
    death of, 744
    Latin American policy of, 658–661
    on muckrakers, 689
    as Navy undersecretary, 650–652, 654
    as New York governor, 655, 657–658
    personality of, 665–666
    photograph of, *666*
    political cartoon on, *705*
    presidency of, 658–661, 690, 695, 704–710, 722
    in presidential election of 1904, 706
    in presidential election of 1912, 713–715, *715*
    and presidential election of 1916, 733–734
    progressivism of, 685, 687, 698, 703, 704–710, 713
    Spanish-American War and, 650–652, 654, *654*,
        662
    sports language used by, 647–648, 663
    as symbol, 666–667
    as vice president, 658
    world tour by, 712–713
    World War I and, 721, 733, 744
Roosevelt Corollary to Monroe Doctrine, 659
Root, Elihu, 658, 666, 704
Roper, Daniel, 823
"Rosie the Riveter," 855
Ross, Edward, 486
Rostow, Walt W., 937
Rough Riders, 651, 654, *654*, *662*
Roughing It (Twain), 673
Round robin, 758
Rowell, Chester, 584
Ruby, Jack, 942, 951
Ruef, Abe, 512, 515, 694
Rural areas. *See* Agriculture
Rural Electrification Administration, 812, 825, 826
Rusk, Dean, 940
Russell, Charles Taze, 886

Russia. *See also* Soviet Union
    civil war in early twentieth century, 770–771
    immigrants from, 773
    Jews of, 576
    military conscription in, 576
    revolution in, *702*, 739, 770, 771, 882–883
    war with Japan, 658
    in World War I, 730–740
    in World War II, 844–845, 847, 860, 866–871, 874
Russian Revolution, *702*, 739, 770, 771, 882–883
Rustin, Bayard, 917
Rutgers University, 680
Ruth, Babe, 764, 767, 961

Sacco, Nicola, 771–773, *772*
Sadat, Anwar, 978, 986, *987*
St. Johns, Adela Rogers, 829
St. Louis, 688
Salaries. *See* Wages
Salk, Jonas, 924
SALT, 978, 987, 1003
SALT-II, 987, 1003
Saltis, "Polack Joe," 777
San Diego, 788
San Francisco, 556, 578, 591, 698, 755, 916, 962
San Juan Hill, battle of, 651, 654
Sandbagging, 513
Sandinistas, 1002, 1007
Sanitation, 596–597
Santa Clara County v. Southern Pacific Railroad, 535
Santo Domingo, 491, 510
Satie, Eric, 904
Saturday Evening Post, 674, 796
Saudi Arabia, 1007
Savings and loan associations, 1000
Scalawags, 487
Scalia, Antonin, 997
Scandals and corruption
    Clinton's sexual behavior, 1026, 1036
    during Grant administration, 490–491
    during Harding administration, 768–769, 785
    Hart's sexual behavior, 1004
    Iran-Contra Affair, 1002
    kickbacks and sandbagging in cities, 512–514
    Lewinsky scandal, 1026–1028, 1036
    during Reconstruction, 487
    upper-class scandals, 558
    Watergate scandal, 980–981
    Whitewater scandal, 1025–1026
    World Series of 1919, 766–767
Scandinavian immigrants, 580
Scarlet fever, 596, 664
Schenck v. United States, 751
Schlafly, Phyllis, 1035
Schlesinger, Arthur, Jr., 969
Schlieffen Plan, 730
Schmitz, Eugene E., 515, 694
Schumann-Heink, Ernestine, 753
Schurz, Carl, 491, 580, 655
Schwab, Charles, 534, 770, 828
Schwarzkopf, Norman, 1007
Scientific management, 687
SCLC. *See* Southern Christian Leadership
    Conference (SCLC)
Scopes, John, 779–780
Scott, Dred, 950
SCUM (Society for Cutting Up Men), 1034
SDI (Strategic Defense Initiative), 1003–1004
SDS. *See* Students for a Democratic Society (SDS)
Seale, Bobby, 960
Sears Roebuck, 588, 664, *794*, 854
SEC. *See* Securities and Exchange Commission (SEC)
Second World War. *See* World War II
Secretarial work, 678–679, *679*
Securities and Exchange Commission (SEC), 1000
Sedition Act of 1918, 751
Seeger, Pete, 833
Segregation. *See also* Civil rights movement
    Carter on, 985
    of education, 672, 918
    in government employment, 687
    Lyndon Johnson on, 947
    in 1950s, 917–918, *917*

I-14 *Index*

Segregation *(continued)*
  progressivism and, 686–687
  of sports, 680–681
Segretti, Donald, 981
Selective Service Act, 746
Selma, Ala., civil rights march, *948*
Senate, U.S. *See also* Congress, U.S.
  election of Senators, 636
  Harding in, 765
  impeachment and trial of Clinton, 1027–1028
  impeachment and trial of Johnson, 485–486, *485*
  Lyndon Johnson in, 946
  League of Nations and, 756, 758
  McCarthy in, 897–898
  Versailles Treaty and, 758, 759, 768
  War Investigating Committee of, 854
  Watergate investigation by, 981
"Separate but equal" doctrine, 672, 918
Sephardic Jews, 580, 672
Serbia, 1017
Serbs in Bosnia, 1017
Serling, Rod, 909
Settlement houses, 585, 587, 686
Seventeen, 914
Seventeenth Amendment, 636
Seward, William H., 483
Sewing machine, 588
Sexual Behavior in the Human Female (Kinsey), 915–916
Sexual Behavior in the Human Male (Kinsey), 915–916
Sexual harassment, 1026, 1035–1036
Sexual revolution, 1031–1033
Sexuality
  birth control and, 988, 1032
  Clinton's sexual behavior, 1026–1027
  homosexuality, 988, 1008, 1025, 1033
  Kennedy's sexual behavior, 933
  Kinsey reports on, 915–916
  in 1950s, 915–917
  in 1980s, 988
  sexual revolution of 1970s–1980s, 1031–1032
Seymour, Horatio, 486
Shanghai, *839*, 840
Sharecroppers, 626–629, *627*
Shaw, Anna Howard, 696
Shawnee Trail, 606
Sheen, Bishop Fulton J., 912
Shellabarger, Samuel, 481
Shepherd, Cybil, 1030
Sheridan, Philip H., 605, 607, 609
Sherman Antitrust Act, 548–549, 637, 704
Sherman Silver Purchase Act, 634, 637
Sherrod, Robert, 863
Shibasaki, Keiji, 862–863
Ships and boats. *See also* Navy; Submarine warfare;
  and specific ships
  ferryboats, 592
  immigrant steamers, 570–571
  Liberty ships, *854*, 855
  Lusitania sinking, 732–733
  yachts, 555, 562
Sholes, Christopher Latham, 678
Shoshone Indians, 603
Sierra Club, 708, 709, 1000
Sihanouk, Prince, 974
Silliman, Benjamin, 536–537
Silver
  mining of, in late nineteenth century, 612, 617, 633
  money question and, 631–634, *634*
  Sherman Silver Purchase Act, 634
  silver certificate, *632*
Silver Shirts, 845
Simmons, William, 775
Simonton, S. R., 628
Simpson, Orenthal "O.J.," 1037
Simpson, "Sockless Jerry," 631, 644, 647
Sims, William S., 738–739
Sinclair, Harry, 769
Sinclair, Upton, 689–690, 698, 707, 830
Singer, Isaac Bashevis, 580
Single tax, 549
Singleton, Benjamin "Pap," 626
Sioux, 608, 609, 611, *611*, 616
Sirhan, Sirhan B., 964

Sirica, John, 981
Sister Carrie (Dreiser), 674
Sit-down strike, 833
Sitting Bull, 616–617
Six Crises (Nixon), 970
Skyscrapers, 594, *594*
Slums, 551, *582*, 595–598
Smallpox, 596
Smith, Alfred E., 685, 693, 699, 785, 792, *792*, 811, 826
Smith, Bessie, 810
Smith, Hamilton S., 672
Smith, Holland, 863
Smith, Jesse L., 769
Smith, Julian, 863
Smith, William A. "Uncle Billy," 537
Smith College, 671
Smuggling, 775–776
SNCC. *See* Student Nonviolent Coordinating
  Committee (SNCC)
Social classes. *See also* Middle class; Poverty; Wealth;
  Working class
  Marxist ideology on class conflict, 550
Social Darwinism, 552–553, 648
Social Democratic party, 692–693, 695, 750
Social Gospel, 551
Social Security, 830, 999, 1021–1022, 1025
Socialism and Socialist party, 550, 689, 692–696,
  706–707, 728–729, 750, 766, 771, 807
Sod house, 624, *625*
Soil Bank Act of 1956, 925
Soldiers. *See* Military
Somalia, 1015–1016
Somme, Battle of, 731
South. *See also* Civil War; and specific states
  agriculture in, 626–629
  consequences of Civil War for, 478
  desegregation of schools in, 918–920, 937
  New South, 628
  readmission of states during Reconstruction, 485
  Reconstruction in, 478–494
  segregation in, during 1950s, 917–918, *918*
  tenants and sharecroppers in, 626–629, *627*
South Africa, 1001
South America. *See* specific countries
South Carolina, 485, 487, 490
South Dakota, 577, 611, *611*, 617, 690, *800*
South Korea, 893–896, *895*
South Pacific, 863
South Vietnam. *See* Vietnam War
Southern Alliance, 630, 634
Southern Christian Leadership Conference (SCLC),
  919–920, 937
Southern Pacific Railroad, 535, 542, 556, 694
Soviet Union. *See also* Cold War; Russia
  Carter's policy on, 986–987
  and Cold War beginnings, 882–888
  collapse of Communism in, 1006, *1007*
  Cuban missile crisis and, 939–940
  Eastern Europe and, 871, 884–886, 896
  Eisenhower policy on, 925–932
  end of, 1006
  glasnost in, 1004, 1006
  invasion of Afghanistan by, 987
  Kennedy's policy toward, 937–940
  in 1980s, 1004
  Nixon-Kissinger policy toward, 978
  perestroika in, 1004
  Reagan's policies toward, 1001–1004
  Truman Doctrine and, 885
  U.S. recognition of, 840
  Vietnam War and, 956
  Warsaw Pact and, 888
  in World War II, 844–845, 860, 866–871, 874
SPAB. *See* Supplies Priorities and Allocation Board
  (SPAB)
Space program, 936
Spain
  Civil War in 1936, 841
  Spanish-American War and, 489, 502, 649–654,
    653, 654
Spalding, Albert G., 679–680
Spanish-American War, 489, 502, 649–654, 653, 654

Spanish flu, 754–755
Spargo, John, 564, 688–689
Sparkman, John, 900
Speculation, 491, 796–797
"Speed" (methamphetamine), 1034
Spellman, Francis, 892
Spencer, Herbert, 552, 648
Spies, August, 550
Spirit of St. Louis, 788
Spock, Benjamin, 959, 964
Sports, 678–681, 764, 766–767, 803, 977–978, 1031
Sprague, Frank J., 592
Spruance, Raymond, 862, 864
Stafford, Jo, 910
Stagflation, 994
Stalin, Joseph, 840, 843, 844, 866, 867, 870, 871, *872*,
  876, 883–885, 896, 900, 927
Stalingrad, battle of, 867
Standard Oil, 535, 537–538, 562, 618, 688
Stanford, Leland, 542, 554, 556, 562, 670–671
Stanford University, 554, 671, 691, 889
Stanton, Edwin, 485
Stanton, Elizabeth Cady, 667, 696
"Star-Spangled Banner," 513, 672, 753
"Star Wars" (SDI), 1003–1004
Starr, Belle, 616, *616*
Starr, Kenneth, 1026
State Department, U.S., 897
States. *See also* specific U.S. states
  admission of, to Union, A-14
  legislatures of, 950–951
  progressivism and state government, 690–694
States' Rights party, 890
Steam engine, 520
Steel industry, *518*, 533–535, *534*, 770
Steel Workers' Organizing Committee, 832
Steeplechase Park, 717
Steffens, Lincoln, 512, 685, 688
Steinbeck, John, 804
Steinem, Gloria, 1034
Stephens, Uriah P., 569–572
Stephenson, David, 775
Stevens, Thaddeus, 481, 484, 485
Stevenson, Adlai, 881, 899–900, 905, 933
Stilwell, Joseph W. "Vinegar Joe," 871, 892
Stimson, Henry L., 838, 839, 840, 846, 877
Stimson Doctrine, 839
Stock market
  bull market, 797–798
  buying stocks "on margin," 797
  crash of 1929, 798–799, *798*, 828
  insider trading, 1000
  in 1920s, 797–798
  percentage of households involved in, 1014
Strategic Arms Limitations Talks (SALT I and II),
  978, 987, 1003
Strep throat, 664
Strikes, 567–568, 572, 637, 695, 696, 705, 729, 750,
  769–770, 833, 854
Strong, Josiah, 648
Student movement, 960–961, 974, 1005, 1031, 1034
Student Nonviolent Coordinating Committee
  (SNCC), 920, 937, 947–948, 949, 960
Students for a Democratic Society (SDS), 961
Submarine warfare, 732, 735, 737, 738–739, 847
Suburbs, *902*, 911–916, 928–929
Success Gospel, 553–554
Suffrage. *See* Voting
Sugar, 548, 549, 649
Sullivan, Ed, 909
Sullivan, John L., 680
Sullivan, Louis H., 594
Sullivan, Tim, 513–515, *514*
Sumner, Charles, 485, 491, 493
Sumner, William Graham, 552–553
Sunbelt, 1020, *1021*
Supermarket, 928–929
Supplies Priorities and Allocation Board (SPAB), 854
"Supply-side" economics, 997
Supreme Court, U.S. *See also* specific justices
  antitrust cases, 704
  Baker v. *Carr*, 951
  Bakke case, 1036

Index I-15

and Berger's conviction, 693
Brandeis as justice of, 718
Brown v. Board of Education of Topeka, 918, 950
Dennis et al. v. United States, 898
Dred Scott v. Sandford, 950
Escobedo v. Illinois, 951
Field as justice of, 525
Hammer v. Dagenhart, 686
Hughes as justice of, 768
"In God We Trust" on money, 711
Johnson and, 951, 972
Korematsu v. United States, 865
list of justices of, A-36 to A-38
Mapp v. Ohio, 951
Miranda v Arizona, 951
Munn v. Illinois, 546
New Deal and, 823–824, 826
Nixon and, 972
Plessy v. Ferguson, 672, 918
pornography decisions, 1032
Radical Republicans and, 485
Reagan and, 997
Reynolds v. Sims, 951
Roe v. Wade, 1035
F. Roosevelt and, 823–824, 826, 950
Santa Clara County v. Southern Pacific Railroad, 535
Schenck v. United States, 751
Clarence Thomas nomination to, 1036
U.S. v. E. C. Knight Company, 549
Wabash case, 546, 549, 630
Warren as chief justice of, 950–951
Westberry v. Sanders, 951
Surplus, government, 502
"Survival of the fittest," 552, 648
Suspension bridges, 594–595, *596*
Sussex, 733
Sussex Pledge, 733
Sweatshops, 588–589
Swift, Gustavus, 562
Swine flu, 755
Swing states, 500
Sylvis, William, 568–569
Syphilis, 664
Syria, 978, 1037

Taft, Robert A., 854, 890, 898–899
Taft, William Howard, 660, 695, 710–715, *711*, *715*, 722, 764, 890
Taft-Hartley Labor-Management Relations Act, 889
Taiwan, 647
Tales of the South Pacific (Michener), 863
Tammany Hall, 500–501, 513
Taney, Roger B., 950
Tank warfare, 731, 867, *957*
Tanner, James "Corporal," 503
Tarawa, battle of, 862–863, 873
Tarbell, Ida M., 688, *689*
Tariffs
   Democratic party and, 510
   Dingley Tariff of 1897, 711
   Fordney-McCumber Tariff of 1922, 786, 787
   GATT (General Agreement on Tariffs and Trade), 1018
   in late nineteenth century, 510
   McKinley Tariff, 510, 655
   NAFTA and, 1017
   Payne-Aldrich Act, 711–712, 716
   Republican party and, 510
   Taft and, 711–712
   Underwood-Simmons Tariff, 716–717
   Wilson and, 716–717
   Wilson-Gorman bill, 510, 649
Taxes
   excise tax, 787
   "flat tax," 1023
   income tax, 636, 786, 830, 998
   Mellon's policies on, 786–787, 806
   in 1990s, 1031
   Reagan's tax cuts, 997–998
   regressive taxes, 787
   single tax, 549
Taylor, Frederick W., 687
Teapot Dome scandal, 769, *769*, 785

Technology. *See also* Inventions; and specific technological developments, such as Television
   farm machinery, 624–625, *626*
   women's employment and, 678–679
   World War I military technology, 730–732
Tecumseh, Chief, 610
Teheran Conference, 871
Telegraph, 521, 525
Telephone, 521–523, *522*, 678
Television, 813, 898, 908–911, *909*, 914, 935, 996, 1024
Teller, Henry W., 633, 655
Teller Amendment, 655
Temperance movement, 699
Temple, Shirley, 810, *811*
Temple University, 554, 671
Ten Days That Shook the World (Reed), 771
Tenant farmers, 626–629
Tennessee, 485
Tennessee Valley Authority (TVA), 825, 826, *827*, 833, 924, 925
Tennis, 764
Tenskwatawa ("The Prophet"), 610
Tenure of Office Act, 485
Terrorism, 989, 1037
Tet Offensive, 956–957
Texas
   dust storms in, 804
   military government of, during Reconstruction, 485
   oil industry in, 628
   "Yellow Dog Democrats" in, 500
Texas Pacific Railroad, 572
Texas State Alliance, 630
Textile industry, 563–567, *563*, 588–589, 696, 795
Thatcher, Margaret, 1004
Thaw, Alice, 556
Thaw, Harry, 558
Thayer, Webster, 772
Theory of the Leisure Class (Veblen), 544
Thieu, Nguyen Van, 974
Third International (Comintern), 771
Third World. *See* specific countries
Thirteenth Amendment, 484
Tho, Le Duc, 974
Thomas, Clarence, 1036
Thomas, Norman, 807–808, 847
Thompson, "Big Bill," 776
Thompson, J. Edgar, 526–527
Thomson, J. Edgar, 533
Three Mile Island accident, 989
Thurmond, Strom, 890, 947, 949
Tilden, Samuel J., 493, 498, *499*, 504, 675
Tilden, William "Big Bill," 764
Tillman, Benjamin "Pitchfork Ben," 489, 686
Tilyou, George C., 676, 716–717
Time magazine, 892, 896
Time zones, 526
Tin Pan Alley, 558
TNT, 884
Tobacco, 548, 628–629, 851
Tocqueville, Alexis de, 542, 581
Tojo, Hideki, 849
Toledo, Ohio, 688, 802
Tonkin Gulf Resolution, 956, 974
Torrio, Johnny, 777
Tourgée, Albion W., 477, 490
Townsend, Francis E., 804, 827–828, 830–831
Townsend Clubs, 828, 831
Toynbee Hall, 587
Toys, 908
Trade. *See also* Tariffs
   GATT (General Agreement on Tariffs and Trade), 1018
   in late nineteenth century, 646–647
   NAFTA, 1017
   during World War I, 732
Transcontinental railroads. *See* Railroads
Transportation. *See also* Railroads
   in cities, 591–593, *592*, *593*
   maps of, *527*, *529*, *530*, *532*
   roads, 913–914, *913*
Treasury, U.S., 502
Treaty of Brest-Litovsk, 739

Treaty of Versailles, 757–758, 759, 768
Treaty of Washington, 768
Trench warfare, 731, *731*
"Trickle-down" economics, 787, 806
Tripp, Linda, 1026
Trolleys, 592–593, *593*
Tropic of Cancer (Miller), 917
Truman, Bess, 889
Truman, Harry S
   atomic bomb and, 859, 876–877, 881, 882
   civil rights and, 889–890, 917
   domestic politics under, 888–891
   Fair Deal of, 889, 892
   foreign policy of, 882–888, 892–896
   Korean War and, 893–896, *895*
   photograph of, *891*
   presidency of, 876
   in presidential election of 1948, 890–891, *891*, 899
   as vice president, 876
   White House repairs and, 819
   World War II and, 876
Truman, Margaret, 890
Truman Doctrine, 885
Trump, Donald, 1030
Trusts. *See also* Business
   money invested in, 549
   regulation of, 542–549, 704–705, 710–711
   T. Roosevelt and, 704–705, *705*
   Sherman Antitrust Act, 548–549
   Standard Oil trust, 538
   sugar trust, 548, 549
   whiskey distilling, 548
Tsongas, Paul, 1008
Tuberculosis, 664
Tumulty, Joseph, 717–718
Tunney, Gene, 764
Turkey, 885, 887, 940
Turner, Frederick Jackson, 601, 649
Tuskegee Institute, *555*, 672, *673*
Twain, Mark, 497, 522, 641, 672–673
Tweed, "Boss" William Marcy, 512–514, 515, 524
Tweed Ring, 487, 515
Twenty-Fifth Amendment, 981, 983
Twenty-First Amendment, 822
Twenty-Third Amendment, 932
Tydings, Millard, 897
Tyler, John, 982
Typewriter, 678–679, *679*
Typhoid, 652, 664
Typhus, 596

U-2 incident, 932, *933*
UAW. *See* United Automobile Workers (UAW)
U-boats, 732, 735, 737, 738–739
UMW. *See* United Mine Workers (UMW)
Underwood, Oscar, 714
Underwood-Simmons Tariff, 716–717
Unemployment, during Great Depression, 802–804, *803*, 833
UNIA. *See* Universal Negro Improvement Association (UNIA)
Union Pacific Railroad, 491, 528, 530–531, 546, 605, 614
Unions. *See* Labor movement
Unitarians, 671
United Automobile Workers (UAW), 808, 832, 833, 919
United Kingdom. *See* Great Britain
United Mine Workers (UMW), 695, 705, 854
United Nations, 885, 886, 893, 978, 989, 1007–1008, 1016, 1017
United States Steel Corporation, 704–705, 766, 770, 786, 828, 832, 833
U.S. v. E. C. Knight Company, 549
United Steel Workers, 832
Universal Negro Improvement Association (UNIA), 774–775
Universities and colleges. *See* Higher education; and specific colleges and universities
University of Alabama, 829–830

I-16 *Index*

University of California, 961, *962*, 1034
University of Chicago, 671
University of Illinois, 671
University of Michigan, 671, 981
University of Mississippi, 937
University of Rochester, 671
University of Texas, 946
University of Wisconsin, 691, 889
Updike, John, 932
Urban areas. *See* Cities; and specific cities and towns
U'ren, William S., 690
USSR. *See* Soviet Union

V-2 rockets, 870
Valentino, Rudolph, 764
Van De Wall, William, 887
Van Doren, Charles, 909–910
Vance, Cyrus, 986
Vandenberg, Arthur H., 885
Vanderbilt, Consuelo, 556–557, *556*
Vanderbilt, Cornelius, 512, 527–528, 536, 542, 555, 556, *557*, 562, 573
Vanderbilt, William, 528, 542, 556
Vanderbilt University, 671
Vanzetti, Bartolomeo, 771–773, *772*
Vaqueros, 613
Vardaman, James K., 686
Vassar College, *670*, 671
Veblen, Thorstein, 544, 555, 793–794
Venereal disease, 664, 1032
Ventura, Jesse, 1030
Verne, Jules, 649, 668–669
Versailles Treaty, 757–758, 759, 768
"Vertical integration" of business, 534–535
Veterans Administration, 769
Viacom, 1031, *1032*
Vice presidents. *See also* specific vice presidents
   list of, A-22 to A-35
   presidential appointment of, in case of vacancy, 983
"Victory gardens," 746, 851
Vienna Summit (1961), 939
Viet Cong, 955–957, 959, 973, 975
Viet Minh, 953, 954
Vietnam Memorial, 976, *976*
Vietnam War
   antiwar sentiment and protest against, *944*, 959–960, 973, 974, 1015
   casualties of, 957, 975–976
   early American involvement in Vietnam, 954–955
   Eisenhower and, 955
   end of, 974–975
   escalation of, 956, 959
   expansion of, into Cambodia and Laos, 974
   financial costs of, 957, 975
   and French involvement in Vietnam, 931, 953–954
   Johnson and, 945, 953, 955–959
   Kennedy and, 945, 955
   map of, *958*
   My Lai massacre, 959
   Nixon and, 945, 972–976
   Tet Offensive, 956–957
   Tonkin Gulf Resolution, 956, 974
   Viet Cong and, 955–957, 959, 973, 975
   Vietnamization of, 973
Vietnamese refugees, 975
Villa, Pancho, 723–724, *725*
Violence
   civil rights movement and, 920, 937, 948, 960
   drug-related violence, 1034
   during Great Depression, 808
   Haymarket riot, 550–551, 572
   against Japanese Americans during World War II, 864–865
   of Ku Klux Klan, 490, *762*, 775, 776
   labor movement and, 567–568, 833, *834*
   lynchings of blacks, 664, 747, 774, 917
   race riots, 747, 959, 960
   violent death among young black males, 1034
   Watts riot, 960
Virginia, 485
Virginian (Wister), 617
VISTA, 952
Volunteers in Service to America (VISTA), 952

Von Hindenburg, Paul, 838
Von Ludendorff, Erich, 754
Von Schlieffen, 730
Voting
   for blacks, 484, 947, 949
   in nineteenth century, 484, 498
   nineteenth-century voter turnout, 498
   political machines and, 512–516
   and presidential elections in nineteenth century, 498
   for women, 668, 669, 686, 696–697, *697*, 698, 719, 748–749
Voting Rights Act of 1965, 947, 949, 950

Wabash, St. Louis, and Pacific Railway Co. v. *Illinois*, 546, 549, 630
Wade, Benjamin, 481, 486
Wade-Davis Bill, 479
Wages
   in 1920s, 792
   of women, 566
   of working class, 562–563, 566
   during World War I, 747, 769
   during World War II, 856
Wagner, Robert F., 685, 699
Wagner Labor Relations Act, 824–825, 832, 889
Wake Island, 655
Wald, Lillian, 587, 668
Walker, Francis, 609
Walker, James J., 776
Wallace, George, 937, 949, 964–965, 971
Wallace, Henry A., 825, 876, 885, 890, 896
Walsh, Thomas J., 785
Wanamaker, John, 506
War bonds, *742*, 752
War Industries Board, 745, 746
War Resources Board (WRB), 853
Ward, Artemus, 497
Ward, Lester Frank, 553
Ware, James E., 596
Warfare. *See also* specific wars and battles
   airplanes in, 730–731, 745, 788, 789, 866
   German *blitzkrieg*, 843
   Indian warfare, 608–609
   Kamikaze, 875
   Pacific Campaign during World War II, 862–863, 871–875
   poisonous mustard gas, 731
   submarine warfare, 732, 735, 737, 738–739, 847
   tank warfare, 731, 867, *957*
   trench warfare, 731, *731*
   World War I military technology, 730–732
Warner Brothers, 810
Warren, Earl, 864, 865, 918, 942, 950–951, 972
Warren Commission, 942, 951
Warsaw Pact, 888
Washington, Booker T., *555*, 667, 672, 747
Washington, George, on cities, 583
Washington, D.C.
   Bonus Expeditionary Force in, 808–809
   Hooverville in, 809
   March on Washington (1963), 937, *938*
   Million Man March in, 1037, *1037*
   White House, 819
Washington and Lee, 671
Washington State, 864
Washington Treaty, 768
WASPs, 578, 685, 773
Watergate scandal, 980–981
Watson, Thomas, 489, 631, 635, 644, 646
Watt, James, 1000
Watts riot, 960
WCTU. *See* Woman's Christian Temperance Union (WCTU)
Wealth
   conspicuous consumption and, 555–556
   "get-rich-quick" schemes in 1920s, 796–798
   Great Depression and the wealthy, 828–829
   in late nineteenth century, 513–514, 536, *540*, 542, 544–545, *545*, 551–558
   marriage between wealthy American women and European nobles, 555, 556–557, *556*, 829
   in 1920s, 1014
   in 1950s, 905

   in 1970s and 1980s, 1014
   philanthropy and, 554–555, 629, 670–671, 675
   in popular culture, 558
   scandals of wealthy, 558
   Social Darwinism and, 552
   Success Gospel and, 553–554
   tax advantages for wealthy, 786, 998, 1031
   and women in late nineteenth century, 555, 556–558
Weapons. *See also* Atomic bomb; Nuclear arms race
   of cowboys, 615
   machine gun, 731
   Nye Committee's investigation of munitions industry, 840, 841
   V-2 rockets, 870
   in World War I, 730–732
Weaver, George "Buck," 766, 767
Weaver, James B., 511, 633, 635
Webster, Daniel, 716
Weinberger, Caspar, 1002, 1004
Weiss, "Little Hymie," 777
Weissman, Solly, 777
Welfare reform, 971, 1021
Wellesley College, 671
Wells, D. A., 533
Wells, H. G., 663
Wesleyan College, 671
West. *See also* Frontier; and specific states
   anticonservation movement in, 709
   cattle industry in, 606–607, *607*, 611–615, *612*, *613*
   economic development of, *612*
   and end of frontier, 649
   Homestead Act and, 530, 625
   Indian reservations in, *603*, 611, *665*
   Indians of, 603–611
   in late nineteenth century, 602–618
   outlaws in, 615–616
   in popular culture, 615–617
   television programs on, 909, 910
   as uninviting land, 602
West Berlin blockade, 887–888, *888*
Westberry v. *Sanders*, 951
Western Federation of Miners (WFM), 728
Western Union, 521, 522
Westerns, 909, 910
Westinghouse, George, 524–525
Westmoreland, William, 956–957
Weyler, Valeriano, 650, 651
Wheat, 622
Wheeler, Burton, 785
Wheeler, Joseph, 650
White, George H., 489
White, Stanford, 558
White, Theodore H., 953
White, William Allen, 666, 685, 687, 707
White Citizens' Councils, 985
Whitewater scandal, 1025–1026
Whitman, Walt, 672, 716
Whooping cough, 664
Why Johnny Can't Read (Fleisch), 910
Whyte, William H., Jr., 916, 932
Wilber, Charles Dana, 624
Wild turkeys, 709
Wild West shows, 616–617
Wilderness Society, 1000
Wildlife. *See* Animals
Wiley, Harvey W., 690
Wilhelm II, Kaiser, 725, 727
Will, George, 1014
Willard, Frances, 699
Willard, Jess, 681
Williams, Gardner, 644
Willkie, Wendell, 846–847
Wills, Garry, 1031
Wilson, Charles, 924
Wilson, Hack, 767
Wilson, Jack (Wovoka), 610–611
Wilson, James (20th century), 704
Wilson, Sloan, 916
Wilson, William B., 695, 717
Wilson, Woodrow
   on automobile, 685
   as baseball fan, 764
   Cabinet of, 717–718

daughters of, 713
on excesses and disorder, 763
Fourteen Points of, 748, 753–756
illnesses of, 755, 758–759
League of Nations and, 753–758, 759
moral diplomacy of, 722–723
New Freedom of, 715, 718–719
personality of, 713, 714
photograph of, 757
presidency of, 686, 695, 715–719, 722–724, 727, 732–740, 746–747, 749–450, 773
in presidential election of 1912, 715, *715*
in presidential election of 1916, 733–734
as Princeton University president, 686–687, 714
progressivism of, 685, 695, 703
retirement of, 760
segregation and, 686–687
Versailles Treaty and, 757–758, 759
World War I and, 721, 727, 732–740, 743, 744
Wilson-Gorman bill, 510, 649
WIN! (Whip Inflation Now!) campaign, 984
Winchell, Walter, 829
Winfrey, Oprah, 1030
Winthrop, John, 520
Wisconsin, 690–691
Wise, Rabbi Isaac Mayer, 580
Wister, Owen, 617
Wobblies. *See* Industrial Workers of the World (IWW)
Wolfe, Tom, 1031
Woman suffrage movement, 668, 669, 686, 696–697, *697*, 698, 719, 748–749
Woman's Christian Temperance Union (WCTU), 699
Women. *See also* Women's rights; and specific women
college education for, 669, *670*, 671
employment of, *522*, 563, *563*, 565–566, *566*, 675, 678–679, 747–748, *749*, 855–856, 914–915
Gibson Girl and, 678
in government employment, 675
in labor movement, *569*, 570–571
in military, 904
in 1950s, 906–907, 914–916, *915*
in 1980s, 988
office work for, 678–679, *679*
in professions, 671
as telephone operators, *522*, 678
in textile industry, 563, *563*
wages of, 566
wealthy women in late nineteenth century, 556–558
during World War I, 747–748, *749*
during World War II, 855–856, 904
Women and Economics (Gilman), 697
Women's Army Corps, 904
Women's rights
abortion rights, 1035
Equal Rights Amendment (ERA), 1034–1035, *1035*
Friedan on, 916, 1034
in 1970s–1990s, 1034–1036
sexual harassment and, 1026, 1035–1036
voting rights, 668, 669, 686, 696–697, *697*, 698, 719, 748–749

Wood, Leonard, 760
Woods, Robert A., 587
Woodward, Robert, 981
Working class. *See also* Industry and industrialization; Labor movement
blacks in, 566–567
child labor, 564–565, 686
hours of factory work, 563–564
immigrant labor, 577, 585
industrialization and, 520–521
leisure and, 676–677
in 1920s, 795
occupational diseases and, 564
size of, 562
and size of factories, 562
taxes and, 787
wages for, 562–563, 566
women as industrial workers, 563, *563*, 565–566, *566*
working conditions in factories, 564
Works Progress Administration (WPA), 821–822, *822*
World Series of 1919, 766–767
World War I
alliances leading up to, 725, *726*
antiwar sentiment during, 744, 750
armistice for, 740
battles during, *738*, 739–740
beginning of, 724
blacks in, 747, *748*, 774
blockade during, 732
casualties of, 731, 739, 740, 754
countries involved in, 725
draft in U.S. during, 744, 746
home front during, 744–761
Lusitania sinking during, 732–733
map of, *738*
name for, 727
naval warfare in, 732
peace conference after, 756–757, *757*
peace mission during, 730
progressivism and, 744–746
propaganda against Germany in U.S., 735–737, 737, 752, *753*
repression and conformity in U.S. during, 749–753
stalemate in, 730
submarine warfare, 732, 735, 737, 738–739
surrender by Germany, 740
trench warfare in, 731, *731*
U.S. entry into, 733–738, *736*
U.S. initial reaction to, 725–730
U.S. involvement in, 738–740
U.S. neutrality at beginning of, 727, 729, *734*
U.S. sympathy for Allies, 727
U.S. sympathy for Central Powers, 728–730
and Wilson's Fourteen Points, 753–756
women during, 747–748, *749*
World War II
African campaign of, 866–867
anti-Japanese hysteria in U.S., 864–866
antiwar sentiment in U.S., 847–848, 849
atomic bomb and, 859, 875–877, *877*, 882
Battle of the Bulge in, 870–871

beginning of, 841–845, *842*
casualties of, 856, 860, 875
chronologies on, 856, 877–878
conscientious objectors during, 865–866
costs of, 853
D-Day in, 869
draft law in U.S., 846, 853
Eisenhower in, 867–871, *869*
end of, 876
in Europe, 866–871
friction among Allies during, 866
German *blitzkrieg* in, 843
German saboteurs in U.S. during, 866
home front during, 850–851, 853–856
invasion of Italy during, 867
invasion of Russia, 844–845
legacies of, 882
Lend-Lease during, 847, 860
maps of, *845*, *868*, *873*
in Pacific, *845*, *858*, 860–866, 871–377, *873*, *874*, 877
Pearl Harbor bombing, *836*, 849, 852–853, *852*, 860
rationing and scrap drives in U.S., 850–851
submarine warfare during, 847
surplus after, 884
U.S. entry into, 849, 852–856
U.S. initial response to, 845–849
U.S. undeclared war on Germany, 847–849
women during, 855–856
World Wildlife Fund, 1000
World's Fairs, 670, 677, 716, 841
Wovoka, 610–611
WPA. *See* Works Progress Administration (WPA)
WRB. *See* War Resources Board (WR3)
Wright, Frank Lloyd, 594
Wylie, Philip, 916
Wynette, Tammy, 1024

Yachting, 555, 562
Yale University, 671, 680
Yalta Conference, 871, 896
Yamamoto, Isoroku, 849, 860, 861, 864
"Yankee ingenuity," 521
Yellow-dog contracts, 573
Yellow fever, 659
Yellow press, 649–651
Yeltsin, Boris, 1006
Yerkes, Charles T., 513
Yom Kippur War, 978
Yorktown, 864
Young, Andrew, 989
Young, Owen D., 790
Young Plan of 1929, 790

Zangara, Joe, 818
Zen Buddhism, 916
Zhou Enlai, 978
Zhukov, Georgi, 869
Zimmermann, Arthur, 737
Zimmerman, Helena, 556
Zukor, Adolph, 752